What the experts are saying about
Choosing the Right College

"ISI's guide to *Choosing the Right College* . . . offers tough-minded analysis of the quality of instruction, the level of academic standards, the campus political atmosphere, and the extent to which the liberal arts tradition is respected and cultivated. It is one of those rare books that cuts through the information glut to the heart of the matter."
— WILLIAM J. BENNETT

"*Choosing the Right College* is head and shoulders above any other college guide."
— THOMAS SOWELL
Hoover Institution, Stanford University

"If prospective students and their families want a critical look at what is taught at America's most powerful and celebrated schools, *Choosing the Right College* may be their only guide."
— *World Magazine*

"American parents (and students) have long needed a reliable 'review' of our nation's universities so they can be sure they will not be supporting the systematic destruction of the values, faith, and worldview they have spent so many years building up. *Choosing the Right College* is the right book for them. It exposes the bad ones and confirms the good ones. My only regret is that it wasn't available as early as the sixties. Think of the administration buildings that might have been spared occupation!"
— CAL THOMAS
syndicated columnist

"[P]rovides as comprehensive a catalogue of the academic skies as is anywhere available. . . . Given the encyclopedic scope of this guide, one can only stand in awe of the consistency with which its editors have been able to grasp what makes each campus tick."
— STEPHEN H. BALCH
President, National Association of Scholars

"A valuable tool that asks more probing questions, and provides far more significant answers, than the typical college guide."

— MICHAEL MEDVED
film critic and syndicated radio host

"What is remarkable about ISI's offering is that it captures the tone of the academic, political, and social life of each school, as well as that school's attitude toward the traditional liberal arts."

— *Crisis* Magazine

"I've got children approaching college age, so I'll be consulting this useful book. I'll even do my best to get the kids to read it."

— WILLIAM KRISTOL
editor and publisher, *The Weekly Standard,*
and Fox News analyst

"A candid, detailed, entertaining, and thoroughly reliable account of what the top colleges have to offer, both socially and academically. It is unmatched in laying out what parents and students have a right to expect from a good college — and which colleges fall short of providing it. Identifying each college's strengths and weaknesses, the guide recommends by name many outstanding teachers and courses, while telling about politically correct but academically insubstantial departments. Definitive and indispensable."

— CHRISTINA HOFF SOMMERS
author of *The War Against Boys: How Misguided
Feminism is Harming Our Young Men*

"At last, parents and prospective students can get an honest, in-depth account of what really awaits them at America's top colleges. This book does not mince words. It provides exacting, no-nonsense assessments of academic life in both its intellectual and moral dimensions. In my opinion, *Choosing the Right College* is an indispensable guide for anyone who wants to make an informed and intelligent choice about one of the most important — and expensive — decisions most of us will ever make."

— ROGER KIMBALL
author of *Tenured Radicals: How Politics Has
Corrupted Our Higher Education*

"A godsend for anyone who wants to know how to beat the academic establishment and actually get an education."

— *National Catholic Register*

"What more can I say? I am using *Choosing the Right College* — actively and appreciatively — as our high-school senior son contemplates colleges and universities. To parents like me, this wise and informative book is a rich blessing."

— WILLIAM MURCHISON
syndicated columnist

"Nowadays there may be no more bewildered people in this land than kids readying themselves to go to college, and no more perplexed ones than the parents who are trying to guide them. In offering this sane, civilized, and at the same time genuinely practical guide to colleges and universities, the Intercollegiate Studies Institute has performed a major service to both."

— MIDGE DECTER
author of *The Liberated Woman and Other Americans* and *Liberal Parents, Radical Children*

"A superb book that will tell you everything you wanted to know, and that the college administrators wouldn't tell you."

— MARTIN ANDERSON
Hoover Institution, Stanford University

CHOOSING THE RIGHT COLLEGE

Introduction by	•	William J. Bennett
Researched and written by	•	the staff of the Intercollegiate Studies Institute (ISI), T. Kenneth Cribb, Jr., President
Project Director	•	Jeffrey O. Nelson
Editor-in-Chief	•	Winfield J. C. Myers
Editor of First Edition	•	Gregory Wolfe
Senior Editors	•	Jeremy Beer, Jeremy Nafziger
Contributing Editors	•	Cory L. Andrews, Lila III Arzua, Kara Björklund, David J. Bobb, Lee Bockhorn, Eric Cohen, Jason E. Duke, Alex Epstein, Amy E. Fahey, Alexandra Gilman, Kyle Harper, Beth Henary, Claudia L. Henrie, Paige E. Hochschild, Robert J. Johansen Jr., Jennifer Kabbany, Ben Kepple, William Keyes, Morgan N. Knull, Marc Levin, Tony Mecia, William F. Meehan III, Scott Rubush, Brent Tantillo, Timothy Byron Webster
Research Assistants	•	Douglas S. Schneider, Benjamin J. Schools

Choosing the Right College

The Whole Truth about America's Top Schools

REVISED AND EXPANDED EDITION

Introduction by
WILLIAM J. BENNETT

Researched and written by
the staff of the Intercollegiate Studies Institute (ISI),
T. Kenneth Cribb, Jr., President

William B. Eerdmans Publishing Company
Grand Rapids, Michigan / Cambridge, U.K.

© 1998, 2001 Intercollegiate Studies Institute
P.O. Box 4431, Wilmington, Delaware 19807
All rights reserved

Published by Wm. B. Eerdmans Publishing Co.
255 Jefferson Ave. S.E., Grand Rapids, Michigan 49503 /
P.O. Box 163, Cambridge CB3 9PU U.K.
www.eerdmans.com

First edition 1998
Second edition 2001

Printed in the United States of America

07 06 05 04 03 02   8 7 6 5 4 3 2

Library of Congress Cataloging-in-Publication Data

Choosing the right college: the whole truth about America's top schools /
introduction by William J. Bennett; researched and written by the staff of
the Intercollegiate Studies Institute (ISI). — Rev. and expanded ed.
     p.   cm.
  ISBN 0-8028-4801-X (pbk.: alk. paper)
    1. Universities and colleges — United States — Directories.
  2. College choice — United States — Handbooks, manuals, etc.
  I. Intercollegiate Studies Institute.

L901.C576   2001
378.73 — dc21

                2001033221

Contents

CONTENTS

CONTENTS

CONTENTS

Acknowledgments

Choosing the Right College was made possible by grants from Arthur E. Rasmussen, Menlo F. Smith, an Anonymous Friend, Mr. and Mrs. J. Bayard Boyle Jr., Claude R. Lambe Charitable Foundation, F. M. Kirby Foundation, and the Huston Foundation. The Intercollegiate Studies Institute gratefully acknowledges their support.

Introduction

William J. Bennett

A question that I am often asked is what colleges I would recommend. It is a reasonable question. But it is also a difficult one to answer, given the vast number of colleges and universities. It simply is not possible for most people — including me — to know what is happening on all, or even most, of America's campuses. What parents and students desperately need is an intellectual road map, a commonsense guide, to help them make their way through the academy.

Choosing a college is a tremendously important — and can be an extremely expensive — undertaking. When done intelligently and thoughtfully, it can be a great investment. After all, a college education can provide graduates with the kind of high-demand skills that can serve them the rest of their lives. But college should provide much more than information and employment skills. Indeed, the undergraduate experience should be more than merely a job-training program. It can also be a time when many young people refine the convictions that will guide and mold their decisions, conduct, and character. The essence of education is, in the words of one philosopher, the transmission of civilization — the imparting of ideals as well as knowledge, the cultivation of the ability to distinguish the true and good from their counterfeits, and the wisdom to prefer the former to the latter.

Yet despite the unparalleled resources American universities offer, there is growing evidence that many American universities are reneging on their duty to educate. The widespread abandonment of academic standards and moral discipline, the politicization of all aspects of campus life, and the deconstruction of academic disciplines have devastated the traditional mission of the liberal arts curriculum. In too many classrooms, radical professors teach their students that Western thought is suspect, that Enlightenment ideals are inherently oppressive, and that the basic principles of the American founding are not "relevant" to our time. The result is not education, but confusion — over the importance of knowledge, the universality of the human experience, the transcendence of ideals and principles. In the end, the central problem is not that the majority of students are being indoctrinated (although some are), but that they graduate knowing almost nothing at all. Or worse still, they graduate thinking that they know everything.

Fortunately, not all universities or professors have bought into this way of thinking. Important and impressive academic departments, professors, and universities still exist; it is simply a matter of finding them. This is no easy task, however — despite the glut of promotional information and bookstore college guides, until now no single publication existed that analyzed and evaluated universities, academic departments, and professors on the basis of principled instruction and intellectual rigor.

ISI's *Choosing the Right College* fills that void. This revised and expanded edition offers tough-minded analysis of the quality of instruction, the level of academic standards, the campus political atmosphere, and the extent to which the liberal arts tradition is respected and cultivated at 110 of the nation's top colleges and universities. It is one of those rare books that cut through the information glut to the heart of the matter. I find it to be authoritative, current, and extremely well written.

The organization responsible for compiling this volume — the Intercollegiate Studies Institute (ISI) — is well-qualified to speak to these issues. Founded in 1953, ISI has worked tirelessly to further a better understanding among American college youth of the principles that sustain a free society. Through conferences, lectures, books, journals, and fellowships, ISI has helped to ensure that real intellectual debates — rather than one-sided indoctrination — take place in academia. In the process of compiling this book, the editors have drawn on many resources — including ISI's network of 60,000 students and faculty members — to produce thoroughly up-to-date portraits of the featured colleges.

The principle of selection in *Choosing the Right College* is eminently practical: of the 110 institutions covered, the majority — about eighty — were chosen according to competitive admissions figures. These are, quite simply, the most selective schools in the country. The guide provides balanced and insightful reports on each one of these schools. The remaining thirty institutions constitute a special list of colleges recommended by the editors as beacons of excellence in preserving the liberal arts tradition.

The ISI guide illustrates and explicates the good, the bad, and the ugly in American higher education. These pages contain a number of real-life horror stories of ideological intolerance, bizarre course offerings, and absurd campus scandals. But the editors have also gone out of their way to search out what is good and commendable, from hard-working professors to dynamic departments and enriching extracurricular activities. The advice you will find in *Choosing the Right College* will provide insights that may save a student from several semesters' worth of trial and error, pointing him or her in the right direction from the start. Best of all, the guide does not hesitate to name names: many of the best faculty members, departments, and special programs in each institution are specifically identified to make it easier for students to make informed education choices.

All too often, Americans treat colleges and universities with a deference that prevents them from asking hard questions and demanding real results. But if there is ever to be genuine, long-lasting education reform, parents and students will have to become shrewder and better-informed education consumers. ISI's *Choosing the Right College* is a powerful tool in this effort. It is my hope that American students will read it, learn from it, and as a result, demand and receive a better university education.

The Importance of the Humanities

Robert Royal

Nearly everyone who has gone to college, or is thinking about going, has experienced the excitement of entering a larger world. That feeling is a clue to something quite important. It is a natural reaction to the prospect of broader social life and intellectual vistas, usually at an age when we are just reaching adulthood. But at whatever age a person decides to pursue serious study, the excitement stems from a sense that personally, socially, and intellectually, institutions of higher learning are places where, if we are fortunate, we may come into living contact with what being more fully human is all about.

The humanities are about being human. In a technological age such as our own, we may decide to study at a college or university so that we can pursue a career in the sciences or get a good job. There is nothing wrong — and much that is right — in these goals. But specialized technical schools or even educational programs sponsored by private companies can do those things for us, and they will probably become the common route for that kind of education in the future. The humanities, however, have always aimed at something quite different, something that many people feel is particularly lacking in twenty-first-century America. *Choosing the Right College* is written to show where you can still find this knowledge on America's campuses.

As the ancient Greek philosopher Plato, one of the great sources of the Western humanistic tradition, once put it:

It is not the life of knowledge, not even if it includes all the sciences, that creates happiness and well-being, but a single branch of knowledge — the science of the good life. If you exclude this from the other branches, medicine will remain equally able to give us health, and shoemaking shoes, and weaving clothes; seamanship will continue to save life at sea, and strategy to win battles; but without the knowledge of good and evil the use and excellence of these sciences will be found to have failed us.

Plato's goal here is not to make a highbrow argument about the need to study ethics or pursue abstruse philosophical investigations, though ethics will inevitably come into the humanities, as will hard thinking. But as Plato shows by comparing it with other kinds of knowledge, the science of the good life is valuable for its own sake as well as for its practical value. It aims at discovering the truths that tell us both who we are and what we need to know if we want to use our other knowledge to make us more fully human. Put briefly and in a modern idiom: at their best, the humanities can teach us how to live.

Human beings are in a unique condition compared with other living things. The higher animals may teach their young a few survival techniques. But we have to teach and learn about many things in order to flourish. No other being that we know of has the intellectual capacity and relative freedom that we humans possess. These two powers make it impossible for us to live by instinct, as most animals do. We have entire ranges of understanding and action that go far beyond anything in the rest of nature. Consequently, both our minds and wills need to be properly formed if we are going to live up to everything that is in us. *Choosing the Right College* will help you find the resources you need to develop your talents fully.

Most talk about freedom today suggests that freedom means liberation from constraints. The older humanistic tradition agrees that we need to be freed from certain external constraints, but even more from internal constraints like unfocused passivity and a slavery to ignorance, habit, emotion, or impulse — our natural condition prior to education. Indeed, without freedom from inner bondage, mere freedom from outward limitations is likely to turn into utter disaster. We need to understand and train ourselves to pursue not only *freedom from* evils and limitations but also *freedom for* what is good. The kinds of human beings most of us typically admire combine a lively spontaneity with well-formed habits of rationality and self-mastery that make it easy for them to both know and do what is good for themselves and others.

How do we make ourselves into the kinds of people we admire? Such things are not achieved without good external guidance and firm internal discipline. Even the very finest university can only offer a beginning to what is, by its very nature, a life-long pursuit. A good college experience may open us up to the prospect of unlimited opportunities and intellectual stimulation; a bad one may condemn us to perpetual frustration and narrowness. The difference is not merely a matter of individual psychology, but the result of a successful or unsuccessful attempt to encounter, and to get some understanding of, the fundamental questions about human existence. Human societies always exist in a state of no little confusion about basic truths. That is one of the reasons why higher learning, which is also a clarification, is necessary. Getting down to basics has never been easy, but in our time it is further complicated by the fact that even many colleges and universities have become confused about what an education in the humanities means. Any student who wants what humanistic studies can give today has to search carefully for guides and work hard with them when they are found. This college guide points the way to a genuine education in the humanities on 110 of America's best campuses.

Contrary to the impression given by most course catalogs, the subjects students need to confront are not very numerous, though they may be approached from many different perspectives and in no little detail. Historically, they have centered around questions about God and man, virtue and vice, heroism and cowardice, tyranny and freedom, truth and untruth. Study of those questions was intended to produce a similarly small number of exemplary human types: the saint, the philosopher, the hero, the statesman, the artist, the scholar, and the scientist.

The basic humanistic subjects — and they must be very basic now because elementary and secondary education today hardly prepare us for them — at any given institution are crucial to whether we will preserve the old authentic thrill of learning to be human beings, or will find ourselves in backwaters of mere information. Most students of the humanities today will have to encounter the essential subject matter in disciplines such as literature, history, politics, and languages. (Philosophy and theology are also crucial subjects. But like mathematics, few people can do the kind of abstract thinking they require to any great extent.) Wherever we choose to begin, however, each of the humanistic disciplines deals with the multiple values a thinking person will encounter over the whole course of life. Hence, they are subjects that can never be outdated, superseded, or finished while we are still alive.

Literature provides us with an imaginative recreation of life that enables us to see things, thanks to the author, that we would be unable to see on our own. A novel like *Moby Dick*, for example, contains a good deal of sea lore and local color. For many readers, that in itself will open their eyes to a larger world. But few people, even those who did whaling in the period in which that novel is set, ever thought as deeply as Herman Melville did about the human struggle with God and nature, good and evil, and what it means for all of us, even landlubbers. After we return from that voyage, we stand on very different ground.

History provides a similar expansion of horizons, but has the added advantage of leading us to reflect on what has actually happened in the human past. Human beings change over the course of their lives and the human race has changed as well. But there are some basic human features that we can observe in the most distant regions of the earth among peoples far remote from us in time. Knowledge about those permanent human things gives us a better perspective on who we are. History also allows us to understand that our own age is not merely the natural order of things. It took great human efforts to build up our civilization, efforts involving intellectual discoveries, backbreaking physical labor, and, often enough, heroic sacrifice of life itself.

For example, every school child has heard the words from the Declaration of

Independence: "We hold these Truths to be self-evident, that all Men are created equal, that they are endowed by their Creator with certain unalienable Rights, that among these are Life, Liberty, and the Pursuit of Happiness — That to secure these Rights, Governments are instituted among Men. . . ." Like any of the truths of the humanities, these principles can be lazily passed over as truisms, only useful for Memorial Day speeches and other ceremonial occasions. But if we begin to look at them carefully, a number of questions of central importance to human life jump out at us. Do we need to refer to a God to understand beings who have rights? What kind of God would that be? Does liberty mean I am free to do whatever I want or, as the Founding Fathers warned, do we need to distinguish sharply between liberty and license? What is this Happiness that we are to pursue? Such questions are the culmination of centuries of struggle to understand individuals in society and to build up a civilized order that makes our relations with one another as productive of the common good as possible.

Just to begin listing such questions helps us to realize how quickly even the most common sentiments lead us out into deep waters. The kind of learning the humanities convey to us is not a matter of knowing a little bit about this and that so that we can take part in polite dinner-table conversations. The range of subjects we encounter in every serious humanistic pursuit goes to the heart of the question of whether we will live well and in good societies, or, like most of the human race for most of history, we will not. As such, these subjects are not a matter of annoying "distribution requirements" or of whimsical "electives" that we can choose at will. Each of us has aptitudes and interests that will lead us to focus on one or more areas in the humanities. But to understand even them well, we need very broad views of human beings and we need to acquire them by looking hard for how and where to get them.

Some people who recognize this have a partly mistaken impression of the problem on the campuses today. The most notorious cases have even appeared in newspapers: an English department that no longer requires students majoring in English to read Shakespeare, or a university with few or no requirements for graduation. An even more difficult problem is the *way* the great humanist thinkers are often taught, even when they are present in the curriculum. The great texts of our culture have endured because they have repeatedly revealed their value to all kinds of people over centuries in very different cultural settings. There is a presumption in favor of ideas with that kind of life in them. But often today they are approached — when they are not merely dismissed — as instances of past prejudices of various kinds. These are alarming signs and the parent or student who wants a concrete evaluation of what such signs mean will want to read the following pages very closely.

Like ourselves, even the greatest figures of the past were imperfect human beings and their prejudices ought to be corrected. But we need to be cautious that our desire to counteract prejudice does not turn into a narrowness and prejudice of its own. One of the ways that often happens today is through a movement called multiculturalism. Basing itself on alleged biases in Western thinking against women, the marginalized, and nonwhite races, it offers non-Western cultures as an antidote. On the surface, this appears utterly benign and even necessary. Who could possibly object to a wider acquaintance with the world or to correctives to our Western ideas from the outside? Properly pursued, these are part and parcel of a true humanism.

Unfortunately, they are not often properly pursued. To understand another culture we have to study its languages, history, great people and events, and then come to a proper appraisal of them, just as we might some earlier period of Western culture such as ancient Greece. Too often, however, multiculturalism stops at the surface, presenting a few selected dimensions of another culture as a weapon with which to attack our own ways and the long social and intellectual traditions on which they are based. Furthermore, on closer inspection, these claims usually prove to be Western values pushed to extremes without proper attention to other truths. Most multicultural approaches to the humanities challenge very little of the culture with which students arrive on contemporary campuses: in fact, they are usually used to enforce ideas already present without opening up any new vistas at all. As such, they should not be allowed to obscure one of the world's great cultural achievements.

So if you want an education in the humanities today it will require work — and vigilance. One reason that the initial excitement of going to college soon dies down for most people is that it seems so difficult to find institutions, departments, or individual teachers that can help in orienting us to the tasks at hand. More typically, our desire for humane learning is thwarted by educational institutions themselves that cannot seem to make up their minds what a humanistic — and human — education should be. The great value of the present guide is that, without concerning itself with any question other than which institutions best provide an education in the humanities or which professors or departments do so in otherwise inhospitable institutions, it provides some practical suggestions for entering the perpetually exciting world of discovering how we may be free, responsible, and ever more human beings.

How to Use This Guide

Winfield J. C. Myers, Editor-in-Chief

You Be the Judge

The first edition of *Choosing the Right College* enjoyed tremendous success, going through four printings to become one of the best-selling college guides in the country. The strengths of that guide — rigorous research, the use of faculty and student sources at each school, a commitment to fairness, and the conviction that the liberal arts best prepare one for life regardless of career choice — have been carried over to this revised and expanded edition. We have added ten schools, substituted several to reflect the fortunes of individual colleges, and updated and revised every essay. This volume is, we believe, the best college guide you can buy.

The earlier edition of this guide brought many comments and questions from its readers; answering some of the questions may suggest how the new edition can help in choosing the right college for yourself or someone you know. Among the most common questions we received were: Why don't you rank institutions? How can one decide which college to attend?

For several important reasons, we deliberately chose not to join the crowd of magazines and other popular publications in ranking schools. The first reason has to do with the close ties between list-making and money-making. College presidents must raise cash to keep their institutions afloat, and few more convenient means of doing this exist than citing a school's rise in national rankings. It is not surprising, therefore, that the public relations offices of our institutions of higher learning are desperate to ensure that their schools are on the correct trajectory (upward). Yet the most popular lists commonly have two failings in this regard. Most simply report what you already know, such as that the Ivies are good and that some party schools are less prestigious. Far worse, they reward colleges for following academic trends — intellectual relativism, moral nihilism, and over-specialized sub-disciplines that cater to professors' careers rather than students' educations. Universities thus have every incentive to recruit faculty whose research is deemed to be on the "cutting edge" of their fields rather than hiring scholars who will strengthen the liberal arts components of their schools. In brief, they often confuse education with indoctrination, permanent substance with ephemeral style.

The second reason is that there is something inherently fatuous about ranking institutions of higher learning, as if such an exercise was as easy as measuring fish. (No surprise that these rankings begin to resemble fish tales.) Education is not a one-size-fits-all commodity. A student who excels at a small liberal arts college might feel overwhelmed at a major state university. Yet that same student's sibling might find solace in the anonymity offered by the larger school. Knowing this, we have written *Choosing the Right College* so that students from a variety of backgrounds and with sundry needs can find a school that's right for them. We include the most prominent state universities, smaller elite liberal arts institutions, all of the Ivies, and many schools with distinctive denominational ties or histories.

Students should exploit the diversity in American higher education and match their own interests, personality, abilities, and expectations with a school that can fulfill most of their needs. *Choosing the Right College* is the best place to begin, because its essays will open the readers' eyes to college *as it is actually experienced* on every campus. The governing philosophy of this guide — that students are best served by a rigorous, diverse, and broad curriculum founded on the traditional disciplines of the liberal arts and sciences — leaves no room for admissions office propaganda or staged pictures in glossy brochures. Our reports are thoroughly researched, frankly reported, and vigorously written.

The Heart and Soul of Higher Education

Some basic information on the size, selectiveness, and cost of each school precedes each essay. Most of this is self-explanatory, but a few of these statistics may require explanation. The "Accepted" line gives the percentage of applicants accepted, and the "Enrolled" line gives the percentage of those accepted who actually enrolled. The "Tuition" line includes two figures, the first indicating the cost of tuition and fees alone at each school, and the second including the amount for room and board. Neither number includes the projected cost of books, supplies, personal expenses, or transportation.

Each essay is divided into four sections. A brief introduction provides a thumbnail sketch of the school. Three longer sections cover the academic, political, and social components of every campus. In the first of these, Academic Life, we examine the curriculum, faculty, and students and compare reality with reputation. Questions we ask in compiling the information for this section include: Do the graduation requirements broadly educate each student regardless of major? What is the quality of intellectual life? Do professors teach, or are they really researchers who employ teaching assistants to deal with undergraduates? Who are the best teachers? What type of student does this school attract? Which departments and programs are strongest and weakest? Our aim here, as elsewhere, is to give you insights formerly available only to insiders and experts.

In the Political Atmosphere section, we judiciously assess the health of academic freedom, free speech, and critical thought. Are professors, backed by administrators and radical students, using their status and power to mislead those entrusted to them? What is life like for students who wish to be educated rather than indoctrinated? We take into account faculty hiring patterns, tenure decisions, course material, and the image projected by the public relations office — the one they want you to believe — in drawing our conclusions. You'll learn what to expect at each campus, and why.

Finally, the Student Life section concentrates on daily living. Rather than echoing received wisdom on how students should live, we present you with information many colleges are unlikely to brag about. Are bathrooms coed? (Yes, they exist.) Are there any single-sex dorms? How widespread is drug and alcohol use? We provide information on crime, student groups and organizations, nearby sources of enrichment and entertainment, and other features of campus life. The result, we believe, is a complete, fair, and rigorously researched assessment of what it's like to live at each school.

Perhaps another use for this book, in addition to its immediate value for parents, students, and guidance counselors, will be as a comprehensive survey of the state of higher education in America. Reading this volume from Amherst to Yale provides a panoramic view of academia today.

As reviewers and customers of our guide point out repeatedly, no other college guide provides the wealth of information, gathered with critical insight and extensive research, found in every essay of *Choosing the Right College*. Among features *unique* to the ISI Guide are lists of the best professors on each campus. Similarly, we tell you the best *and* the worst departments. We pioneered the best/worst lists in the first edition of this guide, and our competition has tried to copy us. But essays written in haste by college students are no substitute for our well-researched book. *Choosing the Right College* is a blueprint to what's best — and what's worst — in American higher education. Used wisely, it will allow readers to decide which college to attend and how to get the most from their years on campus.

ISI and the Student Self-Reliance Project

Choosing the right college is only the first step to ensuring that you will get the most out of your college experience. Once you're on campus, you will face many more choices that will determine the future course of your life. This college guide forms the foundation of our Student Self-Reliance Project, a comprehensive program offering study guides, lectures, conferences, books, graduate fellowships, and other products and services that will help you get the education you deserve. You'll find more information about the Student Self-Reliance Project in the section entitled "Additional Services from ISI," at the end of this guide.

Because the conditions in American higher education are continually changing, we invite you to contribute your thoughts and opinions about the subjects discussed in this guide. You will find a response card in this book that asks you to tell us how helpful *Choosing the Right College* has been and to offer suggestions for improving future editions. Send e-mail to collegeguide@isi.org, or write to us at: ISI, P.O. Box 4431, Wilmington, DE 19807-0431. You can learn more about ISI's extensive educational programming and publications, including the Student Self-Reliance Project, by visiting our website at www.isi.org.

Amherst College

P.O. Box 5000
Amherst, MA 01002-5000
(413) 542-2000
www.amherst.edu

Total enrollment: 1,600
Undergraduates: 1,600
SAT ranges (Verbal/Math): 650-760 (V); 660-740 (M)
Applicants: 5,198
Accepted: 19%
Enrolled: 42%
Application deadline: December 31
Financial aid application deadline: February 1
Tuition: $26,059/$32,400
Core curriculum: No

Some Work for Immortality

Amherst College consistently ranks as one of the top five liberal arts colleges in the country, and thus competes with Ivy League schools for top high school students. Its student body is dedicated and studious and is rewarded with many fine teachers and departments. As a member of a coalition of western Massachusetts colleges, Amherst also offers benefits beyond its own curriculum and social events.

Despite its liberal arts reputation, Amherst has but one general education requirement and nothing approaching a core of mandatory classes. Into this gap recently have come groups of politicized courses: the English department, for example, makes one wonder whether Emily Dickinson is safe in her own hometown. But even the departments that are politicized in comparison to the rest of the school contain good teachers and enough good courses to provide ways around the ideological ones.

The college's administration, though far from traditional in its policies, is fair, and it does not seem likely that Amherst will soon become outlandishly politicized. As long as the college can justly claim that its reputation is still deserved, it will be an excellent choice.

In recent years tuition at Amherst has increased steadily, but college officials say they have balanced costs by giving more financial aid to students. Nevertheless, the rate of tuition increases has outstripped that of many of its elite counterparts and the college is one of only thirty-five in the nation at which tuition and fees for four years exceed $100,000.

Academic Life: One-Hit Wonders

Only one class is required at Amherst, and it doesn't have a name. All students must take a freshman seminar, but twenty of them are offered each year, and the content is left up to the professors who teach them. No college-wide system sets the topics for these seminars. So, not only are students not guaranteed an introduction to Western thought, they aren't even guaranteed basic skills that are required for the rest of their courses.

The remainder of Amherst's general requirements are a total of thirty-one other courses — any courses, any subjects.

Departments have the same lack of structure with regard to the requirements for their majors. In most cases, only one or two courses are designated as required. The remaining seven to nine are chosen by the student; just about any course in the department will count. "The students get no pressure to take certain things, but they also get no guidance," a professor says. That's a little like a basketball coach saying of his team, "Well, we're short, but we're also slow."

It should be said, however, that many of the upper-level courses are designed so as to require the more general introductory courses. "If you have any goals, you're directed to a very integrated system of requirements," says one professor. "The advisors push students into these harder things." This system works as well as it does because of the serious academic attitude of the students. According to a professor, most Amherst students are very ambitious. "Everybody comes in taking math and languages. Kids come in with a serious program. Because of the reputation, [Amherst] attracts the extraordinary: they're imaginative, energetic." A quarter of students choose to double major and a small fraction actually triple major.

They are taught by these outstanding professors: Richard Fink and David Hansen in chemistry; Robert Hilborn in physics; Paul Ewald in biology; Walter Nicholson, Ralph Beals, Frank Westhoff, and Geoffrey Woglom in economics; William Pritchard, David Sofield, Allen Guttmann, and Richard Cody in English; N. Gordon Levin, Jr., in history; Rebecca Sinos, Frederick Griffiths, and Peter Marshall in classics; Antonio Benitez-Rojo, James Maraniss, and Ilan Stavans in Spanish; and Ronald Tiersky, William Taubman, and Hadley Arkes in political science.

Since all Amherst students are undergraduates, opportunities abound for student/teacher interaction. With only nine students per faculty member, the average class size is twenty-two, and only 7 percent of courses exceed fifty students. A new program at Amherst extends freshman orientation by footing the bill for small student groups who want to take their professors out to dinner.

The small size of the college (about 1,600 undergraduates) has kept most departments from the worst excesses of political correctness and multiculturalism, one instructor says. "Here, they're forced to deal with real people, and we have more cordial relationships. The chances of getting a slug are quite small. There aren't that many gut courses, and even the gut courses are pretty good." These "gut courses" are scattered race and gender courses that are still offered, as this professor notes, for an easy A, padding the transcript but not likely challenging the intellect with any rigorous or even valid content.

The school also provides tutoring programs, reading and study skills classes, and supplemental precalculus course. Full-time writing, quantitative skills, and English-as-a-second-language counselors are also available at no charge.

The natural science departments (biology, chemistry, physics, and geology) are widely praised for both teaching and research. For example, Sandra L. Burkett, an assistant professor of chemistry, recently left a tenure-track post at MIT in favor of a job at Amherst. Biology majors in the Honors Program devote about half of their academic effort during the senior year to research, and the resulting thesis is often the basis of their first scientific publication.

Smaller humanities departments, namely, philosophy, fine arts, and Spanish, are also excellent in terms of teaching. One professor adds the classics department to that list, calling it "the best kept secret" at Amherst.

Of the larger departments in humanities and social sciences, economics may be the best. "They tend to be immune to a lot of the vulnerability that other departments have" in giving in to politicization, a professor says. A student points out that, at the very least, "there are no gender studies courses in economics," as there are in many other departments, including ones where they would not be expected. Enrollment in economics has recently overtaken that of English and political science despite the requirement of additional math and statistics courses for majors. Several social science departments have joined economics in demanding tougher quantitative courses, and while "students don't love the stiffer requirements," they are still enrolling in large numbers, a professor says.

History and English have historically been Amherst's strongest, but it appears that past reputation alone is not enough to carry these departments. One professor says history is "probably not as strong" as it used to be. The outstanding professors in both English and history are senior faculty whose commitment to teaching excellence has earned them the respect of colleagues and students, regardless of political affiliation and ideology. The same cannot be said for many of the newer faculty members, the professor says.

Indeed the department seems to be bending over backwards to be perceived as trendy. The English department boasts among its faculty interests feminist criticism, American Indian literature, and sports history. "If we were still teaching English literature the way we did in '64, we'd be the living dead," then-chairman of the English department Kim Townsend told the *Chronicle of Higher Education*.

A noteworthy course offering in English is the seminar "Marxism and Psychoanalysis," which promises to "assess the possibilities and limits of materialist and psychoanalytic criticisms" by studying Marx and Freud, who according to the course description "revolutionized the interpretation of art and literature."

Marxism is also emphasized in the political science department. For example, the course description for "Taking Marx Seriously" begins "Should Marx be given yet another chance?" Perhaps of more concern, the department's seminar on contemporary capitalism is taught by the same professor. Other odd courses offered by the department include "Political Theory and 'the God Problem,'" "Representing Domestic Violence," and "Authority and Sexuality." Political science has also traditionally been one of the most popular majors at Amherst; however, both its popularity and the quality of its teaching have suffered from politicization and a tendency toward deconstructionism.

But this department is faring far better than one that recently split from it, the department of law, jurisprudence, and social thought (LJST). Though independent, LJST still draws heavily on the political science department for professors, students, and courses. Its courses often center around "critical legal theory," the academic term for a deconstructionist view of politics. A student describes it as "a warped and twisted view of political science." Many of the department's faculty are currently on leave, and an unusually high number of those present are visiting professors from other schools.

LJST courses include some with fairly politicized titles: "Law's Madness," "Re-Imagining Law: Feminist Interpretations," and "Race, Place, and the Law." But the department also offers the most popular course in Amherst's history: "Murder." About three hundred students sign up for the course, taught by Professor Austin Sarat, one of the founders of LJST. The course's reading list includes *The Brothers Karamazov, In Cold Blood, Macbeth,* and works by Primo Levi, Hannah Arendt, Agatha Christie, and Albert Camus. "The strategy is, give them a hook — the hook is murder," Sarat told the *New York Times.* "But this is also a way to teach them the great books and moral reasoning." However, course material also includes Michel Foucault, the Marquis de Sade, and popular films like *Pulp Fiction, Natural Born Killers,* and *Psycho,* not to mention screenings of *Geraldo* and Snoop Doggy Dogg videos. The course is rigorous, at least; students say Sarat is a notoriously difficult grader.

The most ideologically driven department at Amherst is women and gender studies (WGS), which, according to one professor, is the only department where "you lose IQ points." It describes itself as "an interdisciplinary exploration of the creation, meaning, function, and perpetuation of gender in human societies." Thus while WGS has its own faculty, it also borrows classes from English, political science, history, psychology, anthropology, and other departments. Cross-listed courses are exceptionally common at Amherst, and, according to some on campus, this practice has encouraged the spread of politicization across the curriculum. "[You have] difficulty finding courses not dealing with race or gender," a student says.

Political Atmosphere: Statements to the Contrary

Amherst's administration tends to give in, at least on smaller issues, to a small group of radical student and faculty activists whose voices seem louder than their actual numbers would predict. Students note that the administration leaves up to student government quite a few important decisions about funding, speakers, activities, and some disciplinary matters. "The administration doesn't step in on any side," says one student. "They leave policing up to student government." Student government consists of a variety of boards, councils, and "subcommittees," with most student members serving in more than one area. The result is a confused sort of decision making, where the personal and political prejudices of the representatives — rather than some sort of overarching vision for the college — hold sway.

For example, Amherst officially recognizes and funds a variety of student publications, all of them with a liberal political point of view. The use or propriety of these funds is rarely questioned. However, the *Amherst Spectator,* the conservative alternative paper (and a rather mildly conservative one at that), was stripped of its funding by the Senate Funding Committee for "not promoting a nice atmosphere" on campus. In addition, its magazines were stolen and its editors were threatened with violence. In 1999, the redesigned *Spectator* became a primarily libertarian magazine focusing on humor.

However, on some bigger issues, some feel that the administration is getting more assertive; that is, the administration is tough when it wants to be, as well as fair-minded. "The president and the dean see through some of this [political correctness]," a professor says. In 1997 the administration canceled its Early Orientation program, which brought incoming students from targeted minority groups to campus early for a series of consciousness-raising and indoctrination sessions. Despite loud protests from some campus radicals, the administration stood firm, despite a one-year boycott of the orientation festivities by the Black Student Union and Asian Students Association.

At the same time, Amherst still sponsors the "Student of Color Open House," a weekend in the fall geared toward prospective minority applicants. The school also maintains an African-American cultural dorm, an English-speaking Latino house, and an Asian house, as well as academic program houses for language study. Undergraduates seem to be highly sensitive to issues of race and gender. Consider this quotation, prominent in the college's viewbook: "I think minority students are comfortable here. Even those that have their problems with Amherst love their institution." Another student is quoted in the viewbook: "Some people who come here worry about 'selling out' — about forgetting where they came from. I've seen that you can socialize with all kinds of people and learn from them without selling out." Obviously, official Amherst gives much attention to race differences, or at least wants to be seen as doing so.

But tensions remain. According to the *Chronicle of Higher Education,* in November 2000 a group of students who claimed they felt marginalized for their race, sexual orientation, or personal convictions held a two-day sit-in at the annex of the dining hall. By taking over the area where athletes usually gather, they hoped to show solidarity and "cultivate unity."

It is a safe assumption, however, that the average Amherst student spends little time worrying over these issues. There is, first of all, the amount of concentration needed for students to handle the academic workload they've taken on. Students also report that the majority of their fellows view political correctness as a nuisance, not as a way of life or as anything they will take with them when they leave college. It is also apparent, however, that the college expects students to speak and act in a politically correct manner while they are enrolled.

The college does not have an official speech code, but the catalogue does contain something called the "Statement of Respect for Persons." It reads: "Respect for the rights, dignity and integrity of others is essential for the well-being of the community. Actions by any person which do not reflect such respect for others are damaging to each member of the community and hence damaging to Amherst College. Each member of the community should be free from interference, intimidation, or disparagement in the work place, the classroom and the social, recreational, and residential environment." According to some on campus, the statement is often used like a speech code, and a rather vague one at that.

However, balancing the "Respect" statement is a "Statement of Freedom of Expression and Dissent" begins by stating: "Amherst College prizes and defends freedom of speech and dissent. It affirms the right of teachers and students to teach and learn, free from coercive force and intimidation and subject only to the constraints of reasoned discourse and peaceful conduct. It also recognizes that such freedoms and rights entail responsibility for one's actions. Thus the College assures and protects the rights of its members to express their views so long as there is neither use nor threat of force nor interference with the rights of others to express their views." A professor reports that while there have been cases of students disciplined for speech outside of the classroom, such cases are now rare.

Student Life: Because I Could Not Stop for Socializing . . .

Amherst is not only in a college town, but in a college region, as it were. West-central Massachusetts is home to the Five Colleges Consortium (Amherst, Smith College, Mount Holyoke College, Hampshire College, and the University of Massachusetts–Amherst), whose members cooperate both academically and socially. This gives Amherst students a chance to deal with peers on other campuses and provides more cultural opportunities than any one of the colleges would be able to offer alone. About half of Amherst students take a five-college class at some point.

Housing is guaranteed for all four years of a student's college career, and 98 percent of students live on campus. Thirty-three residence halls are available (most are coed, but single-sex floors are available), along with what the college calls "former fraternity houses." The college abolished on-campus fraternities in 1984, but several underground groups are still active. A substance-free "Wellness Quarter" is available. Residences are grouped into units called "demes" for the purpose of planning social events and generally getting to know the students in other dorms.

The college offers almost one hundred student groups, spanning a variety of religious, international, and ethnic interests. These include Students of Mixed Heritage and Culture, the teetotaler social club called Alternatives at Amherst, and the Hungry Newt Coffeehouse, a student-run cooperative whose name has nothing to do with the former speaker of the House of Representatives. About 15 percent of the students are members of at least one singing group — a very high percentage. And a group known as The Diversity Educators is dedicated to sponsoring workshops on race in the dorms by using "polarity" and "identity" exercises.

Amherst competes in twenty-seven intercollegiate sports at the NCAA Division III level. In recent years there has been some controversy regarding the academic qualifications of the student-athletes. There are also ten club sports. The college reports that close to 80 percent of the student body participates in club athletics or its intramural program. Workout equipment and a new swimming pool are available for more casual recreation. However, western Massachusetts also offers excellent chances for hiking, canoeing, and skiing.

The college is relatively safe, but students are still appreciative of an excellent and helpful campus security squad. Officers and trained student workers will meet any requests for a safety escort at night.

The University of Arizona

Office of Admissions
P.O. Box 28826
Tucson, AZ 85721-8826
(520) 621-3237
www.arizona.edu

Total enrollment: 34,488
Undergraduates: 26,404
SAT ranges (Verbal/Math): 480-600 (V); 490-610 (M)

Applicants: 17,687
Accepted: 84%
Enrolled: 36%
Application deadline: April 1
Financial aid application deadline: March 1
Tuition: resident: $2,348/$8,236; non-resident: $9,804/$15,692
Core curriculum: No

Raising Arizona

In the last decade, enrollment at Arizona has dramatically increased, in part because of demographic trends which have seen the nation's population move to the South and West. But students have also come because the university has deliberately embarked on a program of expansion and development that has gained it impressive national rankings in both academic publications and more popular measures such as *U.S. News and World Report*'s annual rankings of colleges and universities. It seems that Arizona has been "discovered" by the nation, and many have discovered that one can get a fine and reasonably priced college education there.

The University of Arizona was founded in 1885, and its history reflects some of the "Wild West" quality one might associate with that time. The school may be the only land-grant university that was founded without having any land actually granted to it. The university was appropriated $25,000 by the territorial legislature, but was expected to get the necessary land by appealing to the public-spiritedness of the citizens of Tucson. The citizenry was unmoved by these appeals, and it appeared that the $25,000 grant would have to be returned to the legislature. But at the last minute, two gamblers and a saloon keeper finally gave in and donated 40 acres of land at what was then the outskirts of town. Classes began in 1891, with six professors and thirty-two students in two colleges: Agriculture and Mines. Today, the university has more than 34,000 students and more than one thousand full-time faculty, with 131 programs of study spread over fourteen colleges and eight schools.

The size of Arizona has led to many of the problems associated with the modern multiversity: large class sizes, impersonal undergraduate instruction, and a lack of coherence or vision in the undergraduate programs. However, there are signs that many faculty at Arizona are aware of these problems and are taking steps to deal with them. But the administration, according to some professors, is not yet attuned to these difficulties and is still operating under the "bigger is better" paradigm. Given the science-and-technology focus that characterizes Arizona as well as most other state universities, one might expect programs in the liberal arts to be taking a back seat to the science and tech programs. However the humanities are alive and well here, and it is very possible to get a solid and well-rounded liberal education at Arizona.

Academic Life: Tier Park

The University of Arizona does not have a core curriculum, but the distribution requirements that stand in for a core are relatively strong. The faculty are abandoning the experimentalism and laissez-faire attitude that marked college curricula in the 1970s and '80s. All students are required to take courses in the "University-Wide General Education Structure." These courses are broken down into two tiers, the Tier I courses representing foundational areas such as composition and mathematics, and Tier II courses coming from the arts, sciences, and humanities. There is a writing requirement, and a foreign language is required of all students in the humanities. The overall seriousness of the general education requirement is reflected in the introductory statement to those requirements:

> General education programs provide breadth of knowledge as a balance and complement to the depth provided by the major. General education is designed to accomplish several goals: first, to afford students the opportunity to learn how different disciplines define, acquire and organize knowledge; second, to provide a basis for an examination of values; third, to develop analytic, synthetic, linguistic and computational skills useful for lifelong learning; and finally, to provide a common foundation for wide-ranging dialogue with peers on issues of significance. Taken together, the experiences of general education encourage the student to develop a critical and inquiring attitude, an appreciation of complexity and ambiguity, a tolerance for and empathy with persons of different backgrounds or values and a deepened sense of self. In short, the goal of the general education program is to prepare students to respond more fully and effectively to an increasingly complex world.

While there is a certain amount of "boilerplate" edu-speak jargon in this statement (e.g., the language about "dialogue," "tolerance and empathy," and "a deepened sense of self"), it actually stands out among similar statements from other colleges and universities in its concentration on skills and coherent bodies of knowledge.

According to students and faculty, the "theory" of the general education requirements in the above statement is fairly well expressed in the actual practice of the university. Most students, says one professor, come in with "little or no knowledge or sense of the liberal arts." However, in the course of taking their general education courses, many of them find their worldviews or lives changed. "I hear from students all the time who take our courses [in the humanities] and get hooked into what it means to read," the professor says. "They get a taste of literature or history and they want more," says another.

There is a Western civilization requirement at Arizona, though it is more loosely structured than some faculty would like. But all agree that in practice the system does its job: "The way the program is structured, it is all but impossible for a student to come through here and not get an exposure to the heritage of Western civilization," a professor says.

That exposure to Western civilization is counterbalanced by a non-Western requirement, and in taking the courses designed to fulfill this requirement students are most likely to be the targets of ideological indoctrination of some sort. The university requires that at least one course in a student's program focus on "issues of gender, race, class, ethnicity, or non-Western area studies." In practice, students will in all likelihood be treated to this in more than one class, since professors are encouraged to incorporate such issues into more "traditional" course material. Some departments provide more fertile ground for anti-Western animus than others; the English department is one of the leaders, with offerings such as "The Politics of Memory in Twentieth-Century Chicana/o Literatures."

But the most egregious example of ideology trumping education comes, perhaps unsurprisingly, from the department of Africana studies, in this offering for the Spring of 2001:

> AFAS 304A, "The Social Construction of Race: Whiteness." In constructing this course, the recognition of Whiteness/Blackness is not solely a reactionary response to challenges from persons/non-persons of color; it is also a reflection of the need to provide a narrative of Whiteness/Blackness that intends an understanding of the notion of Whiteness/Blackness as a racial category and the implications of this categorization and association. For example, naming Whiteness displaces it from the unmarked, unnamed status that is itself an effect of dominance. Within the particular disciplines of Anthropology and Ethnic Studies, Whiteness, Blackness and Race have come to be earnest subjects of study. Being White or Black in the 1990s, however, is far from straightforward. It is riddled with ambiguity and marked by a general sense of racial angst as to what it means to be White or Black.

This course description, beneath its dense jargon, has an ideological purport that would be intolerable if offered from another racial group or ideological perspective — even if one lets slide the semantic mess of "non-persons of color."

Luckily, those kinds of courses aren't at all popular. "Most students are going to be turned off" by a course such as that, a student says. "There are plenty of mainstream courses that will fulfill the non-Western requirement." And fortunately most undergraduates receive close attention from advisors when it comes to selecting their courses.

But the fact that courses such as Africana Studies 304A exist at all is a sign of a fracturing of the liberal arts curriculum. At Arizona, the administration's leadership, or lack thereof, is perhaps the cause of this. A common criticism voiced by faculty is the lack, at the administrative level, of an overarching vision or understanding of education. In their rush to expand programs and facilities, it is said, the university's administration has rushed after grants and other sources of money and treat education as a "product-oriented" corporate enterprise. It is seen by many faculty in the humanities as problematic that neither the president nor other top administrators have a background in the humanities. "The administration does not understand the nature and needs of the humanities programs," says a professor. "They can understand when someone wants to spend $20 million to build a new computer facility, but they don't get it if someone needs $20,000 to catalogue a collection of medieval manuscripts." Another faculty member put her criticism even more strongly: "The liberal arts have thrived and done well at Arizona in spite of, and not because of, anything the administration has done."

However, in the boom of fundraising and spending in the past decade, even the traditionally impoverished humanities programs have shared in the wealth. Professors and students alike praise the quality of the facilities. The library is fine, housing a collection of more than four million volumes. The university is building an Integrated Learning Center for freshmen. This will be organized along the lines of a residential college, where students will study and live in the same place, and, it is hoped, develop into a "learning community." Arizona has some excellent programs in the liberal arts: the departments of history, sociology, Russian, art, and classics have all received recognition both within and outside of the university. The departments of economics and philosophy also deserve special mention. Some of the best professors at Arizona include: Heiko Oberman, Richard Eaton, and Roger Nichols in history; Price V. Fishback and John Z. Drabicki in economics; and Lawrence Evers and Robert Houston in English.

The good side of being at a gigantic university is the opportunities for research and learning that smaller schools just can't match. The architecture program offers regular study tours abroad to study the architecture of the classical world. The foreign language departments offer numerous opportunities for students to study abroad. Several different programs allow undergraduates to participate in archaeological digs both in the U.S. and in other countries. Arizona is home to one of the world's best programs in astronomy, and undergraduates can work with leaders in that field at one of the world's best observatories.

Political Atmosphere: No Yelling "Fire" in a Crowded Classroom

Despite the forays into ideology represented by some courses, students and faculty both say that Arizona is a relatively unpoliticized campus — inside the classroom, at least. "I suppose the majority of the faculty here are 'left-leaning,'" says one professor, "but it doesn't get manifested in the classroom." The use of classroom podiums as bully pulpits is rare; students and faculty both find the atmosphere at Arizona to be very open and conducive to genuine debate and discussion. "You have to remember that Arizona is a fairly conservative state, so frequently the students are more conservative than the faculty," a recent graduate says. "But I always found my professors to welcome honest debate and to give a hearing to viewpoints other than their own."

Typically, freshmen courses are very large and are taught once a week by a professor, with other meetings throughout the week in smaller groups led by graduate students. "You can either get really lucky and have a great graduate student, or you can be unlucky like me and get a South American feminist Marxist," says one former student. Honors courses offer some relief: They have smaller course sections. Another student recommends taking introductory courses like calculus at an area community college in order to avoid the crush.

Outside the classroom, students tend to be politically active and liberal. One student who is the former — but not the latter — says it seems that every week is "awareness week" for some cause or another. "It's a 'protest du jour' type of place," the student says. Campus activism tends toward environmental issues, but there are other topics as well.

Arizona students, for example, were active participants in the recent wave of anti-sweatshop demonstrations. Students Against Sweatshops attempted to force the administration to leave the more moderate Fair Labor Association in favor of the radical Workers' Rights Consortium. In an effort to force the administration's hand, eight students blocked access to the main administration building by locking themselves to the doors. President Peter Likins, to his credit, was unmoved and unimpressed. "There is absolutely no way that demonstrating on campus will force me to leave the FLA," he was quoted as saying.

As at many other schools, there is a very active gay, lesbian, and bisexual community. The Committee on Lesbian, Gay, & Bisexual Studies offers a number of cross-listed courses, including "History of Modern Sexualities" and "Lesbian Paradigms." The course description for "Art as Social Practice: Critical Art Practice in the Public Sphere" reads like this:

In the prevailing atmosphere of the disenfranchisement of critical interventionist art practices in the U.S., this course argues for a critical practice that is based on a socio-economic analysis of societal processes but is inclusive of pleasure and desire as well. It aims to create an awareness of different sites in today's United States where critical art practice is taking place. Areas we will consider are gender, queer politics, and race.

There was also a film series called "Lesbian Looks," which recently included such contemporary classics as *Below the Belt*, "an engrossing short film in which two 17-year-old girls explore their budding relationship in and out of the boxing ring." It isn't the only film in the series that focuses on teenagers.

Tucson, at least, is an anomaly in the state's political atmosphere. As one student columnist lamented in the *Arizona Daily Wildcat,* "I found it incredibly frustrating to be a liberal in Arizona this fall. We live in a rare liberal area in a very conservative state. . . . Not so much here in Tucson, but the big smelly city to the north [Phoenix] is teaming [sic] with wealthy conservatives."

Student Life: Just Deserts

The University of Arizona is located in the Sonoran Desert, one of the most picturesque places in the country. Nestled among mountains in a climate which boasts more than three hundred days of sunshine a year, it seems a specially blessed realm. Tucson has grown very rapidly in recent years, emerging to become what is in essence a prosperous college town. There is something for every kind of student. More bohemian types will enjoy the many coffeehouses and shops surrounding campus. There is also a vibrant local music and underground art scene. Mexico is very close, and both students and locals take advantage of this fact by making shopping runs to the border. Both Tucson and the university also host a number of cultural events. And the weather makes outdoor activities attractive year-round.

Then there is the campus, which is as almost as beautiful as its natural surroundings. Built in the classical southwestern style, the buildings are stunning. Students typically congregate on the Mall, an oasis of green grass surrounded by the student union, administration buildings, and the library. The Mall is also the site of the annual Spring Fling, the largest student-run carnival in the country.

Arizona has one of the most expansive Greek systems in the country, with not just older, established houses, but also minority fraternities. For those not attracted to the Greek life, the dorms offer, according to one student, a genuine sense of community — and at Arizona, even the residence hall architecture is beautiful. The dorms also offer an array of living options. There are several all-female and all-male dorms, as well as several honors dorms. For these there are visitation hours, though one former student reports that they are not strictly enforced. The coed dorms maintain separate bathrooms for men and women. Each room has an Ethernet connection.

Except for burglaries and car thefts, of which there were 128 and 37, respectively, in 1999, the Arizona campus is a pretty safe place to be. Major crimes like assault and robbery are comparatively rare (thirteen and eight, respectively, in 1999), but they do happen.

It is reportedly very easy to start your own club at Arizona, but that probably won't be necessary. There is likely an organization that already suits any interest, hobby, or cause you could come up with. There are also many philanthropic organizations and honorary societies.

The Wildcats' athletic teams inspire passion among the student body, particularly the basketball team — which is almost always a contender for the national title — but also the football squad. As might be expected, Arizona maintains a huge rivalry with Arizona State. Arizona also has excellent recreational and intramural facilities.

The size of the school can be a drawback, but some attention is being given to helping students develop "mentoring" relationships with faculty outside the classroom. One effort in this direction is the establishment of "freshman colloquia," in which ten to twelve freshman meet rather informally with a professor, often to discuss his or her current scholarship or research. There are also programs that attempt to bring students and professors together for meals and the like. But at a large university, ultimately the student must be proactive in forming relationships and finding a "niche" for himself. There are simply too many people for anyone to keep track of. "The biggest problem at a place like this," says one professor, "is that it's too big for relationships between faculty and students to develop naturally. Students have to take the initiative. All the faculty I know are open to their students, but when you have 300 of them in a lecture, you just can't seek them out."

Auburn University

Office of Admissions
202 Martin Hall
Auburn, AL 36849-5145
(334) 844-4000
www.auburn.edu

Total enrollment: 21,860
Undergraduates: 19,050
SAT ranges (Verbal/Math): 480-590 (V); 500-600 (M)
Applicants: 11,678
Accepted: 85%
Enrolled: 39%
Application deadline: August 1
Financial aid application deadline: April 15
Tuition: resident: $3,154/$7,794; non-resident: $9,254/$13,894
Core curriculum: Yes

Throwback

Steeped in tradition, Auburn University is also undergoing a lot of change. In many ways, it's a throwback to an earlier American campus: football is king, the Greeks rule the social scene, and radical political activism is next to nil among the mostly apolitical student body. But at the same time, the campus is changing: enrollment is at record levels, and the university is trying to become nationally recognized by drawing on its roots as a public, land-grant institution. This is difficult in Alabama universities, who occasionally suffer from budget cuts as the state legislature tries to address more pressing needs. Some of the academic buildings are in disrepair, some departments are underfunded, and low faculty pay has caused a relatively high turnover.

But compared with other colleges, Auburn's atmosphere is refreshing. When men open doors for women, it's appreciated — not deemed "sexist" and grist for the mill in women's studies classes. "It's a conservative school," says one instructor. "It's just a very Christian, very professional atmosphere. It's dressier than a normal university campus. The girls seem more modest. It just seems cut out of the past, in the good sense."

Auburn administrators are attempting to have the college distinguish itself by reemphasizing the preprofessional departments focused on the practical needs of the state of Alabama. Examples of areas receiving heightened attention include forestry, fisheries and allied aquaculture, information technology, and poultry science. To save money, the university has chopped some programs and merged departments, particularly in the liberal arts, which leaves some professors questioning the university's commitment to a well-rounded education. Nonetheless, Auburn does have a core curriculum, which insures that all students are at least exposed to areas other than chicken reproduction and fish migration patterns.

The Methodist church opened the college in 1859 as the East Alabama Male College but had to close it two years later with the outbreak of the Civil War. It reopened in 1866 in financial shambles. In 1872, the Methodists transferred control to the state of Alabama, making it the first land-grant college in the South to be established apart from the state university. Several name changes later, the school became Auburn University.

Academic Life: Core All Around

Auburn offers undergraduate degrees in more than 130 areas, including many in highly specialized fields. While the university thankfully has a core curriculum that exposes each student to the liberal arts, some professors say that the university's emphasis on the liberal arts has lessened in recent years as the university has tried to distinguish itself in other areas. If true, that would be a lamentable development.

15

Academically, the university is divided into eight colleges (agriculture, architecture, business, education, engineering, liberal arts, science and math, and veterinary medicine) and four schools (forestry, human sciences, nursing, and pharmacy).

All undergraduates, regardless of major, must fulfill the requirements of Auburn's core curriculum. Unlike elsewhere, Auburn's core curriculum is not under attack, and faculty and administrators tend to agree that there is a common body of knowledge worth teaching. University literature proudly proclaims that the core curriculum not only forms the foundation for professional and career programs but also signals Auburn's "traditional commitment to the enhancement of students' personal and intellectual growth and the development of a more responsible citizenry."

To fulfill the requirements of what Auburn calls its core curriculum, students must take some specific courses and have a very limited choice in selecting others. The required courses all students take are two freshman writing courses and two "Great Books" literature courses. The first Great Books course emphasizes ancient, medieval, and Renaissance literature, and the second considers literature from the seventeenth to twentieth centuries. Both involve intensive writing. In addition, students select one of three two-course history sequences (world history, technology and civilization, or "the human odyssey," which focuses on discovery and invention); two science courses (sequences — with labs — in biology, chemistry, geology, physics); a math course; a philosophy course (either logic or ethics); one of four social science courses (in anthropology, geography, psychology, or sociology) and another social science course in either economics or political economy; and a fine arts course.

Just because there's a core curriculum doesn't mean the university is free of political bias in the classroom. Some students single out one of the social science courses, Society and Culture (U101), as one in which sociology professors occasionally harp on their personal political beliefs having to do with the environment, etc. But few core courses suffer from heavy bias. "There are good teachers and bad teachers," says one professor. "It's still possible to get a really good education at Auburn if you pick and choose."

Another professor says that older faculty members tend to be at least fair-minded, while younger faculty tend to be more prone to spouting politically correct offerings in the classroom and not giving students a fair shake. "They're hiring new, younger faculty members, and they bring the virus with them," he says. "But it's moving in the opposite way among students. The students are less politically correct, though they might be forced to mouth the words. I think there's a very healthy reaction to the lies. There are less of the official lies here than other places."

Like just about everywhere, Auburn does have a women's studies curriculum that offers a few political-sounding courses focusing on "gender roles," human sexuality, and "the anthropology of gender." But these types of influences are far less than elsewhere.

There are several truly excellent departments at Auburn, but most are outside of the traditional liberal arts areas; preprofessional programs such as veterinary medicine, agriculture, forestry, and engineering are the strongest on campus.

The shining star of Auburn's social science offerings is its department of economics, which is based in the university's College of Business. The department boasts solid credentials and first-rate professors — all of whom have sterling free-market orientations. The department works in conjunction with the Ludwig von Mises Institute to run reading groups and other programs and provides students with solid foundations in current economic thinking. "If you're market oriented, you want to go to the economics department," one professor said.

The Ludwig von Mises Institute, one of the intellectual highlights at Auburn, is a nationally known educational and scholarly center affiliated with the university's economics department. Named for an Austrian thinker who demonstrated the counterproductive nature of government intervention into the economy, the institute defends free markets, private property rights, and sound monetary policies. It publishes journals and books, awards fellowships, runs seminars and conferences, and makes the public case for limited government. Students interested in free markets and free societies would be advised to look into the institute's programs, as they provide excellent opportunities to learn from some of this country's top economists and political theorists. The institute rolls out the red carpet for interested students.

In addition to economics, the history and philosophy departments are regarded among the strongest, as is the college of engineering. Business is a popular major, though some faculty deride its rampant preprofessionalism. Though these aren't classes, interested students can attend sessions on what to wear to an interview or which utensils to use at dinner — a session that some on campus deride as "The Right Fork."

Some professors to seek out at Auburn include Richard Ault, Roger Garrison, David Kaserman, and Robert Ekelund, Jr., in economics; Rafe Blaufarb in history; Henry Kinnucan in agricultural economics; James Barth in finance; and Susan Fillippeli in the communication department.

The university's honors program, which selects about two hundred freshmen to participate each year, is recognized as one of the university's outstanding programs. The classes are small and designed to provide deep discussions with fellow students and faculty. The program comes with perks: honors students live in separate residence halls, have priority at registration and, in their final semesters at Auburn, have their own library carrels.

In recent years, the university has been trying to reach national prominence by bolstering several of its research programs, particularly in science and technical areas. Under a new "Peaks of Excellence" program developed in 1999, Auburn has dedicated millions of dollars for new research initiatives in transportation, information technology, detection and food safety, biological sciences, fisheries and allied aquaculture, poultry science, and forestry and wildlife sciences. However, many liberal arts faculty feel that the university's emphasis on research in these areas detracts from a liberal arts education. "I would like to see us produce more well-rounded kinds of students," said one professor. "A student who wants a technical education in computers or business would survive here, but they would also survive at the DeVry Institute."

The same professor laments that academics on campus often must compete with other interests. "If we're going to look at the way that football is valued here, it's valued higher than academics, by the alumni, the administration, and everybody else. It's just not very encouraging. It is generally a party school, with athletics emphasized and academics downplayed and grade inflation like you wouldn't believe."

Political Atmosphere: Choices That Shouldn't Have to Be Made

Politically, Auburn is best described as pleasant and noncontroversial. There are virtually no protests, no visible displays of angst, no significant social movements sprouting heads. "There are very few communists here," jokes one student. There are few protests to speak of and the campus atmosphere is quite traditional; students tend to be very polite and friendly, and dress is "preppy," according to one student.

The most visible political debates really don't have an ideological tenor. The most controversial has been the role of Auburn's board of trustees, which some say meddles in the university to too great an extent.

The political situation in the state of Alabama unfortunately tends to play a role in the success of the university in two main ways: first, the trustees are political appointments by the governor and have often been a political hot potato. Second, university administrators believe they do not have the resources they need from the state legislature to sufficiently improve academics. Support for elementary and secondary education in Alabama is often pitted against university funding, and Auburn and the other public universities generally lose. In a March 2000 address, for example, the university president argued against pay increases for elementary school teachers in favor of a modest funding increase for Auburn.

In 2000, much to the chagrin of many professors, the board of trustees instituted what it termed a "forgiveness" policy: an Auburn student may now remove up to three failing grades from his or her grade point average. Before the vote, Auburn president William Muse said the university should "balance the need to protect the academic reputation of the institution with the desire to provide students with some limited means to recover from a bad academic experience." The institution's academic reputation lost.

Like any large university, Auburn attracts the big-name, high-dollar stars from the lecture circuit, such as Maya Angelou, who spoke in April 2000.

Auburn also has separate programs for minority students, which some say serves to keep the races segregated rather than bringing students together. Some of the programs border on the patronizing, such as the Minority Engineering Program, which provides "academic support services to entering minority engineering students," as well as remedial tutoring and mentoring for minorities, according to university literature. The director of the program crows about how the college of engineering retains 2 percentage points more minorities than the university as a whole. Auburn also has an active Office of Multicultural Affairs. Black History Month in February is also a big deal, with a series of lectures and concerts on themes of "diversity," civil rights, and racism. In 2000, the headline Black History Month speaker was hardly a radical activist, but rather basketball great Kareem Abdul-Jabbar, who spoke on the theme of his book, *Profiles in Black Courage,* and signed copies of his new book, *A Season on the Reservation: My Sojourn with the White Mountain Apache.*

Student Life: Sweet Home . . . Auburn

Auburn is the sort of place where generations of families go to, where football runs deep in the blood, and where you wouldn't be caught dead wearing a T-shirt that says "Alabama." (Actually, if you wore one, you might be caught dead.) While the university is trying to diversify itself, Auburn is still a place where college ties run in the family. (Auburn sent out a press release in August 2000 touting a South Carolina family that was graduating its sixteenth family member from Auburn. "We have two more darling granddaughters that I'm sure will go to school here at Auburn one day," the family's matriarch said.)

Students say life at Auburn is serene and collegial. In this state, you're either an Auburn fan or an Alabama fan. There is no middle ground. "My family would have disowned me if I went to Alabama," joked one engineering major.

Football is the major focus of energy in the fall, culminating with the yearly showdown with Alabama, or perhaps a bowl game. Even in the winter and spring, more attention is paid to football recruiting than to basketball.

While fraternities and sororities dominate campus life, there have been some well-publicized incidents of hazing. One Auburn freshman sued the local Kappa Alpha fraternity a few years ago, claiming, among other things, that he had been beaten and forced to jump into a ditch filled with garbage, water, vomit, and human waste. The Alabama Supreme Court ruled in 1998 that the student had no grounds to sue, because he chose to endure the treatment, but the university refused to recognize the local chapter. About half of undergraduates belong to the Greek system, which holds parties on weekends that are popular with many students. Some fraternities have banned alcohol and claim many religious, nondrinking students as members.

Students who live on campus can choose from a variety of options ranging from standard dormitory rooms to furnished, air-conditioned, two-bedroom apartments. There are many single-sex residence halls for women, but none for men. In coed dorms men and women are housed in separate wings or on alternating floors. Visitation hours end at midnight for both sexes.

Auburn offers hundreds of student clubs. There are at least twenty-six different religious organizations — mostly Christian prayer groups and fellowships, but also a Jewish group and Muslim Association.

There are also groups for many different interests, including more obscure ones like amateur radio, equestrian sports, and astronomy. The College Republicans are said to be very active.

Students and professors describe the town of Auburn as a university town that reflects the university's atmosphere. The crime rate on campus is much lower than the surrounding community, which in turn is much lower than national rates. "It's a socially conservative town. It's very church oriented. You see them on every block," says one professor. "There are a lot of very active student Christian organizations, and the Republicans are very active. If a conservative wants to find kindred spirits, there are all sorts of places on campus."

Some students say there's little to do in Auburn, but others claim the town is perfectly suited for study, research, dining, and relaxation. It offers many historical sites and excellent restaurants. Take, for example, the Auburn Chapel, where the first secessionist meeting in the Deep South took place in 1851. Elsewhere in town are barbecue restaurants, Southern restaurants, European-style pubs, and barbers who sprinkle their conversation with talk of moonshine. Ten minutes from Auburn is Chewacla State Park, which has a quiet lake and relaxing picnic spots. It's a local favorite for swimming and hiking.

Bates College

Office of Admissions
Lewiston, ME 04240
(207) 786-6000
www.bates.edu

Total enrollment: 1,706
Undergraduates: 1,706
SAT ranges (Verbal/Math): 620-710 (V); 630-700 (M)

Applicants: 4,240
Admitted: 29 percent
Enrolled: 38 percent
Application deadline: January 15
Financial aid application deadline: February 10
Tuition: $32,650 (comprehensive fee)
Core curriculum: No

The Price of Change

The early history of Bates College is auspicious, even admirable. Founded in 1855 by Freewill Baptists, the school was a center of the abolition movement and admitted women and minorities from its beginning, much like its older Freewill Baptist counterpart, Hillsdale College in Michigan. It did not achieve the financial independence reached by Colby, Bowdoin, and other New England schools for many years, and even today, one faculty member notes, Bates needs to increase its endowment so that it can become less dependent on its high tuition for paying the bills. Nevertheless, the college has become increasingly selective in the past couple of decades. Today it admits 29 percent of those who apply, and 38 percent of those admitted enroll. These are better rates than those achieved at many better-known national universities.

Overall, though, Bates has become less admirable in recent years. Though its 1,700 students can indeed get a very good liberal arts education, they must be aware that some majors and programs are overtly politicized. They must also cope with an administration bent on politicizing both the social life and the curriculum in its effort to win the approval of the liberal forces that now pass judgment on the suitability of colleges. It often seems that a small college wanting to rise in the popular rankings must embrace political correctness, and Bates has fallen into that trap.

While the school's history isn't as illustrious as that of nearby schools like Colby and Bowdoin, Bates does have some good things going for it. Many of these positive aspects are now overshadowed by the multicultural cudgel wielded by its president, but the school has maintained a genuine sense of community and pride. Those considering Bates should also consider the long Maine winter, which is counterbalanced by the scenic beauty of the season. If you don't like the outdoors, you might do better to stay in Boston or travel farther south. And if you don't want to be subject to a good bit of politically correct propaganda, you will find better options. The students don't always pay attention to the PC elements, but they're as much a part of this Maine scene as the lobsters, which certainly leave a better taste in the mouth.

Academic Life: The Wrong Places

It is possible to get a rounded liberal arts education at Bates, but the school's distribution requirements don't guarantee it. These requirements do not compose a true core curriculum; rather, they ask students to take courses within several broad divisions. Students must take any three courses in the physical sciences, two of which are a department-designated set; any three courses in the social sciences, two of which are a set; any five courses from at least two humanities, including history, three of which form a coherent cluster; and one course in which "understanding and use of quantitative techniques are essential."

In addition to these requirements, Bates students must take either two 10-week physical education courses or participate in intercollegiate or club athletics.

An unusual feature of the Bates calendar is a short-term unit offered at the end of spring term in late April. Lasting five weeks, these classes are often offbeat, obscure, and even silly. Courses in the past have included "Philosophy and *Star Trek*," "The Grail Tale: An Annotated Hypertext Version" (including Monty Python's version, of course), and "Representations of Women in Mexican Nationalism."

The most popular majors do not include philosophy or *Star Trek*, however. They are psychology, biology, English, and political science. The number of Bates students who major in biology and the life sciences is almost twice the national average for a school its size, and the number of multi/interdisciplinary studies majors is about two-and-a-half times the national average. Bates offers no business degrees or other professional majors except for education, in which 4.5 percent of students major.

The better departments at Bates are political science, English, psychology, and biology, as well as the sciences in general. Outstanding professors include Douglas Hodgkin in political science and John Cole in history. The philosophy department also features some excellent scholars and teachers, such as David Kolb and Mark Okrent.

Because Bates is not a university, there are no concerns here about courses being taught by graduate TAs — all classes are taught by faculty members. The student/teacher ratio is an excellent ten to one.

That certain departments are politicized can be surmised simply on the basis of their names. According to one professor, "the interdisciplinary programs in women's studies, African-American studies, and American cultural studies are least representative of a spectrum of views." However, this professor adds that "no department is visibly political as an advocacy group in its curriculum or activities. Although departments such as English, sociology, and political science exhibit some political tendencies, each has faculty and course offerings with more traditional orientations."

A close study of course offerings in selected humanities departments reveals an English department that does offer some typically politicized courses, although it is not as fad-bitten as some at other liberal arts colleges or large universities. Freshmen are required to take two 100-level courses during their initial year, and they may select from "Colloquia in Literature" offerings, which are denoted in the catalogue as "especially appropriate for first-year students." Sections are limited to twenty students, and recent topics have included "Reading 'Race' and Ethnicity in American Fiction," "Critical Theory," and "The African-American Novel." Most of the truly odd offerings, though, are found among the short-term classes. These are a telling measure of the professors, because faculty frequently use the opportunity afforded by these succinct springtime classes to teach subjects in which they are particularly interested. Since it appears that some of these classes would scarcely contain enough legitimate material to fill even a shortened class schedule, a close perusal of these courses in every department is always a good idea. In English, for example, they include "Cultural Production and Social Context, Jamaica," "Victorian Womanhood," and "Feminist Literary Criticism."

The history department has a fairly politicized list of offerings as well as a large number of courses (fifteen!) on Asian history — unusually large for a small liberal arts college in Maine. Included among the former are "The Social History of the Civil War," "American Protest in the Twentieth Century," African American History," "Native American History: Contact to Renewal," "Film, Food, and Baseball in Cuba," "The Several Sides of the Cold War," "Colony, Nation, and Diaspora: Cuba, Puerto Rico, and the Dominican Republic." Among the short-term units offered in history are "Origins of the Cuban Revolution," "The Civil-Rights Movement," "Japanese-American 'Relocation' Camps," and "Brazilian Slavery Through Documents."

Since 1991 Bates has offered majors in American cultural studies and African-American studies. The fact that the two departments list an identical faculty and that the catalogue announces that race will be the primary lens through which both topics are viewed is a good indication that these are politicized departments. And consider the department's description of its own subject matter: "Seen as such, the critical study of what it means to be American relies not on fixed, unitary, or absolute values, but rather on dynamic meanings that are themselves a part of cultural history. Respecting diverse claims to truth as changing also allows them to be understood as changeable."

Political Atmosphere: The Sincerest Form of Flattery?

Throughout its history, Bates has been blind to race and gender, even while other schools discriminated heavily. But that distinguished tradition wasn't sufficient for college president Donald Harward and his administration, who have decided that the only diversity worth having is one that is imposed and modeled after the strict codes in place at trendier institutions.

"The president and deans are always talking about multiculturalism and diversity," says a professor. The president, in an address titled "Higher Education in the Nineties," said of his school: "Already emerging are programmatic emphases which will bring greater attention to environmental studies, to international features of the curriculum, and to non-Western languages and culture. Continued attention will be given both to disciplinary areas, which carry the burden of the curriculum, and to interdisciplinary areas of study (such as women's studies, area studies, African American studies, and environmental studies), which complement disciplinary majors and reinforce the value of diversity." From these and other signs, it is clear that the president is determined to move as many of Bates's tents as possible into the multicultural camp. To be fair, it should be said that there has been some resistance, and the student body is hardly among the most politicized in the nation. But the fact remains that much of what the president has done, he has done in lieu of genuine efforts to improve the curriculum and faculty.

Also not unique to Bates is the presence of a multicultural center, which is featured prominently in the college's public relations materials. "The Multicultural Center celebrates and promotes the diverse cultural experiences that each member of Bates College brings to the community," announces college literature. "The Center acts as a catalyst on campus by initiating discussions about class, ethnicity, gender, nationality, race, and sexual orientation."

Among the programs brought in by this center, which the administration clearly sees as a means of wedging its radical and divisive ideology into the college community, are "Black and Brown, Get Down!, a Conversation with Elizabeth Martinez and Elena Featherston," and "The Personal Is Political, Art Exhibit by Marjorie Kramer." The resource room at the center is equally stimulating to the intellect, supplying students with magazines such as *Deneuve: The Lesbian Magazine, Dissident,* and *Covert Action.* Among the student organizations that emanate from the Multicultural Center is the Gay-Lesbian-Bisexual Alliance, which "serve[s] as a support group for gay, lesbian, and bisexual students" and sponsors "a play reading, parties, the Gay and Lesbian Film/Video Festival . . . and comedians." Amandla! supports "better understanding of the many communities of the African Diaspora" by bringing to campus such figures as Sister Souljah, bell hooks, and Sonia Sanchez. Women of Color "confronts issues of racism, sexism, classism, heterosexism, and other forms of prejudice that affect women of color." The group also publishes *Dialectics,* "a literary collective written and edited by women of color."

Given the administration's love affair with things chic, it isn't surprising to learn that it recently attempted to install a speech code. The effort was backed strongly by the dean of students, but a coalition of moderates and leftists defeated it.

Pushing any agenda on any campus is easier when the faculty backs that agenda. Thus, conservative or libertarian candidates are not given a fair shot at job openings at Bates. The administration backs the hiring of ideologically correct candidates for the same reason it created and strongly supports the Multicultural Center: Bates can move up in the national ranks of liberal arts colleges if it imitates national trends started at more prestigious places. A professor says that at Bates, "There have been clear instances of hiring on the basis of affirmative action at the expense of more qualified candidates, especially recently." Another notes that when a search committee came up with a set of finalists, the dean of faculty forced the committee to reconsider on "affirmative action grounds." Says this professor: "It is difficult [for conservative scholars] to make the short list when the pool of candidates contains so few conservatives or moderates."

Student Life: Payment Plans

Compared to those in other schools of its class, a Bates education is among the priciest in the nation, according to U.S. Department of Education information analyzed by Memex Press. Tuition, room, and board totaled $32,650 for 2000/01. The same analysis shows that the school offers the students comparatively little in the way of institutional scholarships, but does provide an unusually large amount of money for student services.

If you can afford it, you'll find a friendly place where students and faculty know each other well. Faculty are quite accessible, and the students certainly benefit from the close contact they have with each other and with their teachers. One professor says that the school has a "friendly atmosphere, with mostly small classes and high student-faculty contact. . . . Conservative faculty such as myself are not ostracized and continue to play a role."

There have never been fraternities and sororities at Bates. Most students live in a coed environment, though there are single-sex dorms available. Most students live on campus in dorms, although some live in university-owned Victorian houses. Most, but not all, residences are coed. The biggest group of students comes from New England, and nearly 90 percent are from states other than Maine. All students eat in the Commons in Chase Hall, a fact that does much to keep the college community coherent.

Social life revolves around a host of student organizations as well as trips to nearby Portland, Maine's ski resorts, and the Atlantic Coast. Excursions to nearby Freeport, home not only to L. L. Bean but also to numerous other outlet stores, allow students to exercise the shopping impulse. Boston is about 140 miles away.

Lewiston, Bates's home, is a fairly working-class town that has seen better days. Crime is generally rare at Bates, though burglaries have been on the rise in recent years. Police also seem to be cracking down more on alcohol and drug use among students, as arrests for these offenses have also become more frequent.

Because of the school's location in one of the most beautiful states in the union, "Batesies," as the students are known, have access to many outdoor recreational activities. The Outing Club sponsors many excursions into the woods and is one of the most popular clubs on campus. More than seventy-five years old, this organization sponsors Winter Carnival and clam bakes, and allows students to check out equipment for their own outdoor adventures.

Bates also has a long history of excellence in college debating. It and Oxford University were the first schools to hold international debates back in 1921, and its debate team is supported by the theater and rhetoric department. Bates came in fourth in the North American Championships in 1992, and in 1995 won the American Parliamentary Debate Association's Second-Place Team of the Year Award.

There are, of course, numerous other student groups, including the Deansmen, a male a cappella singing group with a forty-year history; the Fencing Club; Merimanders, a student-run female a cappella singing group; the Robinson Players student theater group; and rugby, sailing, and riding clubs. The college is served by the *Bates Student*, a weekly student newspaper. WRBC radio culls "one out of every six Batesies" for participation. There is no alternative newspaper in such a small college community, although there might be some need for one. Another college guide with a point of view different from this one notes with approval that the *Bates Student* is "known for its more liberal slant."

Other student groups are predictably political in nature, such as the Women's Action Coalition, Women of Color, Salidaridad Latina, and the Gay-Lesbian-Bisexual Alliance. These types of clubs have become an obligatory presence on America's college campuses, even at small schools such as Bates where the percentage of minority students is very small.

Like many colleges today, Bates requires "sensitivity training" for freshmen during which students are told about the goodness of diversity, homosexuality, and safe sex, and an assortment of the latest politicized bromides. "Sensitivity training" is perhaps one of the factors that contributed to Bates' recent rating as one of the "Top 10 Anti-Male Colleges" by *Men's Health* magazine. According to an article in the *Chronicle of Higher Education*, "Brian McNulty, a Bates spokesman, calls the list 'bogus' and wrong on the facts. He says he isn't losing any sleep over the college's poor standing."

Lest one think that Batesies are overly serious, the college sponsors several good old-fashioned events every year that hearken back to college life before the advent of overly earnest extracurricular activities. The Puddle Jump allows anyone crazy enough to jump into a hole cut in the ice of Lake Andrews on St. Patrick's Day to do so. An ice cream smorgasbord is held twice yearly, as is the school's clam bake (which also features lobsters, of course). The annual Harvest Dinner is a feast for the palate, and the Primal Scream is "a stress-relieving event sponsored and broadcast by WRBC held at 11:00 p.m. the Monday before finals on the Library Terrace." Then there are the Tacky Party and Pubcrawl. The former "challenges Bates students to dress their most 70s-ish and jam to the cheesiest beat around. The Salvation Army's Thrift store is a prime shopping spot for this event." Pubcrawl, held during Senior Week, allows members of the graduating class to "make coed teams of two and run to four local taverns drinking six beers as quickly as they can. The record, set in 1996, is less than sixteen minutes."

As for more conventional sports, Bates fields thirteen men's and fourteen women's NCAA Division III sporting teams and offers intramural opportunities in the standard slate of sports. More than 60 percent of the student body participates in intramural competition. Several years ago Bates was ranked in the top thirty in a national NCAA study on how well colleges balance athletics and academics.

Baylor University

Office of Admissions
Baylor University
Waco, TX 76798
(254) 710-1011
www.baylor.edu

Total enrollment: 12,325
Undergraduates: 11,124
SAT ranges (Verbal/Math): 520-620 (V); 530-640 (M)
Applicants: 7,525
Accepted: 88%
Enrolled: 45%
Application deadline: March 1
Financial aid application deadline: March 1
Tuition: $11,938/$17,176
Core curriculum: No

For Church and State

Baylor is the largest Baptist university in the world, and it acts like it. Baylor defines as its mission the goal of "integrating academic excellence and Christian commitment within a caring community." Still requiring students to attend chapel their freshman year, Baylor's leadership believes that an education is more than advanced reading, writing, and arithmetic — it's a character-building experience.

Founded in 1845, Baylor is also the oldest university in Texas. The university's

27

motto of *Pro Ecclesia, Pro Texana* (for church, for Texas) reflects the emphasis placed on community service in the curriculum, as involvement in church and civic affairs is encouraged.

Despite Baylor's relative isolation in Waco, a small city between Dallas and Austin, the university is no stranger to national headlines. An anachronism in a world of declining values and nihilism, Baylor's administration holds firmly to the traditions of the Baptist faith. In 1996, Baylor became the butt of many jokes by late-night talk show hosts, when for the first time in school history a dance was allowed on campus. More recently, the school has drawn fire from its own faculty for the development of the Michael Polanyi Center, intended to study the ramifications of "intelligent design" theory.

Academic Life: A True Christian College

Baylor's President Robert Sloan, a minister in his own right, is no apologist for those who criticize his university for its emphasis on Christianity in the curriculum. Freshman students are required to take two religion courses, as well as two semesters of Chapel Forum, which not only offers the traditional religious ceremony but also features various lectures and meetings on a variety of topics — for example, a lecture by Margaret Thatcher.

The required religious courses are primarily Christian in focus, with offerings including in-depth studies of the Old and New Testaments, church history, bioethics, archaeology of the Middle East, the history of Roman Catholicism, and Christian ethics.

Beyond the religion and chapel requirements there is no university-wide core curriculum for undergraduates, but the school's comparatively stringent distribution requirements come close to constituting a core. All students seeking the bachelor of arts in the College of Arts and Sciences must take four English courses, including three specific writing courses and either "American Literature" or "World Literature." Students must also complete: a course in mathematics (though a philosophy course in logic may substitute); two to three in the "fine arts" (which area includes courses in art, journalism, music, and speech communication, among other disciplines); three courses in a laboratory science; four courses in "human performance" (i.e., physical education); and six in the social sciences. To fulfill the latter requirement, students generally must complete "American Constitutional Development" and a two-semester history sequence ("World History through the Fourteenth Century" and "World History from 1400 to 1750," or the latter course plus "Modern World Civilizations since 1750"), as well as survey courses in three of the other social science disciplines. They must also take as many foreign language courses as are needed to demonstrate proficiency at the fourth-semester level.

Baylor's Hankamer School of Business emphasizes the importance of the liberal arts by requiring freshman students to take two courses in introductory English and writing, three courses in a foreign language, the aforementioned "American Constitutional Development" course, survey courses in history and economics, an advanced religion course, and five hours of philosophy, art, theatre, foreign literature, or music.

The College of Engineering also supports Baylor's commitment to the liberal arts, requiring two courses in literature, two courses of a foreign language, a course in ethics, and a course in political science.

Two hundred freshman students each year may supplement their education with the Baylor Interdisciplinary Core, a selective program that offers a "coherent approach to knowledge and learning," according to the university. In this program, developed and introduced in 1995 under the guidance of President Sloan, students take courses in three core areas: "World Cultures," "The Natural World," and "The Social World." Courses in the World Cultures section of the curriculum "use texts, works of art, examples of urban design and architecture, and other artifacts that represent the diversity of human voices to explore philosophical, religious, political, educational, artistic, literary, economic, and scientific dimensions of human experience," according to university literature. The aims of these courses are to enhance students' "historical consciousness" via discussion groups and classical texts.

Baylor's academic programs in business, engineering, nursing, law, theology, and music are nationally recognized. In particular, the Hankamer School of Business's entrepreneurship program is widely considered to be among the top five in the nation. The program teaches students how to "manage the family business," as well as *requiring* each of them to "develop a business plan, start, and operate a small business."

Baylor's weakness academically lies in its failure to offer graduate courses in many of its strongest programs like engineering. Besides Baylor's strong law and business graduate programs, the University only offers Ph.D. curricula in Applied Sociology, Biology, Biomedical Studies, Chemistry, Church-State Studies, Educational Psychology, English, Neuroscience, Physics, Religion, and Statistics. This hurts the university not so much directly as indirectly: while Baylor recognizes its strengths are as an undergraduate institution, the university will continue to have difficulty recruiting world-class faculty without an enhancement of its Ph.D. offerings. Without graduate students to assist professors with research, Baylor will never achieve the position of being a great research institution.

But ironically, it may be this absence of research professors that maintains Baylor's charm. Students are almost always taught either by professors or full-time lecturers with class sizes averaging twenty to thirty students. By avoiding the pitfalls of being designated a "research institution," students probably get a better education and have a more enjoyable learning experience.

Despite the school's reverence for tradition, Baylor has still plunged headfirst into some of the typical academic traps. The university offers majors in Asian studies and Latin American studies, and minors in African and Middle Eastern studies. The course offerings for African studies are not particularly politicized — "The

29

Christian Church in Africa" is one course title. While there is one course that explores "African-American Cultural Concepts," the vast majority of the courses focuses on the actual history of African peoples, as well as exploring current social issues, policies, and political institutions of the continent.

The same cannot be said for the Latin American studies program, however. One history course examines "Meso-American and Andean civilizations, the creation of colonial society, and the forces leading to the end of political colonialism in Latin America." Another course offers a feminist critique of the Spanish conquest of Latin America, examining the "changing status of women from pre-Colombian societies to modern Latin America, with emphasis on the last century, emphasizing class and racial stratifications, and cultures as well as regional differences."

The Middle Eastern studies curriculum is fairly straightforward, offering courses in "Archaeology of the Ancient Middle East," "Government and Politics of the Middle East," and Hebrew and Arabic language classes, as well as a fine array of biblical classes that incorporate archaeology, history, and geography. The faculty of Baylor's highly esteemed George W. Truett Seminary often teach these courses.

Many of Baylor's most renowned faculty members, not surprisingly, are professors of religion. Charles Talbert recently finished a term as president of the Catholic Biblical Association of America (CBA). Talbert, a Baptist minister, is only the second Protestant to serve as president of the organization. Thomas Charlton heads Baylor's esteemed Institute for Oral History. Joseph McKinney is widely considered to be one of the nation's foremost experts on international trade.

Political Atmosphere: Right Makes Might

Political controversy at Baylor comes most often in the competition between conservative groups rather than in arguments between opposite political sides — a problem one doesn't see at many institutions, to be sure. The College Republicans and the Young Conservatives of Texas continually bicker and spar over issues more personal in nature than ideological. The College Republicans were kicked off campus in the spring of 2000 for financial impropriety. The Young Conservatives are generally more active politically, assisting local candidates, publishing legislative ratings, as well as printing a fine conservative newspaper called *The Baylor Review.* With these two groups and the general gestalt of the student body, Baylor might be the most active conservative campus in the state. Both the College Republicans and Young Conservatives have brought speakers of national and international import to campus like Margaret Thatcher, Ward Connerly, Steve Forbes, and many others.

The left generally keeps quiet at Baylor — even among the professors. "Most professors at Baylor are conservative," a student says. "A lot of them approach issues of ethics, philosophy, and government from a religious perspective. Yet, we also have a few liberal professors who I have found to be very open-minded." While there is a weak Baylor Democrats chapter on campus, according to a politically active student "the conservatives define the debate, leaving the left to react or do nothing at all." In fact, most students believe the administration leans to the right, citing President Sloan's support of the Michael Polanyi Center, as well as the University's invitation to both Steve Forbes and Lady Thatcher to speak on campus.

But the Michael Polanyi Center has recently been the source of political controversy on the Baylor campus. Established by William A. Dembski, who holds doctorates in mathematics and philosophy, the Michael Polanyi Center's mission was to further scholarly work in the area of "intelligent design," which through mathematical and philosophical (but *not* theological) means seeks to detect evidence for designed structures in the universe. Dembski is a leading and respected scholar in this growing field of research.

Sloan solicited Dembski to come to Baylor to establish the Center without consulting the faculty. When its establishment became public, many faculty — scared that the school would be tarred with the "creationist" brush and that its scholarly reputation would therefore be damaged — questioned the wisdom of the school's association with the Center. Some even loudly demanded that it be closed.

A peer review committee was set up, and with a few minor caveats its report recommended the Center for its advancement of a legitimate form of scientific inquiry. In a press release, Dembski praised the report, saying that "Baylor University is to be commended for remaining strong in the face of intolerant assaults on freedom of thought and expression." This innocuous act was apparently too much for Sloan, who asked Dembski to retract his press release; Dembski refused, and was removed from his post. Said Dembski, accurately enough, "Intellectual McCarthyism, for the moment, prevailed at Baylor."

The administration was also unnecessarily heavy-handed when it employed one of the nation's top law firms to issue a cease and desist order to the conservative student newspaper, the *Baylor Review*. The *Review* was critical of Sloan's handling of the Dembski case. While the university was within its rights to restrict the use of its name, the same ends could have been achieved with considerably less firepower.

All of this turmoil over a fairly small research institute is a reminder of the political rifts that exist just underneath the surface at Baylor. Though a number of faculty embrace the school's Christian identity, many remain concerned that Baylor not do anything that may be perceived as too far outside the academic mainstream — or too "Christian."

Student Life: Waking Up in Waco

It is not uncommon to see cranes towering over the Baylor University campus. The university has over $60 million in new building projects underway or recently completed, including an entirely new law school complex, new soccer and baseball stadiums, an indoor tennis facility, renovations to campus cafeterias, as well as a new museum to house Baylor's art collections and museum studies programs.

Within the last five years, the University has also added the Jesse H. Jones Building to its main library, an impressive state-of-the art facility featuring access to Internet-linked databases, as well as plush study areas for students. This building boom does not obfuscate an already lovely campus executed mostly in Jeffersonian colonial architecture. Some of the standouts architecturally include Pat Neff Hall, the Armstrong Browning Library, and the Burleson Quadrangle. When visiting, one also must not miss the Bear Pit, where the University's mascot — an actual bear — resides. The mascot's home in recent years has become fodder for the fledgling animal rights group on campus. On occasion, the group uses the mascot's home as an example of cruelty and abuse of animals.

Students are required to live on campus their freshman year. Like one might expect from a good Baptist college, there are no coed dormitories. Those women lucky enough to get accepted to Baylor's Interdisciplinary Core may choose to live in Catherine Alexander Hall, a lovely colonial building with spacious rooms and fine amenities. Men should request accommodations in Brooks Hall, which was renovated in 1996. Others may not be so lucky: according to students, many of the dormitories are in desperate need of refurbishment and at times there is a "bug problem."

Most students residing on campus give high marks to the campus cafeterias. An eclectic mix of Southern, Mexican, and traditional American fare is served, as well as healthy cuisine for those concerned with avoiding the "freshman fifteen." The administration has stood firm in requiring freshmen to live on campus their first year. Most students support this policy believing it to be "a great way to meet your future friends for life." Most students leave the dorms after their freshman year, opting for Greek life or an apartment.

Greek life is an important part of Baylor campus life. A quarter of the student population belongs to a social fraternity or sorority. Unlike many other colleges and universities, Baylor keeps a tight reign on Greek activities, having a formal Greek life coordinator in the student activities office. Drinking at rush events is strongly frowned upon (another benefit of being a Baptist university), reducing the likelihood of "Animal House" type parties.

Crime is relatively rare on campus. In the most recent year for which statistics are available, Baylor had thirty-nine burglaries and nine auto thefts. No violent crimes were reported.

Baylor's hometown is perhaps most famous for its proximity to David Koresh's Branch Davidian compound, which went ablaze in 1996. This tragedy has had the effect of obscuring a rather charming small city, which features one of Texas's best downtown historical districts. In recent years, new investment has led to the refurbishment of many of Waco's more historical buildings, including the first headquarters of Dr. Pepper.

Included in this gentrification of the downtown area are new bars and restaurants to approach what Austin and Dallas have had for so long: party spots. Make sure to try out Ninfa's (Mexican), Buzzard Billy's (Cajun), and the Elite Café (where Elvis once ate). Despite these new establishments, most Baylor students, when asked what there is to do in Waco on the weekends, replied, "Get out of town."

While the tuition at Baylor is not cheap, the cost of living in Waco is. Affordable housing is plentiful near campus and meals at some of Waco's finest restaurants average $10 to $15 per person. Because Waco is centrally located between Austin and Dallas, the area is booming as a manufacturing and distribution location, so part-time jobs are plentiful for those students paying their own way through college.

While students often gripe about the lack of activities (i.e., bars, movie theaters, clubs) in Waco, the naturalist student should have no problem. Nearby Lake Waco is the largest urban lake in Texas, offering great fishing, sailing, and water-skiing opportunities. Additionally, since Baylor University is located on the banks of the Brazos River, students may rent small sailboats at the school's marina. Upstream from campus are some of the best mountain bike trails in Texas in the beautiful 416-acre Cameron Park.

Birmingham-Southern College

Office of Admissions
900 Arkadelphia Road
Birmingham, AL 35254
(205) 226-4696
www.bsc.edu

Total enrollment: 1,540
Undergraduates: 1,540
SAT ranges (Verbal/Math): 540-660 (V); 530-640 (M)
Applicants: 867
Accepted: 95%
Enrolled: 40%
Application deadline: March 1
Financial aid application deadline: March 1
Tuition: $15,398/20,791
Core curriculum: No

Subtle Pressures

Stability should never be taken for granted in today's academic climate — there's too much pressure for change, and too many monetary reasons to accept it. But so far, at least, Birmingham-Southern College has managed to hold off the more bizarre forms of political correctness. It has a generally conservative student body with almost no history of political activism; it is situated in a traditional state and region; and it is aligned with the Methodist church. It seems financially healthy.

Most of all, there are good things about Birmingham-Southern that one hopes will be preserved. Students take small classes and have close contact with their professors. The business division has a strong free-market orientation, and more than one-third of the college's students are business majors. Southern (as it is known locally) claims to support a traditional liberal arts education, and though its core is fairly loose in construction, there is little evidence that the school opposes the traditional liberal arts. The faculty is a little shorthanded in some areas — there is only one classicist, for example, and books in those classes are in translation — but students could do much worse.

Academic Life: Thinking Good Thoughts

Birmingham-Southern has no core curriculum to speak of. Instead, it uses a fairly typical set of distribution requirements. All students must take a writing course from the English department, the level of the course being determined by measurement tools like advanced placement tests, application essays, or SAT/ACT scores. Two courses in math are required, as are one lab course in astronomy, biology, chemistry, or physics; one course in philosophy and religion; one in literature; one in arts; and one in either economics, political science, psychology, or sociology. All students must also pass two units in a foreign language (or one at the 200 level or higher). These requirements apply to all students in all disciplines — an admirable policy.

There is also a requirement for one course in history, but it is very general; the catalogue actually says "any course in history." While this is not even close to a requirement in Western civilization, about 80 percent of students do fulfill their history requirement with either a U.S. history or Western civilization course. "The history faculty moans about how most students take a U.S. or Western civilization course," one faculty members says. The students' choice is encouraging, while the department's attitude is not.

The writing requirement, along with the attention paid by faculty to that skill, has been more successful at Birmingham-Southern than at other schools. Says a professor in a field not typically thought of as a strong promoter of writing skills: "I require my students to do a great deal of writing because they must know how to communicate through the written word. It's one of the real strengths of the school."

According to its Web site, "Birmingham-Southern consistently ranks among the top eighty liberal arts colleges in the nation." The strong course offerings and emphasis on writing are part of what makes this ranking deserved.

Birmingham-Southern used to do even more in this area, via a list of common readings and a seminar dedicated to that idea, but that has faded away to a non-required, not-for-credit "freshman reading list" and symposia throughout the year. Predictably, freshman interest is short-lived. "They're really into it the first two months, but by November the grapevine takes over and their peers become their unofficial advisors," a professor says. "You have the students only for a while." However, the college has resisted efforts by its departments to take up more and more of their students' time.

Undergraduates have the option of either obtaining a general education degree or majoring in a particular field. "The provost is very much committed to the idea of a general education, as opposed to concentrating just on the majors," says one educator. B.A. and B.S. general education candidates must take six courses in addition to the general requirements, while eight courses in their subject are required for majors in B.A. and B.S. fields. A general education committee has been instrumental in protecting the core that remains, faculty members say.

Recent additions to the faculty — half the current group have been hired in the last ten years — have placed more emphasis on student research, and this, if allowed to expand unchecked, would also endanger the broad requirements. The research project required on a topic within each senior's major is a good idea, but more might be too much. "There is some predation on the part of the sciences and the business school," says one professor. "At a small college this has a larger impact [than at a large university]. The faculty sometimes want a few more courses; they'll shift to a research university model if they're not careful, and that's not the model for a liberal arts college. It really comes down to the definition of what a liberal education is."

While many professors at Birmingham-Southern pour the majority of their energy into teaching, others are quite active researchers and publishers in their fields. National trends certainly favor those who believe that publication demands should come before teaching, but the president and board of directors at Birmingham-Southern seem to know that the true strength of a small college lies in its ability to offer good teaching to its students. After all, if students want to attend a large research university, they can usually do so for far less money than they pay at Birmingham-Southern. "If anything, we're weak on research," a professor says. "But the atmosphere of publish or perish isn't my favorite. I don't want to feel that my life is dictated by two articles or one book every six months." Professors can't think of anyone who was denied tenure for failure to publish.

"We're a private institution and we must teach well enough so that parents will continue to pay the bills," says one teacher. To this end, the normal maximum class size is thirty-five students, though a few classes have as many as seventy. The student-teacher ratio is approximately twelve-to-one. Because Birmingham Southern has no graduate students, it also has no courses taught by teaching assistants.

One of the best times to see the faculty in action is during "Interim Term," the January session required for four years of all students at Birmingham-Southern. Faculty offer courses either in their own more specialized field of research or, at times, in a very esoteric aspect of their discipline. "A major objective of the curriculum is to encourage all students to develop their potentials for creative activity and independent research," the college catalogue states. "The January interim term provides a unique opportunity for innovation and experimentation on the part of both students and faculty." Students may choose one of the offered courses or design their own, but they are expected to "use initiative and imagination whether their project is a group endeavor or an individual effort."

During Interim Term, for example, business students might study a single industry and take field trips to living examples of that industry — perhaps Delta Airlines in Atlanta or General Motors' Saturn plant in Tennessee. Invited speakers address various elements of business and economics, and students present Harvard Business School cases before the critiquing eyes of outside experts. Other students might travel to Italy and Greece to see firsthand the material remains and cultural descendants of the ancient civilizations they study. Students in the sciences may undertake intensive laboratory experiments under the watchful eye of their professors. This program is seen by most as a resounding success, although one professor notes that "a student may resent the rigor of a lab course versus a business internship. You've got one guy working his tail off in, say, chemistry while another is being taken out for lunch."

A good bit of travel seems to accompany the Interim Term, which is the last remnant of a 1968 curricular reform at Birmingham-Southern. "There is a strong social consciousness on campus, which is reflected in the fact that every January, thirty-five students or so go off to work with the poor in a Third World country," a professor says. A faculty committee must approve every new January course, and the presence of some lesser fare proves that the system isn't fail-safe. Still, the Interim Term is an excellent opportunity for students to broaden their knowledge and experience in myriad fields, and students should take full opportunity of this offering.

Among the outstanding professors at Birmingham-Southern are Paul Cleveland in economics; Dan C. Holliman in biology; V. Markham Lester and Matthew Levey in history; Cecilia McInnis-Bowers in business administration; Michael McInturff in English; Samuel Pezzillo in classics; and Janie Spencer of the Spanish department.

The Division of Economics and Business Administration has four endowed chairs in business and free enterprise, and is considered one of the strongest areas of the college. It is also the most popular division on campus, as more than 35 percent of students select majors in this area — nearly four times the national average. Also very good are the departments of music, history, biology, and the fine and performing arts. Some years ago the college merged with a Birmingham conservatory, and thus the music and arts departments are much more oriented toward performance than at similar institutions.

Birmingham-Southern reflects the values and beliefs of its middle-class, Methodist constituency in that it remains a collection of scholars and not a gathering of ideologues. Most course offerings are traditional at least in title, and the culture that produces most of Birmingham-Southern's students works to rein in radicalized tendencies faculty members might have. The administration has also shown that it is willing to fight for serious courses. Solid offerings can be found in the humanities departments, always the most politicized on any campus. Faculty are, for the most part, politically liberal, "but on the whole they're pretty sensible on academic matters and are committed to old-fashioned standards," says a faculty member.

But while overt radicalism is not tolerated, the generational shift to a more politicized mode of thought can be detected at Southern. "There is bound to be a non-fit with the new people and what the curriculum had been," one professor says. "For example, someone hired to teach eighteenth-century literature may have a different tack, but it is subtle and not overt." This professor tells of a colleague who has been on the faculty for a number of years. When she arrived she taught her humanities courses in a way that was "quite traditional." And yet, now "she does quite a bit of feminist theory along with it. And they [the students] still get all the material with it, so that's OK. The ones who turn it into a religion eventually grate their colleagues to the point that they [the graters] leave."

The college is hardly Duke or Stanford in its level of politicization, although some courses certainly are taught with an advocate's point of view. The catalogue lists several of this type, and though many titles look traditional — okay, except for "Socialism" — the perspectives are not always so. Some examples:

- Sociology 305, "Sociology of the Family," in which one studies "the relationship between the family and the changing external environment as well as the dynamic processes within the family. Historical and cross-cultural perspectives are considered along with alternatives to the traditional family."
- Philosophy 303, "Socialism," which is "an examination of some of the philosophical, political, and economic claims of modern socialists, beginning with and emphasizing Marx, but also moving beyond Marx and Marxism into the work of contemporary socialists who stress the democratic character of socialism and the need for a socialist market economy."
- English 220, "Literature and the Social Experience," which studies "a faculty selected topic (such as African-American Literature, War in Literature, or Androgyny in Literature) focusing on a cultural movement, a social issue, or the perspective of a social group."
- English 230-231 (and cross-listed in history), "Plural America I & II," has as its intent "to recognize the aspects of other cultures appropriated into the West-

ern tradition but often either unacknowledged or glossed over. The end should be an appreciation of the achievements and limitations of our Western heritage, and a heightened sensitivity to the cultural diversity of the world-at-large [*sic*]. Plural America I focuses on Native American and Chicano history and literature and on the European context of American society; Plural America II focuses on African-American and Asian-American history and literature and on the 1960s as a catalyst for multiculturalism."

Political Atmosphere: Nibbling, but Not Biting

A few years ago some feminist faculty at Birmingham-Southern made an attempt to require so-called gender-neutral language on campus, but didn't get much support from their colleagues. Still, the use of this sort of language is unofficially enforced. For example, if a professor brings a course description before a faculty committee for approval, an amendment will likely be forthcoming to change the wording if it is not already gender-neutral. According to one professor, a man who uses conventional English when speaking before the faculty will be politically corrected before the words are halfway out of his mouth. There seems to be little faculty opposition to this imposition, and, indeed, this is the way many radical ideas have found their place in the standard operating procedures at colleges and universities: no one stands up to them.

There was some talk of a speech code at Birmingham-Southern as far back as the Vietnam War, but nothing has been done to revive that idea recently. One administrator did say that there are "no codes, but we would be open to issues of sensitivity as needed." Whether this would include limitations on the speech of those who transgress the current boundaries of "correctness" is difficult to say.

Most departments at Southern host a variety of viewpoints. "There is an emphasis on diversity," a professor says. "I don't see it as much of a threat. It's the kind of diversity you actually want in an academic community. There are some multicultural types here, but the administration wouldn't let them get control of the place."

The composition of the faculty is itself controlled by several layers of administration through which any prospective faculty member must pass before receiving a job offer. "We have forty to forty-five members of the board, and a president [Neal Berte] who's a monarch," a professor says. "We still have an affiliation with the Methodist Church, which of course is itself one of the trendiest institutions in the country. But the particular Methodists who are connected with us are conservative." When a vacancy arises at Birmingham-Southern, the department head nominates three candidates to the provost. The candidates, if satisfactory to the provost, are interviewed by the president, who sometimes vetoes choices. The provost and department interview all three, as does the tenure and promotions committee.

A small school like Southern must be careful to serve its primary constituency:

as one professor notes, though 45 percent of the school's budget comes from its endowment, a drop of ten to fifteen students can cause budgetary problems. The state of Alabama has made significant cuts to the university system budget recently, and the governor has said the state spends too much on higher education and not enough on kindergarten and elementary school. Alabama has quite a number of community colleges and will soon eliminate the meager $600 grant it gives to in-state students who attend in-state private colleges like Birmingham-Southern. With all the cutbacks, public universities have been scrambling for monetary support from the same businesses that donate to private colleges. Despite this, one professor says the future at Birmingham-Southern is promising: "The academic outlook here is good. We have a good age range and mix of ages with our faculty." In the past few years, Birmingham-Southern has received several donations over $10 million, which is a good sign for its financial future.

Student Life: A Pleasant Place

According to the school's literature, Birmingham-Southern is "a 188-acre haven located on a wooded, rolling hilltop." Just three miles away is the city of Birmingham. Birmingham has grown by leaps and bounds over the past few decades, and the presence of the University of Alabama-Birmingham, with its attendant hospitals and world-renowned cardiovascular center, has brought a great deal of new wealth to this city. Birmingham did not exist before the War between the States and thus has no antebellum charm, but it has turned into a dynamic place and has recovered well from the blows dealt it by the demise of most of the steel industry, which gave birth to it. It is by any measure a very pleasant place to live.

Most of Southern's students (nearly 75 percent) are from Alabama, the rest are from twenty-two other states and seven foreign countries.

Somewhat more than half of both men and women at Birmingham-Southern pledge the Greek organizations, and more than three-quarters of all students live on campus. Southern features six men's national social fraternity chapters and seven women's social sorority chapters. There is no coed housing. Southern offers a variety of visitation options for students in dorms: no visitation, limited visitation, and open visitation. For students twenty years old or younger, the choice must be made by both the student and his parents. Students older than twenty may decide on their own.

Southern boasts more than eighty student organizations and enters the big-time sports arena in basketball and baseball but not football, an oddity for any Southern school. There are several academic organizations, including the American Chemical Society, a concert choir, a pre-law organization, and the *Southern Academic Review*, a scholarly journal for the college community. There seem to be very few politically active groups on campus, although the president did ask a faculty member several years ago to serve as an adviser to a gay and lesbian support group. The group is not activist compared to similar groups on other campuses; it once planned a demonstration on campus along with students from the University of Alabama-Birmingham, but according to a professor, "that was headed off before it ever began."

After hours, many students and faculty hang out at The Cellar Coffeehouse, an entirely student staffed and run operation. In addition to steaming coffee, The Cellar features "delectable dessert," live music, judged open-microphone nights, and poetry readings.

Birmingham Southern's campus is surrounded by fencing and the university has no off-campus buildings. On campus, at least, there is little crime, according to official statistics, but off campus, the risk is well above average for a college community according to statistics compiled by apbnews.com.

Boston College

Director of Undergraduate Admission
Devlin Hall
208140 Commonwealth Avenue
Chestnut Hill, MA 02467-3809
(800) 360-2522
www.bc.edu

Total enrollment: 11,722
Undergraduates: 9,188
SAT ranges (Verbal/Math): 590-680 (V); 610-690 (M)
Applicants: 19,746
Accepted: 35%
Enrolled: 33%
Application deadline: January 15
Financial aid application deadline: February 1
Tuition: $23,914/$32,424
Core curriculum: No

Truth and Consequences

Emblazoned on the facade of one of the neo-Gothic administrative buildings in Boston College's quadrangle is a statement that would draw scorn on most campuses: "You will come to know the truth and the truth will set you free." As offensive to secular eyes are the statements that flank the quotation from Jesus: "Right and justice are the pillars of Thy Throne," and "Fear of the Lord is true wisdom and true learning."

At many institutions formerly religious but now secular, such outmoded talk of truth was long ago abandoned. At BC, as well as many other Catholic colleges and universities, the reminders of adherence to a tradition of intellectual, moral, and spiritual search for truth are present, but a battle is waged daily to determine whether this tradition of learning will be rejected or recovered.

BC was founded as a university, and was only ever a college in name only. Retaining a sense of collegiality, or community, is a major challenge for BC, as its concerted efforts to join the ranks of top-tier research institutions have raised the endowment to over $1 billion, and at the same time created some of the tensions between research and teaching that such strivings necessarily bring. Taken together, then, the two most important challenges to BC's identity are very much related: What will be the place of Christianity within an education at Boston College, and what will happen to the liberal arts as BC becomes institutionally more oriented to research? Both challenges are fundamentally about freedom, for with a dilution of the Catholicism that has animated education at BC comes the possibility of new and invasive ideologies taking over.

Academic Life: Holy War

Boston College includes eleven colleges and schools, five of them dedicated to undergraduates. More than fifty majors are offered in the College of Arts and Sciences, the Wallace E. Carroll School of Management, the Lynch School of Education, the School of Nursing, and the College of Advancing Studies (the continuing education school for part-time students). For the undergraduate student interested in the liberal arts, the school of choice would be the College of Arts and Sciences, where about 60 percent of the undergraduates enroll.

Boston College makes a claim to having a core curriculum; it calls its distribution requirements "The University Core," but this is certainly a misnomer. As distribution requirements go, BC's program is quite strong, considering especially that two courses in philosophy and two courses in theology are required. In addition, students must take one course in writing, one in literature, one in the arts, one in mathematics, two in history, two in social sciences, and two in natural sciences. The standard language proficiency is also required. In addition, there is a cultural diversity requirement that may be met with a course that also fulfills another general requirement.

Even with the cultural diversity requirement, which at many institutions offers an escape into the most politicized courses, BC's requirements amount to a fairly rigorous program. The cultural diversity component can feed students some meager intellectual fare, but the extent of politicized courses at BC is still quite limited, compared to most schools its size. All students will find themselves confronting perennial questions as part of the required courses, especially in the theology, philosophy, and history requirements. As one professor notes, the situation is "a lot better than ten years ago," thanks in large part to the efforts of a university core committee to tighten the requirements.

One of the truly outstanding programs at BC is "Perspectives," a program that brings "faculty and students into conversation with the ancient, modern, and contemporary thinkers who have shaped our intellectual and spiritual heritage and who continue to influence the course of our community living." Designed, in the description of one professor, as a "dialectic between ancients and moderns," Perspectives offers four two-semester sequences: "Perspectives on Western Culture," "Modernism in the Expressive Arts," "Horizons of the New Social Sciences," and "New Scientific Visions."

"Perspectives on Western Culture," the two-semester sequence in the classics of philosophy and theology, is by far the most popular of these, with more than twenty sections offered every semester. Starting with Plato, continuing with the Christian fathers, covering the modern political theorists, and ending with Freud, the course seeks, as one professor says, to instill in students an "understanding of who they are — of the part that strives up to God." The hope, the professor says, is that students will "see that there is a beauty in nature and in themselves."

Students in the other Perspectives classes also wrestle with questions of their culture's past and future. As one student says: "It's about freeing your mind." The challenge offered in this program is one of the best opportunities for experiencing the liberation of liberal arts at BC — or any other institution, for that matter.

The honors program at BC, offered in all of the undergraduate colleges, provides another very fine opportunity for qualifying students to study the classics. Open to incoming freshmen with excellent high school records, SAT scores, and recommendations (only about 10 percent of a freshman class gets accepted), the honors program offers courses that satisfy the distribution requirements. BC calls it an "integrated liberal arts education of a kind one can find in few colleges and universities," a claim professors within the program confirm to be true. During the first two years of the program, students take a survey of Western civilization entitled "Western Cultural Tradition," which fulfills the requirements in theology, philosophy, and literature. Primary sources are used throughout the program, and class sizes average only fifteen students.

Another three hundred students or so each year use the "PULSE" program to satisfy the theology and philosophy requirements. The university catalogue describes the program in the following way: "In light of classic philosophical and theological texts, social science, fiction, and poetry, PULSE students address topics such as the relationship of self and society, the nature of community, the mystery of suffering the practical difficulties of developing a just society, urbanism, homelessness and alienation." Students combine the study of great books (though not so much as in Perspectives) with hands-on social work assignments through Boston-area mental health organizations, emergency shelters, correctional facilities, and legal organizations. Though it might sound like some "social justice" programs that dish out more propaganda than anything else, in fact PULSE is a substantial program, quite worthy of its popularity. "It was by far and away the best part of my BC education," one graduate says.

While certain parts of the PULSE program have the potential for politicization, given the wrong professor, the "Faith, Peace, and Justice" program (available as a minor) is thoroughly politicized, according to professors and students familiar with it. Liberal theology, which paints Christianity with thoroughly socialist colors, is a strong component in the program. Other politicized minors include black studies, women's studies, and American studies, which focuses on "American culture past and present, specifically analyzing how American culture has been shaped by the interaction of race, class, ethnicity, gender, and other issues." For a minor in American studies a "theme" is selected; past themes included in the university coursebook reveal its politicized preoccupations: "race in American culture, ethnicity in American culture, media and race, media and gender, colonialism and American culture, poverty and gender, [and] diversity in urban culture."

These areas of politicization point up a question regarding the direction Boston College will now take. Founded by the Jesuits in 1863, BC has as its heritage a four hundred–year tradition of concern for the integration of the intellectual, moral, and religious development of its students. The centerpiece of a Jesuit education has always been a common curriculum that emphasizes the study of the defining works of the humanities, sciences, and social sciences. It seeks, as one current professor puts it, to "take seriously the Catholic priority of the whole soul." While the tradition takes this priority seriously, BC must decide whether it will also do so.

One BC professor warns of two types of changes that could remove this part of the university's soul. The first danger is super-specialization, in which the university is transformed into a kind of shopping mall. Diversity becomes most decisive, and the quest for knowledge and wisdom is supplanted by empiricism and "encyclopediasm" (à la the French Encyclopediasts, who classified knowledge not according to the natural order within the universe, but alphabetically). The second danger is found in a system whose organizing principle is power alone. Multiculturalism runs amok, and reason is replaced by a calculus of power. Both dangers are present at BC, and it's only with vigilance, warns this professor, that they can be combated.

Some departments are losing this fight; English, sociology, and theology have already become heavily politicized. Radical agendas are part of each department, and are quite often manifest in course descriptions. "Love: Literary, Philosophical, Psychoanalytic, Queer," a recent offering in English, promised reading of Fanon, Bersani, and other queer theorists in addition to Plato, Kierkegaard, and Graham Greene. "Contemporary Literary and Cultural Theory" makes no such nod to traditional texts, promising a reading of "major texts within psychoanalytic theory as well as gender/queer theory and post-colonial theory (both of which will have a psychoanalytic slant)." A recent speaker at the "Gender Theories Colloquium," sponsored by the English Department, was celebrated by the department as a "filmmaker, writer, activist, and author of a pioneering essay in gender studies, 'Looking for My Penis: The Eroticized Asian in Gay Video Porn.'" His talk for the forum (no doubt also "pioneering") was entitled "Still Looking: Sexing Gay Asian Men."

Sociology course offerings are also riddled with emphases on race, class, and gender. Few courses, however, are so colorful in their self-descriptions as "Deviance and Social Control," which may be taken as part of the women's studies minor:

> This course represents a social and historical inquiry into the battle between the power of a given social order and its deviant others. It is a story of control and resistance within societies organized according to economic, heterosexist, racial, and imperial hierarchies. It is a story of madness, religious excess, and the pornographic violence of Western Man and his most powerful social institutions. It is also a narrative of the resistance of women, peoples of color, those who desire sex differently and those impoverished by the normal relations of a given social order of things in time. It is a story of how some of us come to know others as evil, sleazy, dirty, dangerous, sick, immoral, or crazy, and how the normative order to which we adhere is disrupted or destroyed by those who know it differently.

The department of theology, one of the largest at BC, is riven with strife, though the ranks of traditionalists have been narrowed over the years as more progressive professors are hired. An emphasis on trendiness within theological scholarship has supplanted the traditional tasks of introducing students to and educating them in the Church Fathers and the foundations of Catholic theology. This trend within Catholic institutions of higher education has taken hold at BC.

The irresoluteness of the department as a whole is seen clearly in its long-standing tolerance of Mary Daly, the radical feminist who only in the last year was ousted from the university. When she was first hired at BC more than twenty years ago, Daly was still nominally Catholic, though strongly heterodox. Since then she has become wildly radical, proclaiming herself an "anti-christ" who wishes to "castrate God the Father."

Daly always denied BC men entry to her classroom, claiming that their presence precluded openness among female students. While the university opposed her discrimination, for years it could not succeed in removing her from the classroom. Only in 1999, with the threat of a lawsuit (and the potential loss of federal financial aid to the institution), did the university finally insist upon equity in enrollment for Daly's classes. That it was potential financial harm — and not damage done to students' minds — that finally prompted the administration to act is an unfortunate commentary on BC's priorities.

Most departments at BC, fortunately, are not politicized, and some offer especially strong and coherent programs of study. The department of political science is especially strong in political philosophy, offering undergraduates the opportunity to consider the classics of Western political thought. The philosophy department offers many fine classes taught by faculty members committed to the Catholic tradition of intellectual inquiry.

Outstanding faculty at BC include William Kilpatrick in the School of Education; Harold Peterson in economics; John Mahoney in English; John Heineman in history; Joseph Flannigan, Thomas Hibbs, Peter Kreeft, Richard Cobb-Stevens, and Ronald Tacelli in philosophy; Nasser Behnegar, Christopher Bruell, Robert Faulkner, Christopher Kelly, Marc Landy, David Lowenthal (emeritus), and Susan Shell in political science; and Stephen Brown, Matthew Lamb, Frederick Lawrence, and Thomas Wangler in theology.

Political Atmosphere: Keeping Square Pegs out of Round Holes

According to several long-time observers of Boston College, the current administration's actions give cause for some measure of optimism. While the rhetoric from certain parts of the administrative upper echelon often includes platitudes of multiculturalism (and assorted other "isms"), the actions of the administration, headed by President Fr. William Leahy, S.J., tend to be more traditional.

On a campus in which the administration does not accord official recognition to the Lesbian, Gay, and Bisexual Community (LGBC) nor to any pro-abortion groups that might wish to be recognized, the pressure exerted by liberal faculty and students to yield to their demands for official sanction has been steady. Leahy, to his credit, has remained steadfastly opposed to such recognition; he also indicated his opposition to adding "sexual orientation" to the university's nondiscrimination clause. "It's my judgment that groups such as LGBC start as support groups for lesbian and gay students, but then become advocates for positions counter to Catholic teachings," he has said.

A recent lecture, interrupted by protesters, some of whom were members of LGBC, demonstrated that Fr. Leahy's concerns were well-founded. An April 1999 lecture entitled "Why Gay Marriage Is Impossible," by Dr. Christopher Wolfe, a political scientist from Marquette University, was disrupted by a noisy mass exodus of thirty students (out of about 120 in the audience). Claiming that Wolfe was purveying "hate speech," they attempted to shout him down. Later, in a letter signed by 150 students and faculty, Wolfe was accused of delivering "a hate-filled speech of bigotry, intolerance, and oppression driven by his extreme religious and sexist views." (Full disclosure: the talk was cosponsored by the St. Thomas More Society and ISI, the producer of this book.)

Particularly remarkable about the accusations brought against Wolfe was that his argument, delivered solely upon natural law grounds (without any appeals to revelation), is fully consistent with Roman Catholic teaching. When Catholic moral teaching is deemed "hate speech" by so large a group of faculty and students who are at a Catholic institution, one need wonder how orthodox a Catholic university can be in the age of ideology that still prevails on university campuses.

This very question has been of some concern to the Vatican, which issued *Ex Corde Ecclesiae* to define the relationship between the Church and Catholic universities worldwide. Several provisions of the document, including requirements that new presidents of Catholic universities pledge fidelity to the magisterium and that the teaching of Catholic theologians be certified by local bishops as orthodox, have led dissenters to all but equate the church with Big Brother. At BC, the shrillness of the debate has been muted by a somewhat noncommittal statement by Leahy, who attempted to calm fears that adoption of the document would diminish BC's commitment to diversity. Leahy's statement was not enough for the chairman of the theology department, however, who stated that he would not abide by the requirement.

The affirmative action program at BC remains strong, but not strong enough for some of the more restlessly liberal student groups. The Undergraduate Government of Boston College (UGBC) has called for a university vice-presidential position to be created to address issues of multiculturalism. Complaining that BC "incorporate[s] a curriculum that reflects the tradition of the dominant culture, and there is a sense that racial issues are constantly bubbling just below the surface," the UGBC has called "for the creation of an alternative to the Western European history core that recognizes the contributions of non–Western European backgrounds." Thus far their requests have not been met, further indication that the administration tolerates only so much of the multicultural agenda.

In addition to much of the UGBC agenda, liberal causes on campus are otherwise advocated by AHANA, or African-American, Hispanic, Asian, and Native American students. The Peace and Justice Coalition sponsors leftist speakers, including Noam Chomsky and Cornell West. The administration has had its own roster of liberal speakers featured at commencement, as the last three commencement speakers have all been members of the Clinton cabinet.

Student Life: Good Odds

There are travel guides that do a much better job of listing all Boston's attractions than we can do here. Suffice it to say that the Boston area has hundreds of things to do and that there are thousands of college students in the area — you do the math.

BC freshmen are assigned a number of years for which they may live in college housing. The university states that "Most receive three years of guaranteed housing with the expectation that they will live off campus [for their] junior year." BC is divided into two campuses (connected by a 10-minute bus ride), and there are four freshman dorms located off of the main campus. Campus housing ranges from traditional residence halls to high-rise apartments to townhouse apartments. All housing is coed by floors.

The First Year Experience, held in seven sessions over the course of the summer, is a freshman's introduction to life at BC. Parents of students attend an orientation program that runs concurrently. In the students' program, themes of diversity and sexuality are bundled with discussions of academic requirements and campus rules.

Campus activities include more than one hundred student-run organizations, including student government, an AM radio station, academic and language societies, performance groups, professional clubs, and service organizations. The primary liberal groups on campus cluster under the heading AHANA, or African-American, Hispanic, Asian, and Native American students. The Office of AHANA Student Programs (OASP) is an official student services organization at BC, with a paid staff that provides numerous programs that "support and enhance the academic performance" of minority undergraduate students.

In all, there are more than one hundred student organizations, including thirty-seven "intercultural groups." Honoraries, musical and artistic groups, pre-professional, and other academic clubs are all represented.

One recent addition to campus is *Crossroads,* a self-described "Catholic newspaper born in love, seeking the truth." Addressing issues of spiritual, political, and social significance, *Crossroads* has engendered debate among students, and according to its editors, helped to contribute to a revivified Catholicism on campus. Not everyone has welcomed the newspaper's presence, however; the editors of *The Heights,* a BC weekly, greeted the publication with suspicion by editorializing about its likely antagonistic tactics. Another conservative presence on campus known for the lively debates and lectures it sponsors is the St. Thomas More Society, whose mission is to "give students an opportunity to discover what it means to be a good Catholic in today's society."

Given its urban location, it is perhaps not surprising that crime is a significant feature of the Boston College landscape. Though most of the crime on campus is confined to burglaries and vehicle thefts — of which there were 195 and 11, respectively, in 1999 — serious physical crime also occurs. There were nine aggravated assaults and eight forcible sex offenses in 1999. All of the sex offenses took place in the dorms.

Sports are not only big at BC, they're also big business. After several major scandals — including allegations of gambling — rocked the campus several years ago, the football and basketball programs are on the rebound. BC fields seventeen

Division I varsity teams for men and sixteen for women. Even a bad season could be considered a success if a team (especially a football team) accomplishes just one thing: beat Notre Dame. Intramural sports are also very popular.

Boston University

Office of Admissions
121 Bay State Road
Boston, MA 02215
(617) 353-2300
www.bu.edu

Total enrollment: 28,487
Undergraduates: 15,469
SAT ranges (Verbal/Math): 600-680 (V); 610-690 (M)
Applicants: 28,215
Accepted: 48%
Enrolled: 30%
Application deadline: January 1
Financial aid application deadline: February 15
Tuition: $25,044/$33,494
Core curriculum: Optional

Silber and Gold

Like so many institutions of higher education in America, Boston University has religious roots; it was founded in 1839 to train ministers for the Methodist Church. Though today its mission has nothing to do with Methodism, BU has not followed the path of many other schools who abandon their religious mission in favor of a politicized gospel. Even as it strives to join the ranks of the top research universities, BU maintains a high level of commitment to traditional ideas of liberal education and the excellence in teaching that is a requisite part of liberal learning.

As the third-largest private university in the United States, with an entirely urban campus stretching for more than a mile along Boston's Charles River, BU affords a wealth of academic and extracurricular opportunities for its almost 30,000 students (more than half of which are undergrads). About the only thing that students won't find among the 250 degree programs in the fifteen schools and colleges at BU is a thoroughly politicized program of study.

BU's generally strong adherence to traditional notions of undergraduate education was shaped in large part by Dr. John Silber. President of BU for most of the last three decades (and now chancellor), Silber forged a faculty and curriculum consistent with his no-nonsense approach to higher education. Academic fads have not found a home at BU, and, to a greater degree than the vast majority of its peers, BU employs relatively few professors bent on propagandizing students with the latest academic ideologies. As important, BU (with a few exceptions) does not abandon its undergrads to the tutelage of teaching assistants, as happens at state schools of similar size.

The opportunity to take a true core curriculum is available to every student at BU. Added to this is an array of programs of study and outstanding professors that make BU an intellectually vibrant institution. Not afraid to dissent from the reigning academic orthodoxies, BU's heterodoxy should place it high on many students' list of places to investigate.

Academic Life: Capitalized "Core"

BU's size allows students to select from many different paths to earning a baccalaureate degree, one of which is the Core Curriculum in the College of Arts and Sciences. This is thanks in large part to the efforts of John Silber. According to one BU professor, prior to Silber's arrival in 1971, BU was in "pretty wretched condition," and the "typical cafeteria situation" in course selection prevailed. While most BU students still select their courses within distribution requirements, 40 percent of the approximately 6,500 College of Arts and Science students choose the Core Curriculum.

Boston University describes the Core Curriculum as "an innovative program of eight historically based, integrated courses providing an in-depth study of classic works (Western and non-Western) in the humanities, important ideas in the natural sciences, and concerns and theoretical bases of the social sciences." Those students choosing the core "pursue a coherent interdisciplinary approach to great works of literature; art and music; and social, religious, scientific, and philosophic thought — works with the power to transcend their own time and to teach things essential and beautiful to any interested human being of our time." We should add that such a curriculum is only "innovative" because of what has happened to university curricula in the last thirty years or so; in actuality, the Core Curriculum is a welcome return to traditional ideas of a university.

The core consists of eight seminars and lectures series taken during the first and second years. It includes intensive historical and literary investigations along with rigorous laboratory work. The reading list includes Homer, Plato, Aristotle, the Gospels, Dante, Montaigne, Shakespeare, and enough other classics to rival any other core save that found at Great Books colleges. According to one student, the core provides a "very good challenge; it's definitely not easy." This student notes that because of the challenge there is some level of attrition, but that students who stick it out "begin to care passionately for the things that are read." There's a "certain camaraderie" that develops around the "commonality of questioning," this student says. Many core students live on special residence floors in Warren Towers, and, according to this same student, the core "becomes a small college."

Core students can work toward any major, as its demands also meet the general education requirements of the College of Arts and Sciences. Students who elect not to take the core (and they are definitely missing out, according to many professors and students) must satisfy the requirements of the Divisional Studies Program.

The Divisional Studies Program is the standard set of distribution requirements whose purpose is easily defeated if a student wishes to do so, according to a professor. The program is made up of four divisions: humanities, mathematics and computer science, natural sciences, and social sciences. Students majoring in a natural science must complete at least six one-semester divisional courses in the humanities and social science divisions, with at least two courses in each. Those with majors in the humanities, mathematics and computer science, or the social sciences must complete at least two courses in each of the three divisions outside the division of their concentration. At least one of the courses in the natural science division must include a laboratory component.

The College of Arts and Sciences is not the only school at BU that offers a core. The School of Management, for example, has its own core, and students also do coursework in CAS. BU is exploring options for vocational programs adopting their own cores and integrating their programs more fully within the liberal arts framework.

Already, the College of General Studies offers a two-year, general education core curriculum and is, according to university literature, "oriented to the student whose traditional admissions credentials from high school may make him or her ineligible for direct admission into the university's four-year liberal arts and professional programs." In other words, it is a second chance for underachievers and nontraditional students. While these programs are now common at U.S. universities (who see them most often as a source of income), this one is rare in that it offers the start of a top-notch liberal education. All courses are team-taught by six professors who represent the various divisions of the undergraduate curriculum: Social Science, Science and Mathematics, and Humanities and Rhetoric. Students take classes in sections of about forty pupils, and extensive academic counseling is provided. Full-time learning specialists are also available and regularly teach classes in "learning how to learn." About 15 percent of BU undergraduates are enrolled in the program, and after completing it, they may proceed to baccalaureate-level studies at

BU. This is certainly one of the best programs of its kind in the nation — it is carefully designed, offers a very real liberal education, and gives the student an opportunity for academic redemption and a better, more informed life.

Another program, this one for freshmen in four-year programs, was inaugurated in the 2000-2001 academic year. It emphasizes the development of writing skills. The first semester works on expository writing, while the second hones the students' writing skills within their fields of concentration. An oratory component to the course is under consideration, evidence of the administration's attention to the classical tradition of rhetoric.

Rhetoric is already a feature of another program designed to encourage more intellectual discourse on campus. Schooling students in the "arts of adult conversation," the lecture and discussion program dubbed "Conversessione" has featured prominent and provocative speakers including David Gelertner and Elizabeth Fox-Genovese. At each program, attended by about fifty undergraduates and a select number of faculty and graduate students, a formal dinner is followed by questions to the speaker from an undergraduate "spokesman" at each table. The goal of the questions is not only to spur discussion at the dinner, but to create, through a ripple effect, more intellectual conversation on campus.

Debate and elevated intellectual inquiry also abound in the highly regarded University Professors Program, which consists of a selection of classes available to any student as well as an invitation-only concentration for the best students at BU. Featuring a distinguished faculty of thirty scholars "who have built their own intellectual bridges between various disciplines of the humanities, arts, and sciences," the program offers a unique and elevated interdisciplinary approach. University literature describes this approach as a response "to the necessity for rigorous and well-founded cross-disciplinary studies apparent in our cultural tradition and reflected tellingly in the work of our major academic centers. This elusive but principal objective is achieved partly by emphasizing the fundamental humanistic values inherent in all academic inquiries." With required course titles like "Interrogating the Universe," and "Idiosyncratic Survey of Modern Literature," the program includes eight required courses, a seminar in which papers are presented by the program faculty (and in which all program students, from freshmen to doctoral candidates, participate), and a thesis.

Outstanding professors at BU are almost too numerous to mention. But they include Brian Jorgensen, Christopher Ricks, and Steven Tigner (also in the School of Education) in the Core Curriculum; Saul Bellow, Bruce Redford, Bonnie Costello, Burton Cooper, Eugene Green, Robert Levine, Robert Pinsky, Michael Prince, and Derek Wolcott in English; Rosanna Warren in English and modern foreign languages and literatures; Peter Berger in sociology; James Collins in biomedical engineering; Walter Clemens, Angelo Codevilla, Walter Connor, and Sofia Perez in political science; Liah Greenfeld in political science and sociology; Wolfgang Haase in classics; Geoffrey Hill in literature and religion; Charles Lindholm, Robert Hefner, and Peter

Wood in anthropology; Glenn Loury in economics; Lucien Richard in theology; Nobel laureate Elie Wiesel in philosophy and religion; Clifford Backman, John Gagliardo, Merle Goldman, James Johnson, William Keylor, and Dietrich Orlow in history; Charles Griswold, David Roochnik, and Stanley Rosen in philosophy; Hillel Levine in religion and sociology; John Daverio and Phyllis Hoffman in the Music Division of the School for the Arts; and Edwin Dellatre, Mary Catherine O'Connor, Roselmina Indrisano, and Judy Schickedanz in the School of Education.

Political Atmosphere: Being BU

BU did not escape the intellectual tumult of the 1960s, and one professor familiar with its history notes that prior to Silber's arrival, BU had a "wildly liberal image." "Run by the faculty for the faculty," the university was "considered to be a weak institution, with no clear identification." Silber, a philosophy professor with a very clear understanding of the meaning of excellence in education, irrevocably changed the school's direction. One faculty member estimates that Silber hired about 80 to 85 percent of the current faculty, and that in this process "he has changed the ethos of BU."

Whether that change in ethos has been entirely positive is still a matter of debate in some campus circles, but no one denies that the president has made an indelible stamp. Even his strongest supporters concede that some of his maneuvers were "very heavy-handed," particularly when it came to dealing with the faculty. Still, according to supporters, these efforts have resulted in a much better situation at BU. Even his most vociferous opponents cannot quibble with the improvement in BU's academic standing and reputation.

Key to that transformation, many would argue, was a dramatic shift in BU's ideological orientation. Politicization of the curriculum is no longer a "particular problem," a professor says. For example, two new scholarly groups unwilling to conform to the ideological politics all too often foisted upon their disciplines have found a home at BU. Both The Historical Society and The Association of Literary Scholars and Critics are based there, and both the university and the organizations are proud that the BU is hospitable to such heterodox efforts to foster scholarship separate from the ideological trends of the day. Furthermore, administration efforts to prevent the adoption of a speech code have been successful, and the university supports none of the "sensitivity courses" taught and even required elsewhere.

If politicization is not a problem at BU, there are many other challenges faced by the school, professors and administrative sources state. Chief among these, according to one administrator, are the "challenges presented by culture." A "generation of students alienated from literature" — because they are hooked on TV and movies — is more averse to liberal education than ever before, this administrator says. The administration sees it as their hard task to convince students that strictly vocational education — absent a liberal arts foundation — is not the best value in the long term. This is not easy, given the financial bind many students foresee and the availability of less expensive public universities.

Another challenge the university faces, according to one professor, is making the rhetoric of BU's commitment to teaching more a reality. There is, according to this professor, "a lot of lip service to teaching," but this is not always matched by results. Some departments farm out their grad students, though BU strictly proscribes grad students from teaching classes (although they may serve as assistants). The pressure applied in certain departments to make more use of graduate students is driven by cost. Students report some problems with teaching assistants, but in general students say that they are able to find small classes with top-notch professors.

Student Life: Urban Delight

If one is looking for a bucolic campus setting, BU is definitely not the place to go. Stretching along the south bank of the Charles River, BU's campus and the surrounding neighborhoods can be described as gritty. What it lacks, however, in architectural splendor BU makes up in urban offerings. Any imaginable ethnic cuisine, the historical tradition and cultural vivacity of Boston, and the youthfulness of a metropolitan area with more than fifty-five colleges and universities combine to make BU abuzz with action. The university buildings and residence halls are spread out over more than a mile, intermixed with other fixtures of the city, so students will became well acquainted with the public transportation system, called the "T," whose cars and buses shuttle students back and forth on campus.

About half of undergraduates reside on campus, and the school has not abandoned the formerly widespread tradition of *in loco parentis*. Students must sign in all guests and escort them at all times; they must show identification to enter dorms; and overnight guests are allowed only for members of the same sex. Freshmen under twenty-one are required to live on campus. The dorms themselves range from Boston brownstones to high-rises, including one 750-bed behemoth that is currently under construction. Resident assistants live in every dorm, and there are faculty-in-residence in most of the large residences and many smaller ones as well. Most dorms are coed, and a huge variety of interest-specific dorm houses and floors are available (running from Earth/Environmental Awareness House to a Classics House).

BU has its own police force, and is very cognizant of the special challenges posed to student safety because of its urban location. Crime and safety awareness programs are offered in the fall and summer to both students and parents.

As with many other schools, the furor over sweatshops has captured the attention of the student government. BU's price tag is of perennial concern, one student active in campus government reports. In general, politicized programs sponsored by the university are not outlandish, but rather more run-of-the-mill multicultural offerings. The "Message for the New Millennium" program, for example, emphasizing peace, humanity, and community, and featuring a bisexual author, was an "ideological and politicized venture," according to a student, but such events are less frequently found at BU than at many other schools its size. Other recent speakers include Patrick Buchanan, who gave a policy address, and commencement speakers Henry Kissinger and Tom Wolfe.

Intramural and club sports are available to students, and the university fields intercollegiate teams in most major sports, although the football team played its final game several years ago. Hockey is the biggest spectator sport at BU, and games are often sold out when the championship-caliber team takes the ice.

There are almost 350 student organizations at BU. Among these are many with a focus on areas of study, including classics, economics, English, history and international relations, modern languages, and philosophy. BU boasts a very large international student population (hailing from more than 140 countries) who form many cultural groups on campus. Students with exotic interests may join the Literary Pipe Smokers, the Medieval Recreation Society, the Friends of Spartacus Youth, or the Friends of the Revolutionary Anti-Imperialist League.

Marsh Chapel offers weekly worship, and campus chaplains are available through the chapel. Hillel House provides the center for Jewish life at BU; the Catholic Center at Newman House does the same for Roman Catholic students. Ministers from various denominations are available on campus.

Bowdoin College

Office of Admissions
5000 College Station
Brunswick, ME 04011
(207) 725-3100
www.bowdoin.edu

Total enrollment: 1,610
Undergraduates: 1,610
SAT ranges (Verbal/Math): 640-720 (V); 640-710 (M)
Applicants: 3,950
Accepted: 32%

Enrolled: 37%
Application deadline: January 1
Financial aid application deadline: February 15
Tuition: $25,940/$32,910
Core curriculum: No

Liberty? Equality? Fraternity?

For starters, Bowdoin is a beautiful college, located just three miles from the sea and not far from Maine's largest city, Portland. The college has a long and venerable history — it's nearing its two hundredth academic year — and there are some excellent classes and programs available to students. The school has a mammoth endowment of around $470 million, and, in one of those quirks of history, graduated both Nathaniel Hawthorne and Henry Wadsworth Longfellow in the same class, in 1825. It is consistently ranked by *U.S. News and World Report* as one of the top ten liberal arts colleges in the U.S.

Bowdoin has long defined "education in terms of a social vision," according to college materials. "Bowdoin's intellectual mission is informed by the humbling and cautionary lesson of the twentieth century: that intellect and cultivation, unless informed by a basic sense of decency, of tolerance and mercy, are ultimately destructive of both the person and society," it states. "The purpose of a Bowdoin education — the mission of the college — is therefore to assist a student to deepen and broaden intellectual capacities that are also attributes of maturity and wisdom: self-knowledge, intellectual honesty, clarity of thought, depth of knowledge, an independent capacity to learn, mental courage, self discipline, tolerance of and interest in differences of culture and belief, and a willingness to serve the common good and subordinate self to higher goals."

These words may be taken in a variety of ways. The administration has found in them justification for politicization of the curriculum, a fact that worries traditionalists on campus who read them quite differently. And to borrow an idea from a Bowdoin alum, traditionalists on campus might just as well be wearing a scarlet letter. While a good student will still be able to sort through the course offerings, choosing the good ones and ignoring the rest, he should expect to run into quite a bit of "the rest."

Academic Life: No Bones About It

Bowdoin requires of its students but two courses in each of three divisions: natural sciences and mathematics, humanities and fine arts, and social and behavioral sciences. The college's view book calls this "a broad and contemporary foundation for a liberal arts education." It is certainly contemporary, but it seems like a stretch to call it broad. And it is certainly not deep enough to be called a foundation. Obviously, the college has made no attempt to implement a demanding core curriculum that would provide a common reading experience for all students.

The educational experience is further narrowed by the mandate that two of these six required courses be in "non-Eurocentric" studies, the very categorization of which gives a good indication that they are at least somewhat politicized. There is, of course, no Western civilization requirement. "Non-Eurocentric courses," as defined in Bowdoin's catalogue, do not include language courses but rather classes that "focus on a non-Eurocentric culture or society, exclusive of Europe and European Russia and their literary, artistic, musical, religious, and political traditions. The requirement is intended to introduce students to the variety of cultures and to open their minds to the different ways in which people perceive and cope with the challenges of life." Whatever contrast there is between the approved cultures and European cultures may of course be lost on students who have not studied the European cultures in the first place.

The college encourages every new student to enroll in one of forty seminars developed to introduce first-year students to college-level study. The purpose of the first-year seminar program is to contribute to students' understanding of the ways in which a specific discipline may relate to other areas in the humanities, social sciences, and sciences. Topics range from the interesting to the politicized, and some are a combination of the two; they include "Writing About Music," "Hawthorne," "Cultural Difference and the Crime Film," "Athens and Jerusalem: Classical and Biblical Sources of the Western Political Tradition," "Racism," and "Magical Realism." Regardless of the topic, most sound more like graduate seminars than like material for first-year students.

Students select courses with the assistance of an academic advisor. Each student is assigned an advisor at the start of his first year, and continues to be advised by the faculty member assigned to him through his sophomore year. After declaring a major (thirty departmental majors and several interdisciplinary majors are offered) at the end of that year, students are generally advised by a member of their major department.

To go with the non-Eurocentric requirement, Bowdoin offers a few entirely non-Eurocentric departments — Africana studies and women's studies, for example. There are more traditional disciplines, of course, and the best of these include economics, chemistry, and government. More than 35 percent of Bowdoin's students major in the social sciences and history, compared to 23.5 percent nationwide at institutions of Bowdoin's class. The percentage of students who major in a foreign language (11 percent) is nearly triple the national average. Also significant are the 7 percent who major in a field related to conservation and natural resources, compared with only 0.6 percent nationally. This latter statistic reflects the growing popularity of Bowdoin's environmental studies major.

Among Bowdoin's best professors are Paul Nyhus in history, John Fitzgerald in economics, John Ambrose and James Higginbotham in classics, and Richard Morgan and Jean Yarbrough in government and legal studies.

About 60 percent of Bowdoin students study abroad as juniors. The opportunities range from the study of Renaissance painting in Florence to ecology in Tanzania to health care in India. Many of these programs include residence with a host family as part of the experience. Bowdoin is also directly affiliated with five off-campus study programs: The Intercollegiate Center for Classical Studies in Rome; The Intercollegiate Sri Lanka Education (ISLE) Program; The South India Term Abroad (SITA) Program; and The Swedish Program in Organization Studies and Public Policy. For those wanting to stay in the U.S., Bowdoin offers a "Twelve College Exchange," which provides Bowdoin students the opportunity to study for a year at Amherst, Connecticut, Dartmouth, Mount Holyoke, Smith, Trinity, Vassar, Wellesley, Wheaton, Williams, or Wesleyan.

A large number of students choose to double-major or to take an interdisciplinary major. Another option: design your own major. And Bowdoin also allows "coordinate majors," which encourage "specialization in an area of learning within the framework of a recognized academic discipline." Currently the coordinate major is offered only in relation to the Africana studies program and the environmental studies program. This option seems little more than a backdoor attempt to get the administration to approve pet projects, eventually fund them, and make them difficult to dislodge.

One highly ideological program already in place is gay and lesbian studies, which is "an interdisciplinary analysis that both considers the specific cultural achievements of gay men and lesbians and takes the experience of lesbians and gay men as a critical perspective on the role of sexuality in culture as a whole." Though the course of study is not formally set, the college recommends courses listed under the departments of anthropology, English, film studies, sociology, and Spanish.

Among departments with full standing, women's studies, Africana studies, and religion are certainly the most politicized, according to a highly regarded professor. English appears to have dropped a few politicized classes of late, and offers a relatively complete slate of literature and creative writing courses — at least, if their titles are to be believed.

One Bowdoin course of study does honor a distinguished alum, Admiral Robert Peary, whose exploration led the college to start a rare Arctic studies program. The program, designated as a "special academic program," offers classes in anthropology and sociology as well as fieldwork through the geology department, both at Bowdoin and points much colder.

Bowdoin College recently received a $21 million gift to pay for the recurring costs of computer and network upgrades and for investments in new technologies from alumnus Stanley F. Druckenmiller, managing director at Soros Fund Management in New York. It creates a $6 million endowment for educational technology and a separate endowment of $15 million to cover rising costs of the college's information technology infrastructure.

Political Atmosphere: The Ministry of Culture

Bowdoin just named a new president, Barry Mills, a lawyer from New York City. Praise for Mills on campus centers on the emphasis he places on "diversity." "Barry Mills is deeply committed to diversity — as exemplified by his efforts in this regard at [his old law firm] — and he believes strongly in the value to Bowdoin and society of making ours a more diverse community," one faculty member told a college publication.

Not everyone seems happy with the college's attempt at diversity. Heather Park, a contributor to the student newspaper, writes: "When dealing with the issue of diversity at Bowdoin, it seems to be very much a black/white issue. I don't want to be misunderstood as saying that diversity at Bowdoin pertains solely to one minority group. I would merely like to point out that this college's commitment to ethnic cultivation and diversity is not evenly distributed. Although there is a significant Asian constituency in the student body, the administration does not heed the economic, academic, and psychological needs of its Asian students. Perhaps Asians do not provide the 'diversity' to raise Bowdoin's standings in the *U.S. News & World Report*."

If he does pursue some idea of diversity, Mills will merely be carrying on what is practically a Bowdoin tradition by now. A senior professor says that the previous administration pursued this notion "obsessively," backing bizarre fields of study and a slew of ranting student groups. In the college's public relations information, various leftist mantras are blended like the ingredients of clam chowder. A few years ago, a young lady featured in an attractive publication sent to prospective students was described as the "minister of culture" of the African-American Society and opinion editor of the *Bowdoin Orient,* the student newspaper. Most officers of student organizations settle for quaint titles like president, secretary, and so on; the appearance of the title "minister of culture" in a publication designed to attract students to Bowdoin gives some indication of the importance placed upon such undertakings by the college and its de facto ministers of culture, whatever their official titles.

Also featured prominently in this publication were the various multicultural groups on campus, including the African-American Society, the John Brown Russwurm African-American Center, the Latin American Student Organization, the Bowdoin Women's Association, and B-GLAD (Bisexual, Gay, Lesbian Alliance for Diversity). Also celebrated is ADAPT (Awareness of Differences Among People Today), whose members "receive intensive training to bring a pluralistic philosophy to other groups on campus. Student groups work together to sponsor such events as a silent dinner and a candlelight vigil to demonstrate their concern for a more diverse curriculum and community." That such atypical groups with small memberships are featured so prominently in a publication blessed by central command and offered to the inquiring public says something important about the image the administration wishes to project.

The same philosophy has been applied to faculty hiring. "At Bowdoin, as at all similar institutions in the Northeast, there is a powerful, but always unspoken, prejudice against conservatives," says one professor. Another recalls that when a young conservative scholar came up for tenure a few years ago, she was rejected. Bowdoin is still not as monolithic in its liberalism as some New England schools (perhaps due in part to the rural setting of the college), but it is obvious that the Bowdoin administration equates quality with conformity to academic trends. For all its good aspects, Bowdoin is likely to remain an intellectual playground for chic intellectuals for some time to come. A politically correct catalogue such as Bowdoin's is impossible without faculty willing to teach such courses. And if those courses are afforded such a place of pride in Bowdoin's public relations material, it seems likely that those who teach them also are given preferential treatment in hiring and tenure.

Bowdoin certainly doesn't need to be politically correct in order to attract funding. Though the cost of attending is very high for a school of Bowdoin's size and rural location, the college's endowment is something in the range of $470 million. There are many new construction and renovation projects on campus, and Bowdoin has some of the finest facilities of any college in its class. A new science facility completed in the summer of 1997 replaced an aged building at a cost of no less than $20 million, a princely sum for a liberal arts college to spend on any building. The libraries are no less excellent. The Hawthorne-Longfellow Library holds nearly 850,000 volumes, a collection that places it near the top of undergraduate institutions in that category. With these impressive figures in mind, one cannot be surprised to learn that the college's expenditure per student on services (admissions, career guidance, health, etc.) is, in the words of one assessment service, "substantially in excess of the norm for institutions of its class." The college also boasts an art museum, a large Visual Arts Center, and several auditoriums used for speeches, plays, and other activities.

Bowdoin's financial future seems secure, as does its ability to draw excellent students from around the country. In the first edition of this guide, one professor gave this assessment of its future: "I am not at all optimistic about the coming decade. . . . Almost every program and department is weaker today than it was six or seven years ago, and I don't see this being reversed. A new president with a new team could do the trick, but that person would have to be a serious academic with strong personal intellectual accomplishments. Given the tendency in recent years for places such as Bowdoin to choose non-academic managers as presidents, the prospect is not encouraging."

It seems that this professor was more right than he knew.

Student Life: In Fine Company

Bowdoin numbers among its alumni President Franklin Pierce (Class of 1824), Chief Justice Melville Weston Fuller (Class of 1853), former Secretary of Defense William Cohen ('62), another Supreme Court justice, sixteen U.S. senators, forty-three U.S. congressmen, eleven governors of Maine, and three current members of the Maine Supreme Court — not to mention Alfred C. Kinsey ('16), author of the famous study of human sexuality. Its student body of 1,610 hails from 48 states and 32 countries.

Even now, the college attracts very bright students, and one would not be surprised to see this honor roll added to by members of the current crop. Bowdoin turned down almost 70 percent of applicants for the class of 2000 (but enrolled only 37 percent of those accepted for admission, a moderate number). That a college in rural Maine could be this selective and attract students from so far away speaks well of Bowdoin's reputation.

Students at Bowdoin may choose from a plethora of club activities and the like. The school sponsors twelve men's and thirteen women's varsity teams, as well as coed golf and sailing. It also has excellent athletic facilities, including the new Farley Field House, which holds a sixteen-lane pool, four indoor tennis courts, and many other exercise areas. All intramural teams are coeducational, which is in keeping with the college's insistence that all students be allowed to participate in all activities, regardless of any detrimental effects this policy may have on the activities themselves.

Among the more popular student organizations is the Outing Club, which hosts excursions into Maine's ample forests and mountains. Bowdoin's debate team was a recent but welcome addition to the choices available to students. Naturally, Bowdoin also has the usual run of socially chic organizations, such as the aforementioned B-GLAD, ADAPT, African-American Society, Bowdoin Women's Association, and Latin American Student Organization, as well as the Asian Student Association, HIV/AIDS Peer Educators, Native American Interest Group, and such. The Catholic Center on campus is reputedly less Catholic than the name would suggest.

What Bowdoin no longer has, however, are fraternities and sororities. Following years of open hostility toward Greek groups, Bowdoin's Governing Board voted in May 1992 to prohibit single-sex fraternities and sororities. The policy applies to all residential and nonresidential single-sex organizations, either local or nationally affiliated. College literature describes such groups as "discriminatory social membership organizations" and proclaims that "single-sex fraternities and sororities are fundamentally inconsistent with the values of this coeducational college." Furthermore, the college has threatened disciplinary action against anyone who recruits for or joins banned organizations.

But even this policy was not draconian enough for the Governing Board. In 1997 it banned the coeducational fraternities that had been set up following the banishment of single-sex Greek letter organizations and ruled that by the year 2000 all coed fraternities will be replaced by a "non-exclusive house system" to which all students may belong. The vote followed on the heels of a report from a Governing Board commission set up to study the matter, and the language of the report can rightfully be characterized as Orwellian. Even as the report calls for the prohibition of free association among individuals of free will, it states that the commission's goals were "building a community at the college; inclusiveness; a need to revitalize the core campus; a desire to focus on the needs of the sophomore class; the importance of identification with a residence in all aspects of student life; and a return to a sense of tradition at Bowdoin." The commission also had the nerve to claim that the new policy would be successful in "fostering an environment of challenge and growth, preserving freedom of expression and inquiry, encouraging mutual respect and civility of discourse and concern for others . . . [and] friendship and fun." All told, the report was yet another indicator that Bowdoin is in the hands of folks for whom tradition is just something to be typed over.

Under the new house system, wholly owned and maintained by the college, each incoming student is assigned (randomly) to campus dormitories. Every student will remain a member of the same house for all four years at Bowdoin, which of course will become a more friendly place open to all, make everyone feel good, and somehow make sure that all students have the right to live exactly where the college puts them.

The "choices" available to students, housing-wise, will at least be above average. There is a high-rise dorm on campus but also college-owned apartments, and discipline- and ethnic-themed houses, though we wonder how these last two can possibly be "nondiscriminatory." All residence hall floors are coed, and in some (but not all) men and women share bathrooms.

The rural setting of the school makes for low crime; it is mostly limited to bike thefts and vandalism. The school is however suing its former controller, alleging that he embezzled about $50,000 from the school. The controller is accused of "using the college treasurer's signature stamp to enable him to make unauthorized transfers from a Bowdoin bank account," according to the *Chronicle of Higher Education.*

Brandeis University

Office of Admissions
P.O. Box 549110
Waltham, Massachusetts 02454-9110
(617) 736-3500
www.brandeis.edu

Total enrollment: 4,405
Undergraduates: 3,141
SAT ranges (Verbal/Math): 610-710 (V); 610-710 (M)
Applicants: 6,103
Accepted: 48%
Enrolled: 30%
Application deadline: January 1
Financial aid application deadline: January 31
Tuition: $25,392/$32,581
Core curriculum: No

Almost Supreme

Colleges and universities generally sell themselves through one of two pitches: "We're small, but we're big," or "We're big, but we're really small." Brandeis makes both claims, noting in its literature: "Brandeis combines two important traditions in higher education: the dedication to teaching that is characteristic of a small, selective college and the facilities and renowned faculty usually associated with a large research university."

In many ways, Brandeis succeeds in striking the balance between commitment to undergraduate teaching and achieving renown in research — both pitches apply. Founded in 1948, Brandeis is the nation's youngest private research university. At the same time, it has kept its undergraduate population small, with an enrollment of about 3,100. Most importantly, students report satisfaction with the commitment of the faculty to the classroom, even as they balance that commitment with widely-recognized research. (A university publication states that Brandeis is ranked ninth in the number of times the work of its faculty is cited by other researchers.)

Named for Supreme Court Justice Louis D. Brandeis, the university celebrates Justice Brandeis as "exemplif[ying] the highest levels of intellectual inquiry." In a description of the student scholarships named in the jurist's honor, the university notes that "He championed broad learning in the arts and sciences as one of the fundamental values of a democracy."

Even as the Brandeis faculty strike a fairly good balance between commitment to teaching and research, the institution as a whole has been challenged in maintaining a fidelity to its stated credo of pursuing "Truth Even Unto Its Innermost Parts." Politicization has eroded certain aspects of a Brandeis education, in the process imperiling the pursuit of truth that is the university's stated objective. Even while the danger is present, there is much to celebrate about Brandeis.

Academic Life: Likely Outcomes

Brandeis has no single course, much less a core curriculum, that all its students must take. Instead, it offers "University Seminars in Humanistic Inquiry," an interdisciplinary program for freshmen, and "clusters," which, while no longer required for graduation, "provide a useful map or guide to some of the many pathways through the curriculum," according to university literature. In addition to the requirements in a student's major, each student must take a quantitative reasoning course, three semesters of a foreign language, what amounts to a diversity requirement, and two semesters of physical education.

Essentially, this amounts to a fairly loose set of distribution requirements. Brandeis refers to the sum total of the requirements as a "core curriculum," but it's hard to conceive of a core in which there isn't even one common course that every student must take to graduate. The only thing the university can offer is the following: "In fulfilling the various requirements of the core curriculum, it is likely that you will have enrolled in at least one course from each of the four schools at the university: Humanities, Social Science, Science, and Creative Arts. If not, you will select a course from any omitted school to complete this requirement."

Even with the lack of a core, the "University Seminars in Humanistic Inquiry" offer freshmen at Brandeis a good opportunity to get off on the right foot in their education. Offered a choice of some forty seminars, freshmen are given, in the university's description, the possibility of exploring "fundamental questions about the meaning of human existence" in courses that "are centered around reading lists that help you see the ways great books and ideas 'speak' to each other."

The freshman seminars arose in the early 1990s as a replacement for what had been a rather traditional humanities core. The school's split emphasis on the liberal arts and the research model of a university ultimately caught up with the humanities, professors report, so while classical humanities themes are still represented, they do not predominate.

With no more than fifteen students in each class led by senior faculty, the program promises much, especially with topics like "Becoming an Educated Person," "Classics of Western Thought," and "Nature and Your Place in It." Other topics, like "Bad Girls," "Everyday Activity," "Revisioning the Classics: Then and Now," "Stigmatized Identities," and "Textual Transformations" hardly inspire confidence that students will be confronted with "the best which has been thought and said in the world," in the words of Matthew Arnold. It's typical of the catalogue that a course like "Bad Girls" is found next to an offering like "Nature and Natural Law," which includes readings from Cicero, Aquinas, Clarence Thomas, and Pope John Paul II.

There is no Western civilization requirement at Brandeis, although a "non-Western and comparative studies course concerning the civilizations of Asia, Africa, Latin America, the Middle East, or Oceania," is now required of all students. Many of these comparative courses are solid, especially given the strength of Near Eastern and Judaic Studies at Brandeis, but some of the courses are heavily politicized.

As with the freshman seminars and the "comparative courses," the "cluster" programs at Brandeis are also a hit-or-miss proposition. There are a fair number of hits, but students must take care to miss the misses, as it were. Until very recently, completing a cluster program was a requirement for graduation from Brandeis. According to the course catalogue, clusters "exemplify the concept of connected learning: that students share an intellectual excitement when courses connect and are related to each other. Each cluster focuses on the multidisciplinary study of a particular topic, theme, problem, region, or period." There are a few clusters with traditional areas of focus ("Greece and Rome, Seen and Seen Again," "The Birth of Europe," "The Renaissance," "The Enlightenment," and "Justice"), but the preponderance of the courses are politicized ("Colonialism and Neo-Colonialism in the Third World," "Cultural Representations of Gender," "Ethnicity, Race, and Culture," "Feminist Perspectives on Society," "Gender and Work," and "Power and Politics: Theory, Literature, and Practice" among them).

With the seminar and cluster concept, Brandeis has at least tried to preserve (or make available) the linking of disciplines essential to genuine liberal education. Still, what matters most is *how* the links are made and whether the curriculum makes it likely that they will be made. Without the proper professorial guidance, the linkages emphasized can become more ideological or accidental than educational and coherent.

Brandeis' founding at the end of World War II — a vastly important time for Western Judaism and the West in general — seems to have left a legacy of intellectual urgency at the institution and to have led the university toward "progressive" agendas. Superficially, this tendency is apparent in the selection of visiting faculty and "celebrity" faculty hires. Anita Hill serves as a professor in the women's studies program, while former Clinton cabinet member Robert Reich serves as University Professor (one of the very few with this honor) and holds an endowed chair in social and economic policy. Former New York City Mayor Ed Koch visited Brandeis (his class was "absolutely horrible," one student says), and former Texas governor Ann Richards taught a class on "The Political Experience," which focused on females in politics and multicultural issues. *Ms.* magazine founder Gloria Steinem has also taught in the women's studies program.

At the same time, Brandeis is home to many scholars whose teaching and research work is very well respected. One student offers high praise for the faculty as a whole, noting that "overall, the faculty is superb." Excellent professors at Brandeis include Eugene Goodheart in English, David Hackett Fischer in history, Anthony Polonsky in Near Eastern and Judaic studies, George W. Ross in sociology, and Stephen J. Whitfield in American studies.

Strong programs include European Cultural Studies and the History of Ideas, both of which stress the integration of disciplines. Sciences, especially biochemistry, biology, chemistry, and physics, are considered very strong, as is the interdisciplinary premed program. The field of neuroscience offers many areas of inquiry to undergrads, and in all of the sciences students are given opportunities to conduct research.

Women's studies, peace and conflict studies, English, and sociology are quite heavily politicized. Women's studies includes courses exploring "Lesbian and Gay Studies: Desire, Identity, and Representation," while a student in the English department can take "AIDS, Activism, and Representation," or "Making Sex, Performing Gender."

Political Atmosphere: Yearly Calendar

According to one Brandeis student, there exists a "substantial left-leaning atmosphere on campus." From the time students arrive on campus until commencement, the administration fosters an atmosphere in which conservative ideas are decidedly not welcome.

Orientation is often seized by universities as an opportunity to initiate its ideological programs. At Brandeis, according to one student's report, orientation is used to disorient students who adhere to a traditional understanding of morality. One presentation in the orientation of 1999, according to the conservative campus publication *Freedom*, featured a kind of celebration of homosexuality. The speaker, a professed lesbian who told of her efforts to wed her partner, proclaimed, "Vermont is our only hope." If students didn't get the message that homosexuality must be accepted by all Brandeis students, the Campus Life Calendar reemphasizes the point by defining homophobia as a "prejudice based on the belief that lesbian, gay and bisexual people are sinful [and] immoral."

The calendar's definition of homophobia points to an ongoing on-campus challenge: the role of religion. Although Brandeis was founded as a secular institution, the student body remains one-half to two-thirds Jewish (depending on who's counting), and issues related to Judaism are at the forefront of campus discussion.

The university as of late has deemphasized its Jewish roots in the interests of attracting a more diverse student body, some say. Ten years ago came the controversial introduction of pork and shellfish into campus dining halls (though the university still has a kosher dining hall), and about the same time the university, while not holding classes on Jewish holidays, stopped printing the names of those holidays on official campus calendars. The university view book makes more prominent mention of Black History Month, the "Chinese Moon Festival," and Kwanzaa than of any Jewish holidays.

On campus, many branches of Judaism are represented, from Orthodox to Reformed. Nevertheless, the emphasis by the administration is most decidedly on diversity — and not the diversity within the Jewish faith. The view book states: "As the only nonsectarian university founded by the Jewish community, we regard these values [i.e., diversity] as vital and seek to engage a diverse body of students who also appreciate their importance." Elsewhere, the view book notes that "The university's principle of diversity and religious freedom is symbolized in bricks and mortar by the Brandeis chapels." Jewish, Catholic, and Protestant, the three chapels, which are all quite striking, were designed by the famous architect Eero Saarinen (the scrolls of the Jewish chapel call to mind the Torah, while the shape of the Catholic and Protestant chapels resemble a Bible). None of the chapels ever casts a shadow on either of the others, in what the university says is a symbol of "the religious freedom and tolerance so valued by the university."

As with so many affirmations of tolerance on university campuses today, the Brandeis endorsement of tolerance has very definite limits, particularly when it comes to tolerating conservatives. In recent years there has been a ferment of activity among conservatives on campus, as students founded several organizations and strengthened other existing organizations.

The College Republicans at Brandeis claim a large membership, and several organizations have sprung from their ranks: People Eat Tasty Animals Club (a play off the well-known animal-rights activist group People for the Ethical Treatment of Animals), and the Second Amendment Club. An attempt to start a group called Preservation of a Male Society, or PMS, was not approved, even though a week later the Feminist Majority Leadership Alliance was granted approval. A Vast Right Wing Conspiracy Lecture Series, featuring conservative speakers, was sponsored on campus by conservative students.

Much of the combat on campus waged by conservatives was spearheaded by *Freedom*, a monthly founded recently that describes itself as "a non-partisan, monthly conservative/libertarian student journal of news and opinion" that seeks to explore subjects "historically denied adequate attention by other campus media." Acting as a thorn in the side of the administration and the student government, the magazine had its student funding cut in half 1998, then yanked altogether in April of 1999 by the student senate. Copies of the magazine were stolen, and the editor of the publication was threatened with physical violence. The magazine as a whole was described by one student government senator as "fascist, racist, homophobic, antisemitic, bigoted, and anti-senate." The charges of antisemitism are especially interesting given the fact that many past and present staffers are faithful Jews.

Despite the obstacles placed in the way of conservative students, one group on campus remained adamant in their quest to bring one of the most recognizable conservative spokesmen in the country, Charlton Heston, to campus. Invited by the Second Amendment Club, Heston agreed to speak on campus, as he does across the country. The announcement of his March 2000 visit was greeted with unprecedented security demands from the university administration, including the presence of ten police officers (in addition to university security), two full-body metal detectors, two metal detector wands, bomb-sniffing dogs, and a paramedic team standing by with four pints of Heston's blood type. Student sponsors were going to be stuck with most of the bill for these mandated items (despite the fact that Heston had spoken in front of university crowds of more than 2,500 without incident). As it turned out, the lecture drew more than seven hundred people (in addition to two hundred protesters). No blood transfusions were needed, and other student groups (including the student senate) helped to defray the costs of the event.

A legal case involving a Brandeis student with important national implications was decided in the fall of 2000. The case, decided by the Supreme Judicial Court of Massachusetts, began when a male Brandeis student was accused by a female of rape. Found guilty of "unwanted sexual activity" and creating a "hostile environment" by a judicial panel of six students and two professors, the student sued the university, claiming that the panel had violated his right to due process. After courts ruled in his favor, Brandeis appealed to Massachusetts' high court, which in ruling for the university stated that "a university is not required to adhere to the standards of due process guaranteed to criminal defendants or to abide by the rules of evidence adopted by courts." Although the ruling applies only to Massachusetts colleges, the court's decision has important ramifications for similar cases elsewhere. While most private universities supported Brandeis, arguing that sufficient safeguards are in place to protect accused students, the current political climate on many campuses — in which kangaroo courts are routinely convened at private universities to prosecute "crimes" as defined by nebulous codes for speech and conduct — casts doubt on the claims of the universities.

Student Life: We Gotta Go Now

Brandeis University is located in the Boston suburb of Waltham, making for easy access to the rich cultural and social offerings of Boston and Cambridge. Trips to both cities are accomplished either by public transportation or the university's free shuttle bus. The suburban location, however, is also conducive to study, and students are said to apply themselves seriously to their academic work. Crime is not a problem.

On campus, two not-too-serious annual events are "not to be missed," according to the view book. "Louis, Louis," the name of which is apparently a rather irreverent play on the university's namesake and the title of the world's most popular party song ("Louie Louie"), comes the week before fall semester final exams. Its spring semester counterpart is "Bronstein" weekend. The view book notes that both are "jam-packed with annual events such semi-formal dances, major concerts, drive-in movies, and many other special events."

More than 85 percent of the student body lives on campus. Along with standard dorms, there is a changing list of special interest houses. In the past these houses have had themes such as international awareness, religious diversity, health issues, environmental awareness, music, and Jewish awareness. There are no single-sex residence halls, and about three-quarters of dorm floors are coed. These floors always have separate bathrooms for men and women.

There are more than 190 student organizations on campus. A number of organizations are oriented toward liberal activism: Activist Resource Center, Brandeis Animal Right Klub (BARK), Feminist Majority Leadership Alliance, Students for Economic Justice, Students for Environmental Action, Triskelion (a homosexual support group), and the Women's Resource Center. Religious organizations include a number of Jewish groups (Orthodox Organization, BaRuCH Reform Chavurah), the Catholic Student Organization, and the Christian Fellowship. A number of organizations are simply baffling: Beastie Boys Syndicate, Boffing Club, Rocky Horror Picture Show Fan Club, and the Zany Bagel Tasters.

In addition to the conservative *Freedom* magazine, there are a number of other publications. *Justice* is the main campus newspaper; other publications include *Louis*, "a magazine of intellectual discourse" (of the liberal variety, it might be added), and magazines *Watch* and *Weathervane*.

For those who are inclined toward athletic events, the university boasts one of the largest multipurpose indoor recreation facilities in the region. The Ford Athletic and Recreation Complex includes a 70,000-square-foot field house that includes the Red Auerbach Arena (where the Boston Celtics used to hold practices until recently). Varsity athletes compete at the NCAA Division III level in ten men's sports and ten women's sports. A total of twenty-three club sports and seven intramural sports are offered.

Brown University

Admissions Office — The College
Brown University
Box 1876
Providence, Rhode Island 02912
(401) 863-2378
www.brown.edu

Total enrollment: 7,333
Undergraduates: 5,777
SAT ranges (Verbal/Math): 650-750 (V); 650-750 (M)
Applicants: 17,000
Accepted: 15%
Enrolled: 56%
Application deadline: January 1
Financial aid application deadline: February 1
Tuition: $26,374/$33,720
Core curriculum: No

They Called It Providence, the One in Rhode Island

Brown University, located in the manufacturing city of Providence, Rhode Island, is New England's third-oldest university. Founded in 1764, Brown is one of the eight members of the prestigious Ivy League. While most of the Ivies are massive research universities, at Brown undergraduates comprise almost eighty percent of the total enrollment. With its relatively smaller size and openness to what in the mission statement is called "intellectual innovation and change," Brown prides itself on "maintaining a university-college of liberal arts."

In seeking to establish the "purpose" of a Brown education, university literature cites Dr. Henry Merritt Wriston, Brown's president from 1937 to 1955: "The central business of the university is the increase of knowledge, the inculcation of wisdom, the refinement of emotional responses, and the development of spiritual awareness." Despite the endorsement of these lofty ends, Brown's commitment to intellectual innovation and change seems to have trumped the concerted pursuit of a liberal education for all of its students.

While many universities have laid aside the traditional core of liberal arts courses and adopted instead a loosely connected set of distribution requirements, Brown has rejected even these anemic standards: there are no required classes except those taken to fulfill a major. Students are free to choose the remaining classes.

69

Moreover, they can choose the manner in which they will be graded — including the option of receiving only pass/fail grades for their entire college careers. In making student choice sacred, and emphasizing the innovative over the eternal, Brown University risks its status as a true institute of liberal learning.

Academic Life: Running the Asylum

The distinguishing feature of Brown's core requirements is that there are none. Required courses are those required by a student's major, a jarring abdication of a university's duty to decide what constitutes learning. Brown doesn't shy away from listing courses that prospective students ought to take, but extends them almost complete freedom once they get to campus.

Brown estimates that around 80 percent of students do take a wide array of classes, but estimating this figure against an essentially standardless basis is rather a waste of time. Besides, a traditional liberal arts education is a lot more than "a wide array of classes." The fact is, students so inclined could graduate with absolutely no education (let alone classes) in the sciences, literature, foreign languages, history, or any of the other liberal arts.

For Brown, the dangers of this abuse of the system are outweighed by the potential benefits: its "unique" undergraduate curriculum, the university claims, "provides bright, self-motivated students the opportunity to become architects of their educational experience." (It should be noted that the Curricular Advising Program is strong, and that faculty take, as one professor noted, an "almost *in loco parentis* responsibility" for the students they advise. Still, not everyone listens to his or her parents.) Students are required to declare their concentration by the end of the sophomore year, meaning they go two years without requirements of any kind.

According to another professor, "the system works well for thoughtful and intellectually mature students who know what they want." These students, the professor says, comprise about 10 percent of Brown's student body. "The remaining ninety percent," he says, "are often attracted to courses by a combination of the instructor's personal style, intellectual or ideological fashion and the nature of the course requirements. Departments compete for enrollment by assigning to the introductory level course charismatic lecturers who can entertain as well as educate and adjust the intellectual content of the course to problems important to recent high school graduates. In this process an invitation to serious academic inquiry may easily be lost."

Still, despite the wide latitude granted students in course selection, another professor praises the program. "It's worked out remarkably well," he says, noting that distribution requirements at many other schools are "quite silly." This same professor also says that the lack of structure spares Brown students from the "diversity" requirements mandated at many other schools; thus there is a "blessing in disguise" in the looseness of the structure. Interestingly, the Old Left (who has backed the Brown lack of structure) has prevented the New Left (with its fads and academic innovations) from imposing a new curriculum. As another professor notes, "How could we enforce a political correctness when we don't force kids to do a single thing?"

The normal course load at Brown is four courses a semester for eight semesters. Only thirty courses are required for a degree, however, in order to "encourage risk-taking in the planning of educational programs" and to "provide a degree of flexibility" to students, according to the university catalogue. Students cannot take fewer than three courses in one semester without the permission of the dean.

The history department, an outstanding department at Brown, for example, requires of concentrators a minimum of eight semester-long courses. Students select an area of history that will be the focus of their program. A series of requirements dictated by the department according to their focus guides students. The program is hardly unstructured, then, a plan several professors interviewed found to be a good balance for the "remarkably good students" that comprise most of the Brown student body. Good professors in the department include Amy Remensnyder (who specializes in European history) and Michael Vorenberg (legal history and the Civil War). Other reliably fair professors include Paul Kellstedt and John Tomasi in political science.

Another excellent department at Brown is neuroscience, which is part of the biology and medicine departments. There are very fine facilities for research, which is encouraged. The overall concentration of biology and medicine, which is divided into several subgroups, is also strong.

Brown is also home to some rare departments. The university boasts the world's only academic department in the history of mathematics, although it has just one professor. It also has North America's only Egyptology department, which has three professors. Brown's Center for Old World Archaeology and Art is an independent academic unit that encompasses a variety of disciplines. The goal of the concentration is to give students a strong background in art and archaeology, supplemented with a series of lectures and special publications. Since 1965 the department has sponsored field activities in southern Italy.

Politicization among the professorate is common, according to several faculty members. There exists a "liberal bias among the faculty — this goes without saying," says a faculty member. Another comments of the atmosphere at Brown, "Political preferences and ideological prejudices are openly expressed in informal talk and this makes professional conversation difficult for a graduate student or faculty member who does not share leftist views." This professor does note that "Older faculty tend to adopt a more balanced and not openly ideological stance. In professional discourse, Marxism (outside the economics department) is not regarded as an obsolete and thoroughly discredited theory but rather as a viable conceptual framework. Postmodernism is commonly considered a useful tool of inquiry."

Academic experimentation at Brown is not limited to its curriculum. Grading policy also offers many options to students. Students may take courses for letter grades (with options for A's, B's, and C's, but not D's and F's). There are no D's or F's. Any grade below a C simply disappears on the way to the registrar's office — the university doesn't place any sort of notation on the student's transcript to indicate that the student even took the course. Without any pluses or minuses available for the three grades that can be given, the net effect has been grade inflation, according to one veteran professor. In addition, students can elect to take all their classes pass/fail — or, in Brown's lingo, "satisfactory/no credit." Or they can request that their instructors provide detailed, written assessments of their work in addition to their regular grades. Finally, Brown students may withdraw from a course until the final exam without penalty, a practice one professor calls "pathetic."

A new program focusing on values education was implementing in the fall of 2000. The Stephen Robert Initiative for the Study of Values, named for Brown's chancellor, entails two new lecture courses aimed at freshmen, along with smaller discussion groups in the university's dormitories. The courses, which will focus on questions related to social justice, morality, character, friendship, and spirituality, will not be mandatory, but instead will be "heavily encouraged," according to a university spokesman. The president of Brown at the time the program was adopted, Gordon Gee, said about the program that the world "needs men and women who can discern and champion the necessary elements of a good life and a just society — citizens who are not easily distracted by the evanescent fads, trends, and materialism of modern culture."

The Francis Wayland Collegium for Liberal Learning sounds promising, but its idea of liberal learning is less like Cardinal Newman and more like the fads that have swept the academy. Established in 1980 to focus on "global and interdisciplinary perspectives on significant issues of human life," the collegium sponsored a 1999-2000 lecture series on "Reflections on Race and Ethnicity." Some of the lectures features included: "The Corn Mother Speaks Through Science About Gender and Race," and "Home Alone: African Notes on Feminism and the Problem of Exclusion." Past series have featured lectures on "Gender Politics and Boyle's Law of Gases," and "Histories of the Present and Future: Feminism, Power, Bodies."

Courses commensurate with the lecture agenda of the Wayland Collegium abound. Among the ideological courses at Brown is "Issues in Gender in Sport," whose premise is detailed in the course catalogue: "Much of the information which shapes our biological and psychosocial knowledge of sport comes from androcentric assumptions. Among the course topics are: biology of gender, origins and causes of male supremacy/female oppression in sport, sexual inequality and distribution of power, and sexuality. Issues of race and socioeconomic class are included."

A "standard concentration program" at Brown that is not so standard at many universities is "Sexuality and Society," "an interdisciplinary concentration that examines the construction of sexualities in social, cultural, political, economic, medical and scientific contexts." In addition to the requirements (one of which is English 115, "Unnatural Acts"), the Brown course guide indicates that "additional structure can be provided . . . by focusing on the formation of a particular kind of sexual identity."

Women's studies is available as a concentration. It's described as an examination of "the construction of gender and the category of 'women' in social, political, economic, and cultural contexts." The English department cross-lists classes with ethnic studies and gender studies. The ethnic studies program includes a class on "Manhood, Masculinity, and Sexuality in Asian American Literature." The American civilization concentration fosters, among other things, the exchange of ideas "within feminism concerning identity politics, queer theory, race, visual pleasure, and mass culture." Another course, in "Theories of Sexuality and Subjectivity," provides "a close reading of theories of sexuality and subjectivity produced by recent feminist theory, psychoanalysis, queer theory, and theories of race and ethnicity. The focus is on the relation between the body and language/representation, hegemony and resistance, the realm of the visual, debates about pornography."

For all of the ideological offerings available at Brown, one professor notes that Brown offers a wide variety of excellent courses that are "academically serious, intellectually stimulating, and ideologically untainted." One course offered by the Portuguese and Brazilian studies department begins with this point of departure: "To many students, an exclusive emphasis on specialized studies fragments the 'world' in which they live. A widespread feeling of loss pervades the minds of students who often come to universities to learn right from wrong, to distinguish what is true from what is false, but who realize at the end of four years that their world has fallen into pieces, for they have deconstructed their freshman beliefs, values and ideologies, but have created nothing to replace them. By attempting to shed light on the process of formation and transformation of world views and their nature, through the utilization of various disciplines, of their discoveries and perspectives, students will recognize that they function within a frame of reference in which facts and values are still tied, and that even though suspending their judgments on questions of truth, they are on a daily basis, consciously or unconsciously, making choices on matters of value."

Political Atmosphere: Incoming Fire

The last three years at Brown have been tumultuous at the top administrative echelons. Vartan Gregorian, Brown's longtime president, left the university in 1997. He was replaced by Gordon Gee, who prior to arriving in Providence had been president of The Ohio State University. During Gee's first full year, Brown enjoyed considerable success, despite the departure of several of its top administrators. Gee raised $109 million in his first full year (no small amount for an endowment that ranks as the smallest in the Ivy League), addressed several financial concerns (alumni giving rates and the question of need-blind admissions), and resolved two lawsuits that had embarrassed the institution (one involved a rape case, and the other involved Title IX funding and equity in funding for women's athletics).

Gee stunned Brown in 1999 by resigning his post to assume the chancellorship at Vanderbilt University. His departure left many at Brown disenchanted with Gee, despite some of the successes he enjoyed. In November of 2000, Ruth J. Simmons, former president of Smith College, was named the eighteenth president of Brown. Simmons is the school's first African-American president. The "commitment to diversity" (read support of affirmative action and multiculturalist programs) that was a focal point of Gee will only be heightened under Simmons, if her past record at Smith College is considered.

The Report of the Visiting Committee on Diversity, convened by Gee and delivered in 2000, sought to place Brown at the vanguard of all American institutions in the promotion of diversity. About the Visiting Committee itself Brown states, "The group itself was diverse, including African Americans, Hispanics, Asian Americans, a Native American, two whites, as well as a white staff person."

The report begins with the assumption that "Diversity became a significant part of Brown's image, culture, and attractiveness" after the release of a 1986 report. The hope of the committee is to further develop the "somewhat diverse ecology" that has developed at Brown. Even more, as Harvard Law School professor Lani Guinier, a committee member, notes, "Brown now has the opportunity to educate the rest of the Ivies that diversity is, or should be, about preparing students and faculty to participate more effectively, knowledgeably, and creatively as public and private citizens in our democracy."

Diversity takes on three meanings in the report, the last of which uses diversity "as a value, the essence of which is a recognition that engagement of our differences potentially enriches us all." Such a nebulous definition hardly precludes the committee from making more than a dozen recommendations on its implementation. Among the sixteen recommendations are an affirmation of what amounts to an expansion of affirmative action programs (for professors and students) and the adoption of "voluntary diversity orientation and education programs" for faculty, administration, and staff. In short, the committee recommends "that the university bring the discussions of race, class, gender, and socioeconomic inequality that now take place in dining halls and dorms into a greater number of classrooms."

One attribute of Brown celebrated by the university is, according to the report, also a source of potential problems: "the high value of individualism." Individualism is extolled when it allows maximal freedom in choosing courses; individualism is a source of concern when it conflicts with the "community" ideals — imposed from the top — regarding diversity and multiculturalism. Diversity programs always pose a danger for a proper sense of individualism, for what serves the collective sense of "diversity" will trump the individual's point of view. The pervasive language of "listening," "learning," and "improving" in the report leaves the reader wondering what enforcement mechanisms will be devised. It also is not a leap to assume that the protection from diversity requirements built into the lack of general education requirements — perhaps the system's greatest benefit — might soon be set aside.

Individualism is swallowed up, in fact, by what the report calls "identity" and "issue" groups, the existence of which it celebrates in a passage worth quoting in its entirety: "[T]he University community must protect and support the choice made by many students to organize and join groups based on similarities of identity, whether they are sexual preference, gender, race, ethnicity, or class. Indeed, with a safe 'home,' students of color, or gay or lesbian students, for example, are likely to be able to more confidently participate in integrated, multi-identity groups. It is only troubling when students make decisions to affiliate exclusively with identity groups because they feel threatened or vulnerable. Unfortunately, flagrant manifestation of prejudice and attacks on affirmative action can have that consequence."

The university's manifesto seems to have been taken to heart by many campus organizations, among which is a very active Lesbian, Gay, Bisexual and Transgendered Alliance (LGBTA). Describing itself as "an umbrella group supporting Queer groups at Brown," the LGBTA includes a number of sub-groups, including the Transgender Group (which include male-to-female or female-to-male transsexuals, crossdressers, transvestites, intersexuals, butches, femmes, or any variety of "genderqueer"), BiTE (Bisexuals Talk and Eat), and an inactive group, RUQUS (Radical University Queers United and Strong, described as "sorta subversive"). Posted on the Web site for the LGBTA is a call for volunteers to work with The Student Center Network, which puts gay and lesbian college students in contact with teenaged students, and a call for both a "female bisexual and butch lesbian" to speak at a panel discussion.

Student Life: The Outside of the Library

First-year students at Brown live on campus in double rooms as part of first-year counseling units. Varying in size from thirty to fifty students, these units are largely coeducational. Upperclass "counselors" live in the units, and minority and women's peer counselors are available in every unit. After their first year, students may live in residence halls, fraternities, sororities, cooperatives, language houses, or other program housing on campus. About 10 percent of students are involved in the Greek system, which holds frequent weekend parties on campus.

In their freshman and sophomore years, students tend to stay on campus for social activities. One professor says of the social scene that Brown offers "the ideal combination of intellectual rigor and an enjoyable social life." Hockey games on Friday or Saturday nights during the season are very popular. Eighteen varsity sports are available to men, while twenty varsity sports are offered to women.

More than two hundred student organizations make Brown a beehive of activity — and activism. Political engagement at Brown is fairly high, one professor estimates. Most of the activism begins on the left, but the College Republicans do have an active chapter. The voices that seem to carry further on campus include those of feminists, who have ample resources at their disposal, including the Sarah Doyle Women's Center and the women's studies department. Also, a sizable chapter of the International Socialist Organization holds many rallies and protest on campus. But one professor cautions against thinking Brown students especially liberal. Another suggests that the "general atmosphere on campus is nonconfrontational, with very few ideologically inspired controversies." The *Brown Daily Herald*, the university's daily newspaper, leans leftward but makes a genuine effort to include many perspectives on its editorial pages.

Many students practice community service while enrolled at Brown. The university estimates that 25 percent undertake some sort of sustained community service project. Volunteering is coordinated by the campus's Center for Public Service, which makes opportunities known to Brown students and faculty.

Brown students have a reputation for earnestness, which is evidenced as much in their studies as in their idea of fun (or fun as understood by denizens of the campus Tech House). *The Chronicle of Higher Education* reported on the creation of what was very likely the world's largest game of Tetris, the Soviet-designed video game in which a player must try to stack blocks without any gaps in the wall. Built on the side of the fourteen-story Sciences Library using more than 10,000 Christmas lights, the game was played by more than two hundred students. For students used to spending hours inside the library, the chance to use the outside of the library — literally — must have been quite a thrill.

When students weary of projects like that, they can turn to the social setting of the city of Providence. Although Providence is not exactly a college town, it is home to a number of colleges and universities, including Providence College, a campus of the University of Rhode Island, Rhode Island College, Johnson and Wales University, and the Rhode Island School of Design. Providence also has many amenities that make it attractive to college students: several good restaurants downtown (especially some Italian eateries), coffee shops, bars, and clubs.

The east side of town, where Brown is located, is the historic area of the city. Crime is not considered a problem on campus, though some areas of Providence have high crime rates. There are no structures still standing from 1636 (the year Roger Williams founded the city and named it Providence because he believed God guided him there), but some houses in the area are more than two hundred years old. Boston, a forty-five-minute trip by car, bus, or train, offers an abundance of historical sites, and many students take advantage of its shopping, professional sports, and social offerings.

Bryn Mawr College

Office of Admissions
Ely House
101 N. Merion Avenue
Bryn Mawr, PA 19010-2899
(610) 526-5152
www.brynmawr.edu

Total enrollment: 1,707
Undergraduates: 1,283
SAT ranges (Verbal/Math): 610-710 (V); 600-680 (M)
Applicants: 1,596
Accepted: 59%
Enrolled: 34%
Application deadline: January 15
Financial aid application deadline: January 15
Tuition: $24,160/$32,500
Core curriculum: No

Several for the Price of One

Bryn Mawr College was founded in 1885 by Dr. Joseph Taylor, a Quaker physician who sought to found a college dedicated to the education of Quaker women. At that time an education in Greek, mathematics, philosophy, and several other fields was open only to men. The college was the first women's school to offer graduate instruction, and today it is still the only predominantly women's college with a fairly extensive selection of graduate programs.

Although the college is no longer affiliated with the Society of Friends, it remains single-sex. However, Bryn Mawr's graduate programs are open to men, and, because many of its 1,200 undergraduates take courses at nearby Haverford College, two Bryn Mawr dorms are made coeducational by male students from Haverford. Bryn Mawr students can also take advantage of other colleges and universities in the Philadelphia area: they may enroll in classes at Swarthmore College, Villanova University, and the University of Pennsylvania, all at no additional charge.

Bryn Mawr is best known for its humanities departments, but the most popular majors are in the sciences. Ironically, those looking for a traditional education will be more likely to find it in the scientific fields; feminist theory has taken over some humanities departments, according to some at Bryn Mawr. Still, students' work in most departments is intense enough that the campus is often eerily quiet during the day, when students are in class or at the library.

Academic Life: A Standard Standard

Bryn Mawr uses a series of distribution requirements, and expects most of them to be fulfilled in the student's first two years at school. Specialization in one's major comes only in the junior and senior years. A bachelor's degree requires thirty-two courses, a quarter of which come in the college's distribution requirements: two courses in the social sciences and three in both the natural sciences and the humanities.

The college also requires two "College Seminars," interdisciplinary "reading-and writing-intensive" programs. One must be taken in the first semester and the other by the end of the student's second year. The topics change from year to year, but recently students have been able to choose from seminars like "The Dance of the Spheres: the Interplay Between the Arts and the Sciences in the Search for Knowledge"; "Human Understanding in a Material World"; "Religion and Public Life in America"; and "The Concept of Time." The descriptions of these seminars, at least, give the impression that many views are considered, including traditional ones — though there is the occasional trendy-topic seminar as well.

Bryn Mawr requires two semesters of English composition, one semester of math, and two years of a foreign language — all of which can be bypassed with good test scores. Students must also complete eight half-semester units in physical education and pass a swimming test.

The college offers twenty-nine majors and sixteen concentrations (multi-disciplinary majors), as well as "independent majors" like American studies, Chinese anthropology, evolutionary studies, folklore and folklife, and linguistics, *inter alia*.

About one-third of the students major in math or science — a high figure compared to the number of women in those fields at other schools. Many students take science courses at Haverford, only a twenty-minute walk or one-mile bus ride away. This high number of science students is not consistent with Bryn Mawr's reputation as a powerhouse in the humanities, but, with the cross-registration possibilities at other local colleges and universities, that reputation has begun to change. In 1998 the National Science Foundation gave Bryn Mawr $200,000 for workshops for professors in the College Seminar program, new courses in math and science for students going in to education, and other projects. The college does have a strong record in the humanities as far as graduate academic achievement is concerned: Bryn Mawr ranks first in the nation in the percentage of its graduates to earn Ph.D.s in the humanities.

Bryn Mawr offers several study-abroad opportunities, both during the summer and during the regular academic year. There are college-sponsored summer programs in Avignon, Florence, and Moscow, all of them requiring language proficiency. During the year students may, with the permission of their major departments and dean, take courses abroad through other universities. The majority of students who study abroad do so during their junior year. In all, there are sixty preapproved programs in twenty-six countries.

In cooperation with the University of Pennsylvania, Bryn Mawr offers two joint-degree programs in which students take classes for five years and graduate with a double major. One is in engineering and applied science, the other in city and regional planning. Another rare program, offered exclusively by Bryn Mawr, is an interdisciplinary major in the growth and structure of cities. Students take courses in a wide variety of fields to learn about "the relationship of urban spatial organization and the built environment to politics, economics, cultures, and societies," according to the college catalogue.

One of the strongest programs at Bryn Mawr is the history of art department. This department boasts a number of outstanding professors and concentrates on Western art, students say. There are courses in the history of architecture, Western art historiography, and European painting and sculpture, and students are encouraged to spend a semester abroad to see firsthand the art they have studied in class.

Another excellent department is classical and Near Eastern archaeology, said to be one of the best in the country. Archaeology majors take courses in several different fields relating to their specialty. Students are encouraged to participate in field projects in North America and overseas, and the department helps find places for them in archaeological digs. Occasionally the department will carry out its own field projects, and undergraduates are invited to participate. Recent excavations have taken place in central Siberia, Greece, and Turkey. Two excellent professors in this department are Richard Ellis and Bryn Mawr alumna Stella Miller-Collett.

The college recently built a $12.9 million addition to its main library that provides space for the archaeology, history of art, and growth and structure of cities departments and their collections.

A few departments have become politicized, at least in part. One of these is English, which, despite offering a number of courses in the foundations of literature, is home to several courses with political themes. For example, "Marginality and Transgression in Victorian Literature" focuses on "poverty, sexuality, revolution, criminality," as well as "the semiotics of transgression [and] the discourses of sexuality." There is also "Queer Literature/Queer Theory," whose description asserts that "feminisms, identity politics, the civil rights movements, human rights discourses, AIDS, technology, law, social/cultural/aesthetic movements and post-modern critical thought has [sic] (de)formed and transformed feminist and queer critical practices to produce new cultural texts that work through and against the binaries of man/woman, hetero/homo, center/margin; first/third world; oppressor/oppressed, subject/object. . . . How do transgender, bisexual, lesbian, and gay identities interact (or fail to interact) with notions of queer, top/bottom, dyke, butch, femme, dramadiva, cyborg, pansexual?" Wow.

Another program, feminist and gender studies, does not offer a major — only a six-course "concentration" that draws about thirty students a year. Most courses are taught by other departments (including some at Haverford).

The comparative literature department is also somewhat politicized, as its own description illustrates: "The study of comparative literature situates literature in an international perspective, examines connections among literary history, literary criticism, critical theory, and poetics, and works toward an understanding of the sociocultural functions of literature. Interpretive methods from other disciplines that interrogate cultural discourses also play a role in the comparative study of literature; among these are anthropology, philosophy, history, religion, classical studies, Africana studies, gender studies, and cultural studies, as well as other arts."

Political Atmosphere: One of Those Stereotypes

Nancy J. Vickers became the president of Bryn Mawr in 1997. An expert in French and Italian literature who edited a scholarly book called *Rewriting the Renaissance: The Discourses of Sexual Differences in Early Modern Europe,* Vickers spearheaded a curriculum revision at the University of Southern California, an experience she described to a Bryn Mawr publication as "a struggle about the nature of disciplinary and interdisciplinary — the residual pull of traditional instruction in a department or area and a sense that it needs to move somewhat beyond that." Traditional observers found the revised USC curriculum to be rather politicized; it did include a new diversity requirement and other politically correct additions.

But if those are indeed Vickers' thoughts on what a modern curriculum should entail, there has been little evidence of it thus far in her stay at Bryn Mawr. She began her presidency by taking the college on a more than two-year-long self-study that resulted in "The Plan for a New Century," approved by the Board of Trustees in 2000. The plan finds that it would be best for the college "to redirect and consolidate our energies rather than to set out into wholly unfamiliar territory," meaning that no large-scale changes are forthcoming. However, the plan does include a proposed "Center for Ethnicities, Communities and Social Policy [that] will increase students' opportunities to learn about and discuss a range of critical issues" and a general desire to "diversify and modernize the curriculum." All told, very tame stuff.

The political atmosphere at Bryn Mawr, however, is generally liberal. The college recently cancelled spring break trips to South Carolina because of the Confederate flag that then flew over the state capitol. It sponsors a diversity week and speakers like Gloria Steinem and Marian Wright Edelman.

The "diversity" on campus, however, rarely includes traditional voices, though *Common Sense*, an independent conservative and libertarian newspaper started by students at nearby Swarthmore College several years ago is available on campus and sometimes includes Bryn Mawr writers.

The most vocal student groups include lesbian and feminist organizations, which, according to students, receive broad support and encouragement from fellow students and administrators. The most prominent group is the Rainbow Alliance, an organization of homosexual students. "Not everyone is out [of the closet] here," a Rainbow Alliance leader told a campus publication. "But it is generally easier here since the community is very comfortable and supportive." Another group leader says one of the "most important things we do" is help students come out to their parents. "The organization has all sorts of other purposes: educational, helping people with coming out issues, safe sex issues, and social issues," this student says. The organization has a small library and its Web page has a section called "What To Do Around Here," where students can find helpful social tips — not to mention directions to, and reviews of, local gay sex shops.

Bryn Mawr also has a socialist organization, Students for Progressive Action, whose members hang lots of posters and prod people with questions every Sunday night as they walk to dining halls. "Nobody really likes them because they're so militant," says one student. Typical issues for the socialists include labor union advocacy and opposition to the death penalty.

But some students claim that the prominence of these radical groups feeds a stereotype that has little to do with reality. "People from other schools think that I'm this militant lesbian feminist, that I'm aggressive and mean," one student says. "It's just one of those stereotypes."

Student Life: Well West of West Philadelphia

Bryn Mawr is only eleven miles west of Philadelphia, but the campus will make anyone forget city squalor. The 135-acre plot is full of trees and gardens, and most buildings are built of graystone in the collegiate Gothic style. According to the college, "architects have described [the campus] as looking like a medieval English village built around an 18th-century town green." Add to that a campus food service recently named the best in the country and dorms that the *Princeton Review* series calls the best in the land, and it isn't hard to see that life at Bryn Mawr can be quite comfortable.

The town of Bryn Mawr, with a population of about nine thousand, is very safe and just a five-minute walk from campus. Although it contains a small variety of stores and restaurants, most social life takes place on campus. Just about all students live on campus in a set of fourteen dorms, two of which are coed (housing Haverford men as well as Bryn Mawr women). One dorm is set aside as a "multicultural residence for students interested in foreign languages and cultures or in the Black Cultural Center," according to the college viewbook.

But, because the academic life at the college is so intense, some students say the social life suffers. "We're not a party school," says one student. "It's not like a state school would have. Students are more concerned about their grades than their social life." A professor in the humanities agrees. "Bryn Mawr's academic environment is a serious and challenging one," she says. "Students work very hard. I suspect that students who are not really interested in their studies are in general not drawn to Bryn Mawr in the first place." The college provides learning opportunities through a wide selection of visiting speakers and performers.

College traditions remain strong at Bryn Mawr. "That's one of the things that really brings us together," says a student. For example, there's "Lantern Night," which hearkens back to a time when no buses connected the Bryn Mawr and Haverford campuses and students would walk between the institutions by the light of a lantern. On Lantern Night, each Bryn Mawr class dresses in a different color, carries lanterns, and sings songs; a big crowd always gathers to watch. The college also celebrates May Day, on which all students wear white dresses, perform medieval dances, and participate in activities such as archery contests. Administrators dress up, too.

Student groups also hold teas, which don't always involve actual tea, but are usually get-togethers with a theme. For instance, one organization recently sponsored a Kevin Bacon tea. Anyone who showed up was treated to a Kevin Bacon movie, free food, and a discussion of the actor. There has also been an Abracadabra Holiday Dinner, with Harry Potter and friends as the subject of readings and activities. Sometimes, depending on the theme, students will dress up.

Despite its small size, Bryn Mawr does have a lot of student groups, including a variety of sports clubs, political organizations, and cultural groups. Many of the clubs include students from Haverford or Swarthmore. These are known as "bi-co" (bi-college, meaning Bryn Mawr and Haverford) and "tri-co" (Bryn Mawr, Haverford, and Swarthmore). Campus political groups are mostly liberal: there are the College Democrats, the Animal Liberation Coalition, Students for a Free Tibet, and several feminist and homosexual organizations, among others. The College Republican group that used to exist is no longer listed as a student group.

Several religious organizations exist on campus, including a Catholic Campus Ministries group, a gospel choir, a Jewish group, InterVarsity Christian Fellowship, several Protestant groups, and the Muslim Student Association. However, students must actively seek religion on campus because its presence is not readily apparent. "If you didn't go out looking for it, you wouldn't be able to find it," a student says.

Bryn Mawr fields varsity teams in basketball, cross-country, field hockey, lacrosse, soccer, swimming, tennis, crew, track and field, volleyball, and badminton, which won a national title in 1995. Club teams include diving, fencing, ice hockey, rugby, sailing, squash, and track. Rather inscrutably, the college athletic department states: "Bryn Mawr makes women players, in every sense of the word."

University of California at Berkeley

Director of Undergraduate Admissions
University of California at Berkeley
110 Sproul Hall, #5800
Berkeley, CA 94720-5800
(510) 642-3175
www.berkeley.edu

Total enrollment: 31,277
Undergraduates: 22,678
SAT ranges (Verbal/Math): 580-710 (V); 620-740 (M)
Applicants: 33,244
Accepted: 26%
Enrolled: 43%
Application deadline: November 30
Financial aid application deadline: March 2
Tuition: resident: $4,047/$12,717; nonresident: $14,661/$23,331
Core curriculum: No

The Beginning and the End

The University of California at Berkeley began as a strong liberal arts school, rooted in a broad and humane understanding of the Western tradition. In 1855 the College of California had a curriculum based on Greek, Latin, English literature, history, mathematics, and natural science. This curriculum was maintained as the institution grew, and when the University of California was created in 1868, the school still had a strong liberal arts orientation.

But today, when Americans think of UC–Berkeley they immediately associate it with the radical movements of the 1960s. Affirmative action pilot programs started here, as did the campus free speech movement. Protesters on other campuses over the years have drawn inspiration from the actions of their fellows in Berkeley. One clear sign that UC–Berkeley has become a byword for campus radicalism is that even mainstream media commentators feel free to snicker at some of the more bizarre, politicized courses the university offers.

But even if imitation is the sincerest form of flattery, and even if that imitation has been largely harmful to traditional education, the fact remains that UC–Berkeley is one of the most prestigious universities in the world. Some even say it may be the best university in the world. At the very least, UC–Berkeley offers an exciting atmosphere and many excellent teachers and departments. It has sent more graduates on to earn Ph.D.s than any other university in America. And even though the school is once again admitting students only on the basis of academic merit, it must turn down several thousand eminently qualified applicants every year. It may be a challenge for a student looking for a true liberal arts education to find birds of his own feather there, but the place is large enough that he can likely find most anything — a superior education and an unforgettable experience included.

Academic Life: Top of the Pops

The largest of UC–Berkeley's fourteen schools and colleges is the College of Letters and Sciences (L&S). This college contains more than sixty departmental majors in the biological sciences, physical sciences, social sciences, and humanities. Almost 75 percent of UC–Berkeley undergraduates enroll in this college, which is also home to more than half of the university's faculty.

Like all other undergraduates at UC–Berkeley, L&S students must fulfill a very basic set of requirements. The first of these is called "Subject A," essentially a literacy requirement met by high school classes, test scores, or a college writing class. The State of California mandates a requirement called "American History and Institutions"; this, too, can be fulfilled with high school classes, tests, or two courses at UC–Berkeley.

The final university requirement, "American Cultures," is the most politicized of the three. Essentially a diversity requirement, it may be fulfilled with what might be described as a course on the culture of American minorities. The class, according to the catalogue, must "take substantial account of groups drawn from at least three of the following: African Americans, indigenous peoples of the United States, Asian Americans, Chicano/Latino Americans, and European Americans." A wide range of courses, almost all of which teach that the human condition can only be understood in terms of race, class, gender, and/or sexuality, satisfy this single-course requirement.

Students in L&S have their own set of college requirements. These include a standard set of distribution requirements: one class in each of seven areas — physical science, biological science, arts and literature, historical studies, philosophy and values, international studies, and social and behavioral sciences. In meeting these requirements, students have most of the catalogue to choose from. Many options are politicized, but many are not.

Three "essential skills" requirements round out the common L&S program. Two courses must be completed in reading and composition, one as a freshman and one as a sophomore. Unfortunately, these choices often suffer from an ideological inflection; the list of departments from which these courses are drawn includes African-American studies, Asian-American studies, Chicano studies, Native American studies, and the radical departments of rhetoric and women's studies. A single course in quantitative reasoning (mathematics, computer science, or statistics) is also required, as is the study of a foreign language, either for three years in high school or for two years at UC–Berkeley. Alternatively, students may take a test to prove their foreign language proficiency.

The university and L&S requirements are a pale shadow of the core curriculum UC–Berkeley had at its founding. The looseness of the current requirements does not ensure that students will graduate with the same education — either in quality or content — and does not create a cohesive intellectual community, let alone one centered on the important works of Western culture.

Though the university is known for its campus and classroom activism, one professor says things are no worse there than at many other colleges in America. "The faculty, overall, are not more liberal than any other academic institution," the professor says. "The residents of the Bay area, in my estimation, give Berkeley its left-wing reputation." Liberal or not, the faculty do teach, and despite the size of the school and the number of graduate students, teaching assistants are used primarily in remedial or language programs and to lead discussions outside the regular class period. As a rule, teaching assistants do not lecture.

Instead, fortunate students are taught by faculty like these: Kenneth T. Jowitt, A. James Gregor, and Nelson W. Polsby in political science; Ann Swidler in sociology; Gerald D. Feldman, Richard M. Abrams, Thomas Brady, Robert Brentano, and David Hollinger in history; Leslie L. Threatte and Ronald S. Stroud in classics; David Vogel in business; and John R. Searle in philosophy.

In addition, Berkeley boasts state-of-the-art research facilities, and has the fourth-largest library in North America, with over eight million volumes.

The university boasts many high-quality departments. A recent report by the National Research Council lists thirty-five of the university's thirty-six graduate programs as among the ten best in the country in their respective fields based on "faculty competence and achievement." Since undergraduates are frequently in contact with graduate students and their professors, this study is worth noting. In L&S, departments making the top ten include classics (second), comparative literature (tenth), English (tied for first, though highly politicized), French (seventh), German (first), history (tied for sixth), mathematics (first), philosophy (fourth), and political science (second).

One professor says economics, political science, history, and — contrary to stereotype — sociology are not politicized: "In fact, they are among the best in the nation." The economics department, though not free market–oriented, promotes a variety of viewpoints with the goal of finding the greatest efficiencies in a mixed economic system. The history department's courses are remarkably devoid of the politically correct or ideological offerings so common in other history departments and in other departments at UC–Berkeley.

Those "other departments" include women's studies, English, and rhetoric, professors say.

The women's studies department literature contains a series of questions: "Although all societies make gender distinctions, how do they differ from one culture to another, how have definitions of male and female roles evolved, how are they perpetuated, and how might they be redefined?" After which, it cites a single answer to them all: the department's goal is to explain why we suffer from "sexual inequality."

A course called "Women and Work" looks at wage inequality, sexual harassment, "individual resistance strategies and collective organizing," class and race differences, and government policy. "Women in Film," another course in the department, "explores feminist approaches to the way women are represented in narrative film, focusing on the problem of how filmic representations of women work to define what it means to be gendered female in our culture."

According to one professor, "The English department has the reputation of being dominated by professors who deconstruct classic texts in order to read into them their own political agendas." The department offers several concentrations to its majors, including sexual identities/gender studies; folklore, popular culture, and cultural theory; and Anglophone and multicultural studies. There are also concentrations in five different historical periods, ranging from medieval to contemporary literature. While quite a few solid literature offerings are listed in the catalogue, the courses required for the trendier concentrations either ignore or attack the texts and ideas of the liberal arts tradition, a professor says. Some of the more politicized courses include "The Romantic Period," whose course description is relatively standard populist fare until its final sentence: "Why did critics come to define Romanticism as the work of six male poets?" The reading list in "Literature and Sexual Identity" includes Plato, Shakespeare, Freud, and Wilde. It is, according to the catalogue, "a course in how to do 'the' history of sexuality." The description continues: "We'll interrogate, first of all, those quotation marks: whose history is it, exactly, and for what purpose?"

But the rhetoric department surpasses both of these. "Of all the departments at Berkeley, I would say that the rhetoric department, by far, is way out in left field," a professor says. The objective of the department is to examine the "rhetorical approach of discourse of all kinds," specifically in the humanities. The fields in which this study is undertaken are diverse: film, law, literature, philosophy, and science being among them. The lenses most often used are sexuality, gender, popular culture, and race. One course offered by this department is "Introduction to the Rhetoric and Theory of Popular Culture," where "race, gender, sexuality, and acculturation, as well as economic and power dynamics are among the issues to be discussed," according to the catalogue. There are courses in "Race and Identity: Performing American Identities" and "Rhetorics of Sexual Exchange." One faculty member is the author of a book that the *Chronicle of Higher Education* credits with helping "to create queer theory."

The lesbian, gay, bisexual, and transgendered studies program at Berkeley, though not a full-fledged department, does offer a minor that includes four "core" courses and two electives. The four core courses are "Alternative Sexual Identities and Communities in Contemporary American Society," "Interpreting the Queer Past: Methods and Problems in the History of Sexuality," "Cultural Representations of Sexualities: Queer Visual Culture," and "Sexuality, Culture, and Colonialism."

Political Atmosphere: Gone, but Not Forgotten

UC–Berkeley had an affirmative action program even before there was such a term; in the early 1960s the school started something called the Educational Opportunity Program, which was designed to promote racial diversity on campus. In thirty years, the school went from an almost all-white campus to one of the country's most diverse universities. In 2000 the undergraduate student body was 40 percent Asian, 30 percent white, 10 percent Hispanic, and 4 percent black. Affirmative action policies meant that only half of the incoming students each year were admitted solely on the basis of test scores and grades; only a tiny portion of students admitted under these criteria were black or Hispanic. The admission of another 46 percent of the 1994-95 incoming class was based on grades, test scores, essays, and "background"; Hispanic students were the largest group in this category, followed by white and Asian students. More than one hundred times as many black students were admitted in this category as were admitted when only test scores and grades were considered.

At the same time, many on campus observed very little mixing of the races, and that there was a stigma attached to black and Hispanic students. "I'm tall," a medical student told the *New York Times*. "If they decided there were not enough tall people here, I'd walk around and people would think, 'Oh, there's one of those tall admissions.' It sounds cruel, but that's how people think."

Affirmative action policies at Berkeley and other California state schools were voted out, however, in 1995 by the state universities' board of regents. The vote was encouraged by California governor Pete Wilson, who had national political ambitions at the time, and regent Ward Connerly, an African-American businessman. Though a serious blow to affirmative action, the vote still allowed university officials to admit 25 to 50 percent of freshmen based on criteria other than grades (although not on the basis of race alone).

Two years after that vote, Californians adopted Proposition 209, which officially ended all public affirmative action programs in the state. The Ninth Circuit Court of Appeals turned away a challenge to the law in August 1997, and once again UC–Berkeley faced an overhaul of its admissions and hiring policies.

The regents' vote and the voice of the state's public has not, however, changed the administration's commitment to diversity. "I can assure you that in implementing this law, the Berkeley campus will remain fully committed to excellence through diversity in every academic and employment program," UC–Berkeley chancellor Robert Berdahl said shortly after Proposition 209 passed.

And there is legitimate reason to believe that affirmative action is not dead at Berkeley, but merely driven underground. According to the student newspaper, *The Berkeleyan*, the university administration has recently reworked its admissions policy so that it now "calls for a more personal, qualitative look at the academic and personal achievements of each student applicant." In short, the admissions office is looking for creative ways to avoid a system based strictly on merit. According to the newspaper, one of the criteria that was recently dropped was the "academic index score," a combination of the applicant's high school GPA and SAT scores. This index has been replaced with "applicants' accomplishments and the context in which those accomplishments have been achieved." The university also considers the applicant's socioeconomic environment, as well as "leadership in non-academic areas." UC–Berkeley even has an "Office of Faculty Equity Assistance" department, which helps implement the campus Academic Affirmative Action plan.

Some point out that UC–Berkeley, because of the excellent applicants it attracts, will never be able to admit students purely on the basis of merit — there are simply too many students with excellent grades and test scores, and not enough spots in the freshman class. However, statistics cited in *National Review* by the late Peter Shaw, past chairman of the National Association of Scholars, indicate that doing away with affirmative action would result in a student body that is 55 percent Asian, 35 percent white, 5 percent Hispanic, and only 2 percent black.

What UC–Berkeley makes of the new laws and how it rearranges its admissions policies may well set the precedent for universities committed to the popular notion of diversity. Just as the university started a trend in the 1960s, it may redefine that trend in the twenty-first century.

Berkeley students, as might be expected, excel at finding something to protest. The fall 2000 semester was no exception, as at least three lecturers were harassed by campus leftists. In September 2000, radical protesters shouted down a speaker who wanted to "lay out the facts" on the case of convicted cop-killer Mumia Abu-Jumal — that is, the speaker wanted to tell Mumia supporters what they didn't want to hear. Students protested with shouts of "Nazi!" and "Fascist!" as the speaker attempted to deliver the speech. Some tried to rip the microphone away, and others burnt supporting literature and handouts.

In October 2000, Nobel laureate James Watson, co-discoverer of the DNA structure, explained his (admittedly peculiar) theories about biochemical connections between skin color and sexual appetite and between obesity and happiness. Some attendees complained that Watson's talk was racist and sexist, and others walked out in protest.

November 2000 brought Israeli diplomat Benjamin Netanyahu to the Berkeley campus; he was shouted down by protesters who claimed that he was nothing more than a war criminal. Meanwhile, 2,000 people with tickets waited for the lecture in vain.

The spring semester brought more attempts to silence unpopular views. After author-activist David Horowitz ran a purposely controversial ad in UC-Berkeley's main campus daily (and many other campus newspapers) called "Ten Reasons Why Reparations for Slavery is a Bad Idea — and Racist Too," leftist protesters stormed the paper's offices with a list of demands, including an apology for running the advertisement. They also stole from the racks, and presumably destroyed, all the newspapers containing the ads. The paper responded by issuing a meek apology for the ad's "incorrect and blatantly inflammatory content" (a response to protesters repeated in depressingly similar fashion on campuses across the land).

Student Life: The Times, They Ain't A-Changin'

It is the city of Berkeley, perhaps even more than the university itself, that gives rise to the aging-hippie image of the place. To walk down Telegraph Avenue is to step into a time warp: from tie-dyed shirts and bongs to books by Herbert Marcuse, the cultural paraphernalia of the late 1960s and early 1970s are on display everywhere.

Some observers argue that nearby Stanford University is far more radical nowadays than UC–Berkeley; still, traditions die hard. But according to one professor, a Louis Farrakhan–Ronald Reagan presidential race, if held at the UC–Berkeley campus, would be a dead heat.

"The people in Berkeley are totally wacked," says a San Francisco resident. "I've seen transvestites walking around in dresses during the middle of the day, and students sitting on street corners yelling out slogans at people, like 'save the animals that are being tortured to death.'" A handful of students walk around and attend classes in the nude, so loath is the university to step on their right to free expression.

Like most top-notch universities, Berkeley attracts a spectrum of students from all over the world. Every state in the country is represented, as well as more than one hundred foreign countries.

The twenty thousand undergraduates and ten thousand graduate students on the Berkeley campus occupy more than one thousand acres in the hills overlooking San Francisco Bay. The city of Berkeley (population about 103,000) caters principally to students. There are trendy restaurants and coffeehouses, but most notably, there are excellent bookstores. A relatively new retail bookstore, Cody's, is very popular. Within one block of campus are several excellent used bookstores, including Shakespeare and Company, Black Oak, Moe's, and Cartesian.

The Bay Area offers a combination of stunning physical beauty and a wealth of cultural attractions. San Francisco and other cities are easily accessible to students via the Bay Area Rapid Transit system (BART).

The campus can accommodate only about five thousand undergraduates, and 70 percent of the dorm space is used by freshmen. Other students live in "theme houses" centered on a language or culture. Single-sex dorms are available to those students who request it. Students can also choose social or quiet dormitories, and there are substance-free housing options. The university also assists students with finding apartments in the campus area.

Sproul Plaza is the campus landmark that perhaps best reflects the liberal and eccentric past of UC–Berkeley. The plaza was named for Robert Gordon Sproul, president of the university for thirty years starting in the 1930s, and connects the César E. Chavez Student Center and the Martin Luther King Student Union.

As early as 1961, the university regents named a fountain on Sproul Plaza for a dog named Ludwig von Schwanenberg that played in the fountain and was a favorite of students. Three years later the plaza became the center of the free speech movement. One day in 1964, student Mario Savio led a protest in the plaza against the arrest of a graduate student who was circulating brochures promoting the Congress of Racial Equality. Savio and his classmates surrounded a police car, and from its roof he delivered a famous speech, telling the protesters: "There is a time when the operation of the machine becomes so odious, makes you so sick at heart, that . . . you've got to put your bodies upon the gears and upon the wheels . . . upon all the apparatus and you've got to make it stop." The squad car was surrounded for thirty-two hours. The university has since erected a plaque in honor of the beginning of the free speech movement, and a series of Mario Savio memorial lectures began in 1997 with a speech by Boston University professor Howard Zinn, a Marxist historian.

As one might expect, conservative activism is minimal on campus. The College Republicans are active with the local party, and some conservative students publish the *California Patriot*, a magazine of unorthodox political opinion.

Extracurricular life at Berkeley thrives, with 380 university-approved clubs, most of which are politicized and socially liberal. Workers' rights groups and minority rights groups have held fasts to honor the death of César Chavez and to protest the abuses faced by strawberry workers in California. Some of the groups include the Queer Alliance, Raza, Solidarity, and Berkeley Campus Democratic Socialists of America. Several groups are organized to promote affirmative action, and the university has a Center for African Studies, described in university literature as "an interdisciplinary research center to support basic research and training of scholars."

Feminist activists at UC–Berkeley have actually called for the murder of Neil Gilbert, an otherwise liberal professor who publicly questioned feminist Mary Koss's contention that 25 percent of all American women have been raped. According to Christina Hoff Sommers's book *Who Stole Feminism?*, Gilbert's reasoning so enraged some Berkeley students that "at one demonstration against Gilbert on the Berkeley campus, students chanted, 'Cut it out or cut it off,' and carried signs that read, 'KILL NEIL GILBERT!'"

At other times, students would be satisfied if their school figuratively killed Stanford. Always an intense rivalry, the football series between the two took on legendary proportions in 1982 when UC–Berkeley beat Stanford with "The Play," a multiple-lateral kickoff return for the winning touchdown with no time left on the clock, the last fifteen yards of which were run through members of the Stanford marching band who had swarmed the field thinking that the game was over. UC–Berkeley also offers twenty-four other varsity sports, as well as a number of intramural opportunities.

Berkeley is consistently among the top five universities in arrests for alcohol, drugs, and weapons. The FBI Crime Index for 1999 reported that 1,125 crimes occurred on campus that year, an 8 percent increase from the year before. Since the university community is so intermingled with the city of Berkeley, the statistics don't say whether the arrests include students or non-students, but crime is certainly a problem in and around campus, despite the university's efforts to curb it.

University of California at Los Angeles

UCLA Undergraduate Admissions and Relations with Schools (UARS)
1147 Murphy Hall
Box 951436
Los Angeles, CA 90095-1436
(310) 825-3101
www.ucla.edu

Total enrollment: 36,351
Undergraduates: 24,668
SAT ranges (Verbal/Math): 570-680 (V); 600-720 (M)
Applicants: 37,794
Accepted: 29%
Enrolled: 38%
Application deadline: November 30
Financial aid application deadline: March 2
Tuition: resident: $3,701/$11,320; non-resident: $14,315/$21,934
Core curriculum: No

L.A. Academic

The University of California at Los Angeles (UCLA) has come a long way since its moved from central Los Angeles to its current campus in the vibrant Westwood district of western Los Angeles some eighty-odd years ago. Back in 1925, when it was still on Vermont Avenue in L.A., its College of Letters and Science awarded 124 bachelor of arts degrees to a class consisting entirely of men. Now, the university has a coed undergraduate student body of close to 25,000 students, an additional nine thousand graduate students, and offers degrees in nearly 120 subjects.

UCLA's campus is not only large, it is quite racially diverse as well — and only slightly less so since the implementation of SP-1, the University of California Board of Regents' directive that ended racial preferences in admissions a few months before the landmark Proposition 209 ballot initiative that killed them in the entire state. The university has a wide array of ethnic studies programs and educational resources for students learning about ethnic studies, and as its Web site proudly notes, "We produce more minority degree holders than almost any other institution of higher education. We are the most multicultural campus in the nation, the new American university for the 21st century."

Of course, as a large research university, UCLA also has some of the downsides of twentieth-century American public universities. Classes can be very large, especially the introductory-level courses. Teaching assistants do a lot of instruction, and the sheer size of the campus means that students can easily feel lost and overwhelmed. But its size also provides advantages: wonderful opportunities for research, access to phenomenal library resources, easy access to a city with just about everything, and a wide variety of campus academic, political, and social opportunities. These may be enough to persuade some bright young people to consider attending UCLA.

Academic Life: Programs upon Programs

Undergraduates attending UCLA can enroll either in the College of Letters and Sciences, home to most liberal arts–based humanities and science programs, or in one of four other schools offering undergraduate degrees: Arts and Architecture; Engineering and Applied Science; Nursing; and Theatre, Film, and Television. Undergraduates have a total of — count 'em — 119 degree programs to choose from. Because of the vast number of courses available, students can pick a schedule containing traditional subject matter or can just as easily end up mired in academic esoterica.

Each college has a broad set of general education requirements, all of which are too general to be of much help in course selection. There are some basic requirements, such as "Subject A" (writing proficiency) or passing a course in American History and Institutions, that are so basic that they can be summarily dispatched even before a student steps foot inside UCLA. Should a student have to complete them on campus, he can pick a course or two from just about any section of the course catalog: the courses that fulfill these requirements come from departments ranging from Chicana and Chicano studies to political science.

The College of Letters and Sciences also has a foreign language and quantitative reasoning requirement, but decent scores on Advanced Placement tests or, for the latter, on the math portion of the SAT get students out of those too. Letters and Sciences has, however, recently added a two-term (UCLA uses a schedule divided into quarters) writing requirement for all freshmen.

Students in the College of Letters and Science must take four courses in the humanities, three courses in the physical sciences, four courses in the social sciences, and three courses in the life sciences. These get mixed reviews from students. "I liked the classes that I took. It gives you a break from your own major," says one student. "I can see why it might be too much though. If you're in a major like [one of the] physical sciences, you have so much to do." The better students consider these general requirements to be "good GPA boosters," he says. UCLA does not require a racial/gender/cultural diversity requirement.

The university's general education cluster program, a five-year pilot program started in 1998, was developed in response to complaints about large class sizes. It allows incoming freshmen students to take a "year-long, team-taught interdisciplinary series of courses," and it has an added bonus of allowing students to get credit for four general education courses over one year. However, enrollment is limited in this program, and only 520 freshmen students were able to get in this year. The university hopes to offer up to ten clusters, each with an enrollment of between 120 and 160 students, for the freshmen entering UCLA in 2001-2002. This would allow half of the incoming freshmen a chance to attend these courses. The fall and winter courses in each cluster are lecture courses with discussion sections; the spring courses are small seminars with less than twenty students.

UCLA is an excellent choice for students who are interested in doing research at the undergraduate level. "There are hundreds of opportunities," says one professor. "Talk to professors about the research you want to do." The university's Undergraduate Research Centers support scholarly, critical, and creative undergraduate research in the humanities and social sciences, and also offers individual research counseling. In addition, the URCs offer the Student Research Program, in which students can participate in research projects with faculty each year. While most of the research opportunities are in the sciences, there are some spots open for research in the humanities. Nearly two thousand students participate each year in the program, and small stipends are available on a competitive basis.

Outstanding professors at UCLA include James Q. Wilson (professor emeritus), Victor Wolfenstein, and Bryan Walker in political science; Sebastian Edwards in economics; Ed Condren, Michael J. Allen, and Debora K. Shuger in English; and Richard Rouse, Carlo Ginzburg, Patrick Geary, Ruth Bloch, Robert I. Burns, S.J., and Joyce Appleby in history. The biology, chemistry, and economics departments are all very strong at UCLA.

Unfortunately, many departments and programs at UCLA have succumbed to the forces of political correctness. Among these are the development studies and the Chicana/Chicano studies majors, as well as the interdepartmental programs in

Afro-American studies, women's studies, and lesbian, gay, bisexual, and transgender studies. Sadly, these programs appear to be little more than glorified exercises in identity politics unduly elevated to be on par with celebrated departments such as the philosophy department. The program in lesbian, gay, bisexual, and transgender studies, for example, offers courses like "Sexual Rights as Cultural Capital" and "Queer Space(s): Identifyin' and Signifyin' in the Fiction of Samuel R. Delany." The program's own description of itself notes that "although the initial focus in lesbian, gay, bisexual and transgender studies is usually on minority sexualities, it is impossible to study minority sexualities in any meaningful way without raising questions about sexuality in general. And questions about sexuality cannot be answered without considering questions of gender, race, class, ethnicity, history, political economy, and the construction of scientific knowledge."

Other identity-conscious departments have similar foci: the African-American studies program offers a course in "The Construction of Sexuality and Gender in African American Fiction," while the women's studies program exists to offer "a holistic approach to the study of fundamental issues of sex and gender . . . [and] how they interact with issues of race, ethnicity, [and] class."

Compare this to the department of philosophy, one of the best such departments in the nation, which notes in its self-description that "'philosopher,' translated from the Greek, literally means 'lover of wisdom.' The term has come to mean someone who seeks knowledge, enlightenment, and truth. The undergraduate program in philosophy is not directed at career objectives. . . . Philosophy is taught to undergraduates primarily as a contribution to their liberal education." The intellectual and academic disparity between sound disciplines such as this and newer, brash pretenders is acute, and even if a student doesn't choose to major in the humanities, there are many fine learning opportunities for them at UCLA in the humanities and the social sciences.

Many classes, whether in the humanities or not, are too large for students' liking. But while most courses enroll less than fifty students, students say that even in the large courses, it usually isn't difficult to get in close contact with your professors. "There are large classes," says one former political science major. "I found that if you go to office hours, there aren't a lot of people there." One professor's syllabus makes that quite clear: "In a large course like (this), the only contact I, as the professor, have with my students is through office hours. I encourage you to get to know me as well as your T.A. by coming to see us during office hours at least once during the quarter."

"Some entering students want professors and not teaching assistants," one professor says. "Fair enough, but remember that a teaching assistant can be the best of all teachers: young, vibrant, in touch with youth, on fire with the subject, and with the full complement of brain cells. The trick is to get a good teaching assistant and a good professor."

"The overcrowding is an issue because a lot of people don't feel comfortable speaking out," says a student. "It's possible to feel anonymous. . . . You have to be aggressive." One professor seconds this advice. "A big class is an opportunity to meet some fascinating peers and to make new friends," he says. "Be adventurous; resourceful; make the first move. The trick is to mix large with small classes to reap the rewards of both kinds."

And UCLA's quarter system can be a tough grind for students, as it packs in a lot of information in a short time. "It's very competitive specifically because it is on a quarter system and you only have ten weeks to learn what they want. It's extra competitive just because of the pace. If you can learn that way, it's a great place," says one student. "If you have to work [in addition to course work], it's probably not the best place to go to school for you."

Political Life: Protest as Recreation

Most students at UCLA are generally apolitical, but all are affected to some degree by an element of loud and vocal student activists. Liberal ideology filters down, frequently, to the classroom, although students say that they're more concerned about how their fellow students will react to what they say rather than their professors' opinions — though that is not always the case.

"One thing I don't like is that if you have an opposing view and you have a teacher with a liberal view, you're not really acknowledged," says one student. "It's like, 'Oh, that's nice — next question.'" And another student goes so far as to say that "in about one-third of the classes [conservative students] feel uncomfortable, but more due to the students than the professors." Indeed, one student believes that the majority of students are sympathetic to liberal views "partly because of the academic atmosphere, and partly because I don't think anyone wants to be thought of as young and conservative."

But one faculty member says that if that's the case, it's news to him. "No one has ever raised this issue with me. . . . I feel completely free [to express my views]," he says.

Liberal and radical students are entrenched in high places in UCLA's student government and are "an almost constant nuisance," according to a graduate student. "The student government frequently uses mandatory student fees to advocate leftist positions — including frequently condemning the university, California, or the United States for something; the mainstream student paper is run by liberals, this making any leftist protest or minor left-wing speaker front-page news, and the racial organizations have created an iron rod. They get their people elected to the student government, then the student government funds their activities (political and social) so that they can build up their membership, so that they can elect their people to office and continue the cycle," he says.

Often it seems that student groups need a radical issue to justify their existence, students say. "There's unionizing and striking grad students. There's various loud rallies and marches usually ending in the takeover of some building or blocking of traffic," a grad student says. "Rules have been altered once it was noticed that conservatives were utilizing them to be insensitive to some preferred group. Essentially, for a sizable portion of the UCLA population, protesting for some liberal cause is their form of recreational/social activity."

Racial and ethnic issues are major sources of controversy. Students continue to protest the recent elimination of racial preferences in university admissions practices. In May 1999, according to the *Daily Bruin,* students protested a University of California Board of Regents meeting and confronted UCLA chancellor Albert Carnesale, demanding he help to reinstate affirmative action at UCLA. (This despite the fact that legally, he can't really do much of anything to restore the old system.) In February 2000, the *Bruin* reported, sixteen people, mostly UCLA law students, were arrested after they took over the Law School's records office with the same goal of restoring racial preferences.

Despite the consternation, UCLA still has one of the most diverse student bodies in the nation. According to the school, 34 percent of the students are Asian-American (an additional 4.5 percent are Filipino); 15 percent are of Hispanic descent; and a little less than 5 percent are black. These numbers have dipped only slightly since the demise of racial preferences in admissions.

"Affirmative action has been huge," one student says, "and it's ongoing." But he notes with bemusement that "the affirmative action opponents won, and these people are fighting a dead issue."

Not that most students care: the majority of them, according to a student, are "mainly apathetic." Another student is more blunt: "Most people just ignore [the protesters]. They don't care." Most students "don't think about politics, and mainly take positions they think won't get anyone to yell at them," a graduate student says. "If you can pin them down to a position, you can easily make them backtrack to a counter position simply by engaging them in debate. Of the politically active people on campus, I think the left dominates. They've got better resources for recruitment and [better] infrastructure. There is a strong conservative and libertarian presence, but we're nowhere near as visible."

Still, all students have to live with the lingering effects of past protests, even if these effects serve only to divert funds from areas where they might be more usefully applied. Perhaps the most visible residue if a protest is UCLA's Chicana/Chicano studies program, which was established after student protests in the early 1990s that involved hunger strikes and campus vandalism. Today, this interdisciplinary program instructs students in "teaching fundamental academic skills such as critical thinking and writing," according to the course catalogue, but also "is committed to . . . the promotion of critical thinking about such issues as gender, sexuality, social action, language, race, ethnicity, class, assimilation/acculturation paradigms, and indigenous traditions" because "the literary and visual arts often function as vehicles for social change and creative empowerment."

This has led to courses like Chicana and Chicano Studies 10A, which explores "labels, [the] colonized mind, sexism, homophobia, stereotyping and alienation." Other courses include "Chicana Feminism" and "Politics of Diversity."

In such an environment, some students feel frustrated, especially those who are devout Christians. There are many religious groups on campus, and a good number of Christian groups, but as one frustrated student says, "It really seems as if a lot of the other religious groups are tolerated" while Christian groups are sometimes given a rough time "because they stand up for certain beliefs." One example of this was when gay student groups organized a "kiss-in" on campus. "Nobody said anything, but the minute any Christian group starts talking . . . then they get blasted in the paper," this student says. "It's hard being a Christian group on campus."

Conservative outlets are rather limited for students, but they do exist. Aside from the conservative party-oriented groups on campus, there is also an Objectivist Club, dedicated to promoting the philosophy of Ayn Rand, as well as a campus chapter of Young Americans for Freedom.

Student Life: 50 Ways to Leave Your College

Going to school at UCLA, says one student, is "like going to school in a big Abercrombie and Fitch ad." One of UCLA's biggest advantages in the social arena of a collegiate experience is that "you have L.A. at your disposal," this student says. "There's not anything that isn't a twenty-minute bus ride away." While Westwood itself is a nice and student-friendly place, there are attractions and diversions, the like of which are unavailable at many colleges, just a few minutes away by car or bus. "Surprisingly few students make full use of the many museums, galleries, and other cultural resources," says a faculty member. In addition, there are spectacular mountains, deserts, and coasts within easy reach of the campus. "Students often find out about the 600-odd miles of trails in the Santa Monica Mountains, for instance, just when they are leaving school," the faculty member says.

First and foremost among these is the Pacific Ocean, which is just five miles away from the UCLA campus. In addition to that, there is shopping and entertainment even closer by in Santa Monica and West Hollywood. In addition, just a few miles to the east, students can visit the Los Angeles County Museum of Art, Chinatown, Little Tokyo, and many other fun destinations. "I think it's good it's not centered around the campus," says one student. "You're not kind of stuck going to fraternity parties."

Not that that isn't an option. There's a resurgent Greek scene on campus. "A big draw for students," says one undergraduate, "happens on Thursday nights — there are fraternity parties on Fraternity Row in Westwood. The frat thing has been, in my book, gaining momentum since I've been going there. They've taken some hits over hazing and things like that, but now I think they're really starting to come back." Students may like the fact, although parents may wince, that "bars are a big deal on campus," according to one student.

But overall, the student scene offers something for everyone, as UCLA has over five hundred registered student groups on campus. "It gets pretty diluted as to what people do," says one student. "There are so many groups. Every other group has their own thing. Everyone has their own little clique."

The range of student organizations is breathtaking in its wide scope. There are ethnic and cultural groups for seemingly every nationality. There are political groups ranging from the Bruin Republicans and Bruin Libertarians to the Youth for a Socialist Action. The latter's stated goal is "to educate our peers about the destructive nature of capitalism, organize protests, and other mass actions, and eventually lead society in a more humane direction." However, students looking to counterbalance such leanings can join either the Bruin Republicans or Libertarians, or the campus chapter of Young Americans for Freedom, whose goal is to "promote conservatism and liberty at UCLA and the surrounding community." The *Daily Bruin* is UCLA's main student-run newspaper; it tilts to the left, but a conservative-oriented student paper is in the planning stages.

With all the activities to choose from, a student offers this bit of advice. "Find people to latch onto. Find something you're interested in. Find a group you can be a part of. If you pour all your time and effort into academics, without taking a break, you'll go nuts. . . . You need to take some time to have some fun."

Housing at UCLA is described in a word by a student as "cramped," but it's also a good place to live. UCLA guarantees two years of housing to incoming freshmen and one year to transfer students, and according to the university's Web site, 90 percent of freshmen live on campus. There are a number of housing options, including four large high-rise dormitories, two buildings that offer "residential suites" (two bedroom apartments without kitchens), three buildings that offer "house" living (in these, there are eight houses to a building) in which each house has its own entrance and living room, and a number of on-campus houses for upper-division students. For upper-division female students, there is the opportunity to live in a substance-free, single-sex house. A fifth high-capacity dormitory is under construction.

In all types of housing, it's almost impossible not to have to live with someone else, as nearly all rooms are doubles or triples. In suites, bedrooms are shared. Single-sex floors are available in a number of halls, but it's typical to live on a coed floor with "designated male and female community restroom/shower facilities," according to the university's Web site. In other housing, private bathrooms may be an option. "The dorms are crowded," says one student, "and they seem to have three kids to a room."

But dorm life is an enjoyable experience. "[Dorms] are fun — if you can afford them," a students says.

Crime on campus isn't much of a concern. One graduate student says he feels safe on campus, but he's a big guy. "Were I a 110-pound female student, I wouldn't walk around campus at 3 a.m. as I commonly do now." Another student notes that streets on and around campus are well-lit, and that campus security officers (in this case, specially trained students) are available from dusk to 1 a.m. to escort fellow students who feel uncomfortable. There is also a campus van service that runs until midnight during the academic year. Another student says that while he thinks the campus is safe, "it was a concern when I was first there," and "most of the criminal activity doesn't come on the campus but on the outskirts."

There are two campus traditions that are notable at UCLA. The first is the school's loyal support of its sports programs, especially its football and basketball teams. UCLA is a member of the Pac Ten conference, and both those teams are quite competitive in the conference and on the national stage. There are eleven varsity-level women's teams and ten men's teams, and the school is also a power in men's volleyball, men's soccer, and women's water polo. In addition, there are extensive in-tramural and club sports available, including lacrosse, snow skiing, rugby, dance, and a number of martial arts disciplines.

The second tradition is known as the Midnight Yell, which is pretty much what is sounds like: each midnight during finals week, every student screams. This is not just a fifteen-second stress reliever, as one student notes, but a celebration that involves general campus-wide revelry and fun. Or at least it *used* to be fun. In the fall of 1999, it metamorphosed into the "Midnight Riot," wherein some students set fire to furniture they had carried into the streets. Twenty students were arrested not only for setting the fires, but for throwing things at the firefighters and police officers who had come to quell the flames and the disturbance. The winter Yell went somewhat better — only nine arrests, according to the *Daily Bruin*.

Still, a student claims that the vandalism was an aberration and that "the media were just as responsible for that as the kids were" because it hyped up the event. However, the students involved with the public disturbance seemed intent on hyping it up themselves. One student told the *Bruin* that this winter quarter's celebration was "pretty boring — there's no helicopters, no fire, no LAPD officers." After talking with a *Bruin* reporter, this student set a fire in the middle of a street and was arrested minutes later by university police. Good plan. Another student complained to the *Bruin* that the university police were "totally out of line" and that "the police had to ruin (the celebration)." She was part of a 150-student mob that taunted police with chants and a bullhorn, and received a citation for setting off a flare, no doubt making her parents very proud.

As for the university, it does not look kindly upon such lawless behavior. "It's been getting a lot more attention since I've been there," says one student. "If you do the Midnight Yell in your dorm you'll be suspended." And school officials thought that while most students were well-behaved, there was enough rowdiness to be disturbing. When a bottle filled with "a combustible liquid" was found on top of an apartment building, it very much concerned the university. "That is a whole different approach than just letting off steam," one administrator told the *Bruin*. "That could hurt people and cause damage to buildings."

Another administrator summed up the university's view to the *Bruin* as follows: "I thought, generally, it was OK. Though I am still disturbed by the fascination with fire, particularly in such a densely populated area . . . I thought the students were generally well-behaved."

As in all things, the majority of students shouldn't be held accountable for the actions of a few bad apples, and UCLA, despite its few flaws, remains an attractive place to go to school. Its top-notch research facilities, impressive academic resources, and plentiful opportunities to get involved with one or more of literally hundreds of student organizations make UCLA an attractive school with a lot to offer any serious student.

University of California at San Diego

Office of Admissions
9500 Gilman Drive
La Jolla, CA 92093
(858) 534-2230
www.ucsd.edu

Total enrollment: 19,918
Undergraduates: 16,230
SAT ranges (Verbal/Math): 560-660 (V); 600-700 (M)
Applicants: 32,547
Accepted: 41%
Enrolled: 25%
Application deadline: November 30
Financial aid application deadline: March 2
Tuition: resident: $3,849/$11,274; non-resident: $14,022/$21,447
Core curriculum: No

The Science of It

The University of California at San Diego, one of the newer campuses in the massive University of California system, has undeservedly stayed in the shadows of its better-known brethren in Los Angeles and Berkeley. Unlike its brethren in Los Angeles and Berkeley, UCSD is not known either for its athletic prowess or its long history as an ideological battleground. As such, it has gone about its business quietly and in the process has built excellent programs in the sciences — programs that science-minded students should not dismiss simply because of UCSD's limited national profile. In addition, San Diego, with its balmy climate, coastal location, and bustling downtown, is a fine place to spend one's college years.

Unfortunately, UCSD has not developed its liberal arts programs as fully as it has its science-oriented ones, and there are a few departments there that should just plain be avoided. These caveats aside, the combination of good science programs and a good place to live make UCSD worthy of consideration by any student interested in science-related fields.

Academic Life

UCSD is divided into five colleges — Revelle, John Muir, Eleanor Roosevelt, Thurgood Marshall, and Earl Warren — the names of which give an insight into the principles that each college was founded on as well as some of the specialties that each offers. (Revelle College is named after Roger Revelle, an eminent scientist perhaps best known for his work on the issue of global warming, and also the founder of UCSD.) John Muir College, for example, offers a minor in environmental studies, whereas Thurgood Marshall offers general education requirements that are heavy on diversity-related issues. The university is planning a "Sixth College" that will begin in 2002 and focus on "art, culture, and technology," according to its Web site.

However, the differences between the colleges are more cosmetic than substantial; students can major in any of the programs offered at UCSD regardless of the school they are in. "The differences between them are really insignificant," a student says. "It's pretty much one school."

The one requirement that all UCSD students have is quite simple: they have to work. Hard.

"This is not a place to go and party," says one student, who adds that UCSD has "a totally different atmosphere. Our school has a semi-professional feel to it, with a lot of people who have taken on a responsibility in their lives and act like it." One professor agrees, saying that "I do think they work hard." In addition, UCSD, like other California universities, schedules its academic year in quarters rather than semesters, making classes "information packaging sessions," in the words of one student.

While each of the colleges has different general education requirements for graduation, Revelle College's program is more rigorous than most. Aside from the general requirements required for all University of California students — a writing requirement and a course in "American History and Institutions" — the Revelle also requires a five-course sequence in an interdisciplinary humanities program with intensive writing in two of those courses; one course in the fine arts; three lower-division social science courses, two of which are in one social science and the other in American cultures; three quarters of calculus; five courses in the natural sciences (four quarters total of physics or chemistry and one quarter of biology); fourth-quarter proficiency in a foreign language, and either a minor or a three-course "area of focus" that is different from the type of major a student is taking.

John Muir College, in contrast, requires that students take two expository-writing courses and four year-long academic sequences (three classes per sequence, for a total of twelve courses) in certain areas. Social sciences and calculus sequences are required, and students choose the remaining two sequences from humanities, the fine arts, or foreign languages. For its part, Eleanor Roosevelt College demands, along with its other requirements, a fine six-course sequence on "The Making of the Modern World," which covers the history of the world from prehistory to the present. Roosevelt College also requires three courses that look at a particular area of the world. Choices include modern Europe, as well as Pan American, the Middle East, and other regions.

The weakest general education requirements are found at Thurgood Marshall College, which offers basically the same general requirements as the other colleges, but forces students to take a year-long, three-course interdisciplinary sequence called "Diversity, Justice, and Imagination." This series, according to the course catalogue, focuses on "socioeconomic diversity in examining class, ethnicity, race, gender, and sexuality as significant markers of difference among persons" in the "Diversity" course and "racial justice, political representation, economic justice, gender, and justice . . . and rights of cultural minorities" in the "Justice" class. And in case some essential politically correct topic somehow got missed in all that, the college also requires students to take courses in both Third World studies and ethnic studies. "They basically teach you that everything that you have been taught is a lie," says one student of the ethnic studies department. "I've had a real problem with that."

In all colleges, the general education requirements are quite broad, which doesn't please those who want students to have a traditional education. "If I had to make a criticism of the education system here," says one professor, "I would say that the students are not getting enough attention as far as general education is concerned. . . . You can ask [students] basic questions about history or the world and they're just ignorant."

Indeed, students at UCSD don't need to take many demanding courses in the area of Western civilization, and the general education requirements, as at many schools today, lack the cohesiveness that is the mark of a true liberal arts education. "All my courses turn out to be general education courses," a professor says, "because I can't assume [students have learned] anything."

These weaknesses aside, UCSD does have a number of excellent programs for its students. The natural sciences are chief among them. "We really have an astounding department of biology," a professor says. "And we have pretty good departments in physics, chemistry, and computer science."

In contrast, only some of the departments in the humanities measure up to this standard. "The humanities departments are variable," the professor says. "There are some very good people here and there in history and philosophy. On the other hand, we can't always keep them." Perhaps most worthy of note are the political science department, well known for its emphasis on Latin American politics, and the theatre department, described by one person as "really quite outstanding." The economics department is not bad either, though not as good as it could be, and psychology and sociology are also pretty good.

And there are plenty of departments at UCSD that don't cut it. Unfortunately, UCSD does not have a strong classics program, and one professor notes that "we're very weak in things like classics. We have [only] one or two people who can teach Greek and Latin subjects with any authority." This professor calls the literature department "a mess," but notes that this is not a problem only found at UCSD.

The ethnic studies department, steeped as it is in left-wing ideology, should be avoided. "It's a very politicized organization," says a faculty member. One student who took an ethnic studies course said that when an unknown party criticized his professor in a letter to the powers that be, "she basically showed how this letter victimized everyone in the room and how it was oppressive."

But even the ethnic studies department produces good instructors, and George Lipsitz in that department is one of many fine professors at UCSD. Others include Peter Irons, Gary Jacobson, Sanford Lakoff, Steven Erie, and Sam Kernell in political science, and Arthur Droge in literature. Professors are also generally easy to get in touch with — as at other campuses, e-mail has become a great way to communicate. "It's made office visits almost unnecessary," says a student.

Students should expect large class sizes. "The general education classes were usually in auditoriums with about two hundred to three hundred students per class, or frequently 150 to 250," says one student. "As for lower division classes for majors, there are eighty to 120 and for upper division courses there are forty to eighty." Another student says that "my classes have ranged from fifty to two hundred [people]."

UCSD is "definitely research-oriented, though not necessarily teaching oriented," one professor says. "On the whole, it's a research school, but there have been and are excellent teachers." This state of affairs has its ups and downs. One of the downs is that teaching assistants do a good deal of teaching, especially at the introductory level, and it's an unpopular fact of life at UCSD. "A lot of people, I think, don't like that," says a student, who points out that language difficulties with TAs who are not native speakers of English can be very frustrating. "I'm trying to learn advanced calculus and I have a TA who just came here four years ago," he says. "It is an issue and it has happened more than once."

However, a very positive aspect of this situation is that student research opportunities are plentiful, especially in the sciences. One of the most highly regarded programs is the Undergraduate Research Conference, in which outstanding undergraduate students present a thesis to faculty. Students can also graduate with honors in a department by completing an honors thesis. "Every year the faculty are very enthused about the theses that are done," a professor says. "There's no question that represents a lot of work." The Scripps Undergraduate Research Fellowship, which focuses on marine and earth sciences, takes place during the summer at the Scripps Institute of Oceanography, and it provides a generous stipend plus housing and travel expenses. A number of scholarships are out there for promising undergraduates, and there are dozens of research centers on campus where cutting-edge research is the routine.

Despite some flaws, UCSD is a great school for serious students who are willing to put in the time and effort to make their education a success. "Be as diligent as possible going through your course work in order to get out of this place in four years or less," advises one student, "because the primary purpose of a UCSD student is to step to the next level." Another student agrees: "It's a true quality education. . . . It's a step behind Berkeley and UCLA at worst."

Political Atmosphere

Like many academic institutions, UCSD is a solidly liberal place, but there is also a good amount of academic freedom on campus. A professors says he feels "far from being unfree." This professor says it's not like how it was "in the Seventies, when you could really get in trouble for not being one of them." This is not to say that there the forces of political correctness have not recently reared their heads at UCSD. But when they have, they have been either defeated in court or simply deemed irrelevant and embarrassing.

Perhaps most awkward for UCSD was the brouhaha that erupted when then–Speaker of the House Newt Gingrich was selected to give the school's commencement speech in 1998. This "was a mistake, because when he came it was very disgraceful," a student says. "There were parents who stood up and yelled at him." It wasn't just some parents who were furious — students protested vigorously in favor and against Gingrich. "That was a bad day for our school," another student says. "What's the point of ruining someone's graduation ceremony just because you have an angry political viewpoint?"

And during 1999, UCSD was forced to settle with a student who had sued the university over its administrative decision to give him three hours of community service for putting up a sign in his dormitory window. Uncharacteristically for situations like this, the sign was from a left-wing perspective and contained obscenities directed at former Israeli Prime Minister Benjamin Netanyahu and former Chilean strongman Augusto Pinochet. But the university argued that the sign was offensive under its rules banning the use of "fighting words." As part of the settlement, the university agreed to revise its rules covering the content of posters and fliers and made a number of concessions regarding its own disciplinary policies.

Despite those defeats, however, the forces of the left wing still maintain a relatively strong hold on certain areas of UCSD life. Groundworks, a so-called alternative book store, is where many students must purchase their books — and it is, according to one student, "extremely . . . radical." He notes, only partially tongue in cheek, that "You know your teacher is a Communist if he asks you to pick up your books there."

The other pseudo-Marxist institution on campus is the Che Café, which one student describes as "a little café that models itself after Marxist and Communist rhetoric and ideology. Everyone who works there is equal; there's no head." As one might expect, this student notes that it is not a real for-profit business, but rather a cooperative.

Also worthy of mention are a number of radical student groups, many of which meet regularly at the school's Cross-Cultural Center. The CCC, according to UCSD's website, "is dedicated to supporting the needs of UCSD's diverse student, staff, and faculty communities." However, the CCC in reality serves as a shelter for left-wing ideologues, as a quick look at its massive 1999-2000 "Diversity Events Calendar" shows. The calendar lists CCC events and others, including meetings for MeCHA, a radical Chicano group; the Student Affirmative Action Coalition; and the Marxist Study Group, which meets nearby at the Student Center.

But for most students, life remains trouble-free from the activist class: they just don't care about politics. "The vast majority of the students are apathetic," says one student. "I would say we have a number of Republican and conservative students, but Democrats still outnumber us 65 to 35." And, it should be noted that religious groups have a powerful voice on campus. "Anytime when religion is involved," says this student, "that's a hot issue. We have a number of Christian conservative students with very strong convictions. They're a force."

Student Life

UCSD has the inherent advantage of being in San Diego, a beautiful, vibrant city on the Pacific coast that has plenty of things to do and see year-round. The campus is just a few minutes from the ocean, and the city has a bustling downtown — both attractions that may not be immediately obvious to those who consider the city merely a glorified naval base.

San Diego has so many attractions and diversions that, while on-campus life "is pretty boring," as one student puts it, UCSD students can easily find things to do. First and foremost, the beach is less than ten minutes by foot. One block away from campus, there is a shopping center with everything, and there are three major malls within a few miles of campus.

UCSD, as one student puts it, "is very anti-Greek. They don't welcome Greeks and they don't have any policies that make being a Greek easy," and he notes that students aren't even supposed to put Greek letters on their houses. In addition, the city of La Jolla — where the university is based — has tight restrictions on housing that would make establishing a Greek system difficult. And, because of UCSD's policy on alcohol — "no tolerance," as one student puts it, there aren't any "real parties in the dorms. But, of course, there's always Tijuana, which a lot of students go to." The Mexican border town is only about thirty minutes away, and thus students are able to indulge in plenty of bad habits: Tijuana has an unsavory reputation and is known mostly for its corruption and violence. Students, especially those who drive across the border, should exercise common sense and caution, and be sure to comply with all Mexican laws and regulations — especially those regarding automobile insurance — to avoid any unnecessary trouble and incarceration. (You can be put in prison if you are in an accident in Mexico and do not have Mexican auto insurance. Consult travel guides for more information. Please.)

Life on campus thankfully does not come close to imitating Tijuana, but nor is it completely dead. There are a number of student clubs and organizations to join, ranging from religious groups such as the InterVarsity Christian Fellowship to political groups such as the College Republicans, along with publications like *The Guardian*, the on-campus newspaper, and *The California Review*, a conservative-oriented newspaper that has recently been re-established at UCSD. Also notable is the Sun God festival, an annual music concert where fun is had by all.

There are no major sporting events at UCSD of the type that one sees at schools like UCLA and USC, and the football team is relegated to club status. But there are a number of varsity-level sports squads at UCSD, including men's and women's teams in basketball, crew, cross country, soccer, volleyball, and water polo. The school jumped from NCAA Division III to Division II in the fall of 2000.

Housing on campus is generally clustered around each college, and there are a variety of options for students living in on-campus housing. The residence halls offer both single and double rooms, along with some suites for eight to ten students, and there are on-campus apartments as well (mostly for returning students). Rooms and suites are, according to the college's Web site, "gender specific in mostly coed buildings." Students who smoke should be mindful of California's strict anti-smoking laws, which UCSD vigorously promotes.

And the dorm food, according to one student, "has gotten better. They're progressing — they're making an effort." But, he adds, "students still get fat."

Crime is somewhat of a concern on campus. While violent crimes and sexual crimes are infrequent, there have been problems with theft, especially involving automobiles. "Auto theft and auto break-ins have been a big issue," a student says. "A lot of cars have been broken into or stolen."

While student life seemingly has a low profile — and this can be said for a lot of things at UCSD — there is no lack of opportunities, whether academic or social, for UCSD students, provided that they go out and find them. Students willing to make that effort should find UCSD to be a rewarding place to go to school.

University of California at Santa Cruz

Office of Admissions
1156 High Street
Santa Cruz, CA 95064
(831) 459-4008
www.ucsc.edu

Total enrollment: 11,300
Undergraduates: 10,269
SAT ranges (Verbal/Math): 520-640 (V); 520-640 (M)
Applicants: 14,485
Accepted: 77%
Enrolled: 22%
Application deadline: November 30
Financial aid application deadline: March 2
Tuition: resident: $4,235/$11,573; non-resident: $10,174/$17,512
Core curriculum: No

Intro

Founded in 1965, the University of California at Santa Cruz has always had a different way of doing things — to the point where it is almost unique among modern-day universities. Perhaps the most public sign of this iconoclasm is its school mascot: the Banana Slugs, immortalized in the popular film *Pulp Fiction*. But UC–Santa Cruz is not merely unconventional in this respect. Indeed, the school seems to take pride in a paradox: it does well what large research universities are supposed to do, but also excels at the things small colleges are supposed to do best.

For example, the university, while a singular unit in many respects, has a strong and well-maintained collegiate academic system in which each college has its own academic emphasis. Not content to build itself near beautiful surroundings, the university sets *within* them — the school is built in a redwood forest overlooking Monterey Bay and the city of Santa Cruz. UC–Santa Cruz places a great deal of emphasis on research, but does not let this interfere with its teaching mission. Undergraduate research opportunities are plentiful, and the school has a number of strong departments, especially in the sciences. The result is an education that both students and faculty at UC–Santa Cruz seem quite happy with. Students concerned about being a cog in the machine of a large university, or who are looking for a relatively close-knit collegiate experience, should consider UC–Santa Cruz.

Consider, that is, with a few caveats: UC–Santa Cruz has several features that might raise some eyebrows, even apart from jokes about the school's mascot. The school, at this writing, uses narrative evaluations (a written report detailing a student's performance), and allows students to choose whether they want to receive a letter grade for a certain course. The personal narrative system, which faces a faculty vote in the fall of 2000, allows some students to slide through four years of instruction with merely "Pass" grades. The school also has a number of courses and disciplines that have fallen prey to modern-day academic trendiness. However, while these factors should be considered by a student interested in UC–Santa Cruz, they should not be enough to disqualify the university.

Academic Life: Three for Eight Ain't Bad

UC–Santa Cruz is made up of eight colleges — with two more being developed — that, while maintaining their own sense of identity, are part of an integrated university. Each has between 1,100 and 1,400 students and between forty and ninety faculty members. The university catalogue describes each college as a "home within a larger university" for students and faculty. "The colleges play a primary role in academic advising and are the center of student life. Students graduate from their college," according to the catalogue. "At the same time, all university academic programs, resources, and student services are open to students of every college." Students entering UC–Santa Cruz are asked to list several colleges in order of preference, and the college does its best to assign students to the college of their choice. However, students who later find themselves gravitating toward a different college may transfer with both colleges' approval. Each college is different architecturally, both in the style of its buildings and in the construction of its general academic program. "A student can go to a big university but still feel part of this tiny community," a student says.

Cowell College, the first at the university, according to the catalogue, encourages "study of the traditions of Western culture and the interplay of those traditions within multicultural American society." Its focus is in the humanities, and is best regarded for its philosophy, classical language, and foreign language departments.

Stevenson College, named for former United Nations ambassador and presidential candidate Adlai Stevenson, is concerned with social sciences, humanities, and natural sciences. It is notable for a three-quarter-long intensive writing course. Its core course focuses on Great Books, from Plato to Gandhi to Marx. Crown College is mainly dedicated to the natural sciences.

Clearly, those three colleges offer the university's best in the way of traditional liberal arts. The other five colleges — Merrill, Porter, Kresge, Oakes, and the as-yet-unnamed College Eight — offer a variety of academic emphases, most of which are enthusiastically given over to multiculturalism. Porter College's core course, for example, considers "the heritage of arts in a multicultural society." Kresge College's core course, "Cultural Intersections," "invites active participation in the creation of new social possibilities. [It] asks: How do we construct our notions of race, gender, class, and sexuality, and how might we?" At Oakes College, the core course "Values and Change in a Diverse Society" "is writing intensive and examines individual and collective responses to issues of culture, gender, sexuality, race, and class." College Eight has a special emphasis on the environment.

Apart from the "core" courses at each college, the general education requirements for all university students are quite broad; they amount to standard, unfocused distribution requirements. There are basic composition and American history requirements that are easily skipped with a decent score on an SAT battery or AP credit. The other general education requirements are a number of courses — between nine and fourteen — in a variety of academic disciplines. Students are to take two courses in the humanities and arts, two courses in the natural sciences, and two courses in the social sciences. Each of the two courses in these categories must be from different departments. In addition, students must take three topical courses, one from each academic area; one quantitative course that involves the use of advanced algebra, statistics, or calculus; two courses in writing, one of which is intensive; one course in the arts, which may come from art, art history, music, film, or theatre; and — of course — one course tagged "ethnic/Third World," which is in essence a diversity requirement.

One professor says that the requirements "are not what I hope to see." But another faculty member says the requirements "are actually quite good," though he'd like to see more writing taking place.

Research opportunities at UC–Santa Cruz are plentiful. "There are strong research opportunities in every department," a faculty member says. "Students are strongly encouraged to do senior research in faculty labs and many publish their results in mainline journals." Some interesting opportunities include marine biology, high-energy physics, and molecular biology. (The university is one of the top two or three RNA research centers in the world.) Almost every psychology faculty member has a team of undergraduate and graduate students working with them.

The university is small enough that students need not compete for time with the professors, nor need they remain anonymous in gigantic lecture courses. Introductory courses may be as large as two hundred students, but "once you hit upper division classes they tend to get smaller," a student says. "Seminar classes are the best, with ten to fifteen students per class." The large classes are still taught by professors, but often have discussion sections led by teaching assistants. "I find sections, most of the time, to be pretty useless as they are too big to individually help students," says one student.

That's not to say that you can't get individual help or guidance from an instructor. "I've definitely been able to get to know the professors well," one student says. "If they have free time they're always willing to sit down and talk with you. They're all really open and approachable. I've gotten the impression that the professors I've come in contact with have really genuinely cared about students."

"We really are committed to [undergraduate education] here," a faculty member says. "All of our senior professors — no matter how distinguished — spend lots of time teaching undergraduates." And UC–Santa Cruz has a number of professors that qualify as distinguished. They include Sandra M. Faber in astronomy; Harry Noller in biology; David Haussler in computer science; David Deamer in chemistry; John Borrego in community studies; Thorne Lay in earth sciences; and Craig W. Haney, Ralph H. Quinn, and Barbara Rogoff in psychology. UC–Santa Cruz's best departments are psychology, biology, linguistics, ocean sciences, earth sciences, and astronomy and astrophysics.

There are also some departments that have fallen victim to political correctness or were spawned from it. These include the women's studies department, which considers "gender as a crucial category for understanding the world." The department offers concentrations in feminist anthropology; gender, race and class; the family; women's work; biology and evolution; feminist theory; language and gender; history and literature; science and technology; sexuality; and women in the Third World, according to its catalogue. Another politicized department is American studies, which "gives special attention to racial, ethnic, sexual, class and regional dynamics in the nation's past and present." The community studies department, which sounds like a marriage of the American studies department and sociology, examines "the intersection of class, race, gender and sexuality in relation to health . . . race and racism, [and] cultural work in social change." And while there is no ethnic studies major as such, UC–Santa Cruz proudly announces that it offers "at least eighty courses each year that focus on race and ethnicity as concepts." These courses are taught by more than forty-five faculty from eighteen departments.

So how can you tell how well you did in any of these courses, traditional or otherwise? This is left to UC–Santa Cruz's personal narrative system of grading. Since 1997, all students have had the opportunity to receive a letter grade along with a personal narrative for a course, or merely a personal narrative. The latter option remains incredibly popular — as one professor says, "80 percent of students voted for narratives with their feet by opting for narratives and pass/fail in any course." While letter grades may become mandatory in a faculty vote in the fall of 2000 (see Political Life, below), the distinctive narrative evaluation has been an important part of UC–Santa Cruz's history and is yet another way that the university does things a little differently.

Political Life: The Narrative Thread

Despite its progressive leanings, students and faculty overwhelmingly say that they feel free to express themselves without fear of intimidation or reprisal, a welcome development not common at other institutions. However, discussion over the past year has revolved around more nonpartisan issues, such as a proposed elimination or modification of the personal narrative system that would include mandatory letter grades, and development on campus.

"It's certainly very politically aware," says one student of the campus. "My guess is that if there were some big issue, there would be huge involvement" on the part of students.

They were certainly active when it came to defending the personal narratives. According to the *Chronicle of Higher Education,* a May 2000 faculty senate vote on whether to institute mandatory letter grades was delayed until the fall of 2000 because about two hundred drum-beating and chanting students blocked the entrance to the senate meeting, which never got off the ground. When the issue was first discussed by the senate in December 1999, nearly one thousand "narrative fans," as the *Chronicle* put it, came out to support it.

Proponents of the change have argued that having narratives instead of grades hurts students' chances to make it into graduate or professional schools and that it also hampers recruiting efforts, but students apparently don't agree.

"I chose the school for its narrative system," says a student. "I think that once the narratives are taken away that the school will go against the principles it was founded on. Some of my narrative evaluations were beautifully written character analyses and I think that they can potentially help me with employment in the future."

"Pretty much anyone who is going to graduate school chooses grades," says another student. If the system is scrapped, he says, "I think it's going to be a real loss."

Professors have mixed opinions. One describes the whole affair "as a non-event blown up by the media," noting that "for three years, UCSC has had a grade option in nearly all courses." Another professor, who says he is "not an advocate of the change," thinks "grades are the Achilles' heel of top-notch higher education. . . . I don't think the atmosphere on campus will be made better by the change." And yet another professor says that "while there are advantages to narrative evaluations used as a grading system, this is not understood by most people and they think narrative evaluations in place of letter grades implies that there is 'no grade.'"

Apart from the grading issue, students and faculty are also concerned about development of the campus. As the school grows, it taxes its available facilities, necessitating more development. But some people at UC–Santa Cruz are concerned with its impact.

"Unfortunately, UC–Santa Cruz has been expanding — too much in my opinion," says a student. "Now, with about five major construction projects going on it is no longer peaceful. Instead, I have bits of sawdust in my eyes and all the paths that I used to walk are closed. . . . We don't want any more growth."

"UC–Santa Cruz has the world's most beautiful campus," one professor says. "But it's threatened by development because there is no automobile-free core as most campuses have."

At least it is this kind of thing that occupies the mind of UC–Santa Cruz students and professors, rather than concerns about academic freedom. "I have a lot of freedom in the classroom. Maybe it's just me, but I never feel intimidated even if a group of students disagrees," says one professor. Another says, "[there's] no problem here. In all situations of life certain statements are inappropriate, but there is as much freedom in UC–Santa Cruz classrooms as there is in chatting with a friend at the supermarket."

"I think students know that they won't be attacked for their ideas, that faculty, with a very few exceptions, are committed to tolerance and openness," another professor says. "This is not a place where a great premium is placed on aggressive, hostile, or nasty intellectual exchange. We are rigorous, mind you, but most of us believe that intellectual growth occurs when people feel the freedom to express themselves without reprisal or humiliation."

Politically, students see the campus, as a whole, as being extremely liberal, but they say that's changing. Those on campus say the school is getting more and more conservative. This annoys some, who think the school may be abandoning its progressive roots. "UC–Santa Cruz is falling into the mold of every other school," a student says. But while the school may be getting more conservative, it is still a fairly liberal place. "I think a lot of [conservatives] become more and more liberal after having been in this environment," another student says.

Student Life: From the Redwood Forests

UC–Santa Cruz is literally in a redwood forest atop a hill over Monterey Bay. The setting is simply spectacular. "I'd have to say the physical environment of the college may be its single best feature," says one student. "A lot of people come here because of the environment and the atmosphere."

Anything near a bay is likely near a beach, and the university is no exception. Students say they enjoy heading to the sand or to Santa Cruz itself. (And one mentions "hot tubbing" as a favorite activitiy.) "The town of Santa Cruz is really nice," says a student, noting a few night spots and a multitude of coffee shops in the downtown area.

On campus, each college serves as a hub for social life for its students, making on-campus living a draw. "Each one of the colleges have their own activities," says a student. "They're all different, and directed towards the people in that college."

About 45 percent of the students live on campus. Housing varies from college to college, but most is in the form of dormitories or apartments. Some colleges, such as Kresge, have only apartments, shared by four to six roommates. Other colleges, like Cowell, offer only dorms. Merrill and other colleges give students both options. In the dorms single-sex and substance-free floors are usually available, as are a number of theme halls, which vary from college to college. For example, Porter College has an Academic Intensive House and a Multicultural House, whereas Crown College has Asian/Pacific Islander floors. Students should be careful in choosing their housing arrangements, however, as there are some facilities with "unisex" bathroom facilities.

Because of the college's unique physical situation, parking on campus is limited, so be prepared. Most students get around campus via shuttle buses. "It could be a little better, but I understand the constraints the university is under," a student says. "Students are always complaining that there aren't enough shuttles and there aren't enough routes."

UC–Santa Cruz is about average when it comes to campus safety, and somewhat safer than most parts of Santa Cruz. The only crimes that occurred in recent years more than occasionally were burglary and larceny, and these were generally around the national average for college campuses.

Among the variety of students groups are those devoted to ethnic or cultural activities, along with a number of groups for homosexual students. There are also branches of InterVarsity Christian Fellowship, Newman Catholic Campus Ministry, and The Upper Room, along with religious groups for Jews, Muslims, Buddhists and other faiths. And there are social groups, such as the Slug Chess and Games Club, as well as ample opportunities for community service.

And no entry on UC–Santa Cruz would be complete without another mention of the Fighting Banana Slugs. Not only does UC–Santa Cruz have an intramural sports program and a sailing, rowing, and kayaking center, it has twelve varsity teams and eight club teams for athletic students. The Slugs compete in NCAA Division III with teams for men and women in basketball, soccer, swimming, tennis, volleyball, and water polo. Club sports include running and cycling. And the Slug Ooze fan club, which exhorts all UC–Santa Cruz students to make the school's opponents "feel the ooze," allows students to support their school's athletic teams — and receive free admission to all home games — for a nominal fee.

California Institute of Technology

Office of Undergraduate Admissions
1200 East California Boulevard
Pasadena, California 91125
(626) 395-6811
www.caltech.edu

Total enrollment: 2,000
Undergraduates: 907
SAT ranges (Verbal/Math): 700-780 (V); 750-800 (M)

Applicants: 2,894
Accepted: 18%
Enrolled: 45%
Application deadline: January 15
Financial aid application deadline: December 15
Tuition: $19,959/$27,825
Core curriculum: Yes

Wish They All Could Be California

The original trustees of the California Institute of Technology laid out the school's mission in this fashion: "To train the creative type of scientist or engineer urgently needed in our educational, governmental, and industrial development." That was in 1921, but it still applies — even though no one at that time imagined the Jet Propulsion Lab (JPL) or other facilities that make Cal Tech voted the best American college, according to *U.S. News and World Report*'s 2000 college rankings — not to mention perhaps the preeminent school of technology in the world. The only institute in its class is another institute of technology, the one in Massachusetts. Its underwhelming mission statement is just something that allows the rest of us to understand what really goes on behind the laboratory and classroom doors.

Only about 18% of applicants are accepted, and those that go must really want to go; they will be somewhat disappointed if they are looking for a traditional liberal arts education. The institute does offer majors in economics, literature, history, science/ethics/society, and social science, but even these students must fulfill the rigorous science, engineering, and mathematics prerequisites required of everyone else. The opposite also applies: engineers and scientists must take several humanities courses. Cal Tech's excellence, however, is not in the humanities but in just about every scientific field that has been conceived. Faculty and graduates have more than twenty Nobel Prizes to their credit, and students get to work with this faculty (whom they outnumber by only three to one) on original research projects to an extent unmatched by any other institution, in any field. As a bonus, many faculty happen to be the top experts in their disciplines. What's more, the institute's Web page loads faster than that of any other college.

What is now Cal Tech began in 1891 as a small school of arts and crafts in downtown Pasadena. It became the California Institute of Technology in 1920, and its growth thereafter was brisk. Guided by men recruited from MIT, the University of Chicago, the University of California, and many other prestigious universities, Cal Tech awarded its first Ph.D.s in 1924, the year after professor Robert Millikan received the Nobel Prize in physics. The institute shed its schools of business and an academy, along with other units unnecessary for the fulfillment of its ambitious goals. It added new programs and departments only when it was certain it had the financial backing and personnel to ensure their quality. Cal Tech, in more ways than one, can take its students to the stars.

Academic Life: As a Matter of Fact, It *Is* Rocket Science

The only type of degree offered at Cal Tech is the bachelor of science, and its requirements are extremely rigorous. To put it another way, incoming students have the nation's highest average SAT scores (about 1500) and they find the curriculum more than a little challenging. Most admitted students rank in the top 5 percent of their graduating class.

The science core curriculum consists of five terms of mathematics (three as a freshman and two as a sophomore); five terms of physics (same distribution); two terms of chemistry (general and quantitative chemistry, including one term of lab); one term of biology; a "freshman menu course," either astronomy or geology; two terms of introductory lab courses (including freshman chemistry lab, plus one other lab chosen from various fields); and one science writing course (a 3,000-word paper written under the direction of a faculty member).

In addition, all students need twelve terms of humanities and social sciences. These include two terms of freshman humanities courses emphasizing writing; two terms of introductory social science courses; two terms of advanced humanities courses; and two terms of advanced social science courses. The remaining four courses may be chosen from any of the humanities/social science offerings. The institute also requires three terms of physical education.

Most all courses are required by name, making this a solid core that guarantees students will receive an uncommonly common grounding to their educations. Cal Tech has owned up to its responsibility as an institute of higher learning to decide what constitutes an education, and has done so with remarkably rigorous standards.

The institute is divided into six different academic divisions: Biology; Chemistry and Chemical Engineering; Engineering and Applied Sciences; Geological and Planetary Sciences; Humanities and Social Sciences; and Physics, Mathematics, and Astronomy. The Humanities and Social Sciences division concentrates on its well-regarded doctoral programs, and thus is probably the weakest when it comes to undergraduate education.

In the other divisions, though, the research opportunities available to undergraduates are perhaps unequaled in the university world. Beginning in their sophomore year, students are encouraged to undertake research projects that they may later expand into a senior thesis. Especially noteworthy is the selective Summer Undergraduate Research Fellowship (SURF) program, which "provides continuing undergraduate students the opportunity to work on an individual research project in a tutorial relationship with a research sponsor, usually a member of the Cal Tech/JPL research community," according to the catalogue.

The ten-week program is especially noteworthy for allowing students to attack complex problems early in their academic careers. About a quarter of SURF participants have their work published in scientific journals. Among the 1997 SURF projects were "Permittivity and Permeability of Ferromagnetic Nanocrystals of Different Chemical Compositions," "Visualizing the Human Body: Art and Medicine in Philadelphia, 1740-1890," "Analysis of Galactic Redshifts from the Hubble Deep Field," and "Is Nereid in Chaotic Rotation?" Obviously, none of these fall into the category of "What I Did During My Summer Vacation."

One class is called Mechanical Engineering 72. Each student is given an identical bag of mechanical gadgets, then must assemble the pieces into a robot in ten weeks. Students don't have to use all the pieces, but they also cannot add outside pieces. At the end of the course, all the robots engage in a remote-controlled magnet-fight that fills Cal Tech's largest auditorium and elicits cheers and screams from Techers watching the game. The robots score points by grabbing magnetic objects and attaching them to a metal wall.

Cal Tech has so many gifted and internationally famous faculty members that anything short of a very long list would miss more people than it includes. And the faculty really do teach the students and are famously available for consultation and — equally importantly — to oversee experiments. Most classes are small; in one recent count, 75 percent of classes had sixteen or fewer students, and even large lecture sections break into small units for lab work. There are less than two thousand students — including only nine hundred undergraduates — but there are some 280 professorial faculty members, giving Cal Tech an incredible undergraduate student-to-faculty ratio of three-to-one. Some other impressive statistics: seventy-four faculty are members of the American Academy of Arts and Sciences; sixty-three faculty and four board members belong to the National Academy of Science; twenty-nine faculty and fourteen board members belong to the National Academy of Engineering; and twenty-three people associated with the institute (including fourteen alumni and double laureate Linus Pauling) are Nobel Prize winners. The new president, David Baltimore, was co-winner of the 1975 Nobel Prize for medicine.

With such a faculty, it is no surprise that virtually every program at Cal Tech is excellent. One faculty member says it is impossible to single out the best departments: "We have so many Nobelists, National Medal Winners, and so on in all the departments." This isn't gross immodesty, just a statement of fact. It is fair to say, however, that physics, engineering, chemistry, astronomy, and biology are very strong in every respect. Departments in the humanities and social sciences are not bad, but do not equal the quality of the engineering and hard science departments.

The facilities for scientific and engineering research at Cal Tech are among the best in the world. As institute literature notes regarding advanced physics, "The comparatively small size of Cal Tech coupled with its great strength in both the pure sciences and engineering make it possible to have a faculty with a wide interest in the application of modern physics to technology, without losing close interaction with 'pure subjects.'" Students in aeronautics may use the Guggenheim Aeronautical Laboratory, the Karman Laboratory of Fluid Mechanics and Jet Propulsion, and the Firestone Flight Sciences Laboratory. For future astronomers, the observatories at Mount Palomar and Big Bear, as well as the Owens Valley Radio Observatory and the Cal Tech Submillimeter Observatory, "together constitute a unique and unprecedented concentration of scientific facilities in astronomy," according to the institute. Included is the two hundred–inch Hale Telescope on Mount Palomar, the largest reflecting telescope in the world. There are six physics labs, not including the Mount Palomar and Owens Valley telescopes, and students interested in this field may investigate particle physics, nuclear and neutrino physics, experimental high-energy astrophysics, infrared astronomy, submillimeter astronomy, computational astronomy, condensed matter physics, applied physics, quantum optics, experimental gravitational physics, neuroscience, theoretical physics, and theoretical astrophysics. There are twelve fields of study in chemical engineering. And then there is the JPL, an internationally famous facility that Cal Tech operates for NASA.

The list goes on and on. Suffice it to say that Cal Tech students don't lack the tools or expert instruction to explore just about every scientific field there is. "People who graduated from here say they did more research here as undergrads than they're doing in grad school," institute literature says. "You're not just a go-fer for the professor and his grad students; here you actually get the hands-on experience. Your adviser is guiding you along in the right direction to make sure you don't blow up anything, but for the most part, it's your project to be successful with, or to really screw up."

Most Cal Tech students use their undergraduate educations as a first step to learning even more. Over half of each graduating class goes on to graduate school in the sciences or engineering.

Political Atmosphere: Empirical Knowledge

Given the tremendous amount of work involved in mastering any of the fields of study at Cal Tech, it is no surprise that there are not enough hours in the day to spend politicizing the institute's curriculum or social life. In addition, the sciences and engineering are not very susceptible to politicization in comparison to the humanities. In other words, the faculty and students at Cal Tech have neither the opportunity nor, apparently, the desire to dabble in social engineering or ideological publications.

To quote its Web site: "We admit that the academic work is demanding, but, again, we have to say that it's not all there is to life at Tech. Actually, you could argue that because the work is so demanding, the break that music or sports or other activities offer is more necessary here than at other places."

Cal Tech tries make sure financial constraints do not prevent any student it admits from attending and awards some merit scholarships regardless of financial need. Applications for admission are evaluated separately from requests for financial aid. Cal Tech practices need-blind admission; that is, with the exception of international students, no applicant is denied admission on the basis of limited financial resources. That said, the institute does employ affirmative action in selecting its student body. It recently received $350,000 from the Andrew W. Mellon Foundation to fund its participation in the Mellon Minority Undergraduate Fellowship Program through the year 2003. When the grant was awarded, Thomas E. Everhart, then-president of the institute, said the money would further Cal Tech's efforts to diversify its student body. Five fellows will be selected each year. They receive year-round mentoring, stipends for conference attendance and summer research, and up to $10,000 toward their undergraduate debts if they graduate and pursue a Ph.D. in fields approved by the foundation.

There is also an Office of Minority Student Affairs. Their mission statement is to "assist the institute in successfully graduating a significant number of undergraduate students who are underrepresented in the fields of mathematics, science, and engineering due to their ethnic and cultural heritage — specifically Native American, African American, and Latino men and women." It does this through counseling, support services, workshops, and outreach. It should be noted that Asian Americans are not considered a minority race at Cal Tech.

But Cal Tech has been blasted in a few publications because this year's freshmen class does not have any blacks. A few years ago it had eight black freshmen, but that was attributed to proactive recruitment. "We are concerned, and we are redoubling our efforts, but recognize that this is simply a statistical fluctuation, that this has nothing to do with something we did," President Baltimore told the *Chronicle of Higher Education.* "We work with numbers, so we know how to treat the numbers, and the numbers didn't mean very much this year." The *Chronicle* noted that out of "roughly 900 undergraduates at Cal Tech, only eleven are black. Forty-nine others — forty-eight Latinos and one American Indian — are considered 'underrepresented' minority students. Asian-American students make up about a quarter of the undergraduate enrollment."

The same problem faces women, who make up 25 percent of the student body. Cal Tech's Director of Admissions Charlene Liebau told the *Chronicle* that Cal Tech is optimistic that it will eventually enroll equal numbers of men and women. "History shows that we reach a plateau every few years before we move up again," Liebau said.

Even before that Mellon Foundation grant, Cal Tech offered special Presidential Scholarships to minority students, and the press release that accompanied the Mellon award notes that "administrative support for minority affairs has been increased with the recent creation of an associate deanship." Cal Tech has an associate dean and director for minority student affairs. There is also a program on race, politics, and region.

The institute does not offer the same incentives to minority faculty. "All we care about is the originality of the candidate, their ability to carry out a top-notch research program, and their published record," a professor says. Minorities are, of course, sought after in all branches of university hiring, but the number of minorities and women in the Cal Tech engineering departments, for example, is quite small.

Cal Tech struggles most with its size, and how to balance enrollment with its considerable resources. "The biggest issue is to overcome the problems associated with being a small school . . . that has to remain focused," a professor says. It is almost a given, though, that very few — if any — departments and programs at Cal Tech will decline in the coming years. The faculty and students seem to be too excellent to permit that, and the vast majority are driven by their work.

Student Life: "Grades, Social Life, Sleep: Pick Two"

Life at Cal Tech is often described as "grades, social life, sleep: pick two." Of course, for students attracted to Cal Tech, long hours of study — especially in the laboratory — are not drudgery, but the opportunity they've always dreamed of. Highly motivated and extremely bright, the average Cal Tech student has probably always stood out among his fellows because of a fascination with science and its application to intellectual problems. What Cal Tech offers these students is a chance to pursue their interests in an atmosphere fully unsatisfied with mediocrity.

The university wants its students to get to know each other and get along. Cal Tech freshmen, during their first or second week of school, go on a cruise together to Catalina, an island off the coast of California, to talk about their upcoming classes, where they are from, and what they aspire to become. Faculty and advisors come along to get to know the students as well. Students get a crash course from instructors about what is expected from them, and what to expect from Cal Tech. Moreover, the students were given each other's e-mail addresses before this freshman orientation to begin communicating over the Internet before meeting face to face.

Cal Tech gives the best students in the country the opportunity to advance as part of the community of scholars who make up the institute. Students claim that in spite of the intense pressure to succeed, there is very little competition among students for grades. In fact, students tend to study in groups and cooperate with one another in the interest of everyone's success. The real competition, it seems, is not with fellow students, but with their own individual projects and goals.

Everyone in the Cal Tech community lives by the honor system, which is boiled down to: "No member shall take unfair advantage of any member of the Cal Tech community." It is taken for granted that students will live by the system and monitor their own behavior. Professors often give take-home exams that are both closed-book and timed. A board of control composed of elected student representatives handles suspected violations and makes recommendations to the appropriate dean.

Cal Tech has a number of activities that allow students to pursue hobbies apart from hard science. The institute publishes a literary magazine of students' submissions, and the student newspaper, the *California Tech,* comes out weekly. For the musically talented (or those wishing to learn), there is a wind ensemble, a jazz band, a symphony orchestra (operated with Occidental College), several choral musical groups, some small chamber ensembles, and musical programs at the college's auditoriums. Other nonscientific endeavors include men's and women's glee clubs, the Cal Tech Flying Team, the Motorcycle Club, the Quiz Bowl, the Folk Music Society, numerous language clubs, the usual assortment of ethnic societies, an amateur radio club, and a bridge club. The Cal Tech Christian Fellowship, Newman Club, and Hillel all operate on campus. In all, there are about one hundred Cal Tech clubs and organizations. Only one, a lesbian and gay club, is noticeably politically correct.

Naturally, there are also professional societies such as the American Chemical Society and the American Society of Mechanical Engineers. Cal Tech sponsors numerous lectures on campus each year, and students can hear some of the best minds in science and engineering speak on their own research.

A favorite haunt is the Cal Tech Y, located on the upper floor of the student center and offering not merely exercise facilities, but also interest-free loans, economical trips and backpacking expeditions, notable speakers, meeting rooms, and a used textbook exchange — all with no membership dues or fees. There is also a student shop in which students may build projects either for classwork or for their own use. "Members not proficient in power tools are limited to hand tools and bench work; however, instruction in power tools is given as needed," the catalogue states.

The institute competes in ten men's and seven women's sports at the NCAA Division III level. There is no football team, but Cal Tech does have varsity fencing, among other sports. Nearly 30 percent of undergraduates are involved in intercollegiate sports, a high number at any school, but especially high at a school so dedicated to academics. More than 80 percent are involved in some form of organized athletics, including the intramural program that pits residence halls against one another in flag football, soccer, swimming, volleyball, tennis, and softball.

Cal Tech is divided into seven undergraduate student houses, each of which has a separate unit with its own dining room and lounge and is home to about seventy-five students. The institute also offers two apartment buildings, two dorms, and a few off-campus houses. There is no Greek system, and more than 90 percent of the student body lives in university housing. All freshmen must live on campus, but they may select their residence hall during "Rotation Week," in which students eat lunch and dinner in each of the houses and get an idea of the character of each. At the end of the week, students submit their preferences in ranked order to the student committee in charge of placing freshmen in the houses. Almost everyone gets assigned to his first or second choice, and no one is required to live in a house he doesn't like. Placements are nonbinding; it's entirely possible to change houses or to live in one house and also be a "social" member of another.

One of the newest on-campus residences is Avery House, a $16.1 million Spanish Colonial structure occupied by undergraduates, graduate students, and faculty members. Certain guests stay in the house with the residents; according to campus literature, "many of the special visitors will be entrepreneurs who have distinguished themselves in a variety of high-tech ventures and whom a young engineer or scientist-to-be would view as inspirations." Avery House allows everyone to "meet informally with entrepreneurs and Cal Tech guests," and "students, researchers, professors, visiting scholars, and industry leaders will live together and think together" and will "embody the spirit of entrepreneurship." In this way, business leaders can learn about the ideas coming out of Cal Tech, and students can make excellent contacts within the business community.

There is not a lot of crime on Cal Tech's campus. But because of the large number of labs and computer science rooms, Cal Tech suffers from a lot of technology theft. Computers, fancy calculators, disk drives, and other techno-gadgets often go missing. Then comes bike theft and vandalism, but those crimes, according to statistics, are relatively rare.

Humorously, the biggest so-called crime facing Cal Tech right now is an accusation from the U.S. government that the university "violated the law by not giving the government free use of automatic gene-sequencing machines, a key tool in efforts by government researchers to map the human genome," according to the *Chronicle of Higher Education*. "Investigators suspect Cal Tech developed the technology using federal funds," the newspaper reported. But in a statement, President Baltimore said Cal Tech did not use federal funds, but rather private funding. The case is pending.

Calvin College

Office of Admissions
3201 Burton St., SE
Grand Rapids, Michigan 49546
(616) 957-6000/ (800) 688-0122
www.calvin.edu

Total enrollment: 4,127
Undergraduates: 4,050
SAT ranges (Verbal/Math): 520-650 (V); 540-650 (M)
Applicants: 1,971

Accepted: 97%
Enrolled: 55%
Application deadline: Rolling admissions
Financial aid application deadline: February 15
Tuition: $14,040/$18,930
Core curriculum: Yes

Redeemed

Calvin College says that its primary purpose is to engage "in vigorous liberal arts education that promotes lifelong Christian service." The College was founded in 1876 by the Christian Reformed Church, and still unashamedly professes its adherence to the Reformed faith. The college "pledges fidelity to Jesus Christ, offering our hearts and lives to do God's work in God's world." The college's statement of purpose goes on to say: "We offer education that is shaped by Christian faith, thought, and practice. We study and address a world made good by God, distorted by sin, redeemed in Christ, and awaiting the fullness of God's reign." The college's statements are not merely pious platitudes: the Christian Reformed Church has a long and vigorous tradition of cultivating the intellect, and Calvin's commitment to a sound liberal arts education continues to advance this tradition.

Historically, Calvin's students and faculty have been drawn mainly from the Dutch, Christian Reformed population that founded and still actively supports the college. But the dominance of the Dutch at Calvin has waned recently as the college has actively sought a broader group of students and faculty. The rationale behind this effort is scriptural: "A commitment of the community is to seek, nurture, and celebrate cultural and ethnic diversity, in obedience to the biblical vision of the kingdom of God formed 'from every tribe and language and people and nation.'"

This effort towards greater diversity has created its own problems, however. Calvin is facing the multicultural temptation that has decimated liberal arts education in many other colleges and universities. Calvin sees the deliverance from this temptation in its unswerving commitment to Reformed Christianity, but there is a tension between the ideal of "diversity" and the ideal of excellence. The faculty and students seem to recognize the tension, and have, so far, successfully balanced it. Calvin College has not given in to the temptation, and indeed shows some signs of being stronger for having faced it.

Academic Life: A Reformed Curriculum

The most significant change to occur academically at Calvin College since the publication of the first edition of this guide (1998) is the adoption of a new, true core curriculum. The new curriculum will take effect in the fall semester of 2001. This core curriculum has been in development since 1997, and was formally approved and adopted in April of 1999. In the past Calvin required a set of courses (a distribution requirement) that conveyed an appreciation of the Western Tradition, but the school came to believe that the requirements were too broadly formulated and that there was a lack of integration between disciplines.

The document that describes the rationale and content of the new core curriculum is impressive. The authors candidly admit the weaknesses of the old system and seek to remedy them. They have identified a set of skills and a body of knowledge that they believe all liberal arts graduates should have, and have structured courses that are designed to provide that skill and knowledge — decisions once thought mandatory for educators, but which have been shirked all to frequently at many institutions of late. Some of the "Core Knowledge" categories include: "The Christian Faith," "Historical Development," and "Our Minds." Among the "Core Skills" identified are: "Cultural Discernment," "The Rhetoric of the Written Word," and "Competence in a Foreign Language." The core curriculum document spells out in some detail what each of the Core Knowledge and Core Skills categories mean and prescribes how courses should be designed to meet the different knowledge and skills objectives.

Most impressive is the way that the Core Curriculum strives for integration between the courses of different disciplines and attempts to sequence courses in such a way that they build upon one another. The program's evident goal is to develop within each student a coherent body of knowledge, which the student can "put to work" with the skills he will have learned: this is the essence of a traditional liberal arts education. While Calvin is not interested in becoming a "Great Books" school like St. John's or Thomas Aquinas, under the new core, its students will have a more unified experience of reading from a common body of great works.

The core specifically requires two years of a foreign language (or competency equivalent to that); two courses in literature and the arts; three courses in math and science; and two courses in Western civilization or history. In addition, the college requires that all students take courses in philosophy and in "Biblical and Theological Foundations." There is also a requirement for one course in the area of "Cross-Cultural Engagement." However, courses meeting this requirement promise not to be the exercise in relativism that characterizes such non-Western courses in other colleges. The guidelines for these courses specifically state that in them students "learn how to distinguish between enduring principles of human morality and their situation-specific adaptations; to witness other cultural embodiments of faith, and thus to reflect on the substance and definition of one's own faith by comparison." In the context of the overall Core at Calvin, such courses could very well strengthen the student's understanding and appreciation of the Western tradition even apart from the obvious benefit of exposing them to other ways of thinking.

The majority of the faculty at Calvin are happy with the new core and feel that it improves the liberal arts program. "This is a true core," one faculty member says.

"We have made the requirements stronger, not weaker. We have added requirements in history and Western civ[ilization] that didn't exist before." Another faculty member says, "The old curriculum had too many options. But we've tightened that and created a sound liberal arts core." Many faculty see the new core as being more integrated across disciplinary lines. Indeed, one of the hallmarks of the new curriculum are Core Capstone courses designed to help third- and fourth-year students integrate the knowledge they have gained both from their core and major courses. These courses are intended to help students formulate a "world-view" that is both Christian and liberal.

While traveling through the new curriculum, students will also want to make time for contact with the stronger departments at Calvin — including English, philosophy, classics, chemistry, religion, and physics — as well as with some of the college's outstanding professors. These include: Edward Ericson Jr., Susan Felch, and James Vanden Bosch in English; Kelly J. Clark and C. Stephen Evans in philosophy; Kenneth D. Bratt in classics; Ronald L. Blankespoor in chemistry; John R. Schneider in religion; and Calvin Stapert in music.

In order to be hired, faculty must sign a confessional statement agreeing to the tenets of the Christian Reformed faith and must belong to the Christian Reformed Church or another church in ecclesiastical fellowship with it. This requirement certainly preserves Calvin from many of the relativist and deconstructionist tendencies that have swept so many colleges. However, it would be fair to say that outspoken conservatives are still made to feel unwelcome in some departments. Several faculty agreed that the history department was the most politicized and liberal department at Calvin, but compared to other schools, this is certainly a relative judgment. Conservatives, says one faculty member, "feel some pressure to prove they're not right-wing crazies." Even so, according to a professor, "conservatives aren't hard to find here." There is a "Conservative Study Group" at Calvin that serves as a forum for ideas and a source of support for conservative faculty.

The faculty share a deep and abiding commitment to excellence in undergraduate teaching. Professors are expected to make teaching their number one priority, and the quality of a professor's teaching weighs heavily in the college's decision to grant tenure. But this commitment to teaching has not impeded the quality or quantity of scholarship produced by Calvin's faculty. One professor said that he was "tremendously impressed" by the scholarship of a number of the Calvin faculty, who, he believed, "would be considered an asset to any great college or university."

The overall intellectual atmosphere of Calvin College is described as vigorous. The professors encourage examination and debate of presuppositions and principles. If one is tempted to think that Calvin's denominational affiliation and confessional commitment stifle debate, think again. Students and faculty agree that there is a lively exchange of ideas in and out of the classroom. There are several different lecture series on campus each year, which bring in noted writers, artists and intellectuals, many of whom are conservative. There is a great intellectual vitality at Calvin, distinguished by the college's commitment to the principle that there is objective Truth to be sought and found.

Political Atmosphere: Nothing to Hide

Calvin College is unreservedly and unapologetically Christian and Reformed. This is the lens through which its policies and priorities must be understood. In order to join the faculty, new hires must sign a confessional statement pledging their adherence to the three principal documents of the Reformed faith: the Heidelberg Confession, the Belgian Confession of 1561, and the Canons of Dort. Faculty are permitted to make minor reservations regarding these articles (for example, they are not required to assent to the blatantly anti-Catholic statements contained in some of these documents), but they must agree to them in substance and principle. Faculty are required, as mentioned above, to belong to the Christian Reformed Church or a church that is in ecclesiastical communion with it. In addition, faculty are required to send their children to Christian schools; non–Christian Reformed schools (such as Catholic schools) are allowed. This final requirement creates the most resistance among faculty, especially among those who were not brought up in the Christian Reformed tradition. There was a movement among some faculty in recent years to eliminate or modify the school requirement, but it failed due to a lack of widespread support. Said one professor, "The resistance to the school requirement is more cultural than theological."

Calvin's Christian commitment is apparent even in courses that appear at first to have little connection to religious issues. Calvin, says one professor, insists that students do three things throughout their education:

- Think about the biblical assumptions concerning human beings, and ask how they apply to the issue being studied.
- Think about the Christian vision, seeing Scripture as a whole.
- Ask: What can we expect from human beings? What institutional frameworks make sense for them?

In taking this approach, this professor said, it becomes readily apparent that "some things, some ideological movements, don't fit" the Christian worldview. "At Calvin," says another professor, "the faculty are constantly being asked how they are bringing a Christian perspective to their discipline."

This concern for communicating the Christian vision does not reduce the educational content at Calvin to simple apologetics for the faith. "We're not fundamentalists," says one professor. "There is no problem here engaging the world, and tackling the toughest intellectual or scientific issues of the day." Another says, "We reject the anti-intellectualism and defensiveness which characterizes too much of the

Evangelical community." And one professor who has taught at other institutions says, "This place is very open to discussing ideas; there is true intellectual freedom. I couldn't do the kind of scholarship I'm doing anyplace else."

In spite of the commitment to Christianity, Calvin was not untouched by the multicultural obsession that began at many colleges and universities in the '90s. However, multiculturalism Calvin style is mild and muted next to that which dominates many secular campuses. "Calvin College is multi-pigmented, not multicultural," says a professor. He says that there is a growing awareness that there is a Christian culture at Calvin that needs to be appreciated and fostered for its own sake. "The Christian Reformed culture is interesting in its own right," he says. Another professor notes that a "a certain amount of 'white guilt'" has motivated the college to expend a great deal of energy recruiting minority faculty and students. But even students recruited from non–Christian Reformed backgrounds are mostly Christians, and therefore are sympathetic to the values of the college.

While Calvin College does officially call for "gender-inclusive language" in academic writing, there have never been any speech codes. There have also been no attempts at introducing any sort of "sensitivity training," either for faculty or students. Radical ideology remains low-key at Calvin. "There are some professors who everyone knows are liberals, but they don't try to use their classes to advance their agenda," says a student.

The overriding principle of Calvin, said one professor, is "coherence" between the Christian identity and educational activity of the college. This is reflected, according to several observers, in the president's style of running the college. The president, Gaylen J. Byker, is noted for calling programs to account for their fidelity to the principles of the college. "He has held people's feet to the fire," says one professor. According to another, the president "tries to rein in the pressures and influences which are not consistent with the identity of the college. He has promoted a greater sense of the need for Calvin to be more self-conscious and deliberate about its identity."

Student Life: Earning Your Keep

Professors at Calvin describe the students generally as "serious." One professor said, "There aren't many programs where you can be a slacker and get through." Given Calvin's whopping 97 percent acceptance rate of applicants, this doesn't at first make any sense. But according to Director of Admissions Dale Kuiper, this approach is deliberate. "We believe in extending the opportunity to receive a good education to as many students as possible. Once the student is here, it's up to him or her to live up to the opportunity and meet the standards of the college."

By all accounts, those standards are high. "The proof of our rigorous expectations is in the lack of grade inflation here," says one professor. "Each year, only two or three students graduate with a 4.0 average." Indeed, some graduate and professional schools are known to add points to the GPA of Calvin graduates to make them comparable to other schools with less exacting standards.

This commitment to providing educational opportunity is also reflected in the amount and variety of sources of scholarships for Calvin students. There are forty-three pages of scholarships listed in the college catalog, some of which are open to all students, and some restricted to students in certain disciplines. There are multiple avenues of support available at Calvin for the diligent student.

All this results in close relationships between students and faculty. "It is the rare student," says one professor, "who feels remote or distant from the faculty." This opinion was echoed by many students. "I've had dinner at a professor's home on a number of occasions," one student says. "The professors are very approachable," says another. "Here at Calvin," says a professor, "you have the opportunity for really wonderful mentoring relationships to develop between students and faculty."

The religious identity of the student body is overwhelmingly Christian, but the Dutch Christian Reformed make up only 55 percent of the student body, a surprisingly small figure given the historical identity and close denominational affiliation of the college. By all accounts, students of non-Reformed backgrounds are made to feel welcome. "We are almost all agreed on the central beliefs of the Christian faith," says one non-Reformed student, "so we get along pretty well."

All students under twenty-one years of age are required to live either on campus or at home with their parents. For most underclassmen, this means living in one of the school's residence halls, which house men and women on separate wings, while juniors and senior typically live in apartments on the other side of the highway. Students in these apartments must adhere to a policy that forbids visitors after midnight (or 1:00 AM on weekends), and restrictions are even tighter for the residence halls. Students are also not allowed to have members of the opposite sex in the bedroom with the door closed.

Even so, Calvin's code of student conduct is fairly relaxed, considering the Calvinist affiliation of the college. Students are not required to sign any pledge of their behavior. "Responsible freedom," is the watchword at Calvin. However, students are expected to refrain from drinking, smoking, sexual immorality, and the use of obscene language on campus. Judicial bodies made up students and faculty enforce the code of conduct. The college takes seriously its role in forming the consciences of the students. An interesting development in recent years is the growing number of students themselves who would like to see the college make stricter demands upon student behavior.

While the student body at Calvin is serious, that seriousness doesn't prevent students from finding diversions from work. Music is important on campus: the school has five different choral ensembles, an excellent orchestra, and a contemporary Christian ensemble. There are numerous intramural sports, as well a variety of intercollegiate athletic teams. Arts organizations include a Writer's Guild and a theater group. There is a campus newspaper, *The Chimes*, though it seems to contain a fair amount material best characterized as adolescent whining. Students participate in a number of political groups as well, such as Amnesty International, College Republicans, and College Democrats. In addition, the city of Grand Rapids offers a surprisingly wide variety of entertainment, from art museums to pop concerts, and the area around Calvin is extraordinarily safe; crime at Calvin, including the areas bordering campus, is pretty much nonexistent.

Carleton College

Office of Admissions
Carleton College
100 South College Street
Northfield, MN 55057
(507) 646-4190 or (800)-995-2275
www.carleton.edu

Total enrollment: 1,880
Undergraduates: 1,880
SAT ranges (Verbal/Math): 640-720 (V); 650-740 (M)
Applicants: 3,642
Accepted: 44%
Enrolled: 30%
Application deadline: January 15
Financial aid application deadline: January 15
Tuition: $23,325/$28,086
Core curriculum: No

Trying Real Hard

Founded in 1866 by the Minnesota Conference of Congregational Churches, Carleton College has established itself as a prominent liberal arts school. To some extent, this distinction is deserved: both faculty and students are dedicated to serious scholarly activity. But reputations have a way of getting in the way of reality.

Carleton College tries too hard at some things and not hard enough at others.

There's something self-conscious in the image the college cultivates — a place too hip for books, but which studies them and learns them so well they can afford some time off to be clever. It's the clever part where Carleton tries too hard. In public relations materials, for example, statistics like the 96 percent of faculty with terminal degrees, the eighty-two National Merit Scholars in the 2000 incoming class, and the half-million-volume library are followed by the noteworthy "fact" that there are 1.797 "Frisbees per capita" on campus.

On the other hand, the college has not tried hard enough to free its campus of ideology. From the admissions office to the curriculum and social atmosphere, Carleton advocates "diversity and cultural pluralism." For example, this is one of the very few institutions of higher learning that has sponsored a drag queen contest (and no, this is not a fraternity thing; fraternities don't exist there). So, we find it odd that male "societies" no longer exist and "closed" groups like fraternities are banned while "diverse" groups such as racially segregated organizations and feminist women's groups proliferate.

Still, say what you will about the campus culture, Carleton students not only work hard and learn quite a bit, but they seem to thrive on the life of the mind, enjoying the "intellectual adventure" on which the college invites them to embark. Students publish in scholarly journals, collaborate with their professors, routinely attend academic conferences, and receive research grants for original scholarly work. Scores go on to graduate school, and Carleton ranks at or near the top of all private colleges in the percentage of graduates who obtain doctorates. The science departments are excellent, and mostly have been spared the politicization that has affected the humanities and social sciences at the college. A mature student capable of withstanding the powerful forces of conformism at Carleton can obtain a fine education there.

Academic Life: Me, a Name I Call Myself

There is no doubt that course work at Carleton is demanding. The curriculum is "pretty intense, with a short list of easy courses," according to a sophomore political science major. But for all the hard work Carleton requires of its students, the college does not require specific courses in some essential subjects, nor does it require mastery of a body of common knowledge. The distribution requirements that it does have are pointedly loose. Coursework in Western civilization is not required, although students must take a course to fulfill the "Recognition and Affirmation of Difference Requirement" (RAD). The RAD course is required, according to the academic catalog, because Carleton "defines itself as an institution that values diversity. This is reflected in the importance and pride the college places in a student body that includes a balanced number of men and women, and includes people from a variety of racial, ethnic, and economic backgrounds." And to what differences does the college refer? "The word 'Difference' in the name of the requirement reminds us that differences do exist, and if we are to create a community that embraces diversity, we must expose ourselves to perspectives that have developed outside of, in opposition to, or in ways only dimly visible to the dominant culture in which most of us have grown up and been advanced."

The phrase "dimly visible" might apply to the so-called dominant culture when it comes to the distribution requirements. Twelve credits in the arts and literature group are required, none of them by name. Students also take twelve credits from history, philosophy, or religion, but since no particular courses are required, a Carleton graduate could be, for the most part, ignorant not just of Western history, but of any history.

Carleton requires students to take three courses in the social sciences (economics, educational studies, linguistics, political science, psychology, sociology, and anthropology). Three mathematics and natural science courses also are required from departments including biology, chemistry, geology, physics, and astronomy; math and computer science; and certain psychology courses. All three courses can be taken without lab work.

Proficiency in writing is required but, unlike some other schools, Carleton does not require a first-year course in composition. Instead, the writing requirement may be met by taking certain introductory courses in just about any department with any professor, or by scoring a "5" on the College Board's AP exam. According to a student, the writing requirement is "not important, and there's talk of eliminating it."

Carleton requires of all majors — including the natural sciences and mathematics — the study of a foreign language through the fourth term or the equivalent competency. There's faculty-driven sentiment on campus, however, arguing that students could fulfill this requirement by taking a linguistics course in which they learn about languages. Foreign language courses do not qualify as RAD courses.

Carlton also requires all students to pass a comprehensive examination (called "Comps") in their major. Students must write a substantial paper or several short ones, and undergo an oral, public defense before a faculty committee. Carleton awards only a B.A. degree.

Despite the construction of the general education requirements, Carleton graduates have amassed an enviable record of achievement over the years. Carleton is second among all liberal arts colleges in graduates who earned Ph.Ds in all fields and first in the number of graduates who earned Ph.Ds. in all sciences and mathematics. In fact, more than half of all Carleton alumni have earned advanced degrees, and more than a quarter have earned doctorates. In the past five years, more Carleton students have been awarded National Science Foundation Fellowships than at any other liberal arts college.

These statistics reveal a highly motivated, selective student body that receives outstanding professional training from the faculty. This is especially true in the sciences (for the class of 2001 and 2002 biology is the most popular major), where the necessary rigor and empiricism serve to block the influences of radical and nihilistic politics. It also speaks well of the faculty's role in giving students the self-confidence and desire to persevere in their fields of study.

Carleton professors are known for permitting their students to collaborate closely with them on research projects, and students who do this are often well prepared for the lab work they will encounter in graduate or professional school. In addition, many professors make sure their students gain some practical experience applying their liberal arts education. Roy Grow, for example, offers his political economy seminar as a volunteer consultant to industry.

Carleton likes nothing more than to seem a place where the nonstandard is standard, where being an "individual" is about as important as being a good student. Carleton's educational philosophy follows from John Dewey, emphasizing the importance of "thinking critically" rather than learning an agreed-upon body of knowledge. The irony is that without the discipline of mastering a common culture, young people have fewer resources, and their individuality is of an extremely limited sort.

Even at an excellent school like Carleton, one can easily find courses and departments that are a poor substitute for the more traditional, rigorous curriculum that they have displaced. In the English department, one of the two courses that fulfills the "advanced seminar requirement" for majors is "Toni Morrison: Nobel Laureate." English majors, however, are not required to study Shakespeare — though there are courses available on The Bard. Sometimes, though, the Shakespeare that appears at Carleton may be distorted: a professor recently directed on campus a rendition of "All's Well That Ends Well" that mixed the "modern with the mythical" and that added scenes not in the original. It's difficult to imagine Carleton's science programs being run with so much disregard of excellence. The practitioners of scientific disciplines agree on what constitutes a fundamental body of knowledge, but in the humanities, and to some degree the social sciences, the hierarchy of knowledge has been abandoned.

Among the most politicized departments at Carleton are history, American studies, English, women's studies, and African/African-American studies. The best departments at Carleton are the hard sciences and political science.

One former political science professor, Paul Wellstone, has taken his politics to the U.S. Senate. Among the better professors are Michael Hemesath in economics; Laurence Cooper, Robert Packer, and Steven Schier in political science; and Owen Jenkins in English, who is retired but frequently returns to the classroom. Harry Williams's African American history courses are "immensely popular," according to one junior, who adds that students would take Williams's courses regardless of the RAD requirement.

Political Atmosphere: A Matter of Pride?

Carleton is known to be generally liberal in both faculty and student leanings, and the same must be said of the administration. The public image projected by the college is one of political righteousness. One of the school's glossy recruiting publications, sent to all prospective students, includes a section entitled "Celebrating Differences." "As in the wider world," the statement reads, "the college is not immune to the anxieties and insensitivities that grow out of racial and cultural differences. But the openness and egalitarian nature of the campus community make Carleton a more receptive place for people of different races, cultures, and beliefs to get to know and understand one another."

Perhaps the most obvious example of Carleton's departure from traditional mores and beliefs is found in its energetic promotion of the gay/lesbian/bisexual/transgendered (GLBT) community. April is GLBT "Pride Month" at Carleton; for those who wish the college would spend more energy on traditional education, it is indeed the cruelest month. Some of the events sponsored by the college during this month include lectures and work on a "Peace Signs" mural that celebrates "diversity and inclusion," according to its artist. According to *The Carletonian,* the first week of the most recent Pride Month included programs by transgendered activist Kate Bornstein, who headed a workshop session with faculty and staff and performed something called "Y2Kate: Gender Virus 2000." In the past, the event has included a Drag Ball and a cross-dressing beauty pageant sort of along the lines of the Miss America contest, although "Miss" may not be the right word in this case. Whether this is truly dangerous or just a colossal waste of time, it clearly has little or nothing to do with a liberal arts education.

Throughout the year, though, Carleton keeps the spirit of Pride Month alive via student organizations like CIAO (Carleton In and Out), billed as a group for lesbian/gay/bisexual/transgendered and "questioning" students. "Once a week that's the place that I go to be fully gay," one student told *The Carletonian.* The college even reaches out to homosexual "students of color" in hopes that they can find a "community to identify with": "The administration is working together to find a way that the students [of color] don't feel that they have to pick one identity over another," a CIAO advisor told the newspaper. And please be sure to label your groups correctly. "People tend to strongly refer to me as 'gay,'" one student said, again in *The Carletonian.* "I object. I'm queer, but I'm not gay. Maybe someday I'll be comfortable with a label, but at this point I'm not sure enough to trap myself in a box. Everyone assumes I'm lesbian, and I don't identify that way at all. I identify as queer. People don't understand that. They think I'm just being inclusive in the term I use and that really I'm a lesbian . . . [but] my experience is not as a lesbian. I usually avoid the topic, because I don't feel like people are willing to talk about really expanding gender and sexuality besides gay, straight and bisexual."

Speaking of images, Carleton may be one of the few places where a student suspects that the 80,000-square-foot, state-of-the-art Recreation Center "will open Carleton to some unwanted cultural phenomena like increased body image issues," according to the college newspaper.

"Unwanted cultural phenomena" indeed.

Elsewhere, Carleton is on the PC bus with a variety of so-called Shared Interest Living Areas each year, such as the Women's Awareness House, where students are invited to "enter a bold new world," and the African-American Awareness group, which was turned down but later approved, perhaps as a marketing tool to be used in the minority recruiting wars. Unfortunately, a program like this undermines Carleton's initiatives to make everyone get along with people from different backgrounds and with different interests. Meanwhile, fraternities and sororities are prohibited, and are described as "closed" organizations.

The dean of admissions publicly announced his "disappointment" that minority enrollment was down for the class entering in 2000, despite the college's use of "differential packaging, a process of offering more desirable financial aid packages" to minorities. In addition, Carlton is participating in an experimental assessment program for minorities that requires the building of a robot using Legos, and several scholarships and fellowships are reserved for minorities.

A small group of minorities on campus has succeeded in forcing the Northfield police department to begin mandatory diversity training, after a couple of Asian students' feelings were hurt when some minors yelled at them and were not "punished."

Carleton has a speech code disguised in a statement called "Discrimination and Academic Freedom." Much to the school's credit, the statement reminds students that in an academic community even "reasoned or evidenced" claims can be "painful" to hear. However, because some "groups" just might be offended by academic speech, the statement undeniably restricts the "unfettered intellectual freedom" it asserts to promote.

Students with opinions contrary to the prevailing orthodoxy at the college know they do not enjoy the free expression of their ideas and opinions. "The message," according to one student, "is that if you oppose affirmative action and homosexuality you oppose Carleton."

In response to some "sexist" and "racist" graffiti on a dorm, the dean of students wrote a "hate speech protocol" and the faculty passed a resolution condemning such things on campus. Some students, however, enjoy more free speech than others. One former columnist for the college newspaper writes, "The most harassed minority on this campus is Carleton's conservative community. We are attacked for our beliefs, shunned for looking at issues from a different perspective, cursed for being who we are."

One would hope that the academic culture at Carleton is strong enough to withstand efforts to totally shut down any who oppose the liberal ethos on campus. After all, the college does not produce so many future scholars by locking them into a prescribed philosophy. But Carleton has a "Statement of Multicultural Education Goals" plus a "Statement on Diversity and Cultural Pluralism," which covers not only hiring practices but also curriculum policies. Given that Carleton is such a small college in such a small town, the threat of social ostracism plays a large role in determining just how far anyone opposed to the school's pet ideologies will go in voicing opposition.

One would not be entirely wrong in thinking that Carleton would be friendlier to liberal and chic faculty than to those who may object to the regnant orthodoxies on campus. However, a faculty member reports that "we have hired conservatives in my department regularly." Whether this is true for other departments remains to be known, but it is an encouraging sign. Clearly at Carleton, as at most colleges, the degree of politicization varies from department to department, with the more humanistic programs more likely to fall prey to the ideologues.

Student Life: It's Your Thing

A recruiting publication claims that at Carleton "people laugh at pretentiousness," but the attempt by many on campus to be smart, hip, grungy, and ironic is a bit too self-conscious for some tastes. Sometimes pretentiousness creeps in the back door.

Like when the same recruiting publication tells the story of a very unofficial campus group called "RAISE," or "Replace All International Symbols with Elvis," which stole the campus's American flag and replaced it with an Elvis banner. According to a ransom note, the flag was only to be returned after the college president sang, in public, at least ten seconds of an Elvis tune. The president belted out "Ain't Nothin' but a Hound Dog" at an assembly one day, and the flag was returned in an attaché case by a RAISE emissary wearing dark glasses. We're pretty sure that with only 1,880 students on campus, someone must have known who he was. We're also pretty sure that he didn't know his prank would wind up as college promotional material, but we suspect he wouldn't mind.

Be that as it may, Carleton students are very active out of the classroom, finding time to participate in extracurricular activities.

According to the school's reckoning, about one-third of them play at least one intercollegiate sport, and nearly three-fourths play intramurals, including football games in the snow, something Minnesota hasn't enjoyed at the professional level since the Vikings moved indoors to the Hubert H. Humphrey Metrodome, about forty-five miles to the north in Minneapolis. Carleton competes in NCAA Division III athletics and fields twelve sports for men and women — common sports as well as the less-common synchronized swimming and ski teams. The school makes a point of telling prospective students that "Carleton coaches understand that academic coursework has priority, and athletes know that they can compete in the intercollegiate arena and still find time to study and to attend afternoon laboratories." Even the football team, however, gets much crowd support from the apathetic students, whose unofficial cheer is "That's all right, that's okay, you'll work for us someday."

The men's and women's Ultimate Frisbee clubs are among the nation's top five in their divisions (yes, apparently there are divisions for that), and the women's rugby club, whose posters around campus promote "Elegant Violence," recently won the Minnesota championship. The cross-country running teams are consistently competitive in the conference and region.

The pretty campus of 950 acres includes a four hundred–acre arboretum, two of Minnesota's fabled ten thousand lakes, a Japanese garden named the best outside of Japan, and new recreation center.

The college staffs a security service but is thinking seriously about switching to a police force. The most common type of crime on campus is larceny, with bicycle theft ranking at the top. According to the 1999 Security Services Annual Report, no assaults or homicides were reported in the years 1996 to 1998 (the years covered in the report), while seven "sex offenses" and seven burglaries were reported in 1998. Fourteen arrests for liquor law violation took place in 1998, a jump from three in 1997 and two in 1996.

Since Carleton students party as hard as they study, it is likely that those fourteen arrests were only a portion of what they might have been. The 1999 Harvard School of Public Health College Alcohol Study gives the college the highest "binge drinking" rate of all colleges and universities surveyed. Nearly half of the students at Carleton who drink do so "to get drunk," according to the study. As a result, the percentage of students at Carleton who have had their sleep or study interrupted by others who are drinking is the highest. At the same time, the Carleton students have the lowest percentage of problems with their drinking: the college has the lowest percentage of students who miss a class, fall behind in their school work, get in trouble with campus or local law enforcement, need medical attention, experience an unwanted sexual advance, and become a victim of sexual assault. As for drug use, Carleton again has the highest percentage of students who have used marijuana and other illicit drugs over the past year, according to the study.

A new set of twelve townhouses, coed units to open in January 2001, will be the only "keg free" student housing on campus. Men and women share bathrooms in the coed dorms, but all dorm rooms on campus are same-sex. There are designated quiet floors around the campus, and the dorms have quiet hours, but most students pulling all-nighters do so in the library.

For all of Carleton's official talk about the college "community," there is a lack of cohesiveness on the campus. "We definitely could use some more school spirit here," says a junior. Perhaps it's because up to two-thirds of the students take advantage of furthering their studies in another culture through the Off-Campus Program. Perhaps it's because the students are "too full of ourselves to have time for anyone else," according to a student writing in the weekly campus "society and culture magazine." Perhaps it's because there's no core curriculum uniting the students around a body of common knowledge. But it's probably because "the academic life here is so hardcore and intense we don't have time for much," says a sophomore.

The college chaplain organized the LGBT Council and heads up the Diversity Initiative Group (DIG), whose task is coordinating campus efforts "to raise awareness and tolerance of diversity." Under her direction, DIG is planning extended training sessions on diversity for student leaders, such as resident assistants, orientation leaders, student wellness advisors, and multicultural peer leaders. The college hosts a variety of religious observances, including Catholic mass, Tibetan Buddhist services, Taizé vespers, and Jewish Shabbat services.

Freshmen are required to show up at orientation having read a book obviously selected by the college to augment its diversity agenda. Known as the Common Reading book, it is discussed in a day's worth of mandatory seminars that send a clear message: this is what we believe and so should you. The students arriving in 2000 had to read *The Spirit Catches You and You Fall Down: A Hmong Child, Her American Doctors, and The Collision of Two Cultures* by Anne Fadiman. Past Common Reading assignments include *The Color of Water: A Black Man's Tribute to His White Mother* by James McBride; *My Brother* by Jamaica Kincaid (who spoke to the students); *Tortilla Curtain* by T. Coraghessan Boyle; *Whose Art Is It?* by Jane Kramer; and *Colored People: A Memoir* by Henry Louis Gates Jr.

Carleton must be admired for its emphasis on community service. During orientation, freshmen are required to partake in a project that benefits the town of Northfield. The college operates Acting in the Community Together for students who want to participate in volunteer programs in the surrounding communities. Carleton ranks fifth among all colleges for graduates who join the Peace Corps. Carleton also has endorsed the "Minnesota Campus Compact," which serves to promote volunteer service and to cultivate "citizen-leaders." For Carleton, however, this has become "service-learning" and "civic engagement" that begins in the classroom. Carleton faculty offer ten courses that provide these components. But "service-learning" incorporated into a course can be misused for political purposes. A new biology course encourages environmental activism, and two students in an Asian-American history course are studying "nationwide efforts" of protests against an alternative rock band, one song of which is perceived as offensive to Asian women.

"Issue-specific activism" is on the rise at Carleton. According to the college newspaper, there's increased student interest in leftist political groups such as the Social Justice Movement, No Sweat, the Green Network, and the Minnesota Public Interest Group (MPIRG). MPIRG, the most well-funded of all groups, automatically gets $7.50 from each student to finance political activity and lobbying unless the student specifically checks "No" on his tuition bill.

Carleton manages to attract the stars of high school classes. Nearly 90 percent of the students who enrolled in 2000 had been involved in community service prior to college. More than 40 percent competed in two or more varsity sports and almost 20 percent were captains of at least one sport; close to 30 percent served on a class or student council; about 30 percent worked on a publication, about half of them as editors; and nearly 40 percent performed in instrumental groups and 25 percent in vocal groups. As with other incoming classes at Carleton, students hail from almost all states, with about a quarter of them home-grown in Minnesota. The other large contingents come from Wisconsin, Illinois, New York, Oregon, Washington, and California.

Participation in traditional political groups at Carleton has decreased, and the College Democrats are defunct. But the long dormant Conservative Union was revived recently because "We want to change the prevailing political attitudes and beliefs at Carleton as well as ensure a free, fair, and vigorous debate takes place on campus," according to the group's chairman, who saw to it that William F. Buckley Jr. lectured on the campus. Among the very few conservative groups are the Newman Club, Pro-Life Organization, and the Conservative Union.

Visiting conservative voices, however are rarely heard at Carleton. George Will spoke at a recent college convocation (the college holds weekly convocations), but other campus speakers are overwhelmingly liberal. Among them have been Maya Angelou, Gwendolyn Brooks, Ramona Africa, Jamaica Kincaid, and President Clinton, the 2000 commencement speaker.

A popular campus tradition is "Rotblatt." Around since 1964, and named after ex–White Sox pitcher Marvin J. Rotblatt, it is an annual marathon softball and "social drinking" event in which just about all students take time to participate. Another campus tradition centers on "The Bust of Schiller," the German poet. A couple of decades ago some students "liberated" the bust from the president's office and, ever since, the "select few" custodians of the bust are expected to make an appearance at a campus event with it.

There are many lectures and performance on campus, including an annual visit by the St. Paul Chamber Orchestra. Students also can drive to the Twin Cities (Minneapolis and St. Paul) for entertainment and the wide range of cultural events held in a major metropolitan area.

Carnegie Mellon University

Carnegie Mellon Office of Admission
5000 Forbes Ave.
Pittsburgh, PA 15213-3890
(412) 268-2082
www.cmu.edu

Total enrollment: 8,514
Undergraduate: 5,106
SAT ranges (Verbal/Math): 600-700 (V); 650-750 (M)
Applicants: 14,475
Accepted: 36%
Enrolled: 25%
Application deadline: January 1
Financial aid application deadline: January 1
Tuition: $24,971/$31,999
Core curriculum: No

Technology — Ain't It Grand?

In today's competitive higher education environment, many so-called liberal arts colleges lure unsuspecting students and their parents with the appeal of ivy-covered halls, an esteemed tradition, and dubious claims about their "commitment to the liberal arts." More often than not, these claims are made despite the fact that many members of the administration and faculty in those ivy-covered halls are actively working to subvert the college's curriculum in ways its founders never envisioned. In this context, there is something refreshing and admirable about Carnegie Mellon's frank articulation of its rather utilitarian aims and mission, and its continued adherence to the dual interests of its founder, industrialist Andrew Carnegie.

The liberal arts are not the primary interest of Carnegie Mellon University (CMU). The university has a reputation for excellence in both the technical sciences (engineering, computer science, robotics) and the arts (especially drama). But it is technology that is the central focus of the university. All CMU students, regardless of the school they enter or the major they select, must take a course in computer instruction, and the university prides itself on being "one of the most progressive, intense, and exciting computing environments in the world." Yahoo ranked CMU as the "Most Wired" U.S. campus for 2000. "Andrew," the campus computer network, links more than 11,000 personal computers and workstations throughout campus, enabling students to register, check grades and course material, and perform numerous other academic functions without ever having to interact with a human being. Indeed, one student looks forward to the annual spring carnival because it is "one of the few times people get out from behind their computers."

Technology has been the school's focus since it began. Originally called the Carnegie Technical Schools, CMU was founded in 1900 to "provide the children of working families with training to move into better careers." In 1912 the school changed its name to the Carnegie Institute of Technology and launched its current reputation as a school that excels in engineering and the performing arts. In 1967 the school merged with the Mellon Institute to become Carnegie Mellon University. Despite the emphasis on computers, many CMU students do have more on their minds than information technology, and Carnegie Mellon can boast an eclectic but uniformly successful cadre of graduates, including Oscar-winning actress Holly Hunter, astronaut Judith Resnik, and artist Andy Warhol.

This college guide does not claim a person cannot be successful without a traditional education — only that such an education, in our opinion, best prepares a person to make his best efforts in his chosen field. In the case of Carnegie Mellon, we submit that the exceptions prove the rule, and that the motivation and skill of a particular student can do much to surmount whatever is lost when the student's education does not include all that we would like. Providing a liberal education has never been Carnegie Mellon's purpose; it has been enough for the school to do well the things that it does.

Academic Life: Useful Things

Carnegie Mellon neither educates its students in the liberal arts tradition nor subscribes to every fad that sweeps academia. Rather, the school boldly proclaims its commitment to training individuals for highly specialized professions: "In a world which has sometimes placed too little emphasis on 'skill,'" says the undergraduate catalogue, "we take pride in educating students who display excellence in application, students who can do useful things with their learning." The cover of the catalogue is emblazoned with only one word: "Achieve." Contemplative students looking for a different type of achievement should go somewhere else.

The university's emphasis on doing, making, creating, and analyzing is reflected in the course requirements for undergraduates. All undergrads have two required courses, one in writing — "because sharp written communication is important to almost every field" — and one in computing, for similar reasons. The freshman English composition course is reputedly heavily politicized, and is considered by many students as one way of ensuring that all freshmen are favorably introduced to multicultural ideology early on. The students must also choose between two courses in "Argument and Interpretation." The courses are taught almost exclusively by graduate students.

Students at CMU enroll in one of seven colleges: Carnegie Institute of Technology (engineering); College of Fine Arts; College of Humanities and Social Sciences (H&SS); Graduate School of Industrial Administration; H. John Heinz III School of Public Policy and Management; Mellon College of Science; and the School of Computer Science. While some students complain that the administration seems largely preoccupied with fund-raising and research, and that some professors aren't as interested in teaching or advising as they should be, the university has many strong departments. According to faculty and students, these include drama, electrical engineering, computer science and robotics, the graduate business school, physics, engineering, music, and industrial management.

One of the best aspects of the engineering program is the low student-faculty ratio. While most engineering schools have their students attend class in large lecture halls, CMU engineers can enjoy a twelve-to-one student-faculty ratio.

The university is nationally recognized as a premier institution for the study of chemical and electrical engineering, but its drama and music departments also have outstanding reputations. But while Carnegie Mellon promotes an unusual blend of science and performing arts, the humanistic disciplines seem to get lost somewhere in the shuffle. Within H&SS are a limited number of departments: economics, English, history, modern languages, philosophy, psychology, social and decision sciences, and statistics. Only about one-quarter of Carnegie Mellon's 5,100 undergraduates choose this college, which stresses "practical skills" as much as — or more than — traditional liberal arts studies. In keeping with its focus on the applied, analytic dimension of education, the college offers two tracks of majors in most areas: a more traditional "disciplinary" major (economics, philosophy, or political science, for instance) and a more specialized "professional" major (usually a compound name, like managerial economics, computational linguistics, or policy and management).

In addition to the writing and computing requirements is a set of general education distribution requirements that all H&SS students must complete, and again, the university has no pretensions that these resemble a traditional core. Students must choose eight courses from among the following six categories: "Cognition, Choice and Behavior," "Economic, Political, and Social Institutions," "Creative Production and Reflection," "Cultural Analysis," "Mathematical Reasoning," and "Science and Technology." There is no formal requirement in Western civilization, though the standard curriculum that all H&SS students must take includes a course in "World Culture." This course "seeks to help students to not only understand cultural differences that exist in the world, but also to value these differences." The standard H&SS curriculum also includes "Writing and Expression" and "Statistical Reasoning." Freshmen are also required to take a seminar. To its credit, Carnegie Mellon does make an honest attempt to give students at least a glimpse of the liberal arts within the professional model of education it espouses. But because of the "progressive" nature of that model — and, of course, the general trendiness of academe — a student's transcript will likely be populated more with courses like "Debates and Controversies: Cultural Differences in Action" or "Cultural and Cross-Cultural Perspectives on the Environment" than with traditional offerings in the liberal arts.

CMU students of all disciplines participant in the university's strong study abroad program. Carnegie Mellon sponsors five university-wide exchange programs (in Chile, Mexico, Switzerland, Singapore, and Japan), and individual departments also have exchanges overseas. The university also has a host of international job, internship, and volunteer opportunities for interested students. For students who prefer to remain on campus, the modern languages department recently launched a way for students to see art of the French Riviera, mainly the Picasso Museum and the Center for Concrete Art, through video teleconferencing. Technology — ain't it grand?

Among the best professors at CMU are: Daniel P. Resnick, David A. Hounshell, and Kiron Skinner in history; W. Robert Dalton and Robert M. Dammon in economics; David Carrier in art history and philosophy; and Alex John London in philosophy.

Political Atmosphere: Noses to the Grindstone

For a variety of reasons, politics generally take a backseat to academics at Carnegie Mellon. The students' drive to achieve usually keeps political and multicultural machinations on campus to a minimum. "About 80 to 90 percent of students are mainly focused on academics," says an undergraduate. The technical nature of the school also plays a role: one professor attributes the general political neutrality, and specifically the absence of serious agitation on multicultural and diversity issues, to the general weakness of the humanities and social sciences on campus. "I think the primary thing that keeps the temperature low here . . . is the fact that the students are either in the hard sciences — where it does not appear to be a hot issue — or in the arts — where it is *de rigueur* and already exists."

Even so, things have on occasion been more than a little unsettled at Carnegie Mellon — just ask Patrick Mooney. The cautionary tale of Mooney, a political science major who repeatedly found himself in litigation against his university, is enough to give any outspoken student pause before enrolling at CMU. It all began in August of 1991, when Mooney was asked to wear a triangle-shaped button, the symbol of gay and lesbian pride, as part of a "Gay, Lesbian, and Bi-Sexual Issues" session conducted as part of the training program for student residence assistants. Although he quietly attended the session, Mooney, a Roman Catholic, refused to wear the gay pride button because it conflicted with his religious beliefs. Four days later he was fired from his position, despite "receiving positive evaluations" on his performance as a residence assistant the previous semester, according to the *Western Pennsylvania Tribune-Review*. Mooney brought suit against the university, "seeking, among

141

other things, an injunction ordering Carnegie Mellon not to discriminate on the basis of religion," according to *Campus* magazine. The suit was settled out of court.

In 1994 Mooney found himself in trouble again, this time falsely accused of harassing a gay professor and facing serious disciplinary action for removing an offensive pro-homosexual poster. The details are admittedly crude, but they illustrate the permissive attitude of Carnegie Mellon's administration toward radical groups and the general intolerance on campus for serious religious conviction. Mooney noticed a flyer with the image of the late Cardinal John J. O'Connor next to a condom with the message "Know Your Scumbags" printed across it. In violation of a campus policy requiring that all flyers bear the name of the sponsoring organization, this poster was unsigned, as it were, except for the pleasant reminder: "We're here. We're queer. We're funded by your student activities fees."

Mooney removed the poster in order to photocopy it and complain to the proper officials. According to Mooney, while he was noticing the poster, he approached a man nearby and asked him "if he could believe that someone would put a poster like that on campus." The man expressed support for the poster, and a brief debate ensued. Mooney later discovered that the man was a homosexual drama professor, and only then because the professor charged him with "harassment on the basis of sexual orientation." After a series of retreats by the university administration, the bogus harassment charges were dropped, but Mooney received a "disciplinary warning" for removing the poster, which turned out to have been hung by a campus gay activist group called CMU-Out.

According to one student, "Pat set a good precedent," proving that truth will win out if you make enough noise, or at least illustrating that universities hate negative press enough to stop persecuting conservative students. Still, the few Carnegie Mellon students willing to stand up for their traditional beliefs and free speech rights often fight an uphill battle. This battle often goes through the University Disciplinary Committee (UDC), which one student calls the "most horrific organization" on campus. A few years ago, according to one undergraduate, a certain female graduate student (nicknamed the "Commissar for Political Correctness") who was heavily involved in CMU-Out and the Pittsburgh Lesbian Avengers, repeatedly brought to the UDC charges against male students. In general, the 3,400 graduate students wield enormous power over campus life, reigning over what one student calls "little fiefdoms."

CMU does have a Political Speakers Forum Board. Although the speakers are predominantly liberal, the College Republicans and Young America's Foundation have, in recent years, successfully hosted such conservatives as Walter Williams and Dinesh D'Souza. Generous university funding for such events is rarely forthcoming, though "if conservatives are willing to do the work," notes one student, "they can have their fair share of the funds." But as one faculty member says, "Hardly any conservative speakers come to the campus."

Because of its strong technical focus, Carnegie Mellon lacks most of the bizarre liberal functions that predominate at other top-notch universities. One exception is the university-funded Women's Center, which claims to represent the women at Carnegie Mellon (only 36 percent of undergraduates are female). This claim would only be true if all the women at CMU were radical feminists. The center sponsors regular meetings such as "Coffee Talk," pledging to discuss the "diverse issues that affect women's lives." For the past few sessions, the "diverse issues" included "Female Misogynists," "Body Image," and "Sex and Masturbation." Over the past few years, some students have expressed disapproval that their tuition and student fees help fund these projects.

Still, things are generally pretty quiet at CMU. The most controversial thing to occur in the last several years was the school's decision, in May 2000, to extend health benefits to same-sex partners of CMU employees. Some alumni reportedly complained about the proposed policy, but evidently not too many: the vote passed the governing board by a 34-8 margin.

Student Life: Away from the Terminal

Carnegie Mellon is located in an attractive area of Pittsburgh, within walking distance of the Oakland, Squirrel Hill, and Shadyside neighborhoods, where students can take advantage of shopping and cultural activities. The campus is bordered by the 500-acre Schenley Park, home to the Frick Fine Arts Museum and the Phipps Conservatory, which is a nice place to jog or, in the winter months, ice-skate. The university reported relatively few crimes on campus for the past few years. Pittsburgh is a thoroughly revamped steel town, partaking in elements of both Midwestern community identity and East Coast cultural activities. The Carnegie, an impressive cultural complex housing the Museum of Art (known for its Impressionist collection), the Museum of Natural History, Carnegie Music Hall, and Carnegie Library, is only a five-minute walk from campus. Although many of Pittsburgh's major cultural activities occur in the summer (the Three Rivers Arts Festival, Three Rivers Regatta, and a Shakespeare festival), CMU students will find plenty of social and cultural opportunities during the academic year.

The campus has retained some tokens of the Scottish heritage of its founder. The main cafeteria, located in Resnik House, is called the Highlander Cafe. The student newspaper is the *Tartan,* the yearbook the *Thistle,* and the drama club the Scotch 'n Soda. The university offers the world's only bagpiping major, and pipers have the opportunity to perform at campus events in the Kiltie Band.

Freshmen are required to live in university housing, but they can choose from a wide range of residence halls, university apartments, special-interest houses, and Greek houses. There are a number of desirable residence hall options for first-year students, including Mudge House, a mansion originally built by the Mudge family but now converted into a coed residence hall. Single-sex accommodations are also

143

available: Scobell Hall houses male residents; the C and D towers of Morewood Gardens (described as what "once was a gracious apartment complex for affluent Pittsburghers") are for women only.

The university attracts students from all over the country, and more than two-thirds of the student population comes from outside Pennsylvania.

The student clubs on campus are mainly technical and/or academic — for example, the CMU chapter for Mechanical Engineers, but the university also has eighteen fraternity and sorority chapters. CMU does have a strong religious presence on campus, and students may choose from Baptist, Methodist, Mormon, Episcopal, Jewish, Lutheran, Orthodox, and Catholic organizations.

Although sports are not the focal point of Carnegie Mellon life, many students become involved in the thirty or so athletic groups the university offers. Carnegie Mellon competes in the NCAA Division III, comprising schools that do not offer athletic scholarships. The university is also a member of the University Athletic Association (UAA), which includes eight other private research universities. The Tartans men's football team holds the Division III record for consecutive games without being shut out. Women's cross-country and both men's and women's swimming are also strong.

In the spring of 1997 the board of trustees elected Dr. Jared L. Cohon as the new president of Carnegie Mellon. Cohon, who previously served as the dean of the School of Forestry at Yale University, replaced outgoing president Dr. Robert Mehrabian, known for his fund-raising skills. Cohon has also served as legislative assistant for energy and environment for Senator Daniel Patrick Moynihan and was appointed by President Clinton in January 1997 to serve as chairman of the Nuclear Waste Technical Review Board. Many faculty speak highly of the priorities of the current administration. As one professor notes, "They have made great efforts, mostly successful, to increase the endowment and have an excellent track record in keeping the physical plant of the university in excellent condition."

Some argue that the university's two predominant interests — the hard sciences and the arts — make for a strange and sometimes volatile blend of "computer geeks" and "artsy types" on campus. One student characterizes it as a "pretty weird environment," but others think the divergent interests are an asset, not a liability. As one professor says, "The atmosphere here is a good one because of the mix of excellent hard science and excellent arts. It's an interesting mix and makes the campus somewhat unusual."

Case Western Reserve University

Office of Undergraduate Admissions
103 Tomlinson Hall
Case Western Reserve University
10900 Euclid Avenue
Cleveland, OH 44106-7055
(216) 368-4450
www.cwru.edu

Total enrollment: 9,237
Undergraduates: 3,423
SAT ranges (Verbal/Math): 610-720 (V); 640-740 (M)
Applicants: 4,346
Accepted: 72%
Enrolled: 24%
Application deadline: February 1
Financial aid application deadline: February 15
Tuition: $20,260/$26,075
Core curriculum: No

The Case for Case Western

Case Western Reserve University, in its most modern incarnation, was the product of a merger in 1967 between the Case Institute of Technology and the liberal arts–oriented Western Reserve University. Despite this apparent dichotomy between the hard sciences and the liberal arts disciplines, it is doing a fine job instructing students on both the engineering and the humanities sides of the academic aisle, and there are plenty of well-regarded departments at CWRU in both divisions, too. Nearly two-thirds of Case's students are of the graduate variety, but that should not cause undergrads to look askance at the university. Undergraduate teaching is a top priority for the school, and while there are some large introductory courses, the university's view book notes with pride that 93 percent of undergraduate credit hours are taught by faculty, not graduate teaching assistants. CWRU has a student-faculty ratio of 8 to 1, and 67 percent of its undergraduate classes have less than thirty students. Enrollment is less than twenty in 53 percent of undergraduate classes, a figure that is improving in recent years.

Case also has the advantage of being centrally located in a major city. It's about four miles from downtown Cleveland, and its campus, on 600 acres in the University Circle area, is close to many cultural and entertainment attractions, in-

145

cluding the Cleveland Museum of Art, the African American Museum and the Cleveland Botanical Garden. It is also a hop, skip, and a jump away from Severance Hall, home of the renowned Cleveland Orchestra. Applicants whose only knowledge of Case is its general location might snicker at the thought of attending university in Cleveland, as the city still tends to suffer from the general perception, among those unfamiliar with its modern recovery, that it is a decaying industrial wasteland. But such criticism is unwarranted: Cleveland is definitely on the rebound, and is moving into the twenty-first century with the best of them. The university view book proudly notes that Cleveland is rated by *Money* magazine as the Midwest's second-best city to live in.

More importantly, students at Case continue to receive, on the whole, a traditional education that forces students to learn. Generally free of political correctness, Case gives students an excellent education; it starts with a batch of very bright students, then demands that they perform academically. Just as there are schools whose reputations are better than the education they provide, the opposite seems true for Case: it hasn't yet gotten the attention that it deserves. Given the importance it places on undergraduate teaching and on challenging students, Case Western Reserve University is worth the consideration of any serious student.

Academic Life: A Case Study in Hard Work

Regardless of your SAT score or class rank, Case will challenge you. Students who survive say they are better for it in the long run. "If you want to party, do *not* come to CWRU. If you want to slack off, do not come here," a student says. "But, if you want a degree that means something, CWRU is a good place for you."

Case offers a number of baccalaureate degrees in programs administered by the various colleges on campus. Each college holds students to a different set of graduation requirements. Candidates for a B.A. from the College of Arts and Sciences, for example, must complete 120 semester hours, which include the General Education Requirements of the College of Arts and Sciences. Students working towards a B.S. must pursue 120 to 131 semester hours, depending on the program. Students aiming for a Bachelor of Science in Engineering (B.S.E.) must take 128 to 133 semester hours and complete the Engineering Core Curriculum as prescribed by the Case School of Engineering. The Weatherhead School of Management has its own General Education Requirements, and so on.

For all intents and purposes, the effect of all of these different requirements, although they are termed "core" curricula, is to impose a variety of distribution requirements on the students. "The general education requirements are very flexible," says one professor. "It is possible for the student to select a solid foundation, but by the same flexibility, however, it is possible to slide through with trendier substitutes."

The Arts and Sciences Core Curriculum, for example, contains an English composition requirement, twelve semester hours' worth of natural and mathematical sciences, twelve hours studying the arts and humanities, nine hours studying the social sciences, and three semester hours in "Global and Cultural Diversity." In this last requirement, students could find themselves taking something reasonable, like Anthropology 352 ("Japanese Culture and Society"), which focuses on modern-day Japanese life, or the more politicized Anthropology 314, which "considers the rich ethnic diversity of the U.S. from the perspective of social/cultural anthropology. Conquest, immigration, problems of conflicts and accommodation, and the character of the diverse regional and ethnic cultures are considered as are forms of racism, discrimination, and their consequences."

The second set of distribution requirements, the Case Core Curriculum, is designed for students majoring in engineering, computer science, and management science. (The "Case" side of the university is the descendant of the Case Institute of Technology, while the old Western Reserve University basically evolved into the liberal arts wing.) This core curriculum is slightly less heavy on the humanities and more focused on the sciences and engineering, as one might expect. It contains the English composition requirement, fourteen semester hours of math, eighteen semester hours in engineering courses, four semester hours of chemistry, eight in physics, and, to make for well-rounded scientists, twenty-one credits in the arts and humanities. The engineers get to skip the Global and Cultural Diversity requirement.

Finally, the Weatherhead Core Curriculum is designed for students pursuing B.S. degrees in accounting or management. It provides a background in the humanities but also mandates a more rigorous mathematics and natural science program for students than does the College of Arts and Sciences — anywhere from five to eight additional semester hours are required. Weatherhead students must complete the Global and Cultural Diversity requirement.

Thought the general requirements are not particularly well-defined, one can in most cases — no pun intended — assume that the courses to meet them will be well-taught. The university places a premium on teaching undergraduates. "CWRU is dominated by faculty who enjoy undergraduate teaching and make themselves easily accessible to undergraduates," a professor says. Students agree with that assessment. Says one, "I've never had any trouble accessing faculty members. They're required to keep generous office hours. And unlike some of the large state universities, there are no lines." This student went on to note that some of his advanced liberal arts courses only contained three or four students. Another student found that his courses improved after he got through the introductory stages of this studies: "A lot of my intro classes and my core classes were pretty lame . . . but once I've gotten into my departments, I've found professors who are really interesting and can convey information well and care about their students."

That caring can come in the form of tough love for many students. "The professors are tough and you can't slack off and maintain a decent GPA," one student says. "There is no grade inflation here, believe me. Also, most of the student body is here to learn, so you aren't dealing with parties at 3 a.m. in your dorm."

Among the best teachers at the university are Theodore S. Gup, William Siebenscuh, Martha Woodmansee, and Thomas G. Bishop in English; Christopher A. Cullis in biology; Chin-Tai Kim in philosophy; Kenneth W. Grundy and Laura Y. Tartakoff in political science; Cynthia M. Beall in anthropology; Robert W. Brown, Glenn Starkman, and Thomas G. Eck in physics; Anthony J. Pearson and Ignacio J. "Doc Oc" Ocasio in chemistry; William S. Peirce and William T. Bogart in economics; Kenneth Ledford, Michael Altschul, and Carroll Pursell in history; and Donald R. Laing Jr., Martin Helzle, and Angeliki Tzanetou — the entire department — in classics.

The economics department is excellent at CWRU, as are all of the departments related to science and engineering. There are very good art history, history, classics, psychology, anthropology, and accounting departments as well.

Case is not resting on its prodigious laurels, either. It continues to energetically promote a strong and rare learning environment. "I really felt the university was picking up," a recent graduate says. "There was a sense of rejuvenation on the campus. There's a real sense that Case is going somewhere. If you're looking for a place with energy and a place where your degree will be worth more in future than it is now, Case is it."

Political Life: Radicals? "I Don't Think We Have Any"

Unlike many schools, where politics is an ever-present facet of university life, Case has a generally open atmosphere. One student argues that, at least unofficially, "CWRU is the sister university of the University of Chicago . . . right down to the rotten athletic programs."

This does not mean that the instructors are completely free of trendy ideas, but it does mean that the general air of the university is apolitical. When asked if radical students were a force to be reckoned with on campus, one student seemed perplexed for a moment, and then offered: "I don't think we have any."

Case has a broad mix of political views among its students, and the university itself seems content to let things go on that way. There isn't much indoctrination of the kind that passes for teaching elsewhere, either — the students wouldn't have it. "If that were the case," says a student, "I'd say about two-thirds of the student body would get up and leave." Other students agree that politics and political correctness are only discussed rarely on campus.

A professor offers that Republican faculty would be rather lonely in most departments, but that Libertarians would find more company. "Because of the large and strong professional schools . . . the political atmosphere here has never seemed crazy," the professor says. "Among the Arts and Sciences faculty the prevailing senti-ment is 'knee-jerk liberal,' but it is possible to express other views and still thrive here." The professor also says that he — and, to the best of his knowledge, other fac-ulty — have never been intimidated such that they avoid certain topics or state-ments in class.

Case has gone through a number of changes at its top levels recently, including the arrival of a new president in 1999. Its vice president of Information Services re-signed in October of 1999, after questions were raised about the university's re-sponses to a Yahoo! Internet Life questionnaire that determined annual college rankings regarding how "wired" a school is.

CWRU received a number-one ranking in this survey in 1999 — and it proudly displays this in its view book. The only problem was, students couldn't figure out how it got to be number one. One student in the know says that the "whole thing was a big joke" because "we didn't and still don't" have many of the things the survey said they did. In April 1999, the undergraduate student government demanded that the university investigate the matter "because of the use of questionable statistics about CWRU's computing facilities and services that were reported in the survey." That call was the result of an April 16, 1999, article in *The Observer,* the student newspaper, that noted that the rise from number sixty-three to number one in the Yahoo! survey was mainly because of the school's implementation of an on-line registration sys-tem. The university's dedication to improving the technological environment on campus was also pointed out. But the paper reported that Case's answer also made claims — regarding the availability of online transcripts, storage space for Web pages, and computer availability — that were problematic at best. Among the points made in the *Observer* article: "Another confusing feature is the aspect of online tran-scripts, which the *Yahoo* article claims are available off of the CWRU network. Ac-cording to the Registrar's office, only the request form for transcripts can be down-loaded off the Web. If students want to view their transcripts, they still need to pay five dollars for the paper version printed by the Registrar's office." This is still the case — students can print out a request form, but they have to make the request in person or via fax because a signature is required to get a transcript.

However, it should be noted that Case has made important strides in this area, and that Web space is now available for all students at CWRU through a partnership with a private firm. Computer labs at the university are not open twenty-four hours, but Case offers students no-cost loans so that they may purchase computers of their own. Every dormitory room on campus is wired with Internet access, and 90 percent of the students own computers; thus, it is unlikely that a student would have trouble finding a computer to use or getting on the Internet.

In a separate controversy, the dean of the Weatherhead School of Management was essentially forced out by the president of the university. The notice was made in the February 24, 2000, edition of the *Campus News,* which noted that the school president announced that after consulting with the dean "and others inside and outside the University about progress towards attaining the school's goals, he had concluded that a change in the school's leadership was necessary." The dean will remain on the faculty, but he concluded his term as dean at the end of the spring semester.

It's as yet unclear what effects this will have on the university. As one professor says, "'New president — looking for a new provost.' The words sound right. We'll see."

Student Life: Hello, Cleveland!

Life at Case offers students many diversions, both cultural or and for entertainment purposes. On the campus itself, students can make use of the Thwing Center, a combination of two buildings that houses the offices of *The Observer*, a post office, two restaurants, and the school bookstore. Students can also take advantage of the proximity of many cultural institutions — there are nearly forty attractions in or near the University Circle neighborhood. Aside from the many art museums and music-oriented institutions, such as Severance Hall and the Cleveland Institute of Music, there is also the Rock and Roll Hall of Fame. It's been open since 1995, and while some have pointed out its flaws, the Hall of Fame has quickly become a landmark and is worth a trip.

Students can also venture downtown to The Flats, a nightlife district along the Cuyahoga river filled with restaurants, nightclubs, and other necessities. They can also visit the Tower City Mall, also located in downtown, popular for its cinema. There's also a student film society that shows recent movies on the cheap at Strosacker Auditorium. The Indians and the reincarnated Browns are Cleveland's favorite sports teams, and Cleveland's Little Italy district and the Coventry area of the city are also close by. They're nice places to grab a bite to eat.

There are plenty of student groups on campus. In addition to eighteen fraternities and five sororities, CWRU has plenty of athletic opportunities for interested students — with a number of varsity sports and club sports in archery, ice hockey, and racquetball. There are also groups for every possible interest, ranging from *The Observer* to the InterVarsity Christian Fellowship to Habitat for Humanity to the Case Engineers Council.

Another campus attraction is still being built: the Weatherhead School plans to open the $62 million Peter B. Lewis Building in 2002. The building is designed in a spectacular modern style by world-famous architect Frank O. Gehry, and if it ultimately looks just half as impressive as the models of it pictured on the school's Web site, it might be worth a trip to campus merely to see it. Gehry recently designed the new Guggenheim Museum in Bilbao, Spain, and the Walt Disney Concert Hall in Los Angeles.

Case requires students to live on campus unless they are living at home with their parents nearby, are seniors, or are twenty-one years of age. Students can get off campus if they're part of a fraternity or sorority, however. The campus itself is divided into two main residential areas: the North Residential Village, which is close to the "cultural area" of campus, and the South Residential Village, which is closer to the science, engineering and administration buildings. The North Village contains ten residence halls, each with double rooms and some single rooms available for upperclassmen. Every building's ground floor has a TV lounge, vending area, kitchen, and laundry room.

In the South Village, there are seven residence halls arranged in suites — six private bedrooms off a single corridor. Each suite has a furnished living room with bathroom facilities located off the living area, and the number of suites on a floor depends on the residence hall. Dining services are provided in centrally located buildings for each village.

Some of the buildings are smoke free, and the Norton House is exclusively for women. There are also quiet study rooms located in each hall.

Students' verdicts on dorm life are mixed. One student says that "you really have no life if you don't live in the dorms or frat houses," and notes that North Side, as the students refer to it, "is a whole lot more social." In addition, the double rooms for North Side freshmen allows students "to meet more people," a student says. South Side also has its proponents: the suites are "a really nice set-up despite the small, small rooms. But, people don't have reason to leave their suite, so you don't get to know everyone in your dorm like on North side," a student says. This student notes that the campus food is "bad," and that living off-campus can be much cheaper.

Crime is something to be concerned about on campus, especially in the North Village. "The North Side, where I lived last year, and where most freshmen live, is not safe," a student says. "It's right next to East Cleveland, which is an absolutely horrible part of town. But, the South Side of campus, where most upperclassmen live, is practically in Cleveland Heights, which is a much safer, more normal suburban area." Another female student says, "As long as I'm not walking alone at night, I feel great." The university does offer a round-the-clock security escort service and all dormitories require a student ID card to open the main door locks, twenty-four hours a day.

The Catholic University of America

Office of Admissions
Cardinal Station
Washington, DC 20064
(202) 319-5305
www.cua.edu

Total enrollment: 5,600
Undergraduates: 2,300
SAT ranges (Verbal/Math): 530-640 (V); 570-620 (M)
Applicants: 2,350
Accepted: 65%
Enrolled: 39%
Application deadline: January 15
Financial aid application deadline: January 15
Tuition: $19,930/$28,003
Core curriculum: Yes

Fides et Ratio

The Catholic University of America is the only institution of higher education founded by the U.S. bishops; its chancellor is the archbishop of Washington, D.C., and Catholic parishes across the country donate a portion of their annual collections to the school. Chartered in 1887 by Pope Leo XIII, the university began as a graduate research institution, one of the first in the nation. In the words of the first rector, Bishop John Joseph Keane, it was anticipated that the university would be a "a living embodiment and illustration of the harmony between reason and revelation, between science and religion, between the genius of America and the Church of Christ."

The tension implicit in Keane's speech — between faith and reason, and between the university's Catholic and American identities — has shaped the university's history. It is a tension that some would argue is deleterious to the effectiveness of the school and that has made unified action and a purposeful mission all but impossible.

The latest president to attempt to direct these forces into coherence is Fr. David O'Connell, the second-youngest president in the school's history. In his inaugural comments, O'Connell made clear how seriously he takes what he calls the school's duties as "the national university of the Church in the United States." He does not shy from recognizing its history of discord, yet he chooses to revel in the richness of plurality, rather than reduce it, while still trying to guide it by the lamp of the Catholic Magisterium: "Our greatest strength is our Catholic identity for it gives form and substance, shape and direction to all we do as a university." He hopes that "academic freedom" will be balanced by "academic responsibility," and that CUA will emerge as a national leader in three specific areas: teaching, research, and nurturing "the heart and souls" of her students.

Such comments seemed to have made an impression on Catholics, as did his public recitation of an Oath of Fidelity to the proper authorities of the Roman Catholic church and his vocal acceptance of papal teachings on higher education. After the first year of his leadership the freshman class burgeoned to eight hundred. One faculty member, however, says that O'Connell's comments "angered some [on campus] and made others nervous," and that the swelling of applications "had more to do with one year of a properly run admissions program than religious orthodoxy; once the money was gutted the numbers plummeted." Indeed, looking at the school year 2000-2001, CUA is the only school in D.C. *not* turning away students; the number of enrolled freshmen dropped approximately 200 from the previous year. Most faculty and students, however, are optimistic in the assessment of O'Connell, yet feel that he will require, as one put it, "stamina and more than stamina — God's abundant grace" to shepherd such a stubborn flock.

The main difficultly facing CUA is its lack of money, caused, some say, by a long history of poor leadership. Several previous administrations had their fate sealed by an inability to secure adequate funding. Recognizing the problem, President O'Connell was recently quoted in CUA's student newspaper as admitting that "he is not proud that we are under-resourced." Yet in the same article CUA's provost argued that the very number and diversity of programs may be a considerable part of the problem. In any case, the University has not been able to shake its reputation for housing talented scholars in a material wasteland. Remaining true to its founding principles and staffed by many professors committed to the restoration of standards, it adds tremendously to true diversity in American higher education.

Academic Life: Coherent Orthodoxy

The Catholic University is primarily a graduate school; fewer than half of the students are undergraduates. It offers, however, a fine undergraduate curriculum and a solid set of distribution requirements. Importantly, CUA is not afraid to stand on its foundation: all students must take courses in religion. Although only 56 percent are from Catholic high schools and the number of clerical students and faculty has dramatically diminished recently, a Catholic atmosphere abides.

The university is divided into the schools of Architecture and Planning; Arts and Sciences; Engineering; Library and Information Sciences; the Columbus School of Law; the Benjamin T. Rome School of Music; Nursing; Philosophy; Religious

Studies; the National Catholic School of Social Services; and the Metropolitan College for nontraditional (i.e., adult) students. Of these, the schools of law, religious studies, and social service are for graduate studies only; graduate students in these and other programs make up 55 percent of the university's enrollment.

The School of Arts and Sciences is the largest undergraduate school and is home to more than eighteen departments and sixty majors. The core requirements in Arts and Sciences underscore the university's prevailing commitment to the liberal arts. In contrast with most general education requirements today, one professor sees "a coherence of vision," in the CUA undergraduate curriculum, which has remained unchanged for nearly two decades. But the traditional set of courses does not necessarily dictate the content of those courses. Another professor says that "[the courses] are very traditional *on paper*, but often not in substance." A former participant in the undergraduate honors program says, "The professors were of high calibre, the approach to religious issues was soft-core political correctness on religious matters, but rigorous in academic standards."

All undergraduates must complete four courses in religion and philosophy. In addition, students take one course in each of these two areas: "Logic, Morality, and Action" and "Nature, Knowledge, and God." One or two courses in composition are required as well as three humanities courses, four in mathematics and natural science, and four in social and behavioral science. CUA has a foreign language requirement, and all students must also complete two intermediate courses in an ancient or modern language, as well as two in ancient or modern literature. The goal of these distribution requirements, according to a recent CUA flier, is to provide students with "an ethical foundation" and "to gain an understanding of the disciplines that are at the core of learning."

Almost without exception, students and faculty rate most of Catholic University's programs of study highly. Political science is frequently singled out as a strong department. Those interested in studying theological matters should be aware that there are two different programs: theology (which is under the aegis of Arts and Sciences) and religious studies (under the direction of the same-named graduate school). Religious studies is slightly more orthodox now than in the days of the iconoclastic Charles Curran, though some say that theology is the better program. There is a separate School of Philosophy, which has had a reputation for rigor and orthodoxy. Within the School of Arts and Science there is a noteworthy separate honors program requiring a sequence of courses from the following areas: "The Christian Tradition," "An Aristotelian Studium," and "Critical Exploration of Social Reality." The honors program's interdisciplinary goals are to provide "an integrated world view based on the interrelation among disciplines of knowledge. It also stresses the traditional values of our Christian heritage." The faculty, explains one student, "tend to be those who really care about undergraduate education and have some notion of the liberal arts as a distinctive project."

Catholic University's strength has traditionally been in medieval studies —

"from Coptic to Canon Law," as a former professor says — and there are small yet excellent programs in Greek and Latin, patristics, medieval, and Byzantine studies. The School of Music "is one the best in the country," according to a faculty member. The School of Architecture, housed in its own building, is well known for giving students opportunities at original and creative work. The School of Nursing also receives high marks from students and faculty. Not surprising given the university's genesis as a graduate institution, graduate programs in most fields remain strong, though according to one professor the dichotomy between graduate and undergraduate has also given the university a "schizophrenic mind" pitting "the champions of undergraduates" against the research-oriented and leading to "a standoff all the time."

English literature has its less traditional courses. A recent article in *The Washington Post* highlighted an English professor's efforts to yoke the "youth culture" and the liberal arts through his course "Poetry and Rock in the Age of Dickey and Dylan." Combining classic rock CDs with printed poetry, and the lecture hall with smoke-filled Allman Brothers concerts in N.Y. (followed by a seminar with the band's drummer Butch Trucks), the professor has attracted students, notoriety, and a variety of outstanding teaching awards from within and outside of CUA. While most of the department's other offerings are much more staid, if not tame ("Intro to Medieval Welsh" or "Milton"), compared to a typical department at a secular university, courses such as "Film Narrative: Woody Allen and Spike Lee" and "Coming of Age in Women's Fiction" jostle cheek by jowl with traditional courses. Still, only history and modern languages are considered weak or easy departments among the conventional liberal arts programs at CUA.

Most teachers, especially those within the honors program, are generally well-rated by the students. While doctoral candidates and graduate teaching assistants can be found, their number is small and they tend to have their instruction carefully monitored to ensure a high standard of work. Classes in the liberal arts typically enroll less than thirty students. CUA professors have received the Carnegie Foundation "Professor of the Year" award for six out of the past nine years. In general, students are happy with their instruction. "I almost feel as though I am at a small college . . . because the faculty are so accessible and willing to go the extra mile for students," one student says.

A professor concurs with this assessment, but adds that the low salaries tend "to demoralize certain faculty" and that the research orientation of the school often comes into conflict with those who wish to concentrate on undergraduate teaching. "There is no way of getting tenure at CUA on the basis on good teaching only," the professor says. This was confirmed recently when one of the more popular professors in the School of Philosophy was denied tenure. "[Students] loved him and thought he was one of the best teachers they ever had," says a faculty member. "He was very generous with his time," a graduate student says, "and committed to excellence in teaching; his publications were solid, but he was outspoken on problems with modern culture, especially those related to technology, and he was not always a 'team player' with fellow faculty."

The faculty are "a mixed bag — as at all institutions," says a former student. "But on the whole, there are enough faculty dedicated to high academic standards, fighting grade inflation, and working the students hard, that it ends up being a good place to get a degree."

One of the greatest weaknesses of CUA's academic program is Mullen Library. "On paper we have one of the finest collections in the country, but over half of the time that I go to collect something that I need, it is missing or stolen," a graduate student says. "The library is in terrible shape," says one teacher, "the holdings are too small, the security is lax — it would be easy to steal anything from the place; it's an embarrassment to the university." Staffing is also a problem: incompetence and lack of interest seem to characterize the lower ranks. It was estimated by the student newspaper that some 15,000 books remained unshelved between the end of the first semester and spring break of the second. One doctoral student complained that it took two hours for the library to issue him a borrower's card and that once he had it, he found considerable theft from the older library resources. Fortunately for those who study at CUA, the university is part of a large D.C. consortium with other research libraries, and it is a easy to gain borrowing privileges at Georgetown University or make use of the Library of Congress or the National Archives for advanced work.

There are many gifted professors at Catholic U., including: Graham Walker, Lee Edwards, Claes G. Ryn, and David Walsh in politics; Jerry Z. Muller in history; Eric Perl, Rev. Kurt Pritzl, O.P., Jean DeGroot, Brad Lewis, Timothy Noone, and Rev. Msgr. Robert Sokolowski in philosophy; Virgil P. Nemoianu in comparative literature and philosophy; Peter Casarella, Robin Darling, and Rev. Neil Roy in theology; Nelson Minnich in church history; Linda Safran in classics; and Stephen Wright in English.

Political Atmosphere: Sense and Nonsense

Just being a Catholic institution does not exempt CUA from controversy surrounding issues of abortion and homosexuality. Although the university has no sanctioned pro-choice group, there is an organization for lesbian and gay student rights. "Things were sad under the previous president," a graduate student says. "Candice Gingrich was invited to speak by a gay and lesbian group. It was squelched, but only because students worked behind the scenes to bring a cardinal in." A faculty member claims that "the Vice President of Student Life was, and is, supportive of homosexual rights and policing hate crimes; sometimes, I believe, he pushes the envelope." Such complaints are common among traditional or orthodox Catholics, but most students seem content with the just-right-of-center atmosphere of CUA.

And things have been different since President O'Connell arrived. "We haven't had that kind of nonsense," says a graduate student. "In fact, Student Life has been quietly curbed, with, for example, the chaplaincy program taken out of their hands and now directly controlled by the president."

Still, The Catholic University does have a very active group of pro-life students and the university is always well represented at the annual pro-life march in D.C. Because of the university's religious orientation, social justice groups like Amnesty International are also fairly active on campus. There are chapters of both College Democrats and College Republicans, although in the past year the Campus Democrats received about 30 percent of the budget of Campus Republicans. There are also broadly conservative groups like the CUA Conservative Union, whose mission is to "stimulate intellectual conservative thought on campus"; "Pro Veritate," dedicated to a "discussion of traditional moral, social, and religious values"; and *Utopia*, a journal dedicated to thoughtful inquiry from an orthodox Catholic point of view.

By and large, the Catholic University administration has not followed academic fashions. "They are *sui generis*," says one graduate student, "sticklers for rules, paperwork, and yet not overly ideological." The disagreements among faculty have more to do with educational and personal philosophy than with political correctness. Perhaps the divided opinion on the dean of Arts and Sciences best illustrates the mixed opinions. One faculty member calls the dean "one of the best . . . college administrators I've seen anywhere." But another professor calls the dean a "technocrat" who went into administration for the wrong motives: "He was fed up with his own discipline." Still, there is a conflict between tradition and modernity, especially as exemplified by the mixed reviews for O'Connell. "It all depends on your receptivity to the compatibility of faith and reason," one instructor says. "Liberals tend to be angry or nervous, conservatives and orthodox Catholics have great hope for him."

Student Life: The End of Degeneracy

Unlike many other Catholic colleges, including nearby Georgetown University, The Catholic University still retains something of its Catholic identity. For starters, there's no getting around its name. But furthermore, the university is adjacent to the National Shrine of the Immaculate Conception and also home to the United States Council of Bishops. The university offers daily mass and a schedule of prayer groups and retreats. How effective such events are at creating a Catholic or even just plain traditional atmosphere is, however, up for discussion. "I have been at secular universities as well as other Catholic institutions," a graduate student says, "and I would not say the university's policies are the reason for any Catholic identity. A small, but committed, number of students who come are serious about their faith; they are the ones who have upheld Christian orthodoxy." A recent undergraduate has stated that he did not "feel much of a Catholic identity — they don't jam the faith down your throat."

"Catholic identity?" says a graduate student. "Spend five minutes looking through the school's own literature: 'Catholic' is a word that modifies 'University.'"

All CUA freshmen and sophomores are required to live on campus in halls of residence supposedly governed by Catholic moral principles. Yet, as one faculty member says, "from my vantage point, student life, in particular the moral culture of the dorms, is the university's weakness." For example, residence hall staff doesn't do much in the way of enforcing visiting hours, according to a student. The consensus on student mores seems to be that there is little consensus: at spring break, bikini and tanning ads jostled for student attention in the campus paper with a notice for a nearby Benedictine retreat. "That sort of sums it up: mainstream America meets residual Catholic traditions," a student says.

The new university president has already begun to make a difference in this area, according to some. "One should look at the history of the school," a doctoral candidate says. "Things have improved; the new president wants an even greater Catholic moral presence. Keep in mind, this is the school a few years back about which actress Susan Sarandon, an alumna, said, 'There's no better place to lose your faith than the Catholic University.' That kind of degeneracy is gone." Indeed, the new chaplaincy established by President O'Connor is highly ranked for such work. Two Franciscans now offer blessings of rooms, traditional spiritual direction, regular in-residence confessions, perpetual adoration, and — as one student says — "an amazing and charismatic presence."

Undergraduate housing is mixed, with some rather shabby older dorms and some attractive settings, especially the hamlet-like Centennial Village. For those who wish to combine the spiritual, intellectual, and social life, there is Engelhard Residential College, a small, self-governing home to about sixty students. Off-campus housing has been mired by high rental costs and a reputation for raucous behavior. This is offset by cheaper opportunities in Maryland and Virginia, easily accessible by the Metro system. Off-campus behavior has also been expensive — for the university's image. Recently, disturbances from a non-sanctioned rugby players house brought the local Brookland community into conflict with the school. Complaints against frequent and debauched parties went without response from the university. "People would be out in their underwear urinating in the streets; it was bad," says a student. A local lawyer who lives in the neighborhood tired of his children being exposed to such behavior and filmed the goings-on and gave the tape to the media. "Then, and only then, did the university intervene, and hard," a graduate student says. "The rugby players don't really represent the student body, but the university handwashing was typical."

Most people at Catholic do not feel threatened by Washington, D.C., crime. "Many people think, given our location, that CUA is a war zone," says a graduate student. "I actually I feel very safe on campus." Indeed, a visit to the Campus Security's

Web site illustrates the progress made in protecting the university community. "Under constant surveillance" is how one student describes the campus. "The place is peppered with emergency phones and is well-patrolled."

Just as it is an island of safety in the midst of a fairly rough part of town, the campus has also retained a kind of pastoral beauty in the midst of urban surroundings. The older architecture is inspiring, and building projects — the first since the completion of the law school in 1995 — are underway for a new residential complex and a university center.

Numerous small clubs and intramural sports are available for students, who take advantage of the offerings and often create their own more novel organizations. Lacrosse, tennis, crew, and the mainstream sports, along with more specialized club activities like fencing, or the Equestrian and Tae Kwon Do clubs have a place at CUA. Official teams at the university offer entertainment on a small scale, though student support is feeble. "Those of us who are regular fans have been disappointed with the small turnout," said the vice president of Student Life in a recent e-mail to the student body. The men's basketball team, for example, has recently become a Division III powerhouse (ranked as high as fifth in the nation), yet still can't draw students. "Even with a powerful team," head coach Mike Lonergan said in the school paper, "who wants to play in front of fifty people?"

Musical recitals and theater seem to be CUA's classiest — and more popular — diversions. CUA's Hartke Theatre has a national reputation for its dramatic performances. "The university makes a genuine effort at providing athletic and cultural activities," a student says. "It just comes down to money. Fortunately, the campus is in D.C., so there is always something to do."

University of Chicago

Office of Admissions
1116 East 59th Street
Chicago, IL 60637
(312) 702-8650
www.uchicago.edu

Total enrollment: 12,327
Undergraduates: 3,917
SAT ranges (Verbal/Math): 650-750 (V); 640-740 (M)

Applicants: 7,396
Accepted: 44%
Enrolled: 33%
Application deadline: January 1
Financial aid application deadline: February 1
Tuition: $24,807/$32,877
Core curriculum: Yes

Sweet Home

The University of Chicago has not only been one of the nation's best universities over the past century; it has been one of the most unabashedly intellectual institutions in the world. When other elite schools took significant steps toward becoming either mere training grounds for industry or centers for careerist faculty members, Chicago stood its ground as a hard-nosed, rigorous alternative for true bookworms. Much of this is still in place, as the legacy of Chicago has helped it maintain its integrity to a greater degree than many other schools that have lost sight of their original missions.

Yet every year brings a further erosion of the older Chicago, whose identity rested on a rigorous core curriculum, a distinguished faculty that proved that teaching and research are not mutually exclusive endeavors, and a belief in the efficacy of education as a means of bettering and reforming both the individual and civilization. A new president, Don Michael Randel, took over in July 2000 after his predecessor, Hugo Sonnenshein, resigned in the wake of alumni and faculty opposition to his plans to remodel Chicago along the lines of the Ivies. President Randel is a scholar of medieval and Renaissance music, a good sign for those who want the university to again champion the humanities and social sciences. Just how effective he will be in attempting to bring the school back to its position of strength remains to be seen, as he faces stiff opposition from faculty careerists and entrenched interest groups.

While the academic world watches as President Randel consolidates his administration, Chicago still has much to offer the serious student. By picking his way carefully through the various core offerings so as to gravitate toward the best and avoid the worst, a student can receive one of the best university educations available anywhere in the world. Unfortunately, that same student, by choosing the type of politicized and trendy classes (including certain choices in the famed core) that were once very rare at Chicago, can emerge undereducated and malformed intellectually. Unless President Randel makes a conscious choice to reverse recent trends, the school's best days lie in its storied past.

Academic Life: Not Common at All

Chicago's Common Core was designed in the 1930s by, among others, Robert Maynard Hutchins, president from 1929 to 1951, and the eminent American sociologist David Riesman. Its purpose was (and, often, still is) to ensure that students matriculating at Chicago are liberally educated regardless of their concentration (as majors are known at Chicago). But more than that, the Common Core allows for the education of students in the manner the university has long been famous for: rigorous, thorough, critical. It made possible the intellectual environment that separated Chicago from virtually every other school. Whether one went on to concentrate in physics or philosophy, Near Eastern Studies or neurology, the Common Core ensured a quality of thought other schools only wished for.

Today, students may still choose to fulfill their core requirements with excellent courses taught by dedicated professors. This means that the campus holds a critical mass of students who are literate enough to carry forward the older mission of the school. However, there are now also plenty of courses in the Common Core that are academically inferior and intellectually trendy.

Other changes have been at work at Chicago lately. The administration plans to increase the size of the undergraduate student body in order to generate more revenue and produce more alumni who might become donors. The fear among traditional professors is that the new students will have just as good SAT scores, but will be "perhaps less attracted by Chicago's previous emphasis on general education and intellectual intensity," says one such professor. "Unlike SATs and class ranks, this is very difficult to measure."

The Common Core takes up much of a student's first two years at Chicago. These general education requirements, which have been reconfigured recently, are divided as follows:

- "Humanities and Civilization Studies," which requires six quarters of study drawn from several three-quarter sequences: two in "Interpretation of Historical, Literary, and Philosophical Texts"; two in "Civilization Studies"; and one in "Musical, Visual, and Dramatic Arts."
- Six quarter-long courses in natural and mathematical sciences, including at least two in the physical sciences, two in biological sciences, and one in mathematical sciences.
- Three quarters in social sciences, which are taken as a sequence.
- Competency in a foreign language. This requirement, which needn't be fulfilled with core classes, reveals a continuing commitment to the liberal arts by at least some administrators.

Students must also take three quarters of physical education.

The first three requirement sets above may be fulfilled by choosing from a large list of classes (really a distribution list) that seems to grow constantly. Many are superb, but others are either politicized and should not be offered at all, or, more commonly, are overly narrow in subject matter and do not help students achieve a broad education in the liberal arts. In the "Humanities and Civilization Studies" requirements, for example, students may take Humanities 140-141-142, "Reading Cultures: Collecting, Traveling, and Capitalist Cultures." Some of the readings for this sequence are important, but as a whole the sequence evinces a commitment less to the liberal arts than to narrower schools of thought in an overly professionalized discipline. According to one professor, this is really a social sciences course gaining popularity "in the hands of the multicultural folks."

Humanities 141, for example, "Focus[es] on the literary conventions of cross-cultural encounter" by reading *The Interesting Narrative of the Life of Olaudah Equiano or Gustavua Vassa the African.* Important works for students of certain cultures, perhaps, but a squandering of one's brief time in the Common Core of Chicago. The same is true of Humanities 160-161-162, "Media Aesthetics: Image, Sound, Text," which asks: "Can artistic media be distinguished in a rigorous and systematic way from non-artistic media? What, for instance, is the relation between artistic and non-artistic use of photography?"

What, students and parents may ask, is the relation between seeking a broad, rigorous liberal arts education at an elite school and taking such a course?

"Many of the humanities courses have become trendy and fragmented," a long-time professor says. "The scaling back of the [humanities] and science core requirements reduces the general or liberal education offered marginally but not radically. It is a bad sign, however, of the lack of enthusiasm for general education among the administration and the younger faculty in the humanities." Young faculty across the nation are less interested in teaching, in general, than were their predecessors. Part of the problem stems from the increasingly indefensible requirements for publishing placed upon younger professors by their elders and peers. Another significant element is the increased professionalization among faculty who define themselves by school of thought, journal allegiances, or conferences attended. In all of this, students are the losers, as they are cast aside as a mere nuisance.

Faculty and students say the following courses are the best way to fulfill the requirements for the General Education sequences. In the humanities group, under "Interpretation of Historical, Literary, and Philosophical Texts," "Human Being and Citizen" garners the highest praise. Students read the very best works of the Western tradition, beginning with Homer and continuing into the last century. There are fourteen sections of this course serving a total of nearly 1,000 students, and about 40 percent of an entering class takes it. Despite the course's popularity, however, one faculty member says that it is difficult to get regular faculty to believe in it, much less teach it. "It runs on postdocs with two- or three-year appointments," the faculty member says. "They teach six sections per year. Almost nobody teaches more than one quarter of these sequences, which is very different from the way it used to be. . . .

It is a great books course, and the humanities faculty would get rid of it if they could, because we read primary sources in this course rather than the secondary sources they're pushing." Other excellent courses in this division include "Philosophical Perspectives on the Humanities" and "Greek Thought and Literature."

Although Western Civilization used to be required of all students, the civilization studies element of the core can now be met with classes focusing on Latin America, Islam, Africa, Russia, South Asia, or East Asia. The "History of Western Civilization" is still "a great course on paper" says one professor, but the percentage of students taking it is down from a high of 60 percent just a few years ago to around 30 percent now. "The continuity is missing," says this teacher, lamenting the retirement of professor Karl Weintraub. Despite his official retirement, Weintraub and his wife, Katie, are the only faculty members still teaching the Western Civilization courses for the entire three-quarter sequence. "But it is still a terrific course, and there are important people who care about it, so it's safe for the next half-dozen years," says this professor.

Classes in music and the visual arts are not stunning, but are "taught well enough," according to a faculty member.

All sciences at Chicago are not created equal, so students should be particularly choosy when fulfilling the largest core requirement — the six quarters of natural sciences. "The physical scientists take teaching very seriously" says a faculty member. "They're extra good citizens, have some excellent courses, and don't have any trouble with staffing." Biology, however, is another matter, according to another professor. "It is budgeted through the medical school, and the college (the undergraduate unit of the university) has no leverage over it" the professor says. "They regard teaching as a burden. But they still have some very good courses, and they can attract some humanists who come there and find that they like what they see." According to a Chicago graduate, the natural science sequences vary in their worth. "In an attempt to interest everybody in the sciences, the university has created several rather flaky sequences in both biological and physical sciences," the graduate says. "My experience here has not been outstandingly satisfying; yet I believe the science core does accomplish the goal of providing true breadth to the liberal education at Chicago."

As for the social science requirements, a professor says that "most, but not all, of them remain directed toward a broad liberal education with an emphasis on basic texts, discussion, and critical thinking." This same source recommends "Classics of Social and Political Thought." That course, along with "Self, Culture, and Society," are the "most successful" and come closest to "exemplifying the 'old core,'" says another professor. On the other hand, "Mind" contains "arcane cognitive psychology with no liberal education. It is no good and has only four sections," says one faculty member.

After finishing the core, Chicago students choose a concentration, which is selected from one of the five collegiate divisions: Biological Sciences, Humanities,

New Collegiate, Physical Sciences, and Social Sciences. In the humanities, the classics concentration is "solid and demanding," but some new hires "are of uncertain quality," according to one professor. Philosophy, while overall fairly rigorous, is a mixed bag in terms of the quality of the classes, according to a professor. The newer faculty members in history have damaged that concentration's reputation; one professor calls the recent hires "just about what you'd expect."

A cross-disciplinary major called "Fundamentals: Issues and Texts," taught through the New Collegiate division, allows serious students to organize their entire major about a single large and fundamental question. A professor says that "The 'old College' spirit also thrives in a couple of programs in the New Collegiate Division," including "Fundamentals" and "Law, Letters, and Society." "But," this person says, "like most such programs, they depend heavily on a few faculty." Examples of the questions treated in Fundamentals include: "How does telling a story shape a life?" and "Is the family a natural or a cultural institution?" The students in this program concentrate on six classic texts and must pass a senior examination on those six books. Students can choose from a huge variety of texts, as up to forty-five classes are offered each quarter on individual books.

"The B.A.s from this program go on to become M.D.s, J.D.s — to everything but experimental physics," says one professor. Two other excellent interdisciplinary programs exist outside the New Collegiate Division: "General Studies in the Humanities" and "History, Philosophy, and Social Studies of Science and Medicine." Another strong department — and home of Nobel laureates — is the economics department, home of the Chicago School of economists and one of the most influential academic departments in the world.

As might be expected, a university with so many outstanding courses and programs is home to a long list of distinguished professors. The list, assembled from the comments of faculty and students, is almost too long to include here. But here it goes: Nathan Tarcov and John Mearsheimer in political science; Ralph Lerner, Mark Strand, Mark Lilla, and Leon Kass of the Committee on Social Thought; Amy Kass of the Humanities division; Karl Joachim Weintraub, officially retired but still teaching history, social thought, and fundamentals; James Redfield and Bert Cohler, who teach "Self, Culture, and Society;" Peter Vandervoort and Paul Sally in mathematics; David Malament, who teaches the philosophy of science; Laura Slatkin in classics; Bruce Redford in English; Gary Becker and James Heckman in economics; Michael Fishbane in Jewish studies; Lorna Straus in biology; Isaac Abella in physics; Jonathan Lear and Robert Pippin of the philosophy department and the Committee on Social Thought; President Emeritus Hannah Holborn Gray in history; Bertram Cohler, who teaches psychology and fundamentals; Jean Bethke Elshtain and Jonathan Smith in religion; Herman Sinaiko of general studies in the humanities; David Powelstock in Slavic languages and literatures; David Bevington in comparative literature; and Lawrence McEnerney of the Little Red Schoolhouse writing program.

Some departments are becoming very politicized, with English chief among them. One professor says that the department is "full of methodologists and ideologues." Some English faculty have even called for a reduction in the core curriculum. "English is politically correct in a big way, and they no longer believe in great texts, but only cultural studies," says a professor. Other politicized departments include African American studies, gender studies, and film studies, which one professor calls "very chic."

Chicago, like most other large research universities, does rely upon graduate teaching assistants for help. Introductory-level classes are often taught by these students, who are themselves working on their dissertations in order to become professors. There are also many "collegiate assistant professors" (who have earned their Ph.D.s either at Chicago or elsewhere) teaching and researching as they search for a permanent academic position. Nevertheless, many senior scholars do teach freshman courses at Chicago, a fact that is a point of pride in the ethos of the school.

Political Atmosphere: Their Loss Is Our Loss

There are more students at Chicago now than in the past, but the professoriate has not grown at the same pace. "The change over the past two decades in the number of undergraduates without increasing the faculty has produced bigger classes outside the core, and some of the students in those larger classes seem less involved, less excited about the substance of the courses, more concerned with grades and getting by," a professor says.

This marks a profound shift among some students (not all) at Chicago, which for decades was known as the kind of place that welcomed intellectually gifted students from all types of backgrounds, including many who were the first college-bound members of their families. "When I first came here [years ago], students seemed more likely to attend class and more likely to regard their classes and studies as central to their lives than they had at [an Ivy League school] where I taught before," the same professor says. "Larger class sizes and perhaps independent changes in the ethos have altered that."

Former University President Hugo Sonnenschein and his administration, however, wanted the university to compete more fully with the Ivies and other elite schools in drawing what one Chicago professor calls "merely the best and the brightest." That is, in order to garner more dollars, the president wanted to expand the undergraduate student enrollment by as many as 1,500 bodies to 4,500 over the next decade. The belief was, apparently, that there can't possibly be that many serious students available — and that the ones that are available will choose Harvard, Stanford, or Princeton, Sonnenschein's former employer. It is an idea that, if carried very far, will certainly change much of what is good about Chicago. And there are signs that the Sonnenschein plan is working even after his departure, in that early applications from crowded (and thus competitive) New England were up an astounding 46 percent in 2000 over the previous year.

A few years ago, the administration even went so far as to discourage students from spending so much time studying — an action unimaginable on any other campus. It seems the administration had worries — utterly unfounded, say numerous professors and students — that students were taking their studies too seriously.

To be clear about our complaint, it seems that this action and others like it reduce the real diversity of higher education in America by despoiling the unique traditions of a singular institution. While there are numerous small liberal arts colleges in the land, only one Chicago has risen, and it is irreplaceable. "What the administration's running into is that when students decide to come to Chicago over one of the Ivies they're picking between attitudes about learning," a student says. "So you're attracting those students who love ideas and discussion, not those bent on career paths." This alone is something worth preserving, no matter what's going on elsewhere. And we're not talking about a tradition like fraternity rush or touching a stone for luck in a football game; a means of preserving the life of the mind is at stake.

"Today, what's best has been diluted through methodology and ideology," a professor says. "Classes are tendentious in some cases. Not everyone teaches in the spirit of liberal education. They're not self-critical and reflective, but professionalized instead. There are some places in the curriculum where trends have crept in — less so than at most places, but more than before."

The erosion of Chicago's proud traditions has caused a great deal of heartache among dedicated faculty members. "The place has been in retreat for a few decades, but the spirit survives because of a living connection to 'that' college of the Hutchins and immediate post-Hutchins era," a professor says. "The old timers here are a living presence who really were the university then. But the new people haven't been socialized in that way — they're not worried about the shape of the place as a whole. They're attached to their field, and their fields are trendy." It has become every professor for himself, says a senior professor. "There used to be much more of a sense of identity with the university as a whole, but now the subfield and the journal to which they contribute or edit draws their allegiance," says the professor. "They no longer consider themselves as belonging to a university community. Today one is rewarded not for teaching but for getting job offers from other places and making a big name for oneself. People are much more concerned about getting ahead in their own field."

Hostility toward the curriculum and university traditions are pretty well expected at other places by now, but are shocking at Chicago. "There is a lot of hatred for the great books among some teachers here," says a professor. "They'll warn students not to take professors who love the great books. And they become apoplectic when they discuss great books teaching." While older programs are under attack, newer ones are sailing along. One very popular program approved as recently as 1983 "might not be able to make it through (the ratification process) today," a professor says. "And yet gender studies flew through."

Though it is not now what it once was, Chicago is still a marvelous place to attend. A professor offers these reasons: "The still striking intellectual seriousness of the place; the still important role of the Core in providing a liberal education through small discussion groups still mostly taught by faculty. The high faculty to student ratio (3,850 undergraduates and a professoriate of more than 1,900) and the general distinction of the faculty. And a greater frequency of independent thinking critical of dominant academic trends."

Some things deserve to abide, and the old Chicago is one of them.

Student Life: Broad Shoulders

Traditionally, students are drawn to the University of Chicago because they yearn to immerse themselves in its tradition of intellectual excellence. While they certainly knew how to enjoy themselves after the manner of all college students, they were not, typically, as committed to extracurricular activity as their peers in the Ivies or other Eastern schools. Indeed, Chicago graduate students who took their undergraduate degree at the Ivies sometimes complain that undergrads at Chicago need to interact with other students more (although not to the point of losing any study time). Part of the work ethic of Chicago's students stems from the fact that many of them are from middle class or working class families and cannot rely on family connections and money to give them a boost (much less allow them to falter).

The campus is mainly Collegiate Gothic, organized into quadrangles, and is located in the Hyde Park neighborhood of South Chicago. Although the area around the school has seen better days, there are still many shops and restaurants nearby, and students report that safety, while always an issue, does not occupy them to the degree that outsiders might imagine. In fact, crime statistics from the Chicago police reveal Hyde Park to be among the safer neighborhoods in the city. Of twenty-five Chicago Police Districts, crimes per 100,000 residents averaged 1,020 in Hyde Park in 1999. Citywide, the average was 2,017, and the worst district (Wentworth) totaled 5,686 crimes per 100,000 residents. Violent crime in the Hyde Park area declined more than 7 percent from 1998 to 1999 and is at the lowest level since the South East Chicago Commission began collecting data in 1975. Since 1989, robberies have declined 41 percent, although nine homicides (off campus) were recorded in 1999 — the most since 1991 and up from only four in 1998. Aggravated assaults in Hyde Park declined 19 percent from 1998 to 1999.

Nevertheless, crime is a concern, and any student should be careful, especially after dark and off campus. There were two forcible sex crimes on campus in 1997, five in 1998, and four in 1999. Robberies on campus for those same years numbered eight, five, and six. In 1997, there were four cases of aggravated assault on campus, five in 1998, and six in 1999. Burglary is by far the greatest crime problem on campus, with about fifty reported each of the last three years. Eight or nine cars get stolen each year. Twenty-nine of the fifty-two burglaries reported in 1999 occurred in residence halls. Other residence hall crimes that year included three robberies and one aggravated assault. (Robberies involve a theft from a person who is present, while theft of objects from a certain place is considered a burglary.)

The university has a police force that is always on duty. As the college handbook says, "Officers are armed and fully empowered to make arrests in accordance with" state laws. More than 150 white emergency telephones are located throughout campus, especially on heavily traveled thoroughfares. Simply pushing a red button alerts police — in fact, the university police recommend that anyone being pursued simply "Continue to use emergency phones along the way so that police can follow your course. An officer or patrol car will come to your aid immediately."

Freshmen are required to live in college houses, although there is no residence hall exclusively for them. A little more than two-thirds of students enrolled in the College live in university-owned housing, and all of them eat in one of three dining commons. All housing is coed, although single-sex floors are available. Of the one-third of students who live off-campus, only four percent live in fraternities. There are no residential sororities at Chicago.

The eleven undergraduate residence halls are divided into thirty-seven "houses," which were created to break up the living system into more personable, community-oriented units. Several of these halls are a bit of a hike (or bus ride) from campus. Broadview, for example, which houses about two hundred students, is "a pleasant fifteen-minute walk from the main quadrangles," according to university literature. Stony Island is a twenty-minute walk, but does offer apartments for upperclassmen. Hitchcock and Snell Halls, among others, are located on campus.

Virtually every religion on earth has a group on campus, an indication of the cosmopolitan flavor of the school: Buddhists, Episcopalians, Roman Catholics, Muslims, Jewish students, and many others can find a spiritual home in on-campus groups.

Among the many student organizations are the Edmund Burke Society, a unique feature of intellectual life at Chicago. The student newspaper, the *Chicago Maroon,* offers opportunities for budding journalists or anyone interested in writing about campus life. Student groups include a College Bowl team, Campus Republicans and Democrats, Democratic Socialists, the Federalist Society, the Outdoor Adventure Club, and numerous clubs organized by professional or academic interest or by nationality.

There are nine women's and eleven men's intercollegiate teams, known as the Maroons. Students may choose from among twenty-one intramural sports, arrayed from archery and billiards to touch football and ultimate Frisbee. There are no less than thirty-four club sports offering a very wide variety of activities, and every member of the university community is eligible for participation in twenty-eight open tournaments in sports like basketball, handball, tennis, and softball. The University of Chicago offers no athletic scholarships or grants-in-aid.

And then there's the city of Chicago, which one Easterner described as "coming closest of any other city in the country to New York." Intended as a compliment, such observations aren't uncommon among visitors. Yet Chicagoans know they have a unique city that needn't look elsewhere (especially eastward) for validation. Home to many of the nation's finest museums (the Museum of Science and Industry is near campus), neighborhoods, architectural treasures, and cultural amenities, Chicago is an ever-present reason for students to recall that genuine education is never the province of mere bookworms. A great university in a livable city — coupled with the school's still-vibrant intellectual life — makes Chicago worth a closer look for any serious and gifted student.

Christendom College

Office of Admissions
134 Christendom Drive
Front Royal, VA 22630
(800) 877-5456
www.christendom.edu

Total enrollment: 356
Undergraduates: 286
SAT ranges (Verbal/Math): 570-720 (V); 530-650 (M)
Applicants: 162
Accepted: 85%
Enrolled: 54%
Application deadline: February 15
Financial aid application deadline: February 15
Tuition: $11,300/$15,870
Core curriculum: Yes

To Restore All Things in Christ

Christendom College was founded by a group of Catholic laymen in 1977 to combat what they saw as the wholesale abandonment of the classical liberal arts tradition. "Even Catholic colleges seemed to be embracing the prevailing culture of utilitarianism and nihilism in their curricula," says one Christendom professor. "Christendom was founded as a response to those trends, to be a place that is solidly Catholic and solidly grounded in the Catholic understanding of the liberal arts."

The college's purpose, according to its handbook, is to provide "a liberal arts education that would fully integrate natural and revealed truth. The purpose of a liberal arts college is to 'educate for life' — to lead the whole man to wisdom, and not just to train a worker for a job." At the heart of Christendom's understanding of truth is the Catholic faith. At Christendom "the truth of the Catholic Faith is seen as central to all other truth: it unifies and illuminates the scientific and humane disciplines." A liberal arts education, according to Christendom, should not just develop intellectual abilities but "form moral character and foster spiritual growth."

The goal of Christendom college is a lofty one, nothing less than "re-Christianiz[ing] the temporal order." Christendom wants its graduates to be "energized subjects of Christ the King." The college's very name signifies this goal: "Christendom" means a Christianized social order. The college's motto is *Instaurare omnia in Christo,* which means "to restore all things in Christ." Christendom takes that "all things" quite literally: there is no natural truth that is not seen as somehow fitting into and leading to the supernatural truth of Christ. This belief in and commitment to truth sets Christendom apart from the great run of colleges and universities today, and has led the school to create a challenging and coherent program that turns out exceptionally well-educated and able graduates.

Academic Life: Uncommon Doctors

Education at Christendom is ordered around a strong core curriculum that begins in the freshman year and continues into the junior year. The core curriculum totals eighty-four semester hours, making up a full two-thirds of a student's course work. In some respects, the core is just what you might expect from any liberal arts college worthy of the name: freshman composition (two semesters), History of Western Civilization (three semesters), and a foreign language (four semesters) form the foundation of the education.

But Christendom's core goes far beyond what even many "good" liberal arts colleges require — take, for example, philosophy: where most liberal arts colleges require at best two or three philosophy courses, Christendom's core requires six semesters of philosophy. The philosophy core is arranged according to the classical Aristotelian order, comprising logic, math (Euclidean geometry), philosophy of man, metaphysics, medieval, and modern philosophy. The "fundamental ordering principle" of the philosophy curriculum was set by no less than St. Thomas Aquinas, the great "Common Doctor" of Catholic philosophy and theology. The purpose of this solid grounding in philosophy is to "assist the student in using reason to understand the nature of reality and to illumine further the truth of revelation."

The truth of the Christian revelation is also a large component of Christendom's core curriculum. There is a substantial dose of Scripture and theology in the core. Students begin with "Fundamentals of Catholic Doctrine" in the freshman year, which is a survey of Catholic teaching, and move into Old and New Testaments in the sophomore year. In the junior year, this segment of the core culminates with courses in moral theology and Catholic apologetics.

One might think that there is a danger of the college becoming a sort of "hothouse" environment that indoctrinates its students, but conversations with a few students quickly clear up that impression. "The people here are very diverse; people have differing opinions on all sorts of things," one junior says. "Actually, in my experience it's the secular universities which are filled with the same sort of people: doctrinaire liberals. People here have made an informed, mature commitment to the Catholic faith."

Faith and reason, the two means of knowing truth in the traditional Catholic worldview, are considered the antidote to the evils besetting modernity, and are at the heart of the Christendom education. According to the "Vision Statement" published by Christendom on the occasion of its twentieth anniversary:

> The student of St. Thomas at once recognizes that much of modern culture has limited the domain of knowledge to the practical order — the effort to remake man and nature — while banishing the speculative order: the discovery of the truth of a given (not constructed) order of reality. In the modern secular and pseudo-Catholic university, the natural, social, and technical sciences are thought to advance man's technical and political liberation, while theology, metaphysics, and ethics languish because they are seen as the products of emotional or religious feelings impervious to rational justification. The twelve courses in theology and philosophy dominate Christendom's core curriculum precisely to help the student overcome this distorted judgment through exposure to the rich Catholic intellectual heritage enlightened by faith and right reason.

In addition to theology and philosophy, the core at Christendom has heavy doses of history and literature. After the freshman "Composition and Literature" sequence, students are required to take three courses in the "Literature of Western Civilization." This sequence leads the student more or less historically through the great books of the West, beginning with Homer's *Iliad* and *Odyssey*, Aeschylus's *Oresteia*, Virgil's *Aeneid*, and St. Augustine's *Confessions*. The student then reads

Boethius's *Consolation of Philosophy,* Dante's *Divine Comedy,* Marlowe's *Dr. Faustus,* and a play by Shakespeare. The literature sequence concludes with Milton's *Paradise Lost,* Goethe's *Faust,* Dostoyevsky's *Crime and Punishment,* and Eliot's *The Wasteland.* The literature program is designed to help the student to see, "through the eyes of the literary artist, both the concrete reality of human life and the ultimate reality of human destiny," according to the college.

The history program takes as its starting point the centrality of the Incarnation of Christ. This should not be surprising to learn that Dr. Warren H. Carroll, known for the widely acclaimed series *A History of Christendom* (not the college, of course), was Christendom College's founding president. According to Dr. Carroll, "for the believing Christian, the Incarnation of Christ — God becoming man — is the most important event that ever happened or could ever happen. Because it was an historical event, the Incarnation gives history transcendent importance." Three semesters of history are required in the core, and many students rate these classes as the best of their Christendom career. "The professors make history really come alive," says one student. "The method they use is sort of a 'philosophy of history,' and it makes you see how history really matters."

The core curriculum at Christendom is rounded out by a modern or classical language: French, Spanish, Italian, Latin, or Greek. Two years of Latin are required of all students majoring in philosophy and theology; other students need four semesters of the language of their choice. Students are required to take two classes in math and science, such as "Euclidean Geometry" and "Introduction to Scientific Thought." Christendom also expects its students to take "Introduction to Political Theory" and "The Social Teachings of the Church." This course is an examination of classical Catholic social doctrine concerning the state, the citizen, the common good, and wealth and poverty using Scripture, the Church fathers, as well as modern papal encyclicals such as Pope John Paul II's *Centesimus Annus.*

Only after completing the core does the student moves into courses in his or her major, which must be declared at the end of the sophomore year. There are only seven majors available to the Christendom student — classical studies, English literature, French, history, philosophy, political science and economics, and theology — and but two minors (in math and Spanish). The college will offer a minor in "Early Christian Studies" beginning in the fall of 2000. This program will focus on the history and literature of the first few centuries of the church. The major programs are designed to integrate the knowledge the student gained in the core, and to bring that knowledge to fruition. "People come to Christendom to learn the truth about reality," says Dr. Robert Rice, Christendom's vice president for academic affairs. "That's *all* of reality, which is the whole of human experience. Truth is One, and we believe that all the truths one learns in the different disciplines illuminate and complement one another. And students see this coherence, and find it exhilarating." At Christendom, education is seen as having a goal, an end. One student sums up this end: "At Christendom, we're taught to know the Truth, desire the Good, and contemplate the Beautiful."

Given the Catholic liberal arts basis of the college, faculty tend to be a self-selected group firmly committed to the principles of the college. The small size of the faculty and the considerable demands of the core curriculum mean that practically all of the faculty teach courses in the core every year. This all but guarantees that students will get to know the faculty early on, and quite well. "The faculty here all understand that our first and foremost responsibility is to teach," said one professor. "We have gotten better and better at 'doing' the liberal arts over the years," says Dr. Rice. "When we founded the college the core was sixty hours. Now it is eighty-four." This commitment to a traditional approach is reflected in the choice of texts and method of teaching those texts. "We are committed to using primary texts whenever possible," Dr. Rice says. "So when we teach Euclidean geometry, we use Euclid's *Elements*. When our students read Chaucer's *Troilus and Criseyde*, they do so in the original Middle English. We use no excerpts or anthologies." This commitment means that Christendom is a remarkably ideology-free zone. Nobody at Christendom is going to be forced to read *I, Rigoberta Menchu* and pretend that it's a good or important book in the great scheme of things.

The strongest departments at Christendom, are, as one might expect, philosophy and theology. The history department is also well regarded. The program in classics is also quite strong, and will get only stronger with the addition of the minor in early Christian studies. Students and faculty both report some weaknesses in the modern languages. "The modern language courses aren't very challenging," one student says. A faculty member says, "We are trying to improve the modern languages here, and we need to." A number of students also expressed disappointment with their courses in political science and economics. "The poli sci courses are the weakest I had here," says one senior. "The poli sci classes don't really seem to fit in to the rest of the program," another student says.

The faculty are all dedicated to teaching, and students generally rate the quality of teaching at Christendom as excellent. With a faculty to student ratio of twelve to one, the students and faculty are close both in and out of the classroom. Students and faculty commonly lunch together on campus, and students are frequently invited to dine at the homes of professors. "With only 260 students and a small faculty, everyone knows each other. It's like being part of a big family," says one professor. Students will find Christendom professors to be very accessible and interested in them not only as students, but as people. "Mentoring relationships develop between faculty and students quite naturally here," one student says. "There is a high level of trust among the students for the faculty," said one professor. Another professor illustrated this high level of trust by relating, "Sometimes a student will ask to see me, and I expect they want to talk about something in class, when what they really want to talk about is their problems with their girlfriend." Professors who can be counted on for exceptional (if sometimes tough) courses include Christopher Blum and Jonathan Reyes in history, William Fahey in classics, William Marshner and Tim Gray in theology, and John Cuddeback and Anthony Andres in philosophy.

Political Atmosphere: Credo

The college's commitment to the Catholic faith is evident not only in its requirements in philosophy and theology, but in its hiring standards. Faculty are expected to be practicing Catholics and assent to official Catholic teaching. To this end, faculty make a "Profession of Faith" and "Oath of Fidelity" to the church upon hiring; both must be renewed annually. Furthermore, faculty contracts "state that public rejection of, or dissent from, the teachings of the Catholic Church as interpreted by the Holy Father, or rejection of the authority of the Pope as head of the Catholic Church, is grounds for the termination of that contract." Christendom is dedicated to the proposition that the Western tradition is good, and that the Catholic faith is true, and therefore has no qualms about requiring its faculty to defend these principles against the relativism and nihilism that are accepted as wisdom in our time.

Students, too, are expected to be committed Catholics, or at least sympathetic to the Catholic faith. This also should come as no surprise at a college whose stated goal is "to help students through their study of the liberal arts to consecrate their intellect and will to Christ." As such, the college aims at feeding the souls as well as the minds of its students. Religious observances, such as daily mass, are an integral part of the college's life. A wide variety of Catholic devotions are popular with Christendom students, such as a daily rosary, or pilgrimages to various shrines. Fittingly, the college's Chapel of Christ the King dominates the campus and is likely to be the first building a visitor notices upon arriving there.

Most of the faculty and students would be considered conservative by the prevailing standards of society. But one does not find anything like lock-step uniformity at Christendom. While socialist or leftist politics don't find a home there, there is genuine disagreement about politics. "There is suspicion about Americanism and the founding among some students and faculty," one professor says. "Some here are inclined to view the whole Enlightenment project as hopelessly corrupt." There is also disagreement about the proper role and scope of government. "The classic Catholic position, as formulated by St. Thomas and others, is that good government promotes virtue among the citizens," says one professor. "But this principle is in tension with our original founding principles of limited government, and certainly contradicts the modern 'values-free' and libertine agenda of the left."

"Coherence" within the curriculum is something of a buzzword among Christendom faculty. With an all-encompassing vision of the liberal arts driving the curriculum, the faculty and administration are at pains to create an educational experience in which each course, major, and rule for community life contributes to an integrated Catholic worldview. The core curriculum achieves that end to a large extent. "By the time students are juniors, they're all talking the same language," one professor says. "The core gives them a common set of categories and standards by which they can measure and make judgments," says another faculty member. But the program falls short of coherence in a few areas, according to some faculty and students. "There is some debate here as to whether political science even belongs in the core of a liberal arts program," says a professor. And the literature department is said to be of lower quality than the others.

Another difficulty is a certain difference of vision between some of the older and younger faculty. The college was founded by people who saw the traditional liberal arts as well as Catholic doctrine being abandoned by the leading Catholic colleges. They saw their mission as one of restoration. "The college was founded to train lay Catholics in the liberal arts who would be loyal to the Church," a professor says. This led to some degree of triumphalism on the part of both students and faculty. One can still catch a scent of that spirit on Christendom's campus, but it has largely dissipated. "The younger faculty have a wider vision of what the college is about," one senior says. "They're less defensive." As times have changed and the grip of the dominant left on the culture has weakened a bit, it seems that Christendom has been able to relax its posture somewhat.

Student Life: Oh, Shenandoah

While the environment at Christendom is certainly ordered, it should not be thought of as controlling. Chapel functions are not mandatory, but, according to a student, "if people notice that you haven't been to mass in a while, they might ask how you're doing." There is an active social life on campus, with everything from intramural sports, limited intercollegiate athletics (men and women play soccer and basketball, and there is a men's baseball team) to numerous dances and parties throughout the year. "The social life was good and healthy and fun," said one recent graduate. People at Christendom certainly rejoice in such expressions of Catholic culture as Oktoberfest and St. Joseph's and St. Patrick's days. One recent graduate said that the atmosphere at Christendom fits the summation of the Christian life expressed by St. John Bosco, "Love, and then have fun."

But that doesn't mean that Christendom is not actively concerned about the morality and virtue of its students. "The faculty here are quite self-conscious about functioning *in loco parentis*," an administrator says. The college enforces a dress code for classes, meals, and the like. Students are expected to dress modestly at all times. Students are also expected to live on campus, and must apply to the dean of student life for an exception. The dorms for men and women are separate and visits by members of the opposite sex are not permitted. The dorms themselves are relatively small (the largest hold about fifty students) and home-like. There is also a high regard for the virtue of courtesy at Christendom. "Visitors are often impressed by the friendliness and courtesy of the students here," says an administrator. "The atmosphere on campus is meant to establish a kind of peaceful order whereby one can more easily be disposed to practice the virtues," a college chaplain says.

Christendom also fosters in its students an appreciation of culture and the arts. The College sponsors the Beato Fra Angelico Fine Arts Program to "offer students a further opportunity to experience directly the higher and more aesthetically praiseworthy fruits of Western Civilization and our contemporary culture." The college sponsors a number of concerts and recitals on campus, and has an active choir and Gregorian chant schola. The college hosts a variety of speakers, both Catholic and political; past invitees include Patrick Buchanan, Russell Kirk, and Alan Keyes. One of the next buildings to be built on campus will be a new library. The Student Activities Council organizes trips to concerts and other cultural events in nearby Washington, D.C. And further afield, in the fall of 2002 the college will inaugurate its Semester in Rome program wherein students will spend a semester of their junior year studying history, art, and architecture in the Eternal City.

Christendom is located in Front Royal, Virginia, in the beautiful Shenandoah Valley, about seventy miles from the nation's capitol. The area is truly a wonder of natural beauty, including the Shenandoah National Park, Skyline Drive (whose northern terminus is in Front Royal), and George Washington National Park. The administration has taken care to make the campus fit in with its setting, but the relative newness and small size of the college means that one won't find any imposing or architecturally striking buildings on campus. While Front Royal itself is a somewhat sleepy town (with the benefit of very low crime, both on and off campus), the students do a pretty good job of keeping life on campus lively. When the need for more excitement strikes, larger towns are only a few miles away, and the District of Columbia is near enough to make a night "on the town" an inviting proposition.

Claremont McKenna College

Admission and Financial Aid Office
890 Columbia Avenue
Claremont, CA 91711-6425
(909) 621-8000
www.claremontmckenna.edu

Total enrollment: 1,016
Undergraduates: 1,016
SAT ranges (Verbal/Math): 640-740 (V); 640-740 (M)
Applicants: 2,827
Accepted: 28%

Enrolled: 32%
Application deadline: January 1
Financial aid application deadline: February 1
Tuition: $22,580/$30,000
Core curriculum: Yes

McKenna — Not McEducation

Claremont McKenna College (CMC) has a lot going for it. Not only is it widely considered to be one of the top schools in the nation for students interested in the study of government, management, and public policy, it has developed a strong commitment to a genuine study of the liberal arts. And that's just what goes on *inside* the classroom. CMC also has the advantage of having a truly peaceful and beautiful campus that, along with the mild and comfortable climate, is an excellent stomping ground for any student serious about his education.

With an enrollment of slightly more than one thousand undergraduates, CMC has many of the hallmarks of a small liberal arts college: a dedicated and accessible faculty, small class sizes, no teaching assistants, and an intimate intellectual and social community. But CMC also has a range of first-class facilities and opportunities that, when combined with its strong academic programs, handily gives its larger competitors in academia a run for their money: eight research institutions, numerous off-campus study programs, and myriad opportunities for undergraduate research.

William F. Buckley Jr. once called CMC the second-most conservative college in the nation (the first being Hillsdale College in Michigan), and certainly many departments at CMC, along with its rigorous academic requirements, make CMC merit such a distinction. Students say that the college is evenly split among conservatives, liberals, and moderates, and that the open academic environment at CMC provides students the chance to freely pursue their studies regardless of their political beliefs. Classroom politicization is minimal, and students are happy — even enthusiastic — about the classical liberal education they are receiving. While some of CMC's programs in the traditional liberals arts are not as strong as one would expect, the seriousness that characterizes CMC's flagship programs runs throughout the school's curriculum.

Academic Life: Required Thought

Claremont McKenna is one of five undergraduate colleges in the Claremont Colleges system. The other four are Harvey Mudd College, which focuses primarily on the sciences and engineering; Scripps College, a women's liberal arts college; Pitzer College, which focuses on social and behavioral sciences; and Pomona College, the oldest college in the system, which focuses on the liberal arts. Each college is independently run in the sense in that each has its own faculty and administration, but CMC students can cross-register with other colleges if they wish to take advantage of courses offered at other Claremont schools.

The college makes no secret of the fact that students arriving at CMC need to be prepared to work. "At Claremont McKenna College, the academic workload is demanding," the catalogue says. But CMC's intellectually rigorous education draws enthusiastic reviews — rather than groans and moans — from its students, 95 percent of whom return to the school following their freshman years. "It's a real solid education," says one student. "It's very focused and very leadership oriented. In terms of education quality, it's very good. I compare notes with friends back east at Ivy League schools and wouldn't trade my education at all. I think I'm very well served." Another student says that she is "absolutely" happy with her CMC education, while a third goes on to proclaim that he "is absolutely thrilled with it. It's a great education." CMC, says one professor, provides an "emphasis on politics and economics, and preparing for responsible leadership — all this in the context of a liberal arts education, not a pre-professional or vocational approach."

CMC also requires that, with few exceptions, each student complete a senior thesis under the direction of a faculty reader. This is, according to the course catalogue, "a major research paper or creative project of substantial length," and is "intended to be a serious exercise in the organization and presentation of written material, in effect an honors course for all students in their final semester or year." This requirement is practically unheard throughout higher education, but again, students at least appreciate what the thesis demands of them. "I think it's wonderful, because it really gives you the opportunity to take what you've learned over the past four years [and use it], and you have a reader who you work with very closely," a student says. While there are some complaints about the thesis, the wailing and gnashing of teeth generally comes from "from people on the eleventh hour," according to one student.

The thesis is just one of CMC's general education requirements, which are an extensive part of a CMC student's academic experience. Students must take one semester-length course in composition and literary analysis, which boils down to an introductory literature course; one course in mathematics, which means calculus — not algebra; two courses in science, one of which must be a laboratory science; proficiency in a foreign language equivalent to passing a third-semester language course; and a course called Civilization 10, "Questions of Civilization." This course is highly regarded by students. "It's not just a Western civilization class," says one, "but it deals with broader themes — it's heavily [focused on] Western civilization, but it also includes Confucius, Lao Tsu, Rumi, and the *Bhagavad Vita*. It's a good program and so that when people talk about Tocqueville or Darwin or St. Paul, or any number of different people, everyone has this common background."

But that's not all. Students must complete one course in three of four social science fields: economics, government, history, and psychology. In the humanities, all students must complete a course in two of these four fields: foreign literature, literature, philosophy, and religious studies. Both of these requirements also stipulate that those majoring in one of those disciplines must take a course outside of it to fulfill their general education requirements — in other words, a history major must take a course in all four social science fields; a literature major must select two courses from the foreign literature, philosophy, and religious studies areas. And as if that weren't enough, students must take three semesters of physical education (with some exceptions). However, some of the above requirements may be met with Advanced Placement credit. According to one professor, the basic requirements amount to "generally sound distribution requirements."

There is no departmental sprawl at CMC — the college has only twelve academic departments, and one of these is a science program shared with several other Claremont schools. But the college's government and economics department are, in a word, top-notch, and its international relations program is also highly regarded. "The government department is arguably the best in the country for providing a sound liberal arts education with a major in government," says one professor. Says another: "The economics and government faculties are outstanding. . . . Many of them have had high-level Washington experience [as] presidential appointees [and] cabinet secretary appointees, and [many have had] extensive involvement in politics at the national and state levels."

"The government department has a wide variety of approaches to the study of politics: political philosophy, political history, constitutional history and constitutional law, institutional history and analysis," the first professor says. "This is not a department dominated by rational choice modeling or multivariate regressions on minutiae."

Among the best faculty at CMC are Charles R. Kesler, Joseph M. Bessette, James H. Nichols, Mark Blitz, Chae-Jin (C. J.) Lee, John J. Pitney Jr., Harold W. Rood, Ralph A. Rossum, and Alan Heslop in the government department; Marcos F. Massoud, William Craig Stubblebine, and Eric A. Helland in economics and accounting; and Robert Faggen in literature.

Unfortunately, not all of CMC's departments live up to the exemplary standards of its government and economics programs. Students report that the history department is the most politicized. "The focus is more on modern history — they've got some people who know their stuff about World War I and World War II, but the history program isn't what it could be," according to one. The history department's liberal leanings would not be as bad if it didn't contain glaring deficiencies in the realm of classical instruction — there were only three courses offered in ancient and pre-modern European history in the 1999-2000 academic year, according to the course catalogue, and these are only wide surveys — *not* the bread-and-butter examinations of Greek and Roman society that one can find at any state university, even a badly politicized one. To its credit, the history department offers numerous and well-thought-out courses on modern European and American history, along with an extensive series of courses on Asian history, but one wonders why a department obviously so committed to poring over modern history in detail ignores the foundations of modern society in favor of courses such as History 131sc, "Working Peoples in the Americas: Race, Labor and Organizing" or History 161sc, "Women in Latin America: Social Justice and Violence." However, it should be noted that these offerings are tame compared to some of the social history courses at some other universities.

The literature department has "got your typical left-wing literature professors," one student says. This student also finds that "psychology is one of our weaker departments."

But in all departments, classes are generally small and inviting, allowing students to interact freely with their professors. While there are occasionally some very large courses — primarily in classes that everyone needs to graduate — "the average class is probably twelve to fifteen students," a student says. "Some introductory general education requirement classes are where you'll have thirty students, but a class bigger than twenty students is an exception."

These classes aren't taught by teaching assistants, either. "Graduate students don't teach at all," a student says. "Frankly, we wouldn't want them to."

This allows for a faculty-student closeness that is downright impressive. "I can basically drop by their office anytime," says one student. "I've had dinner with a number of their families, in fact. It's very easy to get in touch with them, and they really care about the instruction of the students. . . . We're at a teaching college." Another student says, "It's great — you can talk to your professor, and meet them at office hours without any lines. After you've taken one class with them, they know you. They have a rapport with you." This closeness is "not merely a 'feel good' asset — it has practical benefits for students," says a professor. Take the all-important letters of recommendation when it comes time to find a job or graduate school. "We can discuss the students in detail, rather than writing vague generalities," the professor says.

In addition to solid courses, students will find at CMC a multitude of research opportunities. Perhaps most notable are the Henry Salvatori Center for the Study of Individual Freedom and the Rose Institute of State and Local Government. The Salvatori Center "within its general study of freedom . . . focuses particularly on the American Constitution — its founding principles and subsequent construction — and on questions of political philosophy and applied ethics." The Rose Institute allows students to get involved with the political process, working on "election simulations, election analysis, redistricting research, fiscal analyses, studies of California demography, and polling."

"I know people who spend eight hours a day there," in addition to their class work, one student says about the Rose Institute. "They really enjoy it, they really love it." A professor says that the Rose Institute is "especially known for its ability to recruit and retain students . . . and involve them in major research activities." In addition, there are a number of fellowships and scholarships available for students participating in student research.

Last but not least are the diverse off-campus study opportunities that CMC offers its students. According to the school's catalogue, more than 40 percent of students study off-campus during their time in school, and the college provides every opportunity for students to attend these programs. Students can participate in a semester program in Washington, D.C., or in foreign study programs in countries around the globe — from Kenya to Vietnam to Ecuador to Great Britain, or closer to home in Canada and Mexico.

Political Life: A Meeting of Minds

Claremont McKenna's political environment is healthy and open, and regardless of a student's political leanings, he will find his views taken seriously and thoughtfully. Students are evenly split among ideological lines, with one-third considering themselves conservative, one-third moderate, and one-third liberal, according to students. "We have to be one of the most evenly-split colleges in the country," says one student.

Perhaps the best way for students to hone their political knowledge about how the world works is through the Marian Miner Cook Athenaeum, the site of lunch and dinner meetings four times a week featuring lectures by prominent speakers, along with less frequent concerts and performances. "The speakers provide our students with a range of perspectives and interests that most students elsewhere don't confront," says a professor.

Students and faculty, in fact, can't say enough good things about the Athenaeum. Not only does it offer a decent meal — high-quality main courses, always with foreign and exotic foods to collegians known in the outside world as "fruits" and "vegetables" — it allows students to visit with their professors *and* hear a number of incredible speakers. "Recommend everyone go to the Athenaeum," one student says enthusiastically. One professors explains the program as such: "It is a very good adjunct to our education: many prominent and interesting speakers, presented in pleasant surroundings . . . with opportunities usually to talk with the speaker afterwards." Traditionalists will approve of the generally approved dress code as well — "It's a formal setting," says one student, "a coat-and-tie type of thing."

A look at the list of speakers shows an impressive array on both the right and the left, although very infrequently the speakers can be on the fringes. "The two students who help to select the speakers and who introduce the speakers are both Democrats, the first time this has happened in years," says one students. "The speakers have been a little more loopy but there's always a balance." This means that once in a great while, the Athenaeum will feature speakers such as Elaine Brown, former chairman of the Black Panther Party, or Amiri Baraka, a poet whose work is less well known than his past involvement with the Sixties-era Black Nationalist movement.

These infrequent occurrences, however, should not in any way dissuade students from thinking highly of the Athenaeum. The vast majority of speakers at the Athenaeum will be of interest to all students, and with good reason. "We've always had our fair share of Nobel Laureates in poetry and literature," one student says. A look at the full list of speakers during 1999-2000 shows dozens of worthy lecturers: former Independent Counsel Ken Starr, cartoonist Art Spiegelman, Democratic Leadership Council Director Al From, baseball great Reggie Jackson, literature professor Robert Fagles, syndicated columnist Ben Wattenberg; historian Francis Fukuyama, *Weekly Standard* publisher and editor Bill Kristol — and the list goes on.

Students at CMC are a politically active bunch, according to students, and students have been visible in protests against racial incidents in the city of Claremont itself, as well as against various California ballot initiatives. However, much of this is first touched off at the other Claremont campuses, and then trickles down to CMC, students say. "Most of these [protests] are things that come from up on Pitzer," says one student. Campus protests over California's Proposition 22 (an initiative defining marriage as between a man and a woman, effectively eliminating the possibility of gay marriage), Proposition 187 (which would deny illegal aliens certain social benefits), and Proposition 209 (which ended racial preferences in California), end up with both sides vigorously debating the issues at hand. "Students are politically active [but] the mode of Claremont McKenna political activism is different," a student says. "Claremont McKenna's mode of activism is [to] drive down and work on a campaign — not just as a volunteer but help with the campaign; work within the system. The world has plenty of sweaty activists."

CMC recently hired a new chief executive, Pamela Gann, a former dean of Duke University's Law School who has an exceptionally low public profile. She's known as a good fund-raiser — while at Duke, the *Chronicle of Higher Education* reports, she helped raise $17 million for the Law School's first capital campaign. She was also responsible for expanding Duke's international and *pro bono* law programs, the *Chronicle* reports.

"There's a lot of concern among the more conservative folks about what direction she wants to take the college," says one student. But, he adds, "she hasn't done anything controversial — she's really been getting her bearings [this last year]. I'm a little curious to see what she is going to do in the next couple of years."

At the moment, however, the campus remains an open and vibrant place for students to discuss their views, whatever they are. "We're a very politically conscious campus," says one students, "but dissenting with orthodoxy is not a problem." Another student concurs: "From what ever side you come from, you always have allies in the classroom."

"The presence of both liberals and conservatives on the faculty adds a dimension of intellectual diversity that is missing on many campuses," a professor says. "Here, students encounter liberals and conservatives, Republicans and Democrats. They learn to think for themselves."

Perhaps the best indication of CMC's open political environment is the statement that one student made about politicization in the classroom. "The liberal students here don't feel they have a problem with conservative professors." At most colleges in the nation, such a statement would be laughable — but not here.

Student Life: No There There

The town of Claremont is charitably described as sedate, and not inaccurately as boring, at least for college students. "There aren't your normal college town things in Claremont," says one student. However, just because Claremont isn't Ann Arbor or State College doesn't mean that there is nothing to do — just that it takes slightly more effort to find activities.

The Village, Claremont's town center, contains a number of shops, restaurants, and bookstores, but this represents the sum total of entertainment within walking distance of campus. Given this, a car is most certainly helpful, as it allows students the freedom to travel. Los Angeles, about forty miles to the west, is only about an hour away by car — although it can take up to two-and-a-half hours or even longer if traffic is heavy — and many students go there to take advantage of its many cultural and social activities. CMC's Web site prominently lists the many things to do and see in Los Angeles. That list even mentions Los Angeles' horse racing venues, some of which are more seedy than others. (While these can make for a fun day trip, students should, of course, use moderation and common sense when visiting.) Closer to home are the suburban cities of Pomona and Ontario, which are both only a few miles away and offer shopping and other entertainment. Students who want to visit the beach can head for either Los Angeles or Orange County.

Despite all this, life on campus is not lacking in activities. "Everyone has fun to some degree because there's so much going on," a student says. There are dozens of student groups and plentiful athletic opportunities, and the close-knit atmosphere makes it easy to find and make friends.

Students can join clubs that are either exclusive to one campus or available to students from all five campuses, and they range from the far left to the respectable right. As one student says, "We take advantage of what goes on at other campuses, because in a sense we're all one campus." Some recommend joining Civitas, a well-supported community service group; the Hawaiian Club; the Pro-Life Society; or Inter-Varsity Christian Fellowship, the largest student group on campus. There are

183

chapters of both the College Republicans and College Democrats, a pep band, a fencing club, and three publications: *The Collage*, which serves students on all five campuses; the *Claremont Independent*, a conservative-oriented publication also for all five campuses; and *The Forum*, which targets the CMC community. There are also a debate union, a five-campus chapter of Hillel, and a Lesbian, Gay and Bisexual Students' Union.

CMC has an impressive athletics program for such a small campus, although it compensates for its size by running its athletics programs under the aegis of a department that covers Claremont McKenna, Harvey Mudd, and Scripps Colleges. It has nineteen varsity programs for men and women, from football to water polo, and also has a number of club teams, including lacrosse and rugby. There are also a number of intramural programs, and as one student says, "Almost everyone seems to play in a sport."

There is no Greek system on campus, nor is there any push for one. This means that students are left to their own devices when it comes to partying, something that CMC students reportedly do a good deal of — although the campus has become dryer as of late. "People drink, but not nearly as much as when I was a freshman," a junior says. "The climate has changed, and people don't drink nearly as much — the keggers *used* to start at about Wednesday." However, another student says that "student life tends to revolve around alcohol consumption."

Some students are concerned about the campus's seemingly lax attitude towards demon rum. "I almost decided not to come," says one student regarding her reaction to the college's wet reputation. "The drinking policy is really a downfall, and it is, I think, a serious problem." However, CMC does appear to have a relatively tough policy regulating alcohol consumption — the school expressly forbids underage students from touching the stuff, and where alcohol is permitted, it is strictly controlled. Violators of this policy will be subjected to "official action," according to CMC's 1998-99 student guide. The same guide, however, does not expressly discourage alcohol consumption; it only expects that those who choose to drink do so in a responsible manner.

Housing on campus is abundant and adequate. Approximately 95 percent of students live in on-campus housing, and there are twelve residence halls that house approximately sixty to seventy students each. There is also one student apartment complex that houses nearly 150 students. Campus housing, which has single-sex floors and bathrooms (within coed dorms), is clustered in three areas on campus, and the residence halls are only about two to three minutes away from each other at the most. This leads to a camaraderie both within residence halls and between them. "Dorm life is a blast," says one student. "It feels kind of like a family." There is also a central dining facility where students take their meals, and there are enforced quiet hours in dormitory housing.

Crime is not a concern on campus. "I don't think people worry about that at all," says one student. "We're in a sleepy little town." Students say that they don't feel unsafe, but as they say the largest problem is theft, students should always use common sense in safeguarding their belongings.

Fortunately, there is no shortage of that at CMC — whether in the classroom, or outside it.

Clemson University

Undergraduate Admissions Office
105 Sikes Hall, Box 345124, Clemson University
Clemson, SC 29634-5124
(864) 656-2287
www.clemson.edu

Total enrollment: 16,982
Undergraduates: 13,526
SAT ranges (Verbal/Math): 520-620 (V); 540-640 (M)
Applicants: 9,501
Accepted: 68%
Enrolled: 45%
Application deadline: May 1
Financial aid application deadline: April 1
Tuition: resident: $3,590/$7,918; non-resident: $9,784/$14,112
Core curriculum: No

Agriculture Trumps Multiculture

Founded in 1893 as an all-male military school, Clemson University was designed to help lift South Carolina from the ravages of the Civil War. From its roots as a public agricultural and technical college, the Clemson of the twenty-first century now is building itself to be an international university. When the university's new president was inaugurated in April 2000, the flags of seventy-two countries flew to represent the nationalities of Clemson's student body.

Like much of the South, Clemson has strains of old and new that help define its character. In many ways, Clemson's strength is its tradition. Its strongest and most reliable academic offerings remain in the agriculture, business, and engineering-related fields. But as the university has grown into thriving modern university, the humanities and social sciences have also begun attracting attention, though the focus on research in many fields overshadows the emphasis on undergraduate teaching. Students and professors come from around the country to learn and teach at this traditional Southern university just north of the South Carolina-Georgia border.

Two hours north of Atlanta and a half-hour south of the Greenville-Spartanburg area, Clemson lies on what was once the plantation of John C. Calhoun, U.S. senator from South Carolina, vice president of the United States, and one of the most important political thinkers in American history. Clemson's location, as well as its steady and regular influx of tradition-minded South Carolinians, has mostly shielded the university from the radical fringes that have carved their way into the curriculum and social life of other universities. Many alumni remain fiercely loyal to their alma mater and speak admiringly of the friendships they forged in Clemson's small-town atmosphere. It's still a genteel, Southern university that remains surprisingly solid in its academic standards.

Academic Life: The Sciences of It

Today, the university enrolls some 17,000 students, including 3,500 graduate students, in five colleges: Agriculture, Forestry, and Life Sciences; Architecture, Arts, and Humanities; Business and Public Affairs; Engineering and Science; and Health, Education, and Human Development. Bachelor's degrees are offered in seventy-five areas of study, from the usual offerings like English and history to more specialized topics like food science and textile chemistry.

There is no core curriculum at Clemson. Instead, all undergraduates are required to fulfill distribution requirements in several subject areas. Students must take two composition courses, one in oral communication and one course deemed writing intensive; one course in computer skills, which teaches familiarity with word processing programs and spreadsheets; two in math; two in physical or biological science, such as astronomy, biology, chemistry, geology, or physics; two in humanities; and two in social sciences, designed to "introduce students to human social and cultural diversity."

In addition, students must fulfill requirements from their major. And some of the five academic colleges impose additional requirements. For instance, all students in the School of Humanities (part of the College of Architecture, Arts, and Humanities) must complete a minor field of concentration (or a double major), take four humanities courses and four social science courses, and attain proficiency in a foreign language.

One exciting new addition to Clemson's academic life is the creation of a Great Books curriculum. In early 2000, campus officials approved a minor in "Great Works of Western Civilization." Students in this program must take a mandatory upper-level English course and then take one course in each of the following five fields: classical civilization; post-classical literature; philosophy, religion, and social thought; the arts; and the sciences. The establishment of the program met with some resistance from critics who feared a "right-wing takeover of the curriculum," according to the *Chronicle of Higher Education.* (This as opposed to the customary left-wing takeover of curricula, which hardly engenders protest anymore.) But the program seems popular with students. "It makes me think," a junior in a Western Civ class told the Associated Press. "A lot of classes are just memorization — you spit it back on a test. This class is a lot more using your mind." Professors report that the classes are popular with students and that the only problem with the curriculum is finding enough interested teachers for the classes.

Students and faculty seem pleased with the intellectual life at the university. Although professors in the liberal arts and humanities "tend to be of one political ilk," according to one faculty member, the business and science-oriented fields — Clemson's bread and butter — set the campus's no-nonsense tone. "A conservative student would find a comfortable place here," this faculty member says. "It's still a place where women's studies programs don't dominate campus politics."

Though Clemson has no core curriculum, many professors are pleased that the curriculum at least forces all undergraduates to take substantial numbers of courses outside of their major fields. Future geologists must take English, and psychology majors must take math and science. This produces well-rounded students, professors say.

Business is a popular major, and students and faculty members give it high marks. Some of Clemson's strongest departments are in the hard sciences and the more technical fields. Physics, chemistry, and most engineering departments are solid.

Clemson's economics department offers a superior education by giving students a broad view of the discipline while also focusing on its traditional values. Most of the professors are followers of the Chicago school of economics, which favors free markets over government intrusion in the economy. The program emphasizes environmental economics, and its undergraduate curriculum prepares students for careers in business or government by emphasizing problem-solving skills.

The political science faculty is well-regarded, and sources say it has about even numbers of liberals and conservatives. This is a healthy division, since it means that political science students will receive balanced political views.

Among the best professors at Clemson are Thomas Bruce Yandle Jr. and Robert E. McCormick Jr. in economics; Mark Winchell in English (who started the Great Works program); and Joseph G. Louderback in accounting (professor emeritus). Sadly, many of the professors listed as excellent in the first edition of this guide have since moved to other schools or retired.

Despite Clemson's strong array of business and science-oriented fields, there are some whiffs of politics creeping into some courses. Offerings in gender studies and ethnic studies — so popular among elite colleges these days — are remarkably limited at Clemson. Yet they exist. The school offers minors in African American studies and women's studies — fields that look odd among a list of minors that includes food science, horse production, and horticulture.

While many older professors are traditionalists, some of the younger ones have been schooled in the more avant garde. "It's hard to find somebody who hasn't written a dissertation on extremely odd things," says one old-timer.

Political ideologies also make their way into mainstream disciplines. The English department is Clemson's largest, principally because all Clemson undergraduates must take two English courses to graduate. One insider advises treading carefully when selecting English department courses: some professors are first-rate, particularly older professors teaching on topics such as Southern fiction or Shakespeare. But younger graduate students and professors sometimes inject politics into discussions. "You have to walk around land mines there," said one professor a few years ago.

The philosophy and religion department in the School of Humanities is singled out as heavily politicized by many professors. In the first edition of this guide, the following quote from a professor touched off a campuswide debate about the department: "The department is just full of wild men — crazy old Hegelians who believe that Marx was brilliant and crazy post-modernists who can't agree on whether the sun is up these days." In a letter to the campus paper, some professors protested, saying the charge was false. Our source replies: "It's true. It's still true." Whether it was hyperbole or a case of the truth hurting, who knows? But to our knowledge nobody disputed this anecdote: one student told of attending the first day of his upper-level philosophy class. After students waited twenty minutes past the appointed hour for a professor to arrive, a man in blue jeans sitting in the back of the room revealed that he was the instructor and there would be no reading and no lectures for the class — the only assignment for the semester was to keep a journal. And as for class time? "We're just going to come in here and talk about some of the questions you've been thinking about," the instructor said. The department subsists mainly on business students who are required to take its business ethics course. Beyond that, many offerings are limited, and its popularity with students is questionable.

Clemson has an honors program to which prospective students can apply. Members of the honors program are expected to complete at least one honors course each semester and maintain a grade point average of 3.4 or better. Clemson students can also apply after matriculating at the university. The honors courses encourage active student participation rather than passive lecturing and note-taking. Honors classes are offered in many disciplines, and courses include: "Plants in Medicine, Magic, and Murder," "The Arts, Politics, and Technologies of Food," and "Milltowns North and South." Honors participants can also live together and take ski trips and white water rafting trips together.

Though there are many professors who teach at Clemson, some courses are taught by graduate students. A May 2000 report by South Carolina's Higher Education Commission found that Clemson was among several schools that failed to meet standards on the number of hours full-time faculty are teaching in the classroom — an indication that professors spend time researching. In an Associated Press article, Clemson's president explained that the state standards "did not recognize the different missions and challenges of research universities."

Clemson inaugurated a new president in April 2000: Jim Barker, a Clemson graduate and former dean of the university's College of Architecture, Arts, and Humanities. Campus insiders say they expect Barker to carry on most of the university's traditions, since he's familiar with the institution and its practices.

Political Atmosphere: What the Future Will Hold

Compared with other universities, the political climate at Clemson is best described as tranquil. Southern gentility is the norm. There are no protests, even when figures controversial elsewhere visit campus. Newt Gingrich visited a few years back, and no one picketed. When Republican presidential candidates visited before South Carolina's primary in February 2000, nobody shouted them down. On college campuses these days, this is noteworthy.

The flip side is that there's not always very much open and honest discussion of issues on the campus, and the creeping levels of political correctness are met with little resistance and accepted as the norm.

For instance, the university has a Commission on the Status of Women, which has the charge to "discern the status of women at Clemson University and document findings" as well as to "pursue the removal of institutional barriers."

There's also an active Office of Multicultural Affairs, which organizes "awareness months" for Hispanics, Native Americans, blacks, and Asians. The OMA also organizes racially segregated receptions for minority students. And it sponsors a dinner for minority students with a 3.4 GPA or better. Whites with similar academic achievement aren't invited.

The Commission on the Future of Clemson University also recently issued a report calling for more multicultural indoctrination — not, of course, in so many words. It called for a three-credit orientation course on diversity and multiculturalism and encouraged "educating" faculty and staff in diversity issues. It remains to be seen if these will come into place.

Overall though, Clemson is working to expand its image from that of a sleepy South Carolina college to that of an international university. A recent study on Clemson's future concluded that in order to "meet society's compelling challenges in the twenty-first century," the university had to take more of a global focus. It recommended an international education program for humanities majors to "help students appreciate and embrace the cultural differences of our global society." And it recommended that business majors be more exposed to foreign languages and have the opportunity to gain "increased international cultural awareness."

Student Life: Death Valley

Clemson is in a fairly isolated part of South Carolina, lying about twenty minutes off Interstate 85, which connects Richmond and Atlanta. It's a small town dominated by the university, and it has several restaurants and bars that cater mostly to students and others associated with the university. Some students find such an atmosphere stifling, while others find it rewarding because there's a sense of community among students, who aren't going a zillion different directions as they might in a large metropolis. At this writing, a major import from of the outside world — a 204,000-square-foot Wal-Mart Supercenter — is trying to win approval to be built in Clemson. Many Clemson residents oppose the superstore, saying it would destroy Clemson's small-town charm and devastate downtown businesses.

Said one sophomore: "Everybody's extremely friendly. Everybody always smiles. They want to keep the small-town atmosphere. Clemson's the kind of town where you don't have to show ID to write a check."

Some students say the social life on campus changes with the seasons. In the fall, it's football, football, football, with pep rallies, games, and post-game parties dominating weekend activities. "If you haven't been to a Clemson football game, you're missing out on the Clemson experience," says a psychology major. Though Clemson is a small town, on Saturdays of home football games it becomes more like a small city. Alumni from throughout the South converge on the town to root the Tigers to victory. Tailgate parties outside the stadium start early. One student happily reports that unlike many stadiums, Clemson's allows spectators to have their hands stamped at halftime, continue tailgating and return to the stadium in time to catch the second half. The atmosphere and the quality of the Clemson team (in most seasons) led a visiting coach fifty years ago to dub the stadium "Death Valley," and the name has stuck. There's even a rock collected from the Death Valley in California mounted on a pedestal, the touching of which is supposed to endow Clemson players with skill and fortune. Players run from the rock down a grass hill directly onto the field before games.

In the winter, basketball isn't nearly as big. But in the spring, some of the social life revolves around baseball games. Students are known to congregate behind the right field fence. They say you can't really see the game, but you can hear it as you hang out with friends.

One of the most famous off-campus haunts in Clemson is the Esso Club, a gas-station-turned-sports-bar especially busy during football season. The bar itself is made of stadium seats from Clemson's old stadium.

As far as on campus organizations, Clemson has plenty. Particularly popular are religious organizations, such as the Fellowship of Christian Athletes and Campus Crusade for Christ. In addition to the school's main paper, *The Tiger,* there is an alternative conservative paper, *The Tiger Town Observer.*

There are also dozens of active student organizations at Clemson, everything from the French Club to preprofessional engineering organizations, a sports car club (for those interested in sports cars and racing), and a Tae Kwon Do club.

About three-quarters of Clemson students are from South Carolina, though the university draws large numbers of students from throughout the South and a fair number of people from the Northeast. Behind South Carolina, the next-largest states represented at Clemson are (in order) Georgia, Virginia, New Jersey, Florida, and North Carolina, according to university statistics.

Greeks play a heavier role in the campus social scene than their numbers would indicate. About 20 percent of Clemson students are in fraternities or sororities, though Greek parties are fairly big. Fraternities are housed in campus dorms or off-campus. Sororities are must remain in dorms because of an old South Carolina law — designed to outlaw brothels — that forbids large numbers of women from living together. If the law is ever changed, sororities have raised money to build off-campus houses.

Most Clemson dorms are coed, usually with men and women on separate floors, but not always. Several residence halls are, however, single-sex. In university residence halls, visitation hours extend until 2:00 AM; in university apartments, roommates can agree to have no visitation hours at all.

As you might expect in a small college town — or at any college, for that matter — students at Clemson drink. According to the *Chronicle of Higher Education,* Clemson was one of only five schools (out of nearly five hundred surveyed) with 120 or more alcohol-related arrests in 1996-97. Of course, since the statistics cover only arrests, they may indicate that Clemson police take a dimmer view of such carryings-on than do their colleagues in other jurisdictions. In any case, the university is looking at ways to reduce the flow of alcohol around campus. In April 1998, Clemson made headlines when police there arrested forty-two people, including thirty-one students, in an undercover drug sting, according to the *Chronicle of Higher Education.*

Colgate University

Office of Admissions
13 Oak Drive
Hamilton, NY 13346
(315) 228-7401
www.colgate.edu

Total enrollment: 2,778
Undergraduates: 2,773
SAT ranges (Verbal/Math): 630-710 (V); 640-720 (M)
Applicants: 6,050
Accepted: 38%
Enrolled: 31%
Application deadline: January 15
Financial aid application deadline: February 1
Tuition: $25,740/$32,070
Core curriculum: Yes

A Fine Contradiction

In the case of Colgate, the title "university" can be misleading. In essence, Colgate University is a small liberal arts college of about 2,750 undergraduates and only a few graduate students. Other contradictions can be found here, too. For example, many of the faculty seem to despise the fraternity system, but it remains the focus of social life on this isolated rural campus. There is also a contradiction within the curriculum itself: Colgate requires both a core curriculum and a set of distribution requirements, though the core is partially set up as a distribution requirement. Despite these tensions, it must be said that Colgate offers a fine liberal arts education, provided one selects courses from several politicized departments with care.

Admissions are highly selective, with approximately one-third of 6,000 potential students accepted each year. Moreover, the setting is idyllic and the political atmosphere on campus is generally calm. Colgate was chartered in 1819 as the Hamilton Literary and Theological Institution, spent some years as Madison University, and finally in 1890 renamed itself for a New York City soap maker, William Colgate, whose financial support had been crucial to the young institution. The university severed its church ties in 1928 and became coeducational in 1970.

Academic Life: Core Sample

The general education requirements at Colgate consist of distribution choices and what the university calls the "Liberal Arts Core Curriculum." There is also a foreign language requirement that can be met with either high school or university courses. Colgate's distribution requirements mean that a student must take two courses in each of three "divisions": humanities, natural science and mathematics, and social sciences. The two courses must come from different departments within the division; for example, the humanities requirement might be met with courses in English and religion. Any course can count toward the distribution requirement, meaning that students choose from the entire catalogue rather than a selected list.

The Liberal Arts Core Curriculum is more tightly defined and not at all extensive. Four courses are required, with an optional fifth course available to interested students. They may be taken in any order, but are to be completed in a student's first two years.

The Core Curriculum has both strengths and weaknesses. Among its strengths is that it is concerned with central, interdisciplinary, liberal arts themes — according to the catalogue, it is designed to "engage students with some of the persistent, fundamental questions of our culture as posed in classical texts and confronted today as current issues: our relationship to nature, the relationship of the temporal to the eternal, and the definition of the individual within society." Some professors praise the core. "Colgate has a Core Curriculum which is not a hollow joke," says one. "The courses are taught by a broad array of faculty, and the students are exposed to the Great Books." But, another points out, "one must be very selective to ensure that from among this diverse faculty pool, a truly competent teacher is chosen, and this is sometimes difficult."

One of the courses is outstanding. "Western Traditions" covers "the beginnings of Western thought and its resonance throughout the ages" in order to "give students grounding in eras crucially formative of Western traditions and provide them an enhanced appreciation of both the continuity and the diversity of these traditions," the catalogue says. Yet, here too, much depends on selecting a member of the faculty who is truly committed to the goals of this otherwise fine course.

A companion course is often more politicized but, again, that largely depends on the professor teaching it. The course, called "The Challenge of Modernity," has a reputation for being "a bit trendy or politically correct," according to one professor. It can also be rewarding, though, if a student can get in a section led by one of the better professors, some of whom are listed below.

The remaining two liberal arts core courses constitute what are essentially another distribution requirement and, again, they can be highly politicized. The "Scientific Perspectives" portion of the core is satisfied with one of eleven courses — "Psychology of Women" and "Ecology, Ethics, and Wilderness" among them. According to a student, "What Is Science?," "Causality and Indeterminism in Science," and "Critical Analysis of Health Issues: AIDS" are all acceptable choices. The first looks at the methods and practices of science, the next examines the history of the "idea of causality" through the works of philosophers and scientists like Aristotle, Newton, and Schrödinger, and the last critically examines AIDS and explores, through the use of CDC data, the ways in which this disease has become so sadly politicized.

The final requirement in the core curriculum is by a wide margin the most politicized and includes "Cultures of Africa, Asia, and the Americas." Students must choose one course from a list of twenty, each of which focuses on a different culture or country. "The Black Diaspora: Africans at Home and Abroad," "Women in China," and "North American Indians" are some of the options, and none of these are apt to be taught without a well-developed political agenda. Still, with help of a "friendly" faculty advisor, a student can find a decent and rigorously taught class even among this group.

Interested students can take a fifth class, a seminar that includes an extensive research paper on an interdisciplinary theme. Students who complete this course successfully receive the designation "High Distinction in the Liberal Arts Core Curriculum" on their transcripts.

Classes at Colgate are usually small, especially compared to those at large state universities. The average class size is nineteen students. Professors are interested in teaching, but also pursue research. "The faculty are still active researchers, and, as a result, undergraduates get unusual opportunities and greater responsibilities," a professor says. "There is a lot more one-on-one attention that the students get at Colgate than they would elsewhere." Another professor says: "Colgate has a professorial culture where if you are not highly regarded by students it will, of course, affect tenure but, more interestingly, it results in demerits even for tenured faculty." A third professor says, "It is hard to know exactly why the faculty continues to care as much about teaching, after tenure, as they do. It is certainly different at schools like Yale where one's ability to teach has no impact on one's professional advancement. Colgate succeeds remarkably well at maintaining a balance between teaching and research." In fact, it is rumored that the university is weeding out the older faculty who have never published, those who are now considered deadwood, and trying to bring in a vibrant younger group of teacher-scholars.

There are a number of fine departments at Colgate, according to professors. "The best departments in the humanities are English and a small but very serious classics department," one says. "In the natural sciences, the best are chemistry, geology, and a highly rigorous department of psychology. And, in the social sciences the economics and political science departments are both excellent, with a number of relatively conservative faculty."

According to another professor, "The best departments at Colgate examine seriously the classic texts of the traditional liberal arts education." For example, English majors must take courses in British and American literature and in the literature of the middle Ages. The department lists two Shakespeare courses.

Political science has sixteen professors and, according to one professor, "The faculty are representative of an unusually broad range of political perspectives, from socialist to a living and breathing Catholic monarchist, and almost all are excellent teachers." Several people on campus say political science is the best department at Colgate, both in terms of its faculty's research accomplishments, which are competitive with those of some research universities, and its skillful teaching — among the best in the college. Its courses cover government and international relations, but also political theory, with classes in constitutional law, the Enlightenment, America's unique traditions, and political thought from the ancient Greeks to modern times. In particular, the department highlights the close relationship between political thought and institutions and religious thought and institutions.

The department also has a course — "Modernity and Its Conservative American Critics" — on conservative political thought, a very rare offering in American colleges and universities. Its course description reads: "What is wrong with the modern world, especially with the political culture of liberal and progressive intellectual elites? Such questions are explored by studying the radical critique of modernity offered by philosophical, classical and Christian conservatives." But in many other courses taught by the four or five moderate to very conservative members of the department, students are exposed to points of views, texts, and modes of analysis rarely found on today's college campuses. In fact, a student majoring in political science at Colgate is likely to be exposed to serious conservative currents of thought without his or her diploma announcing this to the world. "In a sense," one of the conservative members of the faculty observes, "Colgate's department of political science is a conservative treasure that a student can enjoy without worrying about being marked after graduation as having studied at an insularly conservative college where one might not also be exposed to views on the left."

It also should be mentioned that the natural sciences are particularly strong at Colgate and they offer students an unusual opportunity, almost immediately, to begin conducting research either during the regular academic year or, quite often, during the summer. In truth, the situation at Colgate is very different from that which is found at research universities where undergraduates are often taught by graduate students and, accordingly, have limited contact with the tenured faculty. Instead, at Colgate, students are only taught by regular faculty and, indeed, this same faculty is in a sense dependant on finding undergraduates to help them conduct their research. Without access to graduate students to help in their research, the natural science faculty must quickly develop the skills of their undergrads. And the results are impressive with several departments regularly placing, greatly disproportionate to the size of Colgate, high number of students in prestigious research programs and medical schools.

Because of the strength of its faculty, it is difficult to single out a few for mention. Still, there are few whose teaching abilities or openness to points of view rarely found on college campuses demand recognition. In astronomy, there is Anthony F.

Aveni, recently a national teacher of the year. Aveni also teaches anthropology and directs the school's Native American studies program. In sociology, Gary Urton was this year awarded a prestigious MacArthur "genius" fellowship. In English, Peter Balakian and Frederick Busch are highly acclaimed creative authors and Lynn Staley a noted teacher and scholar. In music, Joseph Swain excels. In philosophy, there are three fine scholars: Maudemarie Clark, David McCabe, and James Wetzel. In the classics, Robert S. Garland is a highly regarded scholar and Andrew R. Keller an exciting teacher. In economics, see Michael R. Haines, Jill Tiefenthaler, and Robert W. Turner. And in political science, we recommend Stanley C. Brubaker in public law; Timothy A. Byrnes and Michael Johnston in comparative politics; Fred Chernoff, Douglas J. Macdonald, and Robert Rothstein in international relations; and in political theory, two prominent conservative scholars, Robert Kraynak and Barry A. Shain.

Like most contemporary colleges, however, there are several highly politicized departments at Colgate. The sociology department, for one, bases much of its teaching on race, gender, and class. Courses include "Power, Racism and Privilege," "Women and Social Change: The Women's Movement," "Gender and the Social Sciences," "Gender and Culture," and "Black Communities in Contemporary America." Another course, "Population Issues," "considers the relationship of population to a range of policy concerns including social welfare and security, the status of women, poverty and economic development, and race and ethnic relations," according to the catalogue. Sociology also offers "Men and Masculinities," which addresses "the symbols and practices through which masculine identities are created; the evolution and forms of male dominance, patriarchy, and fratriarchy; the relationship between masculinity and violence; maleness and the cultural construction of emotion; male heterosexuality and alternative modes of sexuality; the relationship between masculinity, production, and social status; and the impacts of feminism on masculinity in Western societies."

And, sadly, the study of religion in Colgate's department of philosophy and religion, according to one professor, "is dominated by liberation theology and feminism — you know, all the latest trends from the Harvard Divinity School." Despite the fact that about one-third of Colgate's students are Catholic, the religion department, according to this professor, has "a strong anti-Catholic bias." While some philosophy offerings (like "Philosophy of Nature" and "Medieval Philosophy") are in accord with a traditional liberal arts education, others are of a more political nature. "Philosophy and Feminisms," according to the catalogue, "gives special attention to the categories of difference and the Other(s), as these have affected marginalized people, especially women." Topics include "oppressions (e.g. race, class, gender, ethnicity, sexual orientation), violence against women in relation to other forms of violence (e.g., militarism, contemporary colonization, and rape of the earth), women's ways of knowing, friendship among women, barriers separating women [and] women's political activities."

The religion side of the department, though, is even more ideological. "Sexuality and Human Meaning," the catalogue says, "is a critical examination of several religious and philosophical issues dealing with modes of human sexuality in relation to views of the human person." The course description says that "attitudes toward pornography, erotica, marriage, homosexuality, prostitution, and abortion reflect views of the self and its relationships," and that "the perspectives of the major religious traditions and the resources of the empirical sciences" will be studied "in relation to humanizing and dehumanizing dimensions of human sexuality."

Some philosophy and religion courses overlap with the women's studies department. Women's studies is an interdisciplinary program that doesn't have its own full-time staff and therefore offers courses from other departments, including education, economics, English, history, and sociology. Only six courses belong to the women's studies department, including "Biology and Gender," which examines topics such as "evolutionary and cultural models of sexuality, bonding patterns, sex roles and parental behavior; human evolution; [and] sex role stereotypes and gender identification during childhood."

Colgate established its peace studies program in 1970 "as part of the university's response to issues raised by the escalating arms race and the war in Vietnam," according to the catalogue. Peace studies majors take ten courses and must participate in an off-campus project. Like the women's studies program, peace studies makes use of courses from other departments but also has some of its own. An introductory course subtitled "Violence and Nonviolence" covers "positive and negative peace, structural and direct violence, [and] the analysis of conflict" but also attempts to link what it calls "parallel concerns": issues of race, gender, class, and international relations. Another class, "Women and Peace: War, Resistance and Justice," studies the "contributions and aspirations of women toward the creation of a more just and peaceful world."

Political Atmosphere: Greeks at the 'Gate

The most divisive question on Colgate's campus continues to be issues of diversity and the breadth of the Greek system on campus. Over the past several years, there has been a sustained effort on the part of "progressive" faculty to break up the fraternities, and in 1996 about two-thirds of the faculty senate voted in favor of such a policy. Alumni and students protested, and it now seems unlikely that the faculty's wish will be achieved any time soon.

The ban on fraternities would be accomplished with a rule expelling any student who joins one. "It would basically mean that the university would revoke the charters of the fraternities," a student says. However, many fraternity houses are owned by the international foundations that govern their chapter affairs. If fraternities were banned, the foundations and their alumni would be forced to rent out the fraternity house, or leave it empty between reunions. Some fear that if the university disbands the fraternities, it will rent the houses from the foundations and use the residences to set up special-interest dorms. Colgate already has twelve special-interest houses dedicated to, among other things, Asian culture, Hispanic and African-American cultures, and world peace. Many, however, in keeping with the low-key nature of Colgate students, are each year under-subscribed

Complaints about the fraternities include misogyny, elitism, and irresponsible behavior with respect to alcohol. "A powerful minority of the faculty remain committed to destroying the Greek system," a professor says. "They think, with the masculinity that the fraternities represent, they are where all evil lies, especially because the fraternities are not quite as dormant as they were ten years ago." And because of Colgate's reputation as a party school, the administration has become preoccupied with alcohol consumption and is under pressure to develop "alternative social programs that are alcohol-free," another professor says. And, in the mind of the concerned faculty, alcohol consumption, masculinity, heterosexuality, athleticism, sexism, racism, and fraternities all go together. Indeed, you might as well add, moderate and conservative politics too. The frats have responded prudently to these pressures and have become in the past few years a little more subdued.

Colgate recently suspended one chapter for three semesters (starting in November 1997) because of a party that got out of control, according to the student newspaper, *Colgate Maroon-News*. The party not only featured acts of hazing, but the acts of two "exotic dancers" from Syracuse, one of whom was bit by an intoxicated Colgate student. However, more than nine hundred students (about one-third of the undergraduate student body) signed a petition calling the penalty "unjustified and harsh." Other faculty and students supported the sanctions and organized a silent, candlelit march down fraternity row. "The *Maroon* even had a whole issue bashing fraternities following the event," a student says.

Again, it seems unlikely that fraternities will be completely rousted from the Colgate campus. The university has been coed for only about twenty-five years, meaning that for a certain sector of alumni — including some faculty and members of the board of trustees — fraternity life was one of the most important parts of their experience at Colgate. "Many of the alumni are as loyal to their fraternities as they are to their alma mater," a student says. "The fraternities aren't going to just disappear."

Apart from this issue, the Colgate community is rarely given over to political activity. The students are moderately liberal or moderately conservative, according to a professor. Most of the faculty is liberal, and while there are only a few radicals among them, conservative professors are allowed to speak their minds — at least to a certain extent. "Conservatives are not appointed to positions of university governance, but they can teach their courses and, when compared to most other liberal arts colleges, this is a real strength," says a conservative professor.

Most Colgate students are more interested in athletics or social activities than politics. One professor estimates that "maybe five percent" of students are politically active, and says non-fraternity-related demonstrations tend to be small, involving fewer than ten students. "Most students are not liberals, they are sort of mushy Republicans," a professor says. Unfortunately, however, "this means that outspoken conservative students can receive a lot of flak in class." Still, such students can attempt to take classes with moderate faculty and, in addition, will be defended and supported by the openly conservative members of the faculty.

Student Life: Upstate — Not Uptown

Hamilton, New York, is a village of around 2,500 located in the beautiful northern tip of the Chenango Valley in upstate New York. The 1,550-acre campus is particularly attractive, with some buildings dating back to the mid-nineteenth century. Like many remote locations, Hamilton has very little to interest socially minded college students. "Hamilton is dead," a student says. "There are two bars in town . . . but most everybody goes to the fraternity parties." The two nearest cities are Syracuse and Utica, both about forty-five minutes away, but these places are also limited in social attractions and most students tend to stay on campus during their free time, further increasing the social cachet of fraternities and athletic events. "From my perspective, the Greek system is at the center of social life," says one professor. "Of course, sports and sporting events, especially hockey and basketball, are very popular." Says another professor: "The relative isolation and small size of the campus makes for intense and long-lasting relationships between students, which is so different from what I observed in my undergraduate years at the University of California with its giant campuses where it was so difficult to get to know someone really." It also makes for a virtually crime-free environment, at least with respect to more serious incidents.

Despite its location, Colgate has attracted in the past several years some big-name speakers. For example, in 1997 Mikhail Gorbachev spoke to an audience of three thousand on the future of U.S.-Russian relations. Jesse Jackson, Elie Wiesel, and many other prominent liberal personalities have recently visited, as have more conservative voices such as William F. Buckley Jr., Ward Connerly, and Linda Chavez. As well, Governor Christine Todd Whitman of New Jersey gave the commencement address in 1997 and Senator John McCain gave it this past year.

And given its isolation, it is also important to know that for a smallish sort of university, Colgate has a variety of athletic opportunities and facilities. Indeed, it's no secret that Colgate prides, if not defines, itself by its tradition of combining excellence in academics with excellence in athletics. "The combination of Division I athletics and very bright and socially well-rounded students is what makes Colgate a special, if not unique, school — it is this combination which is its signature," says one professor. "Some of my students may be Division I football players, but still they take difficult classes and never ask the question that I most abhor, 'Will this material be on the exam?'"

The university fields twenty-three NCAA Division I varsity teams. Approximately 17 percent of Colgate students participate in varsity programs, while almost 16 percent of the student body participates in almost thirty demanding club sport programs in areas as diverse as alpine skiing, figure skating, martial arts, water polo, and weight lifting. There is also a thriving intramural sports program in which more than 70 percent of the students participate. The university has a gymnasium with a large and superbly outfitted fitness center, a pool and diving complex with a retractable roof and saunas, as well as an ice rink, a trapshooting range, a bowling alley, and an excellent championship golf course (one of the top five among college courses). On nearby Lake Moraine, the university maintains a boathouse. There is also a very active "outdoor education program" that offers recreational activities like backpacking, white-water rafting, rock climbing, and training in wilderness medicine.

Besides athletics and the fraternities, the most important way students escape the confines of upstate rural New York is through participation in Colgate's wide variety of off-campus study groups. These programs offer students the opportunity to live and study abroad or, in the case of the oldest and one of the most highly regarded groups, to live and work in our nation's capital. Each study group is different, with some stressing drama, religion, literature, and the arts, while others focus on science, business, or history. Located in regions as far flung as the Caribbean, Australia, Japan, France, and Russia, they allow students to earn college credit while seeing and getting to know another part of the world and its people.

Back on campus, housing is guaranteed for all four years. Some seniors, however, opt to live off campus and upperclassmen who don't live in Greek houses rent apartments in Hamilton. "Apartment parties are second only to fraternity parties," one student says.

The on-campus options include twelve college houses, eight residence halls, and three apartment complexes. Facilities are coed, with men and women sharing apartments next to each other. The college houses each carry themes around which their residents unite; most are dedicated to a particular ethnic group or political persuasion — uniformly on the left. One house, named for Nobel Peace Prize winner Ralph Bunche, is open to students interested in "world peace." Rather than using the standard university meal plan, its residents have set up a vegetarian cooperative. Another house is called an "ecological living center," where students share household tasks and promote environmental awareness. As one might expect, the theme houses play a minimal role in campus life.

Of the nearly eighty student groups on campus, many are political, but only one might be described as conservative, the College Republicans. Similarly, the university view book lists just four religious organizations: Colgate Jewish Union, InterVarsity Christian Fellowship, Newman Community, and the university church. The university chapel features a stunning pipe organ and is used for orchestra and choir concerts as well as services.

The liberal political groups include the Women's Coalition; Lesbian, Gay, and

Bisexual Alliance; Advocates, a group of gay and straight supporters of the homosexual community; and several multicultural groups. Students for Choice is a pro-abortion advocacy group. Students for Environmental Action (SEA) encourages members and nonmembers to recycle or to use mugs rather than Styrofoam cups — things like that. "The most I have ever seen on campus are posters from the SEA or announcements for the meetings of liberal groups," a student says. "It's not like anyone is in your face on campus. There just isn't anything like that at Colgate."

There are, however, quite a few academic organizations devoted to specific disciplines such as biology or psychology. The view book mentions instrumental and vocal groups, as well as theater and dance troupes. The university operates an FM radio station and a television station, and there are several publications run by students, including the *Maroon,* a satire magazine, a political review, and a literary journal. In short, Colgate's size makes it capable of supporting a wide range of cultural, social, athletic, and academic organizations at a relatively high level of sophistication, but not at such a demanding semi-professional level that students would be incapable of participating in more than one at a time.

University of Colorado at Boulder

Office of Admissions
Campus Box 30
Boulder, CO 80309-0030
(303) 492-6301
www.colorado.edu

Total enrollment: 25,125
Undergraduates: 20,595
SAT ranges (Verbal/Math): 520-620 (V); 530-640 (M)
Applicants: 14,075
Accepted: 85%
Enrolled: 36%
Application deadline: February 1
Financial aid application deadline: April 1
Tuition: resident: $3,210/$8,698; non-resident: $16,392/$21,880
Core curriculum: No

Taking (Birken) Stock

Granola, latte, Birkenstocks — these are just some of the items that compose the grunge culture of Boulder, Colorado. The twenty-five thousand students who attend the University of Colorado at Boulder are generally satisfied with the university's laid-back atmosphere and bucolic setting. Located on a stunning 600-acre campus at the foot of the Rocky Mountains, CU–Boulder has much to recommend itself to outdoor enthusiasts.

Unfortunately, the academic landscape of the university is not as inspiring as its natural surroundings. CU–Boulder has embraced most of the deleterious trends in higher education, from radical environmentalism to a pervasive "multicultural" agenda. All students must take a course in "cultural and gender diversity," and several other requirements are also politicized. There remain pockets of excellence at this large institution, though traditional students must navigate carefully through an undergraduate curriculum littered with lightweight and politically motivated courses.

Academic Life: Dragging a Boulder up a Hill

CU–Boulder consists of seven undergraduate colleges and schools: arts and sciences, business administration, education, engineering and applied sciences, architecture and planning, journalism and mass communication, and music. More than two-thirds of the 20,595 undergraduates enroll in the College of Arts and Sciences, which offers more than sixty areas of study.

Students in this college must attain intermediate-level proficiency in a foreign language, pass two writing courses, and complete courses in both "critical thinking" and "quantitative reasoning and mathematics." The college also has a set of distribution requirements that eschews the standard topical names for "content areas." These include "historical context," "cultural and gender diversity," "United States context," "literature and the arts," "natural sciences," "contemporary societies," and "ideals and values." Most areas' requirements can be met with one course; however, literature and arts requires two, and natural sciences, four.

The goal of the content areas, as stated in the catalogue, usually has something to do with "critical thinking" or "critical evaluation," often with the implicit or explicit objective of undermining or questioning previously held beliefs. For example, the "ideals and values" description states that "ideals and values have usually been determined by long-standing tradition and fixed social practices." Later, the catalogue says the course in this area "will also require consideration of approaches by which value systems are constructed, justified, and applied, especially in regard to the personal, societal, and in some cases cross-cultural contexts." In the "contemporary societies" requirement, students are supposed to develop "new vantage points from which to view their own socio-cultural assumptions and traditions."

However, the curriculum seems predisposed to treat non-Western values less harshly. The general description of the "cultural and gender diversity" area centers on expanding "the range of a student's understanding" and introducing him to "the commonality and diversity of cultural responses to universal human problems."

The saving grace of these requirements is that, occasionally, courses that fulfill them do not carry the ideological impetus ascribed to the requirement. One student, for instance, says a course in ancient and modern democracy (which met the "ideals and values" content area) "was my favorite class." However, some politicization is inescapable: the "cultural and gender diversity" requirement can be fulfilled only with a course in non-Western culture or gender studies. "The feminists are unhappy because students tend to choose the 'culture' rather than the 'gender,'" a professor says. And the more liberal faculty are not satisfied with a single diversity requirement. As one ethnic studies professor, commenting in the campus press, said, "The curriculum is very Euro-American. . . . Students should be taking these [diversity] classes throughout their entire academic trajectory, not just one course."

There is a chance that CU's distribution requirements will soon be changing to some extent, scrapping the old atypical division of courses into areas like "contemporary societies" and "ideals and value" for a more usual division of arts and humanities, social sciences, and natural sciences. But as of this writing the proposed changes have yet to be approved.

With more than 1,400 courses available, picking the distribution courses can be extremely difficult, especially for those who want more traditional course offerings in order to piece together something like a genuine liberal arts education. Such a selection would be difficult even in the "United States context" area; there are few broad survey courses but quite a few specialized, politicized options like "Introduction to Asian-American History" or "Chicano History." The "critical thinking" area can be met with something like "History of Women in Progressive Social Movements."

Many CU–Boulder students rely on student evaluations posted by the university on the Internet when choosing distribution courses. Unfortunately, this process seems to push the faculty toward easy grading and pedagogical theatrics in order to get solid reviews from students. The evaluations have a decidedly political agenda: in addition to rating how much they liked the course, students also assess the professor's coverage of women's and minority issues.

Students will do well to look for these professors: E. Christian Kopff in classics, David Gross and Patricia Limerick in history, Thomas Cech in chemistry, and emeritus professor Edward Rozek in political science. Sociology chairman Gary Marx was recently named a fellow of the Woodrow Wilson Center at the Smithsonian Institution to continue his research on the social implications of new information technologies.

Despite the politicization of many departments and faculties, several departments remain solid. The sciences are generally very good at CU–Boulder; Professor

Cech won the 1989 Nobel Prize in that discipline. The physics department is also considered strong by several students. Some humanities faculty, however, seem unhappy with the disproportionate emphasis on the sciences at the university. "The scientists support the school with federal grants, so basically, anything they want, they get," says one professor. Humanities receive much less outside support, and thus less from the university itself, according to professors.

Among these humanities departments, few are distinguished. "There are a lot of people very committed to mainstream teaching in English and American history," says one professor. Economics is about "average," according to another. However, the most popular departments, psychology and environmental studies, are not well recommended by traditional faculty. English is described as "weak and chaotic" by one professor, though this person adds that "if you're intelligent and resourceful you can make your way through — just ask around to find good professors." One English professor remarked glumly, "If we believed in truth in advertising, we would change the department's name to 'Cultural Studies.'" Political science is considered a radical department by several faculty.

Even a strong teaching department like history, which offers many Western history courses and does well in its ancient Greek and Roman classes, has courses like "Lesbian and Gay History: Culture, Politics, and Social Change in the United States." In that course students investigate "lesbian/gay identity formation, community development, politics, and 'queer' cultural resistance." The economics department has quite a few courses in traditional subdisciplines like "Theory and History of Economic Thought," "Money, Banking and Public Finance," "International Trade and Finance," "Economic History and Economic Development," and "Quantitative Economics," but also covers emerging areas such as "Natural Resources and Environmental Economics." And with more than four dozen faculty members in the English department, specialties and course offerings span the theoretical and disciplinary spectrum. The department, according to one professor, has about "a dozen good professors," but has an equal number of faculty members with specialties in gay and lesbian studies, feminist and cultural studies, and gender studies.

In general, multiculturalism affects much of the Boulder campus, particularly the School of Education, which has a strong reputation in the state but is considered a "big joke" by at least one student. The school is home to the BUENO Center for Multicultural Education, which houses a special Equity, Diversity, and Education Library for elementary and secondary school teachers. The goal of the center, which receives significant funding from the U.S. Department of Education, is to promote "quality education with an emphasis on cultural pluralism." The university also has programs in Afro-American, American Indian, Asian-American, and Chicano studies, all connected to the university's Center for the Study of Ethnicity and Race.

Several programs can land students in smaller, less politicized classes. One is the President's Leadership Class, a two-year program of lectures and recitations for selected students. One student, who landed an internship at the state capital through the program, notes that it serves as a "good way to have a small community in a big place." There is also a small university-wide honors program, in which classes are limited to fifteen students. An honors program member says most of the distribution requirements can be fulfilled through the program. Students can also graduate with departmental honors, which usually requires a senior thesis. There are several in-state internship opportunities, and a fair number of students also opt for programs abroad, though one student says overseas internships (rather than simply studying abroad) have become more popular of late. "You feel like you're not being frivolous," she notes.

When asked to characterize the students, one professor says that "they have a very strong commitment to looking good and skiing." But there are opportunities for solid intellectual advancement at CU–Boulder for talented and motivated students. "The best students are well taken care of," a professor says. "If you're an average student, you're on your own." According to university figures, less than a third of students ranked in the top 10 percent of their high school classes, though 70 percent were in the top quarter.

Political Atmosphere: A Rolling Boulder Gathers No Moss

Persistent, general criticism from faculty and administrators, followed by a 5-4 vote by the university board of regents against asking for her resignation, forced CU president Judith Albino to step down in 1995. Her successor, John Buechner, had been chancellor of the university's night school in Denver. He was forced to step down in 1999 when the campus paper, the *Colorado Daily*, showed that he was paying a thirty-something consultant with no educational experience over $100,000 per year while he "consulted" with her over Valentine's Day weekend at a Washington, D.C., hotel. Even before this story broke, his administration had been described as a "disaster" by one faculty member. It remains to be seen how the new president of the CU system, Elizabeth Hoffman, will work out. The former provost and vice chancellor of the University of Illinois at Chicago, Hoffman was responsible for recruiting the controversial Stanley Fish to be a dean at the school.

A year before the vote on Albino, the board of regents rejected the university's recommendation of tenure for an associate professor of English who specialized in erotic literature. The professor, who taught creative writing and lacked a Ph.D., had authored two books on the use of obscenity in literature. "The people that put me in office would not think that his specialty is very essential to liberal arts education," one regent told the *Chronicle of Higher Education*. "We get enough out of that from *Playboy*." Faculty denounced the decision as a severe breach of academic freedom, and the regents, described by one professor as "Republican but spineless," ultimately reversed their decision.

The state of Colorado has not adopted anti–affirmative action measures such as California's Proposition 209, but a similar bill was considered in 1997. The bill would have officially ended the state's consideration of race and gender in all hiring, educational, and contracting decisions. Although some CU–Boulder students expressed support for the bill, many more rallied outside the state capitol to protest the measure, which they said would devastate the minority student population at CU–Boulder. In any case, the bill was killed in the state legislature.

In 1999, the regents narrowly defeated a "diversity resolution" that would have included sexual orientation in the school's diversity statement. Though diversity is an oft-heard phrase on campus, one professor may not be exaggerating as much as the CU administration would like to believe when he says, "You can count the black faculty and staff on the fingers of both hands, even if you are Captain Hook."

The Black Student Organization has lobbied the university on curriculum matters, and claims that "one of the things we worked on recently was getting the university to diversify the history requirement of the school's core curriculum, which only included courses on European history," according to the *Multi-cultural Student's Guide to Colleges.* (The assertion is not true; the "historical context" course list, though weighted toward Western history, includes courses in Latin America, Sub-Saharan Africa, China, and Japan.)

The most politically active group on the predominantly liberal campus is the Young Democrats Club. There is also an active homosexual group, the Lesbian Bisexual Gay Transgendered Alliance. Yet most students are not involved in political issues, preferring instead their academic and extracurricular pursuits. "There's definitely an individualistic tendency here," says one student.

CU–Boulder has a full calendar of campus speakers — "about three or four speakers every night," according to one student. "There are always signs all over the place." Liberal speakers outnumber conservative ones by a wide margin; recent guests include Dave Foreman, founder of Earth First!; the princess of Burma; and Secretary of the Interior Bruce Babbitt, who spoke on the threat of global warming.

Student Life: Tap the Rockies

Founded in 1876, the CU–Boulder campus boasts many architectural attractions, including the oldest building, Old Main, and many others built in the North Italian Renaissance Style. Freshmen are required to live on campus, and about half elect to stay there for their sophomore year. The residence halls feature a number of special academic programs, which allow students majoring in the same discipline to live together and take some courses in the dorm itself. Unlike those on many campuses, the halls are, for the most part, built in the same beautiful architectural style that marks the rest of campus; some even feature flagstone floors and stone fireplaces. All the halls are coed, with some housing men and women on separate floors, and others on the same floor but in separate wings. There are always separate bathrooms for men and women. "Substance-free" housing is available.

Most upperclassmen move to apartments, although finding one can be frustrating. "Boulder has an ordinance so it can't grow outward," says one student. There is also a four-story height restriction on city buildings. "This is a good thing, because they want to keep the open space around the city, but it makes apartments expensive and difficult to find," the student says. "Every year, the price goes up and the quality goes down."

Even without apartment rent, Boulder is a relatively expensive city. "But the quality of living is good," says a student. Numerous restaurants and shops are within easy reach of campus, including "The Hill," an area where students can get away for a cup of coffee. There is also the Pearl Street Mall, a ten-block pedestrian area. But, according to one undergraduate, "Students don't really hang out there — it's more for the community."

Outdoor pursuits top the list of extracurricular activities among CU–Boulder students. Hiking, mountain biking, and skiing are extremely popular. "It's about a five-minute walk to the mountains," a student says, exaggerating only slightly. "That's probably why a lot of people come here." (About one-third of the student body is from outside of Colorado, but that group represents all remaining states plus eighty foreign countries.) There are numerous outdoor-oriented student organizations, including cycling, flying, and soaring clubs. Not surprisingly, CU–Boulder is also home to many environmental and animal rights groups, including Sinapu, a grassroots organization dedicated to reintroducing the wolf to Colorado. According to the campus press, the organization receives twenty-nine cents per student, which it uses in part to fund wilderness internships that get students involved in conservation efforts. The group has met with resistance from local ranchers, who say wolf reintroduction will devastate their cattle populations.

Those students interested in indoor social pursuits will find informal clubs for each major, as well as Mortar Board, a senior honors group that has been active in community service projects such as a children's literary festival and visits to a senior citizens' home.

When it comes to organized athletics, football is by far the most popular sport. The Buffaloes ("Buffs," to fans) compete in the Big Twelve Conference at the NCAA Division I level. Women's basketball and volleyball have also attracted attention recently, and the university typically competes for NCAA ski championships, battling other skiing campuses like Utah and Vermont.

Greek organizations flourish on campus, often to the dismay of the administration, which doesn't care for the heavy drinking and partying that go on at some fraternities. In 1995 the fraternities banned beer at social events, but allowed members to continue to drink in their rooms. "Colorado is the first campus to go that far in combating alcohol abuse," noted an article in the *Chronicle of Higher Education*. But, apparently, alcohol abuse continued largely unabated, and in the spring of 1997 hordes of partying students in the University Hill section of town (home to fraternities, sororities, and student apartments) got out of control. Police were dispatched after fights broke out and a bonfire was started in the middle of the street. According to the *Chronicle,* police were attacked by four hundred students and had to use tear gas and rubber bullets to disperse a crowd of 1,500, many of whom were "throwing bricks, looting parking meters, and setting fires."

Some students said they were protesting a recent campaign by the university to crack down on alcohol abuse at parties, while others suggested that a large percentage of the crowd were not members of fraternities or sororities, and were not even CU–Boulder students. Both the administration and the Interfraternity and Panhellenic Councils hoped a new alcohol ban would help curb student drinking and preclude similar riots in the future. In an effort to reverse the university's reputation as a party school, the administration also announced it would suspend students who provide alcohol to minors. This decision outraged many students; as one undergraduate told the campus paper, "I think they've extended their bounds. . . . It's like Big Brother — they're out of their jurisdiction." One hopes this student was not considering a career in law. Cooperation between Boulder police and the university administration has resulted in scores of citations against fraternity members, although one police sergeant noted, "Drinking is not just a Greek issue; it's a student issue." In any case, the ill will and tension has not abated. More rioting broke out in the fall of 1999 after police broke up Halloween parties; $100,000 in damage was the result.

Other than alcohol-related crime, Boulder is a fairly safe place, though the campus's reputation does attract a number of drifters and junkies. Drugs are a relatively big part of the Boulder scene.

Many of the organized campus activities revolve around multicultural celebrations (Chicano History Week or Red Nations Cultural Unity Awareness Week, for example). The university also recently began an annual "disability cultural forum" that brings together poets, writers, activists, and artists to "celebrate and raise awareness of disability culture," thus adding another element to the growing body of victimization studies.

Boulder approaches Seattle as a hotbed of grunge music, having sprouted local bands like The Samples and Big Head Todd and the Monsters. The campus has hosted the Gin Blossoms, Blind Melon, and Bush. Those with more refined musical sensibilities will not be disappointed in the university's performance opportunities, which include the Collegium Musicum (an early music group) and an English handbell choir. There are also four facilities for theater and dance productions, although the best time of year for such recitals is the summer, when the city hosts the Colorado Shakespeare Festival and Lyric Theatre Festival.

Columbia University

Office of Undergraduate Admissions
212 Hamilton Hall
New York, NY 10027
(212) 854-2521
www.columbia.edu

Total enrollment: 20,504
Undergraduates: 7,530
SAT ranges (Verbal/Math): 650-760 (V); 650-740 (M)
Applicants: 13,012
Accepted: 14%
Enrolled: 54%
Application deadline: December 15
Financial aid application deadline: February 12
Tuition: $24,794/$32,526
Core curriculum: Yes

Rising with NYC

Columbia is best known, and desired, for two things: its core curriculum and its New York City location. Although the latter might have been a liability a decade or so ago, when New York City was mired in crime and scandal, today both the City and the University have rebounded. In fact, Columbia, which once suffered from a brain drain, can now attract faculty members from other prestigious schools. Academically and physically, it has been rebuilding, and its future looks very bright indeed.

Columbia's dedication to its core curriculum sets it apart from its Ivy League peers, most of which can't seem to decide what every student should know. With its venerable core, Columbia announces that some things must be known by those who attend college. Fellow Ivy Leaguer Brown University, for example, doesn't even impose distribution requirements on its students, let alone construct a standard set of classes on Western culture. There is a considerable difference between a university that says "learn this" and one that says "learn whatever floats your boat."

Not that Columbia is immune to multiculturalism or political correctness — its location in New York City guarantees exposure to winds from many directions. Some politicized classes have indeed entered the curriculum. Columbia's students tend to define themselves along racial lines; gay and feminist groups dominate much of the political discourse on campus. Students at Columbia pride themselves on challenging the status quo, a tradition that dates back to Vietnam War demonstrations. But overall, commitment to the liberal arts tradition has survived better at Columbia than at most places, and much of this is due to the abiding core.

Administrators constantly talk of "revising" and "updating" the core, and a few years ago they did add a foreign cultures requirement. The common curriculum has undergone a number of minor revisions, but today it remains roughly as it was first conceived in 1919. At a time when many schools are desperately searching for ways to make education "relevant," Columbia can rest assured that its core provides its students with knowledge that is both timely and timeless.

Academic Life: Holding the Line

The largest undergraduate unit of Columbia University is Columbia College, which enrolls approximately 3,500 students. The heart of Columbia College's curriculum — which all 3,500 students must take — is the core. It represents a commitment to undergraduate education by a major research university. And if a senior faculty member is correct, this trend may continue: "I suspect that in ten years Columbia will be more oriented toward undergraduate life than it is now and less involved in graduate teaching," this person speculates.

The one constant trait of the core is that it is always under revision — the course list has been altered several times in the last few decades. However, the list still does much to introduce students to important aspects of Western civilization. The university describes the core as its "signature, its intellectual coat of arms." According to the catalogue, the courses in the core "attempt to explore what it means to be human and to provide all Columbia students, regardless of their major or concentration, with a lively inheritance of Western literature, philosophy, history, music, and art."

Core courses are taught in seminars limited to about two dozen students. Each course has a standard reading list, although instructors are allowed a little leeway to inject materials that fit their academic interests. Students are supposed to complete the core by the end of their sophomore years. Says a professor, "Columbia undergraduates today are innately more talented than [my Ivy alma mater's] undergraduates of my era, but perhaps not as well prepared in some specific subjects (history in particular) as those of my generation were."

Core courses, along with some others, are sometimes taught by graduate students. "Columbia makes extensive use of T.A.s to teach sections in lecture courses, but only in rare cases do T.A.s teach courses independently," this source reports. "Except for the core curriculum, part of which is taught by advanced graduate students, all courses for freshmen and sophomores at Columbia are taught by members of the faculty, senior and junior," this person continues.

The catalogue states: "As a result, these courses are, in the best sense, the most practical that Columbia students take: the skills and habits honed by the core — observation, analysis, argument, imaginative comparison, respect for ideas and nuances — are nothing less than a rigorous preparation for life as an intelligent citizen in today's world."

"Contemporary Civilization" first appeared in Columbia's curriculum in 1919 as a course on war-and-peace issues. It has been revised extensively since then, and today this year-long course focuses on the relation of individuals to the state and society, the problems of morality, and "the constructions of concepts like the economy, race, and gender." Students read Plato, Aristotle, Augustine, Machiavelli, Hobbes, Locke, Rousseau, Kant, Smith, Marx, Darwin, Nietzsche, and Freud.

Three core courses are dedicated to the humanities. "Literature Humanities," also a year-long course, was originally designed in 1937. Intensive readings range from Homer, Sophocles, and Euripides to the Bible, Dante, Goethe, and Shakespeare. "Music Humanities" and "Art Humanities," both semester courses, introduce students to the major works and movements in Western art and music. Both make use of the vast resources of New York City's museums and concert halls.

"Logic and Rhetoric" is designed to complement the other core courses. The only text, according to the catalogue, is the students' own writing. Each section has no more than twelve students, instantly making this course preferable to the cattle call style of freshman comp classes offered at many other schools.

The core is popular among students, mainly because they knew what they were getting into before they enrolled in Columbia. "These were all books I wanted to read," says one English major. "Very few institutions offer a type of program like this, and there aren't a lot of people walking around saying, 'This is ethnocentric. Why are we learning the canon?'"

Professors also seem to like the core because they know that all of their students possess a certain body of knowledge. Any lecturer can allude to Dante's *Inferno*, for example, when talking about another subject and be confident that students know what he's talking about. Despite the ongoing revisions to the core, one professor says it remains in roughly the same form it was years ago, though the Middle Ages get less time now and there is more emphasis on feminist topics than in the past. Some younger faculty, the professor says, resent the core for the long, intensive hours of work it necessitates — but not for ideological reasons.

There is some movement on campus to make the core reading lists more inclusive of non-European authors. An assistant professor of Spanish and Portuguese recently told a gathering of Columbia's new Latino studies program that the "Literature Humanities" list should be "flexible and elastic, constantly being revised as the nation changes." Traditionalists at Columbia and elsewhere, however, contend that making a canon "elastic" and "flexible" erodes the meaning of core courses, which are designed to provide students with timeless and lasting insight through the study of the human condition. Says a professor, "In the core, the requirements are very specific, and there is little latitude for individual choice."

In addition to the core, all students must fulfill several distribution requirements. There is a three-course science requirement, to be met with a two-term sequence plus another semester class in a different field. This requirement ensures at least some familiarity with a particular area in science or mathematics.

Additionally, students must demonstrate competency in a foreign language through the fourth-semester level, either via classes or achievement tests. The university offers courses in thirty-three languages.

Beginning with the class of 1998, Columbia instituted what it calls a "major cultures requirement." Students must complete two courses that expose them to different cultures and civilizations throughout the world. They have wide latitude in selecting which courses they will take to fulfill this requirement, which was added because some professors and students thought the Western emphasis of the core was too limited. Such a requirement is not nearly as intrusive at Columbia as at other places since the university does not consider it a substitute for the thorough study of Western culture.

The final general education requirement at Columbia is nonacademic: students must take one year of general physical education courses and be able to swim seventy-five yards without resting.

Columbia has two other undergraduate entities: the School of Engineering and Applied Science and Barnard College. Engineering students are required to take "elements of" Columbia's core along with their own set of scientific courses, according to university literature. However, Barnard, which enrolls 2,200 women, has its own courses, admissions policies, dorms, and diplomas. Barnard women can take some courses at Columbia College, but cross-registration is neither common nor required. All students at the university are allowed to register (provided they are sufficiently prepared) for some courses in other schools, including the renowned Juilliard School of Music and other graduate programs.

Also in conjunction with its graduate and professional schools, Columbia offers accelerated paths to advanced degrees. For example, with approval students can earn a bachelor of arts degree and a law degree in six years. Similar programs exist in engineering, public policy, and international affairs.

Columbia offers qualified students the possibility of spending their junior years studying at Oxford or Cambridge. The university also operates study-abroad programs in Paris, Berlin, and Kyoto, Japan. These latter programs are taught in foreign languages, and most have a language requirement for admission.

Columbia is regarded as having one of the best graduate journalism schools in the country, comparable only to Northwestern. Founded by Joseph Pulitzer in 1902, its goal is to "recognize that journalism is one of the great and intellectual professions," said Pulitzer. "Our Republic and its press," Pulitzer wrote in a 1904 article defending his proposal for a journalism school, "will rise or fall together." In 1984, George T. Delacorte (Class of 1913) expanded the school by endowing the Delacorte Center for Magazine Journalism.

Admission to Columbia is more difficult now than in earlier years. "Columbia has experienced a phenomenal increase in applications in recent years and, along with it, a very noticeable improvement in the already-high quality of our undergraduates," says a professor. "Columbia's admissions process is now more selective than that of any other university's except Harvard and Princeton, although our yield is still lower than Yale's and perhaps others'."

Some of the best professors on Columbia's excellent faculty include Carol Gluck, Sima Schama, Caroline Walker Bynum, Richard Bushman, and Alan Brinkley in history; David Rosand in art history; Elaine Combs-Schilling in anthropology; George Stade, James Shapiro, Andrew Delbanco, Joan Ferrante, and Michael Seidel in English; David Sidorsky in philosophy; Brian Barry in political science; Vijay Modi in mechanical engineering; Richard Brilliant, Joseph Connors, David Freedberg, David Rosand, Stephen Murray, and James Beck in Art History; Samuel Danishefsky in chemistry; James E. G. Zetzel in classics; and R. Glenn Hubbard (who is currently on leave serving in the Bush White House) and Robert Mundell in economics.

Among the best departments at Columbia is physics. Four graduates of this department have won Nobel Prizes in the field, and, in all, twenty-six Nobel winners have been associated with this department as students or faculty. Current professor (and Columbia alumnus) Melvin Schwartz won the Nobel Prize in 1988 and teaches some courses for undergraduates. Scientific advances made at Columbia include the invention of Formica, the smashing of the atom, FM radio, and the element deuterium, according to university literature.

Columbia's department of English and comparative literature is very popular and well known among students for the strength of its professoriate. Because the core familiarizes students with the great works of literature even before they get to English electives, class discussions can be conducted on a high level.

Also excellent is the history department, home to such notable historians as Alan Brinkley and Simon Schama. The department of art history has a long and distinguished reputation and is particularly strong in Renaissance studies.

Other departments start and end with politics. Columbia began a Latino studies department in the spring of 1996 and continues to expand it. Although departmental policies and ideology are still emerging, comments from its director printed in a campus paper indicate that the department's purpose is more political than academic.

Another ethnic-based department, the Institute for Research in African-American Studies, offers a major in African-American studies and other programs that bring speakers to campus. The institute's director, Manning Marable, a self-proclaimed "democratic socialist," led a group of faculty members to Cuba in June 1997 to "examine race and gender issues" in the Communist country. In a university press release, Marable spoke of Cuba in glowing terms. "Cuba has represented metaphorically the ability of an oppressed people to challenge imperialism and colonialism," Marable said. "In the political imagination of black America, Cuba represents the radical possibility of fundamental social change."

The women's and gender studies department at Columbia is also quite politicized, and its interests run to the subdiscipline of gay and lesbian studies. For example, the course "Introduction to Gay and Lesbian Studies" promises to discuss "race, class, gender, religion, and national difference . . . as part of the elaboration of homosexual/lesbian/queer identities." A course called "The Invisible Woman in Literature: The Lesbian Literary Tradition" bills itself as "an interdisciplinary exploration of the lesbian experience." "Women and Science," the course catalogue says, includes "feminist critiques of biological research and the institution of science."

Political Atmosphere: It's a Hell of a Town

The president of Columbia, George Rupp, announced that he will retire at the end of the 2002 academic year. A Presbyterian minister who holds degrees from Princeton, Yale, and Harvard, Rupp was once the dean of Harvard's divinity school. At Harvard, Rupp is credited with spearheading a drive to revise the school's curriculum to "address more directly the pluralistic character of contemporary religious life" and with implementing a women's studies program, according to a Columbia press release. Rupp became president of Columbia in 1993 and raised eyebrows soon after his arrival by replacing some of the university's top deans. Some complained that the steps were taken without proper consultation beforehand with faculty, students, and other administrators; others praised Rupp as a visionary.

Rupp has also helped the university raise $2.74 billion in ten years. With this capital he has improved Columbia's library, built a new business and law building, and established a new undergraduate residence hall, Jewish center, and student center; many other buildings have been remodeled.

The university is currently facing criticism over its new sexual misconduct policy. In 1999, a female student complained about an incident and felt that the administration ignored her. She started a coalition of students and fought for a new, more strict, policy on sexual harassment and assault complaints. She won, but the backlash has been very public, and mostly negative. The *Boston Globe,* for example, saw it this way: "At a time when colleges nationwide feel newly emboldened to replace constitutional due process with their unique brands of discipline, the Columbia policy is seen by some students and civil libertarians as an extraordinary step toward injustice. According to Boston University Chancellor John Silber, the system has elements lifted from a Kafka novel: "No lawyers. No right to face the accuser or listen to witnesses. Complaints can be filed up to five years after the alleged incident. No right to cross-examination, and no recorded transcript of what was said — of the detailed arguments or of the nuances that might influence the jury."

The student newspaper also ran critiques of the new policy. Student Karl Ward writes: "The phrase 'guilty until proven innocent' has never seemed so fitting — the policy as it stands does not state who bears the burden of proof in any allegation. . . . But perhaps the best indictment of the policy has come from the [campus group] Feminists For Free Expression . . . who just this week released a statement condemning it, stating, 'as feminists, we of course applaud the idea of taking sexual assault very seriously and providing for its punishment . . . but it is no service to women to hold that offenses against them require a kangaroo court.'"

The *Globe* reports that Columbia officials, despite the protests, plan to keep the new policy in place and it "will be reviewed regularly. The lack of courtroom-style due process is common in campus judiciaries, they noted, to avoid treating students like criminal plaintiffs and defendants." And columnist Nat Hentoff of the *Village Voice* reported the thesis of an article in the *Columbia Law Review*, of all places, by Vivian Berger and the late Curtis J. Berger, two Columbia Law School professors, that refutes the legal ground upon which the school's reading of contract law, and hence its case, is based. Hentoff complained that Columbia's majority of professors and administrators "who have supported this policy — or remained silent — have taught their students that contracts can be broken and rights trampled for a 'higher good.' And the university's principal teacher, President George Rupp, is in urgent need of a remedial course in fairness with Columbia professor Vivian Berger."

Another recent, public controversy occurred for Columbia when professor Edward Said of the school's English department threw a rock at an Israeli guardhouse from across the Lebanese border. News associations carried a picture of the incident, and there was considerable outcry from some students and faculty. Columbia officials responded in defense of professor Said: "We do not believe in a speech code at Columbia, nor shall we act as a speech police," Jonathan R. Cole, provost and dean of faculties, said in a five-page open letter to the institution's student newspaper and student-government association. "To my knowledge the stone was directed at no one, no law was broken, no indictment was made, no criminal or civil action has been taken against Professor Said."

Yet another problem facing Columbia is what students and faculty call "enlargement and enhancement," which basically means raising tuition and slowly decreasing the number of tenured faculty. "As students here at Columbia we've been witness to the continual growth of the undergraduate student body, while the number of tenured faculty in each department has either stayed the same or decreased," writes student Israel Gordan in the *Spectator*. "But we're all supposed to grin and bear it in overcrowded classrooms, meager course offerings each semester, . . . and diminished advising resources."

Rupp and his administration have also faced strikes by Columbia's clerical workers and support staff. A strike in 1996 disrupted life at Barnard College for five months. Another walkout in October 1997 affected service in Columbia's dining halls, health services, and mail rooms. At issue was Columbia's elimination of many positions and the university's proposed "pay for performance" plan that would have allowed supervisors to reward outstanding employees with monetary bonuses. The union's opposition to the bonus plan was described by one striking employee, who told the *Spectator*: "I'm out here striking because I don't want to see Columbia University return to a racist, sexist, merit-pay system."

Many students and professors backed the union. Professor Eric Foner, a specialist in labor history, and a group of faculty members began rescheduling and relocating classes to avoid crossing the picket lines. Nearly three hundred classes were moved off campus to coffee shops, bars, and other locations in the city.

The strike ended after two weeks with the university raising the workers' pay by three percent and tabling the controversial merit-pay proposal. The money that had been set aside for bonuses is being used on worker training instead.

Student Life: On and Off Broadway

What is today known as Columbia University began in 1754 as King's College, making it the first college in New York and the fifth oldest in the nation. King's College was renamed Columbia College in 1784, and that became Columbia University in 1896. The university moved in and out of several New York City locations before settling in at its current home along Broadway in the Morningside Heights neighborhood of Manhattan's Upper West Side.

Students say that if you don't like New York, you probably won't like Columbia either. A relatively large number of students transfer out of Columbia because they want out of New York City, but a large number of students transfer to the university for the opposite reason.

This New York attitude seems to affect some students in a negative way. Some lament in the student newspaper about how Columbia can seem very intimidating and lonely, despite the millions of people in the city. Some complain that Columbia's student psychological services are severely lacking. In an editorial in the *Columbia Daily Spectator*, it was noted that six Columbians, some students, some faculty, had died in the past year. "When tragedy strikes, it is not a coincidence that the Columbia undergraduate community begins grumbling about the failures of undergraduate advising and support services, saying this university often seems too cold, too intimidating," the editorial stated. "But the common thread in these complaints is a sense that the people charged with overseeing undergraduate life are not listening and not responding."

The editorial continued: "Students receive psychological support from a system that seems visible only after the death of a classmate. Help is available to those who need it, but we need to examine if it is delivered adequately. We need to look at whether there is enough counseling available before the tragedy, to deal with the normal rigors of a Columbia day. Columbia Psychological Services, while staffed with dedicated professionals, simply does not provide the hours to serve each student's needs promptly. . . . This is one area where the university should make strides in helping its students, no matter the cost."

Nearly all students — 90 percent — live on campus because of the high costs of renting in Manhattan (all freshman are required to do so). Columbia has standard dormitory accommodations, but also has "theme houses" dedicated to a particular topic or culture. Some of these include the Pan-Africa House, the Japan House, and the Art House. All dorms have quiet hours, and many floors are designated as non-smoking, but no dorms have visitation restrictions. Most floors are coed, as are many of the suites and apartments; there are some coed bathrooms as well. There are no single-sex residence halls. Dining facilities on campus are limited, students report, and most leave the university's dining plan after the first year in order to eat off campus.

The social aspects of life at Columbia usually yield to the bright lights and big city. Students say New York mostly overrides university social events, and that life at Columbia isn't as clubbish as it is at more secluded, smaller colleges. While some students join the Greek system (twelve fraternities, six sororities, and four coed fraternities) or take advantage of on-campus movies and speakers, many others go to nearby bars and restaurants — or plays or concerts or sporting events or just about any attraction the city can provide. Students are constantly reminded that they're in a big city. "New York is a huge part of everyone's life," a student says. "Even if you try to avoid it, you're still kind of dealing with it."

Columbia has established agreements with several New York arts organizations that allow students free admission with presentation of their student IDs. Some of these organizations, including the Metropolitan Museum of Art, the Museum of Modern Art, and the Lincoln Center for the Performing Arts, also reserve internship slots for Columbia students.

Being located in New York means Columbia's students are cramped in with the rest of the city. But a major effort to create more space was completed last year, and now the $68 million Alfred Lerner Hall, a student center, provides 225,000 square feet for student organizations, the arts, cultural events, recreation and dining.

Columbia has many different student groups, and there's something for everybody, students say. One of the largest groups on campus is the Black Students Organization (BSO), although several other ethnicity-based groups are present as well, including ones that focus on the cultures of China, Korea, the Philippines, Italy, Thailand, Vietnam, Haiti, Greece, Iran, Armenia, Latin America, and Pakistan. While some say these types of groups encourage separatism among people of different backgrounds at the college, the groups' members say they are necessary to keep their cultures alive.

The most vocally politicized groups are the BSO, International Socialist Organization, and Gay, Lesbian, and Bisexual Coalition. Smaller, quirkier groups are also active at Columbia. A student chapter of the National Organization for the Reform of

Marijuana Laws recently asked Columbia's dorm advisers to "rethink their role" in the enforcement of Columbia's anti-drug policies because the university's policies are "ineffectual and counter-productive." Columbia enforces drug laws instead of referring drug abusers to counseling, the group complained. The letter has had no apparent effect.

Another group called Conversio Virium ("exchange of power") is a university-approved organization that dedicates itself to "discussion, education, and peer support concerning BDSM [bondage, domination, sadomasochism] issues." Literature from the group assures interested parties that it "does not promote, support, or engage in violence of any sort. What it attempts to promote and support is safe, sane, and consensual BDSM play." The group says it recognizes that "these activities can become quite intense and observers may misunderstand," but that "they are actually healthy forms of sexual expression as long as they are done in a safe and mutually consensual manner."

Columbia has traditional student organizations as well. There are campus groups for many faiths, including Baptists, Catholics, Episcopalians, Lutherans, Muslims, Methodists, Presbyterians, and others. There are also chapters of nondenominational religious groups, such as Campus Crusade for Christ and InterVarsity Christian Fellowship. Columbia students publish a monthly nondenominational Christian newspaper, the *Columbia Standard*. The university also employs a university chaplain who coordinates events to unify the Columbia community, such as dinners with leaders of different ethnic groups on campus.

Columbia is home to twenty-two libraries, which combined hold more than 168 million volumes, nearly 4 million microforms, and more than 26 million manuscripts — the ninth-largest academic library in the country. Most students use Butler Library, the research library for humanities and history topics.

As for crime, one student says: "Everything has turned around since Giuliani became mayor. Recent anti-police demagoguery does have the potential to change this, though, and a Democratic mayor could mark a regression back to Dinkins danger." Says another, "I feel extremely safe. I have no problem walking home with my laptop at two o'clock in the morning. Many people here from Berkeley and U. Penn., two real slums, say there is no comparison. But I do think this sort of setting is more conducive to happiness for graduate students than for undergraduates. Although a very green campus, it is not an insular community." Indeed, according to official numbers, crime at Columbia amounts to the same on many other campuses: bike theft, vandalism, public drunkenness, and assault are not uncommon. But only the very naïve would wander about New York City without exercising some caution.

Connecticut College

Office of Admission
270 Mohegan Avenue
New London, CT 06320-4196
(860) 439-2200
www.connecticutcollege.edu

Total enrollment: 1,650
Undergraduates: 1,650
SAT ranges (Verbal/Math): 592-688 (V); 585-676 (M)
Applicants: 4,441
Accepted: 32%
Enrolled: 33%
Application deadline: December 15
Financial aid application deadline: January 15
Tuition: $31,985 (comprehensive fee includes room and board)
Core curriculum: No

The Forest vs. the Trees

Connecticut College is a liberal arts school founded in 1911 as a women's college of the traditional New England style. It has a beautiful campus on a 750-acre arboretum not to mention a healthy endowment and fund-raising programs. Its national reputation has risen steadily over the past several years, both as a result of its own comprehensive strategic plan and because of the increase in the number of applicants. With only 32 percent of applicants admitted, it is one of the more selective colleges in the nation. Situated in New London, it has in recent years reached out to that community in a number of ways as it uses its hometown as something of a laboratory for civic improvement.

But another side of the tale is more disturbing. Like many other schools, Conn College, as it's known, is run by savvy people who know that rising in the rankings systems of national magazines requires repeated kowtowing to the dominant politics of the day. And this Conn College has done with abandon. It has initiated a plan known locally as "Academic Initiative #4: Multiculturalism and Diversity," which in turn has a five-year goal: "To transform the campus community and curriculum to engage more closely the diverse and multicultural society in which we live."

Now, this is the kind of thing we hoped most college administrators would at least be too embarrassed to talk about publicly, and perhaps we should be grateful to Connecticut College's rulers for their candor. But the tired old slogans of the academic left — "the college will accelerate recruitment of . . . students, faculty, and staff of color, with special emphasis on historically underrepresented American racial and ethnic groups" — are considered cutting-edge at Conn College. As outlined below, these directives will receive the money and administrative backing necessary to ensure that one's race and ethnicity are the most significant qualities one possesses, supplanting intellect, accomplishment, honor, and hard work as avenues to success and self-awareness.

The school still employs many superb professors and has a hard-working, intelligent student body. Degrees earned there can open doors to good graduate and professional schools, and students who pick and choose their way through the curriculum can get a very good education. As the quality of students entering the school increases, one can hope that they will be able to discern gold from brass. One will last, the other will tarnish.

Academic Life: Only Sounds Sound

There is no core curriculum at Conn College, which places it firmly in the majority of American institutions of higher learning. Students must take one "foundational course" in each of seven areas, normally by the end of their sophomore year. These areas include: physical and biological sciences (though no lab sequence is required); mathematics and logic; social sciences; critical studies in literature and the arts (not necessarily including the study of Western literature and the arts); creative arts; philosophical and religious studies; and historical studies (no U.S. or Western history necessary).

The distribution requirements have not changed much in the past dozen years. "A few years ago the college added a 'General Education' program, on which the jury is, I think, still out, requiring incoming freshmen to read certain texts in common, attend a certain number of designated events, and meet in tutorials during their first year," says a professor. "Like many such programs, I think it probably sounds better than it is." This person also notes that "The distribution requirement itself . . . satisfies nobody completely but does offer some kind of balance."

The strength of the institution is the humanities. The English and history departments are the two biggest on campus, with enrollment and the number of major numbers steady over the last decade. Government, the third-most popular department, is also well thought of. The college seems to want to improve its science offerings; while botany has always drawn strength from its access to the college arboretum, since the college went coed chemistry, physics, and biology have grown stronger.

Worse off is the gender and women's studies department, which includes the usual selection of ideology-driven selections. One source reports that "the athletics department is in a mess right now from personnel issues," although "overall the athletics program, which promotes maximum participation and does not include a football team, has been one of its best features." This source adds that "Child development, which recently changed its name to Human Potential [Development] or something equally silly, has long been on the administration's hit list and has probably suffered some as a result." One can also find several politicized classes in sociology, a discipline that suffers from the same affliction in departments nationwide.

Among the best professors on campus are William Frasure in government; Robert Proctor in Italian; Robert Askins in botany; George Willauer, Blanche Boyd, and John Gordon in English; Catherine Spencer in French; and Perry Susskind in mathematics. These teachers and, no doubt, others offer the aspiring student an excellent education, at least in their own classrooms. But there are many opportunities for the uninformed student to find politicized classrooms that will fail them in the long run.

There are few teaching assistants per se at Conn College, although qualified seniors may be trained to act as writing tutors. "All senior professors teach undergraduates, on a full-time schedule," says a professor. Another adds that teaching assistants are used almost entirely as lab assistants in the science courses. "Senior professors regularly teach freshmen," says another professor. With a student-teacher ratio of only eleven to one, students have access to senior faculty members and mostly small classes. Introductory courses can be larger, however.

When asked about the quality of freshmen, professors agree with the administration's line that each new year brings more qualified applicants. "Many, including myself, feel that our incoming classes have been improving steadily over the last several years. The admissions office numbers bear out this conclusion." Concurs another: "From teaching freshmen I can also say that they are relatively more committed and capable of a faster pace. In general, their writing is vastly superior [to that of earlier classes]."

Political Atmosphere: No Bones About It

In the tradition of New England liberal arts colleges, Connecticut College is status-conscious, left-of-center, and fairly trendy in its general politics. The administration of President Claire L. Gaudiani, who submitted her resignation in the fall of 2000, has been a mixed blessing for the school. Undoubtedly a superb fund-raiser, she made possible the hiring of good faculty members, the retention of those who might have moved to more prestigious schools, and the rise of the school in national rankings. A dynamic, determined personality, she also made the school more concerned with the health of New London, its home — so much so, in fact, that the faculty opposed her efforts to further involve (some would say mire) the school in town/gown relations.

On the other hand, she and the board have launched a new strategic plan for the school that, though it is not without laudable goals, contains many provisions explicitly designed to appeal to national opinion makers who often reward adherence to trends and chic positions rather than academic rigor. The Connecticut College Comprehensive Strategic Plan has a most ambitious goal: "[It] challenges the traditional assumptions of space, time, and the role of student and faculty. The result is a radically different learning experience that will uniquely prepare students for a lifetime as citizen leaders." There are six elements to this new plan: funded internships; TRIP (Traveling Research and Immersion Program); local/global citizenship; multiculturalism and diversity; new majors, new programs, and emerging areas; and visiting scholars, artists and other distinguished professionals. Every element of the plan has a five-year goal.

The two most telling are the plans for new majors and for multiculturalism. The goal of the former is: "To position the college at the forefront of existing fields and at the juncture of new interdisciplinary fields by identifying the most important emerging fields and subfields of study in the sciences, arts, social sciences, and humanities, by developing program initiatives in them, and by establishing new academic majors and programs in subjects of great contemporary significance." In a school that fails to require its students to take U.S. or Western history, this kind of infatuation with the new — with innovation for innovation's sake — is no surprise. Nor is the emphasis on the contemporary significance of academic study, which is oxymoronic — as if knowledge of the past or of good literature is somehow unconnected with contemporary society in a way that no passing academic fad could ever be.

But the real danger to the academic and social integrity of the school lies in the goal of multiculturalism and diversity, which seeks, in five years, "to transform the campus community and curriculum to engage more closely the diverse and multicultural society in which we live." For here the plans of the more activist members of the administration are clear: the transformation of the school into a bastion of political correctness in which sloganeering and posturing will upend academic achievement as the principal goal of education. It's a shame that more administrators don't try mere quality and rigor as routes to fame and higher rankings.

As stated on the college's Web site, "The goal . . . is to create a campus community that reflects demographic trends and is renowned for its pervasive, interdisciplinary commitment to multiculturalism and diversity. . . . To transform these ideals into reality the college will make significant changes in academic programming, student life activities, hiring, and admissions." This grand scheme to make Conn College into a showcase of modern ideologies will involve hiring faculty members whose job it will be to press forward with the transformation by influencing the departments to which they are appointed. "Because increased multiculturalism and diversity are an institution-wide priority, this initiative proposes securing four additional tenure lines, one allocated to each academic division," the plan states. It continues: "A social scientist writing on racial theory, for example, or a scientist researching environmental racism will thus affect the study of multiculturalism and diversity in her or his own division as well as in American studies." Later the description notes that the social sciences will be the first to be reformed, for they already have "a relatively large number of courses, faculty, and students concerned with multiculturalism and diversity." Senior scholars will be hired "whose work focuses explicitly on issues affecting historically underrepresented racial and ethnic groups in the U.S."

Other appointments (read more money) go to administrators and professors who will owe their jobs to the new scheme and who, therefore, can be relied upon for loyalty to those who hired them. "To complement the academic programming, the college will accelerate recruitment of American students, faculty, and staff of color, with special emphasis on historically underrepresented American racial and ethnic groups." To oversee this and more, a full-time director of multicultural enrollment "will be hired and financial aid will be enhanced for accepted multicultural students in the Class of '04." They will even try to steal such students from other schools (which have their own desperate plans for increasing minority enrollment), much as many rich universities already attempt to pull away minority faculty from their peers. Thus, we've arrived at the time when well-off schools such as Connecticut College actively recruit students from other schools to win bragging rights among opinion makers who consider such things intrinsically good. But what, one might ask, of the fate of those schools from which these students are recruited? Having done the hard work of finding them in high school, they'll lose them to a better offer. We wonder if Conn College will soon find itself victim of a similar policy from, say, that other Connecticut school in New Haven.

Once the students are brought to campus by whatever means, the campus will be transformed to suit what the administration deems to be their needs. "The college will undertake a variety of student life initiatives to integrate more fully the intellectual, physical, and spiritual aspects of the campus community in respect to issues of multiculturalism and diversity." Here the matter goes far beyond race: "Among the initiatives . . . are reconfiguring the chaplaincy as the Office of Religious and Spiritual Life and exploring joint academic and religious/spiritual programming." The next sentence: "The college will hire a part-time staff person to support students on sexual orientation issues." But once the official line of the chaplaincy is changed in this manner, what of those whose religious beliefs require them to disagree strongly with this stance? And just what will be the impact on the curriculum of this element of the plan?

Already the college offers a number of highly politicized classes. There are Sociology 404 "Analysis of Research on Sex and Gender" and Comparative Studies 227, titled "Bodies for Sale: Prostitution in Early Modern and Modern Europe." Film 331, "Representing Gender," is "an examination of the construction of gender in mainstream narrative film in the light of contemporary film theory and criticism. The work of independent women and gay filmmakers to deconstruct this narrative tradition and use the cinematic apparatus to narrate their own experience forms a secondary focus of the course," according to the catalogue. And Gender and Women's

Studies 226, "Structure of Opporession [*sic*], Strategies of Resistance," looks at "the intersections among race, class, gender, sexuality, and national origin within the context of globalization and as sites of both oppression and resistance."

The fear here is that these examples will look tame once the five-year plans are carried out and it will be very difficult to say that Connecticut College pays even passing attention to real liberal arts education.

Student Life: Orienteering

The students and faculty at Conn College form a tight-knit community, as New London is a smallish place and 98 percent of the student body lives on campus. The several orientation programs range from fun to harmful. COOP, for example — Conn's Outdoor Orientation Program — lasts four days, during which time freshmen gather outdoors for bucolic recreation and get-to-know-you sessions. On the other hand, Genesis, a one-day program for minority students, "provides the opportunity for first-year students of color and their parents and guardians to familiarize themselves with the campus and interact closely with each other prior to the arrival of the rest of the first-year students." This program is hosted by the director of the school's Multicultural Center, a mandatory feature on self-proclaimed sensitive campuses. This runs contrary to the undoubtedly strong community spirit of the school because it encourages students to think of themselves as members of groups, introduces them only to students like themselves (no diversity in that), and therefore ensures that their college careers begin with a lesson in groupthink. Yet another orientation program, Odyssey, exists for international students. Students who do not fall into any preconceived category of special attention also attend an orientation designed to "ease the transition to college for the first-year student."

All housing at Connecticut College is coed and all students are required to live on campus unless they are living with their parents, guardians, or spouse within commuting distance of the college. Most of the buildings are attractive stone structures, although several modernist creations also house students. Crime is virtually nonexistent both on campus and in the residence halls.

Several specialty houses exist — again, some legitimate, some very questionable. There's the Cooperative House/Abbey House, in which residents are "responsible for the cooking of meals and the cleaning of the kitchen area on a rotating schedule." Earth House is not made of earth, but rather "allows six students to live in a small residential community in which all of the occupants commit to earth friendly living." Multicultural House/Unity House is both a cultural center and home to just four students. The college also offers housing for languages, quiet living ("Contrary to what some people assume, the quiet house is not boring nor is it an isolated house," the college says), and a substance-free house in which students agree to forgo smoking, drinking, and taking drugs.

The college prohibits underage drinking, although private parties are allowed at designated areas and may serve beer from a single keg. This does not so much prevent underage drinking (a very difficult proposition) as it relieves the college from any responsibility resulting from that. Student organizations are to work with the director of student activities "in determining the appropriate amount of alcohol" to be served, according to college literature. There is a campus bar where one must present valid ID to be admitted. In a letter to parents from the dean of student life, notification is made of Conn College's concern for student safety, whether the threat is fire, alcohol, or drug abuse. This is a laudatory step to ensure parents of the college's concern for students' physical safety.

Three programs stand out in residence halls. Adopt-a-Faculty/Staff brings in professors or college staff members as adoptees for a year, during which time they visit the house frequently and participate in a variety of activities with the residents. Dessert and Dialogue invites a faculty and/or staff member for, well, dessert and dialogue. Dine and Dialogue does the same thing, but with a more substantial repast. All are designed to bring students and faculty or staff together in informal settings.

There are many opportunities for students to enjoy themselves by joining clubs or sports teams. There are club and intramural sports, in which over 75 percent of the student body participates; these include baseball, equestrian, women's rugby, team tennis, coed softball, and coed beach volleyball in the spring. There are also a number of intercollegiate teams, including some rare entries like squash, rowing, sailing, and water polo. Student clubs include a male *a cappella* group, the Co Co Beaux; a film society; and the Conn Artists, billed as "the most electrifying coed *a cappella* group in sports-entertainment today."

Then there are groups that cater to (and encourage) students' other pursuits: SEAL, Students Educating for Animal Liberation; C-Green, an environmental movement organization; and SOUL (Sexual Orientations United for Liberation), the school's gay, lesbian, and bisexual support group. A confidential support group associated with SOUL is BAGAL (Bisexuals and Gays and Lesbians and ?uestioning). It sponsors a drag ball in March and operates a Web site on the college's server that, with a few clicks of the mouse, will quickly take a surfer into the world of gay porn. Links on the site include "The Cool Page for Teen Queers," which offers advice on deciding whether one is homosexual; "Being Out, Proud, and Accepted" (again, aimed at teenagers); and "gay friendly" religions.

The more radical organizations are of course attractive to only a few students. But their presence, and their use of the school's Web domain and facilities, lets prospective students and parents know the parameters of behavior and thought at Conn College. Given the propositions for the future implementation of multicultural plans, things are unlikely to change. Peer pressure, always difficult to resist among youth (and their parents), backed by administrative approval in the name of tolerance, ensures a very liberal student life atmosphere.

Cornell University

Undergraduate Admissions Office
410 Thurston Avenue
Ithaca, NY 14850-2488
(607) 225-5241
www.cornell.edu

Total enrollment: 19,480
Undergraduates: 13,422
SAT ranges (Verbal/Math): 600-700 (V); 640-730 (M)
Applicants: 19,860
Accepted: 34%
Enrolled: 47%
Application deadline: January 1
Financial aid application deadline: February 15
Tuition: $24,852/$32,983
Core curriculum: No

Sailing to Ithaca

Cornell University was founded in 1865 by Ezra Cornell, an inventor who became wealthy by investing in Western Union, and Andrew Dickson White, a New York state legislator. Cornell was an earthy man-of-the-people type, while White was well traveled and elegant, educated at Yale and Oxford. Their idea was to start a school on Cornell's farm in Ithaca for all sorts of studies, and with Cornell's donation of $500,000 and substantial state funds, Cornell became the first school in the nation to be privately endowed and publicly supported. Even today, some of its colleges are public while others are private, a distinction that is reflected in a marked difference in tuition.

Cornell would later join the elite Ivy League, and although its degree does not carry the panache of Harvard or Yale, it is highly regarded by the business community and professional schools. Moreover, New York residents benefit from a very low tuition of less than $10,000 at the school's state-supported colleges.

Unlike a more intimate Ivy such as Princeton, Cornell offers both the benefits and disadvantages of a larger school. On the positive side, Cornell boasts a wide range of excellent departments, from astronomy to agriculture. Its superb science departments are particularly noteworthy given the Ivy League's traditional emphasis on liberal arts. On the other hand, the university's official recruiting publication, "The Big Red Book," actually brags that Psychology 101 is "so popular it's taught in a

2,000-seat concert hall." Nevertheless, 72 percent of Cornell's classes have fewer than twenty students, so a more intimate learning environment is not hard to find.

Unfortunately, the campus has in recent times been bombarded by violent student takeovers of buildings and other distracting pressure tactics by radical students. Worse, the administration has caved in to virtually every multicultural demand, creating a fragmented campus, effectively segregated housing, and a badly politicized curriculum. But students who can sort through the most politically correct academic offerings and withstand the barrage of left-wing campus activism can obtain a quality education at Cornell.

Academic Life: Sailing Through Ithaca

Cornell is widely acclaimed for its fine programs in engineering and the natural sciences, but the liberal arts branch of the university, the College of Arts and Sciences, is not quite as distinguished. Beginning with the events of 1969, when armed black militants took over Willard Straight Hall for three days and demanded the creation of a department of Africana studies as well as a special dormitory for black students, the college began to disintegrate into a hodgepodge of special-interest fiefdoms. Not only do both the dormitory and Africana department persist, but the Arts and Sciences curriculum is now checkered with politically correct courses of questionable academic merit.

The distribution requirements in the College of Arts and Sciences attempt to assure that students receive a well-rounded, broad-based liberal arts education, but one professor calls them "meaningless and arbitrary." The college mandates that its four thousand students take a total of nine courses from five groups: physical and biological sciences; "other science courses"; quantitative and formal reasoning; social sciences and history; and humanities and the arts. Four classes must be selected from the first two groups, with at least one in "other sciences." If students take but one science course during their career, they are permitted to apply up to two credits of "advanced placement" toward this requirement. The other five courses come from the remaining three groups — groups that include courses in women's studies, Africana studies, and Asian studies.

In fact, at least one of the required courses must focus on, according to the university catalogue, "an area or people other than those of the United States, Canada, or Europe." Unless of course it's a course in Native American culture: those do fulfill the diversity requirement. Also required is one course on a historical period prior to the twentieth century. While this requirement could be used (if a student is so led) to study a classical Western author like Shakespeare, Plato, or Dostoyevsky, or artists like Michelangelo or Raphael, many of the courses that meet the "diversity" requirement (called a "breadth" requirement by the university) are among the most politically correct in the catalogue. The classes include "Emotion, Gender, and Culture" and "Sex and Gender in Cross-Cultural Perspective." Empirical data indicates that the requirement may be an attempt by the administration to populate these classes, which are often the least popular. Several years ago, the Cornell dean's office released a study showing that of the 111 courses that drew five or fewer students, most were in women's studies, non-Western languages, or other identity-based areas of the curriculum.

Perhaps the most politically correct courses at Cornell are "Lesbian Personae," "Gay Fiction," and "Radical Democratic Feminisms." "Lesbian Personae" examines how "lesbian desire and identity are historically constructed through narrative." It features "a discussion of desire and performativity" highlighted by mandatory screenings of lesbian films. "Gay Fiction" offers "an overview of male homoerotic narratives in literature and film." Topics include "the gay outlaw, decadence, AIDS and desire, sublimation, and sexual encoding." "Radical Democratic Feminisms" focuses on "socialist feminism, radical democratic pluralism, critical race theory, and radical anti-racist and anti-heterosexist multiculturalism."

On the other hand, there are still many traditional courses left in the curriculum taught by superb professors. Among the best faculty are Jeremy Rabkin and Elizabeth Sanders in government; Gail Fine in philosophy; John Najemy in history; and Patricia Carden in Russian literature.

In the College of Arts and Sciences, the departments of physics, chemistry, and biological sciences are considered excellent. Nobel Prize winner Roald Hoffman teaches in the chemistry department, but laureate Hans Bethe is retired from the physics department and astronomer Carl Sagan has passed away. The College of Agricultural and Life Sciences, one of Cornell's three public colleges, is highly regarded for preprofessional students looking at medical school, vet school, or graduate research in the natural and applied sciences. It also houses many students who wish to study engineering but are attracted to the lower tuition of the agricultural school in comparison with the private engineering school.

The marriage of public and private education is one of Cornell's unique attributes: regardless of which college a student enrolls in, he is permitted to take courses in most units of the university. Thus a student may design his own program of study in engineering, the sciences, or the social sciences by enrolling in the public colleges and earning a degree in agricultural engineering, horticulture, rural sociology, industrial and labor relations, or a host of other fields while still taking many courses through the private colleges. While this mixture of private and public education offers tremendous flexibility for Cornell students, there is an ever-present, if subtle, resentment among the students in the private colleges of engineering, arts and sciences, and architecture over sharing their classrooms with students paying the considerably cheaper public college rates.

One of Cornell's overall academic strengths is its reputation for challenging students. Compared to many other equally and more prestigious schools, grade inflation is relatively rare at Cornell. In fact, like the University of Chicago, the academic difficulty of Cornell combined with its depressing weather have created a substantial student demand for mental health counseling.

An unusual feature of Cornell's academic menu is the School of Hotel Administration, the largest and oldest program of its type in the country. Seniors from outside of the program tend to take advantage of the "Wine and Beverages" course served up by the school, but the hotel program has a fine reputation internationally. For practice, students manage the 150-room Statler Hotel and the adjoining J. Willard Marriott Center. The latter houses most of the classroom space and training facilities, while the former is a working hotel for parents, prospective students, and visiting faculty.

While the hotel school welcomes guests to campus, much of the rest of Cornell has invited multiculturalism to take up residence and the politicization of traditional academic departments is well underway. In particular, the economics department gets low marks from undergraduates and faculty, and anthropology, as at many campuses, is described as "very ideologically charged." The history department has been flooded in recent years with younger faculty known for putting a leftist spin on the past, but a recent graduate says, "History is stronger than English because they still require a lot of writing in the history department." Some professors say that while the university used to be strong in history and literature, now there remains only a smattering of good teachers in the arts college, with no department possessing a sizeable group of them. Moreover, a lack of structure in most colleges and faculty allows faculty to teach whatever they want, resulting in a disorganized curriculum full of marginal courses.

And these courses might not even be well taught: most departments and colleges at Cornell place little stock in teaching ability. It is publications, not teaching skills, according to a full professor, that are given almost exclusive consideration in decisions regarding tenure.

The university has taken some steps to protect faculty members accused of campus misconduct. Many faculty were disturbed after sanctions were imposed on the popular psychology professor James Maas when he was accused of sexual harassment several years ago. Maas was extremely friendly with many of his students; in fact, he frequently gave gifts and invited students to his home to visit him, his wife, and children. But after four of Maas's female students took courses with a notoriously liberal feminist professor human ecology at Cornell, they decided that Maas's gift giving and frequent hugs (even in the presence of his wife) constituted sexual harassment. Maas's suit was dismissed by the New York Court of Appeals in November 1999 on procedural grounds, but the College of Arts and Sciences has faculty approved new guidelines following the incident that give professors greater rights to attorney representation and due process.

Political Atmosphere: Resistance Is Not Futile

Cornell's watershed political event occurred on April 19, 1969, when members of the university's Afro-American Society seized the student union and demanded the creation of an independent black studies program, an investigation into a campus cross burning, and amnesty for AAS members who were sanctioned for previous demonstrations. The administration gave up and gave in, and more than eighty AAS members marched out of the student union the next day, carrying rifles and raising their fists in Black Power salutes. The university didn't even reprimand them. A 1999 book, "Cornell '69: Liberalism and the Crisis of the American University," by University of Wisconsin political science professor Donald Downs (a sophomore at Cornell in 1969), documents how many of the leading black activists then now work at the top levels of law, Wall Street, politics, or universities.

The demonstrators' success after college has apparently not been as inspiring to current students as their misguided takeover has been. Hispanic students took over the administration building for four days in 1993 and were rewarded with both a special dormitory and a program in Latin American studies. The university even seems awed by the protest: on the twenty-fifth anniversary of the incident, it closed Willard Straight Hall and posted a banner stating that the hall is closed to commemorate the "courageous struggle and sacrifice" of the 1969 student agitators. The leader of the group (who during the demonstration said, "The time has come when the pigs are going to die") was elected to Cornell's board of trustees. Now a respected pension fund manager, he has said he wishes the 1969 riot had not occurred — and for that, was promptly vilified by today's Cornell radicals for betraying the cause.

These current radicals have at least moved away from armed resistance. It seems that sex is now the hot "issue" that minority rights were in the Sixties. The Intercollegiate Studies Institute bestowed upon the university one of its "Polly" awards in 2000 in honor of one of the most politically correct outrages on America's campuses during the previous year. The award was earned by this: resident advisors at Cornell hosted a "Roman Orgy" party in a campus dormitory with funding from student fees. While organizers suggested that the party would consist of massages and snacks, it was not long before the clothes started to come off. The RAs helped get everyone in the mood with dimmed lights, incense, and a bowl of condoms. To sum up: tuition money sponsored an orgy, the organizers were not punished, and a student said it was "a very positive and good event," according to the *Cornell Daily Sun*.

Sexual liberation is also the theme at the Cornell University Health Promotion Office. Videotapes available to students include "Safe Sex Shorts," described on their Web site as "an adults-only tape that is a series of erotic and explicit short scenarios that include such how-tos as using a condom." Another video in the library is "She's Safe." Its description reads: "an international collection of PSAs, erotic and safe sex videos. Contains explicit sexual imagery. Safe and fun sexual behavior for woman-to-woman relationships."

Meanwhile, the Division of Rare and Manuscript Collections of the University library continues work on its Human Sexuality Collection. The repository brings together "historically important" erotic and pornographic films so that professors and students can study film erotica. The collection includes such cinematic tours de force as *Caligula* and *Deep Throat*, and curators even took contributions from a decidedly nonacademic source, "the people who own Good Vibrations, a vibrator store in San Francisco."

Another example of the left-leaning environment at Cornell centers around the *Cornell Law Review* during the 1996-97 school year. Citing the fact that the editorial board of the prestigious journal is mostly male, the Cornell administration commissioned a "Gender Study Committee" to ask why there weren't more female officers on the *Review* and to investigate trumped-up charges of misogyny. This all came in spite of the fact that two-thirds of the staff earn their positions by merit — top grades or blindly judged writing skills — while another third is chosen by a form of affirmative action based on a written statement of how they will bring diversity to the staff. Then, the total staff of fifty votes in a secret ballot for the editors. Apparently, the administration could not tolerate the election of males, even through a democratic, merit-based process. And ironically, the *Cornell Law Review,* a typically liberal law journal, is anything but a conservative bastion.

Condemnation based on content is reserved for the *Cornell Review,* an independent newspaper published by conservative and libertarian students. In 1997, bundles of the newspaper were burned by student organizations infuriated by the paper's parody of ebonics. The protest blocked the Quad to traffic for an entire afternoon. Despite photographs that clearly identified those responsible, the administration took no action and declared that the leftist students were engaged in protected free speech. The dean of students blamed the victim (who apparently had different rights to free speech), saying the *Review* "performs a rather negative role on the campus." The students who blocked traffic were in clear violation of the Student Code of Conduct, but the university refused to take disciplinary action against them and even refused an offer from the Ithaca Police Department to help control the demonstration.

On the other hand, the Women's Resource Center, an official entity created by the administration, is more balanced than many of its counterparts at other universities. Although its Web site features links to numerous leftist campus groups such as BRIDGES (Bisexuals Reinventing Definitions of Gender and Sexuality), the site also points visitors to the Cornell Coalition for Life.

Cornell has been an epicenter for the anti-sweatshop movement. Armed with financial support from U.S. labor unions, Cornell student activists held a rally last year with more than two hundred participants and collected more than two thousand student signatures on their anti-sweatshop petition. Cornell is one of three Ivy League schools in the Workers Rights Consortium, an organization founded to monitor so-called abuses of workers in foreign countries.

Cornell has a strong affirmative action policy. In a November 1998 statement backing the use of racial and gender preferences in admissions, President Hunter Rawlings opined, "The benefits of affirmative action accrue not simply to the individuals for whom opportunities are expanded, but to the entire university community, which derives much of its vitality from the perspectives of different cultures, races, and individual points of view."

Student Life: Separate, but Separate

Cornell gets high marks for the quality of its facilities and the beauty of its grounds — despite the customary cold weather and overcast skies. Ithaca is located in the center of New York and borders the Cayuga Lake, one of the scenic Finger Lakes. Each of the seven colleges and schools has its own classrooms, libraries, and student gathering areas. In all, Cornell has nineteen libraries housing more than 5.5 million books. The six thousand students who play recreational sports enjoy the first class athletic facilities on campus, including an eighteen-hole golf course designed by Cornell graduate Robert Trent Jones Sr. Interestingly, the university's soccer field sits atop a quarter-mile-round atom smasher. At Schoellkopf Hall, a massage therapist provides half-hour and hour massages by appointment to students, employees, and visitors.

Ithaca has around thirty thousand permanent residents, but caters to a large student population, as Cornell and Ithaca College combined double the nonstudent population. As such, restaurants, pizza parlors, coffeehouses, video stores, and other student haunts are plentiful. Crime, fortunately, is not. Students generally have good reason to feel safe in town and on campus.

Ithaca is four hours to New York City by car and about three hours to Albany or Buffalo. Syracuse is only an hour away and offers the nearest Amtrak station and jet airport. However, U.S. Airways Express provides nonstop propeller plane service from Ithaca to New York La Guardia and its Philadelphia hub.

The pleasant setting of the campus, however, is marred by Cornell's policy of racially segregated housing. The black student dorm, Ujamaa, is by far the largest such house, and Hispanics and Native Americans also have the option to live in separate facilities. As a result, the vast majority of the black students are concentrated on the north side of the campus while the west campus has always been overwhelmingly white. Perhaps because they have not yet mounted an assault on a campus building, gay students do not yet have their own dorm. We aren't really kidding about that: a student leader of the Hispanic dorm told the *New York Times* gay students "haven't presented enough of a threat to the university" to get their own residence.

In the 1999-2000 academic year, Cornell embarked on a new initiative to "reconstruct and reconceptualize" the residential environment. In addition to separate housing for freshmen, which is now being built, a committee of faculty members, administrators, and students has been charged with devising ways to create a unified living-and-learning experience for sophomores, juniors, and seniors, regardless of their major. The goal is to offer undergraduates opportunities for close daily contact with faculty members and graduate and professional students, by offering residence-based classes, seminars, class sections, and study groups, as well as advising and career services in the residences. Faculty members and graduate students will live and eat in the dorms. This initiative emphasizes that learning and intellectual inquiry are not limited to classroom interactions.

However, this initiative will not involve a reassertion of the university's *in loco parentis* function, according to Glenn C. Altschuler, professor of American studies and dean of the School of Continuing Education and Summer Sessions at Cornell, and Isaac Kramnick, a professor of government at Cornell. They write that "Cornell professors have expressed little interest in being moral tutors, let alone moral police, in undergraduate residences. Each spring the Cornell administration attempts to convince faculty members to patrol the campus during the annual Slope Day celebration to help crack down on underage drinking. Each year, only a few faculty members agree to play this role." Altschuler and Kramnick, who are in favor of bringing faculty into the student residences, conclude that the university need not concern itself with acting in place of students' parents and that to expect this would stifle other student-faculty interaction outside the classroom.

Instead, the residence staff has taken to acting just plain *loco*. Orientation at Cornell has become infected with political correctness. The new freshman orientation session assigns students to racial, ethnic, and gender groups for separate instruction. Orientations for peer counselors and resident assistants are dominated by political agendas, the merits of which are not open for debate. One resident assistant who complained about explicit pornographic videos shown at housing staff orientation was told that he had to recover from latent homophobia.

Given this sort of atmosphere, Cornell's website is exceptionally accurate in referring to its two all-female residence halls as "throwback[s] to bygone times." Visitors to these halls are even asked to abide by the old-fashioned tradition of having an escort throughout the building. There are also two residence halls exclusively for men. The rest of the residence halls offer a variety of living options, including some coed floors.

Student organizations at Cornell include Association for Students of Color, Breaking the Silence Collective, Campus Green Vote, Christian Fellowship, Coalition For Life, Coalition for the Homeless, College Republicans, Cornell Democrats, Democratic Socialists of America, Feminist Action League, Direct Action To Stop Homophobia, and the Secular Humanists of Cornell. Cornell also has a student chapter of Movimiento Estudiantil Chicano de Aztlan (MECHA). MECHA advocates returning Texas, New Mexico, Arizona, and California to Mexico and works to combat the oppression Mexicans have suffered at the hands of the white *gringo* and *gabacho* (garbage).

On the other hand, perhaps the most innocuous student organization at Cornell is the International Association of Camel Breeders, a reflection of the agricultural school at Cornell, which is one of the university's public colleges.

Student publications at Cornell include the aforementioned conservative *Cornell Review,* the liberal *Cornell Perspective,* the humorous *Cornell Lunatic,* and the mainstream *Cornell Daily Sun,* the only morning paper in Ithaca and the starting point in the careers of E. B. White, Kurt Vonnegut Jr., Thomas Pynchon, and Dick Schaap.

Cornell's fraternities and sororities attract one-third of the students.

Cornell has much to offer, especially to students seeking a degree in scientific and technical fields in an Ivy League environment. Among the Ivies, its relatively large size, academic standards, faculty reputation, and degree marketability are comparable with the University of Pennsylvania. However, in contrast to the urban and notoriously dangerous setting of Penn, Cornell is perched in bucolic upstate New York. While the maelstrom of politically correct attacks on academic and student life are anything but tranquil, Cornell continues to enjoy a fine reputation and to provide some of the more practical fields of study in the Ivy League.

University of Dallas

Office of Admissions
1845 E. Northgate
Irving, TX 75062
(800) 628-6999
www.udallas.edu

Total enrollment: 3,211
Undergraduates: 1,184
SAT ranges (Verbal/Math): 575-680 (V); 540-650 (M)
Applicants: 1,213
Accepted: 76%
Enrolled: 33%
Application deadline: February 15
Financial aid application deadline: Rolling
Tuition: $15,188/$20,972
Core curriculum: Yes

To the Core

The University of Dallas is not well known in higher education circles. Even among some Dallas-area residents it is best known as an alternative parking lot for Cowboys games at Texas Stadium. But this is not as it should be. The University of Dallas offers an impressive, rigorous curriculum, employs excellent faculty, shapes its students to be serious, committed, and responsible, and, in short, represents the best in Catholic higher education.

Founded in 1956, UD has managed to accomplish this feat with a small endowment of just $40 million. Indeed, the biggest challenge facing the school over the years has been a lack of funds, and President Msgr. Milam Joseph was hired several years ago with a mandate to improve the school's financial status. Msgr. Joseph has tripled the school's marketing and public relations staff, and in October of 1999 he launched a capital campaign to raise $104 million by 2010. At the same time, his efforts have sparked some suspicion and controversy among students and professors who believe that the administration's commitment to bring in large donors and raise the school's profile may come at the expense of fidelity to the school's liberal arts mission.

Whatever friction may exist between the administration on the one hand and the faculty, students, and alumni on the other, the school's atmosphere remains unique. "There is a quiet devotional life here that gives the school a lot of its character as well as a wonderful critical thoughtfulness," a professor says. Students say that Dallas is "warm and open," and that the school "teaches you what true freedom is, the freedom to make good choices." And though alumni admit that a degree from Dallas doesn't necessarily turn the heads of employers or graduate schools ("only alumni know its true value," says one grad), they typically express nothing but satisfaction with their decision.

"I think it may be the best education currently available," says a professor. "There are so many superior faculty here, and so many wonderful students, that as long as they and the core are in place, few colleges or universities can rival the intellectual energy and seriousness of UD."

Academic Life: Uncommon Common Learning

The centerpiece of the University of Dallas education is the core curriculum. Both the faculty and the students rave about the core as at once the best thing about the university and its defining feature. Though according to one professor, there is a "current worry that there are forces at work that may want to get rid of the core," if the faculty and students have anything to say about it, the core is in no danger. The first school accredited by the American Academy for Liberal Education, a group committed to recognizing schools that have solid liberal arts curricula, Dallas boasts

235

a solid core curriculum taken by all students during their first two years, regardless of their majors. The last two years of study are devoted primarily to courses in the major, with some elective credits left for students to use as well. Besides traditional majors, students may complete one of Dallas's preprofessional or dual degree programs (e.g., pre-dentistry or a joint BA/MBA program); additional concentrations (e.g., in journalism or medieval and renaissance studies) may also be added.

The core consists of twelve hours in philosophy, twelve in English, nine in math and fine arts, six to eight in science, twelve to fourteen in ancient and modern languages, six in American civilization, six in Western civilization, three in politics, three in economics, and six in theology. All told, there are more defined hours in Dallas's core curriculum than there are in certain *majors* at other schools. Students have some leeway within these requirements, but not much. Nor do they feed on insipid "survey" courses. All students, for instance, take the Literary Tradition sequence: the same four English classes in the same order. In the first course, students engage in intensive study of classical epic poetry by reading *The Iliad, The Odyssey, The Aeneid, Beowulf,* and *Sir Gawain.* The second course concentrates on the Christian epic poem (especially Dante, Milton, Coleridge, and Eliot), the third on dramatic tragedies and comedies (including the Book of Job, Aeschylus, Euripides, and Shakespeare), and the fourth on the modern novel (including Melville, Dostoyevsky, Joyce, and Faulkner). By the end of this sequence, Dallas students have a far better grounding in the literary heritage of the West than do most Ivy League graduates — or, in all likelihood, some professors.

Many of the same themes and authors are encountered from a different perspective in the three common philosophy courses, entitled "Philosophy and the Ethical Life," "Philosophy of Man," and "Philosophy of Being." Here students tackle the foundational philosophical texts of Plato, Aristotle, Augustine, Aquinas, Kant, Nietzsche, and Heidegger, among others. Not even the American and Western Civilization courses succumb to textbook treatments: students read instead works like Ben Franklin's *Autobiography,* Frederick Douglass's *Narrative,* and *The Education of Henry Adams* in the American civ sequence and Thucydides' *History of the Peloponnesian War,* Boethius's *Consolation of Philosophy,* Thomas More's *Utopia,* Calvin's *Institutes,* Burke's *Reflections, The Communist Manifesto,* and Leo XIII's *Rerum novarum* in the Western civ courses.

The core economics course has a resolutely free-market emphasis. The core course in American politics gives special attention to the *Declaration, Federalist Papers,* and Alexis de Tocqueville's *Democracy in America.* The theology courses comprise an introductory course in biblical scholarship and one entitled the "Western Theological Tradition." There is some leeway in the science and language requirements, in that students can choose which science and language they want to study. But with these requirements, it should be clear that every Dallas student is ensured a rigorous and broad introduction to the liberal arts tradition.

Dallas is also notable for its unique Rome program, which offers students the opportunity to spend one semester of their sophomore year at Due Santi, the university's Rome campus. Roughly 85 percent of Dallas students participate in the program, at least in part because of glowing reports from the students who went before them. Having a year and a half of study of the ancients under their belts, students are well prepared to benefit from the experience (which includes a trip to Greece), and professors agree with their students that the Rome semester is an integral part of a Dallas education. "The semester in Rome is definitely very formative," says a professor. "The students become more sophisticated, cosmopolitan, and appreciative of history, other cultures, and the universality of the Faith."

Students claim that grade inflation is not the norm at Dallas, as it has become elsewhere. "I am so proud of some of the B's and C's I got because I had to work so hard at it," one says. One professor claims that grade inflation is about average, while another claims that it is "present but not rampant. We tend to inflate when students are in their major area, but there are still no easy A's." If Dallas students get about the same grades as their counterparts at other schools, they work much harder to get them. "My friends who went to more prestigious universities didn't study nearly as much as I did. You *had* to study at UD. And you had to *read* — original sources, not a textbook," boasts one recent UD grad.

Politics (which at Dallas means political philosophy) and literature are the most popular majors at UD. These departments are also singled out as strengths by faculty and students, along with philosophy and theology. The science departments must be very good as well: the medical school acceptance rate for Dallas graduates is 90 percent.

Teaching at Dallas is strong across the board, but some of the best undergraduate teachers include Gerard Wegemer, David Davies, John Alvis, and Fr. Robert Maguire in English; Richard Dougherty, Leo Paul de Alvarez, Thomas G. West, and John Paynter in politics; Mark D. Lowery and Margaret Turek in theology; Fr. James Lehrberger, William A. Frank, and Janet E. Smith in philosophy; Thomas W. Jodziewicz in history; Hazel Cazorla and Alexandra Wilhelmsen in Spanish; William Doyle in economics; Richard Olenick in physics; and Frank Doe in biology. Professors in general play a large role in the university community, taking an active part in university social events and other extracurricular programs. Students give them high praise for their accessibility and their consistency. "The professors really lived what they said," one says. "They write what they think, and they behave the way that they preach."

The UD professoriate is actively involved with their respective disciplines. UD expects its junior faculty to publish in order to get tenure, but even tenured faculty usually keep publishing. "There's peer pressure to keep going," a professor says. "Everyone wants to pull their weight." Yet teaching does not suffer, in large part because most of the professors at Dallas really *want* to be there. They believe in the school's mission and are happy to be in a place where open support for the traditional canon of the West is not viewed with suspicion. The visibility and reputation of the faculty is evident in the big-name speakers that are often brought to campus to lecture.

Though class sizes are getting larger, they still tend to be comparatively small; it may not be unusual for freshmen and sophomores to sit in classes of thirty to forty, but the average is more like twenty to twenty-five. One professor warns that with increasing enrollment, class sizes in core courses could continue to rise unless more faculty are added. However, as one faculty member puts it, "the spirit of dialogue reigns supreme over campus," even in larger courses.

As part of its attempt to attract more students, the school recently added a computer science major, and there has been talk of adding a business major. There is some anxiety that in the near future these students will be exempted from UD's core requirements, but for now, at least, all students must take the core curriculum, no matter what their majors.

Political Atmosphere: Everyone's Business?

At a school that proudly states that one of its primary goals is character development, a school that openly claims as its themes truth, virtue, freedom, justice, revelation, and discovery, there is not much room for radical politicization. One could not hope for much better than these words from the UD mission statement: "The core curriculum emphasizes the study of the great deeds and works of Western civilization, both ancient and modern. The majors are built upon the core and invite students to disciplined inquiry into the fundamental aspects of being and of our relation to God, to nature, and to fellow human beings."

Faculty and students take these words seriously. This means that there are virtually no politicized courses at Dallas, nor any devoted exclusively to trendy topics. There are no gay and lesbian theorists among the faculty, for example; nor is there a cultural studies department. In this regard, Dallas is absolutely and refreshingly unique. The education and psychology departments are mentioned as ones not up to par with the university's other departments, but even here they are not so much politicized as comparatively mediocre. As one student explains, education tends to be "where students who had a harder time with the liberal arts end up. It's the easiest program there is."

However, some tension has entered the school atmosphere of late. The administration of Msgr. Joseph, according to some students and faculty, is not fully committed to the school's liberal arts mission. This is reflected in the first goal of Msgr. Joseph's capital campaign, which is to build a new "Global Center for Business and Technology" for the university's money-making Graduate School of Management (GSM). The GSM enrolls almost 1.5 times as many students as does the undergraduate college, but according to some its atmosphere is very different in that it is only nominally Catholic. "They don't give a flip about Catholic virtue," says one student of the GSM.

The Joseph administration is also leaning much more heavily on professional educrats and fundraisers than on the academics of previous administrations. A certain amount of distrust between the administration and the faculty, students, and alumni has been the result. "Msgr. Joseph and others want to make it a much larger school, more versatile — with more computers and majors — and drag it away from the liberal arts. So he's hiring people in administration who share his vision," an alumnus complains.

Furthermore, there is some indication that the administration is trying to silence or intimidate conservative professors or students. Two faculty were recently unofficially reprimanded by the administration for an op ed piece they wrote supporting papal policies toward dissenting theologians. Professors agree that faculty are self-censoring themselves both inside and outside the classroom. "The impression is that those who are outspokenly religiously conservative are an embarrassment to the president," says one. Another faculty member explains that the current administration has trouble distinguishing "Catholic orthodoxy from Catholic fundamentalism and far-right-wing political conservatism." Students have had run-ins with the administration as well. Msgr. Joseph reportedly has chastised some for kneeling to take communion and for questioning some of his policies.

Of course, all of this must be put in context. The university administration is still more open to orthodox Catholicism and a traditional vision of the liberal arts than are the vast majority of Catholic schools, and the more conservative or traditionally Catholic students at Dallas are used to encountering little or no opposition from the administration. But the open-mindedness that characterizes UD is such an asset that many students and faculty are exceptionally wary of any threat to it. Says one professor, "The administration has done such a good job on things like maintenance, increasing the endowment, and improving faculty salaries, that it has to be cautious not to touch the academic program, to leave it to those who are qualified to run it."

One student looks at the current situation rather practically. "I don't think it's going to hell in a handbasket. I think that what they're doing right now is a necessary evil because the school is financially strapped," the student says. "There will be growth but I don't think it will diminish the strengths of the academic departments. And I don't think they will change the core because the faculty give it such support and they'll outlive Msgr. Joseph."

As Catholic as Dallas no doubt is — about 70 percent of its undergraduates identify themselves as Catholic — students and faculty report that non-Catholics generally feel comfortable at the school. There is little proselytization by individuals, and none by the university itself. (Protestant worship services are available on campus.) Says one professor about non-Catholics, "Those I have spoken with have expressed some surprise that no one ever approached them about becoming Catholic."

Nor is the curriculum, though traditional, an exercise in piety; on the contrary, there is a genuine engagement with modern and contemporary thought. Dallas therefore attracts, as one faculty member puts it, "students who are serious about the Western tradition but not necessarily serious about Catholicism." The result is a different atmosphere, one marked by less insulation and less homogeneity than at the handful of other Catholic schools generally considered "orthodox."

"UD is actually quite a mixed place," a professor says. "It is not as uniformly conservative as some of the other Catholic colleges and universities known to be conservative." The university is genuinely liberal and tolerant, according to students. Debate is encouraged instead of squelched, and there is no expectation of uniformity among students. As a result, "There are no true outsiders," says a student, though it usually happens that "if you start out wearing baggy pants and combat boots, you're probably not going to end up wearing the same thing when you graduate."

Student Life: Brick and Block

The good news is that the University of Dallas commands the finest tract of land in Irving, Texas. The bad news is that as a modern suburb that has seen its population quadruple since 1960 to over 175,000 today, Irving has precious little to recommend it, least of all natural beauty. Nor is the university placed in a student-friendly neighborhood, as there are no stores, coffee houses, restaurants, or bars within easy walking distance. "I never really saw Dallas because I didn't have a car," says a recent grad. "If you don't have a car, you're lucky to make it to the grocery store." The university's Dallas Year program tries to overcome this limitation by organizing outings for freshmen to the opera, sporting events, museums, and symphonies, and the convenience of the Dallas–Fort Worth airport is a distinct advantage. But along with its pile-of-bricks architectural style, the university's location is clearly its greatest deficiency.

The students still manage to have fun, though. For all their moral and intellectual seriousness, undergraduates are notable for their lack of puritanical joylessness. Parties in the private apartments adjoining the campus are not infrequent, and the annual Groundhog Day party finds students in the woods at night with a keg or three. Charity Week brings a large percentage of the students together for more constructive festivities. And for those students who have their own transportation, the Dallas–Fort Worth "metroplex" offers abundant cultural opportunities and activities.

The fundamental agreement between Dallas students on core matters is an important contribution to the school's community atmosphere. "You are surrounded by kids who will enforce the school's ideas that there is a truth, it can be known by man, and it is unchanging," a student says. And as another student puts it, "For being such a small school, everyone really finds their niche. There's always someone who has common ground with you, and it's easy to find them." One professor beams that the students are "hard-working, respectful, and bright. I certainly do not see our students as closed-minded or set in their ways and thinking. They are, I think, truly open and unafraid. Many of them are devout Catholics and that does provide a standard for their judgments. They are open to anything compatible with authentic Catholicism."

The presence of the university has contributed to the development of a substantial Catholic community in the area. Students can and often do attend mass at the beautiful Cistercian monastery nearby or the Dominican priory located on campus. Mass is held at the university's Chapel of the Incarnation twice daily; many students attend but there is little pressure, if any, for them to do so. It is possible to "get through UD and not learn anything about your faith," says one student. But "if you want to practice and grow in your faith there is the opportunity to do so and you would never be ridiculed for it."

Athletics at Dallas are improving but are far from top-notch. The university recently added a baseball team in an effort to increase the proportion of men attending the school. (Nearly two-thirds of the 1999 freshmen were women.) During the last couple of years there were discussions of implementing a football program, but this idea aroused controversy and has been shelved, at least for now. Some intramural sports are offered, including football, soccer, basketball, volleyball, and softball, and they are popular. Rugby is a well-liked club sport.

The University Democrats may be the most radical student group on campus. Some graffiti does get scrawled on the campus sidewalks every year — by the Crusaders for Life. There are surely not many other campuses in the United States where such activism would occasion nary a sign of protest or counter-display.

Single-sex dormitory living is available. Coed dorms do not include coed floors or bathrooms. Visitation hours for members of the opposite sex are quite restricted, and students entertaining members of the opposite sex must keep the door "bolted" — that is, extend the deadbolt so that the door cannot shut all the way. Roughly two-thirds of students live on campus; students are required to do so until they are 21 unless they are married, veterans, or living with their parents. Many students find off-campus housing right across the street; other apartments are relatively easy to find in nearby Irving neighborhoods. Students perceive the campus and its environs to be very safe. Crime can be a problem in south Irving, but this ethnically varied area is also more interesting than the standard suburbanity of north Irving.

artmouth College

Dean of Admissions & Financial Aid
McNutt Hall
Hanover, NH 03775
(603) 646-2875
www.dartmouth.edu

Total enrollment: 5,500
Undergraduates: 4,023
SAT ranges (Verbal/Math): 660-750 (V); 670-760 (M)
Applicants: 10,143
Accepted: 21%
Enrolled: 49%
Application deadline: January 1
Financial aid application deadline: February 1
Tuition: $25,653/$33,210
Core curriculum: No

Yet Those Who Love It

Dartmouth College was founded in 1754 as More's Indian Charity School by a graduate of Yale, the Reverend Eleazar Wheelock. The original mission of the school was to educate Native American youth, as well as English children. The school was renamed for William Legge, the Earl of Dartmouth, who financially supported the school.

In 1818, Daniel Webster, himself a graduate of Dartmouth seventeen years earlier, went to the U.S. Supreme Court to plead against a state takeover of the college. "Sir, you may destroy this little institution; it is weak; it is in your hands! I know it is one of the lesser lights in the literary horizon of our country," Webster said. "You may put it out. But if you do, you must carry through your work! You must extinguish, one after the another, all those great lights of science which, for more than a century, have thrown their radiance over our land."

Webster concluded, "It is, sir, as I have said, a small college. And yet, there are those who love it."

He won. To this day, there are those who love Dartmouth, some for its past glories and some for its present achievements. Those fond of the modern Dartmouth laud its inclusion of diversity and ideological instruction in the curriculum and campus life. However, a large group of alumni resent the growing multiculturalism and politicization at Dartmouth and yearn for the campus they once loved. And now, it is the new Dartmouth that is winning.

Academic Life: According to Plan

Dartmouth's basic curriculum requires that students take ten courses covering eight different sectors of the university. As such, the requirements do not force students to learn any foundational disciplines in depth. Instead, a Dartmouth student must take only a single course in art; literature; philosophical, religious, or historical analysis; international and comparative study; quantitative and deductive science; and technology or applied science; plus two courses in both social analysis and natural and physical science.

There are three additional distribution requirements known as "world culture" courses. One course is required in each of three areas: "the culture, ideas, or institutions of the United States, of Europe, and of at least one non-Western society." According to some on campus, the non-Western courses are largely politicized and spend a good amount of time criticizing Western institutions.

Dartmouth freshmen must take an English composition course within the first two quarters, but accomplished students can be exempted from this requirement. Once the English requirement is fulfilled, freshmen choose one of about seventy seminars representing thirty departments and programs. These intimate seminars enroll no more than sixteen students and offer an introduction to the writing and scholarship required in upper-level courses.

Dartmouth operates on a schedule known, not surprisingly, as the Dartmouth Plan. Adopted in 1972 when the college went coed, this calendar contains four ten-week academic terms per year. At the time the plan was implemented, there were roughly one thousand male students and, rather than reducing the male enrollment to make space for females, the college choose this plan to make the most efficient use of its facilities. A typical student spends only two or three terms of each year on campus, but must attend for the first three terms of his freshman year and the final three of his senior year.

Faculty say the Dartmouth Plan makes it easier for students to schedule off-campus study, including terms at overseas universities and internships — and 63 percent of students partake of some form of off-campus study. The disadvantage of the plan is that students can't always register for the classes they want because a particular course may be offered only during a specific term.

Dartmouth offers thirty-eight traditional majors, plus interdisciplinary majors in African and Afro-American studies, environmental studies, Native American studies, and women's studies. In addition to these choices, the college gives students considerable latitude to create their own fields of study or combine existing ones into a double major.

The best professors at Dartmouth include Edward M. Bradley and William C. Scott in classics; Michael Mastanduno and Roger D. Masters in government; P. David Lagomarsino, Pamela Crossley, Kenneth E. Shewmaker, and Heide W. Whelan in history; Robert Fogelin in philosophy; Charles H. Stinson and Ehud Benor in religion; and Peter Saccio in English, whose Shakespeare class is one of the best.

A graduate says, "Students have an opportunity to be very close to their professors at Dartmouth. The teachers are very accessible, and it is truly amazing that undergraduate students can just walk right in and talk with their professors. It is an incredible advantage."

According to professors and students, the best and most traditional departments at Dartmouth are history, government, and classics. Three departments considered highly politicized by students and faculty are women's studies, Latin American studies, and English.

Dartmouth's curriculum has become littered with politically correct courses of questionable academic value. Quite a few English classes (at a school that graduated both Robert Frost and Theodore Geisel [Dr. Seuss]) are devoted to themes of class, race, or gender. However, there are also scores of traditional courses listed in the catalogue, though one wonders from what perspective these are taught. "The English department is pretty notorious for being liberal," a student says. One member of the department reportedly has tried to intimidate advertisers in the *Dartmouth Review*, the venerable conservative student newspaper, into withdrawing their financial support.

The Nelson A. Rockefeller Center for the Social Sciences supports research on public policy questions, visiting scholars and lecturers, off-campus internships, and conferences. The center, named for the former U.S. vice president and Dartmouth alumnus, also offers a public policy minor for undergraduates. Citing forums on "environmental racism" and other topics, many students say the center's courses and events have become overly politicized.

Dartmouth alumni interested in preserving traditions and standards have formed the Hopkins Institute, an unofficial alumni organization based in Arlington, Virginia. "Dartmouth students are no longer required to read Shakespeare, Dante, Plato or even to know the basic facts of American history," says one alumnus associated with the group. The organization has brought prominent speakers to campus, such as William F. Buckley, Jack Kemp, and the late former U.S. Treasury Secretary William Simon. The institute also provides scholarship money to selected students.

Political Life: Family Feud

Dartmouth has been one of the prime battlegrounds in the academic culture wars. This is in part because there have been a number of outspoken conservatives who have summoned resistance to the tidal wave of political correctness. Among them have been English professor emeritus and syndicated columnist Jeffrey Hart and the distinguished string of *Dartmouth Review* editors.

There has been a running feud between the administration and the *Review*, the paper whose student staff has included Dinesh D'Souza, Benjamin Hart, Gregory

Fossedal, and many other prominent conservative scholars and journalists. The *Review* has received national attention for its clever spoofs of academic fads and ludicrous courses. Its message is heard by more than ten thousand Dartmouth alumni subscribers.

However, the administration has done its best to stifle the nation's most prestigious conservative campus newspaper. Two books — *The Hollow Men: Politics and Corruption in Higher Education*, by Charles Sykes, and *Poisoned Ivy*, by Benjamin Hart — document the tactics employed against the *Review*. Students distributing the paper have been arrested. Review writers have been denied information by administrators — even when the information was a matter of public record. Benjamin Hart was even physically attacked by a Dartmouth administrator named Samuel Smith while distributing the paper. According to Sykes's book, Smith punched and kicked Hart and tried to throw him though a plate glass door. Three days after the assault, the university faculty voted 113 to 5 against disciplinary action for Smith, but in favor of censuring the newspaper.

In another incident in the mid-1980s, a music professor unsuccessfully sued the *Review* for libel after a reporter sat in on his class and wrote that the professor "arrived late, left class for periods as long as ten minutes at a time, and spent at least half of his lecture on the 'race question,' castigating students as racist and sexist," according to Sykes. After the article was printed, the professor went to the reporter's dorm room and launched into an obscenity-filled, threatening tirade. In a separate incident several years later, he hung up on a *Review* reporter doing a story about a leftist classroom harangue and broke the flash attachment on a photographer's camera when the paper tried to visit him in person for comment.

The administration took no action against the professor and a campus rally to support him drew four hundred students. However, three *Review* staffers were suspended and another was put on probation. The suspensions were overturned when a U.S. court of appeals judge — himself a Dartmouth alum — found that the disciplinary proceedings were invalid because they "took place against a backdrop of undisguised college hostility to the political views expressed in the *Dartmouth Review* as well as the polemical and excessive terms in which those opinions were sometimes cast."

One more recent indicator of the politically correct atmosphere at Dartmouth was the August 1999 cancellation of a Hawaiian luau planned by the Alpha Chi Alpha fraternity and the Delta Delta Delta sorority. The party was canceled after a student sent an e-mail message to everyone on campus describing the party as an act of "bigotry." Aaron Akamu, a native of Hawaii, wrote a lengthy criticism of the planned party in *The Dartmouth*, the official student newspaper. He groused, "That people feel a right to capitalize on some stereotype of where I am from and the people I feel a cultural responsibility to in the name of fun, angers and hurts me." Senior Whit Warlow responded, "It's pretty ridiculous that this is such an issue. You have to draw a line between political correctness and having fun."

Dartmouth supports institutionalized politically correctness as a matter of policy. Like many campuses, Dartmouth has established a Women's Resource Center. Its video library includes: "Abortion for Survival" (produced by The Fund for the Feminist Majority); "Excited, Angry, Active, Vocal: Women Out Loud" (produced by the Video Virgin); "Hot, Sexy and Safer"; and "Speaking Out for Reproductive Freedom." None of the titles in the library appear to present a conservative or pro-life perspective. The staff of the Women's Resource Center also delivers presentations to campus groups. Topics include: "Being an Ally in the Battle Against 'Isms'"; "Non-Sexist Language"; and "Homophobia and Sexism: Deadly Duo."

The Dartmouth administration recently created the Coalition for Gay, Lesbian, Bisexual and Transgender Concerns. It is composed of faculty, staff, and administrators "dedicated to enhancing life for gay men, lesbians, and bisexuals at the College." This agency also "provides support on an individual basis to those members of the community who have experienced negative affects of homophobia."

Dartmouth also has a coordinator of gay, lesbian, and bisexual programming who "provides individual advising to students with concerns about sexual orientation, and serves as group advisor for the Dartmouth Rainbow Alliance [a student gay/lesbian/transgender group]." The Dartmouth Web site says that "the coordinator also organizes some programming events, particularly in the fall term around National Coming Out Month" and "serves as spokesperson and advocate within the Dartmouth community for the needs and concerns of lesbian, gay, bisexual and transgender students."

Student Life: Greeks Baring Rifts

The forty-one residences that are home to more than 2,800 Dartmouth undergraduates include traditional residence halls and small free-standing units that house students who are interested in academic affinity or special interest housing. Though there are a few single-sex floors, there are no single-sex residence halls, and in fact most suites are shared by men and women (though the bathrooms are not). In addition, more than five hundred juniors and seniors reside in college-owned and affiliated coed, fraternity, sorority, and undergraduate society houses. Dartmouth also offers "substance-free housing," an attractive respite for students uninterested in binge drinking and drug use.

The cultural/racial houses are called "academic affinity programs." They include Cutter/Shabazz, which houses the offices of the African-American Society and twenty-eight upper-level students on coed floors. Dartmouth also offers La Casa for Hispanic students and the Native American House.

Although Dartmouth has long had one of the most vibrant Greek scenes in the Ivy League (beginning with its first fraternity in 1841), the administration has attempted in recent years to social engineer, if not abolish, this institution. First, kegs were banned and campus security were asked to monitor parties. After this rule had the unintended consequence of beer being replaced by hard liquor, kegs were again allowed, but with restrictions. At one point, more than half of the fraternities were on probation for violating the keg policy. The college Greek system consists of twenty-eight organizations. About 50 percent of eligible students participate.

In 1999, Dartmouth attracted national attention when it released the "Student Life Initiative," a document that called for changes that would supposedly improve student life. It proposed more campus housing choices, student-controlled social space, and the elimination of alcohol abuse. However, it was the recommendation of mandatory coed social houses that infuriated Dartmouth's Greek community and sparked a national uproar. The decision and its effects were broadcast on ABC's *World News Tonight* and were even noted in *The Times of London.*

Although the trustees' proposal has not yet been fully implemented, the trustees have placed a moratorium on the formation of new fraternities and sororities. They also deferred rush from the fall to the winter of sophomore year. Taps, bars, and refrigeration units must be removed from houses, but kegs registered with the college are allowed.

However, the Greek controversy at Dartmouth bubbled over again in May of 2000 when the University reprimanded all graduating members of the former Phi Delta Alpha fraternity for "dirty rushing" — that is, joining the organization during their freshman year. Students at Dartmouth are not permitted to become a member of a coed Greek organization until their sophomore year. The students will not face disciplinary action, but the violations will be noted in their personal files. The administration's handling of this incident angered many students, because several of the seniors who received the letter were innocent of the charges, including several who transferred to Dartmouth during their sophomore year.

In addition to its Greek system, Dartmouth is home to a wide variety of independent student organizations. They include Animal Advocacy, Conservative Union at Dartmouth, Students for Choice, The Dartmouth Coalition for Life, Dartmouth Young Republicans, Young Democrats, Ivy Leaguers for Freedom, Model United Nations, Bridge Club, Medieval Enthusiasts, Sewing Club, and Movimiento Estudiantil Chicano/a de Aztlan (MEChA). MEChA is a radical Hispanic group that seeks to expel white oppressors and return the southwestern U.S. states to Mexico. On the other hand, the Conservative Union recently fought successfully to preserve the college's ROTC program.

Dartmouth also boasts a number of artistic student organizations that sponsor theater and musical performances. From the hip-hop of Sheba to the tap dance of Steppin' Out, a performance organization exists to suit almost every artistic taste.

Dartmouth has terrific opportunities for students interested in radio. WDCR and WFRD comprise the only completely student-run commercial broadcast AM/FM station in America. Students are responsible for all phases of radio broadcasting including, news, public affairs, radio engineering, promotion, and programming. More than one hundred students work in some capacity at the radio station.

Dartmouth is a haven for debaters. In addition to the Dartmouth Parliamentary Debate Team, a common fixture in the Ivy League, the Dartmouth Forensic Union is one of the nation's most prestigious cross-examination debate programs, having won four national championships in the past thirty years. Dartmouth even hosts a summer camp that trains high school students in this fast-paced style of debate.

Sports serve as a major social outlet at Dartmouth. More than twenty-five sports are divided into male-only, female-only, and coed leagues. Dartmouth also fields thirty-four "Big Green" intercollegiate sports teams that compete at the NCAA Division I level.

As all of these organizations indicate, the typical Dartmouth student is concerned with being well rounded. "That's the catch word that distinguishes a Dartmouth student from his Harvard counterpart," an alumnus says. "The Harvard student is interested in being the best at one particular thing — such as a world-class violinist — and not really doing much else. The Dartmouth student is well-rounded in that he is playing a club sport like rugby, serving as an officer in his fraternity, and working for a student publication."

Dartmouth is located in Hanover, a small New Hampshire town near the upper valley of the Connecticut River. The 200-acre campus is surrounded by forests and mountains, offering students a beautifully serene setting in which to study. Although Hanover is hardly a transportation hub, there is propeller plane service from the Lebanon/Hanover airport to Philadelphia and La Guardia. Boston is about two hours away by car, and, while not as cosmopolitan, Concord, New Hampshire, is about half that distance.

Dartmouth offers a phenomenal array of recreational activities that are unheard of on most campuses. The Dartmouth Skiway is an official ski area and an exceedingly popular destination for students during the harsh New Hampshire winter. As the temperature warms in the spring, students enjoy the Hanover Country Club Golf Course and riding horses at the Morton Farm Riding Center. The Dartmouth Outing Club, the nation's oldest collegiate outing club, runs outdoor activities for about 1,500 students, about one-third of the student body.

There are also indoor attractions on campus. The Hood Museum of Art, one of the nation's oldest college museums in the country, houses more than sixty thousand objects, most of which are non-Western and modern art. The Hopkins Center hosts movies, art exhibitions, drama and dance performances, and an occasional seminar. "The Hop," as it is known, was designed by Wallace K. Harrison, who was also responsible for the Metropolitan Opera House in New York City.

The Baker Library, one of the oldest in the United States, is accessible to all students via the personal computers with which all of them are supplied. Dormitory rooms and faculty offices are all on the computer network, meaning that the library and other information are within reach from nearly any place on campus.

The crime risk at Dartmouth is rated as moderate by apbnews.com. However, this probably overstates the danger on this rural New Hampshire campus. There were no murders or forcible sexual offenses in 1996 or 1997. The vast majority of the crimes were reported were liquor and drug offenses. While Dartmouth students may need to restrain themselves, there is only minimal danger to life or limb on the placid campus.

Davidson College

Office of Admission
Post Office Box 1737
Davidson, NC 28036
(800) 768-0380
www.davidson.edu

Total enrollment: 1,623
Undergraduates: 1,623
SAT ranges (Verbal/Math): 630-740 (V); 640-720 (M)
Applicants: 2,823
Accepted: 38%
Enrolled: 42%
Application deadline: January 2
Financial aid application deadline: February 15
Tuition: $23,094/$29,666
Core curriculum: No

What Others Can't

Davidson College offers things a major research university can't. It is focused on teaching, rather than driven by research. It is a small school with only 1,600 students, set in a quaint North Carolina college town free of the hustle and bustle of city life. There is a refreshing emphasis on the liberal arts, and students and professors say the small classes and personal relationships make for an excellent educational experience. Davidson's beautiful campus makes one feel cloistered from the outside world: its mosaic of pathways past neoclassical buildings provides the ultimate college setting. And the college has barely scratched the surface of academic trends found in so many other places.

The college was founded by Presbyterians in 1837 as a liberal arts college, and still sees itself as (informally) related to the church. As its statement of purpose says, the college seeks to "assist students in developing humane instincts and disciplined and creative minds for lives of leadership and service." This same statement notes that the college "emphasizes those studies, disciplines, and activities that are mentally, spiritually, and physically liberating." Davidson complies quite closely with its mission statement, even today where other colleges use these things purely as window dressing.

What's more, Davidson has no plans to grow into a large university with graduate programs. "It's got a strong and enduring focus on the traditional liberal arts as its core," said a humanities professor. "It's kept that focus pretty clearly."

Academic Life: Talk About School

Davidson has what it calls a "core curriculum," but its requirements are better described as distribution requirements, as they give students choices within specified areas rather than mandating a certain list of courses. Students must complete one course in literature; one in fine arts; one in history; one in religion and a second in either religion or philosophy; one in natural sciences, a second in mathematics and a third in either science or mathematics; two in social sciences; physical education requirements; and a one-course "cultural diversity requirement." Students must also become competent in a foreign language and complete a composition requirement. Because students choose among classes that are relatively few in number, it is difficult to skirt at least some exposure to Western culture.

There is no getting around the diversity requirement, however, as Davidson has given a nod to this popular curricular addition. Elsewhere, "diversity" has been code for highly politicized, encounter group–like classes that glorify Third World cultures while demeaning Western culture. Such raw politics is largely absent at Davidson, even in these diversity courses, though it appears to be making small inroads here and there.

Davidson students choose among twenty majors, which are all in traditional fields. They may also minor in any of ten fields. The college also has "concentrations" in eight subjects, including oft-politicized fields such as ethnic studies and gender studies, but also in areas like applied mathematics, neuroscience, and Southern studies.

Among the bright lights in Davidson's curriculum is its humanities program, a four-semester course for freshmen and sophomores that aims to help students understand the Western tradition. Students study Western civilization through different lenses: literary, religious, philosophical, artistic. The humanities program attracts a cadre of students enthusiastic about a Great Books–like program, as well as those interested in finding a convenient and coherent way to dispose of several distribution requirements. Unfortunately, the program has come under fire from some quarters, particularly the religion department, for being too traditional and too Western-oriented. Yet it remains one of Davidson's richest and most rewarding courses of study.

A quick review of the college's course catalog shows that at least some of the classes at Davidson have been unfortunately influenced by political trends in academia. For instance, there's Political Science 450, "Contemporary Feminist Political Theory," which explores "some of the most important and provocative feminist political theory" of the last twenty years. One of the course's goals is to "help you practice the skills required in political discussions." The reading list is composed almost entirely by left-wing political rants by the likes of Catharine MacKinnon.

Then there's French 320, "Adultery in the Novel," which promises to study "adulterous desire and female sexual transgression" in French literature of the last three hundred years. In the course, the students have the benefit of examining "the deeply rooted double standard of morality which governs any treatment of male vs. female adultery."

Still, Davidson has far fewer of these types of offerings than other small liberal arts colleges, though it remains to be seen if newer, younger teachers will add more.

Students praise Davidson for its rigorous education, and many say academics are properly at the center of their college experience. "If you're the type of person who wants to go out and party and coast through college, I don't think Davidson is the place for you," says a junior. "Academics are really important to everybody here. It's probably the most important thing to everybody here. Even when you go out on the weekend, people talk about school."

Classes tend to be small — only rarely do they exceed thirty or thirty-five students. Many students say one of the greatest things about Davidson is the relationships they build with professors, who typically invite groups of students to their homes for dinner or a movie or a class discussion. "You get a lot of access to your professors," says one student. "Here, it seems as though the professors are specifically told to allocate a lot of time to just sitting in their offices and being available to students."

Because Davidson is geared toward teaching instead of research, it goes without saying that many of the 150 full-time professors on campus value their time in the classroom with students. There are many highly motivated, excellent teachers on campus. Professors mentioned by their colleagues and students as the best include Peter J. Ahrensdorf in political science; Randy F. Nelson and Paul Miller in English; Hansford M. Epes in German; and Lance K. Stell in philosophy. Particularly strong departments include philosophy, political science, history, mathematics, chemistry, and economics.

Political Atmosphere: Calming Influence

Davidson retains Southern charm, despite the fact that its small student body represents forty-seven states and thirty-seven countries. The campus has a conservative feel, preppy-like and collegial, with few signs of the radical elements that have infested colleges elsewhere. "You don't really have people walking around with purple hair and guys wearing girls' clothing," a student says.

Davidson has long been associated with a genteel element of Southern society whose code of conduct discourages unwarranted personal attack or radical politics. This legacy of Southern manners continues to play a significant role on campus, where, as one teacher notes, "There is a kind of Southern preference for a consensual approach. If someone is too combative, they're thought of as rude and are shunned." Many agree that Davidson is a depoliticized place where the focus remains on teaching.

But within that gentility, others see a disturbing trend. Because political disagreements are typically internalized, many practices fly below the radar and attract no vocal opposition. In the first edition of this book, one professor noted: "The move toward politicization here is not dramatic but it's not glacial, either. There is a definite tendency in that direction. I won't happen merely in five years, but maybe ten to fifteen years." Another professor said he was a little dismayed with the constant addition of trendy ethnic and gender studies programs, though he noted that they are all concentrations, rather than majors: "As most places are experiencing, there are tugs and pulls at the curriculum. These things may or may not stand the test of time. They are definitely fads, but people want them in order to maintain their enthusiasm for what they do."

Two years later, such fads still receive the backing of the administration, but not as wholeheartedly as elsewhere. Since gender and ethnic studies are merely concentrations, not full majors, they'll die an easier death when the trend passes — one hopes.

Even though administrators support the traditional humanities program, some professors say its future is in doubt — though that's more because of a lack of interest among faculty than because of any direct attacks. New professors especially disdain the program, and many don't want to teach in it. Its future, therefore, depends on the quality of hiring decisions made by individual departments. "Some people will come in and say it looks kind of like a Great Books program and roll their eyes," a professor says. "They are socialized [in graduate school] to think making such a comment is cutting edge. . . . They look at the heavy historical orientation and complain about the DWEMs — the dead, white, European males."

In the spring of 2000, Davidson faculty debated a report from a "gender equity study group" that called for the creation of a "gender equity office" — which at other places has meant the installation of a feminist ombudsman to respond to the grievances of any woman on campus. The report offered no evidence of pay disparities or any systematic problems at Davidson, but instead relied on a few anonymous anecdotes that ranged in severity from bad manners to unprofessional behavior. Campus sources say the creation of a gender equity office is unlikely, because it would cost money that could better be spent elsewhere.

Professors report a modest level of mandatory "sensitivity training" when freshmen arrive, in which students hear about the evils of white male European civilization.

While some students are politically zealous in their pet projects — such as gay rights or feminist issues — the vast majority of students on campus are apolitical, professors and students say. There is a very liberal newspaper that tries to prick people's consciences on social issues, but for the most part there's more interest among students in academics. "I think the students by and large are very interested to learn, and I think they're eager students," says one social science professor.

Student Life: "Male Friendly," Whatever That Is

Davidson is about twenty minutes north of Charlotte, North Carolina's largest city (population 521,000), which has grown tremendously in the last decade. As home to two of the country's largest banks — Bank of America and First Union — Charlotte is known as somewhat of a buttoned-down, slightly bland city. But it offers what large cities offer: excellent restaurants, several museums, a performing arts center, plenty of parks, and many, many churches. For a change of pace, Davidson students head to Charlotte's reawakening downtown area for its cluster of bars, restaurants, and night clubs. Charlotte also offers professional sports: the Carolina Panthers football team plays in a downtown stadium, while the Charlotte Hornets (basketball) play a little further south along Interstate 77. Davidson is also just minutes away from Lake Norman, popular with outdoor enthusiasts for hiking trails, boating, and camping. The Lake Norman area is also exploding with growth, particularly of new housing developments, chain restaurants, and the like. For those who want to venture a little farther away, the Blue Ridge Mountains are two or three hours away, and Myrtle Beach, S.C. — popular with spring breakers — is about a five-hour drive.

But students spend most of their time in and around Davidson, a pretty Southern town with several historical markers noting not only the founding of Davidson College, but the fact that Woodrow Wilson studied there from 1873 to 1874. The social life on campus consists chiefly of parties thrown by one of the seven fraternities, by one of the five eating clubs (all but one or which are women-only), or simply by friends. This is convenient, since 96 percent of Davidson students live on campus. Single-sex residence halls are available for both men and women, and the coed dorms divide men and women by floor (unless they are suite-style, in which case men and women still retain their own bathrooms).

Davidson is a small college town, with a two-block business district across the street from campus that has the main B's of a college town: bank, bookstore, bistro, barber, and Ben & Jerry's. A few blocks away, near the train tracks, is a converted mill building called The Davidson Depot — a "restaurant and tap room" popular with students. The campus also has a 24-hour fitness center and a student union. Crime is a rare occurrence on or around the Davidson campus.

In the spring of 2001, Davidson is scheduled to open the new Knobloch Campus Center. It will include a fitness center, 25-foot climbing wall, and a post office, as well as meeting rooms, an amphitheater, and offices.

One of the aspects that sets Davidson College apart from its peers is its honor code. Although the campus has an air of collegiality and friendliness, the honor code in five succinct sentences spells out what the college expects from its students: "Every student shall be honor bound to refrain from cheating (including plagiarism). Every student shall be honor bound to refrain from stealing. Every student shall be honor bound from lying about official college business. Every student shall be honor bound to report immediately all violations of the Honor System which come under his or her observation; failure to do so shall be a violation of the Honor System. Every student found guilty of a violation shall ordinarily be dismissed from the college." Administrators say the honor code creates an atmosphere of trust: professors give exams that students can take at home; students feel secure that an abandoned wallet or purse will be returned; and there is the sense that a person's word is his or her bond. Students give high marks to the flexibility and the value of responsibility given by the honor code. "If you work better in the morning, you can take tests only in the morning," says a student. Or if you drop some money, you can come back an hour later and find it on the floor where you dropped it, he says.

In September 2000, *Men's Health* magazine ranked Davidson No. 2 on a list of the top 10 "male-friendly" colleges in the nation — a ranking the magazine writers compiled by assessing fraternity life; academic programs in math, science, business, and engineering; and whether colleges offered more courses "on the Great Books than on the twelve oppressed women writers of Borneo." The magazine noted Davidson's "refreshingly PC-free" academic focus and its emphasis on Western civilization, and touted the fact that around 50 percent of male students belong to fraternities. The school's unofficial motto is "deep thinking, hard playing," the article said. The campus reaction to being named a "male-friendly" institution was what you might expect. An associate dean told the *Charlotte Observer* that the "whole article is pretty silly." A sophomore told the paper that "it makes it sound like Davidson is a place that supports a male elitist attitude, but it's not like that at all." A recent graduate disagreed, saying: "It's a male-oriented school, and there's definitely a good old boys network. But there's also a niche of really powerful women. I became a feminist there."

Although Davidson places a premium on creating a sense of community — for men and women — it also, like many other colleges, has its share of organizations devoted to making minority students "feel comfortable." Some say these groups only contribute to self-segregation. Davidson has a program called ACES (Academic and Career Enrichment for Students) that offers workshops and seminars to "enhance the academic and vocational experiences of minority students." There's the Black Student Coalition, designed to "maintain a spirit of solidarity" among African-American students. The college also supports special mentoring for black freshmen and sophomores and not one but two black history months (January and February).

Davidson offers a lot in religious life. Its ties to its Presbyterian roots include a chaplain's office with two ordained ministers in the Presbyterian Church (USA). (There are also two ministers from other denominations.) There are ten religious organizations on campus, ranging from a gospel choir to interfaith fellowship to various Christian and Jewish services and groups. There are also a couple of "social justice"–type student groups, which work on issues of homelessness, sweatshops, and other national and international causes.

Although by and large students who attend Davidson are fond of it, at times the routine of a small college and small town can be stifling. "Sometimes it just gets too small and you kinda get fed up with it," says an English major. "It's not, 'Oh my God I hate it so much.' It's like 'I've been doing the same thing all the time and want to try something else.' That's the time to take a road trip." For those who want to get away for a longer period of time, Davidson encourages and sponsors several popular study abroad programs.

Sports is an important part of the Davidson experience. A whopping 90 percent of students participate in intramural or club sports, according to college literature. And about one quarter play on varsity teams. Davidson is one of the smallest NCAA Division I colleges in the country, and it fields teams in twenty-one varsity sports.

Service to the community is also very important to a majority of Davidson students. Professors report that the college tends to select students who have demonstrated a commitment to community service, so Davidson students are very volunteer-oriented even before they arrive. There are plenty of opportunities at Davidson to tutor poor children or build Habitat for Humanity houses, and some professors say the pressure to volunteer can be quite strong.

Overall, students and professors give Davidson high marks for its commitment to teaching and its intimate setting, which inspires close bonds. Says one student: "There's something about this place that just keeps drawing me back."

Duke University

Director of Undergraduate Admissions
2138 Campus Drive
Box 90586
Durham, NC 27708
(919) 684-3214
www.duke.edu

Total enrollment: 10,800
Undergraduates: 6,300
SAT ranges (Verbal/Math): 660-760 (V); 680-780 (M)
Applicants: 13,888
Accepted: 27%
Enrolled: 43%
Application deadline: January 2
Financial aid application deadline: November 1
Tuition: $25,630/$33,017
Core curriculum: No

Ivy South

A T-shirt on sale in the Duke University bookstore proclaims Duke as "the Harvard of the South," and that's not too far from the truth — in more ways than the university probably intends to suggest. Like Harvard, Duke attracts some of the most intellectually promising students from throughout the United States and the world. But it's also guilty of many of Harvard's excesses: Duke fancies itself on the "cutting edge" of scholarship, political atmosphere, and its approach to student life.

Though it's set in the comfortable climate of a mid-sized tobacco town in North Carolina, Duke's political climate more closely resembles that of campuses in the Northeast. In the last twenty years, this university founded by Quaker and Methodist farmers in 1838 has achieved a reputation as an Ivy League–caliber school with decent weather and a place where students' favorite motto — "work hard, play hard" — is more or less true. But with its Ivy-like obsession with multiculturalism, its penchant for offering bizarre courses and strange focuses of study, and its obvious bias against traditional ideals, Duke can suck students unawares into some of the worst problems of academia.

Still, it's possible for students to find a well-rounded education at Duke. There are pockets of traditionalism, which, if not outspoken, are at least resolute in their ideas. Longtime professors report that the radical fervor of perhaps a decade ago has lost steam. In its place: a broad consensus that the study of race, class, and gender is paramount.

Academic Life: Meet the New Boss, Same as the Old Boss

The good news is that since the first edition of this guide in 1998, Duke's curriculum has undergone a wholesale change and that the most notorious of all Duke professors — English professor Stanley Fish — has left for an administrative position at a small college in Chicago. The bad news is that the new curriculum is little better than the original and that the university has continued the business of hiring trendy professors who operate at the margins of society.

In the fall of 2000, Duke debuted new graduation requirements called "Curriculum 2000." It replaces a curriculum that required students only to take courses in five of six areas, the result being that many students avoided any classes whatsoever in, say, science or mathematics or foreign language. The new curriculum is designed to fix that loophole, but it is still far from a core curriculum, as students have tremendous leeway to pick politicized or extremely specialized courses within a given subject area.

By the same token, they are free to pick more traditional, survey-type courses. Course descriptions at Duke are amazingly honest, and a conscientious student can avoid most of the politicized classes by a careful reading of course descriptions. "They can figure out where the real meat and potatoes are," one professor says.

Under Curriculum 2000, students in Trinity College (Duke's division of undergraduate arts and sciences) must take three courses in each of the following areas: arts and literature, civilizations, social sciences, and natural sciences and mathematics (which includes at least two from natural sciences). At least one foreign language course is required. Students must also take a course in academic writing.

Also, undergraduates must take one course involving quantitative, inductive and deductive reasoning, and one course that incorporates "interpretative and aesthetic approaches." They must also take two courses exposing them to each of three "focused inquiries": "cross-cultural inquiry," "science technology and society," and "ethical inquiry." Some courses might count in more than one of these categories. A class on African art, for example, might satisfy the art and literature requirement, the aesthetic approach requirement, and the "cross-cultural inquiry" requirement.

While some might see the new curriculum as an improvement on the old, because it at least requires exposure to unpopular yet important fields such as science or mathematics, others say it's just more of the same. It now requires cross-cultural inquiry without any requirement that the student take a core survey course in Western civilization or any similar course.

For real cross-cultural studies, try Duke's international programs; more than 40 percent of Duke students study abroad for a summer, semester, or year. Duke runs programs in more than ten countries and also encourages students to study elsewhere on other universities' programs if they want to go elsewhere. Credits transfer, and the cost is comparable to studies in Durham.

The new curriculum also reduces the number of required courses from fifteen to as few as thirteen — allowing undergraduates more electives in specialized courses without requiring a basic understanding of the field in question. There may be other unintended consequences, too: though students and faculty members report that the hard sciences remain solid, some worry that, because more students will be taking science and math courses under the new curriculum, professors will water down the more basic courses.

The lack of structure in the curriculum means that, as one student put it, "whatever a student's major, he is going to have at least a couple of very liberal teachers . . . [and] some students do graduate after having taken four years of pure and total nonsense."

Duke does have many outstanding teachers, and serious students should seek them out rather than rely on the curricular structure to land them in classes taught by these professors. According to faculty and students, the best teachers at Duke include Victor Strandberg, Kenny J. Williams, Reynolds Price, Michael Valdez Moses, Buford Jones, Ian Baucom, Jennifer Thorn, Thomas Pfau, James W. Applewhite, and Deborah Pope in English; Bruce Kuniholm, Peter Wood, and Alex Roland in history; Michael A. Gillespie, Ruth W. Grant, Peter D. Feaver, Christopher F. Gelpi, Albert F. Eldridge, John H. Aldrich, and Allen Kornberg in political science; Diskin Clay and Francis Newton in classical studies; Michael Ferejohn and Martin Golding in philosophy; Frank L. Borchardt in Germanic languages and literature; Richard Hodel in mathematics; Craufurd Goodwin in economics; and Ronald D. Perkins in earth and ocean sciences. The departments and programs noted for excellence include political science, economics, Slavic languages and literature, and classical studies.

Apart from these departments and in other professors' classrooms, the bizarre classes of recent Duke history continue. The all-too-familiar political themes are sexuality, Marxism, oppression, etc., which are present not only in classes devoted exclusively to those topics, but also in more traditional disciplines such as history, literature, and art.

Look, for example, at Duke's "Marxism and Society" program, which offers a certificate (similar to a minor) and a lecture series. According to university literature, the Marxism and Society Program focuses on an "appraisal of Marxist methods of analysis and their social implications," and includes topics such as "sexual and racial inequality, alienation, development and underdevelopment in the world system, labor processes, protest movements and ideologies." You get the idea. Indeed, the director of this program, Professor Frederic Jameson, once told *Commentary* magazine that preparing students for the "struggles of the future" was "the supreme mission of a Marxist pedagogy." Those who think a free exchange of ideas is the hallmark of a liberal arts education had best avoid this program. It's worth noting that courses in thirteen Duke departments count toward the certificate in Marxism and Society, which says something about those departments.

The study of Marxism was chic at Duke in the late 1980s and early 1990s, but the near total collapse of the Soviet empire, coupled with the departure of some of the trendiest professors, has taken its toll. "The steam has gone out of the Marxists," says one professor. "They used to have a lot of power, but now a lot of residual people like Fred Jameson are passe."

If studying Marxism sounds boring, students might try to earn a certificate in a topic Duke views as fresh and exciting: sexuality. Duke's "Program in the Study of Sexualities," unveiled in 1996, advertises itself as a "vital and active field of academic inquiry and scholarly research." Study topics include "a wide range from heterosexuality to homosexuality, and include other erotic desires, sexual relationships, and gender roles." Some students have criticized the program for its transparent political activism.

A sister department is women's studies, which is just as strong now at Duke as it's ever been. Women's studies is a field that is probably the most notoriously and routinely politicized. An introductory course, Women's Studies 103, lists the following as titles of readings: "Loving Another Woman," "If Men Could Menstruate," and "Using Pregnancy to Control Women." The class syllabus encourages students to attend political rallies and then "to incorporate these events in your papers or use them as springboards for further study."

Many otherwise academic departments — English, history, foreign language, for example — now routinely cross-list courses with the women's studies program. Nobody has challenged the spread of these courses, which have multiplied like bacteria. "The women have won the battle with women's studies," a professor says. "They've got everything they want, so they're relatively quiet."

Perhaps the most high-profile department at Duke is its notorious English department, which has been featured in front-page *New York Times* articles, *Wall Street Journal* pieces, and scores of academic magazines for its high-dollar, trendy brand of avant-garde "scholarship." Since its heyday as the department to emulate, many of its stars have left for greener pastures. What remains is chiefly a blend between old-guard traditionalists and newer, younger professors who, if not traditional, are at least open-minded and provide a solid grounding in English. Fanatics are still around, of course, but they have far fewer of the perquisites, privileges, and clout they once enjoyed.

Political Atmosphere: Southern Climate?

People who know nothing about Duke might believe that because it's in the heart of conservative North Carolina, a state that has, seemingly since the beginning of time, elected Jesse Helms to the U.S. Senate, that the political climate at Duke is conservative, or at least traditional. It's not. Duke has made a habit of drawing liberal professors and administrations from other parts of the country. The collusion between certain professors and administrators creates a climate that encourages uncritical exploration of other cultures, political activities under the guise of scholarship and value, and judgment-free living while disdaining the study and appreciation of Western civilization.

From the moment eager Duke students set foot on campus to years after they leave, these are the major themes the administration projects.

There are the usual orientation meetings on racism and sexism and rape and "homophobia." As a student makes his way through Duke, wildly liberal professors become unavoidable. Many of Duke's younger faculty members are more willing to politicize their courses than are their older colleagues. "The younger members of the faculty are much more liberal [than their elders]," says one student. "However, the older ones are often scared to be bold in their more conservative views and often present certain things that may oppose their [own] ideas. They are simply scared that they will not be thought to be open-minded. In other words, the older members of the faculty are over-compensating to the left-wing agenda."

And after students graduate, Duke seeks to find out how successful its cultural education has been. In a survey sent to Duke alumni in March 2000, the university asks questions such as how much interaction alumni had with blacks, Asians, Native Americans, etc., while at Duke (none, little, some, substantial, the most) versus how much they have now. Another question asks: "While you were an undergraduate, did you ever seriously question or rethink your beliefs or values . . . about people with sexual orientations other than your own?" The implication is that Duke wants to know how much luck it has had in making students accept homosexuality and have friends of different racial backgrounds — in other words, how it's molded them.

The campus climate is liberal. Rarely does a week at Duke pass without a task force report on racism, a panel on gender issues, a rally against sweatshops, and the like.

The emphasis on "diversity" at Duke has its cost. Students and professors say the student body is racially divided. There's not necessarily any animosity, but students of the same race typically stick together. Student activity fees fund these race-based groups, and the university does its part by holding, for example, prospective student weekends targeting blacks one week and Hispanics the next.

"It's fragmenting into more and more smaller and smaller groups: American Indians, Chicanos, West Indians, Pacific Islanders, and so on," says one humanities professor. "It's sort of like the census. For each box to check, there's an organized group."

There have been several "racial incidents" at Duke in recent years, the sorts of things that speak more to the heightened and irrational sensitivity of the campus than any sort of racism that many non-Southerners associate with Southern schools. In one highly publicized incident, in the spring of 1999, several students had agitated for the formation of a major in Hindi. In response, a Duke freshman wrote a letter to the campus paper saying students should study Western civilization before foreign cultures. According to the *Chronicle of Higher Education,* the writer was then the victim of several threatening and anonymous e-mails, one of which read: "WE WILL BEAT YOU WITHIN ONE INCH OF YOUR LIFE!" He was visited by three Indian students who called him a racist and threatened him with violence. The university claimed it investigated the threats but pressed no charges, and Duke President Nan Keohane later told the freshman that she thought the thugs were "just blowing off steam." (The university later made the study of Hindi a concentration within an existing major.)

A few years earlier, the campus was in an uproar for several days after a Duke employee found a brown doll hanging from a tree near a bench frequented by black students. Campus police began investigating what student activists called a "mock lynching" and a "hate crime." But police dropped the investigation when two black students came forward and admitted to hanging the doll to "make a political statement." The two were not prosecuted, and the university refuses even to release their identities.

The political bias of speakers at the university has come under fire in recent years. In the 1999-2000 school year, the school's major speakers committee brought in Johnny Cochran, Ralph Nader, Al Franken, and Joycelyn Elders. That led one sophomore to complain to the campus paper that "each speaker delivered a message entwined with liberal political views . . . without balancing them with speakers of the opposing ideology."

In the last few years, Duke has been at the forefront at the latest activist rallying cry: opposition to alleged "sweatshops" that produce college apparel. Duke was among the first schools in the country where students demanded that their college change licensing agreements with clothing manufacturers to provide for disclosure of labor conditions in overseas factories. At Duke, a small band of students staged a sit-in in the administration building until the university president acceded to their demands. This earned Duke a rating from *Mother Jones* magazine, in 1998, as the number-1 activist school in the world.

The ranking surprised many students, because it's only a small segment of the student population that worries about such things. Despite the school's left-wing political climate, most students just shrug it off and go about their business of studying or playing sports or relaxing. With the beauty of Duke's campus, the pleasant climate, and so many other things going on, most Duke students realize that there are more important things than paying heed to a small and zealous sect of agitating students.

Student Life: Won't Go Back to Tobacco Road

Though it's home to North Carolina Central University and Duke University, Durham is not a college town in the sense that Chapel Hill and Charlottesville are college towns. Durham is an old tobacco town — it's even home to a tobacco museum, complete with a mechanical farmer who explains how tobacco is grown and old TV commercials featuring the weatherbeaten Marlboro Man. While it's now becoming better known for nearby high-tech Research Triangle Park, Durham lacks a major, centralized strip of bars, restaurants, and shops that cater to the college crowd (although Ninth Street, near Duke's East Campus, is experiencing somewhat of a rebirth).

For that reason, most of Duke's social scene and activities take place on campus, though some upperclassmen favor the bar scene in nearby Chapel Hill (home to the University of North Carolina).

About 90 percent of Duke students live on campus, and the university does guarantee housing for all four years. Freshmen, known at Duke as "first-year students," live on East Campus, home to brick dorms, an auditorium, a library, athletic fields, a gym, classrooms, an art museum, and several of the humanities departments. Upperclassmen have a choice between West Campus dorms and Central Campus apartments, although some unlucky sophomores get stuck in a North Campus dorm somewhat isolated from everywhere else. No matter where they are located, the dorms feature condom vending machines — and it is therefore not surprising that, as one recent alumnus stated, in the dorms "you can see anyone you want at any hour of the day." Single-sex living is available for both men and women; coed dorms usually, but not always, divide the sexes by floor. There are reportedly no coed bathrooms.

West Campus is Duke's main campus; it houses the administration building, the student center, Duke's main library, the towering neo-Gothic chapel, most classrooms, academic departments, and the football and basketball stadiums. Buses connect the campuses.

There's no lack of student groups on campus, and there's something for everyone, from ethnic groups to literary magazines, choirs to a student-run radio station. Duke has an active ROTC program, which awards scholarships to students who commit to joining the military after graduation. Students get most of their information on campus from *The Chronicle,* Duke's daily newspaper whose letters page is often a repository for charges of racism, calls to protest, perceived slights, and often sarcastic political debate. *The Duke Review* is the college's conservative paper, prone to pointing out the follies and excesses of Duke administrators and student leaders.

Duke's student government organization, like that of many schools, tends to take itself seriously yet is paid little heed by most students. Though it divvies up thousands of dollars to student groups, including some with political agendas, it touches most students' lives by overseeing the line-monitoring and tenting policies for Duke basketball games.

If there's one uniting experience among a radically diverse group of students, it's Duke basketball. The team is almost always a contender for the national championship. In the age of rampant NCAA violations, Duke prides itself on running a squeaky-clean program that graduates nearly all of its athletes (except recently, when a handful started to leave school early for professional basketball). The student fans (the "Cameron Crazies") pride themselves on inventing new cheers to taunt the opposition, and it must be said that they are among the country's most inventive (and, sometimes, crass) hands at this. Much of the school's social life between December and March revolves around basketball, from camping out in tents for weeks before the home game (a tent city known as Krzyzewskiville, after coach Mike Krzyzewski) against archrival North Carolina, to the game itself, to the occasional celebratory bonfire afterwards. The bonfire ritual, some say, is becoming less common and less rowdy than in years past. "Every year, the bonfire gets lamer and lamer," a recent graduate complained to the campus paper. "At least my freshman year, there was a hell of a lot of nudity."

The football team is less popular, and less successful. There are also plenty of other intercollegiate, club, and intramural sports at Duke.

In recent years, the university has been taking a harder line on alcohol. In the early '90s, beer flowed nearly every night of the week from fraternity taps. Now, such parties are limited to weekends, and Greeks must hire a university-approved bartender to dispense the beer. At the same, the university has been trying to provide alternative, alcohol-free activities. A student-run movie theater is popular, and there are forums and panels on nearly any topic imaginable most nights of the week.

Despite its efforts, Duke has still had several well-publicized problems with alcohol in recent years. In November 1999, a Duke student died from aspiration pneumonia, which he contracted by inhaling his vomit after a night of binge drinking. Image-conscious administrators at first covered up the role of alcohol in the student's death — saying he simply died of pneumonia — until a second student contracted the same "disease" three months later, again after a night of drinking. She recovered, and administrators fessed up and wrung hands profusely over covering up whole truth and missing a "teachable moment" about alcohol abuse. The same year, a fraternity and sorority were also suspended while administrators investigated allegations of excessive drinking.

There is a substance-free freshman dorm on Duke's East Campus, but administrators rejected requests for a similar upperclassman dorm on West Campus, saying there was insufficient demand.

Besides alcohol violations, crime — even serious crime like robberies and forcible sex offenses — is not a rare occurrence on and around the Duke campus. Durham can be pretty rough, and East Campus, where the freshmen live, is particularly dangerous because of its proximity to the city proper. West Campus, where most of the classroom buildings are, is much safer.

Emory University

Office of Admissions
1380 Oxford Road NE
Atlanta, GA 30322
(404) 727-6036
www.emory.edu

Total enrollment: 11,398
Undergraduates: 6,316
SAT ranges (Verbal/Math): 630-715 (V); 650-725 (M)
Applicants: 9,850
Accepted: 43%
Enrolled: 28%
Application deadline: January 15
Financial aid application deadline: April 1
Tuition: $24,532/$32,400
Core curriculum: No

It's Money That Matters

That Emory University continues to grow in stature and national name-recognition is no accident. For many years its leaders have capitalized on its wealth to attract bright scholars in an array of disciplines to its bustling campus in Atlanta's pleasant Druid Hills neighborhood. While the monetary gifts of former Coca-Cola CEO and Emory graduate Robert Woodruff are legendary, they are as significant for the support they have attracted as for the gifts themselves. Money attracts money, whether in the world of socialites or universities, and today Emory finds that getting attention — and the money that seems to always follow — is easier than ever.

Founded in Oxford, Georgia, as a training ground for Methodist pastors in 1836, Emory today encompasses a broad collection of schools and colleges in virtually every field. While most schools founded in the early nineteenth century are either memories or small colleges, Emory is increasingly a national university. It moved to its current location in 1919, yet the campus seems much younger, with its large number of new buildings and the constant rumble of construction machinery — signs of affluence and ambition. The Centers for Disease Control and Prevention and the American Cancer Society are located on campus, and help to keep the school in the media's sights most of the time. Federal dollars combined with private support maintain excellent facilities in the sciences, and Emory's hospital is the best in the state and a leader nationwide. All of this, combined with Atlanta's dynamic economy, allows the university to attract high-caliber faculty from all over the world.

During the 1990s, Emory spent a great deal of money, some of it unwisely, in purchasing the services of professors whose work put them at the so-called "cutting edge" of their fields. This came at a price far higher than their salaries and perks: their careerism and zeal politicized much of the curriculum and soured the collegiality of both faculty and students. Today there are still plenty of zealots on campus who measure a colleague's worth by his adherence to intellectual fads, yet things have changed for the better in recent years as nihilism has become increasingly stale and the current crop of students seems more bent on making the cut than cutting each other's throats.

Academic Life: The Up and Up

Emory's academic life has never been better in spite of the presence of a coterie of radical professors and students who seek to politicize every element of life. Several years ago these professors seemed to have gotten the upper hand in hiring faculty, awarding tenure, and constructing the curriculum. And they're still there, to be sure, in numbers that should worry anyone committed to learning in an atmosphere free of fear from speech and thought police. Also, students must be vigilant if they are to avoid political indoctrination (and waste thousands of dollars) by taking the wrong classes. Nevertheless, a few recent developments are to be applauded.

Among them is a new requirement for everyone in Emory College (the school of arts and sciences for undergraduates) to take a foreign language. This is true multiculturalism, not the ersatz ideological variety, and strengthens the curriculum. All students must also take a course in Western cultures and history, another positive move. Yet this requirement, for one course only, is matched by the college's requirement for a course in non-Western cultures. The point here is not that the latter courses are unworthy of study, for many of them are. And it's certainly not that students shouldn't study foreign cultures, which they should. It is that students in a Western country studying in a Western institution speaking a Western language should study that culture more.

Other requirements are typical of those found in most modern universities. There is nothing approaching a core curriculum, and the distribution requirements vary widely in both usefulness and degree of politicization. Some are fairly straightforward: a freshman writing requirement; a course in mathematics or computer science; and two courses in natural science. Others that appear to be traditional in nature and scope turn out, on closer inspection, to include very politicized choices. Among this lot are the two courses in the social sciences. While this requirement may be fulfilled with courses in economics or political science, most of the offerings are narrow and often politicized. These include: Education 314, "Education and Cultural Diversity"; Women's Studies 322, "Introduction to Gay and Lesbian Studies"; Sociology 225/Women's Studies 221, "Sociology of Sex and Gender"; African American Studies 101, "Dynamics of the Black Community"; and Women's Studies 100, "Introduction to Women's Studies."

Other questionable courses may be taken in order to fulfill the two-course humanities requirement. Again, there are legitimate courses and others over-specialized, politicized, or both. While an offering such as Art History 101, "Art and Architecture from Prehistory to the Renaissance," have great potential, courses such as Film Studies 381, "Introduction to Film Theory," and 372, "History of Film Since 1938," or Spanish 312, "Theories of Hispanic Theatre and Film," are too specialized to pass as general education courses and should be preceded by less specialized introductions to these fields of study.

Another requirement, "Historical, Cultural, and International Perspectives," has two sections requiring one courses each. The first, "U.S. History," might make one think that Emory is the rare school that believes its students should know something about American history. Yet the requirement description reveals something quite different: "One course [is required] from the list below on the history of politics, society, or culture in the United States providing a perspective on American diversity. This course examines the use of historical methods, offers perspectives on the history of the United States, and relates the United States to the rest of the world." The courses offered back up this pledge. Among them: Sociology 247, "Race and Ethnic Relations"; History 336/Women's Studies 336, "Multi-Cultural History of Women in the U.S."; and Interdisciplinary Studies 112, "American Identities."

The companion requirement, "Historical Perspectives on Western Culture," is much more legitimate, as students may study a number of different elements of non-U.S. Western culture in the one class required. Yet a third area requirement, "Nonwestern Cultures or Comparative and International Studies," is much less appealing, not so much because it is non-Western as because many of the classes that fulfill this requirement are again over-specialized or politicized. They forget that they are supposed to be introductions. These include: Interdisciplinary Studies 113, "The Politics of Identity"; Chinese 360, "Modern Chinese Women in Film and Fiction"; and AFS 282/History of Art 282, "Arts of Eastern and Southern Africa." Yet some of the courses listed under this requirement sound promising: Classics 104, "Ancient Cities and Urban Culture"; Chinese 270, "The Heritage of China"; and Middle Eastern Studies 100, "Introduction to the Middle East." These courses, because of their general nature and apolitical approach, are far more suitable as part of a liberal education.

Although Emory has become a research university at which professors who bring in grant money are valued over those who don't, "teaching is taken pretty seriously here," according to one professor. "I've seen people with mediocre teaching records pay for it" at tenure time, this faculty member says. Among the strongest departments at Emory are political science, English, history, biology, and psychology.

The weakest are the foreign language departments, which one professor describes as "pretty political." Another professor describes these departments as "mere political parties."

Also politicized is a the Interdisciplinary Studies in Culture and Society department, described by one faculty member as "politicized to the tee with gay and lesbian material and postmodern crap." Among its offerings: Interdisciplinary Studies 385H/Women's Studies 384J/African American Studies 270G, "Race, Gender, and the Body: Stereotypes and New Types." The course description reads, in part: "How do such factors as race, gender, class, ability and sexuality influence the popular representations of women that we often see in our society? This interdisciplinary course will explore . . . both literary and visual representations of the body in western culture and focus on the intersections of race and gender in these images. We will begin our study with the black female body, which is often used as the measure difference [sic], specifically in terms of the formation of identities and power relations in western ideology. We will further our study by drawing comparisons between this figure and other figures, including other 'colored' female bodies, the black male body, and white male and female bodies. . . . [W]e will further consider the ways in which social images shape and/or reflect social realities, as well as explore how particular writers and artists revise and interrogate such imagees [sic] — from archetypes to stereotypes to 'new types.'"

Or misguided students can try Interdisciplinary Studies 385K/Religion 329/Environmental Studies 329, "Religion and Ecology: A Theory Practice Learning Approach," in which they "will examine several paradigms of nature as sacred, including ones from Christianity, Buddhism, and Amerindian. Perspectives from Feminism, Deep Ecology, Global Ethics, and poetic discourse will be used for further analysis." What's more, "There will be opportunities for the class to develop consciousness of 'place' including the relationships of 'place' and eco-justice."

Particularly egregious — especially in a school founded by and for Methodists — is the politicization found in the religion department and the Candler School of Theology, both of which employ numerous professors for whom religion is little more than a socially constructed opium for the masses and peculiar to a specific time and place. Along with standard courses on Christian history, ethics, and world religions, students may also choose from a broad selection of topics which place less emphasis on traditional approaches to the study of religion than on gender, class, race, disabilities, and social activism. The religion department expects all students and faculty to adhere to a statement on inclusive language that forbids the use of "man," "mankind," or "he" to denote all persons.

On the bright side of things, among the best teachers at Emory are Elizabeth Fox-Genovese, Kenneth W. Stein, Patrick N. Allitt, and Thomas S. Burns in history; Merle Black, Harvey Klehr, Randall W. Strahan, Robert C. Bartlette, and Carrie R. Wickham in political science; Marshall P. Duke in psychology; Donald W. Livingston, Donald Phillip Verene, and Ann Hartle in philosophy; and Paul H. Rubin in economics.

The work ethic at Emory is probably more developed than at many universities. Many students, aiming at prestigious graduate schools, are quite serious, yet the overall atmosphere is relaxed and Southern. Class sizes are generally small, graduate student teaching assistants are used less than at many large state universities, and professors are available for private meetings. Most teachers consider class discussions as important as written work, and there are many guided research projects and reading programs that further encourage professor-student relationships. A bright student can still obtain a very good education at Emory, but he will need to be forearmed with information on the best and worst the school has to offer.

Political Atmosphere: Moving On

Several years ago Emory was in the grip of a student body leadership that sought to impose, through force, their radicalized vision of the world on the entire campus. This vocal yet small number of student activists sought to use a loosely written harassment code to intimidate into silence anyone who strayed from politically correct speech or action. Yet things have lightened up a bit of late, according to faculty and students. "It's better now than it was a few years ago," a professor says. "There were a few student radicals who graduated, and their successors are less vocal and less harmful."

University President William Chase, the former president of Wesleyan College in Connecticut, has vowed to make Emory a model of multicultural education. This is unfortunate, since in practice it means little more than seeking the approval of the professional education establishment — a group that looks after its own interests with little regard for the well-being of students.

It may also mean that no opposition will be tolerated. Over the past few years the Emory administration has forced — literally — several of its own professors from campus. These disputes involve alleged misdeeds by the professors, who in turn contend that they are being victimized for crossing swords with an administration that allows no one to question its policies. According to the *Chronicle of Higher Education,* three tenured faculty members have been escorted off campus by security guards and told not to return or contact their former colleagues. According to the *Chronicle,* these professors, two from the medical school and one from the business school, claim gross mistreatment by the administration. One medical school professor "was handcuffed by armed security guards at the Emory-affiliated hospital where he worked," the *Chronicle* reported, after he wrote to elected officials and accused the school of putting the health of patients at risk by cutting costs too severely. The next day, Emory sent a message to his home (at midnight) ordering him to stay away from campus and avoid contact with colleagues. Another professor of medicine was ordered to turn over his medical records to the administration and undergo psychiatric testing, a move that was condemned by the National Mental Health Association of Georgia. He claims that "Emory is punishing him for blowing the whistle on the administration's alleged misuse of federal money — a charge campus officials deny," reported the *Chronicle*.

Curiously, the strongest opposition to these actions has come not from the faculty but from students. Given the threat of legal action, it is somewhat understandable that many faculty members would be loath to risk home and savings in the defense of scholarly integrity, although one could wish for a stronger stand. Yet many faculty are cowed by a fear known to adolescents everywhere: social ostracism. Beyond the actions of a few brave souls who, in fact, are often thanked privately by colleagues too fearful to speak up themselves in public, the defense of freedom of speech on campus often falls to students who by their nature are more fearless and transient than their teachers.

Nevertheless, professors say that the general atmosphere, especially in Emory College, where most undergraduates matriculate, is better now than in the recent past. One faculty member says that "things are a little bit less [oppressive] than in the past," because, he says, some of the most politicized offerings are held in check because they lack departmental standing. This source says that "both women's studies and the African American studies program are programs, not departments, so their faculty have appointments in departments," a fact that means that these faculty members must have "departmental legitimacy." "We don't have people who float in a nether world without a discipline," says another teacher. "These departments at Emory are not nearly as politicized as they are at other universities where they've attained departmental status." And the trends in the student body noted above apply to the faculty as well. "Professors still talk about multiculturalism and diversity, but less than four or five years ago," according to a professor. "This is even true with faculty searches. Today, if there's no minority candidate on your search list [for new faculty positions], it isn't automatically assumed that you've failed."

Student Life: The Atlanta Games

Emory's undergraduate student body hails from across the nation and around the world. "They're probably brighter than ever before," says a long-time professor. Yet, this faculty member adds, "they also probably read less than their predecessors, a trait that is true across the country."

These students get to live in the beautiful and relatively safe Druid Hills neighborhood of Atlanta, a city known for its red-hot economy. When students wish to unwind, they have at their disposal the resources of the South's flagship city, itself only two hours from the mountains and five hours from the coast. Atlanta attracts national tours of bands, orchestras, and cultural exhibits to suit almost any taste or sophistication, and its own musical, artistic, and cultural institutions are either already superb (as with the symphony) or up-and-coming. And the city is also home to numerous ethnic minorities from every continent, giving it an international flavor once found only in the large cities of the North.

Although Emory does not field a varsity football team, students enthusiastically support nine intercollegiate and no fewer than forty intramural teams for men, as well as eight intercollegiate and forty intramural teams for women. As a member of the NCAA's Division III, the school gives no athletic scholarships, but the sports facilities are excellent: there are tennis courts, a huge new gymnasium, and an Olympic-sized swimming pool. Nature lovers enjoy Lullwater, a park that adjoins the campus and features walking trails, fields, and a small lake.

The 630-acre campus itself is an attraction with its gentle hills, spreading trees, and generous — though shrinking — green space. Many buildings are colorful and rather grand, with marble facades and red roofs, while others mimic the unfortunate Bauhaus style that seems so dated to everyone but campus-design architects. The new money at Emory has generated a rush of new construction, including a library and new residential halls. Other impressive facilities have also sprouted up recently, most notably a large research/science center, a student center, and an art and archaeology museum.

All this expansion has enabled Emory to inject new vitality into campus life. There are about two hundred groups and organizations, including Amnesty International, College Republicans, Young Democrats, Alternative Spring Break (which sends students on service-oriented projects), various religious, ethnic, and cultural groups, and Emory's Amazing Throwing Up Society, a juggling club. There is also the President's Commission on Lesbian/Gay/Bisexual/Transgender Concerns, the mission statement of which begins: "The [commission] serves as an advisory body to the president, and derives its authority from the president." Members to this body are appointed by the president himself, upon recommendation by the group.

Emory has twenty-five fraternities and sororities to which about half the students belong. The Greeks lead the social scene, but don't dominate it; there are simply too many alternatives. When students want a break from campus life, downtown Atlanta is only five miles away. There they find myriad cultural attractions, as well as cinemas, malls, gardens, bars, and restaurants. The Metropolitan Atlanta Rapid Transportation System (MARTA) goes to all parts of the city. Students can also find many amenities within walking distance of the university. Crime is not a major problem at Emory, and the campus security system is quite good. Drug use stays in the closet; alcohol use does not. "Our biggest problem is dealing with drugs and alcohol," says a professor familiar with the undergraduate social scene. "Students here drink a lot, not unlike other places. On weekends it gets out of hand." This faculty member says that alcohol abuse is a more significant problem than drugs. Bars and nightclubs in the posh entertainment district of Buckhead, just a few miles away, even sent buses to fetch students in the evenings and then poured them back onto campus in an effort to reduce drunk driving.

Housing at Emory has been in shorter supply recently because of the increased

size of incoming freshman classes. Many students prefer to live in apartments or fraternities, however, and almost all students who desire university housing receive it.
Freshmen must live on campus; upperclassmen's housing is determined by lottery.
All dormitories are coed except for one allotted to women. There are no coed bathrooms. Comfort levels range from doubles with no sink to small apartments with
kitchens.

University of Florida

Office of Admissions
201 Criser Hall
Gainesville, FL 32611
(352) 392-1365
www.ufl.edu

Total enrollment: 45,441
Undergraduates: 33,118
SAT ranges (Verbal/Math): 580-670 (V); 590-690 (M)
Applicants: 20,324
Accepted: 60%
Enrolled: 51%
Application deadline: January 16
Financial aid application deadline: March 15
Tuition: resident: $2,300/$7,920; non-resident: $9,810/$15,250
Core curriculum: No

Statistical Anomaly

Florida is a big, land-grant, public research school. As such, it is characterized by a
great deal of heterogeneity, a huge student body (the sixth-largest in the country)
and campus (nearly 2,000 acres), and a wide variety of course and program offerings.

But academically, it's a bit better than all that would seem to indicate, at least
compared to many of its land-grant, state-school peers. Florida is relatively selective
and draws a number of high-quality students, more than the university's sheer size

would itself predict. And, appropriately enough for a university that traces its roots back to the East Florida Seminary, a more traditional, Southern-inspired atmosphere can still be detected here and there. Diversity-mongering at Florida is a bit more muted than at comparable institutions, and there are active and strong religious communities and conservative/traditional voices among the student body and even — gasp! — the faculty. After all, explains one student, "this *is* rural Northern Florida." But even so, the pessimistic might be forgiven for wondering just how long this comparatively balanced, moderate — even, in some ways, idyllic — atmosphere will last.

Academic Life: Gordon Rules

"The liberal arts and sciences form the intellectual core of the university," according to university materials. But there is no core curriculum at Florida. All undergraduates must instead complete a thirty-six-hour "general education" requirement, and it's not a demanding one. It includes three hours in composition, six in mathematical sciences, and nine each in humanities, social and behavioral sciences, and physical and biological sciences. There is also an "International and Diversity" requirement, which may be fulfilled simultaneously with a general education requirement; courses that meet this requirement "focus on diversity among nations (the 'international' component) and/or within a nation (including the U.S.). The latter includes differences such as gender, class, race, ethnicity, sexuality, or culture," according to university materials. Students need six such hours to graduate.

The state of Florida's "Gordon Rule" requires — or intends to require — students to achieve competence in "communication" and "computation." In order to satisfy this rule, students must get at least a C in courses that require, in total, at least 24,000 words of substantial writing. Courses are labeled as requiring either zero, two thousand, four thousand, or six thousand words. The computation component simply requires a C or higher in six hours of math-related courses, one of which must actually be a class in mathematics. This obviously adds nothing extra to the university's mathematical sciences requirement listed above.

With a student to faculty ratio of twenty-two to one, there are a number of large courses at Florida (almost a quarter of the sections in fall 1999 had more than fifty students enrolled). Students, especially upperclassmen, can find smaller classes without too much trouble though. They have more difficulty selecting a major, since more than one hundred are offered.

The Honors Program provides smaller classes, exclusive dorms, special advising, and — it is hoped — a unique social and academic community for elite students during their first two years on campus. Special Honors sections of required courses are particularly beneficial, as the university candidly puts it, "when you are trying to decide whether to take a twenty-five-person honors class or a two hundred–person lecture class to fulfill a Gordon Rule or General Education requirement." The Honors Program also offers courses designed and held for honors students only; the seriousness of these courses varies widely, from "Masterworks of Music" to "Fred's Food Factory." The rigor of honors courses, according to university materials, does not exceed that of standard courses. The program seems designed more with the goal of luring high-quality students to UF than in providing them with a uniquely valuable educational experience.

Former president John Lombardi instituted the Teaching Improvement Program, with the aid of the state legislature, in 1992 (the program applies to all state schools in Florida). Growing explicitly out of his dissatisfaction with the disproportionate weight assigned to research productivity in faculty evaluation, the plan attempts to reward excellence in undergraduate teaching. Faculty are nominated for awards by their committees, department chairs, and deans; winners receive a $5,000 increase in base pay. Those who teach more students and spend more hours in the classroom are more likely to win; faculty must also put together portfolios demonstrating the quality of their teaching. Perhaps not too much should be made of this plan; as one professor states, Florida still "emphasizes research at the expense of undergraduate teaching." And the plan has flaws (e.g., it would seem to create an incentive for departments to offer large classes so that its faculty could demonstrate "productivity") as well as its critics, but it is clearly a step in the right direction and represents a uniquely strong commitment to teaching for a research school, however unsatisfactory this commitment might still be.

In addition, under the university's "bank" system, the budgets of Florida's colleges are tied, in part, to their success in limiting the number of courses taught by adjuncts and teaching assistants; unfortunately, budgets are also tied to items such as research productivity, fund raising, and other monetary factors, which may act to decrease the quality of teaching. This "business model" was also championed by former president Lombardi.

Grade inflation, according to one professor, is "no worse here than in other institutions." One student echoes this, saying that students have to work for A's, "but probably not as hard as we should."

Stephen McKnight and Robert Hatch in history; Sanford Berg in economics; Thomas Auxter and Robert D'Amico in philosophy; William Kelso, Richard Conley, and David Hedge in political science; and Rodman Webb and Gordon Greenwood in educational psychology are among the relatively many good professors at Florida.

Offerings in the philosophy department are generally substantial, traditional, and unpoliticized; it appears that majors in philosophy will get a very good education in that discipline. Political science is said to have strong teaching and, according to one student, while "definitely not top notch" is "certainly above average." Professors in the department, though for the most part avowedly liberal, are said to be generally even-handed. Even the history department is comparatively traditional in its focus and content. The majority of the faculty specialize in either U.S. or Euro-

273

pean/Mediterranean history (something that cannot be taken for granted at other schools), and the history of science is especially well-covered. (Unfortunately, there is but one required course for majors, and one can get as trivial and unsatisfactory education in history as is possible elsewhere.) Economics is also a strong department, though it is unfortunately placed in the College of Business Administration instead of Liberal Arts and Sciences.

It will come as no surprise that the English department contains the usual politicized offerings (do we really need English majors in courses titled as poorly as "Contemporary U.S. Women of Color: (Re) rac-/class-/gender-/sex-ing identities"?). Women's studies, according to one senior, is "incredibly leftist." The social sciences generally are also said to be more ideological than other departments.

Political Atmosphere: People Awareness

Governor Jeb Bush's One Florida Plan and its "Talented 20" provision, instituted before the 1999-2000 academic year, abolished racial preferences in admissions and replaced it with guaranteed admission for the top 20 percent of graduating seniors from Florida high schools. Many university officials, faculty, and students were quite critical, and it was the cause of much recent controversy. However, in the plan's first year, African-American enrollment increased by 33 percent and Hispanic enrollment by 19 percent (some of which, critics said, may have been due to population growth; but it also had something to do with the university redoubling its minority recruiting efforts). However, if such success continues, the controversy is likely to disappear.

There are a number of official university programs to cater to different identity groups. The Office for Student Services runs the Institute of Black Culture and Institute of Hispanic-Latino Cultures. There is a Multicultural Affairs Office and a University Minority Mentor Program as well. The former office administers something called the Gender Awareness Program (GAP), "a peer education program to assist students and student organizations with issues of gender." GAP "peer educators," as they are called, apparently serve as a sort of campus gender police.

The Multicultural Affairs Office also runs the Friends of Lesbians, Gays, and Bisexuals program and the Committee on Sexism and Homophobia, which sponsors "educational programs" to produce right thinking. There is also a Gay, Lesbian, Bisexual, and Transgender Resource Center (from whose Web site the visitor is just one link away from other sites selling "anatomically correct" dolls, among other things), and the GLBT community on campus has called for "sensitivity training" for resident assistants and campus police.

Each fall brings the event with the mind-numbingly banal name, People Awareness Week, "a celebration of the diverse student body, faculty, and staff of the University of Florida," or, as the university material goes on to say, "really a celebration of ourselves." In 1999, noted scholars Woody Harrelson, MTV veejay Kennedy, and others were brought to campus as part of the week's events, where they spoke about, according to the school newspaper, "issues ranging from the medical use of marijuana to the Zapatista movement to free speech and censorship."

It is worth noting that there is a remarkably visible religious presence as well. The Christian Faculty Fellowship regularly sponsors lectures by well-known Christian intellectuals, including philosopher J. Budziszewski, historian George Marsden, and biochemist Michael Behe. It also places an annual advertisement inviting students to "Ask us about our faith and how it has shaped our lives. . . . We are available to talk to you about any matter that concerns you." The 2000 ad had 190 signers. There are also a number of active Hindu, Muslim, and Jewish student groups representing other religious perspectives.

This aspect of the University of Florida environment helps make it unique among large state schools. There are, according to one professor, "active, vocal faculty groups that support conservative causes without stigma." In general, says this professor, "there is a small but effective voice for conservative issues. Moreover, the College Republicans is as large and as active as the College Democrats." Thus, there is a balance to the political atmosphere at Florida that is largely absent elsewhere. Says one student leader, Florida is "definitely not a radical place." Conservative voices are not afraid to speak out; in fact, according to one student, the student government includes perhaps more conservative Republicans than liberal Democrats, and as a body it is receptive to political views from across the spectrum. Even the lecture program is, as one student puts it, "incredibly balanced." The student speakers' bureau, called Accent, has a very large budget, and has in the past brought in speakers such as Mikhail Gorbachev and Steve Forbes. Its sense of fairness was illustrated when, during the 2000 campaign, it sponsored speeches by both Ralph Nader and Pat Buchanan.

Though one professor says that "'free speech' is probably as circumscribed here as at most institutions," and that faculty generally watch what they say in classrooms, the political atmosphere at Florida is much more balanced and less ideological than at its counterparts.

Student Life: Lifetime Gaines

As the accolades it has earned from *Money* magazine and elsewhere indicate, Gainesville is an exceptional place to live; the climate is wonderful, allowing for outdoor activities year-round, and cultural opportunities abound, including several theatres, dance companies, and musical groups. It is, as one student puts it, "strictly a college town. It if weren't for UF the place would collapse." Students generally hang out across campus on University Avenue or downtown, both of which areas feature concentrations of bars, restaurants, and shops.

The northeast corner of Florida's campus is listed in the National Register of Historic Places; the campus also includes an 81-acre wildlife sanctuary. If students get restless, Gainesville is only fifty miles from the Gulf of Mexico and less than seventy miles from the Atlantic Ocean, and as you might expect, on fine days the beach attracts many an undergrad. In addition, serious crime is rarely an issue in Gainesville. Police blotters on- and off-campus are filled with liquor law violations and thefts more than anything else, and faculty and students do not list crime as a major concern. "Things happen," says one student, "but I'm not even close to worrying about it." Perhaps this is one reason why Florida has a remarkably high freshman retention rate: 92 percent. Heck, even Florida's graduates are often loath to leave, one reason the city has, according to *Money*, one of the highest concentrations of single people in the country.

A little more than 80 percent of the student body is from Florida, and about 22 percent are minorities. The students are described as generally liberal but are not, laments one student, "terribly intellectual." According to the student, "People basically go to class and forget about it." Nor are they really very political. Florida's "international faculty and student body, exceptional range of nationalities, ethnic groups, religions, and political outlooks make it difficult for any one ideology to predominate," says a professor.

Only 11 percent of students join the Greek system, a system that at UF has been plagued by a relatively high number of suspensions and probations. Nonetheless, student social life is still said to largely center around the Greek scene. Only 15 percent of students live on campus. All residence halls are coed except one; they are not "dry," but smoking is prohibited. Guests of the opposite sex are not permitted to spend the night, though the degree to which this is enforced is not clear. Every residence hall room is equipped with high-speed Internet ports.

In the Swamp, following the Gators, especially in men's football, is a campuswide passion, and what sense of community exists at this large school centers around coach Steve Spurrier's team. The men's basketball team isn't too shabby either, advancing to the NCAA Final Four in 2000. Generally, the Gators' intercollegiate athletics program, men and women, is one of the best in the Southeastern Conference. The student body is active in more than sixty intramural and club sports as well.

There are more than 450 student organizations on campus, covering the entire political, religious, and cultural spectrum. Both radical and more traditional voices are well represented. Catholic students should note that questions have been raised about the orthodoxy of the St. Augustine Catholic Student Center. Freshman orientation is comparatively sane, according to students.

Florida State University

Office of Admissions
A2500 University Center
Tallahassee, FL 32306-1009
(904) 644-6200
www.fsu.edu

Total enrollment: 33,327
Undergraduates: 24,699
SAT ranges (Verbal/Math): 520-620 (V); 520-620 (M)
Applicants: 21,159
Accepted: 64%
Enrolled: 38%
Application deadline: March 1
Financial aid application deadline: March 1
Tuition: resident: $2,196/$7,356; non-resident: $9,184/$14,344
Core curriculum: No

Beach Week

Florida State University is at the top of its class — the class of partying schools, that is. Both *Rolling Stone* and *The Princeton Review* have ranked the university as the nation's top school for such activity.

While certainly this is a big draw for many students, this college guide seeks to focus on more serious concerns, and in that respect we don't rank it quite so highly. FSU is strong in economics and classics, but as a liberal arts school it is weak. The economics department gathers some of its strength from a $10-million grant to fund the teaching of market economics.

FSU is part of the State University System of Florida, which was founded in 1857. FSU started out as the Florida State College for Women but went coeducational in 1947; many of the first men who enrolled at the university were beneficiaries of the GI Bill. The main campus sits on 418 acres in the state capital of Tallahassee. There is a satellite campus in Panama City as well as a marine laboratory on the Gulf Coast and a joint engineering program with Florida A&M at Innovation Park. The school also boasts its own radio and television stations. Students enjoy the four-season weather of the panhandle of Florida, an unusual trait for the state. The school is also football crazy — the Seminoles routinely challenge for the national championship and have won it several times in the recent past.

Academic Life: Gulf Stream Waters

Florida State tries to provide a broader educational base for its students, and, admirably, states that an education should be more than something "narrowly focused on acquisition of skills needed to secure your first job." However, the school subsequently pushes a rather watered down liberal arts curriculum, and one that is clouded by multiculturalism at that.

The university has sixteen major academic divisions, ranging from social and hard scientific to the arts. As far as undergraduate liberal arts studies are concerned, the two most important are the College of Arts and Sciences and the College of Social Science.

The College of Arts and Sciences is made up of nineteen departments, six institutes, and ten interdisciplinary programs. Along with the usual programs one would expect to find, it also has some unusual majors like meteorology, English with an emphasis in business, and Latin and Caribbean studies (both with and without a business emphasis). The College of Social Sciences, which became a separate school in 1973, is home to twelve departments, including the extremely strong school of economics and a black studies program along with a center for African-American culture. There are also departments that deal with urban planning and public policy, including the Pepper Institute on Aging.

Students in these two colleges, like all the students in the university, are required to take 120 credits of coursework to graduate. Every returning junior must also pass the College-Level Academic Skills Test (which includes sections on vocabulary and algebra) in order to return to the university. There is no core curriculum; in fact, there is not even a set of general education requirements common to all students. Instead, each program has its own set of distribution requirements. Generally, though, each program requires at least this much: two English courses, one course each in history, social science, literature, fine arts, and two natural science courses (including one with a lab requirement). Students seeking a B.A. must also attain intermediate-level proficiency in a foreign language.

The lack of a common set of required courses does not, however, stop the university from requiring of all students two courses intended to compare and contrast Western and non-Western traditions. This sounds like a noble idea, but FSU tends to miss the boat when it comes to providing an enlightened sense of multiculturalism, allowing most courses to shortchange Western tradition to focus on trendier brands of indoctrination.

Then there are the two multicultural requirements — one designated the "cross cultural course" (the "X-requirement") and a second called "Diversity in Western Culture" (the "Y-requirement"). Students are not fooled, and see these courses for what they are: concessions to current trends in academics. "The X and Y requirements are nothing more than indoctrination courses," one student says. "We have to take classes like women's studies, African-American studies, and other courses taught from an ideological point of view."

FSU also enforces the state of Florida's "Gordon Rule," which requires students to write a combined 24,000 words in English, history, or humanities classes. Again, this is a rather noble endeavor, one intended to improve the writing skills of FSU's undergrad population — but the C-minus minimum passing grade raises some doubt as to its effectiveness.

Students can expect to do their work in very large classes, especially in their first two years. Class size only begins to shrink in their third or fourth years — and even fifth years (which 60 percent of incoming freshmen need to graduate). This generally means that close student-faculty relationships are not forged until later in the game.

Still, a student who knows his direction can find enough good classes to forge a decent education, according to some professors. This presumably is not because of the curricular structure, but in spite of it. Certain departments and professors are excellent, and the classics and economics departments are highly regarded in academic circles. Good professors include Bruce L. Benson, James D. Gwartney, and Randall G. Holcombe in economics; Leon Golden in classics; Charles E. Billings in political science; Edward F. Keuchel in history; and Douglas R. Fowler in English.

The economics department features a diversity of approaches, including theories from the Chicago School to the Keynesian School. The classics department also provides an uncommon educational opportunity for students. The courses it offers — including "Greek Drama," "Greek Poetry," "The Roman Historians and Cicero," and "Literature of the Republic" — have been disappearing from course catalogues across the country. The department also has an archaeology program that allows students to travel abroad for several different projects.

Other departments, such as sociology, are not in particularly good shape. The department is divided into technically oriented demographers and ideologues who emphasize race and gender relations above all else.

Political Atmosphere: Furious Enthusiasm

FSU President Talbot "Sandy" D'Alemberte is described by one faculty member as someone who is "not a meddler." This same professor says that "Most of his day-to-day operations pertain to fund-raising and representing the university. FSU is a mega-university that has so many dimensions — it would be hard to mold it from the top down."

This amicable governance is only broken by one issue — hiring and promoting of faculty. FSU has a tendency to hire big-name professors who are published often in hot journals in an effort to boost its academic reputation. The tenure process has fortunately not fallen victim to the affirmative action or politicization that is widespread at other state universities.

In October 2000, D'Alemberte outlined for the faculty Senate his vision for the future of FSU. The president said he expects strong fund-raising to continue, and that the university would be in the top fifty nationwide in terms of endowment within the next five years. Further, he said, "Our student body will continue to be more highly qualified and more diverse each year." One of the biggest and least specific of his predictions: "We will achieve all the recognitions that identify American universities as top institutions." Suffice it to say that the school has a long way to go to get to the top of this guide's list.

In his speech, D'Alemberte mentioned athletics, saying, "Our sports programs, particularly our women's sports, will continue to advance, and we will become a serious competitor for the Sears Cup, which rewards all-around athletic programs." FSU athletics, particularly its football team, are indeed highly regarded and respected, but one has to wonder at the amount of time and resources the university devotes to what is certainly tangential to what should be the school's primary role.

For example, the only regular column in the *Florida State Times*, a magazine produced by the Office of University Communications, is written by Charlie Barnes, legendary executive director of the Seminole (Athletic) Boosters. In a recent column, Barnes argues that the success of the football team — he calls it "the Dynasty" — "would be a magnificent picture window through which America could view the work of our university. Indeed, the lofty profiles enjoyed variously by Notre Dame, Penn State, Texas, Southern Cal, Ohio State, Michigan, and the like, all stand upon original foundations of athletic excellence."

It may be worth noting that the booster club is in the midst of a $70 million "Dynasty Campaign." "There's no conjurer's secret to raising money," Barnes says. "It's simple: all those who love Florida State University must be asked to give however much and in whatever way they can. Every person who shares the powerful vision of what Florida State can achieve must be given the opportunity to help."

This is a common fallacy among sports boosters, who seem unwilling to allow sports to stand on their own as an important extracurricular without subscribing some sort of image-boosting role or imagining that success on a field somehow improves the overall value of a university. While certainly many in the nation know FSU only because of its athletic teams, the school proves the point that an excellent overall university does not necessarily follow from national championships and a highly admirable athletic program.

Given the climate of athletic support on campus, it's no surprise that the school's athletic nickname — the Seminoles — has survived politically correct criticism. Though the use of Native Americans as a nickname for sports teams has drawn widespread criticism, Chief Osceola remains a fixture at FSU, not so much because of the school's desire to keep it, but because of intense public support for the mascot. In fact, the D'Alemberte has argued that the use of the name and a mascot in full

Native American regalia actually advances multiculturalism. "Florida State's historic identification with the heroic Seminole Tribe of Florida is a proud tradition," he wrote in *USA Today*. "Chief Osceola [the mascot], astride his Appaloosa when he plants a flaming spear on the 50-yard line, ignites a furious enthusiasm and loyalty in thousands of football fans, but also salutes a people who have proven that perseverance with integrity prevails."

Student Life: Demanding a Recount

For better or worse, FSU is known on a national basis as a party school. Some feel this reputation has been blown out of proportion by those in the media. Indeed, fewer than 20 percent of all students pledge to one of the school's forty-five Greek organizations. Most student events are held at the Oglesby Union, which houses a bowling alley, a variety of lounges, a bowling alley, a movie theatre, a coffee house, and several restaurants — hardly party central. Also, Tallahassee's relatively small size (250,000 residents and 50,000 students from FSU and two smaller schools) might skew the perception of the school negatively. But one professor does concede that students "seem more interested in the weekend than the weekday."

Students can choose from one of fifteen residence halls and several other living arrangements. The university strongly encourages students to live on campus for at least their first year at the school, offering "the convenience factor" as the best reason to do so. There are a number of theme halls, including some dedicated to honors students, ethnic groups, and substance-free living. There are also options for single-sex floors. Crime on campus is above national averages, according to APB News; most of it involves larceny, but there are more robberies and assaults than at the average school as well.

The large community supports hundreds of student groups ranging from academic societies and multicultural alliances to religious organizations and social clubs. There is both a Federalist Society and a fencing club, for example. The school also offers an ROTC program. And most unusual: the FSU Flying High Circus. Founded in the late 1940s, this completely independent group performs acrobatic acts at a professional level — with no financial support from the school at all.

The school's conservative student groups definitely have a leg up on those that lean to the left. The College Republicans and the Institute for Conservative Studies have brought speakers like Alan Keyes and Ralph Reed to campus. In addition, the Eagle Forum recently started a chapter at FSU and a conservative/libertarian paper, *The Independent Perspective,* publishes every two months. Liberal groups like the Black Student Union and the Florida State University Lesbian Gay Bisexual Student Union are not nearly as organized. The College Democrats only attract about twenty members each year. But, truth be told, students at FSU don't care all that much about politics.

Instead, FSU loves its sports — intramural and club sports are numerous, but football is king. The 'Noles football team generally beats up on its Atlantic Coast Conference competition in its annual march to the Bowl Championship Series. This love of athletics is seen in the more than $100 million dollars the school has poured into its athletic programs, including $90 million to renovate Doak Campbell Stadium, the home of the football team.

The city of Tallahassee is statistically one of America's ten most-educated cities, making lending the capital a progressive and active civic life. Despite the closeness of the Gulf Coast beaches, the campus offers three swimming pools and the "FSU Reservation," a lakeside complex that is home to picnics, water skiing, and concerts. The university is only a few blocks from the state capitol building, meaning that interested students can easily watch their state government at work or even get an internship in a state office. Some enterprising students even tried to rent rooms to reporters covering the 2000 election recount.

Furman University

Office of Admissions
3300 Poinsett Highway
Greenville, SC 29613
(864) 294-3127
www.furman.edu

Total enrollment: 2,700
Undergraduates: 2,600
SAT ranges (Verbal/Math): 570-670 (V); 580-670 (M)
Applicants: 3,600
Accepted: 58%
Enrolled: 31%
Application deadline: February 1
Financial aid application deadline: February 1
Tuition: $19,156/$24,419
Core curriculum: No

In and Around the Lake

Step onto Furman's secluded campus on the outskirts of Greenville, S.C., and you're struck by two things: First, there's the overwhelming beauty of the place, with its modern brick buildings, numerous fountains, and a lake complete with ducks. Second, there's a lot of construction around campus, which seems appropriate since Furman is trying to build itself from a well-regarded regional university into a nationally acclaimed liberal arts school. But while the shape of new buildings is known through artist's renderings and blueprints, no one knows what the finished Furman will look like: Will it stay with its roots and continue to offer students a solid, well-rounded liberal arts education? Or will it adopt some of the bad habits and fanciest trends of academia in its quest for national recognition?

Little at Furman is likely to change overnight. Though the institution likes to tout the fact that it draws students from forty-eight states and thirty-nine foreign countries, 79 percent of its students come from the Southeast, with about one-third of all students coming from South Carolina. This translates to a gentility and a generally conservative feel at Furman, as do the Baptist leanings of administrators, trustees, and alumni. Though the university severed its long-standing ties to the South Carolina Baptist Convention in 1992, many of the practices remain in place: It's a totally "dry" campus — no alcohol allowed anywhere, by anyone — and there's a strict visitation policy for dorm rooms belonging to members of the opposite sex. Many of the academic fads have made far fewer inroads at Furman, and the institution's dedication to the liberal arts and to teaching is genuine. Were it not for a small master's program for certified teachers and a microscopic master's program in chemistry, Furman "University" would be a college.

Some people at Furman gripe that the university's academic reputation lags behind its actual academic performance, and that might well be true. What's undoubtedly true is that Furman is an institution dedicated to giving undergraduates a very good education, while trying to eliminate many of the distractions of college life and keeping the focus squarely where it belongs: on academics.

Academic Life: GER-onimo

Furman has twenty-four academic departments that offer students a total of thirty-six majors. At the heart of all majors, though, are Furman's General Education Requirements, known around campus as GERs. It's not a core curriculum, because students have a choice of courses within the requirements. But the choices tend to be limited, so that students are pretty much assured of graduating with a solid understanding of different fields. Other universities, which offer wide choices, do not always have such assurances.

The GERs include five courses in the humanities (composition; an introductory history, religion, and a choice of language course, or a three-part humanities course focusing on Western Civilization; and a fifth humanities course of choice); foreign language competency through the intermediate level; one mathematics course, usually calculus; two natural science courses; two social science courses (selected from a list of ten courses); one out of four qualifying fine arts courses; and a health and exercise science course called "Wellness Concepts."

In addition to GERs, students must take at least one course in the university's "Asian-African program," which offers about forty courses from which to choose. The catalogue says this program "emphasizes major dimensions of experience from the non-Western two-thirds of humanity." The courses include studies of non-Western history, politics, and philosophy.

Although some students occasionally complain that the GERs involve too many classes, most students seem to realize the benefits. "You're going to be able to stick your toes in a lot of different areas and see what you like and what you don't," said one senior.

One distinctive feature of Furman's curriculum is its Cultural Life Program. Each quarter, the university sponsors dozens of lectures, plays, panels and other outside-of-class learning experiences — just like any other college. But at Furman, students are required to attend nine of these events, known as CLPs, per year. If they don't, they don't graduate. In the fall of 2000, examples of CLPs included a speech on the life of Jesus, a movie as part of Hispanic Heritage Month, and talks on topics like "Religious Pluralism and the U.S.: How Does It Impact You?," "Election 2000 and the Youth Vote," and "Are Women Taking Their Rightful Place in the Political Spotlight?"

Furman's dedication to undergraduate teaching is noteworthy. Its graduate programs are very small and consist mainly of graduate programs for teachers. There are no teaching assistants at Furman — all instruction is done by faculty members, 94 percent of whom hold doctoral degrees. Classes are typically reasonably sized, with most of them enrolling twenty to thirty students. The largest class, according to students, is the general-education humanities sequence course, which has around one hundred students but also meets in smaller sections during the week with a professor. "The professors at Furman are excellent," says a junior psychology major. "They are very approachable. I really enjoy my classes."

Another interesting part of Furman's academic experience is what the school calls "engaged learning." The university encourages students to participate in internships in the Greenville area to supplement their classroom experiences, and the university has also begun offering pre-professional courses in business administration, accounting, and music performance. This is a shift away from Furman's liberal arts focus, and though it's a small shift, one hopes it doesn't grow to supplant what the university is doing in the more traditional areas. The goal of higher education, after all, is to produce well-informed, smart-thinking citizens — not to graduate people who are technically competent in a given area.

Students report that grade inflation is not as bad at Furman as elsewhere. The average grade point average is around 2.5, a B-/C+. Some students say the classes are rigorous, more so than those of friends at other schools. "There is an extremely heavy courseload," says one junior. "I wish I had more time to do fun college stuff. We have to work more than other colleges, but we're better prepared."

The most strongly regarded departments at Furman are chemistry, psychology, and health and exercise science. Though Furman has many good teachers, some of the best, according to students and professors, are David S. Spear and T. Lloyd Benson in history; Stanley J. H. Crowe in English; David H. Bost and Alvin L. Prince in modern languages and literatures; Paul R. Rasmussen in psychology; and Silas N. Pearman III in health and exercise science.

Political Atmosphere: Diverse Airs

One recent and ongoing topic of debate on campus is the perceived homogeneity of Furman students, who have a reputation of being overwhelmingly white, upper middle class, and traditional in their beliefs. In fact, 10 percent of Furman students are minorities, and the university, almost to the point of obsession, is pushing hard to up that number in the usual way: pandering to minority groups with special minorities-only programs, the kinds of which Greenville native Jesse Jackson would approve. "Furman's really doing a lot of things to bring a lot more 'diversity,'" says one student. There's a black student weekend for potential recruits, a minority recruiting specialist in the admissions office, and plenty of blacks-only events on campus. "There are receptions and all kinds of things on campus just for minorities," an admissions officer boasted in a recent session on campus.

Furman has established an Office of Multicultural Affairs to help create "an educational environment in which diversity is understood, embraced, and celebrated." The office sponsors activities at orientation, as well as mentoring programs, a Black Seniors Banquet, and heritage month celebrations for blacks, Asians, and Hispanics.

These activities are not uncommon at universities throughout the country, but are somewhat new for Furman. The university has also adopted another fashionable program: a very limited women's studies curriculum. Students can earn a concentration (but not a major) in women's studies by taking four of nine approved courses such as "Reading Race, Class, and Gender in America" and a philosophy course that examines "liberal feminism, socialist or Marxist feminism, radical feminism, and others."

Students and professors report that while students tend to be fairly conservative, faculty members tilt more to the left, particularly in the religion and sociology departments. But others say political bias rarely makes it into the classroom. "It's usually the sort of thing where you know where they're coming from, but they want to hear all opinions," says one senior. Another says: "A lot of them are more liberal than the students are, particularly the religion faculty. Over there, it's not what you were taught in Sunday school."

A junior history major says he's often disappointed in his classmates for not challenging the traditional interpretations in the field. "You have a lot of people who think very much the same way," he said. "The newest trends and the most revisionist aspects of it aren't what's on students' minds." He says he'd prefer more diverse opinions in classes — the same problem found at other schools throughout the country, but from the opposite side of the coin. Often, it's the new trends and historical revisionism that dominate classes, with nobody willing to support the traditional view.

Still, some on campus say that there's sort of a creeping political correctness — that students know what sorts of things they're supposed to say, even if it contradicts what they really think. "At times it seems real open and that everyone's open to everyone else's ideas," says a sophomore. "But there are also underlying feelings of what's right and wrong. There are certain things that are frowned upon. There are some that are honest about it, but there are others who say things just to be politically correct." Put in perspective, though, political correctness simply is not as large a problem at Furman as at most other universities, where speaking up for disapproved-of ideas can be grounds for scorn or ridicule. If anything, Furman students kill each other with kindness.

Student Life: Wet and Dry

What sets Furman apart from other schools is its beauty and its tradition-minded social policies. The 750-acre campus includes an eighteen-hole golf course, seven fountains, a rose garden, a Japanese garden, and the college's centerpiece, a thirty-acre lake. You could mistake the view of the lake from Furman's student center for one you might see at a resort — were you not surrounded by young women in sorority shirts and standing in front of a Chic-Fil-A. The lake looks suitable for a few windsurfers, maybe even small sailboats. The walking trails around the lake are used equally by joggers and people just looking to study in a scenic setting. In the middle of the lake, on a small peninsula, is a bell tower, and the tradition is that under the bell tower is where you kiss your last love, i.e., the one you'll marry. Another tradition involving the lake: if it's your birthday, your friends could very well throw you in.

While the lake can get you all wet, the rest of the campus is completely dry in that no alcohol is permitted, anywhere. This policy is a sign of the administration's commitment to its religious influences, but as one might imagine, it is controversial among students, particularly among those of drinking age who can face sanctions for having a six-pack in their fridge. Students say the administration enforces the policy strictly — it's not some public relations tool. If resident assistants see you with alcohol, you're in trouble. Period. (It should be noted that alcohol-related violations constitute just about the only measurable "crime" in and around the Furman campus.) "There's still enough of a Christian, Baptist tradition that the effort to make certain parts of campus 'wet' has run up into a brick wall," says one student, who admits to an occasional beer. Of course, just because the school has a policy doesn't mean all students follow it. "Furman isn't completely dry," confides a sophomore. Many students also leave campus for fraternity parties or bars, where they can drink without fear of sanction.

Dormitory floors (and some entire dorms) are single-sex. Members of the opposite sex are permitted in dorms between 10 a.m. and 2 a.m., provided they are escorted to and from the entrance by a resident. This rule, too, is enforced, though bright college students can probably find some way around it from time to time.

Just a few years ago, only about half of all Furman students lived on campus. But the university began building additional housing, and now 93 percent of students live on campus. Freshmen, sophomores, and juniors are required to live on campus, and with the addition of two new apartment complexes, Furman for the first time will be able to accommodate nearly all its students on campus. In the future, the university might require seniors to live on campus once additional buildings are complete.

In interviews with students, one recurring theme is that students are amiable. "The thing I like most about Furman is that everybody is so friendly," says one junior. "They smile and say hi. With all of the stress that we have with classes, it's one of my favorite things." Furman students say they form close friendships with each other, which is somewhat bolstered by the secluded, self-contained campus. "At times it feels really small, but at the same time it's close-knit and you get to know more people better," one student says.

The two most dominant social forces on campus seem to be religion and the Greek system. The university encourages students to participate in religious services. There is a nondenominational service in the university chapel each Sunday, and there are about twenty different religious groups on campus. The largest and most active is the Baptist Student Union. A religious council, composed of representatives from various religions, meets regularly to promote cooperation among the groups.

Fraternities and sororities are the other hub of social life at Furman. About one-third of Furman students join one of the university's seven sororities and eight fraternities. There are no fraternity or sorority houses per se, though Greek organizations sometimes hold parties at a member's off-campus house. One fraternity member says non-Greeks aren't excluded. "Greek life is still the home of the high-end formals and biggest beer parties," he says. "But your average student does other things as well. Most of my social life is not tied in to the Greek system."

Furman's student body comes from almost all of the states and from nearly forty foreign countries, though the school does not draw as many students from outside the Southeast as it would like. About 79 percent of students come from the

Southeast, and about 32 percent of the student body is from South Carolina. The university wants to bring the numbers more into parity.

Greenville, S.C., is about two and a half hours north of Atlanta and two hours south of Charlotte, N.C. Greenville, population 58,000, is a pleasant, fast-growing city that is slowly gaining more things to do. The nearby Bi-Lo Center hosts A-list musical acts such as Shania Twain and Tina Turner. The city has a minor league baseball team, the Greenville Braves. The Blue Ridge Mountains are close, the South Carolina beaches are four hours away, and there are plenty of recreational opportunities within an hour's drive. Popular off-campus hangouts in Greenville include The Funk Yard dance club, Coffee Underground, Barnes & Noble, and The Thirsty Dog.

George Mason University

Office of Admissions
4400 University Drive
Mail Stop 3A4
Fairfax, Virginia 22030-4444
(703) 993-2400
www.gmu.edu

Total enrollment: 24,180
Undergraduates: 15,262
SAT ranges (Verbal/Math): 460-580 (V); 470-580 (M)
Applicants: 6,508
Accepted: 59%
Enrolled: 33%
Application deadline: February 1
Financial aid application deadline: March 1
Tuition: resident: $3,768/$9,218; non-resident: $12,612/$18,062
Core curriculum: No

Patriot Games

George Mason University began in 1957 as a branch of the University of Virginia, back when the state's heart resided more in the rural setting of Charlottesville than in what would become the center of the political and technological boom area of northern Virginia. It became an independent school in 1972, and has grown to fifteen thousand undergraduates and nine thousand graduate students, supported by the enormous growth in Virginia's Washington, D.C., suburbs. In fact, nearly 90 percent of the school's students come from Virginia, though forty-nine states and 118 foreign countries are also represented.

George Mason is similar to other large state universities in a variety of ways, but it has rejected much of the politicization that often dominates such schools. To be sure, some strange courses can be found in the college catalogue, but they represent only a tiny fraction of the curriculum. "Virginia is a relatively conservative state," says one professor. "Even the Democrats who are in the legislature tend to be conservative Democrats." The university's Board of Visitors, chaired by Ed Meese, has already taken steps to strengthen the curriculum.

George Mason, the university's namesake, was the author of the Virginia Declaration of Rights, which served as the foundation for the nation's Bill of Rights, and quite a revolutionary. But the school named after him is not so revolutionary. The liberal arts requirements at the College of the Arts and Sciences are predictably weak: they may be numerous, but are spread thinly and are far from ideal in content or rigor. The university's experimental college program, a small division called the New Century College, is supposed to be a state-of-the-art interdisciplinary college. In reality, it is closer to what college would look like if it were designed exclusively by social workers and psychotherapists.

However, the university has invested much in its fine economics department, which includes Nobel Prize winner James Buchanan. Even the lesser programs at George Mason are a bargain, with tuition around $3,800 for in-state students; after all, the university must remain competitive with the many colleges and universities in the Washington metropolitan area. Out-of-state students must decide if the education at George Mason is worth the $13,000 they pay for tuition.

Academic Life: Stop the Revolution

Of George Mason's twelve graduate and undergraduate divisions, the College of Arts and Sciences is the largest and most directly concerned with the liberal arts. This college contains fifteen departments and about 5,500 students, or approximately 36 percent of the undergraduate student body. Students in this college must take two courses in English composition and one course in oral communication. Those seeking a B.A. degree must take courses in, or demonstrate proficiency in, a foreign language to the intermediate level. Depending on the number of courses a student must take to meet the language requirement, the general education requirements can account for slightly more than half the total number of hours required for a B.A. degree — more than at many similar institutions.

The other general education requirements for a B.A. degree in the College of Arts and Sciences are standard fare at most large universities, and fairly utilitarian in nature. The university makes no attempt to bring students together in a course that would offer readings common to all. Four courses are required in the humanities, but the two courses in literature can be selected from any English courses above the 200 level or any modern and classical language courses above the 300 level. The other humanities requirements are also broad, and include fine arts and philosophy or religious studies. One course is required in analytical reasoning, as are two from among economics, government, geography, and history, and two from the departments of anthropology, psychology, and sociology. Two courses are required in natural sciences; both must include a lab.

Curriculum changes will take effect in the fall of 2001; these will include slightly tougher requirements in writing, public speaking, and computer skills, but will also require two new courses, one in U.S. history and another in Western civilization — a rather bold step in today's academic climate. The U.S. and Western civ courses were insisted upon by the university's Board of Visitors, which is chaired by Reagan administration attorney general Ed Meese and includes Heritage Foundation president Edwin J. Feulner. Faculty had wanted to require only one course — any course — on "U.S. and Western institutions, traditions, and economies," and the change by the board brought a resolution from the faculty senate condemning the board for micromanaging curricular issues and for coming up with a plan that was "academically inferior" to the one they had proposed.

The new plan keeps a requirement for a course on "global understanding, international institutions, and cross-cultural values," according to the university's provost (quoted in the *Chronicle of Higher Education*). This includes anthropology courses on the native cultures, art, politics, history, and religions of most parts of the world. Though this requirement is obviously in place to satisfy the needs of the multiculturalists, the titles and descriptions of the courses that fulfill the requirement are in most cases fairly straightforward, devoid of the usual language about Western "oppression" and "hegemony."

B.S. degree candidates in the College of Arts and Science need only satisfy a writing requirement and take four courses outside of their area of concentration to meet the general education requirements.

George Mason has excellent professors whom students should be able to find given the few constrictions on their choice of general education classes. These include Richard Wagner, Charles Rowley, Walter E. Williams, Karen I. Vaughn, Tyler Cowen, and Nobel Prize winner James M. Buchanan in economics; Robert L. Sachs in math; Peter J. Denning and Kenneth A. DeJong in computer sciences; and Robert Ehrlich in physics.

Economics is clearly the best department in the College of Arts and Sciences, and at George Mason in general. The department is home to several professors with national reputations, and the Chicago, Public Choice, and Austrian Schools are well represented. Constitutional economics has been the particular contribution of James Buchanan. A number of courses examine the Austrian tradition of Ludwig von Mises and Friedrich von Hayek.

Associated with the university is the James Buchanan Center, named for Nobel laureate James Buchanan, who has taught at the school since 1983, three years before he won the prize. Buchanan has written several well-known books, including *Fiscal Theory and Political Economy; The Calculus of Consent; The Limits of Liberty; Democracy in Deficit; The Power to Tax;* and *The Reason of Rules*. The Buchanan Center incorporates the Center for the Study of Public Choice and the Center for the Study of Market Processes. The Institute for Humane Studies is a post-instructional institute of GMU, which, though academically part of the university, is privately funded. The Institute for Humane Studies relocated to Arlington, Virginia, in 1999, although the economics department and Buchanan Center remain in Fairfax. All three are among the leading centers in the country for free-market economic theory.

The Center for the Study of Public Choice, of which Dr. Buchanan is the advisory general director, concerns itself with research into public policy issues, with a special eye toward "public choice" issues. The Institute for Humane Studies describes itself as an organization that "assists undergraduate and graduate students who have a special interest in individual liberty." The institute offers several programs for both graduate students and undergraduates, including a variety of scholarships. The third part of the Buchanan Center, the Center for the Study of Market Processes, is an educational and research nonprofit organization that generates solutions to organizational and social problems.

Three other departments at George Mason are also noted for their high academic standards and insistence on proper, rigorous scholarship. These are the departments of math, physics, and decision sciences (a department in the School of Business Administration).

George Mason does have two especially politicized departments — women's studies and African-American studies — but their influence seems to be limited to their own fiefdoms. "The women's studies department and the African-American studies department do not have a significant presence . . . as they often do at other politicized universities," a professor says. Neither department offers a major, and, as in the courses under the "diversity" general education requirement, those listed under African-American studies at least appear to be light on the political histrionics commonly found elsewhere. Some courses required for the minor include "The Afro-American Experience in the United States: African Background to 1885," "The Afro-American Experience in the United States: Reconstruction to the Present," and "Minority Group Politics and Policies."

Women's studies appears to be more ideological. According to promotional materials, minors in this department will "examine the ways that racism, sexism, classism, and homophobia operate and discuss strategies for social change." The department goes on to state: "Women's studies faculty members share a commitment to addressing the experiences and contributions of women previously excluded from the traditional curriculum — including women of color, lesbians, working-class women, and poor women."

The most politicized sector of George Mason is a division called the New Century College (NCC), which offers degrees in "integrative studies," "individualized studies," "interdisciplinary studies," and "social work." One professor calls the NCC offerings "an experimental education," and does not intend it as a compliment. The program has little to do with the traditional understanding of the liberal arts as the disciplines that foster what Cardinal Newman called the "philosophical habit of mind." Rather, the NCC, with its rhetoric of "learning communities" and "integrative learning," seems like a brainchild of academics who grew up in the sixties.

The Board of Visitors nearly eliminated the college entirely in 1999, saying that the program lacked rigor and was, essentially, a waste of time and money. However, a compromise proposal from Mason president Alan Merten was adopted instead, making the NCC a part of the College of Arts and Sciences starting in July 2000. This eliminated the NCC's financial and administrative independence. NCC administrators agreed to the compromise only because the alternative was the end of their college, and the dean of the College of Arts and Sciences told the *Chronicle of Higher Education* that he hoped that the teaching innovations of the NCC would energize the larger college, and that the larger college could make the NCC offerings more rigorous. The NCC will keep its faculty and will still admit and graduate students, but a joint committee of NCC and Arts and Sciences faculty will make curriculum decisions for the NCC.

At the moment, the NCC curriculum is divided into three parts. The first year, called Division I, consists of "common courses and integrated learning," according to the catalogue. The four mandatory six-week units are on "interdisciplinary issues in education," "the natural world," "the socially constructed world," and the "relationship between the individual and society." Division II "is constructed of learning communities, each of which combines subjects usually taught in several separate courses into a single course of study." Division III, subtitled "Specialization," is said to be the equivalent of a major in "a traditional degree program." It can include "learning communities, independent study, seminars, mentored research, experiential learning, and traditional courses."

In fact, "experiential learning" is another college requirement, meaning that students must obtain at least twelve credit hours through internships, study abroad, or courses that include lots of field trips and other off-campus work. According to the NCC, "integrated learning" includes "collaboration, experiential learning, and self-reflection." Rather than focus on classical literature, students are encouraged, at least in part, to focus on their own experiences — in short, their feelings are considered more important than the great texts. The board of visitors was right: this is not particularly rigorous stuff.

Courses offered by the NCC include these lightweights: "The Socially Constructed World," "Horizons: 2000 — Expanding Awareness/Breaking Gender Barriers," and "Construction of Differences."

Political Atmosphere: Visitors versus Home Team

Alan Merten was inaugurated as George Mason's fifth president in April of 1997, but already some on campus are not confident that he will be successful. In the opinion of one professor, Merten is a "fairly weak president" who has made some errors early in his presidency. Merten also talks a good bit about strengthening the university's technology offerings in order to serve Northern Virginia's burgeoning computer industry — a move that smacks of job training rather than liberal education.

In addition, George Mason has succumbed to the usual politicized hiring processes of larger universities. Departments must have their search efforts for new faculty approved by an "equity office" that enforces affirmative action policies. Departments are expected to advertise in "black publications" and other media directed at the African-American community so as to secure minority professors.

The university administration also welcomes political correctness by hosting several "multicultural" events on campus, including Asian Awareness Week, Black History Month, Hispanic Heritage Month, Martin Luther King Day, and Women's History Month. In order to promote these events, the university has hosted several celebrity speakers, including Harry Belafonte, Julian Bond, Shirley Chisholm, and Susan Rook.

The new administration must have done something to anger liberals, or must have at least been perceived as unfriendly to certain groups prior to taking office. Merten's inauguration was disrupted by a Mason group called Coalition for a Hate-Free Campus and an off-campus group called the D.C. Lesbian Avengers. At an inaugural prayer service in St. Robert Bellarmine Chapel, two self-described lesbians interrupted the service by standing and displaying vests that read "Praying for a Hate Free Campus," while others (wearing T-shirts announcing "We Recruit") handed out pro-homosexual literature.

Recently, there was an effort to create a homosexual center on campus, but the Board of Visitors, as it has several times in the recent past (see Academic Life, above), intervened and rejected the idea. The conservative nature of that board has more than once saved the university from less-than-stellar ideas.

Student Life: Capital Suburb

George Mason is located in Fairfax County, the Washington, D.C., suburb that boasts one of the ten highest per-capita incomes in the nation. The campus is about thirty miles from the District, but isn't far from Interstate 66, which ends beside the Lincoln Memorial on the Mall, and is also close to a Metro (subway) stop where one can board an amazingly clean but not particularly cheap train into the nation's capital. Of course, Washington boasts hundreds of things to do, from the free attractions of the Smithsonian and other governmental tours and buildings to the bars of Georgetown to the fine restaurants all over town. Increasingly, fine dining and entertainment choices have spread to the suburbs as well.

Mason itself boasts outstanding facilities on its 677-acre main campus. Because the university is so young, there is little in the way of classic traditional architecture. Many of the buildings on campus are better inside than out, including the excellent George W. Johnson Center, which houses a library, computer labs, student services, class space for the New Century College, and a four-story open atrium where students can eat or gather. The Center for the Arts includes a 2,000-seat Concert Hall, two smaller theaters, dance studios, and assorted music and fine arts studios. Students have first crack at five hundred free tickets to each Concert Hall performance, some of which have featured internationally known classical artists. The Patriot Center seats ten thousand for indoor sports and rock concerts.

Nearly 90 percent of George Mason's student body is from Virginia. This makes for something of a commuter atmosphere on campus, especially considering the number of nontraditional (i.e., older) students who further or complete their educations at Mason. Still, campus life is active and there are more than 200 officially recognized student groups. Most are recreational or otherwise nonpolitical in focus. There are also sixteen fraternities and ten sororities, though there is no Greek housing.

The university offers both coed and single-sex dorms. In addition to campus apartments, there are Living Learning Programs, described by the university as "intentionally designed residence hall communities that can expand your learning beyond the classroom in many exciting and meaningful ways." These include theme-oriented dorm floors, like the Healthy Living Floor, Quiet Living Floor, Community Service Floor, and Conflict Resolution Floor as well as more unusual ones focusing on ancient civilizations, "The American Experience" — "Experience Enlightenment political theory and true stories of American loggers and paramedics" — and "The Environment" — "Learn how to make a difference, and meet others who appreciate your interests in preserving the natural elements we all share." The Living Learning Programs include not only dorm life, but a list of recommended and required courses.

Given its tony suburban location, the danger of the campus environs is not something about which George Mason students need worry. But the school did report an unusually high number of forcible sex offenses (8) and aggravated assaults (7) in 1999.

Among the political clubs are the College Republicans and two gay, lesbian, and bisexual groups — the Pride Alliance and the Action Committee — which have recently been energized by the rejection of a university-funded campus homosexual center. The Pride Alliance is the more visible of the two. It brings speakers to campus and hosts discussion groups. The Action Committee was founded as a direct result of the board's decision, and is dedicated to activism. It calls itself "an active, grass-roots organizing body" and works with recognized campus groups (including student government) and other local and national homosexual organizations, including the group that helped protest at President Merten's inauguration, the D.C. Lesbian Avengers.

There is also a Women's Coalition at George Mason that publishes a literary journal called *So to Speak,* as well as multicultural groups like the African Student Association, Black Student Alliance, Club Latino, Hispanic Women's Coalition, and the Student Coalition against Racism. Then there are the groups that, if they aren't at the fringe, can certainly see it from where they stand. These include Children of a Dark Eternity, which promotes "alternative religions" like the Church of Satan, the Covenant of the Goddess, and the Pagan Federation; and Thumbs Up for Democracy, which promotes disenfranchised political minorities such as the Black Panthers and the Green Party.

The George Mason Patriots field NCAA Division I teams in a number of sports. The university also has a sports facility open to students that houses basketball and racquetball courts, an indoor 200-meter track, seven tennis courts, and weight rooms. In addition, the university maintains several outdoor athletic fields on the Fairfax campus.

Georgetown University

Office of Undergraduate Admissions
Georgetown University
Washington, DC 20057-1002
(202) 687-3600
www.georgetown.edu

Total enrollment: 12,472
Undergraduates: 6,418
SAT ranges (Verbal/Math): 620-730 (V); 630-720 (M)
Applicants: 13,242
Accepted: 23%

Enrolled: 49%
Application deadline: January 10
Financial aid application deadline: Rolling
Tuition: $24,340/$33,260
Core curriculum: No

The Spirit of Catholicism

Perhaps the problem is that Washington, D.C., does not provide a healthy environment for a university. Georgetown University, for example, seems to have contracted a case of bureaucratic doublespeak and political evasion from its neighbors inside the Beltway. Thus, are Georgetown students hard-core partiers? No, they just have a "robust social life," says the Georgetown administration. Are Georgetown freshmen shown how to use condoms in orientation? No, they are merely exposed to "risk reduction programming." And here's a good one: Is Georgetown a Catholic school? Well, that depends, as one famous Beltway resident (and Georgetown alumnus) recently put it, on what your definition of "is" is.

Georgetown University *calls* itself a Catholic school. But what Georgetown means by "Catholic" — indeed, what Georgetown means by *anything* — is not always easy to determine. Founded in 1789 by John Carroll, the first American Roman Catholic bishop, Georgetown expends a lot of breath attempting to ensure its auditors that the school is rooted in the "Catholic and Jesuit tradition." But Georgetown speaks about its "Jesuit heritage" the way you might expect someone to speak about their German or Filipino heritage. It provides some nice customs and traditions and may even help explain some of their quirks, but it isn't *normative,* for pete's sake.

In fact, Georgetown hosts speakers, employs faculty, enrolls students, and offers classes and programs that are as secularized as those at any college in America.

Yet there is a glimmer of hope on the horizon. With *Ex Corde Ecclesiae,* promulgated in 1990, the Vatican put Catholic schools on notice that they would have to abide by a principle common to Catholics and non-Catholics alike: truth in advertising. The American bishops finally got around to agreeing on new rules to implement *Ex Corde Ecclesiae* last year. It is possible that these rules will be ignored or forgotten, of course, but if they are not (the Georgetown administration is already talking about the "spirit of *Ex Corde Ecclesiae,*" not a good sign), things may improve at Georgetown.

In the meantime, the school will most likely continue to ply its trade in institutional hypocrisy, making little effort to hire Catholic professors or to promote Catholicism among its students while responding to critics with windy talk about the importance of dialogue, the complexities of a religious witness in a secular world, etc., *ad nauseam.* Georgetown describes itself as "a national University rooted in the Catholic faith, committed to spiritual inquiry, engaged in the public sphere, and invigorated by religious and cultural pluralism." It is impossible not to read that "rooted in" as a deliberate equivocation. "The claim that Georgetown is a Catholic school with Catholic values is nonsense," one professor says. "Georgetown is no more Catholic than the University of Maryland."

Academic Life: The Spirit of Liberal Arts

Georgetown talks about its "core curriculum" but, as with so much of the school's verbiage, this is misleading. The "core" is not all that different from the kind of distribution requirements one finds elsewhere, with the important exception that all students must take two theology courses. There are continual rumblings about making changes to the "core," and in fact it has been modified on a couple of occasions during the last few years.

Georgetown has four colleges for undergraduates, including a nursing school, school of foreign service, a business school, and Georgetown College, which is the liberal arts and sciences school. Georgetown College students may choose from more than forty majors, but all must complete two courses in each of the following areas: literature and writing, history, philosophy, theology, math/science, and social science. Students must also complete the study of a foreign language through the intermediate level. In an attempt at breadth, the university does not allow students to enroll in more than two courses in any one discipline during their first or second years; nor may two courses in the same discipline be taken during the same semester during the student's first two years.

Courses fulfilling the literature and writing requirement, according to the bulletin, must be "taught in the English language, must include the close analysis of texts, and must be writing intensive." Certain courses in classics, comparative literature, East Asian, or Slavic may be used to meet this requirement. The history requirement may be fulfilled by survey courses in "European Civilization," "History of the Atlantic World," or "World History." The course description for both European Civilization I and II states that "special attention is paid to issues of class, gender, marginality, and the relationship of Europe to non-Western cultures." Students may test out of the history requirement either partially or completely by scoring at least a 3 on the AP test. A course in United States history is not required.

The philosophy requirement is fulfilled by a course in general philosophy and one in ethics. Many "general philosophy" and ethics courses cover traditional content and introduce students to the work of classical and modern philosophers, and as a whole the philosophy department at Georgetown is less politicized than other departments. The theology requirement is fulfilled by a course in the "Problem of God" or "Introduction to Biblical Literature" and an elective at the intermediate level. The specific content of the former course varies significantly by section: to be safe, students should try to take the section taught by Thomas King, S.J., one of

Georgetown's finest teachers. The content of the course in biblical literature, not surprisingly, is a bit more specified. The math/science and social science requirements may be fulfilled in a myriad of ways.

Besides Fr. King, the best teachers at Georgetown include James V. Schall, S.J., and George W. Carey in government; Jeffrey I. Shulman, Paul F. Betz, Alvaro F. V. Ribeiro, S.J., and Joan M. Holmer in English; Wayne Davis and Wilfried Ver Eecke in philosophy; and Marius Schwartz and George J. Visknins in economics. In theology, Stephen M. Fields, S.J., should be sought out. The government department is regarded as comparatively strong, particularly in its political philosophy offerings and faculty. Classics, psychology, history, philosophy, and economics all contain pockets of strength and are generally solid.

One of Georgetown's strengths lies in the accessibility of professors and in their genuine commitment to teaching, despite heavy pressure to publish. As one faculty member says, "There is strong institutional and informal pressure to be available to students, to grade papers intensively and generally to recognize the dependency of this institution on the good will of students," or to practice *cura personalis,* in the words of the Jesuits. Teaching excellence is even reported to be necessary for tenure, though of course it is not as important as publication.

Georgetown can also boast about its small class sizes. "We have some large lecture courses, but not nearly as many as state schools and many other private schools," says a professor. Indeed, even Georgetown's larger courses are comparatively small, typically enrolling seventy to seventy-five students. These courses are said to be most common in economics and history. English courses, on the other hand, are limited to an enrollment of twenty.

Grade inflation has taken serious root at Georgetown. A 1997 faculty report found that 42 percent of the grades awarded at Georgetown in 1994 were A's, compared to just 26 percent in 1980. It also stated that courses were not challenging enough, as Georgetown students "in a typical week study fewer hours, work more hours for pay, and party more hours than their peers at comparable institutions." New plans to counter this grade inflation were never carried out or had little effect. By 1998, 45 percent of Georgetown grades were A's. The American Studies department is particularly bad — from 1994 to 1998, no grade lower than a C was given to a student in an American Studies course — but economics and chemistry are less inflationary. The important place that Georgetown gives student evaluations of professors has been fingered as one reason for the university's increasing problem with grade inflation.

Political Atmosphere: The Spirit of Tradition

Georgetown says that it "is committed to a view of reality which reflects Catholic and Jesuit influences." Leo J. O'Donovan, S.J., who stepped down as school president in early 2001, has written that "Our Catholic, Jesuit character is our greatest inspiration, enhancing and encouraging us truly to educate men and women for others." Besides their banality and vagueness, the most revealing aspect of these quotations is the phrase, "Catholic, Jesuit." One gets the feeling that the latter adjective is not used in order to be more specific, but to qualify the statement, as in "Yes, we're a Catholic school, but take that with a grain of salt. We're Jesuit, you know."

There's a defensiveness in much of Georgetown's promotional literature. One piece claims that "No secular university makes such a commitment to ensuring that Catholic thought and teaching are not only available, but prominent." (But then, does anyone *expect* a secular university do that?) In any case, students and professors agree that authentic Catholic teaching is not especially prominent at Georgetown, and that alternative views get much more air time. More fundamentally, this statement illustrates Georgetown's belief that mere exposure to Catholic ideas is the essence of a Catholic school and a Catholic education.

Georgetown is clearly worried by critics' complaints that the school is not very Catholic at all. In a document entitled "Georgetown's Catholic and Jesuit Identity," the university lists several ways in which it "expresses and affirms its Catholic identity." It mentions that it employs prominent Catholic scholars, that many of its students say they are Catholic, that there are Jesuits teaching on campus, and so on. There is no mention, anywhere, of how the school attempts to imbue its students with anything more than "the spirit" of Catholicism, or how it attempts to uphold Catholic moral teaching on campus. It does not matter how many self-described "Catholics" Georgetown employs, or how many chairs it endows for "Catholic scholars." As *Ex Corde Ecclesiae* makes clear, these professors must be practicing Catholics committed to the teachings of the church for an institution's "Catholicism" to have any meaning.

The administration's agonizing over the request of some students and alumni to place crucifixes in classrooms is proof enough that Georgetown's Catholicism is of the closet variety. After some "dialogue" (read, "stonewalling"), the university eventually complied, but not without sapping the crucifixes of their specifically religious symbolism by intentionally choosing a wide variety of "significant" styles and placing scholarly descriptions next to each one. At the same time, the administration added a display of "rotating religious symbols" in the Bunn Intercultural Center on campus to give witness to the school's "spirit of religious inclusiveness."

Not surprisingly, many students are getting the message that religious expression and education don't mix. One senior was quoted in the *Chronicle of Higher Education* as saying that crucifixes contradict the Jesuit belief in open-mindedness. A faculty member was quoted as saying that the effort to introduce crucifixes into classrooms was part of an effort by a minority of students to make Georgetown a "more overtly religious place." The problem, according to him, was that he didn't "see much evidence that that [goal] is a widely shared sentiment." He may be right.

And one must wonder how some Georgetown courses fit, exactly, with the

"Catholic and Jesuit tradition." "Unspeakable Lives: Gay and Lesbian Narratives," for example, introduces students to "strategies of representation occasioned by politically problematic sexualities, especially as these intersect with the construction of gender, race — and most recently, as the politics of sex informs a new cultural aesthetic of disease."

"Unspeakable Lives" is an offering of the Georgetown English department, which houses a number of politicized courses, but also a comparatively large proportion of courses bearing on traditional topics of literary study. Georgetown is still smarting from changes in the English department in 1993 that removed Shakespeare from the curriculum. Or at least it was reported that way in the press. While it's true that a Shakespeare course is no longer required of English majors, the school now offers nine Shakespeare courses annually, compared to the average of 2.6 at comparable schools. The English department now offers three concentrations: (1) literature and literary history, (2) culture and performance, and (3) writing. Students must take four courses in their chosen concentration, two outside their concentration, and two in material written before 1850.

The women's studies program is singled out as the most politicized. "It lacks any academic rigor and gives the school a bad name," says one professor. That is an understatement, though at least the department's Web site is up-front about the program's agenda. "Students in the program are strongly encouraged to combine feminist theory with practical applications of their scholarship," the site says. "Majors and minors must also take fourth credit options geared to volunteer efforts in women's organizations or one in which the student uses feminist principles and skills." Given course titles like "Dangerous Women: Prostitution, Women's Sexuality and Public Panic," one can only hope that practical application is not always encouraged.

The theology department is none too special, either. *Ex Corde Ecclesiae,* according to one faculty member, could have no better effect than to improve the theology offerings and faculty. "The theology department is a disgrace, save for two or three people," says the professor. There is certainly nothing in the distribution of course offerings that would make one believe that Georgetown is a Catholic university. Of the 114 theology courses listed by the department, only eleven focus specifically on Catholic theology or Catholic thinkers. By way of comparison, eight are devoted to Hinduism and Buddhism, thirteen to Judaism, and seven to Islam. There are several courses devoted to liberation theology, and the course description for "Womanist Theology" is instructive. This course "serves to provide a critical response to the absence/invisibility of African American women in both feminist and Black liberation theologies and to acknowledge their 'coming to voice' as articulators of a wholistic [sic], communication theology which challenges racism, sexism, and classism."

Georgetown's lecture program has little balance — let alone a Catholic slant — bringing in notably pro-abortion and/or anti-Catholic speakers. The university has also allowed student groups to bring to campus controversial speakers like *Hustler* publisher Larry Flynt, and just plain silly speakers like talk show host Jerry Springer.

Though there is not now an unreasonable speech code on the books, that may soon change. A menorah displayed on campus was vandalized twice in late 1999 by a Georgetown student who was soon apprehended. A group of student radicals called the Georgetown Unity Coalition clamored for a speech code in the wake of this and other incidents, and President O'Donovan called on the university chaplain and dean to "develop ideas and strategies for strengthening inclusion and understanding in our diverse community." But whether the move for a more restrictive speech code is successful, there is an implicit speech code already in place. "It's the mood that prevails that inhibits open debate on issues," says a professor. "It's like a tiger is poised to pounce on anyone who deviates from the PC line." Professors must be wary as well. "It would be easy for a young professor to say something in class that could be exploited and then he or she would be a goner," says a faculty member. "The thing is, though, that most of the professors hired aren't likely to wander off the reservation."

The O'Donovan administration was notable for its fecklessness. In the last several years it has caved on a number of occasions in response to student protests, a regular event at Georgetown. On two occasions, female faculty denied tenure by their departments were reinstated by the administration in response to protesters' demands. Recently, the O'Donovan administration agreed to the demands of students staging a sit-in that Georgetown enforce tougher labor standards on the manufacturers of university-licensed products.

But like many institutions, when academic or intellectual freedom is truly threatened, Georgetown is strangely silent. When three thousand copies of the *Georgetown Academy*, Georgetown's alternative conservative newspaper, were stolen, the administration did nothing. Pressure from alumni and other outside groups finally moved President O'Donovan to issue a half-hearted condemnatory statement, but little attempt was made to find or punish the offenders (even though there were witnesses), and O'Donovan said nothing when the official student newspaper, *The Hoya*, applauded the theft of the *Academy*.

The Hoya itself seems disinterested in free speech. In the spring of 2000, a student writer named Robert Swope submitted his regular column. The subject of the column was *The Vagina Monologues*, a play performed on campus as a commentary on violence and female sexuality. In the play, a 24-year-old woman gives alcohol to a 13-year-old girl, then induces her to participate in sex. Besides making the argument that the administration of a Roman Catholic university should not have allowed the play to be performed, Swope — reasonably, it seems — pointed out that had the older person in the situation been a man, "rational people . . . would consider that rape." Instead, he noted, the mostly female crowd laughed at the scene.

The editors of *The Hoya* not only refused to print the column, they fired Swope. They claimed at first that Swope had written on women's issues in his previous column; this was not in fact true, though Swope had done a piece six weeks earlier that was critical of the women's studies program as an academic discipline. So the editors then complained about the timeliness and length of the columnist's submissions — complaints they had never before made — and finally admitted that the column and its writer were ditched because of content. "That a columnist has devoted two of the four columns . . . this semester [to] ridiculing the women's studies program and condemning the women's center creates the appearance of some personal vendetta that hurts the newspaper's credibility," the editor-in-chief said.

These shenanigans earned *The Hoya* a letter from Georgetown alumnus and *Exorcist* author William Peter Blatty, which read in part: "With all that the demon says and does in my novel, never until I read of the *Hoya*'s and Leo O'Donovan's support of *The Vagina Monologues*, and their suppression of Robert Swope's article, have I truly appreciated the meaning of the word *obscenity*."

Student Life: The Spirit of Convictions

Georgetown enrolls just over thirteen thousand undergraduates. It has a very low acceptance rate of roughly 23 percent, making it one of only eighteen schools to accept less than 30 percent of its applicants, and attracts extremely bright and able students from across the nation. The university's reputation is reflected in the fact that it competes with elite secular schools like Harvard, Duke, and Brown for students.

Georgetown students, in fact, are said by some to be the university's greatest strength. One professor claims that Georgetown undergrads are comparable to those found in the nation's best schools: "As good as you get for the kind of student (politico type) we draw." As bright as they may be, Georgetown's students hardly have a reputation for bookishness. Georgetown is known as a party school — one where, for instance, "drop your pants" parties (don't ask) are said to be frequent. In the mid-'90s the school just barely missed *Playboy*'s list of the top 40 party schools in the nation (but did grab first place in another survey), and professors have complained about hung-over students in their morning classes.

Of course, Georgetown draws more than its share of politically active and ambitious students. Opportunities to work on Capitol Hill abound. Others focus their political activities closer to home. Besides standard student organizations like the College Democrats and Republicans, student groups include the typographically challenged H*yas for Choice (a pro-abortion group that is not officially recognized but is still allowed to meet in Georgetown classrooms and distribute materials on campus) and GU-PRIDE (which, after battling the Georgetown administration in the 1980s, is now officially recognized, given university funding, and has an official campus office). The GU-PRIDE Web site includes links to various homosexual organizations, including those targeting youths like !OutProud! and the Gay Teens' Penpal Connection.

Student orientation is said, by one professor, to be increasingly "a brainwashing experience with great ritual. It's as bad as you will find." The program, called "Peer Education," includes a demonstration of condom use. The university official responsible for the program recently defended the condom demonstration on the grounds that the university only included it in a "thoughtful" way. Dialogue with Campus Ministry resulted. Dialogue always results at Georgetown.

Besides dialoguing with others, the Georgetown Campus Ministry office provides services, events, and chaplains for Catholics, Jews, Protestants, and Muslims. There are a number of opportunities for religious worship on campus. Mass is celebrated three times a day at the beautiful Dahlgren Chapel, and at least once daily at several other chapels on campus. Protestant, Jewish, and Muslim services are also available.

According to one professor, the safety of Georgetown's campus is "bad and getting worse." Indeed, a university employee was shot on campus in December of 1999. In 1996, the administration increased the number and luminosity of lights and placed call boxes around campus. Free escort services are available. Though it may have a crime problem, the surrounding neighborhood is genteel and inviting. Well-kept, outlandishly expensive townhouses line the red-brick streets, small neighborhood pubs, pharmacies, and restaurants perch inconspicuously on street corners, and there are a number of good second-hand bookstores in the area.

Students living in university residences do not have an option for single-sex living. Many apartments are provided for students; all of the more traditional dormitories include coed floors. Several residence halls have been designated smoke free. Students select on-campus housing in an order determined by a lottery.

University of Georgia

Office of Admissions
212 Terrell Hall
Athens, GA 30602
(706) 542-2112
www.uga.com

Total enrollment: 30,912
Undergraduates: 22,835
SAT ranges (Verbal/Math): 550-640 (V); 550-650 (M)

Applicants: 13,400
Accepted: 61%
Enrolled: 49%
Application deadline: February 15
Financial aid application deadline: March 1
Tuition: resident: $3,276/$8,126; non-resident: $10,794/$15,644
Core curriculum: No

Approaching Athens

From its founding in 1785 (although it didn't open until 1801) until the post-war era, the state legislators who fund the University of Georgia were content to underfund the state's flagship university. It was assumed, especially from the 1950s onward, that many of the most talented students might choose to go out-of-state rather than make the trek to Athens, home of the Bulldogs, a large Greek system, and a large school of agriculture. But if your opinion of Georgia is more than a decade or so old, you'll need to update it if it's to reflect today's UGA. For the charming antebellum town of Athens is full of avant-garde bands, chic restaurants, and scholars from all over the world. And its university has never had a higher profile nor been better funded.

Student quality has gone up measurably in recent years thanks to the enormous growth in the state's population (it's now the tenth most populous) and the Hope Scholarship program, which allows in-state students who maintain a B average to attend tuition-free. This makes Georgia an attractive buy for the better in-state students, and out-of-staters looking for an increasingly valuable degree would do well to visit the campus and talk to the professors. Anyone will be impressed by the physical plant, as recent construction projects include a new art museum, school of music, drama headquarters, and many additions to the already excellent science programs.

Yet even as the quality of the student body has improved along with the research facilities and general faculty, many departments are wracked by internal strife, political grandstanding, and a level of intolerance equal to that found on any other campus. Georgia is not the only up-and-coming school that has attempted a shortcut to fame by hiring professors who place careerist style over intellectual substance, and many courses are highly politicized. It's certainly possible to get a first-rate education in Athens, but students must choose their professors not by their graduate institution but by the content of their courses.

Academic Life: Georgia *of* My Mind

As is the case at most large research universities, students at Georgia may choose from a vast array of fields of study. Thirteen schools and colleges, a 3.5-million-volume library, and excellent scientific research facilities provide the breadth and depth necessary for pursing just about any field of knowledge. These attributes, coupled with the Hope Scholarships and remarkable growth in the state's population, allow admissions officers to turn away students who would have been admitted only a decade ago. "The entering SAT scores of freshmen are only a few points below those of UNC-Chapel Hill, and the honors student SAT scores are equivalent with those of Duke's entering freshmen," a professor says.

Indeed, the Honors Program is superb and provides smart, ambitious students with many additional opportunities for academic growth. Smaller classes with the best professors and opportunities for advanced research are only some of the advantages of this 2,500-student program. The quality of the best students also shows in the three Rhodes scholarships awarded to UGA graduates over the past few years. To identify and aid students with great academic potential, Georgia runs the Academic Scholarship Identification Program, which gives students access to additional research and travel opportunities along with cultural activities in order to increase their chances at winning prestigious scholarships.

Rather than a true core curriculum, Georgia has a set of distribution requirements. A typical set of courses must be taken in the humanities, social sciences, sciences, and so on. No study of Western civilization per se is required, although all students must know enough U.S. and Georgia history to pass either an examination or a course in American history; most opt for the latter. Similarly, everyone must know enough about the Constitution of the United States to pass an examination, or they may learn enough in class to pass Political Science 101 or its honors equivalent. These requirements, set by the state board of regents, hardly ensure that Georgia's graduates are liberally educated, but they at least expose students to some of the more important elements of American history and government. Unfortunately, the absence of a Western civilization requirement means that students may not acquire the ability to place this knowledge into the broader context of history.

Unlike many more prestigious schools, Georgia has a foreign language requirement: four courses for A.B. candidates and three for B.S. candidates. Other requirements for the A.B. degree include: a course in fine arts, one in philosophy or religion, and another in either category; two math and four science courses (including at least one two-course sequence); and four courses in social sciences. These course requirements would benefit from the addition of a structured curriculum that demonstrated the administration's faith in the efficacy of the liberal arts. All students must complete an environmental literacy requirement, a bow to a new god of our age, as well as one semester of basic physical education.

Georgia offers its share of politicized courses, usually under the guise of multiculturalism or gender studies. True multicultural studies, such as the study of foreign tongues or deep reading in a foreign culture, require significant intellectual effort. Modern studies that pass for multiculturalism seldom offer more than cliché-ridden tirades against the West written by Western or Western-educated intellectuals. The catalogue lists these courses:

History 4530, "The History of Orientalism." Images and symbolism used by Europeans and Americans to define the Islamic Middle East. The history of the Middle East through representation — stereotypes, myths, fairy tales, novels, films, and news coverage — particularly the ramifications of these images on Western foreign policy towards the Islamic Middle East.

Women's Studies 3100, "Lesbian and Gay Studies." Investigation of same-sex desire, heterosexuality, homosexuality, and the regulation of sexual identities across different racial/ethnic and class/regional communities. Focusing on Native American, African American, Latino, Asian American, and international studies, with texts from law, anthropology, history, film, fiction, and theory.

Women's Studies 4120, "Biology and Politics of Women's Reproduction." Women's reproductive life cycles from the perspective of evolutionary biology and the political theory of radical feminism. Topics include puberty, sexual cycling, menarche, pregnancy, childbirth, and menopause. Feminist critiques of science are explored.

Nevertheless, Georgia is a leader in offering research opportunities for undergraduates. Students will find that many professors are willing to help them pursue projects researching their special interests. Internships are also available and the university's Internship Coordinator of the Career Planning and Placement Center can be a valuable source of information about these opportunities. Students often work with faculty members who have secured grants from the National Science Foundation and other groups, so savvy undergraduates will inquire about such possibilities early in their careers.

This attention to undergraduates is unevenly dispersed over the rest of campus. As at most large state schools, Georgia employs legions of graduate students to bear part of the teaching burden. These are found mostly in introductory courses and in the lab sections of large introductory science classes. The lecture section of such classes can be quite large, with three or four hundred students attending in an auditorium. Generally, classes become smaller once a student chooses a major (or upper-division electives), so that individualized attention is more likely. Much of it depends on the work ethic and personality of the individual professor, since some are anxious to spend hours with their students, while others shun them in order to pursue research. Students should always seek out those faculty members who are willing to spend the time necessary to ensure that students are taught rather than processed.

Georgia does have many dedicated faculty members who are dedicated to undergraduate teaching. These professors include: Jonathan Evans, James Kilgo, James E. Kibler Jr., and Hugh Kenner in English; Bernard Dauenhauer (professor emeritus) in philosophy; Noel Fallows in Spanish; Kirk Willis, William F. Holmes, James Cobb, and John C. Inscoe in history; Thomas M. Lessl in speech communications; Charles Hudson and David Hally in anthropology; Richard LaFleur in classics; Ronald L. Blount in psychology; Allen C. Amason in management; Keith S. Delaplane in entomology; John Pickering in ecology; Daniel Promislow in genetics; and Dwight R. Lee, David B. Mustard, Peter G. Klein, and Richard Timberlake (professor emeritus) in economics. Strong funding for the agricultural programs many decades ago translated into the growth of many fine science departments, and today this research-driven segment of the university is the strongest and most prominent part. Quantum chemistry, environmental studies, botany, forestry, and most other science and agriculture departments rate well consistently, and students choosing these majors also benefit from superb facilities. Other strong departments include economics, political science, art history, and psychology, which is the largest major on campus.

Political Atmosphere: Marching Through Georgia

The story of Georgia's march leftward mimics that of many other universities. After decades of presiding over a middling sort of institution, administrators naturally welcomed the influx of tax dollars gathered from the state's burgeoning population. They built fine new facilities, hired faculty with prestigious alma maters, and eventually were able to raise the bar for admissions. So far, so good. But it's not enough to simply have money; you have to be able to discern gold from brass in order to improve the quality of what is taught. In other words, pedigrees are more important among horses than professors, some of whom resemble a horse in all the wrong ways.

Much of this "progress" came under the watch of former UGA president Charles Knapp, who resigned in 1997 to help run a liberal foundation in Washington, D.C. He instituted the requirement for a course in environmentalism, and during his administration many departments became increasingly politicized. These include women's studies, history, philosophy, African American studies, and Romance languages.

One area of special concern is the College of Education, where the professionalization of knowledge often trumps its dissemination. Students will find hundreds of courses that purport to teach students *how* to teach in lieu of *what* to teach. As if the substitution of methodology for content is not enough, the educrat class also wants to be taken very seriously by professors in the liberal arts (who generally view them with disdain). Therefore, they ape many of the worst characteristics of the modern academy, even if they're a few years behind the curve: political correctness, sensitivity training, and multiculturalism. Concerning the latter, the College of Education has even issued a verbose "Statement of Position for Strategic Planning and Strategic Actions," in which one can find the following statement: "As one of the largest and most prestigious colleges of education in the United States, the University of Georgia College of Education plays a major role in helping provide accurate information and knowledge dealing with issues of diversity. We also intend to play a critical role in influencing the dialogue on race, ethnicity, gender, class, and other aspects of multiculturalism in order to help shape a more democratic society in the twenty-first century." Given the poor performance of so many public schools, a result in part of the inferior education found in colleges of education, we wish that more attention would be paid to mathematics, the sciences, and literacy — what used to be called education.

Other highly politicized departments include women's studies, where advocacy scholarship is the norm. In addition to the classes listed above, the following conference announcement reveals much about contemporary feminist scholarship.

January 12-14, 2001 — 14th Annual Conference on Interdisciplinary Studies, "Social and Economic Justice: Deconstructing Myths and Masks Through Qualitative Research." Georgia Center for Continuing Education. The theme for QUIG 2001 invites participants to explore issues of social and economic justice, particularly the myths and masks we use across the globe to perpetuate injustice and oppression such as racism, sexism, ableism, homophobia, poverty, violence, and illiteracy, as well as ways in which qualitative research has contributed to alleviating injustice.

Virtually every cliché used in so-called progressive circles is used with absolute seriousness in this announcement and, by extension, within the supporting department. Such ersatz intellectual work only pushes the party line, fails to challenge academic norms, and leaves students angry and ill-read.

Women's studies also hosts speakers, including Dr. Claudia F. Card, who delivered the annual Anne Carson Coley Lecture, a series founded to explore recent research in gay and lesbian studies. The lecture was titled "Lesbians, Evil, and Gray Zones," and dealt with "the problem of complicity in one's own maltreatment." Her thesis is that the plight of gays and lesbians is analogous to that of Holocaust victims. As she explained, "The term 'gray zone' comes from Holocaust survivor Primo Levi, who used it to describe the area inhabited by concentration camp prisoners who became kapos (captains with authority over other prisoners) or performed other services for the Nazis in exchange for various privileges." Hence, any homosexual who is pressured to "out" another occupies the same moral ground as a Holocaust-era kapos. This would be laughable, would the comparison be less insulting.

Like many other public universities, Georgia has an official homosexual group, called Lambda Alliance. It claims to serve the interests of the "lesbian, gay, bisexual, and transgendered" members of the university community and to represent their interests and offer them a "safe, secure, and supportive environment." With offices in Memorial Hall, built to honor the university's World War I dead, it carries the imprimatur of the administration. The group also sponsors an "Awareness Week" during spring, National Coming Out Day activities, Valentine's Day activities, and special events during the remainder of the academic year.

Politicization at Georgia also extends to hiring and tenure decisions, as indicated by several recent incidents in departments in the humanities and social sciences. A professor whose students charged that they were verbally abused in class, shown pornographic movies, and had great difficulty reaching the professor for office hour consultations was nevertheless given tenure in her first try. In the same department, the wife of a professor making a six-figure salary received her Ph.D. from his colleagues and was then given a job in that same department — and it was all written into his contract before he took his job, according to sources on campus. In another case, the husband of a female faculty member was offered a tenure-track position (which was never advertised nationally) in the name of diversity; though each is white, she threatened to leave for what in fact was a non-tenure-track job, a move no one would make. This was nothing more than a ploy to get her husband a job, and everyone knew it, but everyone played along like the woman was serious. The bluff succeeded. "It's like a bizarre mating ritual among animals," says a professor.

Such shenanigans cost the university (and students) dearly. A few years ago two young, promising, and accomplished scholar-teachers won university-wide teaching awards while they held temporary appointments in one of Georgia's humanities departments. They were the only department members to receive such awards during those years, and yet neither man was considered seriously for tenure-track positions in their fields. One of them was by that time the author of two books and the editor of another, and yet his personal politics were not what the department wanted. As a result, both men left Georgia at the end of their terms, and students were deprived of the opportunity to be taught by two of the finest young teachers on campus.

For now, though, the university cannot use race and gender in admissions decisions, according to a U.S. district court ruling made in July 2000. A few months after that ruling, the university settled a lawsuit filed by several students who claimed they had been denied admission to UGA because the university "used race as part of an index to decide which borderline applicants to admit," according to the *Chronicle of Higher Education*. The university agreed to admit the students that still wanted to come and to pay the students a total of $63,000 to cover the difference between what they would have paid at Georgia and what they wound up paying at the schools they attended while the lawsuit was pending.

Student Life: Home Grown

Students at today's UGA score higher on standardized tests than their predecessors, graduate at a higher rate, and, if they're in-state, attend tuition-free if they maintain a B average. This makes Georgia one of the better education deals in the country, especially for students with serious interests in the sciences and other high-caliber programs. Regional schools such as Duke, Emory, and Davidson say they've felt the pinch as increasing numbers of Atlanta-area students (or their cash-strapped parents) opt for Athens. The presence of such students is good in several ways: not only is the intellectual level of the entire school raised, but better students are less likely to fall victim to the increasingly dated ideologies spouted by their social climbing professors.

Given these facts, it isn't surprising that approximately 85 percent of Georgia's undergraduates hail from Georgia. If the school is to climb the next rung of the ladder, however, it will face opposition from state legislators and taxpayers, because the easiest way to bring in even more excellent students is to accept more out-of-state students who can bring their higher SAT scores and tuition dollars with them. "There is heavy political pressure to take a large share of students from Georgia. This is true at the undergraduate level and at the graduate and professional schools, like the law school and business school," says one professor. "Consequently, in-state students are of much lower quality than out-of-state students. To improve, the university should reduce the share of in-state students."

One downside to the Hope Scholarship program is the upward pressure it places on grades. This is manifested among the faculty by fear that assigning low grades may cost a student his scholarship and, therefore, chance at a college education. (The *Chronicle of Higher Education* reported that 56 percent of University of Georgia freshmen who had Hope scholarships in 1997-98 retained them this year, down from 65 per cent a year earlier.) As one professor told the *Chronicle,* when he realized that only five of his ninety-six students had a grade above 90 percent, the required minimum for keeping the Hope Scholarship, he gave As to students with an 87.35 percent average or higher, a move that raised the number of A's to twenty-three. "I just weakened," he said. "My TAs and I participated in some pretty wholesale grade inflation."

The university's own Web site is very candid about the pressures placed on students themselves to maintain a B-average, something that can lead to increased incidents of cheating. To address this problem, the school has adopted very strict punishments for plagiarism, including an F in the course in which the violation occurred and a two-year notation on the culprit's academic transcript. An assistant vice president for instruction told a university reporter: "I was really taken aback" by the harshness of the new policy. "If the penalties don't send a strong message that we take academic honesty seriously, I can't imagine what would." This VP continued, "These penalties truly can change a student's life forever. That's why we're running as fast and as hard as we can to get the word out. Students cannot afford to make bad decisions."

Georgia has very few dorm rooms for a huge state school, and only about 6,500 students, a figure unchanged for many years. Some of these residential halls are coed, others single sex. The university offers four different visitation options, ranging from visiting hours of noon to midnight Friday and Saturday (most restrictive), to visitation permitted 24 hours a day, seven days a week (no restrictions). Bathrooms are segregated by sex, and students over 21 may consume alcoholic beverages in their dorm rooms only. Underage drinking is prohibited, but no one denies that it occurs. All dorms save one have controlled access that require a student ID to enter, and security staff are on duty in every hall from 10 p.m. until 6 a.m. daily. Crime in Athens and the adjacent university community is not unknown, and there have even been very occasional murders and rapes on campus. Yet UGA is not a violent or particularly unsafe campus.

Because of the relatively small number of dorm rooms, most students live off campus in abundant (but not always cheap) apartments. Athens is a delightful college town that offers elements of both the Old and New South. Many beautiful antebellum structures remain, since the town was east of the paws of Sherman's army. Athens, like the university it hosts, has become significantly more sophisticated in recent years and is another reason students apply to Georgia in record numbers. Downtown Athens, directly across the street from the oldest section of campus, offers cafes, restaurants of all types, and many bars and stores that cater to student tastes. Students longing for the big city head to Atlanta, about an hour to the southwest.

Football is still the most important sport at Georgia (a fact that the football stadium's location in the center of campus makes hard to deny), but interest in games other than football has grown over the past decade. There is an increasingly wide gap between the levels of enthusiasm for the gridiron "Dawgs" found among graying alumni and the current student body. Today, track and field, swimming, tennis, and other, newer sports claim a larger share of the limelight than in the past. And the university offers many intramural sports for dedicated but non-scholarship athletes.

Like any large state university, Georgia's list of student organizations is long and ranges from the banal to the bizarre. Among the better are the various academic honor societies and fraternities organized around academic disciplines. Many religious groups have campus headquarters, including the Baptist Student Union, the Catholic Student Fellowship, Hillel, and the Wesley Foundation.

Georgia Institute of Technology

Office of Admissions
225 North Avenue, NW
Atlanta, GA 30332-0320
(404) 894-2000
www.gatech.edu

Total enrollment: 14,100
Undergraduates: 10,256
SAT ranges (Verbal/Math): 590-690 (V); 630-725 (M)
Applicants: 7,579
Accepted: 69%
Enrolled: 45%
Application deadline: January 15
Financial aid application deadline: March 1
Tuition: resident: $3,308/$9,008; non-resident: $10,826/$16,526
Core curriculum: No

Rambling Rex

Georgia Tech, as the Georgia Institute of Technology is more commonly known, is one of the nation's leading technical institutes, with scores of undergraduate and graduate programs, impressive research facilities, and a large budget supported by the state's burgeoning population. Like its rival, the University of Georgia, Georgia Tech has benefited from the Hope Scholarship program, which offers free tuition to in-state students who maintain a B average. It has a superb faculty offering courses in five undergraduate colleges: architecture, computing, engineering, Ivan Allen College (non-scientific fields of study), and the sciences.

According to the school, Georgia Tech "enrolls the highest percentage of freshmen National Merit Scholars and the third highest percentage of National Achievement Scholars among publicly supported institutions in the U.S." As difficult as this makes Tech to get into, students should know that it's even harder to get out of. Those planning to attend should prepare for four years of hard work and intensive study. But a degree at this fine school is likely to make it all worthwhile.

Plans call for the school to expand its campus to the east side of the interstates that run through downtown Atlanta. This expansion of a major university in an urban area is a rare move today and further solidifies Georgia Tech as a leading member of the downtown Atlanta community. It's also a leading research center, and in today's complex world of high-tech industry, even undergraduate students need access to top-flight research centers.

Tech students spend long hours at study, and their work pays off in the form of a well-respected degree and a fine education. Obviously, the school is not for students interested primarily in the liberal arts, and it's not for anyone with less-than-stellar SAT scores. But those with the interests and aptitudes can find few places that will serve them any better than Georgia Tech. The best students can even spend half of the academic year working for companies across the country in their field of study. Graduates swear by the institute, and today's technology has been much improved by it. If further enhancements can be made to the liberal arts division of the college without the courses becoming overly politicized, Georgia Tech will remain a technological power for some time to come.

Academic Life: Work Hard and Prosper

Students come to Tech to learn about engineering and science — fields that require long hours of study. Its curriculum is designed to produce graduates well versed in their disciplines, so it is necessarily weaker in the humanities and social sciences than most of the other institutions in this book. Still, students are required to complete about as many hours of course work in the humanities — eighteen — as they are at most other schools. An equal number of hours is required in the social sciences. Statewide requirements include either examinations or courses in U.S. and Georgia history. Most students fulfill this requirement through introductory-level classes in political science and U.S. history. No courses in Western civilization are required, although many are available.

Yet all students must take calculus, physics, mathematics, and several courses in the sciences, so an aptitude for such studies is not so much demanded as assumed. Students report hours of preparation for notoriously difficult exams in many classes, so that even those who enter with perfect records find themselves working harder than ever before, and perhaps for lesser grades than before. Georgia Tech graduates know their fields and develop excellent study habits and other disciplines. Students who fail to do these things seldom graduate.

The College of Architecture, established in 1908, is well-respected in professional circles. It offers undergraduate degrees in architecture, building construction, and industrial design, as well as graduate degrees.

The College of Computing, founded in 1990, grew out of the earlier School of Information Science. Today students selecting a major in this college make good use of highly specialized facilities packed with the very latest computer equipment and run by some of the best computer scientists in the business. The college is located in a 40,000-square-foot facility built in 1989 to the standards required for this burgeoning field of study.

The College of Sciences holds six schools for biology, chemistry and biochemistry, earth and atmospheric sciences, mathematics, physics, and psychology, as well as the non-degree-granting departments of health and performance sciences. In all of these fields, students will find top experts churning out research and working in well-equipped laboratories. Two of the university's best professors — George Cain and Carl Spruill — teach mathematics in this college, and math, along with chemistry, are considered the best in a list of good departments. Other top professors include Charles A. Eckert and Charles L. Liotta in chemical engineering and Rigoberto Hernandez in chemistry.

The Ivan Allen College of Management is less technically oriented than the other colleges and strives, according to the institute, to "educate leaders, innovators, and renaissance engineers." Such a philosophy reflects the complexities of the modern business world, in which disciplinary boundaries have softened considerably and innovative thinking is required. In the New Economy of e-commerce and the fast-paced changes it entails, new solutions must be found to old (and recently developed) problems. The official literature continues: "The Ivan Allen College addresses the three major forces — technological change, globalization, and diversity — that will shape the new knowledge, skills, and values essential to tomorrow's leaders. Through progressive programs geared to the twenty-first century, the Ivan Allen College instills in its graduates the capabilities to succeed in a rapidly changing world." Graduate of Ivan Allen College enter such fields as public policy, government, information design and technology, and technology policy design and implementation.

Students in Ivan Allen College may major in the School of History, Technology, and Society, which, "unlike standard liberal arts degrees . . . requires broad-based training including course work in mathematics, science, and engineering, that is consistent with the overall mission of Georgia Tech as a technological university," according to the catalogue. Classes offered in that department include the "History of American Business," "Engineers in American Life," "History of Electrical Sciences and Technology," and "The Development of Industrial Cities," as well as more traditional historical studies.

Of course, Georgia Tech is best known for its College of Engineering, and it is here that one finds some of the best and largest programs on campus. The programs in mechanical engineering and in electrical and computer engineering are two of the finest departments on campus. There are nine degree-granting schools in this college, and one can study just about any field of engineering with very fine faculty in excellent facilities. Graduates of these programs command high salaries from the companies that recruit on campus (and there were around 550 such companies in one recent year). Classes are very demanding and clearly not for every student, even bright and motivated ones, but for those with an aptitude for technical thought and the discipline to study hard, Georgia Tech offers an extremely attractive degree.

Another excellent program at Georgia Tech is the Cooperative Plan, implemented in 1912 for students desiring to combine "practical experience with techni-cal theory," in the words of the catalogue. Approximately one-third of the under-graduate student body, or more than three thousand students, take the Cooperative Plan, which lasts five years rather than the traditional four. Students are chosen in a competitive process based on high grades and evidence of self-discipline, then work in hundreds of industries around the country for one semester each year and take classes on campus during the other semester. Thus, students are given excellent op-portunities to gain both job experiences and financial aid. According to the univer-sity, "the plan provides, to a substantial degree, the experience most companies re-quire of their employees before promoting them to positions of responsibility." This opportunity is just another way that Georgia Tech provides great chunks of the edu-cation students will need for life in their chosen careers.

Even before students begin regular classes, they receive a model introduction to campus academic life. Within the last decade, Georgia Tech started a rigorous summer program for black and Hispanic freshmen. The five-week program had ex-isted prior to that as a remedial program, and its success was mixed at best. "We were starting off with the idea that the kids were dumb," a university administrator told columnist William Raspberry. "We didn't say that, of course, but the program was set up on a deficit model. We were going to fix what was wrong with these mi-nority kids." This model proved inaccurate, however, and before long the teachers in the program started their sessions with "the idea that these youngsters were unusu-ally bright, that we had very high expectations of them," the administrator said. The students responded well, with those who took the so-called "Challenge" course per-forming better than non-minority students once regular classes began — in fact, the percentage of minority students with 4.0 GPAs in their first semester at Georgia Tech was twice that for white students. The success of the program brought the university deserved national attention, and today, Georgia Tech holds a two-week version of the program for all of its incoming students — further proof that bright students, when challenged with academic rigor rather than patronized by well-intentioned bureaucrats, can excel in their chosen fields.

As for the Hope scholarship program, only 40 per cent kept their scholarships in 1999, down from 45 per cent in 1998, according to the *Chronicle of Higher Educa-tion*. These figures indicate just how difficult it is to maintain a high GPA at Tech.

Political Atmosphere: Nose in a Book

Compared to many other schools in this guide, Georgia Tech is quite free of politi-cized curricula or other forms of noxious activities. Yet it can be found, particularly in some of the classes in the humanities and social sciences offered through Ivan Al-len College. "I don't see much of it, although I do hear that there are some people in the humanities who are pretty bad," says one professor. "It does exist."

Similarly, the administration does push diversity, mainly through structures devoted to recruiting minority faculty and students. "But it's generally pretty tame stuff," the professor says. "The administration practices affirmative action, but in a fairly benign way." Another professor says that in practice, this version of affirmative action means that "if we get one thousand applications for positions in a year, and if there are any blacks or women in the stack, their applications will get looked at."

Georgia Tech does have a "director of diversity" whose job it is to recruit qualified minority students. This is common at many technical institutes because of the small numbers of minority professionals in technical fields. Yet the academic integrity and epistemology of the fields of study taught at Tech keep things more straightforward than at many nontechnical schools. "The hard sciences and engineering are a lot more honest about academics," says a professor. "It's a more serious business here than at many places. Most of my colleagues are ultra-liberal on social issues, but academically we all get along fine. We have very rigorous academics here, and there just isn't the room for nonsense you might get elsewhere." This nonsense includes speech codes and sensitivity training, but such things are rare or nonexistent at Georgia Tech and none are on the horizon.

Student Life: The Atlanta Games

Georgia Tech demands much from its students, so anyone thinking about enrolling should have no illusions about the long haul ahead of them. But the rewards are great for those with the aptitude for such studies, and it is one of the better academic bargains in this book.

But of course even the most studious must have social lives, and Tech's primary asset for that vital element of college life is its location in Atlanta, one of the nation's most dynamic cities. Tech is located downtown, so students have no trouble finding ways to spend their free time. The neighborhood just to the west of campus is on the mend in recent years, but students must still exercise caution when venturing out, as is the case in any urban experience. (Crime on the Georgia Tech campus is actually not that much worse than at comparable institutions.) If your idea of college must include broad expanses of lawn, brooks running along green banks, and mountains on the horizon, then Tech isn't for you. But if you crave the fast-paced life that city living coupled with intensive academics can bring, it might be the right place.

Another fast-paced element of today's society, e-commerce, plays an important role in Tech's academic culture and even its financial well-being. Recently, a "26-year-old computer whiz who dropped out of [Georgia Tech] to found an Internet-security company" donated $15 million to the Institute's College of Computing, according to the *Chronicle of Higher Education*. This act put his name on the new $70 million complex for advanced computing and information technology.

While Tech can't guarantee every student (much less dropouts) such success, this story sheds much light on the potential of this dynamic new culture, of which the nation's elite engineering schools are the epicenter.

Georgia Tech is a member of the Atlantic Coast Conference and competes with other schools that invest enormous sums of money in their sports programs. Even with the high level of competition, Georgia Tech athletes rank among the top twelve NCAA programs in football player graduation rates, and in the top twenty-five programs for overall student-athlete graduation. Other sports also receive their due attention at Tech, which benefited greatly from the 1996 Olympic Games held in Atlanta. Construction for the games resulted in a new Olympic-size pool, new dormitories, and other amenities long desired by the Georgia Tech community. For professional sports fans, the city offers teams in all major sports, including the Atlanta Braves, Hawks, Falcons, and the new hockey team, the Thrashers.

Additionally, the athletics department will receive $50.5 million from the estate of Lee Edwards Candler, which the *Chronicle of Higher Education* claims is the largest gift ever received by an athletics department. The school will use the money to "renovate facilities and improve services for athletes," according to the *Chronicle*.

With about 9,200 undergraduates and about 3,700 graduate students, there are bound to be clubs to suit most interests. Among the 170 extracurricular activities are several publications, a student-run FM radio station, and other low-key sorts of clubs, like a walking and running club and an environmental awareness group. There are, of course, many academic organizations. The Georgia Tech Library and Information Center has more technical reports than many places have books — approximately 2 million. There are also 2.7 million books, 170,000 maps, 700,000 government documents, and a complete collection of U.S. patents. The Georgia Tech Center for the Arts offers relief from numbers and diagrams with several theaters and galleries. The center has hosted the 1992 vice presidential debate, a roundtable discussion with former secretaries of defense, and performers like Itzhak Perlman, Marcel Marceau, Branford Marsalis, and the Canadian Brass.

Freshmen are required to live in one of Georgia Tech's 28 residence halls, a majority of which have been designated as single-sex. The coed dorms usually house men and women on separate floors. Students who are of drinking age are allowed to have alcohol in their rooms. Each residence hall determines its own quiet hours policy, as well as an "open hours" policy for visitors of the opposite sex, though overnight guests are generally permitted.

Grove City College

Office of Admissions
100 Campus Dr.
Grove City, PA 16127-2104
(724) 458-2100
www.gcc.edu

Total enrollment: 2,329
Undergraduates: 2,323
SAT ranges (Verbal/Math): 560-680 (V); 600-690 (M)
Applicants: 2,163
Accepted: 44%
Enrolled: 61%
Application deadline: February 15
Financial aid application deadline: April 15
Tuition: $7,220/$11,426
Core curriculum: Yes

Health and Education — But No Welfare

Grove City College made national news some twenty-five years ago when it refused to allow the Department of Health, Education, and Welfare to, in effect, take control of its administration and policy making decisions. After litigation that went all the way to the Supreme Court of the United States, the college decided to refuse federal funds of any kind, and today it is one of only a few institutions of higher learning (the other notable school being Hillsdale College) that is genuinely free of federal money (including student grants and loans) and hence federal control.

In keeping itself free from meddling bureaucracies, Grove City's educational philosophy can be implemented fully and honestly. At the heart of this philosophy is the desire to offer its students the best liberal education it can muster.

Founded in 1876, Grove City has consistently upheld both high ideals and high standards for its faculty and students. It requires that its faculty be practicing Christians and that its students attend chapel functions a minimum of sixteen times each semester. It is not embarrassed by Western heritage and requires an excellent six-semester sequence in traditional humanities. "In brief, Grove City College aims to be a Christian college of liberal arts and sciences," the college states. "It seeks to help its students to grow as persons, to achieve an integrated overview of reality, and master at least one major discipline of knowledge. . . . Grove City College is not narrowly denominational. The college simply aims to give today's youth the best in the liberal arts and sciences in a wholesome Christian environment." In a day when public af-filiation with a church and ardent defense of tradition can cause the eyes of the lite-rati to roll back in their heads, Grove City has taken a courageous stand for the pur-suit of truth, and has done so with academic distinction.

Academic Life: A Humane Alternative

Grove City requires of its students one class on Western culture each semester for their first three years, and doesn't try to hide the fact that the classes will concern themselves with Christianity, Western culture, and American heritage. The typical Grover is serious about academics and wants to learn from a Christian perspective, without the PC distractions that are typical to other universities. "While many points of view are examined, and comparisons made to other civilizations, the college con-tinues to unapologetically advocate preservation of America's religious, political, and economic heritage of individual freedom and responsibility," the catalogue states. These Western culture courses are the best evidence of the educational phi-losophy at Grove City. "Rejecting relativism and secularism, [the college] fosters in-tellectual, moral, spiritual and social development consistent with a Christian com-mitment to truth, morality and freedom," according to the catalogue. "Rather than political, ideological, or philosophical agendas, objective truth continues as the goal of liberal learning." This type of clear-sighted and principled language is rare in col-lege catalogues, so we'll quote some more: "At the core of the curriculum, particu-larly in the humanities, contemporary perspectives are not emphasized to the ne-glect of books and thinkers and ideas in the West proved across the ages to be of value in the quest for knowledge. Intellectual inquiry remains open to the questions religion raises and receptive to the answers Christianity offers."

This commitment to genuine quality at the expense of the ephemeral marks Grove City as a place in which neither teacher nor pupil need be embarrassed by their beliefs, a place where no one is "beyond" Christianity or the realm of what is true and beautiful. In the humanities core, students study seminal works of litera-ture, art, philosophy, and more, from the ancient Hebrews through the classical world, the Middle Ages and Renaissance, and on to modern times.

These classes constitute a significant commitment on the part of the college to ensure that every student, no matter what his major, will receive a broad liberal edu-cation before graduating. And the fact that it is carried out over a three-year period means that students have a common set of readings for most of their college career — something that is radically different from the intellectually incoherent and frac-tured environment found on most American campuses. "It is a recognition that some prescription on the part of the university is needed," a professor says. "One needs to be an educated person, and you do so by coming in close contact with some of the best that has been thought and written. It works very well."

Other general requirements at Grove City are more properly described as distribution requirements: all students must take two courses in social sciences/international studies, two in quantitative and logical reasoning, and two laboratory courses in natural sciences. Students seeking a B.A. degree must demonstrate second-year proficiency in a foreign language, and that is the only general requirement not made of all students (although some distribution requirements may be fulfilled with courses that also count toward a major). Students must also demonstrate writing competency either by scoring high on their SAT II (Writing Test) or by enrolling in a tutorial geared to that purpose.

Although relatively small (about 2,300 students), Grove City offers a large selection of majors — not as many as a large state or private university, naturally, but with a wide enough range that most interests are served. The most popular fields are in the liberal arts and the sciences, but majors are also available in both electrical and mechanical engineering, many fields of education, and several areas within the broad rubric of business administration. Preprofessional programs (which also require the general education classes) have extremely high success rates when it comes to sending graduates on to further study. One weakness is the absence of a major in classical languages and civilization, although students may take New Testament Greek through the department of religion and philosophy. Also, no majors are offered in art and art history, nor in theater and drama. An unusual major, reflective of the college's history and purpose, is a combined program in Christian thought (religion) and communications.

Not only is the range of courses broad, their content is exemplary. Many essays in this guide list courses that range from the narrowly ideological to the laughably mindless. Grove City, however, offers no such courses. Instead, its courses are conceived of and taught as they ought to be. For example:

- "Literary Criticism and Theory" — "A detailed examination of the major literary critics and theories of Western civilization. Part I is devoted to key figures of the Classical tradition; Part II uses basic tenets of that tradition to critique the 'new wave' of critical theory."
- "Poetry" — "This course explores a wide range of traditional and contemporary poetry; gives insight into ways poets use imagery, rhyme, meter, persona and sound qualities to create meaning in poetry; provides experience with prosody and with problems in translation; and offers in-depth experience with the work of selected poets." This class requires students to read the poets themselves rather than the literary theorists who deconstruct them.
- "British History to 1781" — "A general survey of British history with special emphasis on the development of the common law, the parliament, and the British constitution."

While most professors at Grove City share this commitment to the liberal arts, some even exceed that standard. According to faculty, these include John Dixon in

English, Marvin Folkertsma in political science, John Sparks in business administration, Jeff Herbener and Dirk Mateer in economics, and Paul Schaefer in religion. As noted in the course listings above, the excellent English department has "a faculty dedicated to actually studying the intent of the writers and the background out of which they wrote," according to a professor in another department. Also strong are business; economics, which emphasizes free-market theories represented by Austrian and Public Choice schools of thought; and political science, which offers its students internships in state and national offices.

Political Atmosphere: Having None of It

Given Grove City's love of Western tradition, Christianity, and traditional morality, it comes as little surprise when a professor says, "We have no politicized departments whatsoever." While at some colleges this boast might be seen as an effort at damage control, at Grove City it is believable. Professors are recruited not only for their academic gifts, but for the way in which their teaching and personal philosophies fit with the stated purpose of the school. "There are no pockets of opposition," says another professor. "There are many fine faculty out there with good Ph.D.s. We let them know we're committed to Christian values and we check their references. We don't get bamboozled. There has been no erosion of commitment to the college's core commitments."

Finding people who match the college's requirements and philosophy and "are not tainted by political correctness" is getting more difficult, says another faculty member. "It's especially difficult in literature and theology. We check references very thoroughly. We say right up front that we're evangelical and are committed to personal and economic liberty."

Perhaps the most valuable aspect of Grove City's ideology-free environment is the freedom it gives to both faculty and students. "Because we have a clear statement of purpose and a mission, we attract like-minded people and we're able to concentrate on the intellectual development of our students," says a professor. "People who come here to teach can actually do what they're most interested in."

Many small schools have taken the popular media's bait and tried to raise their standing in the ubiquitous (and largely meaningless) magazine rankings by hiring and promoting faculty who put publishing first and teaching second. Grove City is above all that; it has been wise enough to recognize that the true purpose of a liberal arts college is to teach the next generation to search for truth and to live responsible lives in the light of what reason and revelation have made known. Grove City's "position is that if you produce useful research it's a plus, and that's fine as long as it's not about minutiae," says a professor. "This is not a publish or perish atmosphere, but one geared toward the conveyance of knowledge from one generation to the next. Quite a few of us publish, but basically this is not a publishing place." Publishing does figure in such things as pay and assessment, but it is not the central mission of those who teach first and publish second.

"This is a teaching college, but we do encourage publishing if you have something to say," says one professor. However, given the culture at most large graduate schools today, it is not always easy to convince new Ph.D.s that they can be secure in putting teaching (or any other matter in life) before publishing. "You must deal with this matter when fresh Ph.D.s come on board," one professor says. "They come out of the publishing culture. The majority of people we've hired in the last three or four years are from other colleges, so they already have ten or fifteen years of experience. And they're not left alone here — we evaluate them."

Tenure — often the carrot waggling at the end of the publishing stick — is not an issue at Grove City: no one gets it, ever. Every single employee is hired on a year-to-year contract. While one might assume that this would result in a high turnover rate among faculty, just the opposite is true. "The college has a very low attrition rate among the faculty," says one professor. "We don't dismiss someone for transient reasons. If I ceased to teach they would first try to rehabilitate me, but they wouldn't put up with me indefinitely. There is a great deal of trust here. You don't worry about it if you do a good job." The unusual arrangement was undertaken to prevent the type of abuses of tenure that have of late made news — a professor who stopped writing lectures years ago, or who regards his students as impediments, or who is absent more often than not. At Grove City the absence of tenure acts as a natural braking mechanism for those who would turn the campus into a place of indoctrination.

In another rare practice, Grove City does not accept government aid of any kind. "Grove City College operates on a balanced budget, refuses all federal aid, and remains virtually debt-free, thereby proving that higher education can operate responsibly by providing an affordable, first-rate education without government funding or mandates," the college view book states. According to a faculty member, "Our independence means that the state and federal governments don't have to look beyond our own rationales and reasoning. They don't have to do anything about our needs, and the speed of change on campus and the content of it can be self-determined. Also, we can pay attention to other academic groups and other private accrediting agencies." Even without government money, the cost of tuition and room and board at Grove City is just $11,426. That's much less than the tuition alone at many inferior schools. Included in the cost are new notebook computers and color printers that students keep upon completing their degrees.

No wonder so many people want to get in. Grove City received 1,906 applications for the 525 dorm openings in the freshman class that began school in the fall of 2000 — proof that many students are still interested in quality liberal arts educations. Nearly 65 percent of those accepted were enrolled, a very high number. With all the applicants, Grove City was able to select a freshman class with an average SAT score of 1,258 and an average high school GPA of 3.7, and of whom one in six were valedictorians or salutatorians in their high school classes, thereby ensuring that excellent students will be sitting in the college's excellent classes.

Student Life: Historic Standards

Grove City's commitment to Christian values is apparent in its student life policies. The college's philosophy reflects concepts of dignity, truth, and honor that are ridiculed elsewhere as hopelessly out-of-date. For example, students are required to live in single-sex campus housing unless they are commuters living with families, and there are no coed dorms. All students must attend chapel or convocations at least sixteen times per semester. Similarly, students are warned that certain types of behavior will result in disciplinary action, perhaps even dismissal. Among these are the use of drugs and alcohol as well as premarital sex, homosexuality, or "any other conduct which violates historic Christian standards."

The college catalogue frankly describes what students will find should they choose to attend: "Students in a free society have the right to choose the college which best suits their needs, interests and lifestyles. Students, having chosen their college, have the responsibility to observe the standards and regulations established by the college they have selected. Members of the Grove City College campus community are expected to observe Christian moral standards, as they have been understood by most of the Christian community historically." As the application and enrollment figures demonstrate, many find this structured environment a highly desirable alternative to the anything-goes attitude found on most campuses today.

The college has also preserved architectural traditions, and its stunning Collegiate Gothic campus includes spires, stained glass, and green malls. The campus was designed by Frederick Olmstead, renowned landscaper of New York City's Central Park.

Grove City students compete in twenty intercollegiate sports at the NCAA Division III level and play on four club teams. The Physical Learning Center contains two swimming pools — one for recreation, one for competition — as well as fitness and weight rooms, an "Intramural Room" with four full-size basketball courts, a dance studio, a bowling alley, and racquetball courts.

With more than one hundred student organizations and activities, the college caters to virtually every interest. Because of the school's religious and intellectual orientation, there are no worries about liberal political or activist groups disrupting the campus. Instead, twenty religious groups and activities are available, including organizations for Protestants and Catholics. Two standout religious groups are Salt Company, a Christian Bible study group, and Warriors for Christ, a campus-wide prayer and study club. Many performances are offered throughout the school year. Grove City College also boasts an excellent marching band, 260 members strong, one of the nation's largest marching bands considering the school's small size.

There are nineteen honor societies and as many departmental and professional clubs. Six local sororities and eight local fraternities fill out the social scene on campus. Greek participation has declined over the years; last year just 15 percent of students joined.

Grove City, Pennsylvania, is a small town of only eight thousand. But should students want to reach a big city, Pittsburgh is only sixty miles to the south. Because of its rural location, crime is simply not a problem on campus.

Hampden-Sydney College

Hampden-Sydney College
Office of Admissions
Hampden-Sydney, VA 23943
(800) 755-0733
www.hsc.edu

Total enrollment: 1,000
Undergraduates: 1,000
SAT ranges (Verbal/Math): 500-610 (V); 510-610 (M)
Applicants: 989
Accepted: 72%
Enrolled: 42%
Application deadline: March 1
Financial aid application deadline: March 1
Tuition: $16,500/$22,500
Core curriculum: No

The Men's Rooms

In a time when America wonders if "character" matters, Hampden-Sydney's position remains unambiguous. The founding mission of this small liberal arts college is to "to form good men and good citizens." After 225 years, "Hampden-Sydney has never waivered in its efforts to develop educated men of character," says the dean of students at the college for the past three decades. "That makes this place special." And he means "men" in the literal sense: Hampden-Sydney is one of the few remaining colleges open only to men.

That's not all that makes Hampden-Sydney a special place. Hampden-Sydney still has one of the most thorough set of graduation requirements in the country. Students are offered a thorough and solid education in the traditional liberal arts and in the Western intellectual heritage. In addition, Hampden-Sydney's energetic professors still enthusiastically accept their primary obligation to teach. Perhaps what really distinguishes the college from all others is the campus milieu, which is a blend of honor with "common decency and respect for others."

The college has been in operation since 1775 and is the tenth-oldest in the country. The founders chose the names of two seventeenth-century English states-men who had died in the cause of representative government, John Hampden and Algernon Sydney, then got their own local patriots — Patrick Henry and James Madi-son, among others — to serve on the college's first board of trustees.

One does wish that the college could be more like its namesakes and take a firm stand against one inclination in higher education. Hampden-Sydney has let a few faculty and administrators (not students) wave a small flag in the name of "di-versity." But it is not now a great cause for concern; the college's integrity appears unquestionable. Just as part of this beautiful campus in southern Virginia is pro-tected as a National Historic Preservation Zone, so are the college's standards and traditions. Hampden-Sydney's dedication to its past has served it well thus far, and it is hoped that it will continue to do so.

Academic Life: More than Rhetoric

Hampden-Sydney does not have an actual core curriculum, but its graduation re-quirements are more structured than most. The college has a definite idea of what it wants its students to learn, and that alone makes the requirements preferable to many found at other schools. "The college is committed to the development of hu-mane and lettered men and to the belief that a liberal education provides the best foundation not only for a professional career, but for the great intellectual and moral challenges of life," the college catalogue says. The school's respect for this tradition means that the curriculum has largely resisted the pull of innovation — an upcom-ing curriculum change is the first major one in eighteen years.

The new distribution requirements take effect with the 2001-02 academic year. Ever traditional, though, Hampden-Sydney concentrates its considerable resources on consolidating its strengths, not on adding new majors or departments. The re-quired course of study is divided into seven areas: humanities (three to seven courses); natural science and mathematics (four courses); social sciences (three courses); Western culture (five courses); international studies (one course); religious and philosophic studies (one course); and fine arts (one "appreciation" or history course or two "applied" courses).

Among the language and literature distribution requirements is a mainstay of the Hampden-Sydney curriculum: students must demonstrate proficiency in rhetoric and foreign language. In order to ensure that its students "write clearly, cogently, and grammatically," the college requires two introductory-level rhetoric courses, after which students must pass either an examination or rhetoric tutorial. (College publications print students' spirited testimonials to the rigorous but invaluable rhetoric requirement.) All students also must demonstrate proficiency in a foreign language, by passing either two intermediate level courses or one advanced level course.

The most notable feature of the new distribution requirements is a mandatory three-semester Western culture course that, according to a professor, "blends Western history and civilization with the Great Books." Such a requirement does not exist at most colleges. "We make sure the students know Western culture and civilization," says a senior professor. "We don't leave that to chance."

The other two courses in the Western culture requirement must come from a set of courses designated as American studies. Among the courses that fulfill this requirement are several in U.S. history, English, political science, or religion.

The international studies requirement, new with this new curriculum, aims to introduce students to a course (or study abroad experience) "with a significant foreign cultural component that challenges students to think beyond the parameters of the Western tradition." The courses that fulfill this requirement fall in a number of areas, from biology to religion. Foreign language study, however, does not count in this area.

Hampden-Sydney doesn't just let students pick and choose as their fancies dictate when it comes to the standard curriculum: the distribution areas each contain only a handful of classes that will fill the requirement. For example, four courses are required in the area of natural sciences and mathematics. The catalogue states that two courses must be chosen from a short list of five and that one of them must include a lab. To round out that category, students must take one of nine different math courses, plus an additional course outside the student's major. Similar rigor is found in the social science requirements — two of the three courses must be chosen from about ten offerings.

The classes selected as worthy of being graduation requirements for the most part aren't the politicized nonsense found elsewhere (although a course in postcolonial literature, a highly politicized area of study used to denounce the West, will fulfill the international studies requirement, and multiethnic literature or African-American literature courses will satisfy part of the American studies requirement). The college commendably does not capitalize on the "isms" in its course descriptions, which is rare enough, but it also ensures that art classes are about art, that music classes are about music, and that course offerings pertain to the broader topic at hand, rather than serving as forums for the condemnation of Western culture or the propagation of someone's recent dissertation. The faculty "take the liberal arts seriously, the Western Tradition seriously," a professor says.

Some of the best professors at Hampden-Sydney include James F. Pontuso, William B. Jones, and David E. Marion in political science; James A. Arieti and John L. Brinkley in classics; William A. Shear and Alexander J. Werth in biology; Lawrence H. Martin Jr. in English; Victor N. Cabas and Susan P. Robbins in rhetoric; James Simms in history; and Kenneth N. Townsend, Peter Mitias, and Anthony M. Carilli in economics.

One of the strongest departments on campus is political science, the third-most popular major. At Hampden-Sydney, the political science department sees contemporary political problems in the light of the writings of the great historical Western and American political thinkers.

The classics department, though only three people strong, is also considered one of the college's best teaching departments. From the smallest major we turn to the largest: economics, in which 30 percent of Hampden-Sydney students major. The science departments are strong, with chemistry getting mentioned most by faculty, although biology is the fourth-most popular major.

As in most other schools, Hampden-Sydney's English and history departments lean towards political correctness. The English department, however, is quite good when compared to its highly politicized counterparts at other schools. English majors are required to take the course in Shakespeare, as well as a broad set of courses across literary periods and genres and a "Capstone Experience" in their senior year. But they must fulfill a single-course requirement in "literature of difference." Of the forty courses offered by the department, though, only four are classified in this category: "African-American Literature," "Women and Literature," "Multiethnic Literature," and "Postcolonial Literature." Several single author courses (of the dead white guy type, such as Chaucer, Milton, Faulkner, or Hemingway) are offered, and one of them (in addition to Shakespeare) is required. An American literature course is required, but a recent version of the course covered the period from the Civil War to the present and studied twenty-five authors; ten were women, and none of the twenty-five were named Faulkner, Hemingway, Fitzgerald, or Eliot, which seems like a stretch. Other course descriptions include works by authors who most often see the light of day in politicized courses: Maxine Hong Kingston, Rita Dove, Marilyn Hacker, and Alice Munro. Oddly, these names do not appear in the college catalogue — just in Web page course descriptions. Admirably, a trendy course called "Introduction to Cinema" does not fulfill the distribution requirement in literature. These courses are "not seen as the wave of the future" at Hampden-Sydney, according to a senior professor. Surely, if the department were overrun with feminists and postmodernists, the popular course in "Literature of War" would not still be offered in the curriculum. Still, the English department is worth keeping an eye on. The outgoing chairman, a high-profile sponsor of the "diversity" movement who left the college for another faculty position, is succeeded by a comrade-in-arms who created the department's African-American Literature course. "There's a possibility that the department will become politicized, but right now there are enough people dedicated to the study of literature for its own sake," says a professor.

Similarly, the history department has not resisted the tug of political correctness. It has taken a somewhat revisionist stance on the Civil War. This phenomenon is apparent at other Southern schools, and defies any explanation other than that the professors themselves got their information from politicized graduate schools. Whatever the reason, the attitude is curious at a strongly traditional school just miles from Appomattox Court House and in a state that was the site of nearly two-thirds of all the battles fought in the War between the States. History, however, remains the second-most popular major at Hampden-Sydney.

The modern language department is described as an "embarrassing problem." Clearly, though, its shortcoming is not the result of ideology or of a weakening of standards, but of a high turnover of young, inexperienced faculty. The department lost a well-regarded teacher in recent years and the faculty is predominantly at the junior level. The department seems to be making a comeback under the current chairman, who is praised by her colleagues in other departments. Philosophy, also set back due to the loss of a first-rate teacher, is described as "weak but improving."

The primary responsibility of Hampden-Sydney faculty is teaching, and they are enthusiastic educators. The student-teacher ratio is thirteen to one, and most classes are small. Rarely can a student show up for class unprepared and slip by. Professors expect their students to discuss, argue, and defend their opinions. Professors across the board are known as very tough graders. "I don't think there are any soft or easy routes through the Hampden-Sydney curriculum," says the dean of the faculty. The college awards numerous summer research stipends for students, mostly for work in the natural sciences or mathematics, and at the end of their junior year, students may compete for selection as one of only a few senior fellows. Almost half of each graduating class attends graduate or professional schools.

The faculty has a reputation for sensible research in traditional areas, with only a couple of professors recently undertaking scholarship in academically suspect areas like popular culture, film, and women's studies. A college publication mentions an academic paper with the dippy title "Barbie Doesn't Live Here Anymore," by a rhetoric professor. Another paper, "Male Turf," written by a student in collaboration with his rhetoric professor, "concerns the experience of teaching and being taught Jane Austen's *Emma* in an all-male class at an all-male college." The rhetoric faculty is predominantly female, and some of their research interests are limited to women; the same holds for the foreign language department. The second course in the rhetoric sequence can be "theme based," a type of class that at most schools pertains to the professor's pet ideology such as global capitalism (bad) or race (good), but a professor in another department asserts that these rhetoric courses at Hampden-Sydney are "not politicized." The themes are intended "to excite the students," he says. Another senior faculty member says, "it would be hard to find a professor trying to indoctrinate in the classroom here."

But all told, the Hampden-Sydney student does not have to question whether the school is becoming any less dedicated to the traditional liberal arts, says the dean of the faculty, "because we've made this two hundred–year commitment to liberal education."

"We've been able to keep the demons at the door," says a professor.

Political Atmosphere: Protected Zone

A former president of Hampden-Sydney told in one of his speeches about a foreign languages professor at the college who when asked if he taught French or German said, "Neither. I teach men." The professor had moved on to another college by the time Hampden-Sydney, in the fall of 1996, came very close to admitting women, but we think he would have liked the way it turned out. Despite what others may say or write, that decision to remain all-male kept the world of academe more diverse — not less. And fortunately, the college's new president, who took office in July 2000, seems determined to keep it that way, saying the college's all-male status is "what keeps Hampden-Sydney Hampden-Sydney."

The question about "going coed" still makes its way into the school newspaper, *The Tiger.* Four years after the vote, the paper refers to it, sometimes in an editorial but usually in interviews with faculty and administrators. There appears to be some lingering resentment, on both sides of the argument. The issue is "dead," says one professor, but the mere mention of it stirs the waters of controversy.

In other areas, the politics prevalent in the world outside of Farmville, Virginia, rarely come into play at Hampden-Sydney. There are no radical student groups or activist faculty simply because "the culture of this place just doesn't allow it," according to a professor.

Although a professor says that there is "no movement on campus causing confrontation or polarization with racial overtones," there is an office of Intercultural Affairs with a full-time director, who is involved with student and resident assistant orientations. Unlike the situation at most other schools, the "intercultural" campus programs at Hampden-Sydney are educational and respectful, mostly lectures by authors, civic leaders, and scholars or performances by musicians. The intercultural affairs office at Hampden-Sydney seems very much in keeping with the college's assumption that "common decency and respect for others" exists in the community. Further, two senior professors have suggested that the college may have been forced to create the office of intercultural affairs due to pressure from its accrediting agency. According to the college, "nearly 10 percent of the student body is made up of blacks, Asians, Hispanics, and Native Americans." The new president of the college wants to increase the "diversity of the applicant pool," according to *The Tiger*, but an admissions officer at the college assures us there are "no quotas or goals."

The college recently held a "Race Symposium," forty years after the closing of the schools in the surrounding county as part of Virginia's "Massive Resistance" policy to avoid court-ordered integration. "This was done the way it should be," says a professor, "without the divisive, heavy hand of government. We did this on our own, in a classy, thoughtful, and civil way." Indeed, the college made it clear that the purpose of the forum was to discuss what happened and "move on," not to point fingers. Our hope is that the college's efforts on this front continue in this temperament.

Disagreements among faculty over the curriculum are solved in similarly reasonable debates rather than raised voices. Arguments for black or minority components in the curriculum are rational, a professor says. Make no mistake about it, though, Hampden-Sydney faculty consists of "progressives" and "conservatives," with the latter obviously outnumbered. The vote to change the distribution requirements seems to have fallen mostly along political lines, but at Hampden-Sydney discussions about such restructuring don't occur too often, and thus are taken quite seriously. (The academic affairs committee, which responsible for the distribution requirements, however, has agreed to review the new curriculum "at least once every five years.") Faculty debates may devolve into politics and territorial squabbling at times, but at Hampden-Sydney the question always pertains to academic standards. As with all discussion about the required course of study at Hampden-Sydney, the result of curricular debates is the same: "Western Civilization is not at stake," says a history professor.

The casual observer might also take for granted that the traditionalism of the curriculum and the college's gentlemanly expectations of its students produce well-mannered young men for whom civil debate and general good take the place of agitation.

One of the strongest indicators of the character of Hampden-Sydney students is the high place the school's Honor Code holds in their minds. The Honor Code (and the Student Code of Conduct) is enforced by students, not faculty or administration, and the penalties for lying, cheating, stealing, and other infractions (including not reporting Honor Code violations by fellow students) are stiff: a dishonorable suspension, or even expulsion. "If [President Bill] Clinton were a student at Hampden-Sydney, he'd be thrown out for violating the Honor Code," said the college's newspaper editor said on *The NewsHour with Jim Lehrer.*

Rather than making Hampden-Sydney's atmosphere unbearable, the Honor Code gives the students a certain amount of freedom, since they expect that their fellow classmates will always act like gentlemen and be honest. Certainly the expectation that one's peers will always act with honor and goodwill contributes to the congeniality of the campus.

The John Templeton Foundation recognizes the school for its emphasis on "building character and integrity." *Insight* magazine ranks Hampden-Sydney the third-most "politically incorrect school" and calls it a place "where the faculty act as guardians of the best that has been handed down to us and as competent helpful guides through the inevitable changes society experiences."

"We're not completely immunized to the all the nonsense in higher education," says a professor. "Any of the stuff you see here — in the English department, in intercultural affairs — is standard. There's just no way a place like Hampden-Sydney can prevent it. That we have so little of it, that it has not affected the culture of the place, says a lot about who we are and what our mission is."

Student Life: Rare Club for Well-Mannered Men

Hampden-Sydney students come from thirty-three states, most of them in the South. Over half hail from Virginia, with another 10 percent from North Carolina, followed by contingents from Maryland, South Carolina, Georgia, Texas, West Virginia, and Alabama.

There's no doubt that the decision to attend Hampden-Sydney requires maturity, for the young man who goes there knows what he is doing, and why. "You don't come to Hampden-Sydney in spite of single-sex education, you come because of single-sex education," says a student in a recruiting brochure. "Emancipated from the social pressure and the inevitable distraction of wooing (or trying to impress) classmates, students feel freer to express themselves, to focus on their studies and the task at hand: learning," says another student.

A classics professor (and a graduate of the school) describes the Hampden-Sydney student this way: "We're still getting the same guy here. He's comfortable. He's comfortable knowing what he's headed for, which are the traditional things: business, law, medicine, and, yes, still the occasional calling as a minister. He has nice manners, and is fairly bright. They're just nice guys to be around." Another professor describes the Hampden-Sydney student as "civil and more public spirited than most people their age."

Many years ago, a publication dubbed Hampden-Sydney the "Finishing School for Southern Gentlemen," while another called it one of the preppiest colleges in the country. Hampden-Sydney did not blush. Since 1978, the college has issued "To Manner Born, to Manners Bred: A Hip-Pocket Guide to Etiquette for the Hampden-Sydney Man." It covers all occasions when "others expect traditional social conventions to be observed." The section on "Dress," for example, reminds students that "at Hampden-Sydney a jacket and tie are traditional at football games." Hampden-Sydney football games, to be sure, are major social events. Blue blazers, khakis, button-downs, and topsiders (albeit sans socks) are *de rigueur.*

The leading attribute of the Hampden-Sydney man may be "politeness" (according to a Hampden-Sydney survey), but in athletics he is highly competitive and plays to win. About a quarter of the students join one of the eight NCAA Division III intercollegiate teams, and close to 80 percent take part in at least one of the thirteen intramural athletic programs. There are also eight club sports (including the rugby team, coached for several years by a female economics professor).

The college encourages participation in intercollegiate athletics "because it can be and is a true character-building experience," according to the athletic mission statement. The lacrosse and basketball teams have become national contenders in recent years. The basketball team that reached the NCAA championship game in 1999 had seven National Merit Scholars, as well as the class valedictorian. The biggest football game of the season is always the final one against Randolph Macon College; it has drawn some of the biggest crowds in Division III gridiron history. A long-standing activity associated with "The Game" includes a bonfire with hot chocolate. The college is reconsidering a year-old restriction on tailgating at the football games because "it just hasn't worked," says a professor. Not only did attendance at the games decrease; *esprit de corps* did too.

Weeknights are a time to hit the books. Students respect others' right to pursue their studies, and the college enforces some regulations. Noise level restrictions contribute to an overall atmosphere of studious endeavor during the week.

Weekends are a time to play, and the Hampden-Sydney student will make the most of it. Fraternity Circle is home to the college's Greek organizations, and the center of the weekend social scene. Fraternities practice an open-door policy for most social events, so students roam from party to party, making the college at times seem like one big fraternity. About 40 percent of the students belong to fraternities, and each of the fraternity houses recently has been either renovated or destroyed and rebuilt.

And yes, there are sometimes women at Hampden-Sydney. A popular bumper sticker at the college reads: "Hampden-Sydney. Where men are men and women are guests." On many weekends (especially in football season), the college looks like a coed campus. Students from four nearby women's colleges (Hollins College, Sweet Briar College, Randolph Macon Woman's College, and Mary Baldwin College), as well as from coed schools across the state, arrive by the carload — and even the busload. These women are "a large part of the charm weekends at [Hampden-Sydney] have," writes the news editor of *The Tiger.* At other times, Hampden-Sydney men might pile into cars for a "road trip" to another college. Coed Longwood College is a just a couple of miles away.

Visitation is allowed in the dormitories, and the college will intervene only when the visitation interferes with a roommate's right to privacy, study, or sleep. On big weekends, female guests often outnumber guys in the dorms.

The college has a strict alcohol policy, and drugs are forbidden on campus. Students must obey the Honor Code at all times, on and off campus, so the college is reasonably safe (though according to official statistics there are a few more burglaries than one might expect). "Hampden-Sydney has a wonderful approach to student life in that the institution grants maximum freedom to students, expects responsible use of that freedom . . . and strongly encourages students govern themselves and manage their lives in ways that balance freedom and obligation to live within acceptable norms," the dean of students says. Printed inside the student handbook are Hampden-Sydney traditions — "Hampden-Sydney men are on their honor in all activities on and off the campus throughout the year" and "All men speak to everyone they meet on campus" among them.

Except for the occasional visit to a restaurant, there's certainly not much else to do in Farmville, the small town nearest the college. If Farmville doesn't have what students are looking for — and in all likelihood, it does not — they head to Roanoke, Richmond, or Charlottesville.

The forty or so student groups are generally quiet and serious in nature. These include a few rare listings, like the Madisonian Society and the Society for the Preservation of Southern Heritage, as well as a couple of debating societies (such as the Union Philanthropic Society, the country's second-oldest student debating society) and fifteen honor fraternities, publications, Inter-Varsity Christian Fellowship, The Republican Society, and Rifle Association. "Good Men Good Citizens" is campus organization that coordinates many volunteer community service activites of the students and faculty. Past campus organizations have included student companies formed to serve in the Revolutionary and Civil Wars. The college's colors — garnet and gray — come from the military uniforms worn by its students in the Revolutionary War.

Hunting and fishing, as well as skeet shooting, are popular pastimes at Hampden-Sydney. "Some students have two cars, one nice one, plus one for their hunting or fishing gear," says a professor. The dean of the faculty is a nationally competitive skeet shooter. One of the best bass lakes on the east coast is just four miles from campus.

Students and faculty enjoy frequent contact in and out of the classroom, for many of the professors live on or close to campus. The college's presidents frequently eat in the dining hall, and a past president served brunch to the students in his Sunday School class at his home, after the morning service in College Church.

The historic campus is beautiful, and will hopefully only get more so with a recently announced $77-million campaign for "new buildings, building additions, and landscape enhancement," according to a college brochure. A few of many southern oaks on campus have names (The Constitution Oak, for example), and the community gets attached to them. "When a tree is distressed, the removal of it can be an emotional topic. It has to be thoroughly researched," says the director of the grounds.

Harvard University

Dean of Admissions and Financial Aid
Harvard and Radcliffe Colleges
Byerly Hall, 8 Garden St.
Cambridge, MA 02138
(617) 495-1551
www.harvard.edu

Total enrollment: 17,700
Undergraduates: 6,700
SAT ranges (Verbal/Math): 700-800 (V); 700-790 (M)
Applicants: 18,161
Accepted: 11%
Enrolled: 79%
Application deadline: January 1
Financial aid application deadline: February 1
Tuition: $25,128/$33,110
Core curriculum: No

The King of the World

No other institution in the country is as synonymous with quality as Harvard. The very name conjures up images of smartly dressed students, old families whose names are chiseled in the friezes of campus buildings, fearsome professors with rapier wits, and a clubby atmosphere that defines the world according to who went there and who didn't. According to this view, which was at least once true at America's most prestigious schools, entrée to Harvard was reserved for folks who were simply the best — the best bred, best connected, most fortunate lot that America could produce.

Harvard is still the envy of the world, and rightly so. It remains the richest university on earth, with an endowment surpassing the size of some countries' gross domestic product. Alone among American schools, it can steal faculty from virtually anywhere, and the name-dropping potential of any graduate will put him on the road to success if he's made of good stuff to begin with. All of this is true because Harvard has always embodied the highest aspirations of high culture. Its ear is finely tuned to its progeny's outpourings on topics of concern to this class, and what it plays back to this constituency reinforces that group's self-image. What's more, it goads, pushes, and expects alumni, supporters, and assorted elites to follow its lead.

As long as American high culture defined itself against the vulgar, the common, and the trite, American culture was strengthened by exposure to it. When it scolded or disapproved, society benefited because elite opinion more often than not drew upon Harvard's own motto: *Veritas*, truth. It believed in truth, served truth, and sought to preserve the cultural milieu in which it was discovered and through which it descended. This is the Harvard of reputation, the school that educated the best to be the best in the service of the nation and the world.

But times have changed, and elite culture has shed its skin. Or more pointedly, it has cloaked itself in that which it once abhorred. Rather than provide a space to seek truth, it has denied truth's existence. In place of the best that has been thought and written, it proclaimed a new theory of relativity that rendered all things equal, or equally base, so that no culture is privileged, no knowledge most worthy of attention. And yet, because of the origins of the new cultural relativism and intellectual nihilism — our elite schools — things aren't as equal as the new learning's partisans insist. The old networks still exist, just with different players. Harvard still offers its students unique and fantastic opportunities and will always lead, but its constituency, expanded when merit supplanted birth as the principal criterion for admission, might wonder just where it is being led.

Academic Life: An Abdication

Harvard, along with most other schools, employs the term core curriculum to describe what is actually a set of distribution requirements. "We like to brag, 'Of course we have a core curriculum. It contains over 350 courses!'," a professor says. Others say that what impersonates a core is actually hollow. In short, students can take whatever they want to take. "Our core . . . exists for the convenience of the faculty, who can't decide on what an education is," a professor says. "Harvard provides absolutely no guarantee that a student will emerge with a broad liberal education." Another person says Harvard's distribution requirements "focus . . . on 'approaches to knowledge' rather than on any content in particular."

The university catalogue says (with emphasis added):

[T]he Core differs from other programs of general education. It does not define intellectual breadth as the mastery of a set of Great Books, or the digestion of a specific quantum of information, or the surveying of current knowledge in certain fields. Rather, the Core seeks to introduce students to the major *approaches to knowledge* in areas that the faculty considers indispensable to undergraduate education. It aims to show what kinds of knowledge and what forms of inquiry exist in these areas, how different means of analysis are acquired, how they are used, and what their value is. The courses within each area or subdivision of the program are equivalent in the sense that, while their subject matter may vary, their emphasis on a particular way of thinking is the same.

Certainly other universities are loath to take a stand on what an educated person should know: which books to read, what civilization to study, why some things are more important than others, what is true and what is false. But this is Harvard, after all. As the acknowledged leader among American universities, it can be criticized for failing to construct even a set of distribution requirements that would ensure that every student became familiar with Western and U.S. history, the great works of the Western canon, and other elements of knowledge once assumed among the nation's intellectual elite.

In fact, one of the most common complaints among students is that the structure of the general education curriculum gives them virtually no guidance in obtaining a broad liberal education. With so many choices, nothing stands out as important — especially since the university refuses to say what's important. "The core here is terrible," says one student. "It's perhaps not as lenient as at some other schools, but it is a very absurd system. . . . Usually you get a professor teaching their latest knowledge. Therefore, what you study isn't important — it's the approach that counts. You can get away without learning a scrap of European or U.S. history."

"It can't be papered over that the general scheme of a Harvard undergraduate education is an unfortunate one, given the resources and promise of this university," a professor says. "The core is absolutely onerous in its gobbling up of students' time in courses that often enough are weak fare." Some of the brightest students even forgo writing a thesis (which would lead to an honors degree) in order to take more of the interesting and challenging departmental classes.

What then are the general education requirements at Harvard College, the main undergraduate school? A course in expository writing is required of all freshmen, and students must take one or two courses to fulfill the language requirement. Students then choose courses from eight of eleven subject areas, depending on their major. The catalogue states that the eight subject areas required are the ones "most remote" from the student's field of study. The eleven areas are: foreign cultures; historical studies A and B; literature and arts A, B, and C; moral reasoning; quantitative reasoning; science A and B; and social analysis. As an example, a classics major would be exempt from foreign cultures, and from two of the literature and arts groups. A number of courses can be used to meet a given requirement.

Another complaint about the core is that a student could be well-versed in one of the required areas, yet still be forced to take a class geared to novices. The quality of freshmen at Harvard and other elite institutions is very high, as admissions are more competitive today than ever before. Yet even the best universities must accept students as they emerge from high school, and here the amount of learning such students absorb is a matter of debate. "The freshmen increasingly appear to be more competent and capable in science and math than the humanities," says one faculty member. "We have bright kids, but many aren't well read, or at least not as much as they should be," says another.

Nevertheless, Harvard's unparalleled reputation nets it a growing number of the very best students. "As the quality of high school education deteriorates and SAT scores are inflated by lower standards, Harvard benefits disproportionately," a professor says. "The absence of true discriminations of quality in secondary education compels all the more students to apply to the one school regarded as the best. This argument may well have merit, because the high numbers of applications at Harvard are difficult to account for by means of other explanations." A recent graduate says that "Harvard is more meritocratic than it ever has been, with astoundingly high SAT scores. The 'problem' of the student body is that they are all too groomed, too success-oriented, too hyper. There appears to be a large percentage of the student body on anti-depressants, for example."

There remain many dedicated and superb professors at Harvard. Among them are Richard Thomas in classics; John Sherman in history of art and architecture; Robert Levin in music; John Malmstad in Slavic languages and literatures; Larry Benson, Robert Kiely, Daniel Donoghue, and Helen Vendler in English; Martin Feldstein and Robert Barro in economics; Harvey Mansfield, Stanley Hoffman, Peter Hall, Samuel Huntington, and Steve Rosen in government; Stephen Thernstrom, James Hankins, Ernest May, Ann Blair, Mark Kishlansky Michael McCormick, and Brendan Dooley in history; James McCarthy in earth and planetary sciences; Ruth Wisse in Jewish studies; Peter Rosen in international relations; Roger Porter in American politics; Thomas Scanlon in philosophy; Jon Levenson in the Divinity School; Robert Coles, a psychiatrist who teaches undergraduates; Stephen Mitchell in folklore; and Donald Fanger in comparative literature.

Among the strongest departments are classics, history, music, government, physics, mathematics, earth and planetary sciences, biology, and chemistry. One professor says that philosophy "is beginning to look like a shadow of its former self because of the passing of old greats." Another says that history, though still very good, "has made impressive attempts to get better, but there is often competence where there used to be brilliance."

Among the most politicized departments is religion, which a faculty member says "has its problems with politicization and lack of wisdom." African studies, social studies, the Center for Literary and Cultural Studies, English, fine arts, anthropology, Romance languages and literatures, comparative literature, and women's studies are also quite politicized.

"Many departments, especially in the humanities, are very politicized," a senior professor says. "There are a number of egregiously bad courses, and the way they teach is also politicized. This is pervasive in the humanities, less true in the social sciences. It is not so true in political science or economics. History is in between the humanities and social sciences."

Social studies draws the ire of another professor. "Social studies is a terrible department because they indoctrinate the best of the students with multiculturalism," the professor says. The department didn't fool at least one student. "I found the social studies department especially left-leaning," the student said. "The fundamental premises of the department — the 'social studies method' of approaching social phenomena — seems derived ultimately from Marx. That is, the major historical events . . . are assumed to arise out of economical and social conditions. The independent role of ideas and philosophy in shaping history is underestimated." Political and social theory are introduced at the sophomore level, but the first semester mainly centers on the Continental tradition (Marx, Durkheim, Weber, and Freud), while Postmodernists like Foucault, Habermas, and contemporary feminist theories get the second semester. John Locke and the American Founders, for example, do not appear on the syllabus.

Early in 2001, Harvard named former U.S. Treasury Secretary Lawrence H. Summers as its new president. An economist, Mr. Summers earned his Ph.D. at Harvard and taught there for ten years.

Political Atmosphere: Smart Enough to Know Better

The general political atmosphere at Harvard is left-of-center, an unremarkable observation that applies to most American college campuses. Trends at Harvard are worth watching closely, however, since other schools tend to follow close behind them. With that in mind, there is some reason to hope that a trend spotted by some faculty members is a good omen for the future of American higher education. At the same time, the news is mixed, especially for anyone who values the humanities' role in Western culture.

This new trend is summed up nicely by a professor. When asked if national reports that a majority of college-bound high school students will vote Republican, this person replied: "By no means do I see anything like a majority voting Republican. What I do clearly see, however, is that students are beginning to flock to common-sense courses in Western history and to courses that take the Western religious tradition seriously. I see a seriously decreasing interest on the students' part in race/gender/class/discourse."

Close observers of higher education have sensed such a move for some time, although until now it has been difficult to know just what the repercussions would be. Whatever problems plague it, Harvard, like other elite schools, draws some very sharp students. They're willing to work hard, and many would rather be educated than trained — that is, well read, well rounded, and prepared for the complex world of business that has emerged over the past several years. In that world, the ability to speak and write well is highly valued, especially in the long run. And the best way to acquire these skills is to read (and then write about) the best that has been written. This necessarily requires a curriculum that recognizes and rewards merit, whether in history, literature, philosophy, or other disciplines. A curriculum that is based instead on politics — and the bizarre politics of the academy at that — is bound to bore, for great works cannot be mere political tracts. Just as the socialist (or National

Socialist) novel was a failure, so is the feminist, or hyper-sensitive minority, or any other politicized variation, bound to fail. And the best students see that they're being sold a bill of false goods and say, "No thanks."

Thus, at elite schools across the nation, the best professors are discovered by the best students, and knowledge worth preserving and passing down is once again highly valued. This is bad news for ideologues posing as professors and for the administrators who support them for reasons of public relations and for internal gain, namely money. Highly politicized departments go begging for students, and the per-capita spending for such bastions of trendy thought is much higher than what is found in departments that, while hardly conservative, offer students intellectual stimulation rather than political indoctrination. Trying to gain admission to the classes of a Robert Coles or Harvey Mansfield is much more difficult than getting into a typical women's studies class, where warm bodies are in short supply.

Yet the other side of this coin is less attractive, for if the best students are driven from highly politicized offerings, and if the humanities are the seat of such classes, then these subjects suffer. Asked how Harvard will change over the next ten years, a professor says: "The humanities will have become weaker without the appearance of having done so. This is a consequence, about which it is hard to do anything, of the banality of postmodernism and the particular form of ethnic and racial awareness that is so popular in academia today." In short, the best students, denied the opportunity of reading the best authors, will gravitate to more intellectually challenging fare, leaving the humanities weaker than ever.

The nation's best universities are already producing a generation of leaders who know little history, fail to appreciate the power of literature, and therefore enter the world of business malformed. The beneficiaries are the hard sciences, where politicized work is generally ridiculed and avoided, and schools of business, where innovation and originality are rewarded rather than oppressed. We're seeing a reconfiguration of Harvard and, with it, of America's elite. "The brightest people I knew at Harvard went into investment banking rather than academe," says one alumnus. And while the nation certainly needs bright people to enter the world of business, it also needs those same persons to receive more than a smattering of education in the liberal arts before they do so. "My advice [to freshmen] would be to forget about the Internet and the New Economy," a recent graduate says. "They're going to be Harvard grads, for heaven's sake, so things will turn out well when it's time to enter the real world. In the meantime, they should make the most of the extraordinary intellectual resources available." A professor seconds this advice: "For students wishing to spend their time wisely, I would recommend a traditional major: history, mathematics, and the like. I would also advise them to constantly be on the lookout for new and interesting courses."

Indeed, such an education (available at Harvard if you know where to look), is hardly a liability in the business world. "I haven't encountered one alum five years out of Harvard who finds the English degree an albatross," a professor says. If word of this fact can only influence the offerings of the English department (and other liberal arts departments), Harvard, and therefore the nation, will produce a more humane, insightful, and effective class of leaders.

The upside to being a conservative student at Harvard, according to a senior professor, is that you may get a better education. "They don't lap up what's in front of them," the professor says. "It is better for conservatives to go to a liberal university, because the most valuable thing to be learned in a democracy is to learn to stand up to public opinion."

Public opinion is imposed though speech codes and sensitivity training, another sign that the nontraditional elements are in control at Harvard. Undergraduates are subject to gender-neutral language directives and "mandatory sensitivity sessions which would be a joke were they not such a serious intrusion," says a source. "The program is run by fanatics. It is quite upsetting." This comes at a time when schools and courts have begun to seriously question the propriety and sometimes the constitutionality of speech codes; however, the source says, "the faculty, at the urging or at least with the acquiescence of the dean, actually adopted a set of sexual harassment guidelines that seriously impinge on speech at the Law School." The Derek Bok Teaching Center is the base for sensitivity training, and all residential units at Harvard have "affirmative action and sex tutors," a professor says. "The job of the latter is to help heterosexuals discover they're homosexuals, and to help women who've had sex realize they've been raped." Freshmen face sessions on race and sexual orientation, according to one student. "There are also mandatory safe sex educational sessions featuring instructions on the expert use of condoms (on bananas), dental dams, rubber gloves, and other devices," the student says.

Student Life: Play in the Yard

Undergraduate residential life at Harvard centers around the residential houses, modeled on those found at Oxford and Cambridge Universities. They were established in the 1930s because administrators became concerned that the growth of the university was destroying the close bonds among students and between students and faculty that are supposed to be nurtured in a small liberal-arts college atmosphere. Students live in Harvard Yard, a quadrangle of buildings, during their freshman year and move into the houses for their final three years. Over the years the houses have developed a fair degree of independence.

This excellent arrangement still has much to offer, but observers note two disturbing trends in the house system. In the early 1990s, says a recent graduate, "Harvard became concerned about the concentration of minorities into a few of the houses, more so about the concentration of athletes into one of the houses, and so selectivity of housing decisions was eliminated and the houses were in other administrative ways degraded from their once-primary place in an upperclassman's social life." With this loss of ability to select the type of students that best fit the character and traditions of each house, they became more like standard dorms.

This source says that Harvard has lost some of its distinctiveness because of this effort to reduce the diversity of housing on campus. "This is important because Harvard is big, and it is easy to get lost," says the alum. "One of its best features over the years is its internal structural diversity, which preserved pockets of local traditions: whatever a student's interests and/or proclivities, they very often could find their way to a congenial group to help make it through their years. The administrative rationalization of student life, leading to greater central bureaucratic and therapeutic control, does not bode well for the future." Once again, a centralizing bureaucracy has obliterated local culture in the name of bringing peace where there was no discord. The result is a grayer campus, more uniformity in social customs, and reduced opportunity to become part of a grand tradition.

Another source of distinctiveness at Harvard, Radcliffe College, merged into Harvard recently. Once one of the nation's premier undergraduate colleges for women (but sharing Harvard's faculty), Radcliffe was deemed redundant in a coeducational age. Approximately $150 million of its $200 million in assets went to establish the Radcliffe Institute for Advanced Study, according to the *Chronicle of Higher Education*.

Students occupy suites in the houses that are single sex but on coed floors. Bathrooms are not shared, and Harvard students do not have the reputation for hard partying that their peers at MIT do, although alcohol and drug use are far from unknown. But they're a serious lot with much ambition, and most know better than to jeopardize their future with such behavior.

As for on-campus crime, there were ten forcible sex offenses in 1998; eleven in 1999. Burglary has fallen from 594 reported incidents in 1997 to 502 in 1999; aggravated assault dropped from eighteen in 1998 to eight in 1999. There were 149 reported burglaries in residence halls in 1999. Harvard is relatively safe, but students should remember that they're in a large city and never take their safety for granted.

The other disturbing trend, says a source familiar with the house system, is "the rise of live-together homosexual couples among the freshman proctors. Masters of houses were originally to have the most concrete role of *in loco parentis*, in the place of parents, in guiding their charges. Perhaps they still do, but in ways that most parents would find surprising, to say the least.

Students will find plenty of organizations that peddle ideas rarely found in the middle class homes from which most of them come. A prime example is PCC, or the Peer Contraceptive Counselors, who are volunteer undergraduates. The literature of this service, which is run through the Harvard Health Clinic, notes that students needn't be nervous about speaking in public, for "You can do anything after you've learned to handle Woody the Wooden P — ." They'll also find handy pen and ink drawings on how to use contraceptives, along with numerous campus locations where they'll find free condoms — mostly in bathrooms or laundry rooms in such out-of-the-way places that they sound like pick-up spots.

Some of the more famous student organizations include the *Crimson* (the college's student newspaper), the Hasty Pudding Club, the *Lampoon,* and the Glee Club. Harvard surely has more student organizations than just about any other school anywhere, and a student can find a niche no matter what his interests. In fact, one of the hallmarks of student life at Harvard is the unusually high degree of involvement in extracurricular activities. With As and Bs virtually guaranteed thanks to grade inflation, many students place as much emphasis on their activities as they do their academic work. One can easily immerse oneself in non-careerist pursuits. There are also numerous special-interest groups whose membership define themselves by some sort of minority status, be it race, ethnicity, or sexual orientation.

Harvard does have an alternative, fairly mainstream conservative newspaper called the *Salient.* This paper is mainline Republican in its editorial policies, and "it's respected by at least some of the student body," says a student.

Harvard's football team hasn't won a national championship since 1919 (and don't hold your breath for another one), but it and other varsity level sports still attract the attention of the student body year in and year out. The school fields forty-one varsity teams, which it claims is more than any other college in the nation. Harvard has excellent facilities for recreational sports such as tennis, squash, and the like. There are numerous intramural teams, most of which are formed around the residential Houses. The university's literature says that about two-thirds of the student body participates at some level of sporting activity.

Cambridge offers many cultural incentives for virtually any student, from pizza to excellent restaurants, and its bookstores are numerous and of exceptionally high quality. Harvard Square is a quirky, pseudo-bohemian hang-out for all manner of people and activities, including almost continual chess matches, the serious student or scholar relaxing with a book, and the affected posing of intellectual wannabes. It's a great place to watch people. On the larger scale, Boston is one of the nation's last truly livable large cities, with a vibrant downtown with beautiful architecture and countless stores and shops. And the confluence of other Boston universities, most notably next-door MIT, makes for a large number of college types all over the area. Certainly, the number of speakers, plays, and other events catering to the interests of students is hard to match elsewhere, and students have endless opportunities in virtually every field of study or interest.

Haverford College

Office of Admissions
370 Lancaster Ave.
Haverford, PA 19041-1392
(610) 896-1350
www.haverford.edu

Total enrollment: 1,118
Undergraduates: 1,118
SAT ranges (Verbal/Math): 640-740 (V); 630-720 (M)
Applicants: 2,650
Accepted: 35%
Enrolled: 35%
Application deadline: January 15
Financial aid application deadline: January 31
Tuition: $24,940/$32,850
Core curriculum: No

Main Line Fords

Haverford College is a small, elite institution occupying some two hundred prime acres along the Main Line, one of the plushest areas of suburban Philadelphia. Founded by Quakers from New York and Philadelphia in 1833, it is the oldest Quaker-founded college in the land.

With only 1,100 students — all of them undergraduates — Haverford is able to pay close attention to its students (who call themselves "Fords") and to ensure their immersion in the college's culture. The student-teacher ratio is about nine to one, and more than 70 percent of the courses have less than twenty students. The college offers many fine courses, but little guidance on which ones comprise a solid liberal arts education.

Haverford was an all-male institution until 1980, and it continues to have close ties with neighboring Bryn Mawr College, an all-female institution about a mile down the road. Students at the two schools frequently cross-register in order to fill in the gaps in their curricula by making use of the other college's strengths. Students at Haverford may also take classes at Swarthmore and the University of Pennsylvania.

Academic Life: What Do You Do with All That Leeway?

Haverford's catalogue says many of the right things about liberal education. The curriculum, according to the catalogue, is "designed to help its students develop the capacity to learn, to understand, and to make sound and thoughtful judgments." Liberal education "requires a sense of the breadth of human inquiry and creativity," it says. "The human mind has explored the myriad facets of our physical and social environments; it has produced compelling works of art, literature, and philosophy. Every student is encouraged to engage a full range of disciplines — fine arts, the written word, empirical investigation, economy and society — in order to become a broadly-educated person."

Whether the distribution requirements at Haverford accomplish this is, like at many places, a function of structure rather than course content. And the requirements are too general to guarantee the things the college speaks of so highly in its catalogue. There is a one-semester freshman writing requirement, and the courses that fulfill it seem well-designed — try especially the "L" (literature) sections, which include a reading list full of classic texts. The college also requires foreign language competency through a full year of courses or through study abroad.

But the distribution requirements mandate three courses in each of these areas: humanities, social sciences, and natural sciences. In each area, students must take courses from at least two different departments. One of the nine courses has to involve quantitative reasoning — statistics, math, or the like.

Haverford attributes to its Quaker roots the final distribution requirement: one course in "social justice." The catalogue states that the college "sees education in part as a means for understanding the historical conditions and cultural mechanisms of social injustice, and for questioning the hierarchies and relationships of power which shape society." The courses that fulfill this requirement deal with either "the structures, workings, and consequences of prejudice, inequality, and injustice" or the "efforts at political and cultural change" intended to overcome them. Some of the courses that meet this requirement include "Peace and Conflict Studies," "Disease and Discrimination," and "Literacies and Education."

The Haverford curriculum leaves something to be desired because it gives students too much leeway in choosing which classes are important — a choice few underclassmen are informed enough to make. And the "social justice" requirement is a clearly political move that seeks to substitute ideology for knowledge. On the other hand, in an age when many schools have relegated language study to only those students actually majoring in that language, Haverford's insistence that all students study a foreign tongue is evidence of some commitment to the traditional liberal arts curriculum of generations past.

Another positive aspect of the Haverford curriculum is the absence of preprofessional majors, such as business or education, that have so diluted the curricula at institutions nationwide. Haverford obviously believes that its students should be taught rather than trained. "Haverford is a lot like the University of Chicago," says a recent alumnus. "It attracts genuinely intellectual students but not merely pre-career types. . . . It's institutionally superior to many of today's colleges, but compared to the curriculum it offered in the 1950s, it's quite weak." Says a student: "Haverford has a broad liberal arts requirement, and I took many classes outside my particular field of interest. It most certainly imparted a broad liberal arts background to my education." Good classes are indeed readily available, and many are well taught. "My professors in the humanities are all talented and dedicated," says a student.

Haverford students benefit tremendously from the college's association with Bryn Mawr College, just a fifteen-minute walk or short bus ride away. All students at either college may take classes on both campuses and may even major in a program not available at their home school. This allows Haverford students to take advantage of Bryn Mawr's nationally known programs in classical civilization, languages, and archaeology, as well as its excellent art history department. About 90 percent of Haverford students take at least one class at Bryn Mawr, and most take more, according to college literature. This same literature notes: "You may take any course at Bryn Mawr, even if the same course is offered here — perhaps the time is a better fit to your schedule or you like the professor's sense of humor better." No special permission is needed, and students at both schools have the same chance of getting into any class offered on either campus. Credit transfers are automatic and require no special requests. Says a student: "A lot of men are afraid to take a class at Bryn Mawr, because it's not our campus and we know it. You don't go there alone because there are some really militant types there. Of course, there are some very nice women who go there too. You tend to keep to your own while you're there." A student says that the close association with Bryn Mawr is "definitely a reason to go to Haverford." Students speak of Haverford and Bryn Mawr as the bi-college community; when Swarthmore is thrown in, it becomes the tri-college community.

Students may also take classes at Swarthmore and Penn. Only about 10 percent do so at Swarthmore, however, which is less convenient than Bryn Mawr even though there is a shuttle bus. And even fewer go to Penn, which isn't terribly convenient and lies in a high-crime neighborhood in West Philadelphia.

Despite the social justice requirement, there are not many departments at Haverford that seem to have been conceived in some fit of multicultural yearning. Africana studies is an area of concentration (rather than a major) and offers a number of serious surveys of African and African-American history as well as humanities courses in legitimate areas like the Harlem Renaissance. We're not sure how "Queer Theory/Queer Literature" (taught by the Bryn Mawr English department) got on its course list, however.

Departments with more traditional titles — take English, for example — may be more politicized. The short title of English 347 is "Eighteenth-Century British Literature," but it is subtitled "Love, Sex, and Marriage in Eighteenth-Century British Literature" and it looks at the changing conceptions of masculinity, femininity, hetero- and homosexuality and the relations among these terms," according to the catalogue. "Our readings will allow us to focus on some of the following topics: the rise of the companionate marriage, the role and position of men and women within marriage, the shifting formulations of passion and sentiment, the various debates over the nature of female sexuality, the reformation or disappearance of the libertine rake, the emergence of the (male and female) homosexual, the portrayal and treatment of the prostitute, and the connections between pornography and print culture." The department also offers courses titled "The Queer Novel" and "Sex and Gender in the Middle Ages," along with the interesting but out-of-place-for-undergraduates "John Brown's Body," a survey of writings touched off by Brown's raid on Harpers Ferry. These offerings — tangential at best — appear in the Fall 2000 schedule in numbers at least as often as basic, core English courses.

Students say the political science and sociology departments can be quite politicized, as can peace studies, feminist and gender studies, and intercultural studies.

The sciences are very good at Haverford, and students mention biology and chemistry as particularly strong. "About 95 percent of students who make it into the pre-med program get into the medical school of their choice," says a senior. Bryn Mawr is also strong in the sciences. Haverford recently received a $1.7 million grant "to expand interdisciplinary science classes, student research opportunities, and minority science-education programs." The grant came from the Howard Hughes Medical Institute, which has now given Haverford a total of $4.25 million since 1988.

Among the good professors are Linda Gerstein in history, C. Stephen Finley and Kimberley Benston in English, and Vernon J. Dixon and Richard J. Ball in economics.

Political Atmosphere: Conservative Liberalism

The number of organizations devoted to multiculturalism that the 1,100 or so students at Haverford support is as large as what one would expect in a much larger institution. For example, there is BGALA (Bisexual, Gay, and Lesbian Alliance) Lounge, which, according to campus literature, "provides a safe space and a support network for queer studies on campus. In addition, students of all sexual orientations are welcome at our meetings. We strive to activate and educate the Haverford community about Gay, Lesbian, and Bisexual issues. We also want to throw lots of great parties."

Then there's the Multicultural Center, a "resource and support center for people interested in multicultural issues." According to campus literature, this office is "responsible for sensitizing the Haverford community to the concerns of people of color." Speakers brought to campus by this office include George Stallings, founder of the African-American Catholic Church, a small Afrocentric breakaway group from the Roman Catholic Church, and labor organizer Cesar Chavez.

One shouldn't overlook the Women's Center, which is billed as "nonpolitical space that is meant for the whole community's use." Though many events have to do with sexual assault prevention and other issues, the center also sponsored a talk by someone named Mistress Lorelei. She is a professional dominatrix.

There are also numerous organizations for students of every ethnic group. The Black Student League strives to "provide a comfort zone where black students can be totally comfortable with their black identity in this predominantly white institution." Among the student groups are Women of Color, the Feminist Alliance, and the Progressive Labor Party, described in college literature as "an international revolutionary communist organization."

From the makeup of the faculty, the course offerings, and the general tone of the campus (confirmed by students and alumni), it seems highly unlikely that tradition-minded scholars have much luck obtaining teaching posts at Haverford. Unfortunately, this policy reduces the options available to students, who must often settle for one voice rather than many. Yet a student notes that "This is a quiet, do-your-own-thing campus, and that's part of the Quaker tradition. You don't condemn anyone," and that the political atmosphere "isn't electrified the way it is on many campuses." Students practice what one student calls "a conservative liberalism, if that makes sense." That is, while many students, and most faculty, are left-of-center politically, the campus itself is not rife with political conflict, and politics is not the favorite topic of conversation at the coffee bar or in the classroom.

Students operate under an Honor System, which covers both academic and social life. "The Code is not a list of rules, it is a philosophy of conduct though honesty, integrity, and understanding," the college states. The system is run by the Honor Council, sixteen elected student representatives who "foster discussion and awareness of the Honor Code and [help] to resolve questions and issues concerning the code." The code demands that students take full responsibility for doing their own work on homework assignments, papers, and exams; take-home exams are common at Haverford, and finals have been unproctored since 1898. Socially, the implications of the code are a bit more open to interpretation. "It is expected that students will show concern for others and that problems, when they arise, will be dealt with in a spirit of mutual respect," the college states. "There are no resident advisers in the dorms because students are expected to work out any difficulties on their own."

Student Life: A Walk in the Park

Haverford students get to enjoy a picturesque 216-acre campus located in a highly desirable neighborhood of suburban Philadelphia. Haverford describes its campus as "park-like," and it truly is, mainly because it was originally landscaped by the English gardener William Carvill and includes a nature walk and duck pond. Among the many fine buildings is the newest one: a 50,000-square-foot Campus Center.

Campus life is a bit different from that found at many campuses both because of the small size of the college and the very close relationship it has with Bryn Mawr College. As noted above, over 90 percent of Haverford students enroll for at least one class at Bryn Mawr, and they may eat at any of that college's dining halls and even live in its dorms. Back at Haverford, 98 percent of students live on campus, where most have their own room because 70 percent of the housing is arranged as suites of singles. Nearly two-thirds of freshmen also benefit from this arrangement, which certainly fosters a sense of community at Haverford, where 80 percent of students are from outside of Pennsylvania. Another sort of community sense is developed by the fact that men and women share the same floor in the coed dorms, and often the same bathroom. The campus crime risk is quite low.

The Haverford and Bryn Mawr student bodies are served by the *Bi-College News,* as well as a literary magazine titled *Musomania,* also a bi-college publication. *Common Sense,* an alternative student newspaper for the tri-college community (including Swarthmore), offers a very different and independent editorial and newsgathering voice. *Third Side of the Coin* is a humor magazine, and the *Tri-College Guide* is a weekly events publication.

Students may also participate in any number of extracurricular activities, including the Debate Society, which teams students from Haverford and Bryn Mawr for intercollegiate contests up and down the East Coast. The Zymurgy Club studies "the fine art of homebrew" and allows students to gather to "enjoy the taste and history of beer and its construction." Looney Tunes is a coed a cappella group of the bi-college community, and the Oxford Blues is Haverford's only all-female a cappella group. As a college with Quaker origins, Haverford sponsors the Quaker Action and Activities Committee (QuAAC), which maintains a Quaker influence on the nonsectarian campus. Other religious organizations include the Jewish Student Union; Christian Fellowship, which is associated with the InterVarsity Christian Fellowship; and Catholic Campus Ministries, which ministers to the Haverford and Bryn Mawr communities.

The Republican Club at Haverford has some twenty-five members and is very active, according to a member. 8th Dimension, a volunteer group that coordinates students' activities in the community, "does a great job," says a student. The group's Web page says it was founded by "a group of students [who] felt the college should make a concerted effort to put a program in place that allows the community to become actively involved in an area upheld by Quaker beliefs. . . . Community service was seen as the missing link for a complete education . . . as well as reflecting the college's traditional Quaker social concerns." Less serious is the group called the FABs — "Fords Against Boredom." A student says this is "a cool club organizing trips into the city [Philadelphia] to see the Phillies or attend a monster truck rally, which is a kick." All of its events are alcohol-free.

Sports are very popular, as some 85 percent of the student body is involved in athletic programs, and fully 40 percent plays on Haverford's intercollegiate teams. Student-organized teams play ice hockey, volleyball, and basketball, among many other sports. Intercollegiate competition is available in soccer, track, cricket, and squash, along with most traditional sports (but not football). There are eleven varsity teams for both men and women.

Haverford lies only eleven miles from Center City Philadelphia, which may be reached easily via train. Philadelphia offers numerous restaurants, nightclubs, and other attractions for the work-weary student. The Philadelphia Museum of Art is the largest of many cultural institutions available, and historic sites dating from the founding of the nation are within easy reach. The New Jersey and Delaware beaches are an easy drive away, as are ski resorts in the Poconos. Closer to home, Haverford, Bryn Mawr, and neighboring towns along the Main Line offer a large assortment of restaurants and other centers of shopping and entertainment.

Hillsdale College

Director of Admissions
35 East College Street
Hillsdale, MI 49242
(417) 437-7341, ext. 327
www.hillsdale.edu

Total enrollment: 1,160
Undergraduates: 1,160
SAT ranges (Verbal/Math): 570-690 (V); 520-660 (M)
Applicants: 1,008
Accepted: 84%
Enrolled: 39%
Application deadline: Rolling
Financial aid application deadline: March 15
Tuition: $13,840/$19,540
Core curriculum: Yes

Living On

With many American colleges and universities having abandoned liberal arts education in favor of modern liberalism, one of the most conservative schools in the country, Hillsdale College, has matured into one of the most liberal in the learning opportunities it affords students.

Hillsdale's conservatism is evidenced most famously in its adherence to its tradition of refusing federal money, including (since 1985) federally insured student loans. This refusal allows Hillsdale to remain free of federal affirmative action programs, among other intrusions.

Coupled with the institution's conservatism is its commitment to liberal education. Truly liberated learning teaches responsibilities, and according to Hillsdale's mission statement, "The college considers itself a trustee of modern man's intellectual and spiritual inheritance from the Judeo-Christian faith and Greco-Roman culture, a heritage finding its clearest expression in the American experiment of self-government under law." Liberal learning thus has as its goal "the preservation of that legacy." As the college emphasizes, "The liberal arts are dedicated to simulating students' intellectual curiosity, to encouraging the critical, well-disciplined mind, and to fostering personal growth through academic challenge."

Hillsdale does that.

Academic Life: Yes, There Is in Fact a Meal Plan

Hillsdale has been accused by one writer of being no more than a "conservative think tank with a meal plan" (Emily Eakin, writing in *Lingua Franca*, 1996), but the college is much more than that. Its education is not geared to policy nor to churning out ranks of conservative clones. Rather, through a solid core curriculum and a faculty devoted to teaching, it seeks to confront students with the enduring and controversial questions that have brought the West anything but unanimity in ideas. According to one student, the result of this confrontation is a "true broadening of perspective that gets at first principles."

Hillsdale requires all students to take year-long sequences in Western history and Western literature. The history course is divided into "The Western Heritage to 1600" and "The American Heritage." Each section works from a fine reader created by the department faculty. Also required are writing-intensive literature courses, including two semesters of "Freshman Rhetoric and the Great Books." All nonscience majors must take a year-long, team-taught science course covering topics in biology, chemistry, and physics, though because of the ground it covers, the course is thought too general by some students. Beyond these requirements, all students must take mathematics, philosophy or religion, three semesters of a foreign language, an upper-level literature or classics course, an offering in the fine arts, and two introductory courses in economics, political science, psychology, or sociology. A year-long sequence in the fine arts is being considered, as are other options for further solidifying the core.

This rigorous schedule, rather than repelling students, has attracted them —

and they're good ones. Over the past decade the quality of the student body at Hillsdale has grown considerably, such that faculty believe that a substantial interest in a liberal arts education among those beginning college is "now a given," according to a professor. In addition to this positive trend, the rigor of the core curriculum was strengthened through reforms implemented several years ago. A fine intellectual resonance has resulted, as students are able to share even more of a common foundation in their coursework.

The history department's mission statement typifies the understanding of the role a liberal education plays at Hillsdale. The first stated goal is "to develop the minds and improve the hearts of students by engaging them in reflection upon the ideas, events, cultural patterns, and leaders responsible for shaping our Western heritage, of which the American heritage is a part." The second part of the mission emphasizes the necessity of "critical and free inquiry," while the third points to the "dialogue with the inhabitants of the living past" in which students will be engaged.

Hillsdale's small size contributes greatly to the ability of departments to successfully strive for such noble goals. Many students point to the abundance of small seminar classes as one of the outstanding features of a Hillsdale education. "What gave Hillsdale its identity to me was the interaction with the professors," one student says. Another says that professors there are "genuinely interested in students beyond their academic capacity."

The college offers twenty-seven majors, the best-regarded among them being political science, history, English, biology, and chemistry. Business and education majors are popular; together they accounted for 43 percent of the degrees conferred in 1999 — a statistic that concerns some among the faculty. Efforts to reorganize the business and education programs in order to orient them more toward the liberal arts have met with mixed success. Majors in political economy (with classes taught by the faculties of history, political science, and economics) and American studies (made up of faculty from English, history, and political science) are also strong — not judgments this guide often makes on like-titled departments at other colleges. The classics department has recently witnessed a renaissance: surging enrollment in Latin classes (more than 20 percent of a recent freshman class enrolled in Latin 101) required the hiring of a third full-time faculty member in that department. Also making tremendous strides in the last two years has been the music program, with a burgeoning number of musical groups marking increased student participation. The Honors Program, recently revamped, offers a fine enhancement to the Hillsdale experience for those students who are selected.

Hillsdale's commitment to core principles, dedication to the liberal arts, and emphasis on teaching has attracted a strong faculty with many outstanding professors. These include Lee Ann Fisher Baron and Christopher VanOrman in chemistry; Richard Ebeling and Gary Wolfram in economics; Michael Jordan, John Reist, and David Whalen in English; Thomas Conner, David Stewart, and John Willson in history; Thomas Burke and James Stephens in philosophy; Kenneth Hayes in physics;

Robert Eden and Mickey Craig in political science; Donald Westblade in religion; and Michael Bauman, professor of theology and culture and director of Christian studies.

Classroom offerings are complemented by a lecture series known as the Center for Constructive Alternatives (CCA). Four week-long seminars are held each year, and students must enroll in two of the seminars for academic credit. Topics for the 2000-2001 academic year include "Junk Science: The Political Abuse of Research" and "The Morality of Civility." One of the seminars every year is cosponsored by the Ludwig von Mises Lecture Series (named for the eminent Austrian economist) and focuses on free-market ideas. The "alternatives" suggested by the lecture series are decidedly those provided by conservative thinking, but among the more than one thousand guests are good number of liberals, including Eleanor Clift, Stanley Fish, Gary Hart, Jesse Jackson, George McGovern, and Patricia Schroeder. The roster of conservative speakers participating in the series is vast: Ronald Reagan, William F. Buckley, Jr., George Bush Sr., Dan Quayle, Lynne Cheney, Clarence Thomas, Mark Helprin, and Jeanne Kirkpatrick are on it.

Other excellent programs allow Hillsdale's philosophy to be exported beyond its campus. The Shavano Institute for National Leadership, the school's off-campus lecture series, has sponsored more than one hundred programs for more than ten thousand business and community leaders around the country. A free monthly publication, *Imprimis* (Latin for "in the first place"), featuring conservative lectures that have been delivered to Hillsdale audiences, is sent to almost one million people. The Hillsdale Academy, which recently added a high school to its K-8 program, has become a fine example for many schools around the country through Hillsdale's "A Model for America" program.

Political Atmosphere: Sad but True

The platitudes of the new multiculturalists ring hollow when compared with the policies of inclusion Hillsdale has practiced for years. When it opened its doors in 1844 as a Freewill Baptist school, Hillsdale was the first college in the nation to have a policy of nondiscrimination written into its charter. It admitted women, blacks, and other minorities on a par with white males for two decades *before* the Civil War. During World War I, Hillsdale refused to segregate its ROTC units and won a battle with the federal government over the matter.

Hillsdale had to fight the federal government again in the 1970s and '80s. After the school refused to comply with the federal requirements that it report the ethnic and gender makeup of faculty, students, and staff, the federal government contended that Hillsdale was an "indirect recipient" of government funds because Hillsdale students were the beneficiaries of federal loans and scholarships. When the government's claims were upheld by the Supreme Court in 1985, Hillsdale affirmed its independence by renouncing even "indirect" funding from the federal government. Since then, Hillsdale has proudly proclaimed its independence from federal largesse.

Hillsdale's stand for independence from federal intervention won it national acclaim. Donations poured in, facilitated by the skilled fund-raising efforts of Dr. George Roche, who became president of Hillsdale in 1971. Relishing Hillsdale's status as "the little college that could," Roche raised almost $325 million by 1999, an amount that afforded Hillsdale what today is a remarkable endowment of more than $180 million.

The big financial push was not without controversy. Faculty members critical of what they perceived as all-consuming fund-raising efforts occasionally left the school, claiming that the college was losing its focus on providing a liberal arts education. Both allies and enemies of Roche admitted that he exercised almost absolute control over the institution. Students running afoul of the administration's strict oversight of campus publications and extracurricular activities complained of a heavy administrative hand. "Instead of engendering conversation or debate, they said this is the way it would have to be," one student said at the time. But even then, this student said, the administration did not meddle inside the classrooms; instruction remained an "enclave of freedom."

Roche's impact on Hillsdale went much beyond building its budget, for his efforts transformed a relatively obscure Midwestern college into a conservative colossus with a top-ranked faculty (named in a recent *U.S. News & World Report* as the best in the Midwest). Despite these occasional controversies over means, most students and faculty members were in agreement with the ends pursued by Roche and his administration. All of the students and faculty members — even those critical of Roche — recognized his enormous contribution to Hillsdale College. The tenacity that allowed him to remain steadfast against the federal government led many at Hillsdale to believe that despite nagging health problems Roche would remain as president for many years to come — extending his already remarkable run of twenty-seven years in that post. His tenure, however, would end in tragedy and sadness.

In mid-October 1999, Roche's daughter-in-law, Lissa Roche, committed suicide. As Hillsdale's director of seminars and managing editor of the Hillsdale College Press, she had played an integral role in advancing Hillsdale's message around the nation. Her suicide shocked and saddened the campus and the conservative world in which she had been so active. Then news came that before her death Lissa Roche had admitted to a nineteen-year affair with her father-in-law. The Hillsdale Board of Trustees announced that the president had been suspended, and on November 10, Roche resigned his post, writing tersely that he had "no wish to continue."

The refusal by Hillsdale administrators to discuss any reasons for Roche's resignation or to launch an investigation of Lissa Roche's allegations of an affair led to a firestorm of protest. Some conservatives claimed that Hillsdale was engaging in a kind of cover-up. William Bennett, who had agreed to serve on the search committee for a new president, resigned in the wake of the college's inaction, saying, "The whole thing just reeks." Foes of conservatism, taking the allegations to be true, accused the conservative movement of hypocrisy in its selective moralism. For weeks following Roche's resignation the campus was caught in a tempest for which no one had prepared.

Admitting to no more than ineptitude in dealing with the media onslaught, the Hillsdale administration did not make an inquiry into the actions of its past president. This fact still rankles some on the Right, but even the administration's harshest critics — on and off campus — admit that such an investigation might have dragged on for years without arriving at any conclusions. The trustees' swift actions regarding Roche were followed by a nationwide search for a new president that concluded in April with the selection of Larry Arnn, then president of The Claremont Institute for the Study of Statesmanship and Political Philosophy, a conservative California think tank.

Most media accounts of the scandal surrounding Roche's departure neglected to report how little affected the core mission of Hillsdale was in the midst of the controversy. Classes continued without interruption. Furthermore, some faculty report that students, while conscious of the distraction posed by the media circus, redoubled their efforts in the classroom. Throughout the year, the college continued to do what it has always done, and that is to provide students with the opportunity to engage each other and their teachers in conversation about the highest ideas and ideals bequeathed by the West.

With the Roche controversy now behind them, faculty and students alike are generally optimistic about the college's future under its new president. Several professors note that the faculty has never been stronger, and that combined with the rapid progress made recently in the quality of the student body, Hillsdale is in an excellent position to continue to improve its academic standing. While George Roche's administrative style made him "estranged from the faculty in the last few years," in the words of one professor, there is great hope that Arnn will be able to establish a much better rapport. Students, too, are optimistic that the change in leadership will mean a more open administration.

In several speeches as president-elect, Arnn emphasized the necessity of the liberal arts for freedom and the future of America. The Founding Fathers recognized the necessity of virtue and morality, Arnn has said. The cultivation of the proper habits of mind and heart necessary for protecting natural rights comes in part through an education in the liberal arts. "Colleges of a certain type are necessary to the preservation of liberty. They are necessary to the making of good laws. Without them the laws will lose the spirit of freedom, and then freedom itself will soon be gone," Arnn stated in a speech published in the June 2000 issue of *Imprimis*. "Hillsdale does not take from the federal government. Instead it gives to it lessons in what government should be." A liberal arts education, pursued "first and foremost as an academic task," thus assumes a role surpassing academics: Hillsdale College, in pursuing the liberal arts, is thus "an institution of freedom."

Hillsdale sees its political mission as nonpartisan. But there are certain political consequences of an education in the liberal arts, one of which is that the liberty that comes from the study of the liberal arts is primarily an education in the necessity of self-government. Hillsdale is thus conservative in character, but this does not imply a unanimity of political views among the faculty. Indeed, there is a great deal of debate on campus — but it's a debate that does not get mired in the muck of academic fads. The faculty's statement on academic freedom, drafted originally by Russell Kirk, stands in marked contrast to the notion of academic freedom prevalent at most institutions today. In part it reads: "[A]cademic freedom in particular required attachment to a body of truth, made known through the order and integration of knowledge. Of such truths the college is the conservator and renewer, and the primary function of the college is to transmit, through these truths, some measure of wisdom and virtue."

Student Life: Isolated in Middle America

Hillsdale's campus is "centrally isolated" in a town of about 8,000 in the rural hills of southern Michigan. With Ann Arbor and Lansing each about ninety minutes away and Detroit still further, life in Hillsdale is hard for a diehard city slicker. But the campus offerings are sufficient to satisfy even the most ambitious student.

Clubs and campus organizations are numerous. There are political groups (College Republicans and Libertarians have a presence, but no College Democrat chapter is active on campus); religious groups (more than a quarter of the student body attends the large group meetings of the InterVarsity Christian Fellowship); academically oriented groups (Praxis is a the political economy club, and the honoraries for history and political science regularly sponsor speakers); and even a group dedicated to reading aloud the literary contributions of A. A. Milne. An annual talent show has been a big hit as of late.

The Greek presence on campus is significant, with almost half of the students joining the four fraternities and four sororities on campus. All dorms at Hillsdale are single-sex and have strictly enforced visiting hours.

Because of its small-town location, crime is virtually nonexistent on campus, and students regularly leave backpacks outside the dining hall unattended.

Hillsdale offers varsity sports at the NCAA Division II level in baseball, basketball, cross country, football, golf, soccer, tennis, and indoor and outdoor track for men, and basketball, cross country, soccer, softball, swimming, tennis, indoor and outdoor track, and volleyball for women. A fine sports complex provides ample opportunities for club and intramural sports.

College of the Holy Cross

Office of Admissions
College of the Holy Cross
One College Street
Worcester, MA 01510-2395
(508) 793-2011
www.holycross.edu

Total enrollment: 2,801
Undergraduates: 2,801
SAT ranges (Verbal/Math): 550-670 (V); 550-670 (M)
Applicants: 4,836
Accepted: 44%
Enrolled: 34%
Application deadline: January 15
Financial aid application deadline: February 15
Tuition: $23,815/$31,355
Core curriculum: No

By Tradition and Choice

The College of the Holy Cross (CHC) begins its mission statement affirming its identity as "a Jesuit liberal arts college serving the Catholic community, American society, and the wider world." This identity, its statement says, is upheld "by tradition and choice." While it is true that by tradition Holy Cross has sustained a strong liberal arts education, it remains to be seen whether Holy Cross will choose to adhere to this tradition or to supplant it with new ideas of what an education should be.

Tradition, it's got: CHC is the oldest Catholic college in New England, founded in 1843 by Bishop Joseph Fenwick, S.J. Located in the heart of Massachusetts (fifty miles west of Boston), the college began as an all-male school but became coeducational in the 1970s. The college today is a relatively small undergraduate institution (less than three thousand undergraduates) that, as its mission statement declares, "pursues excellence in teaching, learning, and research."

The pursuit of excellence in education has long characterized the Jesuit tradition. Coupled with this pursuit has been an ethic of service, along with what CHC states is a requisite "promotion of justice." The Jesuit commitment to liberal arts, service, and justice has for centuries been exported to diverse cultures. At their best, the Jesuits were the first multiculturalists, respecting and cherishing the cultures in which they worked. Now, liberation theology and its attendant ideologies threaten the tradition of liberal arts at Holy Cross. The new multiculturalism often demands a leveling of cultures and ideas that ends in an elevation of "toleration" above all.

The frieze of Holy Cross's Dinand Library includes these words: "Ut Cognoscant te Solum Deum Verum et Quem Misisti Jesum Christum" (That they might know you, the One True God, and Jesus Christ, whom you have sent). Perhaps there is no better way to remind the college of its noble mission than by what has been carved into its buildings. Whether Holy Cross will seek the liberty of soul that comes in a study of the liberal arts or the ideological "liberation" that is desired by some politicized administrators and faculty is perhaps the most important question in the institution's future. The Catholic theologian Cardinal Newman emphasized that the primary purpose of education is knowledge for its own sake, not for political purposes. Despite the inroads made by the new multiculturalism, in many areas Holy Cross offers to students a very sound education, one firmly rooted in what is best in the Jesuit tradition.

Academic Life: Distribution, for Now

Twenty years ago, the curriculum at Holy Cross had departed very far from a liberal arts focus — a "bland mish-mash," according to one professor. The curriculum today does not include a core, but is nevertheless on much more solid ground. And against all trends in education, a true core may be on the way: CHC's new president, Rev. Michael McFarland, S.J., has said that he would like "to see the distribution requirements turned into a true core curriculum." As he told CHC's campus newspaper, *The Crusader News,* in early 2000, "That means there should be a clearer definition of their purpose, a sharper focus, and assurance that the courses involved reflect that purpose and focus."

For now, however, the purpose and focus of a student's program of study is largely dependent upon the student's chosen concentration, for departmental missions vary quite widely. Holy Cross offers bachelor of arts degrees in twenty-four majors, including (among the less common for schools its size) Russian, sociology-anthropology, studies in European literature, and the history of visual arts. All students are required to take ten distribution courses spread over six areas of the curriculum: the arts and literature (one course in each), religious and philosophical studies (one course in each — low for a church-related school, though McFarland has expressed a desire to see more philosophy courses), historical studies (one course), cross-cultural studies (one course), social science (two courses), and natural and mathematical sciences (two courses, at least one of which is in a natural science). In addition, competency in a classical language, modern foreign language, or American Sign Language is required. Beginning with the Class of 2004, this language requirement will be replaced by a new, two-course distribution requirement called "Language Studies" (meaning that one year of language study will suffice for the requirement).

The cross-cultural course requirement, as at other institutions, opens the door to the most politicized offerings. At Holy Cross, the program means that a student will "examine contemporary societies and cultures other than one's own. Courses in this area are intended to expand one's frame of reference by providing an awareness of the similarities and differences among the peoples of the world, as well as to foster a sense of belonging to a larger community." The cross-cultural studies program is under administrative review, and one professor notes that the administration has recently been more "stringent" in making sure the course students take to satisfy the requirement has a non-Western emphasis.

The Center for Interdisciplinary and Special Studies "seeks to be a catalyst for innovation and experimentation in the curriculum." Among the current "experiments" offered at CHC are concentrations (which, unlike majors, allow for interdisciplinary selection of electives) in African American studies, international studies, peace and conflict studies, and women's studies.

Among these concentrations, peace and conflict studies and women's studies are especially politicized. Beginning with the premise (shaped by the not-so-much-now-as-in-the-past looming prospect of nuclear conflagration), "Unless we are all secure, none of us are," the peace and conflict program seeks to "educate women and men for the responsibility of citizenship in an age of nuclear weapons. . . . It seeks to give students the motivation and competence to deal effectively with threats to peace, justice, and human survival." Liberationism is laced throughout the program of study.

Women's studies (rather modestly) "seeks to interpret the female experience and transform the female condition. It engenders sociopolitical awareness of women's position in society by critiquing existing modes of thought and by positing alternatives." Noting in its fuchsia-colored brochure that the establishment of the program of study at CHC in 1991 "marks the institution's commitment to feminist, multicultural, interdisciplinary education," the program promises that "through exploring the intersection of female selfhood and ideologies of gender, class, race, ethnicity, and sexuality, students . . . achieve a broad understanding of culture as a social determinant, and learn to question the ways in which society ignores, restrict or diminishes women's contributions." Courses offered to this end include "Women and Gender in Latin America," "Colloquium: A History of Sex," "Sex Role Development," "Feminist Ethics," and "Women Mystics." A Women's Studies Award is granted to the top graduate, in part for "development and articulation of a feminist critical consciousness."

Religious studies departments around the country are notoriously politicized, and Holy Cross's entry is, sadly, no exception. The very supplanting of departments of theology by "religious studies" departments is indicative of the focus of studies; if a Catholic school can't have a department of theology, who can? Holy Cross, at least, does not neglect the Catholic character of religious study as much as at some Catholic institutions, but in reading the courses offered in the department one wonders if the primary concentration is understanding the foundations of faith or comparing world religions within a "pluralistic" context. Yoga is the stated subject of one course in the catalogue, while none of the church fathers merits mention. Students will learn all about economic and political liberationism, but little about medieval theologians. In "Feminist Perspectives in Theology," according to the catalogue, "alternative reconstructions that feminist/womanist/mujerista theologians present" are taught. "Sexual Justice: A Social Ethic of Sexuality" has as its aim the study of "sexuality within a broader system of class, race, gender and disability dynamics."

In addition to these programs of study, the sociology department is also recognized as particularly politicized. Again, this is not an uncommon department on many campuses wherein to find courses that lean to the left. "The Sociology of Men" at CHC is an example of such an offering: "Topics include men's antifemininity, homophobia, inexpressiveness, success-orientation, relations with family, and grandparenting." The new president of Holy Cross has also expressed a desire to see a cross-cultural studies program, which given its likely association with the Center for Religion, Ethics, and Culture may mean more sham multiculturalism than sound scholarship.

Despite these outposts of ideology, there are many fine programs of study at CHC. The First-Year Program, which all incoming students are invited to join (and about 25 percent do), offers special seminars, common readings, and extracurricular events. Organized around a particular theme (which for 1999-2000 was "When self encounters others, how then shall we live?"), the program entails a year-long seminar and three regular courses. Participating students live in the same residence halls and are guided by team-led discussions in their inquiries. College literature promises that in this program, "Artificial barriers between classroom activity and the rest of life quickly collapse." Professors who have led the program corroborate this claim and say that the program is only getting stronger.

The College Honors Program offers a rigorous opportunity to explore issues in depth, beginning in the second year of college for selected students. The college states that the program "helps students to organize their liberal arts education at the highest level of excellence." One professor speaks positively about the "spirit of integration" that pervades the program. Classes are small, averaging eight to ten students. Students take at least two seminars selected from a number of themes. As juniors and seniors, honors students meet for five to seven evening colloquia each semester, and each student writes a thesis during his or her senior year.

The classics department at Holy Cross is one of the largest such undergraduate departments in the country, with thirteen full-time faculty members, more than fifty majors, and more than four hundred non-majors enrolled in classes at any time. More importantly, it is one of the finest classics departments in the country. Courses in Greek and Latin, Greek and Roman history, politics, philosophy, religion, mythology, archaeology, and literature are offered. The classics department has "quite an impact on the college," a professor says. "Students fall in love with the classics." At

CHC, the classics are anything but dead — office corridors are constantly crawling with students. Enhancing the study of the ancients is a very modern study program called the Perseus Project, a digital library focusing primarily on ancient Greece.

Joining the classics department as one of the finest undergraduate departments in the nation is the political science department. It too takes a traditional approach to its discipline. The faculty is "trying to train citizens," a professor says. A rigorous program comprising four subfields (political philosophy, American government, comparative politics, and international relations), has been crafted, and students interested in faddish courses will have to look elsewhere. It is worth noting that the Washington Semester Program (not restricted to political science majors) is an academically challenging offering (rather than a vacation) during which students write a thesis under the tutelage of their advisers.

The biology, chemistry, history, and music departments also enjoy solid reputations on campus, with biology and chemistry majors especially appreciative of the research work they are able to do with their professors.

Outstanding professors at Holy Cross include: Nancy E. Andrews, Thomas R. Martin, and Blaise Nagy in classics; Robert K. Cording, James M. Kee, Thomas M. C. Lawler, and Richard E. Matlak in English; David J. Schap in economics; Noel D. Cary in history; Jessica Waldoff in music; Joseph P. Lawrence in philosophy; and Donald R. Brand, Loren Cass, Caren G. Dubnoff, David L. Schaefer, Denise Schaeffer, and Ward J. Thomas in political science.

Political Atmosphere: What Will Be Tolerated

The new president of Holy Cross has called for a "culture of tolerance, where people are accepted for who they are and valued for the variety of experiences they bring." He said in an interview with the campus newspaper, "People on every side have to be willing to listen to and value one another. That does not mean giving up one's beliefs." And he adds: "You have to change the campus climate, perception of the school, and people's attitudes, none of which yield easily."

As with any such encouragement of tolerance, the challenge is to ensure that the advocates of what is deemed intolerant are not forced by intolerance to give up their beliefs. However, with the recent appointment of an associate vice president for diversity, this administration seems bent on at least some sort of attitudinal adjustment. Just where the demands will be made is yet to be seen. It is clear, however, according to sources on campus, that many of the guest speakers and extracurricular events lean to their left in their political orientation.

The campus appearance of gangster rapper Chuck D, sponsored by the Black Student Union, recently sparked controversy, as faculty and students debated the propriety of the lecture (funded by student fees) by the anti-Semitic rapper. Some faculty members were outspoken in their criticism, noting that the appearance of

Chuck D not only lacked academic merit but also offered a forum for an "artist" whose lyrics are rife with anti-Semitic slogans. Several students responded to the criticisms with a letter to the editor of the campus newspaper. Noting that their "academic major involves [them] in the study of textual analysis," the signatories (who included an associate professor of English) attempted to explain away Chuck D's derogatory use of the term "the big six million" as a reference to the music industry, rather than a vitriolic attack on the Jews who perished in the Holocaust.

Though the campus speaker series tends toward the left, the Hanify-Howland Memorial Lecture has provided some balance. This event includes a a lecture on public affairs followed by student seminars. Recent speakers have included Harvey Mansfield, a conservative professor of government at Harvard, Chris Matthews, host of "Hardball," and Paul Wolfowitz, former foreign policy adviser to President Reagan.

Holy Cross has a homosexual rights organization known as Allies, which "is dedicated to creating a humane campus environment for all persons regardless of sexual orientation." Allies hopes, through "education," to "make the environment of Holy Cross safer and more supportive for gay, lesbian, and bisexual students." The group suggests that members wear an "Allies button," an upside-down pink triangle, which designates the wearer as "a safe person to talk with," presumably about homosexual issues. Stickers with the designations "safe person" and "safe space" adorn faculty offices. The group is also involved in National Coming Out Day festivities.

The majority of political activism at Holy Cross, however, supports a popular version of social justice somewhat informed by liberation theology. Holy Cross joined the Workers Rights Consortium (WRC), known mostly for its protests against sweatshop labor used in the production of college athletic apparel. The Student Labor Action Committee at Holy Cross, which lobbied for the college to join the WRC, has, according to advocates of the campus group, "successfully lobbied to ban the sale of 'Gardenburgers'" from the dining hall "until the company broke with Norpak, known abuser of worker rights," and has also supported an American Farm Workers union campaign for the rights of strawberry workers.

Student Life: The Worcester Shire

Worcester is a college town, with more than fifteen colleges, universities, and academic societies in the area, including Assumption College, Clark University, and Worcester Polytech. Fifteen institutions belong to the Colleges of Worcester Consortium, which affords students at CHC opportunities for taking classes not offered at CHC. More than 36,000 students reside in and around Worcester, the second-largest city in New England with a population of 170,000.

The Holy Cross campus is spread out in a wooded area in several groupings of buildings (quads) set upon a hill overlooking the city. According to official figures,

361

the campus itself is very safe; it is not isolated, however — a large elevated freeway passes by the football and baseball stadiums and the campus is within walking distance of Worcester neighborhoods. Most students (80 percent) live in the nine residence halls on campus; there are no fraternities or sororities at CHC (as the college claims that they are "antithetical to [Holy Cross's] traditions of openness and friendship between all members of this community" and because of the "social separation that such organizations encourage"). Boston is less than fifty miles away, and New York City is a three-hour drive.

A majority of Holy Cross students choose to live in one of the college's eight residence halls. All are coed, with men and women on different floors. There are some visitation restrictions.

Drinking is all-too-common an extracurricular activity at CHC, and the administration has taken steps to cultivate the connection between the intellectual and moral virtues. With more than one hundred student organizations on campus, it seems that there should be no shortage of better things to do.

Service projects are popular at CHC, and students are actively involved in the Worcester community. The Office of College Chaplains supports work within the Diocese of Worcester, sponsors service trips within and beyond the United States (one of the student groups involved is the Appalachia Service Project), and celebrates several masses on campus every day, though attendance is not mandated.

Holy Cross is one of the smallest schools in the country to support a Division I athletic program, and the Crusaders have enjoyed some success against much larger foes. The school offers twelve varsity sports for men and eleven for women. Lake Quinsigamond, home to the men's and women's crew squads, is a fine venue for rowing. With more than thirty intramural sports and several club teams, the college estimates that at least 90 percent of the study body is involved in sports at some level.

University of Illinois at Urbana–Champaign

Office of Admissions and Records
901 West Illinois Street
Urbana, Illinois 61801
(217) 333-0302
www.uiuc.edu

Total enrollment: 36,258
Undergraduates: 27,400
SAT ranges (Verbal/Math): 550-650 (V); 590-710 (M)
Applicants: 17,867
Accepted: 71%
Enrolled: 51%
Application deadline: January 1
Financial aid application deadline: March 15
Tuition: resident: $4,746/$10,590; non-resident: $11,838/$17,682
Core curriculum: No

Urbana Renewal

The University of Illinois attracts some of the brightest students from Illinois and beyond to its sprawling campus in the central part of the state. The university was founded in 1867 as a typical land-grant institution, particularly emphasizing the sciences, technology, and agriculture. However, the university has gone far beyond these humble beginnings to boast not only the third-largest library in the United States (and the largest among state institutions) but excellent programs in several areas in the humanities as well as the sciences among its 150 majors. However, the sheer mass of courses and majors exposes the student to the educational malady that is symptomatic of the modern multiversity: with a plethora of choices available and little direction in the form of a core curriculum, the student is at risk of receiving a disjointed and incoherent education.

The university, in particular the College of Liberal Arts and Sciences, has begun to recognize this problem and has taken preliminary steps toward correcting it. While it is possible for a student to remain anonymous, it is also possible for a motivated student to have an excellent educational experience and work closely with professors. The university's tuition is still a bargain for the in-state student, and the student who takes responsibility for his education can be confident of getting plenty of "bang for his buck."

Academic Life: Reevaluating Its Ills

In the early 1990s, the University of Illinois began to reevaluate its general education requirements, the distribution of courses that all students must take. The feeling was that these distribution requirements had become so general and diffuse as to hardly merit the term "requirement" at all. The College of Liberal Arts and Sciences has done the most to close some of the loopholes and develop a more coherent program, but other colleges (especially the College of Education) have made only minimal progress.

Students in LAS are expected to take three courses in the humanities, and two each in science and math. These requirements represent an increase of one course each from the previous standard. Unfortunately, the humanities requirements can often be fulfilled by something less than essential, like "Women in Prehistory" or "Sex and Gender in Classical Antiquity." Students in LAS are also required to take at least three semesters of a foreign language (or to attain comparable competency). This too is one course more than the previous distribution requirements asked. "The purpose of raising the foreign language requirement was to try to guarantee that students get at least one course beyond the elementary level," says one professor. "We also recognized practically that many students, having taken three semesters of a language, would go ahead and take a fourth." The university requires all students to take a course in a "non-Western" discipline or area, but this is putatively balanced by a requirement that all students take a course in Western culture. Many excellent courses are offered in traditional liberal arts disciplines, and the student who takes the time to inform himself can receive an outstanding liberal arts education — or, at least, a handful of good courses. "I would characterize our distribution requirements as strong but flexible," a faculty member says.

The "flexibility" of the LAS General Education curriculum places a high degree of responsibility on the student to ensure the quality of his own education. "Most students come here with a fairly defined goal or major in mind," says a professor. "Those who don't tend to have problems." According to faculty, most students who arrive at LAS have the general thought that they want a liberal arts education, but they're not entirely sure what that means. If the student is well advised, or sticks to courses dealing with standard topics, he will get a fairly sound exposure to the liberal arts, though obviously the structure of a coherent core would offer much more to those whose idea of a liberal arts education never advances beyond a general conception.

And who will advise the student in such a large and impersonal place? Most departments, especially the larger ones, have designated academic advisors. These are mostly "academic professionals," a hybrid position created by the university in the last few years. They are Ph.D.s hired mainly to do undergraduate teaching and academic advising. "The positions were created as a partial response to complaints of students, parents, and legislators that too many undergraduate courses were taught by teaching assistants," a professor says. "These people . . . are well qualified to teach in their fields. But they don't have the research and publication demands of regular tenure-track professors, so they can devote themselves to undergraduate teaching. As the pool of graduate students has shrunk in the last few years, we've relied more and more on them."

Most students are satisfied with the advising and direction they received from their departments and report good experiences with courses taught by the academic professionals. But having the opportunity to learn from great scholars who are at the forefront of their disciplines can open a student's mind to new insights and make a good college experience a great one. In order to give undergraduates the chance to have such interaction, the university instituted "discovery" courses in 1995. A discovery course is limited to twenty students and taught by regular professors, many of whom are leaders in their fields. A discovery course might be a special section of an introductory course or may deal with more specialized, advanced topics. Students are especially encouraged to "experiment" with these courses and take one outside of their major area. Students generally are impressed with the high quality of these courses, and professors enjoy teaching them. "We get good students in these classes: they're interested and motivated," says a professor. "I think it stretches students' minds. Every year I teach a discovery course, and we always get a couple of students from it who decide to major in our department."

Illinois is well known for the quality of its programs in engineering, the sciences, journalism, and business. The College of Agriculture is one of the oldest in the nation, and its programs are widely respected. Other departments with strong programs are economics, labor and industrial relations, geography, and history. The classics department has a distinguished history and boasts several world-class scholars. The religious studies program is also excellent, surprisingly so for a state university. Some of the outstanding faculty at Illinois are Robert Weissberg in political science; Keith Hitchins in history; Robert McKim in philosophy; Lee Alston and Fred Gottheil in economics; Rajeshwari Pandharipande in religious studies; and James Dengate in classics.

The quality of the education at Illinois is bolstered by its libraries; the collection comprises 14 million volumes. The Undergraduate Library is noteworthy in that it was built underground so as not to cast a shadow on the Morrow Plots, the oldest continuously cultivated experimental farm in the country. The Main Library is vast, but its stacks are open only to faculty and graduate students. Undergraduates must submit written requests for books, and wait while they are retrieved (usually this takes only fifteen to twenty minutes). There are thirty-eight departmental libraries as well.

The university has established relationships with several religious institutions, such as the Newman Foundation, which ministers to Roman Catholic students at the university. These institutions offer courses approved by the university for elective credit. Students can take up to ten semester hours of credit in such courses. The university also has Army, Navy, and Air Force ROTC programs. There is an honors program for the top one hundred cadets, which pairs each of them up with a professor in his field.

In such a large university, it is easy for a student to get lost in the crowd. "When a professor has two hundred kids in a lecture, he couldn't get to know us even if he wanted to," says a student. The situation is worst for students in the sciences and engineering. "I had been here a year and a half before I actually ever had a one-on-one conversation with a professor," an engineering student says. Students in the humanities report a better experience: "My department is fairly small, so we tend to have pretty close relationships with our professors," an LAS student says. Most students say that their professors are receptive and interested in them when they are approached, but that the student has to take the initiative. "Unless you're lucky enough to be in a small program," said one student, "you definitely have to make the first move in getting to know your professors." The problem of distance between students and faculty seems to be one of scale rather than aloofness. There are just too many students for the faculty to be able to get to know many of them.

Political Atmosphere

The large size of the university means that there are people of pretty much any ideological stripe somewhere on campus. "We've got it all here," says one professor. "You can still find communists and socialists, and feminism and gay rights are simply *de rigueur*. We even had, at least for a while, a woman in the psychology department who was a lesbian separatist." The university is generally perceived to tolerate most of the excesses of the left, but there is evidence that that is changing. Activists have, as of yet, been unable to strong-arm the university into establishing a gay studies program. "I think that the moment is passing for the extreme left here," says a professor. "You can find a few holdouts, but everyone knows that Marxism is dead." As one might expect, the departments of women's studies, Latina/Latino studies, and Afro-American studies are filled with leftist ideologues. But efforts to radicalize the curriculum by requiring students to take classes in these departments have been rebuffed. "Students are 'encouraged' by the university to take these courses," one professor says. But this is far from the requirements for such courses levied by other institutions, and another professor says that "students aren't very interested in that stuff, and those programs don't attract many students." We suspect that the same would happen at other institutions, were their arbitrary, politically correct general education requirements dropped.

Many students, though, still have to contend with political correctness in their classes. Students are expected to use "inclusive language" in their papers, and some report having papers marked down for failing to do so to their instructor's satisfaction. The "role of women" is supposed to be taught in all general education classes, and some instructors take that as license to turn their classes into consciousness-raising seminars about the evils of men. A few students report blatantly ideological attempts to punish students who disagree with instructors. "I wrote a paper for my Rhetoric 105 class [one of the basic freshman writing courses] in which I argued against gay marriage," a student says. "The teaching assistant gave me a D on the paper because 'you can't argue for that sort of position without appealing to hate and religious bigotry.' I had to go to the department chair to get the grade raised to a C, and that's all I could do."

The College of Education is regarded as being extremely politicized as well as academically weak. "My education classes are mostly a joke," said one education major. "I look at the education degree as a union card — it's a hoop I need to jump through to be a teacher." The history department also has a significant left-wing bias. But the English department is considered by many to be the most politicized department on campus, on par with programs such as women's studies. A course called "Postcolonial Literatures in English" is an indication of this ideological tendency. According to the catalogue, this course is an "examination of selected postcolonial literature, theory, and film as texts that 'write back' to dominant European representations of power, identity, gender, and the Other." The English department also offers many courses on more standard topics and authors, but one would be well-advised to investigate the instructor and content of the course before taking it. Many course descriptions in the catalogue are not descriptive at all, and one could take a class titled simply "Introduction to Shakespeare" that turned out to be a foray into deconstructing the Bard. As in the marketplace, the principle of *caveat emptor* applies in the academy.

The university's hiring practices put a premium on finding and hiring minority and women candidates for teaching posts. In fact, any department can hire an otherwise qualified minority into its faculty at any time, regardless of whether the department has a budget line open for the position. Furthermore, if departments do not hire enough women and minorities to meet "guidelines" (read: quotas), they will find themselves under increasing scrutiny. "If a department were to go through a couple of hiring cycles without hiring a woman or minority candidate, they'd probably start having some budget lines cut," one professor says.

On the other hand, faculty report that they are able to deny tenure to faculty members who don't meet standards of teaching or scholarship, even if they are minorities. "The university will back up departments in getting rid of minority faculty who don't cut it," says a professor. Another professor says, "We once decided to deny tenure to a woman, and she threatened all kinds of legal action. But the administration stood behind our decision." It seems as though the university, although willing to strong-arm departments into hiring women and minorities, is not willing to lower professional standards simply to keep professors who aren't qualified.

The university also seems to be taking the quality of undergraduate teaching more seriously in making decisions about hiring and retaining faculty. The academic professionals are hired and evaluated largely on the basis of their teaching ability. But even regular tenure-track faculty are expected to show evidence of satisfactory teaching. "We used to truly pay lip service to teaching in making tenure decisions," one professor admits. But departments are finding that they can't get away with that anymore. Hiring someone with no teaching experience, or retaining someone with a poor track record of teaching, is proving an increasingly tough sell. "It's harder to hire these days," says one professor, "because we need to find people who really can teach."

In spite of the prevailing liberal culture on campus, many students and faculty see signs of hope. There are certainly radicals in the university, but they have been unsuccessful, so far, at forcing their schemes upon the university as a whole. "I actually take the continual whining of the left here as a good sign," says one professor. "They are pretty much agitating for the same things they were ten years ago, because they aren't getting them." Most of the professors don't use the classroom as a forum for promoting an ideology. "I've never had a professor who tried to indoctrinate us in class," says a junior in LAS, "and I don't know anyone who has, either." In many departments conservative faculty and students can go about their business without fearing reprisals. "I think most of us [department heads] really try to keep our departments balanced, both academically and politically," said one department chair.

Student Life: Beware! Greeks' Bearing Shifts

The University of Illinois is large enough that most students can explore their interests, whether those interests are intellectual, political, or athletic. There are numerous student organizations, ranging from the College Republicans to the Lacrosse Club to the Illini Union Board. The latter organization runs bookstores, organizes concerts, and brings distinguished speakers to the campus. The Student Government Association is large and active, though it tends to throw its weight behind left-wing causes.

The Greek system at Illinois is the largest of any college in the country. There are more than fifty fraternities and sororities, and they "have a big impact on the social life on campus," according to one student. The fraternities and sororities at Illinois have come under fire, though, in recent years. "The fraternities are seen as the locus of a lot of the underage and excessive drinking on campus," says one professor. This has led to some fraternities being placed on probation. In an effort to protect themselves from such disciplinary action — as well as from civil liability — many fraternities are cutting off the tap. "Our house is going dry next year and a lot of other houses have done it already," says a student.

There is also a great variety of religious groups active on campus. A number of churches located near campus serve student congregations, and there is an active Hillel Foundation serving Jewish students in the heart of the campus. "There is a very large religious presence here at U of I," says a campus minister. "There is a substantial Catholic presence at the Newman Foundation, but also wide variety of Protestant organizations, such as Campus Crusade for Christ and Inter-Varsity Fellowship. The university is pretty good at respecting students' religious prerogatives, and professors are pretty good at respecting students' religious perspectives."

About a third of students live in the university's dorms, which range from the stately Georgian architecture of Busey-Evans Hall to the ugly cinder-block boxes of the so-called "Six-Pack." While a few single rooms are available, most students have roommates. If a student does not express a roommate preference on a housing application, the university pairs him up with someone based on major and interests. "The university instituted a 'racially blind' housing policy a few years ago," says one professor. "There is some special programming geared for minority students, but there are no racially or ethnically segregated dorms." By and large, whatever diversity or multicultural programs the university has have been scaled back in recent years, as there is a growing pool of minority applicants who meet standard admission requirements. "There really isn't much in the way of PC nonsense in the dorms," a student reports. Students have the option of living in single-sex halls, and the coed dorms generally place men and women on separate floors.

Illinois is a Big Ten school, and Big Ten football and basketball are very popular with students and alumni of the university. But there are ample opportunities for intramural athletics as well. There are thirty-two tennis courts, thirty-four playing fields, several gyms, an ice arena, and two eighteen-hole golf courses for the athletically inclined.

The oldest part of the campus, known as the Quad, is quite picturesque and park-like. It is surrounded by imposing buildings that house most of the LAS departments. The area surrounding campus, known as Campustown, has many shops, coffeehouses, bookstores, restaurants, and bars. Crime is relatively uncommon at Illinois, though burglaries are not rare and even serious crimes occur now and again. The Krannert Center for the Performing Arts is home to the performing arts programs at Illinois and mounts several theatrical and operatic productions every year, as well as numerous chamber and orchestral performances.

Indiana University–Bloomington

Office of Admissions
300 N. Jordan Avenue
Bloomington, IN 47405-1106
(812) 855-0661
www.iub.edu

Total enrollment: 36,201
Undergraduates: 28,511
SAT ranges (Verbal/Math): 490-600 (V); 490-610 (M)
Applicants: 20,095
Accepted: 81%
Enrolled: 41%
Application deadline: Rolling
Financial aid application deadline: Rolling (March 1 priority)
Tuition: resident: $4,362/$9,970; non-resident: $13,418/$19,026
Core curriculum: No

Back Home Again

Indiana University is in many ways typical of large state research universities. It has many highly ranked programs (and many, many programs, period), attracts lots of capable students, sits in an attractive college town, and has its fair share of ideological silliness. And like other large state research universities, it has all but eliminated any semblance of a core curriculum in favor of minimal distribution requirements.

One can get a very good liberal arts education at Indiana, but it will take some effort. Powerful radical student organizations and an administration receptive to them have done their best to thoroughly politicize the university. In this environment, the sheer heterogeneity of IU's course offerings and the size of the school become advantages. Furthermore, political shenanigans somehow never seem oppressive at IU, for the school has managed to retain, no doubt unwillingly, some of the rural, provincial ethos of its surrounding environment, including its home state's passion for the game of basketball.

And whatever might be going on underneath the surface, the face of the IU campus is serene and inviting. One student speaks for many when she says that "the campus is the best part of IU. Sometimes I look around, despite all the battles we fight, and I am so glad I am here. It is beautiful any time of year, and it has so many great little hideaway spots, either under a tree, or inside the Beck Chapel for a quiet prayer." The natural beauty of the campus and its old, distinctive limestone buildings contribute to a physical atmosphere that is wholly conducive to contemplation and study. An evening stroll through the arboretum, past Dunn Meadow, beside the Union, across the Jordan River, and through the woods along Indiana Avenue is of great restorative value. So is a basketball game.

Academic Life: TOPICS in Shirking Traditional Liberal Arts

There is no core curriculum at Indiana, plain and simple. Indiana defines its commitment to the liberal arts tradition in terms of its consequences — e.g., "intellectual flexibility and breadth of mind," the ability to "think critically and creatively," the development of "historical consciousness," etc. — rather than with respect to any canon or system of studies.

As a result of this approach, there are only three courses that all students are required to take. Even these so-called "TOPICS" courses — one each in the arts and humanities, social and historical studies, and the natural and mathematical sciences — do not constitute a common education for IU students since the various sections of these courses vary widely. TOPICS classes are not survey courses, but are more specialized. They "usually tend to focus on what the professor is currently researching," according to one faculty member.

Beyond this, students must only fulfill certain minimum distribution requirements, including one course each in English composition, intensive writing, and mathematics, two courses in "culture studies," and four courses (or the equivalent) in a foreign language. The enormous flexibility students have in designing their curricula is best reflected in the range of elective hours that can be used to fulfill the graduation requirement — anywhere from seven to sixty-one.

Even a requirement as seemingly straightforward as English composition may be fulfilled in myriad ways: The intensive writing label is tagged on to a number of courses in almost every major, so students need take no special writing course. A two-semester course in Afro-American studies will even do the trick (and will fulfill the culture studies requirement at the same time, incidentally).

In fact, hundreds of courses fulfill the culture studies requirement. Though many of these deal with non-Western cultures, students can also meet the requirement by sticking close to the Western canon, should they so choose. Politicized and trendy courses bearing titles like "Gender, Sexuality, and Popular Culture" and "Rap Music" share eligibility with courses in ancient Greek philosophy, Renaissance art, and Christian literature.

High-scoring entering freshmen may choose to participate in IU's Honors College. This program makes special courses available to honors students, though there is still no core curriculum. Honors students are encouraged to take one honors course per semester. For freshmen, this generally means a two-semester sequence of interdisciplinary seminars called "Ideas and Experience." Both seminars stick pretty close to the traditional canon in the authors and texts presented, with the fall seminar focusing on ancient thought and the spring seminar on modern. Students should be aware, however, that different professors approach these courses in significantly different ways. Other honors courses are a hodge-podge group, including special sections of fundamental courses — e.g., in physics or political science — as well as courses like "Medicine, Magic, and Mortality." Honors students are assigned student mentors to help them adjust to college life and find suitable courses.

IU's academic reputation rests largely upon its Kelley School of Business and the School of Music. IU also has a reputation as an excellent language school; there are no less than thirty-four languages, including Sioux, in which the student may fulfill the foreign language requirement. Elsewhere, it has a number of highly ranked programs (the university's Web site states that there are one hundred programs ranked in various national top twenty lists), some of which are in the liberal arts and sciences. But as usual, rankings can be deceiving. Because of widespread politicization and complacency, few of IU's departments stand out, in any absolute sense, as excellent, and there are virtually no professors at IU who are outspoken defenders of traditional approaches to the liberal arts or the West. (Indiana, for instance, is one of the few states in the union that has no National Association of Scholars affiliate.)

One emeritus professor is somewhat gloomy about the situation, suggesting to IU students, "If you want to get an education, IU has an excellent library." He is right; IU's libraries include nearly six million volumes. However, there are some good, fair professors in the liberal arts whose courses students should seek out. These include Jeffrey C. Isaac in political science; Irving Katz in history; Tim O'Connor in philosophy; Richard M. McFall in psychology; Allen Douglas in West European studies; and Kenneth Johnston and Lewis Miller in English.

Students report that professors are accessible. "I have never heard any stories of students not being able to get in contact with one of their teachers or professors," says one student. Many introductory courses are taught by teaching assistants, especially in the language departments. University statistics indicate that only 21 percent of its courses enroll more than forty students, but to students this seems low. One senior majoring in political science estimates that most of his classes have had about 150 people. Another upperclassman reports that "90 percent of my classes are typically [more than] one hundred students."

Though grade inflation is as big a problem at IU as at most universities, the school has reportedly taken efforts to curb it. One measure has been to print on semester grade reports not only the student's grade but his rank in that class.

Political Atmosphere: If No One Objects,
Are They Really Protesting?

IU has all the ideological bureaucracies of a University of Wisconsin or a University of Michigan. There are special offices for African-American and Latino students. A new Black Culture Center is under construction. The university maintains an "Office of Student Ethics and Anti-Harassment Programs" to deal with transgressing students. Two teams — the "Racial Incidents Team" and the "Gay, Lesbian, & Bisexual Anti-Harassment Team" — are ready to respond to victims of ethnic, racial, or sexual-orientation insensitivity. There is a "Gay, Lesbian, Bisexual & Transgender Student Support Service" that says it works closely with OUT, IU's active — and, students say, powerful — student organization, and so on.

But though IU's administration is in full sympathy with the radical multicultural and diversity agenda, the acrimonious controversies and in-your-face politics that mark other schools are largely absent at IU. Perhaps there is simply no effectual opposition. But whatever the reason, the biggest controversy in the last couple of years surrounded the administration's plans to cut a couple of hundred acres out of a preserve near Griffy Lake to build a championship golf course. The subsequent public protest forced IU to drop its plans, but this is hardly the stuff of deep ideological division. The political atmosphere is "very muted," says one recent graduate. "It seems that the undergraduates there now are not very passionate about anything."

It could be that they're scared. Indiana maintains what one student describes as "a very biased and ridiculous speech code." Actually, the code employs the kind of language typically found in sexual harassment laws and regulations, but it is apparently used as a handy stick with which to threaten certain groups. As a result, many students are careful to watch what they say. "We always said that the walls have ears," says one alumnus. That sentiment is echoed by a current student. "The Christian groups and pro-life groups are often afraid to be active because of the apparent bias against them." And another says that "The university is very active in punishing people for discriminatory speech. There are many offices and groups on campus to enforce" the speech code.

Unofficial enforcement comes from student organizations like OUT and the student newspaper, the *Indiana Daily Student.* "I have heard bizarre stories of people being punished for ridiculous activities simply because the homosexual organizations have pushed for the punishment," writes an undergraduate. "There have also been cases where the gay and bisexual group has actively pushed for the punishment of people simply because they were Greek or Christian. It is ridiculous how powerful this group has become." Indeed, OUT is repeatedly mentioned as a major player on the IU political scene. The strength of OUT at IU is partially explained by the presence of the Kinsey Institute, a very active and outspoken proponent of radical sexual politics.

Whatever role the thought police play in muting political conflict on campus,

IU is also protected somewhat by its status as a Midwestern outpost. "Indiana is still pretty provincial," says a professor. "There is a cultural lag, and that is of some advantage." Indeed, the state of Indiana is conservative enough that legislative pressure can occasionally be used to good effect. A few years ago, IU was forced to abandon its plans to build a Gay, Lesbian, Bisexual, and Transgendered Students Center with public money when concerned students brought the effort to the attention of legislators. (However, the center was subsequently built with funds from a private donation.)

The most politicized departments include English, anthropology and political science. "The English department is unquestionably the worst," says one faculty member. But because of the department's size, this faculty member says, a student can still carve out a good education. Older professors, according to a student, tend to be much less politicized than their younger colleagues. Nontraditional English courses include ones like "College Sports and Student Life," which includes the viewing of classic films and programs like *Animal House, School Daze, Felicity,* and *SportsCenter.* Students report that many political science professors are not afraid to advance their decidedly left-leaning agendas. The history department has also deteriorated in recent years. There is now no one on the faculty specializing in pre–Civil War U.S. history, and in a given semester there are nearly as many courses offered in Latin American history as in Western European or U.S. history. A course entitled "Medieval Sexuality" indicates the direction in which the department is headed:

> By examining the institutions and ideas that dominated the construction of gender in the Middle Ages, this course will illuminate problems such as the cult of virginity, a clerical gay subculture, transvestite saints, and many others. What will emerge is not one, but many 'sexualities.'

The School of Social Work and the School of Public and Environmental Affairs are also known for pushing political agendas. The School of Health, Physical Education, and Recreation offers a course in human sexuality that, according to students, essentially teaches pornography. "Interestingly enough," says one student, it is "one of the most popular classes at IU."

Student Life: Assembly Hall Ball

Bloomington is the ideal college town. Set amidst the pastoral charm of the forested hills and hollows of southern Indiana, Bloomington combines natural beauty with the friendliness and pace of a small town and the cultural advantages of a university city. Or as one professor states, Bloomington "has just the right mix of provincial coherence and sophistication." Cafes, bars, and restaurants on Kirkwood Avenue just west of campus lure both students and professors on evenings and weekends; for those who want the amenities of a larger city, Indianapolis and its thoroughly revitalized downtown is just an hour away. Biking, hiking, and swimming opportunities abound just off campus at Griffy Lake, the Monroe Reservoir, and the Hoosier National Forest. The autumns are stunningly beautiful.

Although students at large schools like Indiana are rarely united by anything, two institutions at IU nearly succeed in making campus unity a reality. The first is the annual Little 500 Bicycle Race — mythologized by the film *Breaking Away* — which captures the campus's attention in April and provides the excuse for the accompanying "World's Greatest College Weekend." (Thanks to the film, every year there is a race entry from the "Cutters.") In recent years authorities have quelled some of the partying surrounding the race, which, in some cases, had begun to degenerate into little more than rioting.

In a state where Larry Bird holds at least quasi-divine status (even though he originally enrolled at IU, Bird left without ever playing for the Hoosiers and went to Indiana State), it is no surprise that the other focus to student life is provided by the men's basketball team, coached for nearly thirty years by that obstreperous poster child for political incorrectness, Bob Knight. After years of seemingly unending controversy, Knight was finally fired by President Myles Brand just as school began in the fall of 2000 — an act that touched off a night of rioting on campus. (The fact that Knight's teams had not achieved as much success of late probably made his behavior all the more unacceptable.) Students will certainly continue to support the team, even though the administration has for years unaccountably refused to create a true student section in Assembly Hall. Showalter Fountain is the traditional meeting place after big victories, especially ones over Purdue. The men's soccer team has had more success than any other program of late, winning the last two NCAA championships. IU offers an abundance of intramural sports opportunities.

As might be expected at a university of this size, there are student organizations to suit every political, social, and religious persuasion, and some to suit persuasions you didn't think existed. Among the radical groups, OUT is extraordinarily active, commandeering the IU Auditorium for the Miss Gay IU pageant in March during Pride Week; the annual gay and lesbian kiss-in in front of Ballantine Hall shocks some students and amuses others. The Animal Defense League exists primarily to harass animal researchers at the university and maintains pictures of its faculty targets on its Web site.

There are plenty of options for more conservative students to get acquainted as well, including College Republicans, IU Students for Life, and a number of religious organizations. (As the university Web site puts it, without a trace of irony, "While attending the university, [students] may wish to continue in the same faith tradition that was theirs at home.") IU also has its full share of fraternities and sororities; as at most schools, the Greeks and the independents tend to be fairly isolated from one another. The Collins Living and Learning Center is the residential center of the school's alternative scene; it is the host site for OUT's "Lesbopalooza."

There are no single-sex dorms, but most dorms split men and women by floors. Coed floors are for upper-class students only and include separate bathroom facilities for men and women. All floors have quiet hours, voted on by residents; certain floors designated as "academic" have stricter hours that are actually enforced. Some dorms have "open" visitation, in which the only restriction is that students not have a member of the opposite sex stay overnight, and students say that even this is rarely enforced. Other dorms have "limited" visitation, in which case guests must leave by midnight on weeknights and by 2 a.m. on weekends. No dorms are officially designated as "substance-free," though some do have no-smoking floors.

Indiana has built an elaborate bureaucratic structure to support its concerted attempt to indoctrinate its dormitory residents. Besides resident assistants, the university employs "CommUNITY Educators (CUEs)" — undergrads whose job it is to plan and present to dorm-dwellers "a variety of educational programs related to issues of diversity, especially issues related to race, gender, religion, sexual orientation, and ability." These CUEs in turn report to "diversity education specialists" who help establish program "goals" and monitor progress toward reaching those goals.

Many students resent this heavy-handed approach. One student reports that he was told, falsely, that he had to attend a special diversity course for his dorm building. "I was just a naïve freshman, and it took me six weeks to figure out that I didn't really have to be there." Another student reports that he too was told he had to attend a floor diversity presentation until he finally became so disgusted that he just walked out, with the rest of the floor behind him.

The mandatory freshman orientation session is the start of what the university attempts to continue in the dorms. The "Commission on Multicultural Understanding" assists the Office of Diversity Programs in designing "a student orientation session that addresses the topics of racism and diversity" as well as "a welcome reception for diverse students." "Freshman orientation is a wake-up call for most incoming freshmen," says one student. "Alternative lifestyle groups are very active during this time to push their agendas on the incoming freshmen."

Both students and professors generally agree that IU's campus is very safe, and the university's official crime statistics generally back this up. "The university has a top notch police force that does a good job of patrolling the campus," a student says. "In the last three years that I have been a student here, the university has made efforts every year to increase lighting on campus, and most students would agree that they feel safe when walking through the campus at night." There is a safety escort service available to anyone who wishes to use it.

University of Iowa

Office of Admissions
107 Calvin Hall
Iowa City, IA 52242
319-335-3847
www.uiowa.edu

Total enrollment: 28,311
Undergraduates: 19,284
SAT ranges (Verbal/Math): 520-660 (V); 540-660 (M)
Applicants: 11,358
Accepted: 83%
Enrolled: 41%
Application deadline: May 15
Financial aid application deadline: As soon as possible after January 1
Tuition: resident: $2,998/$11,628; non-resident: $10,440/$19,390
Core curriculum: No

A Workshop with No Tools

Located in Iowa City, almost four hours from the nearest major cities (Chicago, Minneapolis/St. Paul, and Kansas City), the University of Iowa is not exactly at the center of the cosmopolitan universe; it was once even described by a university geographer as "centrally isolated." But that hasn't stopped it from playing an integral role in the nation's literary life. Flannery O'Connor studied here, for a time, at the famous Writers' Workshop. So did John Irving, Jorie Graham, Andre Dubus, Wallace Stegner, and a number of famous others.

But whether the quality of the typical Iowa undergraduate education even remotely approaches the quality of the Writers' Workshop is debatable at best. For like virtually all state schools, Iowa maintains only an unimaginative, pedestrian set of distribution requirements for its undergraduates; they will not necessarily encounter the great authors and texts of the West — the Bible, Thomas Aquinas, William Faulkner — who helped form the mind of Flannery O'Connor. Nor will they necessarily encounter Flannery O'Connor.

Academic Life: Planning for Other Things

Well, maybe that's not entirely true. After all, Iowa students may notice that there is a Flannery O'Connor Chair in Letters, currently held by poet Marvin Bell. The school's program in creative writing continues to be highly regarded, as do its studio arts and theatre arts programs. The English, history, political science, psychology, and American studies departments are also highly ranked, but though each certainly contains fine faculty, it is well to cast a skeptical eye on such rankings.

For one thing, it is telling that of the five goals in the Liberal Arts College's Strategic Plan for 2000-2005, none involve the improvement of the understanding or knowledge its students have of the liberal arts. In fact, the primary goal is "to articulate . . . a vision of the liberal arts that demonstrates the centrality of our research to our mission." Other goals focus on technology, diversity, interdisciplinary education, and the development of "a culture of collegiality, service, and good citizenship." The college cites its newest major, environmental science, and certificate programs in sexuality studies and medieval studies as examples of recent successes. (Women's studies, American studies, and African American world studies were also recently promoted to full departmental status.)

Iowa does at least have the liberal arts rhetoric down. Calling the liberal arts "education for life," university materials boast that its General Education Program in the liberal arts "aims to develop in every one of our students these enduring qualities that mark a liberally educated person:

- "a lifetime pursuit of personal intellectual growth and a lifetime practice of social responsibility;
- "open-mindedness, tolerance, and the ability to question and evaluate one's own attitudes and beliefs;
- "sufficient general knowledge and proficiencies to adapt to new vocations and new opportunities;
- "the ability to understand and to cope with the complexity and diversity of contemporary life."

However, the university shies away from suggestions that these (mostly) laudable qualities are best gained through a core curriculum. Instead, as it tells its students, "Over the years, liberal arts institutions have shifted from a consensus about a single 'core curriculum' of specific courses, disciplines, and skills to a more pluralistic view of general education." In practice, this translates to a very loose and amorphous set of distribution requirements. Iowa students must complete four to eight hours in rhetoric, demonstrate competency in a foreign language at the fourth-year high school level, take one course in the "Interpretation of Literature," three in "Historical Perspectives," one in the humanities, two in natural sciences, one in "Quantitative or Formal Reasoning," one in social sciences, and two more courses in two of seven areas, one of which is "Cultural Diversity." Iowa is actually a bit behind the curve in not *requiring* a course in the latter area, but slightly ahead of it in the sheer number of categories into which it has fractured its general education requirements.

The potential for politicization is present in many of these requirements. In some, it's encouraged. Rhetoric courses, for instance, are supposed to challenge students "to consider what it means to speak and write as a member of a community — indeed of many communities." The Interpretation of Literature course is supposed to teach students how to read and analyze texts, and it provides a case in point for how a savvy student can negotiate university curricula to obtain a solid education. Each semester brings more than seventy sections of this course, each, depending on the instructor, with a different reading list and approach. Though most of the courses require students to read worthy texts and authors (Shelly's *Frankenstein,* Bradbury's *Fahrenheit 451,* Morrison's *Sula,* and Shakespeare's *Much Ado About Nothing, Hamlet,* and *Romeo and Juliet* appear to be the most popular), the instructor's perspective can alter the value of the course substantially. Students may be asked to read and evaluate texts through the race/gender/class prism; but in other sections they will find these political concerns to be either absent or of comparatively minor concern in relation to the text itself. It all depends on the teaching assistant, since professors don't teach these courses.

Thus, students have extraordinary flexibility in creating their schedules. But apparently Iowa believes that courses in virtually anything it has to offer will endow its students with the liberal qualities it claims that it intends to instill.

Things may be taking a turn for the worse, as Iowa is considering revising the General Education Program in the next several years. Though some suggestions being considered would be beneficial — the creation of "capstone" courses for more majors, better preparation of TAs to teach, and improvement of facilities for teaching (inadequate infrastructure, facilities, and technology is a recurring complaint within the liberal arts college) — another is to ensure that courses in the General Education curriculum support "internationalization and interdisciplinarity, including understanding of issues related to cultural, gender, and ethnic diversity."

As it stands, students can choose from more than fifty undergraduate majors. The most popular are prebusiness, engineering, and preprofessional majors, which reflects the underlying reality that Iowa's focus does not really lie in the liberal arts anyway. As the strategic plan puts it, its aspiration is to "become one of the ten most distinguished public research universities in the nation." No amount of words about a focus on teaching can serve to hide Iowa's primary dedication to research.

The student-faculty ratio is roughly fourteen to one, with 92 percent of undergraduate courses containing fewer than fifty students, and 79 percent fewer than thirty. Most courses are taught by professors, though TAs typically teach discussion sections and, occasionally, introductory courses. As with many schools its size, Iowa has had to face the problem of students not being able to graduate in four years. Thus, if students meet their responsibilities under the school's Four-Year Plan, Iowa may waive remaining course requirements.

Teaching in the social sciences, at least, according to one professor is "generally balanced and free from political/ideological taint," and there are noticeable pockets of strength in the English department. Good professors in the social sciences and elsewhere include Douglas Madsen in political science, Archibald Coolidge and Robert Kelley in English, Bruce Gronbeck in communication studies, and Jason Duncan in history.

Political Atmosphere: Build It and They Might Come

Diversity and its wonderful accoutrements provide a monotonous mantra for the Iowa administration. But the reality gives the extraordinary energy devoted to the "D"-word a "they protest too much" quality. For, though according to the university Web site Iowa is a "haven of diversity," the truth is that the vast majority of students are white (91 percent), or from Iowa and adjoining states (88 percent).

These are, of course, embarrassing facts for many on campus, and there are any number of efforts and initiatives and plans and discussions underway to fix them. The Liberal Arts Strategic Plan calls for the percentage of women on the faculty to increase to 40 percent (from 31 percent) by 2005, as well as for substantial increases in minority hires. And the university's Subcommittee on Diversity Initiatives recently recommended, in its "Report Card on Racial and Ethnic Diversity," that departments that were successful in recruiting and retaining minority students, faculty, and staff be given extra funding. (The report card gives the university only a "D" for its diversity efforts thus far, despite the rhetorical juice devoted to them on campus.) The university also started a sexualities studies program in 1998, for which, along with the beginning of an "Alternative Prom" in 1999 and its first "Rainbow graduation" in 2000, it has been lauded by the Gay Lesbian Bisexual Transgender Union.

The diversity-mongering reaches fever pitch during "Human Rights Week," held the week of Martin Luther King Jr. Day and ostensibly a celebration of his legacy. The 2001 celebration brought Angela Davis to campus as the featured speaker, and included such events as "Journeys through Diversity," a panel discussion with physicians, as well as a fundraiser called "Choice Dinner Celebration," sponsored by a local abortion clinic to help its poorer "clients" pay for abortions. The appropriateness of this particular way of celebrating "human rights" apparently went unquestioned by the Iowa administration, which provided the building and publicity for the event.

The hypersensitivity betrayed by official Iowa is reflected in the overblown reactions students, faculty, and townsmen have to illiberalism. When a series of racist threats, including a bomb threat, were made in early 2000, more than one thousand citizens, students, and faculty gathered for a "walk the walk" march across campus in a show of protest and solidarity. A black dental student was later identified as the source of the threats. Iowa's Vice President Ann Rhodes later cracked, at a news conference, that she had "figured it was going to be a white guy between twenty-five and fifty-five because they're the root of most evil. . . . But what do I know?"

For this, Rhodes was forced to resign from her administrative post, an apt demonstration of the absence of good humor and proportionality apparently endemic in isolated and insular Iowa. This can make for a brand of quaint, leftist provincialism. For example, law professor Marc Linder, claiming to the *Chronicle of Higher Education* that he was acting as part of the "worldwide struggle of science against tobacco capital," has, during the last two years, made numerous noisy complaints about actors' smoking during plays on campus. The university, acting sensibly for once, has not given in to his demands that actors simply act as if they are smoking. And an innocuous message from Students for Bush, asking anyone interested in helping the Bush campaign to contact them and sent with the aid of the university's communications department, was the cause of controversy in late 1999. The university was forced to explain that it had a neutral policy of providing e-mail lists to every organization who asked.

Iowa students joined in the recent wave of anti–sweat shop demonstrations, occupying a hallway outside President Mary Sue Coleman's office to demand that the university sever its ties with the more moderate Fair Labor Association and join the Worker Rights Consortium. The university met the latter demand but not the former.

The English department is predictably politicized in many ways (though not completely by any means). Who would have thought that novels like *The Great Gatsby* and *The Sun Also Rises* would provoke different critical queries than "Where does queer subjectivity fit into the shift from realist to modernist narratives? How are racial politics mutually constitutive with sexual politics in the modern world?" But what do we know? Not all of us have taken "American Novel II: Sex, Gender, and the American Novel."

Iowa's history department may be even worse. Its primary area of strength is in women's history and the "history of gender," which does not bode well for the student interested in ideologically unbiased history. Nine of the department's thirty-one faculty members specialize in women's/gender history, according to the department's Web page, with thirteen courses in these areas available to undergraduates. The department also offers special "diversity sections" for majors.

Every freshmen has the opportunity to take a First Year Seminar Course, small discussion-style courses, though it is not required. These courses have been purposely designed to allow faculty to teach on whatever research they're currently engaged in. The result, not surprisingly, is that these courses tend to be narrowly focused, insubstantial, and often quite politicized offerings. Capped at fifteen students, examples include "Smoke and Mirrors: The Secrets of Big Tobacco" and "Coolies, Commies, and Spies — U.S. Perceptions and Representations of China." On the other hand, it seems that there is usually one course dealing with Shakespeare each term.

Student Life: No, This Is Iowa

Iowa City is a liberal and tolerant place. As one student puts it, the locals "are nice and polite — almost hallucinatorily so," and like to think of their burg as the "Athens of the Midwest." Though the climate is marked by frigid winters and steamy summers, the surrounding environs are hilly and especially beautiful in spring and fall. It is universally regarded as a good place to live.

It's especially good during one's college years. Iowa City has about 60,000 people and is in many ways typical of the Midwestern college town, combining bohemian lifestyles with cosmopolitan outlooks and a thriving cultural scene. Many students "scheme so that they won't have to leave," says one student, who also laments the city's high cost of housing. Iowa's campus and Iowa City are generally safe places, though a comparatively large number of forcible sex offenses (eleven) on campus have been reported for each of the last two years for which statistics are available (1998 and 1999). The university is situated on a 1,900-acre campus along the Iowa River. Its focal point is the Greek-revival Old Capitol, which served as the territorial capitol building from 1842 to 1846. Students are often informed, entertained, or simply harangued by protesters and speakers (e.g., the Jugglers Against Homophobia) on the Pedestrian Mall.

But for all its pretensions to sophistication, Iowa City is still a fairly provincial place, possessing what one student calls a healthy degree of "heartland skepticism. They don't just believe the latest theory to come out of somewhere." As economist Deirdre (formerly Donald) McCloskey noted when explaining her impending move to Chicago, Iowa City "is not a good place to look for a husband," at least for transsexuals.

There are more than 370 different student groups on campus, including many religious ones (e.g., Campus Crusade for Christ, Orthodox Christian Fellowship, Aliber/Hillel Jewish Student Center) as well as more radical ones like the UI Feminist Union, the GraDykes, and the River City Pagan Community. The *Iowan Daily*, the school paper, takes a typically left-of-center perspective; there is no alternative conservative or libertarian student paper. The Gay Lesbian Bisexual Transgender Union is said to get a lot of attention; but on the other hand, it drew a crowd of only thirty to its National Coming Out Day celebration in October 2000.

As mentioned earlier, Iowa's student body is generally made up of kids from Iowa, though a substantial number also come from the Chicago suburbs. They are not generally of the caliber one finds at Iowa's sister Big Ten schools in Wisconsin or Michigan. Roughly 12 percent of the student body joins one of twenty-one fraternities and eighteen sororities. Unlike the dorms, frat houses at Iowa are officially dry, largely in response to an alcohol-related death of a pledge in 1995.

Iowa offers a bunch of social programs during the first weeks of class called "WOW!" which stands for "Weeks of Welcome." Freshmen are not required to live in the dorms, but about 90 percent do. All residence halls are coed, with men and women on separate floors. The halls are not dry; students twenty-one or older can have alcohol in their rooms. Certain special floors have been designated as nonsmoking, and others as "quiet houses" (there are noise restrictions from 7 p.m. to 10 a.m.) for students more interested in books than the typical undergraduate. Marijuana use in Iowa dorms is also reportedly increasing, according to a *Des Moines Register* report in October 2000. By 2001, all residence hall rooms were to have high-speed Internet connections.

Because Iowa is in the Big Ten, it is not surprising that intercollegiate athletics — especially men's football and basketball — play a central role in the identity of the school. Intramural sports are also popular, and bicycling attracts a number of enthusiasts, as it is a sport especially suited to the state's varied and interesting but not-too-steep terrain.

James Madison University

Office of Admissions
James Madison University
Harrisonburg, VA 22807
(540) 568-6147
www.jmu.edu

Total enrollment: 14,814
Undergraduates: 13,668
SAT ranges (Verbal/Math): 540-620 (V); 540-640 (M)
Applicants: 12,980
Accepted: 65%
Enrolled: 36%
Application deadline: January 15
Financial aid application deadline: February 15
Tuition: resident: $4,000/$9,290; non-resident: $9,850/$15,140
Core curriculum: No

Acting Presidential

Thomas Jefferson has the University of Virginia. George Washington has Washington and Lee. And another Founding Father — the drafter of the Constitution and the nation's fourth president — is memorialized in Harrisonburg, Virginia, at what was once a state teacher's college for women.

Harrisonburg, a small town in the Shenandoah Valley between the Blue Ridge and Allegheny Mountains, is home to James Madison University (JMU). Founded in 1908, JMU has undergone tremendous growth in the last twenty-five years and is now a comprehensive, coeducational university with about 15,000 students. *U.S. News and World Report* ranks it as the number-two regional university in the South.

Undergraduates at JMU cite a number of things when asked why they like being there; among them are the friendliness of the student body, the beauty of the Shenandoah Valley, and the many outdoor activities available nearby. Indeed, a ski resort lies about ten miles from campus; hiking trails and campgrounds also abound.

Both inside and outside the university's classrooms, politics plays less of a role than at many other institutions of higher learning. Student and faculty radicals are few at JMU, and most of the students are conservative in outlook and culture. There is considerable wealth at JMU, but one does not have to be wealthy to attend: Virginians pay around $9,000, out-of-staters about $15,000.

James Madison is growing. It has boosted its student enrollment and launched initiatives to improve its instruction and intellectual climate. The university says that 20 percent of its alumni donate money to the school, good enough to rank JMU twenty-seventh in that category, according to *U.S. News*. It's an institution determined to live up to the greatness of its namesake.

Academic Life: Cluster Bombing?

Academic departments at JMU fall into one of five schools: the College of Arts and Letters, the College of Business, the College of Education and Psychology, the College of Integrated Science and Technology, and the College of Science and Mathematics. Students may choose from more than forty majors.

JMU's set of general education requirements were introduced in 1997 to replace something called the "liberal studies requirements," eleven areas in which students had to take a course or two. The new requirements are slightly more complicated and drew many complaints from faculty, who said they were not adequately consulted about the changes, and from students, who preferred the more flexible liberal studies requirements.

Under the new requirements, students take forty-one to forty-three hours of course work designed to ensure that they acquire skills and knowledge that will help them later in life. Students take courses in each of five clusters: "Skills for the 21st Century," "Arts and Humanities," "The Natural World," "Social and Cultural Processes," and "Individuals in the Human Community." Within each cluster, students choose one of several "packages," a cross-disciplinary or sequenced set of courses.

For example, in the "Arts and Humanities" cluster, students might choose a package called "Past Cultures and Modern Perspectives," which requires three courses: "Past Cultures," which includes Mayan and Aztec culture, ancient Rome and Greece, and the medieval and Renaissance periods; "Modern Perspectives," which covers the years from the Enlightenment to early modernity; and "Cross-Cultural Perspectives," a grab bag for East Asian, West African, and Native American studies.

Those three classes complete the requirements for that cluster. It should be noted that the package described above was just a few years ago called "Greek Experience" and included courses in the foundations of Western philosophy, Greek epic poetry, and the Greek culture circa the fifth century B.C.

So while the scheme of the general education program remains a well-intentioned and well-conceived combination of the elements of a core curriculum and distribution requirements, the contents of the clusters require continued scrutiny. As it stands, a student can get out of an institution named for one of our most influential presidents without a course in American history. The gutting of clusters like the dear departed "Greek Experience" makes it less likely that students will graduate with a grounding in the basis of Western culture, as well.

On the positive side, the requirements structure allows students to examine topics in depth across disciplines and are not forced to pick unrelated courses from thick catalogues in order to meet vague distribution requirements. The politicization of the packages varies widely — some include courses obsessing on race, class, and gender that are commonly found at many universities today — so choosing wisely is now at more of a premium than in the past. For those that do, the general education requirements will prove very satisfactory.

In addition to the general education requirements, the university levies a few more requirements based on the type of degree a student is seeking. A bachelor's degree requires a minimum of 120 credit hours; a bachelor of fine arts or a bachelor of music, slightly more. In addition, B.A. students have to master a foreign language at an intermediate level and take a philosophy course of their choosing. The B.S. degree entails courses in math and social science in addition to university-wide requirements.

JMU has an honors program. Entering freshmen who graduated in the top 15 percent of their high school class and scored better than 1,300 on the SAT are eligible to apply for the 180 spots in this program. Both the minimum SAT score and the number of spots available have gone up recently, a good sign. By offering small, special classes and independent study, the honors program seeks to cultivate critical thinking and creative expression.

The university is also home to a famous Shakespeare touring troupe — Shenandoah Shakespeare. Founded and run by JMU English professor Ralph Cohen, the company reinterprets Shakespeare's plays and performs them in two hours, substantially less time than required for most Shakespearean performances, but approximately the running time promised in the text of *Romeo and Juliet*. Actors sing

Elizabethan songs in the text to the tunes of modern songs. In *A Midsummer Night's Dream*, for instance, actors put the Bard's words to the tune of "Strangers in the Night" and the theme from the TV show *Gilligan's Island*. Cohen says such adaptations are precisely what Shakespeare would have wanted: his works were meant to be entertaining and full of topical references. The company was formed entirely of JMU students when it began in 1988, but today, all are professionals.

James Madison's College of Business has a strong reputation among students and faculty. The college offers degrees in international business, hospitality and tourism management, accounting, economics, finance, computer information systems, management, marketing, operations management, and quantitative finance. Business is one of the most popular majors at JMU.

High marks are also given to the psychology department, which offers both bachelor of arts and bachelor of science degrees. In addition, the department offers a five-year program that leads to both a bachelor of science and a master's degree in psychology. The university also runs the Human Development Center, which offers clinical services to the Harrisonburg community and gives students hands-on training.

The university boasts a large music program for those interested in becoming music teachers, industry professionals, performers, or composers. The School of Music gives its students a solid background in the theoretical, historical, and stylistic aspects of music, and sponsors a variety of concerts and recitals throughout the year. JMU is one of the few universities in the nation to offer a minor in "music industry," designed to provide students whose specialties are in other disciplines a chance to explore career opportunities in the entertainment business. Though not connected to the School of Music, the JMU marching band is excellent and has won several national awards.

Outstanding professors at JMU include: Robert Geary in English, Elizabeth Neatrour in Russian language and literature, Mark Usry in business, Stephen Bowers in political science, Lee Congdon in history, and David Kreutzer in economics.

James Madison lacks the highly politicized academic departments that are found in many of the country's so-called leading universities. Students report that, for the most part, professors stick to the subject matter and do not use classrooms as their bully pulpits. However, some political biases do occasionally penetrate some courses. "If you're politically minded, you can tell they're sometimes leaning one way," says a student. "Generally, the professors are pretty open, but it's tough to get into much discussion and get your point across in a class of forty people."

Students say the politics that does creep into the classroom is often in the social sciences and humanities: history, political science, English, economics, sociology. Both liberal and conservative faculty can be found in these fields. "It's pretty even as far as the number of conservatives versus liberals," one student says.

James Madison does offer a minor in women's studies, a field that at other universities tends to be highly politicized, emphasizing victimization and advocating political activism. JMU minors take two introductory women's studies courses and then select four more approved courses from such fields as sociology, history, English, and economics.

Political Atmosphere: Dynastic Change

The current state of JMU owes much to the twenty-seven-year presidency of Ronald Carrier, who stepped down in 1998 and was immediately named the university's first chancellor. Carrier was often accused of empire building for his relentless pursuit of state and private funding, university construction and growth, and regional and national recognition. Say what one will about Carrier's often brash personal style — and according to those familiar with the situation, it has already been said — there is no denying that his efforts are primarily responsible for the university as it stands today.

Carrier survived — indeed, prevailed — through clashes with a number of parties. The leader of the school's honor board took him to court after he reduced the suspension of two students for honor code violations. Carrier won. In 1995, Carrier announced his plan to eliminate the major in physics and fire the university's ten physics professors, a move that was widely seen as retaliation for criticism of the president by members of the department. Six months later, after a group of professors sued him over the plan and the faculty senate approved a resolution saying it had no confidence in his leadership, Carrier changed his mind, and no physics faculty were let go. Carrier was also subpoenaed to testify at the trial of a woman and her boyfriend accused (and later convicted) of killing a man who had allegedly acted as her pimp. According to the defense lawyer, Carrier — as well as two other members of the JMU Board of Visitors, one of them a Rockingham County supervisor — were to have been among the woman's customers. The subpoenas were thrown out by a judge after Carrier and one of the others signed affidavits saying they had no knowledge that would bear on the case, and the defense lawyer was ordered to pay their legal costs.

Carrier was succeeded by Linwood H. Rose, one of his most loyal lieutenants over the years. Rose's inauguration day in September of 1999, however, became the occasion for the continuation of a protest that had begun in April of that year. In April, the University Council, a group of faculty, students, and administrators, had voted down a request to cancel classes on the holiday commemorating the birth of Martin Luther King Jr. When the university cancelled classes for Rose's inauguration, the issue was revived, and more than sixty-five students held a silent protest on the Quad, the main lawn at JMU. The protest also attracted an assortment of other student activist groups, but remained peaceful and had no real disruptive effect on the ceremonies.

"I hadn't thought of this before, but one of Mr. Madison's Bill of Rights was the

387

right to freedom of speech and the right to make your feelings known," a university spokesman told the student paper, *The Breeze*. "It's certainly not unusual on a college campus that people make their feelings known, and I thought the demonstration was very orderly. I commend the group for that."

The university does address some of the protestors' concerns via a Center for Multicultural Student Services, which, according to its Web site, "serves to encourage students of color to achieve and maintain academic excellence, . . . in making a successful . . . adjustment to university life, to serve as a liaison between students and the university administration, and to act in the role of ombudsperson in resolving issues of concern for students of color." The center has also brought to campus an assortment of liberal speakers, including Julian Bond, Kweisi Mfume, Spike Lee, and Winnie Mandela.

The university's student body is around 5 percent black and 11 percent minority overall. Administrators, including Rose prior to his ascendance to the presidency, have said they would like to increase the percentage of minority students at JMU but that, lamentably, they receive too many applications from whites. "It's a real struggle to try and promote the notion of diversity," Rose said several years ago. "We have an applicant pool that is more homogeneous than we would like to have."

Enrollment at JMU has risen substantially in recent years. A total of 14,814 students were enrolled in the fall of 1999, up from 11,539 just five years earlier. About 3,500 of the new slots were for undergraduates. Some students complain that the availability of classes has not kept pace with the number of students, and as a result, it has been increasingly difficult to enroll in classes required to graduate.

With an eye toward improving health and information sciences, JMU has particularly been developing the College of Integrated Science and Technology, which graduated its first class in 1997 and whose buildings (architecturally underwhelming, it should be noted) are separated from the older main campus by Interstate 81.

Student Life: Oh, Shenandoah

JMU's 472-acre campus in Harrisonburg is located in Virginia's beautiful and historic Shenandoah Valley. Although a small town (population of about 35,000), it's the center of commerce and travel for the surrounding area. Three other institutions of higher education are also located in or near Harrisonburg: Eastern Mennonite University and Seminary, Bridgewater College, and Blue Ridge Community College. Besides education and tourism, the area is known for its poultry industry. Harrisonburg is about a two-hour drive from Washington, Richmond, and Roanoke, and it's just off an interstate highway.

Harrisonburg is near Shenandoah National Park and Skyline Drive to the east, and the George Washington National Forest to the west. The city's downtown was gutted twenty-five years ago when the Valley Mall opened east of town, but is now staging a comeback. An old Woolworth's store on Court Square was converted to a small theater for mostly independent movies and live performances as well as a good restaurant and microbrewery. An old furniture store on the square was converted to a JMU residence hall, and a number of small shops and dining establishments depend on student support.

The crime rate in Harrisonburg is low and students should consider themselves fairly safe but should also take the normal precautions. However, area law enforcement officers had to don riot gear to break up a large party near campus at the start of the 2000-2001 school year. A handful of students were arrested for failing to leave the scene or for throwing bottles and other debris at the line of officers. The incident further strained relations between students and city residents, who have long complained that students litter and otherwise disrupt the neighborhoods around campus.

Around 15 percent of JMU students belong to fraternities or sororities, but the Greeks do not dominate the social scene. Much more common than frat parties are smaller get-togethers in students' rooms, or jaunts off campus to a bar. Students report no excessive pressure to drink at parties and plenty to do that does not involve alcohol. Still, university police average about 130 alcohol-related arrests per year.

The university has thirty dormitories, some of which contain suites for up to six people. There are women-only dorms, but none solely for men. JMU has a few substance-free halls and international halls. There is a housing shortage on campus, and the university has in recent years had to lease rooms in local motels for students. A number of older students live near campus in several massive banks of privately owned town houses.

JMU has many different clubs and activities in which students can participate. The student newspaper, the *Breeze,* is published twice weekly. An impressive number of religious groups are available, including gospel choirs, prayer groups, and organizations for all different kinds of denominations. There's even a break-dancing club, designed to practice and promote the dancing craze of the mid-1980s.

The most prominent groups on campus are the student government association and the College Republicans, which claims to have more members than any other political group at the university. They sponsor forums and debates on current political issues. The student government has an active multicultural committee that plans activities designed to "raise awareness" of minority women on campus, but otherwise seems dedicated to a wide range of student concerns.

Radical groups include Harmony, the gay and lesbian association; Earth, a liberal environmental organization; and the Young Democratic Socialists of America, which describes itself as a "feminist, anti-racist, democratic, Socialist organization." Its issues include "fighting the militaristic and homophobic ROTC on campus" and "taking on the racist [Immigration and Naturalization Service]." The organization's Web page includes photos of Karl Marx.

The Socialists got into trouble recently when several members went into a local clothing store and surreptitiously (and illegally) stuffed propaganda into the pockets of all the pairs of Guess? jeans. In their defense, the Socialists claimed that Guess? uses exploitive labor practices. In recent years, they have also held a Mr. and Mrs. Sweatshop contest, won by Nike's Phil Knight and Disney's Minnie Mouse. In keeping with that, the group disrupted a Disney recruitment meeting on campus and chalked messages around campus saying "Disney uses sweatshops in Haiti."

Though these liberal groups may sound popular, students say their memberships are small and incestuous. Overall, the student body at JMU is conservative.

JMU fields teams in twenty-seven intercollegiate sports, but is considering cutting eight of them — tennis, archery, and gymnastics for both men and women, along with men's wrestling and swimming. The school sponsors approximately forty intramural sports as well as sports clubs.

Johns Hopkins University

Office of Admissions
The Johns Hopkins University
140 Garland Hall
34th and Charles Streets
Baltimore, MD 21218
(410) 516-8171
www.jhu.edu

Total enrollment: 5,230
Undergraduates: 3,904
SAT ranges (Verbal/Math): 620-730 (V); 660-760 (M)
Applicants: 9,495
Accepted: 33%
Enrolled: 32%
Application deadline: January 1
Financial aid application deadline: February 1
Tuition: $24,930/$33,115
Core curriculum: No

Research Opportunities

Johns Hopkins was founded in 1876 as a research institution modeled on nineteenth-century continental European universities, which emphasized research and scholarship at the advanced level. According to a current college catalogue, Johns Hopkins still considers itself loyal to its founding vision as "a graduate university with an associated preparatory college, a place where knowledge would be created and assembled, as well as taught."

Thus, although they outnumber graduate students by over two to one, undergraduates may continue to feel like something of an afterthought at Hopkins, where the emphasis is still largely on graduate research and faculty scholarship. As one cynical graduate student puts it: "Undergrads bring in revenue."

Still, the university's traditional strengths in research and scholarship can work to an undergraduate's advantage. As the university proclaims in its undergraduate handbook, the faculty's "involvement as leaders in their professional fields cannot help but benefit their students." And unlike most universities, where such claims usually translate into distant faculty who are uninterested in undergraduate life, this is often not the case at Hopkins. "One of the best things about Hopkins is the opportunity for research," a student says. "It is very easy to get started on top-notch projects. My ex-roommate, a mechanical engineer, walked down to the med school one day and started doing robotics research the next day. A year later, the person he was working for left and he took over the project — as an undergraduate."

Academic Life: Distribution Blues

Johns Hopkins comprises eight degree-granting divisions: Arts and Sciences, Engineering, Medicine, Hygiene and Public Health, Nursing, the Peabody Conservatory of Music, the School of Advanced International Studies, and the School of Continuing Studies. In addition to requirements for their major, students in Arts and Sciences must complete a fairly broad and unstructured set of distribution requirements. All students must take four writing-intensive courses. In addition, humanities and social science majors must take a total of thirty credits in natural sciences (N), mathematics or other quantitative studies (Q), humanities (H), social or behavioral sciences (S), and engineering (E), excluding the category for their major (H or S). At least twelve of these credits must be in the N, Q, or E categories, in any combination.

This loose set of requirements could hardly be considered a core curriculum; indeed, an undergraduate majoring in history could conceivably fulfill them by taking twelve credits in engineering and graduate without any courses in mathematics or the natural sciences. Students interested in pursuing a liberal arts education will thus have to structure their own program by carefully surveying the courses that satisfy the distribution requirements and selecting those that appear to correspond to the traditional categories of a core curriculum, such as "Science in the Western Tradition: The Rise of Modern Science" or "Introduction to Greek Philosophy."

Some solid programs still exist in the humanities and social sciences, although many disciplines have become increasingly politicized. Political science is considered strong, and the department administers an excellent program in international studies. Advanced students in this program may be able to avail themselves of Hopkins's Paul H. Nitze School of Advanced International Studies (SAIS) for a semester. Located in downtown Washington, D.C., the SAIS campus is primarily for graduate study and emphasizes foreign languages, international law, and diplomacy. Courses in international relations are also offered through Hopkins's campus in Bologna, Italy.

History, it is said, still retains some good faculty. However, the English department is awash in the latest theoretical trends; in the current listing of faculty interests, over a third cite "critical theory" among their specializations. Science and engineering, including pre-med, are strong disciplines at Hopkins. The university has an innovative FlexMed program for entering medical students that offers flexible options regarding admission so that students can pursue "one-of-a-kind, individual learning experiences" such as research, study abroad, or service work between their undergraduate and advanced medical studies. The university's program in biomedical engineering also has an excellent reputation.

The highly politicized areas of study at Hopkins are the recently established Program in Comparative American Cultures and the Institute for Global Studies in Culture, Power, and History, which offers a minor in multicultural and regional studies. The Humanities Center, which administers an Honors Program in Humanistic Studies, also appears to be in the grip of current ideological trends. While the Humanities Center announces that "the coordinated study of Western civilization through its literature, art, philosophy, and history has been one of the oldest continuing concerns at Hopkins," the center's primary concerns are "comparative literature, intellectual history, and feminist theory," and it offers such "advanced" undergraduate courses as "Trauma and Feminism: The Case of Multiple Personalities."

Advising at Hopkins is thought to be fair, and although faculty are frequently preoccupied with research endeavors, many make themselves available to their students. Graduate students, according to one student, are not routinely used to teach undergraduates, perhaps because their own emphasis is on research and scholarship. Bright students may find themselves sharing courses with graduate students at the upper level, and qualified humanities students can participate in honors programs in comparative literature and intellectual or cultural history.

Because of its prime location in the greater D.C. area, Hopkins students have ready access to world-class research and curricular opportunities. Students can easily avail themselves of the resources at the Library of Congress, the Folger Shakespeare Library, and numerous other area libraries. Closer to home, the Hopkins library facilities are described as "excellent" by one student, who also praises their electronic resources. "The library was just recently renovated," notes another, "and if they don't have something you need, they will get it for you through interlibrary loan."

The average Hopkins student is extremely intelligent and hardworking. One student has noticed that "some students here have a chip on their shoulder because they're not at an Ivy League school." Whether or not they compare themselves to Ivy Leaguers, it's clear that most Hopkins students spend more time at the library than at the local bar.

Political Atmosphere: To Each His Own

The political climate at Hopkins appears to be in constant flux, with a lingering core of traditional faculty being rapidly replaced by more liberal and activist professors, and a moderate undergraduate student body existing alongside a contingent of radical graduate students. According to one student, "The undergraduates tend to be much more conservative than the graduate students." And in general, notes another, "politics do not enter the vocabulary of many of the students. They are too busy studying."

Most members of the administration appear to have little interest in undergraduate liberal education. One professor refers to senior administrators as "faceless bureaucrats," and laments that the two presidents preceding the current officeholder, William R. Brody, "had no serious educational interests." Brody, by contrast, has moved his family on campus, and some have interpreted this as a sign that he is serious about his leadership of the university. "He may even have a philosophy of education," says one hopeful faculty member.

Increasingly, faculty members at Hopkins are becoming warriors in the ideological battles gripping American higher education — especially in the humanities, where the qualification of strong scholarship all too frequently translates into the hiring of professors engaged in politicized study. Older faculty members lament the loss of collegiality among the faculty, and complain that there is very little conversation among members of the same department, let alone across disciplines. Speaking of the gradual demise of the Hopkins Faculty Club, one professor notes that it once "played an academic role. . . . You learned things. You got new ideas. You got perspectives on what you were doing. That's not true anymore, and that's a loss. We don't really have a community anymore." Another says (in an article in the *Chronicle of Higher Education*) that "things that are associated with the university as an entity have lost their appeal. The Hopkins spirit is not a real entity. It doesn't exist anymore."

The reasons for this decline of collegiality are numerous: Younger faculty are more interested in pursuing their own scholarship than in exchanging ideas with

393

other professors, and often view faculty gatherings as elitist and unproductive. As one professor notes, newer faculty "are pressed for publishing rather than perishing, and they don't want to be distracted from their pursuit of professional advancement." A junior member of the English department echoes this cynical and utilitarian sentiment: "What one cares most about is being evaluated on one's work. . . . It's much harder for women and minority faculty members to come into a university and be socially incorporated than to be professionally incorporated. . . . You shouldn't require that someone be socially graceful in addition to being very good in their field." Such attitudes have only further devastated an already flagging social and intellectual environment at Hopkins.

As at similar institutions of higher learning, tenure at Hopkins appears to be dictated primarily by publications and research potential rather than teaching ability. And, along with a growing number of universities in our litigious society, Hopkins has found itself embroiled in legal battles over tenure disputes in recent years. A couple of years ago the university was sued by two members of the medical faculty, husband and wife Samuel Ritter and Rebecca Snider. Drs. Ritter and Snider were recruited by Hopkins and left their tenured posts at Cornell and Duke, respectively, with the understanding that they would be granted tenure. Dr. Ritter was denied tenure after both the dean of the school and the school's promotions committee recommended him for it. The couple was awarded $822,844 by a Maryland circuit court, but lost in appeals court, according to the *Chronicle of Higher Education*. The case points up the ad hoc manner in which tenure proceedings are frequently conducted in higher education.

Hopkins hosts numerous special-interest groups, including the Diverse Sexuality and Gender Alliance and Students for Environmental Action, as well as chapters of College Democrats and College Republicans. Regarding campus politics, one student says that "the most politically sensitive issues have been with the gay and lesbian community and the black students organization." The campus student weekly, the *News-Letter*, is considered politically balanced, although it ran afoul of student groups a few years ago after printing a political cartoon considered derogatory to Chinese people.

In general, most of the media attention Hopkins gets is incidental to the political atmosphere of the institution, in contrast to other universities where controversies usually arise out of the radical campus climate. The shooting death of a student by a member of the campus Republican group a few years ago, as well as the tenure dispute of Dr. Ritter, could have happened on any university campus and do not denote any particular political excesses of the students or administration at Hopkins. Indeed, if anything, the undergraduate student body is moderate to conservative, and perhaps one of the few advantages to the lack of a cohesive undergraduate environment is the comparative political apathy of Hopkins students. Learning is thus much easier in a climate relatively free from the activism and multicultural "sensitivity" so prevalent on other college campuses.

Student Life: Studying Wins

Homewood, the main campus of Johns Hopkins, is located on 140 acres in a residential area of Baltimore on the former estate of Charles Carroll Jr., son of the signer of the Declaration of Independence. One student likens the campus to "a little postage stamp." Another comments that "the campus is small — one could walk across it in ten minutes. It is also very pretty, especially in the spring." The east side of campus is what one student calls a "student ghetto," while to the west is a working-class neighborhood bordered by a park and wooded area. In addition to the wealth of cultural opportunities available down the freeway in Washington, D.C., Baltimore offers more than enough to keep students off of Interstate 95. The impressive Baltimore Art Museum is on the edge of the campus. Other prime cultural venues include the Walters Art Gallery and the Peabody Conservatory of Music. The city's Inner Harbor area alone, with fine restaurants, bars, shopping, and the National Aquarium — not to mention Camden Yard and PSINet Stadium, where the Orioles and Ravens play, respectively — may include all the options a student needs.

Hopkins requires freshmen and sophomores to live in residence halls. These coed halls typically house men and women on the same floor (shared bathrooms are the norm). The university also owns a number of apartments, homes, and row houses, which it makes available to upperclassmen. Students can usually find reasonably priced non-university rentals in the neighboring area. Campus safety is a perennial issue, with crimes ranging from petty theft to rape. The university has established several safety measures to reduce the risk of crime, such as an evening escort service to places like the library and a shuttle to convey students to off-campus locations.

Decades of emphasis on research and scholarship have not aided Hopkins in the establishment of a sense of community among students and faculty. "There's not much undergraduate or graduate social life," laments one student. When asked to characterize the social climate of the university, another student says, "Hopkins, summed up in a nutshell, is a place where students spend most of their time studying. Studying has a higher priority than anything else — social life generally takes a backseat." There is a Greek system at the university — if one sorority and two fraternities qualify as a "system" — though it "is not emphasized," according to one student.

More than ninety social, cultural, religious, athletic, and related student groups exist at Johns Hopkins. Religious groups range from the Hopkins InterVarsity Christian Fellowship to the Zen Meditation Society. "Cultural clubs organize events often," according to one student. The university is home to scores of ethnic and cultural associations, ranging from the Association of Thai Students to the European Students Union. There are also numerous activity clubs for everything from chess to bicycling.

Athletics have not traditionally been a focus of extracurricular life, though one student says "sports are gaining ground across the board." Lacrosse is enormous, and the university is home to the Lacrosse Hall of Fame. Until recently men's lacrosse was the university's only Division I sport, but it will soon be joined by women's lacrosse. Men's and women's swimming and men's fencing are also traditionally strong, and field hockey, water polo, and men's soccer have grown in recent years as well. But as with most nonacademic concerns at Hopkins, student interest in athletics remains relatively low. "As an athlete," notes one student, "one complaint I have always had is the lack of interest of the Hopkins community in athletic events. Only a small percentage of the population attends events — they would rather spend it in the library. It's a shame since many of our teams are doing well."

Kenyon College

Dean of Admissions
Ransom Hall
Kenyon College
Gambier, OH 43022-9623
(800) 848-2468
www.kenyon.edu

Total enrollment: 1,550
Undergraduates: 1,550
SAT ranges (Verbal/Math): 610-710 (V); 580-690 (M)
Applicants: 2,420
Admitted: 68%
Enrolled: 28%
Application deadline: February 15
Financial aid application deadline: February 15
Tuition: $26,080/$30,450
Core curriculum: No

Into (and Out of) the Woods

"The first of Kenyon's goodly race/Was that great man Philander Chase." Thus begins Kenyon historian George F. Smythe's charming song telling the history of

Kenyon College, the oldest private institution of higher education in Ohio. Chase, an educator and the first Episcopal minister in Ohio, envisioned not just a college, but a college in the European traditions of curriculum and architecture — and this was in 1824, when Ohio was not far from the new nation's frontier. Chase collected donations from English lords (including Lord Kenyon and a Lord Gambier, for whom Chase named the college and the village next to it, respectively) and built the first Collegiate Gothic buildings in America — along with a program of classical education. Early notable graduates included Edwin M. Stanton, who was Lincoln's secretary of war; Supreme Court Justices David Davis and Stanley Matthews; and President Rutherford B. Hayes.

While it might seem impossible that that a classic college could thrive in 1824 among the uncut woods of Ohio, the roughness of the frontier was less of a distraction to Kenyon's commitment to education than the wildness of today's academic front lines. But more recent graduates — actor Paul Newman, birth-control-pill developer Carl Djerassi, and late Swedish prime minister Olaf Palme, to name a few — received much the same quality of education as did the alums who'd gone before. In that regard, Kenyon has helped to tame two hostile borders in the last 175 years. Its intellectual atmosphere remains as peaceful and idyllic as the surrounding countryside has become.

Academic Life: Grand Kenyon

Kenyon has no core curriculum, opting instead for the less rigorous "distribution" requirements that have become common throughout the country. All students must take one full unit (two semesters) of course work in each of the College's four academic divisions: fine arts, humanities, social sciences, and natural sciences. Working with a faculty advisor, students may choose any courses within each division to meet the distribution requirement. "We believe this offers the 'best of both worlds,' in that there is sufficient structure so that students will be broadly educated, and they still have a great deal of freedom in planning their own program," the college says in admissions materials. Thus Kenyon's notion of the liberal arts focuses more on students becoming "well-rounded" than on passing on a specific body of knowledge that should be common to all students. According to the college, "A loose structure of diversification requirements for the bachelor's degree, along with more focused coursework requirements within individual majors, fosters both breadth and depth of study." This seems on par with saying that to get the best view of the universe, one should only use a telescope and a microscope.

Next year the college will add a one-year foreign language requirement (for those students who cannot demonstrate the equivalent proficiency), as well as a one-course "quantitative reasoning" requirement. (The latter is not necessarily a math course. A social science course in understanding statistical data would suffice, for example.) Each student must also take at least eighteen semester-long courses from an area outside his major. Students may choose either a departmental major (chemistry, French, etc.), an interdisciplinary major (such as international studies or molecular biology), or a "synoptic" (self-designed) major. Approximately 20 percent of students choose a double major or design a synoptic major.

Kenyon does have a concentration called the Integrated Program of Humane Studies (IPHS), which is like a miniature Great Books program without the standing of a major. Instruction in the IPHS consists of small seminars and individual tutorials, with a minimum of lectures. The program is popular and highly regarded; each year sixty to seventy students in the incoming class of about 425 choose the IPHS.

Although Kenyon may have succumbed to the national reluctance to adopt a core curriculum, like most other small liberal arts colleges it shows an admirable concern for teaching its undergraduates. The current teacher-student ratio is ten to one. Average class size for introductory courses is twenty-two, and you can expect around sixteen students in upper-division courses. Since Kenyon is such a small, close-knit environment, there is ample opportunity for students to interact with their professors outside of the classroom. (As one professor puts it, "What else are we going to do here?") Teaching assistants do not teach introductory courses, although native speakers (technically TAs) work with the daily lab sections of language courses.

But while Kenyon's faculty maintains an admirable focus on teaching, some of the other disturbing academic trends in American higher education have established beachheads in Gambier. Grade inflation "is rampant, and has been for quite a while," says a professor. "It hasn't reached the utterly absurd proportions of some coastal schools, but it is a problem. . . . The fact that we have for the first time instituted student evaluations of courses as a part of a professor's review dossier will surely not help."

Outstanding professors at Kenyon include: Harry M. Clor, Fred E. Baumann, Pamela K. Jensen, Kirk R. Emmert, Devin A. Stauffer, and Steve E. Van Holde in political science; Perry Lentz, Timothy B. Shutt, Sergei Lobanov-Rostovsky, Jennifer S. Clarvoe, Adele S. Davidson, and Judy Rae Smith in English; David E. Harrington in economics; Scott Cummings and Rosemary Marusak in chemistry; Carolin Hahnemann in classics; Roy Wortman and Reed Browning in history; Andrew W. Pessin, Juan E. De Pascuale, and Joel F. Richeimer in philosophy; John J. Macionis in sociology; and Paula C. Turner in physics.

The strongest departments include political science, English, and economics, as well as drama and the fine arts. Sciences are good and improving rapidly, and philosophy has also "come on powerfully in recent years" according to one professor. Many of the best departments are also the most popular; English, history, political science, psychology, economics, and biology graduate the most majors.

The English department initially gained fame in the 1940s and 50s under the leadership of the famed Southern Agrarian poet and literary critic John Crowe Ransom. Poet Robert Lowell left Harvard to study with Ransom, and graduated from

Kenyon in 1940. Other famous graduates from this period include poet James Wright and novelists E. L. Doctorow and William Gass. Ransom founded the department's nationally renowned literary journal, the *Kenyon Review.* In both its public relations and recruitment materials, Kenyon highlights the English department's distinguished literary history. However, the New Criticism espoused by Ransom (who actually coined that phrase) has all but disappeared from the department, with recent faculty hiring tending towards postmodernism and non-Western literature. And yet, though one finds occasional odd courses like "Film as Text" and "Queer Shakespeare," the department still boasts an outstanding selection of traditional courses. Indeed, the English department's biggest problem is that its popularity means courses are in high demand and are sometimes crowded or already closed when students attempt to register for them.

Political science is another highly regarded department at Kenyon, both for its faculty and its commitment to the traditional liberal arts. A perfect example of this commitment is the department's year-long introductory seminar, "The Quest for Justice," which features readings from Plato, the Bible, Aquinas, Hobbes, Machiavelli, the American Founders, and many more.

The history department, meanwhile, has long had a reputation for being the most politicized department on campus, even though it had a considerable number of good teachers. But a "recent civil war there has come out, as far as I can see, with the good guys winning and a renewed concern for standards and the traditions of academic freedom," according to one Kenyon professor.

Political Atmosphere: The Important Things

An atmosphere of civil debate and discussion reigns at Kenyon. This has allowed the college to largely avoid the worst effects of emphasizing multiculturalism and diversity. "Overall I have no doubt that the political atmosphere on campus is very good, certainly better than I've ever known it," one professor says. The school did fight in the wars over political correctness in the 1980s, but since then, according to faculty, the institution has moved back to more traditional understandings of scholarship, civility, academic freedom, and standards. "I'm very proud of [Kenyon] right now," says one professor, "allowing for all the necessary effects of the general climate of academia." This positive environment starts with good leadership at the top, and Kenyon's president, Robert Oden, is widely respected among the faculty and students as a true champion of the liberal arts and of intellectual diversity.

According to faculty, politics play little or no role whatsoever in decisions over hiring and tenure. Neither faculty members nor students seem to suffer any noticeable ostracism for their political beliefs. A minimal speech code is on the books, largely concerning ethnic slurs, though apparently no one ever really gets charged. A joint committee of faculty and staff handles grievances under the code.

The college does feature a multicultural center, as well as the expected array of ethnic student groups (Black Student Union, etc.) and race-based scholarship programs. In the past few years, there has been an increased emphasis on "diversity" — though the college is quick to point out that it promotes diversity not through the traditional category of race, but through "geography, economics, religious backgrounds, talents, and experience." After what the administration describes as a "strong effort to increase racial diversity," black, Hispanic, and Asian students now make up 12 percent of the school's enrollment.

Several other groups exist to promote "sensitivity" to ethnic, religious, gender, and racial stereotypes. Among these are the Women's Network, the "Racial Awareness Program" for freshmen, and Allied Sexual Orientations, which (according to the college) "raises consciousness" on issues of sexual orientation. During the 1999-2000 school year, the latter group held "OutFest '99." "We sang, we danced; we shouted, and spoke obscene sexual messages. A great time was had by all," says the group's Web page.

Kenyon also has its share of borderline courses, which are found almost exclusively in the humanities departments like sociology and anthropology. Current examples include "Women, Crime, and the Law," "Race, Ethnicity, and American Law," "Gender Stratification," and the aforementioned "Queer Shakespeare." But even these might be considered run-of-the-mill at other schools, while at Kenyon, they are the rare exceptions to an otherwise solid intellectual atmosphere.

Student Life: No Philandering Here

Gambier, Ohio, is considered the smallest college town in America — its 650 citizens are badly outnumbered by the 1,550 Kenyon students. The location, between Columbus and Cleveland, is rural and quiet. Philander Chase chose this place to remove his students from the influences of cities and villages, where there were "persons who find it in their interest or malicious pleasure to seduce young men from their studies into vice and dissipation." In this sense, Chase succeeded beyond his wildest dreams: vice and dissipation must rank approximately 251st and 252nd in a hypothetical list of things to do in Gambier.

The setting of the campus itself is beautiful. Its eight hundred acres are integrated with the town and sit on a height of land surrounded by cornfields and wooded hills, with a river curving close by. A wide walkway called the Middle Path runs the length of the campus, traversing the village of Gambier and serving as a communal anchor. The lovely Gothic buildings are the first example of Collegiate Gothic architecture in America. One of these buildings, Pierce Hall, noted for the soaring beams, stained glass windows, and massive oak tables of its dining room, houses offices for student groups, as well as Philander's Pub, a popular student eatery located on the lower level. The other centrally located campus building is the

Gund Commons, which houses a second dining hall, a large space for dances and parties, a lounge with billiards and ping-pong, and a twenty-four-hour study area. Elsewhere, the Red Door Cafe serves as the requisite campus coffeehouse.

Kenyon takes seriously the concept of a "residential college": all students are required to live in college housing (unless they are married or older than thirty), and to participate in the college dining plan. After their freshman year, groups of up to ten students may elect to live together. There are thirteen residence halls and four groups of apartments. One residence hall is reserved for women; the others are coed. Some dorms do not divide men and women by floor, but they always maintain separate bathrooms for each sex.

Juniors and seniors may live in campus residences as part of officially recognized organizations, which include fraternities and sororities. Recently, there have been rather quiet discussions on campus about fraternities' alleged insensitivity toward women. "The remarkable thing about this is that some of the feminist students have begun to challenge the men to live up to their professions of gentlemanliness and, not surprisingly, when it is put that way, the fraternities have begun to respond," a professor says. "This seems very hopeful to me."

Off-campus entertainment options are limited unless one is talking about *way* off campus. Columbus, the nearest big city, is one hour away. Mt. Vernon, a nearby town of about 15,000, features "a great Chinese restaurant, a new six-screen theater, shopping, and any fast-food franchise you can imagine," according to the school's admissions materials. While this may not get one's heart pumping, it's important to also recognize another advantage of being located in a small, quiet, rural town: Crime at Kenyon is virtually nonexistent. However, the college does have a Safety and Security Office, and asks its students to take the usual common-sense precautions when walking at night and so forth.

The majority of students — 40 percent of the most recent arriving class — are Midwesterners, with about a quarter of them home grown in Ohio. But Kenyon's fine programs and reputation also attract a substantial number of students from all regions of the country. All fifty states are represented, as are twenty-five foreign countries. Female students, who weren't even admitted until thirty years ago, now outnumber male students 55 percent to 45 percent.

Though Kenyon was founded under the auspices of the Episcopal Church, it is not a particularly religious campus. There is an Ecumenical Board of Campus Ministries, which includes Roman Catholic and Jewish chaplains. Episcopal students are welcomed by the local parish, which is nearly as old as the college itself. Many religious services are held in the college's historic Church of the Holy Spirit, built in 1869. Student religious groups include the Christian Fellowship, Hillel, the Newman Club, and various other Buddhist, evangelical Christian, and Muslim organizations.

In addition to these groups, Kenyon boasts more than 150 student clubs and organizations, including academic fellowships, service groups, ethnic societies, and performing troupes. Athletics have played a large role at Kenyon since 1859, when the college's first baseball team was formed. Twenty-two varsity teams currently compete at the NCAA Division III level, including the powerhouse swimming and diving teams, of which the school is justifiably proud. The men's team — the "Lords" — has won an amazing twenty-one consecutive national titles (the longest championship streak in any sport, in any division, in the NCAA), and the women — the "Ladies" — have won seventeen in a row. Kenyon also offers a full variety of club and intramural athletic teams.

Kenyon features several examples of the kind of tradition you can only get at a small school. For example, during Senior Week, members of the senior class take on the faculty in a spirited game of softball. During orientation, each entering class of students gathers on the steps of Rosse Hall to sing Kenyon songs, and four years later the graduating members of the class gather on the same steps to sing on the afternoon preceding their commencement.

Lafayette College

Office of Admissions
Lafayette College
118 Markle Hall
Easton, PA 18042
(610) 330-5100
www.lafayette.edu

Total enrollment: 2,283
Undergraduates: 2,283
SAT ranges (Verbal/Math): 560-650 (V); 600-690 (M)
Applicants: 5,038
Accepted: 40%
Enrolled: 28%
Application deadline: January 1
Financial aid application deadline: February 1
Tuition: $22,929/$30,035
Core curriculum: No

Historical Attractions

In 1832, the citizens of the small industrial town of Easton, Pennsylvania, saw one of their dreams come to fruition — the establishment of a college dedicated to the study of "Military Science with the course of Literature and General Science pursued in the Colleges of our Country." They had started their labor back in 1824, and the college's catalogue notes that due to popular excitement over the farewell tour of the Marquis de Lafayette, the Revolutionary War hero, the founders named their nascent college in his honor.

At the time, Easton was a thriving industrial center, thanks to its proximity to the Lehigh and Delaware rivers, as well as a number of canals and railroads. As northeastern Pennsylvania became heavily involved in anthracite coal production, and then later as that industry declined, Easton found it necessary to reinvent itself — and it is now perhaps best notable for its many historical attractions, ranging from the National Canal Museum and a number of local historical exhibits.

Like Easton, Lafayette College has also done a bit of reinventing, in order to stay current with the times — but many of its old focuses haven't changed. Like the town, the college is notable for its historical attractions — namely liberal arts and solid teaching. First founded as a liberal arts college for men, Lafayette is now coeducational — but it is still a small liberal arts college, where graduate students are unheard of and teaching is still given its due. One of the first colleges in the United States to offer courses related to engineering, the field remains one of Lafayette's prime foci — and along with its economics and business major, it is perhaps what Lafayette is best known for. These strong programs, its small and inviting atmosphere, and a beautiful campus all make Lafayette worthy of consideration for high schoolers interested in pursuing either engineering or business, or a number of up-and-coming liberal arts disciplines.

Academic Life: Marquis Attraction

Lafayette's small size and its focus on undergraduate education wins applause from students. "I'm very happy," says one student. "It's been very challenging — they made me work a lot and it hasn't been a lot of busy work. I've learned a lot in my four years." Barron's *Profiles of American Colleges* rates Lafayette as one of the fifty "most academically competitive colleges" in the nation, and the college's Web page proudly lists students who have received Fulbright grants and other major awards. According to the Web site, fifty-nine students are members of Phi Beta Kappa.

Lafayette, while it doesn't have a core curriculum per se, does have what it calls a "Common Course of Study," basically a number of required courses every student must take plus a distribution requirement. For the distribution requirement aspect of the Common Course of Study, every student must take at least one course in mathematics, two natural science courses that have a laboratory component (such as physics or chemistry), and at least three courses in the humanities and the social sciences. There's also a foreign culture requirement for students pursuing a Bachelor of Arts degree, in which students must either show intermediate proficiency in a foreign language, complete a semester abroad, or complete a three-course "cluster" dealing with any foreign culture, ranging from Africa and the Middle East to France to Latin America.

However, students all have to take certain courses, regardless of their major. The First-Year Seminar class, which according to the school's catalogue is to be taken in the fall of a student's freshman year, is, as one professor puts it, "a kind of introduction to college life." The seminar classes, each limited to sixteen students, are affiliated with Lafayette's College Writing Program. The other mandatory courses also have to do with writing. There are five in all — a lot compared to other colleges, where one or two are required at best. Aside from the First-Year Seminar, students must take College Writing, an intensive writing and reading course; a Values and Science/Technology Seminar, which looks at ethical issues surrounding developments in science and technology; and two upper-division writing courses, one in the junior year and one in the senior year.

The workload can be heavy, but at least students will not have to face it in a class of four hundred students. "There's a small student-faculty ratio," says one professor. One student notes that "with the exception of one class, I've never had a class size greater than 30."

There also aren't any graduate students at the school, which presents a two-fold advantage for students attending Lafayette. First, professors do all the teaching, and students are happy with the close relationships and easy accessibility that their professors are willing to give. "Professors are usually pretty easy to reach," says one student. "A lot give their home phone numbers in case a student has a problem with a paper they are writing or something. They also have a decent amount of office hours." Another credits personal attention from faculty with making the education received at Lafayette truly extraordinary.

The second advantage is that bright students can also engage in research opportunities with instructors. One program in particular, the EXCEL Scholars program, provides selected students with a chance to work on collaborative research projects with faculty members. Not only can students work full time for ten weeks during the summer on an EXCEL project, they can work during the three-week Interim Session between terms and eight to ten hours a week during the school year. Students are even paid for their work — $8 per hour — and receive, if they're working when class isn't in session, on-campus housing.

"It's very, very popular," says one faculty member. "In the summertime we must have one hundred students working on EXCEL [projects] with a professor."

Students also use the summer and Interim Session to participate in Lafayette's many study-abroad programs (although there are also five semester abroad programs run by Lafayette faculty during each school year). Lafayette's study-abroad program has a number of advantages, including the fact that there's no extra cost to the programs during the school year. Credit for courses taken abroad is transferable to Lafayette, and during the school year, so is the financial aid, making the programs accessible to a lot of people who might not have been able to study overseas otherwise. "I enjoyed it," says one student who participated. "I thought it was very well done. It was a great opportunity, and you can do it and still graduate in four years."

The intensive Interim Session courses are becoming more popular. "They bring more and more people every year," says one student who participated in an Interim Session trip to Israel recently. "You get a full semester course in three weeks," he says, complete with guided tours, readings, and exams — and "the classwork didn't make it not fun — it added to [the experience]."

Lafayette's strengths lie in the economics and business department, as well as in the engineering department, but there's also an increasing emphasis on the natural sciences, like biology, chemistry, and physics. Lafayette's English department is also highly regarded, and psychology is gaining strength. "We've gotten a lot more students and a few more professors [in psychology]," notes one student.

Among the best professors at Lafayette include Wendy Hill in psychology; John F. Greco and Ismail Jouny in electrical and computer engineering; Elizabeth W. McMahon, Derek Smith, and Gary P. Gordon in mathematics; Howard J. Marblestone in foreign languages and literatures; Ilan Peleg in government and law; and Susan L. Averett in economics and business.

Political Life: Calm Instead of the Storm

Lafayette's a rather quiet place politically, and when controversy has arisen, it has handled it in an appropriate and reasonable fashion. While a few departments do have a liberal slant to them, politicization of the classroom is kept to a minimum for both faculty and students. While students — being students — tend to have liberal views at Lafayette on an overall basis, they're also generally apathetic when it comes to politics.

"Definitely the religion courses are very liberal," says one student, explaining that "every view can be right" in them. "In other courses I've taken, they haven't had a chance to be conservative or liberal," this student says. "I don't get the sense that current political issues come up much. Another student agrees with this assessment, and says that "as a rule, the students on campus are more apathetic to the state of things."

"We don't have a real reactionary student body," one professor says, adding that issues relating to academic freedom have never been an issue. "I never really thought about it," she says, after seeming surprised as the question, "so I must be free to [speak my mind]. I think they're pretty serious about academic freedom."

Anyone wondering whether Lafayette tolerates conservative speech on campus need look no further than its selection of George F. Will as its 2000 commencement speaker.

Lafayette has been the scene of some racial controversy during the past year. The college, acutely aware that its black student population hovers around 3 to 4 percent of its enrollment, actively recruits black and other minority students to attend Lafayette. The school offers a number of programs for its black students, including the Portlock Black Cultural Center, and there are black student groups on campus such as the Brothers of Lafayette, but the low minority enrollment has been a concern for students and administration alike. Throw into this mix, in February of 2000, two white students' project from Lafayette's "Protest Art" class — which consisted of about twenty posters plastered around campus, that featured the picture of a black student from a financial aid brochure combined with denigrating racial stereotypes about blacks. To make matters worse, the posters were put up during Lafayette's "Prologue" weekend — when the college invites minority students and their families to attend classes.

Hanging the posters to coincide with that event was, depending on one's point of view, offensive, incredibly stupid, or merely unthinking. "I just don't think they were thinking," says one student. The *Allentown Morning Call* reported that many black students were offended by the posters. But the college has, so far, acted admirably. At many colleges, such an incident would have paralyzed the institution for days while charges of racism and intolerance were thrown back and forth. But the two offenders, described by the *Morning Call* as "heartbroken" over the incident and who said they made the poster in an (obviously failed) attempt to condemn racial stereotypes, were not pilloried by the Lafayette community. The *Morning Call* noted that Lafayette did not take any disciplinary action against the students, that their identities weren't released (although they were later identified in a later story about the affair), and that their professor in the Protest Art class, who is black, came to their defense. Instead of degenerating into an ideological free-for-all, the campus started up a dialogue on racial issues that by all accounts seems healthy. Thus, Lafayette managed to keep a potentially ugly incident in perspective — something that very rarely happens on college campuses these days.

Student Life: Even the Athletes Study

Students say that the city of Easton doesn't factor much into the social life of Lafayette undergraduates. Lafayette, located on what is popularly known as "College Hill," not only has somewhat of an emotional detachment from the surrounding area when it comes to student life, but it is physically removed from the town as well. "Easton is at the bottom of the Hill," says one student, "and no one comes up. . . . People go there just to get cash and food, but the area of Easton that's at the foot of the Hill really isn't that great." That's not to say that there's no reason to go into Easton — the city does offer a number of cultural attractions like the National Canal Museum that will appeal to history buffs and the Crayola crayon factory. And one student notes that "bowling is pretty popular around here. There are two alleys about ten minutes away." But overall, students say that life at Lafayette is pretty quiet. "On campus, there isn't that much to do," says one — but there are still enough activities so that students can have a fun time while at school.

First and foremost among these is the school's Greek system. Unlike many schools, where the Greek system is a pale shadow of its former self, Lafayette's remains a vibrant and prevalent force on campus. "The Greek system is declining, but it's still pretty popular," says one student. "It's not small." Consequently, a major source of entertainment for students is that oldest of collegiate traditions — the party. "Partying is the major thing here — many people party on the weekends," says one student. Another student adds that "fraternity and sorority nights are pretty crazy around here."

There are also a variety of clubs and organizations students can join. The InterVarsity Christian Fellowship, a staple of collegiate life, is here, and there are clubs for sports ranging from crew to ice hockey and chess.

Lafayette also has an outstanding intercollegiate athletics program for a school its size. A competitor in the Patriot League, Lafayette fields a total of twenty-two NCAA Division I varsity teams — something that is both surprising and cherished. "It's kind of amazing since we are such a small school," a student says. When the college discussed moving from Division I to Division II — where it would face smaller schools — the students were infuriated. And it's not like the athletes are academic slouches either: Lafayette is the only Division I school in the nation that can claim a perfect graduation rate for both men's and women's basketball players who entered school in 1989 to 1992. Football players graduate at a rate of 81 percent — one of the ten best rates in the country. There are also thirty-five intramural teams for students who don't quite rise, athletically, to the Division I level.

Dorm life at Lafayette is given an enthusiastic thumbs-up by students. "I really like dorm life here," says one student. "Some people opt to stay off-campus, and I can't see myself doing that." The close atmosphere makes it easy to find friends; one student says it's important to "find a group of friends who are involved in what you're doing." He also noted that his experience "could have been bad if I hadn't found a good group of friends."

There are a variety of living options on campus, with a number of single-sex dormitories for both men and women, although, thanks to college policy, incoming freshmen will end up living with a roommate. In addition, there are also a number of houses with live-in faculty members.

Lafayette is also a rather safe campus. According to one student, crime is "not at all" a problem on campus. "I always can walk around at night," he says, "and it's very well lit and security is prevalent."

A final aspect of Lafayette campus life is that, in short, they despise nearby Lehigh University. "The big [tradition] is that we hate Lehigh," says a student. "That's our only real tradition at the school." It may not be the finest tradition to have, but it's also another unifying force on a campus that exemplifies what small college life is about.

Louisiana State University

Office of Admissions
110 Thomas Boyd Hall
Baton Rouge, LA 70803
(225) 578-1175
www.lsu.edu

Total enrollment: 30,977
Undergraduates: 25,922
ACT ranges (English/Math): 21-27 (E); 19-26 (M)
Applicants: 9,382
Accepted: 82%
Enrolled: 63%
Application deadline: May 1
Financial aid application deadline: December 15
Tuition: resident: $3,398/$7,668; non-resident: $8,698/$12,968
Core curriculum: No

A Dollar Short

The origins of Louisiana State University can be traced to a state-chartered college whose first president, in the years just ahead of the Civil War, was William T. Sherman, of all people. But in modern times, as Louisianians never tire of boasting, Huey Long's vision had the more profound effect on the university. It was Long who relocated the school to its current location just south of Baton Rouge, on a 2,000-acre campus adjacent to the Mississippi River, where he sought to build a first-class university with prominent faculty and winning athletic teams. Now, as in the King-fish's own day, that grand aspiration remains only partially fulfilled, providing a lesson about the effects of chronic underfunding by state government and of a populist tradition that sometimes overwhelms academic excellence.

LSU enjoyed its greatest renown during the middle decades of the twentieth century. The school was a leading outpost of the southern agrarian revival that had local practitioners in Robert Penn Warren, Cleanth Brooks, and the *Southern Review*. In political philosophy, too, LSU had a stream of distinguished professors, including Eric Voegelin, Willmoore Kendall, and Charles Hyneman. Among the notable persons who spent time in graduate study at LSU during this era were Hubert Humphrey, Richard Weaver, and Robert Lowell — a sample that amply demonstrates LSU's then-dazzling intellectual environment. Today, there is some reason to hope that the school may be recovering some of its former luster, as admissions standards are progressively tightened and several academic initiatives for advanced undergraduates are introduced.

Academic Life: Attempts at Resuscitation

All incoming freshmen are admitted to the University College, the academic division that serves as gatekeeper to the seventy-three major fields offered by LSU's ten specialized colleges. While enrolled in the University College, students complete general education requirements that are preliminary to all majors. The requirements take the form of a loose distribution schema, in which students are required to complete thirty-eight hours of course work spread among English composition, analytical reasoning, arts and humanities, natural sciences, and social sciences. One student cautions that the survey courses that fulfill the general education requirements can result "in a disappointingly shallow education," and for that reason serious scholars should seek out more challenging classes.

During their sophomore year, students typically apply for admission to the college in which they wish to complete their majors. The specialized colleges include Arts and Sciences, Agriculture, Basic Sciences, Business Administration, Engineering, Education, and Engineering. Some colleges, such as Design, have rigorous GPA requirements, meaning students need to work for good grades as freshmen if they hope to be admitted.

As with any research university, LSU's institutional commitment is divided between the undergraduate teaching that sustains the budget and the faculty research and graduate student instruction that many professors prefer. But LSU offers programs — more and more in recent years — designed to accommodate those students — and professors — who seek a liberal arts–type education. Part of the impetus behind these initiatives is the recognition by the state that Louisiana has been losing many of its brightest high school students to out-of-state institutions.

One such academic stronghold at LSU is the Honors College, to which outstanding high school students may apply. Housed in the historic French House, the

Honors College offers smaller class sections taught by faculty in an interdisciplinary, liberal arts approach. Classes in such areas as ancient civilization, philosophy, religion, history, law, and some sciences count toward the general education requirements and draw the brightest undergraduates together. Although the reading lists and homework load for honors courses are greater, the benefits offered to students include more faculty contact and priority course registration. One honors student describes the professors in the program as "adherents to the old-school classical approach to education." Another student praises the honors seminars as places where "students can voice their opinions," with the result that "they tend to work harder in those classes." Students complete a traditional major within one of the regular academic colleges, which means that participation in the Honors College can — and, in practice, often does — coincide with studies in fields outside the humanities. During their senior year, students can elect to complete a thesis under the Honors College's sponsorship.

In fall 2000, LSU launched a Residential College that advertises itself as "a comprehensive living-learning community." Students live together in Hergot Hall and take common class sections in English, theater, history, and science. Upperclassman mentors and several faculty members reside in the dorm with the students. In a departure from LSU's otherwise sex-segregated dorms, the Residential College provides housing that is coed by floor. Although currently it is just a freshman-year experience designed for about three hundred students, the Residential College offers greater intimacy to students who might feel overwhelmed by the university's size.

Each spring, LSU invites top high school graduates to attend a special testing session at which they can test out of freshman academic requirements and take advantage of early class scheduling. In addition to a merit aid program known as Tuition Opportunity Program for Students (TOPS), for which all Louisiana public high school students are eligible, LSU offers other merit scholarships "awarded mainly on the basis of standardized test scores and high school academic record," according to the school. These can cover full and partial tuition, room and board, and provide campus employment. Most notably, the Chancellor's Alumni Scholarships offer students, including those from out-of-state, the opportunity to be assigned to work with faculty members on research projects.

To increase selectivity and hold down enrollment, LSU is raising admissions standards (currently set at a minimum 2.8 high school GPA) and phasing out remedial classes. As with any large university, however, students express concern about large class sizes and report difficulty registering for certain required courses — even at a place where more than 3,400 course sections are offered each academic year. LSU's student to faculty ratio of 18:1 translates into average lecture hall sizes of thirty-two students and science labs of twenty students. Class sizes vary in practice, although freshman English courses average about twenty to twenty-five students, and freshman math sections are capped at forty students.

Although upper-level course enrollments are generally smaller, introductory-level courses sometimes try to serve more than two hundred. "LSU's biggest problem right now is booming enrollment," one undergrad says. "One class I took last fall was supposed to have three hundred people in it, but ended up having 426 on the first day of class. It was a mess." Classes with larger enrollments can be cramped, impersonal, and less academically demanding. Some freshman- and sophomore-level courses, another student notes, are "dumbed down" by professors who "seem to grade on the level of the worst in the class" rather than teaching to the better students.

Students report that instructors are accessible in person and by e-mail, and some professors even lament that too few students take advantage of office hours. "The key to receiving a good education at LSU is to be assertive as far as taking challenging courses and engaging in discourse with professors," a student says. Graduate teaching assistants teach some course sections, particularly in areas such as English, math, and the basic sciences. "TAs at LSU teach rudimentary concepts well, though students complain about difficult-to-understand foreigners," says a recent graduate.

In order to prioritize resources, LSU has designated twelve departments for "enhanced" funding, which has caused quiet discontent among the departments that were passed over. In truth, underfunding by the State of Louisiana, compounded by LSU's inexpensive tuition, is perhaps the greatest obstacle that the university faces in improving academic excellence. Not only classroom instruction suffers from a lack of resources; many of LSU's stately Italian Renaissance style buildings are in obvious need of renovations. An accreditation report recently described LSU's historic theater (executed in Art Deco decor) as "dirty, depressing, dilapidated, and demoralizing."

Given such financial constraints, LSU offers an impressive number of strong academic programs. In the humanities, English, political science, history, philosophy and religious studies, music, and theater are notable for their quality instruction. The business and engineering colleges are well-regarded and place graduates with both in-state firms and those located in Atlanta and Houston. LSU's design school, particular the architecture program, earns praise from campus observers. Students from throughout the southeastern United States and Latin America enroll in agricultural programs. The mass communications school is growing in size and reputation. And the geography department is one of the finest in the country. The economics department is free market–oriented, although professors use econometric rather than theoretic approaches to the subject.

Students at LSU have some wonderful scholars at their disposal, many of whom present their subjects free of ideological bias. Among those often cited by people on campus are John R. May, Kevin Cope, James L. Babin, David Madden, Jean Rohloff, Peggy Prenshaw, Bainard Cowan, and Anna Nardo in English; Robert J. Edgeworth and Emily E. Batinski in foreign languages; John R. Baker, Edward Hugh Henderson, and Mary Sirridge in philosophy and religious studies; Paul F. Paskoff,

Victor L. Stater, and Gaines M. Foster in history; Caye Drapcho and Marybeth Lima in biological engineering; O. Carruth McGehee and Charles N. Delzell in mathematics; Jules d'Hemecourt in mass communications; and Amanda B. Bower in marketing. LSU's Eric Voegelin Institute is directed by G. Ellis Sandoz, who one of three outstanding political theorists (along with Cecil L. Eubanks and James R. Stoner Jr.) in the political science department. In the Honors College, Robert McMahon, James D. Hardy Jr., and Drew Lamonica stand out from a faculty that is strong across the board.

Courses on Louisiana politics and history are perennial favorites on campus, as is a fundamental issues of politics course offered as a survey of political ideas. In addition, LSU offers a variety of lesser-known but worthy classes, such as one in religious studies on the Holocaust that is taught by a local rabbi and an introductory course on oceanography. Some students admit disappointment in the outdated equipment used in basic lab courses in chemistry, physics, and biology.

Political Atmosphere: Cajun, but Not Spicy

Despite being located in Louisiana's capital city, LSU is not a hotbed of political activism, due in part to the prevailing Southern conservative tradition that holds sway over the campus. There is a "Free Speech Alley" adjacent to the Student Union that sometimes attracts political or religious speakers, but students mostly are preoccupied with academics, social activities, and outside employment. "There is no campus repression of any particular viewpoint but that does not mean there is a tremendous amount of political diversity," a student says. "The majority of students would fall into the category of being politically apathetic."

Race is perhaps the most highly-charged political topic on campus, and LSU remains under a 1970s-era desegregation order. The administration cites the court order's precedence as its basis for ignoring the recent *Hopwood* decision, in which the Fifth Circuit Court of Appeals ruled that affirmative action admissions programs are unconstitutional at state institutions. Although LSU's student body and faculty is predominantly white, an active NAACP chapter (whose membership overlaps with LSU's African-American Cultural Center) has been successful in wresting some concessions from the administration. A vice chancellor for diversity was recently hired, and in the summer of 2000, the university renamed the "Plantation Room" at a banquet facility in the Student Union. One undergraduate claims that certain black students are "loud and demanding" on campus, a style of engagement that seems to yield results.

The faculty senate created a permanent Commission on the Status of Minorities to study racial issues on campus, but the administration soon overshadowed such efforts by announcing an initiative that calls for increasing black student enrollment by 20 percent and increasing full-time minority faculty by 73 percent. The plan promises these numerical results "without compromising increasingly high admissions requirements, academic standards, and the criteria for the selection and evaluation of faculty." Some campus observers are skeptical of that assurance. "LSU has gone the way of the politically correct university," says one student.

Students identify the mass communications and the women's and gender studies programs as places where politics unduly intrudes on classroom learning. More generally, it is a good rule to read course descriptions and, if possible, course syllabi in advance of registering for classes. One sociology course, for example, distributes a sheet of "assumptions" that govern the readings and discussions, and among the assumptions is this: "The larger social environment within which families are embedded is the product of three interlocking hierarchies of power: class, race, and gender." To LSU's credit, however, there are professors with more traditional approaches to be found in nearly every department, if the student is willing to locate them and develop a rapport.

"Generally speaking, I would describe LSU students as conservative and religious but grounded in common sense and decency rather than fanaticism," one professor says. The easygoing South Louisiana ethos, which is almost Mediterranean in its earthy appreciation of living, coexists easily with filial and religious piety. One student expresses fear that LSU is not welcoming to racial minorities and homosexuals, but neither is it a place where such students need fear for their safety. Despite heavy-handed attempts by the administration to "diversify" campus, most students hold traditional views, but also tolerate those with different perspectives.

Student Life: Southern Comfort

The Greek system is deeply ingrained on campus, and LSU was recently named by the *Princeton Review* as America's "Number 1 Party School" — a designation the administration swiftly disavowed. But the greater social organizer is athletics: just as Louisiana's society once was governed by the planting season, LSU's student life takes its cue from the athletic calendar. "Football reigns, basketball when successful is a hot ticket, and baseball at LSU is the best in the country," a student says. There are eighteen intercollegiate teams at LSU and another forty-six intramural sports. The men's and women's intercollegiate teams consistently shine on the field and court, often to boisterous fans that exude "Tiger Mania."

As with other Southeastern Conference schools, football season at LSU is about more than just the game. The fall months are dominated by football games that fill the oversized LSU stadium with students and alumni and spawn related rituals such as tailgating, fraternity activities, concerts, away-game road trips, and the marching Tiger Band. The library even closes early on game days. The only student demonstration that occurred at LSU during recent years was caused by student fears that not enough football tickets would be available for their purchase.

413

For those whose interests encompass more than athletics, LSU's 2,000-acre campus along the Mississippi River offers a variety of natural and cultural activities. In addition to concerts and recitals provided by the School of Music, a visiting artists series sponsors concerts by internationally known musicians and ensembles. There is a strong theater department that stages works from both the classic and experimental repertoire and a professional theater company is in residence on campus. Downtown Baton Rouge is just up the road, offering jazz and blues clubs, a symphony orchestra, and two riverboat casinos (for those twenty-one or older). Most students prefer to stay closer to campus, with the Chimes Restaurant being a favorite watering hole for professors and students.

There are more than two hundred service, political, ethnic, preprofessional, and religious student groups on campus. Student government is visibly involved with university affairs, as are service groups such as Rotaract and the LSU Ambassadors. A daily student newspaper, the *Reveille*, provides basic campus coverage though little investigative reporting. The NAACP is active on campus, as is an International Cultural Center that sponsors film nights and coffee forums. Barnes & Noble recently assumed operation of LSU's campus bookstore, adding a coffee shop and expanding the hours in the process.

Religious life is important at LSU. Catholics constitute 50 percent of the student population, and evangelical and mainline Protestants also make up a hefty percentage. Muslim students have access to a nearby mosque. Student groups such as the Baptist Collegiate Ministry and Catholic Student Center are particularly active, but a large number of denominations have churches adjacent to campus and engage in campus outreach. "Religion is alive at LSU but when you get down to it, it is not dominant," one student says. For example, there was little controversy when a student group calling itself Sexual Health Advocates showed up at every campus dorm in the fall of 2000 to promote "safe sex."

"Like any other university, drinking is a favorite pastime," one student says. Since a fraternity pledge's death in 1997 from alcohol poisoning, the administration has clamped down on on-campus alcohol consumption. An annual "Greek Assessment" by the administration has resulted in the suspension of one fraternity and the imposition of sanctions of others. Only 15 percent of the student body belongs to fraternities and sororities, but that number does not reflect their considerable prominence in campus life. It is often said that Greek students are affluent, and at LSU they seem to consciously cultivate that image. The fraternities and sororities are segregated in practice, with separate governing councils based on race. In addition to the social benefits of pledging, there can be tangible material rewards. "The networking tactics of most Greek organizations serve them well, not only aiding members in job searches and social circles but also in finding previous exams for their courses," one non-Greek says.

Joining a fraternity or sorority is not necessary to enjoy social life at LSU. But making friends is essential, which is why many non-Greek freshmen choose to live

in campus housing, in close proximity to other students. There are nineteen residence halls on campus. Most are air-conditioned, and suites, private bathrooms,
common kitchens, and computer labs are among the features found in some dorms.
Private bedrooms can be had for a higher price. Data ports are being installed in all
dorms. Although the campus is nominally "substance-free," several residence halls
have explicit twenty-four-hour quiet floors or substance-free rooms. The key to finding suitable lodging is to apply early, and to investigate the amenities and ethos of
individual dorms. Kirby-Smith, for example, is a dumping ground for freshman boys
(there are six all-male and seven all-female residence halls). East Campus Apartments are highly sought after because of their newness and condo-style suites. The
Lavilles are largely filled by Honors College students and high academic achievers.

One student describes campus housing as "spartan yet adequate." There is no
residency requirement for students, but LSU says that 65 percent of new students
(including those in Greek houses) live on campus. Often looking for greater freedom
and to save money, most upperclassmen and graduate students live in nearby apartment complexes or in group rental homes. The one cautionary note about off-
campus housing is that commuter parking is found at LSU's peripheries and the on-
campus transportation system is poor. "To get to class you walk," a student says. On
top of that, some areas of campus are not well lit or paved, although the university
has installed call boxes in the darker recesses. Still, the campus reports crime statistics well above the national averages in the categories of rape, assault, robbery, and
larcenies of all kind, including car theft.

For students who want to get away, New Orleans is just a ninety-minute drive,
and there are also the Gulf Coast beaches of Mississippi and the Florida panhandle.
LSU provides a Mardi Gras holiday each year, although Cajun culture can be enjoyed
year-round in local restaurants and in the friendly spirit of native Louisianians.

University of Massachusetts at Amherst

Undergraduate Admissions Office
University Admissions Center
University of Massachusetts
Box 30120
Amherst, MA 01003-0120
(413) 545-0222
www.umass.edu

Total enrollment: 23,570
Undergraduates: 18,214
SAT ranges (Verbal/Math): 500-610 (V); 510-620 (M)
Applicants: 19,499
Accepted: 67%
Enrolled: 28%
Application deadline: February 1
Financial aid application deadline: March 1
Tuition: resident: $5,212/$10,002; non-resident: $13,366/$18,155
Core curriculum: No

Unholy Thoughts

In the University of Massachusetts at Amherst view book, the first photograph is of an unidentified stained glass bearing the inscription "Idea of a University." One wonders what Cardinal John Henry Newman, from whose 1873 book the quote is derived, would think of the Massachusetts haven for ideological excesses.

Despite improvements in the overall standing of the university as measured by admissions competitiveness, UMass remains a deeply politicized university. As with any school of its massive size, however, there are good possibilities — isolated though they may be — for truly liberal learning. Nonetheless, the overall tone fostered by the school's administration and pet departmental projects and programs is not conducive to a liberal education. An especially weak set of distribution requirements is matched only by the administration's bowing before the totemic triad of race, class, and gender.

In late 1998 a university report was presented to the chancellor's office. Its subject was "A New Approach to Promoting Community, Diversity, and Social Justice," and its preamble affirmed the celebration of differences in areas including "age, class, culture, ethnicity, gender, ideology, language, nationality, political beliefs, race, religious affiliation, sexual orientation and varying ability." The rhetoric affirms a diversity of ideas, but the reality at UMass is all too often an enforced ideological conformity. Students wishing to break free from the university's concerted efforts in enforcing "diversity" can find some worthwhile studies, but their dedication to "the idea of a university" must be especially tenacious.

Academic Life: High Marx

The undergraduate portion of the University of Massachusetts at Amherst is composed of ten schools: the College of Humanities and Fine Arts, the College of Natural Sciences and Mathematics, the College of Social and Behavioral Sciences, the School of Engineering, the College of Food and Natural Resources, the Isenberg School of Management, the School of Nursing, the School of Education, the School of Public Health and Health Sciences, and an honors program known as Commonwealth College.

Like many big state universities, UMass requires that students fulfill a set of distribution requirements rather than a traditional core curriculum. Its distribution requirements are especially anemic; even less is required of students at the flagship campus in the distribution requirements than is required of students at the University of Massachusetts–Boston, a school that has been criticized for its weak academic standards.

The general education requirements comprise only a quarter of the 120 credits required for graduation. Despite the university's affirmation that "an undergraduate's general education should encompass some reasonable fraction of the totality of human knowledge, insight, and interpretation," the distribution requirements fail to provide assurance that students will have a common core of knowledge or that it will even cover a reasonable fraction of all the areas of knowledge.

All freshmen must take a writing course; another writing course is required in the junior year, this one related to the student's major. A total of six courses must be taken in what is called the "Social World." This includes one course in literature, one course in the arts or a second course in literature, one course in historical studies, two courses in the social and behavioral sciences, and one additional course in any of these areas or an interdisciplinary course. Two of these six courses must meet the university's diversity requirement. Three courses are required in the sciences; basic math skills must be demonstrated either by one course or by exam, and one course in analytic reasoning is required. Among the different areas, there are sixty-three offerings that satisfy the literature requirement, thirty-three courses that meet the requirement in arts or a second literature class, and thirty-three courses that meet the history requirements. As is obvious, this hardly assures a common body of knowledge on which a liberal education can be built.

No course in Western civilization is required. As is often the case with diversity requirements, there are plenty of courses that might be classified as "oppression studies," but there also exist legitimate courses of study, such as in Chinese history, that fulfill the requirement.

UMass–Amherst has for years been a bastion of Marxist studies. The postmodern permutations on the Marxist theme have produced a variety of courses that focus on race and gender, in addition to class. A comparative literature seminar on "Medieval Women Writers and Feminist Theory" looks at old texts through the eyes of current feminist theory. Another English course, "Introduction to American Studies," which fulfills the diversity requirement, provides a "focus on issues of race, class, gender, and ethnicity."

Women's studies is, true to its politicized origins in the late 1960s, one of the most ideological programs at the university. The program also offers, among other things, "The Social Construction of Whiteness and Women" and "The Philosophy of Gender and Sexuality," which provides an "introduction to theories of the relations between sex, gender, and sexuality from a feminist perspective. Topics include: biological determinist, social constructionist, historical, and performative theories of gender and sexuality, sexual identities (hetero-, gay, bi-, trans- and intersexualities, and race, class, ethnic differences), and the politics of sexuality (identity politics, conservative politics, queer theory)." These courses too tough? The department also gives credit for participating in the Lesbian, Bisexual, Gay, and Transgendered Lecture Series or serving a practicum at the campus Everywoman's Center.

The W. E. B. DuBois Department of Afro-American Studies bills itself as "one of the largest such departments in the country." The courses offered there are boilerplate identity politics: for example, "Race, Ethnicity and Gender in U.S. History" and "The Political Economy of Class and Race." One course description on the life of Du Bois hails him as "perhaps America's greatest intellectual activist."

Of all the politicized programs, departments, and courses of study mentioned in this guide, none is more thoroughgoing in its leftward tilt than the Social Thought and Political Economy (STPEC) program at UMass. A virtual minefield of ideological courses, the program is also a practical training ground for young leftists, as an internship is required for graduation with the STPEC major. Organized in 1972, the program has become, according to one professor, "a Marxist bailiwick."

STPEC courses, the university bulletin notes, "may deal with issues such as freedom and the state, structural inequality in the economy, work and work relations, the relationship of Western to non-Western cultures, the interrelationship of racism, sexism, and class oppression, the psychodynamics of politics, and theories of social change." Courses are drawn from various departments in the humanities and social sciences, including Afro-American studies, anthropology (itself a very politicized department), economics, history, Judaic and Near Eastern studies, legal studies, philosophy, political science, sociology, and women's studies. About half of the professors are drawn from Umass–Amherst, while the other half come from the other four colleges that are part of the Five College Consortium (see below).

Four STPEC seminars are required, and among the recent seminars offered for seniors are the following programs: "Latino Politics and Identity"; "Queer Theories/ Social Realities"; "Race, Ethnicity, and Nationality"; "Marx and Post-Colonial Discourses"; "Capitalism and Patriarchy"; "Race, Radicalism, and Culture in the Twentieth Century"; and "Community Organizing in Big Cities Around Issues of Poverty." One course title accurately sums up the philosophy of the program of the whole: "They Taught You Wrong," which seeks to "dispel misconceptions and stereotypes of Native Americans."

One of the benefits of a university in which there are over 17,000 undergraduates is that a student need not be forced into the worst of the politicized programs. Students report, in fact, that there are many fine teachers and scholars at UMass. Among the outstanding faculty members are John Palmer in biology; Herbert Gintis, Robert Costrell, and Dale Ballou in economics; Vincent DiMarco, Robert Keefe, William Kerrigan, Arthur Kinney, and Paul Mariani in English; R. Dean Ware in history; Jeffrey Sedgewick in political science; and Daphne Patai in Spanish and Portuguese.

Particular praise is offered for the English department by one student, who notes that despite some of the politicized course offerings there are many excellent literature classes. Otherwise, the strength of UMass is generally thought to be in the sciences, particularly polymer science and engineering.

Commonwealth College, the university's 2,000-student honors college, boasts high entrance requirements that are being strengthened each year, along with the academic performance of students in the program. "Pizza & Prof" nights feature informal gatherings for lectures, and one student notes that the program as a whole is succeeding in creating a small institution within a very large one.

One student offers high praise for the Five College Consortium, an exchange program in which UMass students may take classes at nearby Amherst College, Hampshire College, Mount Holyoke College, and Smith College. Expanding the range of choice a UMass student has, the program is one of the "best features" of the university program. "Where else are you going to get five colleges for the price of one?" the student says.

Political Atmosphere: Chapter and (Di)verse

The highly politicized character of many of the academic programs is not an accident arrived at in defiance of the administration. In fact, the university administration has been at the vanguard of the multicultural movement, on campus and even around the country.

UMass–Amherst endured several campus uprisings (complete with takeovers of administrative buildings) in the early and mid-1990s that, because the university so quickly caved in to student demands, prompted the Massachusetts legislature to act. Only under the direction of new president William Bulger was a stricter policy against appeasing campus demonstrations implemented.

419

Sometimes criticized for maintaining the same autocratic style as he did when leading the Massachusetts senate for seventeen years, Bulger since his inauguration in 1995 has succeeded in at least improving the reputation and financial standing of the UMass system as a whole. In a statistic the university is fond of citing, UMass–Amherst has risen fifty-nine notches on the *U.S. News & World Report* rankings. In addition, the university system's endowment has tripled under Bulger, and the budget increases approved by the Massachusetts legislature have far outpaced their previous level (owing in large part to the influence Bulger still exerts on Massachusetts legislators, many of whom benefited from the patronage he regularly doled out).

An aggressive advertising campaign has been launched aimed at improving the standing of the system as a whole and especially the prestige of the flagship Amherst campus. A program called by the *Boston Globe* "Bulger's pet project," the University Scholars program, has attracted more than one hundred high school valedictorians each year for the past several years to UMass-Amherst. In addition, Bulger was instrumental in pushing for the establishment of the honors college, Commonwealth College. Overall, endowed positions are up considerably, from four in 1996 to twenty-two as of July 2000.

Faculty grousing about Bulger's salary increase (which, at $238,000, only raised him to a middling level among comparative university presidents) is sometimes accompanied by complaints about underfunding of faculty positions (some claim that more than 250 faculty positions are vacant) and a sorely neglected physical plant.

Less often heard are complaints about the ideological direction in which UMass–Amherst continues to head. But they should be: money can pour into a university's coffers, but what it does with the money is ultimately more important. And UMass–Amherst seems bent on taking itself into the brave new world of the multiversity.

A 1998 report titled "A New Approach to Promoting Community, Diversity, and Social Justice: Aspects of *Strategic Action*" took as its starting point the assumption that the university could do even more to promote multiculturalism than it already does — not a small leap to make. "At its core, the University continues to be, as it has always been, a community of inquiry and dissemination of knowledge," the report states. "We now pursue this historic mission, however, in a broader setting. We need to understand and serve ever more diverse and inclusive interests, responsibilities and constituencies."

As is so often the case when a group expresses the desire to better a traditional mission, the reality of the situation is that the new ideas trump the old. Vestiges of the old order — antiquated ideas like academic freedom — are often discarded. Daphne Patai, UMass–Amherst professor of Spanish and Portuguese, has written widely on the influence of feminist ideology on campuses. In an editorial in the *Chronicle of Higher Education,* Patai quotes a UMass–Amherst professor of women's studies, who in 1997 (while director of the program) summed up the sacrifices often made in the name of new thinking: "We can't lose track of the wider goal in order to defend some narrow definition of academic freedom, which might amount to a right not to have to respond to new knowledges that are relevant to someone's own field of expertise."

The "new knowledges" animate the 1998 report and dictate a plan of action that has largely been implemented, according to administration officials. One of the "strategic principles" articulated in a previous report, and endorsed in the 1998 report, calls for the university to "foster the continuing evolution from a monocultural to a multicultural and eventually to a trans-cultural community, valuing the richness of diversity and differences of individuals and cultures, yet affirming our common humanity."

Written in the almost impenetrable language of educratese, driven by every recent fad that has swept through the university, the report is replete with code words that signal to the initiated the necessary actions. The report calls upon the university to "work toward blurring boundaries and rendering barriers permeable to make the university more integrative."

Instead of relegating this task to specific offices set up for the promotion of diversity (and there are a multitude of such offices on campus), the university wants departments to take on the task of promoting social justice. Because "both the problems of diversity and social justice and proposed solutions have been ignored by the majority of the campus community as not relevant to them," efforts will be made to raise the consciousness of those not on board, the report says. This agenda is accurately summarized in the report's definition of social justice: "efforts to eradicate exclusion and promote full and equal inclusion and participation for all social groups."

Stymied in its efforts to continue its aggressive affirmative action plan for undergraduate admissions, in January 2000 UMass–Amherst announced a plan that would ostensibly limit the use of race in its admissions criteria. In an effort to sidestep court rulings that have found strict quota systems unconstitutional, the university adopted a new ten-point system to be used for students with lower grades and test scores. Under the new plan, considerably less weight is placed on SAT scores; diversity counts for one of the ten points.

Recommendations of the Task Force on Undergraduate Admissions, convened by the chancellor in the spring of 1999, include the following: the implementation of a plan (similar to that adopted in California and Texas) to admit any Massachusetts student who is in the top ten percent of his high school graduating class; the appointment of an associate vice chancellor for diversity; the creation of a diversity Web page; the convening of a committee on diversity; the expansion of ethnic studies to include full-fledged academic departments; and the establishment of an African American, Latino, Asian, and Native American (ALANA) resource center (in addition to the cultural centers already in place). The report also suggests that the following questions might be used to determine the potential contribution of an applicant: "Has the applicant worked as an advocate of or volunteered to promote diversity?" and "Does the applicant understand, and know how to deal with, racism?"

Common sense says that this is *not* "the idea of a university." Common sense says, rather, that this is a bad combination of social engineering and identity politics. For example, here's how the administration justifies the need for more ethnic study programs: "ALANA retention rates will be enhanced is more classes related to cultural diversity are offered. We recommend that more classes in the areas of Asian American, Latino, and Native American studies be taught by qualified faculty members. In addition, having this curriculum on campus benefits *all* students, or whatever race, who desire to expand their knowledge of different ethnic groups. Courses in these departments should be classified as 'diversity' general education requirements, to encourage students of all backgrounds to take them. This would create UMass graduates who are highly prepared for the working world, since the more a student knows about the world and those in it, the better prepared they are for their future."

Elsewhere on campus, students are substituting radical activism for actually preparing themselves for their futures. In an interesting variation on town and gown relations, voters in the town of Amherst recently approved a referendum asking local police officers to ignore the state laws prohibiting marijuana possession. The university's Cannabis Reform Coalition almost certainly made the difference in the count with a determined get-out-the-vote effort.

Gay activism is common on campus, and not only among students. M. V. Lee Badgett, an economist at UMass–Amherst, directs the Institute for Gay and Lesbian Strategic Studies. Badgett's research "focuses on race, gender and sexual orientation discrimination in the workplace and on gay family issues," while the institute seeks to "create an equal and integrated society for people of all sexual orientations and gender identities."

There was no word from the institute when a UMass–Amherst professor with a penchant for pornography set up a Web site featuring photos of him with bare-chested strippers. The author of *Unspeakable ShaXXXspeares,* Professor Richard Burt, a tenured English professor, posted a picture of him fondling the breasts of a blonde. He also offered links to "Porn Stars I Have Known." To the university's credit, it shut down the Web site, which was set up using a university account.

Student Life: Belle Amherst

UMass–Amherst is located in the picturesque Pioneer Valley in western Massachusetts. Offering plenty of biking and hiking opportunities for students with outdoor interests, the area also features several fine college towns, including nearby Northhampton, which one student describes as a "jewel" rich in restaurants and cultural offerings. The valley is also within decent driving distance of Boston and New York City.

Despite its setting, the crime rate at UMass is astonishingly high. In 1999, for example, 27 forcible sex offenses, 25 motor vehicle thefts, and 101 burglaries were reported. The numbers for 1997 and 1998 were similar. Students are advised to take care.

Housing on campus is mandatory for a student's first two years. Students can choose to live in single-sex or coed residence halls. Most of the coed dorms house men and women on the same floor while maintaining separate bathrooms for each sex, though a few house men and women on alternate floors.

In addition to the standard dorms, the residence system at UMass reflects the politicization of the school it serves. The system offers special interest residential programs that "enable [students] to live with smaller groups of students who share [their] interests and concerns," according to the university. Among the choices are arts communities, language houses, and "ethnic and cultural affinity housing," including special cultural centers. "House cultural centers" in residence halls, according to university literature, provide "homes-away-from-home for students of common heritage as well as students interested in a culture other than their own." These centers include the Anacoana Caribbean Cultural Center, the Dr. Josephine White Eagle Memorial, the Native American Cultural Center, the United Asia Cultural Center, the Martin Luther King Jr. Cultural Center, the Malcolm X Cultural Center, the Latin American Cultural Center, and the Sylvan Multicultural Center. Almost all residence halls are coed, but single-sex living areas are available.

In addition to these programs the Housing Assignment Office runs a program called "2 in 20" that "provides a supportive community living experience for gay, lesbian, bisexual, and transgender students and their heterosexual allies." The name "2 in 20" is taken from the dubious assertion that 10 percent of the general population is homosexual. In a *Chronicle of Higher Education* article, one student called the "2 in 20" floor a "gay fantasy world." According to the *Chronicle*, "On a walk down the hall, [one] would know that the doors featuring sultry photographs of Sharon Stone and Madonna had been decorated by women, and that the door with pictures of shirtless male models belongs to a man." In 2000, about forty students lived on the floor.

There are more than two hundred registered student organizations on campus, including a variety of musical organizations, honor societies, performing arts groups, political organizations, and religious groups. University literature gives special mention to the *Third World* community weekly newspaper, and notes that the *Massachusetts Daily Collegian* is the largest daily campus newspaper in the East. One student notes the particular strength of Christian fellowships on campus, including InterVarsity Christianity Fellowship, Campus Crusade for Christ, the Navigators, the Newman Club, and the Lutheran Group. (The university calendar is, of course, inclusive to a fault, noting the holidays not only for Christians and Jews, but also for Buddhists, Baha'is, Hindus, Muslims, and Sikhs. Thus Durga Puja, the Worship of Divine Mother, is given special note in the "University Policy on Class Absence for Religious Observances.")

The university offers fifteen women's and fourteen men's athletic teams, which compete at the NCAA Division I level. There are many club and intramural sports available for students, and more than ten thousand students, faculty, and staff participate in the intramural sports program.

Massachusetts Institute of Technology

Office of Admissions
Room 3-108
77 Massachusetts Avenue
Cambridge, MA 02139-4307
(617) 253-4791
www.mit.edu

Total enrollment: 9,972
Undergraduates: 4,300
SAT ranges (Verbal/Math): 660-760 (V); 730-800 (M)
Applicants: 9,136
Accepted: 19%
Enrolled: 60%
Application deadline: January 1
Financial aid application deadline: January 11
Tuition: $26,050/$33,225
Core curriculum: Yes

Gravity's Rainbow

In a garden at the Massachusetts Institute of Technology (MIT) grows a tree said to be a distant relative of the one that dropped the apple that provided Sir Isaac Newton with the correlative for gravity. Regardless of the truth of that tree's lineage or Newton's mode of innovative thought, MIT itself is directly descended from the great scientists and thinkers of the past; the things discovered there today will change our future.

MIT is the nation's premier institution for the study of engineering, science, and computer science, and its faculty includes ten Nobel laureates and eight recipients of the so-called MacArthur "genius" grants. The institute's renown does not extend to the humanities and social science programs in which only 6 percent of the five thousand undergraduates enroll. However, the institute has of late made serious efforts to bring its humanities departments closer to the standard set by its scientists, and has had some success.

According to some on campus, MIT in recent years has become less of a technical college and more of an Ivy League college, with a decreased emphasis on math and science and a new emphasis on diversity, multiculturalism, and humanities. MIT might be responding to what the *Boston Globe* calls the "quickening pace of technological change (that) sparks a surge in social questions." The *Globe* contends administrators at technical colleges are realizing they need to address humanities and ethics in science; MIT, as in its scientific programs, is ahead of this curve.

Still, not many students choose MIT for a liberal arts education. The emphasis there is definitely on scientific research, and faculty double as the leading inventors and innovators in their fields. Students, likewise, are driven and highly intelligent — MIT application materials talk about holding on to SAT scores "until you've seen those 800s." Graduates, in addition to procuring a fine education, are instantly credible and respected upon mention of their alma mater, which is one of the finest compliments a school can receive.

Academic Life: Engineering Solution

Nearly two-thirds of MIT undergraduates major in engineering, and one quarter enroll in the sciences, leaving only 450 or so students to be divided between the schools of Humanities and Social Sciences, Architecture and Planning, and Management.

All students, however, are subject to MIT's harrowing basic curriculum, the General Institute Requirements. In their first semester students are advised to take Calculus I, Physics I, Chemistry, and a course in the humanities/arts/social sciences (HASS). Most students also participate in an optional freshman seminar. The course list for the spring term includes Calculus II, Physics II, Biology, another HASS course, and an optional undergraduate seminar. About half of the students receive advanced placement for one or more of the science requirements, and can thus move on to a course in their prospective major or an elective.

MIT no longer has a foreign language requirement, but students do need to accumulate eight "physical fitness points": two points are allotted for a quarter-length class, four points for playing on an intercollegiate team. However, all students must prove their ability to swim — despite the fact that after they graduate from MIT they will likely be able to create a makeshift boat out of baling twine and flotsam.

All told, the General Institute Requirements amount to six science courses, eight HASS courses, two electives in science and technology, and a laboratory requirement. About 15 percent of students are involved in special programs with modified core course lists. These programs, entitled "Concourse," "Experimental Study Group," and "Integrated Study Program," stress "individual initiative and close student-faculty relationships." Professors interviewed for this guide recommended the "Concourse" program, a year-long, highly structured group of courses that, according to the huge institute catalogue, explores "both the unity and the conflict of technical, scientific, and humanistic viewpoints and ideas." According to the catalogue, "The objective, possible only because of the unique combination of assets offered by MIT, is not only to achieve competence in the separate disciplines but also to examine the mutual relevance of freshman-year calculus, physics, chemistry, biology, and humanities."

Because of their heavy interest in science, some students undervalue the humanities and social sciences forced upon them by the MIT curriculum. Writing in the journal *Counterpoint*, MIT student Min-Hank Ho notes that "by lumping humanities with the other requirements, it becomes just another chore that needs to be completed before graduation." He reports that many MIT students take their HASS courses on a pass-fail basis just "to get them out of the way." Unlike in the rigid science requirements, students are allowed to choose which HASS courses they will take — although some complain that scheduling conflicts constrict their choices. Others select the most science-oriented courses, such as "Microeconomics" or similarly analytical courses, in order to fulfill the requirement. While some on campus suggest that the HASS course list should be adapted to fit students' tastes, a better suggestion might be to institute a humanities core that is as well thought out as the science core seems to be.

The humanities courses at MIT remain generally free of politicization, and science courses are all but immune to such intrusions. (Obviously, it's difficult to teach "Feminist Physics" or "The Calculus of Oppression.") To fulfill the HASS requirement, students will find many courses on Western civilization, but a few non-traditional selections as well. There is a class called "Gender and Science" and another called "Riots, Strikes, and Conspiracies in American History." But, as one student says, "No one department at MIT is particularly politicized. A handful of courses deal with social issues such as homosexuality and gender relations, and multicultural classes do exist, but none are required or particularly biased." As a general rule, the curriculum is "certainly unpoliticized," according to one professor, who notes that linguist Noam Chomsky is a "colorful exception." Chomsky, the best-known humanities professor at MIT and essentially the inventor of modern linguistic study, has written numerous books on linguistics, mass media, and foreign policy. All but the linguistic ones are somewhat notorious for their controversial political theories.

MIT students can enroll in courses at nearby Harvard University and Wellesley College, but for the most part they find all they need at MIT, where the list of Nobel laureates is longer than the list of good faculty at other schools. Strong departments at MIT are what one would expect from a blue-ribbon technological institute: mechanical engineering, electrical engineering, computer science, and physics. Surprisingly, about one-quarter of undergraduates come to MIT to major in premed.

MIT will soon have a $350 million neuroscience complex. "The multiple new connected buildings will be devoted to a newly created institute within MIT — the McGovern Institute for Brain Research — plus three existing departments or centers, and the new Martinos Center for Functional and Structural Biomedical Imaging," according to the *Boston Globe*. In addition, the institute is in the midst of a $1.5-billion capital campaign and the campus will soon undergo a $300-million renovation.

The Sloan School of Management also has an outstanding reputation. Though most of its programs are directed toward graduate study and research, the school does offer a B.S. degree in management science, heavy on the use of mathematical, statistical, and computer technology.

While MIT has a world-class reputation for scientific research, the school has brought its reputation to bear on efforts to strengthen its humanities and social sciences programs as well. More undergraduates — though still not a lot — are coming to MIT for liberal arts disciplines; programs in economics, political science, philosophy, linguistics, and biology are also considered excellent. The research emphasis of the rest of the school seems to have manifested itself in the humanities departments as avant-garde creativity. Among the distinguished faculty members in the arts, humanities, and social sciences are several with interests in such areas as media arts, creative writing, architecture, and linguistics. Professor Tod Machover, for instance, is the creator of computerized hyperinstruments; Nicholas Negroponte is founder of *Wired* magazine; and MacArthur fellow Evelyn Fox Keller is the author of *Reflections on Gender and Science*.

Faculty are generally very pleased with their jobs at MIT, where they get to pursue their own research, work with some of the best in their field, and teach bright, motivated students. Although tenure decisions are based almost exclusively on research, most faculty take their teaching seriously. According to one professor, "Senior faculty often teach introductory courses."

Political Atmosphere: Measuring Stress

The stereotype of MIT students is that of extremely serious, hardworking "computer geeks" who study excessively and rarely take time off to enjoy their college years. While this characterization certainly did not come about out of thin air ("the dorm lights burn late here," notes one professor), in truth, students' academic motivation is fueled as much by the rigorous nature of the school's curriculum as it is by personal disposition. Indeed, many in the MIT community have questioned the wisdom of the institute's frequently excessive workload. According to one professor, some faculty have made efforts to "relax" the academic program, but "students resist" because they want the challenge and want their degrees to be valuable.

However, there were enough complaints from students, deans, housemasters, and athletic coaches about the workload that in the spring semester of 1997, the chair of the faculty issued a statement calling on faculty to be more realistic and fair in making assignments and formulating exams.

According to that statement, it is not unheard of for professors "to schedule classes on Saturday mornings," hold "evening quizzes or exams without either canceling a class or a problem set during the same week," or extend assignments into reading week, exam week, or January term. Frequently, it is the professor's travel or research schedule that forces changes to the class calendar. The institute's Faculty Policy Committee has drafted guidelines that specify reasonable requirements, grades, and other aspects of the academic calendar, and the institute is trying to enforce these rules. Even if the rules were applied to the letter, an MIT education would still be extremely challenging and demanding. The administration also wants greater integration of residential and academic life and more out-of-class activity between professors and students. The institute would like to create dorms that include faculty members, much as the residential colleges at Harvard do.

The academic work leaves little time for much politicking, and students and faculty alike report that MIT is not a strongly politicized campus. One professor notes that "the kind of students attracted to MIT are usually not politically inclined." According to one student, "An atmosphere of political apathy among most MIT students prevails."

However, MIT has not been immune from debates about affirmative action and quotas. There has been pressure on MIT to increase minority enrollment (even though one-third of the student body is Asian-American) and to diversify the faculty. In one very public gesture, a mechanical engineering professor fasted and camped outside the president's office every Wednesday to protest the underrepresentation of "faculty of color." He was joined at one point by one hundred students, and, according to *The Multicultural Student's Guide to Colleges*, "the president of MIT has instructed heads of departments to look for more minority faculty members, and his office will provide financial help for the search."

MIT's president, Charles M. Vest, told the *Boston Globe* recently that "The toughest hill to climb is building diversity in the faculty." The newspaper reports that of MIT's 913 faculty, 144 (16 percent) are women, and that fifteen of the women and 106 male professors are minorities (a total minority representation of 13 percent).

The institute usually makes a public reaffirmation of its dedication to equal opportunity and affirmative action at some point during Black History Month, a student says. Recently, President Vest did so in a public address on the legacy of Martin Luther King Jr. "Whatever its imperfection," said the president, "affirmative action has improved access and opportunity for women and minorities in America." He cited numerous statistics illustrating MIT's progress toward a more diverse faculty, but said, "Clearly, we have far more work to do."

Although he argued that diversity would continue to make MIT a better institution, Vest also seemed prepared to sacrifice quality in academics for the sake of political correctness. "In the end, we must pursue these policies in spite of their cost and regardless of their benefits," Vest said. "We must pursue them because they are right and just."

The president, who generally has good rapport with faculty, has disturbed some professors with the mandated diversity plan and the possible negative impact it may have on standards at MIT. On the whole, though, the faculty at MIT are too busy to "get involved in administrative squabbles," according to one professor.

There has been a movement on campus to ban the institute's ROTC program on the grounds that military policy on homosexuality violates the school's nondiscrimination statement. This has not caused concern on campus, either by those opposed to or in favor of such a move. "ROTC has been a topic of discussion in the campus media for quite a while," says a student, but so far no formal actions have been taken to remove the campus chapter.

The daily paper at MIT is the *Tech,* but there is also something called the "Alternative News Collective" that publishes a progressive biweekly newspaper, the *Thistle.* The *Tech* also "tends to be PC," according to one professor, "but no one really reads it." Another campus paper, *Counterpoint,* is published jointly ten times a year by MIT and Wellesley and calls itself a "Journal of Rational Discourse and Campus Life." Recent issues have included stories on MIT's dining situation and the inadequacies of campus child care at Wellesley. Although the journal has a reputation for being conservative, recent issues show few signs of a distinctively conservative viewpoint. However, the *Tech* endorsed Ralph Nader for president and is considered a left-leaning publication.

Campus lectures at MIT usually have a distinctively scientific tenor to them. Several recent discussions addressed intersections of science, technology, and culture: "The Impact of Computers on Children's Lives," "Do We Need NASA?" "A Discussion of the Ethical and Scientific Implications of Cloning," "On the Question of Stupidity," and "Technologies of Freedom? Emerging Media in Modern Culture." A panel discussion, cosponsored by the Program in Science, Technology, and Society and the Program in Women's Studies, addressed recent challenges to feminism and included such speakers as feminist Katha Pollitt, columnist for the *Nation.* Other speakers of note have included Coretta Scott King, Lani Guinier, and Salman Rushdie. A lecture by Charles Murray, noted libertarian and author of the controversial book *The Bell Curve,* was protested by a small group.

The majority of lectures, however, appear to cater to a much more specialized audience: "Hot Electrons in Quantum Cascade Lasers," "Interactions between Manganese and Freshwater Algae," "Centrifuge Modeling of Immiscible Flow Processes," and "Estimating Attractor Dimension for a Simple Permixed Flame Propagation Model."

It's not hard to see how the stereotypes about MIT students got started.

Campus Life: No Tea Party

MIT is located on a 150-acre campus in Cambridge, across the Charles River from Boston. The area might have one of the highest concentrations of students in the nation: Harvard, Wellesley, Radcliffe College, Boston University, Boston College, and Brandeis University are all nearby. All these schools are within easy reach of the Boston Museum of Fine Arts, Gardner Museum, the New England Conservatory of Music, the Boston Symphony Orchestra, the Boston Pops, and the Boston Ballet Company.

Because of its prime New England location, the MIT campus is also an excellent port of embarkation for scenic and historic day and weekend trips to places like Cape Cod or the villages of Lexington and Concord.

However, getting around by car in the Boston area is nothing but a hassle. MIT students largely rely on their feet or their bicycles for local travel. But lock your bikes: they are stolen from bike racks with some regularity. Increasing petty crime also extends to labs and residences, from which computers and memory chips are sometimes lifted. The urban setting also means lots of people unconnected to MIT may wander through the campus. In fact, during the first nine months of 2000, vigilant MIT police officers conducted routine checks and inquiries of 319 suspicious people on MIT property. Of these, 231 were given trespass warnings; six were student problems; two were psychiatric cases; one was an employee problem; and seventy-nine proved to be no problem.

Roughly two-thirds of MIT students choose to live in campus dormitories, where they can choose from numerous single-sex or mixed-sex residences. The remaining students live in the thirty fraternities or six sororities, or off campus. Housing is guaranteed for all four years (a real plus given the Boston market) and mixes all classes (freshman through senior). The school's push for diversity has resulted in the presence of a "Women's Independent Living Group" and a black campus residence called by its inhabitants (in what might, from another source, be considered racist terms) "Chocolate City."

MIT freshman Scott Krueger died with a 0.4 blood-alcohol level after a night of hazing in September 1997. This created a wave of bad press for the college, which revamped its alcohol policies on campus. MIT will no longer allow its money to be spent on alcohol at university-related functions; it will strictly enforce a no-alcohol policy in the dormitories; it will work to promote an alcohol-free lifestyle for college students. All freshmen will live on campus in a $40 million dorm, expected to be completed fall 2001.

Men still outnumber women at MIT (about 60 percent to 40 percent of the student body), but the institution is trying to make incoming classes more equal in balance. One professor says female students are not only as bright and motivated as their male peers, but also have "the same nerdish demeanor" — not considered a bad thing at MIT. Apparently, most men at MIT are dying for some women, since male students dominate the school's population. But not all men. MIT has four homosexual student groups, including the MIT GLBT Coffeehouse, sponsored by the MIT Graduate Student Council. It's a social organization that "supports the needs of the MIT gay, lesbian, bisexual, and transgendered community," and hosts monthly Coffeehouse socials.

Though MIT students are preoccupied with their academic performance, they are not too busy to keep more than two hundred student organizations up and running, including many research-specific societies, some divided along ethnic and gender lines (American Indian Science and Engineering Society, Society of Women Engineers, etc.). More than sixty intramural and club sports programs are offered, as are more than a dozen musical and theater groups, including the Guild of Bellringers and the Gilbert and Sullivan Players. One professor says student musical performances are "extremely professional" and observes that there is a "serious avocational interest" on the part of students when it comes to fine arts pursuits. Political groups range from the subdued College Republicans to the more active Radicals for Capitalism/Objectivist Lyceum. According to one undergraduate, the College Republicans Club hasn't even asked for university funding in recent years due to its inactivity. MIT has had a pagan student group since the 1980s. On Halloween, the group uses the campus chapel to commune with the dead. Perhaps this provides a nice break from the sciences.

There are numerous other student religious groups, representing everything from Campus Crusade for Christ to MITAAH (MIT Atheists, Agnostics, and Humanists), which proclaims itself "the only Freethought group at a leading scientific institution." A founding member, writing in *Counterpoint*, bemoaned what she considered to be the fact that "Christianity underlies the accepted world view of the majority of MIT students," and sought an alternative to "world views based on blind faith and superstition to the exclusion of skepticism, reasoning, and analytical skills."

The University of Michigan

Office of Undergraduate Admissions
1220 Student Activities Building
Ann Arbor, MI 48109-1316
(734) 764-7433
www.umich.edu

Total enrollment: 37,846
Undergraduates: 24,493
SAT ranges (Verbal/Math): 570-670 (V); 600-710 (M)
Applicants: 21,132
Accepted: 64%
Enrolled: 41%
Application deadline: February 1
Financial aid application deadline: February 1
Tuition: resident: $6,526/$12,336; non-resident: $20,356/$26,166
Core curriculum: No

First of a Flourishing Breed

Founded in 1817, twenty years before the state of Michigan officially came into exis-tence, the University of Michigan was the first truly huge institution of higher educa-tion in the United States. Michigan is not the oldest state school in the nation, but it has been one of the largest state schools since the middle of the nineteenth century. While many other state schools a hundred years ago were small colleges catering to their homegrown social elites, the University of Michigan, financially well off, was spending its dollars on a wide array of programs and on faculty research.

The momentum of this mammoth undertaking continues to the present day; thanks to thanks to its sheer size and massive budget, Michigan is able to provide opportunities that smaller schools simply cannot. The university doesn't have one library — it has twenty-eight of them. The libraries don't just have a few special col-lections — they have vast holdings in everything from Asian to European rare books and manuscripts, not to mention one of the largest collections of papyrus fragments (ten thousand pieces) in the world. It spent nearly half-a-billion dollars on research in 1998. It has specialists in every field from early medieval Indian art to nuclear en-gineering. And its football stadium can hold more than 111,000 people.

As such, Michigan can overwhelm even an experienced research professor, let alone an eighteen-year-old freshmen. The campus is so large that it requires a bus system to shuttle students around campus, generally between Central Campus, the oldest and most populated part of the school, and North Campus, a newer, more spread-out campus primarily geared towards the sciences that was constructed a short distance north of the city center. You can get lost navigating the campus, but you can also be waylaid somewhere in the curriculum, which includes a number of revisionist- or multiculturalist-type courses posing as core requirements. But while politics permeates the classroom, those attending Michigan can easily find a serious education if they are willing to look for it. Part of that will undoubtedly come as they form their own opinions about and deal with the reigning orthodoxies on campus. There are enough opportunities at Michigan so that a student, no matter what his interests, can find what he is looking for.

Academic Life: To Be Determined

Instead of a rigorous core curriculum, Michigan requires that all students complete a number of courses distributed over a wide variety of subject areas. These distribution requirements vary among the different colleges the university comprises, and the university does leave a lot of the choice to the students' discretion. So while the university makes it possible for students to take engaging, thoughtful classes on more traditional subject matter, it also allows students to study the obscure, the trivial, and the politically correct. "The potential breadth is gigantic," one professor says. "You can take a course on anything. You can branch off in every direction."

Some advice on selecting courses at Michigan: Each term, consider the choices with a great deal of thought, read course descriptions closely, and always know what exactly you're getting into. Like Indiana Jones in *The Last Crusade*, faced with picking the true Holy Grail among many, don't be distracted by the more glitzy, worldly prospects. Students who choose wisely can make even the seemingly most politically correct of requirements into a wonderful learning experience. But students who choose poorly may find themselves stuck in a course like Women's Studies 240 that examines, for example, "the new feminist scholarship of women" and how "capitalism, racism, imperialism, and heterosexism affect women's lives."

Students looking to earn an A.B. or B.S. degree from the College of Literature, Science, and the Arts (LS&A) must complete a total of 120 credits with a cumulative GPA of 2.0 or better, and must receive a 2.0 overall GPA in the courses that make up the student's concentration (Michigan's word for a major). "The difference between the A.B. and B.S. degrees," according to the College's Bulletin, "is that the B.S. degree requires sixty credits of approved courses in the physical and natural sciences and/or mathematics." In addition, the LS&A now offers academic minors; these involve fifteen credits of work outside the department of concentration. These minors must be planned out in conjunction with and approved by an academic advisor — a wise way of doing things, whether it's required or not.

LS&A mandates that its students complete an "area distribution plan," which accounts for thirty out of the 120 minimum credits. Students must take seven credits worth of courses in the areas of natural science, social science, and humanities, for a total of twenty-one credits. In addition, students must also complete three credits in three out of these five areas: natural science; social science; humanities; mathematical and symbolic analysis; and creative expression, for a total of nine credits.

All students pursuing the A.B. and B.S. degrees must also complete:

- An English composition requirement, consisting of one introductory and one upper-level course.
- A quantitative reasoning requirement that consists of one or two courses, depending on the weight given to a course. (Two courses in introductory astronomy, for example, fulfill this requirement, but so does one term of calculus.)
- A foreign language requirement, in which students must master a fourth-term language course with a grade of C-minus or better. High school courses that advance the student beyond the first term or terms of language study (as determined by an exam) count toward this requirement.
- Finally, students must complete the "Race and Ethnicity" (R&E) requirement, which stipulates that each student must take a course focusing on "(1) the meaning of race, ethnicity and racism; (2) racial and ethnic intolerance and resulting inequality as it occurs in the United States and elsewhere; (3) comparisons of discrimination based on race, ethnicity, religion, social class, or gender," according to the college bulletin.

While the writing and foreign language requirements are generally solid, students who sign up for the wrong English 124/125 section (an introductory composition course) or choose a lesser-known language such as Ojibwe may find themselves in for a surprise. But it is the R&E requirement where students are usually sucked into taking courses of dubious value. Even the seemingly benign courses course called First Year Seminar in Cultural Anthropology has a syllabus concentrating on "Race and Power in the Americas," which discusses "how 'race' is implicated in relations of power and is tied to distinctions based on class, ethnicity, gender, and nationality," according to a college course guide.

Fortunately, students generally have a wide array of options when it comes to choosing a concentration. These concentrations take up between twenty-four and forty-eight credits, most or all of which usually fall outside the general degree requirements listed above, and there are dozens of them to choose from, ranging from physics to oceanography to French and francophone studies. Such a range is also, unfortunately, bound to include both the excellent (history and political science, for example) and the bizarre (like women's studies and American culture).

Within LS&A, students can pursue an A.B. or a B.S. degree, a bachelor of general studies degree, or a specialized bachelor of science in chemistry degree. The general studies program is an interdisciplinary approach to earning a bachelor's degree which, according to the college's bulletin, "encourages students to take responsibility for structuring their own multidisciplinary academic programs within guidelines emphasizing upper-level courses elected in three or more departments." A well-disciplined student could use it to gain mastery of many broad areas of learning — say English, history, and political science — but others could use it simply to get out of the requirements (such as they are) of the A.B. and B.S. degrees.

The university's curriculum plan is a double-edged sword, one that allows a thoughtful student to receive a traditional, old-style education along any number of paths, but also avails the possibility of cutting oneself on the sharp and glinting blade of modernity. A trusted academic advisor, instructors, and friends can go a long way in helping a student determine what courses will best serve his needs. A new student should study the course guide carefully and make use of his session with an academic advisor at orientation, remembering all the while that the university, with its failure to pinpoint and require what makes for a decent education, will not be doing it for him.

Michigan places a premium on research, although students taking upper-level courses can easily find small classes where the sole instructor is the professor teaching the course. As one faculty member says, "although the University of Michigan is primarily a research institution, the acquisition and dissemination of knowledge — research and teaching, respectively — are two sides of the same knowledge coin [here]."

Students have varied opinions regarding class sizes. "From what I have learned, almost all of the introductory classes are large, but beyond them await much smaller and more interesting classes," says one. One undergraduate said that his courses have included "large, professor-directed lecture sections" of fifty to five hundred students, and "then smaller discussion sections." Depending on the department, classes can range from "small and inviting," as one student says, to situations where the department "loves to put you in eighty-plus-person classes with a little figure in the distance flapping lips, expecting you to take worthwhile notes," according to another. As at most places, the smaller classes are usually a student's best bet. "Classes are, on average, too large," a student says. "The most fulfilling courses I've ever taken . . . have been classes with a class list of less than twenty."

"The big courses can be too damn big," a professor says, "but they can be good." He adds that, "if you want to reach out and do something one-on-one, you have to reach out." This can easily be done by attending office hours, exchanging e-mail with professors, and participating in "living-learning" programs. This professor also recommended courses known as "first-year seminars" for freshmen looking for small courses with a professor. "If you don't know about them," this faculty member says, "you're missing something." A former instructor at Michigan agrees, saying the first-year seminars are good for students and professors alike "because you get to know the student and can pay attention to their individual problems with the subject matter, as opposed to letting them swim and sink."

Michigan is also an incredibly computer-intensive campus, with computer labs spread throughout campus and the dormitories. This greatly improves communication between faculty and students. "If a student's on spring vacation in New York, that's absolutely no barrier," a professor says. "Even if you are reluctant to come to office hours or you don't know where the office is or something, you can always send off an e-mail."

Among just a few of the outstanding professors at Michigan are Gary Solon and Klaas Van 'T Velt in economics; Ralph G. Williams, Ejner Jensen, John Knott, Robert Lewis, and Robert Weisbuch in English; H. Don Cameron, Ludwig Koenen, David O. Ross, and Charles Witke in classics and great books; Scott Spector in Germanic languages and literatures; William Rosenberg, John Fine, Sidney Fine, Thomas Tentler, Diane O. Hughes, David Lewis, and Rudolf Mrazek in history; Ronald Inglehart and Raymond Tanter in political science; and Chris Peterson in the psychology department. Michigan boasts more excellent departments than some colleges and universities have departments, period. These include political science, history, classical archaeology, classical civilization, classical languages and literatures, anthropology, chemistry, physics, all engineering concentrations, Judaic studies, Chinese language and literature, Greek language and literature, Latin language and literature, the Medieval and Renaissance Collegium, philosophy, psychology, economics, business administration, mathematics, Near Eastern studies, neuroscience and art history.

Of course, Michigan also has its fair share of politicized departments: women's studies, African and Afro-American studies, American culture, education, social work, and cultural anthropology. Many of the courses that can be used to fulfill the R&E requirement fall into these disciplines, and some of these courses are politically and advocacy-oriented. One wonders how well many of these courses would fare if they were not endorsed and filled by the college-wide basic requirements system. Occasionally, some courses will not even try to hide their political bent, as shown in this course description from African and Afro-American Studies 203, which as of the fall of 1999 could count toward the social science distribution requirement:

> There is a great concern that all the rights gained in the sixties are now being eroded by legal challenges to affirmative action rules. Indeed there is a hue and cry that there is now reverse discrimination and that preferential treatment is illegal. The African American community in particular appears to be greatly alarmed by these challenges and is looking for ways to respond to these setbacks. This course will address the dilemma of the response and attempt to shape some thinking about the fight for affirmative action. The cases at the University of Michigan and the University of Texas will be examined not for their legal construct but for their meaning as a social construct. In addition Proposition 209 will be discussed as an important watershed in the anti–civil rights movement. The anti–affirmative action forces, and the dilemma of African-Americans and

other minorities against affirmative action will be seriously addressed. Some attention will be paid to Justice Clarence Thomas and Mr. Ward Connerly, two major figures against affirmative action. The objective is to begin the process of cogent action and to develop the language to articulate affirmative action as a right and not a benefit.

In other courses, the potential for indoctrination at the expense of instruction is severe. A principal example offered in the Fall of 2000 was English 317: Literature and Culture, Section 001, which focused on "How to Be Gay: Homosexuality and Initiation." It should be noted that this course can be used to fulfill the humanities distribution requirement, and that it costs the student a laboratory fee of $35; what the lab fee is for exactly, the description does not say. "This course will examine the general topic of the role that initiation plays in the formation of gay identity," the course guide says, and will examine "a number of cultural artifacts and activities that seem to play a prominent role in learning how to be gay: Hollywood movies, grand opera, Broadway musicals, and other works of classical and popular music, as well as camp, diva-worship, drag, muscle culture, style, fashion, and interior design." In addition, it will focus on whether there are "a number of classically 'gay' works such that, despite changing tastes and generations, ALL gay men, of whatever class, race, or ethnicity, need to know them, in order to be gay? What roles do such works play in learning how to be gay? What is there about these works that makes them essential parts of a gay male curriculum?" The class engendered considerable opposition within the state, and concerned taxpayers obtained 15,000 signatures on a petition asking the University not to offer the class again. The class was dropped from the Spring 2001 catalogue, but word is that it will return when the professor who teaches it returns to campus.

Michigan's English department has perhaps the widest range of courses on a scale of outstanding to academic esoterica. For example, compare English 124 and 125, "Writing and Literature" and "College Writing," respectively, which are staples for students completing introductory composition requirement. Each offers dozens of sections for students to choose from. In the winter term of 2000, they ranged from English 124's Section 004, which helped students "develop clear, effective, and convincing writing "and included works by Agatha Christie, Poe and A. C. Doyle "in order to explore different methods of creating interest, revealing information, and drawing conclusions from the evidence at hand," to Section 059 of English 125, "Representing Violence," which takes "an anthropological lens to examine how and why different 'violences' are imagined in different genres and media: TV news report and paperback novel, historical narrative and public testimony, horror movie and radio gangsta rap. As we encounter distinct representations, we will consider how gender, language and culture contribute to our ways of grasping this slippery, many-sided phenomenon."

They got the "slippery" part right, anyway.

Political Atmosphere: Ignore Them, and Still They Won't Go Away

Most students arriving at Michigan, like most college freshmen, have yet to make up their minds regarding their political beliefs. At Michigan, new students will find themselves on a campus marinating in politics. With an administration that generally doesn't stand up to student radicals, the university's racial preferences in admissions under attack in the courts, and a student government with a large leftist contingent, the political atmosphere is extremely thick. These attitudes sometimes seep through into the classroom, and even the most nonpolitical student will be touched in some way by university politics.

Racial preferences in admissions is The Big Issue at Michigan, as the university is currently being sued by two white applicants to the LS&A and a white applicant to the Law School for allegedly admitting less-qualified minority students at their expense. Oddly enough, the university changed its admissions criteria in 1998 so that the school relies *even more* on race as a factor in admissions now than it did in past years. In fact, according to student media, applicants to the University of Michigan will find that even a perfect SAT score, a great essay, and oodles of extracurricular or leadership activities will count less towards their admission than their race or socio-economic status.

The university's obsession with diversity is only begins with the application process; it continues until a student walks out the door with his degree. This is manifested in the large number of programs and services Michigan offers minorities and other special-interest groups, along with its refusal to crack down on those special-interest groups when a few agitators cause disturbances. This is not to say that these programs do not offer worthwhile services, or that they are entirely run by ideological cadres. But when underclassmen suffer through huge lectures with four or five hundred students and some students may not receive all the financial assistance they need, one wonders whether parts of Michigan's considerable budget could be more wisely spent.

The University's Office of Multi-Ethnic Student Affairs, Office of Academic Minority Initatives, and the Trotter House offer a variety of services for minority students. Each dormitory also has a minority peer advisor and a multicultural hall council, along with multicultural lounges. And at graduation time, the university holds Black Celebratory and Celebracíon Latina functions for its black and Hispanic students.

Michigan's Office of Lesbian, Gay, Bisexual, and Transgender Affairs, another university division catering to a slim minority of students, announced a conference in 2000 called "Moving Beyond the Rhetoric." According to the office, the conference is "committed to a philosophy of social justice in the struggle against racism, sexism, homophobia, and classism." Its goals are numerous, including to "develop a vision of and action plan for creating a multifaceted movement for creating social change that incorporates Race, Class, Sexual Orientation, and Gender," as well as to "promote discourse on how to raise consciousness at the local, national, and international levels, and how to trigger social reform needed to eradicate race, class, sexual orientation, and gender injustice."

Students at Michigan say that politics enters into the classroom, although not all the faculty interviewed agreed with this view. One frustrated student says that "politics, wholly and completely, almost inevitably permeates the classroom" and that she faced "a non-stop barrage of slanted, biased, politically charged propaganda." Another student complains that his instructor told him "he hurt the class" because "when other students made poor arguments, I would disagree and prove them wrong. This, in [my instructor's] view, 'intimidated' people from raising their voice."

Faculty, on the other hand, say that the classroom is an open place, and one professor says that the "revolution on political correctness" is "not all that worrisome from a teaching perspective."

However, another professor says that he is aware that he has to avoid making "offensive statements." "I've never had complaints, but I feel like I'd better watch it," this faculty member continues. He says he needs to be careful especially when making examples that could, without clarification, be taken the wrong way.

As for students, the small but vocal radical element gets away with a lot: other students say this faction isn't controlled by the university when it steps over the line. "It coddles them, plain and simple," one student says. Every few months, the student says, these groups "organize a 'Day of Action' in defense of affirmative action. Each time, about twenty students show up until fire alarms mysteriously go off around campus. Instantly, hundreds of students flood out of the buildings onto the center of campus, unwittingly becoming part of the protest."

In addition, the university has been in the national news thanks to protests over its use of sweatshop labor and for the allegedly anti–American Indian practices of a student secret society called "Michigamua." Both incidents involved protestors occupying offices — the dean's office, in the case of the sweatshop demonstration. The latter incident received a great deal of attention because the protestors, known as the Students of Color Coalition, spent thirty-seven days occupying Michigamua's office and because of the support of public figures like Rev. Al Sharpton.

The university's response to the sweatshop protestors was to accede to their demand that it affiliate itself with the Worker's Rights Coalition, a factory monitoring group that a student publication described as "extremist." As for the Michigamua incident, the university president issued a declaration claiming "practices that negatively stereotype groups in our society cause unjust pain and humiliation," and that such practices "are not acceptable behaviors." It is also looking into the "assignment and use of the Michigan Union tower" — where Michigamua's office is located — "and any other exclusively assigned space."

However, despite these high-profile incidents, the radicals don't have much influence. "[They have] basically no influence on campus life," this student says. "Most students, quite frankly, don't give a damn."

Student Life: The Victors

With around twenty thousand Michigan undergraduates in and around Ann Arbor, it is easy for every student to find people with similar interests, beliefs, and hobbies in the midst of a cosmopolitan and vibrant urban environment. While the university itself can be intimidating at first, there is a plethora of opportunities to make friends and pursue one's favorite activities all over campus.

Orientation is not all that bad for incoming students, and aside from a bit of politicized indoctrination, its greatest crime would appear to be cheesiness. "It wasn't that bad," says one freshman student, although he says it was "boring and pointless."

"We got there, were led around like sheep, heard a bunch of soapbox speeches, ate sub-edible food, slept in a room the size of a shoe box in East Quad, and endured the peppy (read: annoying) orientation leaders," this student continues. "They addressed all of the sensitive issues in a play, but it seemed more like a Chinese propaganda thing. But it was more comfortable than it could have been." The play, this student adds, covered issues relating to alternative sexual lifestyles "as well as the extremely helpful 'how to drink and not die' portion."

Michigan's dormitories range from old-fashioned, stately houses to complexes that resemble high-rise apartment buildings. The dorms are generally good places to live. "I love my dorm, amazingly," a student says. "It's easy, and comfy, and a lot better than dealing with an off-campus hell-hole." When choosing a place to live, keep in mind that most courses offered by LS&A are located on Central Campus and courses for other schools (Music, Architecture, and a good number of Engineering courses) are located on North Campus. However, the two campuses are linked by a university-run bus system, usually pretty good but less reliable on weekends.

Most students live either on the University's Central Campus or on the Hill, where four dormitories are perched over Palmer Field, a facility consisting of a track, tennis courts, and a large field used for pick-up football games and Frisbee tossing. Occasionally, LS&A students will find themselves in Bursley Hall on North Campus, bad because it is far away from the Central Campus, but mitigated by the fact that Bursley is generally regarded as the best dormitory at Michigan. "They felt bad for sticking you up in the middle of nowhere, but getting to live in the nicest dorm is somewhat compensation," a former student says. Certain buildings contain academic programs within the building; for example, East Quad on Central Campus is the home of the University's Residential College, while Alice Lloyd, located on the Hill, houses the Lloyd Scholars program. These programs allow students to learn in a smaller, more close-knit environment.

Within the dormitories, life can vary widely from hall to hall. Some corridors and rooms are substance-free or non-smoking. Likewise, most dormitories offer floors or corridors solely for males or females, although there are also halls where men and women live side-by-side, although not in the same rooms. Females-only Stockwell Hall is the only large single-sex dormitory.

Freshman women who wish to live in a more traditional environment can apply to live in the Helen Newberry House, the Betsey Barbour House, or the Martha Cook Building. Newberry and Barbour are small all-female dormitories, whereas Martha Cook offers "traditional living in a historic building." The Martha Cook Building offers sit-down dinners served by waitresses three nights a week, a number of faculty dinners, and a quiet atmosphere. In addition, Martha Cook also has male visitation hours. However, space is limited in these buildings.

Campus crime has declined 30 percent from 1995 to 1998, the last year for which statistics are available, according to Michigan's Department of Public Safety website. However, students attending Michigan, especially if they are new, should use common sense when it comes to protecting themselves from crime. After all, the university is a decent-sized town unto itself, what with 11,000 campus residents, 37,000 total students, and 22,000 faculty and staff. The most common crimes on campus, by far, are larceny and burglary, with 1,348 and 111 cases reported, respectively, in 1998. Sexual crimes are rather infrequent, with three cases of forcible rape and fifteen cases of lesser sexual crime reported to police during that year. Students report that they do not worry about their safety at Michigan. "[This is a] completely safe campus," a student says. "Crime is not an issue." Just to make sure, the university also has a police force of thirty full-time officers (in addition to support staff), a series of emergency telephones around campus, and walking services, shared-taxi services, and shuttles that operate in the evenings.

Since it's such a big place, the university can occasionally appear unfeeling at times: as one writer at a student publication cracked, Michigan is the *a la carte* university: "Oh, you want that? That's extra!" However, Michigan has such a rich collection of people and resources that students can easily find a group of friends that share their beliefs and concerns, regardless of what they are. There are a number of fraternities and sororities on campus, along with a number of minority and ethnic student groups, such as the Indian American Students Association. There are also dozens of politically oriented or hobby-centered student clubs, ranging from the College Democrats and Republicans to the Musicians for Christ.

Student publications regularly stir things up on campus and keep readers aware of the happenings around Michigan and the outside world. The left-leaning *Michigan Daily*, founded more than a century ago, is the established student paper. Its principal rivals are the conservative *Michigan Review*, a biweekly campus affairs journal, and a number of smaller publications such as the *Michigan Independent* that also offer interested students a chance to voice their opinions.

The campus and Ann Arbor offer more than enough attractions to keep students occupied. The State Theater and the Michigan Theater are within walking distance, offering current and classic films at a reasonable price. The Borders bookstore chain got its start in Ann Arbor, and its store on Liberty Street is a veritable treasure trove for book-lovers. And restaurant lovers needn't despair in Ann Arbor — students can find great Italian food at Gratzi, wonderful sandwiches at

Zingerman's Deli, and a phenomenal pizza at the Cottage Inn restaurant on East William Street.

But no mention of life at Michigan is complete without mentioning perhaps the coolest facet of being a student there: the sports programs. The games are always a great deal of fun, whether one is in the stands at Michigan Stadium watching the legendary Wolverines football team or helping fellow hockey fans heckle an opposing team's goalie. Even if you don't go to Michigan, you've already heard the school's classic fight song, "The Victors," hundreds of times. Michigan is extremely competitive in most of its sports, and with their national reputation, Michigan's sports teams are the great uniting force on a campus that can often seem preoccupied with that topic.

Michigan State University

Office of Admissions and Scholarships
250 Administration Building
East Lansing, Michigan 48824-0590
(517) 355-1855
www.msu.edu

Total enrollment: 43,000
Undergraduates: 34,000
SAT ranges (Verbal/Math): 490-610 (V); 490-630 (M)
Applications: 22,623
Accepted: 71%
Enrolled: 41%
Application deadline: December 1
Financial aid application deadline: January 1
Tuition: resident: $5,472/$9,980; non-resident: $13,096/$17,604
Core curriculum: No

Behemoth University

Michigan State University is one of the oldest land-grant universities in the country. Founded in 1855, the university has grown from a primarily agricultural school to a huge "multiversity" with fourteen colleges and 34,000 undergraduates populating more than 150 programs of study. While the university's promotional literature tries to portray its size in a positive light, assurances such as "You won't get lost — we'll give you a map!" (found in university admissions literature) are a rather silly attempt to calm the reasonable fear that Michigan State is an institution grown beyond human scale.

The late author and scholar Russell Kirk, himself a graduate of MSU, coined the term "Behemoth University" to describe his alma mater. For him the term characterized an institution grown bloated, ponderous, and destructively out of control. MSU symbolized to Kirk all that was wrong with the modern multiversity: the abandonment of liberal learning for the pursuit of narrow utilitarian programs and ideological agendas. Unfortunately, over the years Kirk's characterization has become more and more apt, and there seems to be no sign of the trend's reversal.

In spite of the university's mass-production approach to education, there are opportunities for students to get a good liberal arts education at MSU. In the College of Arts and Letters, some solid programs flourish. For students who wish to pursue the sciences while at the same time chasing a well-rounded education, the Lyman Briggs School offers excellent programs. Finally, special notice must be given to the James Madison College, a nationally recognized college within the university that concentrates on public policy and government while maintaining a strong liberal arts component.

Academic Life: Muddled State

Michigan State does not have a core curriculum. There is a loose collection of distribution requirements that includes basic competence in writing and math. The writing requirement can be met by taking either writing courses or by taking specially designated courses in other disciplines (such as English or philosophy) that have strong writing requirements. The math requirement can be met with courses in either college algebra, calculus, or statistics.

Beyond the basic competencies in math and writing, the largest group of classes the MSU student will take outside of his major are those of the Integrative Studies Program (ISP). This program consists of seven or eight courses in the arts and humanities, the natural sciences, and the social sciences. The goal and purpose of the program is certainly lofty; the university claims:

> The program . . . provides students with a sense of the interrelatedness of knowledge, especially the intersection of liberal learning with the professional, technical and specialized knowledge of the major. . . . The Integrative Studies Program encourages the development of analytical skills and the use of a variety of methods of inquiry. . . . The program fosters the student's sense of responsibility as an effective citizen of a diverse yet interdependent world.

However, the number and kinds of courses that meet these requirements are so broad and diffuse that there is an element of wishful thinking in calling it a "program." Indeed, apart from some faculty advisors, students are essentially on their own and can devise a curriculum to suit their own fancies. There is nothing approaching a coherent introduction to an identifiable body of knowledge proposed in the ISP.

What there is an abundance of in the ISP is left-wing ideology. The courses in the humanities, for example, are replete with overt references to multiculturalism. For example, Humanities 211, "Area and Multicultural Studies in Africa and Asia," is, according to some students who have taken it, a semester-long tirade against the West and extols the virtues of socialism and collectivism. In fact, courses in the ISP are all scored for their "diversity": courses are designated with an "I" for international diversity, a "D" for multicultural diversity, and an "N" for national diversity. Students are required to take at least one course from either the "I" or the "N" category. There is a requirement that students take at least one "non-Western" course, but a degree from Michigan State doesn't depend on whether the student takes a course in Western civilization.

The one course that all MSU students take is "Integrative Studies in the Arts and Humanities 201: The U.S. and the World." This course, according to one student, was "a primer in understanding that America is the cause of most of the world's problems. Anything wrong with the world — war, poverty, you name it — it's America's fault. And especially the fault of white, male Americans." Another student called it "leftist political reindoctrination." So at MSU, the one educational experience all students share is an attack upon the Western cultural heritage.

The key to understanding the real thrust and purpose of the ISP might be found in the final sentence of a description in a brochure sent to prospective students. The program, it says, "fosters the student's sense of responsibility as an effective citizen of a diverse yet interdependent world." This high-minded purpose, however, acquires a different meaning in the light of the actual situation at MSU and the meaning of the code words in it. "Responsibility," in the language of the left, is guilt, particularly white guilt. The "effective citizen," to the leftist ideologue, is an activist for left-wing causes. "Diversity" is, in academia, a diversity that excludes whites, males, Europeans, and people of traditional religious beliefs, especially Christians. These together make the ISP's goal not only liberal, but counter to a traditional liberal arts education.

For the student interested in that liberal arts education, only three of MSU's colleges offer relevant programs. The College of Arts and Sciences is home to the traditional liberal arts disciplines such as history and foreign languages. The College of Social Science has excellent programs in economics and politics. But the clear standout for many students wanting a well-rounded, coherent education is the James Madison College. This is a "college within the university" that attempts to create a close-knit learning environment, aimed at providing a "liberal education in public affairs."

The James Madison College at MSU offers majors in international relations, political economy, political theory and constitutional democracy, and social relations. It was established in 1967 as a school of public affairs, but now constitutes a real intellectual community within the larger university. Its residential setting creates close relationships between faculty and the one thousand students who meet in smaller-than-average classes as well as outside the classroom.

JMC aims at a self-contained educational experience and largely succeeds. Students in the college take a year-long JMC version of the university writing courses, in which the readings examine issues such as "the individual in society, the search for selfhood, or identity, and the social circumstances in which decisions and identities are shaped." Students in these courses also read and write on various topics in American history.

JMC also has its own versions of classes designed to meet other university requirements. These courses enable the JMC student to avoid some of the nonsense and indoctrination that he might find in the university's ordinary distribution courses. For example, students in the college can enroll in a two-semester sequence titled "Introduction to the Study of Public Affairs," which fulfills the university's social science requirement. These two classes focus on the political, economic, and social aspects of American society, and the readings are drawn from a variety of sources in the fields of history, political science, economics, and sociology. JMC also requires its students to take two courses in economics, as well as an internship in some sort of public policy organization such as government agencies, legislative offices, or nonprofit organizations.

The best departments at MSU outside of JMC are economics, political science, biology, and most of the other programs in the Lyman Briggs School. The Lyman Briggs School is similar to the James Madison College in that it offers a residential, smaller-scale learning environment, dedicated to the study of the natural sciences. The foreign language programs at MSU are also quite good.

Some outstanding faculty at Michigan State include Louis Hunt, Constance Hunt, and Richard Zinman at James Madison College; William Allen and Jerry Weinberger in political science; Paul Segerstrom in economics; and Daniel Ilgen in psychology.

The most radical faculty at MSU are to be found, not surprisingly, in the women's studies department and in the Latin American and Caribbean studies and Latino studies programs. In women's studies, for example, one can be treated to such offerings as Women's Studies 204, titled "Lesbian, Bisexual, and Gay Studies: Psychological and Cultural Issues," or Women's Studies 321, "Lesbian Culture and Identities," which is an introduction to "lesbian history, lesbian culture/communities, and the construction of lesbian identity." The English department also has its share of radical agendas. English 102, "Everyday English," promises an introduction to "genderlects," among other things. Even if that course can explain what the heck "genderlects" are, we doubt it can make a decent case for including them in a low-level college English course. Because of courses like these, the student at MSU needs to seek out a good adviser to guide him through the ideological minefields that await him in many of the undergraduate programs.

Political Atmosphere: Middle of the State

MSU has a relatively middle-of-the-road reputation, especially when compared to its rival, the University of Michigan. The president of MSU, M. Peter McPherson, was a member of the Bush administration, and he has gained national attention for espousing conservative principles in his administration of the university. He created a great deal of controversy several years ago by opposing the extension of benefits to the partners of gay and lesbian MSU employees.

Politically, many students at MSU could be classified as "apathetic," a student says. "Most students here totally don't care" about politics, says another. The student body could be described as moderately liberal; the majority voted for Bill Clinton in both 1992 and '96. "MSU has a reputation as a blue collar school, and most students are interested in getting through and getting a good job," says one professor. "They're not the crusader types."

While most students may not be "crusaders," there is still no shortage of leftist activists. These activists tend to be concentrated in the Division of Residence Life (the department that manages the residence halls), the university's newspaper, *The Spartan*, and in student government. The student government was embroiled in controversy during the 1998 election year for violating its own constitution — not to mention state election laws — by making contributions to the campaign of Democratic gubernatorial candidate (and infamous attorney for Dr. Jack Kevorkian) Geoffrey Fieger. "The student government is extremely corrupt," one student says.

The Division of Residence Life has acquired a reputation for liberal activism as well. "The Residence Life office is captive to the gay activists," a junior says. "The dorms are peppered with pro-gay posters and banners," another student says, "and PRISM (a gay activist organization) has managed pretty much to cow the university into endorsing whatever it demands." For example, each year, the Division of Residence Life, along with PRISM and several organizations, sponsors a university-wide event known as "Segregation Week." This event features rallies, demonstrations, and "consciousness-raising" sessions in the dorms all designed to indoctrinate students in the gay rights agenda as well as other leftist political concerns.

The Spartan is also well-known as an organ of radical opinion on campus. It is said to bar its writers and contributors from using "religious language" in their submissions. Most recently *The Spartan* was embroiled in controversy for its summary firing of a columnist who wrote a column critical of gay-rights pressure tactics. This columnist was not accorded a hearing or any other recourse regarding his dismissal, which had been demanded by several gay organizations on campus. "They [the gay organizations] threatened to boycott the paper," a student says. When the student columnist retained legal counsel, he was told by a university official that his attempts to defend himself were "unacceptable" and would not be tolerated by the university. "The university has a pattern of 'looking the other way' when it comes to the excesses of the left," a professor says.

Another source of campus activism comes from the student Xicano (i.e., Chicano) organization. The unusual spelling is itself a political statement, rejecting any hint of Anglicization. After several years of unsuccessfully attempting to make MSU "grape-free" as a show of solidarity with oppressed Latino agricultural workers, the organization created a firestorm of controversy with a new protest in the 1999-2000 academic year. A number of group members checked out four hundred university library books each — the maximum number allowed. They condemned the books for being of "European" origin, and the thousands of tomes were padlocked in a semi-trailer and guarded by organization members. The group then announced it was "holding the books hostage," and would not return them until the university met their demands. "It was a real circus," says a senior. "Lots of people were really angry," says another student. "They couldn't get books they needed for papers and such because they were locked up in that trailer." The situation dragged out for weeks until the university finally retrieved the books.

Amidst the occasional circus, most students remain politically apathetic. And many faculty members complain that their students are also academically apathetic. Many, however, are not apathetic to partying: besides the normal college-town drinking problems, the school got national attention in 1997 for the on-campus "Gunson riots," so named because they started on Gunson Street. What started as a drunken brawl between a few rowdy students ended with crowds burning furniture and cars in the street and smashing the windows of police cars. The university is still suffering from the public relations fallout of the incident.

Student Life

The university's campus is sprawling, but quite pleasant, with wooded areas, and a park-like feel to parts of the campus, complete with hiking trails and bike paths. East Lansing has an active cultural and night life; indeed, it is a haven for student-socialites with a plethora of bars, restaurants, and fraternity parties. Unique to East Lansing are the bars, including the always-packed and smoky Silver Dollar and The Riv, a favorite of fraternity brothers (in terms of employment — the majority of employees at the Riv are MSU frat boys). Sparty's (which plays off the MSU nickname, the Spartans) is one of the most popular nightclubs in town. The city is also easy to get around in, with an inexpensive bus system that makes travel both on and off campus quick and convenient.

Perhaps students' entertainment options are one reason faculty complain that the biggest problem they face is student apathy. One professor says "30 percent of students don't come to class on a regular basis. The problem with the students at MSU is not one of intellect, but of motivation."

Apathy is not a problem when it comes to athletics, especially when a contest against the University of Michigan Wolverines is concerned. MSU has fourteen intercollegiate teams for men and eleven for women, and boasts that it has the largest intramural program in the world: more than 2,300 teams involved in more than two dozen sports. The sports facilities are immense. For example, the football stadium holds seventy-two thousand and the basketball arena seats more than fifteen thousand. MSU also has an ice hockey venue, an eighteen-hole golf course, and a baseball field, among other facilities.

Other campus structures are also built to the scale of a large state university. The MSU libraries house more than 4 million volumes, plus an additional quarter-million rare books in a special collection. The Wharton Center for Performing Arts contains two theaters: the Great Hall and Festival Stage, which can hold 2,500 audience members, and a smaller theater with 600 seats. The Kellogg Hotel and Conference Center, named for the Kellogg's of cereal fame in nearby Battle Creek, hosts more than 400,000 guests each year at more than a thousand conferences and meetings. The center also allows MSU hotel and restaurant science majors a chance to practice.

MSU is also home to the Kresge Art Museum, which contains more than five thousand works of art, as well as classrooms and art studios.

Crime at MSU is about what should be expected for an institution of its size. Serious offenses are relatively uncommon; burglaries and thefts are not, and arrests for liquor or drug violations are routine.

The residence hall system at MSU is the largest in the country. There are 23 undergraduate dorms (each of which houses about 1,000 students), one graduate dorm, and three university-owned apartment complexes. Each room comes equipped with cable, ethernet, and voice mail services. All dorms are coed, with men and women living on separate floors in all but a couple, in which the sexes are separated by suite.

There are hundreds of registered student organizations at MSU. These include unique groups like Bombsquad Productions, which "plans and implements programs that cater to students of color," the Complementary and Alternative Medicine Club, and the In Your Face Reality Troupe — Virtual Sexuality, which claims as its purpose the production of "dramatical [sic] presentations to educate students on sexual behaviors." For students interested in other forms of in-your-face reality, there are many pre-professional, athletic, and religious organizations.

Middlebury College

Admissions Office
The Emma Willard House
Middlebury, VT 05753-6002
(802) 388-3711
www.middlebury.edu

Total enrollment: 2,200
Undergraduates: 2,200
SAT ranges (Verbal/Math): 680-730 (V); 670-740 (M)
Applicants: 4,869
Accepted: 26%
Enrolled: 42%
Application deadline: December 15
Financial aid application deadline: December 31
Tuition: $32,765 (comprehensive fee includes room and board)
Core curriculum: No

Been Through the Wars

Middlebury College was for years a good liberal arts college in the New England tradition, but it suffered under a reputation as a rich kids' paradise, complete with its own ski area and mountainous surroundings worthy of a resort. The professors were known to be dedicated, but the student body seemed more interested in personal pleasure than in the life of the mind. "Our main debit is our reputation of being a club," one professor says. "Middlebury's primary challenge is to emphasize the importance of intellectual work."

Over the past several years Middlebury has labored mightily to meet this challenge, and has had a good deal of success. Today the student who matriculates at Middlebury will find a rigorous curriculum taught by some extremely gifted and dedicated professors in a setting that is the quintessence of New England.

This move into the world of top-notch colleges was not accomplished without a few philosophical battles — not all of which were won unanimously, or finally. Still, the supporters of traditional education who have held out against radicalizing forces have every right to feel proud of the result. Even though it is forced to compete with reputable schools in its own region, Middlebury has done an admirable job in preserving a sense of the importance of the liberal arts. While no small number of faculty members would be happy to see the college become more ideological, they are,

449

for now, balanced and counteracted by scholars who have won what today amounts to a rare victory in academia.

Academic Life: Good Choices

Middlebury has no core curriculum, instead allowing its students to choose courses from seven out of eight distribution areas: literature, arts, philosophical and religious studies, historical studies, physical and life sciences, social analysis, foreign language, and deductive reasoning and analytical processes. There is also a two-season physical education requirement. Though this setup is hardly a shining example of the liberal arts tradition, Middlebury makes up for the looseness of its requirements with fine teaching. Of course, it is also possible to fulfill the distribution requirement with tangential courses. But, as one professor says, "With careful choosing and good advice, a student can obtain an excellent, broad liberal arts education."

In addition to the seven classes that make up this requirement, students must also complete a three-course "cultures and civilizations" mandate. As is the case for the distribution courses, the students make the choices here, though they must come up with one class on the United States, one on Europe, and one on "a part of the world other than the U.S. or Europe."

"We have some pretty loose and undemanding cultural literacy requirements," says one professor, who along with other faculty is working on a proposal for a required humanities core. Faculty interviewed for this guide were divided as to whether Middlebury needs a core, not because they weren't committed to the liberal arts, but because some saw the present curriculum as strong enough to accomplish the goals of such an education.

Middlebury also requires two intensive writing seminars of all students. The first must be taken during the student's first semester on campus, and the second falls prior to the end of the sophomore year. The first-year seminar is taught via a thematic, interdisciplinary method, and the instructor chooses the theme and reading list. Each student's instructor for that seminar becomes his adviser for his first year at Middlebury.

Though many of the writing seminars are very well taught, and the list of offerings is generally very encouraging, some focus on topics more conducive to politicization. Recent examples include "Global Popular Music," "Environmental Controversies in the U.S.," "When People Work Together, Communities Change," and some fluffy, upper-level options in sociology and anthropology.

Middlebury's majors — forty-three of them, including five area studies in the international major — involve ten to sixteen courses, making them of slightly more than average bulk. Students can also opt for a major known as the "Independent Scholar," in which, according to college literature, "outstanding students with clear educational goals that cannot be fulfilled within the framework of normal departmental requirements may plan their own curricular programs with the assistance of a faculty advisor."

Several special programs are designed to prepare students for professional careers, yet Middlebury offers only the B.A. degree — no B.S. degrees, and no bachelor's degrees in education or other nonacademic subjects. A pre-med course list exists, but not as a major. Other preprofessional programs are cobbled together for students with, say, business or nursing interests, but the same degree requirements that apply to other students also apply to those choosing these paths.

Middlebury operates on a semester schedule, but offers a Winter Term each January. During that month students elect a single, intensive program of study that involves an independent project overseen by a member of the faculty.

Among the best professors at Middlebury are Richard Wolfson in physics; Murray Dry and Paul Nelson in political science; Kirsten Powell in history of art and architecture; Robert Hill, David Price, John Bertolini, and Marion A. Wells in English; and James Ralph and Travis Jacobs in history.

As for the most recommended departments at Middlebury, faculty rate these as the best: history, political science, English and American literature. Physics, economics, classics, theater, and foreign languages are also well respected. More than one-third of the student body majors in the social sciences and history, fully ten percentage points ahead of the average for similar institutions.

Middlebury's English department is best known for its association with the Bread Loaf Writers' Conference, a summer program in literature and creative writing it hosts each year. The best Middlebury undergraduates are permitted to enroll in Bread Loaf courses in the summer between their junior and senior years. The conference brings well-known writers to Vermont (and a few other locations) to teach courses and work with individual students. It is an excellent opportunity for students to become acquainted with the world of professional writers, editors, literary agents, and publication.

Even without Bread Loaf the department is strong. "They have as fine an undergraduate creative writing program as you'll find anywhere," a professor says. "It is insisted that all writers be grounded deeply in the Western tradition. English literature here is also very strong." Middlebury is among only a handful of top colleges to still require a Shakespeare class of its English majors, who must also take several period courses and pass a comprehensive senior exam. The Program in Literary Studies has a required reading list drawn from the masterworks of eleven national literatures.

Bread Loaf is not the only summer program for which the college is known. Its summer language schools, founded in 1915, offer students from Middlebury and elsewhere the chance to immerse themselves in one of the eight languages offered each year. Each participant must promise not to speak English during the entire session, and the credits earned can be applied to a Middlebury degree. Even during the regular school year, a large group of students study foreign languages, among other things, at Middlebury: nearly 12 percent of the student body majors in foreign languages and literatures, a rate almost four times the national average.

Some professors caution, however, that Middlebury's reputation for foreign language studies is overblown. "The summer programs [in foreign languages] are great, but that's a whole new faculty," one says. Says another: "The irony is that the reputation of the college is built on the language instruction. But language instruction here per se is not that good. Most of their best students are French majors. They're just not good teachers."

Nonetheless, students may put their language skills to work through the Middlebury Schools Abroad program, which offers study in several European cities. In addition to the language students, Middlebury's international relations majors also make good use of this program, as well as other college-approved programs in the Far East and Latin America. Closer to home, Middlebury offers semesters in Washington, D.C., or at the Williams College–Mystic Seaport Program in American Maritime Studies, where students delve into coastal history, literature, culture, and oceanography.

Middlebury is also heavily involved in the Center for Northern Studies, located about an hour away in Wolcott, Vermont. Students majoring in geography, environmental studies, or biology and who hear the call of the wild may spend a semester or a year in residency there. The program involves many field trips in the nearby woods and bogs, as well as a month of field study in northern regions such as Newfoundland, Alaska, or the Scottish Isles.

Environmental studies attract about 5 percent of students, a large number for that field, and Middlebury is noted nationwide for its environmental programs. But, like the college's other acclaimed program, language studies, it's not all it's cracked up to be, according to some on campus. "The administration is promoting this department very hard, and it will be the biggest department very soon," a professor says. "They get the big dollars, and they get a bunch of kids who after four years wonder, 'What did I do?' There's still a battle here over it, because enough of the hard scientists are opposed to it."

Students preferring wood paneling to the actual woods use the Geonomics Institute at Middlebury, described in college literature as "a dynamic international organization of business executives, policy makers, lawyers, bankers, and regional specialists." At the institute, leaders in government, business, and academe hold symposia on economic, political, and social problems — and students are invited. Recently the institute considered ways to create private-sector economies in the former Soviet Union, East Asia, and Latin America in cooperation with the West.

Despite its strengths, Middlebury has several politicized programs. Chief among these is women's studies, which one professor describes as "very weak with almost no majors, and everyone is afraid to debate it." The program does not have a lot of respect on campus, and the administration is not afraid to stand up to it; according to another professor, a radical member of the department was recently approved for reappointment, but the president of the college overrode the decision and fired her.

"There have been efforts to politicize the curriculum, but these efforts for the most part have been successfully resisted," says a professor. "Often, the most politicized courses, a relatively small number, are recognized as such by the students and do not attract large enrollments; usually it's a case of preaching to the choir." The school has recently added an interdisciplinary African-American studies minor, but there is no indication that it is any more politicized than other programs.

Political Atmosphere: The Sun After the Storm

Middlebury is a rarity in higher education today in that multiculturalist talk seems to be waning rather than gathering strength. "There's a fair amount of talk about multiculturalism and diversity [but] not as much as there used to be," a professor says. Several years ago the college endured a skirmish over the curriculum, but because several faculty stood up for the principles of liberal learning, the most politically correct proposals were defeated. For example, the required reading list for English majors disappeared temporarily several years ago, but has since been brought back.

It seems that Middlebury has pursued a more reasoned version of diversity than that found at some of its competitors. "Multiculturalism is such an elusive term," says another professor. "Nathan Glazer has recently argued that we are all multiculturalists now, and his assessment probably defines campus life at Middlebury. We value diversity here. There is no question that the trend at Middlebury is to cultivate a greater awareness of traditions outside of the U.S. and western Europe." The college does have an Office of Institutional Diversity, which has proposed a multicultural center and curriculum changes and which makes the standard request for increased "dialogue," but one imagines that these ideas will be debated on campus in the same considered manner as their predecessors.

Middlebury has also toned down an early-1990s version of a speech code described by one faculty member as "absolutely atrocious." The original code was employed briefly on campus before the faculty voted in a more sensible one. However, one professor who refused to comply with the rules of the original code was not offered a position the following year; he was, though, reinstated shortly after the new code was adopted, a faculty member reports. "Things are better now," a professor says. "We've turned the corner, partly because of the organizations that have taken up [the cause of free speech]." The current policy contains enough qualifications and protections that "it does not seem to be too powerful a censoring force," another faculty members says. "Of course, how much self-censoring it produces is difficult to say."

This conflict is still alive and well, however, for the Christian Fellowship at Middlebury. As in a similar recent controversy at Tufts University, a Middlebury

Christian Fellowship member announced that he was gay and was refused a leadership position in that organization. He sued on the grounds that this violated the college's nondiscrimination policy. In the spring of 2000, the Middlebury Community Council ruled that even religious groups cannot discriminate on the basis of religion, and the dean informed the Christian Fellowship that they must comply or be stripped of their status as a student organization. To date, the matter has not been resolved.

The faculty hiring process at Middlebury is often a battle between the administration's preference for more politicized candidates and a department's wish for solid scholarship, some say. "It's a political battle every time they go through a search," says one professor. "But some of us are determined to hire a real scholar instead of an ideologue. . . . The gratification is that the students know it."

According to professors, the college puts a great deal of stock in a professor's publishing record, but also considers his teaching abilities when making tenure decisions. "Excellent teaching is an absolute at Middlebury," says a professor. "Substantial publishing is required for tenure. In general now, a candidate for tenure needs to have a book published or under contract with a reputable press." College president (and history professor) John McCardell Jr. has been known to intervene and deny tenure to professors with insufficient publications, professors say.

For their part, students abide by the honor system as a condition of matriculation. Under that system all quizzes, tests, and finals are unproctored. At the conclusion of each, students must write and sign the following statement: "I have neither given nor received unauthorized aid on this examination." The student-managed Judicial Council hears allegations of code violations, and penalties can be as severe as indefinite suspension from the college.

Student Life: The Only Game in Town

Faculty at Middlebury tend to become involved in the lives of their students. The college maintains a "commons system" (similar to the college system at Yale University), in which students and faculty are assigned to residential communities to share cultural and "fellowship" experiences beyond the normal rampages of a typical college student weekend. In all, there are five residential commons, or dormitory clusters, each intended to be "a microcosm of Middlebury College as a whole," according to the school's Web site. The commons system replaced the Greek system of fraternities and sororities and, according to a faculty member, "offers students social options beyond weekend drinking bouts." This is especially important because of Middlebury's rural setting, giving students a structured kind of living that makes the formation of friends easier than the typical "cliquishness" of Greek life.

On the whole, this system seems to be an excellent way for students and faculty to relate to one another as adults, as one professor puts it. In turn, it is highly successful in attracting the best and most mature students. The common system includes a number of largely self-governing, coeducational "houses," some of which are intended for students who share a particular academic interest.

Middlebury, Vermont, is a very small, isolated town of eight thousand people. Serious crime is virtually unknown; campus crime mainly consists of the occasional burglary. It is two and a half hours from Montreal, four from Boston and Hartford, and about five from New York City. Because of this, the manner in which students and faculty interact is even more important than at urban campuses — there really is no other game in town. A faculty member says that relationship is "always predicated on the belief that the faculty and students can approach each other as adults." The campus hosts, according to the college view book, "four hundred films, one hundred twenty-five video presentations, one hundred professional or student concert and dance performances, twenty theatrical productions, twenty readings of fiction or poetry, ten gallery exhibitions, ninety dances and parties, and five hundred club meetings" each year. Appropriately, all students are expected to live on campus, with very few exceptions for upperclassmen.

The student body of about 2,000 will increase to around 2,350 over the next several years if college projections are correct. Middlebury intends to hire additional professors to keep up with the increase in enrollment, and plans call for the student-teacher ratio to remain around its current level, approximately eleven-to-one. The new faculty positions are earmarked for what are already the college's most popular and well-known programs, including literature, language study, international studies, and environmental studies. With the increase in the student body will come major construction projects, including a new science center, a new dining hall, new dorms, and an expansion of Starr Library (already home to about 1 million items).

Middlebury is in a gorgeous valley, with the Adirondacks to the west and the Green Mountains to the east; naturally, many students pursue outdoor activities in their free time. But the college also offers numerous student organizations, the best of which are reported to be the International Students Organization, the Political Forum, the Thomas Fellowship, the Christian Fellowship, and the Newman Club. Like most colleges of any size, Middlebury also has the usual gamut of radical student groups, but these are not considered disruptive to the community.

Both students and faculty look forward to Winter Carnival, a three-day event with ski trips, parties, concerts, and ice shows. No one need travel very far to ski: Middlebury is not only close to, but owns the 800-acre Snow Bowl ski area near the Bread Loaf campus. Snow Bowl is the largest college-owned ski facility in the nation.

Of course, both alpine and Nordic skiing figure in Middlebury's intercollegiate sports programs, as does ice hockey, a sport in which the school has won multiple NCAA Division III national titles. More common (i.e., warm-weather) sports are also offered, including baseball, basketball, cross-country, field hockey, football, golf, tennis, squash, and soccer. Club teams compete in crew, cricket, cycling, martial arts, rugby, softball, and other sports.

University of Minnesota–Twin Cities

Admissions
240 Williamson Hall
231 Pillsbury Drive, Southeast
Minneapolis, MN 55455
(800) 752-1000
www.umn.edu

Total enrollment: 45,481
Undergraduates: 26,972
SAT Ranges (Verbal/Math): 540-660 (V); 550-670 (M)
Applicants: 15,319
Accepted: 73%
Enrolled: 46%
Application deadline: December 15
Financial aid application deadline: February 15
Tuition: resident: $4,878/$9,791; non-resident: $13,463/$18,377
Core curriculum: No

Big House on the Prairie

Founded in 1851, the University of Minnesota–Twin Cities is situated on more than two thousand acres and is one of the largest campuses in the country, with an undergraduate enrollment of 27,000 and a total student body of close to 46,000. Because of its size, the U of M can be an anonymous and overwhelming place. This is a particular danger for students with a more traditional cast of mind, for they will find themselves surrounded by scores of politicized faculty, courses, programs, and student organizations.

Minnesota, the "Land of Ten Thousand Lakes," has a strong regional flavor, best articulated by Garrison Keillor, whose stories from the fictional Lake Woebegon tell of quirky, honest, Lutheran small town folk. The state is politically progressive, but also known for its independence in electoral matters: the governor is former wrestler Jesse Ventura and, until recently, it sent to Washington both the most liberal and one of the more conservative senators. However, students at the University of Minnesota are more apt to encounter more radical activists than conservative Lutheran farmers. In fact, because of the powerful influence of the university, the Twin Cities has been rechristened "Land of Ten Thousand Liberals" by some conservative wags.

"The U of M is one of the most politically correct campuses in the nation," says one professor. "It has relentlessly and aggressively pushed the entire PC agenda: affirmative action, multiculturalism, radical feminist studies, separate minority facilities, and so forth." The university, generally, does not try to mask its radical agenda and ideological predilections, and it should be said that UM's diversity does have some positive aspects. The university has nineteen colleges, and undergraduates can choose from more than 161 degrees, from horticulture to biochemistry to journalism to performing arts. But its general education requirements — required for any major — are fraught with liberal classes and left-leaning subjects.

Academic Life: The Liberal Meaning of Liberal Arts

The College of Liberal Arts is the largest college at the University of Minnesota's Twin Cities campus, one of nearly a dozen colleges that grant bachelor level degrees and one of seven that admit freshmen. Regardless of the college they call home, students are required to meet a set of general education requirements; the university calls them "liberal education" requirements. They include one course in physical science and one course in biological science, both with laboratories; one course in social sciences and one course in historical perspectives; one course in literature and one course in humanities; and one course in mathematical thinking (often met with a calculus or statistics class).

The university also requires one course in each of four "Themes of Liberal Education" areas: environment, international perspective, cultural diversity, and citizenship and public ethics.

There are is also a writing requirement: one or two writing courses (depending on the student's proficiency) during the freshman year.

Students enrolling in the College of Liberal Arts can choose from a wide range of majors — everything from traditional disciplines such as English, philosophy, and history to more obscure or recently established programs like Chicano studies, cultural studies and comparative literature, and Scandinavian languages and Finnish. In addition, students can apply for a "Bachelor of Individualized Studies" degree, essentially a major of their own design.

Though the general requirements are called "liberal education," the university does very little to ensure that the courses that meet them constitute anything of the sort. Worse, many of the choices are not the traditional introductory survey courses, but are instead tangential or politically motivated. "There are probably fifty [to] sixty courses which fulfill the 'cultural diversity' requirement," says one student. And one professor says that some of the politicized courses are the result of departments' competition for students. So instead of a standard introduction to American literature, for example, students get their "liberal education" through courses like "Literature of American Minorities," "Introduction to Women's Literature," and "The Harlem Renaissance."

457

Much of the U of M curriculum has been eroded by the domination of ideological agendas, according to conservative students and faculty. "This is especially true of the College of Liberal Arts," says one professor. "However, it is a mistake to generalize about the university as a whole because large sections of it — the hard sciences, the medical school — are relatively free of these developments." Indeed, students and faculty alike praise the chemical engineering and materials science programs, which also enjoy top national rankings. Most science departments are highly regarded, with the biochemistry and microbiology programs being described as "outstanding" by one professor. Economics has a strong reputation, but students should be prepared for enormous class sizes. Journalism and political science are also recommended.

Literary studies at Minnesota are particularly disappointing. English is characterized as "a disaster" by one professor, despite a few excellent teachers. The English department does offer many courses with traditional titles and reading lists, and all majors are still required to take a survey of English literature and a course in Shakespeare. But undergraduate survey courses satisfy only the literature category of the general education requirements, while courses like "Gender and the English Language" or "Literature of American Minorities" also satisfy the cultural diversity requirement — guess which ones nonmajors are more likely to take. Undergraduates could take a course in "Figures in Anglophone Literature: Ken Saro-Wiwa," for which the description reads:

> We will read some of Saro-Wiwa's writing, and will discuss his experiment with "broken English" in *Sozaboy,* but this will not be a purely literary course. . . . I want to explore the whole of Saro-Wiwa's "case," including such questions as: the role of the various human rights organizations that were finally unable to stop his execution; cultural survival for small ethnic groups like the Ogoni; failure of the post-colonial state in Nigeria . . . ; the effect of the post-colonial "nation" on marginal groups; the place of multinationals like Shell in the destruction of the Ogoni and their environment; the effectiveness of Saro-Wiwa's tactics of resistance; the politics of international responses to his execution.

While there is a course dedicated to this writer, there are none devoted exclusively to the works of Chaucer or Milton, according to the Spring 2001 course offerings.

Comparative literature, French, and the department of discourse and society are all dominated by advocates of "cutting-edge" theory ("the latest fads from Paris") and a multicultural agenda. Indeed, cultural studies and comparative literature, grouped into a single department, is perhaps the department most driven by leftist ideological assumptions. Students majoring in this program must take introductory courses in "Rhetoric, Power, Desire" and "Knowledge, Persuasion, and Power," as well as "advanced" courses selected from such categories as "Social Construction of the Subject," in which students will analyze "gender, sexuality, race, and class as discursive constructions productive of human subjectivity and cultural difference." Indeed, it is not difficult to find courses in these radicalized departments that are largely void of intellectual content. "Sexualities — from Perversity to Diversity" and "Gay Men and Homophobia in American Culture" are but two of the recent offerings there. The course description for the former reads:

> Contemporary constructions of Western sexuality (heterosexuality, homosexuality, lesbianism, romance, pornography, erotic domination, and lynching), institutions that constitute or compel them, and moral discourses. Materials include fiction, personal narratives, manuals, ads, journalism, and scholarship and theory from several disciplines.

As far as class size is concerned, one student notes that his language classes were small, with from fifteen to twenty students on average. Other introductory classes had upwards of two hundred students, but were broken into smaller "recitation" groups led by graduate students. Honors students often take upper-level courses in their major department along with graduate students. Advising at the university seems to be adequate for most students, and with a little effort undergraduates find their professors approachable. "Professors are pretty accessible, especially with e-mail," says one undergraduate.

Ultimately, undergraduates at Minnesota will continue to get the short end of the stick, as resources and energy are predominantly focused on research and graduate and professional education rather than teaching or the liberal arts. U of M faculty and other researchers competed successfully for $455 million in research and sponsored awards in fiscal year 2000, up 25 percent from 1999. Research expenditures are also up 12 percent to $376 million. As one professor laments, "Despite the usual ceremonial statements about dedication to teaching, the university has little interest in undergraduate education. It defines itself as 'research oriented,' which inevitably means concentration on graduate study and research." However, the university still retains many faculty who are committed to their teaching. One professor says: "There are many outstanding professors, both as teachers and scholars and occasionally both." These outstanding professors include Thomas J. Bouchard Jr., Matthew McGue, William Grove, and Paul Meehl (emeritus, but seek him out anyway) in psychology; James B. Serrin in mathematics; Bernard Bachrach, Deborah Bachrach, David Kieft, and James D. Tracy in history; John Dolan in philosophy; Oriol T. Valls in physics; and Ian Maitland in the Carlson School of Management.

For students seeking a more rigorous educational experience, the honors program in the College of Liberal Arts is highly recommended. "Any student who can get in, should," notes one professor. "Class sizes are small, and the instructors mainly excellent."

Political Atmosphere: Full Court Press

The University of Minnesota has for the last two years suffered a large amount of bad press due to the revelation that one of its academic counselors, who tutored men's basketball players, wrote more than 400 papers for at least twenty players from 1993 to 1998.

Shortly after this information surfaced in March 1999 came another damning allegation that since 1993, U of M athletics officials, sometimes with the cooperation of campus police, intervened in sexual misconduct and assault investigations of athletes and helped settle agreements in cases that were not given to prosecutors. University investigators, soon after the second claim came up, filed a report that stated there was evidence of favoritism toward student-athletes accused of assaults. The university's president then ordered a review of university police procedures and student discipline. A few months later the university moved much of its athletic oversight to faculty divisions.

To this day investigations are still ongoing, mostly concerning professors giving favoritism to athletes, especially basketball players. Four top sports officials at the university have left since the scandal broke.

The university has other legal problems, including a lawsuit recently settled for a reported $80,000. It was brought by an academic adviser who said he had been harassed by athletics-department employees, made to work in a hostile environment, and paid less than his peers because he was homosexual.

This lawsuit must have especially troubled university administrators who, according to insiders, are primarily concerned with pursuing politically correct policies and garnering favorable public attention. "The main priorities for the past decade," according to one professor, "have been to satisfy the demands of women and minorities, to hire as many as can reasonably be done given the constraints of minimum qualifications, and to attract as much favorable publicity for itself as possible." Tenure appears to be based largely on publications, research, and political factors rather than excellence in teaching. "Of course there are teaching awards," says one professor, "but that is mere window dressing." Another faculty member notes: "I have good reason to believe that search committees are highly politicized. The pressure is constantly on to hire more women and minorities."

Tensions between faculty and the Minnesota Board of Regents have been particularly high in recent years, as the regents sought to implement a new set of policies regarding tenure. According to the *Chronicle of Higher Education,* the controversy initially began in the spring of 1996, when the regents recommended cutting the base salaries for tenured professors with poor performance records and retaining the right to fire tenured professors "if their programs were eliminated or restructured and the university was unable to retrain or reassign them."

In the fall of 1996 faculty organizers garnered enough support to hold a referendum on forming a collective-bargaining unit, but professors voted 692 to 666 against the union in February 1997. After plenty of ill will on both sides, faculty politicking, and mediation by then-Governor Arne Carlson, the regents backed down on their stringent tenure code. The experience was an exhausting, if ultimately heady, one for faculty opponents of the code, many of whom put into play the radical organizing and protesting tactics usually reserved for their student disciples. After the Faculty Senate approved the revised tenure code, professors sang an adapted version of an antiwar ballad they dubbed the "Tenure Song," according to the *Chronicle.*

In the midst of the tenure dispute, the university's president at the time, Nils Hasselmo, announced that he would step down to return to his faculty position. The university has thus recently ushered in a new president (Mark Yudof) and dean of the CLA, and although their public statements have been "the usual boilerplate about excellence in teaching and research," a professor says, the verdict is still out on their actual leadership and vision for the university.

There is no formal speech code at the U of M, but, as one professor notes, "woe unto any student who strays from the straight and narrow in speech or writing." There have been some well-publicized incidents of discriminatory behavior, notably an attempt a few years ago to prevent the student Republican group from distributing materials critical of President Clinton and the Democratic administration during Freshman Week. "There was a public outcry and the university had to back down," says a professor. According to one student, the university is continually trying to put through formal "sensitivity training" in freshman orientation.

There are numerous political clubs at Minnesota, most of them liberal. Recognized groups include the Association of Gay, Lesbian, Bisexual, and Transgender Student Organizations and Their Friends; Minnesota College Republicans; Minnesota Public Interest Research Group; Student Organization for Animal Rights (SOAR); and Students against Fee Excess. The campus Republican Club is fairly active and visible. In the fall of 1996 several members of the group demanded the removal of a poster of Planned Parenthood founder Margaret Sanger from the main library, arguing that she was a racist who had spoken at Ku Klux Klan rallies. They also were critical of birth control literature distributed from the campus student center, which encouraged students to "Be Like Margaret Sanger." A *Chronicle of Higher Education* story noted that campus feminists dismissed the Republican Club members' demands, arguing that the group members "are against birth control altogether."

As one faculty member says, "The campus paper is way over on the left and it is very influential." Speakers on campus are also predominantly liberal, and, according to students and faculty, conservative speakers are rare and have been shouted down in campus appearances.

Student Life: Winter and August

The Twin Cities campus is actually two campuses, one in Minneapolis where most liberal arts students take courses, and one about three miles away in St. Paul for students studying agriculture, biology, human ecology, natural resources, and veterinary medicine. The "East Bank" area of the Minneapolis campus is the most attractive, boasting the university's original buildings and traditional architecture. One student describes it as a "pretty campus" and praises its proximity to the Twin Cities as its most viable social feature.

The campus is described as "absolutely beautiful" by one visitor. But, the university is going through major construction that is hampering student life. Said President Yudof recently: "I do really apologize to the students for the inconvenience. There are days, with my sense of direction, that I really believe, as we used to say in Texas, 'You just can't get there from here.'" Delays in construction have prolonged the agony.

In recent years the Twin Cities area has earned national recognition as a highly "livable" area, a peculiarly Midwestern blend of cosmopolitan vitality and historic charm. Those of a more artsy bent have found the local music and theater scene to have much to offer, while the Minneapolis Institute of Art, Walker Art Center, and Minnesota Museum of Art serve up more traditional cultural fare. As one professor says, "The Twin Cities of Minneapolis/St. Paul are a treasure house of cultural resources: theater, music, museums, and so forth — and all easily accessible."

Crime on campus is about average for a large university. Bicycle and vehicle theft are the biggest threats, and there are fair number of drug and alcohol citations handed out. The biggest two crimes over the last few years are the basketball scandals and the vandalization of an animal research lab, both of which ended up costing the university millions.

Students who live in one of Minnesota's residence halls have a number of living options. Several dorms have been designated as substance-free, and a few halls have especially strict quiet hours. Visitation restrictions range from an "open guest" policy in which guests may be present at any time, to a "no guest" policy in which no member of the opposite sex is ever allowed in the resident's room. All dorms, however, are coed, with men and women residing on different floors or in different wings or blocks of rooms. Men and women have separate bathrooms.

There are numerous extracurricular clubs on campus, everything from ballroom dancing to fencing, chess, juggling, tae kwon do, paintball, and cycling. About three-quarters of the students hail from Minnesota, and despite the wide range of minority and ethnic groups on college campuses these days, the university has to be one of the few in the country with a Norwegian student organization.

On a campus so large, it would be unusual if athletics were not conducted on a grand scale as well. The Minnesota Golden Gophers field Big Ten teams in ten women's and eleven men's varsity sports. The football team plays in the vast Hubert

H. Humphrey Metrodome, sharing that venue with the Minnesota Vikings and Twins.

If you're looking for a location that offers year-round fun in the sun, the University of Minnesota–Twin Cities may not be for you. Although plenty of outdoor activities are available to students, such as rollerblading, sailing, and cycling, the cities' northern clime makes ice skating and cross-country skiing the activities of choice during much of the year. "The winters are brutal and very long," says a professor. (A local joke divides the year into two seasons: winter and August.) Still, opportunities abound for dipping into cafes or bookstores for a hot drink, studying, or socializing in the neighboring commercial districts, such as the "Dinkytown" area on the campus's northwest edge.

In general, the intellectual landscape of undergraduate education at the U of M has been so thoroughly politicized, and traditional liberal studies have become — in the university's lingua franca — so "marginalized," that it is a formidable prospect for entering undergraduates to piece together a true liberal education, at least from the general education offerings. As one professor notes, "When 'Destruction of the Brazilian Rain Forest' will satisfy the science requirement, why take a tough course like biology?" Still, the sheer size of the school ensures that, at least for the short term, some good professors, courses, and programs remain. The key to accessing them is determination and resourcefulness. "It is easy for a determined student to find out who has won awards for excellence in teaching, which courses actually teach something, which professors really care about their students," the professor says.

Morehouse College

Office of Admissions
830 Westview Drive, S.W.
Atlanta, Georgia 30314
(404) 681-2880
www.morehouse.edu

Total enrollment: 3,012
Undergraduates: 3,012
SAT ranges (Verbal/Math): 440-680 (V); 470-680 (M)
Applicants: 2,785

Accepted: 66%
Enrolled: 41%
Application deadline: February 15
Financial aid application deadline: April 15
Tuition: $11,618/$18,588
Core curriculum: Yes

The Morehouse Man

While Washington, D.C., may be the nation's capital, Atlanta, Georgia, is widely regarded as the capital of black America, and with good reason. Not only is the city famous as the "cradle of the Civil Rights movement" and as a dynamic center for international trade, but it has proven to be a major arena for the development of black leadership in business, academia, and government.

As the nation's only historically black, all-male, four-year liberal arts college, Morehouse College has been a major contributing factor to Atlanta's success. In 1867, two years after the end of the Civil War, Augusta Institute was founded in the basement of a Baptist church in Augusta, Georgia, to prepare black men for the ministry and teaching. The college moved to Atlanta in 1879 and in 1913 became Morehouse College.

Morehouse's alumni roster reads like a list of the most famous and successful black men of this century. Foremost of these, of course, is Dr. Martin Luther King Jr., whose memory is prominently honored on campus by the Martin Luther King Jr. International Chapel. But the alumni roster also numbers former secretary of Health and Human Services Louis Sullivan, filmmaker Spike Lee, actor Samuel L. Jackson, businessman Robert Johnson, and former Atlanta mayor Maynard Jackson, all of whom (despite their differences) share in the near-mythic identity of the "Morehouse Man" and the attendant "Morehouse Mystique." Accordingly, unlike at many small liberal arts colleges, a sense of pride and decorum pervades the atmosphere at Morehouse, where many young men wear coats and ties to class and where one professor from the North confessed, "When I first arrived, I was called 'sir' so often I thought it was part of my name."

Perhaps Morehouse's climate of respect is due to the fact that — again, unlike other colleges that have wandered from their roots — it embraces a keen sense of its history, in both religious and secular arenas. Though the college is now independent of any religious body, it maintains close ties to the historically black churches, and there's a quality to the campus rhetoric, in official publications and campus landmark inscriptions, that can be described as nothing less than inspirational. Furthermore, its very campus encompasses the highest point of Atlanta, where the Battle of Atlanta was fought during the Civil War, and underneath Graves Hall, at the hill's summit, black Confederate soldiers are buried.

That black Confederates are buried in the heart of the campus is an unintentional but resonant irony for those who maintain that the placidly traditional face of the institution covers a significant degree of internal turmoil. One professor who has since left Morehouse noted that the college has been in a "kind of malaise," coasting on the reputation of its illustrious graduates and stuck in the era of Benjamin Mays, the famous educator and legendary president of the school during the forties, who greatly influenced Dr. King. Progress, however, did not keep pace with time. "My assessment," this same professor stated regarding the Morehouse of ten or twenty years ago, "was that there was a great discrepancy between what Mays had created and what one would want [of a college now]."

Some critics have charged the college with "academic incest" in hiring Morehouse Men to chair departments and programs. Others have complained that the administration has maintained an official "climate of secrecy" regarding decisions that concern both faculty and students. Even during those years, however, "the benefits [of a Morehouse education] far outweighed the problems," one parent held. "The whole symbolic notion of the 'Morehouse Man' was still in place," inspiring young black men to confidence and academic attainment, even when other areas at the college needed work — in 1994, for example, Nima Warfield became the college's first Rhodes scholar. And since the 1995 appointment of Dr. Walter E. Massey as president, Morehouse has begun a process of self-evaluation and modernization and, in the words of the *Brief History of Morehouse,* "embraced the challenge of preparing for the twenty-first century and the goal of becoming one of the nation's best liberal arts colleges."

Academic Life: The Head That Wears the Crown

In keeping with the decorous campus demeanor, where signs at the entrances of buildings request that "Gentlemen: Please remove your hats," one distinction of Morehouse's curriculum is that it is, comparatively speaking, highly structured. While the core curriculum of most colleges consists merely of loose distribution requirements that give students considerable latitude in choosing courses, Morehouse requires a series of specific courses. "There is no leeway allowed in completing the courses," a professor says. "Students are encouraged to finish the core before the junior year, so they are eligible for Phi Beta Kappa."

The core consists of fifty-three semester hours of required course work. For starters, Morehouse demands two composition courses and two health and physical education courses, as well as a year of freshman orientation.

Prior to 1998, students had to take two world literature courses, but one of these courses was dropped and replaced with an additional humanities course, meaning students must now take four humanities courses as part of the core curriculum. A previous public speaking requirement in the core was replaced with a computer competency course, though public speaking is still a requirement of each major and is taught by the individual departments.

The school still requires two courses in the "World History: Topical Approaches" sequence, in which, according to the college catalogue, "One-third attention [is] given to the United States, including the African-American experience; one-third attention given to Europe; one-third attention given to Africa." Such a seemingly balanced approach has not always been popular. A faculty member who has taught the courses complained of the sequence as little more than a "pastiche of Western civilization and African civilization" that was "poorly thought-out. . . . What it turned out to be was a course where one would go in and teach his or her expertise." The caliber of the material has also received criticism. Regarding the sequence, the same faculty member said he'd heard students remark that "they'd had more interesting classes in high school."

All students must take the "Biological Science" course (except for majors in biology, who take a two-semester "General Biology" sequence). Similarly, students must take the introductory "Physical Science" course from the physics department, which emphasizes, in addition to basic principles of physics, "the interplay between technology and science, and the influence of technology in the world community." In addition, the catalogue course entry notes that "the approach is primarily conceptual, and physics is presented as a historical and humanistic development of the human intellect." Such a course description bears witness to a couple of the phenomena with which Walter Massey, himself a well-known physicist, has been credited in his tenure as president: an increased emphasis on real-life application of pure science to the business world, and a recognition of the interdisciplinary nature of study.

In mathematics, students choose two out of four possible courses in order to fulfill a sequence requirement; there is a track for non–science majors as well as one geared toward business and engineering.

In language, Morehouse men must advance to and complete six hours at the intermediate level of a modern foreign language; choices include French, Spanish, German, Japanese, Russian, and Swahili. There is no classics department, a rather large gap for a liberal arts institution, nor are any classical languages available. The most extensive departments are of course French and Spanish, both of which offer electives in French and Spanish "Diaspora" literature alongside the full complement of traditional readings.

Another core curricular area in which students have some latitude in course choices is humanities, where they must take four courses out of a list of eleven. For some reason the list is heavily weighted toward music courses, with only two offerings of "Introduction to Religion" and "Introduction to Philosophy." In social science, students must choose two out of seventeen courses, which include the popular sociology class "Men in Society" and "Psychology of the African-American Experience," offered by the psychology department.

The final and most characteristic feature of the core is that students earn at least twenty-four units of "Crown Forum" during their time at Morehouse. Crown Forum is basically chapel, though its focus appears to be inspirational and empowering rather than directly theological. The forum meets only eight times a year, which means that a student must log a full three years of attendance in order to fulfill the requirement. Its title derives from a statement by theologian and Morehouse alumnus Howard Thurman, who said that as Morehouse men, "A crown is placed over our heads that for the rest of our lives we are trying to grow tall enough to wear." One student says, however, that "Some students feel it's a waste of time," and there is a certain cynicism in some quarters about the college's ever-present "Morehouse mystique" rhetoric.

While neither a traditionalist academic nor a leftist radical would be completely happy with Morehouse's approach (the aforementioned "radical" professor registered dissatisfaction about how "conservative" and "pretty religious" the college is), the strength of Morehouse's core is its coherence and the very fact that it is a common experience to which all students subscribe.

The college is sensitive to student learning or opportunity deficits, and has, for example, "since 1939 . . . sponsored a Reading Program for freshmen and upperclassmen who need and/or desire to improve their reading skills and abilities in college . . .-level reading." Extensive tutoring is also available in the Frederick Douglass Commons, a large and quiet study center at the middle of the dormitory quadrangle.

Outstanding professors at Morehouse include Alton Hornsby Jr. and Marcellus C. Barksdale in history; Harold Braithwaite, Duane Jackson, and Madge Willis in psychology; Aaron Parker in philosophy and religion; Aakhut Em Bak in physics; Emmanuel O. Onifade in economics and business administration; and Melvin Rahming in English.

Among the strongest departments are psychology, religion ("but not philosophy," a professor says — the two disciplines are grouped together but are considered separate departments), history, sociology ("on the verge of being strong," according to a professor), and business administration.

For years, a main concern at Morehouse has been the desire for a more African American–centered curriculum, but it wasn't until President Massey arrived that the college instituted an African-American studies major. Most courses, however, had been already specifically geared to the needs of an African-American student population: "I teach my courses from an African-centered perspective — period," one professor says, and this seems to be the case with most members of the faculty. The same professor also complains of the philosophy department, of its tendency to be "old school," and that "there isn't any philosophy that comes out of the African tradition."

One distinctive way in which some Morehouse faculty attempt to make their courses "African-centered" is to mandate community service hours as part of course requirements. In one course, fifteen hours of community service were stipulated for the semester, roughly equaling one hour per week, in addition to other assignments.

While traditionalists might complain that such requirements only pad a syllabus, one professor maintains that the practice helps to fulfill the college's mission: "I came to Morehouse because the mission statement says to build leaders for the community."

The "community," at Morehouse, is not far away — although the campuses of Morehouse and the other Atlanta University Center colleges are manicured and safe, this is not the case in general with the West End neighborhood in which they are located. "Some of the worst drug trade and highest incarceration rates [in Atlanta] are in the area around the Atlanta University Center," a professor says. Such a requirement makes coursework "real," he explains, because the students then "have to go out and . . . put what they know about black folks into action." Upwards of one-third of the faculty now include some sort of community service in their syllabi. The practice is predominant in departments such as sociology and psychology that naturally lend themselves to social activism.

Beyond the given that an "African-centered" slant to the curriculum more or less exists throughout the departments, Morehouse otherwise appears to have much less political and theoretical strife than other liberal arts institutions. Whereas at most colleges the English department is the site of great political high jinks, arcane critical theory, or touchy-feely therapeutics, Morehouse's English offerings largely consist of survey courses. The one course that has even the faintest hint of trendiness, a post-colonial literature course entitled "The West Indian Novel," is taught by the highly respected professor Melvin Rahming, who is universally acclaimed for being challenging, hard, and fair — "a phenomenal teacher; a wise man," says one of his colleagues. One student says he knows "a lot of seniors" who, if they could get into Dr. Rahming's class, would "rather take a C as opposed to taking another course and getting an A."

The reason for the relatively apolitical academic atmosphere at Morehouse is unclear: a former faculty member says there is simply "not that kind of debate," but rather there has tended in the past to be "a lot of pressure [on the faculty] to conform and be quiet." There apparently are old-style radicals at Morehouse — not everyone is wildly enamored of the free market, for example. However (and especially since Massey has become president), Morehouse has strengthened its already excellent corporate connections, and its curriculum emphasizes the global nature of business. As would seem proper to the nation's only all-male, historically black college, a sense of community spirit pervades all programs, but a couple are particularly notable. Since 1990 Morehouse has been home to the Morehouse Research Institute, whose stated objectives are, according to the college's Web site, to "increase the availability of scholarly work on issues concerning the status of African-American men and boys, and increase the visibility of researchers . . . who work on solutions to problems that threaten not only the vitality of the black community, but also the social and economic health of the nation." As well, under the aegis of the history department, Morehouse is home to the noted *Journal of Negro History*.

Political Atmosphere: Paradoxical

The political atmosphere at Morehouse is paradoxical. Since the college is historically black and male, one might be inclined to regard the campus's political character as left of center. Indeed, as one professor says, there is "almost a proliferation of student organizations focused on the African and black community," but this seems to be a testament to bonds of faith, blood, and loyalty rather than a commitment to ideology. Rather, outside the classroom, the general conclusion of many faculty is that Morehouse men tend to be conservative. "Kids aspire to be bourgeois," the same professor notes.

Gender relations are one area in which Morehouse has been characterized as conservative, and gender has been a hot topic of conversation in the last couple of years. "Morehouse men [have] needed to rethink gender," one professor says. "[There's been] a kind of male identity that smacked of the worst form of patriarchy." The problem has manifested itself particularly with regard to female faculty members, who have traditionally "felt a little bit uncomfortable" in the midst of this all-male environment. "You don't find many women in prominent positions," one faculty member said of the college in the pre-Massey era, and the general atmosphere led to the creation of an organization called Black Men against Sexism to draw attention to the issue.

Furthermore, the issue of gender is brought even closer to hand because, as part of the Atlanta University Center, Morehouse allows cross-registration, which brings women into the classroom, especially those from nearby Spelman College. "A lot of students at Spelman . . . come in and bring a lot to the table," admits one student. Some students, therefore, see a movement toward coeducation as inevitable: "The all-male institution is going to be challenged," he says. Still, faculty response to the prospect consists largely of amusement. "Not unless Sherman marches through Georgia again," quips one. "The alums would probably have a conniption fit if anybody even spoke about it becoming coed," says another, although he admits the possibility that "in ten years the mentality would be quite different."

Other problems concerning Morehouse's political atmosphere revolve around what many see as the administration's stony refusal to debate controversial issues facing the community. "Morehouse [has] had a horrendous problem with the school newspaper," one professor says, and once even "put it out of business" when it raised some questions the administration didn't want to answer. "The paper was not allowed to publish, under the pretext that a faculty advisor could not be found," he says. Much later, after a savvy faculty member agreed to step in as adviser, the paper went on to "win top prize in two categories at a regional convention." Another faculty member says President Massey is a strong supporter of freedom of speech and that the university makes no move to review or censor the paper prior to publication. Still, when the paper was prevented from publishing, it raised few eyebrows or voices around campus, which disappointed more than one professor.

Morehouse does host some sensitivity training, and there has been some nebulous controversy on campus concerning homosexual students. One year, it was a matter of comment when "a couple of the guys went out dressed as women" to Freaknik, a music festival that used to be held in Atlanta annually. "I know a couple of students on campus who are obviously gay and flamboyant," admits one student, but "on campus they should behave and dress as men." There are also rumblings concerning an incident in which a gay student sexually harassed a fellow (straight) student, but "the heterosexual guy was punished," the same student complains. Another student, however, mentions that while there was "some upheaval" when "a homosexual organization tried to rally support . . . there's a large range of acceptance at Morehouse as long as you don't go overboard into the extreme."

Since Massey's arrival in 1995, the college has reportedly put a premium on hiring talented young scholars who are involved in original research, although the focus remains upon teaching. Everyone, as well, agrees that Morehouse's campaign of modernizing and improving itself would not have occurred without the inspirational example set by Dr. Johnnetta Cole, former president of Spelman College, who led Spelman through a capital campaign and a major program of modernization during the late '80s and the '90s. What Cole was doing was "light years ahead of what Southern black colleges were thinking of at the time," says one professor, and "Morehouse felt embarrassed." The hiring of Massey, a nationally known figure as well as a Morehouse alumnus, and the burgeoning efforts to modernize are predicated on the "perception that we can do better," one faculty member says.

Student Life: Brotherhood

Students — as well as Morehouse promotional material — submit that while the classroom portions of the Morehouse experience are important, the strongest aspect of four years at the college is the sense of brotherhood that develops in the dorms and outside of class. "It's about trust and support, respect and lifelong friendships," a student said recently in a college brochure. "You really have to live it to understand it."

Accordingly, the college has a rich campus life, and a multitude of student organizations that serve as the ground for cultivating the close ties and loyalties for which the college is known. Many of these focus on areas of particular and historical interest to black students: there are chapters on campus of both the NAACP and the Southern Christian Leadership Conference, as well as the National Student Support Council for Africa. A surprising number of clubs are available for students from various states, such as the D.C. Metropolitan Club and the Pacific Northwest Club, and many preprofessional and business organizations.

In the realm of religion are the Fellowship of Christian Athletes, a gospel choir, and the Morehouse Gospel Theatre Ensemble, but two Muslim student organizations also exist on campus, one under the aegis of the controversial Nation of Islam. While Christianity is a strong cultural presence at Morehouse, its effects are gentle and diffuse. And, as Muslims are making some strongly evangelistic efforts at Morehouse and in the Atlanta University Center as a whole, playing upon black desires to find in Islam a unified heritage, Muslim influence will likely increase. During the fall of 1997, for example, a sign in the student post office asked students: "Did you know that nearly all those West and North Africans enslaved in the U.S. who could read and write, spoke, read, and wrote in Arabic? Why not follow their example?

In the fall of 1997 the Morehouse College Republicans joined the College Democrats group on the campus political scene. When the founder decided to start the club, he got "a lot of sneers here and there," but went ahead anyway, as "one professor said, 'Do it!'" There are a lot of Republicans around Morehouse, he claims. Still, the Morehouse ethic of brotherhood predominates, and there is apparently a lot of good-natured debate: reportedly, Democrats also attend the meetings of the College Republicans.

There are two student-run publications on campus: the Torch, which is the school yearbook, and the *Maroon Tiger*, the student newspaper. There are intramural sports, in addition to varsity teams in football, basketball, tennis, cross-country, and track and field, which are part of the Southern Intercollegiate Athletic Conference and the NCAA Division II.

The most controversial area of student life concerns the fraternities. There is a strong fraternity tradition at black colleges, most famously illustrated in Morehouse alum Spike Lee's film *School Daze*, but it is the *School Daze* image of the fraternity that Morehouse would like to get away from.

As recently as the Fall of 1997, the charters of two of the most famous black fraternities, Kappa Alpha Psi and Alpha Phi Alpha, were suspended. The reason for the suspensions is not commonly known, another testament to the college's zealous PR; those on campus presumed it had to do with excessive hazing. Whatever the problem was, it has apparently been resolved: a professor says that all suspended fraternities will be restored to the campus by the spring of 2002. Whatever else is said of the fraternities, it was they who popularized the classic image of the Morehouse man — bow ties, sport coats, etc. — and provided the college's most ritualized social scene. The campus now has a bit more of a Northeastern urban look than in the past, with the bow tie–types not as prevalent.

Crime on the Morehouse campus is very infrequent, though the number of car thefts has increased in recent years.

A final note regarding student life at Morehouse concerns the expense of attending the institution; a number of students interviewed spoke of having dropped out at various times in order to raise money to attend, even though Morehouse has generous funding available. The cost for tuition, room, and board approached $19,814 in 2000-2001, cheaper than many comparable liberal arts colleges but impossibly expensive for many. The difficulties students have in attending seem only to increase the loyalty that Morehouse men have for the college.

Mount Holyoke College

Office of Admissions
Director of Admissions
Mount Holyoke College
College Street
South Hadley, MA 01075-1424
(413) 538-2000
www.mtholyoke.edu

Total enrollment: 2,192
Undergraduates: 2,192
SAT ranges (Verbal/Math): 580-680 (V); 550-650 (M)
Applicants: 2,613
Accepted: 59%
Enrolled: 34%
Application deadline: January 15
Financial aid application deadline: January 15
Tuition: $25,380/$32,790
Core curriculum: No

A Lyon Among Women

The nation's oldest institution of higher education for women, Mount Holyoke has a reputation — not wholly undeserved — as one of the nation's most distinguished liberal arts colleges for women. Founded in 1837 as the Mount Holyoke Female Seminary, the college has always combined a liberal program of studies with a dedication to public service, and has retained its founding emphasis on the natural sciences. Still, the definition of what constitutes both a liberal arts education and a concern for civic welfare have been dramatically redefined at the college over the years and is now something more unconventional and radical than it used to be. Despite the considerable lip service paid to the liberal arts in Mount Holyoke's promotional literature, both the curriculum and social atmosphere at the college have taken on a radically politicized nature.

Mount Holyoke is proud of its progressive heritage and regularly trots out the achievements of its foundress Mary Lyon in crafting a "demanding curriculum conspicuously free of domestic pursuits." The college is proud to proclaim its affinity for Mary Lyon's "renowned" dictum: "Go where no one else will go. Do what no one else will do." Still, after researching the educational and social landscape at Mount Holyoke, prospective undergraduates and their parents will likely be convinced that there are sometimes good reasons why no one else has "gone there" or "done that," and that Mount Holyoke would be better off sticking to a legitimate liberal arts course than pursuing its penchant for the innovative and experimental.

Academic Life: For the Good of Your World

Traditionally, the focus at Mount Holyoke has not been only on the cultivation of the life of the mind, but on educating young women to reform society. That emphasis continues today. "There is a strong sense of social mission," says one professor, who indicates that students at Mount Holyoke pursue education not only for self-fulfillment but "for the good of the world." In this sense, the professor adds, Mount Holyoke continues to be "the opposite of a party school. . . . There is a place for personal, academic, and social seriousness here."

Departments and programs at Mount Holyoke range from African American and African studies to programs in complex organizations and critical social thought. More trendy programs such as environmental studies or film studies rest alongside majors in art, classics, history, and medieval studies.

Among the many requirements for the bachelor of arts degree at Mount Holyoke (as at so many of its sister institutions) is a multicultural requirement; as college literature states, "All . . . students are also required to take one of the approved four-credit courses that offer exposure to a multicultural perspective by focusing on some aspect of Africa, Asia, Latin America, the Middle East, or the non-white peoples of North America." This is somewhat offset by a required year-long course "examining Western heritages." The curriculum also mandates a course in qualitative reasoning, a first-year writing course, proficiency in a foreign language, and six credits in physical education.

There are also distribution requirements at Mount Holyoke. Students must take three courses in the humanities, two in the social sciences, and two in science and mathematics. To its credit, the college specifies that these seven credits must be from different categories within each division: for instance, students could choose one course in music, one in philosophy, and one in history from the humanities, rather than selecting three courses in religion. Still, as with all distribution requirements, there is a danger of students selecting only courses that only of tangential

473

value rather than those with lasting virtue. Many courses come with a politicized agenda, and students are thus advised to peruse course descriptions and reading lists carefully and to consult trusted upperclassmen for advice.

Although Mount Holyoke frequently invokes the spirit of a classical liberal education in its promotional literature, much of the curriculum is politicized. There are lots of course titles that begin "Women and . . ." There are also ones like "Women, Girls, and Mathematics"; "Buddhism, Feminism, and Ecology"; "Racial Identity in Teens"; "Women's Rights"; "Gay Issues"; and "Reproductive Ethics." Mount Holyoke faculty include such unconventional personalities as Susan D. Scotto, lecturer in Russian language and literature and a comedic performer in a film series entitled "Big Bitch." Scotto declares in an online interview that "there's no right answer to anything in life," and inspires her students by advertising a Russian literature survey that promises "Sex! Sin! Avant-garde hijinks!" and coming to class dressed in such unacademic garb as a faux alligator-skin vinyl miniskirt.

The well-known (and good) professors at the school include Anthony Lake, a professor of international relations who was nominated by President Clinton to head the Central Intelligence Agency; Professor of Sociology Richard Moran, a criminologist whose comments appear regularly in newspapers and public radio; and Professor of History Joseph Ellis, winner of the 1997 National Book Award in nonfiction for his biography of Thomas Jefferson. The women's studies department boasts professor Martha Ackmann, a noted feminist who criticized feminists for supporting President Clinton during the Lewinsky scandal.

Mount Holyoke students have always enjoyed a high degree of freedom in both their academic life and their social options. The college encourages independent study projects and offers students great flexibility regarding prescribed courses and final examinations. The college's Junior Year Abroad program is very popular, and many students opt to spend either a semester or a year studying overseas. Mount Holyoke is also a member of the Twelve College Exchange Program, which allows its students to take classes at other member schools (including Amherst, Bowdoin, Connecticut College, Dartmouth, Smith, Trinity, Vassar, Wellesley, Wesleyan [Conn.], Wheaton [Mass.], and Williams).

Mount Holyoke also offers a January Term during which students participate in some form of internship or self-study. This program is academically lightweight — "more fun than serious," one student says. "The formal academic aspect of it has faded," says a professor, who adds that because most faculty are preoccupied with administrative duties (hiring, for example) during that time of year, "they don't have time to teach January term."

The college has also recently announced an innovation in their application procedure: starting with the class entering in the fall 2001 academic year, SAT scores will be optional for college admission. Arguing that standardized test scores do not necessarily reflect the qualities the college is looking for in prospective students (attributes like "intellectual curiosity, thoughtfulness, leadership, creativity, civic engagement, and social conscience"), the college has decided to make such test scores optional, and rely instead on a variety of indicators that reflect "the culture and values" of Mount Holyoke. Under the new policy, it appears that students who attended prestigious prep schools will be at a decided advantage, since the admissions process will include a thorough review of the student's high school record "within the context of extensive data on the quality of that school." While the college is probably sincere in its motivation behind such an endeavor, it is difficult to avoid the suspicion that the arrangement was the brainchild of some clever development officer, since the move to make test scores optional is part of a grant program supported by the Mellon Foundation, who will underwrite a "study of how this change affects our applicant pool and our matriculants' success," as well as fund college efforts "to build a climate of achievement for all students."

Political Atmosphere: Two Sides

The current president of Mount Holyoke, Joanne Creighton, is a literary scholar by training (she has published books on William Faulkner, Margaret Drabble, and Joyce Carol Oates), and thus sympathetic to the college's liberal arts mission. Indeed, her public pronouncements would generally find favor with this guide and people interested in pursuing a traditional liberal arts education. In a recent editorial, Creighton defined a liberal education as "the disinterested pursuit of knowledge as its own end without immediate application" and declared that a "liberal arts education fosters what John Cardinal Newman called a philosophical habit of mind." She further asserted that "we still need havens where the serenity of a contemplative mind can be mastered; where the joys of learning for learning's sake are appreciated; where students can ponder great books without regard for their vocational application."

With her conservative rhetoric, Creighton invokes inspiring images of young women reading and discussing the classics. Yet it is difficult to square these images with the curricular, social, and political realities of a Mount Holyoke education. Indeed, Creighton's claims of "disinterestedness" in liberal education seem to be in direct conflict with the often radical social mission of Mount Holyoke. This conflict between "learning for learning's sake" and social activism is imbedded in the college's mission statement, which is to educate "a diverse community of women at the highest level of academic excellence and to foster the alliance of liberal arts education with purposeful engagement in the world."

For many Mount Holyoke women, "engagement in the world" begins the first semester of their freshman year, when they join radical campus political groups and focus more on activism than academics — or, more commonly and less knowingly, engage in activism disguised as academics. The college certainly does not want for left-leaning political and "cultural" student groups, such as FREE (For Rights Equal and Empowering), Movimiento Estudiantil Chicano de Aztlan (MEChA), Massachusetts Students Public Interest Research Group (MassPIRG), the Student Organization for Animal Rights (SOAR), Amnesty International, Students for Free Tibet, and the AIDS awareness coalition, among many others. Several of Mount Holyoke's student groups are organized around "women's issues," such as the Helping Overcome Problematic Eating (HOPE) group or the campus chapter of Women Against Sexual Harassment (WASH). "A lot of the students see themselves in leadership roles," a professor says. "There is a long tradition of political involvement here."

Similarly, the college's repeated mantra that it is a true liberal arts college, and "will not redefine its nature to meet the expectations of those who may, legitimately, seek an education in something other than the liberal arts," appears laughable in light of recently introduced majors and interdisciplinary programs in "critical social thought," environmental studies, and computer science, as well as programs "to study the administration and management of complex organizations: government, colleges and universities, public school systems, hospitals, businesses, and international and transnational organizations."

The president's admirable speeches are further laid aside for numerous college-sponsored lectures on activist and feminist concern. A quick glance at a typical lecture calendar reveals such talks as "Toward a More Activist Economics"; "The Truth that Never Hurts: Thirty Years of Writing and Organizing for Justice and Social Change"; "Adolescent Girls and Power"; "Antiracism Activism"; "The State of Asian America: Activism and Resistance." There are also campus workshops dedicated to hunger awareness and civil disobedience training.

When it comes to issues concerning sexuality and reproduction, the campus is clearly supportive of every conceivable nontraditional passion. Groups such as SYSTA, Lesbian, Bisexual & Questioning Women of Color, True Colors (the Lesbian/Bisexual Alliance), and Spectrum (a support group for lesbians and bisexuals) dominate the scene. Perhaps the most pernicious group is the so-called "Student Health Educators" (SHE): interested students can log on to the SHE home page through the Mount Holyoke Web site and learn about the wonders of the female condom and masturbation.

Conspicuously, there is no pro-life group on campus, and the college is home to a number of activist pro-abortion faculty, including Professor of Anthropology Lynn Morgan, who published an op-ed piece in the *Dayton Daily News* in 1999 entitled "Extremists Trafficking in Fetal Remains." The piece argued that opponents of abortion have been "exploiting" fetal remains for propaganda purposes.

Although the college declares that a "compassionate understanding" must co-exist alongside the "search for knowledge" at Mount Holyoke, tolerance for dissenting (read "conservative") viewpoints on issues like abortion and sexual orientation is low. Ironically, the college declares in its statement of principles that it is "a fellowship whose members are gentle of spirit and tolerant of human failing, but maintain unrelenting hostility toward any destruction of human dignity." Unfortunately, the reigning definition of "human dignity" at Mount Holyoke is synonymous with radical notions of autonomy and sexual libertinism, and the "unrelenting hostility" is more likely reserved for those with conservative views.

Minority issues have become a concern at Mount Holyoke in recent years. The college has several minority-oriented student organizations, including Asian American Sisters in Action, a Black Student/Alumni Conference, Association of Pan African Unity, as well as a minority group for those women studying science (Sistas in Science) and one for lesbian minorities. Although 17 percent of students are from minority groups and the college has had a black studies department since the 1970s, Mount Holyoke still has not been able to shake its image as a four-year haven for overprivileged white girls. In recent literature, the college insinuates that the influx of minority students has not been easy on the Mount Holyoke community, noting that "while increased diversity enriches the community, it has also raised issues about the meaning of community. The college is actively engaged in educating students, faculty, and staff to understand and appreciate personal and cultural differences, and to be sensitive to the traditions and needs of others." Toward that end, the college has formed an Advisory Committee on Multicultural Community and College Life. Composed of students, faculty, and administrators, the committee "provides oversight for policies impacting students outside the classroom."

Student Life: Members Only

Mount Holyoke women have numerous options regarding residence life, with choices ranging from classic Victorian structures to modern apartment-like dwellings. All dormitories have pianos and grandfather clocks. Particularly attractive dwellings include "The Rockies," a set of large Tudor-style buildings; Ham Hall, which has beautiful views of Upper Lake; and MacGregor, where all the rooms have bay windows and window seats. There are several traditions surrounding dormitory life: all halls house members of all four classes; students typically change residence halls every autumn; and hall life includes occasional afternoon teas. Another tradition, known as "elfing," involves a junior "Big Sister" who is assigned as a "secret elf" for an incoming freshman. "Most of my social life is in the dorm," says one student. Although Mount Holyoke is free from the concerns about coed dormitories that plague other colleges and universities, overnight guests of the opposite sex can be a problem, so incoming freshmen will want to be clear about their rooming preferences.

There is definitely a country club quality to some of the choices available to students at Mount Holyoke. The college has one of the finest equestrian facilities anywhere in the country — not just in academia — and students may board their horses there. The college has an award-winning Donald Ross–designed golf course as well. The popular intercollegiate and club athletic offerings are typically upperclass pursuits — tennis, squash, field hockey, lacrosse, water polo, rugby, cro-quiet, and fencing, along with the "Boots and Saddles" equestrian club and the "Combined Training and Dressage" group. (Of course, volleyball, basketball, and other common sports are also represented.) The arts are also popular extracurriculars at Mount Holyoke. More than two hundred students participate in some form of vocal performance, including Concert Choir and several *a cappella* groups.

Even this idyllic setting is not immune to societal dangers: campus safety is a perennial issue at Mount Holyoke, since crime is no stranger to the community of South Hadley. While most reported crimes — such as theft of storage items, annoying phone calls, or car vandalism — are routine campus issues and nothing to be particularly concerned about, fear of sexual assault is perhaps more heightened on this all-female campus. But Mount Holyoke's campus is considered quite safe, and the campus and community police are quite vigilant in patrolling the campus and immediate environs. Still, many Mount Holyoke students take classes at other nearby colleges, and students were alarmed in the autumn of 1999 by a series of assaults against female students at the neighboring University of Massachusetts. Mount Holyoke's Office of Public Safety conducted several residence hall workshops and self-defense programs in response to the assaults. During this spate of assaults at UMass, a Mount Holyoke student narrowly escaped an attacker in Northampton, Massachusetts, near the entrance to Smith College.

Although it began as a missionary school, Mount Holyoke phased out its seminary curriculum in the late nineteenth century and abandoned required chapel in the 1960s. Vestiges of religious expression are on a purely extracurricular basis. There are campus chapters of InterVarsity Christian Fellowship, the Newman Association, and the Jewish Student Union, along with a Muslim student organization and one called Sisters of Hinduism Reaching Inwards. Eliot House is the campus spiritual center, and the site of the Wa-Shin-An Japanese Tea House and meditation garden. The tea house, whose name means "Peace-Mind-House," was built in 1984 by architect Teruo Hara, who noted that his main purpose was "to create a very quiet space which somehow shows people that there are different solutions."

With an endowment of $364 million, Mount Holyoke is certainly more financially secure than in the early days when foundress Mary Lyon traveled the byroads of Massachusetts by stagecoach, according to the college Web site, "to fill her green velvet bag with contributions . . . from six cents to a thousand dollars, sometimes consisting of scraps of fabric for students' quilts and feathers for their pillows." Still, prospective undergraduates will need to come up with quite a bit more than fabric scraps and feathers in order to finance their education at Mount Holyoke today: tuition hovers at $24,200, while room and board is estimated at $7,110. Over two-thirds of Mount Holyoke students receive need-based financial aid. Nearly a fifth of Mount Holyoke students have "legacy" connections (mothers, sisters, aunts, or other relatives who graduated from the college).

New York University

Office of Undergraduate Admissions
22 Washington Square North
New York, NY 10011-9191
(212) 998-4500
www.nyu.edu

Total enrollment: 37,000
Undergraduates: 18,204
SAT ranges (Verbal/Math): 620-710 (V); 610-710 (M)
Applicants: 28,794
Accepted: 32%
Enrolled: 40%
Application deadline: January 15
Financial aid application deadline: February 15
Tuition: $24,336/$33,562
Core curriculum: No

Hip to Be (Washington) Square

New York University (NYU) was founded in 1831, and counter to the practices of the time, it offered courses in the practical sciences and arts, such as business, law, and medicine rather than instructing the sons of privilege in Greek and Latin and the liberal arts. The first president of its board of trustees was Albert Gallatin, once an adviser to President Thomas Jefferson, who endeavored to provide "a rational and practical education for all."

New York City is an excellent place to attempt such an effort — the "all" Gallatin mentions can definitely be found there. NYU is located on Washington Square, in the middle of Greenwich Village, which might be the most likely site in the world to find just about anything.

Unfortunately for the modern NYU, a little too much of the Village has entered the college. The 18,000 undergraduates there must negotiate the politicized curriculum with the same caution they need to pass safely through the city's streets. "A major influence of the political correctness on the university campus comes from being in the city," a professor says. Moreover, undergraduate classes are often large, and not always well taught.

It must be said, however, that the city has also benefited the university. Opportunities for internships and exchange programs for faculty and students that simply could not be offered in a smaller setting are available at NYU. The university makes good use of its $1 billion endowment to make the best of life in New York City. But the challenge now is to keep the bad stuff at bay.

Academic Life: A Gallatin Attempt

There are thirteen divisions of NYU, ranging from the schools of medicine, dentistry, and law to schools of business and social work. The most important colleges for the student interested in the liberal arts are the College of the Arts and Sciences and the Gallatin School of Individualized Study.

The College of the Arts and Sciences is the largest of the undergraduate colleges. The curriculum is expansive, and the choices on the general education list (known as the Morse Academic Plan after Samuel Morse, the one-time NYU faculty member who invented the telegraph) are many. The Morse Plan is a set of distribution requirements, though it was once intended to be a core curriculum taught only by full-time faculty in small seminars that debated the classics of Western literature. Unfortunately, NYU did not create the necessary faculty slots and the program sprawled; many courses are now taught by junior faculty or teaching assistants, and sections originally planned for twenty-five students are now as large as two hundred. The school's Web page has been reduced to touting the program's diversity, as in: "The college [of Arts and Sciences] is one of the most diverse communities anywhere."

The Morse Plan includes four components: Foundations of Contemporary Culture, Foundations of Scientific Inquiry, Expository Writing, and Foreign Languages.

The first of these, Foundations of Contemporary Culture, comprises a four-course sequence usually completed during the student's first two years at NYU. The four courses are called "Conversations of the West," "World Cultures," "Societies and the Social Sciences," and "Expressive Culture." All courses are interdisciplinary, and are ordered so as to expose students to intercultural similarities and differences.

The Foundations of Scientific Inquiry requirement is also a sequence: three courses called "Quantitative Reasoning," "Natural Science I (An Introduction to the Physical Universe)," and "Natural Science II (Our Place in the Biological Realm)." These courses are taught using solid quantitative and analytical methods.

The final requirements demand one year of expository writing classes and the equivalent of two years of foreign language study.

Morse requirements are usually completed in the first two years of study — before a student moves on to the more specialized courses required for a major. On paper, the courses form at least an approximation of a traditional core curriculum, but the reality is that they are often taught by professors more intent on their own research than on undergraduate teaching, faculty say. "The undergraduate courses are large and anonymous," one professor says. "The undergraduate curriculum does not meet the standards of higher education," says another.

An alternative for students looking for smaller classes and a different setup is the Gallatin School of Individualized Study. The school describes itself as "an innovative college that encourages individual exploration." Most notably, the Gallatin School offers students the opportunity to study the seminal works of the Western tradition. One professor characterized the Gallatin School as a "splendid program that emphasizes the great books with a small setting."

The requirements of the Gallatin School are looser than those at a prototypical great books program, such as that found at schools like Thomas Aquinas College. According to the school's Web site, "When students choose Gallatin, they take on the exciting challenge of creating their own curriculum and unique plan for learning." Students need thirty-two credit hours in liberal arts courses in the humanities, social sciences, mathematics or science, and expository writing. The courses can come from virtually any college of the university and are not required by name, only by category. Once this "core" requirement in the liberal arts is completed, Gallatin students declare a concentration, the bounds and requirements of which are not even loosely defined. Consequently, students are able to declare almost anything as a concentration, including women's studies, environmental studies, performing arts, pre-law, or any other field that interests them.

The Gallatin School also requires participation in a "First-Year Seminar." These seminars are limited to about twenty students and involve discussions on the fundamental questions of liberal education. There is a rhetoric requirement (two expository writing courses, limited to fifteen students per section), and all seniors face a "Senior Colloquium," an oral examination conducted by three professors covering texts related to the student's concentration. The exam not only tests students' knowledge of their field, but also explores "ways of integrating their academic, professional, and personal experiences with the great books they have been reading and the ideas they have been examining in their Gallatin courses," according to the university catalogue.

The best courses at the Gallatin School are "Interdisciplinary Seminars," which cover great works by classical authors like Shakespeare, Plato, Homer, and Nietzsche, as well as modern works by Toni Morrison and Elie Wiesel. However, the school also teaches a few more dubious courses, such as "African Queens and Harlem Slaves" and "Gender and Resistance, Race, and Rebellion." And the trend in the school is toward greater politicization. "What has happened to the Gallatin School is a great tragedy," says one professor. "They are exploring crazy, post-modern studies. If they had notable professors . . . that would be one thing. But the professors are not very good at what they do." Another professor notes that the quality of students in the program has increased over the last few years, and this has made the student less susceptible to the political ideology that often appears in their classes.

A student says that, overall, NYU's program lacks both intellectual urgency and the proper focus. "Intellectually, the program is very soft. It is as if there is nothing to learn, but there is emoting to be done," the student says. "The recurrent question is 'how do we feel' about this or that. Students aren't studying literature, as much as they are studying themselves."

Exceptions to this observation are the classes taught by these fine professors: Herbert London in the Gallatin division; Israel Kirzner and Mario Rizzo in economics; Paul Vitz in psychology; Norman Cantor in history; James Steven J. Brams in politics; Angela D. Dillard in history and politics; Larissa Bonfante in classics; Evelyn Birge Vitz and Seth Benardete in medieval and Renaissance studies; and Wolf V. Heydebrand in sociology.

One of the best departments at NYU is economics, where Ludwig von Mises, one of the fathers of the Austrian School, once taught. Today's department is home to both free-market proponents and welfare-state types, but these distinctions are virtually invisible in the classrooms, where the department is unified on methodology and well-published in its research. Teachers tend to ignore public policy questions and ideological debates in order to concentrate on the deeper questions of economics: What is science, and what is the contribution of economics?

Two other good departments are psychology and medieval and Renaissance studies, both of which have avoided the encroachment of politicized courses.

NYU has an enormous library that is of benefit to all departments. The Elmer Holmes Bobst Library, one of the largest open-stack research libraries in the nation, stands twelve stories high and occupies an entire city block. Its collection of 2.5 million volumes includes, according to the university, strengths in "American and English literature and history, economics, education, science, music, United Nations documents, Near Eastern and Ibero-American languages and literatures, and Judaica and Hebraica." The library also has a special collection in labor history.

Among the most politicized departments at NYU is French, said by one student to have been "captured by a certain sect of literati that is enamored with feminist and deconstructionist theories." The classes that examine nineteenth- and twentieth-century French thought are the most politicized. Jacques Derrida visits the department each year.

The Africana studies department, according to the catalogue, covers "black consciousness, black feminism, and questions of class and gender dynamics within black communities." The department offers two concentrations within the major: Pan-African history and thought and black urban studies. Students in the Pan-African concentration study feminism and communism from an African-American perspective, and examine literary and political movements like "the Harlem Renaissance, the Negritude movement, black consciousness, black feminism, and black intellectual leaders such as W. E. B. DuBois, Zora Neale Hurston, C. L. R. James, Malcolm X, Angela Davis, Leopold Senghor, and Kwame Nkrumah," according to the catalogue. Students in black urban studies look at, among other things, "music and sports industries, mass media, the police, and public schools."

Some of the politicized courses in the Africana studies department include "Race, Power, and the Postindustrial City" and "20th-Century Black Feminist

Thought and Practice in the U.S.," which, according to the catalogue, "examines various forms of social/sexual policing, larger social narratives about black women's sexuality, black women and urban poverty debates, class politics within feminism(s) and gender, and class tensions within black social protest movements." There are seminars in "Pan-Africanism" that vary from semester to semester, with topics that include "African unity, black rebellion, colonialism and racism, the black diaspora and culture, and relationships between Pan-Africanism and movements such as nationalism, Marxism, and Afrocentricity," according to the catalogue.

The comparative literature department spells out its ideology in the university catalogue: "What also makes this study of literature comparative is that it examines texts not ordinarily seen as literary for their uses of language and traces the effects of such literature on cultural representations of gender, race, and class." A look at the course list shows that the department is not exaggerating.

Political Atmosphere: The Village People

The outgoing president of NYU, L. Jay Oliva, is like many modern university presidents in that he concerns himself more with fund-raising than with academics, according to professors. The president and his administration have not taken a hard line against political correctness, nor have they gone out of their way to encourage it. However, according to one professor, "The administration would be hospitable to innovations in the curriculum, especially those that would attract new students."

The NYU administration has encouraged the departments of the university to hire more minority professors and has set goals for affirmative action hires, according to professors. Like other universities, NYU has had difficulty retaining black professors; because of the scarcity of black academicians in a time of affirmative action hiring pushes, other schools have offered NYU professors more money, a professor says. Women have also been historically underrepresented on the NYU faculty, but the administration has not pushed departments to hire on the basis of sex. "Women faculty would rather hire excellent colleagues than just people of the same sex," one professor says.

Recently, the most publicized employment issue on campus has to do with the push by teaching assistants to unionize. In late 2000, the TAs were on the winning side of a decision by the National Labor Relations Board, which held that there was "no basis to deny collective bargaining rights to statutory employees merely because they are employed by an educational institution in which they are enrolled as students." The 1,400 TAs voted to form a union, the first of its kind at a private U.S. college. University officials worried over the impact the ruling would have at NYU and around the country. "Who teaches what courses and how the courses are taught and what is taught — the notion that that's decided in collective bargaining instead of in the faculty-student consultation process is very worrisome to the university," Robert

Berne, NYU vice president for academic and health affairs, told the *Chronicle of Higher Education*. Already campaigns for unions are underway at Columbia and Brandeis universities, and the ruling gave new strength to a ten-year campaign by Yale TAs for similar consideration.

The union drive is just one of the liberal aspects of the Greenwich Village campus. "The diversity here is as wide as the rainbow, and there are protests all the time," says one student. "The problem is when you are walking around NYU you can't tell what is a student protest, and what comes from the Village." Campus activists post scores of advertisements for rallies and events held both on and off campus. "The protests are usually pretty large," a student says. "At a minimum, you will see about twenty students holding placards or screaming out some slogans." One hot topic is animal rights, and students have demonstrated for it on campus and in Washington Square. A march to a Manhattan furrier was organized to protest fur coats. Homosexual activism is common, and, reportedly, a sizable sector of the student body is homosexual. The university funds an Office of Lesbian, Gay, Bisexual, and Transgender Students, which supports the many officially recognized student homosexual organizations, including Queer Union; the AIDS Awareness Club; Out-Artists; Lesbians, Gays, Bisexuals, and Transgenders in Public Service; Lesbian, Gay, and Bisexual Association of Business Students; Lesbian, Gay, and Bisexual People in Medicine; Bisexual, Lesbian, and Gay Law Students; Fluidity, a group for bisexuals; and "Campgrrrl," something for bisexual and transgender women. The office posts a "Gender and Sexuality Course Guide" on its Web page, which includes these courses offered in the Spring of 2001: "Wild Women in German Drama"; "Sexual Rights and Wrongs: Porn, Sexwork, and Other"; "Queer Theories: Queering Visual Cultures"; "Gay White (Virtual) Way: L&G Plays on Bway"; and "Witchcraft, Magic, and Social Power." The last one is from the school of continuing and professional studies, making a mockery of Gallatin's idea of practical education.

The Office of Student Life also hosts the Office of African-American, Latino, and Asian-American Student Services, which provides minority students with academic and professional services, including counseling. The office works to increase the number of minority students who graduate from NYU and to help these students find employment after college. Along with the university's Office of Career Services, the multicultural office holds an annual "Job Fair for Students of Color," which gives minority students exposure to recruiters from various firms.

Student Life: Bright Lights, Big City

NYU students face both the advantages and disadvantages of life in one of the world's most fascinating cities. The possibilities for entertainment, eating, and shopping are unlimited; traveling by subway or taxi, students can catch Broadway musicals and plays, watch a taping of David Letterman's show at the Ed Sullivan

Theater, or tour the United Nations, the Statue of Liberty, the Empire State Building, the World Trade Center, and hundreds of other places. Many students spend their free time in bookstores, including Strand Books, one of the largest in the city and specialists in out-of-print and used books; Gotham Book Mart, good for literature and philosophy titles; and Patelson's House of Music, noted for its selection of musical scores and books on literature.

The most obvious drawback of life in New York is crime. Greenwich Village is the scene of a lot of drug trafficking, but the area around NYU is considered safer than the neighborhoods around Columbia University, for example. "Crime in general is improving in the city," an NYU professor says. "Of course, you have to be very careful at, say, two in the morning — which, ironically, is when students are usually out on the town." There are usually police officers in Washington Square, and the university grounds are said to be comparatively safe.

Students, more than half of which come to NYU from the mid-Atlantic region, live in residence halls or in off-campus apartments, though the latter can be very expensive. About 60 percent of the student body lives on campus. Although the administration inquires each year about interest in theme houses, so far the only housing with a designated issue are "health conscious" floors whose residents oppose alcohol and drug abuse. Many residence halls were formerly hotels, and, as a result, students enjoy the benefits associated with fine residential living. One alumna found some of the antique hotel furniture and was permitted to use it in her room. A number of celebrities, including Al Pacino and Jerry Garcia, lived in these buildings before they were converted to student housing.

There are fourteen active fraternities and twelve sororities at NYU, but only seven frats have residential houses. Because of the innumerable options in the city, Greek life is not the focus of NYU social life, except perhaps for fraternity members. "Sure, students will go to fraternity parties, but they don't live and die for them," a student says. "There are plenty other places to party."

The list of more than 250 student groups includes ethnic organizations, several publications, performance groups, and social clubs like the Society for Creative Anachronism and the Outdoors Club. There are a few religious organizations, like the Baptist Student Union, several Jewish groups, a gospel choir, and a couple of Christian organizations. Most unusual name: "The Friends of Spartacus Youth Club," an explicitly Trotskyite organization. Overall, the list of official student organizations is fairly short considering the size of the university, but this is likely another result of NYU's location in a city with so many other things to do.

NYU athletes compete in nineteen intercollegiate sports, with the university's most recent success being a national Division III championship won by the women's basketball team. Historically, NYU can boast of its win over Manhattan College in the first-ever intercollegiate lacrosse game, played in 1877 in Central Park. Also, the model for the stiff-arming figure atop the Heisman Trophy is former NYU star Ed Smith, who posed for the statue in 1935. The university has eighteen club sports and

485

seventeen intramural choices as well. Recreation facilities on campus include tennis, squash, and racquetball courts; fitness rooms; and a track.

State University of New York at Binghamton

Office of Admissions
Enrollment Services and Management
State University of New York at Binghamton
P.O. Box 6000
Binghamton, NY 13902-6000
(607) 777-2171
www.binghamton.edu

Total enrollment: 12,473
Undergraduates: 9,858
SAT ranges (Verbal/Math): 540-640 (V); 570-660 (M)
Applicants: 16,507
Accepted: 42%
Enrolled: 28%
Application deadline: Rolling
Financial aid application deadline: March 1
Tuition: resident: $4,416/$9,932; non-resident: $9,316/$14,832
Core curriculum: No

What's Past Is Past

In recent times the State University of New York at Binghamton (SUNY–Binghamton) has been hailed as a "public Ivy," the most prestigious state university in New York and one of the nation's leading liberal arts institutions. But that was then, and this is now: although it still enjoys a strong national reputation, and does retain a number of good professors and programs, Binghamton is gradually shedding the rigorous liberal arts tradition that once distinguished it from the other universities in the state system.

The school began as a branch of Syracuse University in 1946, but was incorporated into the state university system four years later as Harpur College (after local Colonial patriot Robert Harpur). Harpur College was led by a cadre of East Coast intellectuals eager to implement an innovative liberal arts curriculum. Its first dean envisioned an Ivy League–caliber liberal arts institution modeled on small, prestigious colleges like Swarthmore College (as it was then, of course). High-ranking professors from Princeton were brought in, among them noted Augustinian scholar Bernard Huppe and Aldo Bernardo, a distinguished expert on Petrarch. The faculty were charged with implementing a rigorous cycle of required undergraduate courses, with a broad-based liberal arts curriculum that stressed language and the tutorial system of teaching, a curriculum and method that according to one of the original faculty were "second to none for that period." Students worked their way through a three-year series of courses on the nature of language, the history of ideas, the natural and social sciences, foreign languages, and the fine arts.

But within twenty years the program began to unravel amid a general spirit of student dissatisfaction with what they viewed as faculty dogmatism and curricular constraints. Today the noble plan on which the college was founded continues to crumble; in fact, Binghamton seems to be running, not walking, from its past. Sadly, one won't find Binghamton boasting about its prestigious intellectual heritage in its current promotional literature. Although the university still considers itself a premier liberal arts institution, the attack on the solid core of studies that once distinguished Binghamton as an innovative, intellectually rigorous school has intensified in recent years, and, according to more traditional faculty and students there, it seems only a matter of time before the radical ideologues finally win the day. State budget cuts and faculty and graduate student activism threaten to undermine the years of good work accomplished by many of this century's finest scholars. As one wistful faculty member observes, the fine reputation Binghamton now enjoys is based on "what it once was" rather than what it currently aspires to be.

Academic Life: Out with the Old

The Harpur College of Arts and Sciences at SUNY–Binghamton is the academic home for about 70 percent of the university's nearly ten thousand undergraduates. There students pursue majors in the humanities, sciences, and social sciences. The remaining Binghamton students are divided among four other schools: the Decker School of Nursing, the School of Management, the School of Education and Human Development, and the Thomas J. Watson School of Engineering and Applied Science.

Within Harpur College, a limited number of distribution requirements must be met by all liberal arts students. According to the university, these are intended to instill "an appreciation of and capacity for effective personal expression; knowledge about various intellectual traditions; [and] an understanding of and respect for dif-

ferent peoples and civilizations" along with some other phrases about logical thinking and an appreciation of the arts and the natural world. In short, it's a very nontraditional rundown of the purpose of the liberal arts.

The list of courses intended to teach these nebulous powers has recently been
expanded, though at the same time, the college made it easier for just about any
course to count toward a given a requirement. The requirements are one course in
each of these: oral communication, composition, natural sciences, social sciences,
humanities, "Pluralism-American History," "Global Interdependencies," a science
laboratory course, "Mathematics/Reasoning," and "Aesthetic Perspective." Obviously, some of these are there for reasons of multiculturalism. There is also a two-
credit physical education requirement. The courses used to fulfill these requirements need not have anything to do with the central concepts of the discipline (for
those areas that actually encompass a something traditionally considered a discipline) or with the point of liberal arts education. "Film and Society" can take care of
the "Global Interdependencies" part, and "Principles of Photography" is good
enough for one of the science courses.

In addition, Harpur college students must take two courses in each of three areas — humanities, social sciences, and science and math — plus four courses outside their major area of study. These courses can focus on just about anything; in
2001, for example, courses that could count toward the Harpur humanities requirement include "The African Novel"; "Multiculturalism"; "Derrida"; "Ancient Sexuality
and Gender"; "Women Who Fight Back"; "The Colonized Body of Literature";
Witches, Scapegoats, and Disorder"; and "Ecofeminism." Again, these count toward
the *humanities* requirement.

At least one campus source finds the whole setup underwhelming. Writing in
the *Binghamton Review,* student Nathan Wurtzel says, "How does B.U.'s General Education requirement rate? It doesn't stack up to Buffalo, Cortland, or Geneseo. It isn't
as good as Plattsburgh, Potsdam, Purchase, or any other SUNY that begins with a 'P.'
The University Center at Stony Brook has a better core curriculum and so does the
small campus at Old Westbury. Binghamton University requires less credit hours in
general education than any other SUNY. Of course, we do have a nice new diversity
logo and those other schools don't. So there!"

Binghamton also offers several programs and degrees in minority studies.
While there are currently no women's studies or Asian and Asian-American studies
majors, students may opt for a concentration in these areas (or a minor in the case of
women's studies); majors are, however, offered in Latin American and Caribbean
studies and in Africana studies.

These programs are, as one might expect, slanted to reflect a single political
viewpoint. An offended Jewish student complains that the head of the Africana studies department compares Zionism to apartheid. Women's studies courses also tend
to be highly radicalized. One student related an incident in which a male student
disagreed with the perspective of the professor and argued that "we only study left-

wing professors" in the class. The professor's response to this student dissident? Calling the campus police on him.

The university is also home to the Fernand Braudel Center for the Study of Economics, Historical Systems, and Civilizations, established several years ago to study Marxist thought. Though one student characterizes the economics department as "mainstream," some course offerings tend to stray far to the left: one freshman-level course offered to undergraduates is Econ 129, "Radical Political Economy," in which students study "mainstream thought and capitalist structure from [a] radical perspective," including the "nature and function of private property, class exploitation, and economic crises" from the standpoint of reformist and revolutionary ideology. The sociology program, considered "highly politicized" by one professor, also receives low marks from conservative students. "It's really just consciousness-raising," says one.

Several excellent faculty and programs do exist at SUNY–Binghamton, in spite of the pall that ideological multiculturalism has cast over the campus in recent years. Many faculty, regardless of their political affiliation, are able to teach courses without bias. Students give high praise to philosophy professor John Arthur, Judaic studies professor Alan Arkush, and classics professor Saul Levin, to mention just a few. Students and faculty alike praise the biology program for its professionalism.

In addition to the more traditional humanities and social science majors, Binghamton also offers some innovative study options and degree programs that are in keeping with the traditional liberal arts ideals upon which the university was founded. One such program is "Philosophy, Politics, and Law," a course of studies offered to both liberal arts and pre-law students. Administered through the philosophy department, the program is premised on the idea that a study of law should be part of a general liberal education, since law "leads far beyond the narrow confines of legal cases to perennial questions of law's origins, operation, and justification." For this major, students take a broad span of required courses in philosophy, political science, and history. They also have the opportunity to study for a semester or a year at the University of East Anglia in Norwich, England.

The "Languages across the Curriculum," or "LxC" program, was developed with one eye "toward the global village of tomorrow." The wording of that description may make one skeptical, but the program itself is worthwhile and well conceived: it involves students reading from foreign language textbooks and secondary material in selected nonlanguage courses. The premise is that students who are proficient in a foreign language should be using that language throughout their curriculum of studies. The ambitious long-term goal of the program, as expressed in university literature, "is to bring about a situation where students can use any foreign language they know in any class at any level anywhere in the university curriculum." To facilitate movement toward this goal, the university trains a corps of language resource specialists whose job is to help students assimilate foreign language materials into their courses of studies.

The university also has a medieval studies major, in which all students are required, among other things, to take either two courses in medieval Latin or one in a medieval vernacular language. Additionally, Binghamton offers more than a dozen interdisciplinary courses in which students can major, minor, or earn certificates.

Although some of its liberal arts programs are solid and admirable, Binghamton's love affair with the experimental and the politically correct is increasingly at odds with its foundation of liberal arts studies. Perhaps because students, parents, and employers in today's competitive job market seem more impressed with the utilitarian than with meaningful statements about the value of a liberal education, Binghamton has begun stressing aspects of the school that would impress these constituencies, such as low tuition (*Kiplinger's* ranked it fifth in a list of best buys in U.S. public education) and an emergent reputation for research. In this environment, it is difficult to say how much longer Binghamton can preserve its stated commitment to undergraduate teaching and a true liberal arts curriculum.

Political Atmosphere: Inequality and Oppression

In the spring of 1997 a brewing controversy over a proposal to require two politically charged courses on race and gender came to a head. The courses, "The Social Construction of Inequality" and "The Nature of Oppression," had the support and sponsorship of a number of faculty, including an anthropology professor who saw them as "an opportunity to address diversity in an in-depth way." More savvy students and faculty, however, saw the proposal as yet one more attempt by the doyens of multiculturalism to indoctrinate all Binghamton students into the ideology of power and oppression. A bitter feud erupted between the two sides, resulting in protest marches, sit-ins, a student takeover of the administration building, and the exchange of pleasantries between conservative and liberal factions in campus publications. Writing in the conservative *Binghamton Review*, political philosophy major John Carney warned, "Force me to bow down and study 'The Nature of Oppression' and I will reach for my longbow."

No actual arrows flew, and student and faculty representatives on the College Council voted 21-16 to drop the proposed courses. While many students were elated, the proponents of the courses on oppression and inequality had sour words for the victors. "With this vote," the Graduate Students Organization president complained dramatically in the mainstream campus paper *Pipe Dream*, "the right wing has consolidated its hold on this campus, and the neo-fascist takeover is complete." Despite the vote, the "oppression" studies requirement, at this writing, continues to be debated, and one professor laments that the process will inevitably be of a highly charged nature. "The whole thing," the professor says, "will be flawed by political issues that should never be a part of the discussion."

490

Of course, the university kept its seat on the multicultural bandwagon. Most announcements for faculty jobs include the phrase "who share our commitment to diversity," and there are organizations on campus whose only purpose is the promotion of multiculturalism. A state university system trustee, Candace de Russy, was quoted in the conservative *Binghamton Review,* as saying: "Where politicization exists at SUNY and elsewhere in the academy, it is to be found primarily in departments of humanities and social sciences. Therein disinterested intellectual inquiry is subordinated and even abandoned in favor of 'liberatory political' goals. For those thus politicized, academic and scientific inquiry is not open-ended but geared to justifying pre-determined conclusions — conclusions having everything to do with politics and power."

Politics of this sort are introduced to incoming Binghamton students in a two-day summer orientation session. A concurrent seminar is held for their parents. Some students have complained recently about the "sensitivity training" introduced by university staffers during the orientation, saying it amounts to little more than multicultural indoctrination. The corny titles of some games do little to hide the activities' real agenda. For example, in recent years, students have been asked to play "Wheel of Oppression," in which they break into small groups and talk about the roots and evils of oppression. They also have played "Cultural Pursuit," a game modeled on Trivial Pursuit but with categories like "Experience being stereotyped," "Is white, male middle or upper class," or "Has a friend or relative who is gay, lesbian or bisexual." One student dismissively refers to the whole experience as "Kindergarten 101" and advises opting out of it if at all possible.

Some balance is provided by the *Binghamton Review,* which acts as a thoughtful alternative to the liberal *Pipe Dream* and monitors radical happenings on campus. However, the *Review* is not welcome in some quarters. It survives even though the student assembly voted to cut its funding a few years ago because of "offensive cartoons." Since then, the *Review* no longer solicits or accepts funds from the university. Staff members face a chronic problem of the newspapers being stolen from campus distribution points. And during the 1997 academic year a furor erupted when the interim director of women's studies allegedly sent an ultimatum, written on official university stationery, to the campus bookstore: either stop advertising in the *Review* or face a boycott from the women's studies department. The bookstore yielded to the threat and withdrew its advertising from the conservative paper. After some sleuthing, Review staffers discovered the existence of the letter, and the letter writer was subsequently condemned by the Harpur College Council.

The majority of speakers brought to campus have political agendas to promote. Binghamton has hosted Leonard Jeffries, Louis Farrakhan, Bob Abrams, and Ralph Nader. But conservatives have also appeared on campus, though usually without any financial support from the university. Jeremy Rabkin, Erik von Kuehnelt-Leddihn, and National Association of Scholars member and professor of Austrian economics Barry Smith have all spoken on campus as well.

Student Life: Whereas There Are a Lot of Great Titles out There . . .

SUNY–Binghamton is nestled on more than 600 wooded acres near the Susquehanna River, bordered at the southern tip by a 117-acre nature preserve. Students expecting ivy-covered spires will be disappointed, though: All buildings postdate 1958 and are for the most part typically soulless modern constructions. The housing environment, however, is designed to take advantage of the beautiful natural surroundings — none of the campus residences stands higher than three stories. Undergraduates are required to live on campus for their first year, and can choose from among four residential colleges (Hinman, Newing, Dickinson, or College-in-the-Woods). The individual halls that constitute these colleges are all coed, and the vast majority of floors are coed as well, though men and women have separate bathrooms. Residents may also select one of several special-interest living situations. Current options include things like dance, fitness, "Diversity Circle," and "Maintaining Eating Alternatives Together (M.E.A.T.)."

Crime is infrequent but not unknown on and around the Binghamton campus. Burglaries are the most common type of violation. Most of these occur in the dorms, as do most of the reported forcible sex offenses (there were four in 1998 and three in 1999).

SUNY–Binghamton's Colonials, the university's sports teams, proudly wear the school's green and white colors in a variety of intercollegiate athletics. For those with more modest athletic activity in mind, there is a wealth of student-organized or intramural sports, including crew, cycling, equestrian, Frisbee, lacrosse, rugby, snowboarding, and karate clubs. The university also sponsors "co-rec" touch football, played on the lawns outside the residence halls. This popular pastime involves six-player teams (three men and three women); one of the women must play quarterback.

The university recently opened a 4,000-square-foot exercise facility called FitSpace, which offers air-conditioned workout and aerobics rooms to students for a modest fee. The university also completed construction of a million-dollar track and soccer complex, and has articulated a commitment to the continued support and expansion of the college athletic program.

In addition to athletics, some 130 student organizations operate on campus, including some rather vocal political groups like the Gay People's Union, the Black Student Union, the Democratic Socialists of America, and others. These groups reportedly have a large influence on Binghamton's student government group, the Student Association. The Student Association, though somewhat radical, sometimes mixes its politics with humor, as was the case in a recent resolution asking the student union to stock pornographic films in its video store. The resolution read in part:

> Whereas, students engage in a lot of promiscuous sex on this campus (granted, not as much as at Albany . . .), and if students had another way to release their

sexual energies, they might find themselves with less of a need to participate in sex acts themselves.

Whereas, Health Services would most likely laud the notion of porn in Take One Video.

Whereas, there are a lot of great titles out there. . . .

No word on whether the store acquiesced. But in any case, there are other things to do around the campus, which is not actually located in Binghamton, but across the Susquehanna River in the small town of Vestal. Binghamton, though, is home to two professional sports teams (the Binghamton Rangers hockey team and the Binghamton Mets baseball team), as well as a professional opera company, symphony and pops orchestras, theaters, and shopping malls. The downtown Arena is a popular music venue, as is the excellent Anderson Center for the Arts on campus, which also hosts plays, recitals, and other performances.

University of North Carolina at Chapel Hill

Office of Undergraduate Admissions
CB #2200, Jackson Hall
Chapel Hill, NC 27599-2200
(919) 966-3621
www.unc.edu

Total enrollment: 24,180
Undergraduates: 15,321
SAT ranges (Verbal/Math): 570-680 (V); 570-680 (M)
Applicants: 16,022
Accepted: 39%
Enrolled: 55%
Application deadline: January 15
Financial aid application deadline: March 1
Tuition: resident: $2,768/$8,508; non-resident: $11,934/$17,674
Core curriculum: No

Going to Carolina

One of the oldest universities in the country, the University of North Carolina's flagship campus in Chapel Hill has a proud history of educating many of the state's leading political figures and businessmen. But since its founding in 1789, this large, public university has also acquired a national reputation for its high-quality academics, exceedingly low tuition, and dominant sports teams.

Professors want to teach there — its educational program is solid; the campus is beautiful, and the intellectual community, both in Chapel Hill and the famous Research Triangle Park, is vibrant, supportive, and challenging.

For those outside of North Carolina, admission to the Chapel Hill campus is nearly as competitive as that at many elite private schools. But the tuition for out-of-staters — $11,934 — is about half the price of those colleges. If you happen to live in North Carolina, tuition is the biggest bargain around, a mere $2,768 per year. But administrators hope to double that figure over the next five years to support an increase in faculty salaries. Of course, as a state university, UNC is not the most selective institution around. And despite its prestige, there are students who would rather party than pursue excellence.

Some of the best academic things UNC has to offer get wasted on some of the students. Many say that academically, they have little guidance and tend to get lost in a major research university that also has more than 15,000 undergraduates. The school's curriculum does little to help, since it gives teenagers the ability to choose any number of courses, good and not-so-solid, to fulfill general education requirements.

Life outside of the classroom is similar to academic life: there's plenty to choose from. Whatever the time of year, there's always plenty going on in Chapel Hill, a quintessential college town with a lively main drag. In 1999, one of the university's most revered former students, basketball legend Michael Jordan, even opened a restaurant there.

Academic Life: "Perspectives" of a Large School

At a university as large as UNC, there is naturally a wide number of courses available, the quality of which varies widely. The university offers more than fifty majors and forty minors, but there is no core curriculum, and students are given a wide range to choose the classes that will count toward the general requirements that do exist. Many students complain that the advising system is weak. Others say the real strength of UNC is not so much its courses per se, but rather the contacts one makes with fellow students and the creation of a bond with alumni. Others complain of rampant pre-professionalism, which might be expected at a state university where degrees in journalism, business, and other vocational-type majors are popular.

With the right guidance, students can carve out for themselves a quality liberal arts education. But a diploma from UNC does not guarantee that one has undertaken such learning. UNC once required students to spend their first two years studying the best-known literary and philosophical works of the Western tradition, as well as the history of the West. Those days are now twenty years gone: the university settled for a set of distribution requirements back in 1981, when traditional faculty were outvoted by those who found the value of various "perspectives" to outweigh the substance offered by the core.

Today, students must fulfill basic requirements in English composition (two courses), foreign languages, and mathematics. Other requirements are called "perspectives," and thus the requirement for a literature and a fine arts class is called the "aesthetic perspective." There are also requirements of two science courses ("natural sciences perspective"); one course in philosophy, religion, or political science ("philosophical perspective"); and two courses from two different social science departments (the "social sciences perspective").

"The question in my mind about the requirements is that there are ways of getting around it with very little 'perspective' being gained," a faculty member says. "Students see it a little bit like pieces of a puzzle they're putting together. They don't always see the whole puzzle."

Says one senior: "The requirements are really lax. It's a weakness. It's like a cafeteria: you can get whatever you want."

There is also a "Western Historical/Non-Western Perspective" consisting of two courses: one on a pre-1700 Western history topic and a second on either a Western or non-Western historical theme. The first course must be chosen from a list of twenty-eight offerings, including standard Western history survey courses. But to fulfill the requirement, students can elect instead to take "Women of Byzantium" or "Women and Marriage in Medieval and Renaissance Europe" — courses that are better suited toward in-depth graduate study following a proper introduction to the historical milieu.

Another requirement, instituted in 1994, mandates a "cultural diversity requirement" that gives them "the opportunity to gain a better understanding of cultural diversity," according to the university catalog. Among the more than two hundred options for this requirement are "Sex and Gender in Antiquity," "Performance of Women of Color," "Leisure in a Diverse Society," and a drama course, "Non-Western Costume History."

Some students dread one final requirement: the swim test. To graduate, students must tread water for several minutes. Swimming classes are available for those who are more likely to sink than swim.

Administrators are hoping that a new computer requirement will change campus life. Beginning in the fall of 2000, entering freshmen are required to own a laptop computer for their undergraduate careers at the university. Although this adds a couple thousand dollars to the cost of attending the university, administrators say it will encourage the use of technology and allow students to have easy and instant access to course syllabi, online class discussions, and research. UNC is among a handful of colleges nationwide to have such a requirement.

The long list of excellent professors at UNC means that many good courses are there for the taking. Professors to look for include: Judith B. Farquhar in anthropology; Jean S. DeSaix, William M. Kier, and Patricia J. Pukkila in biology; James Jorgenson in chemistry; Kenneth J. Reckford, Sara Mack, and George W. Houston in classics; Doris W. Betts and Michael McFee in creative writing; Barbara Day in education; Michael K. Salemi in economics; Richard D. Rust, George S. Lensing Jr., Trudier Harris, Christopher M. Armitage, Weldon E. Thornton, Thomas A. Stumpf, Joy Kasson, A. Reid Barbour, Robert G. Kirkpatrick, James Seay, and Theodore H. Leinbaugh in English; Risa Palm in geography (and dean of the College of Arts and Sciences); Roger W. Lotchin, Jacquelyn D. Hall, Jay M. Smith, Judith M. Bennett, E. Willis Brooks, William L. Barney, W. Miles Fletcher, Peter A. Coclanis, and John F. Kasson in history; Robert Lauterborn in journalism; Sue Ellen Goodman in mathematics; Michael Zenge, James Ketch, and Thomas A. Warburton in music; Richard A. Smyth (professor emeritus) in philosophy; Laurie E. McNeil and Lawrence G. Rowan in physics and astronomy; Jeffrey Obler, Steven Leonard, Joel Schwartz, Jurg Steiner, and Michael Lienesch in political science; Richard King (professor emeritus) in psychology; Ruel W. Tyson Jr., David L. Halperin, and Peter I. Kaufman in religious studies; and John Shelton Reed in sociology.

UNC has an equally impressive list of highly regarded departments, including English, biology, history, chemistry, journalism, economics, political science, business, classics, religious studies, French, German, and philosophy. Each department has good and bad — the best advice, here as everywhere, is to choose courses wisely.

The English department is noted for its attention to teaching, its traditional curriculum, and its freshman composition program. The classics department and the program in journalism and mass communication also are among the best in the nation. The art history department's strength is teaching, but it is also boosted by the university's impressive art collection.

UNC has a highly regarded honors program, popular with many of the students winning full academic scholarships to the university. Students praise it for its rigor in liberal arts, and prospective students can apply before they matriculate or try to transfer into the program after arriving on campus. The program offers about 120 honors courses a year in about thirty areas of study. The courses stress writing and student participation. Honors students spend their senior year working on sixty-to-eighty-page papers that must be defended before a faculty panel.

Despite all its solid programs, UNC has its share of politicized and lightweight alternatives. "A big university is like a city," one professor says. "You have all sorts of upper class as well as slum areas." Students and faculty report that most professors have a liberal outlook but are honest about it and truly appreciate differing points of view. A student paper recently looked up the political party affiliations of professors in the humanities and social sciences and found that about 80 percent of those registered were Democrats.

Many consider the communications studies department the most politicized at UNC. It regularly offers Marxist slants on subject matter, students and professors say, and favorite topics are exploitation of the masses by large corporations and media conglomerates. It's a popular major, but one professor says the classes are "trendy and showy."

A relic from the 1960s, Peace, War, and Defense is a major at UNC. Students report that many of its classes are left-leaning, but there are so few majors in this field that nobody takes it seriously.

UNC's department of women's studies, like similar programs at other schools, has its roots in politics. It offers a major and a minor. Its courses are regarded as simple — provided that students regurgitate the party line that women are unjustly treated in society. Many courses that count toward the major are cross-listed in other departments. The more bizarre examples of courses (and these titles sound relatively tame compared to those found elsewhere) include "Gender and Imperialism," "Women's Spirituality across Cultures," and "Practicum in Women's Studies," the latter being a supervised internship where students can earn credit working for, say, Planned Parenthood or other abortion-rights groups.

Beyond the realm of the political are the lightweight courses. There are several courses in Leisure Studies, in which students spend semesters examining the role of recreation in society. And a recent course to gain notoriety is "The History of Rock Music," in which more than two hundred students file into an auditorium to listen to the Beach Boys and Elvis Presley tunes. One student told the local paper that she signed up for the class because she thought it would be "something a little more fun to balance out English and foreign language requirements."

Freshmen and sophomores can expect to attend large courses, as well as smaller ones taught by graduate students. Class lists of more than two hundred students are common in survey classes. Such classes are usually taught by a professor two or three times a week, with a small section of the class meeting once a week to answer students' questions and go further in-depth. As students begin taking higher-level classes, the class sizes shrink and students have a better opportunity to get to know professors. UNC also offers a wide variety of freshman seminars designed to expose freshmen to the small-class experience.

One longtime faculty member says teaching has declined at UNC over the last two or three decades because of the emphasis on faculty research. Research is now the primary criterion for tenure decisions, the professor says. "You have to be terribly inept to be turned down for bad teaching."

The university has taken steps recently to reverse the slide in teaching. A Center for Teaching and Learning is there to help to professors and teaching assistants. Alumni and several departments sponsor teaching awards that include money, and the university has started some short-term chairs that are filled solely on the basis of teaching excellence.

Many on campus hope the administration will soon give the same attention to the university's academic advising system.

"Students here don't put a lot of faith in their advisors," one student says. "Most students I talk to have complaints about their advisors." A professor says UNC students have a great will to succeed, and since their assigned advisors aren't helping, they seek advice from older students and spend time making connections that could help them once they graduate. "A bright kid can get good training with good people," the professor says. "But the average people tend to get lost in the crowd." Honors students and athletes get the best assistance, another professor says.

Students don't always make the most of their opportunities for advising. "Students will tell you their advisers only give them 10 minutes and rubber-stamp stuff," a professor says. "Advisors will tell you they hold office hours regularly, and nobody comes to see them until panic pre-registration. Both reports are correct."

Political Atmosphere: Carolina on My Mind

Although UNC's professors and administration tend to be far more liberal than the residents of the state of North Carolina, a generally traditional student body — and traditional state — keep things from getting too out of hand. Administrators are, after all, ultimately responsible to the North Carolina General Assembly, and anything making too many waves could catch the eye of legislators. UNC is nowhere near as politically correct as neighboring Duke University and is less politicized than today's average large state research institution. One student reports that the most visible multicultural events are along the lines of "awareness" weeks or months for gays and lesbians, Asian-Americans, women's history, and African-American history. It is true that the university has welcomed many aspects of the modern multiculturalist and diversity agendas. For example, a North Carolina newspaper has documented, using publicly available admissions information, the use of racial preferences in undergraduate admissions.

There have been some controversies in which administrators have bucked tradition in favor of cutting-edge academic trends. But they're certainly not blazing new trails in propagandizing.

Some students say the university's obsession with race and diversity issues promotes ethnic separation, a complaint echoed at other universities. It's not uncommon to walk into a cafeteria and see one table of black students, another table of white students. (Other ethnic groups such as Hispanics and Asians are relatively few in number at UNC.)

Many of the organized ethnic and gender groups have taken it upon themselves to attack much of the traditional status quo, with varying degrees of success.

498

The most successful, clearly, has been the drive to form a Black Cultural Center — a move that started about a decade ago, when administrators succumbed to student protests, over objections of many who thought such a center emphasized racial division over racial unity. But now, that controversy is settled, and in 1999, BCC backers finished raising the $9 million needed from private sources. Construction is scheduled to begin in January of 2001.

Then there are the occasional attacks on UNC's history. In 1913, to honor Civil War veterans, university alumni erected a monument of a Confederate soldier on the northern boundary of campus. The director of the Black Cultural Center, followed by several students, called for the removal of the statue, likening the situation to statues of Lenin in post-Communist Russia or the Confederate battle flag atop the South Carolina statehouse. The university replied that it had "no consideration now" of removing the monument. Nor does UNC plan — for now, anyway — to rename any of its buildings named for people who once owned slaves. Activists sometimes grumble about that one.

But, breaking with tradition, the university in 1999 did allow women to begin living in the oldest building on campus, Old East. The building had been men only.

One of the latest activist causes has been the "anti-sweatshop" crusade to ensure that UNC paraphernalia is produced in overseas factories where workers earn a "living wage." In 1999, about twenty activists staged a four-day "takeover" of the administration building to protest abuses. The sit-in was hardly confrontational: students brought sleeping bags and crammed for finals on laptop computers. University officials brought them bagels and praised their dedication. Administrators finally buckled to the pressure and agreed to monitor where and how clothing and other items are made. UNC's provost told the protesters: "I like the guts, I like the class, I like the compassion."

Although administrators rarely stand up to left-wing protesters and activists, students on the campus stress that in most protests, it's the same small group of activists that come up with these issues. "Most people don't care," says one junior. "They're off playing basketball or working out or they're in the orchestra. Everyone has something that they do, and politics is just one thing you can pick from."

A small group of dedicated conservative students at UNC has worked with national organizations to bring big-name speakers to campus and provide a political balance. Recent speakers include Al Sharpton, Bill Buckley, Armstrong Williams, Star Parker, Antonin Scalia, and Ward Connerly.

UNC has no formal speech code. One professor says: "There is a lot said here about sensitivity, but it has not gone so far as a formalized speech code or sensitivity training for freshmen of the sort I read about elsewhere."

Faculty and administration do exert some control over politics in the classroom through hiring practices and tenure evaluations. "You couldn't get a job here, even if you're great in your field, if you're not politically correct," a professor says. Another professor says some departments will not accept traditional scholars, but if one should be hired, factors other than politics (i.e., research and teaching) are more important when it comes to keeping one's job. Another professor has found the situation in Chapel Hill to be a bit better than that: "In the range of my experience, at UNC a candidate's personal political position is not taken into account in hiring or tenure. It is possible for a scholar favoring a more traditionalist approach to make the short list."

In April of 2000, UNC Chapel Hill named a new chancellor, a music professor who had been the head of the University of Nebraska. Upon his selection, he said he had the goal of making UNC into the best public university in the country, though he also expressed strong interest in expanding the "quantity and quality" of diversity at UNC. He did not elaborate, and at this writing it remains to be seen how he will change the campus.

Student Life: The Sky Is Carolina Blue

Chapel Hill is one of America's most idyllic college towns. The town's downtown has an old, small-town feel, while sprawling apartment complexes and malls lie off in the distance, reached easily by bus. The town's main drag, Franklin Street, looks historic and is almost always bustling with activity, with students and residents frequenting the seemingly endless strip of bars, restaurants, upscale shops, bookstores, cafes, and the like.

Chapel Hill is just about the intellectual and geographic center of North Carolina. Its proximity to Durham (home of Duke University) and to Raleigh (home of North Carolina State University) makes the area attractive to high-tech companies, visiting lecturers, and all sorts of other cooperative academic ventures. The town's proximity to both the mountains (four hours) and to the coast (three and a half) make it attractive to potential students.

The historic and prettiest part of campus borders Franklin Street and contains some of the university's most recognizable spots. Gardens and sprawling lawns make the university's campus an ideal place to stroll or sit and read.

The main part of campus also includes several administrative buildings, classrooms, libraries, the student union, student bookstore, and "the pit" — a concrete quad that's always the site of demonstrations, petition drives, and other student activities.

As underclassmen, many students live in high-rise dormitories ten to fifteen minutes away from the main campus. Though the university guarantees housing for four years and encourages students to live on campus, most juniors and seniors move off campus, a trend found at virtually every state university. Each of the twenty-nine on-campus residence halls is wired for Internet access and cable television. Living arrangements include single-sex halls, single-sex floors, and coed floors.

As mandated by statute, 82 percent of UNC students are from North Carolina, with the rest from out of state. The groups tend to mix and get along just fine.

The few crimes that do occur on campus are generally car break-ins and thefts from unlocked dorm rooms. Serious crimes are rare and receive heavy attention in the media. As at other campuses, women are advised not to walk alone at night. Some areas on the fringes of campus are poorly lit, though the university is working to improve lighting. Chapel Hill is generally a safe town with few undesirable areas. The main drag has a few beggars.

There are several churches within walking distance of campus.

There are hundreds of student organizations on campus — everything from ethnic identity groups to religious clubs to all forms of campus media. Most UNC students aren't bookworms, but rather tend to be active and well-rounded. "Everyone I know is pretty much involved in one activity and is waist deep in it," said one senior.

For all the talk about diversity at UNC, many women undergraduates say it could use a little more diversity between the sexes. Women undergraduates outnumber men nearly 2-to-1, causing interesting effects on the campus dating scene. Many women say there aren't enough men to go around. The men say too many women are discouraged by the on-campus prospects and that too many look off campus when the man of their dreams might be right under their nose.

About 18 percent of the student body joins Greek organizations. UNC has twenty-eight fraternities and nineteen sororities, but because UNC is so large and Chapel Hill is so vibrant, Greeks don't play an overwhelming role in the campus's social life, as is the case elsewhere. But fraternity parties are still popular, particularly among freshmen and sophomores.

The *Daily Tar Heel* is Carolina's award-winning student-run daily paper. It's a highly read source of campus news, though some students complain that its reporters-in-training focus too much uncritical attention on identity politics, multiculturalism, and related subjects. The *Carolina Review,* a monthly conservative journal, dissects campus news and often provides a refreshing take on campus orthodoxy.

UNC fields twenty-eight varsity teams in the most common women's and men's intercollegiate sports. Although the women's soccer team has won fifteen national championships in seventeen years, UNC Chapel Hill is most famous for its men's basketball team — a perennial contender for the national championship made great by the recently retired Coach Dean Smith. Unlike other big-time sports programs, UNC has a reputation as a squeaky-clean, above-board operation. When UNC is playing a big game against rival Duke or in the Final Four, the whole town comes to a halt and everyone finds a spot in front of a television. Tickets to home basketball games are free but can be hard to come by. Even after graduation, UNC basketball remains a special bond among alumni (who can be found in sizable numbers in nearly every major city on the East Coast). Football is less popular, and less successful.

There are also plenty of intramural sports: sixty in all, including baseball, bowling, crew, golf, rock climbing, and tae kwon do. The Student Recreation Center is a large state-of-the-art gym in the center of campus, and very popular with students.

Northwestern University

Office of Undergraduate Admissions
1801 Hinman Avenue
P.O. Box 3060
Evanston, IL 60204-3060
www.nwu.edu

Total enrollment: 17,500
Undergraduates: 7,698
SAT ranges (Verbal/Math): 640-730 (V); 660-740 (M)
Applicants: 15,460
Accepted: 32%
Enrolled: 39%
Application deadline: January 1
Financial aid application deadline: February 1
Tuition: $24,648/$31,968
Core curriculum: No

Unfamiliar Territory

Northwestern University will celebrate its 150th anniversary in 2001. Established in 1851 to serve the people of what was then called the Northwest Territory, Northwestern has swelled over the years from its initial group of ten male students and two faculty members to its current size of 13,700 full-time students on its lakefront campuses in Evanston and Chicago.

Still considered politically moderate, if not conservative, by many observers, Northwestern has swung to the left in recent years as campus activism, ideologically motivated courses, and liberal programs and speakers have shown significant increases. Undergraduates at Northwestern are still more conservative than at similar institutions, but they are often overshadowed — or worse, indoctrinated — by an increasingly radical professoriate and graduate student population. In addition to its lingering reputation for political moderation, the university still enjoys a reputation for academic excellence; many think of it as one of the "non-Ivy Ivies." But this too is an area in which leftover suppositions do not reflect the current state of the university. Some insiders say the university's proclamations of teaching excellence have become more rhetoric than reality, and that Northwestern's interest in major research grants outpaces its will to maintain solid liberal arts programming for undergraduates.

Northwestern is desperately attempting to retain its status both as a rigorous undergraduate college and a cutting-edge research institution. In its mission statement the university proclaims "its unique potential for combining the best features of world-class research institutions with the advantages of smaller, teaching-oriented schools." But this, now, is fast on the way to becoming only a statement. The verdict is still out on how much longer Northwestern will be able to preserve what remains of this balance.

Academic Life: Days of Weinberg and Roses

Approximately 7,700 undergraduates are enrolled in Northwestern's six undergraduate schools: the College of Arts and Sciences, the School of Education and Social Policy, the McCormick School of Engineering and Applied Science, the Medill School of Journalism, the School of Music, and the School of Speech.

The Weinberg College of Arts and Sciences, the main liberal arts school, has numerous specialized multicultural programs, including separate departments in African-American studies, African and Asian studies, and African studies. In a spirit of true diversity, the university also offers a major in European thought and culture, and has an American studies program as well.

There is no core curriculum either across all colleges or within a given college. Even the distribution requirements that stand in for a core vary from school to school, and each major of course has its own requirements as well. At the College of Arts and Sciences, students must demonstrate proficiency in a foreign language and in basic writing. They are also required to take two quarter-long courses in six different areas: natural sciences; formal studies; social and behavioral sciences; historical studies; values; and literature and the fine arts. The college does offer Western civilization courses that can count toward requirements in the last three areas, but attaches special stipulations to these courses which seem designed to ensure that students will receive only a limited number of distribution credits for such courses.

All freshmen take two freshman seminars designed to give students the experience of small class sizes, intimate discussion, and close contact with good professors. The topics of these seminars, however, range widely from academically challenging to very lightweight, and most are so specialized that they would be more appropriate for graduate seminars than for introductory college courses. Indeed, according to a former graduate student, many of them are taught by graduate students who select topics related to their doctoral dissertations. "Children and Television," sponsored by the psychology department, explores the "relation between modern media and children's cognitive and social development"; "Tolstoy and the Bible," offered through the Slavic languages and literature department, analyzes *War and Peace* as well as the books of Genesis, Samuel, and Matthew; while "Language, Race, and Gender," from the women's studies department, examines "the structure and function of sexist and racist language." In many of these seminars, class participation counts for nearly a third of the final grade, taking much of the burden off of the instructor.

While the small classes are a nice idea, the freshman seminars, like the distribution requirements, are no substitute for a real liberal arts education. The descriptions of some of the seminars read like parodies — and would be hilarious spoofs, at that, but for the fact that parents and students have given the university significant money thinking that the students would obtain a genuine education. For instance, one might suspect from the title that in "Crossing Classes: The Role of Romantic Comedy," students might read Shakespeare, Austen, or related works. The description, however, reveals otherwise:

> Course Description: Societies are divided into a variety of social classes, arrayed in a hierarchy from least to most desirable. Romantic love implies a personal choice, which can be viewed as a threat to the maintenance of class boundaries. A variety of strategies are employed to increase the likelihood that people will date and marry people "just like us." One essence of romantic comedy films in the U.S. has been that "love conquers all," including obstacles to pursuing love across existing social boundaries (economic, ethnic, racial, or otherwise).

> Teaching Method: The course will consist of a series of films, which we will view together, and then discuss in the following class period (the class time is set at two hours primarily to permit the viewing the films [sic], a few of which might stretch into the lunch hour.

> Reading: There will be some readings on stratification in society, and some on the roots of commercial films in general, and romantic comedies in particular.

In this course, then, Northwestern freshmen receive credit for a semester spent viewing what most of them will undoubtedly term "chick flicks," with half of the class time spent watching movies and virtually no outside reading. Numerous other freshman seminars are equally appalling when it comes to instructor preparation ("this course will be based heavily on group discussion" is a common refrain in the descriptions) and intellectual rigor. A course on "Scandals and Reputations," for instance, includes writing assignments analyzing "the reputation of a friend or classmate" as well as — unsurprisingly — "the effects of the scandals of the Clinton administration on the construction of his reputation." While some of these issues certainly make for interesting discussion, they do virtually nothing to foster the "philosophic habit of mind" that Cardinal Newman considered the object of a true liberal education. There is thus an acute need for Northwestern students to select their freshmen seminars with great care, especially since there is often a connection between these seminars and academic advising in the early stages of one's under-graduate career. "Whoever you end up with for your seminar is your advisor for the first two years before you declare your major," says a student.

The seminars are likely the smallest classes students will see in their first couple of years. For most undergraduates, lecture courses are the exception rather than the rule at Northwestern. Introductory courses in popular majors can have between 120 and two hundred students. "A couple maxed out at 400 students," says an under-graduate of his introductory science courses. Teaching assistants play a significant role in these larger lecture courses. "TA's are the ones you approach" in large courses, says a student, who adds that he has been generally pleased with the quality of in-struction from the teaching assistants.

On the plus side, at least the university has not yet imposed a diversity course requirement. "Different student groups and departments like women's studies have been pushing for it," says one student, but so far the administration has not yet ca-pitulated.

In response to contemporary concerns, the College of Arts and Sciences offers a minor in "Science in Human Culture," the purpose of which is to "prepare students to confront the impact of science, medicine, and technology on society and on their own lives," according to the catalogue. Students select seven courses from a list of offerings and develop their own "theme" such as "technology and social change" or "science and gender." The courses in this program are cross-listed in other depart-ments, and include such solid topics as early European medicine and the "History of Western Science and Medicine," as well as more tangential courses like "Human Re-production," "Human Sexuality," and "The History of Abortion."

Good departments include history, English, and psychology, while physics is considered relatively weak. Library facilities are first-rate, and the McCormick Li-brary of Special Collections contains such gems as unpublished letters of T. S. Eliot.

The Medill School of Journalism has produced forty Pulitzer Prize winners and is easily one of the most acclaimed journalism programs in the country. Recent de-velopments within the School of Journalism include a $1.5-million Knight Founda-tion grant in order to hire a senior broadcast practitioner for an endowed chair — someone who, according to Dean Ken Bode, "will lead our efforts to maintain and expand news values and ethics in the powerful yet troubled medium of TV." The journalism school also recently hired NBC news veteran Joe Angotti as program chair.

Among the better professors at Northwestern are: Edward Muir and T. H. Breen in history; Joseph Epstein, Mary Kinzie, and Joshua Weiner in English; Richard Keickhefer in religious studies; Sarah E. Fraser, Sandra L. Hindman, Lyle Massey, David Mickenberg, and O. K. Werckmeister in art history; Kenneth Seeskin in philosophy; Robert Wallace, James Packer, Martin Mueller, John Wright, Ahuvia Kahane, and Reginald Allen in classics; Stefano Mula in Italian; Saul Morson and Andrew Wachtel in Slavic language and literature; and Stephen Presser, a law professor who has a joint appointment in history.

Political Atmosphere: Hate Strikes Close

According to students, there has been "increased activism" on Northwestern's campus recently. But perhaps the most explosive political situation on campus in the 1999-2000 academic year was really a non-issue that spiraled out of proportion. In October of 1999, racist literature from an organization called The World Church of the Creator was distributed on campus, purportedly at the behest of the group's leader, white supremacist Matthew Hale. Students were understandably outraged: in July of the previous summer, Benjamin Smith, one of Hale's followers, had shot and killed former Northwestern basketball coach Ricky Byrdsong as well as a Korean student. Smith, who later killed himself as police closed in, chose his victims at random based on race. (Byrdsong was an African-American man.) According to one student, campus police booted the literature distributor off campus. Hale then wrote a letter of complaint to the *Northwestern Daily*, claiming that five Northwestern students had approached him about granting his organization religious status on campus (only fifteen members are needed for campus recognition) and vowing to make a personal visit to campus.

At the end of the third quarter, Hale made his appearance on campus and was greeted by a "We Hate Hale" rally and virulent protests by the campus Marxist group and the NAACP. The incident brought bad press for Northwestern and a public relations victory for Hale, who ended up acquiring near-martyr status amongst his followers after having rocks thrown at him and being punched by a student activist.

Other hot-button political issues at Northwestern are similar to those inspiring activism on campuses nationwide. Topping the list are sweatshop protests and labor protests, such as those against Starbucks for underpaying their coffee pickers. "Some of the activists are pretty sincere; many of them are just along for the ride," an undergraduate says. "We had students running around nude in the Student Center" to protest sweatshop practices, says another.

Northwestern hosts numerous high-profile speakers, most of them of a decidedly liberal persuasion. Many of these speakers are sponsored by the journalism or law schools. Recent speakers included Tom Brokaw, actor Danny Glover, Illinois Gov. George Ryan, and George McGovern, who spoke on the "war against hunger."

Other well-publicized events included a lecture on "Feminism and the New Millennium" by *The Nation* columnist Katha Pollitt, who served as the Kreeger Wolf Distinguished Visiting Professor at Northwestern, and a talk on "The New Millennium and the Partnership of Men and Women" by UN Ambassador Linda Tarr-Whelan, who serves as chairwoman of Northwestern's Center for Policy Alternatives.

The campus also hosts a number of debates and symposia on contemporary issues. During the most recent academic year, the campus sponsored a "teach-in" on wrongful death convictions featuring Jesse Jackson and wrongfully convicted Rubin "Hurricane" Carter. The teach-in was one of the first public events sponsored by the recently created Center on Wrongful Convictions, a joint effort of the law school and the journalism school. The center was formed to identify and rectify "wrongful death convictions and other serious miscarriages of justice in criminal cases." One of the faculty members of the center is journalism professor David Protess, whose research along with that of his students into the cases of several wrongly convicted death row inmates was instrumental in persuading Gov. Ryan to declare a moratorium on the death penalty. The university also presented a debate on legal animal rights co-sponsored by the Animal Defense Fund and the Federalist Society. The debate featured Steven M. Wise, a well-known animal rights professor at Harvard Law School, as well as University of Chicago law professor Richard Epstein and U.S. Circuit Judge Richard Posner. In addition to these events, the university also sponsored a symposium on "Compensating for History: Restitution and Retribution for World War II Crimes."

Student money was also used to bring controversial rapper Ice-T to campus by the student group Colors as part of its "racial sensitivity" initiative. Charlton Heston also spoke at Northwestern; "He was the best-attended speaker the entire year," boasts one conservative student. Two students protested during his talk, but Heston received a standing ovation.

The Alice Berline Kaplan Center for the Humanities has as its expressed purpose to "foster development of a broad, highly innovative humanities culture at Northwestern," though the lineup of speaking events sponsored by the center reveals the very loose application of the word "culture." Recent lectures include "Protesting through Acquiescence: Young Senegalese Women's Discourse on Sexuality and Marriageability"; "No Place Like Home: Relationships and Family Life Among Lesbians and Gay Men"; "Sleeping with Mr. Collins: The Eighteenth-Century Invention of Sexual Disgust"; and "We are the World, But Who Are We? Globalization and the Politics of Representation."

The university has a multicultural center (in case the Center for the Humanities misses something, we suppose), but students complain that the center has not effectively fostered multicultural awareness on campus. "We're not feeling like this center is our place," a Hispanic student told the *Daily*. "Then, do we even have a place in the university?" The center recently had to cancel a campus barbecue because of a lack of funds.

But the university as a whole has not had trouble raising money. Indeed, Northwestern's fund-raising efforts have been so successful that the university recently increased its goal for Campaign Northwestern from $1 billion to $1.4 billion after 90 percent of the original goal was committed only halfway into the planned five-year effort. Another question may be where this money is going. According to one faculty member, one of the biggest obstacles to traditional education at Northwestern is what this professor calls a "reserved soap-box policy," in which certain faculty appointments are earmarked for left-wing scholars in order to further the radical hegemony on campus.

Given the strength of the journalism program, one can at least be confident that events on campus will be well-covered by the student press. The main student newspaper, the *Northwestern Daily*, has had competition in the form of the more conservative *Northwestern Chronicle* since 1991. According to a student involved with the *Chronicle*, "We cover things the *Daily* doesn't — more politics, more in-depth coverage, a larger entertainment section." The paper has been fighting an uphill battle against campus antipathy, financial mismanagement, and faulty student government procedures. "We didn't get any respect when we first started," says one student editor. The paper does not enjoy any faculty support, and was formally "derecognized" as a student group a couple of years ago. According to a student, normal procedures were not followed when the student government took this action, and the paper has since been reinstated as a student group. But the paper receives no campus funding, and advertising funds have been scarce recently as the *Daily* allegedly has undertaken a covert campaign to lure away the *Chronicle's* advertisers. All things considered, the paper has it better than similar ventures on other college campuses. "We receive no hate mail; no one is threatening to assault us," says a student.

Student Life: Sweet Home, Evanston

Located on the shores of Lake Michigan in Evanston, Illinois, Northwestern is only twelve miles from downtown Chicago. Everything one hears about Chicago's harsh climate is confirmed by Northwestern students, who complain about severe winters and strong winds on campus. They also complain — oddly, given Chicago's proximity — about the lack of readily accessible social and cultural opportunities. "Evanston is kind of boring," says one student, and even though Chicago is within striking distance, many students "are pretty land-locked" and do not make frequent trips into the city. "When I got here I thought I'd be there [Chicago] all the time," says a student, "but I'm not." "Northwestern's social scene isn't that active," says another.

We're not sure what they're complaining about, as there does seem to be a considerable number of options on campus and off. On campus, there is the Ditmar Gallery, which recently hosted a Holocaust exhibit, and the School of Music, which frequently hosts jazz musicians from Chicago and also features a popular senior recital. In addition, there is a very active thespian community on campus. The range of activities in Chicago is so vast and well-known that we won't even bother to list them here.

Perhaps because of the perceived threat of social isolation, fraternities and sororities are popular options. Almost half the campus is a member of a Greek organization, and students says that the relationship between the Greek system and the administration is a fairly harmonious one. One fraternity, Psi Upsilon, was shut down last year and the building it inhabited was condemned, but this incident was described by a student as "an aberration."

Other students recommend applying to live in one of Northwestern's residential colleges. Eleven of the college's twenty-nine residence halls are dedicated to such themes as the arts, public affairs, or international studies. "The colleges are organized around interests," says a student, who is extremely pleased with his selection of a building housing all film or communications majors. "It's like my home — there's lots of camaraderie." Overnight guests and alcohol — for those over 21 — are allowed in all halls. Single-sex living is available for both men and women; in coed dorms, men and women are separated by floor or wing so that each sex has its own bathroom.

The university has been relatively successful in reducing campus crime in the last couple of years. The Evanston campus saw a 21 percent decrease in overall crime between 1998 and 1999, a drop that university police attribute largely to stricter alcohol policies. "I think the university has really put the kibosh on the students," a campus police sergeant told the *Daily*. "The university police are very efficient," a student says. However, while crime as a whole as declined of late, burglaries in student dormitories were up 47 percent between 1998 and 1999.

The Northwestern Wildcats are members of the Big Ten Conference. Varsity sports at Northwestern include men's and women's basketball, golf, soccer, tennis, and swimming, men's baseball, football, and wrestling, and women's fencing, field hockey, softball, and volleyball. The football team boasts seven "Big Ten" championships and one Rose Bowl Championship; the team's recent performance has been inconsistent at best, though, and it must be said that in the major men's sports of football and basketball, the university has spent much of its recent history as the conference doormat.

Apart from losing basketball games, campus traditions include the "Primal Scream," an end-of-the-term vocal emission of tension in the plaza outside the campus library, and Armadillo Day, a day of festivities such as face painting, musical performances, and the occasional appearance of a live armadillo.

Northwestern has an aggressive building expansion agenda underway, including a new $70-million high-tech medical research facility in Chicago, supported by the state of Illinois and a $40 million grant from university trustee Ann Lurie, as well a proposed life science research pavilion on the Evanston campus. The Norris University Center, which houses student group offices and other services, gets high marks from students. "There's a good diner there," a student says.

When asked why he selected Northwestern, one student responded that three factors — location, reputation, and financial aid — influenced his decision. The school was close to home and close to Chicago, and financial aid and work-study programs were readily available. However, it's the middle factor that university supporters should worry about. The university's reputation as a politically neutral environment and as a solid undergraduate teaching institution appear to be overrated. There are, however, enough pockets of academic excellence and political sanity for students to navigate their way through Northwestern's undergraduate program.

University of Notre Dame

Office of Admissions
Notre Dame, IN 46556
(219) 631-7505
www.nd.edu

Total enrollment: 10,200
Undergraduates: 8,014
SAT ranges (Verbal/Math): 620-710 (V); 640-720 (M)
Applicants: 10,052
Accepted: 34%
Enrolled: 57%
Application deadline: January 9
Financial aid application deadline: February 15
Tuition: $27,950/$33,700
Core curriculum: Yes

Beneath the Dome

The University of Notre Dame has long been the most visible and prominent Roman Catholic university in the United States. Well known for its football program, in which athletes capable of reading and commenting on complex texts nevertheless take on and usually defeat the best teams in the country, the university has also made possible an excellent education to the broad Catholic middle class whose children were often excluded, either by bigotry or financial lack, from the most elite universities. The WASPs had their Ivies, and the Catholics had Notre Dame. Although the university for years has had an excellent law school and many professional and graduate divisions, its primary strength throughout most of its existence has been the high caliber of its undergraduate curriculum.

In years past students could rest assured of both the authentic Catholic identity of the school and the personalized attention of the excellent teaching faculty. But this was before a meeting in 1967 of Catholic colleges and universities held at Notre Dame's retreat in Land O' Lakes, Wisconsin, during which it was decided that the Catholic identity of these schools was a liability in a secular age. As the Land O' Lakes statement puts it: "To perform its teaching and research functions effectively, the Catholic university must have a true autonomy and academic freedom in the face of authority of whatever kind, lay or clerical, external to the academic community itself." This is a rather Protestant reading of the Catholic tradition in higher education, and its consequences are everywhere visible at Notre Dame today. Its president has publicly criticized *Ex corde ecclesiae*, the Vatican's statement on the centrality of the Catholic faith to Catholic institutions.

Today, many at Notre Dame want the school to be move toward the research university — something that would presumably come at a cost to its unique, historic identity as a purveyor of the liberal arts. In the past, Notre Dame has been identified not with acceptance of worldly trends but with a willingness to change the world. There is evidence that some scholars and administrators at Notre Dame believe the secularization of the university has gone too far, and that its Catholic identity needs to be protected and cultivated. While the outcome of this identity crisis remains uncertain, it is still possible to carve out a challenging — and Catholic — liberal arts education under the shadow of the Golden Dome.

Academic Life: South Bent

Freshmen at Notre Dame must enroll in a year-long program called College of First Year of Studies before they choose a major and academically go their separate ways. The college, which has its own faculty and dean, is one of only four of its kind in the United States. A total of ten courses are required, five per semester. They include a freshman seminar, as well as grammar and composition — classes one student calls "pretty remedial. You have TAs [teaching assistants] who are not first-rate." Students must also complete distribution requirements that include two courses each in theology and philosophy.

Overall, the first year at Notre Dame is not as strong as it could be. A faculty member says: "The core course reflects faculty compromises and is not exclusively devoted to the reading of great books. Now even *this* core course is under attack."

Another professor notes: "It's possible to do a pretty good job in general by picking and choosing your courses, but the offerings are quite uneven." Certainly, it is possible to find some very good professors. Says one of them: "A qualification [to criticism of the university] is that Notre Dame still hires a core of substantial scholars. Because of its tradition and the high quality of the applicant pool in all areas you can find solid people."

Following their freshman year, students enroll in one of four colleges (Arts and Letters, Business Administration, Engineering, and Science), according to their majors. The College of Arts and Letters is the oldest and largest on campus. One excellent choice there is the Program of Liberal Studies, known around campus as the "Great Books" major, which features seminars conducted in the Socratic dialogue method. Tutorial courses augment these seminars, and students read closely and write extensively about the books covered. This program offers what at one time not so far past was the standard liberal arts education at most of the country's colleges — an education that has for the most part been replaced by a smorgasbord from which students select the things they like. By choosing the Great Books program, however, students ensure that they will be educated for life rather than merely trained for a particular job.

Outside of this program, a student takes his chances. Though the degree of politicization in the curriculum is less at Notre Dame than at the major research universities, it is significantly more than one might expect from what is arguably this nation's flagship Catholic university. As one professor says, "Like any mantra, multiculturalist education is not an experience but an experiment. And like any experiment, the money is deposited where you have the most need to keep up certain appearances." This teacher continues: "Diversity makes people very prickly. It entails performance anxiety. We take our pulse too often. We ask ourselves every day, 'How diverse are we today?'"

The most politicized department is arguably theology. As one professor says, theology at Notre Dame "is awful. The president always rushes to their aid and says things that are completely incompatible with the teachings of the Holy Father." This faculty member notes that *Ex corde ecclesiae* is meant as a governing guideline for Catholic universities and colleges and calls on them to remember whence they came and by whose authority (namely, the Holy See's) they call themselves Catholic. And yet, says this faculty member, "They really don't know what that means any more. Their ecclesiology is so fragmented they don't get it. And once their ecclesiology fell apart, the theology department was transformed." A longtime professor notes that the department's problems are "probably not too well known among the alumni. A lot of people in their fifties and sixties probably don't know what's going on. They see a good life in the dorms and think it's OK."

Some professors say that orthodox Catholics are much less likely to be hired by the theology department — or given leadership positions if they do manage to get on campus — than are their lukewarm brethren. A student remembers that a professor in one theology course lectured on ancient creation myths and questioned the veracity of the Old Testament. This student defended the Bible, although "the professor's position was that she was innocent until proven guilty, and the burden of proof was on anyone who defended the Bible."

Also politicized is the English department. Religion is not generally broached in the hiring of English faculty, but, as one professor notes, "They'll ask [prospective hires] about T. S. Eliot and get them to play their cards."

Aside from theology, however, the most overtly politicized unit is the Gender Studies Program. Offered through the Gender Studies Program is an introductory class in which are examined, among other things, the "history and theory of sexuality and queer theory." The program also offers courses with only a minimal connection to undergraduate higher education, like GSC 462, "Sex and Gender in Cinema"; GSC 448, "Anthropology of Reproduction"; GSC 428, "Race, Gender, and Women of Color"; and GSC 418, "Witchcraft and the Occult." The program also hosted an event called "Dante's Queer Nature." It may or may not be worth noting, however, that while the program's Web page used to contain links to pornographic Internet sites, those links have been removed.

The push for professional education may pose the biggest danger to Notre Dame. "The careerist drive is the greatest threat," says a longtime professor. "The drive for excellence is the engine of secularization. We hire faculty who we see as qualified not because they add to the Catholicity of the school but because they help in our quest for greatness."

Of course, Notre Dame still boasts many outstanding professors, including John Matthias, James Dougherty, and Thomas Werge in English; Ralph McInerny and Alvin Plantinga in philosophy; Marvin O'Connell, George Marsden, James Turner, and Jay Dolan in history; Charles Rice, John Finnis, and Gerald Bradley in the Law School; and Walter Nicgorski in government. Besides the Program of Liberal Studies (whose professors include Frederick J. Crosson, Walter Nicgorski, and Mary Katherine Tillman), Notre Dame is home to excellent departments of philosophy, history, and government. However, many undergrads will find themselves being taught by teaching assistants. "Most of my colleagues wouldn't be here without their graduate students," says one professor. "Those students are necessary for the operation of the university — they're the heart of the place, because they do so much teaching."

Political Atmosphere: Only as Catholic as the Rest of the Country

In considering the various problems troubling Notre Dame at the moment, one professor says the greatest concern for many traditionalist faculty members is the moral values promoted on campus. "There is almost no discussion open or private of values here," the professor says. "The idea is 'don't bring up values or we won't get along,' and therefore we can't discuss it." Notes a student: "The defining ethic is that we all need to do a lot of social service and be nice to everyone."

A significant change in the faculty has occurred in the years since the Land O' Lakes conference removed Notre Dame from the direct control of the order of Holy Cross priests who founded and, theoretically at least, still run the school. Every year since, the percentage of faculty who are Catholic has declined; today it is about 65 percent. However, only 29 percent of new faculty hires over the last several years have been Catholic. The rate dips to 25 percent when the most Catholic division of the university, the Law School, is factored out. Says a professor: "Those who are hired say they're never asked about their religion, that it just never came up, that they could have been at an interview for a position at Berkeley. And when you consider that 26 percent of the U.S. is Catholic, that's not much effort on Notre Dame's part." Given Notre Dame's close identity with the Catholic Church and the image it markets to the public and alumni, the numbers are surprising.

A number of students who apply to Notre Dame and the parents who help them go are probably expecting something more Catholic than they get, those on campus say. Alumni aren't especially aware of what's going on at the school, either, professors say. "The alumni need to see that Notre Dame is a cultural treasure and not merely an institution," a professor says. "I haven't met a single parent all year because they don't come to talk to the teachers — they only hear about dollars from the administration. But no university can go on for long by just selling football tickets."

The university's president, the Rev. Edward A. Malloy, has been a frequent critic of *Ex corde Ecclesiae*. With the Rev. J. Donald Monan, chancellor of Boston College, he wrote in the Jesuit magazine *America* that the rules outlined in that encyclical were "profoundly detrimental to Catholic higher education." Other criticisms by this pair included the document's suggestion that theology professors "make a profession of faith and take an oath of fidelity." Also objectionable was the suggestion that Catholic institutions "condition a professor's appointment on integrity of doctrine and good character."

As the school moves closer and closer to the secular model of elite Eastern schools, an array of ideologies is rushing in to fill the void left by the retreat of the church's influence on campus life. "I would advise any young faculty member who comes here to keep quiet about any religious beliefs," a professor says. "Don't make your faith a matter of general knowledge, because it's much, much harder to be hired if you're an orthodox Catholic. There isn't much debate on this any more — it's been this way for twenty years."

In 1999 a gay, tenured professor of medieval studies resigned from Notre Dame because the university refused to include sexual orientation in its anti-discrimination policy. In 1998 a homosexual priest, who says he keeps his vow of celibacy, resigned his post as well. The Faculty Senate and a committee appointed by the vice-president for student affairs had both recommended amending the policy to include sexual orientation, but the Board of Fellows, consisting of lay people and priests who ensure the university's Catholic character, voted against a change. Malloy earlier had issued a statement called the "Spirit of Inclusion," which said that homosexuals were welcome on campus but did not attempt to extend the anti-discrimination policy.

Like at most universities, the students at Notre Dame are more conservative than their liberal faculty. In 1999 the student government presented the Board of Trustees with a report that argued that the university wasn't doing enough to ensure the institution's Catholic identity. Students wanted Notre Dame to highlight its "intense Catholic character" in admissions. The students also were worried by the decline in the percentage of Catholic professors. They also wanted the mandatory theology course include "a serious study of Catholic dogma and doctrine."

The school is at a crossroads, according to a senior professor. "Notre Dame is salvageable, but it could be lost [to the Catholic tradition]. It's possible that in a generation it could be like Georgetown." Says another professor: "Any politicization of the university is dangerous, because you create a vacuum and open the door for ideologies."

Student Life: Prayer Request

Student life at Notre Dame has much to commend it, because the student body is more conservative than the faculty. People can always be found at the Grotto, a replica of the shrine of Our Lady of Lourdes. Masses are held several times daily in the basilica, and most dorms have their own chapels with daily mass. As a former student says, "They're a well-scrubbed student body. Most are from professional families and most are headed for the professions. There's not a lot of counter-cultural stuff there."

There are no coed dorms, and a priest or a nun lives in every dorm. These rules, which would appear draconian on most college campuses, have long been a part of life at Notre Dame (at least since women were first admitted in 1972). Former president Fr. Theodore Hesburgh, who governed the university for some twenty years, is said to have remarked that Notre Dame would have coed dorms only over his dead body. While some students agitate for a general loosening of social policies at the school, others say that indicate that the enforcement of these regulations is not particularly tight anyway. Alcohol is officially prohibited in the dorms, for example, but lots of drinking occurs there, students say. It's also not that difficult to get around the visitation rules in the dorm if a student — as they are apt to be — is so inclined. Other rules are more closely followed: freshmen are not allowed to have cars on campus, and hazing is prohibited.

There is a pro-life movement on campus that is now active again. A few years ago the movement's leader pressured a reluctant administration into speaking up publicly in favor of life. As a former student says, "They just sort of went to the administration and said, 'Why aren't you more openly pro-life?'" That got them moving on the issue."

Other student groups include ROTC, several chorales (including a liturgical choir), Habitat for Humanity, an undergraduate investment club, and Humor Artists, a comedy troupe.

Campus crime is very low, according to statistics reported by the school. Reports of burglary, not very common in the first place, have been declining over the last three years; there were only twenty-seven such incidents in 1999 — a third as many as there were in 1997. The university reported only six forcible sexual assaults over the last three years, and only one aggravated assault.

Naturally, athletics (as well as a lot of social activities) at Notre Dame revolve around football, a tradition since 1887, and the school gets precious national exposure thanks to an exclusive contract with one network to carry all of their home games. But other sports have also been quite successful, including baseball and women's soccer. In all, there are thirteen men's teams and thirteen women's teams. But, unless a high school senior is a highly regarded football player in search of a spot in the NFL, other criteria will determine whether he should attend Notre Dame. Much of it has to do with the maturity of the student in question. "A reasonably well-informed 18-year-old who has access to one good professor and is told to select his classes with care will be OK," a professor says. "There are a lot of good groups with kids who get together and pray, read, or just hang."

Oberlin College

Office of Admissions
Dean of Admissions
Carnegie Building
Oberlin, OH 44074
(216) 775-8411
www.oberlin.edu

Total enrollment: 2,928
Undergraduates: 2,905
SAT ranges (Verbal/Math): 630-730 (V); 590-700 (M)
Applicants: 4,855
Accepted: 50%

Enrolled: 30%
Application deadline: January 2
Financial aid application deadline: February 15
Tuition: $25,355/$31,719
Core curriculum: No

Missionary Zeal

Oberlin College was founded in 1833 by two missionaries to train teachers and missionaries for excursions into the still-wild West. Just four years later, Oberlin became the first college in the country to admit women, and one of the first to admit African-Americans.

Though the school is now entirely secular, the zeal of the early mission workers lives on — albeit in ways they probably didn't intend. Political correctness is the religion today, and at Oberlin it's not so much debated as instilled. In fact, the widespread acceptance of modern ideologies makes the place rather calm in its overall political activity, although students and faculty with traditional beliefs certainly feel otherwise.

The academic program can be rigorous, despite a recent curriculum revision. "It makes you a great contestant on 'Jeopardy,'" a recent graduate says. Carefully selecting the best of Oberlin's classes makes all the difference, regardless of the radical ideas that preoccupy much of the campus. Certainly, politics is a major force on campus, but a force mostly unopposed causes few ripples.

Academic Life: The Open Field

Oberlin College abolished its core curriculum in the early 1970s, a time when such steps were not uncommon among highly rated schools. Until the early 1980s there were no required courses: students merely had to choose a major and collect a certain number of credit hours in any manner they wished. But in the 1986-87 school year Oberlin began to restore "bits and pieces of requirements," according to one professor.

Today there is next to no support on campus for a return to a traditional core curriculum. Distribution requirements are general, mandating 112 hours of credit for graduation, with at least nine credits in each of the college's three divisions: Arts and Humanities, Social and Behavorial Sciences, and Natural Sciences and Mathematics. The selected courses must represent at least two departments within each division. "Beyond this minimal expectation the college encourages its students to explore the growing scope and substance of human knowledge by taking additional courses outside the area of their primary interests," the catalogue states.

Oberlin does have a two-course writing requirement and a "quantitative proficiency" requirement, both of which may be satisfied with high scores on standardized tests or by designated courses. The writing courses must come from two different departments, and choices include "Traditional African Cosmology" in the department of African-American studies and "Sexually Transmitted Diseases" in the biology department, among others. Quantitative proficiency requirements are similarly interdisciplinary — courses in American history and politics (including the fringes thereof; for example, "American Sexualities") will suffice, along with other more substantive options, like an art course entitled "The Technology of Greek and Roman Architecture."

Formerly a nine-credit "cultural requirement," the catalogue now states that "the undergraduate course of study should include non-Western, minority, and women's studies as well as European and American studies." The requirement was ostensibly designed to expose "students to several minority cultures," in the words of a humanities professor, but because of lobbying by foreign language departments, the study of a language other than English satisfied this requirement. Because of the latitude permitted in fulfilling the expectation of cultural diversity, it is "neither onerous for students or really clear in what it's accomplishing," says the humanities professor.

All students must take at least three Winter Term classes while at Oberlin. This four-week January session is designed to "afford students an opportunity to devise and pursue programs of independent study or research," the catalogue states; independent study, it says, is intended to "encourage and enable students to discover the value of self-education." During Winter Term, students can select a course offered by the college or create their own. The possibilities can be worthwhile, and usually are as taxing as the student wishes to make them. One student analyzed her extensive childhood diaries and wrote an analytical paper on what she had learned. The same student, during another Winter Term, obtained half of her credit for working at the local historical society and the other half for putting together a schedule of physical exercise, which previously had not been a priority for her. Professors have some guidance over independent studies, but there has been controversy on campus over the latitude permitted by some professors in interpreting the requirements.

While many colleges allow some form of independent study, few have a program that is entirely student-run. Oberlin's "Experimental College" (EXCO) is just that, offering short courses taught by either faculty or students. These courses count in small bits toward the hours needed for graduation, and while they don't replace regular classes, students do use EXCO offerings "to pad our schedule a little bit," one student says. In the past, courses have included "Football Appreciation" (taught on Sunday afternoons by members of the football team) and "Essential Films of the 80s" (featuring *Ferris Bueller's Day Off,* among others). Other courses are activity-based, such as knitting and self-defense. There have been courses in soap operas. While the media classes are designed to stimulate critical discussion, most are not taken very seriously.

"Private reading," one-on-one tutorials with a chosen professor, is available when the regular curriculum does not offer in-depth study of a particular topic.

These professors teach more traditional courses, and do so very well: Robert Longsworth in English; Jeff Witmer in mathematics; David Benzing, Yolanda Cruz, and Roger Laushman in biology; Norman Craig and Martin Ackermann in chemistry; and Robert Warner in the physics department. The natural sciences, especially biology, chemistry, physics, and neuroscience/biopsychology, are considered very strong, as are the departments of mathematics, philosophy, politics, and classics. The religion department has evident strengths in Judaism and Eastern religions, but tends to treat Christianity in terms of the phenomenology of religion and the "construction" of narratives.

One of Oberlin's best-known programs is the Conservatory of Music, separate from the College of Arts and Sciences, which encompasses all other disciplines. The conservatory, which shares the college campus and enrolls more than 550 students, was founded in 1865 as a private music school and became part of the college two years later. Oberlin says it is "the only institution in the country to combine a leading liberal arts college and a world-renowned conservatory on one campus." Many Arts and Sciences students take courses at the conservatory, and double majors are possible if the student can gain separate admission to both entities (conservatory admission is very competitive). The conservatory is one of the best in the nation, and its undergraduate program is a match for some graduate programs. Its 188 Steinway pianos constitute the largest collection under one roof outside the Steinway factory. There are three major performance halls, including Finney Chapel, named for the nineteenth-century revivalist whose support was critical to Oberlin's early years.

The natural science departments' stature on campus is compared by one professor to that of the conservatory's. "I think natural science at Oberlin is a little-known jewel — it has a crucial function in maintaining [Oberlin's] academic caliber, and does attract some of the best students," the professor says. "It's comparable to having the Conservatory of Music, one quality of uniqueness which is inarguable." Probably the strongest of the several strong sciences at Oberlin is chemistry, according to a professor from another department. "It's worked very hard to build and maintain a coherent identity," the professor says. "I've heard rich testimonials from students about how valuable this experience is. The department is, without question, crackerjack." Two chemistry professors, Norman Craig and Martin Ackermann, have won the Catalyst Award of the American Chemical Society. Craig, now professor emeritus, is a former Oberlin student, and both are noted for making strenuous efforts to involve students in their research, both during the summer and throughout the year.

Biology is known for several superlative teachers. Physics is also highly regarded; its strengths lie in its teaching rather than its professors' reputation for research outside the Oberlin community. The physics department has been successful in serving both its most advanced majors and students taking a course to fill out their distribution requirements.

There is considerable politicization among the humanities departments, but philosophy and classics have escaped much of it. Art history, though radical, is known for its strenuous academic requirements. In other humanities departments students will find varying degrees of politicization. In general the social sciences are Oberlin's least traditional area. English and history are in close to the same predicament, their faculties representing the full spectrum of radical positions. English is the largest major on campus, claiming one out of every five members of the average graduating class. In the Oberlin catalogue, English department course descriptions are terse and sober, but, nevertheless, the titles give some indication of their teachers' leanings: for example, "Domestic Violence in Early Modern Drama" and "Reading Victorian Sexualities." Even apart from the subject matter, many survey courses are politicized by a tiresome preoccupation with sex and gender issues rather than with the great books themselves.

In history, the same tendency toward theory prevails. In one course titled "The Body as Historical Subject," students "explore the use of the body both as a site of symbolic representation and as a site for the construction of experience, gender, and sexuality," through readings that include libertine French philosopher Michel Foucault. "Roots of Feminist Analysis" and "History of Latinas in the United States" were recently offered during a year in which "American Intellectual History" and "Machiavelli and the Renaissance" were not. While the catalogue does list traditional survey offerings in American and European history, a professor in another department says no history professors are specialists in European history. When the European history position came open not long ago, the department hired a specialist in South Asian history, the professor says.

Oberlin's women's studies program is, according to a professor from another department, internally divided into various feminist camps, and its pedagogy "is a matter of deep dispute among warring factions in the students and faculty." This professor says disputes within the department have become distractions for the college community, and for that and other reasons the program has yet to gain standing as an official department. African-American studies, on the other hand, is a department and has a very "clear sense of self-identity," the professor says. Oberlin does not have a gay and lesbian studies program, but a handful of humanities courses pay significant attention to homosexuality. Asian students have recently begun to lobby for more courses on Asian history and culture, and on the Asian experience in America.

Political Atmosphere: Going Underground

Traditional and conservative students and faculty can have a tough time at Oberlin. One professor says segments of the Oberlin community are "ideological and aggressive." Another person familiar with the campus estimates that as many as one-fifth of the students are "unbelievably intolerant" of traditional beliefs. The pockets of political conservatives and evangelical Christians on campus, including the Oberlin Christian Fellowship and Ecumenical Christians at Oberlin, use the hostility to their beliefs as a source of self-strengthening and challenge, a student says. Some Christian faculty have placed fish symbols on their doors, perhaps unconsciously using the sign as early Christians did: in the face of persecution.

"The whole public atmosphere is pretty much confined to the left," a professor says. "In the rhetoric that is constantly used at this place, in questions of sexual orientation and racial divides, there is a real balkanization that has taken place in recent years." This, the professor says, is over and above the mere leftism of the past.

The most prominent radical group at Oberlin is the gay community. "I don't think any accurate depiction would avoid the fact that the gay presence is strong and vocal," one professor says. Another calls the college "a haven" for gay, lesbian, and bisexual students. All agree that the groups are politically shrewd: Oberlin's homosexual community schedules its "Gay Pride" festival to coincide with a program for incoming students. This has "caused a good deal of administrative consternation," a professor says, but the events have occurred during the same week for several years running. The Drag Ball held every spring is easily the most popular social event on campus. About 1,600 of the college's 2,800 students attend, and recently they have been joined by college president Nancy Schrom Dye. Even students who begin college opposed to these activities often give in to social pressures and eventually attend, a recent graduate says. This person recalls that a friend of hers who was "Republican and very religious" refused to go to the Drag Ball his freshman year but changed his mind as a sophomore and went.

Other sexual issues attract Oberlin's attention. Since homosexual couples may live together in college residence halls, the administration has been pressured — unsuccessfully — to allow heterosexual couples the same privilege. Some residence halls have coed bathrooms. One bizarre incident occurred in 1997, when, as part of a student's composition recital at the conservatory, two masked students entered the recital hall and one began performing fellatio on the other. Though this was considered extreme even by Oberlin standards, the administration took no disciplinary action and said only that the display fell under the license of artistic expression normally granted performers.

Oberlin has also debated "program houses," student residences dedicated to common interests or ethnic backgrounds. The college has four houses whose residents are interested in a particular foreign language, as well as an Asia House, Afrikan Heritage House, the Women's Collective, Hebrew House, and Third World House, each of which offers events for residents and sponsors programs for the community at large. Lately the program houses have objected to being located in an isolated section of the campus and have asked to be placed elsewhere so as to become better integrated into the campus community.

Despite the predominance and acceptance of radical policies and groups, one professor says the college's nihilistic image is more hype than substance. While it's true that the multicultural issues "tend to stimulate a good deal of conversation," and that Oberlin tends to "harbor" and value its reputation for politicization, the professor says that, lately, students have been "much less politically interested or perceptive" than in the past. "The number of relatively passive students and faculty members has grown in the last decade." While the dominant voices on campus may be given to sensational rhetoric, there does exist a sort of underground comprised of a variety of opinions and ideas, the professor says. A recent graduate says she was pleasantly "surprised at the number of conservative students" and glad to find that she and they did not feel "like they were hunted down." Within the college's more moderate elements, this graduate says, "you can find people like you, even if you might not be in the majority, or of the opinion Oberlin's known for."

Still, it is more practical to keep quiet and not offend the more powerful campus radicals. Oberlin's campus judicial proceedings are said to be secretive and particularly vicious when dealing with sexual harassment charges. The college has a sexual offense officer who "operates totally in an atmosphere of confidentiality," one faculty member says. As a result, there are "relatively few formal proceedings" of a high-profile sort, and the hushed hearings tend to contribute to a subtle paranoia in the college community, the professor says. The college has an elaborate sexual offense policy that spells out "what are regarded as linguistic misbehaviors to faculty, students, and employees," a professor says. Once someone is accused, there is an "elaborate grievance process — almost grotesquely elaborate," particularly in the application of parliamentary procedure, the professor says. "Plagiarism is nothing in comparison with that."

Student Life: . . . and the Wisdom to Know the Difference

Many things are not permitted at Oberlin, but smoking marijuana "is, if not countenanced, then at least tacitly permitted," says a graduate. And, unlike ideological transgressions, recreational drug use does not normally result in campus judicial proceedings, "unless it's a big problem," the graduate says. "It does give Oberlin the reputation for being a little bit of a 'druggie' school."

According to the student newspaper, the *Oberlin Review*, some students feel comfortable enough around drugs to advertise their use. In 1997 an anonymous group of students sent out flyers announcing "Trip Saturday," intended, in the words of the *Review*, to "create a community atmosphere and to explore the options created by use of psychedelics throughout the country." The campus was not sure what to make of this, but the administration was: it responded not with statements on the moral or ethical implications of illicit drug use, but with advice from the counseling center on "how to deal with a 'bad trip,'" the *Review* reported. Several students were quoted anonymously in the article, with one admitting that "it's known I sell psychedelic drugs" and another saying it is "really, really easy" to obtain drugs at Oberlin.

(As for the *Review,* it also feels free to flout societal taboos, making liberal use of the f-bomb in articles on subjects as mundane as a women's lacrosse tournament.)

The town of Oberlin is officially dry, although some liquor licenses have been issued to various establishments, including the Oberlin College Inn. In addition to harder drug use, some "people drink a lot of beer," according to one student. Crime statistics indicate that Oberlin has a very safe environment for students, excepting of course the dangers of drugs.

Fraternities and sororities are absent at Oberlin. Students live instead in either traditional dormitories, the aforementioned program houses, or cooperative houses. The dorms are either single-sex or coed, sometimes by alternate rooms. In coed sections, each floor holds an anonymous vote as to whether bathrooms should be coed as well; one "no" vote is allegedly enough to keep the bathrooms separate.

Student organizations include the Lesbian, Gay, and Bisexual Union; College Democrats; Oberlin Christian Fellowship; Students for Free Tibet; and Oberlin Zionists. There are 11 women's and 10 men's varsity sports at Oberlin. There are also 14 different club teams, including equestrian and an Ultimate Frisbee squad, and a number of intramural sports, including bowling, basketball, and volleyball.

Oberlin, a town of eight thousand, is thirty-five miles southwest of Cleveland. Its tree-lined streets include some charming clapboard houses. Among the many cultural perks of life at Oberlin are good bookstores (the Co-op and Miranda Books) and great coffee shops (the Feve; the Java Zone, where faculty and staff hang out; and the more elegant Main Street Mercantile Store and Tea Room, known locally as the Merc). Another architectural gem in the downtown area is the Apollo movie theater, an art deco building that features current films (as opposed to the more vintage and artistic film series shown on campus). And admission at the Apollo is only three dollars — two dollars on Tuesday and Thursday nights.

The Ohio State University

Office of Admissions
Lincoln Tower
1800 Cannon Drive
Columbus, OH 43210-1200
(614) 292-3980
www.osu.edu

Total enrollment: 48,003
Undergraduates: 36,092
SAT ranges (Verbal/Math): 500-620 (V); 520-640 (M)
Applicants: 19,805
Accepted: 74%
Enrolled: 42%
Application deadline: February 15
Financial aid application deadline: February 15
Tuition: resident: $4,383/$10,190; non-resident: $12,732/$18,539
Core curriculum: No

Its Own Weight

There's one thing that can be said with complete certitude about Ohio State and its 1,644-acre campus (one of the world's largest): It's big. And because it's so big — the second-largest student body in the nation, behind the University of Texas at Austin — that may be about the only thing that can be said about the school without quali-fication. Except, perhaps, that it's not the place to go for a liberal arts education, if you have a choice.

Not that the university will tell you any such thing. But that certainly seems to be a common view among OSU liberal arts faculty, who agree that students looking for a serious liberal arts education would be better served elsewhere. Only "focused, savvy undergraduates" interested in going on for a graduate or professional degree, according to one professor, will be well served at OSU. Another cites the University of Miami and Ohio University as better state schools for the liberal arts–inclined, and Michigan and Wisconsin as better Big Ten choices.

But if that doesn't convince you, take a look at the university's own materials and self-description. OSU is the epitome of the new corporate-style — and corpora-tion-catering — mega-university, so much so that the *Chronicle of Higher Education* noted that if you glanced quickly at one piece of school literature, "you might think the newsletter is published by the Amoco Corporation, not the Ohio State University." Everywhere you look or read, university attention is lavished on research, technology, and diversity — but not education, and certainly not the liberal arts. If you go to OSU looking for a more traditional education, well, the only thing to do is to read on.

Academic Life: Turfgrass Science?

OSU's Academic Plan, published in October 2000, amply demonstrates where its priorities lie. The school's goal is to become "the nation's leading public land-grant university." Its plan to do this includes attracting "world-class faculty" (i.e., star scholars who bring in grant money) and to increase faculty pay. It also has specific goals tied to National Research Council and *U.S. News* rankings, wanting ten programs in those organizations' top ten lists and twenty in their top twenty by 2010. A ton of money is being poured into certain programs in order to reach this goal, including research and library facilities. Perhaps some of this effort will actually benefit students; OSU is aiming to increase course accessibility and reduce class sizes, and the creation of ten new "scholars programs" by 2003 will attempt to place top students in like-minded communities.

The hope is not only that these programs will attract better students, but also that it will help curb student attrition, which the administration considered a big enough problem (probably because of its concerns about maintaining racial/ethnic diversity) to hire a high-priced consultant to help it identify at-risk students and ways to keep them on campus. This initiative resulted in the creation of a "personal contact program." Of course, only a mega-university like OSU would need to ensure that it had "personal contact" with its students.

The student to faculty ratio at OSU is fourteen to one, but 17 percent of classes have fifty or more students, and 20 percent of classes are taught by graduate teaching assistants. The comparative unimportance of teaching excellence was demonstrated rather dramatically in 1998, when Howard Fleeter, an assistant professor of public policy, was denied tenure even though he had won three teacher of the year awards in his department since his arrival in 1989. His department had even voted for his tenure, but higher-up administrators disagreed.

Rather than a core curriculum for all students, OSU has different distribution requirements depending on the student's school. If a student is seeking a B.A. in the College of Arts and Sciences, the student will have to complete ten units in "writing and related skills" (each course is generally worth five units), nine or ten units in quantitative/logical skills, twenty units in natural science, fifteen units in social science, twenty-five units in the arts and humanities, and five units in "contemporary world issues." Students must also demonstrate language proficiency equivalent to what is expected in a fourth-quarter language course.

These "requirements" are easy to fill. For instance, "Textiles and Clothing,"

"Family Resource Management," and "Rural Sociology" would satisfy the social science requirement, although, on the other hand, students could easily choose a more traditional route to fulfilling the requirement as well. But they don't have to. Students can easily get away without taking, say, a survey course in political science. To fulfill half of the writing requirement, each student must take English 110, an introductory composition course. But any one of forty-one other courses will complete the second half of the requirement, including "Agricultural Communication" or "Theatre." The quantitative/logical skill requirement is similarly loose. It does not even require, necessarily, a course in mathematics. To fulfill the arts and humanities requirement, students must take a two-course "historical survey" sequence in one of four areas: philosophy, economics, history, or African-American and African studies. One course must also be selected from long lists of eligible courses in literature, visual/performing arts, and "cultures and ideas." The contemporary world issues requirement, like virtually all of the requirements, may be fulfilled in myriad ways and within myriad departments: courses in agriculture, crop science, geodetic science, food science, etc., all may work.

There are also "Diversity Experience" and "International Issues" requirements, which are normally fulfilled with classes that also meet other general education requirements. The university's stated reasoning for this requirement is as follows:

> A liberal education should foster an understanding of American institutions and the pluralistic nature of American society. Only with such an understanding can citizens appreciate the significance of diversity in our society and the importance of the values of tolerance and equality. You must select a course that gives significant treatment to the pluralistic nature of institutions, society, and culture in the United States, with special attention to issues of race, gender, class, and ethnicity.

The lists of courses fulfilling these requirements are also long.

The quality of one's peers at OSU will vary widely. As with all large state schools, there are many very bright students; however, only 29 percent of the 1999 crop of freshmen graduated in the top tenth of their class. OSU, which had an open admissions policy until 1987, has become steadily more selective ever since, but it is still far from difficult to gain admittance: about three-quarters of those who apply, get in. Because OSU's admission is nearly open to all Ohio kids, classes — as one professor euphemistically puts it — "have to be structured for a heterogeneous clientele." As a result, the quality of the faculty is said to be more impressive, by and large, than the students. The aforementioned Scholars Program does draw some quality in-state students, and according to one professor "compares favorably with a decent middle-of-the-road Ivy League education."

Students complain that one way in which OSU is attempting to achieve greater selectivity is by continually raising tuition. The state legislature has capped tuition increases at 6 percent per year, and the OSU administration has raised tuition costs just that much in each of the last three years. President William E. Kirwan has also tried to circumvent the cap by attempting to implement new fees, and he is reportedly now lobbying the state legislature to increase or drop the tuition cap.

OSU's engineering and business majors consistently rank highly nationally. Psychology and English, however, are the largest majors. The school offers more than 170 degree programs, covering everything from jazz studies to turfgrass science. Though, according to one professor, none of the departments "specialize in undergraduate education," nearly all have some excellent teachers. Still, undergraduate teaching is not a specialty, and it is frequently conducted by graduate students. Some reliable (i.e., nonpoliticized) teachers include Howard Marvel, Gene Mumy, and Eric Fisher in economics; Edward Crenshaw in sociology; In Jae Myung in psychology; Janet Box-Steffensmeier in political science; and Phoebe Spinrad in English.

Grade inflation, as a problem, varies from professor to professor and department to department. Says one professor, "there are some instructors . . . who routinely fail underperforming students, but there are just as many faculty members who refuse to fail people." In other words, according to another professor, "I've seen worse at other schools." English and other courses in the humanities are said to be easier than those in the sciences and business school.

Getting the courses you need at OSU can be problematic. Only 20 percent of students enrolling at OSU graduate within four years, and only 48 percent within five.

Political Atmosphere: We Have a Plan

As the "Diversity Education" requirement suggests, OSU's primary institutional concern could well be said to be political, not educational. In fact, according to the university's Diversity Action Plan, a major topic of discussion on campus for the past two years at least, OSU's goal is not to become known for, oh, say, *education*, but instead to become a "national model for diversity." As the final report, issued in June 2000, makes clear, this is nothing short of a call for full-scale campus politicization. The report proposes (1) the establishment of a multicultural center, (2) diversity training workshops for student leaders, (3) the elimination of housing policies that discriminate against same sex partners, (4) that faculty search committee chairs submit reports regarding the methods they used to attract women and minorities, including documentation of the rationale for their exclusion (or inclusion) in the final pool of candidates, and (5) the addition of "diversity dialogues" to University College classes. (The University College is a non–degree granting college enrolling many freshmen and transfer students who have not yet gained admittance to their program of choice.)

The Diversity Plan is being spearheaded by President Kirwan, and his aggressiveness in doing so worries some faculty. "It's very discouraging, and I fear OSU may turn into a 'people's republic' if something doesn't change," says one.

Not that there isn't plenty of politicization already. There are the usual suspects — African American and African studies and women's studies, most notably, but also psychology. The English department also includes its fair share of nontraditional and sometimes bizarre courses, including one titled "Chickflicks," whose course description claims that "'The woman's film' plays against major assumptions of both film criticism and mainstream cinema, both of which often prioritize 'the man's film' (horror, film noir, the Western, the war film) and the canon of male directors. Chickflicks thus raise critical questions about spectatorship and Hollywood formulas in relationship to gender and sexual identity, topics which will be emphasized in our discussions."

And yet despite courses like that, the English department — not unlike many others at OSU — retains some traces of a more traditional past; this constitutes the primary advantage of a large school like OSU. There is even something approaching an English core: all majors must take courses in British literature (one on works written before 1800, a second on those written after 1800), either the pre– or post–Civil War course in American literature, and "Critical Writing." Students must further be sure that they complete at least one more course in literature before 1800, literature after 1800, and, alas, in an area of English studies that is *not* literature (e.g., critical theory, film, etc.). Majors may focus in one of sixteen areas, including everything from medieval lit to poetry to feminist studies. A similar core-plus-distribution-requirements system characterizes the history major as well.

Unapproved speech can bring trouble at OSU. A cartoonist for the student paper was fired after one of his "Stillman" cartoons poked fun at women's studies majors. There were swift and angry protests from the Feminist Majority and a number of newspaper thefts. Said the unfortunate Bob Hewitt to his own paper, "As far as I'm concerned, it looks like [the protesters] are looking for diversity, minus my opinion." The state of diversity drives on campuses nationwide has rarely been better expressed.

In the classroom, professors must engage in self-censoring, often, if they are to keep their jobs. Says one faculty member, "Some topics are relatively taboo, and right-wing activism is definitely frowned upon." This professor says that an "activist Christian colleague" of his was recently denied tenure for political reasons. Those professors on the "wrong side" of things must be particularly productive to keep their jobs.

According to one student, the atmosphere at OSU is "definitely left of center but not radical liberal." In fact, the campus as a whole is fairly apolitical, with the vast majority of students uninterested in political matters. Only about 10 percent, for example, vote in student elections.

Like an increasing number of college campuses, OSU has a mainstream left-of-center daily and an alternative right-of-center newspaper. At OSU, these are *The Lantern* and *The OSU Observer*, respectively.

Student Life: Not So Quiet Riot

The most distinctive aspect of student life at Ohio State may be the disturbing fact that student riots are an annual, and sometimes even semi-annual, feature of the landscape. Many, if not all, of these riots follow big football games — wins *or* losses — and the police now routinely plan for them, despite extensive administration efforts to end them, including door-to-door visits by then-president Gordon Gee and then–head football coach John Cooper. In 1999, the city of Columbus spent an extra $80,000 for police protection following the Ohio State-Michigan game (a heated rivalry) — and the game was played in Ann Arbor. After the 2000 loss to Michigan, one student was stabbed, three police officers were injured, eleven students were arrested, and 129 fires were started. Tear gas and wooden bullets were used by police. The university's efforts are obviously not paying off.

The riots usually occur at big parties in off-campus students' residences where the host has little control over who attends, much less their behavior. Ironically, these mammoth house parties are the direct result of the university's own greed; according to a student reporter, the university, in collaboration with the city government, has used the power of eminent domain to drive out several bars on High Street, ostensibly in the name of revitalization. This has moved the college drinking scene to less centralized and less watched areas. The closing of close-to-campus bars, says one student, has severely dampened campus nightlife and increased concerns about drunken driving.

Columbus is a fairly large city, with more than 1.5 million people living within the borders of its metropolitan sprawl. The part of the city surrounding campus is notable for its heavy crime. The three police patrol zones that border OSU are the most crime-ridden in the city, and this fact is reflected in the official crime statistics reported by the school (1999 saw four murders or non-negligent manslaughters and thirty-seven forcible sexual assaults in these areas, not to mention 592 burglaries and 403 motor vehicle thefts). The head of the campus police department told the *Chronicle of Higher Education* recently that only 20 percent of the student body lives in these areas (which is still roughly 10,000 students), while 60 percent choose to live as far as ten miles northwest of campus in a low-crime neighborhood. He also said that just one mile east of campus there are "rows and rows of crack houses," which isn't particularly comforting.

The university tries to brush off concerns about crime. One spokeswoman was quoted as saying that, "Sociologically speaking, the more people you have, the more crime you'll have." But an equally large institution, the University of Texas, doesn't have nearly the crime problems that OSU does. Though crime, according to one professor, "is not epidemic by any means" on and around campus, another faculty member admits to being "a little worried. The campus area has a bit too much crime for my tastes." However, this same professor maintains that despite the crime and the sketchy areas near campus, Columbus is generally a friendly and livable place.

Students echo this sentiment. One gushes that for such a large school, OSU retains a genuine sense of community and school pride. "People here are friendly. I come from New Jersey, but the people here are ready to start a conversation with anyone."

As the rioting attests, Buckeye football is huge. Says one student, if the Buckeyes lose "it looks like a funeral around here." But so are intramurals and recreational sports; 90 percent of the student body participates in some sport or other, from gymnastics to water polo to squash. (The women's rugby team is not quite as unruly as the student rioters, but thirteen team members did get in trouble for posing topless for a team picture on the steps of the Lincoln Memorial during a trip to Washington, D.C.) Columbus offers further opportunities for spectator sports, including a AAA baseball team, a major league soccer team, and the brand new NHL Columbus Blue Jackets. For the athletically uninclined, Columbus has a symphony, several art museums, and a ballet troupe. Students ride the local bus system for free.

The vast majority of students — 93 percent — are from Ohio. Only about a quarter of them live on campus, and 13 percent join sororities or fraternities. Of the twenty-six residence halls, none are male-only, though two are exclusively female. The rest house women and men in a variety of ways, sometimes on different floors, sometimes on the same floor but in different wings, and sometimes on the same floor and same wing. In the latter situation, men and women often share bathrooms. Six floors on campus have been designated as substance free. Many dorms have special programs, like the African-American Living-Learning Program or the First Year Experience Program. Visitation hours in all dorms are subject to minimal restrictions. As of 1999, students no longer had the option of living under the football stadium in the Stadium Scholarship Dormitory, which was torn down when the stadium underwent renovations.

OSU makes no bones about "diversity education" being one of its primary goals among the denizens of its residence halls. Its explicit objectives include "building communities of students with an increased sensitivity to differences in race, ethnicity, sexual orientation, gender, ability, religion, etc." and "designing learning communities focusing on diversity as a competency area." It is hard to imagine how one can be "competent" in diversity, but there you have it.

Perhaps inspired by OSU's diversity education efforts, Students for Freethought, a secular humanist organization, has pushed for the removal of prayer from commencement proceedings and for the deletion of the phrase "The Year of Our Lord" from diplomas. There are at least two groups for gays, lesbians, and bisexuals, as well as a Pagan Student Association. But then OSU has student organizations of every imaginable type — roughly 550 of them, including thirty-six honor societies and thirty-seven religious organizations.

University of Pennsylvania

Dean of Admissions
University of Pennsylvania
1 College Hall
Philadelphia, PA 19014-6376
(215) 898-7507
www.upenn.edu

Total enrollment: 17,854
Undergraduates: 9,770
SAT ranges (Verbal/Math): 640-730 (V); 670-760 (M)
Applicants: 17,666
Accepted: 26%
Enrolled: 54%
Application deadline: January 1
Financial aid application deadline: April 15
Tuition: $25,166/$33,242
Core curriculum: No

Philadelphia Freedom

The University of Pennsylvania was founded in 1740 as a charity school for Philadelphia children. In 1750 American patriot Benjamin Franklin merged the Public Academy of Philadelphia with this charity school and named the new institution the College, Academy, and Charitable School of Philadelphia. Due to its early founding, Penn claims to be "the nation's first university [but not the first college], the nation's first medical school, its first collegiate business school, the first journalism program, [and] the first university teaching hospital."

As an Ivy League school with impressive origins, Penn has had a lot going for it. But increasingly the version of freedom celebrated by this Philadelphia institution is one based not on tradition but on the new multiculturalism, which dictates freedom for some and straitjackets for others. In the hands of recent administrations, the university's motto — "Leges Sine Moribus Vanae" (Laws without morals are useless) — has been stretched, twisted, and occasionally even contradicted.

Along with an aggressive ideological regime has come, predictably, an abdication of the principles of liberal education. Penn is rapidly abandoning these traditions, and in the new century Penn is looking to have students even more engaged in job training and service projects than the extensive degree to which they presently are on campus. Penn's attempt to redefine the meaning of freedom — the "liberal" in "liberal arts" — has made it one of the more controversial Ivy League schools, and may well haunt it in the twenty-first century.

Academic Life: Undergraduates, Underdogs

Penn has nothing even remotely resembling a core curriculum, even going so far as to refer in its catalogue to classes in "The General Requirement" as "electives." Students enrolled in one of four undergraduate schools (the School of Nursing, the School of Engineering and Applied Sciences, the Wharton School, and the School of Arts and Sciences) must take ten General Requirement courses distributed among seven "sectors." The university makes little effort to direct the students along any particular path, and even states in the course catalogue that "it is also recognized that the plenitude of university courses is in itself bewildering; informed choice is only possible if the number of General Requirement alternatives is reasonably contained."

Philly's own Rocky Balboa may not have been as big an underdog as are students forced to discover a solid liberal arts education at Penn. Their choices are contained only by the sectors, which include society (I), history and tradition (II), arts and letters (III), formal reasoning and analysis (IV), the living world (V), the physical world (VI), and science studies (VII). Students must take two courses from each of the first three sectors, and one from each of sectors IV, V, and VI, and another course in either IV, V, VI, or VII.

The problem is that the sector with the shortest list of possible courses, formal reasoning and analysis, contains sixteen courses in seven departments. The longest list, arts and letters, permits seventy-four courses in any of dozens of departments. Lists contain a mixture of Western and non-Western topics, in traditional and non-traditional fields, ranging from "Understanding the Cult Controversy" and "Male-Female Communication: East and West" to "History of Ancient Philosophy" and "Shakespeare." Students are told to take what interests them, period. The number of courses offered in the General Requirement makes it quite possible to avoid all of the texts and issues that once constituted a traditional liberal arts education, a student says.

But with the right choices, the General Requirement can be used to select an extraordinary education. In a highly politicized academic environment such as Penn, a loose curriculum is a better alternative than a required partisan multicultural curriculum.

Undergraduates must also complete a minimal foreign language requirement by demonstrating proficiency in one of the thirty-nine languages offered, either by taking classes or by passing a test. A writing requirement was added to the general requirements in 1993, which also can be satisfied by taking one writing course, a class with an attached writing lab, or two classes affiliated with the "Writing Across the

University" program. Some courses that have counted in the latter category include "Writing Multiculturalism," "Weird and Eccentric: Unusual Individuals in the History of the Philadelphia Area," "Student Movements and the Political Process," and "Star Wars: The Cosmology." Penn recently added a quantitative skills requirement, which requires students to select one course that has to do with analyzing data.

The general requirements apply to all Penn undergrads who choose one of the more than fifty majors under the School of Arts and Sciences. The other schools have their own general requirements, each more focused on the area of the school's specialization.

The Wharton School, usually thought of as a graduate school, also offers prestigious undergraduate degrees in business fields. *Business Week* ranked Wharton's MBA program the best in the nation, and *U.S. News & World Report* gave Wharton's undergraduate business program its top ranking. Its departments of accounting, marketing, nonprofit management, quantitative studies, business ethics, and global management are all considered among the top six in the country.

Penn students who want to get out of Philadelphia for a time can choose from a range of sixty-three programs that reach twenty-six countries on all six inhabited continents. In 1997-1998, 503 Penn undergraduates participated in study-abroad programs for credit.

In addition to its 9,700 undergraduates, Penn enrolls more than 8,000 graduate students in twelve graduate and professional schools. Besides the Wharton School, the School of Arts and Sciences, the Law School, and the School of Medicine are thought to be among the top ten nationwide. Penn is home to the only veterinary school in Pennsylvania, and its highly regarded School of Nursing offers bachelor's, master's, and doctoral degrees. The university also is home to the Annenberg School for Communication, the School of Dental Medicine, the School of Engineering and Applied Science, the Graduate School of Education, the Graduate School of Fine Arts, and the School of Social Work.

Several good professors are available to undergraduates at Penn. Among them are Al Filreis in English; Alan Charles Kors, Walter McDougall, Ann Moyer, Arthur Waldron, and Thomas Childers in history; Gary Hatfield, James Ross, and Zoltan Domotor in philosophy; and Mark Adams in history and the sociology of science.

The best departments on campus are the ones least touched by ideological fever. That doesn't leave many to choose from, but psychology is said by a professor to be "rigorous, and deeply grounded in both biological science and in humanistic study." Mathematics, physics, and other sciences are also highly regarded. "The hard sciences are good in terms of academics," a student says. Despite these comments, most conservative members of the Penn community are silent when asked to name exceptional departments at Penn.

Quite a few departments are dominated by a politicized atmosphere, however. "Most departments in the School of Arts and Sciences are hostile to traditional political views," says a student. "One student reported getting a paper back that said,

'Maybe you would have gotten a better grade if you had not learned how to write from *The Red and Blue*' [the campus conservative newspaper]."

English is one of the most politicized departments at Penn; one professor calls the curriculum there "politicized, self-indulgent, and intolerant," while a student says the department's take on literary criticism resides "on the cutting edge of wackiness." A recent graduate calls the department a "haven for Neo-Marxists." One professor, Nina Auerbach, has written a book entitled *Our Vampires, Our Selves,* which is based on the thesis "that vampirism springs not only from paranoia, xenophobia, or immortal longings, but from generosity and shared enthusiasm."

Political Atmosphere: Can Anyone Here Play This Game?

Penn has suffered from recent university administrations committed to surfing on the multicultural wave now sweeping over the academy. The current president, Judith Rodin, a Penn alumna, took office in 1994. Rodin came to Penn from Yale University, where she served as provost and as the dean of the Graduate School of Arts and Sciences. Rodin's Yale years had their share of controversy. In fact, many Yale students and alumni blame her for the loss of Lee Bass's $20 million grant for the establishment of Western civilization studies. When Rodin was provost at Yale, a committee set up to determine the implementation of the Bass grant recommended to Yale's president that some of the money be used to hire four new junior professors to teach Western civilization. Rodin strongly advised against this. The president sided with Rodin, and the $20 million was returned to Bass, a move that led to the loss over nearly $100 million in donations from other disgusted Yale alumni.

It is possible that Rodin has learned her lesson. "[She] is very savvy when it comes to public relations," a student says. "Over the past year she has tried very hard to do away with Penn's image of ideological policing and intellectual intolerance." Rodin recently admitted that "Campus speech codes and similar regulations were not able to reduce the level of intolerance or incivility, as we found so painfully at Penn, and . . . I abolished the speech code at Penn because I believe that such measures fundamentally send the wrong message, a message that reinforces the sense of powerless individuals and of monolithic institutions, of cultural orthodoxy and paternalistic authority, and of ideological conformity and political correctness." Rodin has also stated publicly that she wants a diversity not only of race but of opinion, including both conservative and liberal ideas.

There is no doubt that damage has been done to Penn's reputation, damage that began during the tenure of Sheldon Hackney, who left Penn briefly to serve as director of the National Endowment for the Humanities under President Clinton. (He is now back at Penn as a professor of history.) Students at Penn came to call Hackney "the Pope of Political Correctness," and two incidents among many that occurred during his term as president help explain why.

Several years ago, a conservative columnist for a university-recognized student publication, the *Daily Pennsylvanian,* wrote an editorial critical of the university's hate-speech code, admissions policies that favored minorities, and over-the-top multiculturalism. A group of black students accused the writer of racial harassment, but the charge was dropped by the administration when the journalist pointed out an official university policy that expressly forbade investigation of students for opinions published in school papers. In retaliation for the dismissal of charges, a group calling itself "The Black Community" stole an entire pressrun of the newspaper. Even after the students proudly confessed to vandalism, Hackney refused to discipline them. "After the event, the number of reported newspaper thefts on campuses quadrupled," says an alumnus. "There was no question that Hackney's unwillingness to punish the students was a green light to copycat cases of newspaper thefts around the country. The message at Penn was clear: if an article insults you, feel free to steal and destroy the paper."

Then there was the so-called water buffalo incident, a classic episode in the annals of political correctness. In January of 1993 a group of female African-American students were chanting and making other noises outside a dormitory where several students were studying and sleeping. It was around midnight, and the students in the dorm, disturbed by the noise, gathered at the windows to shout at the women to be quiet. Eventually police were called. Based on the complaints of the students outside, the police interrogated dormitory resident Eden Jacobowitz, who admitted to shouting, "Shut up, you water buffalo." The Judicial Inquiry Office of the university charged Jacobowitz with racial harassment under the hate-speech code. A publicity storm ensued, and the unfavorable publicity caused the board of trustees to order the speech code scrapped.

Student Life: The Broad Street Bullies

Located in West Philadelphia, Penn's campus is an oasis of prosperity in an area wracked by urban decay. The wealthy university is sandwiched between run-down buildings and a major expressway. In order to improve the surrounding areas, the university runs a program called the West Philadelphia Improvement Corps, where Penn students "incorporate real-world research into their academic studies" by providing classes and educational opportunities to community residents and public-school students.

Despite these depressed surroundings, it is still expensive to go to Penn, where the undergraduate tuition is more than $25,000 a year and room and board fees are more than $8,000. (Keep in mind that the average freshman aid award was more than $21,600, according to the university.) Still, Penn received a record-high 17,666 applications for admission to the Class of 2004. Of those applicants, 26.4 percent were offered admission. The university notes that 36 percent of the most recent incoming freshman class was from ethnic minorities — a credit to the multiculturalist objectives of the administration.

The 262-acre campus includes attractions such as Houston Hall, the nation's first student union; the University of Pennsylvania Museum (established in 1887, its one-million-item collection includes artifacts from Egypt, Mesopotamia, Africa, Asia, Polynesia, and the Americas, and it is considered one of the finest university archaeology and anthropology museums in the country); and Franklin Field, the oldest collegiate football field still in use and the country's first double-decked college stadium. Victorian buildings are intermingled with modern structures on the campus. Locust Walk, once a city street but now open only to nonmotorized traffic, is perhaps the most beautiful part of the campus. "During the day, Locust Walk hosts an on-going ballet of people, coming in and out of class," says an alumnus.

While virtually all underclassmen live in West Philadelphia, many upperclassmen and graduate students live across the Schuylkill River in Center City, the heart of Philadelphia. One benefit of living away from campus is comparative safety. In 1996 a Penn student was shot on campus. This was the last straw for students tired of panhandlers on campus (around the intersections of Thirty-eighth and Spruce and Thirty-sixth and Chestnut) as well as residents of West Philly who run red lights, roll through stop signs, and throw trash on the ground. Public drunkenness has reportedly been a problem, and graffiti can be found on the buildings of local businesses. The administration has now allowed campus security personnel to carry semiautomatic weapons. Other students have requested "a police officer on every corner" and a "big wall around campus." One recent alumnus characterized the Penn campus as "extremely unsafe." Last year there were some sixty burglaries and half a dozen forcible sexual assaults on campus.

The administration did recently install floodlights on top of three high-rise dormitories on campus, but has done or can do little about the surrounding streets. "When it comes to safety, the Rodin administration has a very fuzzy definition of what is 'on campus,'" a student says.

Those undergraduates who do decide to hunker down on campus live in one of twelve "college houses," which are residential communities designed to bring students in day-to-day contact with faculty and graduate advisors. Accomodations in the architecturally diverse college houses range from traditional dormitories to apartments. All are coed, with men and women sharing the same floors but not the same bathrooms.

Students enjoy the ever-popular South Street (site of bars, restaurants, stores, coffeehouses, and booksellers) and can visit Philadelphia's rich array of museums and historic sites. Undergraduates who crave a party but wish to avoid the dangers of the streets can usually find something going on at one of the several fraternities or sororities on campus.

Several conservative groups are active on campus, including the *Red and Blue* magazine. There is also an active chapter of the College Republicans.

One of the most politicized student groups on campus is the Lesbian, Gay, Bisexual Center (LGBC), an official university office with a budget over $100,000.

The administration sponsors the highly politicized Penn Women's Center, which provides advising, advocacy, counseling, and referrals regarding contraceptives and abortion. The organization networks with a number of feminist student groups, including Women for Equal Opportunity at the University of Pennsylvania; Penn Women's Alliance; Sister, Sister, a black women's group for students, staff, and faculty; Voyage Out (a publication of the Women's Alliance); Women United for Change; and Multicultural Women at Penn.

Under the Hackney administration, the Women's Center was the focus of several politically correct campus outrages, and its radicalism has not subsided under President Rodin. One of the groups sponsored by the Center is White Women against Racism, a group of "white women struggling with our own racism and speaking out against racism on the Penn campus and in the larger community." At one meeting of the group, the center's director ejected a student from the group, telling her that her presence was inappropriate. The student was black. The incident made the PC headlines, but Penn refused to reprimand the center's director. One Penn professor described the White Women fiasco as "one of those moments when you can't tell the difference between parody and the real thing." A year later Rodin increased the Center's budget and staff and moved the offices into one of the most prized locations on campus — an evicted fraternity on Locust Walk.

Penn runs a very active sports program at both the varsity and intramural level. Its basketball and football teams were Ivy League champions in 2000.

Pennsylvania State University

Admissions Office
University Park Campus
University Park, PA 16802
(814) 865-5471
www.psu.edu

Total enrollment: 40,571
Undergraduates: 34,406
SAT ranges (Verbal/Math): 530-640 (V); 550-660 (M)
Applicants: 26,100

Accepted: 49%
Enrolled: 39%
Application deadline: Rolling
Financial aid application deadline: February 15
Tuition: resident: $7,068/$11,982; non-resident: $14,540/$19,454
Core curriculum: No

Join the Crowd

Pennsylvania State University, known more commonly as Penn State, is one of the oldest land-grant state colleges in the country. Founded in 1855 as The Agricultural College of Pennsylvania, it has led the way in many of the developments which have come to typify large-scale state universities. The university embraced education in engineering and the sciences early in its history and has long had a reputation for outstanding engineering programs. The university also led the way in the liberal arts, and in the 1880s became the first college to offer a course in American litera-ture. In the 1930s the university began to establish branch campuses throughout the state. During the 1950s and '60s the university exploded both geographically and in terms of enrollment, as the baby boom generation went to college. The university's reputation as a first-tier research institution also was established during the '60s and remains today. In some ways, Penn State can be considered a bellwether for the trends in American public higher education: trends, good or bad, that affect big state schools often get their start at Penn State.

Despite its history, Penn State boasts excellent programs in several areas of the humanities as well as the sciences. It is distinguished by the quality and size of its li-brary and other facilities. And there is a wide array of programs available: more than 160 majors are open to undergraduates. The variety of courses and majors, however, exposes the student to the educational malady that is symptomatic of the modern multiversity: so many courses, so little direction in which ones to take. At Penn State and elsewhere, the risk is an idiosyncratic and incoherent education.

At Penn State, many students will also feel lost in the crowd. Last year's fresh-man class alone included more than 5,600 students, and most students will have to take many large lecture classes during their first two years. It is difficult to obtain any sort of academic relationship with a professor when you are one of four hundred students in a lecture hall. However, while it is possible for a student to remain anon-ymous, it is also possible for a motivated student to have an excellent educational experience and work closely with professors. The university's tuition is reasonable for in-state students, and the student who takes responsibility for his education and receives good guidance can eke out a good education.

Academic Life: Things Fall Apart

If you're like most Penn State students, you will begin your academic career with your major already declared. It is becoming increasingly uncommon for students to go to the university with an "undeclared" or "general curriculum" major, hoping that something will pique their interest along the way. "Most students here have a pretty good idea of their direction when they come here," says one freshman. "Students may change their major along the way, but usually that's because their goals become more clearly focused," a professor says. Admissions requirements are fairly stringent. The average incoming freshman had a high school GPA well over 3.5 and a combined SAT score in the 1200s.

The academic competition at Penn State tends to produce serious students. "You have to be pretty studious to survive here," one undergraduate says. "This is definitely not a big party school."

Even so, Penn State, like most large state universities, does not have a core curriculum. Instead, there is a set of distribution requirements. The idea behind such requirements is that they allow students more freedom while simultaneously ensuring that they acquire basic skills and receive exposure to similar bodies of knowledge. In theory this system sounds fine, but in practice it can create problems. In order for a distribution system to work, it is necessary that there be a coordinating vision and authority that harmonizes the disparate parts into a coherent whole. At Penn State, as at most other large universities, that coordinating vision is lacking.

The problem is that too many — way too many — different courses are allowed to satisfy different requirements. At Penn State, students are required to take a total of five courses in two skills areas: writing/speaking (three courses) and quantification (two courses). They must also complete three credits in "Health and Physical Activity" (which typically consists of completing two courses), three courses in the natural sciences, two in the arts, two in the humanities, and two in the social and behavioral sciences. They must also complete one credit of the First-Year Seminar, and a course in "intercultural and international competence."

Courses that fulfill the skills area requirements vary widely. In the writing/speaking area, technical writing, business writing, rhetoric, composition, and speech will do the trick. So will a first-year seminar in earth and mineral sciences or a course in English as a second language. The quantification requirement can be met through courses in calculus or logic or computer programming, among many other options.

In the so-called "knowledge domains," the number of courses that fulfill the requirements is so large as to bring in to question whether these are requirements at all. The undergraduate bulletin lists 197 courses can be taken to fulfill the health and physical activity general education requirement, 117 are available in the natural sciences area, 128 in arts, 261 in the humanities, and 120 in the social and behavioral sciences.

As one might expect, with this kind of system it is completely possible to meet the general education requirements by taking nothing but entirely trivial and/or politicized courses. And it is also possible to get a fairly traditional education, for the range of courses offered is staggering. In arts, for instance, a student could take either "Italian Renaissance Art" or a workshop called "Theatre in Diverse Cultures." In natural sciences, there is both "Experimental Chemistry" and "Out of the Fiery Furnace," "a history of materials, energy and man, with emphasis on their interrelationships." In social and behavioral sciences, it's difficult not to see the difference between the basic educational value of "Principles of Economics" and "Gender Dynamics in Africa." In the humanities, the university approves both "Philosophy and Literature in Western Culture" and "The Theme of Identity in World Literature: Race, Gender, and Other Issues of Diversity." Penn State leaves these choices completely up to its young students.

One course is also needed to meet the "Intercultural and International Competence" requirement. Asking that students take a course that focuses either on issues of gender, race, or non-Western cultures is, in and of itself, not especially problematic; indeed, it would be hard to characterize an education as "well-rounded" if it did not expose the student to other cultures and viewpoints. But in the contemporary academy this concept has frequently been politicized, and either indoctrination or trendy pabulum is offered in place of serious instruction and inquiry. Penn State has, unfortunately, its own share of this academic version of Gresham's law. Courses that meet this requirement include "Spirit, Space, Survival: Contemporary Black Women," which investigates "how recent black women have used spirit and space to survive," and "Gender and Geography" (geography?), which enlightens students as to "links between gender relations and spatial structures."

The first-year seminar courses vary tremendously as well. Some are as good as an introduction to art history, and many are as inessential as "Introduction to Health Aspects of Human Sexuality."

Penn State should perhaps be given some credit for maintaining comparatively solid writing and math requirements. And Penn State should also be lauded for requiring almost all students to take two years of a foreign language. But on the whole, Penn State's general education curriculum does little to ensure that students are actually educated.

The philosophy department at Penn State is said to be excellent. Students should seek out Rick Lee, Douglas Anderson, and John Christman. Here as elsewhere, though, students are warned that they must actively seek curricular advice from professors, who are usually more than willing to help. Other exceptional professors include Philip Jenkins in history and religious studies, Stanley Rosen in philosophy, and D. Douglas Miller in music.

Political Atmosphere: Politicization Without Representation

Students and faculty agree in describing Penn State as a relatively unpoliticized campus. "While the faculty here are predominantly liberal, most are very good at separating the classroom from their political views," a professor says. The large size of the university ensures that one can find people of pretty much any political leanings. "We've got communists and socialists and feminists and gay activists here," says one student. "You name it, and you can find it here."

Nonetheless, the student body remains largely uninterested in participating in the sort of radical activism that is endemic at some of Penn State's sister Big Ten schools. "What passes for a rally here is rather pathetic," says one student, who explains that "the people here are more interested in quiet sorts of things, like service groups."

Penn State's rural location and engineering/science focus probably keeps a lot of more radical types away. But even those activists who do end up at Penn State reportedly do not feel very comfortable with either the student body or the faculty. "We're in the midst of a very conservative area," says a graduate student, "and that affects the campus whether they like it or not." This student agrees that a lot of faculty keep their political agendas to themselves. "I don't see a lot of what you would call activism on the part of the faculty, even in the classroom." Faculty in some of the traditional disciplines are said to have maintained a spirit of free inquiry.

There is, in fact, a substantial conservative community at the school. The College Republican chapter is large and active, and there is also a sizeable Libertarian presence. During the recent political campaign, many Penn State students were involved in campaigning for candidates of both parties. One student says that "the honors dorms were dominated by posters for Bush/Cheney." There are numerous opportunities for politically motivated students to work in both state and national political offices as interns.

But sometimes there opens a troubling gap between Pennsylvanian conservatism and trendy campus radicalism. Earlier this year, a state lawmaker denounced the student-run Sex Faire, which included activities like "Orgasm Bingo" and "pin the clitoris on the vulva." Representative John Lawless had earlier complained about a "Womyn's Concerns" art festival called "C***fest." Lawless's presence on the state's appropriations committee may give his outrage a little oomph.

As one might expect, the departments of women's studies, Latin American studies, and African and African-American studies are dominated by leftists. Many other departments, such as English and sociology, offer plenty of politicized courses. But most students report that they get along well with even the professors they disagree with. "I had a professor once who was openly Marxist," said one student. "He and I got into several arguments in class, and I was worried that he would take it out on my grades. But as it turned out, he was very fair in grading me, and very helpful in going over my papers and that. He really wanted to help me better express my beliefs."

The Penn State administration, on the other hand, does a world-class job of diversity-mongering. Diversity initiatives abound, and the school devotes a good deal of hot air — not to mention Web site bandwidth — toward exclaiming its right thinking. The Web site prominently displays a quotation from President Graham Spanier, which reads: "We must join forces to deplore racism, sexism, homophobia, and anti-Semitism and other religious harassment. We must combat sexual violence. We must ward off all forms of discrimination that seek to find a home here."

For its talismans, the university employs not only anguished press releases, but also an event called Unity Week. Last year's events included a "Transgender Discussion Panel," a talk on "Living Between Danger and Love: Violence in Same-Sex Relationships," and a "Tolerance for the Millennium" forum. There was also a "Hate Crimes Awareness Day," complete with personal testimonies.

There is a large ideological bureaucracy to disseminate the doctrines of the diversity-and-tolerance cult, including a Multicultural Resource Center, a Center for Women Students, a Commission on Racial/Ethnic Diversity, a Commission on Lesbian, Gay, Bisexual, and Transgender Equity, and a Commission for Women.

There are also a number of programs targeted specifically at minority students. These include Fast Start, which provides mentoring services, and "A Guide for Minority Students," written by "Penn State professionals working in minority student recruitment and retention." Like-minded student groups include Project Growth, "a group of undergraduate students from a kaleidoscope of beliefs and backgrounds who have committed themselves to work for increased campus awareness of diversity." Penn State has produced a video series to train its faculty and staff how to be aware to issues of race, sex, gender, and sexual orientation. And there is a Campus Environment Team, a sort of roving band of ideological informers "that works intensively and proactively to address diversity issues, acts of intolerance, and related issues. The team meets once a week to review ongoing issues and make recommendations about handling them to appropriate university administrators and faculty."

There is even a five-year plan called the "Framework for Diversity," which requires each administrative unit to report on what it has done to "expose students to a variety of cultures and international perspectives," and to "develop a shared and inclusive understanding of diversity."

All of this indoctrination seems to have provoked a truly regrettable backlash, as in fall 2000 there were a number of violent and threatening incidents, including racist e-mails and an assault directed against lesbian students.

Student Life: How Happy Was My Valley

Penn State is in a rural and fairly isolated area of Pennsylvania; former Indiana University basketball coach Bob Knight once complained that going to State College was like going on a "camping trip." That riled up the Penn State student body, but many reportedly share his assessment. Some students used to big-city attractions and nightlife complain about the relative boredom of Happy Valley.

But in fact there is plenty to do. Penn State enjoys a vibrant and active cultural life. The performing arts program brings in top-notch musicians, dance groups, and theater troupes. Recent performances have ranged from Alanis Morissette to the Backstreet Boys to the St. Petersburg State Ballet. The Central Pennsylvania Festival of the Arts arrives in July. Furthermore, students themselves organize and participate in a wide variety of cultural and artistic events — there are hundreds of registered student organizations. There are also superb athletic facilities for those who are so inclined. Of course, Penn State is a Big Ten Conference school, so Nittany Lions basketball and football — especially football — as well as a dozen other NCAA Division I sports provide an abundant source of diversion for students and residents.

And there are advantages associated with Penn State's rural and agriculturally blessed location. The natural surroundings are beautiful, and skiing is just twenty minutes away. Hiking, mountain biking, and drives through the nearby Amish country are popular, and there is a farmer's market in town throughout the summer and most of the fall semester. Several recreational areas and parks are within easy driving distance; these are popular cites for picnics and boating. One student describes the physical campus as "not extraordinarily beautiful architecturally, but I've seen worse. The grounds are wonderful, spacious, and well kept." But it also sprawling.

Crime is relatively infrequent. "My impression is that people are not really concerned," says one student. "There is an on-campus escort service, but large numbers of residents don't even lock their doors here." However, given its comparatively peaceful location, it should be noted that Penn State is the site of a high number of forcible sex offenses, according to official statistics. There were seventeen of these crimes in 1999 (eight of which occurred in the residence halls). Otherwise, the crime rate on and around campus is rather low. Town-gown relations, however, are reportedly strained.

As freshmen, Penn State students are required to live in the university dorms. There are dorms organized according to gender or ethnicity, such as all-female, all-male, or all-Latino dorms, and according to special interests, such as engineering; the coed dorms are coed by floor. "In general, the university and especially the university housing office bend over backwards catering to minorities," says one student. "The residence hall staff are careful to acknowledge every possible ethnic or religious holiday," another student says. Not surprisingly, then, the residence hall orientation program is politically correct, but relatively low key. Furthermore, a student's personal morals or principles are generally respected by residence life staff. "If I had a problem with a roommate whose lifestyle I found offensive or immoral," one student says, "I could go to the residence hall staff and complain, and be given a new room or roommate within a day or two."

543

The so-called "east halls," where most of the freshman are placed, are said to be pretty raucous. There is also a large Greek system; it, along with football games, is the center of the campus drinking scene.

Pepperdine University

Seaver College
24255 Pacific Coast Highway
Malibu, CA 90263-4392
(310) 456-4000
www.pepperdine.edu

Total enrollment: 7,885
Undergraduates: 3,230
SAT ranges (Verbal/Math): 570-670 (V); 580-680 (M)
Applicants: 5,219
Accepted: 35%
Enrolled: 30%
Application deadline: January 15
Financial aid application deadline: April 1
Tuition: $24,050/$31,340
Core curriculum: Yes

Surf and Turf

In its relatively short existence, Pepperdine University has gained a reputation for being a conservative liberal arts school steeped with a healthy respect for religion — in today's academic world, it is often viewed as one of the traditionalists' shining cities on a hill while larger institutions suffer under the darkness of political correctness. This view is not entirely accurate, as some of the overwhelming influences of the academy at large have infiltrated Pepperdine over the years, but the school remains an attractive place for students interested in a relatively strong curriculum, a place where religion is valued, and a warm, friendly atmosphere in which to pursue their studies.

It also doesn't hurt that Pepperdine has one of the most beautiful campuses of any institution of higher education in the nation. Located about a half-hour away from the hectic environs of Los Angeles, the college is secluded from the fast-paced city in Malibu, where the university's undergraduate college and two of its four graduate programs are located. The campus is close to the beach, and the climate and the surf are added bonuses for students interested in pursuing their studies seriously.

The founder of Pepperdine also had that in mind. The university got off the ground in 1937 thanks to George Pepperdine, founder of Western Auto Supply Company. It was originally located in Los Angeles on thirty-four acres of land, but thanks to the support of a wealthy donor, the school was relocated to an 830-acre campus in Malibu that now serves as the home of Seaver College, its undergraduate arm, the School of Law, and the School of Public Policy. Mr. Pepperdine's vision for his namesake institution was "to help young men and women prepare themselves for a life of usefulness in this competitive world and to help them build a foundation of Christian character and faith which will survive the storms of life."

The emphasis on religion cannot be overstated; Pepperdine has a far more religious atmosphere than most schools today, and it has remained firm in its religious roots. George Pepperdine was a lifelong member of the Church of Christ, and the school not only remains affiliated with that denomination, but continues to assert that these Christian principles are central to its work — even though religious commitments on the part of students are not as common or steadfast as in the past.

While Pepperdine certainly advocates a traditional education, it is not as solid in that commitment as one might expect, compared to institutions like Hillsdale College, for example. But that notwithstanding, Pepperdine continues to offer students an enjoyable setting in which to learn, with small classes, ample opportunities for close instruction, and an atmosphere in which teaching is still considered the most important task of an instructor.

Academic Life: Pepperdine and the Salt of the Earth

Pepperdine University consists of five institutions — Seaver College, the undergraduate institution; the School of Law; the School of Business and Management; the Graduate School of Education and Psychology; and the School of Public Policy, the last of which opened its doors in 1997.

Seaver College offers a variety of disciplines in which to major; these are divided into seven divisions. The Division of Business Administration offers majors in accounting, business administration, and international business studies. The Communication Division offers, among others, majors in journalism, advertising, public relations, French, German, and Spanish. These two divisions are also the most popular.

The other divisions at Seaver are Humanities and Teacher Education; Natural Science; Religion; Fine Arts; and Social Science. Pepperdine is well known for its programs in business administration and sports medicine, and it offers a good economics program as well. Students may also pursue a bachelor of arts in international studies, specializing in one of the following areas: Asian studies, economic studies, European studies, international/intercultural communications studies, international management studies, political studies, and Latin American studies.

In order to graduate, students must complete the General Education Program, a major program, and elective courses for a total of 128 "semester units," according to Seaver College's catalog. Forty of these units must be in upper division courses, and a minimum of twenty-four upper-division units in the student's major must be earned from Seaver College.

The General Education Program is a far-reaching and intensive part of a student's experience at Pepperdine, and includes anywhere from seventeen to twenty courses plus two units of physical education, for a total obligation of sixty-five to seventy units. The catalog recommends that students complete these courses in their freshman and sophomore years, and for the most part, the courses cover traditional subject matter. There is a two-course sequence in English composition and literature required in a student's freshman year; a three-course religion sequence, with two of those courses covering the "History and Religion of Israel" and "Early Christianity"; a three-course sequence on Western heritage; three semesters (or the equivalent) of a foreign language; and one course in behavioral science (psychology or sociology).

But that's not all. The college also requires that students take two out of three courses in American heritage, selected by the student from "Economic Principles," "The United States of America," and the "American Political Process." In addition, students need to take one course in non-Western heritage. Even this last requirement, which at other institutions might be designed merely to plant trendy ideas into the heads of students, maintains a principled, traditional focus. Most of the offerings in the non-Western area are Asian studies courses.

The General Education Program also demands one course in a laboratory science course, such as "Principles of Biology"; one course in mathematics; one course on "Public Speaking and Rhetorical Analysis"; and a freshman seminar, designed to "build community among a small group of freshmen" and "provide academic and personal advice," according to the college catalogue.

The General Education requirements, according to one professor, "are heavy," but they do "provide the students with a balanced liberal arts education." This is especially noteworthy for students who major in business or communications-related fields, and who at other institutions might be exempted from whatever core curriculum exists.

Students also have the opportunity to participate in Pepperdine's Great Books Colloquium, "a four-course sequence on masterpieces of Western civilization," as described by the college. Enrollment in the program is limited, and prospective students should apply prior to their freshman years, but the requirements for getting in are easy enough: all one has to do is be eligible for English 101 (the beginning introductory composition course) and to possess "a willingness to commit oneself to the time and effort required by the courses," the course catalog states. "Students should be advised that the reading load is much heavier than that for the freshman composition courses, and that the writing assignments are comparable. However, past students have testified that the greater challenge has given them precisely what they desired from a university education: an opportunity to read fine works, rigorous training in writing and discussion, a forum for sharing ideas, and a close-knit group in which to grow intellectually."

Students who take these colloquium courses fulfill their English composition and literature requirements, the freshman seminar requirement, as well as portions of two other requirements. And the Great Books program is one of the highlights of a Pepperdine education — faculty *love* this program. "I think that, in addition to our international programs, that this is one of the jewels of the Pepperdine crown," says one. Another professor says with enthusiasm that the Great Books program is "where I have found the best students I've had."

Thanks to Pepperdine's small undergraduate population and close setting, getting to know the professors is much easier than at a larger school. "If you're a motivated student and you find professors who you hit it off with," a professor says, "you can do a lot of one-on-one." Students are similarly enthused about the close relationships they can have with faculty members. "I was able to go to his office hours and shoot the breeze about politics for hours," a student says of one of her teachers. "The faculty members are extremely accessible. I really feel spoiled; the personal attention available to every student is staggering. All of my teachers know my first and last name, and I maintain a personal relationship with many of my teachers."

Indeed, there are a number of truly outstanding professors at Pepperdine, though many, including James Q. Wilson and Ted V. McAllister in the School of Public Policy, generally do not teach undergraduate courses. Some of the best undergraduate faculty at Pepperdine include Ronald Batchelder in economics, Michael Ditmore in English, Darrel Colson and Michael Gose in Great Books, Don Thompson in mathematics, Stephen Monsma, Jeanne Heffernan, and J. Christopher Soper in political science, and Ronald Highfield in religion.

Only a few courses — primarily ones in religion and humanities — are taught in large lecture halls. Most of the courses at Pepperdine are quite small, numbering from between fifteen and forty students. The college boasts on its Web site that the average class size is seventeen, and that there is a student-to-faculty ratio of 13 to 1.

This undoubtedly has something to do with the fact that teaching, as opposed to research, is job one for Pepperdine faculty. While research is valued, two out of the four evaluations used when considering tenure and promotion have to do with teaching. "Here at Pepperdine, teaching is the priority," a faculty member says. "There's an increasing emphasis on research, but the teaching part is more important than ever."

In addition to the personal teaching available in Malibu, students can also participate in one of Pepperdine's many study abroad programs. Seaver College offers year-round residential programs in Germany, England, Italy, and Latin America, along with summer programs in Spain and France. There are also a number of special programs during the summer that students can participate in, including study in Israel. "The curriculum has been designed so that students may complete a substantial portion of their general education requirements while enrolled [in international programs]," the catalogue states. This allows, according to the catalogue, a "serious adventure in study and scholarship."

Political Life: Few Waves, but Some Ripples

Perception, it seems, isn't always reality. "The popular perception is that Pepperdine is a conservative place," one faculty member says. But then he adds, "that's pretty much the [perception of the] donors." One prominent alumnus who says he has "heard the horror stories for years" from conservative students says that "despite its conservative reputation, a host of conservative donors, and lavish alumni and Law School banquets featuring prominent conservative speakers, the fact of the matter is that conservative professors are nonexistent at Pepperdine when it comes to the courses that really affect a student's view on politics and government."

So while Pepperdine is notable for its traditional education, certain departments — notably political science and sociology — are known by those who notice such things to lean left. One student relates that in a sociology class, most of what the professor presented in class was "strictly liberal" — and among the exercises included watching the film *Roger and Me*, which was then used as the basis for an assignment to write about class structure. Another exercise in this course included playing Monopoly where there "were different standards for different classes of people, the moral being that as the rich get richer, the poor get poorer." She added that despite this, she has "not had any bad courses" during her time at Pepperdine.

Pepperdine's convocation requirement for graduation, in which students must attend fourteen lectures or concerts per term, features events that "are usually religious, sometimes political, and always liberal in nature," according to a student. "If there are conservative speakers, they never talk about politics, only religion." A case in point: Linda Chavez came to give a talk and spoke about religious issues, whereas Pepperdine also hosted a convocation with Elaine Brown, a former high-ranking member of the Black Panthers with an extremely controversial past, and she spoke entirely about politics, although she did quote the Bible a few times.

These influences aside, Pepperdine still is a very traditional campus where the faculty have near-total academic freedom. "I think it's pretty free," one professor says. "I never get harassed. . . . You can argue for whatever you want and you won't get fired. . . . People are too busy [for that type of thing]. You don't have that type of infighting."

Pepperdine faculty are also more free than at most colleges when it comes to discussing religious themes and values. "Students need to take three courses in religion," says a faculty member. "I would say that, in addition, many of the courses in the humanities also try to look at relevant issues from a Christian world view. But this is not done in an artificial manner. I would say that there is a greater freedom to discuss matters of morality and ethics with reference to traditional Christian values than you would find in a public university setting." The school, this professor says, has a "Christian mission, which is strong, but not stifling." Students report that many professors find ways to work Christian ideals into their disciplines naturally, without being overbearing.

Pepperdine is by no means a hotbed of political activity like Berkeley. Students on campus tend to be pretty apolitical. "Pepperdine is a noncontroversial, nonconfrontational kind of campus. It is politically boring," a student says. "The general attitude outside of religious hot topics is almost complete apathy." An alumnus says that "there aren't many organized liberal groups on campus as there are only about 2,500 students," and that "many students are from wealthy Republican families who sent their kids there to protect them from the ravages of popular culture. . . . Their views tend to reflect a hybrid between popular culture and the Republican views of their parents."

Student Life: Life's a Beach

Pepperdine, as one faculty member says, has no "town-gown relationship." For one thing, there's no town there; students have to drive most anywhere they want to go off campus. But Pepperdine does have many activities to keep students occupied — perhaps too many. "Sometimes there are too many social distractions, along with the beach, which keep students from studying," the professor says.

However, since most students are not looking for their college years to be like a monastic retreat, this will come as welcome news. West Los Angeles is only about thirty minutes away in light traffic (although that time can increase considerably if there is traffic and/or construction work) and is easy enough to get to: just hop on the Pacific Coast Highway and head south, and you'll eventually run into the city.

Plenty of Pepperdine students do just that. "Malibu is not exactly a college town, but Los Angeles has a lot to offer," one says. In Santa Monica, slightly closer than Los Angeles, students often go to the Third Street Promenade, home to all manner of stores, bars, and restaurants, and not far from the beach. Further to the east, students frequent bars and restaurants in the Hollywood area. Los Angeles itself has a host of cultural exhibits, sports teams, and other activities — enough so that no one will ever get bored. In Malibu itself, there are a lot of nice local restaurants, including the Malibu Inn, and the Malibu Yogurt shop is a popular student destination.

Pepperdine is one of the most crime-free campuses in the nation. Serious crime is unknown; reported burglaries have been decreasing and liquor and drug violations are substantially less frequent than at comparable institutions.

There's also a healthy attitude towards community service on campus, represented by Pepperdine's Step Forward Day. Students help pick up trash in Malibu, clean up local schools, and pack lunches for the homeless. "It is truly a thrill to see so many people involved," says a student.

Housing at Pepperdine is limited, but freshmen and sophomores under twenty-one that aren't living with their parents are required to live on campus. The university believes that "students profit more from living on campus than from living off campus," according to the catalogue. Life on campus is a comfortable existence, despite strict rules — no alcohol, no firearms, no candles, no pets, and no one from the opposite sex in your living area from 11 p.m. to 11 a.m. These rules are enforced by a regiment of resident and student advisors.

Incoming freshmen live in suites shared by eight students, each suite having a double bathroom (two showers, two sinks, two commodes), a living area, and four double bedrooms. The suites are clustered six to a hall surrounding a main lobby with a fireplace, television, and laundry room. Out of the twenty-three residence halls on campus, twenty-two are designed along these lines. The remaining residence hall is a tower complex reserved for sophomores and upperclassmen. This complex holds about 275 students, and has six wings — two for men, four for women. The tower has all double rooms, and each two doubles share a bathroom.

While many upperclassmen live off-campus, they also have a shot at homes in two apartment complexes offering two-bedroom apartments for four people, with a shared kitchen, living/dining area, and bathroom.

For on-campus activities, there is a the Howard A. White Center, a twenty-four-hour recreational facility where students can play Ping-Pong or billiards, or watch television on a big screen.

Pepperdine also has a number of competitive athletic programs. The Waves, as Pepperdine's teams are known, are well known in water polo and volleyball circles, and its basketball team performed admirably in the 2000 NCAA Division I. For lesser athletes, there is also a variety of club and intramural sports that students can participate in. And of course, spectatorship is popular as well. "The homecoming basketball game is huge — everyone from the school goes, packs into the Firestone Fieldhouse, and the camaraderie is amazing," a student says. "We all stormed the court when we beat Gonzaga this year."

But it is Pepperdine's religious side that draws many students, and Pepperdine expects its students to pursue religious interests. The college strongly encourages students to join a church, and it offers Seaver-wide worship assemblies, devotionals, small-group Bible study, and an on-campus ministry. Recent freshmen orientation programs even made a number of references to students meeting their future spouses at school. "There were a few faculty members who gave speeches and mentioned over and over the possibility that our future spouses were here at college," says one freshman. "They did not advocate or push this idea of marriage, exactly, but the mention of it so many times was a little bizarre."

This student notes that "the first three questions many students ask when they meet you are, 'What is your name?,' 'What is your major?,' and 'What church do you attend?'" We can answer the latter of these: 80 percent of the students at Pepperdine say they come from a Christian religious background, with Roman Catholicism the most prevalent (17.6 percent), and the Church of Christ close behind (16.9 percent, and increasing). The university is careful to note in its student catalogue that services are held every Sunday and Wednesday at the Malibu Church of Christ, but also points out that other religious groups maintain congregations nearby and welcome students.

Pepperdine's strong religious tradition is one of its many strengths. The quality of its general education requirements, the close relationships it fosters between professors and students, and that religious tradition combined with what one professor terms as a "healthy mix between the devout and the not-so-devout" makes Pepperdine, while not as conservative as one might expect, a good choice for a student looking to receive a traditional education.

Princeton University

Admission Office Box 430
Princeton University
Princeton, New Jersey 08544-0430
(609) 258-3060
www.princeton.edu

Total enrollment: 6,350
Undergraduates: 4,600
SAT ranges (Verbal/Math): 680-770 (V); 690-770 (M)
Applicants: 13,654
Accepted: 12%
Enrolled: 70%
Application deadline: January 2
Financial aid application deadline: February 1
Tuition: $26,160/$33,613
Core curriculum: No

What More Can Be Said

Founded in 1746 as the College of New Jersey, Princeton University occupies a unique position in American higher education. The lovely town of Princeton, equidistant from New York City and Philadelphia, is easy on the eyes if hard on the wallet. The campus itself is among the most beautiful in the country, with stone Gothic buildings, Georgian brick structures, and a smattering of modernist creations scattered among hardwood trees and ubiquitous ivy. Along with Dartmouth College, Princeton is an undergraduate's Ivy League school, as students have access to many full professors from their first days on campus.

Princeton is leading the way in doing away with the burden of debt from student loans that many undergraduates carry with them into the business world. The school has announced a new program that will replace student loans with scholarships. According the school's Web site, "Princeton is the first of its peer institutions — and, except for the service academies, possibly the first American university — to announce that aid recipients will not be required to borrow to pay for college." This is marvelous news for undergraduates not only at Princeton, but across the nation. As a trend-setter, Princeton's move will most likely be followed by other institutions.

The school also has a reputation as being a bit — just a bit — more traditional than its peers, although campus politics are overall left of center. But for a top-flight student with the necessary credentials and luck to be admitted, it provides a valuable degree along with plenty of intellectual and moral challenges. As at other elite schools, Princeton harbors a small yet vocal faction of radical students who can rely on the "tolerant" ethos of the modern university to bully their colleagues into silence. Yet, as one professor says, students who "seek out small courses, of which there are plenty, and departments that are not overburdened" will "get an absolutely first-rate education." The key is to know where to look, what to avoid, and what to expect. The place is, after all, Princeton.

Academic Life: Bright Minds on Their Own

Princeton abandoned its core curriculum many years ago and now follows the standard plan of distribution requirements common in American universities. "Princeton still has a fair number of requirements intended to provide students with a broad liberal arts education," a professor says. "How well the requirements work is another question." The catalogue states: "There are no required courses; instead the areas encourage students to make choices that best suit their intellectual curiosity and academic goals." A student notes: "Princeton is perceived to be somewhere between Brown, without any core requirements, and Columbia, with a solid core curriculum. Students work out a distribution of classes to fulfill requirements — hence the element of choice within a set of requirements."

Students must take courses in seven groups: Epistemology and Cognition (one course selected from anthropology, philosophy, psychology, and linguistics); Ethical Thought and Moral Values (one course in philosophy, politics, or religion); Historical Analysis (one course in classics, East Asian studies, history, Near Eastern studies, or religion); Literature and the Arts (two courses); Quantitative Reasoning (one course in mathematics, computer science, operations research, or financial engineering); Science and Technology (two courses, with labs); and Social Analysis (two courses). There is also a foreign language requirement.

None of the requirements is terribly specific. For example, no American history is required, nor is the study of Western civilization stipulated, although most students will study some element of it at some point. Still, students may fill much of their academic record with classes that are either unimportant (if not potentially damaging to naïve students) or so marginal as to be useless in a program of general study. The Epistemology and Cognition requirement may be fulfilled with "Race, Class, and Intelligence in America." The Historical Analysis requirement can be taken care of with "Sex, Sexuality, and Gender" or "The Transatlantic Sixties: Culture and Politics in Europe and the United States." In the Literature and the Arts group, one could take "Women in Film," "Sexuality and Desire in Modern Japan," or "The Literatures of U.S. Women of Color."

The Social Analysis component, which the catalogue says is "designed to familiarize students with different approaches to the study of social life and to introduce them to modes of thinking about social institutions and cultural norms and their interconnectedness with forms of human behavior," also includes its share of courses taught with a point of view rather than with a point. Examples are "Law and the Politics of Race" and "Inequality: Class, Race, and Gender." Note though, that there are also solid offerings in all required areas, and that the looseness of the requirements makes it possible to avoid politicized courses, for the most part.

Among the most respected academic traditions at Princeton are the junior papers required of each liberal arts major and a senior thesis that must be written by most every undergraduate. (Some departments require two papers, and other require just one. Science departments usually require some sort of research project from juniors.) Students work with a faculty member of their choice to complete the papers, which average about thirty pages. This emphasis on independent study, which colors the upperclassmen's experience at Princeton, makes choosing a good concentration (major) and professor all the more important. With a good faculty member who is genuinely concerned about his student's intellectual progress, such a curriculum can give a tremendous boost to one's career and life.

The honor code, adopted in 1893, is another respected, time-honored Princeton tradition that still receives almost universal student support. Students must sign the code as a condition of admission. Under the terms of the code, students must write on each examination paper: "I pledge my honor that I have not violated the honor code during this examination." And the code seems to work: exams are not proctored, yet cheating is extremely rare, students and faculty say. Violations are the province of the undergraduate Honor Committee, a rather secretive body that recommends penalties to the university president. Punishment can include suspension or permanent expulsion.

Nationally, the best students apply to more schools than ever before. This means that highly competitive schools like Princeton are more difficult to get into than at any time in their long histories. While freshmen are still very good, the increased competition stems largely from an increase in numbers. This means also that, at the top of the application pile for any Ivy (and especially for Princeton, Yale, and Harvard), many applicants are round filed rather than accepted more as a result of chance than merit. "Some freshmen are extremely well prepared, while some — many — are not," says one professor. Princeton has plans to add an additional five hundred undergraduates over the next few years, but it remains to be seen if the new slots will indeed go to the most qualified applicants. "If the statistics are correct, it is already the case that classes have been getting stronger academically for years now," the professor says. "I must say that this improvement is not obvious to me." Another professor says freshmen of late have been less prepared in the humanities, but that many arrive with better science and computer skills than in the past. A third professor has not noted a decline in students' preparation, but says that "the admissions office seems to give a good deal of weight to accomplishments in athletics and the arts."

A prominent professor worries that additional undergraduates will exacerbate the trend away from emphasizing undergraduate teaching found at so many other schools but, until now, held more at bay at Princeton than at its peers. "One way in which Princeton has changed dramatically from [twenty years ago] is in the diminished contact of faculty with undergraduates. Princeton has claimed to have the virtues of both a small liberal arts college and a great research university. [Years ago], the small liberal arts part was honored more than it is now." Unfortunately, the professor says, "undergraduates are increasingly likely to have graduate students as their [teaching assistants], and it is not unusual for students to have no real contact with faculty until their junior year when they already have a major." Another professor agrees: "I expect that in ten years Princeton will have moved even farther from the small college part of its self-image."

But for now, says a student, "Princeton's main strength academically is the emphasis the school places upon undergraduate education. This means that undergraduates receive instruction from the most notable faculty members here." On the other hand, this source continues, "Students must remember that most notable professors are known for their scholarship and not necessarily for their teaching."

There are many superb professors at Princeton. Professors and students name the following as among the best: Peter Lake, James M. McPherson, Anthony Grafton, Steve Kotkin, Peter R. Brown, and William C. Jordan in history; Steven F. Cohen, Robert George, Patrick Deneen, Stephen Macedo, Keith Whittington, and Paul Sigmund in politics; Aaron Friedberg, Jeffrey Herbst, and Henry S. Bienen with joint appointments in politics and the Woodrow Wilson School of Public and International Affairs; Viviana Zelizer, Paul Starr, Thomas Espenshade, Sara McLanahan, and Robert Wuthnow in sociology; Burton Malkiel, Alan S. Blinder, and Harvey S. Rosen in economics; Martha Himmelfarb, R. Marie Griffith, and Leigh Schmidt in religion; John Fleming, D. Vance Smith, Oliver Arnold, James Richardson, and Joanna Picciotto in English; Saul A. Kripke and Harry Frankfurt in philosophy; Robert Hollander in comparative literature; and Michael Sugrue in humanities.

Among departments, the strongest include history, which is among the best in the nation, economics, mathematics, physics, philosophy, religion, classics, and the Woodrow Wilson School of Public Policy. One person on campus says "the physics, mathematics, and philosophy departments are the best in the world, period." A professor says that history, "despite its faculty, is far less politicized than one might expect." The most politicized include English and comparative literature.

An exciting recent development at Princeton is the establishment of the James Madison Program in American Ideals and Institutions under the Directorship of Robert P. George, an outspoken conservative professor in the Department of Politics. The Madison Program does not offer a major, but will host lectures and conferences to which undergraduate students are invited. It will also develop courses to be offered by George and others in Politics.

On a less encouraging note, grade inflation is a problem at Princeton, as it is at most universities across the country. A graduate student reports: "The greatest academic difficulty at Princeton is grade inflation. Because Princeton students have done well in high school, they desire to maintain their standing through their college career." This person adds that, given the high expectations from both students and parents, the pressure for students to attain high grades "even when unmerited, is constant." Also, says this source, "The university has a number of cumbersome structures in place to force graduate students and faculty to justify grades below C-given to any undergraduates. In fairness, it should be noted that professors are faced with a difficult dilemma: assign grades strictly on merit and watch as their students are denied entry to the better graduate and professional schools; or go along with the now-accepted practice of grading everyone as above average. Students may opt for a "Pass/D/Fail Option" in up to four classes, a strategy intended to allow students to take riskier classes but that, in fact, merely allows them to work less in difficult math or science classes. Still, the opportunity for earning a "D" will give some students pause when choosing this option.

The school offers advisors in the residential colleges and among the faculty of a student's concentration, but students must be prudent, ask trusted friends about professors, and of course follow their instincts. Students should "choose courses carefully and get advice from faculty members who have proven their love of learning," says one professor. A graduate student adds that "faculty members advise students, but the quality of advising is uneven."

A graduate student observes: "Princeton's student population is bright and gifted, though their motivation is largely pre-professional. Each one is smart but wants to make something of himself or herself in commerce, public affairs, law, or medicine." Given this, many professors say that students at Princeton should take advantage of the liberal arts opportunities there, even at the expense of resume-building professional training. (A degree from Princeton itself goes a long way toward opening career doors of any kind.) "This is college; forget about your career," a professor says. "Nobody from Princeton starves and they should seek truth." Says another: "I'd advise them to use the best things Princeton has to offer — small classes, ample opportunity to work closely with a distinguished faculty, great academic and intellectual resources — as fully as they can, and let the New Economy take care of itself until they're ready to leave the university." Only students drawn intellectually to the more technical concentrations, such as computer science, should pursue them in college, this person adds.

Yet another professor advises new students to seek departments that aren't too crowded already. "Students seem to feel that to get the right finance job they need to be economics majors," this person says. Yet "this has left the economics department terribly overenrolled, with predictable results for the quality of teaching and advising." Students desiring to make themselves more marketable might consider adding a certificate program, or minor, in a more salable field. "It may be that the certificate programs in finance and computer science will allow students to major in other fields while still making themselves competitive for the kinds of jobs they hope for," this professor says.

Political Atmosphere: Generally Princely

Princeton, along with a handful of the very best universities, offers so much that is good that the 12 percent of students who are admitted should attend in spite of the number of radicals among the professoriate and student body. The radicals, powerful though they may be, are far from a majority and can be avoided if one knows where to look. But the student who arrives unprepared and naïve, or who is more a follower than leader, can be very badly damaged, spiritually and intellectually, by some of the forces one finds there.

Harold Shapiro, Princeton's president, will retire soon after this essay is published. When asked what they would like to see in his replacement, one professor says: "I'd like to see a view of the world that values scholarship that won't necessarily land us in the *New York Times*." Adds another, "All I ask for is for someone open to a bit of *intellectual* diversity." This is seconded by a closer observer of Princeton's recent history: "Harold Shapiro is leaving, but the prospects for the future are not looking bright for a diverse set of viewpoints being expressed on campus. Although President Shapiro was maligned by his critics, there are far worse possibilities looming." As these comments reveal, the dominant stance among professors is a *Times-*

editorial stance — a common mentality among academics. Yet even *Times*-style intellectuals can teach well; it's their intellectually less critical colleagues, in cahoots with various university administrators and students, who can cheat their charges of an education.

Nowhere has this situation become so clear as in the appointment of Australian bioethicist Peter Singer to the Ira W. Camp chair in bioethics at the University Center for Human Values. Because he holds very controversial views on euthanasia and infanticide, and believes that humans are not privileged creatures, his appointment was greeted with much criticism. The *Newark Star-Ledger* reported that Singer "has said that it may be more humane to kill a disabled newborn than to let the infant live." The paper continued, "This would extend to infants with treatable diseases such as hemophilia." This report is affirmed in Singer's book, *Practical Ethics,* excerpted in the *New York Times,* in which he asks: "[I]f the hemophiliac child is killed, will his parents have another child whom they would not have had if the hemophiliac child lives? If they would, is the second child likely to have a better life than the one killed? Often it will be possible to answer both these questions affirmatively." He continues, "The main point is clear: killing a disabled infant is not morally equivalent to killing a person. Very often it is not wrong at all." Carrying his thoughts to their logical conclusion, Singer also wrote a positive review on a book about bestiality. Writing for a soft porn site, the ethicist claimed that "mutually satisfying activities may develop" between owners and their pets — i.e., bestiality.

On Singer's first day of class at Princeton, some 250 demonstrators, many disabled and in wheel chairs, showed up to voice their fears that his appointment would lend intellectual respectability to a philosophy that would see them as something less than fully human. The administration has stood behind its appointment of Singer and had the demonstrators arrested — even though the more common administration response to protests by radical student groups is a promise to remedy any wrong, whether feigned or real. In the Singer case, Princeton pleads "academic freedom."

On the other hand, the embarrassment caused by Singer's presence seems to have played a role in the university's decision to allow the creation of the aforementioned James Madison Program in American Ideals and Institutions. Headed by conservative politics professor Robert P. George, this program will serve somewhat as a counterweight to the radicalism at the University Center for Human Values.

The Office of Student Life includes, among other things, Health Services, which not only refers students for abortions, but provides contraceptives and offers the controversial "morning after pill." There are allegations that the university uses a secret fund to pay for abortions; one Texas organization that provides abortion malpractice litigation support has even advertised in the *Daily Princetonian* to let students know that if they are injured during an abortion paid for by the university, they might have grounds for a lawsuit. The Office, however, is said to be fairly even-handed in giving money to student organizations.

Health Services also runs the Sexual Harassment/Assault Advising, Resources, and Education (SHARE) Program. SHARE puts out a booklet called "The Source: A Resource Guide for the Lesbian, Gay, Bisexual and Transgendered Community and Friends," and also sponsors a peer education program entitled "Sex on a Saturday Night," which incoming freshman are required to attend. After seeing graphic depictions of sexual practices and a condom-use demonstration, one student tried to walk out of one of these required meetings. She was physically barred from leaving by one of the residential advisors.

Students at Princeton, as at most other modern universities, can define themselves just about any way they choose. One student wrote about his "coming out" as gay on the university's gay organization's Web site:

> I thought that would be impossible [as Princeton] was considered by many to be the most conservative Ivy of them all. Fortunately, that has not been the case. My experience here has been an overwhelmingly positive one, and although the coming out process itself was difficult due to a fairly small campus community, those that were here were very supportive, as were, to my surprise, most of my straight friends. To be sure, there are some scary incidents — but fortunately, they have seemed much milder than those which occur on other campus [sic], and are mitigated by the very strong support of the administration for the LGBT [Lesbian/Gay/Bisexual/Transgendered] community.

As the last line of his statement indicates, the administration at Princeton takes not a hands-off approach to this sensitive topic, but a proactive stance that affirms students decisions to engage in risky behavior.

Student Life: Members of the Club

Princeton is as ideal a college town as one is likely to find, but with a genteel twist. Unlike, say, Ann Arbor or Berkeley, Princeton is small, very upper class, and colonial in origins. Only a short train ride from New York and Philadelphia, it offers easy access to major metropolitan areas, but is a pedestrian-oriented town filled with upscale shops and several fine restaurants (although residents say it needs more of the latter). Pedestrians can generally assume that automobiles really will stop and allow them to cross the road — an assumption that could have drastic consequences in many locales.

All housing in Princeton's residential colleges is coed and 97 percent of undergraduates live on campus. Underclassmen dine at their residential colleges, but about 75 percent of juniors and seniors eat at one of the eleven private eating clubs. In fact, much of the social life at Princeton is centered on the eating clubs housed in the beautiful mansions of Prospect Street. "Campus life if centered around Prospect Street and the eating clubs there," says one student. Admission to five of the clubs is highly competitive; several of them use a "bicker process" to select their members. "The bicker process is similar to a fraternity rush," a student says. "The various eating clubs throw parties, and occasionally they will host bands to play for their guests. . . . Once you have decided which club you would like to belong to, you put your name on a list. However, not every one gets in. . . . A lot depends on who you know." Groups of friends have been known to split up when some are chosen above others. Even acceptance into the nonselective clubs is not guaranteed, as remaining membership slots are given out via lottery. Once student notes: "People may not realize that all eating clubs do not include the "bicker" process. I myself joined a 'non-bicker' club with several of my friends, where by signing-in early we assured that we would all be in the same club. Our club has brought lots of big bands this year and it's a lot of fun."

The university's undergraduate and graduate students are the beneficiaries of the university's massive endowment — the largest per capita endowment of any college or university in the country, and one that has doubled from about $4 billion to $8 billion in the last five years. This money has bought some of the country's best facilities for housing, athletics, research, and social life, in addition to the most generous financial aid packages in the Ivy League. Among Princeton's finest assets is the Firestone Library, which was one of the largest libraries in the world even before its recent expansion. The university's art center and museum have just been completely renovated, and a new molecular biology building ranks among the nation's top undergraduate research facilities in that field. Computer facilities at Princeton are abundant and easily accessible to students. And a new student center, the First Campus Center, "appears to be helping draw together faculty, graduate students, and undergraduates into a common space with a variety of culinary options," says a student.

A whopping 65 percent of alumni donate money to Princeton, an indication of the value they place on their experience there. This is the highest rate of alumni giving in the country — only one other college (Dartmouth) has more than half its alumni as financial contributors.

Athletics at Princeton is strongly supported by the administration; one student says the admissions policy is designed to favor "the perfect athlete-student." Besides the thirty-eight intercollegiate teams, the university sponsors forty club teams and many intramural sports. Again, the facilities are excellent. They include a superior aquatics center, a golf course, an ice rink, an Olympic-level water course for crew and sailing races, a 6,500-seat gymnasium, and a new 30,000-seat football stadium, packed for games against rivals Yale and Harvard. The athletic program claimed fourteen Ivy League championships in one recent year.

Crime is not a serious problem in Princeton because it is an upscale community. Students are advised to be careful and to look after their belongings, however.

Professors say that Princeton's students generally vote Democratic and are very sociable. "Opinion at Princeton is quite varied, but the majority seem to be mainstream Democrats," says one teacher. Another adds, "Despite Princeton's reputation (probably deserved) for being less liberal than the competition, I would be extremely surprised if students didn't vote Democratic by a large majority." Still, conservatives are well represented and the pro-life voice is louder than ever. "Princeton always has a good group of active conservative students," says another professor. "Many of those in the group are among the intellectually strongest undergraduates in the university. Their wits have been sharpened by intellectual battle."

Providence College

Office of Admission
Harkins Hall 222
549 River Avenue
Providence, RI 02918-0002
(800) 721-6444
www.providence.edu

Total enrollment: 5,442
Undergraduates: 3,751
SAT ranges (Verbal/Math): 540-630 (V); 540-630 (M)
Applicants: 5,328
Accepted: 60%
Enrolled: 31%
Application deadline: February 1
Financial aid application deadline: February 1
Tuition: $18,750/$26,375
Core curriculum: Yes

A Different "PC" — The One in Rhode Island

Providence College is an up-and-coming small liberal arts college that deserves a larger national reputation than it currently enjoys. Founded in 1917 (and opened two years later) by the Order of Friars Preachers, or Dominicans, it offers its students a rigorous liberal arts education, a true core curriculum, a faculty that actually teaches its students, and a tradition of higher learning dating back to St. Dominic, the thirteenth-century monk. Yet students matriculating there are not transported to a museum of Catholicism or a place in which piety trumps intellectual merit; they attend a modern college that prepares them for life in the world by schooling them in timeless truths.

Providence College's mission statement reads: "The college actively cultivates intellectual, spiritual, ethical and aesthetic values within the context of the Judaeo-Christian heritage. These values are nurtured by the unique tradition of the Dominican Order, which emphasizes quality teaching and scholarship." And the message from the president on the school's Web site deserves attention: "[W]e believe that education is much more than the curriculum and the classroom. Knowledge alone is not enough. Some of the worst atrocities in history have been committed by people who were learned, cultured, and patrons of the arts. Learning must be combined with moral and spiritual growth, must be joined to moral choices that affirm the human and foster community."

The school is known colloquially as PC — letters that have recently come to stand for "political correctness." There is rich irony in this shorthand, for PC is generally politically *in*correct if that term means a place where the Western tradition is taught, argued over, and presented in its fullness rather than facilely dismissed. There are very few shallow options at Providence, and students can expect to find an accessible and concerned faculty that expects great things from them both inside and out of the classroom. The school is a unique institution that deserves a closer look by students from beyond its native New England. If you're looking for an education for life rather than a high-priced vocational school, or a place where PC has a different meaning, Providence College deserves to be on your short list.

Academic Life: What You Need to Know

Unlike most of America's 1,855 baccalaureate institutions, Providence College has never abandoned its core curriculum. This represents a faith that every student can be provided a broad liberal arts education and that this education will prepare them for life and for any career. This educational philosophy might be summed up: students are taught; employees are trained. The centerpiece of the core is a two-year series of team-taught classes called the Development of Western Civilization (DWC).

The syllabus for these classes leaves little room for doubting either their academic rigor or the integrity of their content. Under "Policies and Procedures," students will find: "It is expected that those assignments will have been completed before the class, and that you will bring the appropriate textbooks to the class. Failing to do either of these diminishes the course for yourself and others." And, "Attendance at all lectures is expected," along with "Quizzes and examinations must be taken when scheduled. Only serious health, personal reasons, or legitimate school-related activities" will result in an excuse being given.

Once in class, students study Western civilization from ancient Mesopotamia through the Byzantine and Islamic Empires during the first semester, and the Middle Ages through the seventeenth century in the second. During their sophomore years, their studies take them from Absolutism in France until the late nineteenth century in the fall, and the end of spring semester finds them all the way to the collapse of communism and the pontificate of John Paul II.

These classes are quite comprehensive in their efforts to cover a variety of disciplines — history, art, philosophy, theology, and literature — which is one of the reasons they're team taught. Such an approach draws upon the strengths of four professors rather than searching for a polymath to cover every field of knowledge over the past several thousand years. "[It is] one of the truly outstanding courses in American higher education," a professor says. "The staff works consciously to integrate the disciplines so that students are getting political history, intellectual history, and cultural history all at once."

Having said that, we would like to see Providence drop its use of secondary source textbooks in DWC and adopt primary sources as the principal means by which students are exposed to the West. No textbook can substitute for the real thing, and Providence would take its curriculum up several notches if it simply assigned Homer's *Iliad,* say, rather than snippets of it culled from a textbook. Such a move, modeled on the curricula of Columbia University's readings of previous decades, or the University of Michigan's Honors College Great Books classes, would give reason for taking PC's academic claims more seriously. In an otherwise strong course, the omission of primary sources is a self-inflicted and unnecessary wound.

Requirements for the course are fairly extensive, though not backbreaking. Says a faculty member: "All students are required to do ten pages of writing every semester. There are no graduate students teaching or part-timers or anything of that sort. Senior professors make up a sizable percentage of the staff. Each professor attends all the lectures . . . so in their own lectures they can play off their colleague's work and . . . be prepared to lead a discussion in the seminars. Integration of the material is a prime concern." Students learn what any good student of Western culture knows: that the West is far from the hegemonic, homogeneous force caricatured by its critics. "Along the way we show how truly diverse Western Civilization is," notes someone who teaches the class. "There is nothing triumphalistic about the course; we show the majesty and the madness."

As for student quality, Providence, like many other institutions, has benefited from the tendency of high school students to apply to an ever-growing number of universities and colleges. This has spread the wealth of good students among the non-Ivies even as it has, some argue, consolidated their hold on the most competitive students. "The quality of the students has improved substantially over the time I have taught here," says a professor with several decades at Providence. "They are mentally quicker, more broadly aware, and they write better." This teacher notes, however, that today's high schools still do not prepare students for college as well as they did thirty years ago.

In 1994, Providence began awarding only merit-based scholarships while simultaneously greatly increasing the amount of money available. "The results have been dramatic, as the rising tide has lifted a good number of boats — which is to say that the merit scholarship students have had a strong positive effect in the classroom and on academic life more broadly conceived," a professor says.

As for the best options, sources recommend the humanities major, which requires two years of a foreign language and twelve courses in the traditional humanities disciplines. The strongest departments are biology, chemistry, history, English, political science, and theology. Among the weakest are education (a sure bet on most campuses to be among the least challenging majors), marketing, and management.

Excellent teachers include Rodney Delasanta, Anthony Esolen, Terrie Curran, Brian Barbour, Ellen Goodman, Alexandra Mullen, and Stephen Lynch in English; David Lewis Stokes and Patrick Reid in theology; Joan Branham in art history; Mario DiNunzio and Richard Grace in history; Joseph Guido, O.P., in psychology; William Hudson in political science; and Donald Kehew in philosophy.

Providence is conservative in another important way: It has not joined the legions of small liberal arts colleges that expect professors to produce major publications at a research-university pace and at the expense of teaching. Tenure remains a teaching decision, though promotion is in some cases a publication decision. "We are blessed with many fine, serious teachers, and it is possible to rise to the [tenured] associate professor level largely, though not exclusively, on the strength of teaching and service," a professor says. This is in keeping with the school's mission as a teaching college first and is a welcome sign of administrative sanity.

Political Atmosphere: Providentially Strong

Providence College is not immune to political pressures, but it withstands them better than most schools do. It has maintained its Catholic character to a greater degree than many other nominally Catholic schools. There have been significant, tense debates on the curriculum, hiring, and the general mission of the school, according to a professor. "At the end of the '80s, some of us brought to the fore the question about the college's Catholic identity," this professor says. "Was it going to be maintained? If so, how? For about a year there was a good deal of wrangling; speakers were brought in, symposia were held, attempts were made to learn from other 'models,' such as Notre Dame of the Jesuit schools. The issue of hiring was a central one and caused a good deal of rancor." Yet things turned out well. "A vote of the entire faculty showed an overwhelming desire to remain Catholic in a serious way. There is of course a minority who would have it otherwise."

The curriculum was debated in the late '90s, and many members of social science departments were and are determined to water down the DWC core courses. The push failed. "Last year a group of largely the same people were determined to put through a 'diversity' requirement," a professor says. "This effort also failed for two reasons: those pushing the idea were unable to define 'diversity' in any coherent and satisfying way; and the president said that any requirement would have to be consistent with the College's mission statement. This last requirement led to the collapse of the effort."

How has PC remained Catholic in spite of the general hostility among academics to any traditional intellectual life and internal opposition by social scientists? "Leadership has been generally — one might say, providentially — strong," a professor says. "While it is true that it was lay initiative that first forced the issue, the presidents have been committed to being Catholic in an integral way." Furthermore, the college community recognized that "the college has a right to exist in that way and that hiring would have to in some way be involved," the professor says. All candidates for full-time positions must give a written response to the college's mission statement in order to be considered. Laymen played a large role in these decision, says another source: "There is a solid group of lay Catholic intellectuals who want the college to be both genuinely Catholic and academically excellent. And the Dominicans still retain a great deal of power at the level of the trustees."

One area that the Dominicans could exercise more control over is the Balfour Center for Multicultural Affairs, which bills itself as "A Tapestry of Cultural Diversity at Providence College." The opening line in the Web site's description: "Imagine a place where all are welcome, accepted, and valued. In this place, each individual's contribution is encouraged and becomes a part of the tapestry needed to enlighten and inform others . . . A place to celebrate differences." This cliché-ridden description is meant to imply that the remainder of campus is somehow less sensitive, less open to "each individual's contribution," less enlightened — hence the need to spread their tolerant view of the world.

The Balfour Center, founded as the Office for Minority Student Affairs and renamed in 1994, also awards a number of scholarships, some set aside for minorities. This gives it some degree of power on campus, because it makes those students beholden to it and obligates the administration to turn a blind eye toward its more activist mission. It's a simple trade-off: the administration can show off some minority students, virtually cost-free, and the center can rest assured of significantly less interference in its internal affairs than its politics might otherwise attract at a school such as PC. Sources report that the center is cause for worry because it is a rallying point for faculty members and administrators who want to bring about fundamental change to the college's character and mission.

And yet there are indeed behavioral boundaries on campus, as three students discovered when they plastered the campus with blue pro-abortion fliers that pictured a marble statue of the Virgin Mary (blue is the color associated with her) with the inscription: "How's this for an immaculate concept: Keep Abortion Safe and Legal." The students were expelled and fined $1,000 each — a very gutsy move on the part of the school's president, the Rev. Philip A. Smith. Fr. Smith issued a statement that was reported in the *Chronicle of Higher Education:* "Their action was determined to be a deliberate misuse of the image of the Blessed Virgin, a venerated person important to Catholic and Christian belief, to promote an activity that is morally offensive and contrary to the teachings of the Catholic Church and the mission of Providence College." According to the *Chronicle,* campus administrators and students tore the fliers down "immediately after they were posted." While such actions on the part of the administration would have been commonplace forty years ago, the homogenization of higher education in America has undermined the sense of identity that makes such actions possible on most campuses. It is an indication of PC's commitment to its mission — and the courage of its president — that moral limits still exist on his campus.

Unfortunately, some agencies know no limits when it comes to strong-arming colleges and universities. The national accrediting agency, without whose imprimatur no college is taken seriously, requires every department and program, as one professor puts it, to "engage in the kind of 'assessing' that one used to associate with education departments and other bastions of non-thought, seat warming, and time wasting." This mandates that professors "draw up a long list of outcomes [from each class] and then draw up more lists of how these outcomes will be measured. And then we must write reports about how these measurements measured up!" This process, described by the professor as an "endless, fruitless, aimless process that wastes enormous amounts of time and energy and has nothing to do with the life of the mind," is typical of the types of regulations even small schools like PC must adhere to in order to remain "legitimate." Perhaps it's time for such schools to look for a new accrediting agency that cares more about the life of the mind than busy work to justify its own existence.

Student Life: No Man Is a Rhode Island

The small size of Providence College and the commitment of the faculty to the welfare of their students makes for an inviting atmosphere. The college lies on 105 acres in a residential section of Providence, Rhode Island. The 3,700 students hail from forty-two states and nine foreign countries, an indication that the school does seek a national student body.

Residence halls (there are nine) are guaranteed to freshmen and sophomores, who (except for commuters and married students) are required to live on campus. Halls are both coed and single sex. There are also apartments for students beyond their freshman year. Juniors and seniors wishing to live off-campus must obtain the permission of the school. There is no browbeating involved in student orientation.

However, because of a larger than expected influx of freshmen in the current year, more than 170 students who applied to live in campus apartments were turned down, according to the campus newspaper, *The Cowl*. According to the paper, the one thousand students in the class of '02 filled on-campus housing very quickly, a move that sent juniors scrambling for the apartments in greater numbers than usual. The increase reveals a greater percentage of students accepting admission to PC than the admissions office anticipated, which is a good sign of the school's increased prestige. In earlier years juniors regularly moved into on-campus apartments and were, according to the paper, told by tour leaders during their campus visits that this would occur. Some thirty to thirty-five seniors were required to live off-campus because of this unprecedented crunch.

Crime statistics reveal a fairly safe campus. On the campus itself, one robbery occurred in 1997 and none in the following two years. There were six aggravated assaults on campus (but none in residence halls) in 1998 and three in 1999; ten burglaries on campus in '98 (none in dorms) and fifteen in '99 (including 8 in dorms). One on-campus arson was reported in 1998. Three motor vehicle thefts occurred in both 1997 and 1998 and 6 in 1999. There were no murders or forcible sex offenses in those years.

Providence is a vibrant city with a good cultural life. Brown University and the University of Rhode Island share the colonial city with PC, and both schools have active speaker programs and cultural events that are open to others. The Providence Performing Arts Center hosts national touring groups for plays, ballets, and other events.

For those looking for other forms of entertainment, the Bruins, a top-level farm team for the NHL's Boston Bruins, offer hockey. The International Tennis Hall of Fame in Newport reflects the region's genteel traditions. PC students, of course, needn't venture off campus to find excellent sports teams, particularly the men's and women's Friars basketball teams. Other intercollegiate teams include hockey, lacrosse, field hockey, swimming, tennis, and track. There are a host of intramural programs as well.

Rhode Island, the nation's smallest state, is also one of its most beautiful, with one hundred miles of beaches. Unspoiled coastline, inland bays, forests, and countless attractions are within easy reach of PC. Narragansett Bay is one of the country's most spectacular bodies of water. Newport, with its mansions from the Gilded Age, retains its charm and offers visitors a glimpse of life as only the wealthiest knew it. Boston is only an hour and a half up the road; New York City is approximately four hours to the southwest. Providence is served by Amtrak and has a good airport, so getting away is easy even for students who don't own a car.

Reed College

Office of Admissions
Portland, OR 97202
(800) 547-4750
www.reed.edu

Total enrollment: 1,385
Undergraduates: 1,366
SAT ranges (Verbal/Math): 630-730 (V); 590-700 (M)
Applicants: 1,716
Accepted: 74%
Enrolled: 28%
Application deadline: January 15
Financial aid application deadline: March 1
Tuition: $25,020/$31,840
Core curriculum: Yes

Majoring in Academe

Reed College, founded in 1907, requires its students to read some of the great texts of Western civilization, which is more than can be said for other institutions, even many small liberal arts colleges. But while the best colleges in the country ask their students to read so that they will become truly and liberally educated, Reed seems more interested in providing students with raw material that can later be consumed in the fires of the ideological furnace.

Moreover, Reed College, despite the vaunted individualism of its students, seems to encourage them to acquire knowledge with the goal of one day getting into graduate school, picking up an advanced degree, and finding a job somewhere in academe, teaching the hot topics that future Reed students will then study. If Reed has a characteristic fault, it is that there is too much learning for learning's sake, and not enough for the sake of truth. At times even the administration exhibits a perplexing form of intellectual snobbery, as exemplified in Reed's refusal to submit information for *U.S. New and World Report*'s annual college rankings on grounds that the survey is too simplistic.

Though Reed students enter their educations through the right doors, they can end up sidetracked by passing fads. A Reed education virtually assures a student acceptance in graduate school, which is indeed a great privilege. But the more urgent question is whether Reed can assure its students a profound understanding of the ideas and principles that have shaped our civilization.

Academic Life: But What Does It Profit a Man . . .

One could argue that Reed College is a mirror of the intellectual world of academe in that it simultaneously insists that its students work very hard at acquiring a classical education even as they subject that education to radical critique. As one professor says, "We read the Greeks because it just so happens that they wrote about how to think about complex issues in a way that doesn't presume too much foreknowledge." The point of education at Reed is not, this faculty member says, "to introduce people to the roots of Western culture, but to get them to think about the most important human questions with the best writers."

Reed's philosophy of education demands of students a genuine commitment of time and effort in order to graduate. All students must take Humanities 110, which requires that they read carefully, write about, and discuss many of the most important primary sources of the Western tradition. Thus, Reed requires of its students a familiarity of the West much stronger than that found at many colleges and universities with larger reputations.

The reading list for the two-semester humanities course includes Greek and Roman classics and ends with St. Augustine's *Confessions*. It is taught by what one professor termed the "conference method," in which lectures are followed by smaller weekly conferences limited to sixteen students per section. About twenty faculty members teach the course, taking turns lecturing. "We rotate all of the lectures, and they are meant to be taken very critically," says a faculty member who teaches the course. "They are a critical engagement with the texts and with each other."

Humanities 110 was instituted in 1943 and has remained the foundation of a Reed education ever since. After taking the course, students are encouraged — though not required — to take one of three other humanities courses. Two of these cover Renaissance and modern Europe, and a third, instituted in 1995, covers classical Chinese civilization. The latter should not be seen as a move away from rigorous studies, since it does not fit the typical multiculturalist mold of substituting Western-inspired radical works for the foreign culture supposedly being studied. Rather, it was conceived, says one professor, as a means of "dealing with a non-Western humanities subject with rigor. We decided to do a classical, and then an Early Modern, Chinese course. It's important that things be done really well. We don't jump on band wagons, and some students are disappointed because they're trendier [than the faculty]."

The humanities course, one professor says, "gives everyone a common language." He continues: "From the faculty's perspective, teaching the humanities course is great, because we all go to each other's lectures, and everyone updates their lectures yearly." Nothing makes an academic sweat like having to perform in front of his colleagues, and these public performances certainly help to quell any faculty apathy that might arise.

And yet, as one professor notes, it is quite possible, in the atmosphere created by Reed's offbeat culture, for faculty to deliver lectures on the Greeks or Romans that are themselves a bit off center. "Because most faculty come from literary backgrounds and are themselves trendy, we have a fair share of rather wacky lectures," the professor notes. And yet, there still remains in the required humanities course a balance, for, as a faculty member says, "No narrow specialty group can control it, and this exerts a conservative control. The lunatics are largely compensated for by conservative faculty."

The college also has distribution requirements of a full year of literature, philosophy, or "the arts"; two credits in history, social sciences, or psychology; two courses in the natural sciences; two courses from either mathematics and formal logic or foreign language, and three semesters of physical education. However, the connection between the courses that could be used to satisfy the distribution requirements — not to mention those that count as electives — and the serious study of the Western canon varies from close to barely perceptible. Studying the course catalogue at Reed, one surmises that many classes in the humanities and social sciences are geared to an exploration of methodology and theory rather than a close reading of primary sources.

Such courses include Classics 314, "Gender and Sexuality in the Classical World," in which students are introduced to "feminist theory, gender theory, and theories of sexuality and will generate a variety of valid ways in which to examine and understand the issues of gender and sexuality raised by the products of classical culture." In the history department, there are courses dealing with "Peasants and the State in China" and "Gender and History" alongside more traditional offerings such as "The Making of the Atlantic World: Europe and the Americas, 1500-1800" and a conference course on the French Revolution that explicitly looks at the revolution from both "traditional historiography and contemporary revisionist historiography" perspectives.

The English department's offerings are replete with courses top-heavy with theoretical and methodological approaches, including English 338, "Representing Mothers: Contemporary Fiction and Theory," which examines motherhood as a social institution particularly through the eyes of writers responding to Adrienne Rich's *Of Woman Born: Motherhood as Experience and Institution.* Students explore "how the categories of gender, race, ethnicity, sexual orientation, and class shape the institution, experience, and representation of motherhood." English 365, "Image and Gender in Victorian and Modern Poetry," focuses on "how the representation of gender is linguistically, culturally, and socially construed" by examining images of women in texts and paintings.

However, one searches the Reed catalogue in vain for courses covering the European Middle Ages, the Renaissance, the Reformation, or — surprisingly for a college located in Oregon and founded by money from the estate of pioneer Simeon Reed — the American West.

Despite the examples given above, English and classics are not among the departments listed by faculty as Reed's weakest. Those departments include Spanish, German, economics, sociology, and anthropology. There are several strong departments on campus, including the sciences, especially physics, mathematics, chemistry, and biology (probably the best department on campus). Also well regarded are the art history and philosophy departments. Philosophy ranks number one in the country in majors who go on to graduate school. Outstanding teachers can be found at Reed, including Peter Steinberger in political science, Lisa Steinman in English, C. D. C. Reeve in philosophy, Peter Parshall in art history, Walter Englert in classics, Robert Kaplan in biology, and David Griffiths in physics. Students also benefit from a ten-to-one student-to-faculty ratio and classes that average only fifteen students.

In all classes, professors assign grades to students, but the college does not actually tell a student his grades unless he requests them. An exception to this rule is made if a student scores below a C in any class; the student is then told of his grade and meets with his professor. The college does this, it explains, because "Reed College encourages students to measure academic achievement by self-assessment of their grasp of course material and intellectual growth. . . . The college does not wish to divide students by labels of achievement. While a conventional letter grade for each course is recorded for every student, the registrar's office does not routinely distribute grades to students, providing work continues at satisfactory . . . levels."

This philosophy is one of the most important pillars supporting what is known around campus as the "Reed ethos." In other ways, however, Reed requires that its students bare their minds, if not their souls. All students must pass a junior qualifying examination before moving on to their senior years. In this exam, administered by the major division or department in which the student will work, weaknesses are identified and students who are not yet ready to work independently on their senior theses (also required of all students) are encouraged to either bone up or choose another major. The senior thesis itself is a "sustained investigation of a carefully defined problem — experimental, critical, or creative — chosen from the major field and considered as one part of an overall senior-year program," according to the college catalogue. Finally, before graduating students must sit for a comprehensive two-hour oral review given by the major division or department. Focusing mostly on the senior's thesis, "the committee of examiners will include faculty from the student's own department and division, a second division, and, on occasion, professionals from outside the college." As noted above, Reed requires a great deal of work from its students, and a degree is by no means assured by simply enrolling at this little school in Portland.

Political Atmosphere: A Farm Team for Graduate Schools

The student body and faculty at Reed College tend to be left of center in their politics and social attitudes even as they defend a strong core curriculum and work ethic.

There is at least a minimal degree of tolerance for those who depart from the norm. As one professor who has taught at Reed for decades notes, "There has been something of a distancing of the faculty from students of the opposite sex. There has been a chilling effect on frankness and openness on campus — people are less willing to speak their minds these days."

The process of politicization has become more entrenched as older professors retire and are replaced by younger radicals. "A big disappointment is how poorly we've capitalized on the buyers' market for professors," a faculty member says. "We have tenured mediocre people when we could have gotten better." According to another professor, "Tenured radicals are really very dull people because they think they know the answers to all the biggest questions. Here just ten people is 10 percent of the faculty, so it's easy for them to change things even if they're not the majority." Recently, some faculty have been unhappy about what seems to be a toning down of the intellectualism on campus in an effort to avoid losing students. "Reed looks more like any other college now," says one teacher. This relaxation of standards, which is by no means peculiar to Reed, occurred because college marketers decided that the image of a school where students read even more than they are assigned, study late into the night, and argue great books with their peers over dinner does not sell to the great American middle class.

Yet the type of community that results when colleges are run like businesses can be undesirable from the standpoint of those who champion quality education. A Reed professor notes that some twenty faculty members, out of about one hundred total, are adjuncts, i.e., temporaries or part-timers. Yet, he notes, "They have a huge effect. They can all vote, and they were all politicized, so they have a big influence on our students." Those professors cannot contribute long-term to the Reed ethos because they will move along soon. Without the continuity derived from a stable academic community, the college (and students) will suffer.

But teaching is still taken very seriously at Reed, and the imbalance between teaching and research that plagues so many colleges and universities has not taken hold. "The single most important criterion [in tenure decisions] is teaching, and we are evaluated by students and by faculty," says one professor. "No matter how many books one has written, no tenure is awarded without good teaching. Most faculty do publish, but they're also very good teachers."

Much pride is taken at Reed because it was named the "most intellectual college in the country" in a recent book on higher education. Whether or not one agrees with this claim, it is certainly true that many Reedies, as they are known locally, see their undergraduate education as a primer for graduate school and a career in academe. Reed proudly trumpets statistics showing that over the past several years it ranks third in the nation among all institutions of higher learning in the production of future Ph.D.s. Categorically, Reed ranks first in percentage of life-science graduates and third in the percentage of science/engineering graduates who go on to earn Ph.D.s. Overall, in percentage of graduates who go on to take doctorates, Reed trails only the California Institute of Technology and Harvey Mudd. The graduate, medical, and professional schools most frequently attended by Reed graduates include Harvard, Stanford, the University of California at Berkeley, and the University of Chicago. The thirty Rhodes scholars produced by Reed since 1915 is equaled by only one other liberal arts college.

This impressive record is both a result of and a defining factor in the Reed ethos, which, as we have seen, seeks to maintain very high academic standards while exposing students to the very latest methods of research in every field. And while it is certainly an achievement of which everyone in the Reed community can be proud, it goes a long way toward explaining why so many of the courses at Reed reflect the dominant trends in the academy, whatever they may be. More than most colleges and universities, Reed is a farm team for the better graduate schools. Its graduates, in turn, excel in their fields because the stuff of the graduate schools is what they were fed as undergraduates. This gives them a leg up on their colleagues from most other institutions.

Student Life: A Good Reed

Alongside the rigorous courses at Reed is a very strong and quite trendy culture that is all but required of anyone who would matriculate there. As one professor says, "The '60s Berkeley look is very big here, but we work them very hard." Ironically, today this look is not so much countercultural as it is mainstream.

Be that as it may, it may still be fitting that Reed is located on Woodstock Drive. Life at Reed is intensely academic and a bit different from similarly sized schools across the nation. Most notable is the total absence of a Greek system: there are no fraternities or sororities at Reed. There are numerous student organizations, however, ranging from arts groups like Shoestring Theatre, which has used student funds to stage plays such as David Mamet's *Oleanna* and hold a lecture on Madonna videos, to Christian Fellowship and Chaverim, a Jewish student organization, to groups that cater to more avant-garde interests. Among the latter are environmental groups, Pagan Circle, Queer Alliance, and the Safer Sex Society, which proudly "provides you Reedies with condoms, dental dams, personal lubricant, and safer sex literature. For free! We're the nice people who give you condoms!" Reed is also home to a Women's Center (a "safe, queer-friendly, women-only space"); the Reason, Egoism, and Liberty Forum (a libertarian group); Chunk 666, which is dedicated to helping individuals "prepare for the upcoming apocalypse"; and the Fetish Student Union, which hosts a "Fetish and Bondage Ball," wherein one may explore personal fetishes, "whether you fancy household appliances, deep sea mammals, Velveeta fondue, or just the classic leather and cuffs. Things we believe contribute to a successful ball include a whipping room, jello pit, various take-home inflatables, prizes for OutRageUs dress, and lots-O-latex."

The most scientifically curious students can toy with the Reed Reactor Facility's 250 kW (thermal) TRIGA Mark I nuclear reactor, the only such device with no associated nuclear engineering department or graduate school. The device exists chiefly to serve the "curiosity of anybody interested," and more than 1 percent of the student body holds an operator's license.

About 60 percent of Reed's 1,300 students live on campus, a rather low number for a small liberal arts college. Housing is said to be a problem, since not enough dorms exist to take care of all who would like to live in them. Some of the dorms are quite nice, while others are aging and spartan. Freshmen, almost as many of whom come from the Northeast as from the Northwest, are "encouraged" to live on campus for their first two semesters, and they alone are guaranteed campus housing. A lottery determines which students get dorm rooms in subsequent years. The Residence Life Office also allows students to create "theme houses" in the different residences on campus. The theme houses for 2000-2001 were the English House, which houses students bored with "American life" who have an interest activities such as "politeness, tea, and croquet," and the Outhouse, a coed dorm that works closely with the Reed Outing Club to provide organized outdoor activities for Reedies (including faculty) with serious interest in recreation in the wild. All dorms are coed, though there are some all-female floors. On the other floors, men and women share bathrooms.

All community affairs at Reed are governed by the Honor Principle, which dates from the college's founding and is taken very seriously. Students are not required to sign a code, but everyone in the community is expected to abide by the principle, which states, among other things, that "we declare our commitment to responsible and honorable conduct in academic and community affairs." The Community Constitution, which applies to all students, faculty, and staff, adds that "we further declare that dishonesty, intimidation, harassment, exploitation, and the use or threat of force are incompatible with the preservation of this freedom." A student judicial board enforces the principle among students. The Honor Principle allows faculty to leave tests unmonitored, which is certainly laudatory. Yet its sweeping definition of harassment could leave the door open for the prosecution of those whose sensitivity level is deemed unfit.

Portland offers not only scenic beauty but an increasingly sophisticated cultural life. When they're not reading, students can take advantage of the numerous attractions found in this burgeoning city. A poster child for New Urbanism, Portland was named *Money* magazine's Best Place to Live in 2000. Center city diversions such as the Portland Art Museum, local rock clubs, and java joints abound, and outstanding bookstores such as Powell's offer Reed students almost unlimited titles. The flourishing high-tech community centered around Hewlett Packard and a transportation authority that has implemented an extensive light rail system are often cited as reasons for Portland's recent metropolitan maturity. The area of Portland around Reed is comparatively safe, according to official crime statistics.

Rhodes College

Office of Admissions
2000 North Parkway
Memphis, TN 38112
(800) 844-5969
www.rhodes.edu

Total enrollment: 1,510
Undergraduates: 1,499
SAT ranges (Verbal/Math): 590-690 (V); 590-690 (M)
Applicants: 2,283
Accepted: 77%
Enrolled: 25%
Application deadline: February 1
Financial aid application deadline: March 1
Tuition: $19,503/$25,174
Core curriculum: Yes

Standards Bearer

Of the 110 institutions reported on in this guide, Rhodes is among the most distinctive and distinguished. From its insistence that every new building on its leafy campus follow the original collegiate gothic architecture its unfashionable adherence to rigorous academic standards, Rhodes bucks every trend in American higher education — a move we find both courageous and promising. After changing its name from Southwestern to Rhodes in 1984, the college has taken steps to ensure that it makes a name for itself in circles that count: students and parents seeking one of the best liberal arts educations in the nation, and donors who recognize the importance of upholding educational and moral standards in an era of intellectual nihilism.

Rhodes, in short, has done things right, and most signs indicate that it will continue in this way. Faculty, supporters, and new administration appear willing to shoulder the responsibilities inherent in maintaining and strengthening the liberal arts education that Rhodes offers. This is not to say that there are not pockets within the faculty that would move the school away from its moorings if given the chance, for there are. However, they are outnumbered by professors whose dedication to teaching their students well outweighs the temporal attractions of a politicized classroom.

Yet the philosophies of the world's modern educators ensure that the pressures to conform to relativistic doctrines will always be strong, and vigilance must be maintained if Rhodes is to keep its academic integrity. Most troubling is the obvious toning down of the college's relationship with the Presbyterian church. Whereas in recent years this relationship had been strengthened, the college's Web page make no mention of the school's church affiliation other than to note that Rhodes became Presbyterian in the late nineteenth century when it broke its ties with the Masons. You may download (or request a hard copy of) the college's catalogue, which still trumpets this relationship, however: "The College's Christian commitment and Church relationship are more than assent to a set of vague values or sentimental emotions. They represent a view of existence and reality based upon faith in God as creator, sustainer, and redeemer of life." The effect of this public relations move is to make the school's relationship with the church less obvious and more difficult to find while maintaining that relationship in the official literature of the college. Rhodes is still an excellent institution, however, and deserves a close look by students who wish to spend four years acquiring a high-quality liberal arts education.

Academic Life: Old Time Religion?

If academic excellence is compatible with religious truths, and it certainly is, then Rhodes's decision to lower the profile of its relationship with the Presbyterians is puzzling. The college's "Statement of Christian Commitment and Church Relationship" used to state: "Too many colleges today, lacking a clear identity and direction, have become imitative. The prestige image they follow is often a secular pattern since most of the well-established private institutions in this county are secular in outlook. For church-related institutions the problem is especially serious because imitation draws them away from their own distinctive purposes." That this statement has been removed could indicate the loss of some of its tradition and identity that have made it unique.

A professor says that the college's change of heart regarding its relationship with the Presbyterian church is due to the new administration's desire to distance itself from its predecessor. "Though the new administration [of president William Troutt] affirms that Rhodes is a church-related college, the symbolic and rhetorical trappings of church relatedness have been gradually disappearing," this professor says. The new president doesn't talk about this publicly, perhaps not wanting to run afoul of many college trustees. "But it is my sense," this professor says, "that Troutt is wagering that one of the best ways to gain the trust of the many faculty that disliked [his predecessor] is to do away with the vestiges of what many saw as an imposition of religion from above."

At the same time, another professor says the new administration "has generated a very widely spread enthusiasm for the further development of the college, based both on the tradition of the college and shared visions of where we go from here." A student compliments the new administration's open-door policy: "He [president Troutt] took his door off when he arrived. You can e-mail or call his secretary and get a 15-minute appointment to see him — just go right in and talk to him. He's not in the ivory tower looking down on everyone."

So far, these changes have not affected the curriculum: no one questions its rigor and general integrity. One professor says of Rhodes's qualities: "The Rhodes approach to broad liberal arts education is as good as you are going to see. The college is committed to it and so are most of the faculty." This person continues, "How well it works in practice varies widely from student to student. For those who want it, they can get it here. For those who are determined to remain narrow, they can succeed as well."

Many courses are rigorous, and class sizes are small. Most classes have fewer than forty students, with the largest number enrolling between ten and nineteen students. The student to faculty ratio is twelve to one. There are no teaching assistants. "The big-name professors teach freshman classes," a student says. The intimate atmosphere created by the school's small size and beautiful campus is a central element of the Rhodes experience. "The professors know you (and you know them) on so many different levels," says the same student. "It's very open, and we can talk about anything."

The curriculum at Rhodes exposes students to the Bible and to the Western tradition. As the catalogue says: "[T]he educational purpose of the college is expressed in its maintenance of an environment for the pursuit of truth in which it is ensured that the Christian faith is clearly articulated, that its formative role in Western civilization is carefully considered, and that honest intellectual and moral questions are articulated and responded to intelligently and sensitively." Freshmen are required to choose between two core curricula: "The Search for Values in the Light of Western History and Religion," and "Life: Then and Now." Each program involves twelve credit hours earned over a two-year period. Either choice requires a great deal of reading in primary sources, as well as extensive discussions and writing assignments.

"Search," as it is commonly called, has been taught at Rhodes for fifty years. The college catalogue quotes from an early description of the program: "Our . . . Christian background is traced and analyzed, and the pageant of Civilization is viewed from its beginning to present time." Students read the Hebrew Bible while they simultaneously study Mesopotamian civilization, and they study the Gospels as they learn about Graeco-Roman culture and history. "This course is a basic foundation in the college's commitment to Christian higher education," the catalogue states. In the second year, students continue this intellectual adventure by reading primary sources from one of four disciplines: religious studies, history, philosophy, or literature. One professor describes it as the best approach for students who want to read widely in the liberal arts.

The other option, the so-called "Life" program, is more concentrated in the Hebrew-Christian tradition per se, and to that end students study the Bible in detail during their first year. Their options during the second year are, once again, described best in language now removed from the school's Web site, for they still "may choose among a variety of ways to approach an understanding of the meaning of faith, belief in God, religion, knowledge of the ultimate, ethical responsibility." The three sub-disciplines offered are "Studies in the History of Religion," "Philosophical and Theological Studies," and "Studies in Ethics." Students are free to choose from any of these areas in fulfilling the third and fourth courses in the Life program. Most of the courses in the Life sequence are offered through the religious studies department, although a few are offered by philosophy.

The college also has a set of distribution requirements for all students. These include three courses, chosen by the student, in each of three areas — humanities, social science, and natural science — and two courses in the fine arts. At least one of the humanities courses has to be in literature or film, while one of the natural science courses must include a lab.

The Honors program, open to seniors who maintain a 3.5 GPA, allows participants to engage in intensive, independent work. It is seen by the college as an excellent introduction to graduate study because it is of a "scholarly and creative nature." Thus, the best students can work closely with a professor on a specialized topic of interest even as they complete a broad, liberal arts education. All majors require a senior seminar that "both reviews and integrates important areas within the discipline." This seminar may carry from two to six hours of credit and may be one or two semesters long. And, in a policy that illustrates the college's belief that a student's formal educational experience should occur within a definite framework — during the student's years on campus — attendance at commencement exercises is required in order to receive a degree.

Teaching is still valued at Rhodes. One professor says that "there is no more pressure to publish" at the expense of good teaching than in the past, when there was very little. "There has been no sudden or higher imposition of research" demands, this person says. "I'm still confident that our primary mission is teaching." This claim is backed up by a student: "The big professors teach freshman classes. And you [and your professors] know each other on so many levels. It's very open, and you can talk to them about anything."

Among the best teachers at Rhodes are: Mark McMahon in economics and business; Kenneth Morrell in classics; Horst Dinkelacker and James M. Vest in foreign languages; Larry Lacy in philosophy; Julia Ewing in theater; Dan Cullen and Stephen Wirls in political science; Michael Drompp in history; Cynthia Marshall, Brian Shaffer, Jennifer Brady, Tina Barr, and Debra Pittman in English; Karl Kaltenthaler in international relations; Steve Haynes, F. Michael McLain, and Ellen Armour in religious studies; Victor Coonin in art; Carolyn Jaslow and Terry Hill in biology; and Bradford Pendley in chemistry.

Departments and programs rated best by faculty and students include the foreign languages, business, economics, political science, international studies, English, biology, chemistry, and physics. One faculty member says that English and economics are "very strong." A professor notes that "the departments that attract the best students are the sciences." Unfortunately, the departments considered weaker — history and social sciences — accounted for almost a quarter of a recent graduating class. "History is still weak and offers too much social history," says a professor. "And anthropology/sociology is weak, both in its personnel and within the disciplines."

Political Atmosphere: Redefine and Refine

Rhodes is no hotbed of political activity. It's fair to say that many students are moderate to conservative, while most faculty members are liberal but not radical. Yet a student says that "the student body is much more liberal than often portrayed." This student continues: "There's a big diversity debate now. Troutt has formed a diversity task force to find out how to bring more diversity to the college. But, do we have to lower our standards? I hope not." Another student notes that there have been activities to call attention to hunger and homelessness this year on campus, a rather new development that mostly consisted of "signs up . . . everywhere."

Under the new president, "the college is moving toward a redefining and refining of its curriculum, faculty policies in general, and so on," a professor says. "It's hard to say at this point where it's going. If there are strong agendas being pushed by anyone, I don't know about it." Other professors says that the diversity committee created by Troutt will look into ways to increase the ethnic diversity of the faculty and student body. "He's either doing it as a sop to the left, and a dangerous one, or it's a way of ingratiating himself to the faculty without any intention behind it," says one. "He has to be aware of the difficulty of a place like Rhodes at attracting minority faculty." Indeed, smaller colleges, even those as financially sound as Rhodes, must attempt to lure the small number of minority and female faculty members from larger, more prestigious research universities, a job that the over-professionalization of higher education (which awards politicized research over teaching) makes very difficult.

Rhodes does have an Office of Multicultural Affairs, which seeks to aid minority students. One student group, Focus, which solicits homosexual members, maintains a Web site accessible from Rhodes's own pages. On this organization's Web site are links to pornographic pages elsewhere on the Internet. "In past years there was controversy over the status of gay and lesbian groups, but at the moment that has been pushed to the back burner," a professor says.

Student Life: Going to Graceland — and Other Places

Rhodes lies in Memphis, Tennessee, a large and unique city on the banks of the Mississippi. Known as the cradle of the blues and a home for jazz, it boasts many cultural attractions (beyond Graceland) that students take advantage of. The college is very much a part of the city, and the mayor recently declared one summer day "Rhodes College Day" in Memphis. "Many students go to the inner city to work with kids" says a student. "We were the first college in the U.S. to have a Habitat for Humanity chapter." In fact, about 80 percent of the student body participates in community service projects.

Residential life at Rhodes isn't too different from that at most other liberal arts colleges. Freshmen are required to live on campus, and 70 percent of the student body resides in campus housing. The housing shortage forces some juniors to live off campus against their desire, as more students request campus housing than space permits. Dorms are single sex, although 24-hour visitation is the norm. Although the college states in its literature that it "does not provide residence hall rooms for both undergraduate men and women students in the same residence hall," a student says that the dorms "are de facto coed." "We have very liberal dorm policies," the student says. "Only one dorm is officially coed, and that's only because of a housing crisis." The student says there is no cohabitation going on, but only one floor of a single dorm is restricted to a single sex after quiet hours (normally midnight). Alcohol is allowed in dorm rooms and designated campus locations for students age twenty-one and older.

Fifty-seven percent of the men belong to fraternities and 55 percent of women join sororities, as Greeks are "the predominant social group," according to a student. "They're truly a large community," this person says. "Greeks are a good part of the campus and are learning to work with others."

Rhodes's scholars, nearly three-quarters of which come from outside of Tennessee, enjoy a variety of student organizations. About 65 percent of the student body participates in intramural sports, and 21 percent are involved in Rhodes's eight men's and eight women's intercollegiate sports teams. There are club teams in rugby, equestrian events, and lacrosse, among other sports, and more than 60 registered student organizations, very few of which are frivolous or radical.

"There's always something to do" says a student. With such a large number of student groups and the city of Memphis at their disposal, it's no wonder students love Rhodes College. "I have no regrets" about attending Rhodes, says a recent graduate, who adds: "There's so much here that I love." One thing that is conspicuously absent at the school, though, is crime. If official statistics can be believed, few college campuses are as safe as Rhodes.

The percentage of students who enroll at Rhodes once accepted is less than 23 percent, which is rather low for a college of Rhodes's credentials. This figure shows that a fair number of those who apply to Rhodes make it their second choice and see it as a "safe" application for admission. Yet this low number should not lead anyone to think that, once on campus, those who do come show themselves to be anything other than first-rate. The college's own statistics show that almost a third of the student body scored over 700 on the verbal portion of the SAT, and nearly half scored over 600. Additionally, nearly 60 percent graduated in the top tenth of their high school class, and 11 percent were first or second in their class.

Recent graduates were very successful in applying to graduate and professional schools. The school reports that 100 percent of grads seeking admission to law or business schools were accepted, and that 85 percent of those applying for medical school were successful. Overall, 93 percent of applicants to graduate schools are accepted.

Rice University

6100 Main Street
Houston, TX 77005-1892
(800) 527-6957
www.rice.edu

Total enrollment: 4,285
Undergraduates: 2,724
SAT ranges (Verbal/Math): 650-750 (V); 680-770 (M)
Applicants: 6,375
Accepted: 27%
Enrolled: 40%
Application deadline: January 2
Financial aid application deadline: February 15
Tuition: $16,444/$23,294
Core curriculum: No

Death and Texas

Rice University in Houston, Texas, is the university that almost never was. William Marsh Rice, a wealthy New Yorker with frequent business in Houston, became enamored with this one-horse, mosquito-infested swamp by the sea. Much to the dismay of his Yankee friends, Rice had decided to use his personal fortune to establish an institute of higher learning upon his death. Having made the arrangements with his Houston attorney, Capt. James A. Baker, the grandfather of the future Secretary of State, Rice returned home to New York.

Rice's butler and New York attorney, however, had other plans for the Rice fortune. After forging a new will that naming the butler as the heir, they poisoned Rice in 1900. Captain Baker uncovered the plot, recovered the money, and the Rice Institute was founded.

The estate was so large that Rice didn't even charge tuition until 1965. While no longer free, Rice University has consistently ranked as one of *Money* magazine's "best college buys." With its excellent academic reputation, Rice has become nationally known as a (somewhat) more affordable alternative to its Ivy League counterparts.

In Rice's eighty-year history, Houston has been transformed by growth of the city's petrochemical industry and, just as importantly, the advent of air conditioning. While the mosquitoes still remain, Rice's location is difficult to beat. The campus, blanketed by more than five thousand trees, is located minutes away from almost every Houston attraction. Although located in the nation's fourth-largest city, Rice is the smallest NCAA Division I school, with approximately 2,600 undergraduates. Unlike most campuses located in urban environments, Rice's insular design gives it a true campus feel. Whether you are looking for the community of an isolated campus, the excitement and opportunities of a large metropolis, or simply an excellent education, Rice has something for everyone.

Academic Life: One Giant Rice Bowl

Most students at Rice take on two or even three majors. While this phenomenon can, in part, be seen as a consequence of the student body's quality and competitive nature, it is more likely the result of a near-complete lack of core requirements. Basically, a student is required to take twelve hours of course work in each school outside his major, meaning that an economics major (in the School of Social Sciences) would have to take twelve hours in the humanities (history, art, literature, foreign languages) and twelve hours in the sciences (chemistry, computer science, math, etc.). The classes that fulfill these minimal standards are selected entirely by the student. In addition, students must take two or three additional courses selected from a "restricted" list (the university's term) that come from outside his area of concentration. For instance, the aforementioned economics student would also need six more hours from the assortment of courses in the natural science restricted distribution list. There are also requirements for minimal English competency and for two courses in health and physical education.

While most students enjoy the freedom this system offers, the system indicates that Rice has, for the most part, handed over its responsibility to name the courses that are important for a true liberal arts education. The quality of the educational choices depends on the quality or awareness of the student. The university does offer some assistance in the form a academic advisors in each department with whom majors are required to meet at least once a semester. Nonetheless, the university will do very little hand-holding. If your desire is to study engineering while mastering French, don't count on core academic requirements making you the well-rounded person you've always wanted to be.

Whatever the students wind up taking, they are in for a tough time: in terms of academic rigor and realistic grading, Rice has defied the national trend toward artificially buttressing a student's self esteem. While Rice ranks near the top ten universities nationally, many students, jaded by their Harvard friends' inflated grades, feel these rankings are low. Grade inflation at Rice is nonexistent and strongly discouraged. While it may not be difficult to make a B in most social sciences and humanities classes, rarely will more than two to three As be given out of a class of twenty. Science classes, especially the larger, introductory classes, usually set the mean at a C or C+. With a student body of lifelong over-achievers, academic egos often take a bruising.

In exchange, Rice students get excellent, easily accessible professors and small class sizes. All professors are required to have set office hours every week, and most are a short phone call, e-mail, or walk away the rest of the time. Teaching schedules are comparatively light, leaving professors with extra time for research and student interaction. While exceptions always exist, most professors, even the university's Nobel laureate, chemist Dr. Richard E. Smalley, are more than willing to spend an afternoon helping a student out.

Although professors are required to conduct research and publish scholarly papers at a frequency comparable to most major universities, Rice is not generally known as a research institution. With few exceptions, most notably engineering, architecture, and linguistics, its graduate programs are generally ignored by most national rankings. This means that Rice is primarily an undergraduate teaching university. And good professors are ubiquitous at Rice. Some favorites include J. Dennis Huston in English; Richard J. Stoll in political science; Miguel A. Quinones in psychology; John S. Hutchinson in chemistry; and Stephen L. Klineberg in sociology.

Good and bad departments are more difficult to discern. A person serious in pursuing a doctorate would most likely avoid Rice's graduate departments. This, however, does not mean that the undergraduate part of the department is inadequate. Most students, once they find a major that truly interests them, rave about their department. Other students, regardless of their major, will always find faults. Among undergraduates, engineering and hard sciences majors are considered the most difficult, while majors like sociology and English are thought to be easier. This, however, has little to do with the quality of the department.

Is a department good because of the research of the faculty? The rank of their graduate program? Their reputation for being difficult? Or because they have dedicated, caring professors and challenging classes? If the last question is what matters to you, almost all Rice departments are to be considered good — with the possible exception of economics.

While introductory classes can be large (two hundred or more students in the hard sciences classes, fifty-plus for social sciences), they are nearly always taught by professors. Teaching assistants may lead study groups or grade papers, but except when a professor is ill, they rarely teach. Introductory language classes, however, are often taught by teaching assistants.

Most upper-level lecture courses have between ten and twenty-five students. Seminars rarely exceed ten, unless the course or professor is unusually popular. Most majors require that one take a combination of lectures and seminars, and most larger classes have smaller study sessions that meet regularly to allow for more student participation and individual attention.

Unlike most universities, Rice has a strict honor code, which is vigilantly enforced by students. Penalties for cheating on an exam, besides most likely resulting in an automatic F, could result in expulsion. For merely falsifying some data on a lab report, a two-semester suspension would not be unusual.

Over the past few years, Rice has tried to increase the opportunities and financial aid for students who wish to study abroad. Rice now has its own summer program in Spain and semester abroad in Chile. While most students choose not to study abroad, Rice is trying to find ways for more study abroad credits to transfer to its own departments.

Political Atmosphere: A Side Dish

For better or worse, Rice is as about as apolitical as college campuses come. The majority of students' time is occupied by their course work and most would rather spend their free time watching *The Simpsons* or drinking a beer than picketing an abortion clinic or saving a sea turtle. Campus Republican and Democrat groups exist nominally, but they hardly register a blip on the radar screen when compared to, say, intramural sports.

Poorly thought-out political activities on both sides of the spectrum occasionally surface before quickly retreating whence they came. If your goal in college is to become a political activist, Rice is probably not the place. Regardless of your position, you will either be ignored or jeered by the majority of your classmates.

Rice professors, while undoubtedly more liberal than the average Houstonian, tend to keep their political opinions to themselves and out of their classes. Aware of the conservative climate, most professors, if anything, censor themselves to be more conservative. Most faculty are more interested in presenting their subject in an honest, thoughtful manner than pushing a particular political philosophy. Freedom of speech, or lack thereof, is rarely an issue. "Unapproved speech" is generally considered anything that would be considered slanderous in a court of law. Few, if any, feel discouraged from expressing their opinions.

While Rice does not have a speech code, it does have an overly broad sexual harassment policy. For example, Rice considers "unwelcome suggestive or insulting sounds or whistles" to be an example of sexual harassment. Rice also classifies "unwelcome sexual propositions, invitations, solicitations, and flirtations" as sexual harassment. If one student asks another student out on a date but is rejected, one could certainly say that the student who demurred had received an unwelcome proposition or invitation. In fact, the inclusion of the flirtation makes the policy even more sweeping, so as to seemingly include a stare, a wink of an eye, or a love note. Woe be Shakespeare if he were a Rice student today and attempting to write a sonnet for a female student who caught his eye in class.

The Fifth Circuit Court of Appeals, which has jurisdiction over Texas, has outlawed affirmative action in academic settings. Rice has no affirmative action policy, but instead works to "attract highly-qualified students of all backgrounds," according to the university. Rice's admissions process is thorough and extremely selective.

No department at Rice could be considered overtly politicized. A political science class on property rights and institutions probably would not attract the most liberal student, nor would a history class on labor relations necessarily attract the most conservative student. To say, however, that these classes or departments are unjust in their presentation of the materials would be inaccurate. And what is arguably the most conservative department, economics, is generally considered to have the worst professors.

The hiring of faculty and awarding of tenure depend largely on academic reputation and students' reviews, with the professor's political activities playing no discernible role. Professors are expected to publish quite frequently. As Rice is foremost an undergraduate teaching university, student feedback is also taken seriously.

Invited speakers run the political gamut. The Baker Institute on Foreign Policy, named after former Secretary of State James Baker III, attracts many speakers from all over the world. Besides Secretary Baker, who can frequently be spotted around campus, other notable speakers include Henry Kissinger, Jack Kemp, Mikhail Gorbachev, and Yasir Arafat.

Rice, like most top-tier universities, has a range of student groups. Most reflect no more than a common interest in having fun — take for example the soccer club or the Marching Owl Band. Religious organizations range from the Baptist Student Union, the Muslim Students' Association, and a Wicca group. Two of the most active student groups are a different ends of the spectrum: the conservative Campus Crusade for Christ and the not conservative Pride, the gay/lesbian/bisexual association.

Although Rice tends to be less political than its Northeastern counterparts, the Women's Resource Center (WRC) is unabashedly so. Their Web page features links to Emily's List (a fundraising group for Democratic candidates), Feminist Majority, the

National Organization for Women (NOW), Isle of Lesbos, A Dyke's World, and many other left-wing, feminist groups. No links to conservative or libertarian women's groups are provided.

At the WRC's 1999 Women's Conference, all of the speakers advanced a decidedly left-wing agenda. Tamara Jones, introduced as an AIDS and police brutality activist, lamented, "the critical mass strategy reduces political impact to the individual and presumes that individual voters know their self-interest and react. This conventional view of women as an aggregate of individuals overlooks the obligation of resource-rich women to rescue resource-poor women." Jones advocated solutions such as socialized medicine, government child care, and a living wage, but concluded, "Liberal, democratic institutions may be fundamentally incapable of improving the position of the most marginalized groups. Inequality is at the heart of liberal democracy so feminist politics in a liberal democracy can only serve some women at the expense of others."

However, the most bizarre remarks were delivered by Rice alum and Houston City Council Member Annise Parker. Parker, the first lesbian to serve openly on the Council, said, "Women in office are different than men in office; we are socialized differently. We work with each other more cooperatively. I have never seen women on the City Council, even those I disagree with, react with ego. I call it testosterone overload when I see men on the council oppose things they actually support."

Left-wing activism also surfaced at Rice when students organized to protest former President George Bush's 2000 commencement address. Citing alleged human rights abuses at the hands of the Bush administration, these radicals vowed to disrupt the commencement, but reports indicated Bush was able to complete his remarks without any conspicuous disruptions.

Student Life: Village People

There are lots of things to do in Houston, and most of them are within easy distance of the university. Rice Village, a collection of shops, restaurants, and bars, is a short walk. Hermann Park, with its recently remodeled public golf course, and the Houston Zoo are literally across the street, as is the world-renowned Texas Medical Center. The Museum District, home of the Houston Museum of Fine Arts, the nation's sixth-largest, is also within walking distance. Five miles away is Houston's revitalized downtown, replete with theaters, concert halls, and the city's best night life, easily accessible by car or frequent buses. Enron Field, the new home of the Houston Astros, is located just to the east of downtown. Churches of almost every denomination are located nearby, many accessible by foot.

Rice University has no Greek system. In its place, Rice has adopted the residential college system based on those at Oxford and Cambridge. The residential college is the basic social unit at Rice. All students are assigned to a one of the eight colleges (with two more on the way) prior to their arrival and remain members of that college, well, for the rest of their lives. The first question one Rice alum asks another is inevitably, "What college are you from?" While students can live off campus whenever they wish, most prefer to live in the colleges. Housing there is guaranteed to all freshmen and first-year transfer students. Most other students are guaranteed on-campus housing for three out of four years.

Each college is headed by a master and two residential associates. A master is a tenured professor who lives in a house adjacent to the college. Residential associates (RAs) can be either professors or staff members. Masters serve for terms of five years. RAs, while they have no fixed term, cannot serve longer than eight years. Masters and RAs are chosen by a committee of students from the college. Their function is not one of disciplinarian, since each college has its own student-run judicial system; rather, masters and RAs help organize social events, college outings, and other activities, and are more trusted counselors or friends than anything else. Should you have roommate problems, school problems, or any other concern, the masters and RAs are always available.

Besides masters and RAs, most colleges have at least one associate from every department, in addition to members of the community, including doctors, astronauts, business leaders, and even diplomats who serve in various supporting roles.

Each college has its own dining hall, computer labs, kitchens, library, and quadrangles. Intercollege sports competitions, especially women's football, draw more spectators than some Rice teams do. Each college has at least one rival college, and pranks, such as stealing the rival's silverware right before lunch, are common. Colleges also organize outings to restaurants, concerts, and sporting events. Each college throws two to three campus-wide parties each year and also produces several plays.

All colleges are coed. Students at the college determine how rooms are to be divided up, and most often, students with common interests (for example, absolute quiet or extensive partying) tend to get blocks of rooms together. While some areas might be mostly guys or mostly girls, there is no *de jure* single-sex living. On floors that have inhabitants of both sexes, men's and women's restrooms are separate, but there are no restrictions on whom you can have in your dorm room and when you can have them there.

No colleges are alcohol-free, and Rice has one of the most liberal drinking policies to be found. Rice treats the colleges more like independent apartment complexes than traditional dormitories: what is consented to behind closed doors is none of the university's concern. While many students do not drink, free-flowing alcohol and intoxicated students are commonplace on the weekends. Some floors or areas of the college, due to their residents' preference, are more substance-free than others. The thorough roommate questionnaire reliably places freshmen in rooms and areas where they will feel comfortable.

Rice has two on-campus bars: Willy's Pub for undergraduates and Valhalla for graduate students. Thursday night is "Pub Night" at Willy's, and the undergrads flock there. Any student can get in, but only those twenty-one or older are given wristbands that allow them to drink.

Alcohol figures prominently into the two most visible social events: Night of Decadence and Beer Bike. Night of Decadence, known as NOD, is a Halloween party with a twist. Party themes tend to be sexual in a juvenile sort of way, such as "James Bondage" or "Lust in Space," and the costumes tend to be minimal. For obvious reasons, this party causes perennial controversy. The Campus Crusade for Christ hosts a Night of Innocence opposite NOD, where people gather in pajamas to eat ice cream and watch Disney movies. Truth be told, most students skip them both.

Beer Bike, however, is generally revered and universally attended. Beer Bike is a competition between colleges, consisting of a chug team and a bike team. The bike team bikes around a track; the chug team downs either water or beer to signal the start of the next biker. Intercollege pranks reach an apex at this time of year, and the pre–Beer Bike parade consists of perhaps the world's largest water balloon fight. More alums return for Beer Bike than for Homecoming.

Student Orientation, known as O-Week, precedes the first week of classes. O-Week is most comparable to summer camp. Students have to take a few placement examinations and attend seminars on the honor code and other university policies. Besides that, most waking hours are spent on activities designed to facilitate getting to know one another, the campus, and the city.

The Rice campus, although located in the middle of a large city, is generally safe. The campus police force is large in comparison to the size of the university, and emergency phones are located throughout the campus. Crime rarely gets more serious than the occasional stolen bike or backpack.

As Rice's national reputation grows, so does its geographic diversity. While many students are from Texas, students come from all areas of the nation, from all backgrounds. The main unifying factor among Rice students is intelligence.

Excellent professors and challenging courses make Rice tough to beat academically, especially when one factors in the cost of comparable private universities. Although Rice has hardly proven to be immune from the scourge of political correctness, it is a fine choice for students seeking a rigorous education unaccompanied by an enforced left-wing orthodoxy.

Rutgers University

Office of Admissions
Assistant Vice President for University Undergraduate Admissions
Rutgers–The State University of New Jersey: Rutgers College
P.O. Box 2101
New Brunswick, NJ 08903-2101
(732) 445-3770
www.rutgers.edu

Total enrollment: 48,000
Undergraduates: 36,291
SAT ranges (Verbal/Math): 520-640 (V): 540-660 (M)
Applicants: 25,100
Accepted: 62%
Enrolled: 34%
Application deadline: December 1
Financial aid application deadline: March 15
Tuition: resident: $5,000/$11,519; resident: $10,178/$16,697
Core curriculum: No

Law School?

Rutgers–The State University of New Jersey has many characteristics of an Eastern state university, including a sprawling campus in an urban environment and a tendency among students toward anonymity. "Diversity" is not just a cliché (though it's that, too, of course), for the campus is home to people from a variety of social and ethnic backgrounds and to a faculty and student body with wide-ranging interests. One faculty member describes the atmosphere at Rutgers as "intellectual permissiveness," which can work to the advantage of motivated students, including those who want a strong liberal arts education.

According to faculty and students, Rutgers has suffered in recent years from an intrusive and inept administration that is more interested in self-aggrandizement than in the interests of students and faculty. As a result, the Rutgers faculty and administration have an adversarial relationship that has resulted in some faculty resignations and more than a few lawsuits.

Faculty and students agree, however, that despite the frequently inhospitable political climate, Rutgers students can obtain a good undergraduate education. There are numerous fine professors and many solid courses from which to choose. The areas around Rutgers's several campuses are considered by many to be, odd as it may sound, "cultural meccas," and, according to one professor, "there are few places you can get access to really good faculty for such a cheap price." The key to success at Rutgers, according to another professor, is to be an "informed consumer."

Rutgers is "not a place for the weak-minded," cautions a faculty member; another warns students to be prepared for heavy consequences if they express "unfashionable opinions." Rutgers is "also a place where you can disappear and be as lonely and alienated as possible," says a student. However, there are myriad challenging courses and professors, and strong support for undergraduate research. Students must thus weigh the pockets of excellent faculty, courses, and programs — and the low tuition — against the heavy bureaucratization and radical student politics, and decide whether they are motivated and resilient enough to make the most out of a Rutgers education.

Academic Life: Jersey Barriers

Since 1945 Rutgers has been the official state university of New Jersey and has evolved into a mammoth institution, enrolling roughly forty-eight thousand students on campuses in Newark, Camden, and New Brunswick. Each campus has liberal arts programs in addition to more specialized areas of study. Camden houses the School of Business, for instance, while the College of Nursing and the School of Management are located in Newark. At the New Brunswick campus is Cook College for agricultural studies, as well as the College of Engineering, the College of Pharmacy, another School of Business, and the Mason Gross School of the Arts. This essay focuses almost entirely on the New Brunswick campus because of its liberal arts emphasis, and particularly on Rutgers College, which is located there.

The New Brunswick campus, the largest and oldest in the Rutgers system, comprises more than 2,800 acres and caters predominantly to liberal arts students. The campus is divided among four liberal arts colleges: Douglass, Livingston, Rutgers, and University. Each has its own distinct identity and focus, but they share many of the same resources. University College is for "nontraditional" students, those typically older students who are pursuing an education part-time while holding a job or raising a family. Livingston was founded thirty years ago "to foster an understanding of an involvement with complex social issues" and is considered the most progressive of the liberal arts colleges; its motto is "Strength through Diversity." Douglass College was founded in 1918 as the New Jersey College for Women, and is currently the largest women's college in the United States, enrolling nearly three thousand undergraduate women. Douglass women are considered intellectually strong, and the dean of the college, Barbara Shaler, is a trained classicist who receives high marks from students for her professional and personable demeanor.

The largest of the liberal arts colleges, Rutgers College, enrolls nearly nine thousand undergraduates. It is also the oldest and most distinguished of the New

Brunswick liberal arts colleges. Chartered in 1766 as Queen's College by Benjamin Franklin's son William to train Dutch Reformed ministers (in a building that was once a tavern, no less), its name was changed in 1825 to Rutgers College in honor of Revolutionary War veteran Colonel Henry Rutgers. The college has long since shed any vestige of its Dutch Reformed heritage, although it still makes a verbal commitment to "maintaining its long-standing tradition as a liberal arts institution."

Rutgers College does not have a core of courses that all students must take; rather, students are asked to satisfy a series of "general education requirements" that the college has deemed essential to a liberal arts education. As the college's literature explains: "General education is . . . the common denominator of the liberal arts experience. It is knowledge that, as the twenty-first century dawns, continues to provide students with the possibilities for common educated discourse, and that continues to prepare them for citizenship and for leadership in a democratic and pluralistic society."

Unfortunately, there is little to distinguish the Rutgers general education curriculum from that of the many other so-called liberal arts colleges that have weakened curriculum and standards. All students must take an expository writing course and one additional writing-intensive course; they can bypass the former with high advanced placement test scores. One math course is required (again, students may place out of it), along with an additional course chosen from among other mathematical disciplines such as computer sciences, statistics, and logic. Students must take two courses in the natural sciences and two courses in both social sciences and the humanities. There is no foreign language requirement, although Rutgers "recommends that its students establish proficiency in a foreign language."

Rutgers makes no requirements involving European history, literature, art, or music, but all students must take one course "about the non-Western world." Within the social science and humanities requirements, students can find excellent courses in history, classics, philosophy, and other traditional offerings; however, they can also bypass these altogether by choosing from courses in Africana studies, Puerto Rican and Hispanic Caribbean studies, women's studies, African languages and literatures, or Chinese. An emphasis on diversity might be partly defensible considering Rutgers's high minority student population (more than 35 percent), but to have no formal requirement in the humanistic areas of Western thought comes close to intellectual fraud (not to mention false advertising).

According to one professor, three efforts in the last ten years have been undertaken to reform the general curriculum at Rutgers; after much "politicking" among faculty, the result is characterized by one faculty member as the "Chinese menu" approach (one from column A, one from column B . . .).

In its promotional literature, Rutgers proudly points to frequent undergraduate involvement in both self-designed and faculty research. This advertising is true: in a recent student survey, the university reports, more than 40 percent of graduating students said they had the opportunity to participate in a faculty-sponsored re-

search project. The experience helps prepare students for graduate school and professional research projects.

In addition to more traditional disciplines, students at Rutgers can major in
such emerging fields (or pseudofields) as Africana and Afro-American studies,
Puerto Rican studies, or women's studies, and can choose from a dizzying number of
multicultural courses. Rutgers is a hospitable environment for anything promoting
the modern notion of diversity: the university was recently chosen by the African
Studies Association (ASA) to be its official home for African research for the next several years. The student newspaper, the *Daily Targum*, highlighted the event with the
headline "RU Embraces Africana Studies" and quoted elated Rutgers faculty, one of
whom said the ASA's presence "will be very helpful for putting Rutgers on the map."
As a result, students have the privilege of choosing from more than sixty courses
along the lines of "Issues in Afro-Brazilian History" and "The Black Woman in Political Context."

Despite its frequent obeisance to the gods of multiculturalism, Rutgers has not
forsaken all allegiance to traditional education. There are still many good professors
and courses to be found both within and outside of the mainstream programs.
When asked to name the finest departments, faculty, and courses, students and faculty are hard-pressed to narrow their preferences, so generally enthusiastic are they
about the quality of academics at Rutgers. There are good faculty in modern philosophy, although this department is weak in the study of the history of philosophy.
Rutgers offers an undergraduate medieval studies major, a commendable course of
study if rounded out by a complementary minor like classics, philosophy, or English.
The English department is characterized by one student as a "repository for people
who don't know what else to do," although it boasts some good faculty as well, including Richard Poirier, editor of the Library of America (a series of classic American
authors). They offer an excellent array of courses in all periods of English, American,
and medieval literature.

Classics, history, political science, and archaeology are all thought to have
pockets of excellence. The departments of modern languages, especially German
and French, offer excellent courses on culture and literature for majors and non-
majors on topics such as the Enlightenment. The biological sciences, especially microbiology, are world-class. Disciplines that typically have a radical slant today, such
as sociology and anthropology, still retain some excellent faculty, including one sociology professor who does research on "critical perspectives on family issues" and
has argued the importance of fathers in family relationships.

Although the majority of professors are described as liberal, there are also a
considerable number of traditionalists, and ideology doesn't seem to be an overly
significant player at the curricular level. Undergraduates seeking to major in traditional liberal arts disciplines will generally not be disappointed with Rutgers, so long
as they choose they courses carefully.

Class size varies at Rutgers, although with the variety of traditional and newer majors offered, some upper-level undergraduate courses have only a dozen students. Introductory courses naturally tend to have a larger enrollment, but the large number of students who enroll in traditional courses is a testament to both the solid advising system at Rutgers and the good instincts of the student body. A lower-level Greek civilization course, for instance, can attract upwards of seventy students. Undergraduates should expect to find graduate student teaching assistants playing a role in large, introductory courses and occasionally teaching lower-level courses as well.

Faculty and students alike give high marks to the Rutgers College Honors Program, the benefits of which include, in the words of one faculty member, "excellent advising, small classes with very bright students, and an environment where intellectual ambition is encouraged."

Political Atmosphere: See You in Court

According to one professor, Rutgers University is probably the largest academic litigating body in the country, with around eighty lawsuits pending against the university at any given time. The Rutgers administration is said to be "heavily bureaucratized," and operates in an "adversarial and custodial" manner, according to one professor. Like those at similar institutions, Rutgers administrators are handsomely paid and possess a great deal of power. According to one source, many administrators are "out of touch with the needs of the students" and are often so lacking in intellectual sophistication that "they couldn't even be students at Rutgers." Thus, their job often amounts to "enforcing low expectations for the university," and faculty consequently feel demoralized. "Our administrators don't know what a faculty looks like," says one dejected professor.

Rutgers faculty have suffered in recent years from New Jersey governor Christine Whitman's budget cuts and the lack of a faculty contract. Low faculty morale has led to what one professor describes as the "I'm here, I'm doing my time, I'm getting out" syndrome. In the spring of 1997 the *Daily Targum* published a series on "The Downsizing of Academia," which reported widespread faculty unrest and a distressing loss of top-drawer faculty. According to the article, the number of Rutgers faculty has fallen from 2,640 in 1985 to about 2,400; enrollment over that period, however, had remained fairly consistent. (The university says that the faculty now numbers 2,600.) One professor was quoted as saying he was leaving for another institution because "it is such a mess here. . . . The administration is so bad here, and Gov. Whitman's cuts just add to the complications."

The administration seems to be universally reviled by faculty, and the disciplinary code is said by a faculty member to be "Byzantine and unfairly administered." While the actual written regulations concerning such matters as sexual harassment and academic freedom are quite good, they are enforced indiscriminately.

Treatment of sexual harassment allegations, for instance, is described as "capricious": One professor may be unduly interfered with because his course material is considered offensive by a female student, while another who has actually performed an overt act of harassment goes uncharged. Recently, Rutgers President Francis Lawrence recommended the dismissal of William K. Powers, a professor of anthropology, because of pending sexual harassment charges by university students. According to the *Daily Targum*, Professor Powers claims that "the trouble began when a female graduate student filed false sexual harassment charges against both him and his wife," the latter an anthropology professor at Seton Hall. Since the charges were lodged, several students have organized the Student Coalition against Powers's Expulsion.

There also appears to be race-related tension on campus. In 1995 President Lawrence came under fire for a public remark that implied the genetic inferiority of minorities. Although he apologized for the statement, which he claimed was misinterpreted and taken out of context, student activists called for his resignation. In one widely reported protest, a group of students swarmed onto the court in the middle of a Rutgers basketball game in order to express their displeasure.

While Lawrence got in trouble for opening his mouth in that case, some members of the Rutgers community say the administration's silence has allowed other ethnic tensions to simmer unaddressed. There are many Jewish students at Rutgers, as well as a sizable contingent of Jewish faculty. In recent years the Jewish population has suffered from an "anti-Semitic undertone" and an "inhospitable atmosphere," according to one professor. Racial tensions are also said to exist between Jewish and minority students.

Lawrence did resist intense efforts to suspend the university's ROTC program in September of 1999. Campus activists had called for the end of the program to protest President Clinton's "Don't ask, don't tell" policy on gays in military service.

There are currently no conservative newspaper nor active conservative student groups at Rutgers. Chapters of the Intercollegiate Studies Institute and the Young Americans Foundation have cropped up at irregular intervals, but have had difficulty sustaining interest because of the heavy study load, not to mention the opposing nature of the student body. Conservative faculty have fared little better: a chapter of the National Association of Scholars never made it off the ground, although there is a Rutgers Committee on Academic Freedom. Conservative speakers come to campus infrequently, while left-wing programs such as the Center for Comparative Study of Civilization have richly funded lecture budgets. President Bill Clinton and actress Susan Sarandon are among the recent speakers the university has publicly touted, although Steve Forbes also came to speak to a political science class.

Student Life: Which Exit?

More than 90 percent of Rutgers students hail from New Jersey, although the university's view book contains facts and tidbits about the state (it has the nation's second-highest per capita income; the steam locomotive, the motion picture, the electric guitar, and the submarine were all invented there; etc.) that are seemingly designed to make New Jersey more appealing to students from other states.

About 60 percent of Rutgers students live on campus (high, considering how many are from New Jersey, the fifth-smallest state in the land), and housing is guaranteed for the freshman and sophomore years. On the New Brunswick campus, first-year students are assigned to one of eight halls. Special-interest housing is also available. Dorms are coeducational and visitors are permitted without restrictions. All first-year halls are officially dry. Off-campus housing is expensive (the downside of a high per capita income), and students should thoroughly research the surrounding area before committing to a living arrangement. About 20 percent of Rutgers undergraduates are members of fraternities or sororities, although all Greek housing is off-campus.

Safety is also a consideration when finding somewhere to live. Although students can reduce the risk of crime by adopting safe living habits, there is consistent petty theft and the occasional mugging. "New Brunswick is kind of a dicey town," says one student. The campus itself doesn't seem to have any safety issues out of the ordinary for a large university, although the *Chronicle of Higher Education* reports that Rutgers has the second-largest number of drug-related arrests in the country.

Students at the New Brunswick campus take advantage of the shops, banks, and ethnic restaurants (including a sushi bar) on George Street, as well as the many social and cultural opportunities on College Avenue. Well-heeled students can take the train to New York or Philadelphia to enjoy world-class museums, ballets, and orchestras; popular weekend and summer hangouts include the many seaside resorts on the Jersey Shore.

According to both faculty and students, the "logistics" of New Brunswick pose one of the primary difficulties in navigating Rutgers. The campus is sprawling, and auto congestion is acute. "Organizing the day is difficult for students," says one professor, who notes that many work to make ends meet, primarily on off-campus jobs. For these and other reasons, Rutgers is sometimes affectionately referred to as "RU Screw" by frustrated students.

Rutgers boasts hundreds of intramural teams and nearly fifty NCAA Division I and III varsity sports (between the three campuses, which field their own teams). High-ranking teams in recent years include the Lady Knights women's golf team, which took the 1996 Northwest Intercollegiate Championship, as well as women's lacrosse and tennis, men's baseball, and gymnastics, crew, and track. To its credit, Rutgers values high academic performance in its athletes.

Rutgers is also home to more than four hundred student organizations, including everything from Campus Crusade for Christ to lesbian, gay, and bisexual support groups. Its high minority enrollment ensures a wide variety of student organizations divided along racial and ethnic boundaries, many with activist intentions. An increased amount of public space is also set aside for minority students. The Rutgers Asian-American Coalition for Equality (RACE) is an umbrella organization for thirteen smaller Asian and Asian-American groups, and publishes a biweekly paper focusing on Asian-American interests on campus. Rutgers also has a Latino Student Council, representing sixteen different Latino organizations, as well as a Latino Center for Arts and Culture.

A few years ago African-Americans on campus received their own "cultural space" next to the Busch Campus Center. The $1.1 million Paul Robeson Cultural Center is named for one of Rutgers's most famous graduates. (The third African-American to graduate from Rutgers, college football star Robeson gave the 1919 valedictory address before becoming a well-known actor and singer.) The center "provides office space for fourteen student organizations, two conference rooms, a computer room, reading and lounge areas, and a suite for the staff of the center's *Black Voice/Carta Boricua* paper, according to the university. While minority students hail such coalition building and the acquisition of "cultural space," others worry about the further balkanization of the Rutgers student body.

St. John's College

Annapolis campus
Director of Admissions
Post Office Box 2800
Annapolis, MD 21404
(800) 727-9238
www.sjca.edu

Santa Fe campus
Director of Admissions
1160 Camino Cruz Blanca
Santa Fe, NM 87501
(800) 331-6003
www.sjcsf.edu

Total enrollment: Annapolis: 530; Santa Fe: 525
Undergraduates: Annapolis: 480; Santa Fe: 425
SAT ranges (Verbal/Math): 660-750 (V); 580-680 (M)
Applicants: 366
Accepted: 82%
Enrolled: 44%
Application deadline: March 1
Financial aid application deadline: February 15
Tuition: $24,770/$31,346 (both campuses)
Core curriculum: Yes

Meet the New Program, Same as the Old Program

St. John's College thrives on being a different kind of school. It has no intercollegiate athletic teams or academic majors and departments. The SAT is not required for admission and grades are not reported to enrolled students unless they request to see them. Some newer faculty — who, in another peculiarity of the college, are called "tutors" — lack campus offices, so they work out of the coffee shop instead. It is not uncommon for tutors and students to leave notes for one another using chalkboards adjacent to the mailroom. Yet, as unorthodox as all of this may sound, St. John's can justly claim to offer one of the most traditional curricula in the world.

The trend in higher education often seems to be one-directional: toward less rigor and more fluff, toward training rather than educating. St. John's, however, has taken a different path. Originally founded in 1698, the college had a respectable if unremarkable tradition until it fell on hard times during the Great Depression. Bankrupt and with its accreditation in jeopardy, St. John's took a drastic step. It invited two former Rhodes Scholars under the spell of the Great Books renaissance then regnant at Columbia and the University of Chicago to assume leadership of St. John's. These two men, Stringfellow Barr and Scott Buchanan, established in 1937 what came to be known as the New Program. Its heart: a four-year passage through the seminal texts of the West.

Soon St. John's began to attract an odd assortment of characters: European refugees like Jacob Klein and Leo Strauss, the philanthropist Paul Mellon (who attended St. John's as an adult and corresponded with Carl Jung about the difficulties he had studying mathematics), and visiting lecturers like Bernard Knox and Mortimer Adler. In 1964, the college opened a new campus in Santa Fe, New Mexico, moving west in order to expand access to the St. John's program without sacrificing the intimate learning environment. Today the two campuses operate under one governing board but with separate presidents and faculties. Students are able to freely transfer between campuses, as do some faculty. Like the academic program, this structure is a unique arrangement that reflects St. John's mission, which is classical in spirit and innovative in practice. "St. John's seeks to restore the true meaning of a liberal arts education," the academic bulletin declares forthrightly. That in itself is unorthodox in today's academic climate.

Academic Life: To the Core

All students and tutors at St. John's study the same core texts. Students spend their freshman year with Greek philosophers and writers, the sophomore year immersed in the Roman, medieval, and Renaissance periods, the third year grappling with the Enlightenment, and the senior year coming to terms with modernity. Tutors at St. John's tend to teach there for many decades, and the best can boast of having taught every class offered, including the Greek and French language tutorials. This isn't just a good set of coursework, this is the essence of liberal arts education.

St. John's promises students a dialogue with civilization's great ideas. (For this, the *Chronicle of Higher Education* has dubbed the college "a bastion of Western culture.") The literature reading list, for example, includes works by Aeschylus, Virgil, Dante, Chaucer, Shakespeare, Racine, Moliere, Tolstoy, Rimbaud, Kafka, and Faulkner. "St. John's is persuaded that a genuine liberal arts education requires the study of great books — texts of words, symbols, notes, pictures — because they express most originally and often most perfectly the ideas by which contemporary life is knowingly or unknowingly governed," the academic bulletin explains. The books "change our minds, move our hearts, and touch our spirits."

All students begin the St. John's program as freshmen, even those who have begun or completed studies at other colleges. The advantage of this approach is that students and their classmates read the same texts together, which affords a common reference point. Each year, student-initiated study groups spring up, devoted to examining certain ideas in depth or to augmenting the official reading list with related texts.

The heart of the academic program is a twice-weekly seminar (in all four years) in which philosophy, theology, political science, literature, history, economics, and psychology are considered. The ground rules for discussion are basic. "Reason is the only recognized authority," the college explains. About twenty students and two tutors gather to consider an assigned reading. They address one another by last names, so as to put every participant on an equal footing. References to earlier readings can be made, but students and tutors are discouraged from citing texts that would be unfamiliar to other seminar participants. There is no set agenda, beyond fleshing out the reading. Although tutors are charged with concluding seminars at the appropriate time, classrooms at St. John's do not contain clocks; great conversations, the college believes, are not bounded by time.

Nor by architecture: conversation spill outs from seminars into the open air. "Discussions here take place — endlessly, it seems — beneath the quadrangle's trees, in the busy coffee shop, over meals," the *Chronicle of Higher Education* has noted. A "take your tutor to lunch" option permits students to invite tutors to dine with them, and the eight-to-one student-faculty ratio assures ample access to faculty outside of class. As a reflection of the importance given to dialectical inquiry, no tests are given at St. John's.

Separate tutorials and laboratories explore more specialized subjects and material. Each year Johnnies take a mathematics tutorial in which geometry, astronomy, algebra, calculus, and relativity are covered. The thrice-weekly classes are led by one tutor and enroll about fifteen students, who together work with short but challenging readings or proofs. Likewise, tutorials in Greek language are offered for freshmen and sophomores and in French for juniors and seniors. Language tutorials are primarily concerned with translation, and the class works through texts together. During the sophomore year, students also take a tutorial in musical theory and composition.

A third component of the curriculum is science laboratories. These are aimed at studying biology, chemistry, atomic theory, and physics through replicating the famous scientific experiments, such as William Harvey's work on the human heart. Because all students take science, the laboratory exercises are integrated into texts being read simultaneously in seminar. Thus laboratory may cover genetics at the same time the seminar is reading Darwin.

Finally, juniors and seniors choose from a list of fifteen to twenty preceptorials that are offered by tutors each year. These are the only "electives" at St. John's, and students usually can select from a range of authors and texts that are outside of the standard reading list.

Because tutors are assigned the role of Socratic midwives — drawing out conversation rather than directing it — students are assigned to seminars, tutorials, and labs and thus do not "choose" tutors. St. John's uses this system because it discourages the elevation of individual tutors' personalities over the texts. Nevertheless, students confess to having favorite tutors. At the Santa Fe campus, David Bolotin, Joshua Kates, and Cary Stickney are standouts; in Annapolis, Leo Raditsa, David Townsend, Mera Flaumenhaft, Elizabeth Blettner, Anita Kronsberg, Erik Sageng, and George Russell are commended by students. "The tutors I didn't like were those who talked too much and who seemed too interested in their own topics," a recent graduate says. "Overall, the tutors have a good breadth of knowledge, work hard at asking good questions to stimulate discussion, and are available for private consultation."

Tutors are intimately involved with assessing the academic progress of students. Each semester, students sit for an oral exam that takes the form of a conversation about recent readings and their connection to the liberal arts in general. Another form of student appraisal occurs when freshmen and sophomores attend a "don rag" session at which a student's tutors will discuss his performance in the third person, with the student listening as an observer. By the junior year, the don rag gives way to a student-tutor conference, at which the student offers a self-analysis of his work.

In addition, during their first three years, students submit reflective essays (in the spring term in Annapolis, at the end of each semester in Santa Fe) based on the seminar readings. The essay and oral exam at the end of the sophomore year is especially critical, as they used to determine whether a student will be permitted to advance to third-year studies. Tutors expect the student to be familiar with the prescribed texts and to demonstrate critical thinking.

During the spring semester of their senior year, students are furloughed from classes for a month to write an analytical paper on a subject of their choosing. Each paper is then defended before a panel of tutors at a session open to the public. The seriousness with which St. John's regards the senior thesis was demonstrated several years ago when it was discovered that a recent graduate's paper contained plagiarized material. After an investigation, the faculty voted not only to rescind the student's degree but to impose expulsion as a punishment, meaning that the student was unable to finish a degree at the college.

If all of this sounds intimidating, the success with which many students navigate the four-year regimen should be reassuring. "When I talk to friends of mine at other schools, the difference between our educations is astounding," a current student says.

St. John's claims that its students are self-selecting, because it attracts those eager to obtain the kind of education once reserved for royalty and today largely replaced by preprofessional and elective-based studies. Whatever the secret of their success, St. John's graduates are passionate boosters of their college. "The program fulfilled every expectation I had about reading and discussing the Great Books," a young alumna says. "The individual must read a primary work and wrestle with its meaning for herself, not rely on expert opinion. There she must be able to express some of her opinions and questions to others and response to their comments. Such a method of leaning builds community and emphasizes the skill of active listening, two things that don't happen in a typical lecture hall."

Objections to the Great Books are predominantly offered by political liberals who dislike the curriculum's focus on Western civilization and suspect the approach of elitism. To answer such criticism, a black alumnus recently wrote an article in which he declared that "St. Johns is what a college ought to be, and blacks, as well as all races, should not be put off by the general homogeneity of the curriculum." He added that the Great Books "lengthen our attention span, teach us to cultivate humanity, help us to fully appreciate what it means to be human and to exist." Those virtues may be cultivated by Western texts but they benefit people from all cultures and backgrounds.

Conservatives, too, have sometimes been wary of the Great Books approach, fearing that it encourages either relativism (because, in the face of so many persuasive, yet conflicting, arguments students may succumb to collecting ideas rather than evaluating them) or progressivism (by concluding that modernity has overcome the timeless questions facing man). In practice, however, these concerns are allayed by the enduring appreciation that most Johnnies have for ancient philosophy and by their relentless search for truth. One student allows that "the strength of the program, however, is also its weakness — no secondary sources, no 'context' " to help put ideas in perspective.

Many parents and high school students have more fundamental concerns about the vocational applications of a St. John's education. The college offers, in reply, the opinion that attending St. John's will prepare a student for a lifetime of intellectual and professional challenges. "Despite daily assertions to the contrary, there is no educational device for assuring worldly success to students," the academic bulletin states. "To cultivate the rational human powers of the individual so that, armed with the intellectual and moral virtues, he or she may hope to withstand the vicissitudes of outrageous fortune — that is liberal education."

At the same time, St. John's has aggressively sought opportunities to better prepare students for graduate studies and professional employment. The Annapolis campus recently received a $1.1 million grant to start a summer program in which selected students receive an internship and stipend designed to offer practical applications of their learning. A survey of the post-graduation activities of Johnnies is also reassuring: 20 percent go into law or teaching and another 20 percent pursue business careers. Others pursue more unusual occupations; a recent alumna has become a successful romance novelist. "We will not prepare you for careers, but we will give you the chance to discover a vocation," a long-time tutor says.

Political Atmosphere: Think Bohemian, Live Bourgeois

The small size of St. John's and the intellectual rigor there conspire against the kind of student activism prevalent elsewhere. Johnnies are likely to have strong opinions about current events, but few students have the time to agitate when Greek or French translations beckon. The college is not so much disengaged from the world — after all, both Annapolis and Santa Fe are state capitals — as it is a self-contained community in which political questions are timeless. No visitor who attends a Friday night lecture on campus, which attract hundreds of students and tutors and sometimes stretch past midnight, can miss the profound spirit of common intellectual inquiry that animates the college. One alumnus, writing about the St. John's spirit, has reached back to Gustave Flaubert's remark about how it is well to live as a bourgeois but to think like a bohemian.

Owing perhaps to their respective terrains and surrounding communities, the Annapolis and Santa Fe campuses have a reputation for being somewhat different. Annapolis is a quintessential Mid-Atlantic seaport town, neatly maintained and taking its character from the legislators, naval officers, and affluent professionals who share it with St. John's. It is rich in history, with many street names and buildings reflecting its British colonial past. While Annapolis sits on the Chesapeake Bay, Santa Fe saddles the Sangre de Cristo mountain chain and was home to Spanish settlers and later to artist communes. Santa Fe has a reputation as more free spirited than Annapolis, and tends to attract students who would find East Coast culture confining.

Not surprisingly, Johnnies from campus tend to look askance at the other. "Santa Fe is for the weed-smoking hippies to hang out in the mountains!" one Annapolis student says. Meanwhile, a Santa Fe undergrad recently posted a comment on the Annapolis campus's Web site lamenting the latter's reputation for political apathy. Yet each fall some students exchange campuses and thus experience first hand how geography influences the culture within which learning takes place.

Because the academic program of St. John's is well-known to students who choose to attend, the school has been spared the ravages of the culture war. There is periodic discussion about whether the curriculum should be revised to include more recent works, including more by women and minorities, but a curriculum that already includes Homer, St. Augustine, Cervantes, Spinoza, Lobachevsky, W. E. B. DuBois, and Flannery O'Connor does not lack for "multicultural" credentials.

Since tutors ideally function as participants in classroom discussions rather than as proponents for particular ideological viewpoints, there is little opportunity for political advocacy to seep into teaching. In many ways, St. John's is more focused on the process by which knowledge is apprehended and evaluated than it is on fostering agreement about the great questions of mankind. "St. John's is probably one of the few places in this country where you have the ability to study texts on their own terms — without professors' bias (for the most part) and a certain 'accepted' interpretation of what the books say," an undergraduate says.

One of the recurrent complaints of students is that reason is so highly esteemed at St. John's that the influence of other human instincts, such as passion and faith, are implicitly devalued. Some students speculate that the importance given to rationality in classrooms encourages the Bacchic excess that sometimes prevails among students on weekends and at social occasions. "Religion and aesthetics are viewed as subordinate to the holy 'reason' by the majority of students," one undergrad says. "There is quite a lot of hostility toward religiosity in general among the student body. At the same time, there are many conversions (particularly to Catholicism) that I have seen happen as people make their way to their senior year."

The Bible and several medieval and modern theologians are included in the curriculum and generally receive a respectful reception from tutors and students. "Tutors seem to have a basic respect for Christian beliefs, if dealt with in an intellectual rather than personal manner," a recent graduate says. She adds that students would be well advised to approach religious texts within a framework of searching for the truth rather than constructing a "brief for certain points of theology."

Student Life: Crossing the Continental Divide

With its intense academic program, St. John's recognizes the important recreational purpose that social activities serve. Each campus makes the most of the surrounding terrain. In Annapolis, a boathouse allows students to sign out college-owned sailboats and dingies and houses a crew team. An annual croquet match against neighboring Naval Academy midshipmen attracts an enthusiastic audience who come dressed in linen to munch on cucumber sandwiches while watching the competition (Johnnies have prevailed in fifteen of the past eighteen matches).

The mountainous environs of the Santa Fe campus are conducive to rafting trips down the Rio Grande and ski outings to Taos, two hours away. A student Search and Rescue Team trains and cooperates with New Mexico authorities in emergency operations.

Fencing and soccer are popular at both campuses. The Annapolis student newspaper is called the *Gadfly* and the Santa Fe equivalent is called the *Moon*. Other clubs and activities include film clubs, madrigal and theatre groups, Sunday concerts, and student government.

As with any campus, organized parties run the gambit from elegant to debauched. Each campus sponsors a series of waltz parties that feature swing music and themes such as the Halloween Masqued Ball, Mid-Winter Ball, Spring Cotillion, and Commencement Waltz. Upperclassmen and tutors are eager to teach newer students how to waltz, with the result that dances are well attended. More earthy entertainment occurs at annual events such as the Seducers and Corrupters Party (freshmen wear white; upperclassmen black) and Reality Weekend (organized by the junior class each spring). The Pink Triangle Society in Annapolis sponsors an annual "J. Edgar Hoover Memorial Ball."

Although St. John's strives to enforce prevailing state laws, alcohol is as much a regular component of social life on campus as it was in ancient Greek society. This may disappoint students from more conservative backgrounds. "I can't say that St. John's is as much of a community as I had originally hoped," one student says, while otherwise expressing satisfaction with the college.

Six traditional dorms in Annapolis house students, whereas the Santa Fe campus has constructed sixteen townhouse-style units for student lodging. The rooms are functional but not always spacious, and some of the Annapolis buildings show signs of aging. Unmarried students are required to reside on campus and purchase the meal plan, unless a dispensation is obtained from the dean. About 75 percent of students live on campus, and parking is generally accessible.

The brick-style Annapolis campus, which is located in close urban proximity to both the state capitol and public housing, has experienced some muggings in recent years, and the campus security has responded by offering safety tips and providing students with police whistles. Santa Fe's adobe-style campus is located two miles from the downtown and is more separated from the adjoining community. Both offer students twenty-four-hour computer access and have libraries with collections and furnishing designed to aid serious readers.

"The small size of SJC I found to be pleasant and agreeable, the library to be well-stocked in support of the program, the facilities to be adequate, and the overall intellectual atmosphere to be outstanding," one senior says. It is, as the lousy rock song goes, hip to be (somewhat) square. For example, at the long and rigorous lectures and discussions on Friday nights, which showcase both visiting scholars and favorite tutors, students and tutors have been known to display their knowledge much as peacocks do their plumage. But such antics should not scare off prospective students. Like any community, St. John's has its own style and its members are quick to point fun at "Johnnie Jargon" — stock seminar questions such as "What is the Greek on that?" and "Who has another translation?" The intense intellectualism of a school like St. John's is thus balanced by rhetorical playfulness and an appreciation of human folly. For some of America's brightest high school students, that proves to be an appealing combination.

Seton Hall University

Office of Admissions
Seton Hall University
400 South Orange Avenue
South Orange, New Jersey 07079-2680
(800) 843-4255
www.shu.edu

Total enrollment: 10,700
Undergraduates: 4,800
SAT ranges (Verbal/Math): 480-580 (V); 480-580 (M)
Applicants: 4,858
Accepted: 82%
Enrolled: 31%
Application deadline: March 1
Financial aid application deadline: February 15
Tuition: $16,990/$22,440
Core curriculum: No

Mirror, Mirror

The history of Seton Hall University mirrors the evolution of Catholicism in the United States. Founded in 1856 to provide "a home for the mind, the heart, and the spirit," the university historically has drawn its student body from Catholic families in New Jersey and the New York metropolitan area. But the school's Catholic identity partially was submerged during the mid-twentieth century by the national tide of radical theological and political change. In the years since, Seton Hall has moved to reemphasize its Catholic tradition, with the pace quickening under president Msgr. Robert T. Sheeran's leadership. The result: a Catholic university evolving from being a regional treasure to a national resource.

Academic Life: Coming Soon

The oldest diocesan Catholic university in the United States, Seton Hall University encompasses nine academic divisions, including the College of Arts and Sciences, Stillman School of Business, School of Diplomacy and International Relations, College of Education and Human Services, College of Nursing, and several other graduate-level divisions, including the School of Law and a seminary. One professor says that Seton Hall "definitely has the feel of an undergraduate campus."

All undergraduates, regardless of which academic division they enter, must complete a distribution scheme that requires two semesters of English, one semester of math, one semester of oral communication, two semesters of social sciences, two semesters of natural sciences, three semesters of philosophy and religion, and two semesters of history. Arts and Sciences students additionally complete at least two semesters of a foreign language. All told, it's a rather standard scheme of distribution requirements.

All first-year students complete a Freshman Studies program in which a professor or administrator is assigned to be a student's mentor. Mentors teach a related freshman course that addresses time management, study habits, and like topics. An upperclassman is also assigned to each course section to serve as a peer advisor to the new students. One professor confesses that the program "tends to infantilize the incoming class rather than challenge them to reach maturity," but faculty agree that Freshman Studies has improved student retention. To eliminate it, then, would be to throw out the infants with the bath water, as it were.

Students considering Seton Hall should explore some of the features it offers to gifted students. Merit scholarships, including some targeted toward alumni offspring, racial minorities, and females, are available by application. Other students may wish to pursue funding through Army ROTC, which is sponsored on campus.

Applicants with long-term professional plans already in mind will want to consider the dual admission program with Seton Hall's School of Law or the five-year engineering program offered in conjunction with the New York Institute of Technology.

One scholarly gem at Seton Hall is the Honors Program, which draws its students from among freshman applicants with SAT scores of 1,200 and higher. It consists of four semester-long colloquia devoted to the history of civilization, from ancient through medieval and early modern cultures to contemporary civilization. Each student then completes two honors seminars before writing an honors thesis under the direction of a faculty member. The faculty, who are drawn from across the humanities disciplines, foster a liberal arts spirit and have considerable contact time with students because of small class sizes. One professor commends the program as "an important part of the intellectual life of the place." Another professor describes it as "a very strong attraction for high-performing applicants," although he cautions that it encourages the search for philosophic truths rather than an appreciation of Catholicism.

But that is where the interdisciplinary Center for Catholic Studies, directed by Msgr. Richard Liddy, fits in. It aspires to engage students "in the imaginative and sacramental expressions of Catholic life in literature, the arts, social systems, and personal experiences." The center offers both an undergraduate minor and courses that are cross-listed with other departments (thus counting toward distribution requirements). Many courses examine the relationship between Catholicism and history, politics, art, literature, and music. "Its interdisciplinary nature allows students to encounter the beauty and vitality of Catholicism as it is expressed across the disciplines," Liddy has written. "By examining the role Catholicism has played in various cultures, students are challenged to take seriously its influence in every aspect of intellectual, spiritual, and social life." The center sends thirty students to Italy each year to study "The Emergence of Christian Rome," and there are plans to introduce a major in Catholic studies in the coming years.

Students headed in a business direction should look into the Institute for Leadership Studies, which integrates business and financial skills through courses in which regular faculty are augmented by visiting lecturers drawn from the business community. Business majors are eligible for mentoring by corporate leaders, as well as for summer internships, overseas studies, and a co-op program.

One faculty member says that the Seton Hall student body "has a lot of first-generation college students from ascendant working and lower middle class backgrounds whose families typically have to be convinced of the virtues of a liberal arts education." Although some students invariably view college as only a practical, vocational endeavor, others awaken to the liberal arts tradition during their four years on campus. Another professor favorably contrasts "the real learners" present in every class with "the great middle" who are more vocationally motivated.

The student-to-faculty ratio at Seton Hall is fourteen to one, with an average class size of twenty-five. Enrollment in freshman English sections is capped at fifteen, and specialized programs such as the Honors College have similarly limited enrollments.

More than sixty majors and concentrations are available to Seton Hall students. Faculty speak highly of the English department, which includes poets Jeffrey Gray and David Rogers. The history department is strong in American social and constitutional history and European intellectual history, and is open to considering the Catholic dimensions of the subjects. Notable history faculty include Dermot Quinn, William Connell, Ralph Walz, and Patrick Caulker. The philosophy department is anchored by Rev. John Ranieri, David O'Connor, and Robert Mayhew. A new Italian studies program, drawing 150 students a semester to its classes, offers on-campus cultural activities and a summer program in Italy.

Faculty report that the religious studies department is divided between liberationists and traditionalists, although recent appointments provide reason for hope. Msgr. Liddy in the Center for Catholic Studies and Fr. Larry Frizzell in the Institute for Judaeo-Christian Studies merit the attention of students who are interested in approaching orthodoxy seriously.

The sociology and anthropology department emphasizes cultural interpretations of global problems, and students recommend Baron Pineda as an especially gifted teacher. The publication of Richard Rhodes's *Why They Kill* brought national attention to criminal justice professor Lonnie Athens, whom a colleague describes as "very smart and well read."

As distinguished Seton Hall professors such as Stanley Jaki, Edward S. Shapiro, and Robert Herrera retire or take reduced teaching loads, they are being replaced by rising scholars who are "very impressively credentialed," according to one faculty member. Another professor joins in this assessment: "In my opinion the younger faculty represent real hope for the university." This is not something one hears on most campuses, and bears note.

Political Atmosphere: Counter Statements

"A university is Catholic in many ways: by instruction, by the creative faith and love of its members, as well as by living the Catholicity proclaimed," Seton Hall's Catholicity Statement observes. A Seton Hall education therefore involves "a constant challenge to be a witness to the Christ whom we believe has come to liberate and fulfill every person coming into the world, and it is an exploration of the consequences of that faith." A copy of the statement is furnished to all newly hired faculty, along with a request that they conduct their teaching and research in harmony with the underlying philosophy of the university.

In recent years, however, political strife has arisen over competing understandings of Catholicism's implications for a university community. "There are crucifixes on building walls and on the green, and we do have several very public religious events," one longtime professor remarks. "But there is a strong, very liberal group of faculty who would challenge many of today's Church teachings. So Seton Hall University continues to be a bifurcated institution with an administration that doesn't want to make drastic changes." At the same time, the university has not hesitated to oppose unsound innovations, as was shown in the early 1990s when the administration refused recognition to a homosexual student group called "Wilde!" despite repeated entreaties to do so from the student senate.

Although geographically removed from the main campus, Seton Hall's School of Law has developed a reputation for fomenting religious dissent. Supreme Court justice Clarence Thomas once cancelled a scheduled appearance at the law school after feminist students and faculty vowed to stage a protest. Then, in November 1998, three law student groups announced that New Jersey governor Christine Todd Whitman would be presented with an award honoring women who have promoted public policy. The annual Sandra Day O'Connor Medal of Honor, so named after the Supreme Court justice who was an early recipient of it, was previously awarded also to Hillary Clinton and Barbara Jordan. Msgr. Sheeran, who had newly assumed responsibilities as Seton Hall president, swiftly barred the awards ceremony for Whitman from on campus. "Seton Hall has a clearly stated policy that no public recognition is given to those espousing positions contrary to our Catholic mission," he said. "This includes those publicly supporting pro-choice views."

Some faculty at the law school remain unpersuaded by Sheeran's statement.

Shortly after the fiasco with Whitman, the law school hosted an American Civil Liberties Union conference that featured a lawyer who had litigated in court against New Jersey's partial-birth abortion ban. The proponents of such social activism cited in support of their position the Catholicity Statement's declaration that "Seton Hall exercises its mandate of service to humanity first by providing high quality education, and by committing its resources to address the complex problems of church and society: hunger, war, poverty, racism, sexism, all forms of injustice, and environmental degradation."

In response, Seton Hall has sought to reemphasize its Catholic identity through the Center for Catholic Studies and the Institute for Judaeo-Christian Studies. One faculty member explains, "Significant persons among both faculty and students are actively engaged in evangelizing this campus." This trend was visibly demonstrated when Msgr. Sheeran invited the G. K. Chesterton Institute to relocate to campus, adding Rev. Ian Boyd and his *Chesterton Review* to the Seton Hall community. "Fr. Ian Boyd is an internationally recognized scholar with an enormously wide range of contacts," a humanities professor notes. "Indeed in a real sense, he has made the institute into not only a national but an international resource." In addition, the university is developing a relationship with the Newman Institute in Ireland.

The university has hosted a variety of guest speakers, ranging from Sinn Fein leader Gerry Adams to Wendy Shalit, who authored *A Return to Modesty*. Poetry-in-the-Round has brought top-drawer literary figures to campus for twenty years.

Student Life: Tragedy Strikes Home

Seton Hall's 58-acre main campus is located in South Orange, about a dozen miles west of New York City. The setting is suburban and, beyond the sporadic burglary, quite safe. A downtown, within walking distance of campus, features shopping and restaurants and has a train station that connects South Orange with Manhattan and beyond. The Meadowlands and the New Jersey Performing Arts Center in Newark are also nearby.

Although most students commute to school from their homes or off-campus apartments, 40 percent of Seton Hall undergraduates live on campus in traditional dorms or apartment-style buildings. Many freshmen live in the Boland dorms, which are coed by floor and organized according to shared interests. Boland houses students in doubles and in four-person suites. Another option is Aquinas Hall, in which both freshmen and upperclassmen reside. Each two-room suite in Aquinas features a shared bathroom, with a common kitchenette available on every floor.

The nation mourned with Seton Hall after a January 2000 fire swept through several floors in Boland, causing three deaths and a number of injuries. Following the fire, Msgr. Sheeran moved into the dorm for the rest of the school year, providing reassurance to students. Priests and other counselors were made available to students. (Nearly fifty priests live on the Seton Hall campus, some in residence exclusively at seminary while others are engaged in undergraduate teaching and campus ministry.) The university also spent more than $500,000 to assist victims and their families, and announced that sprinklers would be installed in all student rooms.

Lawyers for the families of the dead and injured students complained that the university had not done enough to prevent the fire in the fifty-year-old dorm and was not doing enough in its aftermath to assist the families and students. "I am not naïve about the law and tactics used in the pursuit of justice," Sheeran said in response. "However, when attorneys question our compassion, and the care and support of this community, I take umbrage. We will continue to do whatever we can; but in the face of such loss it will never be enough. It cannot be enough — how could it be? We will do what we can, because it is right — it is the compassionate thing to do and it is what our faith calls us to do."

Seton Hall has dormitory space for 2,100 students, and a data connection is provided for each resident. The Mobile Computer Program, the cost of which is included in tuition, offers every student the use of a laptop computer, and many professors have incorporated computer applications into their teaching. Public data ports are available in library carrels, lounges, and even outdoor park benches. The laptops are updated on a two-year cycle.

Although the *Princeton Review* has rated Seton Hall as a "top party school," the freshman residence halls are officially substance-free. About 15 percent of undergraduates join one of twenty-two fraternities and sororities that have campus chapters. Rush occurs during the second semester, after freshmen have become accustomed to college life.

Nearly 30 percent of Seton Hall students are ethnic minorities. A Puerto Rican Institute reflects a longstanding relationship between the university and Puerto Rico. There are more than seventy student groups, including the nationally ranked Brownson speech team, a campus radio station and newspaper, and many volunteer organizations. A student organization known as CAST organizes lectures and events connected with Catholic studies.

The Seton Hall Pirates athletic teams play in the Big East conference and draw fervent student crowds. In addition to the eighteen varsity teams, a variety of intramural and club sports are available to amateur athletes, and an indoor recreational center offers a pool, running track, courts, and other facilities.

Sewanee, the University of the South

735 University Ave.
Sewanee, TN 37383-1000
(800) 522-2234
www.sewanee.edu

Total enrollment: 1318
Undergraduates: 1318
SAT ranges (Verbal/Math): 570-660 (V); 560-660 (M)
Applicants: 1,642
Accepted: 73%
Enrolled: 33%
Application deadline: February 1
Financial aid application deadline: March 1
Tuition: $20,130/$25,740
Core curriculum: No

Arcadia Shared

One of the purposes of this guide is to highlight institutions that are unique and academically challenging. More than most, Sewanee, as the University of the South is commonly known, fits this description. Geographically isolated yet not too remote, The Domain (as the campus is known) is adorned with beautiful buildings and thousands of acres of forest and fields. Yet it also boasts a tradition of academic excellence and adherence to the liberal arts that attract talented teachers and students.

In 1941, the Southern poet William Alexander Percy wrote of Sewanee, his alma mater: "It's a long way away, even from Chattanooga, in the middle of woods, on top of a bastion of mountains crenelated with blue coves. It is so beautiful that people who have once been there always, one way or another, come back. For such as can detect apple green in an evening sky, it is Arcadia — not the one that never used to be, but the one that many people always live in; only this one can be shared."

Established by the Southern dioceses of the Episcopal church just before the War Between the States and grandly named the University of the South, the school saw decades of hard times both during the war (when Federal troops blew up the cornerstone of the chapel) and afterwards, when it closed for a time. Its first convocation was held in 1868, with nine students and four professors present. Oxford and Cambridge Universities in England sent books to help stock the struggling school's library, and with time and dedication Sewanee became a seat of learning and maturation for generations of Southern men. It became coed in 1969 and abolished mandatory Saturday classes in the 1980s.

A few years ago, the school's traditions and Southern identity seemed at risk. The former vice chancellor (who acts as a president), Samuel Williamson, tried to reconstruct Sewanee in the image of a larger New England school by attempting to increase enrollment and emphasizing interdisciplinary programs and academic and social diversity. Yet, as one professor puts it, the administrator "discovered that a school with a significant history such as Sewanee cannot be fundamentally changed in a decade." Says another faculty member: "The outgoing vice chancellor clearly regarded the Southern identification of the school as a handicap to its national prestige, and there are those who would be happy to lose the name 'University of the South' and become simply 'Sewanee,' believing that the official name discourages some applicants." But, this professor says, "these attitudes are mistaken — for every student repelled by [the official name], there's at least one who's drawn by it." Speaking of Sewanee's particularity, this professor says, "Those qualities are remarkably stubborn here and don't seem to be particularly responsive to administrative fiat." Adds another teacher, "We are not the Williams or Amherst of the South. We have our own identity."

Today a new administration led by Joel Cunningham seems more interested in maintaining Sewanee's traditions while strengthening its core strengths in the liberal arts — very good news for anyone who favors the availability of diverse choices in American higher education. Cunningham's "personality and social skills seem the opposite of the outgoing president's," says a professor. "I think the new vice chancellor is the kind of person we need right now: honest, direct, moderately frugal, even a bit humble, appreciative of our past but aware that we cannot be the kind of school we were in the '60s, '70s, '80s, or '90s." Hence, the wishes of professors, students, and alumni to keep Sewanee a unique, high-quality university have had an impact on the direction of the school. As the essay below reveals, this is a great good, for there is much to cherish at this remote yet justly famous Southern institution. As a professor says, "Teachers whom I know at other institutions are envious" of the quality of the intellectual and social life on "the mountain."

Academic Life: A 'Liberal' Definition of a Core

The definition of a core curriculum has changed over the past few decades, so that what was once considered a core (twenty or more courses) has all but disappeared. Today, universities sometimes claim a set of ten or more courses required of all students as a core, and Sewanee follows that development. This stretches the definition a bit, especially when — as at Sewanee — the students have choices within the so-called core. Still, the program at Sewanee does a good bit to ensure a broad liberal education for all students. "The 'core requirements,' though not amounting to a core curriculum in the strictest sense . . . are quite extensive and in several respects quite rigorous," one professor says.

So Sewanee has a better-than-average set of distribution requirements, and other institutions would do well to adopt this approach if a core curriculum is for some reason out of the question. Among the courses required of all students are a course in English literature and two writing-intensive courses; a foreign language at the third-year level or above; one course in mathematics; two courses in the sciences; one course in history and another in either anthropology, economics, or political science; a course in either religion or philosophy; a course in the fine arts, music, or theatre; and two semesters of physical education. "Sewanee has maintained a remarkably traditional curriculum in comparison with competing institutions and certainly . . . with the Ivy League schools," a professor says. "We still have a serious language requirement!" Another professor notes the number of course hours each student must take outside his major, saying it has the effect of "precluding excessive specialization."

But this list of required courses has been watered down over the past several years. Once, students were required to take classes in both philosophy *and* religion, whereas now they may take one or the other. One semester of mathematics is required now, down from two. The same is true in some majors: it was once thought that English majors needed a full year of Shakespeare, whereas now they take only one semester — still better than some places where The Bard is just another option. The same major used to require one year on the great works of literature, but that has now been cut in half. There are no majors in the usually politicized fields of women's studies or ethnic studies, although there are "concentrations," which do not have departmental status.

Still, Sewanee's refusal to become a professionalized training school for particular industries is sound educational philosophy, as well as good business. Today's world of commerce moves, literally, at the speed of light, and snap decisions require quick learning and agile judgment. These qualities are nurtured by broad reading and learning, and quality students usually prefer to read and write rather than fill in case study books. Sewanee has no trouble filling its liberal arts classes. "The liberal arts still garner far more majors than do the social sciences and pure sciences" says a professor. Says another: "I think we are very well situated as a school with appeal to those who seek a traditional liberal arts education in a serious academic environment. I've told many parents and prospective students that the best way to judge the academic seriousness of a school is to visit the bookstore . . . and see what books are really being taught in classes. In that kind of comparison, we look very, very good."

This tradition is borne out in a look at the strongest departments. The English department — the most popular major on campus — has been home over the years to many literary figures of national note, including Monroe Spears, Andrew Lytle, Allen Tate, and Caroline Gordon. It is the home of the nation's oldest and most prestigious literary quarterly, the *Sewanee Review,* edited by George Core. "The English department continues to attract the most majors and . . . recently received enthusiastic reviews from a visiting evaluation committee composed of teachers from Princeton, Kenyon, Davidson, and Rhodes," a professor says. The department's commitment to traditional courses focusing on historical fields rather than trendy (and passing) subjects "was singled out for particular praise from teachers whose [home] departments have lost sight of the center, as one reviewer put it," the professor says.

In addition to English, history, political science, and the natural sciences are all considered strong. While other departments might not be as strong as those, one faculty member says, "I'm not sure that any Sewanee department is 'politicized' in that it is dominated by an intolerant leftist agenda." Religion is said by some to be a weak department, in part because of the small size of the faculty.

Among the best teachers at Sewanee are Susan J. Ridyard, Woody Register, Charles R. Perry, and William Brown Patterson in history; James R. Peters in philosophy; Eric W. Naylor in Spanish; Gayle E. McKeen in political science; and Robert G. Benson, Dale E. Richardson, John Grammer, Pamela R. Macfie, Thomas M. Carlson, and Wyatt Prunty in English.

Students tend to get more attention at Sewanee than at other places. The student-teacher ratio is eleven to one, and the classes are small and never led by teaching assistants. The impact of this attention, of course, depends on the student's state of mind. "If by age eighteen, you know you want to be a chemist or an M.D., you might do OK to go to Cal Tech or some such highly specialized school," a professor said a few years ago. "But 85 percent of undergraduates out there are still very young and still need a liberal arts education. They need to grow up a little bit, and they need to be taught by professors and not graduate students. A small liberal arts college offers a lot to grow morally and ethically. Here they can also absorb the history of the South and the fact that people do make mistakes."

Sewanee offers students the opportunity to take some courses on a pass-fail basis. To be eligible for pass-fail grading, a student must have a 2.0 GPA, and no required courses designated as prerequisite for a required course may be taken on a pass-fail system. The grade "pass" does not affect a student's GPA, but a "fail" counts as an F.

There are several interdisciplinary programs, including pre-law. The college says that 95 percent of its graduates who apply to law school are accepted. Med school applicants are successful at a rate of 89 percent. There is an engineering program that allows students to complete three years of work at Sewanee and finish their degree with two years at selected engineering schools, after which they receive a bachelor's degree from Sewanee and another in engineering from their chosen institution (the list of which includes Columbia University, Rensselaer Polytechnic Institute, Vanderbilt University, and Washington University in St. Louis). There is also a cooperative degree program in forestry with Duke University, and many study abroad programs.

Students matriculating at Sewanee tend to be quite good, although faculty members say that some of them require a little academic polishing. "Our best students are superb — on a par with the very best anywhere, as our Rhodes, Fulbright, and Watson scholars indicate," a professor says. "Our average students seem to me somewhat less prepared to handle a freshman" class than those of a generation ago. This is confirmed by a colleague: "The students I teach are not particularly well-prepared intellectually when they arrive, though most come with willing hearts and some genuine interest in learning. I'd say they're neither better nor worse" than in previous years. "It is indeed disappointing to see how little difference the improved SAT averages of our entering classes actually make in the classrooms," this professor says.

As for any old money still lying around The Domain, a professor says: "Sewanee has many affluent students but could hardly compare with Washington and Lee in that category because we remain the only school in our area that guarantees financial aid to those who meet the guidelines. [Whether] we can afford to remain 'need blind' . . . in the future remains to be seen. I strongly hope so."

Political Atmosphere: Flags in the Dust

With the change of administrations mentioned above, Sewanee seems to have regained its footing such that it can now concentrate on academics rather than politics. Most observers agree that some damage was done by the former administration, but that the school's traditions and academic excellence proved too strong for mere administrative meddling. The key is to find a balance between tradition and the need of all institutions to change in order to remain vibrant and alive. "I don't believe there's a necessary contradiction between what Richard Weaver calls 'reflective provincialism' and genuine cosmopolitanism, though reconciling the two requires imaginative leadership and a recognition that both are valuable," a professor says. "Here's hoping that our new vice chancellor will see it the same way."

The center of Sewanee, both physically and spiritually, has long been All Saints' Chapel, a large neo-Gothic church with stained glass windows, statuary, and a lovely choir in the chancel. Along the nave used to hang the flags of the Southern states whose Episcopal dioceses founded the university. These were removed by the Williamson administration, lest someone be offended by their presence. "People thought there was an unreconstructed element in Sewanee that refused to admit that chattel slavery was a tragedy," a professor commented not long afterwards. Taking down the flags "was done for outsiders. A central symbol of the school is the chapel itself. The Southern part of the school's identity gives it great wisdom, but the people who were against the flags didn't see it that way. The Southern tradition gives the school a humility that is missing in other parts of the country." This professor continues, "A symbol mediates between the people who read it and what it stands for. It [was] easier to simply take the flags down than to try to explain what they really meant."

Another professor says: "I'm not complacent about Sewanee's ability to maintain what I see as its real and rare virtues. We have a relatively senior faculty, much of which will retire in ten or fifteen years. A great deal could change very quickly after that, and I might be giving very different answers for the tenth edition of *Choosing the Right College.* But for now Sewanee is a good and valuable place."

There is no speech code masquerading as a sexual harassment code, as the latter is really just that: a ban on sexual harassment. The extent to which the code words "multiculturalism" (read cultural relativism) and "diversity" (read acceptance and not simply tolerance of just about anything) are used is a subject for some disagreement. One professor notes that these terms "are seldom heard and affect the curriculum in minor ways if at all. Most efforts to import cultural diversity actually originate with the students involved in a handful of extracurricular groups." Yet another faculty member disagrees: "The terms 'multiculturalism' and 'diversity' are more than 'bantered about.' I dislike the terminology whether applied to the curriculum or to student life at Sewanee, but the ideas behind the words are having an impact on weekly if not daily life."

Yet both professors agree that the buzzwords have stayed out of the curriculum. "Our liberal arts curriculum is still strongly oriented toward the cultural legacy of Europe and toward canonical texts in most disciplines," a professor says. "This is a campus where the most popular major is English and where the two most popular classes in that major are Shakespeare and Chaucer," says one professor. Another notes that Western civilization is still at the core of all departments, and that the English department "does not offer courses on women's issues in literature, American Indian literature, or even Hispanic-American literature." This person says, "We will never abandon the historical core courses — and we cover all of them."

Sewanee has resisted, for the most part, the creep toward becoming a research-oriented school. Good teaching is still very important in faculty culture there. "The standard here is high, and most of my colleagues pride themselves on their teaching and work hard at it," a professor says. "Even at the present moment, when the faculty is being pressured to do more research and publishing than in the past, bad teaching is probably the only sure-fire way to be denied tenure."

Students looking for grade inflation had better go elsewhere, for the older standards in that area still apply. Grade inflation is just one topic that is a big issue elsewhere, but excluded by the atmosphere at Sewanee. "There are so many arguments you don't have to have here," a professor says. "You aren't constantly defending the idea that there are great books worth everyone's time, or the value of liberal arts as opposed to vocational education, or the recognition that students should be held to a standard and not everyone can get an 'A.' Those ideas are shared by most faculty and students."

Student Life: Come In and Stay a While

In order to understand some of the traditions peculiar to the University of the South, both its isolation as well as its Southerness must be taken into account. Perched high atop a flat-topped mountain in the Cumberland Plateau of Southern Tennessee, Sewanee is far from the urban scene; Chattanooga is fifty-five miles to the east and Nashville is sixty-five miles in the other direction. Students must, therefore, create much of their own fun, and this they do with a vengeance. Long known for their work-hard, play-hard tendencies, students find that the isolation creates a close-knit community unthinkable in heavily populated areas.

The school provides so many outlets beyond the classroom that four years isn't enough to sample them all. "The *joie de vivre* [is now] remarkably similar to what I remember" a generation ago, says one alumnus. "So many events are scheduled not only during the weekends but during the week that we are not likely to become a suitcase college" says a professor. In fact, another professor says, the Residential Life office faces problems each Christmas and Spring Break in getting students to vacate their dorms. "And many of [the students] do anything they can think of to remain on campus during the summer," says this professor.

Another key element in the school's personality is found in the beauty of its grounds and architecture. Wide, expansive lawns are ringed with huge trees and numerous flowers, and most of the buildings are built of native sandstone. These include a new dining hall, which looks as if it was constructed a century ago, when collegiate gothic enjoyed wide popularity. All of this adds to the aura of the place and makes a campus visit a must for anyone considering Sewanee.

Students at Sewanee voluntarily adhere to (or, a pessimist might say, choose to ignore) a dress code that stipulates jacket and tie for men and skirts or dresses for women in the classroom. Although some professors report that most students follow this tradition, others note slippage over the past decade. "Most students dress well for class," says a professor. "T-shirt and jeans really are not acceptable in a class with a serious subject matter. Some students still believe you dress to honor the subject, not the teacher or school." Another professor says that on most days, only half of the students follow the dress code and that "these disproportionately are freshmen who soon learn that their compliance isn't really required or expected."

Some who do stand out by their dress are members of the Order of Gownsmen, the most prestigious student organization and the primary student governing body whose members, by all accounts, wear academic gowns to class today just as they have for years. Some 20 percent of the student body belongs to the Order. They also have special privileges, such as the ability to forego final examinations for classes in which they have an "A" average. Perhaps the fact that membership in this elite group is an honor helps explain their adherence to tradition. All students must sign and observe an honor code, which is upheld by a student-elected Honor Council.

Over the past decade enrollment grew from one thousand to 1,300, an expansion mandated by the Williamson administration. Yet "the friendliness and civility of the place seem to be undiminished," according to a professor, who adds that "students who witnessed the expansion have complained that they no longer know *everybody* on campus." Another expansion has been planned for the coming decade, although this one may find more opposition. "I do worry that at some point the general cordiality of the place, which really is our distinctive stock in trade, will begin to suffer," says a professor opposed to the move. Still, today students are frequently invited to the homes of professors, and any visitor will experience the best that Southern hospitality has to offer. Relations both among students and between students and faculty are genuinely warm. It's another consequence of the school's mannerly traditions and geographical isolation.

A few years ago some faculty worried that the expansion of the school would cause some faculty members to move miles away, nearer to Chattanooga, where their spouses could pursue careers. Yet that fear has been allayed, partly because of the Internet and its decentralizing effects on the nation's work force. "The commuting faculty member is a comparatively rare bird, though I'm sure less rare than he used to be," a professor says. "It must be said that Sewanee has been much more alert than most universities to the problems of spousal employment and works hard to solve them."

The community of Sewanee is unincorporated and is managed by the university, a fact that allows students to participate in the volunteer fire department and many other community activities. Students live as members of the community rather than as temporary residents with little connection to the surrounding population. Crime in Sewanee is very rare.

With no town available for off-campus living, nearly all students live on campus. There are both single-sex and coed dorms. There are no shared bathrooms. Students may choose substance- or smoke-free halls if they wish. There are also language houses in which those studying French, German, Russian, or Spanish may live. The true center of campus is All Saints' Chapel, a magnificent structure which, though technically a chapel, would be a sizable church in most towns. Also important to student life is the Bishop's Common, in which are housed a pub, dining room, snack bar, the student post office, lounges, meeting and game rooms, and offices for student organizations. The university operates a student-run radio station and a student newspaper, *The Sewanee Purple*. An alternative newspaper, *The Sewanee Legacy*, sees its mission as defending the university's traditions against attack.

Many national honor societies, such as Blue Key and Phi Beta Kappa, have chapters at Sewanee. More than 60 percent of the student body joins one of the eleven national fraternities or seven local sororities. Fraternities have their own houses and sororities have rooms in the Women's Center, although members live in dorms with the rest of the student body.

There are well over one hundred clubs and organizations for students to join, an amazing number for such a small school. Included in the long list is the Sewanee

Outing Program, the most popular organization. Its members take part in the school's hugely successful canoe team, which has won twenty-two intercollegiate championships, and have access to outdoor equipment, a matter of some importance on a 10,000-acre campus on top of a mountain in a rural part of Tennessee. There is also an equestrian program that offers riding along miles of trails and thirty acres of pasture. About 70 percent of the student body participates in an intramural sport. The college also fields nine NCAA Division III sports teams for men and an equal number for women.

The Sewanee Performing Arts Series sponsors six major theater, music, or dance performances each year. Sewanee also hosts several annual academic events, including the Sewanee Writers' Conference (founded with money from the estate of Tennessee Williams) and the Mediaeval Colloquium, both of which draw nationally known scholars and writers to campus. Those with singing talent may join the University Choir, which sings for the services in All Saints' Chapel.

Smith College

Garrison Hall
Northampton, MA 01063
(413) 585-2500
www.smith.edu

Total enrollment: 2,750
Undergraduates: 2,500
SAT ranges (Verbal/Math): 590-710 (V); 580-670 (M)
Applicants: 3,000
Accepted: 56%
Enrolled: 40%
Application deadline: January 15
Financial aid application deadline: January 1
Tuition: $23,400/$31,560
Core curriculum: No

Keeping Up with the Smithies

From its modest beginning in 1875 with fourteen students, Smith College has swelled to a current undergraduate enrollment of 2,500, making it the largest private women's college in the United States. Traditionally, Smith has been known for its strong liberal arts programs and its emphasis on women's issues. The college was founded with a bequest from Sophia Smith, who stated in her will her intent to "furnish for my own sex means and facilities for education equal to those which are afforded now in our colleges to young men." Famous graduates of Smith include poet Sylvia Plath, feminists Gloria Steinem and Betty Friedan, and chef Julia Child. When Smith alumna Barbara Bush became the first lady, Smith students (known to each other as "Smithies") paraded around in T-shirts emblazoned with: "There must be a better way to get a Smithie in the White House."

Smith women are considered an independent and motivated lot who often combine high academic achievement with a good measure of social activism. Some students and faculty, however, suggest that Smith's commitment to the liberal arts — particularly the humanities — has dwindled over the years, with an increased interest and emphasis on the sciences and the addition of majors in such areas as computer science and childhood education. And despite the college's commitment to academic freedom and free speech, students of a more traditional cast of mind may find the feminist perspective — which creeps its way into nearly every course by professorial design, student demand, or both — narrow and stifling.

Academic Life: Liberated Women

In keeping with the high level of independence and responsibility attributed to Smith undergraduates, there are no specific course requirements beyond the major. Instead, the college offers "just a few guidelines," according to one professor. Not surprisingly, Smith's abandonment of distribution requirements occurred in 1970, at a time when a general relaxation of social and academic standards was taking place in higher education nationwide. Although there has occasionally been talk of instituting more comprehensive general education requirements, nothing has come of it.

However, Smith has exhibited a renewed interest in encouraging a broad liberal arts education. The college guidebook advises students to take courses in seven fields of knowledge: literature, historical studies, social science, natural science, mathematics and analytical philosophy, the arts, and foreign language. In order to graduate with honors, students must now take at least one course in each of these areas. In addition, every student is now required to have one writing-intensive course during her freshman year, and must complete sixty-four credits outside her major to graduate.

Because many students want to graduate with honors, they avoid narrowness in their curriculum choices. And students note the advantages to the absence of a core curriculum, such as the option of taking upper-level classes at an early stage in one's studies. "I liked the freedom of being able to take whatever classes interested me," says one. But a recent graduate in mathematics expresses regret that she completed her degree "without taking a single science class."

The commitment to teaching is high among Smith faculty. With a student-faculty ratio of ten-to-one, the college boasts small courses — averaging fifteen students per class — and accessible teachers. (The small population of grad students on campus does not teach any classes or sections.) One student says that she never had a class with more than twenty-five students. Although they fall victim to the same pressures to publish as at other colleges, professors are very focused on teaching, and it is not uncommon for professors to invite students over for meals. Most welcome conversations with students in their offices, and 96 percent of the faculty holds doctoral degrees.

For the most part, Smith students are studious and disciplined. Unlike huge state schools and other colleges where her friends attended, "everybody does their reading for class," notes one student, and the academic environment is described as "pretty competitive." Popular majors include government, psychology, economics, biology, and art. Nearly a quarter of Smith students pursue the sciences. The new, scholarship-rich Picker Program in Engineering and Technology is the first such program at an undergraduate women's college. Interestingly, this program emphasizes the liberal arts and requires its participants to fulfill honors distribution requirements.

Rigorous interdepartmental majors and minors in medieval studies and ancient studies are also offered at Smith. Medieval studies, offered as a major and a minor, is described as a "vibrant program" by one professor, while ancient studies has almost been swallowed up by the languages and literature department and is only available as a minor. However, medieval studies may be the program at Smith most approaching a traditional liberal arts education. All students enrolled in the major are required to have a working knowledge of Latin and to gain in-depth knowledge of the history, religion, and art of European civilization of the era.

Recommended faculty at Smith include J. Patrick Coby and Donald C. Baumer in government and Carol G. Zaleski in religion and biblical literature.

Smith also boasts one of the best college art museums in the country, and one student describes how, in her drawing class, students were given assignments to trace some of the works in the impressive collection. "The studio art facility is right in the Smith art museum — it was a fantastic experience," she says. And it's about to get even better: The college's fine arts center is undergoing a $35 million expansion and renovation.

In addition to a number of interdepartmental emphases, Smith still offers programs of study in the major liberal arts disciplines: art, classical languages and literatures, economics, history, philosophy, and religion and biblical literature, for a total of forty-five majors and more than fifty minors. The college also has a major program in Afro-American studies, as well as an interdepartmental major in women's studies. As one might expect, many of the courses inevitably evoke women's issues, and courses with some variation on the title "Women and . . ." are all too common in the curriculum. The women's studies program is unabashedly radical, asserting in its program description that it will "encourage students to reconsider traditional interpretations of female experiences in many cultures and periods of history. The program is committed to examining the intersections of gender, race, class, ethnicity and sexuality." The description of their professors further suggests that they "share a desire to teach interdisciplinary courses rich in diversity, courses that might be considered too radical for traditional majors, courses that empower Smith students to think in new and exciting ways."

The department offers special concentrations in queer studies and women of color. In addition, Smith (in conjunction with Wesleyan University) recently launched a new scholarly publication, *Meridians,* which is "by and about women of color in a U.S. and an international context." Championed by Steinem herself, the journal has the subtitle "feminism, race, transnationalism."

Since 1994 — a virtual eternity in the capricious world of women's studies — comparative literature professor Thalia A. Pandiri has been teaching a course titled "'Unnatural' Women: Mothers Who Kill Their Children," often referred to at Smith as "Murdering Moms." "The more people realize that their assumptions are based on very specific cultural, socioeconomic, and historical accidents, the better it is," Pandiri told the *Chronicle of Higher Education.* "That's what I aim to do in anything I teach."

Currently the women's studies department is also hawking T-shirts: "Because women's lives matter," they say, "I study women in a major way."

Smith is a member of a five-college consortium, enabling students to enroll in classes or use facilities at Amherst College, Hampshire College, Mount Holyoke College, and the University of Massachusetts. Most Smithies take advantage of the five-college system, enrolling in two or three courses at one of the other four schools during their undergraduate career. Thirty percent of Smith students also participate in some kind of Junior Year Abroad (JYA) or exchange program. There are four college-sponsored JYA programs, in Florence, Hamburg, Geneva, and Paris, all of which require at least two years of foreign language. Students without the formal language skills opt to go abroad through the JYA programs of other colleges, and, as one student notes, "Smith will pretty much let you do anything, as long as it's reasonable." In fact, more than one hundred study-abroad programs are preapproved by the school.

Despite its focus on undergraduate education, Smith does provide research opportunities, particularly through things like the Smith Scholars Program, which provides students with credit and research funds for self-designed projects. For nontraditional or mature students, the college offers the generous Ada Comstock Scholars Program to allow women to complete their undergraduate study. About 230 women are enrolled in the program at any given time, and, according to one student, most courses have a couple of Ada Comstock scholars in them. Most students are pleased by this: "It is good to have someone with that kind of maturity and life experiences in class," notes one student, although she suggests that the college administration occasionally questions the structure of the program because they are nervous about giving so much financial assistance to just a few women. The college also offers a small number of graduate programs — including education, fine arts, and social work — enrolling about 150 graduate students. Interestingly, these programs are open to both men and women.

Unlike many comparable elite schools, Smith offers an array of merit scholarships for its students. The school also provides the multi-faceted Jacobson Center, with services like writing assistance, student tutoring, and workshops on time management, study skills, and other academic issues. And a successful new program called Praxis guarantees that every Smith student a paid summer internship during her college career.

Political Atmosphere: The Feminist Mystique

Smith has a firmly established and well-deserved reputation as a liberal campus, particularly when it comes to women's issues. But one recent graduate notes that "the political climate is hard to describe. . . . It is not as radical as the impression everyone has of it." Still, one student concedes that nearly every course at Smith, "even something like the 'History of British Literature,' is bound to have a feminist element." Feminist concerns certainly dominate the political landscape at Smith, and the college's active lesbian community is well known. One student notes that there are occasional rifts between the College Republicans and the campus Lesbian Bisexual Transgender Alliance, but that they usually involve only a handful of students.

A group calling itself Feminists of Smith Unite holds weekly meetings, and the Women's Resource Center is stocked with more than 250 unabashedly liberal books. The "transgendered" community recently put out a pamphlet discussing the role of its members at a women's college. And perhaps as a result of student pressure, Smith is one of the few colleges to offer health insurance benefits to students' domestic partners.

When Smith inaugurated Ruth Simmons as president in 1995, she was the first African-American female to head an elite college. President Simmons has been committed to increasing minority enrollment at Smith, though in a *New York Times* interview she argued, "I don't want people to be the object of experimentation. . . . I don't want them to think they're here to be a part of an exotic mix. I always resent feeling that way." Simmons established a very good rapport with students and faculty: "You'd feel comfortable going up and calling her Ruth," says one student, who adds that the president usually gets standing ovations when she addresses groups of students. As a result, Smith may undergo a period of transition when Simmons departs to assume the helm of Brown University effective July 1, 2001. The provost and dean of faculty John M. Connolly will serve as acting president until a new leader is selected.

Despite the high degree of social autonomy in Smith's living arrangements, campus residence life can be highly politicized. The Office of Institutional Diversity is dedicated exclusively "to facilitate diversity efforts and reduce conflicts."

According to a recent report on multiculturalism in higher education, each of Smith's residence houses has a "Managing Diversity Plan," designed to "discourage racism." Under this plan students can be reprimanded for breaking set guidelines on diversity, and "disciplinary action can be taken, such as requiring violators to attend race sensitivity workshops," according to *The Multicultural Student's Guide to Colleges*. One professor says the college's rigid "rubric of diversity" has had the deleterious effect of making it a "more homogeneous place," where the only opinions expressed are those of the left. "Smith would be a better place if there actually was a greater diversity of opinion," says this professor.

Still, the school describes itself as "diverse by design," and in addition to enrolling women from all fifty states, also has a relatively large population of international students. The thirty-year-old Bridge Program is "specifically designed for students of color to gain a further appreciation of their own and others' cultures." In addition to academic and career development, this "Pre-Orientation for Women of Color" features cultural awareness workshops such as "Rebirth of the Black Latina," "Living La Vida Loca," and "Affirmative Action: Past and Present." The college promises that Bridge will be "one of the best Smith traditions that you will remember."

Indeed, Smith College seems thoroughly in thrall to the ideological spirit that has stigmatized every view and opinion as a narrow "ism": heterosexism, classism, and others have become disturbingly common pejorative terms in campus workshops and official statements. One professor notes that Smith is "caught in the throes of PCism." In a document drafted several years ago, entitled "The Smith Design for Institutional Diversity," the college identified "specific manifestations of prejudice," such as "ableism," "classism," and "heterosexism." In true feminist theoretical fashion, the college also targeted the dreaded transgression of "lookism — the belief that appearance is an indicator of a person's value; the construction of a standard for beauty/attractiveness, and oppression through stereotypes and generalizations of both those who do not fit that standard and those who do." Smith also cancels classes to sponsor an annual day of workshops in honor of the college's first African-American graduate, Otelia Cromwell. Rather than being dedicated exclusively to race issues, however, the event's speeches and performances have turned it into a field day for the proponents of the ideology of oppression: "During the workshops, which get decent turnouts, we discuss almost all of the isms you can imagine, heterosexism, racism, ageism, sizeism, you name it," said one student to the editors of *The Multicultural Student's Guide.*

The college administers a lecture series through the five-college system, so prominent speakers rotate between Smith and the other four campuses. But even big-name lecturers take a back seat to studies: "The question," notes one student, "is always whether or not anyone has time to go to talks." A recent sampling of student meetings and lectures indicates the range of interests and activities represented at Smith, which includes Michael Dukakis speaking on mental health care and a series of talks on "Race, Science, Fiction." The Kahn Liberal Arts Institute held a three-day symposium on exile and alienation.

One student admits that "going to Smith as a conservative would be difficult." Yet despite its liberal political tenor, Smith is "a very civil place," notes one professor, and "free speech is upheld," according to a student. Another professor concurs, noting that "People treat each other well, and the college takes academic freedom very seriously."

Student Life: House Bands

The Smith College brick and ivy campus, spanning a modest 125 acres in Northampton, Massachusetts, is small but attractive. The campus includes a beautiful botanical garden complex open every day of the year. It includes the prestigious Lyman Conservatory and a Campus Arboretum above the scenic banks of Paradise Pond. The pond also becomes a skating rink in the winter. Northampton is considered a nice college town by most students. "There are two great movie theatres, the Iron Horse Music Hall, which has lots of live music, four or five coffee houses," and numerous shops and eateries, according to a student. UMass, Amherst, and Hampshire are all an easy bus ride away.

Almost all students live on campus in the Smith housing system, which is composed of thirty-five self-governing houses accommodating from twelve to one hundred students each. Most of the houses are attractive and full of history (and perhaps even a ghost, according to the Smith Web site); many date back to the nineteenth century, and it is not uncommon to find a Smithie living in a house once inhabited by her mother or grandmother when she was a student. Each house is equipped with its own kitchen and dining room, its own piano, and its own cook. The atmosphere at meals ranges from casual breakfasts in pajamas to Thursday night candlelit dinners with invited faculty guests. Houses generally have an equal number of women from each year, and students benefit from the mix of lower- and upperclassmen.

Despite these advantages, the housing system "can be kind of overwhelming for people," one woman says. Students are assigned to houses for their freshman year, and one notes that they are expected to live in the house for all four years, although many end up changing. Because students have little to no choice in the housing system, personality conflicts frequently arise. "It's kind of like a sorority without the exclusivity," says a student. Although some students like the autonomy of the living arrangements, a professor says students live entirely "by themselves, with no adult supervision," which can create problems for those with traditional social mores. And some of the houses are unattractive, such as the 1970s living quarters (affectionately dubbed the "Howard Johnson dorms") on the edge of campus. One resident sums up the living arrangements by suggesting, "It's what you make of it."

Perhaps because of the sheltered nature of the area, Smith takes a rather hands-off approach to campus security, emphasizing personal responsibility rather than official services. While the Department of Public Safety provides twenty-four-hour security on campus, the college stresses that "all students share the responsibility for house security" and requires an evening "house watch" whereby residents of each house monitor the building.

The campus social scene is not as quiet as one might think for a women's college. There is no Greek system, yet the keg parties found elsewhere are also found here. With the college's vast female population, there appears to be no lack of college males from nearby UMass, Amherst, and Hampshire inundating the campus on the weekends, and all three colleges are easily accessed by a free all-night bus system. Some women also make a tradition out of taking weekend trips to visit friends at nearby Ivy League schools such as Harvard, Yale, and Dartmouth.

Athletics are an important extracurricular pursuit for many Smith students. The college competes in the NCAA Division III in fourteen intercollegiate sports, and also offers numerous club sports, including badminton, croquet, fencing, riding, rugby, sailing, synchronized swimming, tae kwon do, and water polo. An ice hockey club, marathon club, and outing club also attract students. The high-tech Ainsworth/Scott Gym Complex has a plethora of modern athletic equipment, and even maintains a "human performance laboratory" where athletes can monitor their aerobic power, flexibility, nutrition, and body composition.

The fine arts are promoted at Smith, and many students are involved in art, drama, dance, or music at the academic or extracurricular level. Noon concerts are held once a week or more in the newly renovated Sage Hall for Performing Arts, and other classical music events abound. The Mendenhall Center for the Performing Arts, named for former college president Thomas Mendenhall, houses impressive music, theater, and dance facilities, including a studio theater with movable seats and a television studio. Students can chose to participate from more than 100 campus organizations. The wide spectrum of options ranges from a thriving campus Republican club that is more than fifty years old to an active Association of Smith Pagans. Under the umbrella of the official college chaplaincy, ASP organizes several rituals a year and sponsors a book exchange. Its Web site also offers a wide selection of chants, such as the pagan version of "Amazing Grace" (including the phrase ". . . that bore a witch like me").

A recent graduate describes her experience at Smith as "unusual" and "peculiar," embodying a uniqueness derived from a combination of its all-female student body, unfettered academic program, energetic political climate, and lingering sense of institutional pride and collegiality. The college's refusal to become coeducational affirms its commitment to women's education. But this brand of distinction may not be for every young woman, especially those who do not embrace the ideology of feminism that has long gripped the campus.

University of Southern California

University of Southern California
Office of Admission and Financial Aid
University Park Campus
Los Angeles, CA 90089-0911
(213) 740-1111
www.usc.edu

Total enrollment: 29,094
Undergraduates: 15,594
SAT ranges (Verbal/Math): 570-670 (V); 590-700 (M)
Applicants: 15,594
Accepted: 37%
Enrolled: 31%
Application deadline: January 31
Financial aid application deadline: March 1
Tuition: $24,104/$31,714
Core curriculum: No

Believing Its Own Press

TIME magazine and the *Princeton Review*, in their annual joint college guide, declared in 1999 that the University of Southern California (USC) was the "College of the Year," an honor that electrified USC alumni and received media attention around the world — even the *South China Morning Post* saw fit to mention the distinction. The reason for the accolade, the publication noted, was that USC was a worthy example to other institutions because of its model of "service learning" — the school's students and staff volunteer heavily in the neighborhoods surrounding the campus and throughout the Los Angeles metropolitan area.

The award may be a sign that USC is finally entering the big time in the eyes of the public, an image that the university, naturally, is actively courting. In the college's view book, top administrators speak loftily about USC's inclusion into the very select club of "world-class" universities and about how far the university has come since its humble inception in 1880, when Los Angeles was a provincial backwater of merely 10,000 inhabitants. As one professor says, "one of the things that USC is doing is moving from being a loose constellation of professional schools to being a real university." It's an image shift that some students find rather puzzling. "USC is a great school, but so full of itself that students get sick of it by their sophomore year," a student says. "If you come here, expect to love it, but also expect to see a university trying to be what it is not — Ivy League."

Although, given the academic degeneracy of certain portions of Ivy League institutions, this may not be a bad thing. USC has a number of excellent — and truly world-class — professional programs, and it more than adequately prepares its students in these programs to compete in the outside world. Classes are usually small and inviting, and there is a truly close-knit sense of community. But, as with all schools, there are certain parts of USC that are weaker than others.

Academic Life: Categorically Denied

Many of USC's strong professional programs are known throughout the world: the school has an incredible School of Cinema-Television, and its Marshall School of Business is also very highly regarded. But while the serious student will find that the sky is the limit at USC, the basement is also an option: as one student says, "you can just slide through one of the easier schools . . . and get no education."

USC's general education requirements mean only that all students must complete a few required elective courses in the liberal arts and sciences. Aside from an introductory and upper-level writing requirement, which consists of two courses, and a foreign language requirement for some students (which requires students to pass a third-term course in a foreign language or otherwise show proficiency in a foreign tongue), these GE requirements are wide in scope.

The college's catalogue describes the six major categories of its general education requirements — from which students must take one course within each category — as such: "the first part, called 'Foundations,' presents courses that give you the 'big picture' about (I) the development of western European and American culture, as well as (II) alternative cultural traditions and (III) the basic principles of animating scientific inquiry. The second part, called "Case Studies," provides particular opportunities for you to sharpen your critical intelligence by considering specific

627

(IV) applications of science and technology, (V), works of literature, philosophy, and art, and (VI), contemporary social issues of urgency and importance."

Certainly the courses that can fulfill these requirements, according to the course catalogue, are often exceptional in their choice of topic. On the other hand, a few of the courses are so steeped in academic triviality that one wonders whether students will come away from them with any useful knowledge at all. Category I ("Cultures and Civilizations"), for instance, only has a few less-than-solid courses, and offers an excellent array ranging from "Ancient Greek Culture and Society" to "Chinese Civilization." On the other hand, Category II ("Cultures and Civilizations II") has a few less-than-seminal courses, such as Anthropology 250, "Race and Sexual Politics in Southeast Asia," but again has a number of excellent offerings.

Category III ("Scientific Principles") offers science courses, which are all relatively solid. The same goes for Category IV ("Investigations in Science and Technology"). Category V ("Arts and Letters") gives students the option to take one of two survey courses on general themes relating to the liberal arts.

But it is Category VI ("Social Issues") that is troubling. The selection there includes helpful and useful courses such as Judaic Studies 211, which focuses on the Holocaust, but also a veritable laundry list of the politically correct esoterica found at so many large schools. For example, History 245, "Gender and Sexuality in American History," is "an investigation of the nature of femininities and masculinities over the course of U.S. history," according to the catalogue. History 265, "Understanding Race and Sex Historically," introduces students "to historical consideration of the difficult contemporary topics of sexuality and race globally." And Multidisciplinary Activities 167, "Marginal Groups in America," covers not just racial minorities — but "teenage mothers, drug abusers, criminals, and the mentally ill."

Also undermining the GE requirements is the fact that students may pass out of Categories I and III, the two most sound requirements, with Advanced Placement credit, but are forced to take Categories II, IV, V and VI regardless of their high school achievement. All told, USC does little to demand that students take much of anything, let alone even an approximation of a core curriculum.

"I don't know anyone who didn't just consider them . . . a thing that you have to do," one student says of the distribution requirements. This students says that the prevailing attitude toward the requirements is "just get an A and get it over with." But one professor cautions not to judge this book by its cover, and notes that the current general education requirements allow a smaller number of courses than they did several years ago. Course titles and descriptions of general education courses "can be misleading," this professor says, adding that in some courses with titles that don't inspire confidence, students can "get in a classroom, and find it's a very good, solid course." Part of the problem is in the marketing of the courses. "In many departments and among many faculty, there is an effort to avoid looking traditional or canonical," the professor says. "The titles [of these courses] look like conference titles, and whether that's a healthy thing is a whole nother question."

There is an alternative. A highly recommended program that the College of Letters, Arts, and Sciences offers is the Thematic Option, an alternative way to complete one's general requirements. "I doubt that there is any Ivy League school that has as tough an academic challenge as there is at USC," says one student who went through this program. USC describes the Thematic Option as "an alternative to the usual ways in which freshmen meet their general education requirements. Its curriculum is arranged around four core courses which focus on the history of Western civilization through the close reading of primary literature and philosophical texts." It is heavy on reading and writing, and it focuses on all the right things — according to the USC course catalogue, it involves "close reading of major texts within the Western tradition; Biblical and classical through contemporary sources"; looking at "critical problems in the development of scientific thought" as well as an "analysis of historical change; social and political theory." Unfortunately, the program is very limited in scope — only 180 to 200 students get in each year, and the average enrollee has a high school GPA in the A range and a 1420 SAT score.

In addition to the above requirements, students face a mandatory diversity requirement — one course selected from a list of many that will find that won't help students that are dedicated to learning about other cultures to gain useful knowledge about them. One wonders, for example, how useful students will find (especially in the absence of prerequisites) courses like Anthropology 371, "Cross-Cultural Research on Urban Gangs," which examines "youth gang dynamics and their effects on institutions," and proposes to do "comparative analysis of Asian-, African-, and Mexican-American gangs." In a similar vein, it seems unlikely that students will use the theories and practices presented in Comparative Literature 445, "Eurocentrism" in the real world.

Just as with the school's general education requirements, USC has strengths and weaknesses that vary with each school and department. The music program, for example, is excellent, as is the cinema program. There is an excellent program in linguistics, and the department of Slavic languages and literature is also well regarded. USC's School of Cinema-Television deserves a special note for being one of the best, if not the best, in the world. "I'm twenty-one, and give me $40 million and I could make a feature film better than the one I saw last week in the theatre," a student in that program says. "I realize how well prepared I am."

Among the outstanding faculty at USC include Gene Bickers in physics and astronomy; Peggy Kamuf in the French and Italian department; James R. Kincaid and Leo Braudy in English; John E. Bowlt in Slavic languages and literature; John Furia Jr., Ronald Austin, and Don Hall in the School of Cinema-Television; Thomas H. Greene and Howard Gillman in political science; Jack Ryan and Ed Cray in the Journalism School of the Annenberg School for Communications; and Richard Sundeen, Juliet Musso, Robert Biller, and Gary Painter in the School of Policy, Planning, and Development. However, one professor notes that "things are uneven," and that "a lot can depend on what faculty you get, and what departments and what courses."

That's an analysis one student agrees with: "USC, in a lot of ways, is really school-by-school," he says.

USC also offers opportunities for undergraduates to get involved in research, not just in the sciences but in social sciences as well. "The president and the provost have continually pushed faculty — and I think they're serious about it — and the faculty have begun to respond," to this call to include undergraduates in research, a professor says. Among other programs, Thematic Option students can participate in an annual undergraduate research conference, and there are also opportunities for undergraduates to conduct research in the Summer Undergraduate Research Internship Program at the Southern California Earthquake Center.

Class sizes at USC are generally small, and while not as small as those at some private colleges, they are generally less than thirty students in upper-division courses. Students are concerned about the teaching quality. "Some professors I've had have made me question the tenure program," a student says. "At a university like USC, tenure is mostly based on research, and not teaching. Sometimes, unfortunately, it shows." But there is no dearth of excellent professors, and while some courses are larger — especially the lower-level courses — professors are generally quite reachable. "They're usually accessible," says a student. "E-mail is professors' life-line. You can send an e-mail to a professor and get an answer within an hour." Professors are expected to keep at least four office hours per week. "The administration tells us to be there for your students," a professor says.

Serious students praise USC as a good place for serious students. "There is no limit to the excellence I can achieve at USC," one says.

Political Atmosphere: The Little Chill

While USC is more conservative than most other Western schools when it comes to the political beliefs of its students, there is no denying that both students and faculty have experienced problems when it comes to expressing themselves in the classroom.

"The politicization of speech in the classroom is clearly confined to certain humanities departments — English, comparative literature, and somewhat in political science and history," says one professor. Some students would add the religion department to that list. "Although most professors are willing to listen, there are issues which will cause a person to be made a fool of," a disillusioned student says. "If a student wishes to discuss religion, and he does not agree with the professor, that student will be made to look like a fool." Another student with a conservative and Christian perspective says, "I think you can see a humanistic, liberal secularism to everything on campus."

One professor says he's concerned with how students will take remarks he makes in class. "I generally speak my mind, however — well, it's not that I feel my

Constitutional rights have been abrogated or that there is anything approaching a legal definition of censorship," he says. "[But] I worry. I have to be very careful about everything that I say, because someone might go off and complain. . . . Some of my colleagues say the same thing." While this professor can't name a single instance where he or a colleague got into deep trouble, "I think that with the very broad interpretation of politically correct speech and sexual harassment . . . there's a chill there." The social pressure comes from other instructors, he says. "If you articulate certain viewpoints, then [other instructors] edge away from you . . . but there aren't any repercussions other than social ones."

Another problem for professors is that the university allows for students to contest their grades if they feel that a professor has treated them unfairly. "Students can file a grade appeal," says one professor. "Most of the panels I have been on have been even-handed and fair," he says, but he adds that the existence of the panels amounts to giving students "free litigation."

These problems don't stop students from pointing out that USC is more conservative than many comparable institutions. "USC is a little more conservative than UCLA or the University of Washington or [the University of California at] Berkeley," says one student. "You can be a Republican at USC." Another student notes that "most students would either be liberal Republicans or conservative Democrats. There are very few party line members, and those who are party line are looked upon with contempt."

Student Life: Have Your People Call My People

Student life at USC is typical of any large school, with plenty of activities, clubs, and sporting events that students enjoy and that foster a sense of community within the school.

Since USC is located smack-dab in the heart of Los Angeles, it is easy for students to take advantage of its diversions. "It's L.A., you know," says one student, who seemed amused by the question "What do USC students do for fun?" "There are unlimited things to do," he says. Another student says that those attending USC can do "anything and everything," primarily because of the short distance to the city's major attractions.

"There isn't too much of a night life around USC," says a student. "Thus, students with cars flee campus for Westwood, Hollywood, Santa Monica, Pasadena, Huntington Beach, and so on," referring to various Los Angeles suburbs known for their night life. Most of these destinations are a short car trip away, between half an hour to an hour depending on traffic, and they offer everything that a college student could want — restaurants, shopping, bars, and, of course, Los Angeles's greatest asset: the warm, sandy beaches and the Pacific Ocean.

Night life aside, students who don't have handy access to a set of wheels can find that there is plenty to do on campus as well. The university sponsors movies and dorm events, and students find good times just hanging around their dorms with their peers.

To fill in the cracks, there are loads of student groups catering to nearly every interest. Students recommend being involved with Troy Camps and Spirits in Action, two of USC's prominent philanthropic organizations. There are numerous ethnic clubs and various preprofessional societies, as well as an extremely active contingent of religious groups. According to one student, because of the dynamic Christian religious groups on campus, "a lot of Christians on other campuses look to us and say, 'that's what we want on our campus.'"

Athletics are also very highly regarded on campus. USC's principal rival, hated crosstown foe UCLA, is always a welcome target for its partisans. "Even if you are not a major sports fan, it's hard to avoid being pulled into Trojan pride and whipping out your victory sign when USC beats UCLA or Notre Dame," a student says. There are thirteen varsity teams at the school, seven for men and six for women, not to mention a number of club and intramural sports.

USC also has a well-entrenched Greek system, with forty-eight recognized Greek organizations on campus. Greek life is pretty much confined to Fraternity Row. "The Row is generally open only to people in the Greek system," says a student. "They only very infrequently have open parties to which everyone is invited." Another student, who estimates the Greek population at about 20 percent of the student body, calls it "a world unto itself," but he also notes that it does carry weight around the college: "The Greek system is so huge at USC."

Housing on USC is "primarily coeducational," according to the school's Web site, although men and women are assigned to different wings or floors of certain buildings and they have their own restroom facilities. Seven residence halls are primarily for freshmen, who make up the vast majority of the dorm population, although many of USC's school-run apartments are also set aside for new first-year students. While the university says on its Web site that 10 to 15 percent of the spaces in university housing is set aside for returning students, students say space is sometimes hard to come by, even if you want to live on campus. "There are some nice dorms on campus, and none of them are infested or particularly dirty," a student says. "But USC does have a housing problem now, which has caused some four-person apartments to now hold five people. Also, it is almost impossible not to share a room if you stay in USC housing, and many students move out of USC housing after their freshmen year."

But the dorms *do* have at least one draw: the Ethernet connection in each room. This fast, reliable Internet gateway has led to many USC–based hits on Napster, a music-sharing site that has come under recent fire from universities for clogging up network resources (and even provoked litigation by record companies against some schools). "I know students with thousands and thousands of .mp3 files," a students says, referring to the standard file format used for music, "and they're living in the dorms next year because of it."

Despite these advantages, the dorm life gets mixed reviews from other students. "The dorms here are not nice, and are basically boxes in a building," says one student. "People are often learning how to operate without their parents around." This can of course lead to behavior that isn't exactly the most conducive to studying.

Even the housing options intended for students who prefer quieter quarters get tepid marks from some. "I lived in the honors dorms my freshman year, which made me understand why, when the recruiters were wining and dining the scholarship recipients, they only mentioned the camaraderie and not accommodations in the Deans' Halls," a student says.

The Deans' Halls are one of many special-interest housing facilities on campus, and are open to students who are the recipients of various university scholarships and those participating in honors programs. Other special-interest housing includes three residential colleges that allow students to have close relationships not only with their fellow students but with faculty members who live there too. There are also a number of special-interest floors for students interested in business, cinema, substance-free living, or limited visitation. There are floors devoted to programs or groups such as Women in Science and Engineering. There is on-campus housing for Jewish and Muslim students that allow them to prepare kosher and *halal* food, respectively, and there are also special floors for black and Latino students in Fluor Tower.

The food is generally good, and it is available at numerous restaurants on campus and at one central dining facility. Freshmen in the dorms should expect to be forced onto the college's meal plan.

Crime on campus is not as large a concern among students as one might think, although because of USC's proximity to a relatively bad area of Los Angeles, students need to be cautious. "I feel very safe on campus, even at night, because we have a good Department of Public Safety here," a female student says. The north side of campus, where most students live, is generally very safe. However, avoid the south and west sides of campus, especially at night. "Crime is not a concern," another student says. "Being that we are in a bad neighborhood, we do get some muggings now and then, but no more than a rural university would." A third student points to the good relations that the school has with the surrounding University Park neighborhood and says that "even because USC is where it's at, the awareness and security are so amplified" that crime is kept low.

Students can't complete their USC experience without brushing up against tradition. This university has plenty of them, including kicking the light poles on the way to the Coliseum for a football game, the crosstown rivalry with UCLA, the annual Skull and Dagger prank, homecoming, the famous Fight Song, and taping up Tommy Trojan — the school's mascot — to save him from pranks at the hands of interloping UCLA students. "USC is nothing," says a student, "if it's not tradition-rich."

Spelman College

350 Spelman Lane, SW
Atlanta, GA 30314-4399
(800) 982-2411
www.spelman.edu

Total enrollment: 2,065
Undergraduates: 2,065
SAT ranges (Verbal/Math): 490-590 (V); 470-560 (M)
Applicants: 3,300
Accepted: 53%
Enrolled: 34%
Application deadline: February 1
Financial aid application deadline: March 1
Tuition: $11,135/$18,015
Core curriculum: No

Money Makes It Happen

It is nearly impossible to speak of the modern Spelman College without mentioning the name of Johnnetta B. Cole, the immensely charismatic and beloved president of Spelman from 1987 to 1997, under whose aegis Spelman advanced from its already respected status as one of the best historically black colleges to become a nationally known academic liberal arts college and research center, as well as an entry point for young black women into the corridors of power. Under Cole's guidance, Spelman successfully conducted a $113-million capital campaign. Not only was the campaign "by far the most successful ever undertaken by a historically black college," according to the *Journal of Blacks in Higher Education,* but it "ranks among the most accomplished campaigns ever mounted by any liberal arts institution." Contributors included not only such high-profile members of the African-American community as Camille and Bill Cosby, who donated a landmark $20 million, and Oprah Winfrey, who logged a $1 million gift, but also foundations and corporations to whom Cole made individual solicitations.

Yet Cole's influence at Spelman extends far beyond her ability to raise money. An already respected anthropologist, Cole came to Spelman with "a concept of how to modernize a university and make it competitive," says a former Spelman faculty member admiringly. "Her watch was very inspirational." Cole took the lead in helping to raise faculty salaries and to attract new research-focused faculty, in particular more black women. The emphasis on research has yielded positive results: "One of the things Johnnetta Cole has not been recognized for are the notable books written by faculty" under her tenure.

Cole's tenacity paid off handsomely for Spelman. By 1996, its faculty ranked 21st in the nation among top liberal arts colleges in *U.S. News and World Report*'s rankings, and in the same rankings, the college improved its simple "regional" status to that of a "national" institution. Perhaps the most prestigious index of the college's rising academic star is the recent bestowal of a Phi Beta Kappa chapter, which has come much more belatedly to Spelman than to neighboring brother school Morehouse, even though Spelman has outpaced Morehouse in many areas for a number of years.

From its tenuous beginnings, Spelman has survived and thrived on both practical hard work and optimism. As was the case for many early black institutions, Spelman was founded by philanthropic whites — two women were commissioned by the American (read Northern) Baptist mission board in 1881 to "study the living conditions 'among the freedmen of the South.'" Barely two years after arriving, Sophia B. Packard and Harriet Giles established a school with a first class of eleven, "mostly ex-slaves," the college *Bulletin* notes, "determined to learn to read the Bible and write well enough to send letters to their families in the North." (With respect to the college's religious origins, Spelman amazingly continues even now to maintain its motto, "Our Whole School for Christ," despite high multicultural interest on campus and a growing Muslim student organization.)

Many historically black institutions had similar origins, but Spelman was fortunate at the outset to secure the support of John D. Rockefeller — in fact, the school's name derives from the name of Rockefeller's wife's mother, and several campus buildings bear the names of Rockefeller family members, which can seem something of a WASP–like cultural oddity to an uninformed observer on campus.

The next great advance for the college was in 1929, when Spelman joined the consortium of historically black colleges that make up what is now called the Atlanta University Center (AUC), which also includes Morehouse and provides the "center-wide" Robert W. Woodruff Library. Shared by all the AUC colleges, the library holds over 827,000 volumes and possesses major African-American collections and archival materials, such as the Countee Cullen Memorial Collection, which focuses on the arts, and the Thayer Collection, which contains items associated with Abraham Lincoln.

Academic Life: It Takes a College

To the casual observer leafing through the Spelman College *Bulletin,* one of the most striking features, right at the front of the volume, is the college's "Statement of Purpose," and in particular two corollary lists of "institutional goals" and "behaviors." While the goals are fairly standard for an academic environment, the "behaviors" extend far beyond academic and career achievement to mandate that a Spelman woman will conform to some rather ambiguous categories, such as "10. Demonstrate self-confidence and self-respect" and "11. Demonstrate pride in her own culture." Such an emphasis on character and spiritual formation places Spelman squarely in the old *in loco parentis* role that most colleges once assumed for students' moral behavior, although in this case the formation is of a pretty clearly liberal, activist variety.

One way Spelman seeks to inculcate its desired "specific behavioral objectives" is through the Assessment of Student Learning and Development Program, which requires that all students take a bizarre and dizzying array of tests at almost every level, from freshman to senior year. The practice seems a little intrusive; not only are students required to take the Watson-Glaser Critical Thinking Appraisal twice, they also must take the Myers-Briggs (personality) Type Indicator, again clearly showing that Spelman conceives of itself as far more than an academic institution, and truly more of the "family" it purports to be.

Equally structured are the general education requirements. Like most selective colleges, Spelman conceives of its basic requirements in pragmatic or mechanistic terms; one of the purposes of the general education requirements is "to prepare students for the challenges of living in a multicultural, highly technological, and information-based society" with a specific emphasis on "the study of African-American and other cultures and a focus on gender." To achieve the latter, Spelman requires a two-semester sequence of courses entitled "The African Diaspora of the World." ADW, as it is called, is the only set of courses required of all students, and is taught from a truly radical perspective: required readings for the course include *Words of Fire: An Anthology of African-American Feminist Thought,* the writings of black lesbian poet Audre Lorde, and works by communist activist Angela Davis. While the first course in the sequence is limited strictly to Africa and the experiences of Africans outside the United States, the second half deals with Africans in America. "The focus is more on slavery, politics, economics, music," a student says. The same student reports that the culminating activity in the course is not an essay or an examination, but an oddly termed "ephemeral project," which "has to be some type of presentation," possibly dramatic or poetic, the purpose of which is unclear. Such an attitude is further confirmed by one student's testimony that the "course is not so much tested; it's a dialogue."

There is one other common experience required for Spelman women: attendance at Convocation, which is more or less a required chapel (though its function is inspirational rather than doctrinally religious) serving to build the close community and shared notion of "sisterhood" for which Spelman is famous. Convocation generally includes music, prayer, a speaker, and chances for students to ask questions of the speaker. Previous speakers have included Children's Defense Fund activist Marian Wright Edelman and First Lady (now Senator) Hillary Clinton.

Otherwise, the general education requirements lack specificity: "computer literacy," math, English composition, and physical education. There is a foreign language requirement; Spanish, French, and Japanese are available at Spelman, but cross-registration is available at other AUC institutions for choices as varied as Arabic (which appears to be rising in popularity, thanks to Muslim evangelism), Chinese, Swahili, German, and Russian. What goes under the heading of a multicultural or non-Western requirement at most colleges is specified as an "International or Women's Studies" elective at Spelman, which offers a pleasantly surprising latitude of choices, from many interesting African electives ("African Politics," "South Africa in Transition") to very traditional art history surveys and studies of French and Spanish literature. Then there are the sorts of distribution requirements that are standard at most colleges: four hours, or one course, in the areas of fine arts, humanities, social sciences, and natural sciences.

With respect to politicized courses or departments, it is hard to say exactly what *would* constitute academic politicization at Spelman, given that the academic perspective from which faculty teach is almost uniformly left wing and "postcolonial." This is expressed perhaps most succinctly in a college *Bulletin* note that is attached to the signature ADW course: the course is taught, it is said, "within a global context and from perspectives that are both interdisciplinary and gender-informed."

Outstanding professors at Spelman include Charnelle Holloway in art, Pamela Gunter-Smith and Victor Ibeanusi in biology, Judy Gebre-Hiwet in English, and Beverly Guy-Sheftall in women's studies. Strong departments include biology, chemistry, economics, English, psychology, and comparative women's studies.

Spelman has several notable special programs, and there are a couple of likely reasons why. Given that Spelman is one of only two historically black, all-female colleges, it is keenly aware of having a kind of stewardship role toward its students as black women "redressing the balance" of historical inequities, and toward the African-American community in general. In addition, and especially since Cole's presidency, Spelman has established links with corporations and groups outside the AUC network with the clear intention of forming Spelman women as business and professional leaders in the world at large.

Like its brother school, Morehouse, Spelman is intensely committed to student counseling and preparation, and, if necessary, remediation. The Summer Science Program is specifically geared toward entering Spelman freshmen who are interested in health professions. Accordingly, freshmen chosen for the program arrive on campus during the summer before the academic year begins for an eight-week program that explores a number of areas in the sciences and includes attention to reading, problem solving, and study skills specific to the sciences. This program appears to be highly regarded by students. Science programs in general are commended by students for their emphasis on research and "real-life" applications.

In addition, a similar Summer Science and Engineering Program for students more interested in engineering and technology-focused science than in pure science or research gives more attention to mathematics and computer science skills.

In a similar vein, for older entering students Spelman offers a service called the Gateway Program, which is specifically geared to women who have been away from school for some time, are "mid-twenties or older" and "financially independent of [their] parents/guardians," and show evidence of having "multiple responsibilities."

Furthermore, the Dow Jones–Spelman College Entrepreneurial Center seeks to enhance opportunities in business for black women, in particular empowering them through resources such as a business library, language courses, and "video and teleconference–style executive courses."

But for every emphasis Spelman places upon the world of global business and trade, there is an equally balanced emphasis on the maintenance of ties to tradition and an understanding of one's context as a black woman in the societal framework. As such, Spelman is also noted for its Women's Research and Resource Center, which, according to college sources, is "the only women's research center of its kind on a historically black college campus," and which focuses not only on pure academics but also on curriculum development and community service.

Perhaps the most impressive of all of Spelman's special programs, however, is the Ethel Waddell Githii Honors Program, which is constituted similarly to other colleges' honors programs for high-achieving students, but which seems to have significantly more structured requirements. All freshmen entering Spelman with a combined SAT of 1,160 are eligible, as well as any freshmen who earn a cumulative GPA of 3.2 for thirty-two credit hours or more. Students who elect the program are required to take "Honors Math" and "Honors Freshman Composition," both of which afford greater independent work than the ordinary course sequences. The *Bulletin* notes that the honors math course requires "independent study papers" in addition to "readings . . . focused on race and gender issues." The honors composition course requires "a spectrum of writing experiences" as well as "research." Most surprising, however, of the honors program requirements is the "Honors Philosophy Seminar," in which students focus "intensively" on six selected Platonic dialogues and Descartes's *Meditations on First Philosophy*. The course is a true rarity in these days when students are almost never asked to take philosophy. Finally, the honors program culminates with the student writing and defending a thesis.

Political Atmosphere: The Call

As is the case at brother school Morehouse, Spelman College's history and achievements occupy a place of near-mythic reverence in the minds of faculty, students, and alumnae, tending to suffuse just about everything the college does with a kind of inspirational and exalted significance. This tone is especially reflected in the college's publicity materials, which also serve, in both design and copy, to give a good indication of Spelman's common values and conventional wisdom. The cover of one brochure from the office of admissions displays a photo collage of attractive women caught in contemplative poses, surrounding what appears to be an African sculpture, and inside, the copy on the first page reads: "This is not coincidence. You do not receive this publication by chance. You may be graduating in the top tier of your class. You may long for your history, your culture, your roots. You may wonder what you could be if you spent the majority of your waking hours being affirmed. You are being called to Spelman."

Effectively, therefore, the college's promotional materials avail themselves of the rhetorical patterns and cadences of traditional black preaching. Practically speaking, what all this rhetoric translates to is a strong emphasis on the notion of "Sisterhood" (even President Johnnetta Cole referred to herself as the "Sister President"), and an emphasis on service to the community.

The biggest area of political controversy, according to one student from the Northeast, may well be in the socioeconomic arena. This student lamented widespread competition for Spelman's numerous scholarships and the animosity that tends to exist between scholarship and nonscholarship students. There also might be a kind of "thin line that's drawn" around international students, who tend to stand out on campus.

But another potential agent for change, if not a source of current controversy, is the burgeoning amount of Muslim activity and — there is no other word for it — evangelism on all the AUC campuses. A few years ago, Muslim students lobbied for a prayer room of their own. Muslim women on campus also have to seek special permission to attend services on days when classes are in session. "The overall feeling is that you don't get encouragement from Spelman, but from the student body," states one student involved with the Muslim group. (At the same time, it ought to be noted, there are also evangelical Christian groups more or less operating outside the Spelman chaplaincy structure, and bulletin boards in the dorms advertise the resources and contact numbers for groups such as the Arise Christian Fellowship.)

In sum, beyond the standard academic-feminist notion of "the personal as political," Spelman women appear to be pretty apolitical — one college guide quotes a senior as saying, "It has been my experience that Spelman students are not very politically motivated, i.e., not concerned with the ramifications of their actions and beliefs outside the microcosm of Spelman." There certainly are no overtly conservative organizations of an academic or cultural bent, as one might find at other colleges, even Morehouse. Nevertheless, Spelman remains true to its history as the preeminent corridor to power for young black women, and a giver of service back to the community, an admirable goal most eloquently expressed in one of the college's brochures: "If we are successful in our academic endeavors, you will be successful. And if we are successful at touching your heart, you will understand that it is your responsibility to hold the hand of your brothers and help them be successful, too."

Student Life: The Rent You Pay

Spelman's commitment to community service has a strong influence on student life. According to a fact sheet entitled "Spelman Synopsis" from the office of public relations, "Over 45 percent of our students engage in some form of community service, which resulted in Spelman being designated as a Point of Light," referring to President Bush's famous program that honored major volunteer contributors to their communities. The West End neighborhood where Spelman is located has one of the highest poverty, incarceration, and AIDS-infection rates in the city (though the college itself is sufficiently policed, beautifully manicured, and the site of very little crime). Spelman women feel a particular burden to aid in this regard — another commonly repeated quotation on campus derives from alumna Marian Wright Edelman: "Service is the rent you pay for living on this earth."

To put Edelman's dictum into practice, Spelman's Office of Community Service matches students with volunteer opportunities in the community and works with faculty to design the service components of academic courses. One exemplary program is the "Star Team," a project of the drama department that uses drama and oral history to help youths deal with and analyze the issues that confront them.

Although only about 15 percent of the students actually pledge a sorority, Greek life plays a major part in the social scene, and even in the service life of the college. Traditionally, black sororities such as Delta Sigma Theta and Alpha Kappa Alpha have been at the vanguard of service to the community, much more so than white sororities, a legacy from days of segregation when few recourses to respectability and security were open to black women. Still, Greek life at Spelman offers more attractions than just community service and, with Morehouse being right across the street, tends to give the campus the air of 1950s-style social courtliness and decorum.

Despite the fact that most Spelman women openly identify themselves with leftist politics, one college guide notes that the other items included on a list of "What's Hot" at Spelman included "old-fashioned dating, student government, religion, and music associations." The same guide noted, in addition, the propensity for Spelman women to be religious (though theologically thoroughly mainline) and socially conservative (drug use and homosexuality are generally frowned upon). Some of these conservative attitudes manifest themselves in campus life in ways practically unheard of at other nonreligious colleges: while the dormitories allow male visitors, they must sign in, and be signed out by 11:30 p.m. — "not 11:31 or 11:35," as a notice from the counselor at one women's residence hall emphasizes.

Spelman women also tend to dress rather well, and more formally than students on most campuses — even in an all-female environment, dresses, makeup, and carefully arranged hair are the norm, a testament not so much to femininity as to Spelman women's desire to appear polished and professional at all times.

The college recently established the first endowed, need-based scholarships in its history: the Giozeuta Foundation Scholars Program, named for the late Roberto G. Guizueta, once CEO of Coca-Cola, provides money for incoming freshmen (renewable for four years) "who face severe economic hardship and who display exceptional leadership potential," according to the college. The program, called Bridging the Gap & Building 21st Century Leaders, was started with a $1 million grant from the foundation.

Stanford University

Office of Undergraduate Admission
Stanford, CA 94305
(650) 723-2300
www.stanford.edu

Total enrollment: 14,084
Undergraduates: 6,591
SAT ranges (Verbal/Math): 670-770 (V); 690-780 (M)
Applicants: 17,919
Accepted: 15%
Enrolled: 65%
Application deadline: December 15
Financial aid application deadline: February 1
Tuition: $24,716/$32,746
Core curriculum: No

It Started Here

Perhaps one day at Stanford University there will be a monument that says: "The culture wars started here." Many people credit a 1987 antiracism demonstration led by the Reverend Jesse Jackson on the Stanford campus with launching a thousand multicultural ships. The crowd's famous chant of "Hey, hey, ho, ho, Western Culture's got to go!" has echoed since then on many other campuses, and Stanford has remained in many minds the epitome of the modern politically and culturally correct institution.

The students that day were referring to a course called "Western Culture," but even though the Reverend Jackson did remind the crowd that they were a part of this culture, many of the demonstrators wanted to jettison more than just one course. The course was replaced by a weak series of courses on ideas and values, and that series has now been replaced again — needless to say, without provision for the teaching of Western culture.

The change in Stanford's reputation and academic fortunes was almost as rapid. Always known as a leader in both the sciences and the liberal arts, the university's undergraduate liberal arts programs are now losing students. It's as if some were scared away by the politicization of the curriculum. Today Stanford seems on the verge of becoming, as one professor recently warned, "Stanford Tech." Located in the heart of Silicon Valley, Stanford is certainly in a position to capitalize on the demand for its well-qualified graduates in the technological and engineering fields. However, the fate of the university's liberal arts disciplines is less easy to gauge. Stanford still has many fine professors, and it consistently recruits its faculty in all areas from the most prestigious graduate schools. While it is still possible to receive a superior liberal arts education at Stanford, the question is, will there be anyone left to receive that education?

Academic Life: Western Culture Went

Multiculturalism is the new standard in the Stanford curriculum, and it is mandatory for all students. The university's distribution requirements make it more than likely that students will be exposed to feminist scholarship and race-based critiques, while at the same time giving short shrift to the Western tradition.

Stanford students choose a total of eleven distribution courses, including an introduction to the humanities and a two-quarter thematic humanities sequence (known as Area 1); a three-course sequence in natural science, applied science and technology, or math (Area 2); and three courses in the humanities and social sciences (Area 3). There is also a foreign language competency requirement and an English composition requirement.

The courses that meet these requirements are an uneven mix (especially those outside the hard or applied sciences), dominated by ideology. Though some of the courses may offer worthwhile material, few of them reflect the traditional purpose of a liberal arts education: transmitting the fundamental values of the Western heritage.

Then there is Area 4, where the choices often come down to the lesser of evils. Area 4 requires a course in two of these three fields: "World Cultures," "American Culture," and "Gender Studies."

Though the *Stanford Bulletin* says that general education requirements are "intended to introduce students to the major social, historical, cultural, and intellectual forces that shape the contemporary world," not one course in the world cultures subarea deals with politically incorrect cultures. The university finds Chinese, Japanese, and Jewish cultures worth studying as world cultures, but not English, French, Russian, or indeed any European culture. The American cultures subarea is similarly beset by multiculturalism. Courses focus on ethnicity; the very idea of the melting pot is discarded. This area offers courses on minorities in America, though the definition of "minority" does not extend to groups that are not currently considered aggrieved, like Irish- or German-Americans. Also missing are courses on pivotal eras of American history — westward expansion, for example. Gender studies is even worse, with course titles like "Gay Autobiography," and "Gender Specific Perspectives on Birth Control." One student said that her understanding of one of the courses in the gender studies subarea was that it was "all about having sex."

The good news, one might think, is that Area 4 (along with Area 1) replaced the notorious "Cultures, Ideas, and Values," or CIV, requirement that sprang up after Western Culture "had to go." The bad news is that the new requirements are only slightly better.

The old CIV forced students to select one of nine three-course sequences on traditional-sounding topics, but with the caveat that each track include works discussing race, gender, class, and religion, and at least some works by female and minority writers. It was a nod in the direction of Western culture, but little more than that. In a 1995 survey, 60 percent of seniors said CIV had "little or no value."

The new requirements began in 1999. The freshman course "Introduction to the Humanities" addresses only four to six major texts, rather than the fifteen to twenty authors found in each quarter of the previous CIV system. The two-course Area 1 humanities sequence that follows it resembles the old CIV, although the hard quotas on numbers of female and minority writers and gender, class, and race issues no longer exists.

Supporters of the new system argued that it would allow smaller departments to participate, since a three-quarter sequence in one area is no longer an option. Furthermore, they claimed that the fewer number of texts would alleviate the "peep-show" feel that was the bane of CIV. These supporters said that when the race and gender quotas were dropped, students would take the material more seriously, since they can no longer complain that they are reading a text only to satisfy a race or gender requirement.

Others on campus viewed the new requirement as a defeat. The new course's lack of quotas has provoked consternation amongst faculty in feminist studies, anthropology, English, and other humanities departments. One professor who doesn't agree with the complainants says their exceptions are based on matters of turf and survival, rather than any pedagogical argument: "English would wither on the vine except for the distribution requirements," the professor says. "The same for philosophy and the languages and literatures." Indeed, as about 90 percent of Stanford's incoming classes choose hard sciences or engineering (what one professor calls "voting with their feet"), any reduction in mandatory classes in certain disciplines is sure to threaten if not the survival of, then the continued expansion of humanities departments that need the distribution requirement to get students into seats.

Some Stanford professors named as outstanding by others on campus are John Taylor in economics; Roger Noll, John Cogan, and Judith Goldstein in political science and public policy; Norman Naimark in history; Richard Cushman, who teaches "Introduction to the Humanities" courses; Maureen Harkin in English; William Durham in anthropology; John Bravman in material science; Kathleen Eisenhardt in industrial engineering; Brad Osgood in mathematics; Douglas Osheroff in physics; George Springer in aeronautics; Eric Roberts in computer science; Michael Bratman in philosophy; and Robert McGinn in the "Science, Technology, and Society" program.

While the politics of the humanities departments gets more headlines, the engineering, natural sciences, and applied sciences departments are Stanford's real strengths. This demonstrates more than anything how Stanford has changed over the past several years. Because of the university's proximity to Silicon Valley, the demand for its engineering and computer science graduates and, to a lesser extent, physics and chemistry graduates is acute. "Silicon Valley fights over these people," one student says.

The physics department is strong in both teaching and research opportunities. Two professors who recently won Nobel Prizes in physics have also in recent years won university teaching awards.

The premed program in Stanford's biology department is also excellent, and faculty from the graduate medical school teach some undergraduate courses. About three-quarters of premed upperclassmen also conduct research under the direction of medical school faculty.

While all of Stanford's science departments are strong, the same cannot be said for humanities. The one department that receives high marks all around is economics, which appears to be dominated by quantitative work. Despite (or perhaps because of) the department's emphasis on econometrics and other highly sophisticated mathematical models, economics maintains the highest undergraduate enrollment on campus; the only departments even close are psychology and biology.

Another department credited with excellent undergraduate teaching is political science, which has benefited, along with the departments of economics and public policy, from its affiliation with the Hoover Institution on War, Revolution, and Peace. The Hoover Institution, a privately endowed think tank housed on the Stanford campus, has become increasingly aggressive in recent years in recruiting research fellows, many of whom share joint appointments in the social science departments, thus providing those departments access to prominent specialists.

Apart from these few good departments, though, the humanities picture is rather bleak. "Good teachers are the exception," a student says. "Departments like anthropology, sociology, history, are not top-notch in terms of teaching," a professor says. A student includes English in that list. Comparative literature, according to a student, is "horrible." Another student says the languages and literature departments have turned toward wholesale political correctness and deconstructionism. What's more, grade inflation is rampant in most humanities courses, students say.

Stanford offers a host of politicized majors, including urban studies, feminist studies, Latin American studies, African and Afro-American studies, and East Asian studies. The good news is that relatively few students choose to major in these areas.

Political Atmosphere: Grapes Make Whine

Some have called the politicization of Stanford University the worst in the nation. The philosopher Allan Bloom wrote in 1989: "Stanford is a trendy place and it responds to trends. Its shameless self-congratulation about this is sufficient to render it ridiculous in the eyes of serious people no matter what their political persuasion." A book entitled *The Diversity Myth* delivers a stinging account of Stanford's descent into multiculturalism. The authors, David O. Sacks and Peter A. Thiel, are Stanford alums and founders of the *Stanford Review*, a conservative journal. The book chronicles a horror show of multicultural excesses, hypersensitivity, and intellectual fascism in the course of college events in the ten years prior to its publication.

While Sacks and Thiel allow that former President Gerhard Casper, who inherited much of the mess from his predecessor Donald Kennedy, did a better job resisting multiculturalism, they say his policies have, in effect, only slowed its growth at Stanford. As another writer quoted in the book says, Western culture will recover; Stanford may or may not.

The new president of Stanford, John Hennessy, was well known as a professor in the computer architecture field before becoming president. He has had success as a fundraiser, landing a $150 million grant last year from James H. Clark, and has proposed a $1-billion money-raising campaign over the next five years. Hennessy plans to use the money to create a series of undergraduate programs called the Stanford Introductory Studies, which would include "freshman and sophomore seminars taught by tenured professors, the sophomore college — an intensive two-week program in which groups of twelve students work closely with a professor — and independent study and research projects that provide support for students working on tutorials related to faculty research and summer-research fellowships," according to the *Chronicle of Higher Education*. Such a program would be a welcome addition to the undergraduate program, assuming it can be taught in a rather nonpoliticized manner, and Hennessy's plans for such a big investment in it are an encouraging sign.

Meanwhile, the politicization that exists in many Stanford classrooms — one statistics exam asked students to figure out the probability that a hypothetical man would be upset if his boyfriend left him, for example — is carried on outside of class in the form of protests. Stanford students have spent time protesting just about everything: racism, sexism, homophobia, intolerance, human rights abuses abroad, logging, the oil industry, etc. Among the stranger activist moments is the annual "Grape Debate," in which students vote, dorm by dorm, on whether grapes will be served in their dining hall. There is actually a Grape Education Committee to provide information to students prior to the vote. The committee was formed after a hunger strike — for crying out loud — in 1994 by students opposed to grapes on campus. The grape boycott goes back to 1965 and Cesar Chavez, who wanted better wages and working conditions for farm workers. The boycott was renewed in the mid-1980s by the United Farm Workers Organizing Committee to protest non-union grapes, and now the debate includes the pros and cons of pesticide use as well.

Student protesters on all issues, however, are vastly outnumbered by non-activist students. Only about 12 percent of students even voted in recent government election. "The media plays up the three to four hundred radicals," a professor says.

Although most students seem not to take the constant protests very seriously, the administration does — though less now than in the past. Former President Casper's office turned down a proposal by the radical group Students for Environmental Action to establish a "Socially Responsible Endowment Fund," which would have been used to support efforts and ventures that environmental activists deemed "responsible." However, the presence of activist student government leaders could make it difficult at times for Casper and his provost Condaleeza Rice (George W. Bush's new national security advisor) to turn away all requests. Hennessy's position on these issues remains to be seen; he took office in November of 2000.

Casper did have some success in removing some of the politicization from the tenure process, making teaching a more important factor in tenure decisions. Stanford has always had the reputation as a tough place to get tenure, and several professors agree that this is still the case — it's just that factors other than research get more consideration now. "Ten or eleven years ago, undergrad teaching counted for nothing," a professor says. "Today, there's a hurdle — you have to be adequate." Although Stanford still hires ten to fifteen registered Democrats for every one Republican for its faculty, according to a report in the *Washington Times,* the two most controversial tenure decisions in recent years have involved professors working in what are considered politicized fields (cultural anthropology and labor history).

Student housing is perhaps the most radical wing of the administration. Stanford has one of the most intrusive "residential education" systems in the nation. It includes resident fellows (sometimes professors, but usually graduate students) and resident assistants (usually upperclassmen) who are dedicated to conveying a political agenda to their charges. Several students who opposed the multiculturalism they were being handed were scorned publicly by the resident fellows, and in some cases even punished. The punishments came even after Stanford's speech code had been ruled unconstitutional by a federal court. Some campus observers report, though, that the university seems to have become more tolerant of traditional viewpoints recently.

Student Life: Suburban Subsistence

The typical Stanford undergraduate lives on campus for all four years, mostly because rent is so expensive in the Bay Area. Almost all freshmen live on campus, and about 85 percent of upperclassmen stay. This makes the campus rather "insular," as one student puts it. "Social life is all pretty much on campus." Trips to San Francisco are rare, even though the trip from Palo Alto to downtown takes less than forty-five minutes on most days. The university is surrounded by suburbs, which offer some attractions that negate the need to go into the city, but much of this stay-at-home attitude is due to the fact that most students take their coursework seriously.

Stanford hosts a number of theme houses or dorms, including houses officially dedicated to certain ethnic or racial groups (e.g., blacks, Chicanos, Asians, and Native Americans). In these official houses, the university attempts some degree of integration by requiring that no more than one-half of a house's population be members of the titular ethnic group. A student reports that there are also a few "de facto" theme houses, such as those for gay students and vegetarians. There is one all-female house. Some, but not all, of the coed dorms place men and women on the same floor; separate bathrooms are maintained. Married couples get special consideration in apartment assignments — as do committed homosexual couples. Committed heterosexual couples do not.

At the same time, the residential education division has led efforts to shut down fraternity houses. One student reports that the leaders of residential education found the frats "too independent," and that the number of fraternities dropped from twelve to just five in a span of five years.

Stanford enrolls about 6,600 undergraduates and more than 7,500 graduate students. This population is enough to support a long list of student organizations covering virtually every conceivable field of interest. There are more than one hundred official student groups, not including intramural athletics. Though many groups are politically inclined, there are academic clubs, musical groups, ethnic groups, and several religious groups, including True Love Waits, Asian American Christian Fellowship, Campus Crusade for Christ, various Catholic organizations, InterVarsity, Lutheran Campus Ministry, and others. Services are held each week on campus for Jews, Catholics, and Protestants.

Students on campus are relatively safe from physical assault, but as on most campuses, there are a fair number of burglaries and car thefts reported each year.

Stanford's athletic program has collected nearly seventy national championships in the school's history, including many in typically Californian sports like water polo, golf, tennis, and swimming. The university's students and alumni won eighteen medals at the 1996 Summer Olympics.

Swarthmore College

500 College Avenue
Swarthmore, PA 19081-1397
(610) 328-8000
www.swarthmore.edu

Total enrollment: 1,448
Undergraduates: 1,448
SAT ranges (Verbal/Math): 655-770 (V); 660-750 (M)
Applicants: 3,993
Accepted: 23%
Enrolled: 39%
Application deadline: January 1
Financial aid application deadline: early February
Tuition: $25,200/$33,004
Core curriculum: No

Reaching an Understanding

Swarthmore College is one of the most selective and rigorous small liberal arts colleges in the country. It is consistently ranks among the top three such schools in national polls, and statistics show that getting in is a difficult proposition for even very good students. The middle half of freshman SAT scores range from 1,300 to better than 1,500, and only about a quarter of those who apply are accepted. Once there, students face challenging courses without the "benefit" of grade inflation. Alumni, three of whom have won Nobel Prizes, support the school generously and are thankful for what they received there.

Swarthmore has a whopping endowment of $610 million, and it uses its wealth to keep the student body small (less than 1,500) and the student-to-faculty ratio very low (nine-to-one). The hefty endowment, enhanced recently by a $30 million donation from alumnus Eugene Lang, also allows Swarthmore to admit qualified students regardless of financial need, which heightens the quality of the school and the value of the education it offers.

Though quite a few courses are structured around various ideologies, there is nothing easy about them. One could look for more structure and cohesion in the general education requirements, but Swarthmore decided two decades ago that if all of its classes were good, no education derived from them could be bad.

Academic Life: Good Choices

In a 1967 study of its own curriculum, Swarthmore came out in favor of "a curriculum that leans sharply toward specialized diversity, and away from uniform generality." The college chose to emphasize "encounters with special topics and problems at a comparatively high level of competence, and . . . student programs that reflect individual constellations of diversified interests." This theory, common among modern liberal arts colleges, means that Swarthmore defines a liberal education by the process through which it is gained, rather than by what it includes.

In practice this means there is no core curriculum, and that the minimal distribution requirements are only loosely defined. Swarthmore students must take three courses from each of the college's divisions: natural sciences, social sciences, and humanities. The courses are supposed to be taken in the first two years of study. Two of the courses in each division must be "primary distribution courses," or PDCs, which, according to the college catalogue, are limited to twenty-five students and "place particular emphasis on the mode of inquiry in a particular discipline." The two PDCs in each division must come from different departments.

Apart from those parameters, there are few restrictions on the way a student may fulfill the general education requirements. "I've run into a few people who seemed a little unfocused," says a student. "But I've found it very good on the whole."

Many of the PDCs are fairly traditional general survey courses, but others are more narrow or ideological in nature. For example, many history PDCs (which meet the social science rather than humanities requirement) concern Europe or the United States, but courses in "Latin America" or "The Formation of the Islamic Middle East" are on equal footing. "It's pretty rare that you would get a course that would be a survey of the Western canon," a graduate says. Many courses emphasize methodology instead of providing an overview of the subject matter. "There tends to be some experimentation with content," the same graduate says. Another student tells of selecting as a PDC a course on modern Europe, only to find that "it turned into a history of modern gender conflicts and issues, which was really deceiving."

The PDCs cover a variety of time periods, cultures, and current critical theories. But not one such course in the English department, for example, surveys classic Western literature — not even from a revisionist point of view. English instead offers courses like "Cultural Practices and Social Texts" and "Illicit Desires in Literature." There is also a PDC called "Portraits of the Artist," which covers Dante, Salman Rushdie, and others, but also "contains videos by or about African griots, Glenn Gould, Julie Dash, Maya Deren, and Ed Wood Jr.," according to the catalogue. A class entitled "Ways of Seeing" involves popular films and television shows, including *Blade Runner, Seinfeld,* and *The Simpsons.*

"Some of the [English] classes are a little flaky," one student says. "[But] they [also] teach perfectly standard kinds of things," such as a Shakespeare survey and a

Chaucer seminar. However, while those courses could count as the third selection from a division, neither is considered a PDC.

Swarthmore does have a foreign language requirement for all students. It can be met with three years of high school language courses, a satisfactory score on a standardized test, or one year of language study at the college level. Students must also take four quarter-length classes in physical education and pass a survival swimming test. And, although politicized courses can count toward the distribution requirements, Swarthmore does not require a multicultural or "diversity" course.

Outstanding professors include Richard Schuldenfrei in philosophy; James Kurth in political science; Rosaria Munson in classics; Maribeth Graybill in art history; and John Boccio, Michael Brown, and Amy Bug in physics. The departments acknowledged as the college's strongest are physics, classics, art history, psychology, and economics. However, one professor cautions against a hierarchical arrangement of departments. "They're all strong," the professor says. "You can't even survive here unless they're strong."

Some departments are also strongly politicized. Beyond its PDC offerings, the history department has a tendency to focus on "very, very obscure" time periods and subjects, a student says. Political science is also said to be highly politicized, and does not have "much tolerance for free-market ideas," a student says. Upper-level courses in that department center on theoretical jargon and the common race-class-gender triumvirate. These courses include "Difference, Dominance, and the Struggle for Equality," "Gender, Politics, and Policy in America," and "Multicultural Politics in the U.S." Though not many upper-level political science courses are offered in European politics, quite a few concern the politics of China, Southeast Asia, and Africa.

The English department's politics are displayed in the titles of upper-level courses — "Lesbian Novels Since World War II," for one. The department also tends to offer courses because students like to take them, one student says. It does require its majors to take courses on periods both before and after 1830, but the student says both sides of the divide are not welcomed equally. "Whenever you get into a class with pre-1830 stuff, people in the class are only in there because of the requirement, and are pretty unenthusiastic," the student says.

The leftward political bias is even more apparent in the department of modern languages and literatures, where a professor's text selection is often an excuse to reinforce the cherished political fixations of race, class, and sex. Course offerings include "La Frontera: The Many Voices of the U.S.-Mexico Border" and "Scandal in the Ink: Queer Traditions in French Literature." But a student who reads the catalogue carefully will also find rather traditional and worthy literary content even in courses with titles that at first hearing sound trendy; "Literature of Dissent," for example, is apparently a way to encourage students to read Turgenev, Tolstoy, and Dostoyevsky.

Interdisciplinary special programs, including black studies, women's studies, environmental studies, and the nebulously named "interpretation theory," are not full-fledged departments and do not offer majors, but students can study in these areas in addition to their majors. Courses in black studies and women's studies appear to be on the radical side, while environmental studies' course titles range from scientific to issues-oriented. The concentration in interpretation theory is not aimed at any particular subject matter, but at deconstructing things through a study of language, film, psychology, sexuality, and religion. Special programs such as these are a recent development at Swarthmore, and the college sees them as a sort of try-out for full degree-granting status, a professor says. After five or ten years the programs will be evaluated, at which point they will disappear completely, become true majors, or be subsumed into another department, as was the case with an international relations program that eventually joined the departments of political science and economics. If these programs do become majors, it would represent a further politicization of Swarthmore's curriculum, which to this point has at least kept its political classes within the confines of traditional departments.

Whatever politics do exist on campus, there is no question that most courses are well taught and are concerned with traditional subjects. Several faculty maintain that the liberal arts departments have kept their essential academic integrity, despite courses like several listed above. "It depends on what you mean by politicized," a professor says. "Professors tend to be liberal-to-progressive, but this does not usually affect the content of courses."

The economics department is said to be open to a variety of views. The department has a free-market emphasis, and is "open to raising a voice for conservative issues," a student says. "They would not only tolerate the expression of those views, they would help you formulate those ideas." Classics is much the same way, according to another student. "It's kind of a small department," the student says. "[But] the reason I found it attractive is that it's particularly immune to individual spur-of-the-moment intellectual trends."

Students in classics can select, among others, an excellent and intensive major in Greek. Both majors and non-majors are encouraged to participate in a special semester at the Intercollegiate Center for Classical Studies in Rome. The philosophy department offers some unusual seminars on topics such as ethical issues in biotechnology, but their course listings demonstrate a weakness in many areas of the history of Western philosophy. The religion department offers vastly more interesting seminars on non-Christian religious topics than on Christian ones, and in general is committed to a comparative, phenomenological approach to its discipline.

Swarthmore has an unusual honors option, the "External Examination Program," in which students attend eight selective and rigorous seminars in their last four semesters. These seminars are only graded at the end of the senior year, and the extensive writing projects required for these seminars — along with oral examinations — are evaluated by faculty from other universities.

Overall, though, Swarthmore's courses are academically rigorous, regardless of the department in which they are taught. "A lot of our attention here is focused on working with students, [having] the best teaching and research availability," a professor says. Grade inflation does not exist at Swarthmore, and a B-plus is considered a very good grade by most students, who must average at least Cs to graduate. "It's still very difficult to do well," one student says. The college bookstore even sells T-shirts that say: "Anywhere Else It Would Have Been an A, Really." All first semester grades are pass/fail.

Political Atmosphere: Can't We All Just Get Along?

Like many small liberal arts colleges founded in the nineteenth century, Swarthmore came from Christian roots. Although it has not been officially aligned with a church for nearly a century, this heritage still influences the campus's atmosphere. Swarthmore was founded in 1864 by members of the Religious Society of Friends, the Quakers, as a coeducational institution, something rare at the time. The college catalogue indicates that, though a secular school, it still "seeks to illuminate the lives of its students with the spiritual principles of the Society of Friends."

These principles, in practice, are more ethical than spiritual. The catalogue speaks of "the individual's responsibility for seeking and applying truth, and for testing whatever truth one believes one has found." It notes the Quaker concerns for "hard work, simple living, and generous giving; personal integrity, social justice, and the peaceful settlement of disputes," but immediately adds that "the College does not seek to impose on its students this Quaker view of life, or any other specific set of convictions about the nature of things and the duties of human beings."

The result is a campus predominantly liberal, "but with tolerance for all kinds of views," says a conservative student. "I find it a very comfortable place to be." There is political diversity and, for the most part, factions accord one another proper respect. Another conservative student says she chose Swarthmore over several other competitors because of its "openness to the expression of a number of differing views, including mine." This student speaks highly of Swarthmore's emphasis on a serious examination of one's own values, saying this practice is a direct legacy of the school's Quaker heritage. One example of the college's commitment to social justice is the Office of Community Service Learning Programs, which co-sponsors projects in the greater Philadelphia area, such as tutorials in public schools and assistance for the homeless.

Another student thinks the college is sometimes too devoted to consensus at the expense of healthy discord. "I sometimes would have preferred a little more room to remain dissenting," the student says. "There could be more emphasis on the right to disagree."

Another T-shirt available on campus reads: "Anywhere Else It Would Have Been an Issue." For the most part, this phrase is correct: If students can't come to an agreement, they likely don't have the time to become involved in further arguments, let alone more radical political activities. There are controversies at Swarthmore, usually involving multiculturalism and diversity issues, but these don't normally get far. "Most of the controversies are sort of silly," a student says. "They're usually issues about having issues."

One recent example involved the American flag, which some students claimed was representative of imperialism. Further, they argued that political allegiances had no place in an educational community, and asked that the flag not be flown on campus. The group was small but vocal; however, the student body voted to keep the flag.

Other groups are also small but vocal — and radical. There are many debates about race, but the most influential groups on campus include the College Democrats, Civil Liberties, Earthlust, and the Feminist Majority. Gay rights are also discussed frequently, both by campus groups and visiting speakers. A former assistant dean returned to the college in 1997 and spoke about the troubles he and his partner had encountered in their attempts to adopt a girl. Swarthmore provides space for a Women's Resource Center, a Black Cultural Center and an Intercultural Center, with the latter "devoted to developing greater awareness of Asian/Asian American, Latino/Hispanic, Gay/Lesbian/Bisexual contributions to Swarthmore College as well as the broader society."

Swarthmore promises to protect freedom of expression, and though a hate speech code was once proposed, it was not adopted. Tenure decisions are said to be objective and based on both excellence in teaching and the adequate production of research. Nevertheless, there appears to be a subtle campus undertone regarding "correct" beliefs, even though the college is nominally open to traditional opinions. A student remembers a peer who was counseled not even to write an essay opposing affirmative action, as well as a professor's public pronouncement that students arriving at Swarthmore from Catholic high schools needed to be rid of their "dogmatism." As part of first-year orientation, students participate in a safe-sex workshop that, one student says, is "a bit on the edge."

Still, traditional students say they are generally comfortable at Swarthmore. One student says, however, that Swarthmore is a place where traditional students will "get a lot of skills, but your values and beliefs as a conservative will not be bolstered." Conservative groups do exist on campus, and have cooperated with liberal groups to sponsor debates; recently Wendell Primus and Robert Rector took opposite sides on the topic "Welfare: Safety Net or Web of Dependency." A conservative newspaper, *Common Sense*, receives funding from the college, but some students say the paper is not particularly good.

Student Life: Life's a Beach

Swarthmore is located in the western suburbs of Philadelphia, a region dense with outstanding colleges and universities. The campus is certainly one of the most beautiful in the nation, with wide lawns and tree-lined roads and paths that can be stunning when fall colors are at their best. Stately Parrish Hall is the center of the campus, containing not only the administrative offices but also five residence halls and the campus newspaper and radio station. In good weather the lawn in front of this building becomes "Parrish Beach," where Frisbee and other collegiate pastimes are pursued.

All new students are expected to live on campus in one of the college's lovely residence halls, and upperclassmen may elect to do so. About 85 percent of the housing is coeducational and, according to the catalogue, single-sex housing cannot be guaranteed to those who request it. Students in single-sex arrangements are expected to set their own visitation policies. There are two small fraternity houses that rent quarters on campus.

Philadelphia and its myriad social, historical, and cultural attractions are only a half hour away by train or car. Swarthmore students thus have easy access to a major city while being able to live in suburban comfort and safety.

Given what's been said about Swarthmore's political atmosphere, it will come as no surprise that many of its student clubs are on the left-hand side of the political spectrum. These include the environmentalist Earthlust and *The L-Word*, a sophisticated, student-edited "Journal of Liberal Thought." But one can also find on campus the College Republicans, who often sponsor speakers, including recently a representative from Feminists for Life; the Swarthmore Conservative Union; and Swarthmore Students Advocating Life.

Several Christian groups, including evangelical ones, are represented on campus, but there is no Newman Center for Catholic students. Religious and moral issues are plumbed in debate nonetheless, and religious conservatives are not always silent — one student even responded to an atheist's complaint by appealing to logic and the thoughts of C. S. Lewis, and his editorial was posted on the *Swarthmore Phoenix*'s Web site. Despite the obstacles, conservative students do attend Swarthmore. Says one: "I like the place a lot. I've been very happy there. The teachers are very committed, and the underlying ethic is one I can really respect."

Swarthmore offers varsity competition in twenty-two sports, with most of the competition taking place in the Centennial Conference. Intramural and club teams extend the range of student athletic opportunities. However, one former sport is now missing: the college board recently voted to dissolve the football team, arguing that the small size of the freshman class made it difficult to fit in all the bodies such a team requires.

Swarthmore has recently become the beneficiary of one of its most famous alumni, the late novelist James Michener. Upon his death, Michener named Swarthmore the main beneficiary of his estate (estimated to be worth many tens of millions of dollars). Though Michener was neither a scholar nor a literary novelist, his big, sweeping novels about various parts of the world have served to educate, as well as entertain, millions of people about places near and far. Perhaps it is in the quietly educational value of his novels that Michener paid his greatest tribute to the education he received at Swarthmore College.

University of Texas at Austin

Office of Admissions
Main Building, Room 7
Austin, TX 78712-1111
(512) 475-7440
www.utexas.edu

Total enrollment: 49,000
Undergraduates: 37,159
SAT ranges (Verbal/Math): 530-640 (V); 550-660 (M)
Applicants: 18,930
Accepted: 63%
Enrolled: 59%
Application deadline: February 1
Financial aid application deadline: March 31
Tuition: resident: $3,575/$9,075 ; non-resident: $10,025/$15,525
Core curriculum: No

Size and Other Matters

During the last five years it would be hard to find a campus that has seen more acrimonious controversy than the University of Texas at Austin. The Fifth Circuit Court of Appeals' decision in the 1996 *Hopwood v. Texas* case, which effectively struck down the university's use of racial preferences in admissions, touched off an endless string of protests, speeches, press conferences, and general moral indignation strong enough, at one point, to even draw Jesse Jackson to campus. The storm around *Hopwood* is only now truly beginning to die down.

The school's hometown, Austin, often suffers from a similar suffocating atmosphere of liberal moral earnestness and self-righteousness. But it seems that nearly everyone is willing to pay the price. For many, the university's location in Austin is its primary advantage. Austin has a booming economy, and UT graduates are loath to leave. At its best, Austin exudes a friendly, bohemian, decadent, fin-de-siecle, devil-may-care, tomorrow-we-die atmosphere. And if that doesn't sound good to you, UT may not be your cup of tea. "Austin is wild, interesting, diverse, unique," says one professor. "Not really typically Texan, but not typical anything else, either."

Surprisingly, both students and faculty regard UT's mammoth size as another major advantage. Founded in 1883 on the forty acres north of the state capitol, the University of Texas at Austin is the largest single-campus university in the United States, just shy of fifty thousand students. The result is that no matter how stultifying

655

the school's (and city's) political atmosphere may sometimes be, there are nooks and crannies where those students and faculty more focused on education than political agendas can survive. The upshot is that UT provides a fine education — if you know where to look. UT is "large enough that some very good teachers and some very good students have slipped through the cracks," says a faculty member. "They aren't always able to locate one another, but when they do, the educational experience can be as rich here as anywhere else."

Academic Life: . . . and That's Why I Reside in Tennessee

Like virtually all state universities, the University of Texas has instituted distribution requirements as a substitute for a core curriculum. Though at first glance it appears that there are some common courses required of all students, further investigation reveals this to be a smokescreen. Still, UT isn't as bad as many state universities. As one professor notes, "There is no way that distribution requirements can compensate for the lack of a really strong core curriculum. But you could do worse than the University of Texas. There is some substance left in the distribution requirements."

All students must take courses in four areas: language arts, social sciences, natural sciences, and general culture. The language arts requirement consists of two components: writing and foreign language. The writing component is met by two courses required of all students: "Rhetoric and Composition" and "Masterworks of Literature." The content of the latter course varies tremendously by section, but it is noteworthy that students can in fact choose sections with traditional, classical subject matter. As for the former, there isn't as much "systematic indoctrination" as there at times in the past, according to a professor, but a definite political slant remains. The foreign language requirement consists of a four-course sequence in the student's chosen language (or testing to an equivalent level of proficiency).

In addition to these classes, students must also make two selections certified as "substantial writing component" courses, at least one of which must be upper-division. Courses acquire this label if more than 50 percent of the student's final grade is dependent upon written work. Since every department offers some of these courses, students usually fulfill this requirement while simultaneously fulfilling major or minor requirements.

Thanks to the Texas Legislature, all students must take two courses in American Government (one of which focuses on Texas government) and two courses in United States history (one covering the period before the Civil War, the second covering the time since) as part of the social science requirement. There is some leeway in the U.S. history portion, as some alternative courses also fulfill the student's obligation, but in any case these courses do not educate UT students in a common body of historical knowledge. The numerous sections of these courses are wildly divergent. In some sections of the first course in American government, students read

Hobbes's *Leviathan* and Locke's *Second Treatise*. In others they get standard text-book treatments or else focus on contemporary public affairs. There is even more diversity among sections of "Issues and Policies in American Government," the second core government course; here the ascription of common course numbers borders on the fraudulent, as different sections bear different subtitles. Some sections cover constitutional law, while others may focus on "Race and Ethnicity in American Politics" or "Women, Gender, and Politics." The sections of the two core history courses also differ greatly. The rest of the social science requirements can be met by a three-hour course in anthropology, economics, geography, linguistics, psychology, or sociology. The best that can be said for all this diversity is that if a student chooses carefully, he can avoid excessive politicization and even find a few excellent courses.

To meet the natural sciences requirement, students must complete eighteen hours of math and the natural sciences, six of which must come in one of the "hard" sciences. The general culture requirement obligates students to take six hours in architecture, fine arts, classics, or philosophy. Some heavily politicized "culture studies" courses are approved as alternatives.

UT's distribution requirements, then, do a comparatively good job in ensuring some minimal breadth of education among students. Despite allegedly common courses, the content of this education will vary widely according to students' course selections, but the sheer number of these courses gives savvy students the opportunity to avoid the most trendy and politicized of the offerings.

A much finer education is offered in UT's "Plan II" Honors Program, available to select students. Founded in 1935, Plan II is the jewel of UT's undergraduate education, attracting students comparable in ability to those found at the nation's elite private institutions. And it is really the only place at UT where students can find a rigorous core curriculum. Plan II students do not "major" in anything, ordinarily, because Plan II is both an honors program *and* a major in and of itself. Plan II freshmen take a year-long course in world literature, two semesters of a foreign language, two semesters of non-U.S. history, math, logic, "Modes of Reasoning," and a first-year tutorial consisting of seminars from professors across campus. In their sophomore years, there is a year-long sequence in philosophy, two more semesters of a foreign language, the legislature-required government sequence (two semesters), physics, biology, and a special Plan II social science course. The junior year brings two Plan II seminars, the two-semester course in American history, a semester of physics, and two semesters of humanities/fine arts (chosen from art history, classics, literature, or philosophy). A thesis is required for all senior Plan II honors students. There are increasing opportunities to take electives as the student progresses.

Plan II isn't perfect. One professor says that the freshman and junior seminars must be chosen with care: "Some are quite substantial, and others are incoherent postmodern ramblings." And though the philosophy and hard science classes are stellar, the social science and math offerings are also said to be a bit suspect. As one professor says, Plan II students "are not given as rigorous a curriculum as they could benefit from." And it seems to be a nearly universal opinion among both students and faculty that Plan II students are snobs who expect to be given high grades unrelated to the extent of their effort. Plan II students are "absolutely full of themselves," according to one professor.

The Liberal Arts Honors Program, developed by psychology professor Joseph Horn, is in many ways just as rigorous. Open to many more students than Plan II, students in this program take three special upper-division courses in the College of Liberal Arts and usually participate in departmental honors programs, which allow them to enroll in tutorial courses with professors and to write a senior thesis.

Although UT's reputation has been made in business, engineering, and the natural sciences, there are some social science and humanities departments that add to the university's strengths. The philosophy department is well-regarded, as are psychology, classics, linguistics, and Germanic studies. The history department is said to include a number of good teachers, though they must compete for time with some rather politicized colleagues. In the hard sciences, physics, math, chemistry, and computer science are exceptionally solid.

At a university of this size there are bound to be a number of exceptional teachers. At UT, these include David G. Martinez and Thomas G. Palaima in classics; William T. Guy Jr. in mathematics; Austin M. Gleeson in physics; William R. Louis, George B. Forgie, and Michael B. Stoff in history; Robert D. King and Lars Gustafsson in Germanic studies; Robert H. Kane, Louis Mackey, David Sosa, Daniel Bonevac, Robert C. Koons, and Alex Mourelatos in philosophy; John Ruszkiewicz and John Trimble in rhetoric and composition; Joseph Horn, Robert Josephs, Randy Diehl, Phil Gough, and Tim Schallert in psychology; Marvin Olasky in journalism; Timothy High in art; Elizabeth M. Richmond-Garza in English; J. Budziszewski and David Prindle in government; Carlota S. Smith and Manfred Krifka in linguistics; Martin Poenie in biology; Stanislav Zimic in Spanish and Portuguese; and Alan Campion in chemistry.

Some of these professors are on the university's official "distinguished teachers" list, but students searching for excellent instructors shouldn't put too much stock in that compilation. UT makes a painstaking effort to make sure the right gender and ethnicity balance is represented, according to one professor.

Not surprisingly, classes at UT tend to run large. "Many classes are huge," says one professor, "but there are also many opportunities for small seminars, especially for those in honors programs or who major in serious subjects, like classics or philosophy." Class size also varies much by major, even at the upper-division level, with classes in, say, physics, much smaller than those in English or computer science. Grade inflation is rampant, as at most universities, though this too varies by department. English and the language departments are said to be in particularly giving moods, with others, like philosophy or psychology, containing both "very strict graders and irresponsibly lax ones," according to one faculty member. The chemistry department actively curves grades to keep inflation down. But lofty grading is more or less a school policy. "The administration encourages grade inflation indirectly by identifying courses that they think are critical courses for minorities and encouraging faculty to grade these courses more leniently," says one professor.

UT's control over the quality of its graduates' education is further compromised by state legislative rules requiring that state universities accept transfer students from any Texas junior college, as long as these students have completed thirty hours with at least a 3.0 GPA. The effect of this rule is that the university admits roughly half as many transfer students as freshmen each year. Says one professor, "it really dilutes the quality of the student body." It also makes for an almost impossible range of student ability. "You could make a Rice out of UT; but there are many more students who are very marginal," a professor says. "And so somebody who comes to UT has to deal with the fact that you're going to encounter a wide caliber of students and faculty who have to deal with that in their planning." That is, many professors pitch their courses to the lowest common denominator of students, or not much higher.

Furthermore, because UT does not have the resources to teach all 37,000 of its undergraduates, it readily accepts credits its students complete at Austin Community College. Many UT students bail out on the more difficult UT courses, especially in difficult subjects, in favor of these comparative joy rides.

More concerning, though, is the fact that UT focuses more on research than on providing quality undergraduate education. Like other places, it employs PR people to tell you that these two are one and the same. But professors say that UT's narrow-minded research focus is one of its greatest flaws. "One of the deficiencies here is that UT does not believe in nurturing young faculty coming up," one says. "Instead what they want to do is to buy big name faculty with prestigious reputations — that is, they don't have to be excellent but only have a reputation for excellence. UT wants to be 'on the map,' to be 'visible' and 'known.' That's a great weakness here and it's going to take a lot to overcome it."

Political Atmosphere: The Blooming Rows of Texans

For a while, it seemed that something called "Hopwood" was to blame for just about everything except for the blazing summer heat at the University of Texas. The controversy that arose after the 1996 *Hopwood* opinion holding that the Law School's use of racial preferences in admissions decisions was unconstitutional engulfed campus for several years, further politicizing a school that had already moved quite a way down the road.

But the sky didn't fall after all. Black and Hispanic students still found their way to the university, and thanks largely to new legislation guaranteeing admission to Texas high school students graduating in the top 10 percent of their classes, black and Hispanic admissions levels now approach their pre-*Hopwood* levels. And so, ironically, the biggest effect of *Hopwood* has been to galvanize and energize campus radicals. In 1998 they persuaded the administration to erect — with student fees — a Martin Luther King Jr. statue on the East Mall as a counterpoise to the statues of Confederate-era heroes — including Robert E. Lee and Jefferson Davis — who line the university's oak-shaded South Mall. It's a legitimate question, and anyone's guess, as to how long the Confederate statues will last. It's genuinely confounding that they have not yet been defaced. In the last couple of years, campus radicals have staged sit-ins, hounded law professor Lino Graglia for statements on race and culture that didn't suit the party line, succeeded in shouting down Ward Connerly during a speech he gave at the Law School, and made Henry Kissinger cancel a scheduled speech on campus because university officials said they could not vouch for his safety.

The administration's response to these and other disruptions has been — in its more spiny moments — meek; often, it verges on downright solidarity with the protesters. With the cancellation of the Kissinger lecture, for instance, there were not even *pro forma* anguished statements from the administration about how sorry they were to see the threat of violence preclude the free exchange of ideas. But that's not surprising, as since *Hopwood* the administration has imitated an elephant cornered by the campus radicals' mice. *Mother Jones* even named UT one of its top ten most-activist campuses in 1999, specifically applauding a protesters' sit-in in November 1998 that persuaded the university president to agree to a series of "town meetings." Ah, progress.

Campus radicals and free speech zealots love the university's West Mall, where during the day student organizations set up information tables and where any person can caterwaul (with a university-provided megaphone) on the Main Building's terrace steps to his heart's content. At times, it seems virtually impossible to escape the racket of loudspeakers and cheering followers; high-minded rhetoric about free speech aside, the West Mall seems to serve notice that UT is more about the life of the mouth than the life of the mind. One professor sees the West Mall as a carefully orchestrated administration charade. "The administration likes it chaotic, but they really don't care about free speech, because when somebody's free speech rights are taken away, they won't defend it," this professor says.

This kind of radical chic most students and professors could do without. One faculty member says that the worst thing about UT is "its aspiration to become a second Berkeley." Another says "the 'distinguished speakers' program should be named the 'retired liberal Democrat politicos' program." But here again, the size of the university is helpful. As one professor says, "Although UT remains almost as PC as any other major state university, the fact that it is embedded in a very conservative state with a very conservative government provides a certain measure of protection to the few conservative voices on campus." Says another, otherwise critical, professor: "As I go around the country, I think the Eastern schools are so much worse, primarily because they have a higher concentration of radical faculty. At places like Brown, the pressure is just relentless, so people just bow their necks and endure it. At UT you can still teach your material."

The English, economics, French and Italian, ethnic studies, women's studies, and education departments are singled out as among the most politicized and/or mediocre. In these areas "our reputation is pretty poor," one professor says. "And we live down to it." Besides Dr. Budziszewski, the government department is described by one professor as "politically correct and boring." Anthropology is also highly politicized, though the small cadre of physical anthropologists are at least partially exempt from this charge. The religious studies department, predictably enough, does not give fair treatment to matters touching on Christian religion. The department once refused to cross-list a philosophy course in Western theism because its focus was too narrow. English, though, is most often mentioned as the single worst department on campus, in terms of politicization and trendy silliness.

As for hiring, "to get hired, a political conservative or a religious believer has to be awfully lucky, terribly subtle, or, preferably, both," laments one professor. The range of political opinions represented among the faculty is terribly skewed. "Out of a faculty of three thousand, I can count the outspoken conservatives on my fingers," says one faculty member. Many don't speak up out of fear. "Junior faculty really run scared" of crossing entrenched chairmen, says one professor.

There seems to be a consensus among faculty that, unless a student is looking into Plan II or the Liberal Arts Honor Program, or has already managed to acquire a solid enough outlook toward the liberal arts tradition that he knows what to look for, he may be better served elsewhere. And religious students need to be particularly wary. "If you are religious, and you don't want to do the homework necessary to provide an intelligent defense of your faith, then don't come to UT, or if you do, avoid the humanities and social sciences — including, above all, the 'religious studies' program," one professor says.

Student Life: Austin, La Vista, Baby

A few years ago Austin was named by *Girlfriends* magazine as the best place in the country for lesbians to live. That's one side of Austin, a city where the prevailing ethos of pretentious radicalism can become tiresome. But aside from its political and moral manifestations, that same atmosphere gives rise to an inviting array of bohemian delights. Though technology companies and their yuppies are moving in at an alarming rate, much of "old Austin" remains, with its down-home, low-key, informal neighborhood shops, bookstores, barbecue joints, taquerias, and bars. Formalities are rare; in Austin, "dressing up" simply means keeping the Birkenstocks in the closet.

Austin is also unique among Texas cities for its natural beauty. The sprawling, sparsely populated Hill Country to the west of the city makes for any number of out-door activities and inviting day trips. Closer to home, the Barton Creek greenbelt to the west of campus provides hiking and biking trails and, when there's water, oppor-tunity to engage in the popular Texas summertime recreational activity of floating down a river on an inner tube with a six pack.

As for the university itself, student social life tends to split along typically Greek/non-Greek lines, but there is something for everyone. When the legislature is in session, politically ambitious students make copies and coffee for representatives and senators at the Capitol. There are hundreds of registered student organizations. The Longhorn Hellraisers paint their faces burnt orange and white, take off their shirts (it's men only: women can join the Hellraiser Honeys), and scream a lot at foot-ball and basketball games. On the radical side of the ledger, MEChA militates against displays of Texas patriotism on the grounds that it is insensitive to Hispanics (Texas took the land from them, you know). The Radical Action Network protests just about everything. The Pagan Student Alliance exists "to protect the interests of Pagan stu-dents on the UT campus, and to promote a common meeting ground for Pagan stu-dents," according to their own information. The Knighthood of BUH specializes in sophomoric shock techniques, including trading pornography for Bibles on the West Mall; it seems that as long as it's a *trade*, this is OK with the administration.

At times, it seems like everyone at UT is from Dallas or Houston. The student body consists largely of white students from these large Texas metropolitan areas, with, as one professor notes, "a sprinkling of minorities and rural kids." As one fac-ulty member puts it, the majority of UT students "are postmodern nihilists, looking for the quickest and easiest road to money and pleasure." Another notes that the school lacks a strong intellectual tradition: "This isn't one of the campuses where there are a lot of students with the intellectual spark."

UT does have a sizable contingent of active conservatives and Christians and therefore has many religiously oriented student organizations. Christian students wanting to remain so should avoid the churches adjoining campus. Catholic stu-dents should be especially wary of the Catholic Student Center; Veritas, a student-led Catholic apologetics group, is a better bet. Other religious groups include Hillel and InterVarsity Christian Fellowship. The Young Conservatives of Texas have a rep-utation for charismatic, fiery leadership and usually manage to stay embroiled in controversy. The University Life Advocates promote the pro-life cause and regularly hold "baby drives" to gather material aid for women with crisis pregnancies.

Football is king in Texas, and in an age of mushy sentimentality, a healthy, hearty hatred still manages to persist between the Horns and the Texas A&M Aggies. The game is traditionally held on Thanksgiving Day morning. UT holds a "Hex Rally" in the week preceding the game; in the wake of the tragic bonfire construction acci-dent at A&M that killed twelve people, it is unclear whether this will continue. Per-haps the most successful intercollegiate sport at UT in recent years has been the men's swimming program, though the basketball and football teams are usually among the nation's best as well. Intramural sports are quite popular, though some of the playing fields are unfortunately situated a couple of miles north of campus.

Freshman orientation consists of the typical diversity-and-alternative-lifestyle-mongering, complete with distribution of condoms. But one professor says that orientation is not taken too seriously, nor is it mandatory. Many students leave once they see what they are in for. Somewhat surprisingly, UT does not have a gay/lesbian center or a student government group specially devoted to gay and lesbian students.

Residence hall living is not the norm at UT. The university's ten residence halls have a combined capacity of just over five thousand, even with the mammoth Jester Hall that can hold just shy of three thousand residents. The vast majority of students live off campus, many in private dormitories adjoining the forty acres. Others live in apartments to the west and north of campus, mostly within walking distance, or in places spread out across the city in various apartment complexes and rented houses. For those who do live on campus, single-sex dormitories are available for both men and women.

Students report feeling quite safe on and around campus, although there are occasional incidents on Guadalupe Street (the "Drag"), which borders the west side.

Texas A&M University

Admissions
Texas A&M–College Station
College Station, TX 77843
(979) 845-3741
www.tamu.edu

Total enrollment: 44,026
Undergraduates: 36,082
SAT ranges (Verbal/Math): 520-630 (V); 550-660 (M)
Applicants: 14,447
Accepted: 74%
Enrolled: 62%
Application deadline: February 15
Financial aid application deadline: April 1
Tuition: resident: $3,374/$8,538; non-resident: $9,824/$14,988
Core curriculum: No

"This Isn't Your Father's Texas A&M"

This sentiment embodies the rapid changes that Texas A&M University at College Station has undergone in the last forty years. Many alumni believe perhaps the greatest change occurred in 1963 when the school converted itself from an all-male military academy to a full-fledged coeducational university. Interestingly, despite this important conversion Texas A&M has retained much from its military school past. The university still sponsors the Corps of Cadets, which is the largest uniformed body of students outside the three U.S. service academies. But while Texas A&M is cultivating liberal arts and business programs, it is still agriculture and mechanics — that is, "A" and "M" — where the university excels.

Texas A&M's school spirit is legendary, some might say even to the point of being destructive. In 1999, twelve Texas A&M students died while building a massive bonfire more than fifty feet high. The bonfire has always been intended to symbolize the school's "burning desire" to beat its arch rival, the University of Texas Longhorns, in their annual football game. But the deaths have many asking whether the price of the tradition is too dear. And A&M has nothing, if it has not tradition.

Academic Life: The Other Way Around

Like the other state universities in Texas, A&M requires students to complete something called a "core curriculum." It's not a core curriculum at all, but rather a set of distribution requirements. And it isn't particularly demanding. In fact, the university even suggests that it be used to supplement or find a major rather than preparing a student for studies of any kind.

"The Core Curriculum provides breadth to any degree. When you have the opportunity to select among various courses, select those that will give you the opportunity to explore a possible major, or make selections that enhance your degree goals," the university Web page states. "For example, if you have thought about being a petroleum engineering major, you can select HIST 360, 'History of the American Petroleum Industry' rather than [another history course]. ENDS 150, 'Architectural History,' would give you the chance to see if your interest holds for an architecture major."

The core, such as it is, requires two communications courses (including one composition and rhetoric course required of all students), two courses in math and logic, two lab courses in science, and two social science courses. One humanities course is required, as is another one in the visual and performing arts. All students must take a physical education class. Finally, there is a three-course citizenship requirement, including required courses in U.S. and state government.

The lists of choices, especially in the social sciences and two humanities categories, are long and wide-ranging. Social science includes everything from agricultural economics to "Sociology of Sport." Courses in "Agricultural Ethics," anthropology, archaeology, classics, history, "Science Fiction Past and Present," and "The American Renaissance" count equally toward the humanities requirement.

While long, the lists don't contain overtly politicized courses. But neither do they provide, in their entirety, anything resembling a traditional liberal arts education. One Web page even contains the history of the term "liberal arts," perhaps by way of explanation for the use of the "L-word" at all.

Given this, it probably should come as no surprise that the traditional agricultural and mechanics programs at Texas A&M still remain the finest academic programs on campus. Nearly one quarter of Texas A&M's undergraduate population majors in some type of engineering. Virtually every engineering program offered from aerospace to petroleum engineering ranks among the top twenty in the nation, with several in the top five.

The university's offerings in the College of Agriculture and Life Sciences are impressive. A student interested in this area can major in areas as specific as agricultural journalism, dairy science, fisheries science, and many others. Somewhat related, the College of Veterinary Science is widely considered to be one of the finest in America. Recently, that college was the birthplace of the first animal specifically cloned for disease resistance. After testing hundreds of cattle, Bull 86 (the name of the cow) was found to be naturally disease-resistant to brucellosis, and under laboratory conditions resistant to tuberculosis and salmonellosis — all serious diseases in veterinary and human health.

The Lowry Mays College and Graduate School of Business has also received high marks by many, with its programs in accounting, management, and marketing ranked among the top twenty-five programs in popular surveys.

And Texas A&M does have a College of Liberal Arts, though it has only twelve departments and offers just sixteen bachelor's degrees (and five interdisciplinary majors). However, there about 5,200 students majoring in these programs, which include anthropology (home to an unusual nautical archaeology program), economics, English, history, journalism, modern and classical languages, philosophy, political science, psychology, sociology, and speech communication. Recently, the college added a department of performance studies (that is, music and theater), the first at the university "dedicated solely to the arts," according to the college Web page.

In its long-range planning document (entitled "Vision 2020"), the university states its intention to add courses and departments in the liberal arts. The college's Web site already claims that "during the past ten years, the College of Liberal Arts has moved from the periphery to the center of Texas A&M University" — though the engineering departments would probably dispute that. The lack of a strong liberal arts department has hurt A&M's standing in the academic community, but students, many of whom see little worth in a liberal arts or fine arts degree, have not complained so much. The college is already modernized its liberal arts offerings in one way: it has a women's studies program, though the course list appears tamer than those found at most other colleges.

A&M houses many capable professors. These include Morgan Reynolds in economics, Walter Bradley in mechanical engineering, D. Bruce Dickson in anthropology, and Douglas Slack in wildlife science.

Political Atmosphere: Missteps

Any school with nearly half of its student body comprised of students in the top ten percent of their high school graduating class is going to have "intellectuals" (read, "liberals"). In fact, many of these sorts have found refuge in the offices of *The Battalion,* the school's daily newspaper. "The Batt," as it is known, has engendered its fair share of controversy in recent years as it has supported the administration's pursuit of a multiculturalism requirement, as well as endorsing candidates who do not believe in the student body's conservative beliefs.

In response to The Batt's liberalism, a conservative newspaper called *The Aggie Review* was created to offer the largely conservative student body an outlet for its views. This newspaper often exposes to shocked alumni the administration's plans to gut traditions like the bonfire of their uniqueness as well as their goal of using liberal mantras like "diversity" to enhance the prestige of the school among other academics.

The Aggies are also proud to claim the largest College Republican chapter in the United States. The organization is particularly active; it campaigned for President George W. Bush in Arkansas, Tennessee, Missouri, and Louisiana. The College Republicans also work in tandem with the Young Conservatives of Texas (YCT) on protests, debates, and campaigns. "YCT is College Republicans with an edge," a student says. Recently, YCT sponsored "Straight Marriage Pride Week" and "Second Amendment Day."

It is only appropriate that Texas A&M have an engineer and alumnus at the helm. Dr. Ray Bowen assumed the presidency in June 1994. Most alumni universally heralded him — until three things happened.

First, Bowen released the Vision 2020 report, a set of twelve recommendations designed to make Texas A&M one of the top ten public universities in the nation by the year 2020. One of the goals posited by the plan was to "diversify and globalize the A&M community."

To achieve this result, Bowen made his second mistake, according to many alumni and students. In the summer of 2000, Bowen adopted a "plan that will require students to take six hours of international or cultural diversity classes." Conservatives contend that the plan was implemented merely to pacify critics who say that A&M students suffer from their culturally deficient surroundings. One conservative student said the multiculturalism requirement is "just one step in a larger plan to sacrifice the values that make A&M special" for greater academic reputation and prestige. And the student followed it with the worst accusation one can make against an A&M president: "He wants to make us just like the University of Texas."

Bowen's third mistake — according to many alumni and students — was the decision to cancel the bonfire for two years after eleven students and one graduate died and twenty-seven more were injured when it crashed to earth because of structural and design deficiencies. Traditionalists believed that if the students died making the bonfire, the last thing they would have wanted was its cancellation. The bonfire had been built every year since 1909. In light of the tragedy, however, it seems prudent to reconsider the design of the structure and to implement safety precautions; two years is not such a long hiatus. The university Web page already features prominently a link to "Bonfire 2002," a page that shows the planning being done for the next bonfire, offers a place for public comment, and includes a memorial to the victims. Despite the decision, Bowen is considered the university's biggest cheerleader, often criticized or complimented for doing whatever it takes (e.g., the multiculturalism requirement) to enhance the school's reputation.

Student Life: Lots of Yelling

To Aggies, College Station is Mecca. Most Aggies each year make at least an annual pilgrimage to this city to visit campus and watch their beloved football team at Kyle Field. The intellectual and avant-garde sort might find College Station boring or even stifling because of its conservatism and miles of strip malls. However, students who attend Texas A&M generally are not the type to worry about the absence of coffee houses with "open-mike" nights or drama department productions of nude Shakespeare; rather, most students at Texas A&M would prefer to tailgate and drink beer before football games or attend College Republican meetings, according to the ones we talked to.

The absence of coffee houses in College Station looks to be Anheuser Busch's gain, as the city is full of terrific pubs, dance halls, and restaurants. Favorites include the Dixie Chicken, which proudly proclaims "more beer sold per square foot than anywhere in the world." The owners of the Dixie Chicken have done so well they have a virtual monopoly on the nightlife in College Station; they also own the Chicken Oil Company, Dry Bean Saloon, Shadow Canyon Dance Hall and Saloon, and Alfred T. Hornback's. Another Aggie favorite is Wings 'N More, which serves up some of the nation's best wings in varying degrees of hotness.

It's a good thing food is available off campus, though, as the food and residence halls at Texas A&M leave much to be desired, according to students. For spartans, Texas A&M offers Hart Hall, which has no air conditioning. While room rates are nearly half those of air conditioned facilities, living there cannot be fun in August. On the other hand, nearly all of Texas A&M's 41 residence halls have been outfitted with Ethernet portals, so that students may access the Internet easily. Thirty of these halls are for non-Corps students; 21 (amazingly) are single-sex. The coed dorms split men and women by floor. The university's Department of Residence Life also offers higher-end options through apartments, graduate, and married student housing. A two-bedroom apartment rents for only $400 a month.

While there are many opportunities for political involvement at Texas A&M, student life is better defined by one's involvement in organizations that enhance the "Aggie Spirit." Thousands of students each year are proud to consider the building of the bonfire to be their primary extracurricular activity. Many students also join the Corps of Cadets because of its esteemed status on campus. Because almost all of Texas A&M's many traditions have their genesis in the school's military past, the Corps serves a vital role at football games. For example, to be a member of the "Fightin' Aggie Band" one must be a member of the Corps of Cadets, as the band wears military uniforms and marches military style.

Instead of cheerleaders, the Aggies have "Yell Leaders." Students and alumni gather at Kyle Field at midnight before the game to practice school yells. These midnight yell practices often attract as many as 30,000 people. Another remnant of Texas A&M's all-male, military past is the tradition of kissing one's date after each touchdown, extra point, or field goal.

The corps serves also as somewhat of a fraternity, but as the university has grown and changed, the number of students involved with Greek sororities and fraternities has increased. Currently, 20 percent of Texas A&M students are involved in Greek life.

Texas A&M also boasts the largest student-union program in the nation, with approximately seven hundred university-recognized clubs and organizations. If you can't find one that interests you, you aren't looking: the groups range from "Malaysians in Aggieland" to a group dedicated to Nordic skiing.

Like most other large universities, students at Texas A&M are occasionally victims of petty thefts in the residence halls. Remarkably, though, there were only thirty-one such occurrences reported in 1999. Campus police are most active in citing underage drinkers, handing out 268 such tickets in 1999.

If College Station options run out, students can always try the social life in Houston, eighty miles away.

Thomas Aquinas College

Admissions Office
Thomas Aquinas College
10,000 North Ojai Road
Santa Paula, California 93060
www.thomasaquinas.edu

Total enrollment: 267
Undergraduates: 267
SAT ranges (Verbal/Math): 610-710 (V); 570-660 (M)
Applicants: 151
Accepted: 85%
Enrolled: 67%
Application deadline: Rolling
Financial aid application deadline: March 2
Tuition: $15,900/$20,400
Core curriculum: Yes

And the Truth Will Make You Whole

Thomas Aquinas College opened in 1971. Its enrollment remains tiny by current university standards — 267 students — but its mission and philosophy are great. Great Books, in fact. The college is, as the name suggests, rooted firmly in the Catholic intellectual and social tradition. Its patron saint is no quaint mascot but an inspiring guide and teacher.

With its Great Books program, the Thomas Aquinas curriculum is virtually unparalleled for providing its students with a rigorous liberal arts education. In an age where the term "traditional liberal arts" gets used for curricula where two or more core classes are defined, this college is one of the few that actually has the right to use it. The guiding principles of Thomas Aquinas are enumerated in its founding document, a monograph entitled, "A Proposal for the Fulfillment of Catholic Liberal Education." Drafted by the college's first president, Ronald P. McArthur, and Marcus Berquist, still a tutor at the college, the document outlines a powerful vision of Catholic liberal education that has scarcely been changed in the last twenty-five years. According to the document, a Catholic college differs from its "secular counterparts" in two essential respects: "First, it will not define itself by academic freedom, but by the divinely revealed truth, and second, that truth will be the chief object of study as well as the governing principle of the whole institution."

It is the end result — the attainment of truth — as much as the *pursuit* of truth that defines the Thomas Aquinas curriculum and method. There is an ordering of knowledge, a set curriculum pursued by all students at Thomas Aquinas, one that moves through progressively more difficult and challenging works of Western literature, math, science, philosophy, and theology, and culminates in the achievement of a higher understanding. "The goal of the curriculum is wisdom," an alumnus says. "The primary teacher is St. Thomas."

Many students come to Thomas Aquinas College after becoming discouraged with their college experience elsewhere. One female freshman, who transferred to Aquinas after attending a well-known Catholic college, observed in the college bulletin that at her previous school, "there was so much 'fooling around' going on and without any thought that their actions were inconsistent with their faith." Transfers are impressed with the superior intellectual environment at Aquinas as much as the exalted moral climate, but above all, students are impressed by a set curriculum that allows for true intellectual development. "I had a friend [at another college] taking metaphysics his freshman year," says a student. "Plato had over the door to his school, 'No one can enter here until he's studied geometry.' Here one thing builds upon another."

Academic Life: The Old Ways Today

As one of the few true Great Books programs in the nation, Thomas Aquinas College boasts a curriculum that would impress the most rigorous of medieval schoolmen. There are no electives and no majors; rather, all students pursue the same four-year sequence of courses, constructed along the medieval divisions of the *trivium* (logic, rhetoric, and grammar) and the *quadrivium* (geometry, astronomy, arithmetic, and music). All of these disciplines are interrelated and oriented toward the same intelligible truth, and all of them culminate in the study of the "queen of the sciences," theology. Structuring the curriculum around the seven liberal arts "helps move the mind from things imagined to being able to think about things more universally," says a professor.

For each of their four years, students take year-long tutorials in mathematics, laboratory science, philosophy, and theology, along with a Great Books seminar that begins with Homer in the freshman year and ends with St. Thomas in the senior year. Students take a two-year language tutorial in which they study Latin grammar; a one-year logic tutorial; and a year of music (Plato's *Timaeus,* Boethius's *On Music,* Mozart's *Sonatas,* and Gustin's *Tonality*). Students must give considerable attention to the math and sciences during their course of study. Each year of the curriculum includes an extensive laboratory course in which students progressively work through scientific studies by Aristotle, Linnaeus, Pascal, Galen, Archimedes, Galileo, Newton, and Einstein. In mathematics courses, students begin with Euclid's *Elements* and conclude with Lobachevski's *Geometrical Researches on the Theory of Parallels.*

Of course, just because a work is considered a "great book" does not necessarily mean that it is a "good book," and one will thus find several works, particularly in the senior seminar when more modern authors are read, whose intent and meaning is in contradiction to the very truth the students are in the process of seeking. Thus heavy doses of Mill, Marx, Engels, Darwin, Nietzsche, and Freud precede the students' examination of several papal encyclicals and Vatican II documents in the senior seminar. As the college view book notes in defense of such selections, they "merely serve as sources of opinions that . . . make the truth more evident by opposition to it." The result is that students do not flee conflicting ideas, but grow from them.

Any list of great books is bound to cause questions; there are scores of great books, and a list can only be so long. Even in a curriculum as well-conceived as that at Thomas Aquinas, a certain latitude of preferences exists, particularly in the realm of literature. One student interviewed didn't quite see the value of reading Flaubert's *Three Tales* in the senior seminar, while a faculty member acknowledged that while all curricular decisions are carefully considered, the best choices are not always made. But to be uncertain about one text in the course of four years of education is hardly cause for concern, given the disappointingly ephemeral nature of much of the reading material at other colleges and universities. And both faculty and students vigorously defend the integrity of the curriculum. When one tutor was asked why students read the Lincoln/Douglas debates, he responded that it exposes the students to a work of American practical politics, adding that it was also a "work of ethical thought," one that considers "what are the goods, what is the best republic, what is man's end," and thus emphasizes the need for theology. One tutor says that "the seminar aims to fill in holes in human experience" not covered by the math and philosophy portions of the curriculum. Even the lesser books in the curriculum make sense and have a use in the whole scheme, simply because the scheme is that good.

Because the college believes that "thinking begins with the imagination," works of imaginative literature do play an integral role in the curriculum, though they are included in the seminar rather than tutorial classes. As one faculty member says, "If you are not well-ordered in your passions and imagination, you will not be well-ordered in your intellect." Consequently, students are required to read works like Jane Austen's *Emma,* as well as more profound works of philosophy and theology, in order to develop an imaginative appreciation for the good and beautiful in preparation for a greater receptivity of the truth found in more difficult texts.

The program is also distinctively Catholic because, according to a student, the studies "culminate in theology, in the study of the Blessed Trinity." This student says that unlike with other Great Books programs, "you don't end up in skepticism. . . . Tutors agree on the fundamental things." The result, says another student, is an "atmosphere of wonder and dialogue."

Indeed, the guide to the curriculum at the college proclaims that "knowledge begins in wonder." In order to foster that sense of wonder, the college places great emphasis on student preparation and initiative. The pedagogical method for most courses, with the exception of an ongoing lecture series, is tutorial, with students participating in a discussion in which they are questioned by the tutor and other students about the works they have read for that class period. The college thus does not consider its faculty to be "professors" in the literal sense — people whose job it is to dispense their own learning to students — but "tutors," men and women who serve to facilitate and guide discussion of the great books. The college asserts that the true teachers are the authors of the books themselves; as one tutor says, "Ideas are best presented by the best minds." And thankfully, the tutors have the sense to recognize that the minds behind the books are indeed greater they their own — something missing in the ego-driven classrooms of many an institution.

The logic behind the pedagogical method is well thought out. "Students generally learn better when they're actively engaged," a professor says. "The method leads to greater engagement." The result is usually not the verbal free-for-all one may encounter at other colleges: tutors are expected to guide the discussion, and most are adept at knowing when and how to participate. "Even when the tutor is doing the 'hands off' thing, he's guiding you with his questions," a student says.

Thomas Aquinas does give letter grades, but underplays their importance. Instead, it has instituted a British form of evaluation called the "Don Rag." Described as "extremely formal" by one student, the "Don Rag" is a twice-yearly event in which a student meets with all of his tutors and receives a verbal "progress report." During the Don Rag, an alumnus says, the faculty "talk to each other about you in front of you. . . . It is an opportunity to tone people down and boost them up."

The final requirement at the school is a senior thesis. The paper must be roughly twenty to thirty pages, and the topic is one of the student's own choosing (though according to one student, faculty recommend selecting "some question in the program or that naturally arises from the program, or that would be in the program if there were more time"). A quick review of students' senior thesis titles reveals the emphasis at Aquinas on general, speculative inquiries rather than specialized, historical studies. Recent topics include such broad, speculative titles as "Whether Purity of Heart Demands the Gift of Understanding or Only Asks for It" or "Whether It Is Ever Moral for a Man to Act in a Way that is Contrary to His Natural Inclinations." There is something refreshing about a college senior possessing enough confidence (and maturity) to select an ambitious thesis topic like "The Origin of Knowledge," when most so-called scholars have eschewed such fundamental considerations in favor of highly specialized, pseudo-scientific inquiries.

Despite the highly impressive nature of the curricular and pedagogical program, not all proponents of the liberal arts consider the Great Books approach the last word in liberal education. Common criticisms of the college's distinctive method and curriculum lodged by onlookers include doubts about the success of the classroom tutorial method, complaints that such a curriculum looks at texts without considering their historical context (and thus somewhat removes them from their true intention and meaning), and the criticism that all Aquinas graduates "think alike" because they all take the same courses year after year. Still, the college stands up to such criticisms, and both students and faculty offer a vigorous and sophisticated defense of their institution's program.

One student notes that they do study history "in a sort of 'accidental' sense, but something in the work has to transcend the present moment and our present culture. . . . The effects of the culture on a work are secondary" to these higher truths. "It is so refreshing to meet these authors simply as men, not as men of a particular time and culture. . . . It can be deadening for students to be saturated with background material." As one alumni notes, "it is the error of [the twentieth] century to be too historical."

And there is certainly a default amount of context surrounding each book in the curriculum because of its location in the curriculum — and this context is easily more apparent than, say, the context provided at other institutions that offer "History of Oppressed People"–style courses to incoming freshmen. As for the criticism that all the students come out of the college thinking alike, while it is true that colleges have a big impact on the way a student views the world, it has to be better for students to emerge with a broad understanding of the foundations of that world than for students to go out into the world having only been indoctrinated into a narrow understanding or field whose star though bright at the moment will crash and burn just a few years hence. With the learning that Aquinas delivers, its students should be able to separate the trends from that which will last, which is not only the point of liberal education in the first place, but which is also worth a great deal more than simple certification of any kind.

Political Atmosphere: The Complete Opposite

The political atmosphere at Thomas Aquinas is vastly different from that of most other colleges today. When asked whether "political correctness" exists on campus, one student said, "We have the complete opposite."

Conservatism is the dominant political preference at Thomas Aquinas. Rather than putting to work the activist precepts gleaned from womens' studies courses, as are her peers at other institutions, the Aquinas woman is more likely to get worked up defending the integrity of gender-specific language or participating in pro-life activities. "Some students come to TAC as non-Catholics and don't convert," says an alumnus. "But no one comes to TAC and stays a Democrat." Still, many students and faculty are not mainstream Republicans, either; one student noted that in the 2000 presidential election, most students he knew were voting for either Pat Buchanan or Alan Keyes rather than George W. Bush.

Despite — indeed, because of — the college's set curriculum and rigorous adherence to the Catholic church, academic freedom is not a burning issue on campus. All Catholic faculty begin the teaching year by making a Profession of Faith and taking an "Oath of Fidelity" to church teachings. Indeed, President Thomas Dillon takes great pride in the college's obedience to church dogma, noting in the college newsletter that while other Catholic colleges are scrambling to implement (or avoid) the prescription of Pope John Paul II's *Ex Corde Ecclesiae* (a document designed to ensure that American Catholic colleges observe the principles of Catholic doctrine), "For us at Thomas Aquinas these efforts are superfluous." President Dillon also notes that, because of the college's distinctive religious and academic identity, there is "no conflict" between Church teaching "and the academic freedom of our teaching faculty. Indeed, we declared our beliefs as Christians that Christ Himself is the Truth, and that if we will be His disciples we will learn the truth and the truth will make us free."

While there may be unanimity among the faculty regarding the curriculum, there are a considerable number of non-Catholic students at Aquinas, and there are even non-Catholics on the teaching faculty (though they do not teach the theology portions of the curriculum). Many of the non-Catholic students end up converting before graduation, and according to students and faculty alike, even those who remain non-Catholic are seldom troublemakers in or out of the classroom. "Non-Catholic students won't let you get away with anything too easily" in the classroom, says one student. "It is good that the truth is tested in the classroom, and beautiful to see that the truth of the faith stands up to the test." A Chinese national, Hui Liu, was even among the entering freshmen in 1999, the first Chinese citizen to attend the college. "I thought I would be challenged here and would be best exposed to the Western culture," he wrote in the college newsletter.

Campus activism at Thomas Aquinas is kept to a minimum; as the college view book boasts, Aquinas "aim[s] at the intellectual life instead of at activism." In keeping with its Catholic character, the most active organizations on campus include apologetics groups and pro-life organizations. Unlike most other colleges and universities across the country, there is no student government at Aquinas. "Student representatives should function in the capacity of advisors to the administration, not as policy-makers," states the college literature. There is no student newspaper, though there is a student journal, called *The Demiurge* (after the god in Plato's *Timaeus*), which features articles, poetry, and other literary offerings by students.

All students and faculty attend an ongoing campus lecture/concert series. The speakers are largely recognizable luminaries in the Catholic intellectual, social, and political realm, and have included Alan Keyes, Henry Hyde, Ralph McInerny, Peter Kreeft, and Scott Hahn.

Faculty hiring at Thomas Aquinas is not subject to the ideological constraints that so often attend such decisions at other institutions — other than, of course, the faith requirements. Although immune to certain pressures, faculty hiring could be accused of a kind of "inbreeding" insofar as it shows a marked preference toward hiring graduates of Thomas Aquinas or other similar Great Books schools, such as St. Mary's College of California or St. John's College in Annapolis and Santa Fe. Roughly two-thirds of the faculty are graduates of these institutions.

The value of such a practice, of course, is that the faculty are already familiar with the pedagogical and curricular format of a Great Books program. Indeed, it's not surprising. Faculty at the college must exhibit a high degree of unity of purpose and approach; all must be prepared to teach any part of the college curriculum. Once hired, tutors remain at Thomas Aquinas under a virtual "permanent appointment" system that dispenses with the usual process of tenure review. Consequently, great care is taken in the search and interview process for new faculty members.

Student Life: Formal Composition

Since 1978, Thomas Aquinas has been located on a beautiful site in southern California, between the cities of Santa Paula and Ojai and a comfortable forty-five miles northwest of Los Angeles. Rugged mountains provide a stunning backdrop to the college's mission-style architecture. While the college is on the site of the former Ferndale Ranch, very few of the buildings predate the college's existence. The college is essentially still under construction: There are still several temporary buildings, but the rate of new buildings completed each year is probably surpassed only by the rise in college enrollment. Since 1995, the college has completed the St. Bernardine Library, a chapel, the Albertus Magnus Science building, and new dormitories. The college continues to move toward its eventual goal of 350 students, admitting its largest freshman class in the 1999-2000 academic year.

Dormitory life is highly civilized, with most students residing in one of the campus' four permanent residence halls and the remainder living in temporary trailers. The most recently completed dormitory is the St. Therese of Lisieux Residence Hall, a 12,300-square-foot residence completed in 1999 to house female students. There are no coed dormitories at Aquinas; indeed, members of the opposite sex are not allowed any visitation privileges in the residence halls. Crime, in the dorms or elsewhere, is nonexistent.

Civility and decorum reign in the social demeanor of Aquinas students. College rules stipulate that "formal dress," including skirts or dresses for women and trousers and collared shirts for men, is "to be worn throughout the week in the chapel, offices, classrooms, laboratories, dining hall, and library." In class, students are to address each other as "Mister" or "Miss," and may not chew gum or consume food or beverages. There is a high degree of student/faculty interaction at the college, and students appreciate the fact that the tutors usually eat meals with the students.

Athletics, though popular among many students, are organized largely on an ad-hoc basis, but there is a soccer club, and students regularly go jogging together or play basketball. The campus choir (including a *scola* trained in Gregorian chant) is active and the Friday lecture series occasionally includes musical performances from area groups such as the Los Angeles Philharmonic.

When their schedules allow, students can make the ten-minute trip into Santa Paula or visit the beach in Ventura, twenty minutes away. Opportunities for hiking, fishing, and backpacking abound in the Los Padres National Forest, which borders the campus. Occasional group outings to the Los Angeles area are organized around cultural events such as performances by the Los Angeles Opera. Still, the college can seem rather isolated at times — or a bit "dull," according to one student — though regular campus social activities complement the students' vigorous intellectual life. At the beginning of the year, every class throws a party for the incoming freshman class, while at the end of the year, every class throws a party for the graduating seniors. There are numerous parties and dances scheduled around the liturgical year, such as the annual Palm Sunday barbecue.

The sacramental and devotional life of the college is, as one might expect, particularly rich. While religious observance is not compulsory, mass is offered daily, as are opportunities for eucharistic adoration and recitation of the rosary.

The college appears to be in healthy financial shape, though it receives no federal or church funds. The college has a generous financial aid policy, stating in its literature that it is "committed to making attendance possible for any qualified student who desires it, even if he and his family are unable to pay the full charges for tuition, room, and board." The college also suggests that parents might view their tuition payments as a kind of charitable contribution, noting that "many parents consider what they pay toward Catholic education a part of their charitable giving." Many students supplement their financial package by participation in a work/study program, in which students engage in a variety of campus work arrangements (food service, library, janitorial) for roughly thirteen hours per week.

Graduates go on to pursue careers in law, medicine, and teaching, and about 10 percent of graduates pursue religious vocations. As one student notes, "we joke about the uselessness of a liberal arts degree, but generally speaking, graduates of Aquinas go on to do important things." Future employment prospects aside, most students select Thomas Aquinas because they desire to know the truth and to obtain what Cardinal Newman called "the philosophic habit of mind." When asked why he decided to come to Thomas Aquinas, one student says that he found "a place that would really screw my head on straight before I go out into the world."

Tufts University

Office of Undergraduate Admissions
Bendetson Hall
Medford, MA 02155-7057
(617) 627-3170
www.tufts.edu

Total enrollment: 9,191
Undergraduates: 4,926
SAT ranges (Verbal/ Math): 600-690 (V); 630-700 (M)
Applicants: 14,192
Accepted: 26%
Enrolled: 33%
Application deadline: January 1
Financial aid application deadline: February 1
Tuition: $25,714/$33,394
Core curriculum: No

Crowded Boston Market

Tufts University was founded by members of the Universalist Church in 1852, but is now a secular school with almost 5,000 undergraduates and 4,000 graduate students on its campus five miles from Boston. The school has always had a rather progressive outlook, beating other colleges to several punches throughout its history. To take just one example, Tufts had many students in preprofessional programs years before such schools were fashionable.

Today the university prides itself on its large number of interdisciplinary and multicultural programs, as well as its aggressive affirmative action hiring and admissions policies. It has some fine liberal arts programs, but its College of Engineering and other preprofessional programs are still among its strongest. Multiculturalism is seeping into the liberal arts curriculum, and more and more that curriculum is coming to resemble the ones at other schools in the United States, not to mention New England and Boston. It remains to be seen whether this likeness will make Tufts just another Boston-area college, lost in the shuffle of its better-known and better-endowed Northeast neighbors.

Academic Life: To Each His Own

Students in Tuft's College of Liberal Arts must take a relatively large number of general education classes, which are divided into two categories: foundation requirements and distribution requirements. The general education courses are not mandated by name, but by subject matter. "There is no rigid program of courses that must be taken by every student," the catalogue says. "Students are regarded as individuals and each student is encouraged to pursue a course of study appropriate to his or her training, experience, aptitudes, and plans for the future."

The foundation requirements include two semesters of writing, a number of courses in foreign languages and cultures, and an elective course in world civilizations. The writing requirement can be reduced by a number of testing-out procedures, and because of that, one student calls it "weak" and "counterproductive." The foreign language and cultures requirement is more substantial: take three semesters in a foreign language (or test out to that level), and then take either a fourth semester in that language, another language to the third-semester level, or three courses dealing with "a single cultural area not native to the student," according to the catalogue. Combinations of language and culture studies can also fulfill the second part of the requirement, but the "single cultural area" rule still applies.

However, many of the cultural studies courses are taught with an ideological bias that slights Western and American culture. The one-course world civilizations requirement is much the same way; some traditional students and faculty refer to it as "anything-but-Western-civ." Previously, these were team-taught, interdisciplinary seminar courses. But they were "roundly despised by the students," according to a professor, and, according to a student, "full of preaching about multiculturalism." The requirement has recently been altered: students now choose from a wider selection of courses offered by the humanities and social science distributive areas. The offerings from both of these divisions, however, are noticeably light on European or American history, philosophy, and literature. "Revolution in Latin America" and "Armenian Arts, Architecture, and Politics," however, could count toward the culture courses in the language requirement.

Tufts's distribution requirements are simpler: two courses in each of five areas, including humanities, arts, social sciences, natural sciences, and mathematical sciences. Students may choose from such departments as "Peace and Justice Studies" or "Urban and Environmental Policy."

One professor says the administration has discussed requiring introductory courses in both Western civilization and world civilization, but he does not expect much to be done in that direction. "What results will probably not be more coherent," he says. Another professor says the natural science and mathematics requirements can be met without truly hard science. The requirements are "stacked towards taking humanities and social sciences," the professor says. For example, several psychology courses count toward the natural science requirement. The professor says that because of this comfortable approach to the distribution requirement, many students do not get the math or science background necessary for advanced coursework. By the same logic, the efficacy of an advanced history or philosophy course is lessened because the student was not required to take a basic survey course that would have provided the context for further study.

Beyond these general requirements, most students work toward a major in the liberal arts (history, classical studies, political science, physics), but there is also the "plan of study" option that is more interdisciplinary. Plans of study recently deemed legitimate have included environmental effects of urbanization, aspects of dance, bilingual education, and nutrition and population in national development. Since one of Tufts's greatest values is its research side, students in the liberal arts and engineering are urged to develop strong analytical skills. Tufts advisors even encourage students to pursue joint degree programs with some of the professional schools.

Outstanding professors at Tufts include George E. Smith and Hugo Bedau in philosophy; Marcelo Bianconi, Linda Loury, and Gilbert Metcalf in economics; Gregory Crane and Dennis Trout in classics; Gerald Gill and George Marcopoulos in history; Eric Todd Quinto in mathematics; and Mingquan Wang in the Chinese department.

The 800-student College of Engineering, separate from the College of Liberal Arts, is very highly regarded by those on campus. A professor in a liberal arts department says he is "impressed with the engineering students — they are among the best students I have had." The College of Engineering and the physics department (in the College of Liberal Arts) jointly offer the well-regarded physics major. According to a professor in another department, physics has "distinguished faculty, and few majors," meaning that students get plenty of access to their fine teachers.

The College of Liberal Arts, with the largest number of departments and about 80 percent of Tufts's 4,900 undergraduates, is more varied in the quality of instruction it offers. Economics and philosophy are probably the best departments in terms of commitment to undergraduate teaching. Both departments are small by outside standards, but the majority of professors in both are described by their peers as "fair," "objective," and "balanced." One professor says the graduates of the philosophy program are "impressive." Both departments, as well as religious studies and economics, have succeeded despite a limited number of professors. Another department noted for its solid teaching is biology.

The most popular programs and majors at Tufts are in international relations, biology, political science, and English. However, a professor says, based on conversations with students, that the curricula of English and political science are highly politicized. Course listings in political science include traditional topics in American and international politics, but many focus primarily on current events or a specific subject; there are few courses in social science statistics, econometrics, or other topics with wider applications. The strengths of international relations, meanwhile, can only be measured by "what [students] make of it," a professor says. "[There are] so many ways to fulfill the requirements."

Tufts expends many of its institutional resources in promoting and expanding interdisciplinary study programs like ethnomusicology, peace and justice studies, world civilizations, and communications and media studies. Some on campus say most of the programs in this classification are overtly political in nature. As one professor puts it, they are "dominated by the literary theory types," which "weakens" the quality of the instruction and curricula.

Tufts students are generally more internationally conscious than are students at other universities. About 40 percent of undergraduates study abroad during their junior year, and the university shows a strong commitment to international learning by encouraging students to study overseas and at Tufts with the university's strong language program.

Political Atmosphere: Preceded by Its Reputation

For the most part, Tufts students don't get involved in campus or national politics. One student active in conservative causes says "there is a small, very loud group of radicals." The rest, according to this student, "are apathetic. They're pro-choice, but don't know why; they're pro-welfare, but don't know why."

But the ones that are involved must be deeply and loudly involved. Tufts has appeared on *Mother Jones* magazine's list of the most politically active campuses, and given that publication's political inclinations, some students must have done something to earn that reputation. Indeed, a professor says he has "a feeling that Tufts is more aggressive in political correctness" than most other schools.

Political activism plays a definite role in the intellectual atmosphere, as well as in the hiring process. One professor says Tufts has "a strong form of affirmative action, even to the point of directed faculty searches." Tufts, like many institutions, advertises in university trade publications for a specialist in, say, African-American politics or women in literature, with the unspoken assumption that the successful candidate will represent the particular group mentioned, in these cases African-Americans or women. This policy, although technically illegal, is rather common in higher education, and is based on the assumption that only a member of the group in question is qualified to address the issues confronting that group.

A professor says that at Tufts there is "a sense that departments are rewarded or punished for hiring the right or wrong color." Administrators never explicitly define diversity, but the word is used constantly when they discuss their goals. "Prizes are given to students for activity and multicultural stuff," another professor says. "There seems to be a slant in the few initiatives coming out of the administration."

Tufts, like many schools, has endured a controversy over a speech code. The university's original speech code, adopted in 1989, was scrapped several years later after similar codes at Michigan and Stanford were ruled unconstitutional. In its place the university instituted, very quietly, a vague "bigotry policy." Few students know about the policy, since it appears in neither the course catalogue nor the student handbook. Those interviewed for this guide were not aware of any recent disciplinary actions resulting from the policy, but nothing prevents its use in the future by someone wishing to attack another he finds nonsupportive of his cause.

Political activism has already affected freshman orientation and student government matters. Orientation is "an indoctrination session, with silly skits about date rape and racism," says a student. "It's degrading." A lecture on date rape, "Why No means No," is meant to intimidate rather than inform, a student says. Another event, "Many Stories, One Community," is a panel of "every race, ethnicity, and sexuality on campus, except white, American, and straight," according to the student.

In the student senate, some representatives are appointed by designated cultural groups, although a recent move to give those special senators voting powers failed because students thought it unfair. Call it Tufts's version of the Boston Tea Party.

The Transgendered, Lesbian, Gay, and Bisexual Community at Tufts is one of the most mobilized and politically active groups on the Tufts campus. During the Spring 2000 semester, a Tufts judicial panel stripped the Tufts Christian Fellowship of campus funding because they refused to allow an openly lesbian student to be the group's president. Since the evangelical student organization views homosexuality as a sin, its members felt they were denied religious liberty, all under the university's definition of discrimination. One student was quoted as saying that the Tufts administration was, "trying to legislate our religious beliefs." After the affair made headlines nationwide, the judicial panel rescinded its previous judgment, and allowed the Christian group to remain a university approved group, but still on probation. Even after that decision, about twenty students staged a two-day sit-in at an administration building, demanding that the university clarify its nondiscrimination policy. The protest ended with a statement from the university president, which did not assent to the demands, but rather said decisions on how the policy is applied should be up to the student judiciary system.

Gay students at Tufts have long been lobbying for coed housing on campus, claiming that homosexual students have faced "awkward situations" with their straight roommates. Tufts administrators rejected the proposal, but are still open to the option of coed suites.

Occasionally, all the available copies of the *Primary Source,* Tufts's independent conservative journal, have been dumped into recycling bins, presumably by those who oppose the paper's positions. A former staff member of the paper says Tufts administrators routinely refuse the *Source's* interview requests.

Tufts was in the news not long ago for admitting a student named Gina Grant. Grant had been accepted at Harvard, but was denied entrance there when it was discovered that she had lied on her application. More exactly, she had omitted the fact that, as a teenager, she had murdered her parents. (Oops.) But Tufts stepped in and not only accepted Grant as a student, but gave her not only a large financial grant package but also a single room — unheard of for freshmen but in this case somewhat understandable.

Student Life: The Greatest Show on Earth?

Social life at Tufts is not centered on campus, but in nearby Boston. "There's not a big Greek system, not a lot of school spirit," a student says. Freshmen and sophomores, unless they live at home, are required to live on campus, and overall, about 70 percent of undergraduates live in university housing — dormitories, apartments, and special-interest houses. The latter includes language houses, international groups, an African-American house, an environment house, and a "substance-free" house. There is one all-female dorm; in the others, men and women sometimes live on the same floor but do not share bathrooms. Eleven fraternities and sororities have chapter houses on campus.

The campus is located in Medford, five miles northwest of Boston, beyond Cambridge, home to Harvard and the Massachusetts Institute of Technology. Though newer university buildings are constructed in modern architectural styles, much of the hilltop campus is composed of older buildings, and the overall effect is quite traditional.

Crime at Tufts has been fairly low compared to other universities of comparable size, perhaps due to the campus police's commitment to safety. Safety phones are located all over the campus; the campus is well-lit; and Campus Police assist with student shuttle and escort services.

Tufts offers the usual array of student organizations. College publications list an impressive portfolio of arts-related activities, including drama, art, and music produced and performed by students. There are also many political organizations, including several feminist groups, Burma Action Group, Vision of Tibet, and the Transgendered, Lesbian, Gay, and Bisexual Community. The campus has religious centers for Catholics, Eastern Orthodox, Protestants, Jews, and Muslims.

Campus speakers represent a variety of philosophies. They have included former president George Bush, historian Arthur Schlesinger Jr., writer Doris Kearns Goodwin, filmmaker Spike Lee, author Alice Walker, former surgeon general Joycelyn Elders, NOW leader Patricia Ireland, activist Jesse Jackson, and author Maya Angelou. Well-known artists like the Boston Camarata, Dave Brubeck, Wynton Marsalis, and the Empire Brass have also appeared at Tufts recently.

P. T. Barnum, who donated $50,000 to Tufts in its early years, also gave the school the preserved hide of his most famous elephant, Jumbo, after the pachyderm was hit by a train and killed. The hide was displayed for years in a natural history museum on campus, but was destroyed in a 1975 fire. Jumbo, however, lives on as the namesake for Tufts's athletic teams. The Jumbos compete on twenty-nine intercollegiate sports teams in all three NCAA divisions. There are also a number of club sports and intramurals.

Tulane University

Office of Admissions
210 Gibbon Hall
New Orleans, LA 70118-5680
(504) 865-5731
www.tulane.edu

Total enrollment: 11,945
Undergraduates: 7,170
SAT ranges (Verbal/Math): 600-700 (V); 590-690 (M)
Applicants: 8,227
Accepted: 78%
Enrolled: 25%
Application deadline: January 15
Financial aid application deadline: February 1
Tuition: $25,390/$32,298
Core curriculum: No

Penny (Tu)lane

For over a century, Tulane University has remained one of the South's premier private universities. Despite some troubles, financial and otherwise, Tulane continues to attract accomplished students and scholars from across the country. After a sluggish period in the 1970s during which the university actually spent some of the capital in its endowment, it recovered sufficiently to construct several excellent new buildings during the 1980s and 1990s and now boasts new engineering, science, and technology buildings, new law and business schools, a very large recreation center, and several apartment-style dorms for undergraduates.

Yet today Tulane is again in financial need, and has yet to fully recover from the disastrous tenure of its radical former president, Eamon Kelley, who resigned in 1998. Tulane's new President, Scott Cowen, is the former dean of the School of Management at Case Western Reserve. It had been hoped that President Cowen's background in management would help him confront some of the school's pressing problems, but thus far he has been slow to reverse the trends set in place by his predecessor.

Leadership is particularly important at this stage of Tulane's history because the past few years have witnessed a precipitous drop in the number of faculty at Tulane's main uptown New Orleans campus. In some ways, then, Tulane can be seen as the victim of its own limited success, as its most distinguished (and intellectually stylish) faculty members leave to assume endowed chairs or to head departments at other institutions. Yet much of the exodus is clearly due to the university's inability to compete with the salaries offered not just by nouveau rich schools like Emory and Duke, but even by second- and third-tier institutions. Perhaps, ironically, its poverty may turn out to be a friend to those who favor a traditional education over trendy indoctrination, since it has often been the most politicized members of the faculty who are lured away. Just as New Orleans herself has kept her charm and architectural beauty in no small part because she has been too poor to replace the venerable buildings of her past with the more ephemeral styles of recent decades, so Tulane itself, ever a part of this city, may weather recent absurdities of academic fashion and emerge stronger for having been behind the times.

Academic Life: The Big Easy

Tulane has no core curriculum, and there will not likely be a sudden push for one — at least not from the scholars dedicated to traditional education. There is a widespread belief that implementing a core at this juncture in the university's history would be quite dangerous given the number of radical faculty on campus, and that the potential for mistakes is too great to risk revamping the curriculum now.

The current system, which a prominent faculty member calls "totally insane . . . [and] so tied up in a large set of distribution requirements that is Byzantine," requires, among other things, one Western culture course and at least one course in a non-Western area. The rest of the distribution requirements include three courses in the humanities and fine arts, three in social sciences, and three in sciences and mathematics — but many courses can count toward the requirements. Because of this archaic and confusing system, concerned faculty try to carve out some niche for students interested in rigorous, non-ideological courses even if the courses are not required. The university does offer an honors program in which students can construct their own curricula, but it doesn't appear to be particularly rigorous.

Despite the best intentions of some professors, Tulane is not exactly fertile ground for courses with a traditional liberal arts focus. "It's a political minefield to try to introduce new courses," says one professor, citing the heated opposition to any classes that may be deemed "elitist." Thus, when a proposal was made to introduce a great books–type course a few years ago, it was opposed by forces led by a particular faculty member who argued that such a course would, through its challenging nature, attract the best students, and that it is bad to bring the best students together in such an elitist way. The course was never taught. "No deliberate policy gives a student a good education here," a senior faculty member says. And things are unlikely to change, given that the new provost has approvingly described higher education as a cafeteria.

An existing program targeted by the anti-elitists is the Air Force ROTC program. Some students have turned to ROTC out of necessity as tuition costs continued to skyrocket. While this is not only harmless, but noble in many ways, it seems that at Tulane — as at many of America's college campuses — the controversy that surrounded the ROTC and similar organizations in the '60s and '70s has yet to fade away. Today at Tulane not a few of the men and women who serve their country and earn their tuition through this corps are afraid to wear their uniforms to class for fear of being mocked by the professor. In some classes membership in ROTC has lowered a student's grade. The students affected cannot usually afford to forgo their scholarships and call home for money, and even those who can should certainly not have to quit serving their country in exchange for equal treatment by their professors.

Similar politics are obvious in the sensitivity training to which freshmen especially, and the rest of the student body as well, are subjected. The office of the dean of students, which a nationally known Tulane professor calls "one of the really bad sub-units at the university," launches various politically correct harangues at students. Over the past several years this type of propaganda has become quite widespread, and the results can be seen in what is less a chilling of free speech than a growing cynicism on the part of students and faculty alike. "Students learn to dissemble, to parrot, and to please, but they don't learn how to think," says a professor who has seen enrollment in his classes increase sharply because he continues to offer rigorous, challenging courses that buck the politicizing trends at the university.

Among the most politicized departments is English, which is now "beyond redemption," according to a teacher in another discipline. The university does host a Shakespeare festival, however. Sociology is also very radicalized, a development that will surprise few who agree with another scholar who says that left-wing views are "just an assumption of the discipline." The Department of Spanish and Portuguese is ideological, as is communications, which is run by faculty enamored with "cultural studies" — an academic euphemism for cultural relativism. History is experiencing tremendous hemorrhaging at the moment, and the loss of senior faculty members to other institutions has opened the door for closet radicals to emerge from hiding to attack their more moderate and professionally accomplished colleagues on both political and personal grounds.

One of the best departments is philosophy, which has done a remarkably good job of hiring and promoting scholars devoted to their research and students rather than any political position. Among its star members are Ronna Burger, John D.

Glenn Jr., and Eric Mack. In history Samuel Ramer, George Bernstein, Kenneth Harl, and Colin MacLachlan are all dedicated teachers. Political science is less politicized than most departments, and Paul Lewis, Robert Robins, Martyn Thompson, W. David Clinton, and Gary Remer require their students to read primary sources rather than secondary literature. Michael Kuczynski in English is very popular with students for his clear presentation of difficult medieval literature, and William Alworth in chemistry is said to be very capable and willing to dedicate a great deal of time to his students. In anthropology Harvey and Victoria Bricker have for years made Tulane a leader in the study of Mesoamerican culture. The university's links to that region (the president's house, a mansion on St. Charles Avenue, was donated by United Fruit) are also reflected in its excellent internationally recognized Latin American studies program, which boasts over sixty allied faculty from numerous disciplines and schools. The Murphy Institute of Political Economy offers an undergraduate degree, and the economics department tends to be libertarian. Judith Schafer stands out as a dedicated and hardworking teacher in the Murphy Institute.

Political Atmosphere: The Off-Target Search

Even though in recent years Tulane's enrollment has increased modestly and the number of courses taken has gone up by 20 percent, the faculty has decreased by no fewer than thirty-five positions, or almost 15 percent. This sounds bad, and it is. The administration compounds the problem because it will rarely fund a new or replacement faculty slot except through what it calls a "target search." This program, run by the dean for multicultural affairs, is dedicated to curing what the administration terms the "racism" at Tulane by giving money (most of it from the Ford Foundation) only for jobs that will go to minority candidates.

Given the shortage of faculty in most departments, this means, in practice, that any department will have a hard time filling a vacancy unless it conducts a target search. Otherwise, the dean is unlikely to approve the department's request for funds, and the shortage will continue — much to the detriment of the students, who will have a smaller choice of classes taught by Ph.D.s, and of the professors themselves, who must continue to offer a selection of courses smaller than what is necessary to attract serious undergraduates to their disciplines. These target searches are conducted by employing a new version of the "good old boy" network that has been so maligned in recent years. To wit: once the target search is initiated according to the normal methods (advertising in national publications), a word-of-mouth search is launched to discover whether anyone already on the faculty, or in the faculty's network, knows of any minority candidates in the final stages of his or her graduate career. This word-of-mouth campaign goes well beyond the requirements of the law; its sole purpose is to serve blatantly political ends.

While Tulane is not the most oppressive place in the country, freedom of expression is still embattled there. A well-known professor notes: "Higher education is increasingly about acquiring attitudes and opinions one puts on like a uniform." This demand for conformity weighs heavily on both faculty and students. Thus, faculty are increasingly reluctant to speak up in opposition to radical theories for fear of being denied tenure, socially ostracized, or even sued. More than one faculty member has looked into purchasing insurance not unlike that acquired by medical doctors for malpractice.

Conservative faculty members have in the recent past been hounded and persecuted on purely political grounds. Some well-known and highly regarded scholars have come ridiculously close to being denied tenure after being attacked by colleagues. Personal jealousies, always present among professionals judged on their output and intellectual capabilities, are often combined with philosophical differences to drive from the profession those who in earlier times would have excelled in their careers. As one professor puts it, "There is still a tolerable degree of intellectual freedom, but you have to be willing to pay the price of social ostracism. You get used to it."

During the spring of 2000, a large student protest against the campus bookstore made national headlines. To rally support for what they termed "sweatshop issues," a group of students staged a sit-in at the administration building and constructed a shanty town in the middle of the campus quad, all while prospective students and parents were visiting the campus for orientation. In the end, President Cowen largely capitulated to their demands and defused the situation.

Campus Life: New Orleans, a Second Education

A significant element of Tulane, at least in its proud history, is Sophie Newcomb College for women. Predating Radcliffe and Barnard, which were modeled upon it, Newcomb College was the source of Newcomb Pottery, which today is extremely valuable. Graduates of Newcomb College receive diplomas with the name of their college on it, but in fact both Newcomb, for women, and the Paul Tulane College of Arts and Sciences, for men, share the same curriculum in what is a thoroughly coeducational arrangement.

Students at Tulane hail from all over the nation, with a particularly strong contingent from the Northeast. The uptown campus (the medical school is downtown) is pretty and is situated in a very desirable neighborhood. Living in New Orleans is itself an education, and students who go to Tulane get to experience firsthand one of the most interesting and eclectic cities in the nation. Just across St. Charles Avenue from the campus is the Frederick Law Olmstead–designed Audubon Park, with its public golf course, jogging and walking trails, and lagoons. Across Magazine Street at the opposite end of the park is Audubon Zoo, one of the nation's finest, with exhibits that mimic the animals' home territory. The Mississippi River flows by the zoo just on the other side of a huge levee that keeps New Orleans dry. The St. Charles Avenue streetcar runs up and down that street, providing an easy and enjoyable way for Tulane students to visit the French Quarter. The food and entertainment found everywhere in New Orleans are hard to match, and the beaches of the Gulf Coast are only a few hours away.

Unfortunately, New Orleans is also one of the most violent cities in the nation, although in recent years index crimes have declined slightly. Students should not avoid coming to Tulane for fear of crime, but they should be extremely careful once they arrive.

Of course, there are plenty of safe and interesting things to do on campus. Tulane has dozens of student clubs and organizations, ranging from the political (Tulanians Against Leftism; Bisexual, Gay, and Lesbian Alliance; Celebrate Difference) to the cultural (Tulane Literary Society) to service-oriented and religious groups (Community Action Council of Tulane, Green Club, InterVarsity, and Hillel). Sports are a major part of everyday life at Tulane. The football team has its loyal supporters, but the men's basketball team claims the devotion of a horde of passionate fans. And many of the women's teams are at the top of their divisions. In addition, there are twenty-seven club sports and dozens of intramural teams.

All nonlocal freshmen are required to live in the residence halls. Freshmen must double up, but upperclassmen can request single rooms, apartments, or suites. All rooms are equipped with cable and Internet connections. Opposite-sex guests are prohibited from staying overnight in residents' rooms, at least officially. Women may elect to live in single-sex accomodations, and the coed dorms place men and women on different wings.

Vanderbilt University

Director of Admissions
401 24th Ave., South
Nashville, TN 37212-9976
(615) 322-2561
www.vanderbilt.edu

Total enrollment: 10,194
Undergraduates: 6,037
SAT ranges (Verbal/Math): 600-690 (V); 620-710 (M)

Applicants: 8,494
Accepted: 61%
Enrolled: 31%
Application deadline: January 7
Financial aid application deadline: February 1
Tuition: $24,712/$33,036
Core curriculum: No

Unrealized Qualities

Over the past several years, Vanderbilt University has worked very hard at improving the quality of both its undergraduate and graduate components. This is not unusual for universities that seek to improve their standings nationally, as all ambitious schools have done. Such efforts involve raising more money, hiring the most qualified professors, improving facilities, and attracting better students. All of these goals are laudable, of course, but since they are being attempted in today's intellectual climate, results are often mixed.

First, the good news: Vanderbilt is a fine university with a dedicated, knowledgeable faculty and an increasingly qualified student body. It is financially sound and significantly less politicized than most higher-ranked (and many lower-ranked) schools. And students who attend will find themselves among smart classmates, professors eager to teach, and facilities that are first-rate.

And yet, Vanderbilt, like most other schools that seek to improve their image, often follows the lead of more elite schools, a habit that means, in the words of one professor, "that we shall continue to misuse our resources." Money that could be used to hire professors with rigorous educations in the liberal arts often winds up in the pockets of those pursing ephemeral subjects poor in intellectual content by riding waves of temporary popularity. This is hardly peculiar to Vanderbilt. But its widespread application won't help the students who come to this venerable Nashville institution expecting more.

Academic Life: Railroaded

Vanderbilt's largest undergraduate component, the College of Arts and Sciences, enrolls most of the school's nearly 5,900 undergraduates. The distribution requirements for graduation are typical of large American universities — a range of classes in the humanities, social sciences, sciences, and electives. There is nothing approaching a core curriculum, and it is unlikely that students will do much reading in common.

Those seeking a B.A. degree in one of the college's twenty-three majors must pass 120 hours of classes. A freshman seminar is required before a student can advance to sophomore standing. Limited to no more than twenty students per section, seminars introduces freshmen to scholarly methodologies and problems. Depending on the quality of the professor teaching the seminar, this required class can be a worthwhile experience. After the freshman year, students begin the Arts and Sciences "Program in Liberal Education," which entails distribution requirements in writing, mathematics, foreign language, history and culture (both American and international), humanities, natural sciences, and social sciences. And that is where students really start to go their separate ways, despite the fact that they all choose from the same list of courses.

That undergraduate education is so routine at most large universities is not accidental. Modern schools exist more as centers of research than as teaching — a fact not negated by the undeniably large number of professors at Vanderbilt who are dedicated teachers. "If current trends continue, Vanderbilt will probably become more of a research institution and less of a teaching institution," says one professor. "This reflects our successful attempts to beef up our national reputation, which usually requires an emphasis on publication." National reputations, as compiled by approved opinion-makers, privilege research over teaching; the quest for new knowledge takes precedence over the dissemination of tradition. Ironically, this new knowledge often goes unread by all but a tiny handful of specialists even as undergraduates are taught more and more about less and less.

Vanderbilt does a better job than many of its peers in exposing freshmen to senior professors rather than only teaching assistants. "Senior professors teach a good many freshman seminars and many undergraduate courses," says one professor. Teaching assistants are used quite often in basic freshmen courses, however. Another professor says: "Senior professors teach freshmen as well as their own advanced undergraduate courses, and since these courses are almost always limited to forty-five or fewer students, we come to know many of the students personally. This is a great strength at Vanderbilt: small classes and accessible professors."

Another bright spot is the quality of recent freshmen, which one professor says "has improved noticeably in the last few years." Again, a bit of irony is in play here, as schools like Vanderbilt — which have traditionally been considered second tier — have gained greater recognition (and therefore more qualified applicants) by following the national trends that increase their rankings even as they harm undergraduate education. Nevertheless, new students will find colleagues who are very bright and eager to get ahead in life. Class performance is up, too, as another professor notes: "The more important trend [among freshmen] is in the quality of their performance in class, and that, too, has improved noticeably. They write better, speak more effectively and more often in classes, and seem more engaged by intellectual discourse than they were ten years ago. I expect more from them now, and they deliver."

Vanderbilt offers majors in all the traditional fields, and has thus far eschewed the temptation to offer majors such as gender studies or women's studies. However, it does offer interdisciplinary majors in African-American studies and urban studies, as well as minors in environmental studies and women's studies. Given recent decisions by the administration, including the appointment in the English department of a chair of gay and lesbian studies, it seems likely that the number of agenda-driven courses, and perhaps even majors, will grow.

Much of the shortfall in Vanderbilt's academic quality can be blamed on the ascendancy of politically correct ideology at the school. In the English department, for example, not even the South, which for so many years lent Vanderbilt its character, young people, money, and gentility, is safe. "The principal teacher of Southern literature hates the South and chooses his texts to show what's wrong with the South and Southerners," a professor says. "People who teach American literature hate America and show the same in the books they use and the way they teach. The cry of racism is a refrain that runs through much of what is taught."

And English used to be one of Vanderbilt's strongest non-science programs. Though the department is not now the pillar it once was, it still is home to some of the university's best professors, namely Mark Jarman, Chris Hassel, John Plummer, Emerson Brown, Roy Gottfried, Walter Sullivan, Harold Weatherby, and Leonard Nathanson.

Joel Harrington of the history department is also an excellent teacher, but the history department as a whole, like others on campus, suffers from the same misguided patterns of thought now affecting English. "I know that the man who teaches Southern history thinks of the South as a problem which he must try to repair through his teaching," says a professor. "I think it's pretty much the same story everywhere except in the hard sciences."

Political Atmosphere: I Don't Hate the South — I Don't, I Don't

Vanderbilt came relatively late to the ideological wars, and even now there are sectors at the school where the bullets have not yet begun to fly. Some on campus note that despite the deteriorating political climate the majority of students remain unaffected. "During my last two years there were noticeable attempts to become more trendy and offer a politicized curriculum," a recent graduate says. "It very much depended on your department and your course of study. You can have excellent professors in some courses, politically correct ones in others." Vanderbilt students tend to gravitate toward courses that ask them to read timeless books rather than the latest in radical political manifestos. It's a pity more of the former are not offered. The reason: the faculty is considerably more liberal than the students, according to representatives of both groups.

Vanderbilt does subscribe to the notion that multicultural initiatives somehow bring about harmony on campus, though the university embraces the tenets of multiculturalism in a more abstract manner than most places. As one professor says,

"We're supposed to all get along and be nice to each other so that no one's feelings will be hurt." University literature on freshman programming has a section entitled "Commitment to Diversity," which states: "Vanderbilt is a geographically, ethnically, and culturally diverse community composed of people of different ages, sexes, races, socioeconomic backgrounds, sexual orientations, religious beliefs, and physical abilities. In order to prepare our students for the future, we nurture this community and encourage our students to develop an understanding of and appreciation for the differences among individuals. While at Vanderbilt, students will have the opportunity to examine the ways in which racism, sexism, religious intolerance, and homophobia act as divisive forces within our democratic society. Students will also have the opportunity to evaluate critically their own beliefs, attitudes, and values in light of their exposure to and contact with persons with different beliefs, attitudes, and values."

This critical evaluation is apparently supposed to be helped along by a speech code, although the speech code at Vanderbilt is not always enforced. A former teaching assistant says that he ignored the university's inclusive language directives in his classes and was not admonished. Of course, the reverse is also true: more trendy TAs who use or enforce the speech code even beyond what the university asks are not likely to be reined in either.

A main control mechanism, though, for the so-called critical evaluation expected of all students is the Office of Housing and Residential Education and Student Health. All freshmen must undergo three residential life programs sponsored by this office. In the first, they are taught about "health issues such as HIV infection, as well as the use and abuse of drugs and alcohol." A second residential life program discusses dating and sexuality, with a focus on "sexual coercion, acquaintance rape, and sexually-transmitted diseases." And the third, as might be expected, centers on "the value of diversity in the residential community." This final program is clearly an effort to enforce an orthodox view of diversity, and the irony resulting from such an attempt is certainly not intended.

Many Vanderbilt faculty believe that the South itself is something of an anachronistic backwater, and overall, it seems that many younger faculty are ashamed of Vanderbilt's Southern, conservative traditions. More than a few would be elated if the school were to become more like Duke University, where multiculturalism is deeply ensconced.

As at other institutions, recent faculty hires at Vanderbilt favor those who teach intellectual trends rather than the great books. In many cases, senior professors who leave Vanderbilt are simply not replaced. One professor recalls asking a younger colleague what kind of literature the younger man enjoyed. Much to the professor's surprise and horror, the man said that he didn't read literature of any kind. The senior scholar thought the man had to be kidding, but he was adamant in his statement. He didn't read literature, he said, because he didn't have time to read such stuff and found it boring anyway. He read theory and cultural studies instead. Both men were English professors.

However, at least one scholar believes that Vanderbilt has a chance to salvage some departments, including English. But concerned alumni and students had better make their demands now. "Those of us retiring now and within the next ten or fifteen years will not live to see the damage that is being done now repaired," says a professor. "The politically correct will not give up the universities, one of their last bastions of power, easily. The wrong people are in control. The universities are not going to heal themselves. They will have to be cleaned up from the outside, but it's terribly difficult to make people outside the academic community believe what goes on within that community."

Student Life: Side Tracks

Commodore Cornelius Vanderbilt, the New York railroad and shipping magnate, industrialist, and banker, donated $1 million in 1873 to build and endow the university that now bears his name, yet he died shortly thereafter and never visited the school. Nevertheless, students who come to Vanderbilt today benefit from a name recognition that cannot be bought. More than 6,000 undergraduates and 4,000 graduate and professional students attend the Nashville school. Almost one third of the undergraduates major in the social sciences and history, a percentage that is double the national average for similar schools. This impressive statistic owes much to another impressive fact: the lack of an undergraduate business major at Vanderbilt.

While for most of the university's past, its students were mainly from the South, for more than two decades now the university has enrolled an increasing proportion of its students from states that never belonged to the Confederacy. Fifty-three percent of all students now hail from outside the South.

Once in Nashville, freshmen must live on campus unless they can obtain special permission to live off-campus. There is a set of freshman dorms set aside for the incoming class, and overall, about 85 percent of the undergraduate student body resides on campus, a very high percentage for a school of Vanderbilt's size. The Greek system at Vanderbilt is large and well established (but not residential, except for up to six officers per chapter), with over half the men and a third of the women as members.

The dorm students at Vanderbilt are allowed to vote on some of the rules for life in each dorm. Decisions left up to the student residents include quiet hours, the hours the dorm will be open to visitation by members of the opposite sex, and the attendance requirements for and frequency of dorm meetings. Vanderbilt also leaves one other issue to the students' young minds: whether the condom machines in certain residence halls will be stocked that year.

Another less than thrilling program at Vanderbilt is the "Mayfield Living/ Learning Lodge Program," in which ten students live together in a one of six lodges and spend the year working together on a chosen project. The projects are described by the university as "self-directed, year-long program[s] of educational activities," and while one can easily see that they are indeed "self-directed," finding a college-level "educational" component is a much greater challenge. The 1999-2000 projects included "A Living History: Nashville's Multicultural Past," "Building Relationships with the Homeless," and "Urban Poverty." Each lodge must make monthly reports to the college, hold weekly meetings, and host lectures with professors and other staff and educational programs for the campus.

Vanderbilt also offers the McGill Project, described as "a unique living-learning experience at Vanderbilt." In fact, it sounds a lot like the Mayfield Living/Learning Lodges. This dorm, which one student calls "the most liberal group at school," is premised on the university's belief that "if students who live together focus around an educational purpose, their residential experience will have a more significant meaning." According to the university, McGill is host to "fun, interactive programs [that] have included making slime with a chemistry professor and learning how musical instruments from Africa are used to convey feeling and emotion."

While these residence halls certainly attract the liberal students at Vanderbilt, their atmosphere does not seem typical of the university. The campus and its community are described perhaps more accurately by one professor in this way: "Vanderbilt is a very expensive school which enrolls many rich students. Most of these are interested in getting into good professional schools and in having a good time when they're not working. Like all student bodies, ours breaks down into a number of interest groups, but we are not an intensely intellectual or political community."

While by no means pervasive, crime is not infrequent at Vanderbilt. Ten aggravated assaults and six sexual assaults were reported at the school in 1999, as well as a number of automobile thefts, burglaries, and other offenses.

Sports are an important element of life at Vanderbilt. The school is a member of the Southeastern Conference, which is known principally as a football conference. Yet Vanderbilt's best teams tend to be in basketball, and it stands out for its commitment to maintaining its membership in the SEC even as it retains the educational requirements for its players. There are also numerous intramural sports formed by dorms and other groups, including the Greeks. Twenty-three club sports are also available.

Off campus, one can do much worse than Nashville. Home of the Grand Ole Opry and the country music industry, Nashville also provides a huge assortment of restaurants, bars, and attractions. Nashville, like much of the South, has grown a great deal in recent years, and the job opportunities for graduates who want to remain in the area are now quite impressive. Students looking to get away from the city can drive four hours to the Great Smoky Mountains.

Vassar College

Office of Admissions
Director of Admissions
Box 10
Poughkeepsie, NY 12601
(845) 437-7300
www.vassar.edu

Total enrollment: 2,276
Undergraduates: 2,276
SAT ranges (Verbal/Math): 640-730 (V); 610-700 (M)
Applied: 4,777
Accepted: 43%
Enrolled: 31%
Application deadline: January 1
Financial aid application deadline: January 10
Tuition: $24,940/$31,880
Core curriculum: No

Tea and Activism

Founded in 1861 as a pioneer institution in women's liberal arts education, Vassar was long considered one of the "Seven Sisters" — the elite, all-women institutions of higher learning in the eastern United States. Vassar did not become coeducational until 1969, after turning down an invitation to merge with Yale University. When coeducation arrived, social regulations were relaxed and student voices became more prominent in campus decisions. Today Vassar is proud of its image as a "liberal" liberal arts institution with an individualistic and activist bent.

In its view book, Vassar proclaims its mission of "nurturing in its students certain lifelong habits of mind and timeless values: respect for human dignity and freedom, concern for society as well as for oneself, faith in reason, and commitment to action." "Vassar generates a genuine feeling of freedom of inquiry," says one professor. But critics of Vassar's unstructured academic program argue that some of this freedom comes at the expense of a broad liberal arts background.

Despite its adoption of a cutting-edge pose, Vassar still maintains some holdover traditions from its glory days as an elite women's college. All professors are still referred to as "Mr." and "Ms." rather than "professor" or "doctor," and afternoon tea is still served in Vassar's historic Main Hall.

Academic Life: The Bold and the Flexible

As the college view book proclaims, "The Vassar curriculum has always been characterized by boldness, breadth, and flexibility, and curricular innovation has been constant in the history of the college." In keeping with its atmosphere of individuality, there is no core curriculum at Vassar, although a few distribution requirements are mandated, including a course on numeracy (statistics, logic, math, psychology) and a demonstrated proficiency in a foreign language. In addition, all freshmen must select at least one course from among a number of "Freshman Courses," introductory courses with enrollments of fewer than twenty students. Topics in these courses range from "Russia and the Short Story" to "Reimaging America," but one common focus, according to the view book, is "the effective expression of ideas in both written and oral work." The college also "strongly" recommends that students take courses in each of Vassar's four divisions (arts, foreign languages and literatures, social sciences, and natural sciences).

Students also can avail themselves of something called the College Course Program, which offers broad, interdisciplinary courses. The language describing this program is vaguely reminiscent of the justification for a liberal education, though Vassar always falls short of championing the liberal arts: "The College Course Program was established to ensure that students can have direct exposure in their years at Vassar to some important expressions of the human spirit in a context that is both multidisciplinary and integrative." Again, however, these are entirely optional — and thankfully so, for offerings range from "The Evolution of Everything" to "Work, Gender, and Social Change" and "Literary Theory."

As far as the general offerings are concerned, "the curriculum is strongly multicultural," says one professor. Strong programs, majors, and departments include history, philosophy, biology, and art. English is considered "excellent in spots," and programs in the Romance languages provide fine opportunities for study abroad. The economics department offers the full range of disciplinary courses, including introductory and advanced courses on Marxian economics along with a couple on neo-classical economics and game theory. Emphasis, however, seems to be on policy-oriented courses such as "The Political Economy of Health Care," "International Monetary Theory and Policy," and "Environmental and Natural Resource Economics." There are also politicized courses like "The Economics of Gender," in which students discuss "controversies over sex and reproduction as market goods."

Indeed, the radicalization of Vassar's curriculum spans several disciplines, and many course descriptions are characterized by a narrow examination of a particular issue. The multidisciplinary program in American culture, for example, offers courses such as "Technology and the American Music Industry" (which "examines cultural dimensions and historical development of sound recording and reproduction technologies") and "From Natural History Museum to Ecotourism."

Interest in the fine arts abounds at Vassar. The Frances Lehman Loeb Art Center, which opened in 1993, houses an impressive collection including nineteenth- and twentieth-century European and American art, Greek and Roman sculpture, and ceramics. Vassar students are often characterized by their artistic flair; consequently, the college dramatic performances are frequently bold and avant-garde. The college has a proscenium theater as well as the recently completed Hallie Flanagan Davis Powerhouse Theatre. The latter structure could be considered an embodiment of Vassar's experimental philosophy; as the college catalogue states: "Created by the reconstruction of an old powerhouse, the theater is a model of flexibility."

To its credit, Vassar still maintains an emphasis on small class sizes, and most faculty are willing to serve as both professors and mentors to their students. "Except for Art 104 — a classic and famous survey — and a few introductory courses in astronomy, chemistry, and physics, all classes are under forty, most are under twenty, and most seminars are about ten students," a faculty member says. "There is a lot of effort to keep classes small, so learning can come from discussion and joint endeavor."

Many faculty live on campus, and students are generally pleased with the level of attention they receive from their professors. One professor notes that "faculty and students work closely together. . . . Inquiry and accomplishment are more valued than rote memorization and 'following rules.'"

Extracurricular academic opportunities are numerous, and interested students should comb the catalogue and discuss with faculty and other students the unique internship, research, and study-abroad possibilities. "There are lots of internships from the Ford Foundation available in the summer for humanities students," one professor says. There are also research opportunities in the sciences under faculty guidance, along with a host of impressive semester or year-long study programs. Vassar participates in the Twelve College Exchange Program, so students may spend a year or semester at schools like Amherst, Bowdoin, Dartmouth, Wheaton (the one in Massachusetts), and Williams. Vassar also has a seven-week summer program in Münster, Germany; internships at British primary schools or at the Clifden Community School in Galway, Ireland; and many junior-year-abroad programs.

Among the better professors at Vassar are: James Merrell, Robert K. Brigham, Nancy Bisaha, and Michaela Pohl in history; Beth Darlington, H. Daniel Peck, Mark C. Amodio, and Everett K. Weedin in English; Nicholas Adams, Susan D. Kuretsky, Eve D'Ambra, Brian Lukacher, and Andrew M. Watsky in art history; Rob Brown in classics; Giovanna Borradoro, Michael McCarthy, Mitchell Miller, and Douglas Winblad in philosophy; Peter Stillman in political science; Alexis Klimoff in Russian; and Debora Dash Moore in religious studies.

Political Atmosphere: Spectators and Participants

Vassar hosts a variety of political student organizations, ranging from the College Democrats to the Young Socialists Club. There are also a number of special-interest clubs, including the Women's Coalition, the Black Student Union, the Student Activist Union, the South Asian Students Alliance, and Queer Coalition.

Students serve on a host of college committees alongside faculty and administration. The college boasts in its promotional literature that when it became coeducational, "students acquired more opportunities for self-government and a greater share in the processes by which college decisions are made." Indeed, a partial listing of joint committees intimates the extent to which mammoth bureaucracies drain valuable time and resources at Vassar and other small institutions: the Master Planning Committee, Student Curriculum Committee, Health and Counseling Committee, Financial Aid Committee, Residential Life Advisory Committee, Security Advisory Committee, Buildings and Grounds Advisory Committee, Admissions Committee. Probably formed in no small part to head off student protest of unpopular administrative decisions, the committees frequently seem mired in confusion and inactivity. A few years ago in the campus newspaper, students complained that their role was often advisory and thus ineffective, and that their opinions weren't valued by senior committee members. In general, though, relations between students and administrators are very cordial. "The administration is fair, competent, and hard-working, and thus popular with faculty and students," a professor says.

Inter Cultural Center facilities for Asian, black, Latino, and Native American students are impressive. As has been the case at most colleges and universities, other "marginalized" groups are likewise scrambling to get a piece of the minority pie. Recently some students and alumni indicated support for the establishment of a separate cultural space for Vassar's homosexual community. Writing in the campus newspaper, a 1996 graduate argued: "Vassar recognizes other minority cultures, like African-Americans, Asian-Americans and Latinos. They have a cultural center on campus, receive funding for educational, historical and pride purposes. They have become specific disciplines. . . . [Vassar needs to] give the queer community what we have been living without: financial support and full acceptance as a community and culture. . . . My suggestion: a queer center on the Vassar campus."

Vassar does have an alternative newspaper, called the *Vassar Spectator,* which had been considered one of the leading conservative student papers until recently. Subtitled the "Journal of Neglected Ideas," the *Spectator* was once edited by Marc A. Thiessen, press spokesman for Senator Jesse Helms at the Senate Foreign Relations Committee. It received support from such conservative stalwarts as William E. Simon and was featured in *Rolling Stone* magazine for its brashly conservative viewpoint. But the current editorial staff thinks the newspaper's conservative image was "giving the wrong impression and being divisive," according to one student, and it has thus recently abandoned its traditional tenor in favor of a consensus approach.

More than anything else, the *Spectator*'s shift in image may have come about because of fear and intimidation. Nearly ten years ago the paper was "de-authorized," thrown out of its office, and denied the use of school facilities for failing to abide by a student government censorship order. Commenting on the decision of the Vassar Student Association (VSA) to withhold funding from the *Spectator*, one administrator remarked, "I think VSA did act responsibly. I have felt for a long time that we have to work against those who will be destructive . . . to the Vassar community." Two years later, in 1990, three editors were charged with "political harassment" and threatened with dismissal for publishing an editorial criticizing the vice president of the student government. A group of students formed the Vassar Coalition for Free Speech and collected more than four hundred signatures on behalf of the beleaguered editors. Charges were dropped two days before the trial, and the clause pertaining to "political speech" was dropped from Vassar's harassment policy — though one wonders how it even got there in the first place.

Indeed, despite its public emphasis on academic freedom, the limits of free speech are continually being redefined at Vassar. In the spring of 1997, for instance, two student editors of the *Vassar Daily*, a small campus newsletter, resigned amidst student outcry over the publication of a controversial satire on ebonics, the vernacular spoken by some black people. While the satire was arguably in poor taste (in addition to demeaning blacks, its language was offensive to women), student reaction was swift and extreme. According to the *Chronicle of Higher Education*, "The student government froze the newsletter's budget until rules for the publication could be reviewed."

The president, Francis Fergusson, receives mixed reviews generally, but, according to one faculty member, "is outstanding, and has great rapport with colleagues and faculty." Tenure decisions at Vassar have not been without controversy in recent years. According to one professor, "Tenure decisions are rigorous and scrupulously fair, and very exhaustive." Still, publishing and administrative activity seem to be given uneven priority in tenure decisions, considering Vassar's commitment to undergraduate teaching. "A candidate must show evidence of more than competent teaching," one professor says. "Scholarship counts a great deal, as does service." Indeed, Vassar's tenure review process has been under legal scrutiny ever since a high-profile discrimination suit was filed twelve years ago. Dr. Cynthia Fisher, a biology professor, argued that Vassar denied her tenure because she was a married woman and had taken time away from her profession to raise her children. In 1994 she was awarded over half a million dollars and a tenured position by a federal district court; that decision was overturned in 1995 and upheld on a technicality in a 1997 appeal. In 1998, Dr. Fisher appealed the case to the U.S. Supreme Court, which declined to hear the case, and let a ruling in Vassar's favor stand, stating that Dr. Fisher had not proved intentional discrimination on the part of the college. Vassar claimed that Dr. Fisher's "absence from the field had left a major gap in her knowledge," yet the biologist had more peer-reviewed articles in prestigious journals than her three male, tenured colleagues and had been awarded grants from the National Science Foundation. In an interview with the *Chronicle of Higher Education,* Dr. Fisher "called the Supreme Court's action disappointing. 'It sends a message that it's almost impossible to win any discrimination cases, particularly in the academic world.'"

In general, "diversity" seems to permeate all aspects of Vassar life, although conservative students would argue that such diversity rarely extends to an inclusion of and tolerance for their views. Indeed, conservatives are conspicuously absent from a sampling of recent high-profile speakers at Vassar, which includes Angela Davis, Hillary Clinton, Meryl Streep, Paul Theroux, Billy Joel, and James Earl Jones.

Student Life: From A to Zeitgeist

Vassar's campus is classically beautiful, with scores of mature trees and monumental buildings. Its oldest and largest building, Main Hall, boasts a facade designed by James Renwick Jr., and was declared a national historic landmark in 1986. Part of Main Hall was renovated and expanded a couple of decades ago to create a mammoth College Center that houses, among other things, computer facilities, a snack bar, a cafe, a post office, a bookshop, a radio station, and the college pub, Matthew's Mug.

Over 95 percent of Vassar students live on campus in one of nine residence halls housing from 130 to 300 students each. There is only one remaining single-sex dormitory, Strong Hall. Among other amenities, each dormitory has a parlor equipped with a Steinway piano for students' use. In 1992 the university began a "Substance Free Corridor" program to offer students a smoke-, alcohol-, and drug-free environment. About 330 students take advantage of this opportunity, in which strict rules regarding smoking, drinking, and noise levels are enforced.

Vassar students compete at the NCAA Division III level in twenty-four intercollegiate sports, ranging from lacrosse and field hockey to baseball. The college also recently welcomed rowing as a varsity sport after purchasing a ten-acre site on the Hudson River and constructing a new dock and a three-building rowing complex.

The college also makes a number of vocal and theatrical organizations available to students, ranging from the Renaissance Singers and the Serenading Club to Improv and the Ebony Theatre Ensemble. A limited number of nonvarsity athletic clubs are also available, including cycling, ski, sailing, and equestrian clubs.

In recent years, the permissive atmosphere at Vassar has led to a few concerns among the local community and even students themselves. In 1999, the college's Queer Association decided to voluntarily discontinue a campus event known as the "Homo-Hop." This "celebration of sexuality and pleasure" had been held annually for more than a decade, and featured dancing, drag queen pageants, and pornographic films. After the November 1999 Homo-Hop, *The Miscellany News,* Vassar's student newspaper, "reported that two local hospitals requested that the party be shut down after they were inundated with medical emergencies" relating to alcohol abuse, according to the *Chronicle of Higher Education*. Indeed, the crime statistics available on Vassar College show thirty-four violations of liquor laws and twenty drug offenses for 1999 — but there was very little crime besides that.

Perhaps one of the few aspects of the college to remain constant over the years is its secure financial health. During the past couple of decades, the college has exceeded expectations in a number of capital campaigns and managed to build endowments for scholarships, faculty salaries, visiting professorships, and curriculum and building development. The college annually awards $13 million of its own money for need-based scholarships. With tuition alone hovering around $25,000, this is welcome news to students without an easy means of financial support.

In sum, the Vassar zeitgeist seems to be one of unfettered freedom and exploration conducted in an atmosphere of academic permissiveness. As one professor notes, "Risk-taking, independence, and difference are cherished here. . . . Vassar is not for the timid or totally conventional student." Vassar assumes that her students are wise and mature enough to chart their own course, although some would contend that this is a rather sentimental assumption to make regarding most of today's college youth.

Villanova University

Office of Admission
800 Lancaster Avenue
Villanova, PA 19085
(610) 519-4500
www.villanova.edu

Total enrollment: 9,952
Undergraduates: 7,144
SAT ranges (Verbal/Math): 550-640 (V); 570-670 (M)
Applicants: 9,826
Accepted: 57%
Enrolled: 30%
Application deadline: January 7
Financial aid application deadline: February 15
Tuition: $22,060/$30,060
Core curriculum: Yes

Most Responsible

If Villanova University seeks to mold a certain type of student, it is the very well rounded, professionally competent, civilly and religiously minded, "whole" person — this, over and against on the one hand the academically brilliant student or on the other the lackadaisical "fraternity" type. Roman Catholic in origin and ethos, the spirit of "Christian humanism" the school so proudly announces as its educational mission is in fact most responsible for Villanova's success as a university and perhaps for the students' successes afterward. At first or second glance, some may (and do) question the Christian dynamic of this large school's educational program, but Villanova on balance lives up to its stated mission. Consequently, there exists a healthy tension between its commitment to contemporary standards of academic excellence and its Catholic Christian values. From the types of courses offered to the various philosophical perspectives of the professors to the assortment of campus speakers, this equilibrium is expressed both in the curriculum and in the campus life at large.

Founded more than 150 years ago, Villanova's beautiful 222-acre campus just eighteen miles west of Philadelphia is situated on the historically affluent Main Line. Still run by the Augustinian Order of priests, the university draws approximately six thousand undergraduates and four thousand graduate students, many of whom are Catholic (about 80 percent) and from the northeast, tri-state area. However the university welcomes students of all faiths and from all places — in fact, forty-eight states and more than fifty foreign countries are represented at the school. In an effort to manage the enrollment and quality of the students, Villanova has capped its undergraduate acceptance rate; recently the freshman class profile had the highest combined SAT scores of any entering class in the school's history.

When politicization manifests itself in the classroom, it is often in the form of fashionable, "subversive" theories — ideologies really — like deconstruction, cultural studies, and a commitment to attend to heretofore "marginalized voices." But there is much good to report at the university on this front: following on the heels of instituting hotly debated diversity requirements and the lessening of religion course requirements, such positive developments as the Core Humanities freshman seminar program, writing intensive requirements, and a thesis requirement for English majors, for example, have also been introduced.

Academic Life: Read It First

An admirable dimension of Villanova's academic program is the many efforts made to uphold the humanities at a time when numerous schools have begun to disregard traditional Western heritage. "Rather than thinking it progress for freshman to walk around with Foucault and Derrida in their back pockets, the top professors here know that *even* Foucault and Derrida were steeped in the Western tradition *before* they deconstructed it," a graduate student says. The renowned and infamous Derrida may be studied later, but first comes some focus on the classics.

The general education requirements at Villanova are complex and demanding and, yes, even reflect the old-fashioned idea of a core curriculum. While there is still a healthy amount of flexibility in the curriculum, the core requirements for students in the College of Liberal Arts and Sciences and the College of Commerce and Finance constitute roughly half their courses, and it is only slightly less than that for students in the Colleges of Nursing and Engineering. All four colleges ask students to take at least one course in religion and to meet requirements in the humanities, ethics, science, and math.

The crowning feature of the College of Liberal Arts and Sciences is the Core Humanities program. All freshmen must take two semester-long seminars that expose them to great works of literature and develop their critical thinking and writing skills. During their first semester, students take "Ancient, Medieval, Renaissance Thought." Professors select the reading list for the course, but one text from each of several categories must be represented: Old Testament, New Testament, classical Greece, St. Augustine, medieval Europe, and Shakespearean drama. In the second semester of Core Humanities, students take "Modern Thought: Enlightenment to the Present." In this class professors choose an "Augustinian theme" and assign readings on that theme from five different time periods (early modern, Enlightenment, romantic, modernist, and contemporary) and in at least three different genres.

These humanities courses are taught by professors in a variety of departments, meaning that each section is slightly different and can be structured to take advantage of the professor's area of expertise. Increasingly this program is taught by Ennis Scholars, a group of talented non-tenured professors singularly committed to this program. Students are expected to write at least thirty pages per semester. "The core is one of the major positive aspects of our university," says one humanities professor. A student gives one possible reason for this: "These two courses become the background for the rest of what we will learn in college. Plus the fact that everyone on campus has read Saint Augustine's *Confessions* means there's always something to talk about in class or in the dorm." Thus the learning is communal as well as rigorous.

In addition to the humanities seminars, liberal arts students must take one ethics course, one fine arts course, two intermediate-level foreign language courses, two history courses, two literature courses, two mathematics or computer science courses, two philosophy courses, two religion courses, three social science courses, and two courses in the natural sciences (with labs). Among these courses, at least four must be designated "writing intensive." Four others must be designated "writing enriched." Villanova has a diversity requirement, and students must also pick up two courses that focus on ethnic minorities, women, or non-Western civilizations.

Overall the highest quality of teaching and learning can be found in Villanova's honors program. Would that the rest of the school was held to these rigorous standards and introduced to the level of intellectual life that flourishes in this department. One need only talk to any of the students, alumni, or professors to recognize the intellectually and socially rich community of scholars that has been created here. The downside of the honors program, as at many other universities, is that the sometimes pretentious intellectualism among the smartest of the smart can breed a good deal of "progressive" thinking in faculty and students alike. The honors program is known to set the academic trend at the school; most recently Villanova's honors program received national attention for an infamous undergraduate course dedicated entirely to the topic of homosexuality.

There are other outstanding academic programs at Villanova that seek to foster a sense of community among interested students, such as "The Villanova Experience" and the new Templeton Visions of Freedom project. Generally, students in such programs take classes together, live together, and attend special lectures and other events with faculty members. Students report that this kind of a program shapes their present and future at the school in a very positive way — the spirit is reminiscent of what we imagine colleges to have been like in days past. Unfortunately, spaces in these programs are very limited, and all such programs are not all academically oriented: some small group seminars address such matters as gender roles and substance abuse. One student says that teaching these kinds of "life skills" is not what she came to college to learn. "But apart from the condescending stuff, the program has been a fantastic educational experience," she adds.

Further excellent features of Villanova's academic program include its very popular Irish studies department, the special courses offered in Arab and Islamic studies, Augustinian studies, the renowned astronomy department (and its professors), the philosophy department, the business school, economics, political science, the NROTC program, and all the comprehensive sciences. Villanova's English and political science departments have remained untainted by the now nearly out-of-vogue academic trends that have so plagued Villanova's philosophy department (among others). From all reports, it is possible, especially in the first two years of school, to take literature courses where literature is still read and not deconstructed according to social class, sexual orientation, or political persuasion. Though the philosophy department is of an extremely high quality (the famous scholars there constantly attract more famous scholars), it's current existence at the university expresses Villanova's internal quarrel between Christian humanism and secular humanism quite clearly.

With rare exception, the professors at Villanova must be considered one of the school's strongest assets since they are present, available, teaching, and willing to mentor undergrads. Their teaching load is substantial — the majority of professors teaching six courses a year, the student to faculty ratio is low (roughly thirteen to one), and even the star professors are in the classroom and on campus. The use of teaching assistants is quite limited. Part of this dynamic results from intelligent university policy but part is simple good will on the part of many professors. Some professors report that their most difficult "problem" is the intellectual faintheartedness of the student population. Students are said to be smart and successful, but the "value of knowledge for knowledge's sake; the sheer joy of the pursuit of truth" that animates the faculty does not, through and through, animate the student body. According to students and professors, some outstanding teachers include William Werpehowski in the peace and justice program; Thomas Smith, Lowell Gustafson, John Schrems, and Colleen Sheehan in political science; Marc Gallicchio in history; Sterling Delano, James Kirschke, Patrick Nolan, Hugh Ormsby-Lennon, Robert E. Wilkinson, and Charles Cherry in English; John Caputo and Daniel Regan in philosophy; John Wojcik in chemistry; Thomas F. Monahan in accountancy; and Richard M. Jacobs in education and human services.

In each department, students and professors report finding at least some politicized classes. Students often use these to fulfill the diversity and multicultural requirements. Courses like "Chaucer: Gender, Narrative, and Authority"; "Feminist Theology"; "Liberation Theology"; "Inscribing Gender in the Middle Ages"; "Race, Class, and Gender"; "AIDS and Social Justice Lab"; and "Eco-Feminism" may not be the best choices for a student seeking an authentic education in the arts and sciences. However, it's not too difficult to steer away from these frequently less substantive class offerings so long as one avoids too many classes in the peace and justice program or women's studies and Africana studies departments. The peace and justice program has a dual nature, serving also as an umbrella organization for groups like Villanova Feminist Coalition, Villanovans for Life, Villanova Environmental Group, International Coalition against Racism, Democratic Socialists of America, and other social outreach/activist groups, which may explain the tendency toward politicized courses in this department.

Political Atmosphere: Beauty So Ancient, Beauty So New

The fundamental reality of Villanova's political atmosphere could be expressed in terms of its campus architecture. The campus's beautiful gothic structures are numerous, and the rich, old stone reflects an elemental conservatism, the imposing double-spired church at the heart of campus championing theology as the queen of all sciences and the importance of religion in society. But then, if one looks carefully, there in the middle of campus sits a sculpture commonly referred to as "The Oreo" because it so resembles the black-white-black structure of the famous cookie. And next to that is what appears to be a large ski lodge that serves as the student center, Connelly Center. A little departure from the traditional gothic? Indeed, and so the same goes for the political climate — moderately traditional with some pull toward a more progressive liberal side. Still, much of this makes Villanova a lively place for the politically interested student.

The politics at Villanova can be found not so much in campus life as in the administration and faculty. They involve matters such as curricular decisions, hiring selections, and the school's mission. Villanova is led by Fr. Edmund J. Dobbin, a Catholic priest of the Augustinian Order, and several other administrators at the university, as well as more than one-third of its board of trustees, are also Augustinians. While one professor describes the administration as "politically neutral," another says they are "left-leaning like most universities, but fairly reasonable." On the positive side, administrators encourage instructors to talk about values and morals in their classes. While the university retains a strong religious influence (religion requirements, crucifixes on most classroom walls, and a lively sense of Catholic social teaching), according to some students and professors its rhetoric is occasionally stronger than the true picture. Perhaps many of the value-free social experiments conducted elsewhere don't fly at Villanova, but professors do voice their liberalism in class, the mainstream newspaper often reflects a secular, liberal mindset, and campus-wide lectures often feature stronger speakers from those on the left of the political spectrum than from those on the right.

Some of these outside visitors, to be fair, are eventually rejected, like Planned Parenthood or Anna Quindlen, the famous author who sits on the board of NARAL, but not without great debates. Nonetheless postmodern, deconstructionist guru Jacques Derrida and others do make their way to the campus. Furthermore, the administration has recently made it difficult for students to bring conservative speakers to campus. In the fall of 2000, some students wanted to bring NRA president Charlton Heston to campus; but the administration blocked their every move, refusing to pay for the basic fees it had always paid for in the past (Heston waived his speaking fee), and even requiring *The Villanova Times,* the campus newspaper that sponsored the event, to pick up the tab for the "extra security" the administration required be on hand. The extra security was apparently necessary to protect Heston from protesters from the university's — ready for this? — Center for Peace and Justice.

Usually, the Villanova administration is kept somewhat in check by a fairly conservative board of directors and a largely traditional alumni base. And now also holding the mainstream student newspaper to account is the aforementioned *Villanova Times,* formerly *The Conservative Column.* This rabble-rousing paper has recently received a great deal of attention for its conservative, Catholic, pro-life stances on issues. Considering Villanova's overall moderate political climate, this paper is as little at home on campus as the Villanova Feminist Coalition.

Student Life: St. Thomas for All

At how many schools would St. Thomas of Villanova Day attract as many people as a Big East basketball game? Yet these comparably attended events are integral to Villanova's student life. The first begins with a grand academic procession into the Pavilion followed by awards, speakers, mass, and a "big feed," described as "very medieval" by one professor. The latter event occurs numerous times a year at the Pavilion as the Villanova Wildcats strive to try to get back to the level that made them the 1985 NCAA champions. Basketball is not to be underestimated at Villanova, and it was perhaps the national attention the school received in 1985 that elevated its status and consequently allowed for more selectivity among applicants. Both the religious and athletic dimensions of campus life build a special unity among students that lives on beyond their undergraduate years. Over and over again alumni attest to this with unfettered enthusiasm.

Dedication to charity work and social outreach programs is also important to campus life at Villanova. Students report that the abundance of volunteerism is firmly rooted in the school's Christian principles and commitment to Catholic social thought, making the students lovers of "human persons" as opposed to lovers of an abstract "humanity." Habitat for Humanity garners an unprecedented amount of student participation, as does Special Olympics — Villanova is the only university in America where such an event is exclusively student-run. Long-running literacy and education programs in prisons, the Blue Key Society, New Student Orientation, numerous charity activities by the fraternities and sororities, Balloon Day, and Martin Luther King Day are other outlets for volunteer service.

Fraternities and sororities attract about 30 percent of students, but these groups do not dominate the university's social life. Other campus activities include many fine theater productions, various and numerous music recitals, art exhibitions, Republican and Democratic groups, several excellent literary publications, and an active student government. In addition to the enormous attention directed toward the talented men's basketball team, Villanova's football team has excelled recently, dominating the Yankee conference in recent years. Also renowned for many years is Villanova's outstanding track and field program, which has produced thirty-three of Villanova's forty Olympians.

The Campus Ministry reflects the traditions of Roman Catholic and Augustinian spirituality through many of its programs, which include, according to university literature, "prayer, liturgy, community service, leadership development, and pastoral care." Mass is offered on campus three times daily during the week and six times on the weekend; Sunday mass remains, for most students, a highlight of the week. One professor describes Sunday mass at Villanova as an event that "harkens back to the old frontier that you used to see in westerns — where church was the center of everything." The services offer both inspiring music and a relatively sound liturgy, though there are grumblings about the "lack of kneeling and missing parts of the mass — like the Creed." The Campus Ministry Office also provides information on nearby churches, temples, and synagogues for students of other faiths.

Rules for student life are not now as traditional as they were even five years ago. At present, only freshmen live in single-sex halls; however, upperclassmen may also ask to live in a single-sex hall. The remaining single-sex residence halls are open to members of the opposite sex from 10 a.m. to midnight on weekdays and from 10 a.m. to 2 a.m. on weekends. This policy is spelled out in the university's "Code of Student Conduct," which also states: "Villanova University believes that a genuine and complete expression of love through sex requires a commitment to living and sharing of two persons in marriage. Consequently, overt sexual behavior and/or overnight visitation by a member of the opposite sex in residential facilities represent flagrant violations." The strong language remains in the Code of Conduct, but Villanova's student government won the war for the rather lengthy visitation hours.

A very attractive feature of Villanova is that campus crime is minimal, leaving students with a feeling of safety and security. Campus safety officers are easily available; boxes with "panic buttons" are plentiful outside and inside buildings; card entry is required for building entry after dark; and better lighting was provided by the removal of some large shrubs and trees a few years ago. The worst and most frequent incidents with the campus police involve drunkenness and vandalism, as at most colleges.

Social life at Villanova is full, and full of parties. But the important question follows: is it possible for a Villanova student to graduate with only a limited exposure to an intellectual life outside the classroom but with an inordinately full social life? Yes, this happens in many circles. But is it also possible for a student to attain more than that: an authentic and broad liberal arts education that prepares him for life? But the student must be willing, an idea clearly expressed at the entrance to Villanova's Falvey Memorial library where there appears a grand mosaic quoting the illustrious St. Augustine: *Tolle lege* — "pick up and read."

University of Virginia

Office of Admission
PO Box 400160
Charlottesville, VA 22904-4160
(804) 924-0311
www.virginia.edu

Total enrollment: 18,550
Undergraduates: 12,489
SAT ranges (Verbal/Math): 590-700 (V); 610-710 (M)
Applicants: 14,145
Accepted: 39%
Enrolled: 53%

Application deadline: January 15
Financial aid application deadline: March 1
Tuition: resident: $4,335/$9,135; non-resident: $17,585/$22,385
Core curriculum: No

The Students Are Declared Independent

There are two things one must realize about Thomas Jefferson's university: It isn't what it used to be, but it isn't too bad, either. If it often fails to live up to its founder's expectations, it still retains enough respect for those expectations and the liberal tradition represented by Jefferson to provide a first-rate educational experience.

The University of Virginia enrolls approximately twelve thousand undergraduates and offers sixty-one majors — perhaps more than even the polymath Jefferson had in mind. But, unfortunately, the school offers little guidance to its students, leaving them largely to their own devices to navigate through U.Va.'s extensive curricular course.

This situation is made worse by the university's distinct preference, in recent years, for funding its professional schools rather than the arts and sciences. Many professors in the College of Arts and Sciences are unhappy with the situation and are pushing to keep a greater share of the tuition money generated by their college. (They currently get $17 million less in budgeted funds that the tuition revenue they produce.) As it stands, though, the high costs associated with starting labs means that there is not enough money to hire enough new faculty in the sciences. And throughout the arts and sciences there is an increasing student-teacher ratio, which leaves some students unable to take the courses they want or need.

Aesthetics have also been increasingly ignored. "The main problem here is that the physical plant in arts and sciences is fairly dismal," a professor says. "You wouldn't think this with all that majestic Jefferson architecture but classrooms are generally unattractive. This is not a problem in the law or business schools, but arts and sciences just gets the crumbs."

Despite these problems, U.Va. could be a lot worse. In many ways it endures less politicization than most elite public and private schools. And as one professor points out, the student-teacher ratio problem in the liberal arts is because U.Va. has a comparatively large number of liberal arts students, not a comparatively small number of faculty. (U.Va., for instance, has fifty faculty members in history; a school thrice its size, the University of Texas, has just fifty-one.) Therefore, if they can get in their courses, "a student is bound to find some good professors in such a large pasture," one professor says.

This commitment to the liberal arts, however tenuous and ill-defined, is rare among state universities and affords the possibility, at least, of an excellent education. "This really is a good school, and it can be a fantastic school if the student is willing to put some effort into choosing the right courses and getting to know professors," a student says. "It's possible to get a first-rate education here, but it doesn't just come to you. Unfortunately, too many people learn this too late."

Academic Life: Submitted to a Candid World

With unintentional irony, the University of Virginia view book juxtaposes rhetoric about the "absolutely central place of the liberal arts" at U.Va. with descriptions of three courses — "A Digital History of the Civil War," "African Dance and Drum Ensemble," and "Environmental Choices" — that one might be forgiven for thinking were not, really, "absolutely central" to a liberal arts education. But for U.Va., a commitment to the liberal arts does not equal a commitment to a core curriculum. The view book, for instance, waxes about the expansion of the curriculum to include both "biochemistry and Buddhist thought" and "marketing and medieval studies." Proudly, it proclaims that "students enjoy great freedom in charting their course through this landscape of ideas."

Here the viewbook is absolutely correct. The course requirements at Virginia are so loose that, with the exception of the foreign language requirement, even a student who randomly fills his class schedule is all but guaranteed to have met them at the end of four years. From an institutional perspective, these loose requirements mean that students' inability to enroll in the courses they want isn't such a problem after all.

"You may as well have no requirements," says a professor. "As is, the requirements present no core body of knowledge."

At U.Va., students must complete three hours in basic English composition; an additional writing course; fourteen credits in a foreign language; six hours in "humanities" (literature, the fine arts, political theory, philosophy, or religious studies); six in social sciences; twelve in natural sciences and mathematics (from a minimum of two departments); three hours of historical studies; and three hours in "non-Western perspectives."

Students can place out of the basic English composition requirement, and there are a number of ways to fulfill the requirement for a second writing course. Every course in English literature qualifies, as do thirty-six other courses scattered across several departments.

The historical studies requirement is essentially meaningless. Not only can it be filled by taking any course — any course at all — in the history department, but by taking any one of seventy other courses listed by a total of eleven other departments. These courses range from surveys of classical, Western art and religious history to more specialized classes like "The Gospel and Letters of John and the Book of Revelation" or nonseminal offerings like "Archaeology of Virginia." However, it should be noted that the vast majority of the courses fulfilling this requirement bear nonpoliticized titles and seem to deal with important topics.

710

With courses like "The Religions of China" and "Archaeology of the Ancient Near East" — not to mention every single history course — fulfilling the historical studies requirement, it is hard to see why a requirement in "non-Western perspectives" is needed. But it is there nonetheless; it is as ill-defined as the historical studies requirement, with 174 different courses eligible to count toward it. These range from numerous history and anthropology courses dealing with non-Western cultures, such as "Modern African History," to religious studies courses dealing with non-Christian religions and Asian studies courses like "Women, Nature, and Society in Modern Japanese Fiction." Not surprisingly, courses that fulfill the non-Western perspectives category tend to be more politicized than others.

The Echols Scholar honors program exempts its students from even these minimal area requirements, amply demonstrating U.Va.'s philosophy that the key to a liberal arts education is the freedom to choose from among the university's one-thousand-odd courses without restrictions or guidance. Not all Echols Scholars are enamored of this approach. As one says, "They still need to emphasize that we should take core requirements."

U.Va.'s emphasis upon student freedom has its advantages, however. If students succeed in getting some direction or are prepared enough to know which courses to take and which to avoid, the education available at U.Va. is still stellar. "The university is a 'big ideas' institution," says a professor. "Faculty are well-known for working on the important ideas of the day. . . . There are always exceptions, but U.Va. is not an especially ideological university or one oriented toward impossibly narrow disciplinary specialization. One of its great strengths is its interdisciplinary character."

One example of an interdisciplinary success, and one way in which students can receive guidance, is through U.Va.'s "Jeffersonian curriculum." This curriculum, the goal of which is to demonstrate the unity of the arts and sciences, tends to guide students toward more traditional course offerings. Departments in the arts and sciences designate certain courses as appropriate for the curriculum; students pursuing this designation (it is not a degree program) must take a specified number of these courses in their first two years and then pursue one of the school's interdisciplinary majors (e.g., "Political and Social Thought," or "Studies in Women and Gender") after that. It is interesting to note that this more traditional approach to education is not given much publicity by the university itself, and many professors and students on campus apparently do not even know it exists.

Though U.Va. has no core curriculum, at least, as one professor explains, the school emphasizes the liberal arts in general. As a result, the liberal arts faculties are much larger than other universities of comparable size, and students can not only shape for themselves an excellent undergraduate education but can also avoid politicized offerings.

This is not as difficult an undertaking at U.Va. as it would be at many places; courses, on the whole, are less politicized and more serious than those found at

711

other state or even private schools. The religious studies, English, history, and government and foreign affairs departments are said to be particularly strong. Excellent professors include George A. Garrett, Gordon M. Braden, Paul Cantor, and Martin C. Battestin in English; Jenny Strauss Clay and Edward Courtney in classics; Jon E. Lendon, Edward L. Ayers, Gary W. Gallagher, Michael F. Holt, Joseph F. Kett, Stephen Innes, and Thomas F. Noble in history; William Wilson, James F. Childress, and Harry Y. Gamble Jr. in religious studies; Kenneth G. Elzinga in economics; Larry J. Sabato, John M. Owen, and James W. Ceaser in government and foreign affairs; Christopher M. S. Johns in art history; Julian W. Connolly in Slavic languages and literature; Roberto Triggiani in math; and James Davison Hunter in sociology.

As usual, class sizes in survey courses are said to be huge, and the lack of enough arts and sciences faculty has made even discussion sections, according to one student, "overflowing." Still, departments like history and English have small seminars for majors in which enrollment is capped to quite reasonable levels (twelve to fifteen students). But as one professor says, "students don't always take them because you have to work in them."

Then there are the courses students want to take, but can't get into. "There are stories of people who can't get into the classes they need and actually have to switch majors," says a student. "More professors are desperately needed." This need also affects professor accessibility. "Students here are yearning to know professors," says one undergrad, "but because of the high student-to-professor ratio, profs just don't have enough time." But another student reports that he has had many opportunities to speak with and even socialize with his professors. "I have had — and this is not a rare thing for any student who is at all motivated — many opportunities to associate with professors in less rigidly academic settings such as coffee houses," he says. These opportunities are made more frequent by the fact that many faculty live very near the university; some even live on campus.

U.Va. often likes to compare itself with Ivy League schools. According to one professor, the primary differences are that U.Va. requires less writing in its courses and has a smaller proportion of intellectually serious students. "Hence I suspect that students do not learn as much from each other and are not as pushed by competition with their peers as are Ivy League students," the professor says. As for grade inflation, there is considerable variation among and within departments. According to one student, "because we're a college of overachievers, there are an inordinate amount of A's and B's given, and not all of these are necessarily earned." Some students believe that professors do not challenge their high-ability students enough.

Political Atmosphere: Prudence, Indeed, Will Dictate

The subject of race has permeated U.Va. news during the last two years, and not only because new DNA evidence revealed that Thomas Jefferson could have fathered one of Sally Hemmings's children. There have also been controversies surrounding racial discrimination in admissions and what many at the school perceive as the inordinate amount of self-segregation among black and white students.

Racial preferences in admissions had been blatant and obvious for years, with black applicants given "booster points." In 1999, fearing a lawsuit, President John T. Casteen III made a unilateral decision to eliminate this system (although race is still said to be one of many factors taken into account). Predictably enough, President Casteen's decision sparked quite a bit of controversy, including protests, teach-ins, and the like. While the faculty was mostly in favor of affirmative action, students were more divided, and many students on both sides of the issue chose to speak out. However, students report that the supporters of racial preferences have managed to silence their opponents through intimidation; one member of the Board of Visitors who suggested that the university had lowered its standards to recruit black students was denounced as a racist. ("I concluded that free speech is alive and well here, at least among students," says one professor.) On the whole, though, the acrimony was something short of the kind of chaos that might have been seen on a more thoroughly politicized campus.

Self-segregation among black and white students has been seen as a problem by both the administration and the students. There is a "black bus stop" where black students traditionally hang out, as well as self-segregation in the dining halls, in the stands at football games, and so on. The university has focused on the need for "racial reconciliation" and, as one student puts it, "there are forums all over the place." Ironically, U.Va. has traditionally been a good school for blacks, and not just in terms of racial preferences in admissions. Blacks constitute 10 percent of the undergraduate population, graduate at almost the same rate as whites, and at the highest rate among public universities.

Though one professor states that "freedom of speech is a fetish at this university," the controversy surrounding the change in admissions policy demonstrated that speaking your mind at Virginia can come with severe social costs. "You can say pretty much what you want in a lecture, but watch out on race," a professor says. "It's very PC here," says a student. Conformity is expected, especially for female students, this student says. "Here you are expected to be a feminist and expected to accept anyone else's lifestyle. You're a horrible closed-minded hypocrite if you don't."

Anthropology, women's studies, and the modern language departments are said to be very politicized. "Hiring decisions in my department have grown increasingly contentious," says one professor, adding that the gender of the potential hire is usually the point of conflict. The hiring process in the modern languages departments is said to be especially politicized, but professors from other departments say they don't have this problem. "Woman are denied tenure just as [often] as men are," says one.

Despite problems, there is no question that the jealous cultivation of the school's peculiar traditions and customs by both faculty and students puts a check on the most radical ideology at Virginia. If Jefferson was a radical in 1776 he is hardly one now, and his name still holds cachet; as one faculty member says, "you've got Thomas Jefferson to invoke against know-nothings." Even more conservative professors, therefore, generally feel free to speak their minds about politics or religion in the classroom.

Student Life: Light and Transient Causes

Charlottesville and the surrounding Blue Ridge Mountains region are picturesque. Charlottesville itself is a quiet, small college town with a population of just 38,000, situated approximately two hours south of Washington, D.C., and an hour west of Richmond. Downtown Charlottesville consists of a pedestrian mall lined with shops, restaurants, and theatres; students often hang out in the bars at "The Corner." The surrounding countryside, accessible in any direction via a ten-minute drive, is ideal for outdoor activities and history buffs.

The original, Jeffersonian campus — that is, the Grounds — with the neoclassical, proportional beauty of the Rotunda, pavillions, and "academical village" (where live selected students and faculty) is magnificent. The Lawn, where students relax and study, was listed as one of the most beautifully landscaped campus sites by the American Society of Landscape Architects in 1999.

The distinctive campus architecture contributes to U.Va.'s distinctive environment, in which peculiar school customs help create a sense of tradition, history, community, and stability. For instance, students refer to U.Va. as simply "The University." Professors are not referred to as "doctor," but as "Mr.," "Ms.," or "Professor," freshmen are "first-years," the campus is "the Grounds," and the school's founder is, simply, "Mr. Jefferson." (The mystique surrounding Jefferson, says one student, borders on the idolatrous. "We have myths about him.") Students dress up for football games, and there are two, one-character secret societies (7 and Z). U.Va. is so tradition-laden that it reminds me of an Ivy League school," says a professor, who studied at two of them. "But unlike at those schools . . . it doesn't seem 'cool' at U.Va. to disparage the traditions, except among a few."

Furthermore, U.Va.'s students' tradition of self-governance, with its famous and still enforced Honor System, remains, in principle at least, a big part of student life. This system has recently been criticized for its secrecy, and proposed changes, critics charge, would only exacerbate the situation. According to the *Washington Post*, the proposals would "strip students of the ability to confront witnesses against them and to refuse to testify against themselves. Witness testimony from transcripts or audio tapes would be admissible, with no chance to clarify, question or challenge its validity. Prosecutors would instruct the jury to interpret an accused student's refusal to testify as evidence of guilt."

Another big part of student life is alcohol. "Virginia's long had a reputation, a deserved reputation, as a party school," says a professor. This is an aspect fed by the popularity of the school's Greek system, which includes about 30 percent of the student body. "For many students, academics seems to be a secondary priority to partying and enjoying the social scene," a student says. "The title 'Wahoos' alludes to the long tradition of heavy drinking associated with U.Va." Some students, not so enamored with this tradition, are trying to end practices like the "fourth-year fifth," in which fourth-years drink a fifth of alcohol before the final football game.

Aside from the partying, U.Va. students are extraordinarily active and ambitious. Says one student, "The campus is a comfortable environment in which to be intelligent. Nobody thinks you're weird if you discuss philosophies of life over coffee." The typical U.Va. student is from Northern Virginia, white, preppy, academically well-prepared, and economically well-off. The latter fact is at least partly explained by U.Va.'s practice of affirmative action for the rich and well-connected. The university recently admitted that the likelihood of an applicant's family donating money to the school was considered in the admissions process.

Quality student groups include InterVarsity Christian Fellowship, Hillel, Madison House (an umbrella service organization), and the Jefferson Debating Society. Intramural sports are very popular, and the Cavaliers (a.k.a. "Wahoos") usually field decent football and men's and women's basketball teams and an exceptional men's soccer team.

The administration has taken steps to improve campus safety, including the installation of emergency phones at various locations on the Grounds and making cell phones available for loan at campus libraries. But crime, especially thefts and muggings, has been on the increase. "The campus is not as safe as you might think," says one faculty member. "It is probably safer than Yale and some other universities in larger cities, but it is not paradise." Some female students are wary of walking at night alone, and the student escort service is said to be so inefficient that people don't like to use it. There has been talk of starting a walking escort service, but no action has yet been taken. Says one jaded student, "It'd probably be understaffed like everything else, anyway."

There are no options for single-sex living at Virginia. All dorms are coed, though there are no coed floors or coed bathrooms or showers. There are no substance-free dorms nor are there visitation hours for the opposite sex.

Wabash College

Admissions Office
PO Box 352
Crawfordsville, IN 47933-0352
(800) 345-5385
www.wabash.edu

Total enrollment: 800
Undergraduates: 800
SAT ranges (Verbal/Math): 530-650 (V); 550-660 (M)
Applicants: 746
Accepted: 75%
Enrolled: 40%
Application deadline: April 1
Financial aid application deadline: December 1
Tuition: $18,294/$24,055
Core curriculum: No

Male-ing It In

Wabash College's motto — "for wisdom and for righteousness" — is suggestive of its origins in 1832 as a college dedicated to the Trinity for the purpose of civilizing what was then the western border of the United States. For the first century of its existence, its presidents were drawn from the ranks of Presbyterian clergy. Wabash produced a famous general and novelist (Lew Wallace of *Ben Hur* fame), a vice president (Thomas R. Marshall, the Democrat remembered best for his advocacy of a 5-cent cigar), and a movie czar (Will Hays, whose Hays Commission regulated the content of Hollywood films). The poet Ezra Pound was briefly on its faculty before being run out of town for indiscretions that rubbed against the austere Calvinist temperament still reflected today in the campus's unostentatious buildings and furnishings.

In other respects, however, today's Wabash is guided by a different philosophy. The official motto is not included in admissions material, and a mission statement newly minted by college trustees promises only that "Wabash College educates men to think critically, act responsibly, lead effectively, and live humanely."

In this case, "men" does indeed mean men only; Wabash remains one of the few all-male colleges in the country. But just as the college long ago left its Christian roots, it seems that it might not be long before that part of its identity is tossed away as well. Conservative-minded alumni and students have helped to keep the single-sex policy so far, but the school has seen aggressive agitation by prominent faculty members for coeducation. The chairman of the economics department even maintains a Web page that upbraids Wabash for "its policy of gender discrimination in admission."

Academic Life: Culture and Tradition(?)

In spirit, Wabash is deeply devoted to educating undergraduates in liberal arts tradition. With the exception of introductory-level classes, which can enroll as many as sixty-five students, most lecture courses and seminars at Wabash have small enrollments. It is not unusual for upper-level seminars to consist of a handful of students and a professor sitting around a small table. Even the largest academic departments have only four or five faculty members, which fosters considerable intimacy once students declare a major and minor during their sophomore year and begin working more intensively with particular departments.

Although it has no core curriculum, Wabash requires that all freshmen complete a one-semester tutorial during their first year on campus. The tutorials have no more than sixteen students, and the course is designed to allow a faculty member to have intensive contact with new students. In recent years, tutorials have surveyed such various topics as World War I, rap music, baseball, and Roman Catholic encyclicals. Incoming students rank the tutorials in order of their interest in them, and most are placed in one of their top choices. Grades for tutorials typically consist of class discussion and a series of written papers related to the assigned texts.

In the sophomore year, students must take a year-long course known as "Cultures and Traditions" (C&T). Perhaps the most ridiculed class at Wabash, C&T offers a case study in how an overly ambitious and not ignoble concept can flop in practice. The interdisciplinary idea of the course is a commendable idea, but to get at that idea, each semester of C&T is fragmented into modules organized around an idea (e.g., friendship, the individual and society) or a region or ethnic group (like Eastern religion, Latin America, black history). C&T meets three times a week, with the sessions divided between small seminar sections led by a professor or staff member (administrators and even librarians are sometimes assigned C&T sections) and large lectures featuring a Wabash professor or visiting lecturer. One student recalls his C&T experience as "dominated by fads; at times we read works not because of their true historical or cultural importance, but because of the skin color of their authors." Another student echoes this view: "When I took the course, we spent two days on Aristotle and Plato, and a week on Malcolm X." In addition to being a vehicle for multiculturalism, C&T shifts from text to text and from subject to subject, providing only the most superficial of knowledge and never really tying the several parts together.

The good news is that C&T is the exception, and the college's relatively liberal distribution requirements allow students the discretion to take challenging courses. Students are required to take three courses in literature and the fine arts; three in the social sciences; three in natural science and mathematics; two in history, philosophy, or religion; and a quantitative studies course. All students, including those in the sciences, take at least two semesters of an ancient or modern language.

Since these choices are made by the students, those who are self-directed and arrive on campus already knowing what they wish to study do very well. "Academic rigor is readily available for those students who seek it out," says a recent graduate. "The faculty, in my experience, were ready to take me wherever I wanted to go, and they were extremely helpful in advancing intellectual creativity and excitement." Some students, however, express regret over the lack of comprehensive focus to Wabash's curriculum. "Students can fulfill their distribution requirements without having read Shakespeare, solved a calculus problem, or studied American history," says another recent graduate.

With the exception of some tutors employed in foreign language instruction, full-time professors (97 percent of which hold the terminal degree in their field) teach the classes at Wabash. Faculty readily meet with students outside of class and many make their e-mail addresses and home telephone numbers available. Extensive faculty-student interaction also occurs at campus lectures and concerts and through colloquia that discuss such topics as medievalism and gender studies. "You can find yourself over at a prof's house for dinner, playing basketball with a prof in the gym, or even drinking with one at a party," a student says.

The small size of Wabash and the importance given to faculty teaching (the student-faculty ratio is ten to one) mean that even large lecture classes usually feature a research paper or essay component that allows students to practice writing. "What particularly impresses me about Wabash is the premium it places upon writing," a recent graduate says. "In most classes, students regularly are assigned ten- to fifteen-page reports; tests are in essay format, almost never multiple choice." And some professors do not actively proctor their exams; they trust their students to uphold the standard of honesty set in the Wabash's Gentleman's Rule. (The Gentleman's Rule — that a Wabash man is expected to conduct himself at all times as a gentleman — is no longer the only rule on campus, but it still enjoys a special status among students.)

Students are divided about the rigor of classroom discussions. "Professors expect you to come to class prepared, and most of them can tell pretty quickly whether you are," a student says. But a recent graduate complains that some courses "place a premium on personal feelings, resulting in classes that resemble the Oprah Winfrey Show, with students acting as panelists, professors as hosts." And students can be fast studies about what opinions the professor as host is most eager to entertain. "Critical thinking isn't consistently rewarded," a student says. "Academic success at Wabash almost always entails learning what the instructor wants to hear and how to repeat it accurately." Another student holds a more nuanced view: "Critical thinking is rewarded to a certain degree but it always helps to regurgitate at least a few of the professor's perspectives."

Among the outstanding departments at Wabash recommended by students are biology, classics, chemistry, economics, and philosophy and religion. Philosophy and religion faculty are particularly impressive and include David Blix, William Placher, and Stephen Webb. Students rave about the department's "History of Christianity" courses. Classicist David Kubiak teaches a much-admired course on literature and mythology, political theorist Edward McLean specializes in constitutionalism, and psychologist Charles Blaich stands out in an otherwise mediocre department.

In contrast, the history department seems to have enshrined the least appealing aspects of postmodernism — relativism, identity politics, and whatever else has recently come down the pike — and recently hired an open admirer of Fidel Castro. While one departmental major insists that the English department offers courses that "cover the gamut of English letters, with a particularly strong focus on early modernism and its relation to our postmodernist age," other students express apprehension about remedial English classes being used to promote leftist causes. Above all, some classes "seem to try and compensate for Wabash's single-sex status," a recent graduate says.

Students who itch to get a break from Crawfordsville can join the 25 percent of juniors who opt for off-campus study or internships, which Wabash is generous about granting (although it sometimes tries to corral students into attending established programs — for example, study abroad in Scotland is supposed to occur at Aberdeen). The college recently received a $20-million grant to build a liberal arts center on campus that promises to provide research opportunities for undergraduates. And some professors, especially in the sciences, employ advanced students during the summer months to assist with research.

Political Atmosphere: Save the Males

The student body at Wabash is noticeably more conservative than the faculty, as was illustrated with some passion a decade ago when the college's trustees last considered the possibility of coeducation. Although the faculty supported coeducation nearly unanimously, students and alumni prevailed in the battle to maintain Wabash as a men's college. The fallout from the controversy continues to this day.

Recently, two women professors ejected students from their classrooms for wearing T-shirts that derided a rival college by declaring, "At Wabash we don't need women." Despite the existence of a faculty "Statement of Principle Concerning Diversity" that announces "our community should embrace both freedom of speech and tolerance for diversity," the aggrieved professors insisted that the T-shirts were offensive to women and thus had no place in the classroom. The resulting student outcry, which lead to national media coverage, seemed to undermine the observation of a *Washington Post* reporter that Wabash is "proudly, unapologetically one of the last all-male institutions of its kind." That observation held for students, at least.

Students explain that it's necessary to distinguish between the balanced class-room teaching of most professors and the same professors' out-of-classroom political activism. Even then, it's hard to escape the conclusion that C&T is not alone among courses that serve political rather than academic purposes. In 1998 the faculty adopted areas of concentration (similar to minors) in multiculturalism and gender studies. The academic bulletin's description of the gender studies program pledges to investigate "strategies that aim to transform unjust or coercive social systems based on gender." That kind of program appears out of place at a school such as Wabash — until one learns that a faculty report not long ago blithely concluded that Wabash students are "angry and intolerant toward those different from themselves."

Students disagree with this assessment. "Most students recognize that true diversity is diversity of viewpoint, not diversity of skin color," one says. "The faculty and staff aren't so sure." Funds laundered through faculty departments and committees routinely underwrite guest lectures — on topics such as the "Gay Farm Boy Experience" — that elicit skepticism and mild bemusement from students. "Wabash pretends to champion free expression, but it is firmly seated in the PC bandwagon," a student says.

One of the beacons of sound thinking on campus is a student-published alternative magazine called the *Wabash Commentary*. The *Commentary* is Wabash's most award-winning publication, but that hasn't prevented it from drawing cackles from leftist faculty that object to the essays and investigative pieces published there. Lauded by the *Indianapolis Star* for "regularly lampooning political correctness," the *Commentary* has a strong readership among students and alumni. Not only did the magazine galvanize opposition when Wabash decided to stage *Angel in America*, the aggressively pro-homosexual play, but the Marxist playwright Tony Kushner responsible for *Angels* later complained to the *New Orleans Times-Picayune* that the *Commentary*'s "very industrious right-wing students got the alumni worked up."

In addition to the *Commentary*, a weekly newspaper called the *Bachelor* varies in quality but often just rewrites college press releases. WNDY, a radio station run by students, features different styles of music and several locally originating talk shows. There also are several student literary journals that, according to students, no one reads.

Surprisingly, considering the political intrigue that occurs around campus, electoral politics is not a popular pastime at Wabash, although the College Republicans and College Democrats have clubs on campus. The city and county surrounding Crawfordsville is so staunchly conservative that the real election usually occurs during Republican primaries. Several small, ideological groups also have a presence at Wabash, including a gay student group, an environmental concerns club, and an Amnesty International chapter.

Student Life: Bachelor Pad

Part of Wabash's charm is that it can be a little rough-hewn and scrappy precisely because college-aged women are not around campus during the week. Historically this has translated into fewer rules than are found at comparable schools, and a greater toleration for men to be themselves. An anecdote recalled by an aged alumnus captures this spirit. At a new student orientation during the Great Depression, the then-president declared: "I know you boys come from different places and backgrounds and you all have habits — some good and some bad; just don't develop any new bad habits while you are here."

Wabash students enjoy greater freedom than many of their contemporaries. All students may bring vehicles to campus, and the college does not require registration or permits for them. Students living in dorms and fraternity houses are permitted to remain in them over holidays and Christmas vacation. There is little crime on campus, and many dorm residents leave their doors unlocked without fear of suffering theft.

In recent years the college has funded extensive dorm and fraternity renovations, in part because it imposed an on-campus residency requirement for freshmen and sophomores. About one-third of Wabash students are not members of Greek organizations and can choose from four dorms in which to live: Martindale, Wolcott, Morris, and College Hall. One of the dorms is nominally substance and noise free. The rooms consist of two-man suites and a smaller number of single rooms, and all have a telephone and ethernet connection for each student. Wabash has invested heavily in telecommunications resources, with the result that each student is assigned a personal telephone number and access to several computer labs.

The rest of the students pledge one of the ten nationally recognized fraternities with chapters on campus. Rush occurs during the summer before freshman orientation and during the week that precedes the start of classes in August. Fraternities are, according to a non-Greek student, "part of the fabric of life here." Although each fraternity has its own personality, several have strong academic reputations on campus and most students who desire to pledge a fraternity will receive one or more bids during rush. "They pursue academics with some intensity," a current undergraduate notes of fraternities, "but not to the degrees of independents."

Fall weekends essentially revolve around football games, with the high point being the annual Wabash-DePauw match that draws thousands of fans and national coverage on ESPN. The basketball, swimming, and soccer teams also figure prominently into athletic life on campus, along with other intercollegiate and intramural sports. A newly completed athletic center serves the whole campus. "Athletics are very popular and important, but they are not given undue attention or inordinate emphasis," a former football player says.

The Sphinx Club, which upperclassmen may pledge, serves as the official booster for Wabash athletics and as guardian of college traditions that include the freshman Chapel Sing and Homecoming rituals. A Pan-Hel week each spring features dances and parties. Other popular student groups are the Glee Club, Parliamentary Union, Malcolm X Institute, and religious fellowships.

Located in a west-central Indiana city of 20,000, Wabash is forty-five miles from Indianapolis and three hours from Chicago. Some students tire of Crawfordsville's semi-rural character, so road trips are common on weekends, with the University of Illinois at Champaign, DePauw, Butler, and Purdue within an hour's driving distance, and Indiana University just a little further. The surrounding community includes an all-night supermarket, several discount retailers, a movie theater, local and chain restaurants, and many churches. Because public transportation is nonexistent, it is helpful to bring a car.

Wabash is a regional school that attracts students who value a liberal arts education, contact time with faculty, and the intimacy of a small college. The generous merit- and need-based financial aid packages that the college offers incoming students often persuade young men from coed Midwestern high schools to give a single-sex college a try. Most don't regret their choice. "Wabash was the school I expected, although I often had to meet it halfway," a recent graduate says.

Wake Forest University

Office of Admissions
Box 7305
Reynolda Station
Winston-Salem, NC 27109
(336) 758-5201

Total enrollment: 6,147
Undergraduates: 3,898
SAT ranges (Verbal/Math): 600-690 (V); 610-700 (M)
Applicants: 5,333
Accepted: 47%
Enrolled: 40%
Application deadline: January 15
Financial aid application deadline: March 15
Tuition: $22,410/$28,750
Core curriculum: No

Sleepers' Wake

Founded by Baptists in 1834, Wake Forest originally sought to mold men's minds and characters for church leadership and other professions. From those humble beginnings, it has evolved into a coed campus, severed formal ties to the North Carolina Baptist Convention in 1986, and transformed itself from a sleepy Southern school in a tobacco town to a powerful private university that embraces some of higher education's most fashionable trends. The school has a strong reputation for academic excellence, and its Division I sports and lovely campus make it even more attractive to students.

Today, Wake Forest is almost a paradox: It's set in an old tobacco town, but embraces new technology and has been named one of the most technologically advanced campuses in the country. It's in a Southern conservative and religious setting, but the university has permitted homosexual marriages in its chapel. It has religious roots but has eschewed religious values.

Wake Forest has become more and more like other large private institutions throughout the country, adapting itself to prevailing intellectual and political trends, rather than attracting to itself people interested in a specific set of beliefs, as it once did. Some professors who were at the school before 1986 have become disheartened by it all and lament the departure from tradition.

Many good professors remain at Wake Forest, however, and even though the curriculum has grown more ideological, the undergraduate student body of about 4,000 is largely conservative. Wake Forest is still a fine school, though no longer is it what it once was.

Academic Life: Strength in Numbers

Wake Forest has no core curriculum, no standard and uniform pieces of knowledge that it seeks to impart to its students. Its requirements instead are distribution requirements, which require students to select from an approved list of courses.

There are two types of requirements: the "basic" course requirements and the "divisional" course requirements. Most students complete the requirements in their freshman and sophomore years and focus their remaining two years on one of the school's thirty majors. The basic course requirements are one freshman seminar, one course in English composition, one foreign language course, and two courses in health and sport science. The divisional requirements mandate courses in English literature, American literature, and foreign literature; courses in two math and science areas (biology, chemistry, physics, and mathematics); one course each in history, religion, and philosophy; three courses in social science (anthropology, economics, politics, psychology, or sociology); and one course in the fine arts.

The requirements are noteworthy for their number, depth, and attention to

723

Western history and literature, if not for their coherence and structure. "In terms of the [time spent on] the required courses, this remains a very traditional school," a professor says. Even students in the school of business must fulfill the arts and science categories required of everyone else. However, the catalogue contains pages of courses that can count toward the requirements, and this waters down the effectiveness of the general education component. "Students take the most popular courses, and often repeat what they took in high school," a professor says.

Top professors at Wake include Helga Welsh in politics, Robert Utley in humanities, Charles Lewis in philosophy, James Barefield in history, J. Daniel Hammond and John C. Moorhouse in economics, Mark Leary in psychology, Edwin Wilson in English, and J. Ned Woodall in anthropology.

The philosophy department has produced several Rhodes scholars. "Philosophy remains a bastion of good, solid academic tradition and is quite Christian," a professor says. "They're unwilling to go along with faddish multiculturalism. They're not all Christians, but they're respectful of one's beliefs." The classics department is also said to be strong. "They are quite solid . . . and rigorous," says a professor. "There is no aim to propagandize." Other excellent programs include politics, economics, biology, chemistry, physics, mathematics, and accounting.

Professors say the most politicized departments are religion, English, psychology, women's studies, and history and speech (which several years ago hired a specialist in rap music). Politics is considered an academically vital department, but it is rather politicized in its outlook. "They brought in a bunch of Ph.D.s from the best schools, and now they've ousted the old leftists who were in control," a professor says. "It's backfired on them." History teaching is said to be revisionist, such that Christopher Columbus is attacked for "killing the Indians," a professor says. "History is particularly uniform and one-dimensional," the professor adds.

Traditional professors also complain that Wake Forest, since dropping its associations with the Baptist church, has been bent on catching up with the multiculturalism promoted by neighboring Duke and the University of North Carolina. While Wake (like most places) still has a long way to go to match Duke, the university recently started a minor in American ethnic studies, and feminist theories are becoming more prominent in several departments. "There's a slow movement toward strengthening those kinds of programs and a increasing awareness of them among students," a professor says. To that end, the university has commissioned studies on "how to improve the multicultural atmosphere on campus," a source on campus says. The findings of the studies are expected to be implemented over the next decade.

There are several concrete examples of bizarre and political topics entering Wake Forest's classrooms, all of which seem to be supported by the administration. The women's studies program sponsors lectures on the following topics: "African Storytelling Frees Us! A Tale of Human Rights," "Sexual Orientation Human-Rights Issues," and "Love — Power — Domination."

There's Women's Studies 359, titled "Fathers and Daughters," designed for "juniors, seniors, and graduate students who want to explore their relationships with their fathers." An interview with and a paper about the student's father accounts for 20 percent of the student's grade in the course. Students ask their fathers a list of about thirty questions, including "What are some of the saddest and some of the happiest experiences you've had with me?" and "How did you feel when I started dating and when I first fell in love?" Responses students gave to the course, posted on the Internet, include: "I don't usually feel this relaxed in class." "As a result of this course, I have learned to see my dad as another human being." And "This class has been therapy for me. I feel truly changed." Some dads might wonder why they're spending $30,000 a year so their daughters can talk to them instead of learning something that universities ought to be teaching.

Then there's Education 359, "Adolescent Psychology," in which students watch a series of documentary films and talk about them. (All the films are shown in class, except for the feature-length movie *Hoop Dreams*.) Other films include *Period Piece* in which "women and girls discuss their feelings about menstruation"; *Your Name is Cellulite,* described as "a very funny cartoon" about "why females hate their bodies"; *Tongues Tied,* in which "black gay men discuss their relationships"; and *Torch Song Trilogy,* the "story of a gay man, his homophobic mom, his lovers, and his adopted gay son." Wrote one student in response to the class: "This is the only seminar class I've ever had where I haven't fallen asleep."

And they call the place "Wake" Forest?

One of the things that sets Wake Forest apart from its peers is its emphasis on technology. The university gives all students, upon enrollment, an IBM Thinkpad computer, the cost of which is included in students' tuition and fees. The student keeps the computer after graduation. In 1999, Wake Forest was named the third "most wired" campus in the country by *Yahoo! Internet Life* magazine. The magazine based its ratings on ubiquity and accessibility — "students being able to jack in from anywhere on campus, and making things available to as many students on campus as possible."

Some professors applaud the laptop requirement, but others say it is just another marketing ploy by the administration, done in lieu of offering a true liberal arts education. Some see the computer distribution and the multicultural additions as cut from the same cloth: the university wants to be on the cutting edge of all things and is more concerned with the latest trends than with the greatest.

Political Atmosphere: The Deacons' Demons

Once a school that trained Baptist pastors, Wake Forest has moved far away from that mission and now embraces an "anything goes" philosophy that has angered some local Baptist leaders. The few ties that remained were completely severed in

2000. Some politics, particularly of the women's studies and multicultural kind, also enters the classroom. While most of the students who attend the university lean toward the conservative side, those in power at the university — the faculty and administration — most assuredly do not.

The year 2000 saw the first homosexual "marriage" in the university's Wait Chapel. After a year or so of wrangling, the university finally decided that the church that performed the ceremony could use the chapel for such a purpose. After "uniting" two lesbians, the pastor told the Christian News Service: "The trustees didn't agree and wished we hadn't performed the ceremony. But they respected our rights as an autonomous body."

Such a value-free mindset also creeps into the school's curriculum. In debating the issue of same-sex marriage in the classroom, the dean of the university's divinity school told the Baptist Press: "Is homosexuality a sin? That's for everyone to sort out individually."

"You cannot characterize Wake Forest as a Baptist school now," says a faculty member. Much of what made the university unique has now been made over to resemble the programs and ideologies found at literally hundreds of other schools. The tradition of Wake Forest and the founding mission of the school are now less visible than ever, diluted by the administration and faculty's haste to conform with what they see around them. And, as one professor says, in order to keep pace with the newest intellectual trends, the school has "compromised excellence for mediocrity."

The university's aggressive racial preference program in admissions and its determination to pursue racial and "gender" diversity has, ironically, resulted in the ideological homogenization of the faculty. Departments that once contained a broad array of intellectual positions, such as history, English, and religion, are today home to one point of view.

A review of the school's freshman orientation also shows that incoming students are exposed to political influences upon arrival in Winston-Salem. Not only does Wake Forest hold separate information sessions for minority groups, which contributes to the segregation of such groups on campus. It also forces students to attend something called "Mosaics," described as a "comedic/dramatic presentation examining diversity issues on campus designed to strengthen our relationships with one another." Unlike many other orientations activities, attendance is mandatory, suggesting that the presentation is little more than political propaganda recommending that students suspend their critical faculties when it comes to racial issues.

Student Life: TobaccoRoad.com

Wake Forest sees itself as a small school with substantial resources. Brochures describe it as offering the close-knit community of a small school, but with the resources of a large university in areas such as technology, study abroad, and athletics.

It hosted one of the 2000 presidential debates, and is the second-smallest school in the country with Division I athletics.

Students at Wake Forest are typically very bright, and a majority — 57 percent — come from the South. The school is evenly split between men and women, and the student body includes 11 percent "multicultural students" — blacks, Asians, Hispanics or American Indians.

One professor says that many of the students are sharp but that there's a prevailing pre-professionalism among the student body. "We have some really excellent students," says the professor. "They're very goal oriented, but only a minimum are really intellectually serious about ideas for their own sake. That's the reason why we've failed to cultivate a broad intellectual environment."

Intellectual life does exist in pockets on campus, though, and can be found by students willing to seek it out. Among the student groups noteworthy in this regard are the Philomathesian Society and the Euzelian Society. Both are literary/cultural societies that died out at Wake Forest many years ago but have recently been resurrected by students looking for ways to advance the life of the mind on campus.

Other campus groups include the Baptist Student Union, a still-living remnant of Wake Forest's historical ties to that church. This group lines up students with service projects, including work in retirement homes, prisons, and soup kitchens. Other religious groups, such as the Presbyterian Student Fellowship and the Wesleyan Foundation, are involved in similar projects.

The university encourages students to become involved in service organizations, and there are plenty on campus: Alpha Phi Omega, BACCHUS (alcohol awareness), Habitat for Humanity, Harbinger Corps, Peer Health Educators, PREPAR (rape prevention awareness), Safe Rides, Student Alumni Council, Student Union, and the Volunteer Service Corps. There are also plenty of opportunities to volunteer in Winston-Salem.

The university does fund many student organizations, including the College Republicans and the Gay, Lesbian, and Bisexual Issues Awareness Group.

The Greek system is the chief social outlet for students. About 40 percent of the student body chooses to join one of the thirteen social fraternities and nine sororities. "The Greeks are very much in charge of social life on campus," a professor says. However, the university administration is not favorably disposed toward the Greeks. "The Greek system is under attack," says one student. "The administration blames the Greeks for alcohol abuse on campus. Since the Greeks rent university houses, they have little power to fight back." Recently the administration shortened the pledge period and raised the grade point average required to join a Greek organization. Fraternities occasionally run afoul of these alcohol crackdowns. The Kappa Alpha order recently faced a suspension for giving alcohol to underage students during rush.

Winston-Salem, North Carolina's fourth-largest city, has about 174,000 people. The town was founded on tobacco but is trying to move away from that image by advertising itself as having transformed into a place for high-tech companies and top-notch medical facilities. The city has a minor league baseball team, the Winston-Salem Warthogs, a Class A team affiliated with the Chicago White Sox. The city's location is prime for outdoor enthusiasts: The Blue Ridge Mountains are only an hour or two to the west, and there are plenty of parks in the area. There are also many concerts in the surrounding area, particularly in nearby Greensboro. Sports fans will also delight in the fact that Wake Forest plays in the Atlantic Coast Conference, a perennial basketball powerhouse.

Freshmen are required to live in university dorms unless they're from the immediate area. Student housing is guaranteed for a student's entire four-year tenure. There are still a few single-sex residence halls, although most are coed by floor. Some dorms are called "substance-free," meaning that the prohibitions on drugs, alcohol, and tobacco that once went for all dorms now apply to just a few. There are also several theme houses that are geared toward student interests or language study. Official statistics indicate that in the dorms and elsewhere, serious crime on campus is negligible, except for burglaries.

Wake Forest encourages its students to study abroad and owns study centers in London, Venice, and Vienna. If those choices seem too limiting, students can participate in programs from other universities at sites throughout the globe.

The University of Washington

Office of Admissions
Executive Director, Admissions and Records
University of Washington
1400 Northeast Campus Parkway
Seattle, WA 98195
(206) 543-5150
www.washington.edu

Total enrollment: 35,108
Undergraduates: 25,273
SAT ranges (Verbal/Math): 500-630 (V); 530-650 (M)
Applicants: 13,330
Accepted: 66%
Enrolled: 48%

Application deadline: January 15
Financial aid application deadline: December 15
Tuition: resident: $3,638/$9,842; non-resident: $12,029/$17,873
Core curriculum: No

Processing and Production

The University of Washington is proud of its status as a mammoth state research university. The university boasts a faculty of more than 3,500 and a total enrollment of more than 35,000 undergraduate and graduate students. The university has several factors to recommend itself to a prospective undergraduate. Many students select the University of Washington for its location in the beautiful, vibrant city of Seattle, and for in-state students the tuition is eminently affordable. Its prodigious size does have several advantages, including impressive library resources, several outstanding faculty, and ample extracurricular opportunities. And among state schools, the university enjoys a strong reputation, making future employment prospects brighter.

Still, radicalism abounds in both the social and intellectual life of the university; the high cost of living in Seattle continues to rise. (Seattle is now the second most expensive city on the West Coast, after San Francisco.) The undergraduate requirements are so diluted that one can easily graduate without ever having encountered any of the works or ideas essential to a well-rounded liberal arts education. "A student who wants to escape an education can do so just as easily as a student who wants to pursue one," says a professor.

The president of the UW since 1995 has been Richard McCormick, who, despite his doctorate in history, articulates a rather utilitarian attitude toward higher education. McCormick has described students (to the *Seattle Times*) as "knowledge workers" and has said that he hopes to find ways to cycle even greater masses of students through UW in an effort to "open much wider the doors of higher education in Washington state." One might question the value of a degree from an institution that seems to value production statistics above educational process. And even apart from the herd-'em-through mentality, the main priorities of the current administration do not involve traditional educational issues, but center instead on such items as minority rights, affirmative action, ethnicity requirements, and labor issues, according to students.

Academic Life: With No Direction Home

As with all else related to the University of Washington, the key word that describes the courses available to undergraduates is "big." Reviewing the mammoth University of Washington course catalogue can be a dizzying experience for many freshmen; gone are the early days in the late 1800s when the fledgling university had only one faculty member who was responsible for a curriculum consisting of "Latin, Greek, English, history, algebra, and physiology." Students can select from more than 130 majors and 1,800 courses each quarter. They would do well to seek out guidance and opportunities early on — and should not expect the help to seek them out.

"Even course descriptions are often misleading," says one student, who suggests that students "look for buzzwords" in such descriptions and combine such reading with recommendations from trustworthy upperclassmen and faculty. Students also recommend checking the course reading list for a clue to the course content and slant. "It takes a lot of initiative for a student to get a good education here," one student says. A professor says, "Classes are big, and too much of the teaching is done by visiting faculty or graduate students. Thus, it is not easy, unless one makes an effort to get to know our regular faculty."

All freshmen are given advisors, but these are seldom drawn from the ranks of full-time faculty members. A graduate student notes that graduate students are frequently hired as undergraduate advisors, and "handle almost all of the advising contact with students." One student had a friend who went through his first two years at the "U-Dub" (as UW is nicknamed) without ever talking to his advisor. "No one approaches you and asks, 'Are you interested in doing this?'" says an undergraduate. "You have to be self-motivated and keep your eyes open for opportunities."

As far as undergraduate requirements are considered, "they are meaningless," according to one student. "There are basically no undergraduate requirements," another says. Undergraduates must take twenty credits (usually four classes) in three different "areas of knowledge": The Natural World; Individuals and Society; and Visual, Literary, and Performing Arts (VLPA). Students must also select fifteen additional credits from any courses in these fields, for a total of seventy-five "areas-of-knowledge" credits. There are literally hundreds of courses that satisfy these requirements, and students are thus left to their own devices to try to craft an education. The so-called requirements outline an education the way the map of a large city limits your choice of routes; that is, hardly at all. Indeed, in a recent curriculum study of Washington state universities published by the Washington Association of Scholars and the Washington Institute Foundation entitled "Lowering the Bar: The Lack of Rigor in Core Curricula at Publicly-Funded Institutions of Higher Learning in the State of Washington," UW ranked the lowest of all state schools surveyed.

For the past several years, a vocal contingent of faculty, students, and administrators have been trying to implement a five-credit "diversity" requirement (which would do nothing to address the lack of rigor), but as of this writing no such requirement has been approved. Still, the university boasts several trendy, unconventional, politically correct programs: students can major in such areas as American ethnic studies, social welfare, society and justice, and women studies. There is an abundance of politicized or ephemeral courses, most of which fulfill "areas of knowledge" requirements. Students can satisfy part of the "Ideas and Society" distribution requirement, for instance, by taking "Feminist Legal Studies" through the society and justice department. The course considers topics like "women in prison, public assistance, the sex industry," according to the catalogue. Or they can take "Philosophy of Feminism" through the political science department, where they consider "intersections of the sex-gender system with other systems of oppression." In the American ethnic studies department, students can count "Race in the American University" toward the I&S requirement, wherein they will study the "entry to, and impact on, American universities by people of color." The same department offers, toward the same requirement, "Political Economy of Race in the United States," which "asks the question, 'Why do people accept unequal status?'"

A far less controversial, though equally ephemeral, choice in the I&S area might be "Scandinavia in World Affairs," in which students consider "Nordic security, international economic pressures, and global conflict resolution." Such a course would hardly give one a grounding in the basic principles of political theory, and students can graduate from the UW by taking just such a smattering of courses without ever encountering fundamental works and ideas. The university does nothing to guarantee basic knowledge, but rather lets students choose the (likely) unrelated specifics that fit their fancies.

"The more I come into contact with different departments, the more disappointed I become," says a graduate student. The university has strong engineering and science programs, and good humanities divisions include foreign languages and classics, according to students. "The language departments are universally reviled by those pushing a multicultural requirement," says one student. Which is probably a good sign. There are several good courses in history and political science, though these areas are increasingly dominated by professors espousing liberal ideology. "The level of commitment to teaching in the history department is, on the whole, pretty high," says one professor. "We have several professors who take it quite seriously." Excellent history professors include Jon Bridgman, James Felak, and R. Tracy McKenzie. One student advises exploring concentrations in various disciplines, such as Eastern European history or American history, though they should avoid any course emphasizing the history or theory of labor practices. One student expressed extreme disappointment with the economics department, and the recent death of noted classical liberal economist Paul Heyne has left that department bereft of conservative or libertarian voices. Even though most faculty at UW could be described as politically liberal, there are nonetheless "many political liberals who still take a traditional educational view," according to a student.

The university is also losing good faculty because of low salaries. Although faculty salaries are comparatively quite low, administrative salaries continue to rank among the highest in the nation, a disparity that has not gone unnoticed by UW faculty. Last year alone, four members of the classics department left UW for other institutions.

Because of the enormous size of its faculty, the UW is able to maintain an average undergraduate class size of thirty-five, but freshmen will still encounter quite a few teaching assistants. According to one student, the majority of lower-level classes are large lecture classes in which smaller, TA-run sessions meet once or twice a week. "Some TAs can be real duds," a student says. One student recommends taking courses in the summer, when classes are smaller and actually taught by a professor. But in many instances this is not possible, and students must bear with the large lectures as best they can. "In some classes I would have been better off getting the reading list and doing it on my own," says one undergraduate.

In order to minimize feelings of isolation or intimidation amongst undergraduates, the university offers both "Freshman Seminars" and something called "Freshman Interest Groups" (FIGs), which are courses targeted specifically to small groups of freshmen. Like the distribution requirements, these are also missed opportunities to provide students with a basic, shared educational experience. While the number of students involved in these experiences is intentionally kept low (no more than fifteen for the seminar and twenty-five for the FIG) and thus conducive to an intimate liberal arts learning environment, the content of the courses, though occasionally interesting or engaging, is not fundamental. An example of a freshman seminar is "Experiential Worlds: From Shared Space to Cyberspace." A student who selects the "Land and Sea" FIG takes a course called "Introduction to Fisheries Sciences."

There is a university Honors Program that admits 150 students each year, but again, there is no set curriculum, though the university describes the experience as a "rigorous, intensive course of study." Traditional-minded students might be at a disadvantage when applying to the Honors Program, as their views will be blatantly apparent in the Honors Essay required of all applicants, which has the following topic: "It is the year 2020, and you are a reporter with the *New York Times* whose assignment is to write an editorial addressing a major issue of your time. Write that editorial." Never mind that reporters aren't customarily in the business of writing editorials: *Wall Street Journal* readers probably need not apply.

In sum, the size of the UW is more of a disadvantage than an advantage for those wishing to pursue an undergraduate education in the liberal arts. One student cites the use of computer facilities on campus as indicative of the problem with such a large institution. "You have wonderful facilities," he notes, "but no one to instruct you." Basically, the UW "has all these resources, but no guide to using them. . . . The university is simply too big."

Political Atmosphere: The Grunge of University Life

It would not be much of an exaggeration to suggest that many activists at UW (both students and faculty) seem to engage in activism just for the sake of being rebellious. In one recent incident, for instance, the student paper, *The Daily*, printed a joke on affirmative action in its humor supplement. The irony of the cartoon was lost on several readers, and irate students and faculty staged a "newspaper burning" on campus, publicly torching copies of the paper. One assumes that they were appalled by the paper's lack of tolerance.

There is no help from university higher-ups when these situations arise. The university president gets low ratings from conservative and liberal students alike. "He's a real slick politician," one student says. "He won't take a stand and panders to everybody on anything."

One of the issues currently consuming the administration is how they can circumvent Initiative 200, a referendum that prohibits preferential treatment based on race, sex, color, ethnicity, or national origin in public employment, education, and contracting. Passed by state voters in 1998, the initiative has sent university officials, particularly those in the Office of Minority Affairs, scrambling to seek "creative" ways to maintain levels of minority enrollment at the university. "A big issue here is diversity, especially since the state's voters outlawed affirmative action," a professor says. "Diversity at the UW is defined very narrowly — it mainly means a few select ethnic groups, along with homosexuals."

Indeed, in a recent update on the effects of Initiative 200, the administration boasted that "for thirty years UW admissions decisions have taken race and ethnicity into account," and acknowledged that only two-thirds of the freshman class "gained entry on the basis of grades and test scores alone," while the other third "was reviewed and admitted on the basis of several additional factors, of which race or ethnicity was one." Commenting on life after the end of affirmative action, the administration warned, "the early signs are not good." In order to maintain the practice while attempting to stay on the sunny side of the law, the university plans to admit one third of the freshman class on the basis of a "supplemental process" that considers both academic standing and "personal factors" such as "economic and educational disadvantage, cultural awareness, overcoming personal adversity, a school adversity factor, and leadership awards and achievements." The university will couple this with an extensive "outreach" effort aimed at targeting potential minority applicants, recruiting at community colleges, high schools, middle schools, "and in some cases elementary schools."

While expanding access to education is no doubt an ostensibly laudable goal, the UW's disinterest in the academic component to admissions standards for minorities is not. Of course, the range of minorities targeted under such initiatives does not appear to extend to Asian-Americans, as they currently make up about one quarter of the freshman class. Indeed, in its published report on "Maintaining Diversity" after Initiative 200, the administration notes that enrollment by African American, American Indian, and Hispanic/Latino students was down from 20 to 40 percent, while Asian American enrollment increased six percent. The conclusion reached by the administration is that "these reductions dramatically underscore the need for aggressive and intensive activities of outreach and recruitment." The president has appointed a Committee on Diversity to "think creatively" about increasing the multicultural presence on campus. "Dealing with the immediate effects of Initiative 200 has been a difficult and painful endeavor for the University of Washington community," the report concludes.

The attempt to circumvent Initiative 200 is blatantly evident in the current college application, which includes revealing essay topics in the "Personal Statement" section required of all applicants. The section stresses that "the university wants you to discuss those aspects of your life that are *not apparent* from information provided on your application or high school transcript" (emphasis theirs). In addition to writing a description of an event in his life that reveals his character, a prospective student may add paragraphs on optional topics if they are "relevant to their life experience." These topics include: "1. Describe any personal hardships or barriers you've had to overcome and explain how they have affected your education," and "2. In the context of your life experience, describe your understanding of cultural differences, how this awareness was acquired, and how it has affected you." These questions clearly have less to do with admission to an institution of higher education than with the administration's determination to continue racial preferencing in its admissions.

Once on campus, students face a number of liberal student activist groups. Out of its four hundred student groups, there are "at least a dozen hard-left student organizations," according to one student, who numbers the College Anarchists and the Students for Global Justice among the worst. These groups frequently have a great deal of overlap in student membership, but the core members are strong and active, frequently combining to form "cells" that pursue particular issues, such as abortion advocacy, anti-sweatshop activities, or protests against the World Trade Organization. "I thought socialism was dead until I came to the U-Dub," one student says.

One of the recent burning issues on campus is the concern for "sweatshop" conditions in the garment industry. While one might wonder why young men and women who are supposed to be concentrating on their education would spend so much time and energy on fair labor practices, the answer is not hard to see when one realizes the fact that the UW is home to a radical Center for Labor Studies. "You can get history credit for organizing a union," one student complains. In May 2000, the campus chapter of Washington Students Against Sweatshops (WSAS), along with sixty-eight professors (including Margaret Levi, head of the Center for Labor Studies), petitioned the university president to join the Worker's Rights Consortium (WRC), an apparel industry watchdog and the brainchild of the United Students Against Sweatshops. The president, as of this writing, was waiting to make a decision on membership in the WRC until he obtained more information about the fledgling organization and instead proposed the creation of a "licensee advisory group" to advise the administration on affiliation with the WRC. "The UW administration will not take the high moral ground," Levi said in the pages of *The Daily*, while other faculty weighed in with their support for the WRC. In comments revelatory of the petitioners' ideological biases, a geography professor argued, "What we need is globalized institutions, to create a higher level of regulation," while a political science professor had these enlightening words on the subject: "Decision making over moral issues requires satisfying informational needs, and I think there is a threshold that has been passed for informational needs on this moral issue." The issue remains a highly sensitive one on campus, and one student predicts that "the administration will probably break contracts with Nike in the coming year" because of pressure from anti-sweatshop groups.

Indeed, UW appears to be an easy target for union recruitment. "The unions run summer training camps" for UW students, a student says. These one- or two-week-long, all-expenses-paid events are basically designed to indoctrinate young people into the wonders of labor unions, according to this student. The teaching assistants at the UW recently voted to unionize, a move that one conservative graduate student described as more about revolutionary tactics than "oppression of the worker," since salaries for TAs are about $26 per hour when one factors in health insurance and an excellent benefits package. Many UW student participated in the highly-publicized Seattle protests against the World Trade Organization. "Most of the students went down [for the protests] just out of curiosity," one student says, adding that "some came back rubbing pepper spray out of their eyes."

With all this going on, UW can thus be a hostile or lonely place for a conservative student. "A lot of students buckle or become isolated," says one such student. Still, there are certain "safe havens" for conservative students, including the campus chapter of the College Republicans. There is also a fledgling conservative paper, *The Right Turn*, which intends to publish monthly in the 2000-2001 academic year to provide a perspective not offered by *The Daily*.

Student Life: The Seattle Experience

Most University of Washington students commute from Seattle and nearby community, and only a small percentage of undergraduates live in residence halls. Both students and faculty complain about the rising cost of living in Seattle and their difficulties in finding affordable off-campus housing. Because of the commuter atmosphere, students may find it difficult to foster a sense of community on campus. As one student reports in the freshman admission packet, "I can walk through the middle of campus and not necessarily see anyone I know." (We're not sure why this is considered worth bragging about.) Many take refuge in fraternities and sororities, which serve as popular social outlets. "If I had to do it over again, I would have joined a fraternity," says an upperclassman. "They provide a sense of community." The university tolerates its vibrant Greek system, though since 1993 all residential fraternities and sororities have been asked to sign a "Recognition Agreement" with the university, committing to "certain well-defined rules," including a pledge to keep their residences alcohol-free.

Besides the fraternities and sororities, UW offers a number of on-campus housing options. Married couples or "same-sex domestic partners" may live in one of the university's family housing buildings. Each of the nine dorms is coed. Men and women sometimes live on the same floor in alternate rooms.

Seattle is a mecca for caffeine junkies: Starbucks Coffee and Seattle's Best are two popular coffee chains (though one no longer has to go to Seattle to find them), and most UW students are well-versed in the java jargon of "lattes," "grandes," and the like. Seattle is also the birthplace of grunge music, so the city and university have their fair share of youth in unconventional clothing and innovative forms of body piercing.

As one might expect from an institution of its size, athletics are an essential part of university life at the U-Dub. Football dominates the athletic scene: as one student notes with considerable understatement, "Huskie football up here is pretty big," and students can get tickets at the bargain rate of $60 per season. Men's baseball, men's and women's tennis, crew, and golf are all popular as well. Students praise the Intramural Activities Building, which has top-quality athletic facilities for the less accomplished athletes on campus.

For those with more elevated cultural tastes, numerous activities are available at both the university and in downtown Seattle. The university has a 1,200-seat theater in the Meany Hall for the Performing Arts, and the School of Drama also stages productions in three smaller theaters. Pike's Place Market, located on the pier in downtown Seattle, is a popular place to buy produce, fresh flowers, and crafts produced by local artists.

But the beautiful state of Washington calls many students away from the city during their free time. With the Cascade Range just out the back door, UW students tend to be ardent nature lovers. Students enjoy biking, hiking, camping, skiing, and other outdoor activities, and it is a well-kept secret that it doesn't rain in Seattle nearly as much as outsiders are led to believe. (New York, Atlanta and Boston all have a higher average rainfall.) The gorgeous Victorian port town of Vancouver, British Columbia, is easily within the realm of weekend possibilities.

The campus, although located in an urban area, is considered quite safe, and the university has a number of campus escort and shuttle services, as well as an impressive fleet of campus police. In 1995, the UW Police Department was awarded the Jeanne Clery National Safe Campus Award, and the university prides itself on its reputation for safety. As one professor notes, "The best thing about the UW is the location. Seattle is a wonderful town, and the campus, though in a city, is safe, has lots of greenery, and its buildings are readily accessible."

Yet for those interested in pursuing a liberal arts education, many of the advantages of studying at the University of Washington (natural beauty, resources, reputation, cost) are easily surpassed by the educational experience provided at smaller, more traditional institutions. As one student advises prospective undergraduates, "if they're interested in liberal arts, I would encourage them to go someplace smaller."

Washington University in St. Louis

Office of Admissions
Campus Box 1089
1 Brookings Drive
St. Louis, MO 63130-4899
(314) 935-6000
www.wustl.edu

Total enrollment: 12,088
Undergraduates: 5,403
SAT ranges (Verbal/Math): 610-700 (V); 640-720 (M)
Applicants: 17,100
Accepted: 34%
Enrolled: 24%
Application deadline: January 15
Financial aid application deadline: February 15
Tuition: $24,745/$32,469
Core curriculum: No

Introduction

Washington University in St. Louis was founded in 1853 by William Greenleaf Eliot to instruct youth in "the principles of morality and reverential regard for truth." The university was originally called Eliot Seminary but was renamed Washington University in 1869, meaning that it took its name prior to the founding of the state university with which it is so often confused. Originally located in downtown St. Louis, the university received an attractive hilltop campus west of the city as part of the planning for the 1904 World's Fair. The university now enrolls more than 5,000 undergraduates, with as many in graduate and professional programs.

Washington University is traditionally known for the strength of its undergraduate education, but the reasons for this are slowly being eliminated. The university appears to be in the throes of an identity crisis. No longer content to be an institution valued primarily for its teaching commitment and solid programming in the liberal arts, the university seems eager to assert itself as a high-profile research institution, garnering massive government and private grants to finance high-tech projects in the sciences and cutting-edge interdisciplinary programs in arts and sciences.

The university appears well-equipped to finance its transformation. Washington University has outlined four areas as "priorities for future development" as part

737

of its "Project 21" development plan: cancer research and treatment, biomedical engineering, visual arts and design, and plant sciences. Each of these four areas is receiving considerable support: a $35 million gift came in for the new Alvin J. Siteman Cancer Center, while plans are underway for a new Visual Arts and Design Center, a new hall for Biomedical Engineering, and the $75-million Donald Danforth Plant Science Center. In 1999, Washington University's top-ranking School of Medicine received the largest grant in the university's history: more than $218 million from the National Human Genome Research Institute to sequence portions of the human genome.

The publicity that accompanies such plans has excited rather than repelled prospective undergraduates, and the recruitment of "top" faculty and unprecedented building projects appear to have been successful in putting Washington University on the popular map. Applications have doubled in the last four years, and more than 17,000 students applied for 1,379 freshman positions in the incoming class of 1999-2000. But while its national status is not a question, its commitment to the practices of its past is.

Academic Life: Meet the New Curriculum, Same as the Old Curriculum

Washington University is divided into five schools: the College of Arts and Sciences, the School of Architecture, the School of Art, the John M. Olin School of Business, and the School of Engineering and Applied Science. The College of Arts and Sciences is home to more than three thousand undergraduate students, or roughly two-thirds of all undergraduates.

Beginning in the 2000-2001 school year, undergraduates in Arts and Sciences will have a new curriculum. The old curriculum consisted of the following distribution requirements: three courses in physical and life sciences, three courses in social and behavioral sciences, and three courses from among at least two of these areas: language study, art forms, aesthetic and ethical values, and modes of reasoning. Under the new curriculum, students will select from "clusters" of courses in four areas: language and the arts, natural sciences, social sciences, and textual and historical studies. There are also basic skills requirements in composition and quantitative reasoning. All told, it's hard to see any improvements inherent in the new system.

The university has had a diversity requirement since 1993, and that will not change under the new curriculum. Undergraduates in Arts and Sciences must take two courses from among three categories: minority groups in the United States, non-European societies outside the United States, and gender studies.

For those wishing to formally counter that requirement, Washington University has a minor entitled "Text and Tradition" that approaches something like a core of classes in the study of Western Civilization. Directed by an associate professor of classics and taught by a handful of faculty from English, philosophy, and classics, the minor entails a sequences of courses in "the basic texts in such diverse areas in Western history as paganism and Christianity, the rise of science, modern consciousness, and varieties of social theory." These courses also fulfill distribution requirements, so students can theoretically avoid more politicized course offerings in these areas. The sequence consists of the following six courses: "Classical Literature"; "Early Western History"; "The Emergence of the Modern Mind"; "Individuals, Community, and Institutions"; Puzzles and Resolutions"; and "The Great Economists." The conception is certainly a solid one, although, according to one student, some of the courses are taught from a perspective not necessarily favorable to the Western tradition, finding more to censure than praise.

Washington University also has a number of interesting interdisciplinary or specialized programs, including programs in "Literature and History," "History and Philosophy of Science," "American Culture Studies," and "Social Thought and Analysis." There is a special "problem solving" set of studies called the Hewlett Program, in which students can choose from among "Environmental Studies," "Earth and Planetary Sciences," or "Study of the Mind-Brain." The university also offers the "International Leadership Program," designed to give first-year students "a good introduction to international studies with key focus from the disciplines of political science, economics, anthropology, and history." All these alternative topics are subject to politicization; check them out with a trusted upperclassman before enrolling.

Prominent faculty at Washington University include novelist and literary philosopher William Gass, winner of the National Book Critics Circle Award; essayist Wayne Fields, author of *Union of Words: A History of Presidential Eloquence* (Free Press, 1996) and director of the American culture studies program; Gerald Early, author and director of the African and Afro-American Studies Department; and Douglass C. North, winner of the 1993 Nobel Prize for economic science. Robert Pollak, professor of economics, is a noted "game theory" expert who applies a "bargaining approach" to family interactions. He commented in a recent university magazine that "I hope to influence the way people think about important things — things such as price indexes, the family, and the environment." Pollak recently received an award from the Population Association of America for his "contribution to the mathematics of population growth" and his work on "fertility, marriage, household, and intergenerational relations."

There are still good faculty in such areas as classics, literature, and history, according to students, although even in these traditional disciplines one will encounter courses that emphasize the triad of race, class, and gender, such as the advanced seminar in "Modernism and Masculinity" offered through the history department. As one might expect, some departments, such as women's studies, are thoroughly radicalized; the purpose of that program is, according to departmental literature, to "emphasize the importance of gender and issues of dominance and subordination, frequently in relation to age, class, race, and ethnicity." The department offers such courses as "Masculinities: Challenge and Reaction," which studies such topics as "sexuality, fathering, male-female relationships, male-male friendships and homophobia, power and dominance." Still, there remain numerous courses and professors that steer clear of such gender politics.

The Olin Library is the university's main research library; this and twelve other departmental and school libraries house nearly three million volumes. Likely because of its creative writing program, the university also has an impressive special collection of the correspondence and manuscripts of several modern authors, including Elizabeth Bishop, Samuel Beckett, and Ford Maddox Ford.

Political Atmosphere: Learning by Example

In the past, Washington University has generally kept a low political profile; what campus activism did exist was conducted by a few faculty or graduate students rather than undergraduates. This appears to be changing, however, and increasing numbers of undergraduates are taking the time to protest everything from sweatshop conditions to the dwindling amount of green space on campus. Indeed, the last issue of the campus paper in the 1999-2000 academic year praised the rising rate of activism among undergraduates that year. Chronicling the political highlights of the year, the paper noted: "'The Vagina Monologues,' abortion-related demonstrations and events, the week of dialogue on race, protests over the paving of the Givens green space, the Campus Crusade/Philosophy Club debate, STOMP forums, opposition to the Amadou Diallo verdict, movements against sweatshops, the boycott of Starbucks, environmental demonstrations — whatever political standpoint these events represented, they all contributed to slowly making Washington University a forum for the exchange of ideas." The article acknowledged that campus activism was still largely the work of relatively few undergraduates, and encouraged these activists to recruit larger numbers: "It is their duty to approach their silent friends and enemies and produce assertiveness from the power of personal challenge," the paper claimed.

In February of 2000, the Conservative Leadership Association sponsored (along with the national organization Operation Save America) a pro-life rally in a campus area called Oak Walk. The demonstration was almost squelched by Associate Vice Chancellor and Director of Campus Life Jill Carnaghi because she was told there would be a speaker on the lawn near the Women's Building, and instead protestors lined the Oak Walk with signs and flyers. There was clear administrative antipathy to the group, but even the campus pro-life organization, Students for Life, was not fully supportive of the rally because of the use of graphic signs. The Students for Life president told the campus paper, "An event like that is something we are not comfortable with at this point." A month later, a newly formed Washington University student group entitled Students Against Gun Violence (SAGV) held a silent protest of gun deaths, lining the Oak Walk with 729 pairs of shoes to signify the number of gun deaths in Missouri. And in April, students planned to participate in a protest of Starbucks Coffee on "the Loop" to protest Starbucks' practice of buying coffee from large plantations in Guatemala rather than smaller plantations where the bean-pickers receive more profit. The university's students drink an estimated one thousand pounds of Starbucks coffee on campus each week, so the issue hits close to home. But when Starbucks agreed to offer "Fair Trade" beans at two thousand of its cafes, the student protestors backed down, though they hope to demand that the student food service purchase the politically correct beans as well.

All this is not to suggest that those with more conservative political, social, and religious views will not find any fellows on campus: there are active chapters of College Republicans, a pro-life organization, and Campus Crusade. Still, with an increasingly liberal faculty and administration, the university does not offer much institutional support for such viewpoints.

Why are students becoming more active in politics? It seems that some professors are teaching them to be.

The most publicized protest of the 1999-2000 academic year occurred off-campus and involved faculty rather than students. A prestigious downtown hotel, Adam's Mark, was to be the site of the Organization of American Historians (OAH) annual conference. But the Adam's Mark chain had recently lost a discrimination lawsuit, paying out $8 million in damages to hotel guests and four black colleges after allegedly racist behavior on the part of the company during a Black College Reunion in a Tampa Bay hotel. The OAH decided not to use Adam's Mark for their conference, and instead OAH member and Washington University Associate Professor of History Leslie Brown organized a protest, gathering two hundred professors and supporters at the downtown courthouse to demonstrate against the hotel's allegedly racist practices. "We brought pressure as historians — quiet, respectable people," Brown said. "Nobody ever thinks of us as being radical."

But perhaps they should. In an April 7, 2000 *Student Life* interview, Brown revealed that she is anything but "quiet" in her political views, and that her protest of the Adam's Mark was but a natural extension of previous activist engagements and a sign of things to come. "I'm sure that after this OAH conference, I'll be active in many more things," she said. Brown said that prior to coming to Washington University, she organized a group of students attend an early pro-choice rally, and that she has been "active in gay and lesbian issues." She told the interviewer: "I see myself as a political activist, but I take most of my politics to the classroom and do things through history."

Unfortunately, "taking politics to the classroom" and recruiting radicals from among the ranks of students is becoming increasingly frequent in Washington University classrooms. It should seem obvious that it dangerously compromises both the intellectual integrity and political neutrality of the institution's academic program. But as Brown said in her interview, "One of my beefs about the ways that we've taught history is that we teach this sort of great-man history and we've convinced a whole generation of students that they have to wait for a leader to come along and tell them what to do and that's actually not true. I see lots of folks with good ideas around race issues, around women's issues, around ethnic issues, around class issues, around environmental issues, and doing all kinds of stuff around campus, and I would like to see WU students do more in taking that enthusiasm and taking that organization off campus."

Even before the Adam's Mark protests, the university administration and faculty have traditionally been far more liberal than the undergraduate student body. Indeed, Washington University has offered full benefits to heterosexual and homosexual "domestic partners" since 1994, several years before other institutions began considering full benefits for gay employees. Chancellor Mark S. Wrighton, formerly a provost at the Massachusetts Institute of Technology and a scientist by training, appears to be interested in turning whichever way the political winds are blowing. In November of 1999, for instance, he voiced his support for the recently established Workers' Rights Consortium, a national student watchdog organization devoted to monitoring the working conditions of those who produce college apparel. Wrighton told the campus paper that "we don't have a policy in place for that assurance that our collegiate apparel is sweat-free." The campus chapter of Amnesty International urged the him to join the national movement and sponsored two Haitian sweatshop speakers in October of 1999.

Overall, Wrighton's administration is a bit more hip than that of his staid and esteemed predecessor Bill Danforth, Purina heir and brother of former Missouri senator John Danforth. Still, Danforth's influence looms large at Washington University, and his name and words are repeatedly invoked by Wrighton. It is largely due to Danforth's clout that Washington University was selected to host the October 17, 2000 presidential debate, the third time it has received such a commission.

Student Life: Gateway

Washington University's hilltop campus is in a lovely suburban part of St. Louis, just minutes from the downtown area. The main university architecture is neo-Gothic, replete with visually appealing arches, gargoyles, and other attractive features, and the university has put considerable funds in recent years into upgrading its older campus buildings, including the impressive Graham Chapel. The university abuts Forest Park, one of the country's largest municipal parks and home to the St. Louis Zoo, Art Museum, and History Museum. Students and faculty alike use the path that runs along the periphery of the park for jogging, cycling, and rollerblading.

Residential life presents numerous options for Washington University's undergraduates. New students live in one of nine residential colleges in an area on campus known as the South 40. Residential colleges consist of one to three buildings with a common community aspect — one college, for instance, features a faculty associates program, while another is a "healthy living" community featuring a program for healthy living and a quieter environment. Three new residential houses were recently dedicated, including the Howard Nemerov House, named for the late poet laureate and director of the university's writing program. All floors in the residential houses are coed, though there are separate bathrooms for each sex.

The Greek system is also thriving at Washington University. Nearly a quarter of all students join one of the university's twelve fraternities and six sororities, which are considered a focal point of campus social and leadership opportunities. Still, Greek life is not immune from controversy, particularly regarding the excessive partying many houses are said to indulge in. As one student said in the campus paper, "For the majority of students, especially for underclassmen who live on the South Forty, fraternities are a place to get drunk." In order to dispel that image, the campus chapter of Beta Theta Pi recently began its "Men of Principle" initiative, which included a vote to make all of its social events alcohol-free.

There is certainly no dearth of social opportunities at Washington University; indeed, by some accounts the university is well on its way to establishing a reputation as a party school. Popular events include "Thurtene," an annual carnival on the front lawn of campus complete with fair rides and concessions. There is also the raucous end-of-semester event appropriately entitled WILD (Walk In, Lay Down), which features bands and a day-long list of activities.

Off-campus, favorite local eateries include Ted Drew's frozen custard, the (original) St. Louis Bread Company, and various ethnic restaurants on a commercial strip of Delmar Avenue known as The Loop. St. Louis hosts a variety of social and cultural activities: students can watch the Cardinals, Rams, and Blues or hear the world-renowned St. Louis Symphony Orchestra at Powell Hall. Other attractions include the famous St. Louis Gateway Arch, which all but the most weak-kneed should ascend at least once.

Despite its almost prosaic setting, safety is a perennial issue for Washington University students, particularly those who live off-campus or frequent nearby "borderline" areas such as The Loop. Armed robbery of students is an occasional problem, though the vast majority of incidents have occurred off campus and the university takes a variety of measures to ensure student safety.

Athletics, both intramural and varsity, are a vital part of the social climate. Washington University is a founding member of the University Athletic Association (UAA) and the Bears compete against other NCAA Division III teams in sports like men's and women's basketball, cross country, soccer, swimming, tennis, and track and field, as well as women's volleyball and men's baseball and football. The women's basketball team is the pride and joy of the Washington University community, especially since an undefeated 1999 season that ended with its second consecutive NCAA Division II national championship.

Announcing his retirement as chancellor of Washington University in 1994,

Bill Danforth said, "I believe that great universities are to the modern world what gothic cathedrals were to the late Middle Ages, symbols of our ideals and of our deepest aspirations." The current academic architecture of Washington University, however, is looking more like a high-tech skyscraper or an eclectic Bauhaus structure than an ordered, purposeful cathedral. Only time will tell whether or not the university's current direction brings a decline in the quality of its undergraduate programs.

Washington and Lee University

Office of Admissions
Lexington, VA 24450
(540) 463-8710
www.wlu.edu

Total enrollment: 2,096
Undergraduates: 1,733
SAT Ranges (Verbal/Math): 630-710 (V); 640-720 (M)
Applicants: 3,057
Accepted: 36%
Enrolled: 42%
Application deadline: January 15
Financial aid application deadline: January 15
Tuition: $17,105/$22,005
Core curriculum: No

The Care and Feeding of Tradition

Tradition is something that requires preservation, but tradition can also preserve the institution that brought it to life. Such is the case at Washington and Lee University (W&L), a liberal arts school whose namesakes are matched only by Thomas Jefferson in the illustrious history and culture of Virginia.

The university was founded in 1749 as Liberty Hall, then saved from financial ruin in 1786 by a gift from George Washington. After more hard times during the Civil War, it was the reputation of Southern general Robert E. Lee that redeemed the school. Although Virginia's revered general was university president for only five years — from the end of the war to his death in 1870 — his brief tenure saw the institutionalizing of some of the cultural and intellectual traditions that to this day give W&L its reputation as a conservative institution. This legacy has kept the school from much harm, and kept its academic program rigorous.

This heritage survives today, though not completely intact. W&L went coed in 1985 after more than 230 years as a men's school. The honor system is still prized, but the speaking tradition — the practice, instituted in Lee's day, of greeting everyone one meets while walking on campus — is dissipated. The next several years will indicate just how much the university is willing to do to preserve its tradition, and how much the traditions can still do for it.

Academic Life: Distributed, but Not Widely

On paper, W&L's distribution requirements appear fairly standard, though perhaps more numerous than at some other schools. They include a composition component (usually one course or a proficiency exam), two years of a foreign language, two courses in literature, four courses in the humanities (fine arts, history, philosophy, and religion, with at least two of the areas represented), ten credits in science and math (including a lab), three courses in the social sciences, and five physical education units (plus a swimming proficiency test).

As at many universities, these requirements are too undirected to offer a traditional liberal arts education — even though the list of courses that meet them is somewhat delimited. However, two factors make W&L's requirements better than they might otherwise appear. First, the university offers very few politicized courses. Among the classes that can fulfill the distribution requirements, most are solid, survey-style courses not given over to the ideologies of the day. As one professor puts it, "There are not a lot of garbage courses in the distribution requirements." Another professor sees a "certain integrity to the general education requirements." This is due in part to the second factor: W&L students themselves. Having selected W&L largely because it is a liberal arts institution, they gravitate toward the more serious courses. "There are no tight requirements, but you have to work at finding alternatives" to the canon of Western history, literature, and philosophy, an alumnus says.

The students, however, disappoint at least one professor, who says less than half of them take the European history or American history introductory sequences offered in fulfillment of the general requirements. Neither course is mandated, either by the requirements or by the history department, which considers class standing the only prerequisite for upper-level history courses, and it is difficult to see how students can be prepared for further study in history without these classes. In the end, it is the student who determines whether he will take these solid introductory courses, though the intellectual tenor of W&L does much to induce him to give them a try.

Indeed, W&L tends to be fairly straightforward in its academic mission: it offers majors in most of the traditional disciplines, but there are no identity-style programs, at least not at the level of a full department. (Gender studies is not an official program, but a few courses are taught in this and other trendy subjects across several departments.)

The English department has an excellent reputation for rich courses and fine teaching. "It's not like departments elsewhere," an alumnus says, noting that race and gender studies are not stressed in the department. A professor in another department says the English faculty "take writing seriously, emphasizing teaching students how to write." He notes that English "is not overrun with political correctness, though there is some." Another professor says the English curriculum is "difficult" and "superior." A review of the course catalogue bears out these observations, as only a few politicized courses appear in the listing.

The School of Commerce, which includes economics, accounting, business management, public policy, and politics, has an even more difficult and challenging curriculum than English — it is perhaps the most rigorous division on campus. A professor describes it as "less vocational than most business schools," although he also notes that accounting, due in part to the nature of the discipline itself, tends to be more focused on the day-to-day technical skills required for a career than are other majors in the school. The other four departments in the school do a fine job of blending theory and practice — a rare mixture at most business schools, which tend toward the latter.

The presence of the politics department in the School of Commerce lends a certain sense of the humanities to the other business disciplines, a professor points out. This department has as its goal "educating citizens and providing a liberal arts education," including "an emphasis on the Founding Fathers and a solid foundation in American political thought." A colleague concurs, noting that the School of Commerce prepares "students for professional work and graduate school." However, a recent graduate says not all the professors are of the highest quality, and that most of the faculty in economics are "not out-and-out socialists, but they're not free-market-oriented either."

W&L's Journalism School (actually a department within the College of Arts and Sciences) is well regarded by those on campus as well as those who hire reporters. The natural sciences, according to one professor, are "in a renaissance" since the building of a new science center and the accompanying expansion of faculty research projects. The university's premed program has been outstanding in placing its graduates in medical school.

Other departments get mixed reviews from those on campus. The history department's reputation as "a conservative outpost" is "undeserved," according to one professor, since some of the most vocal feminists at W&L are professors in that department. However, it is pleasant to know that at a school named in part for Robert E. Lee, the Southern history and Civil War sections of the department are well taught. Perhaps the most politicized department at W&L is art history, where, according to a recent graduate, most of the professors have "very definite political agendas."

On a more positive note, there are professors here doing good work and excellent teaching who would be good directors of study across different fields of interest. They are: Mark Rush, Lucas Morel, and William Connolly in politics; Jefferson Davis Futch in history; Robert Johnson in math; and Suzanne Keen and Dabney Stuart in English. And in the Journalism School, the nationally recognized columnist Edwin Yoder also teaches on the Washington and Lee faculty.

Political Atmosphere: General Orders

The atmosphere at W&L is dominated by the two traditions instituted by General Lee himself more than one hundred years ago: the speaking tradition and the honor system. While the latter is still going strong, the former has begun to fade away. The speaking tradition holds that everyone — faculty, students, and staff — must acknowledge and greet each other as they walk through the campus. One professor reports that the "speaking tradition is 50 percent intact," and he attributes its partial demise to a growing divide between older, less politicized faculty and their more politicized, younger replacements. Indeed, as at many campuses, W&L has had its share of New Dealers who see traditional education, rather than political or social indoctrination, as their responsibility.

A professor says most of these older faculty members have died or retired in recent years. The result, for both W&L and many other institutions, has been increased politicization of the curriculum and campus life. As an alumnus says, "The faculty is liberal, and moving further to the left." At the same time, other professors report that the conservative tendencies of the students and the relative isolation of Lexington provide some motivation for the more overtly politicized faculty to seek positions elsewhere.

While the speaking tradition may be on the wane, campus observers report that the honor system is alive and well. It is entirely student-run: all regulations are written by a student committee, and all honor trials are conducted by a student panel. The "single penalty" provision of the system means that the panel has available only one choice — expulsion — if a student is found guilty of violating the code. Even before students arrive on campus, the honor system has the effect of weeding out those who would prefer not to live under its requirements, a professor says. And those who do attend W&L do so in part because of this rare code. The result is a system of "socially enforced norms," according to one professor. However, another professor believes compliance is just as often "driven by fear, rather than morality or ethics." Whatever the reasons, the result is "a certain element of peace, tranquility, and order," a professor says. Campus crime is negligible, and nearly all the cars, doors, and dorms on campus can be left unlocked. A long-standing campus story has it that a ten dollar bill was found on the floor in the library, tacked to a bulletin board near the building's entrance, and left unclaimed for weeks. Although no one interviewed for this guide could confirm the truth of that story, all agreed that it fit the category of "useful myth" in that it provided a standard to which all W&L students are expected to adhere. And in truth, it might very well have happened.

As uncomplicated as this approach to campus discipline might appear, there have been challenges to the student-run system. In the late 1980s and early 1990s W&L instituted the Confidential Review Committee (CRC), which was responsible for enforcing a new, vaguely defined speech code. Free speech advocate Nat Hentoff (who is politically liberal on most issues) called the CRC the "most tyrannical, arbitrary, most fanatically ideological body of its type" in a 1991 speech at W&L's Lee Chapel. Pressure from alumni and trustees, combined with court rulings that held similar codes at Michigan and Stanford to be unconstitutional, forced the administration to disband the CRC a few years later.

More recently, the student-run Intra-Fraternity Council, which regulates the Greek system on campus, has had its powers curbed by a new faculty board that oversees its operations. Many campus conservatives, including most of the editorial staff of the alternative newspaper, the *Washington and Lee Spectator*, view such moves as assaults on conservative students and their institutions, although one professor notes that binge drinking and hazing can hardly qualify as traditional gentlemanly behavior.

The *Spectator* itself was the target of radicals back in 1991, when two female junior professors wrote letters to its advertisers — on university letterhead — threatening a boycott of their businesses and accusing the *Spectator* (which receives no university funding at all) of being "blatantly racist, sexist, and offensively conservative." The *Spectator* demanded an apology from the university for allowing its stationery to be used in this manner, but its request was denied by Dean John Elrod, now the school's president. Both of the professors involved in this incident have since left the university, but no disciplinary action was taken against either for misuse of university resources.

Just as multiculturalism has yet to gain the ascendancy in W&L's curriculum, so too have ideological inserts into campus life been largely ignored by the majority in the university community. The W&L administration recently attempted to create a dorm with an environmentalist theme as well as an all-black fraternity, but both ideas died for lack of student interest. The administration's wishes have prevailed, however, during freshman orientation, where incoming students are given "sex kits" containing the usual paraphernalia and literature about "safe sex."

Though many faculty at W&L are active politically, the vast majority of students are not. There is no campus chapter of the College Republicans, and even the "Lee" in the university's name doesn't mean there are chapters of the Daughters of the Confederacy or the Society for the Preservation of Southern Heritage. There is a small gay and lesbian group, which is disproportionately noisy. But the only political activity for which W&L is noted is the quadrennial mock presidential convention, held every election year for the party out of power, which on most occasions accurately predicts that party's nominee.

Student Life: Fancy Dressers

Although student political life is fairly dormant, social activities, especially those involving Greek organizations, are numerous. "Fraternities drive the place," says one professor. Nearly 80 percent of W&L's male students are fraternity members. W&L only has a small number of sororities, but then again, it has only admitted women since 1985. One of the most famous campus events is the Fancy Dress Ball (dating back to 1908 or 1871, depending on which version of the story one believes), which brings together students, alumni, professors, and dignitaries for an annual party centered around a particular theme, chosen annually.

Social life apart from the fraternities is described by those on campus as "small," "congenial," "collegial," and "intimate." As far as extracurricular activities are concerned, one thing stands out immediately: W&L seems to be a veritable hive of journalistic activity. In addition to the *Spectator,* mentioned above, are two other newspapers, the *Trident* and the *Ring-tum Phi,* as well *Southern Collegian* magazine, cable television programming, and a radio station. Add to all that a chapter of Sigma Delta Chi, otherwise known as the Society of Professional Journalists.

W&L's preoccupation with words and using them well can also be seen in its successful Forensic Team and Debate Society. Other student organizations include the College Libertarians, G&L (the gay, lesbian, and bisexual group), InterVarsity Christian Fellowship, and the Environmental Awareness Committee.

All freshmen and sophomores are required to live in the dorms. These are all coed, with men and women housed on alternate floors.

Lexington is a small, picturesque town in the scenic Shenandoah Valley that is dominated by two colleges (the Virginia Military Institute is the other one), with the usual array of fast-food restaurants and shops but few other social attractions. Outdoor activities in the Blue Ridge Mountains are popular, and include winter sports at several nearby resorts. Also popular are trips to Washington, D.C., Richmond, and the many other colleges and universities located in central Virginia.

With a name like Washington and Lee, the university had little choice but to call its sports teams the Generals. The teams compete in twenty-three sports — twelve for women, thirteen for men — at the NCAA Division III level. More than 75 percent of the student body participates in a variety of intramural sports. Club sports include equestrian, lacrosse, rugby, softball, and water polo.

Wellesley College

106 Central Street
Wellesley, Massachusetts 02181-8292
(781) 235-0320
www.wellesley.edu

Total enrollment: 2,300
Undergraduates: 2,300
SAT ranges (Verbal/Math): 630-720 (V); 630-720 (M)
Applicants: 2,891
Accepted: 46%
Enrolled: 46%
Application deadline: January 15
Financial aid application deadline: January 15
Tuition: $23,320/$30,554
Core curriculum: No

The Hazards of Modernity

Wellesley is a highly selective college, nearly unparalleled in the types of connections and support it can offer to young women, with an idyllically beautiful campus designed by the architect of New York's Central Park in one of Boston's most pleasant suburbs. By all accounts, Wellesley's faculty are considered competent and rigorous.

"Wellesley is more than any group of people, faculty, and students, gathered at any one time," said Caroline Hazard, president of the college from 1899 through 1910. "It is the resultant power of the effort, the endeavor, the inspiration of all who have lived in it, and of those who shall live; a stream of life; a continuity of thought which has in it the elements of eternity."

Her reverence is characteristic of Wellesley College alumnae, but one cannot predict whether her thoughts on the college — especially the part about "elements of eternity" — as it celebrates its 125th anniversary would have been the same. In Hazard's day, the college was still strongly religious; now it praises multiculturalism and diversity as its religion. Bible course requirements are replaced with "race, religion, and ethnicity" classes.

But despite this trend, students who can discern truth amidst the rantings of liberal professors can get a great education from one of the most prestigious women's colleges in the country. The majority of students accepted at Wellesley were in the top 20 percent of their high school classes, and the college loves to boast about its student body, which, in addition to having top-quality students, is also said to be the most diverse on the East Coast. The college uses a need-blind admission policy and guarantees financial aid to anyone accomplished enough to get in, regardless of her ability to pay. In fact, Wellesley gets away with a lot of its multicultural follies precisely because it still manages in many cases to give excellent students an excellent education. Perhaps Hazard might still see the continuation of that "stream of life."

Academic Life: Dispatches from the Front

Wellesley's relentless focus on "diversity" is manifested in its notion of a core curriculum — distribution requirements, in reality. While its departments are, for the most part, acknowledged as the home of excellent teachers, and the general education requirements are fairly intensive, the school is infatuated with the interdisciplinary approach to education. A recent edition of the Bulletin takes pains to state that "central to the curriculum is the concept of diversity, the concept that the student should pursue a number of disciplines during her four years at the College." In practice, what such an emphasis tends to translate to is exemplified in one student's statement about her major: "I wanted to take two majors — sociology and women's studies — and people were absolutely happy to work together with me. I also wanted to write a thesis focusing on Jewish Studies, sociology, and women's studies, and teachers from the different departments made sure I had the resources to pursue it."

Thos resources include more than nine hundred courses, each designated as introductory, intermediate, or advanced. From these, students must select courses that fulfill the college's distribution requirements, which one professor approvingly calls "fairly stiff." The requirements call for students to take three courses in the areas of language and literature and visual arts. In another category, they pick one in social and behavioral analysis plus two from groups called epistemology and cognition; religion, ethics and moral philosophy; and historical studies. Then there are three courses (including a lab course) in natural or physical sciences and mathematics, problem solving, and computer science. Any of the distribution courses may be used to meet the college's requirement for one course in quantitative reasoning.

The laboratory courses in the latter groups are said to be difficult. "Wellesley's best known for the humanities, but I've found science wonderful here," a student says. In fact, those with a bent toward the sciences should take note: the same student (a biochemistry major) mentions that science graduates are "wanted everywhere" by companies and corporations. "They're snapped up because of their good lab experience."

Beyond the distribution requirements are a language requirement (proficiency at the fourth-semester level). This requirement was recently retained by the college, though not without challenge, according to a professor. Since many Wellesley students come from rigorous secondary-school backgrounds, these students may fulfill the requirement by completing one "unit of language study above the second year college level"; one can also fulfill the requirement with sufficient scores on either an achievement or an advanced placement test.

There is also a writing requirement, fulfilled by the only course required by name, Writing 125. But even that course is not the same for all students. Departments offer their own versions of it or combine with other departments to offer shared sections. Despite this, most Writing 125 courses are thankfully serious, solid, and noncontroversial. The Writing 125 philosophy course focuses, amazingly, only on Plato and Aristotle, and a political science section is "a study of political conflict and consensus through comparison of democratic and authoritarian systems . . . designed to teach critical writing on political topics." Even more "modern" alternatives such as "Writing about Science" and "Great Essays" still require serious reading. There are, however, a couple of lightweight options: in the catalogue entry for "Women and Memoir: A Revision of Life," appended to a reading list that includes Mary McCarthy and Alice Walker, is the disturbing addendum that "students will have the opportunity to use their own journal entries as raw material for critical essays." That would seem to lessen greatly the opportunities for learning critical objectivity. Then there are the standard movie courses that have become ubiquitous college fare; "Strong Women in Film" is one Wellesley-spun version of these.

Far and away, though, the most controversial part of the distribution requirements is the "multicultural" requirement, which was instituted in 1990 — around the time Stanford was beset by marchers chanting that Western culture "had to go." Wellesley's "multicultural" requirement has since undergone a major overhaul. The original requirement stated that students had to take one course primarily concerned with "1) the peoples, cultures, and societies of Africa, Asia, Middle East, Oceania, or Latin America and the Caribbean; or 2) the peoples, cultures and societies of North America that trace their historical origins to these areas; or 3) Native American peoples, cultures, and societies." The new statement of the requirement mostly keeps the first list of world cultures, but changes the last two to read this way: "2) a minority American culture, such as those defined by race, religion, ethnicity, sexual orientation, or physical ability, and/or 3) the processes of racism, social or ethnic discrimination, or cross-cultural interaction." The student chooses the course, and must write a statement justifying her choice.

Apparently, the way the original requirement was phrased bothered members on both the left and right sides of the Wellesley community. For one thing, an enormous number of courses fulfilled the requirement, including such unlikely offerings as "Introduction to the Hebrew Bible/Old Testament." Furthermore, as a 1996 article about the issue in the *Chronicle of Higher Education* noted, some professors were not satisfied with the spectacle of students "taking courses about their own cultures." "People from Asia didn't need to be taking courses on Asia," said one professor involved in the "big curricular revision" a couple of years ago. Even the new compromise version hasn't been popular across the board — faculty members with varying ideologies spoke against it, both because it is politically correct and also because, given the vast increase in multicultural approaches in most departments, it simply isn't needed anymore. The catalogue states that the requirement must be reviewed by Wellesley's Academic Council no later than 2004.

The fact that the multicultural requirement is controversial at all should be seen as an encouraging sign. Thought politicization among the various departments at Wellesley is widespread, those on campus say that it is not extreme. Even Africana studies, which produces "some absolutely radicalized nonsense," according to one longtime Wellesley observer, still has "some good courses." In English, a hotbed of trendiness at many colleges, "most of the courses are on the usual stuff," a faculty member notes; indeed, Wellesley, unlike many colleges today, still requires a Shakespeare course — as well as two courses in literature written before 1900 — of its majors. Political science is known for having some politicized faculty members, but as a whole the department lacks a radical tone. "There are certainly plenty of moderates," a faculty member assures, if not exactly conservatives. One solid conservative is Mary Lefkowitz, the Andrew W. Mellon Professor in the Humanities and an esteemed faculty member in the departments of Greek and Latin. Lefkowitz is widely acknowledged to be one of the most respected classics scholars in the world, and in recent years her efforts as a classicist have placed her in combat against spurious scholarship from Afrocentric scholars. She is the author of critically acclaimed 1996 book *Not out of Africa: How Afrocentrism Became an Excuse to Teach Myth as History.*

At the other end of the scale is, for example, is Tony Martin, a professor of Africana studies who wrote *The Secret Relationship between Blacks and Jews,* a book that purports to uncover the major role that Jews had in promoting the African slave trade. The book is published by the Nation of Islam. According to the *Chronicle of Higher Education,* "many critics view [the book] as anti-Semitic." The chairman of the Africana studies department has been quoted as saying that "the book is both anti-Semitic and bad scholarship, not because it suggests Jews had a role in the slave trade, but because its conclusions about Jews are politically driven." Martin's experience following publication of that book is discussed in his next book, *The Jewish Onslaught: Dispatches from the Wellesley Battlefront.* In it, he talks about alleged attacks on his writing by Lefkowitz. The official attitude of Wellesley to all this instability has been embarrassment, and a recognition that, as Wellesley president Diana Chapman Walsh said, "this is the kind of challenge facing many American colleges and universities as they start down the road to multiculturalism."

In addition to Lefkowitz, outstanding professors at Wellesley include Jonathan Imber in sociology; Marshall Goldman and Karl "Chip" Case in economics; Edward Stettner and Marion Just in political science; and Andrew Webb in biological science.

Wellesley has two major assets that enhance its academic programs: a distinguished alumnae network that is nonpareil among American colleges, and access to seemingly unlimited funding sources, both internal and external. Among the many programs for students is the Washington Public Service Summer Internship Program for junior-year students, which offers "ten-week internships, including a living expense stipend and housing in local university dormitories." Given that the first lady of the United States and now senator from New York (Hillary Rodham Clinton), secretary of state (Madeleine Albright), and novelist Judith Krantz are all Wellesley alumnae, it would seem that the internship offers a likely lead-in to a first job, and certainly a plethora of networking opportunities. The Stone Center for Women, Hestia Institute in Wellesley, and the Wellesley Center for Research on Women also increase opportunities for the college's students, through research opportunities and networking.

Wellesley is also proud of its Elisabeth Kaiser Davis Degree Program, which allows women beyond typical college age to pursue degrees there. The program instills the notion that it's never too late to learn, and the older women are usually mentors to the younger students.

For those students interested less in personal advancement and more in community outreach and service, Wellesley has "a long-standing tradition of reaching out into the world beyond the College," and even offers Service Opportunity grants so that they can afford to spend summers taking advantage of "unpaid community and public service positions."

Wellesley offers the Center for Work and Service, which helps students find paid jobs and community service opportunities. One thing the college did to celebrate its 125 years was "A Day To Make A Difference," one day of community service. More than four hundred students, faculty and staff and sixty-five alumni groups across the nation participated. The local chapters went to the Boston Food Bank, helped clean a women's homeless shelter, and cleaned up a couple of beaches on the north shore of Boston.

Political Atmosphere: A Reasonable Conclusion

As at most other elite colleges today, campus debate is dominated, a source close to the Wellesley community complains, by "perceived issues of racism or sexism, which sometimes I think are overreactions to people's stupid mistakes." A few years ago someone on campus wrote a racist graffito on the dry-erase board of an African-American student, which led to escalating campus controversy over the issue, rather than, one faculty member complained, just "saying 'this is stupid.'" This same faculty member spoke approvingly of how the faculty group enlisted to look into the issue handled it. The group was chaired by Marcellus Andrews, an African-American economist, who rendered the very reasonable conclusion that, in the words of another faculty member, "You can't infringe upon free speech," no matter how misguided.

Most of all, it appears, members of the Wellesley community would like to maintain the fragile peace that has been effected in the past years, and are amenable to reasonable dialogue — for the most part. Unlike at other institutions, where grandstanding and publishing put one on the fast track, tenure at Wellesley is based on good teaching as much as research. Faculty from across the political spectrum tend to respect the scholarship and teaching of others, even when they do not agree with them. There is sensitivity training at Wellesley, but, one faculty member says, "people are getting impatient" with that kind of thing.

True to its multicultural mission, though, Wellesley does manage to provide lots of its resources to its "mosaic of faces." The Slater International/Multicultural Center sponsors programs for a number of groups, while other groups focus on African-American, Latina, and Asian students. African-American students are headquartered at their own Harambee House, whose name comes from "the Swahili word for 'working together.'" The student organization for African-American students is called Ethos; it has its own choir, dance troupe, and theater. There is a chapter of the historic black sorority Alpha Kappa Alpha, which includes students from MIT and Harvard. Among the religious organizations, there is a Ministry to Black Women and a pagan student club. As might be expected, Mezcla and Alianza center on the Latina communities and give particular attention to human rights issues, both in the United States, as in the case of migrant workers, and "in Central and Latin America."

There are even a couple of conservative organizations. There's the Wellesley Republicans, and even the Wellesley Alliance for Life, a companion group to the Wellesley Women for Choice. But while accepted, conservative organizations tend to have a harder time of it than their more progressive peers because "they have a great deal of trouble finding faculty willing to be their advisors," according to one faculty member. An alternative student publication called *Counterpoint* is put out as a joint venture between Wellesley and MIT, but while it tends to be more open than the *Wellesley News* (the official student newspaper), it plays the role of general gadfly rather than a forum of specifically conservative opinion.

Student Life: Sisterly Support

One of the features of Wellesley about which both faculty and students seem to agree enthusiastically is the availability of support networks for the students, and the unusually close relationships that students appear to have with faculty members. Whereas the atmosphere at many colleges, even selective ones, can be somewhat fearsome and alienating, Wellesley faculty and students alike maintain a sisterly watch over one another. Each of the college's twenty-one residence halls has its own governing structure and a "house associate, generally a faculty or staff member." One faculty member fondly recalls being amazed recently when a student was in the hospital for surgery, "at how well the machine worked" in people's willingness to get the student's assignments to her and help out in any way they could. "When I've taught elsewhere," the same faculty member maintains, "if students are in trouble, there's no one to call."

A number of campus traditions are localized in the dormitories. "Each dorm has a long tradition of parties and get-togethers with students from other Boston-area colleges," according to the campus newletter *Voices of Wellesley.* A small community atmosphere is preserved as well, with first-year students sharing both dorms (if not rooms) and meals with members of the other classes. Despite the fact that the college is single-sex, Wellesley women are reported to have an extensive social life with men from the plethora of colleges around Boston, and men are welcome visitors on campus. And, unlike almost every other college in America, one faculty member notes incredulously, "There's no drinking problem. It's the most sober campus." Every now and then, there is a drunk in public citation, but Wellesley has little crime beyond the occasional stolen bicycle.

Wellesley has more than 170 student organization, including such unlikely options as a Rugby Club and the amusingly named Archaeologists Anonymous. There are three a cappella singing groups, one of which includes students from MIT; a glee club; an orchestra; and choirs and jazz groups. Also available are the Dead Serious Improvisational Comedy Troupe, a student-run radio station, and a college dance troupe.

A full range of opportunities exists for students to get involved in college government, and, in a similar vein, a number of political and preprofessional societies help them tap into Wellesley's alumnae network. The fact that Wellesley is located in one of the most prosperous suburbs in the United States might have something to do with that. There's a surfeit, however, of organizations under the heading of "ethnic/cultural awareness."

One persistent but compelling feature of extracurricular life at Wellesley is the "society houses." These buildings are not residences, but have dining facilities and social spaces where groups sponsor lectures and gatherings. Shakespeare House, obviously, is for "students interested in Shakespearean drama," and there are three others with Greek names that focus on art and music, "modern drama," and "intelligent interest in cultural and public affairs." Students may join society houses as early as the second semester of their freshman year. These organizations do not receive funding from the college.

Wellesley provides a full range of standard athletic options, such as NCAA Division III basketball, volleyball, cross-country, and tennis. The college is especially proud of its crew team, established in 1876.

Wesleyan University

Office of Admissions
237 High Street
Middletown, CT 06549
(800) 653-3000
www.wesleyan.edu

Total enrollment: 2,950
Undergraduates: 2,745
SAT ranges (Verbal/Math): 610-720 (V); 610-700 (M)
Applicants: 5,727
Accepted: 32%
Enrolled: 38%
Application deadline: January 1
Financial aid application deadline: February 1
Tuition: $25,130/$31,760
Core curriculum: No

From Methodism to Multiculturalism

Wesleyan was founded in 1831 by the Methodist Church to educate ministers. Recruitment of non-Methodist scholars began in 1888 with Woodrow Wilson, who taught history and economics there for two years before moving on to Princeton. Today Wesleyan offers instruction in forty-one departments and programs and fifty major fields of study. Students may choose from about more than nine hundred courses each year and may be counted upon to devise, with the faculty, some 1,500 individual tutorials and lessons.

While Wesleyan's high selectivity in admissions, productive faculty, and superb library justify its reputation as one of the best small liberal arts schools, it has come a long way from its Methodist origins. Indeed, Wesleyan has become a shrine of modern academic fads such as multiculturalism, racial and gender preferences, political correctness, gender studies, and radical environmentalism. Which is a shame, as the university also offers many fine courses taught by dedicated professors to small groups of students, many of them extremely bright.

All in all, Wesleyan is a college rich in physical and intellectual resources, but it has allowed some of these resources to go to waste. The campus has become deeply politicized and divided. Although a largely pristine education in the classics can still be found in several of Wesleyan's academic programs, the leftist political atmosphere is likely to make most conservative, moderate, or non-political students uncomfortable. Moreover, the embrace of sexual promiscuity and perversion seen in many of Wesleyan's courses and in certain sections of the library may send chills down the spines of many traditionally minded parents and their children.

Academic Life: The Wesleyan Method

Wesleyan proudly espouses the notion that students should direct their own education without the burden of course and curriculum requirements. Wesleyan's vision of higher education also emphasizes self-discovery over knowledge and instruction. According to a report by the administration, "The opportunity for students to engage in research and discovery becomes all the more valuable when learning capabilities rather than content will be the most abiding legacy of a liberal education."

Thus, Wesleyan has no core curriculum. Students need not master any particular body of knowledge. Instead, all students must, in their first two years, take two courses in each of three areas, all from different departments: social and behavioral sciences, humanities and the arts, and natural and mathematical sciences. Over the following two years, one more course in each of these three areas must also be completed.

Freshmen take special classes in the First-Year Initiative Program (FYI) that are designed to improve their writing and rhetorical skills. Taught in small seminars, most of which contain fewer than twenty students, FYI's are "entirely optional," although "students are advised to consider taking at least one of these courses during their first year," according to the catalogue. There is no English composition requirement because "writing skills are emphasized and developed throughout the curriculum."

Wesleyan boasts an outstanding eleven-to-one faculty-student ratio, and 63 percent of all courses have twenty or fewer students. Although most of the faculty are well published, this ratio indicates a strong commitment to undergraduate teaching.

Some of the better departments include history, medieval studies, art history and architectural history, theater, classics, molecular biology and biochemistry, biology, and physics. Wesleyan also claims a strong literary tradition, something that is embodied in the university press and the prestigious summer workshop for writers. The school's most famous literary figure is Pulitzer Prize winner Annie Dillard, who teaches an occasional course in the English department. Other standout faculty members include Martha Crenshaw, Marc Allen Eisner, and John E. Finn in government; Stephen Crites in philosophy; John Bonin in economics; and Joseph Reed and Richard Slotkin in English. Peter Rutland, who teaches Russian and Eastern European studies, is also notable for his books on Soviet economy entitled *The Myth of the Plan* and *The Politics of Economic Stagnation in the Soviet Union.* While these Soviet policies probably remain overwhelmingly popular on the Wesleyan campus, Rutland offers students another perspective.

Wesleyan offers two interdisciplinary programs that combine a seminar/colloquia setting with dedicated professors. Indeed, the programs offered by the College of Letters and the College of Social Sciences are so good that one might call them the true intellectual heart of the university. Although not immune to political correctness, the former is an excellent choice for the ambitious student who wishes to pursue studies in the humanities. It is, according to the catalogue, an "interdisciplinary major program for the study of Western literature, history, and philosophy. The core of the program is a series of five colloquia designed to acquaint students with works of literature, history, and philosophy in the ancient world, the Middle Ages and Renaissance, the 17th and 18th centuries, the 19th century, and the 20th century." The catalogue description says, "Our general goal is the cultivation of 'the educated imagination.'" Sophomores who have completed at least two years of work or its equivalent in a foreign language may apply, and all students must spend a semester abroad studying the language they select.

The interdisciplinary program of the College of Social Sciences is also a very attractive major. Like the College of Letters, it requires students to pursue their studies in a structured academic setting.

Both of these colleges deserve serious consideration by students, as they go a long way toward maintaining true academic integrity at Wesleyan. They offer small classes, intense interaction with faculty, and a coherent approach to the subjects under study. They are indeed colleges within a college.

Despite the administration's fondness for chic studies, many Wesleyan faculty members offer rigorous coursework in traditional and important areas of study. Students wishing to avoid the more politicized elements of the curriculum should peruse the course offerings and find a trusted faculty member upon whom they can rely for advice. Wesleyan has a great deal to offer the serious student in spite of the best efforts of the administration and its favored faculty members: excellent facilities, dedicated professors, a fine library, and small classes.

Departments and programs with a large number of politicized courses include African-American studies, American studies, queer studies (a subunit of American studies), and women's studies. The Center for Humanities, an interdisciplinary program that offers a collection of the most politicized courses from departments across campus, is also a magnet for the propagation of Marxism and feminism.

Among the most politicized (or just plain bizarre) courses are:

- American Studies 180, "Critical Issues in Contemporary Society: Approaches to Radical Change." According to the catalogue, this course "confronts the traditional character of teacher-student relations by rotating teaching responsibilities. The course challenges the hierarchy, oppression, and exploitation in modern American culture with a variety of critical analyses and alternative proposals." The class is divided into groups of eight to twelve students, who with the help of "facilitators" then "plan and read the course's agenda." Yes, they really call it a course agenda. Agenda items may include "current trends in leftist thought, including anarchism, ecology, feminism, Marxism, and ethnic perspectives," according to the catalogue. Furthermore, the catalogue says, "the class will deepen its understanding of these views with an analysis of sexuality, heterosexuality, gender, family, race, community, society, and liberalism. The course integrates the personal with the political. Projects have included guerrilla theater, community organizing, and campus activism."

- College of Letters 290, "Pornography: Writing of Prostitutes." Obviously a course without which no liberal education would be complete. The catalogue says: "This course investigates pornographic literature as a body of discursive practices whose 'materials,' according to culture critic Susan Sontag, comprise 'one of the most extreme forms of human consciousness.' The pornography we study is an art of transgression which impels human sexuality toward, against, and beyond the limits which have traditionally defined civil discourses and practices. . . . Our examination . . . includes the implication of pornography in so-called perverse practices such as voyeurism, bestiality, sadism, and masochism, and considers the inflections of the dominant white-heterosexual tradition by alternative sexualities and genders, as well as by race, class, age, and mental and physical competence."

- Women's Studies 248, "Race, Sex and the History of Normal People." Apparently, the Inquisition, religions, and governments throughout history made no judgments on what constituted normal. For as the course description for this course tells us, "'Normal People' have existed only since the last century. The course considers how scientists have historically related the idea of 'normal' to notions of the superior, good, beuatiful [*sic*], healthy and natural in the context of struggles for power by dominant and marginalized communities. Themes, involving questions of equality and inequality, inclusion and exclusion, include: scientific theories of essential 'race,' 'sex,' and 'culture'; conceptions of the body as physically or mentally healthy or diseased; and classifications of normality and abnormality concerned with sexual behavior."

Political Atmosphere: Peep Show

The politics of Wesleyan may be more left-wing than any other American campus. Perhaps the best evidence of this can be found in the library of the "Queer Resource Center." There, students can watch or check out videos including "How to Female Ejaculate," "Goat Boy and the Potato Chip Ritual," "Dress up for Daddy," "Female Misbehavior," "Party: A Safer Sex Videotape for Black Gay Men," "Macho Dancer," "Stop the Church," and "Two in Twenty: A Lesbian Soap Opera."

In addition to video pornography, the Queer Resource Center library serves up a number of highly provocative books. In addition to their catalogue of titles on

AIDS and gay liberation, the library houses a section entitled "Erotica." Its offerings include *Erotic Naiad, Noir/Black Erotica, Flesh and the Word,* and *Singlehanded.*

In the event the videos and books are not sufficiently stimulating, the Queer Resource Center Web site assures "free condoms and lubrication are available."

Of course, the Queer Resource Center is only the beginning of gay and lesbian, and even transgendered, programs at Wesleyan. The "Queer Alliance" is "a student group that plans queer-related social and political activities to address issues on campus and in the world." The Wesleyan Alliance "is a group of students, faculty, staff, and administrators committed to examining and understanding how social conditioning of gender and sexuality as well as sexism and homophobia affect our lives and relationships. The Allies are trained as nonjudgmental and supportive listeners for people wishing to share their experiences or discuss their issues regarding gender and sexuality."

There is also a "queer positive theme house" on campus in which gay, lesbian, and transgendered students live and host parties. "Queer Youth Outreach" is a group through which Wesleyan students transmit their agenda to area high schools. The organization states that it was "formed to dispel stereotypes and ignorance in Connecticut high schools over queer issues." The group has "participated in and coordinated with area youth groups, queer youth conventions, and hosted youth events on campus. "

But gay activism is only one of the many left-wing causes that dominate the Wesleyan campus. The very active student organization E3 (Earth, Equality, Education) organized a campus rally against the World Trade Organization (WTO) to coincide with the riot in Seattle. In the minutes of their meeting, the group's secretary waxed, "I went in to work this morning and as soon as I got there my supervisor said that she saw me on the news and wanted me to explain the whole issue to her. I did, and now she thinks the WTO sucks."

Another member of the group described her experiences in Seattle in what she described as a poem. She spoke and wrote, in part:

> wto bad not democratic, transparent, nice is dictatorial, secretive, mean fucks over workers, environment, 3rd world peoples, indigenous peoples, butterflies and other things that breathe oxygen because only cares about - profit- for big corporations . . . . . protestors - sitting peacefully - pepper sprayed by heartless police. . . . Action Revolution a better world for All. that means you! pretty cool, huh.

Let's all be thankful that E3 makes no claim that it is a literary group. Instead, in addition to swooning over others' juvenile delinquencies, E3 has also launched a crusade against the automobile. The group "put fake tickets on cars fining people for all the external costs of driving an automobile." They also put banners up on campus promising to push a sports utility vehicle off a cliff if enough people committed to not driving.

In the Spring 2000 semester, a coalition called "Justice for Janitors" formed to clamor for higher pay and better treatment for the custodians and other workers at Wesleyan. The administration caved in to most of the group's goals by agreeing to a minimum total compensation package for all workers of at least $10.20 per hour, full health insurance for all part-time workers, and job protection for employees of a contractor when Wesleyan changes contractors.

Perhaps most revealing were the open letters of support for "Justice for Janitors" sent by various student and faculty groups to the school president. Wesleyan Latino student group La Casa weighed in:

> We . . . promise you that we will not stop until Wesleyan understands that the Latino community is a force that will be reckoned with. Our existence and our strides will not be taken in vain. Until you recognize that a bland admissions process and financial aid is not enough to keep us complacent with whatever policies you are implementing, we will not stop. The Latino community will never be complacent. The janitors are a part of our community. You have no idea what these hard working people, and we recognize them as people, how much they contribute to this institution. We will not tolerate the treatment of this important part of the Latino community and the Wesleyan community with any less respect than what we give you. If it weren't for them, you would be cleaning your own facility with your own hands. Racism and prejudice come in many forms. These days they can be more subtle and more institutionalized. Surely you do not believe that they are long gone nor that the present situation is not an example in itself?

A leader of the student group Ujaama opined, "This situation embarrasses us to a great degree and also challenges the integrity of this institution, displaces the students of color on this campus, and clouds Wesleyan's own vision of diversity as we move into the next millennium." Another Latino activist student group, Ajua Campos, commented:

> How are we, as Latino students, to feel pride towards our community, when this institution continues to allow poverty wages for Latinos? How are we to feel unified when the ideologies of this institution perpetuate racial hierarchy in our community? How are we to feel strengthened, when this institution does nothing to alleviate the situation for its lowest paid employees?

The faculty of the American studies and Latin American studies departments were not about to be left out of this crusade. Their joint message blustered, "Respect for the dignity of all labor has a strong tradition in American studies and Latin American studies programs throughout the hemisphere. . . . We, the undersigned faculty and staff urge the administration to provide the resources necessary to provide equal pay for equal work, and to cease any impediment to the unionization of workers who so desire it."

Wesleyan's political atmosphere is also reflected in its segregated student housing system. There are five special interest (i.e., ethnic) residential houses, including the Asian/Asian-American House, the Intercultural House, Malcolm X House, and the Women of Color House.

In 1996, a controversy arose when very few students chose to live in the Malcolm X House. As a result, the administration allowed nine of the dormitory's rooms to be entered into the campus-wide housing lottery, and they were filled by white students. More than four hundred students launched a protest, observing ten minutes of silence "to symbolize the silencing of the students of color community." They demanded an official policy reserving the house for black students. What could have been a welcome opportunity for close and fulfilling interaction among the races fell prey to a reactionary leftism that rejects the integration so forcefully advocated by liberals in past decades.

Student Life: Connecting in Connecticut

Middletown is a mostly blue-collar community of about forty-three thousand. It is very much a slice of the "old economy," as it is replete with boarded-up factories and businesses. (Crime too, both on and off campus, is not as uncommon as one would like.) However, there are still many shops and eateries for students. New Haven and Hartford are about thirty minutes away, and New York and Boston are each two hours by car or longer by a combination of buses and trains.

Among the student organizations at Wesleyan are about a dozen fraternities and sororities, the Black Women's Collective, the InterVarsity Christian Fellowship, Step One (A Confidential Resource for Students Questioning Their Sexuality), Eight to Eight confidential student listening program, five a capella groups, numerous theater and improv societies, Clinic Escorts (provides escorts for women going to abortion clinics), Student Alliance to Reform Corporations (STARC), Wesleyan Cannabis Coalition, Wesleyan Democrats, Wesleyan Republicans, Wesleyan Scrabble Club, and Wesleyan Knitting Club. Some of these actually have a good reason to exist.

The student body is made up of approximately 2,700 full-time undergraduates and 620 graduate students, including part-time students in the Graduate Liberal Studies Program, which has its primary enrollment in the summer. Only 6 percent of students hail from Connecticut, but the largest group comes from all around the northeastern U.S. All told, students at Wesleyan represent forty-three states and twenty-five countries.

Freshmen are housed in residence halls and houses. Some housing is single-sex, although most is coed. Clark Residence Hall, next to the Olin Library, is reserved exclusively for freshmen. About 95 percent of the undergraduate student body lives on campus, and housing is guaranteed for all four years.

Wesleyan pledges to meet the demonstrated financial need of all students it admits, although, like almost all colleges, parents' and applicants' appraisal of their financial need often differs from the evaluation made by financial aid officers.

Athletic facilities at the school are stellar, thanks to the Freeman Center, completed in 1990. The $22-million complex offers just about any diversion one could imagine, including a 25-yard pool, a 5,000-square-foot exercise room, and an ice-skating arena. About seven hundred of the university's 2,700 undergrads participate in intercollegiate competition on Wesleyan's Division III varsity teams — fourteen for men, fourteen for women, and one coed (golf). Popular varsity sports at Wesleyan include baseball, basketball, football, ice hockey, lacrosse, and tennis. Among the intercollegiate club sports are cycling (men and women), sailing (men and women), and water polo (men and women). Intramural sports include badminton, floor hockey, and racquetball.

Wheaton College

Admissions Office
501 College Avenue
Wheaton, Illinois 60187-5593
(800) 222-2419
www.wheaton.edu

Total enrollment: 2,300
Undergraduates: 1,950
SAT ranges (Verbal/Math): 610-720 (V); 600-700 (M)
Applicants: 1,964
Accepted: 54%
Enrolled: 55%
Application deadline: January 15
Financial aid application deadline: March 15
Tuition: $14,930/$20,190
Core curriculum: No

A Statement of Faith

Wheaton College is considered the intellectual heart of American evangelical Christianity, and many call it the finest college of its type in the United States. The foundation of the college is its commitment to the Christian faith, and that commitment has remained steadfast throughout its history. Wheaton College identifies its purpose as building the church and improving society by "promoting the development of whole and effective Christians through excellence in programs of Christian higher education. This mission expresses our commitment to do all things 'For Christ and His Kingdom.'"

Wheaton College stands out in the sea of relativism and nihilism that has swept over so many colleges in the last decades. The college teaches its students that there is truth, that it is objective, and that it is knowable, and that it is revealed by God. Furthermore, Wheaton promotes the idea that the liberal arts education is the best means of teaching people the truth they most need for their lives. The college sees itself as training Christians who are prepared to meet the needs of the world today.

But Wheaton College sees education as more than intellectual training. While one purpose of a liberal arts education is "to enable students to apprehend truth, . . . beauty, and order," another is to teach the pursuit of "righteousness in the life of both the individual and society," so that they will be prepared "for the responsible use of their freedom." Wheaton's educational goals are lofty: they aim at preparing the whole person intellectually and morally.

Wheaton's evangelical identity is readily apparent to anyone who visits the campus. There are the restrictions one might expect at such a place: no alcohol or tobacco are permitted on campus, and students pledge to forswear the use of these substances entirely while they are enrolled. But these restrictions, and the generally temperate lifestyle of the students, have preserved Wheaton from many of the social problems that have plagued more liberal colleges.

Wheaton offers a high quality liberal arts education for the committed Christian. Students who go to Wheaton say that their intellect is sharpened and their faith is strengthened by the experience. For the student who wants a solid education and feels comfortable with the evangelical environment, Wheaton is an excellent choice.

Academic Life: Amazing Grace

Although Wheaton cannot be described as having a true core curriculum, it does have a fairly solid set of distribution requirements. Students must demonstrate competency in a foreign language equivalent to two years of college study. Wheaton requires several English and composition courses, a demonstrated proficiency in writing, and an oral communication course. Students are required to take two courses in philosophy and two in literature, as well as two courses in fine arts. All students must take three science courses, with at least one four credit-hour lab course. And given the central importance of the Christian faith in Wheaton's identity, it should come as no surprise that the college requires a substantial amount of coursework (fourteen semester hours) in theology and the Bible. The curriculum is structured in such a way as to virtually guarantee the student a solid foundation in the Western tradition, while allowing some flexibility. "It's impossible for a student to come here and not learn what Western Civ. is," says one professor.

Wheaton includes in the introductory paragraphs of its undergraduate catalogue a detailed "Statement of Faith." This statement must be reaffirmed by all faculty annually, and defines "the biblical perspective which informs a Wheaton education." Enforcement of this confessional has helped to preserved Wheaton from most of the destructive impulses in modern academe. "The faculty here take an unapologetic stance against relativism," one student says. There is little or no evidence of any faculty using their classrooms to advance personal or political agendas. There is a certain suspicion of the free market among some faculty, motivated primarily by the Christian concern for social justice. There have been some flirtations with multiculturalism, but at Wheaton that manifests itself primarily in efforts to reach out to ethnic minorities. Some students expressed concern that was evidence of "some liberalization in the understanding of gender roles." According to one student, "Even here people are reluctant to say it's a good thing for a woman to stay at home with her children."

The strongest departments at Wheaton are history, math, economics, biology and chemistry, and biblical and theological studies. The music program deserves special note: It is the second most popular major at Wheaton, and the Conservatory at Wheaton College is widely regarded as one of the finest undergraduate music programs in the country. Many non-majors also participate in the music programs, giving the college a decidedly cultured atmosphere. The outstanding faculty at Wheaton include Peter J. Hill and Seth Norton in business and economics; Jill P. Baumgaertner and Sharon E. Coolidge in English; Mark A. Noll in history; Raymond J. Lewis in biology; and E. John Walford and Joel Sheesley in art. The most popular majors at Wheaton are English, then the aforementioned music, followed by biology and biblical and theological studies.

The college has a reputation for being demanding both in its entrance requirements and in its expectations of students once they do get there. "The academic structure is pretty tight here," one student says. Another student says, "The application process is strict — slouches don't get in here." Thus, the college starts with students who are serious about their studies. Faculty members describe students as generally committed and self-motivated. "Students here have a genuine intellectual curiosity, but are also very goal-oriented," one student says.

The facilities at the college itself are first rate: The Center for Applied Christian Ethics sponsors lectures and symposia on various moral problems of the day.

Wheaton's libraries hold the papers of some of the foremost Christian writers of the past century including the private papers of C. S. Lewis, J. R. R. Tolkien, Dorothy Sayers, and G. K. Chesterton. Wheaton is also the site of the Billy Graham Center, named after the college's most famous alumnus. The Graham Center has a museum and sponsors research and training programs aimed at promoting world evangelization. The Graham Center also holds the archives of a number of prominent mission organizations.

Away from campus, Wheaton offers study-abroad programs in Asia, England, France, Germany, Spain, Mexico, and the Holy Land. If they don't want to leave the country, Wheaton students can join college programs in Washington, D.C.; Aspen, Colorado; or Wheaton's Black Hills Science Station in South Dakota.

Political Atmosphere: How to Be Born Again

Faculty must affirm a confession of faith in order to be hired at Wheaton, and are expected to renew this commitment every year. The college's commitment to evangelicalism stresses four points: First, "the Lordship of Christ over all of life and thought"; second, the authority and inerrancy of Scripture; third, the "responsibility to pursue righteousness and practice justice and mercy to everyone"; and fourth, the necessity of preaching the gospel to the world.

Applicants for teaching posts are examined as much about their adherence to Evangelical principles as to their academic qualifications. Someone who is a good candidate otherwise but does not subscribe to the College's Statement of Faith "simply wouldn't be hired," one professor says. While there has been a push in some quarters to relax the religious standard in hiring to in some cases "diversify" the faculty (read: hire more professors from ethnic minorities), the faculty and administration as a whole have successfully resisted this urge. Recruitment of faculty is done by each department, but the hiring decisions of each department are reviewed by a college-wide committee, and potential hires are interviewed by the college provost and president. You simply "won't find any secularists or relativists" on the faculty at Wheaton, a student says.

Wheaton's faculty are overwhelmingly committed to teaching. There is little of the "publish or perish" mindset which has taken over much of academe. The faculty at Wheaton are not "library rats" who have as little to do with students as possible. Class sizes are generally small, and students form close relationships with professors. This commitment to teaching, however, has not prevented a number of Wheaton faculty from producing outstanding scholarship.

There are some faculty who have reputations as radical feminists, but what seems radical at Wheaton would be considered "just part of the landscape" at most secular colleges, according to one professor. According to another faculty member, who taught at a secular university before going to Wheaton, it is "refreshing to be in an environment where you can say you're pro-life without being vilified as a woman-hating fascist." Says one female student, "anyone who thinks Christianity promotes the inferiority of women hasn't been here. There's nothing like that going on here."

Wheaton expects that its students, as well as faculty, are committed Christians, seeking to put their knowledge to the service of faith. "All truth is God's Truth," is a favorite saying at Wheaton. The college sees the educational endeavor as not merely developing the intellect but as forming the whole person to be an "ambassador of Christ." There is a conscious effort on the part of faculty, says one student, to "integrate your learning with faith." But this focus on integration does not necessarily imply indoctrination. "People are really respectful of differences of opinion around here," a student says. "They don't just tell us, 'This is what you have to believe.'"

"The faculty share a common faith, and that shapes a worldview, which we try to communicate to our students," a professor says. "But we disagree on things, of course. We all understand the importance of honest debate."

Student Life: How Dry I Am

Wheaton's evangelical commitment is lived out by students in submitting to the "Statement of Responsibilities" that they are required to sign upon enrollment. This statement requires, among other things, that students will refrain from the use of tobacco and alcohol while they are enrolled. Wheaton also prohibits gambling, but one has the impression that the college sometimes looks the other way regarding the occasional dorm football pool. The restriction that creates the most resentment among students is the prohibition on most forms of "social" dancing (other than square dancing or folk dancing). Most students actually welcome the structure the statement provides, even though they may chafe against its specifics at times. Some students complain that the rules promote a sense of legalism, but the majority seems to recognize the need for *specific* rules and prohibitions, if there are to be any at all.

Wheaton College expects that all students will belong to a church and attend services regularly, but does not have a specific denominational requirement. There are chapel services on campus three times a week, and students are expected to attend these. These campus services are very engaging, and the college frequently attracts world-renowned preachers to lead these services.

The school also requires its students to live in university housing, which includes traditional dormitories as well as university-owned houses and apartments. Many dorms are single-sex. Those that are coed house men and women in separate wings. Opposite-sex visitors are allowed for a limited time during the evenings, but may not spend the night. According to a recent alumnus, this visitation policy is strictly enforced.

Expectations for a wholesome lifestyle come as no surprise to students arriving on campus. These are made clear enough on the college's application form, which asks students to complete an essay (described by one student as "intimidating") about their faith and relationship with Christ. All in all, students find that there is "spiritual freedom" at Wheaton, but that their spiritual growth is encouraged and fostered.

All of this makes Wheaton College a very pleasant place to live and study. The college has managed to preserve a rare innocence among its students and on its campus, and students seem to love the friendly atmosphere. There is no "mad rush to get away on weekends" that one can find at other colleges, a student says. The dorms become close communities, and students tend to form close relationships with their peers in the same majors. This tight community also makes for very close relationships between faculty and students. "The professors are very willing and involved with us," said one student. "They really try to get to know us." Another says that "the faculty go out of their way to form relationships with students." It is not uncommon at all for professors to invite groups of students home to dinner. "They really are our mentors and role models," the second student says.

Wheaton's park-like campus is beautiful, and the college takes creating that beauty seriously. There is a range of architectural styles represented on campus, but nothing seems out of place or out of relationship. There is ample evidence of planning for future growth. Very little crime is reported on campus or in the immediate area, yet Wheaton's setting in the suburbs of Chicago make the cultural and intellectual resources of that city readily available to students. But students don't need to go away to find diversion. There are numerous events planned on campus, from concerts to movies to intramural sports. There are dozens of student organizations, such as Amnesty International, the Gross Anatomy Club, and the musical groups. Students will also find opportunities to put their learning and talents to work through the outreach ministries offered through the college.

The College of William and Mary

Office of Undergraduate Admission
P.O. Box 8795
Williamsburg, Virginia 23187-8795
(757) 221-4223
www.wm.edu

Total enrollment: 7,560
Undergraduates: 5,560
SAT ranges (Verbal/Math): 620-710 (V); 610-700 (M)
Applicants: 6,878
Accepted: 45%
Enrolled: 42%
Application deadline: January 5
Financial aid application deadline: February 15
Tuition: resident: $4,687/$9,783; non-resident: $16,904/$22,030
Core curriculum: No

Royalty

The College of William and Mary (W&M) is the second-oldest institution of higher learning in the United States, and is the only institution in the country to have a Royal Charter (granted in 1693 by namesakes King William III and Queen Mary II). Phi Beta Kappa was founded there the same year as the United States, and the largely honorary title of college chancellor has been held by George Washington, John Tyler, Warren Burger, and, currently, Margaret Thatcher. The school has scores of reasons to be proud of its past — and unlike a lot of other colleges, it is.

But W&M has ample reason to be proud of its present, too. The college, private until 1906, is one of best state schools in the country, and its faculty is famously dedicated to undergraduate teaching. For the third year in a row, *U.S. News & World Report* ranked W&M as the best small public university in the country. State funding has gone down in recent years, but the college continues to improve. It is a genuine bargain, especially for Virginia residents, even without throwing in the small-college ambiance one feels on this university's campus.

The college attracts an excellent student body, well rounded and focused on its studies. The 7,560 students (5,560 undergraduates) enjoy a student-faculty ratio of twelve-to-one. The beautiful campus includes the oldest academic building in continual use in the country, and it is thought to have been designed by none other than Christopher Wren.

Academic Life: A Glorious Revolution

William and Mary uses distribution requirements rather than a core curriculum. A revised general education curriculum went into effect in 1996, and while at other schools that might have meant a looser, more politicized set of requirements, faculty say the new standards actually closed some gaps in the old curriculum. They "make it more likely that all undergraduate students get a taste of a broad range of intellectual experiences, including creative endeavors, before they leave," a professor says. "The older system was good, but left some loopholes through which many students could slip if carelessly advised, whereas the new system specifies in more detail what a good adviser and well motivated student would have come up with under the old system."

The revised curriculum requires eleven courses distributed among mathematics and quantitative reasoning; natural sciences (including a laboratory course); social sciences; world cultures and history; literature and history of the arts; creative and performing arts; and philosophical, religious, and social thought. Students must also demonstrate proficiency in a foreign language, writing, and physical education. Each entering freshman must take one freshman seminar; these are offered in most of the college's departments. There is also a Western civilization requirement.

While the general education classes are mostly solid liberal arts courses, enough is left up to the instructor that someone so inclined could taint the course with the ideology of his choice. "The only risk [under the new system] is that, under our system of classroom freedom, some instructors will deviate from catalogue descriptions of courses far enough to make a course inappropriate for the requirement that it supposedly fulfills," a professor says.

A student says advisers encourage students to take a range of classes, and especially ask them to explore areas outside their majors. "They don't usually have an agenda — my advisor is a campaign manager of the Democratic Party, but he doesn't try to steer me toward liberal professors," the student says. "And they try to get students to take courses from a wide variety of departments, so that if you're a humanities major you're encouraged to take science courses."

Although some professors and administrators would like to see W&M become more politicized in both its course offerings and faculty makeup, it has resisted the onslaught of politicization more adamantly than many other schools of comparable quality. "The issue here is well under control at present," a professor says. "Students are made aware of the real injustices which have been done in the past, but none of this has been done in such a way as to disrupt the process of true liberal education; attempts to do that have failed quite quickly because the many women and minorities in the administration are, for the most part, realists who know how to work within the system." In general, administrators have no radical agenda or politically correct bias, a student says.

The professors who teach some of the best courses at W&M are George Grayson and Clayton Clemens in government, Robert E. Welsh and Hans C. von Baeyer in physics, Dale E. Hoak and James L. Axtell in history, Kim Wheatley and John Conlee in English, Lewis Leadbeater and James Baron in classical studies, Thomas Finn in religion, Gerald H. Johnson in geology, and Lawrence L. Wiseman in biology.

According to faculty and students, the college's strongest departments are biology, classical studies, economics, geology, physics, and religion. Government has some excellent professors, but has become increasingly politicized in recent years. Philosophy demonstrates a not unusual weakness in ancient and historical approaches to its subject matter.

Despite the college's best efforts, ideological teaching has crept into several departments. These, according to faculty and students, include public policy, English, and the department of literary and cultural studies.

Some of the freshmen seminars reveal an agenda beyond merely expanding the intellectual horizons of students. In the past, some have centered upon themes such as gender, race, and political power. The idea of the freshman seminar is perfectly valid: give new students the opportunity to learn in a small setting from an experienced faculty member. And many of W&M's seminars do just that. Students must pay attention, read the material, and be ready to contribute to class discussions — even in the politicized offerings. Yet the more radical seminars miss out on another educational chance: the pursuit of broad knowledge rather than narrow ideology. This lack is especially unfortunate when the participants are freshmen and still in the process of training their minds toward the manner in which they will be educated for the rest of their lives.

There are also some radical classes beyond the freshman seminars, though these are more rare than at similar institutions. The English department teaches "Modern Black American Literature," which addresses "the problem of patronage, the 'black aesthetic,' and the rise of black literary theory and 'womanist' criticism." Nevertheless, it should be said that the English department currently offers an impressive range of courses on topics elsewhere considered taboo, such as Shakespeare, Chaucer, 18th-century literature and the English of the King James Bible. The literary and cultural studies department offers an introductory course whose topic varies each year, and some of these get a little too recent and popular to be considered of lasting educational value. This program on the whole seems designed to give students a false sense of worldly "cultural" exposure.

Political Atmosphere: Teaching Fit for a King

Faculty at William and Mary value the teaching role of the college, and those who want it to remain true to its original mission have kept the institution from the problems that arise in trying to become a major research university. According to a faculty member, during the 1980s and into the early 1990s the administration wanted the college to become a research institute along the lines of a Johns Hopkins. "They encountered considerable resistance from most of the faculty, although the chemistry, physics, and history departments always have been dominated by people who thought that way," the professor says.

Other factors beyond the school's control have played a part as well. "What really saved us during those years was the tight budget," a professor says. With no money to escape its tradition, W&M did its best to keep alive the better portions of its rich past. Another benefit came from a new post-tenure review procedure demanded by the Virginia Council of Higher Education. This directive "made it very clear that research was third behind teaching and service in what the state expected to have reviewed," a professor says.

Typical professors at W&M teach a heavier load than do their counterparts at similar schools, although full professors often teach less — "often for good reason," a professor says. A few years ago the college eliminated eight graduate programs, including the popular M.A. in English, so fewer teaching assistants are available, those on campus say. But since professors no longer had to spend as much time with graduate students, there was increased pressure to produce research. However, the steps taken by W&M to emphasize teaching prevented the situation from becoming unbalanced.

The college has also tamed the growth of business and other professional programs that sometimes overshadow the liberal arts departments. Part of this was by design, part by accident: "Business deans have had a talent for shooting themselves in the foot," a professor says. But the professional programs still attract the largest donations, mostly because alumni of those programs are in better financial shape to dispense their largesse.

Although Virginia, home to about two-thirds of the students, is a conservative state, the student body is less conservative than the college administration and more similar politically to the faculty. "The general ideology is liberal," a professor says. "Most students are knee-jerk liberals, and there are more leftist groups on campus that do a lot of programs, but they're no more favored by the administration than conservative groups."

W&M does have several well-promoted "diversity weeks," and the administration seems solidly in favor of these. However, according to a student, "no one pays attention to [multicultural groups] beyond these weeks. This is not so much a conservative school as one where everyone on both sides is relaxed and less vocal." The diversity weeks are organized by the college's Office of Multicultural Affairs, whose other events range from ethnic dinners to entire months dedicated to selected groups. Some examples include Hispanic Heritage Month, Chusok Festival, Expressions of India, Pre-Kwanzaa Celebration, Lunar New Year Celebration, Black History Month, Women's History Month, and Taste of Asia. The college sponsors the Multicultural Leadership Retreat each August for presidents of cultural organizations like the African American Male Coalition, Global Nomads, ESSENCE — Women of Color, Empowerment Network, and the Latin American Club.

The Office of Multicultural Affairs also offers such services as "Multicultural Student Advocacy," through which "professional staff are available to provide information and advice on personal and social matters, to make referrals to other campus and community resources as appropriate . . . and to serve as a catalyst if you feel you have been offended or the victim of discrimination." The office also runs "Diversity Training," designed to "break down barriers, challenge the stereotypes, and strive to learn from differences in people, cultures, and the global community."

The college has no formal speech code, and freshmen face only a light dose of instruction upon arriving on campus: a one-hour seminar preaches the merits of safe sex, getting plenty of sleep, and eating well. After this, according to a student, "there is no more propaganda."

Student Life: Restoration

William and Mary stands at one end of Duke of Gloucester Street, the heart of exquisitely and meticulously restored Colonial Williamsburg. Essentially a large, open-air museum, Colonial Williamsburg includes scores of period houses, shops, mansions, and buildings used by the colonial government, all explained by costumed guides and craftsmen. Some W&M students work in the shops and museums, and the restored buildings of the colonial town are architecturally similar to the college's oldest buildings. The 1,200-acre W&M campus has the oldest continually used academic building in the nation; built in 1697, the Christopher Wren Building is named for its presumed architect. Even the more recent additions to the campus reflect the influence of colonial brickwork and proportions.

The Tidewater region of Virginia includes many other historical attractions such as Yorktown and Jamestown, but also offers beaches and the Chesapeake Bay. The Outer Banks of North Carolina are only three hours away. Williamsburg is about 150 miles south of Washington, D.C., and fifty miles from both Richmond and Norfolk, Virginia.

The student body is mostly Virginian. Recent statistics show that 54 percent of in-state applicants were accepted, while only 32 percent of out-of-staters made it in. Students appreciate the atmosphere and the quality of teaching at W&M. "I visited campus and really liked it," a student says. "It's moderately sized, mostly an undergraduate school, and there are good professors. I like the lower key atmosphere here. It isn't an all-consuming school." For the quality of education offered, W&M is a bargain for in-state students, who paid around $4,700 in tuition for the 2000-01 academic year. Out-of-state students pay around $17,000.

The Earl Gregg Swem Library holds more than 1 million volumes and houses special collections of documents from a number of historical figures, including former chief justice Warren Burger.

W&M was the first school in the country to institute an honor code, and this code survives today; no doubt it is one reason, besides the school's setting, for the absence of crime on campus. Students are also responsible for governing their own residence halls, deciding open hours, smoking policies, and quiet times. Both coed and single-sex dorms are available, and all freshmen are required to live on campus unless they reside both with their families and within thirty miles of the school. Housing is guaranteed for three out of four years, but most upperclassmen who want rooms can get them. Only juniors and seniors are allowed to keep cars on campus.

There are 260 student groups at W&M, ranging from performing ensembles to religious and service organizations. The college says that about two-thirds of students participate in some form of community service. The campus also has fifteen national social fraternities and thirteen sororities.

The largest group on campus, however, is the College Republicans. Other conservative groups include the Thatcher Society, which sponsors debates, and the *Remnant*, an alternative student newspaper.

W&M has twenty-three intercollegiate sports teams, and its student-athletes are noted as students as frequently as they are as athletes. The graduation rate for W&M athletes is in the top 3 percent of all NCAA Division I programs. There are also 29 student-run club teams, including fencing, surfing, and croquet. Almost 90 percent of students participate in a sport, including intercollegiate, club, or intramural activities.

Williams College

Office of Admissions
Director of Admissions
Williams College
P. O. Box 487
Williamstown, MA 01267
(413) 597-2211
www.williams.edu

Total enrollment: 2,101
Undergraduates: 2,052
SAT ranges (Verbal/Math): 650-760 (V); 650-750 (M)
Applicants: 5,007
Accepted: 23%

Enrolled: 47%
Application deadline: January 1
Financial aid application deadline: February 1
Tuition: $24,790/$31,520
Core curriculum: No

No Small Advantage

When Henry David Thoreau visited Williams College in 1844, he remarked that "It would be no small advantage if every college were thus located at the base of a mountain." Nestled in the idyllic Berkshire Mountains in western Massachusetts, Williams College has a long and distinguished history as one on the nation's best liberal arts colleges. Chartered in 1793, the college was created to educate "young gentlemen from every part of the Union . . . in all branches of useful and polite literature."

Alas, much has changed in recent decades — and much of it for the worse. A century ago, all incoming students were required to demonstrate proficiency in Latin and Greek and to write a series of essays on Homer, Virgil, and Shakespeare. Today, students often graduate with little or no knowledge of these authors or their significance. Once proudly dedicated to the "moral and intellectual cultivation of future leaders," the moral fiber of the school has withered — evidenced in things like the recent school-sponsored "Queer Sex Jam," a residential policy of coed dorms and bathrooms, and myriad courses that promote transgression rather than sober, serious, honest inquiry. The weak leadership of the past decade — culminating in the resignation of the college president in fall 1999 — has resulted in what one faculty member called "institutional drift."

In relative terms, however, Williams still has much to boast about — a gigantic endowment, loyal and successful alumni, superb athletics, and a core of brilliant teachers and scholars. As one student put it, "You can get a great education here — but not just by showing up. You've got to know how to sift through the foolishness. And there's a lot of it."

Academic Life: Equal Footing, Little Traction

There is no core curriculum at Williams, only a very broad set of distribution requirements. All students must take at least three courses in each of three divisions: language and the arts, social studies, and science and mathematics. But these requirements do very little to shape what students actually study, and they do nothing to bring coherence to the maze of majors, clusters, concentrations, and special programs that make up the Williams curriculum. For example, students get the same humanities credit for taking "Greek and Roman Epic" or "Dostoyevsky and His Age" as they do for courses like "American Genders, American Sexualities" or "Feminist Theory and the Representation of Women in Film."

"The study of Western civilization is given no special place in the curriculum," says one student. "Sure, the courses in history, literature, and philosophy are often there — or at least seem to be. But it is entirely possible to leave here without reading any really great books or learning any history beyond that of race and gender."

Yet while students can graduate with little or no knowledge of ancient Greece and Rome, Shakespeare or Chaucer, the *Federalist Papers,* and the Civil War, all students are required to take a course in the "non-Western, non-European experience." This one-course "peoples and cultures requirement," as it is officially called, is intended "to help students to begin to understand the cultural diversity of American society and the world at large." The course must be "primarily concerned with the peoples and cultures of North America that trace their origins to Africa, Asia, Latin America, Oceania, or the Caribbean." This means that courses in Chinese language, black radicalism, and the economics of sustainable development count toward the requirement while courses on the history of Irish immigration, the Evangelical movement, or the Polish economy after communism do not.

More than one hundred courses fulfill the "peoples and cultures requirement" (called the "PC requirement" by many students, both for its initials and content). "The requirement is so representative of the bean-counting mentality," says one student. "Certain groups count, other groups don't. Some groups are part of the 'diversity rainbow' and others aren't. It's that simple and that ridiculous." Because it is only one course and because many courses — including, it must be noted, a few excellent courses — fulfill the criteria, the requirement is only minimally obtrusive.

The general philosophy among administrators is a do-your-own-thing version of "student-centered education," and the curriculum represents more the particular interests of particular professors than it does any encompassing vision of what constitutes a truly liberal education. The result is that most departments are a mixed bag — with some excellent courses and some trivial courses. With the exception of the hard sciences and mathematics, most departments are riddled with disagreement and dissent, which has led to the elimination or watering down of departmental requirements for those who major in the humanities and social sciences.

For example, history majors are required to take at least one course in three divisions: "American and Canadian History," "European History," and "African, Asian, Latin-American History." But these divisions are so open-ended that they do not really define anything. The "American and Canadian History" requirement is equally fulfilled by taking "Urban Theory," "U.S. Latino Studies," "Cultural Encounters in the American West," "A History of the United States Since 1865," and other courses of greatly varying value. With only a very few exceptions, none of the history courses have prerequisites, which means students are not constrained by what they may or may not already have studied. A major in history often amounts to nothing more than a random selection of nine courses in any order on virtually any historical or quasi-historical subject. English and political science have only slightly more structure; thus, like history, the major requirements in those departments are next to meaningless because they are so general.

The economics department is more rigorously organized, but the focus is largely on modeling solutions to economic problems rather than on economic thinking. This means that there are a lot of courses on the World Bank and the IMF, on game theory and other mathematical approaches to economics, and on sustainable development but very few courses on the relationship between free markets, rule of law, and a free society. Economics is by far the most popular major: roughly one fifth of every class at Williams gets this degree.

In general, the humanities and social science departments each have a handful of great teachers. James Nolan and Robert Jackall are both brilliant sociologists who teach courses on American culture, crime, religion, and politics. Michael Lewis is a gifted teacher and scholar of American art and architecture. Stephen Fix's courses on English literature — especially Samuel Johnson — are superb. Gary Jacobsohn's courses on American government and James McAllister's courses on international relations are excellent. The programs in Chinese and Japanese are very strong. The art history program, which works closely with the world-renowned Clark Institute of Art, is among the best in the nation — especially the year-long survey course in the history of Western art.

Williams's programs in the sciences are extremely good. Biology, chemistry, physics, geology, mathematics, and a rare undergraduate program in neuroscience are all recommended. The college just finished a multi-million-dollar renovation of its Science Quad, which improves these programs even more. The premed program is also excellent — Williams students enjoy one of the highest medical school acceptance rates of any undergraduate program in the country.

"The key is finding and working with the best professors," said one student. "They're out there, and you can usually build a strong major around one or two of them." "Sometimes courses are not what they seem," said another student. "You've got to do your research. You've got to find good advisors — whether it be good professors or older students who know the ropes."

For example, the introduction to American government course — called "Power, Politics, and Democracy in America" — changes drastically depending on who is teaching it. Sometimes it centers around a study of the Constitution, *The Federalist Papers,* and Toqueville's *Democracy in America;* sometimes it focuses on competing models of political behavior; and sometimes students have to settle for the "inherent inequalities in the American political system." The same is true in the introductory English course required of all English majors, which ranges from "Thinking and Writing About Television" to "The Space of Literature" to "Forms of Revenge."

In addition to the major academic disciplines, Williams has endless combinations of course clusters, concentrations, and multi-disciplinary majors, which are, according to one professor, mostly "politicized fiefdoms." These include Afro-American studies, women's and gender studies, and gay, lesbian, and bisexual studies. The largest and most influential of these is women's and gender studies, which includes courses like "Gendering Social Movements," "Feminism, Race, and Culture: Women of Color and the Politics of Representation," and "Chickflicks: The Women's Movement and Cinefeminism."

Far more promising is the recently created program in leadership studies, which combines courses from sociology, history, art, political science, and psychology to "explore the phenomena of leadership in a wide range of historical, cultural, organizational, and intellectual domains." Williams also has a "Contract Major" option, which allows students to propose their own academic program. Recent contract majors have included everything from "Social Thought" to "Architecture" to "Sex Studies."

Another unique element of the Williams curriculum is the Winter Study program — where students in the month of January take a single course or complete a self-designed project. The courses and projects range from what amounts to Club-Med ed ("Glass and Glassblowing," "Principles and Techniques of Cooking," "Hawaii Field Geology") to the more serious ("An Introduction to Greek Philosophy," "Joyce's Art of Memory," "English Rhymes and Rhythms"). Grading is on a pass/fail basis and is usually based on a single ten-page paper. The majority of students stay on campus, but many do "research projects" in places like Las Vegas, Vail, and San Francisco. Some students do internships — especially those in pre-med, who spend at least one of their Winter Study terms following a doctor around each day. The idea is that the January term allows students to explore new intellectual interests without the distraction of grades and other courses, but the reality is usually more of an extended winter break.

Williams has some excellent off-campus programs, including "Semester at Sea" in which students study the history and literature of the oceans, along with practical marine skills, while living in historic cooperative houses at the Mystic (Conn.) Seaport Museum. In addition to learning boatbuilding, shipsmithing, sailing, and celestial navigation, students take courses in maritime history, literature of the sea, oceanography or marine ecology, and marine policy. Located further from Massachusetts is the Williams Oxford Programme, in which students spend a year at Oxford University, taking courses in the tutorial system.

Political Atmosphere: A Local Malaise

Williams is still suffering from the exodus or retirement in recent years of some of its best professors — especially in the areas of political theory, philosophy, and history. While the exiting professors all give different reasons for leaving, the last few years at the college have been, as one professor put it, "something of a malaise." Both professors and students tend to blame the weak leadership of the outgoing president — Harry Payne — described by most as a fair, decent, and intelligent man, but as visionless and weak-willed. Payne resigned in Fall 1999 after alienating faculty over a $20 million alumni gift for a performing arts center that he accepted without consulting the faculty.

Both students and faculty are optimistic about the incoming president — Morton Schapiro, a former Williams faculty member, who was the dean of the College of Letters, Arts, and Sciences at the University of Southern California. An economist, Schapiro's research has focused on the economics of higher education — in particular, the question of student aid and affordability — which leaves some fearing that he will be, as one prominent member of the alumni put it, "more focused on than the means of education than the ends." But his record at USC is impressive. There, he helped to create a rigorous General Education program.

Williams made the front page of the *New York Times* in 1997 after a radical, armed, left-wing organization recruited members on the college's campus. And not just in dorms and abandoned buildings: members of the Provisional Communist Party, a paramilitary organization planning a takeover of the United States, not only recruited, but spoke in political science classes under the auspices of a local labor organization. Some Williams students left school and joined the organization, and one was arrested in Brooklyn when a cache of weapons was discovered in an apartment there.

Even more shocking is that even after the raid and the arrest, political scientist Alex Willingham continued inviting members of the organization to his classes. Willingham is no marginal figure at Williams: He is the director of the Multicultural Center (MCC), which has a gigantic budget for sponsoring speakers and conferences and funding student groups and activities that are part of the Minority Coalition. Some recent MCC events include "Coming Out/Queer Pride Days"; a multi-college conference on multicultural, feminist, and queer issues called "Beyond the Box"; a five-week "consciousness raising" project called "Whose Responsibility Is It?"; the annual "Feminist Seder," which instead of recounting the plagues God imposed on Egypt recounts the plagues the male patriarchy has imposed on women; and, perhaps most telling, a separate pre-orientation retreat for "African, Latino/a, Asian, and Native-American" freshmen prior to orientation exercises for the rest of the incoming students. The program — called "Windows on Williams" — guarantees that the first experience these students have at Williams is as member of a particular identity group. "In the name of diversity and multiculturalism, the program splits students up by race from day one," says one student.

The Minority Coalition (MinCo) includes the following student groups: Asian American Students in Action, the Bisexual, Gay, Lesbian, and Transgendered Union, the Black Student Union, the Chinese American Student Union, the Queer Straight Alliance, Students Organized Against Racism, Students of Mixed Heritage, the Williams Feminist Alliance, and others. These groups get special activity funding through a separate budget and separate budget process — creating a MinCo vs. non-MinCo split. The MinCo groups get special centers, offices, and houses. And so, not surprisingly, social and political life on campus is dominated by these groups, who apparently perceive their purposes in life to be raising awareness, fighting prejudice, and pressing grievances against the administration, which are almost always listened to and met.

Despite this, the majority of the student body is not politically active. Most go along with the loudest groups or finding the myriad Pride Week activities mildly amusing. "Most students just go along with all the political correctness even if they think it's ridiculous," says one student. "The intellectually ambitious but apolitical students avoid the politically charged classes, while the lazy ones take easy classes wherever they can find them."

There is a strong if small conservative voice on campus. It is most easily located in the Garfield Republican Club (named after President James A. Garfield, a Williams graduate) and in the conservative newspaper, *The Williams Free Press*. "The *Free Press* is always provocative — sometimes sophomoric — but it raises important issues, often brilliantly," says one professor. The newspaper regularly runs afoul of the faculty and administration and frequently receives angry letters. But no one doubts the paper's influence: It has an alumni readership of about 700, which has prompted the Williams Public Affairs Office to regularly attack the *Free Press* in its alumni briefings. Well-known conservative writers and leaders serve on the paper's advisory board — including William Bennett (Williams class of 1965), George Gilder, and Dinesh D'Souza. And many former *Free Press* editors have become rising stars in the conservative intellectual world.

In addition, the Garfield Republican Club regularly sponsors conservative speakers on campus — including in recent years Charles Murray, Robert Novak, William Buckley, Michael Medved, and Alan Keyes.

Student Life: Party Policy

The vast majority of Williams students live on campus. Certain dormitories are set aside for freshmen, while other housing is assigned by lottery. Several of the old fraternity houses — fraternities were banned in the 1960s — are considered the best places to live, while there are also "some monstrous 60s and 70s buildings," according to a student. Residential life at Williams gets ratings all across the board, from "miserable" to "excellent." Some students complain that they get "thrown into houses with a few of their close friends and thirty-five people they have nothing in common with."

All dorms — including freshman dorms — are coed. And students wishing for some measure of privacy will be disappointed to learn that many of the residential hall bathrooms are also coed. This coed bathroom policy made national headlines a couple of years ago when now-famous student journalist Wendy Shalit attacked the college in an article — "A Ladies' Room of One's Own" — printed or excerpted in *Commentary, U.S. News and World Report,* and *Reader's Digest.*

An ongoing controversy is the "Party Policy," the set of rules and regulations for campus parties. Party restrictions have gotten more and more stringent in recent years in an effort to clamp down on underage drinking, and many students contend that these steps have ruined social life, which revolves around large registered parties and events, a handful of local bars, and sports teams, which have become surrogate fraternities. Perhaps the school should concentrate more of its energy on preventing burglaries, which is the one other crime that occurs with some frequency on campus.

Outdoor activities are also an integral part of student life — camping, mountain climbing, fishing, and so on. Williams is about 150 miles from both Boston and New York, but the campus itself is rural and somewhat isolated — though absolutely beautiful and perfectly set for those who love the outdoors.

Both intramural and varsity sports are big at Williams, with over half of the student body participating in some competitive form of athletics. There are thirty-one varsity, fifteen junior varsity, and seven club teams. Nearly every program, men's and women's, finishes at or near the top of its division, and for the last five years Williams has either won or been a runner-up for the NCAA Division III Director's Cup, a competition that honors the nation's best athletic department by assigning points based on the achievements of all the sports teams from a college. Williams is extremely proud of the high academic performance of many of its athletes, and annually honors those carrying strong academic records. The athletic facilities are excellent, and the Taconic Golf Course is one of the best in New England, recently hosting the U.S. Senior Amateur Open. All students are required to fulfill a physical education requirement by participating in intramural sports, taking sports or dance classes, or participating in a conditioning program.

Although Williams has dumped several of its grand traditions, some remain strong — especially the bitter rivalry between Williams and Amherst College. The rivalry began in the nineteenth century when some members of the Williams community petitioned to move the college into the Connecticut Valley because of the remoteness of Williamstown. In 1821 Williams president Zephaniah Swift Moore left with a group of student to found Amherst. Williams-Amherst games have always been "absolutely wild affairs," as one student puts it. "Full-fledged wars," says another.

The Hopkins Observatory at Williams, the oldest astronomical observatory in the country, dates from 1838. There is also a beautiful chapel, which unlike Swarthmore, has escaped being turned into a student center — but just barely. There is a new student center — complete with offices, computer rooms, a coffee shop, and lounges for chitchat.

The college has kept up with the high-tech age: Williams Students Online was one of the first and remains one of the best all-purpose student Web sites in the country, and many Williams graduates (including AOL Chairman Steve Case) have gone on to play important roles in the high-tech boom. In addition, many professors have integrated online components to their classes. A few classes are "webcast" live, and Williams has been sought after by a number of outside companies to contribute classes to new online universities.

Graduates go on to many different careers, but investment banking, consulting, and high-tech companies are the most popular, with all the leading firms coming to campus to recruit. In addition, a number of Williams students teach (both at prep schools and Teach for America) or go to medical or law school.

A Williams education carries a hefty price tag — just under $32,000 for tuition, room, board, and fees in 1999-2000. Williams made national headlines this fall when it announced that it would freeze its 2000-2001 cost — a nearly unprecedented move in recent years for selective private institutions — and instead tap into a larger share of its endowment income. The endowment hovers around $1 billion, making Williams one of the wealthiest schools per student in the nation. The college maintains a need-blind admissions policy — 44 percent of student receive aid, with the average award at $22,000.

Admissions is very competitive — with annual acceptance rates hovering around 20 percent. New York, Massachusetts, and California send the greatest number of students to Williams.

University of Wisconsin–Madison

University of Wisconsin–Madison
Office of Admissions
3rd Floor
UW-Armory and Gymnasium
716 Langdon Street
Madison, WI 53706-1400
(608) 262-3961
www.wisc.edu

Total enrollment: 1,219
Undergraduates: 28,476
SAT ranges (Verbal/Math): 550-660 (V); 580-700 (M)

Applicants: 16,853
Accepted: 74%
Enrolled: 46%
Application deadline: February 1
Financial aid application deadline: February 15
Tuition: resident: $3,780/$9,250; non-resident: $13,920/$19,390
Core curriculum: No

The Heartland's Hotbed

One of the nation's first land-grant colleges, the University of Wisconsin–Madison still proclaims loyalty to its original mission: to be, "through teaching, research, and community service, an asset with offerings for every corner of the state." With students enrolled from every county in Wisconsin and roughly a third of its approximately 300,000 alumni living in-state, the university can make strong claims to having an effect throughout the state.

But what impact does it have? The university competed with Berkeley in the 1960s for campus protests, and some observers contend that the school has become a haven for strident activism and a laboratory for social engineering. The university campus and the state capitol building are connected by the mile-long State Street, which has become a kind of ideological conduit for the transfer of liberal ideas. Dubbed "The Heartland's Progressive Hotbed" by the *Utne Reader,* Madison earned a place among the liberal magazine's "ten most enlightened towns," a place where people can "sip latte, watch foreign films, visit naturopaths, join kayak clubs, browse used-book shops, buy organic chevre, or find meditation centers."

It seems though, that this modern "enlightenment" has come at the expense, many times, of the Enlightenment and other hallmarks of Western society. The rhetoric employed by the university to describe its curriculum is frequently not matched by the reality of the courses of study. Recent political correctness has yielded the "Madison Plan," an aggressive multicultural initiative designed to increase the number of minority students and faculty and to raise "diversity" awareness among the student population. Speech codes have been used to restrict the flow of ideas.

Fortunately, ideological impositions are not the whole story at UW–Madison. There is a very fine program called Integrated Liberal Studies, emphasizing Western culture, and thanks to the sheer size of the institution, there are pockets of traditional academic excellence throughout the university. Pursuing a program of solid liberal studies remains a good possibility for the determined student.

Academic Life: Words, and Some Deeds

The University of Wisconsin–Madison is made up of nine separate colleges: the College of Agricultural and Life Science, the School of Business, the College of Engineering, the School of Education, the School of Human Ecology, the College of Letters and Science, the School of Medicine, the School of Nursing, and the School of Pharmacy. The university enrolls more than 28,000 undergraduates, two thirds of them in the College of Letters and Science.

In its undergraduate bulletin, the university outlines the components of a liberal education in a remarkably traditional fashion, admirably free from the political and utilitarian emphasis found at most state universities. A degree from the College of Letters and Science will provide students with four things, according to the catalogue: "education of the whole person" (including the "capacity to think critically"); "education for citizenship"; "education for a productive life" (emphasizing not just a formal work setting, but such activities as "participation in the arts" and "community service"); and "education for the love of learning."

The guide continues in words that would make Cardinal Newman proud: "Education for the love of learning" is described as "the cornerstone of liberal arts . . . the joy of learning to satisfy human curiosity." The catalogue continues: "Although this may appear to go against the practical, bottom-line grain that is often so prevalent, in truth the practical world is shaped by the ideas and devices whose origins were in the love of learning for its own sake. The students of the liberal arts benefit from, and pass on, this legacy."

Turning from this noble rhetoric to the general education requirements, then, is a somewhat disappointing experience. On the positive side, as one professor says, the requirements are "in considerably better shape than they were ten years ago." Emphasizing the necessity of "breadth" within a liberal education, for a bachelor of arts degree the university requires four courses in the humanities (two of which must be in literature), four courses in the social sciences, and four courses in the natural sciences (including at least one physical science and one biological science course). The "breadth" courses must be survey-type courses; specialized topics won't count. No more than ten credits from any one department may count toward the breadth requirement.

Specifically, the university requires up to two writing courses, up to two courses in quantitative reasoning (math or logic), four to six credits in natural sciences (either one course with a lab or two without), two courses in the arts and literature, and one course in social studies. There is also a requirement for two years of a foreign language. There are also minimal mathematics requirements for both B.A. and B.S. students, with more courses required of the B.S. candidates.

Finally, all students are required to take one course in ethnic studies. The ethnic studies requirement "is intended to further a student's education for citizenship and: (1) increase students' understanding of and capacity to value the unique cultural and ethnic backgrounds and contributions of groups not integrated into the mainstream; (2) facilitate an understanding of what it means to live in a society that may display hostility to the individual on the basis of stereotypes of . . . race, religion, sex, or national origin; and (3) equip students to respond constructively to problems of our increasingly pluralistic American society." As might be expected, some of the courses that satisfy the ethnic studies requirement are soft.

Although a liberal education is hardly guaranteed at Wisconsin, the vast resources of the university mean that with concerted effort a student can cobble together a very good liberal course of study. One of the best ways to do this at UW–Madison is a program called Integrated Liberal Studies (ILS). Offered as a certificate (as opposed to a major), ILS is described by the university as a "flourishing interdisciplinary program, focusing on Western history, literature and the arts, social, political, and economic thought, and the nature and history of science." Established in 1948, ILS is one of the oldest continuous interdisciplinary programs in the United States. It owes much to Alexander Meiklejohn's Experimental College, founded at UW–Madison in 1927.

Even as UW has grown into a massive research university, ILS has managed to retain its identity as a kind of collegium within the university. The program has a "good community feeling," one participating student says. With smaller classes, students excited about what they're studying, professors who have chosen to be part of the program, and teaching assistants who are described as "some of the best on campus," ILS facilitates the exploration of what this same student calls "excellent and alternative ideas."

In a university without a requirement to study Western civilization, an exploration of the contributions of the West can indeed become a kind of alternative study. Within ILS, the pursuit is sure to be rigorous. "The purpose of the program," according to a university description, "is to counter the fragmentation of undergraduate education by providing a common ground of learning." The university's distribution requirements, themselves rather fragmented, can be wholly satisfied with ILS courses.

The general course offerings within ILS are organized historically. Each of the following is offered in a two-semester sequence: "Western Culture: Science, Technology, and Philosophy"; Western Culture: Literature and the Arts"; "Western Culture: Political and Economic Thought"; and "History of Western Culture." In addition, a "Critical Thinking and Expression" course is offered. Advanced courses offer a more modern approach, and include such topics as "Contemporary Physical Science," "Heroes and Scoundrels in Western Culture," and "Literature and Science." All courses are constructed to integrate a number of disciplines. Some classes meet in the living room of the Meiklejohn House, while others meet in dorms.

About two thousand students are enrolled in ILS classes each semester, and waiting lists can be found for almost every class. "It is definitely alive and flourishing," says a professor in the program. Says a student: "I really don't know anyone that has been dissatisfied with the program."

Pathways to Excellence is another strong program at UW–Madison. The description of this program, largely geared to honors students, notes that "a truly outstanding liberal education cannot be earned in the lecture hall alone. The capacity to think critically, engage with others in spirited debate, and make sense of the world around us is fostered coequally by the informal activities that take place outside the classroom." Based on "support for the values of engagement, empowerment, and community," Pathways is described as "providing undergraduates with the opportunity to discover their own capacity for excellence."

Outstanding teachers at UW–Madison include: Donald Downs in political science; William Cronon, Stanley Payne, and Robert Frykenberg (president of the Wisconsin Association of Scholars) in history; Lester Hunt in philosophy; Patricia Fennell and David Becker in art; Lloyd Blitzer (emeritus) in communication; and James Baughman in journalism.

For a large university, there are surprisingly few politicized programs at UW–Madison. Women's studies, however, is one of them. This department offers a course in "Lesbian Culture," which focuses on "the history, meanings, and representations of relationships among women; critically analyzes the concepts of lesbian perspective, theory, aesthetic, and sensibility." Another course is entitled "Goddesses and Feminine Powers."

Political Atmosphere: Shalala, You've Got Me on My Knees

The University of Wisconsin–Madison has earned its reputation as one of the most progressive universities in the nation. At the same time, the sheer size of the university ensures that in all of the competition between departments, programs, and organizations, UW is, in the estimation of one professor, a "reasonably free place."

The freedom enjoyed by professors and students has been hard-fought, for UW–Madison has a history of speech codes and excursions into multicultural experimentation that is perhaps unrivaled in academia. What might be considered a cult of tolerance was set in place by Clinton cabinet member Donna Shalala in the late 1980s during her term as chancellor. Its legacy is still felt on campus.

Emblazoned on every piece of UW literature is a kind of credo: "True learning requires free and open debate, civil discourse and tolerance of many different individuals and ideas. We are preparing students to live and work in a world that speaks with many voices and from many cultures. Tolerance is not only essential to learning, it is an essential to be learned. The University of Wisconsin–Madison is built upon these values and will act vigorously to defend them. We will maintain an environment conducive to teaching and learning that is free from intimidation for all."

Tolerance has become the chief virtue from which all others emanate, it seems. However, like so many of the top research universities, tolerance is sometimes pursued above truth. "There are all kinds of worlds here, and if someone believes that there will be a common curriculum or common faith, that is totally irrelevant," a professor says. The silver lining, according to this professor: by and large, people leave one another alone.

Despite the university's carving out considerable leeway to faculty and students to pursue their own endeavors, there are important limitations placed upon the academic freedom enjoyed at UW. The university was at the vanguard of early efforts to impose politically correct speech codes. The introduction of such a code in the late 1980s resulted in the mobilization of forces in favor of free speech. In 1991 the "hate speech" code was found unconstitutional, but a faculty speech code remained intact.

The battle against that prohibition continued, and in 1999 the twenty-year-old faculty speech code once again came under fire. The Faculty Committee for Freedom and Rights scored an unexpected victory in the ensuing debate, citing evidence of professors hauled before hearings because of supposed insensitivities (one incident involved the use of the word "niggardly"). The opponents of the faculty speech code dramatically changed the rule: instead of establishing the nebulous standard of "demeaning" language for which a professor might be liable for disciplinary action, the code now stipulates that "all expression germane to the instructional setting — including but not limited to information, the presentation or advocacy of ideas, assignment of course materials, and teaching techniques — is protected from disciplinary action." The new code also affirms the importance of academic freedom, no small victory in a university where, according to one professor, "if you criticize diversity, you will be labeled a racist." The code states: "The maintenance of intellectual freedom through the open expression of ideas will sometimes be unavoidably hurtful."

Despite this win for free speech, some students continue to clamor for programs by which they can drag faculty members into kangaroo courts for failing to observer the cult of tolerance. Flyers announcing the formation of a "speak-up program" called Making for a Respectable Campus (MARC) were distributed in the fall of 2000. The program would allow students to file anonymous complaints against professors (and students) for alleged discrimination. One professor reports that the program already has administrative backing. Noting also that all of the previous battles have resulted in the "galvanization" of one of the strongest faculty free speech groups in the nation, this professor predicts that the program will not be adopted without a fight.

One other free speech battle that made it all the way to the United States Supreme Court involved a controversy over student fees. In a case that came to be known as *Southworth,* for the UW law student who brought the original suit, the Supreme Court ruled that UW did not violate the First Amendment rights of students to fund campus groups to which students object. Among the organizations to which the students who brought the suit objected were the International Socialist Society, the Ten Percent Society (which lobbied for same-sex marriages), the Campus Women's Center (which lobbied for abortion rights), the UW Greens, and the Madison AIDS Support Network. In ruling against the students, the court let stand the funding mechanism for student organizations at UW and set an important precedent for universities around the country.

Efforts to implement the "Madison Plan" for diversity have enlisted a virtual army of diversity bureaucrats, among them the Multicultural Academic Programs and Services, the Multicultural Student Center (governed by a fifteen-member faculty, staff, student, and community advisory board), and the Race Relations Education Program, which "conducts workshops that provide a critical understanding of how racism and other oppression works in U.S. society, challenges participants to recognize their own racial biases and misinformation, and facilitates a healthy awareness of the dynamics of racial and cultural differences." Or so it claims.

Plans proposing ambitious "diversity" goals seem to mushroom in Madison. Plan 2008 lists as its first goal to "increase the number of Wisconsin high school graduates of color who apply, are accepted, and enroll at UW." Another goal is to "foster institutional environments and course development that enhance learning and a respect for racial and ethnic diversity." The plan also calls for bolstering the ethnic studies programs, continuation of "diversity-related strategic hiring of faculty" (read, "affirmative action"), and the establishment of a "campus celebration of Martin Luther King Jr. Day as a national Day of Diversity" in coordination with the City of Madison.

Along with these goals for the future, the university has recently gone for more immediate results — and one of these backfired badly. Admissions officials doctored a photograph of white football fans to include the face of a black student, and put the picture on the cover of the undergraduate application for 2001. The officials, after being found out, admitted their error, but explained that they were attempting to project a more diverse image to the student body.

Student Life: Whatever the Weather

The University of Wisconsin is pleasantly situated in a vibrant location that combines a fine urban area with two large, glacial lakes, Mendota and Monona. Although some students complain about the long, harsh winters, most find the inclement weather offset by the myriad social opportunities Madison has to offer. State Street is a popular student venue, with shops, cafes, bookstores, and plenty of opportunities to hear live music. From May to September the town hosts an impressive Saturday morning farmers market. Affording all of the opportunities of a large metro area, Madison is not so large as to overwhelm students with distractions.

Housing in Madison is not a major problem, despite the fact that the university has rooms for only one-sixth of the total student population. Undergraduates are not required to live on campus, although most freshmen choose to live in residence halls. Single-sex housing is available, as is housing with limited visitation privileges. Other options include special-interest housing such as honors student houses, fraternity and sorority houses, and off-campus apartments or homes. Crime is not considered a problem in Madison.

With more than 530 student organizations on campus, there is no shortage of extracurricular opportunities. Progressive groups abound — we'll blame cabin fever for some of these — including Billionaires for Bush (Or Gore), which sponsors the Million Billionaire March; Friends of the Spartacus Youth Club ("a revolutionary socialist organization in the tradition of Marx, Engels, Lenin, and Trotsky"); One in a Minyan (a Jewish lesbian and gay group); Sex Out Loud (Boy O Boy, an affiliated group, is "for men who are attracted to men"); Students Helping Others Understand Tolerance (SHOUT), which is dedicated "to teaching acceptance and celebrating diversity"; and the Wisconsin Public Interest Research Group (Big Red, Go Green! is their slogan). The Lesbian, Gay, Bisexual, and Transgender Campus Center serves "as an open meeting place for all queer students and organizations"; it publishes the *q-cumber* magazine.

The Homebrewer's Organization for the Promotion of Zymurgy (HOPZ) and the Ethno Pharmacology Society are two unique organizations. The Greek system is strong, as about 10 percent of undergraduates are members of fraternities or sororities. InterVarsity Christian Fellowship has a strong presence on campus, as do other religious groups.

As a member of the Big Ten, the university fields several high-profile athletic programs. Fans from the university and around the state are extremely loyal to the Wisconsin Badgers football team, which in 2000 became the first Big Ten team to win back-to-back Rose Bowls. Basketball is also very popular of late, and hockey has always been so. A new athletic facility is popular among students.

Yale University

PO Box 208234
New Haven, CT 06520
(203) 432-1900
www.yale.edu

Total enrollment: 11,017
Undergraduates: 5,266
SAT ranges (Verbal/Math): 690-780 (V); 690-770 (M)
Applicants: 13,270
Accepted: 16%
Enrolled: 65%
Application deadline: December 31
Financial aid application deadline: February 1
Tuition: $25,220/$32,880
Core curriculum: No

This Much Remains

As much as this guide derides modern tampering with traditional liberal arts educations, the fact remains that superb educations can be found at some of America's
most elite schools despite the higher-than-average degree of politicization found
there. That's certainly the case with Yale, which is simultaneously highly political
and excellent. It's a matter of knowing where to look once you arrive on the campus
of the third-oldest university in the country. As Yale celebrates its three-hundredth
anniversary in 2001, it faces many internal problems with its curriculum, physical
plant, and the continuing decline of the city of New Haven. Yet undergraduates will
discover a vibrant intellectual life, the best political clubs in the nation, and the prestige that comes from earning a degree from one of the most respected schools on
earth.

Part of Yale's allure stems from the less professionalized curriculum. It produces fewer high-income graduates than many of its peers because it has traditionally concentrated its undergraduate efforts on the liberal arts and sciences rather
than on business, and its professional post-graduate schools of law and medicine,
while esteemed, are much smaller than those of arch rival Harvard. It also has fewer
research institutes than huge research universities like Michigan. All of this benefits
the undergraduate body, which remains the central focus of life on campus.

Academic Life: First a College

While Yale's commitment to undergraduate education is stronger than that found at many other elite schools, it nevertheless leaves it to students to determine what an education is and which courses should be taken to achieve it. This open approach, common among most American universities, is summed up by the university:

> One of the distinguishing features of a liberal education is that it has no single definition. Yale consequently does not prescribe any specific course to be taken by a student, but instead urges each undergraduate to design a program of study suited to his or her own particular needs and interests from the multitude of courses available to college students in a university.

By this means Yale cedes the responsibility for answering a complex question — "What should an educated person know?" — to eighteen-year-olds living away from home for the first time. This is both unnecessary and harmful: unnecessary because this key question can in fact be answered and needn't be treated as a riddle of the sphinx; harmful because, left to their own devices, students tend to follow trends set by their predecessors and superiors. Today, such trends are likely to be intellectually nihilistic and morally vacuous.

Hence, students arriving in New Haven should immediately seek out the professors and programs recommended in this guide as well as those recommended by trusted faculty advisors and sensible peers as they seek to complete the distribution requirements set forth by Yale College, the largest and oldest component of the university. The distribution requirements include an assigned number of courses in four distribution groups: the humanities, fine arts, the social sciences, and the sciences. The college also requires foreign language competency through the intermediate level.

"[The distribution requirements] do not in themselves produce a broadly educated person," a professor says. "This is because courses in every group tend to be narrow rather than broad. The long-ago demise of the survey course is a primary reason for the lack of a broad education, but more currently of concern is the pseudo-scientific methodology that has infected not only the social sciences but even the humanities, and this 'scientism' insists that all studies be narrow."

Among the many outstanding teachers employed by Yale are the following: Ian Shapiro, Steven Smith, Norma Thompson, and John McCormick in political science; Jonathan Spence, Frank Turner, Joanne Freeman, Paul Kennedy, Henry Turner, Donald Kagan, David Brian Davis, Paul Freedman, Gaddis Smith, John Lewis Gaddis, and Thomas Arnold in history; David Quint, Sarah Winter, Laura Green, Ruth Bernard Yeazell, Alexander Welsh, Nigel Alderman, Matthew Giancarlo, Ramie Targoff, and David Bromwich in English language and literature; Karsten Harries in philosophy; Serge Lang and Peter Schultheiss (professor emeritus) in mathematics; Eric

Denardo in operations research; Maria Rosa Menocal in Spanish; Cyrus Hamlin in German studies; Maria Georgopoulou, Walter Cahn, and Creighton Gilbert in art history; Carlos M. N. Eire, Harry Stout, and Brevard Childs in religious studies; Guiseppe Mazzotta in Italian; Vladimir Alexandrov in Russian; David Gelertner in computer science; and Sidney Altman in biology.

Students and faculty rank the following departments as particularly strong: history, humanities, art history, biology, biochemistry, genetics, mathematics, music, neuroscience, physiology, and a specialized major known as ethics, politics, and economics, or EPE, that admits only forty students each year. About 42 percent of undergraduates at Yale major in the arts and humanities, 33 percent in the social sciences, and 24 percent in the biological and physical sciences.

The "Directed Studies" program should be on the agenda of ambitious freshmen — assuming that he or she can get into the program, which is no small task. Those wishing to take part in it must apply to it the summer after they are accepted at Yale. The program now accepts 120 students each year, up from eighty just two years ago. More than two hundred students apply out of the freshman class of approximately 1,100. Still, it is one of the most attractive options for students of the highest caliber. The curriculum consists of close reading of primary sources of the West, from the Greeks to the modern world, in seminars of eighteen students or fewer.

It is, in the words of one professor, an "elite course." "Directed studies is a good choice because it is the only chance these students have at Yale to immerse themselves in a coherent syllabus," the professor says. "They do have the opportunity later on to fashion a coherent discipline, but often even the majors are very wide. Directed studies gives them a broad base they don't get elsewhere except for certain areas of math and science." The program requires a great deal of writing from the students, and is, according to another faculty member, the "crown jewel of Yale College. It is a truly outstanding program — there is no matching its quality. Professors can pick out these students later because they are better writers and speakers."

How can such a program thrive at a modern university? In part, faculty who might be hostile to the authors taught — Homer, Herodotus, St. Augustine, Machiavelli, and Mill, among others — know that it is but one option among many, professors favorably disposed to the program say. The administration, say sources on campus, knows that many alumni favor such offerings, and they can point to Directed Studies as proof of the vitality of studies in Western civilization without having to require it of every student. One professor notes that the program's ability to "keep a low profile" hasn't hurt, either.

Whatever it does, it stands in contrast to the handful of politicized departments at Yale. "Almost all departments at all top-ranked research universities are weak and politicized because almost all are held captive by the barren and useless methodologies of the pseudo-sciences," claims one professor. Among the most politicized at Yale are American studies, women's studies, African-American studies, and ethnicity, race, and migration, or ERM. Of ERM, a professor says: "ERM is trying to model itself on EPE [ethics, politics, and economics], which is very solid. It attracts the best students, and requires a senior essay. They produce most of the winners of the senior essay contests. It has an obvious coherence and is modeled on an Oxford program. So, ERM, which is pure leftist propaganda, has tried to ride on the success of EPE."

A professor says that American studies is "notoriously easy. Students there don't have to know anything" to get good grades; they need only "swallow a very big political pill" to move along. This professor calls American studies Yale's "worst department." And although the history department contains several excellent scholar/teachers, a professors notes that the stylishness of social history means that they "have people who under the guise of social history are really teaching ethnic and feminist studies." Of women's studies, a faculty member says: "It's so predictable. It's the same old bunch you'd expect."

Even less-than-stellar departments do not detract much from the good choices Yale offers. "For those students who wish to find Old Yale in the course catalogue, it's there," a student says.

Beware the teaching assistants, however. At Yale, as at most universities, teaching assistants are more likely to be radical in their politics and pedagogy than the faculty. "In sections [taught by TAs], less judicious and more politicized TAs would attempt to quash the conservative viewpoint [of students]," a student says. "Yet the seasoned professor is willing to hear all sides, regardless of his own persuasion." This student says that such an issue arose in his directed studies course during his freshman year. "Being the lone conservative student in a seminar of twelve students, my conservative beliefs were often discarded by my peers. The professor, though himself a man of the far left, was always willing to call on me and debate my views with intensity. He often complimented my willingness to be iconoclastic in that environment." When a fellow student actually called this student a fascist, a term used so often by the campus left that is has been vacated of meaning, "The professor sternly cautioned the class about in fact being the real fascists by trying to silence me."

Professors find their incoming students somewhat better prepared for the rigors of college than they were, say, a decade ago. But, says a professor: "Neither then nor now could they be considered rigorously educated. This is because . . . American high school education seems to focus on 'issues' of current concern such as recycling, the death penalty, social security, etc. This is not education." Yet students seem to be better prepared in mathematics, while informal outlets expose them to the humanities. "More students seem to be getting some exposure to the 'great books' not from their formal schooling, but from aunts or uncles or friends of the family who steer them toward ideas and works they are not getting during classroom time," the professor says.

While at Yale, though, students are said to take their educations more seriously than at its rival Ivies. "I had visited Harvard and others and found them more focused on the graduate level," says a student. "These [other] schools, following the German *Wissenschaft* model, sought to produce specialists receiving M.A.s. My assumption was that a school which focused on the college [i.e., undergraduate students] would be dedicated more towards producing leaders educated in the liberal arts." According to a student, a professor has said that "Yale students go to work to do various activities and study in their free time." Extracurricular commitments do take up a lot of students' time, but students find that their peers have a less competitive attitude than at other Ivy League schools, which makes it easier to develop an intellectual and social community.

For their part, faculty at Yale work with students, meet with them during office hours, and seek to develop and advance their own teaching skills. Of course, Yale does use teaching assistants in its larger introductory courses, but, says the student, "Yale is first a college, then a university." Grade inflation, a national problem particularly pronounced at the Ivies, is found in some courses, but less so in seminars.

Political Atmosphere: Too Bright for Tolerance

A low point in Yale's history came when the administration first solicited a $20-million gift from alumnus Lee Bass for teaching Western Civilization courses and then caved in to radical faculty members who blocked implementation. When Mr. Bass learned of this two years after the fact from press accounts, he demanded that his donor intent be honored. Yale refused and was forced to return the money. The shallow and convenient prejudice against Western Civilization this episode reflected has not abated, although some report that the tone of campus radicals has grown less shrill. Unfortunately, that's because the campus radicals no longer need to subdue the opposition — that's already been done.

The first casualty in this conflict is academic freedom. Harassment codes, which on the surface appear to be innocuous protections from misogynists to which only a barbarian could object, in fact act as speech codes used to silence faculty and students who dare to speak their own minds. At Yale, as at other elite schools, radicals have honed their skills so that their operations are smoother and less noticeable. In this manner, they get their way without risking ridicule by the media.

Academically, this situation is revealed through the establishment, little by little, of an atmosphere in which disagreement with the established order of things is simply not tolerated. "No clear case of the denial of academic freedom has or is likely to occur," says a Yale professor. "Those who wish to suppress academic freedom are far too accomplished for that. Instead, there is a pervasive, continual, all-enveloping atmosphere of praise for some (those who work on black lesbian women's health care), and they look askance at anyone who, for example, might take Aristotle seriously. It's working beautifully." One student found this atmosphere so off-putting that he "soon grew to despise the liberal hegemony on campus" and, after reading Allan Bloom's *Closing of the American Mind,* "began to prioritize my interests, understanding why it was important that I study the West and Great Books."

Another means by which ideologues exert control on campus is through the manipulation of faculty hiring. The philosophical make-up of younger faculty members reveals who's in charge of the hiring process. If radicals constitute a minority of current faculty members, they'll need to raise hell to get noticed and ensure that their own kind are hired. But when they make up either an outright majority or, more likely, a majority of those who take an active interest in their department, they needn't voice their demands quite so loudly.

This situation manifests itself through the epistemology and pedagogy employed by professors. If everyone in a department is, say, a cultural relativist, then what seemed to be a political question can be passed off as one of scholarship. The same criteria can be applied to race and ethnic studies, studies of gender and sexuality, or just about any other matter now addressed on campuses. And indeed, this is what one finds at Yale. "Faculty hiring is based not on ideological purity but on methodological purity, which is a far more powerfully sophisticated version of the same thing," a professor says. "Regression analyses, dealing with what already is, always defeats thinking about, for example, virtue. 'Ideology' is out of date; today, over 90 percent of professors share the same leftist ideology without even thinking about it."

And it gets into the Yale catalogue, as evidenced by these courses:

American Studies 406b: "Race, Ethnicity, and Sexuality in Twentieth-Century America." "An examination of cultural productions that deal with race, ethnicity, and sexuality during the twentieth century. Special attention to repression and expression of sexuality in a variety of cultural, social, political, and economic contexts. Topics include prostitution, homosexuality, heterosexuality, marriage, and miscegenation."

Sociology 308b/Women's and Gender Studies 354b: "Sexual Diversity and Social Change." "Survey course examining the notion that sexuality is socially constructed, constrained, and contested. Focus on theory and history of sexual variations, cultures, and politics of sexual minorities in the United States; relationship between sexual minorities and institutions; and phenomena such as transvestitism and bisexuality."

Women's and Gender Studies 361b/Sociology 317b: "Sociology of Heterosexuality." "The course begins with the assumption that heterosexuality is socially produced and reproduced. Examination of heterosexuality as it is produced through a binary gender system; through structures such as law, religion, and psychiatry; through texts such as television, fiction, magazines, and movies; and through rituals such as weddings."

This sort of "education" starts with freshman orientation, which is, for the most part, an effort by the administration to exert sufficient peer pressure on impressionable young students to cause them to fall into line with acceptable forms of behavior and speech. A student publication, *Light and Truth*, describes the sessions as "run by a small clique of administrators and students" and "designed to convince you that there is one accepted set of views on race, sex, and rock 'n roll. But political and cultural temperaments of every type are found at Yale, and neither universal respect nor approbation is accorded to anyone."

During these orientation sessions, the language used by authority figures is chosen carefully in order to influence the thought (and speech) of new students. *Light and Truth* notes that, "Educators, when speaking of relationships between students, always make certain to employ 'gender-neutral' language," so that no one might be offended by normal language. "The educators," the magazine continues, "wishing to avoid the unacceptably intolerant terms 'boyfriend' and 'girlfriend,' speak instead of 'partners.'"

After being shown every form of contraception known to man, freshmen are then required to take part in the "condom race," in which each person is given a condom and broken up into groups. Each group, in turn, gets a wooden phallus, and students sit in a circle passing the phallus around to see which group can place all of its condoms on the phallus first. *Light and Truth* notes that "No one seriously suggests abstinence as a viable option, and the whole sexual ordeal is presented as a great joke." (This attitude is reinforced by the health services department, in whose waiting room an undergraduate reports being met "with the harrowing sight of a Christmas tree decorated entirely with contraceptives.") New students should consult the fall issue of this useful magazine for an intelligent rating of which orientation events to attend and which to avoid — that is, if they can even find the issue. Recently, hundreds of copies of the annual *Survival Guide* published by *Light and Truth* were removed from freshman mailboxes around campus.

Then there is the annual Gay Pride Week, a period during which students are expected to march in lock step with the administration's sympathetic (some would say libertine) view of the small yet vocal homosexual lobbying groups on campus. Recently, members of that lobby covered the campus with posters announcing S&M workshops and pornographic chalkings on campus buildings. The week culminates with an "Access to Flesh Conference," consisting of two days of workshops on drag queens and so forth. "Toleration" long ago became synonymous with "acceptance" on American college campuses, a fact driven home by some students who decided to lampoon the annual Pride Week by hanging some small posters announcing "Celebrate Gay Lust," "Celebrate Gay Gluttony," and the like. In reaction, Pride Week leaders ripped down every satirical poster and the administration promised to get to the bottom of this act of intolerance. This action won Yale a coveted Polly Award from ISI.

Still, there is no speech code at Yale, and even the best efforts of vocal administrators working in cahoots with student activists cannot stifle debate among such a talented student body. "Yale escaped the whole speech code trend of the '90s," says a recent graduate. "There's a lot of free-wheeling debate there. You can say almost anything" if you're willing to stand up for what you believe and can withstand the peer pressure to conform. "The orientation sessions are forceful, but classes and peer pressure do the most damage. There's always subtle pressure, and everyone knows the PC thing to say." Another former student says that "The main thing is to have courage. If you're courageous, you can be pretty happy at Yale. Life can be very rich there, and I don't mean just activism, but the intellectual life."

A current student concurs with these judgments. "It is quite amazing the extent to which conservative students have an outlet for activity on a dominantly liberal campus," this person says. This results less from any type of conservative activism, the student says, than from "a society dedicated to intellectual debate and fraternity. The conservative organizations become centers of debate, discussion, and friendship that complement the course work and the rest of the Yale experience."

Student Life: Colleges Within College

Student life at Yale College is centered around the residential college system, a hallmark of life at Yale since 1932. The catalogue states the basics of life in the residential colleges succinctly: "Each college has its own dining hall, where the students eat together, as well as its own library, common rooms, and athletic teams; each college offers courses for which academic credit is given; and each college celebrates the progress of the academic year with various festivities, concerts, and dramatic presentations."

Each college has developed its own personality over the decades, and graduates are almost as loyal to their college as to their school. Headed by a residential master and a dean, each college has its own courtyard. Freshmen are assigned to a college and begin living in one their sophomore year. All freshmen and sophomores must live on campus, and most undergraduates choose to live in their colleges throughout their four years at Yale; only 10 to 15 percent live off campus.

This historic element of student life is one of the most distinctive and beneficial experiences for Yale undergraduates because it creates a tighter circle within an otherwise daunting 11,000-student university with no unifying infrastructure. A professor notes that the level of civility in the colleges is higher than would be the case in most dorms, both because of the presence of the master and because of the degree of responsibility expected of the students themselves. A student says that the residential college system is "certainly a high point of the Yale life." The residential colleges provide some degree of shelter from the stresses of college life, this student says, by allowing students the luxury of "a long dinner or relaxing in a common room."

Privacy isn't to be expected, however. A student notes that "Yale students live in suites of up to ten people, so they gather with many people in the common room or can be alone in their rooms." Even the most private room there is — the bathroom — isn't private. "In fact," says a student, "all bathrooms are coed. Frankly, I do find the prospect a bit repulsive."

As for drug and alcohol use, a student says that "There is definitely the presence of alcohol on campus. . . . Alcohol [is used in] a very traditional, social form." Students say there is the regular measure of frat-house drinking, but that no one is pressured to drink if he or she wishes to abstain. As for drugs, "There is a very small (almost nonexistent) group of drug users who largely keep to themselves," a student says.

Substances like these definitely don't get in the way of what is perhaps the most intellectually vigorous undergraduate political scene in the nation. "Conservatives and libertarians have highly active parties and publications available to them and are perhaps the most lively and self-confident political groups at Yale," a professor says. "The brightest new students, even including those who arrive with pre-inserted leftist political views, are attracted to these parties because that's where the brightest upperclassmen seem to have gravitated."

The parties are part of Yale Political Union, which is the largest student organization on campus. It has more than 1,400 members (or some 25 percent of the undergraduate student body), and is the only group of its kind in the country. It is home for six political parties — Conservative, Independent, Liberal, Party of the Right, Progressive, and Tory — all of which are debating, social, and fraternal organizations. The Political Union is nonpartisan and invites guests from across the philosophical spectrum. Students interested in lively debate, nationally known guest speakers, dinners with like-minded students, and more should look into these unique groups. Membership is invitation-only, but students may associate with any party. Says one student member of the Conservative Party, "It offers fantastic opportunities for debate and friendship. The party eats dinner as a group four nights a week, meets at Mory's [a legendary local pub] for lunch on Fridays, and has a weekly debate caucus, which is the highlight of the week."

Many other student groups add to the vibrant social life for which Yale has long been known. These include the aforementioned *Light and Truth,* along with the *Yale Free Press,* another alternative newspaper; the *Yale Record,* a humor monthly published since 1872; and the *Yale Daily News,* Yale's so-called mainstream student daily. A student calls the *Daily News* "notoriously left-wing, but a fine Yale tradition."

Among the large variety of student groups are the *Yale Angler's Journal,* which features serious writing about the hallowed sport of fly fishing; the Whiffenpoofs, a male a cappella group; the Yale College Entrepreneurial Society; the Allan Bloom Forum, which invites nationally known speakers to address cultural and scholarly issues; and many academic and social groups. Yale fields intercollegiate teams in all of the major sports. Like other Ivy League schools, it requires that its athletes maintain high academic standards and does not award athletic scholarships. Among the many intramural sports, organized by residential college, are golf, soccer, football, tennis, basketball, swimming, squash, softball, and billiards.

Yale brims with cultural institutions, including the Center for British Art, one of the finest of its kind in North America; the University Art Gallery; the Peabody Museum of Natural History; and the huge library system. Centering around the Sterling Memorial Library, Yale's collection of over 10 million volumes is second in size only to Harvard's and is one of the great collections in the world.

A campaign to repair and update Yale's beautiful campus is well under way. Fifteen architectural firms were retained to help renovate one hundred of the 224 buildings — a project that will take $500 million to complete. Yale has traditionally been known for its humanities and social science departments, but that balance of power could shift as it prepares to spend half a billion dollars on a new medical school and an equal sum on new science buildings.

New Haven has long been regarded by many Yalies as the weakest element of life at Yale. While the city does have its defenders, crime is a concern around campus, and new students should learn their way around before straying too far from the Gothic towers and green lawns for which the school is known. Boarded-up row houses line streets only a few blocks from campus — a remarkable sight in a town that's home to one of the world's richest universities. By far the most common crime on campus is burglary, with reported incidents totaling 92 in 1997, 57 in 1998, and 66 in 1999 (the latest year for which statistics are available). In 1999, 13 of these burglaries occurred in residence halls.

There are many local institutions in New Haven without which Yale would simply not be Yale. These include the aforementioned Mory's Temple Bar; the Yale Co-Op, which has sold books and Yale paraphernalia since 1886; the Yankee Doodle, which a student magazine describes as serving "world-class burgers and other excellent food" faster than McDonalds; and J. Press, originator of the Ivy League look now popular among non-grungy young people everywhere. A student says, "I feel very safe in New Haven, which really is no worse than any other city. If you stay out of the ghetto to the west of campus, you'll be fine." Many Yale students volunteer their time to help tutor area youngsters or to do what they can to improve New Haven's housing. New York City, the shore, and the New England countryside are all within easy reach by train or car.

Additional Services from ISI

Choosing the Right College has been produced by the staff of the Intercollegiate Studies Institute (ISI), a non-profit, non-partisan educational think tank founded in 1953. For nearly five decades, ISI has supported efforts to strengthen liberal arts curricula at colleges and universities nationwide. As we approach our first half-century of service, our programs and publications are stronger and more influential than ever before.

ISI's Student Self-Reliance Project, of which *Choosing the Right College* is the foundation, is a comprehensive program designed to ensure that every student has access to the intellectual tools they need to make the most of their education. After choosing a school that is right for you, you can also consult this guide to navigate your path through the academic, political, and social life at your school. Beyond *Choosing the Right College*, ISI offers numerous programs and publications to make your studies both easier and more productive.

Turn first to *A Student's Guide to Liberal Learning* for wise counsel on reading well, maturing intellectually, and gaining insight into the nature of your education. Then use *A Student's Guide to the Core Curriculum* to build a foundation for your studies. By choosing your electives carefully, you can obtain the education you deserve even at schools that abolished their core curricula decades ago. ISI's guide to designing your own core will show you how.

As you progress through your college years, you will find that our unique study guides will keep you ahead of the class. Titled *A Student's Guide to U.S. History* (or to *Economics, Literature, the Study of History, Philosophy,* or *Political Philosophy*), these guides, by nationally known scholars, are superb introductions to the most important fields in the liberal arts. You'll learn the principal works and ideas that animate each discipline so that you will be able to approach each class with a degree of sophistication that will surprise your professor. More important than pleasing your professors, however, these guides help you to really grasp each subject, to make it your own.

Conferences, lectures, fellowships, and other publications round out the benefits that ISI brings to tens of thousands of students and professors. ISI organizes conferences on important intellectual problems as well as career development seminars throughout the nation each year. Lecturers sponsored by ISI speak on over two hundred college campuses annually on a vast array of topics. Graduate students in the humanities and social sciences may apply for our prestigious fellowships. And ISI publishes and distributes a range of scholarly and opinion journals, as well as at least a dozen serious books of non-fiction through its national trade imprint, ISI Books, each year.

Whatever your stage of education — home school, high school, college, graduate school, or life-long learner — ISI offers programs and publications designed to help you make the most of your talents. Whether you are a student or teacher, professor or parent, you can benefit from our resources and expertise.

Finally, you will find an attached reply card at the end of this book. Because we are interested in your opinions, we hope you will take the time to fill out the card and mail it back to us. Your evaluation is an important part of our ongoing efforts to offer you the best college guide in America — and because we appreciate your feedback, we'll send you a complimentary copy of *A Student's Guide to Liberal Learning*.

To learn more about the Intercollegiate Studies Institute, a non-profit 501(c)3 organization, or to make a donation to ISI, visit our Web site at www.isi.org or e-mail us at collegeguide@isi.org. You may also call us at (800) 526-7022; or mail us at: ISI, P.O. Box 4431, Wilmington, DE 19807-0431.

Choosing the Right College — *Revised Edition* Reply Card

ISI values your opinion of its college guide and hopes you will help it better determine the effectiveness of this book by completing and returning this **reply card**. ISI will in turn send you a free copy of *A Student's Guide to Liberal Learning* by Georgetown University professor James V. Schall.

Name: _____ E-mail Address: _____

Address: _____

Schools in which you are most interested: _____

Check all that apply: I am a ☐ homeschooler ☐ student ☐ grandparent ☐ parent ☐ professor
                               ☐ guidance counselor ☐ other _____

Please circle your answer from 1 to 5, with 1 being of no help and 5 being extremely helpful.

1. How helpful was this guide in choosing your school? 1 2 3 4 5

2. Did the use of this guide change your mind about a given institution? 1 2 3 4 5

3. How satisfied were you with the range and number of schools considered? 1 2 3 4 5

4. How strongly would you recommend this guide to others? 1 2 3 4 5

5. Please rate the following features of each essay, from 1 to 5: Academic Life _____ Political Atmosphere _____ Student Life _____

BUSINESS REPLY MAIL
PERMIT NO. 44   WILMINGTON, DE

INTERCOLLEGIATE STUDIES INSTITUTE, INC.
PO BOX 4431
WILMINGTON, DE   19807-0431